International Business Transactions

ASPEN CASEBOOK SERIES

International Business Transactions

Problems, Cases, and Materials

Third Edition

Daniel C.K. Chow

The Frank E. and Virginia H. Bazler Chair in Business Law
The Ohio State University Michael E. Moritz
College of Law

Thomas J. Schoenbaum

Harold S. Shefelman Distinguished Professor
University of Washington School of Law

Wolters Kluwer

Published by Wolters Kluwer in New York.

Wolters Kluwer serves customers worldwide with CCH, Aspen Publishers, and Kluwer Law International products. (www.wolterskluwerlb.com)

To contact Customer Service, e-mail customer.service@wolterskluwer.com, call 1-800-234-1660, fax 1-800-901-9075, or mail correspondence to:

Wolters Kluwer
Attn: Order Department
PO Box 990
Frederick, MD 21705

Printed in the United States of America.

1 2 3 4 5 6 7 8 9 0

ISBN 978-1-4548-4941-4

Library of Congress Cataloging-in-Publication Data

Chow, Daniel C. K., author.
  International business transactions : problems, cases, and materials / Daniel C.K. Chow, The Frank E. and Virginia H. Bazler Chair in Business Law, Ohio State University Michael E. Moritz College of Law; Thomas J. Schoenbaum, Harold S. Shefelman Distinguished Professor, University of Washington School of Law.—Third edition.
      pages cm
  Includes bibliographical references and index.
  ISBN 978-1-4548-4941-4 (alk. paper)
  1. Export sales contracts—United States—Cases. 2. Investments, Foreign—Law and legislation—United States—Cases. 3. Arbitration and award—United States—Cases. 4. Export sales contracts—United States—Problems, exercises, etc. 5. Investments, Foreign—Law and legislation—United States—Problems, exercises, etc. 6. Arbitration and award—United States—Problems, exercises, etc. I. Schoenbaum, Thomas J., author. II. Title.
  KF915.C48 2014
  343.7308'7076—dc23
                          2014040802

About Wolters Kluwer Law & Business

Wolters Kluwer Law & Business is a leading global provider of intelligent information and digital solutions for legal and business professionals in key specialty areas, and respected educational resources for professors and law students. Wolters Kluwer Law & Business connects legal and business professionals as well as those in the education market with timely, specialized authoritative content and information-enabled solutions to support success through productivity, accuracy and mobility.

Serving customers worldwide, Wolters Kluwer Law & Business products include those under the Aspen Publishers, CCH, Kluwer Law International, Loislaw, ftwilliam.com and MediRegs family of products.

CCH products have been a trusted resource since 1913, and are highly regarded resources for legal, securities, antitrust and trade regulation, government contracting, banking, pension, payroll, employment and labor, and healthcare reimbursement and compliance professionals.

Aspen Publishers products provide essential information to attorneys, business professionals and law students. Written by preeminent authorities, the product line offers analytical and practical information in a range of specialty practice areas from securities law and intellectual property to mergers and acquisitions and pension/benefits. Aspen's trusted legal education resources provide professors and students with high-quality, up-to-date and effective resources for successful instruction and study in all areas of the law.

Kluwer Law International products provide the global business community with reliable international legal information in English. Legal practitioners, corporate counsel and business executives around the world rely on Kluwer Law journals, looseleafs, books, and electronic products for comprehensive information in many areas of international legal practice.

Loislaw is a comprehensive online legal research product providing legal content to law firm practitioners of various specializations. Loislaw provides attorneys with the ability to quickly and efficiently find the necessary legal information they need, when and where they need it, by facilitating access to primary law as well as state-specific law, records, forms and treatises.

ftwilliam.com offers employee benefits professionals the highest quality plan documents (retirement, welfare and non-qualified) and government forms (5500/PBGC, 1099 and IRS) software at highly competitive prices.

MediRegs products provide integrated health care compliance content and software solutions for professionals in healthcare, higher education and life sciences, including professionals in accounting, law and consulting.

Wolters Kluwer Law & Business, a division of Wolters Kluwer, is headquartered in New York. Wolters Kluwer is a market-leading global information services company focused on professionals.

To my wife Ching and our son Alan

DC

Summary of Contents

Contents   *xi*
Preface to the Third Edition   *xxvii*
Acknowledgments   *xxix*

1 *Introduction*   **1**
2 *International Sale of Goods*   **49**
3 *The Sales Contract*   **165**
4 *Letters of Credit*   **225**
5 *Non-Establishment Forms of International Business: Agency
   and Distributorships, Technology Transfer, Contract
   Manufacturing, and Franchising*   **283**
6 *Foreign Direct Investment*   **349**
7 *Protecting Intellectual Property Rights*   **525**
8 *Dispute Resolution*   **587**
9 *Corporate Social Responsibility*   **713**

Table of Cases   *767*
Index   *773*

Contents

Preface to the Third Edition   *xxvii*
Acknowledgments   *xxix*

1 *Introduction*   1

I.   Some Background Considerations   1
      A. Scope and Approach of This Book   1
                 Note on IBT and International Trade Legal Skills   3
      B. Counsel in International Business   4
          1.   Issues Faced by Lawyers   4
          2.   Role of Counsel for an MNE   4
          3.   Challenges for the International Lawyer   7
                 Notes and Questions   8
                 Problem 1-1   8
                 Problem 1-2   9
      C. Cultural Concerns   9
                 Notes and Questions   10
                 Problem 1-3   11
                 Problem 1-4   12
II.   The Growth of International Business Since the Second World War   12
III. Modern Forms and Patterns of International Business and Commerce   14
      A. Trade in Goods   14
      B. Trade in Services   15
      C. Foreign Direct Investment   16
      D. Technology Transfer   17
IV.   Some Important New Developments   18
      A. The Rise of China and East and South Asia   18
      B. The Role of Multinational Enterprises   19
      C. Globalization   20
                 Notes and Questions   21
                 Problem 1-5   22
      V. The Legal Framework for International Business Transactions   22

A.   Introductory Considerations   22
B.   International Conflicts of Law and Choice of Law   22
C.   The New Lex Mercatoria ("Law Merchant")   24
D.   Sources of Law for International Business Transactions   24
E.   International Forums and Institutions   26
     1.   UNCITRAL   26
     2.   UNIDROIT   26
     3.   The International Chamber of Commerce   27
F.   Major Categories of International Business Law   28
     1.   Public International Law   28
     2.   Regional Supranational Law   29
     3.   Uniform Codes and Other Harmonizing Measures   29
     4.   Domestic Law   30
          Problem 1-6   30
G.   Relationship of Sources of International Law to Domestic Law   30
          Problem 1-7   32
          Problem 1-8   33
VI. International Economic Law: The Public Law Institutions and
     Rules That Facilitate and Regulate International Business   33
          Problem 1-9   34
A.   The World Trade Organization   35
B.   Preferential Trade Agreements   37
C.   The North American Free Trade Agreement   38
     1.   NAFTA Objectives   39
     2.   NAFTA Administration and Dispute Settlement   39
D.   The European Union   40
E.   Free Trade in Asia   42
     1.   ASEAN   43
     2.   APEC   43
F.   Free Trade in the Americas   43
G.   Developing Countries   44
H.   The Organization for Economic Cooperation and Development   45
I.   Trade Institutions and Policy in the United States   45
          Notes and Questions   46

2   *International Sale of Goods*   **49**

I.   Overview of the International Sales Transaction   49
A.   Expectations of the Parties   49
B.   The International Context   50
          Note on Trade Financing   52
     1.   The Sales Contract   53
          Form 2-1 Letter of Inquiry   54
          Form 2-2 Pro Forma Invoice   55
          Form 2-3 Purchase Order   56
          Notes and Questions   57

	2.	Letter of Credit	57
		Notes and Questions	58
		Form 2-4 Commercial Letter of Credit	59
	3.	The Bill of Lading and the Contract of Affreightment	60
		Form 2-5 Bill of Lading	62
		Notes and Questions	63
	4.	Overview of the Entire Documentary Sale Transaction	63
		Notes and Questions	65
		Note on International E-Trade	66
		Problem 2-1	66
C.	Commercial Terms Under the ICC Incoterms		67
		Problem 2-2	70
		INCOTERMS 2010 ICC Rules for Use of Domestic and International Trade Terms	70
		FOB	70
		Problem 2-3	73
		CIF	74
D.	Interpretation of Commercial Terms		78
		Problem 2-4	78
		Biddell Brothers v. E. Clemens Horst Company	78
		E. Clemens Horst Company v. Biddell Brothers	81
		Notes and Questions	82
E.	Documents of Title		82
		Problem 2-5	83
		Comptoir d'Achat et de Vente Du Boerenbond Belge S/A v. Luis de Ridder Limitada (The Julia)	83
		Notes and Questions	87
		Problem 2-6	89
F.	Contracts of Affreightment, Bills of Lading, and Insurance		89
	1.	The Contract of Affreightment and the Bill of Lading	89
		Hague-Visby Rules	92
	2.	COGSA: A Thumbnail Sketch	95
		Norfolk Southern Railway Co. v. Kirby	97
		Kawasaki Kisen Kaisha Ltd. v. Regal-Beloit Corp. (The "K" Line Case)	102
		Notes and Questions	108
		Problem 2-7	110
		Anvil Knitwear v. Crowley American Transport, Inc.	111
		Problem 2-8	113
		Steel Coils, Inc. v. M/V Lake Marion	114
		Notes and Questions	120
	3.	Marine Insurance	121
		American National Fire Insurance Co. v. Mirasco, Inc.	121
		Notes and Questions	127
		Problem 2-9	128
II.	The International Sales Contract and International Trade Law Considerations		128
A.	Export Trade Matters		129
		Problem 2-10	129
		Problem 2-11	129
		Problem 2-12	129

U.S. Regulation of Exports: The Export Administration
Act, The Office of Foreign Assets Control, Antiboycott
Laws, The Economic Espionage Act, and The Foreign Corrupt
Practices Act   130
Notes and Questions   134
B.   Import Trade Matters   134
Problem 2-13   135
Problem 2-14   136
Problem 2-15   136
Problem 2-16   137
U.S. Regulation of Imported Goods: Classification, Valuation,
Rules of Origin, Marking, Free Trades Areas and Customs
Unions, and Other Import Restrictions   137
Notes and Questions   147
1.   Classification Issues   148
North American Processing Co. v. United States   149
JVC Co. of America v. United States   150
Better Home Plastics Corp. v. United States   152
Notes and Questions   154
Problem 2-17   154
2.   Valuation Issues   154
Century Importers, Inc. v. United States   155
Notes and Questions   157
Problem 2-18   157
3.   Rules of Origin   158
Zuniga v. United States   158
Notes and Questions   159
Problem 2-19   160
4.   Marking   160
Bestfoods v. United States   160
Notes and Questions   162
Problem 2-20   163
Note on International Trade Law and the Import/Export Sales
Transaction   163

3   *The Sales Contract*   **165**

I.   Choice of Law   165
Kristinus v. H. Stern Com. e Ind. S.A.   165
Notes and Questions   167
II.   The United Nations Convention on Contracts for the International
Sale of Goods   168
A.   Basic Features of the CISG   170
B.   Historical Origins   170
C.   Cases on the CISG   170
Note on the UNIDROIT Principles   171
D.   Sphere of Application of the CISG: Articles 1–6   171

1.	Article 1(1)(a) and the Test of Internationality	172
	Problem 3-1	172
2.	Article 1(1)(b)	173
	Prime Start Ltd. v. Maher Forest Products Ltd.	173
	Notes and Questions	175
	Problem 3-2	176
3.	Other Issues Relating to Scope	176
	Problem 3-3	176
	Problem 3-4	177
	Amco Ukrservice & Prompriladamco v. American Meter Co.	177
	UNCITRAL CLOUT Case 131	181
	UNCITRAL CLOUT Case 122	181
	Notes and Questions	182
4.	Interpreting the CISG: Articles 7–13	183
	Notes and Questions	184
	Problem 3-5	185
	GPL Treatment, Ltd. v. Louisiana-Pacific Corp.	186
	Notes and Questions	186
	Forestal Guarani S.A. v. Daros International Inc.	187
5.	Part II of the CISG: Formation of the Contract	189
	a. The Offer	190
	b. Acceptance, Withdrawal, and Revocation of an Offer	190
	Problem 3-6	191
	Problem 3-7	192
	c. Acceptance	192
	Problem 3-8	194
	Filanto, S.p.A. v. Chilewich International Corp.	195
	Notes and Questions	198
	Problem 3-9	199
	Notes and Questions	200
	d. Formation of the Complex Sales Contract Under the CISG	201
	Problem 3-10	201
	United Technologies International Pratt & Whitney Commercial Engine Business v. Malev Hungarian Airlines	202
	Notes and Questions	205
6.	Performance of the Contract	206
	a. Delivery by Seller	206
	Problem 3-11	206
	Notes and Questions	206
	b. Conforming Goods	207
	Problem 3-12	208
	Problem 3-13	208
	Medical Marketing International, Inc. v. Internazionale Medico Scientifica, S.r.l.	208
	BP Oil International, Ltd. v. Empresa Estatal Petroleos de Ecuador	210
	Notes and Questions	212
	c. Payment by Buyer	212
	Problem 3-14	213
	Problem 3-15	213
	Unilex, D. 1995-1	213

Problem 3-16   213
   d. Excused Performance   214
      (1) Article 79   214
Problem 3-17   215
Tsakiroglou & Co. Ltd. v. Noblee Thorl G.m.b.H.   215
      (2) Performance Delegated to a Third Party   217
Problem 3-18   218
Unilex, D. 1993-3.4   218
Notes and Questions   219
  7.   Remedies   219
    a. Remedies of the Seller   220
Dingxi Longhai Dairy, Ltd. v. Becwood Technology Group, LLC   220
Problem 3-19   221
Notes and Questions   221
Problem 3-20   222
Problem 3-21   222
    b. Remedies of the Buyer   222
Problem 3-22   223
Problem 3-23   223
Problem 3-24   223
Problem 3-25   224
    c. Anticipatory Breach and Installment Contracts   224
Problem 3-26   224
Problem 3-27   224
Notes and Questions   224

4   *Letters of Credit*   **225**

I.   Sources of Letter of Credit Law   225
II.   Letter of Credit Basics   226
Problem 4-1   230
Problem 4-2   230
Problem 4-3   231
Problem 4-4   231
Problem 4-5   231
Problem 4-6   232
III. Basic Principles of Letter of Credit Law   232
  A. The Independence Principle   232
Problem 4-7   232
Urquhart Lindsay and Company, Ltd. v. Eastern Bank, Ltd.   233
Notes and Questions   236
Maurice O'Meara Co. v. National Park Bank of New York   236
Notes and Questions   240
  B. Strict Compliance   241
Problem 4-8   241
J.H. Rayner and Company, Ltd. v. Hambro's Bank, Ltd.   242
Hanil Bank v. PT. Bank Negara Indonesia   246

	Notes and Questions	249
	Problem 4-9	251
	Problem 4-10	251
	Note on Electronic Communications	251
	Problem 4-11	253
C.	The Fraud Exception to the Independence Principle and Enjoining the Letter of Credit	253
	1. The Problem of Fraud	253
	2. Sources of Law	255
	3. Different Types of Innocent Parties	256
	4. Fraud Cases Not Involving Innocent Third Parties	257
	Problem 4-12	258
	Mid-America Tire, Inc. v. PTZ Trading Ltd.	258
	Notes and Questions	265
	5. Enjoining the Standby Letter of Credit	265
	a. The Standby Letter of Credit	265
	b. Sources of Law for the Standby Letter of Credit	267
	Notes and Questions	268
	Problem 4-13	269
	American Bell International, Inc. v. Islamic Republic of Iran	269
	Harris Corporation v. National Iranian Radio & Television	275
	Notes and Questions	280
	Problem 4-14	280

5 *Non-Establishment Forms of International Business: Agency and Distributorships, Technology Transfer, Contract Manufacturing, and Franchising* 283

	Beyond the Sales Transaction	283
	Non-Establishment Forms of Business Abroad	284
I.	Agency and Distributorships	285
A.	Control	286
B.	Competition Law Issues	287
C.	Termination Issues	287
D.	Intellectual Property Issues	289
E.	Other Considerations	289
	Problem 5-1	290
	Problem 5-2	291
	Problem 5-3	291
	1. Local and Regional Legal Requirements	296
	a. German Law	296
	Problem 5-4	297
	German Statutes Relating to Agency Agreements	297
	b. The European Union	300
	Problem 5-5	302
	Problem 5-6	302
	Treaty on the Functioning of the European Union	303

		Commission Regulation (EC) No. 330/2010 on the Application of Article 101(3) of the Treaty to Categories of Vertical Agreements and Concerted Practices	304
		Notes and Questions	306
II.	Technology Transfer and Licensing		307
		Beyond the Agency/Distributorship to Technology Transfer	308
	A.	What Is Technology Transfer and Why Is It Important?	308
		1. Technology Transfer in International Business	309
		2. Intellectual Property and World Economic Development	310
		3. Intellectual Property and Related Topics	311
		Notes and Questions	311
	B.	The International Intellectual Property Legal System	312
		1. Patents	313
		International Patent Treaties	314
		2. Trademarks	316
		International Trademark Treaties	317
		3. Copyright	318
		International Copyright Treaties	319
		4. Know-How and Trade Secrets	320
		International Treaties	321
		Notes and Questions	321
III.	Selected Issues in Licensing: The Patent License Agreement		322
		Problem 5-7	322
		Problem 5-8	322
		Problem 5-9	323
		Problem 5-10	323
		Patent License Agreement	324
		Commission Regulation (EU) No. 316/2014 of 21 March 2014 on the Application of Article 101(3) of the Treaty to Categories of Technology Transfer Agreements	330
		Notes and Questions	333
IV.	Business Format Franchising		334
		Notes and Questions	336
		Problem 5-11	336
		Franchise Agreement	337
		Problem 5-12	343
		Pronuptia de Paris GmbH v. Pronuptia de Paris	343
		Notes and Questions	346

6   *Foreign Direct Investment*   **349**

I.	Introduction		349
	A.	The Decision to Invest: Medtech Reaches a Crossroads	349
		1. Market Penetration	351
		2. Management and Control	351
		3. Intellectual Property	351
		4. Research and Development Abroad	352

	5.	Global Competition	353
	B.	Mergers and Acquisitions (M&A)	353
II.		Global Trends in Foreign Direct Investment	355
	A.	Recent Growth	355
	B.	Role of FDI in Economic Development	356
		Notes and Questions	356
		Problem 6-1	357
III.		International Investment Law	357
	A.	The Traditional Framework for Protecting FDI: The International	
		Court of Justice	358
		Anglo-Iranian Oil Co. Case (U.S. v. Iran)	358
		Case Concerning Barcelona Traction, Light and Power	
		Company (The Barcelona Traction Case) (Belgium v. Spain),	
		Second Phase	359
		Case Concerning Elettronica Sicula S.p.A. (The ELSI Case)	
		(U.S. v. Italy)	360
		Notes and Questions	360
	B.	Multilateral and Bilateral Treaties	362
		Modern International Investment Law: Bilateral Investment	
		Treaties, Free Trade Agreements and Customs Unions, and the	
		Convention on the Settlement of Disputes Between States and	
		Nationals of Other States (the ICSID Convention)	362
		Notes and Questions	366
		Problem 6-2	367
		Lanco International, Inc. v. Argentine Republic	368
		Notes and Questions	374
		Wena Hotels, Ltd. v. Arab Republic of Egypt	374
		Notes and Questions	379
		LG&E Energy Corp., et al. v. Argentine Republic	380
		Notes and Questions	385
		Note on Enforcement of ICSID Awards	386
	C.	An Example of a Regional Trade Agreement: NAFTA	387
		Marvin Feldman v. Mexico	389
		Notes and Questions	395
		Problem 6-3	396
	D.	Investment and the World Trade Organization	397
		Notes and Questions	399
IV.		Limits in Corporate Conduct in International Investment: The Foreign	
		Corrupt Practices Act	399
		Problem 6-4	400
		Problem 6-5	401
		Problem 6-6	401
	A.	Overview of the FCPA	401
		1. Persons Subject to the FCPA	402
		2. Nexus with Intestate Commerce	402
		3. Corrupt Intent	403
		4. Proscribed Payments	403
		5. Persons to Whom Payments Are Made	403
		6. Purpose of the Payment	403
		Notes on the OECD Bribery Convention and Other International	
		Treaties	403

Notes and Questions 404
B. Basic Issues Under the FCPA 405
Problem 6-7 405
United States v. Kay 405
Stichting Ter behartiging Van de Belangen Van Oudaandeelhouders
in Het Kapitaal Van Saybolt International B.V. v. Schreiber 413
Problem 6-8 419
United States v. Kozeny 419
Notes and Questions 422
Note on the U.S. Foreign Investment and National Security
Act of 2007 422
V. The Transactional Aspects of FDI: Establishment in the European Union,
China, and Brazil 423
A. Introduction 423
Conceptual Outline and Checklist of Foreign Direct
Investment Issues 425
B. Foreign Investment in the European Union 427
1. Access to the Internal Market of the EU: The Four Freedoms 427
Problem 6-9 428
Rewe-Zentral AG v. Bundesmonopolverwaltung für Branntwein 428
Notes and Questions 430
Problem 6-10 430
Centros Ltd. v. Erhvervs-og Selskabsstyrelsen 431
Notes and Questions 432
Note on Protection of Intellectual Property in the EU 433
2. Establishment in the EU 433
Problem 6-11 433
An Overview of Company Establishment in Three European
Legal Systems: The United Kingdom, France, and Germany 434
Note on Employee Co-determination in Management Issues
in France and Germany 437
Notes and Questions 438
3. EU Competition Law Affecting Foreign Direct Investment 439
a. Abuse of a Dominant Position 440
Problem 6-12 441
United Brands Company v. Commission of the European Communities 442
Microsoft Corp. v. Commission of the European Communities 445
Notes and Questions 450
b. The EC Merger Regulation 451
Tetra Laval BV v. Commission of the European Communities 452
Notes and Questions 455
Note on the Extraterritorial Application of EU Competition Law 456
C. Foreign Direct Investment in China 457
1. China's Economic System 457
Daniel C.K. Chow, *The Legal System of the People's Republic of*
China in a Nutshell 457
Notes and Questions 463
2. China's FDI Legal Regime and Foreign Investment Business
Vehicles 464
a. The Joint Venture 464
b. The Wholly Foreign-Owned Enterprise 465

			Notes and Questions	465
			Note on a Gamble by an MNE That Paid Off	465
	3.		Establishing the Joint Venture	466
		a.	Approval Process	466
			Problem 6-13	467
		b.	Capital Investment	468
		c.	Management Structure	468
			Problem 6-14	469
			Problem 6-15	469
			Problem 6-16	470
			Problem 6-17	470
			Problem 6-18	471
			PRC Equity Joint Venture Law (2001)	471
			Equity Joint Venture Law Implementing Regulations	472
			Joint Venture Contract Between Beijing Seagull Detergent Group Corp. and Acme (China), Ltd.	474
			Notes and Questions	490
D.			Foreign Direct Investment in Brazil	492
	1.		Brazil's Approach to FDI	493
		a.	Policy Objectives	494
		b.	Some Background Economic History and Considerations	494
		c.	The Enactment of the Profits Remittance Law	496
	2.		The Business Climate in Brazil	497
			Problem 6-19	497
			Brazil's Environment for Doing Business and for Foreign Direct Investment	497
	3.		Brazilian Laws Relating to Foreign Direct Investment and Business Organizations	509
		a.	Brazilian Business Organizations	509
			Problem 6-20	509
			Overview of Business Entities Available for Use in Foreign Direct Investment in Brazil	510
		b.	Brazilian Laws Applicable to Foreign Direct Investment	513
			Problem 6-21	513
			Problem 6-22	514
			Profits Remittance Law	514
			Notes and Questions	520
			Note on Sovereign Debt Collection	521

7 *Protecting Intellectual Property Rights* 525

I.			Overview of Commercial Piracy	526
	A.		Rise in Commercial Piracy	526
			Problem 7-1	528
	B.		Categories of Commercial Piracy	529
		1.	Copyright Piracy	529
			Notes and Questions	531
		2.	Trademark Counterfeiting	532

		Notes and Questions	534
	3.	Patent Infringements	534
		Notes and Questions	535
C.	Counterfeiting and Commercial Piracy in China		537
		Statement of Professor Daniel Chow Before the Senate	
		Government Oversight and Management Subcommittee	537
		Notes and Questions	538
		Problem 7-2	540
		Problem 7-3	542
		Problem 7-4	542
		Daniel C.K. Chow, *Organized Crime, Local Protectionism,*	
		and the Trade in Counterfeit Goods in China	543
		Notes and Questions	551
		Note on Responses by MNEs and Foreign Governments	552
		Problem 7-5	552
II.	TRIPs and the Protection of Intellectual Property Rights		553
A.	Intellectual Property, TRIPs, and the WTO		553
		Notes and Questions	555
B.	Enforcement Obligations Under TRIPs Against Commercial Piracy		555
	1.	General Enforcement Obligations	555
		Notes and Questions	556
	2.	Provisional Measures	557
		Problem 7-6	558
C.	TRIPs and the Access to Medicines Debate		558
		Notes and Questions	563
		Problem 7-7	564
D.	TRIPs and the Biopiracy Debate		564
		Problem 7-8	566
		Problem 7-9	566
III.	Gray-Market Goods and Parallel Imports		566
A.	What Are Gray-Market Goods and Parallel Imports?		567
		Notes and Questions	568
B.	Gray-Market Goods Under U.S. Law		568
		Problem 7-10	571
		K-Mart Corp. v. Cartier, Inc.	571
		Lever Brothers Co. v. United States	574
		Notes and Questions	576
		Problem 7-11	577
		Quality King Distributors, Inc. v. L'anza Research International, Inc.	577
		Kirtsaeng v. John Wiley & Sons, Inc.	580
		Notes and Questions	584

| **8** | ***Dispute Resolution*** | **587** |

I.	Introduction		587
		Overview of International Business Dispute Resolution Issues	587
		Preliminary Issues	588

		Choice of Forum		588
		Choice of Law		589
		Jurisdiction		589
		Sovereign Immunity and the Act of State Doctrine		590
		Resolving Preliminary Issues by Agreement		591
		Dispute Resolution Other Than by Litigation		591
		Other Issues		593
II.	Arbitration			593
	A.	Choosing Arbitration		593
		Susan Karamanian, *The Road to the Tribunal and Beyond: International Commercial Arbitration and the United States Courts*		594
		Note on Expanding Grounds to Vacate Arbitration Awards		597
		Negotiating and Structuring International Arbitration Transactions, Using Model Arbitration Clauses, and Practical Matters in Arbitration		597
		Notes and Questions		600
	B.	Enforcing the Agreement to Arbitrate		601
		Problem 8-1		601
		Mitsubishi Motors Corp. v. Soler Chrysler-Plymouth, Inc.		602
		Notes and Questions		607
	C.	Judicial Review and Enforcement of the Award		607
		Problem 8-2		607
		Problem 8-3		608
		Polytek Engineering Co., Ltd. v. Jacobson Companies		608
		Stolt-Nielsen SA v. AnimalFeeds Int'l Corp.		612
		Stolt-Nielsen SA v. AnimalFeeds International Corporation		617
		Notes and Questions		619
III.	Litigation			619
	A.	Choice of Forum		621
		Problem 8-4		621
		M/S Bremen v. Zapata Off-Shore Co.		622
		Gita Sports Ltd. v. SG Sensortechnik GmbH & Co. KG		626
		Notes and Questions		630
		Problem 8-5		631
		Problem 8-6		631
		Problem 8-7		632
		Note on the Hague Convention on Choice of Court Agreements		632
	B.	Choice of Law		633
		1.	Choice of Law Approaches	634
			Amco Ukrservice v. American Meter Co.	634
			Notes and Questions	638
		2.	Choice of Law Clauses	639
			Problem 8-8	639
			Problem 8-9	639
			The Restatement (Second) of Conflict of Laws (1971)	640
			Notes and Questions	640
	C.	Jurisdiction		641
		1.	International Law	641
			Kathleen Hixson, *Extraterritorial Jurisdiction Under the Third Restatement of Foreign Relations Law of the United States*	641
			Notes and Questions	643

2. Adjudicative Jurisdiction: Subject Matter and Territorial
  Jurisdiction 644
    Problem 8-10 645
    Asahi Metal Indus. Co., Ltd. v. Superior Court 646
    Goodyear Dunlop Tires Operations, S.A. v. Brown 651
    Glencore Grain Rotterdam B.V. v. Shivnath Rai Harnarain Co. ... 653
    Notes and Questions 656
3. Sovereign Immunity 657
    Problem 8-11 658
    In re Arbitration Between: Trans Chem. Ltd. & China Nat'l Mach.
      Import & Export Corp. 658
    Note on Restrictive Immunity 660
4. The Act of State Doctrine 661
    Problem 8-12 661
    Optopics Lab. Corp. v. Savannah Bank of Nigeria, Ltd. 661
    FOGADE v. ENB Revocable Trust 665
    Notes and Questions 667
    Problem 8-13 668
5. International Comity and *Forum Non Conveniens* 668
    DeYoung v. Beddome 668
    Notes and Questions 672
6. Service of Process 673
    Conax Florida Corp. v. Astrium Ltd. 673
    Notes and Questions 676
7. Jurisdiction over Parent and Affiliated Companies 677
    Problem 8-14 677
    Itel Containers Int'l Corp. v. Atlanttrafik Express Serv. Ltd. ... 678
    Notes and Questions 682
    Problem 8-15 682
8. Conflicts of Jurisdiction: Multiple Proceedings in Different Forums ... 683
    Goss International Corp. v. Man Roland Druckmachinen AG ... 683
    Notes and Questions 686
    Finanz AG Zurich v. Banco Economico S.A. 686
    Ibeto Petrochemical Indus. Ltd. v. M/T Beffen 690
    Notes and Questions 693
D. Evidence and Discovery 694
  1. Obtaining Evidence Abroad 694
    Problem 8-16 694
    Tulip Computers Int'l B.V. v. Dell Computer Corp. 695
    Notes and Questions 698
  2. Obtaining Evidence in the United States for Use in Foreign
    Courts 699
    In re Clerici 699
    Notes and Questions 702
E. Recognition and Foreign Enforcement of Foreign Judgments ... 703
    Problem 8-17 703
    Somportex Ltd. v. Philadelphia Chewing Gum Corp. 704
    Society of Lloyd's v. Siemon-Netto 708
    Notes and Questions 711

| 9 | *Corporate Social Responsibility* | **713** |

I.	Introduction	713
	Problem 9-1	713
	Problem 9-2	714
	Jonathan I. Charney, *Transnational Corporations and Developing*	
	Public International Law	714
	Jordan J. Paust, *Human Rights Responsibilities of Private Corporations*	715
	Doe I v. Wal-Mart Stores, Inc.	719
	Notes and Questions	722
	Problem 9-3	723
II.	Codes and Standards of Conduct	724
	Problem 9-4	724
	Problem 9-5	724
	Organization for Economic Cooperation and Development:	
	The OECD Guidelines for Multinational Enterprises, 2011	725
	Note on Implementation of the OECD Guidelines for	
	Multinational Enterprises	729
	Note on the "Polluter Pays Principle" as the Basis of	
	Encouraging Multinational Companies to Engage in	
	Sustainable Development	730
	Problem 9-6	732
	Instituting a Corporate Environmental and Safety	
	Management System	732
	Environmental Liability Disclosure Obligations of	
	Public Companies	735
	Notes and Questions	736
	A Guide for the Perplexed: Creating a CSR Program for	
	Your Company	737
III.	Exporting Hazard: Legal and Ethical Considerations	737
	Problem 9-7	737
	H. Jeffrey Leonard, *Confronting Industrial Pollution in Rapidly*	
	Industrializing Countries: Myths, Pitfalls, and Opportunities	738
	Maureen A. Bent, *Exporting Hazardous Industries: Should*	
	American Standards Apply?	739
	Treaties Restricting Trade in Hazardous Materials	740
	Organization for Economic Cooperation and Development:	
	Council Recommendation on the Application of the Polluter-Pays	
	Principle to Accidental Pollution	741
	Note on U.S. Controls on Exports of Hazardous Wastes	742
	Notes and Questions	743
IV.	Liability for Industrial Accidents	743
	Problem 9-8	743
	Stephen C. McCaffrey, *Accidents Do Happen: Hazardous*	
	Technology and International Tort Litigation	744
	Problem 9-9	745
	In re Union Carbide Corp. Gas Plant Disaster at Bhopal,	
	India in December 1984	745

	Shyam Divan and Armin Rosencranz, *The Bhopal Settlement*	748
	Note on the Bhopal Settlement and Its Tortuous Aftermath	752
	Notes and Questions	753
V.	The U.S. Alien Tort Statute	754
	Abdullahi v. Pfizer, Inc.	756
	Kiobel v. Royal Dutch Petroleum Company	763
	Notes and Questions	765

Table of Cases   767
Index   773

Preface to the Third Edition

We take pleasure in offering our colleagues and friends and law and business students an updated third edition of our book, *International Business Transactions: Problems, Cases, and Materials*. Our purpose remains to offer in the most compact format possible primary materials on the laws of international business operating in our increasingly complex world. In the years since the publication of the second edition there have been many new developments, which we try our best to include in this edition, but the overall framework of the law remains the same. Thus users of this book will find much that is familiar, but we have endeavored to update all the chapters of the book.

We continue to believe—more than ever—that law students interested in business law are remiss if they do not take a course in international business transactions law. International business operations are no longer exotic or uncommon. Virtually all business enterprises now engage or will engage in some international activities, and there is no bright line distinction between domestic and international business ventures. Thus, the law or business student and practicing lawyers need familiarity with the expanding corpus of relevant international laws and practices businesses must cope with in their international operations.

For pedagogical reasons in this book we distinguish international business transactions law from international trade law, which we cover in a companion book, Chow and Schoenbaum, *International Trade Law: Problems, Cases, and Materials* (2d ed. 2012). We believe that international business law, which is mainly private international law and the international dimensions of private law, is conceptually distinct from international trade law, which is mainly public international law. Despite the fact that the practicing lawyer may deal in cases that combine both trade and transactional law, we believe it is confusing for law students to study both of these subjects together in the same course. In addition, the corpus of law in both these areas is now so vast that it is impossible to cover them both in a single course. Of course in this book we do cover a modicum of trade law, especially customs law, which is essential to import and export sales of goods.

We include in this edition, as in prior editions, many short problems that are designed to allow the student to apply his or her knowledge of international business law to concrete situations. We have designed the materials and the problems to fit together so the book will function as a learning tool. We believe, however, that the materials stand on their own, so the instructor has the flexibility to omit some or all of the problems or to substitute his or her own problems for ours.

We also include in this edition an updated Document Supplement that is designed to be used in conjunction with the Casebook itself.

We are always happy to receive comments from colleagues or students on how we can further improve this book as a learning tool.

Dan Chow
Ohio State University School of Law
Email: chow.1@osu.edu

Thomas J. Schoenbaum
University of Washington School of Law
Email: tjschoen@uw.edu

Acknowledgments

"Accidents Do Happen: Hazardous Technology and International Tort Litigations," by Stephen C. McCaffrey, 1 The Transnational Lawyer 41 (1988). Reprinted with the permission of the University of the Pacific McGeorge Law Review and the author.

"The Bhopal Settlement," by Shyam Divan and Armin Rosencranz, 1989 Environmental and Policy, 166. Reprinted with the permission of IOS Press B.V. and the authors.

"Confronting Industrial Pollution in Rapidly Industrializing Countries: Myths, Pitfalls and Opportunities," by H. Jeffrey Leonard, 12 Ecology Law Quarterly (1985). Reprinted with the permission of the Regents of the University of California and the author.

"Council Recommendation of the Application of the Polluter-Pays Principle to Accidental Pollution," Organization for Economic Co-operation and Development, 28 I.L.M. 1320 (1989). Reprinted with the permission of the American Society of International Law.

Exporting Hazardous Industries: Should American Standards Apply? By Maureen A. Bent, 20 NYU J. Int'l L. & Politics, 777, 78-81 (1988). Journal of International Law and Politics. Reprinted with the permission of the NYU Journal of International Law and Politics.

"Extraterritorial Jurisdiction Under the Third Restatement of the Foreign Relations Law of the United States," by Kathleen Hixson, 12 Fordham L. Rev. 127, 129-37. Reprinted with the permission of the author.

"Human Rights Responsibilities of Private Corporations," by Jordan J. Paust, 35 Vanderbilt Journal of Transnational Law, 801, 802-12 (2002). Reprinted with the permission of the Vanderbilt University Law School.

Lanco v. Argentine Republic, 40 ILM 457 (2001) March 2001, Vol. XL, pp. 457-473.

"The Legal System of the People's Republic of China in a Nutshell," by Daniel C.K. Chow — excerpt (words only) and p. 33—Chart: GDP of Top Ten Countries. Reprinted with the permission of Thomson West and the author.

LG&E Energy Corp. v. Argentine Republic, 46 ILM 40 (2007) January 2007 Vol. 46, pp. 40-76.

Marvin Feldman v. Mexico, 42 ILM 625 (2003).

"The OECD Guidelines for Multinational Enterprises," Organization for Economic Cooperation and Development 2011 Edition, OECD Publishing.

"The Road to the Tribunal and Beyond: International Arbitration and the United States," by Susan Karamanian, 34 George Washington International L. Review 17, 19-21. Reprinted with the permission of the George Washington University.

"The Role of Organized, Crime, Local Protectionism and the Trade in Counterfeit Goods in China," by Daniel C.K. Chow, Text pp. 473-481, Table p. 482, Map p. 477. Reprinted with the permission of Elsevier Science and the author.

"Transnational Corporations and Developing Public International Law," by Jonathan Charney, Duke L.J. 748, 762-69 (1983). Reprinted with the permission of the Duke University School of Law.

Wena Hotels Ltd. v. Arab Republic of Egypt (ICSID Case No. ARB/98/4), p. 129, 41 ILM 881 (2002).

International
Business Transactions

1   *Introduction*

We first discuss the scope of this book and the major themes of the developing field of international business transactions that we will be exploring in subsequent chapters.

I.   *Some Background Considerations*

A.   Scope and Approach of This Book

International business transactions (IBTs) are private business transactions that are international in character. The international element exists when the parties have their places of business in different nation-states; when these transactions involve the movement of goods, services, technology, or capital across the boundaries of different nations; or when transactions between parties of one state have a direct effect in a different state.

    IBTs may be categorized, at least in general terms, according to the extent of penetration in international markets. The first level of penetration is a simple export-import transaction, for example, a sale of goods involving a seller from the United States and a buyer from Germany. If this is successful and the company finds a sufficient demand for its products, the seller may establish an agent in Germany or a distributor of its products who will attempt to increase the seller's penetration of the targeted markets. After this step, the U.S. seller may decide to engage in contract manufacturing, the third level of penetration. This can involve licensing a German entity to manufacture its products in Germany for sale and distribution in Germany and other European countries. A significant issue in such a licensing transaction is technology transfer because the seller will need to allow the German manufacturer some access to the seller's intellectual property rights. Alternatively, or after the term of the licensing agreement, the U.S. seller may decide to set up its own operations in Germany by establishing a business entity of which it is the sole or part owner. The U.S. seller would have the choice of setting up its own operations from scratch by establishing a German subsidiary or of buying an existing German business entity. In either case, this would be what is termed "foreign direct investment."

    If there is sufficient demand for the U.S. company's products, not only in Germany and Europe, but around the world, our imaginary U.S. company may employ similar strategies in many nations. If it is successful, our company will become a world-class business known as a multinational enterprise (MNE). A similar scenario would exist if the seller in the example above were selling services, such as financial services or insurance, instead of products.

    This book will examine all of these transactions and trace this progression from the simple contract of sale to the establishment of foreign direct investment. Of course, each IBT has its own particular character, and real IBTs are variations on the themes just described. Nevertheless, we believe this progression is a useful way of studying the subject in an academic setting. After this introductory chapter provides some background considerations, the next five chapters of this book will trace this progression. Chapters Two, Three, and Four concern the international sales transaction and Chapters Five and Six examine agency/distributorships, contract manufacturing, and foreign direct investment. Although we weave intellectual property issues into most of the earlier chapters, we devote all of Chapter Seven to the protection of intellectual property rights, an issue of fundamental importance in international business today. Chapter Eight then turns to dispute resolution in an international business context. Finally, Chapter Nine concerns corporate social responsibility and examines the obligations of MNEs concerning issues of human rights, labor conditions, and the environment.

The transactions that are the focus of this book are private transactions that affect the interests of private or nongovernmental parties. The parties to most of the transactions examined in this book are business entities, companies, or MNEs. We want to distinguish the transactions that are the subject of this book from international transactions that affect public rights (such as where government entities engage in business activity that may affect the rights of its citizens as a whole) and the rights of other nations (such as when one nation engages in the sale of military equipment to another or when one nation assists another in rebuilding its economy and industry after some calamity, such as war).

The IBTs that we examine in this book not only involve private parties but they also involve areas of commerce traditionally deemed as areas of private law such as contracts, property, and torts. Public laws that affect IBTs such as antitrust, securities, customs, exchange controls, and general economic regulation will be discussed by way of background but will not be the focus of this book. One of the hallmarks of private law is that the parties have the freedom to contractually alter private law rights and obligations. By contrast, public laws are generally mandatory in nature and do not permit parties to alter their impact or effect. The distinction between private and public law brings us to another important point about the focus and orientation of this book.

We want to distinguish the scope and subject matter of this book from another field, international trade law or international economic law. While this field is related to the field of IBT that is the subject matter of this book, we believe that it is fruitful to view international business transactions and international trade/economic law as separate although related fields that should be the subject of separate courses in the law school curriculum. International trade/economic law concerns the attempts by nations, acting in their sovereign capacities, to regulate economic and commercial activity between themselves and the conduct of such activity by their nationals through mandatory public laws. For example, export and import controls such as customs classifications, quotas, tariffs, and other customs controls belong to the field of international trade/economic law. Laws governing unfair trade practices that allow importing nations to impose sanctions on unfairly priced imports also belong to the field of international trade law. The principal organization that is involved in the regulation of international trade/economics is the World Trade Organization (WTO), with its headquarters in Geneva, Switzerland. Another important body in the regulation of international trade is the European Union (EU), consisting of 28 states (as of this writing), including virtually all the nations of western and central Europe. On trade and economic issues, the EU is charged with the complete economic integration of its member economies by eliminating all trade barriers and by adopting a common economic policy, including customs duties, with respect to nonmember states. While we consider the WTO, the EU, and other international and regional economic institutions in this book and how they impact the private transactions that are the subject of this book, these institutions will not be our focus as in a course on international trade law. Of course, international trade law is an important course of study in its own right. To this end, we have authored a separate casebook, Chow and Schoenbaum, *International Trade Law: Problems, Cases, and Materials* (Aspen 2d ed. 2012), which treats the field of international trade law in detail and is intended as the international trade law companion to this book.

To be sure, we do cover topics relating to international trade law in this book and some of this coverage will be in depth because all IBTs operate against the background of international trade and economic regulation. In many chapters, we blend and interweave topics of international trade law into our materials on private transactions. Our approach is to select those topics of international trade law that are most immediate and pertinent as the necessary background for understanding the progression of topics that we cover: the sales contract, distribution, licensing, and foreign direct investment. However, our coverage of international trade is selective as it is for the primary purpose of understanding the private transaction.

To give you a sense of how we use and select international trade law topics in this book, consider that in our coverage of the international sales transaction we cover the importer's compliance with U.S. customs laws, a trade law topic, in detail. We believe that this is the trade law topic that is most closely connected to the transactional issues related to the sale of goods and that affects the IBT practitioner at a micro level on a day-to-day basis. Our assumption is that when our students go on to represent one of the parties in an international sale they are most likely to represent a U.S. party. The trade law issues of most importance to the U.S. party will generally occur when the U.S. party is the buyer-importer. The buyer must satisfy U.S. customs laws, which will determine the amount of the tax or customs duty that must be paid by the buyer-importer. As the amount of duty that must be paid is a significant issue for most buyers, we cover this topic in depth. On the other hand, we believe that the trade law issues are generally less complex when the U.S. party is the seller. In this case, the U.S. seller must comply with U.S. export controls and related laws, but these issues are generally less complex so we cover this topic in less detail. Our approach to treating the trade law issues in a sales transaction reflects how we treat the trade law issues in all of the areas covered in this book: We cover selected trade law materials that are most important to the private transaction.

We believe that a book focusing on the private business transaction against a carefully selected set of materials relating to international trade law offers enough substance and challenges for a separate course. We also believe that a fruitful course of study for the student interested in international business law would be a course on IBT followed by a separate, advanced course on international trade law. This casebook along with its companion book, Chow and Schoenbaum, *International Trade Law: Problems, Cases, and Materials* (Aspen 2d ed. 2012), are designed to be a complete and concise package for the study of international business law as far as these vast and complicated fields can be studied in law schools.

NOTE ON IBT AND INTERNATIONAL TRADE LEGAL SKILLS

As the fields of international business transactions and international trade law are different, will a lawyer practicing in both fields need different skills? If so, how do the skills necessary for IBTs differ from those necessary for international trade law issues? In IBTs, the focus is on *negotiating, structuring, and implementing* transactions against a background of private laws that allow for bargains altering rights and obligations by contract.

The party sitting across the table is usually another private party. In international trade law, the focus is on *compliance* with mandatory public laws, and the party that one normally deals with is a governmental authority with regulatory and enforcement powers. Both types of skills are necessary to help clients take full advantage of business opportunities.

B. Counsel in International Business

We now consider the role of the lawyer in IBTs. It should not be surprising that the growth of international business and trade of all kinds in the latter part of the twentieth century and the first part of the twenty-first century has also transformed the legal profession. As MNEs expand abroad, many will require their company lawyers to spend extended assignments overseas and advise their overseas businesses. As many of the world's most successful law firms have MNEs as their clients and as their clients have expanded their reach around the world, law firms have also expanded their capabilities and offices in order to meet their clients' changing needs. We are now in the era of the multinational law firm as many firms believe that it is essential to have international capability in order to compete in the global marketplace. Some of the world's largest law firms have branch offices around the world similar to those of MNEs.

1. Issues Faced by Lawyers

The issues confronting a lawyer in IBTs can be divided into two categories: issues of competence and issues of ethics. No lawyer can be expected to be competent in all of the legal issues that can arise from IBTs. A lawyer will often be faced with foreign laws and foreign languages. How should the lawyer best advise his or her clients in this situation? Where the lawyer is a partner in a law firm, the client is often an MNE; where the lawyer is "in-house" counsel, the client is usually top management such as the chief executive officer or a vice president of a business division. The role of the lawyer in these situations may be to manage a group of local foreign lawyers and experts.

Issues of ethics can be complex in an international setting. Most nations, including the United States, have codes of professional ethics for lawyers. In an international setting, one issue is whether the lawyer is subject to the ethics rules of the foreign nation in which the client is doing business. How should the lawyer advise a client when dealing with a culture in which corruption is rampant and where bribery of government officials and private parties is commonplace? Does a lawyer have any duty to consider larger economic and political issues in representing MNEs that are doing business in a developing (poor) nation? These are also issues that we will be exploring in this book.

2. Role of Counsel for an MNE

As the most important actors in IBTs today are MNEs, as further discussed in Section IV.B of this chapter, we now provide an overview of the legal department of an MNE and the work and challenges of an in-house lawyer. Our hypothetical MNE is Acme, an MNE based in the United States and engaged in the consumer products business around the world. Acme has a large legal department headed by a general counsel. Large companies have in-house lawyers because these lawyers, as employees of the company, are viewed as being more loyal and as having a greater familiarity with company business. Many companies like to know that a business manager can simply walk down the hall and chat with a company lawyer or pick up the phone and ask a lawyer to attend a meeting or to answer a question. Business managers are less likely to enjoy this level of service or have such access to legal services if they must depend only on outside law firms.

Today, the general counsel may be called the "global general counsel" to reflect the realities of the modern corporation. Most general counsels are members of the elite top-management group of the MNE and are at the level of a vice president or senior vice president of the corporation, which is usually one level below that of the most senior executives (often called presidents who head up entire important regions or business units of the company, such as "President of Acme, North America" where geographical divisions are used or "President, Acme Hair Care" where business divisions are used). Presidents are usually one level below and the general counsel is usually two levels below the chief executive officer.

In most companies the legal department is viewed as "support" because the main business of the MNE is the product or service that it sells. The main business of Nike is producing athletic shoes and sports apparel and the main business of Coca-Cola is producing soft drinks; the role of their legal departments is to provide support for the main business of the company. This is one major distinction between an in-house lawyer and a lawyer at a law firm where the main business of the company is providing legal services.

The reporting structure for in-house lawyers is generally divided along two lines. On legal work, in-house lawyers often report to business managers. The general counsel would report to presidents of regions or business departments and to the CEO. Each lawyer would also report functionally to his or her superior in the legal department hierarchy with the general counsel at the top.

Our hypothetical MNE has a U.S. headquarters where the global general counsel will be located. In addition, the MNE has regional general counsels, such as a "General Counsel, Asia-Pacific" or a "General Counsel, Europe." These lawyers report to the global general counsel and are one level below the general counsel (but who aspire to attain that position eventually) and are either vice presidents or directors. A country with major business operations will also have a country general counsel, who is generally one level below the regional general counsel in the hierarchy (e.g., "General Counsel, Greater China"). A country general counsel is usually a director or an associate director within the company. The country general counsel will have a legal staff of lawyers who are senior counsels or below.

To give you a sense of the legal work of an in-house lawyer, let's take a look at the work of the legal department of Acme-China, our hypothetical foreign investment enterprise in China that is further examined in Chapter Six on foreign direct investment. Acme is a world-class company that manufactures famous brands of shampoo, soap, skin lotion, cosmetics, and other household products for the booming China market. China's growing middle class seems to have an insatiable appetite for premium international brands. Acme has an in-house legal department in China. What are the types of tasks that these lawyers are expected to undertake?

Acme's lawyers in the China legal department had helped to set up the initial joint ventures engaged in the various consumer products industries by drafting the legal documents when Acme first entered the China market. For the very first joint venture established by Acme in the late 1980s, Acme hired an international law firm to draft the joint venture documents and to work with Acme in securing all of the approvals required by China's government authorities. After the first joint venture, Acme's in-house lawyers in China had acquired a set of joint venture documents and familiarity with the approval process, so Acme's management then internalized all of this work to save on costs. Recently, Acme's lawyers have advised management to eschew forming joint ventures with local Chinese partners in favor of establishing wholly foreign-owned enterprises (WFOEs).

(For a detailed discussion of the joint venture, WFOE, and various business entities in China, see pp. 464-465.)

Although Acme's joint ventures and WFOEs are now well established in China, Acme must still have contacts with China's many government authorities on a regular basis and the contacts are usually done through the legal department, which is designated as the single point of contact within the company (although sometimes the government affairs department is also involved). Acme's joint ventures, although given managerial autonomy by law, are still formally under the supervision of a government authority with regulatory power over Acme's industry. Acme must file reports with supervisory authorities once a quarter on its business activities and must regularly consult with tax authorities on the amount of the company's tax liabilities and submit tax invoices to the government. All of these contacts between Acme and Chinese authorities will be conducted through the legal department. As Acme is planning to establish new joint ventures in other product lines, to reorganize and combine some of its joint ventures as wholly foreign-owned subsidiaries of Acme, and to increase the capital of some of its existing joint ventures, Acme's lawyers are very busy meeting with Acme-China's managers to review and plan all of these changes. Acme's lawyers must also meet with Chinese government authorities on a regular basis to keep them apprised of the planned changes, as their approval is needed. Chinese authorities will also provide Acme with their input on whether such changes are feasible and how to structure the transactions. All of this work, of course, requires that Acme's lawyers be intimately familiar with China's laws, legal system, and political system. While Acme's lawyers can now handle most issues, they occasionally seek help from outside law firms and accounting firms on issues that require special expertise, such as tax or reorganization and merger issues.

As Acme is an aggressive and ambitious company, it is always offering new products for the China market and actively promoting existing products. Acme's legal department needs to file new trademark applications with China's national trademark authorities for each new brand that is introduced and for each new variation on an existing trademark, which the marketing department is constantly proposing as it changes the style and appearance of the products to keep them fresh and appealing to changing consumer tastes. Where products involve new patents, Acme's lawyers must also file patent applications with China's national patent authority. Acme's legal department also works closely with the marketing department, which is organized with brand managers in charge of each brand such as Seagull Shampoo. Acme's brand managers work closely with international advertising agencies to promote new commercials, and Acme's in-house lawyers must review all advertising to see that it complies with China's stringent advertising laws. The legal department also works with the marketing department to secure approvals from China's Ministry of Telecommunications in Beijing for all new television commercials. Acme's lawyers also review sales and purchasing contracts from their purchasing department, which must buy a large amount of raw materials from local suppliers in order to manufacture its products. In addition, Acme's lawyers are busy offering advice to Acme-China's human resources department on the many personnel and labor issues that arise on a daily basis.

Acme also currently has a serious commercial piracy problem in China as many counterfeit Acme products have appeared on the market. Acme's in-house lawyers protect their intellectual property rights by hiring private investigation companies and outside law firms specializing in intellectual property to pursue counterfeiters and enforcement actions. Counterfeiting in China is a major problem that we will examine in detail in Chapter Seven.

3. Challenges for the International Lawyer

The picture presented above shows Acme's lawyers and its business managers working busily and harmoniously and as a team in promoting Acme's business and earning profits, but there are opportunities for conflicts and challenges in the workplace as well. One of the important tasks of Acme's lawyers is to ensure that Acme is in compliance with all of China's laws and this may involve reining in some of the more aggressive tactics of Acme's business managers. This role sometimes casts the company in-house lawyer in the role of a "naysayer" who is perceived as always saying "no" and bringing negative news to the company's business managers. In some companies, lawyers may even be disliked by the business departments if they are viewed as too risk averse and as constantly creating obstacles to business plans or frustrating the "can't miss" strategies of an up-and-coming star manager.

Of course, in-house lawyers occasionally experience similar conflicts with business departments in a domestic setting as well, but these conflicts can be especially acute in an international setting. Business managers who are assigned abroad are usually given three- to five-year assignments with the understanding that a promotion awaits them after a successful performance there and a return to the MNE's headquarters in the United States. Managers are judged on what they have accomplished, that is, how many new joint ventures they have established, how many new products were introduced, and how much sales revenues have increased during their assignments. These business managers feel pressure to perform and produce within a short period of time during their overseas assignment, which is now often considered to be critical for long-term advancement within many corporations. Some business managers have been tempted to pursue very aggressive strategies, knowing that they will be rewarded when their assignment is over and that problems with their risky strategies may not arise until years later—long after they have departed the foreign branch and have been promoted. In this situation, conflict can arise between ambitious business managers who seek business results (and professional advancement within the company) and the in-house lawyer whose job is to protect the company from unnecessary risks.

Another reason for greater potential conflict in the international workplace is that often the laws of developing countries are incomplete or unclear and the legal system less than predictable. For example, like that of many other developing countries, China's legal system contains many gaps and ambiguities and is subject to rapid change. There are many gray areas in China's legal system where the legality of certain actions is subject to legitimately differing opinions and where, as a result, risk is more difficult to assess. But China is not alone in having an undeveloped legal system. The lack of a mature, predictable legal system and the general absence of the rule of law are common problems in developing countries all over the world. Conducting business in an environment that lacks a mature legal system can give rise to greater uncertainty and more frequent and serious disagreements on the degree of risk involved than in a developed legal system, such as that of the United States.

A developing country's lack of a mature legal system also creates challenges in dealing with local foreign lawyers. For example, in China the ranks of the legal profession have increased dramatically with the opening up of China to foreign business and trade in 1978. The prospect of undreamed-of riches for the elite of the legal profession, intense competition for a handful of multinational clients, and a nascent awareness of legal ethics all contribute to a professional environment in which sharp practices and improper conduct are all too common. For many Chinese lawyers, the goal is to achieve the result desired by the client by whatever means necessary so as to retain the client's business rather than to use independent judgment to offer candid and objective legal advice that may not always be what the client wants to hear. Using illegal tactics such as bribing a judge, a prosecutor, or other government officials without the client's knowledge is made easier in a legal environment that is often inaccessible to foreign clients. Lacking Chinese language skills and contacts within the Chinese legal system, many foreign clients have no means to independently check on the work done by local lawyers. Of course, these issues are not unique to China by any means. Issues of legal and business ethics are common problems in developing countries.

NOTES AND QUESTIONS

1. Large law firms are routinely engaged in international transactions and some firms have branch offices in many different countries. While a typical large firm may have separate departments for corporate, tax, intellectual property, and litigation, these firms generally do not have an international business transactions department. Why? Which department handles international business transactions?

2. Given the realities of law firm practice, would you counsel law students to present themselves to law firms as aspiring IBT lawyers?

PROBLEM 1-1

Foreign investment laws in China currently provide that applications to establish joint ventures with a capital investment of over $100 million in certain industries must be submitted to the Ministry of Commerce (MOFCOM) in Beijing for approval. Joint ventures with investments below $100 million can be approved at the local level. In the 1990s, some local approval authorities began the practice of allowing joint venture applicants to split a single application to establish a joint venture of over their approval limit into two or more applications on the theory that local approval is legal so long as each application is under the approval limit. The local authorities allowed the splitting of applications even though all of the applications really concerned a single joint venture and even though the total capital invested in the joint venture that was finally established was over their approval limit. Some lawyers viewed this tactic as an artifice to circumvent central-level requirements, but many parties favored this approach because it avoided an application to Beijing with all of the delays and more intense scrutiny that would follow.

A senior finance manager in Acme-China comes to you, Acme's in-house counsel, and says, "Can we just split our application to establish our new $100 million joint venture into two $50 million applications and submit them to the local authorities who have promised to approve the deal in 30 days so that we avoid the hassle and the two-year wait for approval in Beijing? You know that I need to get this done because I am going back to the United States next year when I'm up for Vice President. I'll also put in a good word with your boss in the United States who says that he is looking for a new General Counsel, North America. Look, I know that you have some reservations but you admit that the law is unclear. Anyway, the local authorities have already told us that they will approve the application so we are covered. If MOFCOM raises any questions we can just say that the local authorities approved the application and told us that this procedure was lawful. So please draw up the two applications and get them to me by the end of the week. Let's get a beer after work at the White Swan Hotel and talk about this further. My treat." As you leave work that evening for the White Swan, you remember from your professional ethics class in law school that you are to represent your client zealously and within the boundaries of the law but then realize that this axiom isn't very helpful in this situation. You also think about how nice it would be to move back to the United States and get a promotion. What do you tell the finance manager?

PROBLEM 1-2

You are in-house counsel at Acme's subsidiary in Russia and have a disagreement with a business manager over the legality of certain payments that are being made to the local government authorities in connection with some needed approvals. You are concerned that these payments might be considered to be illegal bribes under local law and may also raise problems under the U.S. Foreign Corrupt Practices Act (see Chapter Six at pp. 399-422), but your business manager argues that these are lawful administrative fees and that this is a "gray area" as all of Acme's competitors are paying them. You have a meeting with the business manager and lay out the five reasons you think that the payments are illegal, but the manager says, "Okay, you've done your job by laying out the risks for me. I'm willing to take the risks so let's make the payments." As you are opposed to the payments, you then suggest that the company get an opinion letter from an outside local counsel. You can see that the business manager is irritated with you (and you worry momentarily about your annual review from the manager), but the manager finally agrees to abide by the opinion letter. You hire one of a number of newly established local Russian law firms specializing in foreign investment and you explain your position and the position of the business manager on the payments. One week later, you get an opinion letter signed by the local firm stating that, under local law, it is absolutely clear that the payments are illegal, and listing the five reasons that you stated. You also get a bill for $25,000 and a letter with a long list of other areas in which the law firm is eager to help you. Do you give the opinion letter to the business manager? How would you suggest getting an opinion letter from outside counsel in this situation? What cautions about dealing with outside law firms does this episode suggest?

C.   Cultural Concerns

In an age where people, goods, services, capital, and technology now routinely cross national boundaries, issues of differences and clashes in culture that affect IBTs have also become more common. By culture, we refer to the values and norms shared by a group and the group's economic, social, political, and religious institutions. Although consideration of cultural issues may not have been traditionally considered part of the work of an international transactions lawyer, a lawyer who ignores cultural issues in an IBT today does so at his or her own peril.

Cultural differences between countries have a direct impact on particular IBTs in two ways. First, cultural issues should be part of the background "business case" for a private transaction, but unlike economic, legal, and marketing issues (all part of traditional business and legal analysis), cultural issues may be ignored to the detriment of the transaction. For example, when the Walt Disney Company bought a tract of land near Paris to construct Disneyland Paris, Disney's management team in the United States assumed that the promise of jobs and economic development would result in widespread local support for the new theme park. Instead, the local populace valued its traditional rural lifestyle over economic development and offered spirited resistance to the Disney project, much to the surprise of Disney's management. In addition, a Disney theme park had been a spectacular success in Japan, but the Japanese were far more receptive to U.S. culture than many of the French who, if anything, were lukewarm toward American culture. Although these were important considerations, the experienced business and legal officials at Disney never considered the cultural factors. *See* Jeanne M. Brett, *Negotiating Globally* 8 (2001). One explanation for the failure of the Disney officials to fully consider the cultural factors is that these factors are not present in the United States, the business environment to which Disney officials were accustomed, and so were ignored in the company's initial forays into the international market.

A second way that differences in culture can affect IBTs is in negotiating styles. Lawyers are often called on by their clients to negotiate across cultures: A lawyer might negotiate a sales contract with a German buyer and a joint venture with a Brazilian partner for the same client. Understanding differences in negotiating styles can be advantageous to the lawyer or business executive. Failure to understand cultural differences might result in "value being left on the table," that is, in a deal where both parties are not as well off as they could be if barriers in culture and negotiating styles could be overcome. Cross-cultural negotiation skills have become highly sought after in the modern age as we have acquired a better understanding of cultural differences. According to one view, there are certain prevalent cultural categories that are reflected in negotiation strategies and styles: individualism versus collectivism, egalitarianism versus hierarchy, and low-context versus high-context communications. *See* Brett, *supra*, at 15–21. Most countries fall into these categories. Individualist cultures place the interests of the individual above those of the collective; hierarchical cultures, unlike egalitarian cultures, emphasize differentiated social status and deference to social superiors and associate social power with social status; negotiators from low-context-communications cultures emphasize direct, explicit exchanges, whereas those from high-context-communications cultures emphasize indirect exchanges that must be understood against a complex and unstated background of social values. *See id.* Negotiators from individualist, egalitarian, and low-context-communications cultures, such as the United States, use direct, confrontational styles, whereas negotiators from collectivist, hierarchical, and high-context-communications cultures, such as China, prefer to use indirect negotiation styles that avoid confrontation. Where there is a negotiation between persons with clashing negotiation styles, such as from the United States and China, the difference in styles could lead to poor communication and misunderstanding that results in a less-than-optimal result for both parties. Another, perhaps even greater, concern to lawyers and their clients is that they may be disadvantaged and exploited by the other party's skillful negotiators who are used to working in cross-cultural contexts. From the viewpoint of the lawyer negotiating on behalf of a client, the goal is to avoid both results that can arise from the pitfalls of culture.

NOTES AND QUESTIONS

1. A large literature on cultural issues in international business has emerged. In particular, experts urge caution in dealing with non-Western cultures that may have deeply embedded cultural norms that differ from Western values. Take the following example dealing with the Chinese:

A U.S. company had a contract from a German buyer to sell bicycles produced in China. When the first shipment was ready, there was a problem. The bikes rattled. The U.S. buyer did not want to accept the shipment, knowing that they would not be acceptable to the German customer, whose high-end market niche was dominated by bikes that were whisper quiet. What to do? In U.S. culture, the normal approach would be to tell the manufacturer that the rattling bikes were unacceptable and that the problem had to be fixed. In China, such a direct confrontation would be extremely rude and cause much loss of face. Knowing this, the U.S. manager went to the Chinese plant, inspected the bicycles, rode a few, and asked about the rattle. "Is this rattle normal? Do all the bikes rattle? Do you think the German buyer will think there is something wrong with the bike if it rattles?" Then he left. The next shipment of bikes had no rattles.[1]

We believe that the suggested approach has a number of pitfalls. For example, under the suggested approach, when does the U.S. manager find out whether the problem has been resolved? How much time must the U.S. manager spend in following this approach? Do you see any other issues with this approach? How would you suggest handling this problem without causing "loss of face"?

2. How should managers handle cross-cultural negotiations? Here is one suggestion:

> Be prepared for interests and priorities to have a cultural basis. If you are proposing to bring economic development to a region, find out how people in the region feel about economic development before you get to the negotiation table. Prepare for the negotiation by understanding the culture. See how the culture is classified according to the cultural values of individualism versus collectivism and egalitarianism versus hierarchy. Do some background research so you have a good understanding of the other negotiator's political, economic, and social environment. Make sure you have your own interpreter. Use your interpreter to help you understand the cultural factors influencing the other party's interests and priorities.[2]

Suppose that you are advising a senior vice president in charge of international business development who is scheduled to fly to Japan for a three-day meeting with Japanese officials on establishing a joint venture and then to travel to Chile to negotiate a foreign direct investment deal the following week. Would you advise the business executive to follow this prescription? What would you suggest?

PROBLEM 1-3

In light of the success of fast-food franchises such as McDonald's and Pizza Hut in China, Joe's Blue Collar Burgers, an Ohio company with locations around the Midwest, is considering expansion into China. Joe's has been able to successfully compete against famous fast-food chains in the Midwest based on its no-frills, working-class image, offering burgers at half the price of more flashy fast-food chains. Joe's decor also reflects its image and approach. Joe's founders grew up during the Great Depression and have consistently stressed frugality in the company's corporate philosophy. Food is served in clean but plain and somewhat austere surroundings. Joe's has signs in various places in its restaurants stressing thrift in daily life, a return to the simple non-materialistic values of

---

1. Brett, *supra*, at 8.
2. *Id.* at 204-205.

rural America, and the rejection of a wasteful, luxury lifestyle. Joe's has developed a niche in the U.S. market and has been earning modest but steady profits for many years. Joe's management sees no reason why using the same strategy to compete against fast-food competitors in China will not be just as successful as it was in the United States. Do you see any issues relating to culture with Joe's approach to China?

PROBLEM 1-4

Texas Barbecue Ribs, a successful Houston-based restaurant chain, is considering an expansion into Europe. Texas Ribs serves supersized portions of smoked ribs, southern-style coleslaw, and crunchy fries with its slogan "Everything Comes Bigger in Texas" in an interior setting with bold colors, a southwestern motif, and loud Texas country music. The restaurant has been quite successful in the Southwest and the South. What cultural issues might Texas Ribs face in European markets? How would Texas Ribs do in China?

II. The Growth of International Business Since the Second World War

This section explores some of the important developments in the international arena that form the modern historical background for international commercial and business transactions. The second half of the twentieth century, particularly the last two decades of the century, was marked by a surge in international business and trade of all kinds and the integration of the economies of the world to a greater extent than ever before. Today, the immense flow of business and trade across national boundaries on a daily basis is a distinguishing feature of the modern world. International trade in goods, technology, services, and investment across national boundaries are commonplace.

FIGURE 1-1
Exports of Goods and Services as a
Percentage of Gross Domestic Product
(Measured at Current Prices)

Country	1960	2010
Canada	17.2	29.4
France	14.5	25.6
Germany	19.0	47.0
Japan	10.7	15.2
Netherlands	47.7	78.2
Sweden	22.8	49.7
Switzerland	29.3	51.7
United Kingdom	20.9	30.5
United States	5.2	12.7

Source: OECD National Accounts Volume 2009; OECD Key Tables 2013.

This surge in international business and trade can be traced to several major historical events. First, at the end of the Second World War, the United States and some of its allies met at the Bretton Woods Conference in New Hampshire, which led to the creation of the legal institutions that would create the postwar legal framework for world trade: the International Monetary Fund (IMF), the World Bank, and the General Agreement on Tariffs and Trade (GATT). The world economy had just endured a decade and a half of immense turmoil and disruption. Protectionist trade measures in the form of excessive tariffs and protective currency regulations had triggered hostilities among nations, a worldwide depression, and an immensely destructive world war. The United States and its allies wanted to put into place a set of international institutions to prevent the economic policies that led to world tensions and hostilities. One of the lessons affirmed by the Second World War is that when economic conflict exists among nations, military conflict may not be too far behind. The IMF was established to create restrictions on national regulation of currency and foreign exchange controls. The IMF also became a lender of last resort for those developing nations that were unable to repay their foreign loans. The World Bank was created in 1944, first to aid in the reconstruction of Europe and then to provide loans to support the developing world. A third organization, the International Trade Organization (ITO), was proposed to encourage free trade by reducing tariffs, the customs duties imposed on imported goods. While the ITO was still being discussed, a group of nations negotiated the GATT, a package of tariff reductions, which was designed as an early boost to trade liberalization after the Second World War. Due mainly to opposition by the United States, the ITO was never approved. After the demise of the ITO, a small staff was created in Geneva to handle basic administrative tasks for the GATT. In 1995, the World Trade Organization was established to administer the GATT and to assume the role originally intended for the ITO.

Although these international institutions helped to increase international business and trade, there were limits on its expansion after the Second World War. First, the existence of the Soviet Union and its satellite countries and the People's Republic of China and its sphere of influence in Asia meant that the expansion of international business and trade excluded a significant portion of the world as the Cold War froze in place the barriers to business and trade that had existed between the West and the East at the end of the Second World War. After the Second World War, China purposefully isolated itself by shutting its doors to the world (with the exception of trade with the Soviet Union until China split with the Soviet Union in the 1960s) in a fervent, if misguided, attempt at self-sufficiency. Second, because GATT was viewed as a rich nation's club, many developing nations did not wish to participate in GATT. Third, until the 1980s, many developing nations, some freed from colonization only at the end of the Second World War, did not trust developed nations and, as a result, erected restrictive laws against international business and trade.

In the past several decades, a number of significant developments have vastly accelerated the pace of international business and trade. The disintegration of the Soviet Union and its satellites in Eastern Europe removed the barriers to trade and exchanges that had existed since the end of the Second World War. In 1978, China adopted economic reforms and created one of the world's most active and important markets for international business and trade. In conjunction with this vast sea change in the political arena, the information technology revolution, started in the United States in the 1990s, created new opportunities for trade and world integration that seemed impossible only a decade before. Developing nations began to view economic development as a priority, and now aggressively compete for investment dollars from developed nations. During the last round of GATT negotiations that led to the establishment of the WTO, developing nations played an important role. Today, about three-quarters of WTO members are developing countries. A major development of the fourth Ministerial Conference of the WTO held in Doha, Qatar in November 2001 was the explicit recognition of the needs of developing countries in the future work program of the WTO. This Conference resolved to open a new comprehensive trade negotiation, the Doha Development Agenda, which, although stalled, is still ongoing at this writing, to address not only traditional trade issues, but also the need to open world markets to products and services produced by developing countries.

III. Modern Forms and Patterns of International Business and Commerce

There are four principal channels of international business and trade in the modern world: trade in goods, trade in services, technology transfer, and foreign direct investment. Our focus in this book is on the private transactions in each of these four channels and not the international trade law aspects that we will examine only by way of background. Each of these topics will be the focus of one or more chapters or sections of this book.

A. Trade in Goods

Traditionally, states engaged in international business and trade principally through trade in goods. Since the end of the Second World War, international trade has been driving the process of globalization and integration of the world's economies. Merchandise exports have jumped from $1.9 trillion in 1980 to $18.4 trillion in 2012.

FIGURE 1-2
Growth of World Merchandise Exports in the Past Three Decades (in $ Billions) and Percentage Share

Year	World	Developed Countries	EU	USA	Developing Countries
1980	2,049	66.2	41.5	11.0	33.8
1990	3,496	72.5	44.7	11.3	31.6
2000	6,449	71.7	38.0	12.1	28.3
2005	10,500	68.0	38.7	8.6	32.0
2010	15,283	63.0	33.8	8.4	37.0
2012	18,402	56.3	31.5	8.4	43.7

Source: UNCTAD Handbook of Statistics (2013).

International trade statistics show a number of remarkable trends: (1) global trade is expanding in both relative and absolute terms; (2) the U.S. share of world exports is in decline; (3) the global share of developing countries is increasing—the nearly 44 percent share recorded in 2012 is the highest in history; and (4) international trade is an increasingly important part of every nation's economic activity and well-being—for the United States in 2013, international trade amounts to over 25 percent of all economic activity.

The traditional measure of trade competitiveness has been determined by share of world exports. Under this criterion, until about two decades ago, 20 economies, consisting primarily of developed countries led by the United States, Germany, and Japan, maintained about a two-thirds share of world trade. However, starting from about 1990 to the present (2014), developing countries, led by China, have emerged to take a leading role in world exports. Of all countries, China stands apart in merchandise exports. In 2009, China became the world's largest exporter of goods, surpassing the entire membership of the EU, and China has far exceeded other countries in export growth. This trend foreshadows a greater role for developing nations in international business and trade in the future.

Another significant trend is that the growth in exports is tied directly to the level of technology involved. In this context, technology refers to knowledge (often protected by intellectual property rights). Exports grow faster the higher the level of technology involved in the product and the less the reliance on natural resources as a source for the product. In the area of technology-intensive exports, developing countries are growing faster than their developed counterparts. High-technology products are now the largest source of foreign exchange for developing countries. In 2012, exports of technology-intensive products by developing countries reached 18 percent of total manufactured exports. *See World Development Indicators: Science and Technology,* World Bank (2014), *http://wdi.worldbank.org/table/5.13.* The role of technology (intellectual property) as an engine of international business and economic development for developing nations is another emerging world trend.

B. Trade in Services

Unlike the trade in goods, the international trade in services involves no packages crossing a national boundary and a customs frontier. The intangible nature of the trade in services makes it inherently more difficult to measure in concrete terms. Some trade in services can be defined by a physical activity such as transport, hotel, or insurance services, but other types of services such as consultancy or education are more intangible and may be more difficult to define and measure. While the measurement of the trade in services is subject to greater difficulties than the measurement of the trade in goods, trade in services has been growing on a rapid basis paralleling the growth in the trade in goods.

In 2013, services accounted for almost three-fourths of the gross domestic product (GDP) of developed countries, the world's principal export markets for services. By 2011, services had surpassed almost 51 percent of GDP in developing countries. *See UNCTAD Handbook of Statistics 2013,* 434 (2013). Examples of major services exports are sea and air transportation, travel, communications, insurance, financial, computer and information, legal, and other business services. Although services trade has lagged behind trade in goods, services trade is growing rapidly. Among developed countries the export of commercial services has grown at a faster rate (7.0 percent) than the growth of export of goods (6.1 percent) for the period 1990 to 2012. *See UNCTAD*

Handbook of Statistics 2013, 274 (2013). Global services trade is growing at about 10 percent annually and in 2012 amounted to $8.700 trillion. Services trade includes such
matters as sea and air transportation, travel, communications, insurance, banking and
financial services, computer and information services, legal and a wide variety of business services.

Lawyers in particular have a large stake in the liberalization of trade in services.
Lawyers have long been barred by regulations forbidding transborder legal services.
Although some of these barriers have been eliminated, many still remain. For an exhaus-
tive treatment of this important subject, see Gilles Muller, *Liberalization of Trade in Legal
Services* (2013).

As the tradeability of services increases as a result of modern information and communication technologies, it can be expected that the production of a growing number of
services will shift to developing countries as was the case with manufacturing. The growth
in foreign direct investment fueled primarily by MNEs, further discussed below, may fore-
shadow an expansion in the export of services. As companies expand their operations on
a global basis, they will also move research and development, marketing, sales, accounting, human resources, and other services abroad as well. A number of MNEs are relocat-
ing these services to lower-cost sites and are exporting them back to the United States. In
the developing world, Asia appears to be more advanced than other regions in attracting
the relocation of services.

C. Foreign Direct Investment

Foreign direct investment (FDI) refers to the creation or acquisition by a business entity
resident in one nation of a lasting ownership interest in a business entity resident in
another nation, usually obtained through the investment of capital, technology, and other
resources. Up to the mid-1980s, foreign trade in goods was the most significant channel
of international trade between states. Exports grew much faster than FDI in the 1950s,
1960s, and 1970s. In the 1980s, however, this pattern began to change and the growth
rates in FDI began to exceed the growth rates in merchandise trade. Coinciding with the
disintegration of the Soviet Union and its satellites, FDI began to rise dramatically in the
1980s and has now become the principal impetus behind the deepening of world economic integration. During the 24-year period from 1980 to 2004, world real industrial
production rose by 60 percent, or by an annual growth rate of 2 percent. International
merchandise trade as represented by export figures increased by 210 percent over this
whole period or by 4.8 percent annually, more than twice as rapidly as industrial production. An even more dramatic increase occurred in the area of FDI. From 1973 to 1997,
FDI increased by 780 percent or by an annual growth rate of 9.5 percent, twice as large as
the merchandise growth rate.

FDI reached an historic peak in 2007, touching a record almost $3 trillion, before
falling back to about $1.2 trillion in the global recession year 2009. Since 2009, global
FDI has again steadily increased, rising about 15 percent per year. In 2012, global FDI was
$1.6 trillion, and total global inward FDI stock stood at $20.4 trillion.[3] The rebound of
FDI was widespread, covering all three groups of economies, developed, developing, and
economies in transition.[4]

---

3. UNCTAD World Investment Report 2-3 (2012).
4. *Id.* at 6

The two main categories of FDI are mergers and acquisitions (M&A) of existing businesses and greenfield investments. An example of FDI through M&A is when an MNE acquires an existing company in a foreign country. An example of a greenfield investment is when the MNE sets up a brand new business entity in a foreign country. In value terms, greenfield investment exceeds M&A; in 2011, for example, greenfield investment projects totaled $904 billion. Greenfield investment and M&A differ markedly in their impacts on host economies. At least in the short run, M&As do not bring the same development benefits as greenfield investment projects, in terms of the creation of new productive capacity.[5]

The source of most FDI continues to be from developed countries—$1.24 trillion in 2011—with the EU, North America, and Japan in the lead. But FDI outflows from developing and transition countries are increasingly significant.[6]

According to UNCTAD, the United Nations Conference on Trade and Development, the following forces are the main drivers behind the surge in FDI:

> The first is policy liberalization: opening up national markets and allowing all kinds of FDI and non-equity arrangements. In 2001, 208 changes in FDI laws were made by 71 countries. More than 90 percent aimed at making the investment climate more favourable to inward FDI. In addition, as many as 97 countries were involved in the conclusion of 158 bilateral investment treaties, bringing the total of such treaties to 2,099 by the end of 2001. Similarly, 67 new double taxation treaties were concluded.
>
> The second force is rapid technological change, with its rising costs and risks, which makes it imperative for firms to tap world markets and to share these costs and risks. On the other hand, falling transport and communication costs—the "death" of distance—have made it economical to integrate distant operations and ship products and components across the globe in the search for efficiency.
>
> The third force, a result of the previous two, is increasing competition. Heightened competition compels firms to explore new ways of increasing their efficiency, including by extending their international reach to new markets at an early stage and by shifting certain production activities to reduce costs.

UNCTAD *World Investment Report* at xv–xvi (2002).

D.   Technology Transfer

In the modern era, technology (i.e., knowledge that is usually protected by intellectual property law) serves a vital role in international business, trade, and economic development. The legal issues that arise from the transfer of technology (intellectual property) will be one of the key themes that we explore in this book. How is technology transfer related to the issues discussed so far in this book? Improving export competitiveness and attracting FDI are important goals for all states in the world today, but these goals are not ends in themselves. Rather, they serve as the means to a more overarching end: economic development. For developed nations, this means improved productivity and higher standards of living; for developing nations, this means modernization and industrialization in order to overcome backwardness and poverty. For all nations, technology is critical to achieving these goals.

---

5. *Id.* at 3.
6. *Id.* at 4.

Because of their importance in promoting economic development, intellectual property rights are the source of some of the sharpest disagreements between developed and developing nations. Developed countries dominate in the creation of technology; developing nations tend to be importers and consumers of technology created in developed countries. Many developing nations believe that intellectual property rights are unduly restricting their access to technology by denying access altogether or only through the payment of burdensome royalties and licensing fees. On the flip side, developed nations argue that strong intellectual property laws are needed to protect their innovations.

As we have seen in the discussion of exports, the higher the level of technology the faster the growth in exports. In the area of FDI, in many instances the most important contribution of the FDI that is critical to its success is not the capital investment but the technology contributed in the form of intellectual property such as patents, trademarks, copyrights, trade secrets, and know-how.

As an indication of the growing importance of intellectual property in international business and trade, technology transfer, as measured by payments for royalties and licensing fees, increased dramatically at about the same rate as FDI in the past two decades. Technology payments rose from $92 billion in 2000 to $289 billion in 2012; the annual growth rate for technology payments in the decade of the 2000s was 10.7 percent, even exceeding the growth rate for FDI at 9.9 percent. *See UNCTAD Handbook of Statistics 2013; UNCTAD World Investment Report 2010.* It should not be surprising that developed countries dominate in the area of technology transfer. In 2012, 85 percent of all of the royalties and licensing fees on a worldwide basis were received by the United States (43 percent), the leading states of the European Union (31 percent), and Japan (11 percent). *See UNCTAD Handbook of Statistics 2013,* 300 (2013).

In this book, we will focus on intellectual property in international business, not on intellectual property as such. For a comprehensive treatment of international intellectual property, see Chow and Lee, *International Intellectual Property: Problems, Cases, and Materials* (West 2d ed. 2012).

IV. Some Important New Developments

A. The Rise of China and East and South Asia

During the past two decades the economies of Asia have emerged to lead the world in economic growth. Of these economies, China stands apart. From a low economic base at the time of economic liberalization in 1979, China in 2010 surpassed Japan as the second largest economy in the world, and is on track to surpass the United States as the leading world economy in the 2020s. In 2012, China's GDP (the measure of gross value added by resident producers in a country's economy) was $8.230 trillion, 13.27 percent of the world economy. The United States' GDP in 2012 was $15.685 trillion, 25.3 percent of the world economy. Japan, the third ranking economy in 2012, had a GDP of $5.960 trillion, 9.6 percent of the world economy. The GDP of the European Union (28 countries) was $17.001 trillion in 2012.

What is striking about the world economic situation in 2014, however, is the uneven growth of various countries' economies. While Latin America, North America, Europe, and Japan exhibit very low economic growth rates, Asian economies have increasing vitality. While the United States is growing at a modest rate of between 2 and 3 percent (barely keeping up with population increases), Japan and the EU are growing at less than 1 percent. On the other hand, for the rest of the decade of the 2010s, China is forecast to grow at an average rate of over 7 percent; India (GDP $1.842 trillion) at over 6 percent, and Asia without China at over 5 percent. Africa has averaged over 5 percent growth since 2004 and is expected to continue at that rate. This state of affairs could signal a change in the world economic order that has existed for hundreds of years: a shift in the economic dominance of the West for the first time in recorded history. The United States and the West (with Japan) have dominated world trade and international business in the modern era, but this could change in the middle years of the twenty-first century. The rise of China and Asia is a theme we will explore further in this book.

B.   The Role of Multinational Enterprises

A multinational enterprise, or MNE, is a profit-making organization that performs activities of production, distribution, and research and development in more than one country. The multinational enterprise is the major vehicle for promoting all four of the channels of international business and trade (goods, services, technology, and investment). MNEs play a major role in increasing the export competitiveness in the area of goods and services of host countries, especially developing countries, by providing additional capital and know-how as well as access to global, regional, and home markets. Over one-third of all worldwide trade takes place within MNEs and about 80 percent of all world trade involves at least one MNE. *See* Jorn Kleinert, *The Role of Multinational Enterprises in Globalization: An Empirical Overview* 24–25 (2001). FDI is tied directly to MNEs as they serve as the foreign investor and provide the capital and resources in the vast bulk of FDI transactions in the world today. MNEs are now also the owners of the world's most valuable patents, trademarks, copyrights, and other forms of intellectual property and dominate the transfer of technology on a worldwide basis.

   A sense of the importance of MNEs in world trade and business is provided by the following UNCTAD summary:

> Recent estimates suggest that there are about 78,000 [MNEs] today, with about 780,000 foreign affiliates across the globe. Their economic impact can be measured in different ways. In 2001, foreign affiliates accounted for about 73 million employees, compared to 24 million in 1990, for an estimated 3% of the global workforce; their sales of almost $25 trillion were almost twice as high as world exports in 2006, compared to 1990 when both were roughly equal; and the stock of outward foreign direct investment increased from $1.7 trillion to $12.0 trillion over the same period. Foreign affiliates now account for one-tenth of world GDP and one-third of world exports.

UNCTAD World Investment Report at xv (2004). According to the most recent UNCTAD World Investment Report, foreign affiliates of MNEs employed almost 72 million people in 2012, their sales reached approximately $26 trillion, and their nearly $7.5 trillion in exports accounted for about one-third of total world exports. As an indicator of the influence of some MNEs in the world economy, according to some economic measures the largest MNEs are larger than many countries. In a comparison of the sales volume of firms with the GDP of countries and major cities in 2009, of the world's 100 largest economies 53 were countries, 13 were companies, and the remaining 34 were major cities. *See The*

World's Top 100 Economies, WORLD BANK (2010) *http://siteresources.worldbank.org/INTUWM/Resources/WorldsTop100Economies.pdf.*

As MNEs have assumed a major role in globalization, a host of new issues has arisen. Should MNEs be subject to ethical or legal obligations because of their importance in the world economy? Do MNEs have affirmative obligations to assist in development as well? We will explore these issues in this book, but for now consider the role of MNEs in the context of the following debate concerning globalization.

C.   Globalization

The term "globalization" has become a watchword of our time, a word that provokes debate and controversy. For some, globalization is a benign and inevitable development. For others, it represents the summation and cause of all social and economic ills. For most of us, however, globalization is something in between these two extremes: It brings us benefits but also creates problems that have to be dealt with and managed. What is globalization? There are many definitions, but we prefer a short and simple one. Globalization, at least in the economic sphere, is the relatively free movement of goods, services, technology, capital, information, and people over the entire planet. Globalization has happened in the lifetimes of many who witnessed a world of nations that were separated by rigid physical, political, and technological boundaries; the pace of change has been stunning. It is beyond the scope of this book to consider the full range of issues surrounding globalization, but we would like to make the following two points.

First, we believe the debate between the "globalizers" and the anti-globalizers does not capture what is at stake and adds only heat not light. The so-called anti-globalizers simply miss the point; in fact, the anti-globalizers themselves have gone global and air their criticisms as global values. As Robert Howse in his essay, *The End of the Globalization Debate*, has stated: "There is no longer an anti-globalization side in the debate, coherently representing the position that the territorial nation-state should remain the locus of control over economic activity and should retain a monopoly on legitimate governance. Today the protestors who march against globalization are not marching in favor of the state. Instead they are mostly advocating a set of values that transcend state boundaries and that require global action."[7]

Second, we believe that the real debate over globalization concerns concrete problems that have emerged in the present age of globalization that cannot be addressed by the individual action of even the most powerful of the territorial states of the world. Collective action by many states is required. For example, MNEs are able to organize their corporate structures, usually consisting of a parent company and various holding companies and subsidiaries, to evade national laws on protection of the environment, human rights, and workers' rights by locating their most dangerous operations in developing countries with lax regulatory or enforcement schemes. As Joseph Stiglitz has pointed out, economic globalization has outpaced political globalization so "we have a chaotic, uncoordinated system of global governance without global government, an array of agreements dealing with a series of problems, from global warming to international trade and capital flows."[8] The real problem in such a situation is that the world needs new rules and regimes to deal with global problems that are beyond the ken of any one state; but

---

7. 121 Harv. L. Rev. 1528, 1530 (2008).
8. *Making Globalization Work* 21 (2006).

often the international political order is loath to formulate and to deliver such rules. So the urgent need is for the nations of the world to establish and enforce global rules that adequately address the very real problems that are exacerbated by globalization: protection of environmental values, human rights, employment and workers' rights, income inequality, and a host of other problems. In other words, we must establish globalization with a human face. This book cannot address all of these important issues, but in Chapter Nine on Corporate Social Responsibility, we treat impacts of globalization that are integral to international business transactions.

NOTES AND QUESTIONS

1. While globalization has powerful proponents, see, e.g., Thomas L. Friedman, *The World Is Flat* (2007), it also has passionate opposition. One group of objectors to globalization can be categorized as "nationalist-protectionist." This group tends to blame globalization for certain social, economic, and political ills affecting their home countries. Political figures such as Pat Buchanan in the United States condemn neoliberal internationalism, free trade, and MNEs for loss of jobs at home and moral decline. *See, e.g.,* John Gray, *False Dawn* (1998). A second group of anti-globalists, such as Ralph Nader, argue that economic globalization has undermined the democratic accountability of MNEs and that they are free to exploit workers and damage the environment around the world. Intergovernmental organizations such as the International Monetary Fund, the World Bank, and the World Trade Organization are said to be the not so secret tools of MNEs. *See, e.g.,* Ralph Nader, *Free Trade and the Decline of Democracy in the Case Against Free Trade* (1993). A third group, which includes academics like Amy Chua, denounces globalization for causing instability and social turmoil among developing countries and for its exacerbation of the economic disparities between the developed and the developing worlds. *See, e.g.,* Amy Chua, *World on Fire* (2004). Most opponents of globalization concede that reversal of the process is impossible and that the further deepening of this process is probably inexorable. The real battleground is over how to control the damaging effects of globalization and who should bear these costs. We explore these important issues in depth in Chapter Nine, but for now consider these issues in light of the following questions that are currently being debated.

2. What kind of corporate social responsibility or obligations do MNEs have in meeting the harmful effects of globalization? Bill Gates, the founder of Microsoft, argues that MNEs should undertake projects in the fields of education, health, protection of the environment, and the alleviation of world poverty in order to supplement the efforts of governments and international agencies. Gates calls this "creative capitalism." The arguments in favor of this idea are based on the concept of "social compact" — that society grants corporations unique powers and privileges, such as limited liability, and they in turn should act to benefit society. An additional argument is that MNEs have a stake in long-term profitability and will thrive only if societal ills are addressed. Arguments against the idea that MNEs should undertake such projects are that if an MNE does not try to maximize profits it is unfair to shareholders and employees. In addition, the argument can be advanced that MNEs do not have the expertise to carry out societal projects, and they will not be accountable to any organization if they do such work. For an in-depth account of Bill Gates's ideas and the objections of his critics, see Michael Kinsley (ed.), *Creative Capitalism* (2008).

3. What responsibility do states and intergovernmental organizations have to manage the process of globalization so as to reduce its harmful impact on civil society?

PROBLEM 1-5

Assume that you are the foreign trade minister of Z, a developing country that has a host of serious economic and social problems. You are the leader of a group of developing countries that will attend a world economic summit with a group of advanced industrialized countries. At the summit, you will give a speech arguing that historical events have created a moral duty on the part of developed nations and their MNEs to provide financial assistance and compensation to developing countries. The second part of your argument is that developing nations should be exempt from stringent international environmental controls on industry and from intellectual property laws. As trade minister, can you make these arguments on behalf of the developing nations? Now assume you are the leader of a developed nation that is home to powerful MNEs. How do you respond?

Not my place

V. The Legal Framework for International Business Transactions

A. Introductory Considerations

As we now turn to the legal framework for IBTs, we start with a basic question: Is this an international law course? The answer to this question is "yes and no." IBT is not a traditional field of law like torts, contracts, or even competition and securities law or public international law. Rather, the international business lawyer must be familiar with many specialized fields of law. IBTs cut across and concern many legal fields. Frequently, an IBT will concern both international law and domestic law, sometimes of the lawyer's home country, but perhaps also the domestic laws of several countries.

IBTs also cut across and concern both private law, which governs legal relations between private individuals and firms, and public law, which deals with regulation by governments. Moreover, IBTs cut across many legal subjects, including commercial law, torts, administrative law, and a number of regulatory law fields.

Although the international business lawyer deals in both international and domestic law, in this course we will, of course, emphasize the international aspects of international business practice since the domestic laws frequently encountered are covered in other law school courses. We emphasize, however, that there is no bright-line distinction between the international and domestic aspects of the practice. With this caveat in mind, we now turn to an overview of the legal framework in which most IBTs occur. This framework consists of the choice of law principles and substantive rules of law that apply to a particular transaction and the primary legal institutions and forums that create and interpret the law.

B. International Conflicts of Law and Choice of Law

One of the most basic tasks for any lawyer engaged in IBTs is to determine what substantive laws apply to the transaction. This can be a complicated task in an IBT because a number of different applicable laws from both national and international sources may apply. Moreover, various aspects of a single transaction may be governed by different laws. How is the choice of law determination made in an international context and what principles govern this choice?

International law is traditionally divided into two fields: *public international law*, which is the system of laws governing the relations of nation-states, intergovernmental organizations, and, to a limited extent, the private conduct of individuals; and *private international law*, which refers to the use of domestic choice of law rules by domestic courts to resolve issues of conflicts of laws and the recognition and enforcement of judgments in an international context. We now discuss private international law, as IBTs have traditionally been associated with this field.

A transaction that involves the movement of goods, services, technology, or capital across the boundaries of country A and country B creates a choice of law issue of what substantive law governs the transaction. In a situation where the parties themselves had not made an effective choice of law in a contract, or where the transaction was not governed by a superseding law such as an international treaty, the choice of law among the domestic law of country A, country B, or a combination of the two to govern the transaction was called private international law. The underlying assumption of this traditional approach was that all IBTs were governed by private law (i.e., national or domestic law not international law) and the rules of private international law helped to resolve which national law applied to the IBT.

Thus, the term "private international law" is really a misnomer. Private international law is really a field of domestic law because it refers to use of domestic choice of law rules by a domestic court to resolve international conflicts of law issues involving the choice between the laws of two or more nations. The end of the process is domestic law as well because the application of the choice of law rules leads either to the use of local domestic law or to the use of foreign domestic law in national courts.

In applying its own domestic choice of law rules in an international conflicts of law context—which becomes an application of private international law—a domestic court typically weighs a number of factors, including:

(a) the needs of the interstate and international systems,
(b) the relevant policies of the forum,
(c) the relevant policies of other interested states and the relative interests of those states in the determination of the particular issue,
(d) the protection of justified expectations,
(e) the basic policies underlying the particular field of law,
(f) certainty, predictability, and uniformity of result, and
(g) ease in the determination and application of the law to be applied.

Restatement, Conflicts of Law (Second) §6 (1971). These factors are broad in scope, and courts will inevitably use their discretion in weighing them, leading to a lack of predictability in results. Moreover, the Restatement factors set forth above are a restatement of the approach of U.S. courts, and the domestic courts of each nation will apply their own version of international choice of law principles. To deal with the lack of predictability and uniformity in the area of private international law rules, the Hague Conference on Private International Law was established in 1893 in order to promote uniform private international law rules as a major part of its work program. The Hague Conference is a self-standing intergovernmental organization created under a statute adopted by a treaty in 1955 and currently has 45 members, including the United States, which did not join the conference until 1964. The conference has prepared conventions prescribing choice of law rules for testamentary dispositions, products liability, matrimonial property, and contracts for the international sale of goods. The United States is not a party to these conventions, but is a party to two well-known procedural conventions promulgated by the Hague Conference, the Convention on the Service Abroad of Judicial and Extrajudicial Documents in Civil or Commercial Matters, 20 U.S.T. 361, 658 U.N.T.S. 163, entered into force on February 23, 1969, and the Convention on the Taking of Evidence Abroad in Civil or Commercial Matters, 23 U.S.T. 2555, 847 U.N.T.S. 231, entered into force on October 7, 1972.

C.   The New Lex Mercatoria ("Law Merchant")

In medieval times before the rise of the nation-state, business transactions were carried on across the existing frontiers of Europe. However, international conflicts of law did not arise in the modern sense because merchants in different European kingdoms employed common legal rules to resolve disputes. This body of law was known as the *lex mercatoria* or medieval law merchant and was a special type of supranational common law applicable to business transactions among European merchants. Special international commercial courts were created to deal with international business problems. This situation had a long history in Europe; the medieval *lex mercatoria* was the successor to the ancient *jus gentium* of Roman law. Thus, the traditional conflicts of law approach to IBTs is exceptional; it dates back only to the rise of nation-states since the seventeenth century and the creation of national bodies of law. *See* Filip De Ly, *International Business Law and Lex Mercatoria* (1992).

During the last 60 years and continuing today at an accelerating pace, a new *lex mercatoria* has developed that functions in a similar fashion to the *lex mercatoria* of old. We have now and are continuing to create a truly international body of rules to govern IBTs. As a result, the body of domestic law known as private international law is diminishing in relevance and importance. We no longer need conflicts of law principles if we develop and use a uniform body of substantive law that is the same for each nation. Of course, it is too strong to say that conflicts of law are now rare. They still arise and private international law is still needed. What we have now is a hybrid system of the *lex mercatoria* and private international law.

There are three reasons for the new *lex mercatoria* and the diminution of private international law. First, for many years sustained efforts have been made by both nations and private entities to harmonize international business and commercial law through the promulgation of international treaties and uniform codes. These and other law creation methods have given us a vast body of doctrine that is truly international in character. Second, courts now freely allow parties to choose the applicable law that will govern their transactions. Third, the availability and popularity of arbitration as a dispute resolution technique means that many disputes are now resolved by international bodies, not by national courts. These international arbitration bodies are comfortable operating outside the parameters of national laws and forums. Traditional private international law analysis does continue to be applicable, however, where no superseding international law is applicable or where the parties have not chosen a source of law to govern the transaction. In these cases, a private international law analysis would result in the application of the domestic law of one of the nations involved in the transaction.

D.   Sources of Law for International Business Transactions

The Hague Conference discussed above is an attempt to harmonize international commercial law through the adoption of uniform rules of international choice of law that would lead to predictability in the choice of a substantive law by domestic courts. During the latter half of the twentieth century, however, many additional approaches to harmonization gained extensive support from the international community.

Professor Roy Goode of St. John's College, Oxford, has written on the currently accepted sources of international business law as follows:

The Instruments of Harmonization

The Range of Available Instruments

There are at least nine methods by which harmonization may be either effected or in some measure inducted, namely:

(1) a multilateral Convention without a Uniform Law as such;
(2) a multilateral Convention embodying a Uniform Law;
(3) a set of bilateral Treaties;
(4) [European] Community legislation;
(5) a Model Law;
(6) a codification of custom and usage promulgated by an international non-governmental body;
(7) international trade terms promulgated by such an organization;
(8) model contracts and general contractual conditions;
(9) restatements by scholars and other experts.

The characteristic of the first four is that they have the force of law, subject to such constitutional acts as may be necessary to give them force in the territory of a particular Contracting State.[9] The Model is, as its name implies, a model which can be adopted in its entirety, adapted, or simply used as the basis for ideas; it has no legal force as such. The next four instruments depend on their efficacy upon incorporation into contracts.

Roy Goode, *Reflections on the Harmonization of Commercial Law* reprinted in Ross Cranston and Roy Goode, *Commercial and Consumer Law* 6–7 (Oxford 1993). In the discussion below, we will categorize the sources of international law applicable to IBTs. Professor Goode's nine instruments of harmonization fall into two of the three categories of the sources of law for international business transactions that we further discuss below.

We should note that there is a historical precedent for a uniform supranational law applying to commercial transactions, the *lex mercatoria* discussed in the previous section. As we have noted, the *lex mercatoria* was a set of international legal rules created by custom and usage that supplemented what was at that time the often-incomplete commercial law of states. By the nineteenth century, as most nations had absorbed the medieval *lex mercatoria* into their national laws or had replaced it by their own national commercial law and IBTs became largely governed by national law, some legal theorists rejected the very notion of a supranational merchant law altogether, stating instead that all IBTs were necessarily governed by national law. However, some vestiges of the *lex mercatoria* as a set of customary legal rules still remain, and it is possible that courts may still refer to long-standing rules of international commerce that differ somewhat from national laws. The concept of a *lex mercatoria* has been given new life by the many harmonizing codes, model laws, and systems of terms, further discussed below, which were created in the latter part of the twentieth century.

---

9. Authors' Note: A nation that is a signatory to a treaty is referred to as a contracting state, which underscores that the treaty is a legal text, whereas a nation that belongs to an international organization is a member. Thus, the original GATT had contracting parties, whereas the WTO has members.

E. International Forums and Institutions

We now turn to some of the principal institutions that are the sources of the harmonization of the law applicable to IBTs. Perhaps the most important are the following:

1. UNCITRAL

The United Nations Commission on International Trade Law (UNCITRAL or the Commission) is the core legal body of the United Nations in the field of international commerce and trade. Today, UNCITRAL is the most prolific source of proposals for the unification of commercial law. UNCITRAL was established by the United Nations (UN) in 1966. The Commission is dedicated to formulating modern rules on commercial transactions and to furthering the harmonization and unification of the law of international commerce. The Commission is presently composed of 60 member states elected by the UN General Assembly. The states are elected for a term of six years with the terms of half of the members expiring every three years. Membership is structured so as to be representative of the world's various geographic regions as well as its principal legal and economic systems. Some of the current members of the commission include France, Germany, Cameroon, Rwanda, Russia, Lithuania, and Mexico. The United States has been represented on the Commission since its inception. The Commission's secretariat, its main administrative body, is located in Vienna, with working sessions held in alternative years at the UN headquarters in New York and in Vienna.

One of UNCITRAL's most important tasks is to create multilateral conventions or treaties on international commerce that have the force of law. Conventions drafted by UNCITRAL are formally approved as official UN instruments at a diplomatic conference convened by the General Assembly. The convention then is open for signature for those nations that wish to adopt the treaty. In some cases, the conventions provide by their own terms that they do not enter into force unless a minimum number of nations adopt and ratify the treaty. Among the major results of the Commission is the Convention on Contracts for the International Sale of Goods (1980) (CISG), which has established a comprehensive code of legal rules governing contracts for the international sale of goods. Another notable example is the Convention on the Carriage of Goods by Sea (concluded 1978, entry into force 1992)—the "Hamburg Rules"—which establishes a uniform legal regime governing the rights and obligations of shippers, carriers, and consignees under a contract of carriage of goods by sea. The United States has yet to ratify this treaty although it has already come into force for some 20 countries. UNCITRAL was instrumental in promoting the ratification by nations of the influential New York Convention on the Recognition and Enforcement of Foreign Arbitral Awards (1958), which is examined in Chapter Eight of this book.

UNCITRAL also drafts model laws for incorporation by states such as the UNCITRAL Model Law on Procurement of Goods, Construction, and Services (1994), designed to assist developing countries in reforming their laws on government procurement. UNCITRAL also creates legal rules that parties can directly incorporate by contract to govern their transactions. Examples are the UNCITRAL Arbitration Rules (1976), which parties may agree on for the conduct of arbitral proceedings arising out of their commercial relationships, and the UNCITRAL Conciliation Rules (1980). UNCITRAL also provides technical assistance for states on law reform projects and legal and legislative guides.

2. UNIDROIT

The International Institute for the Unification of Private Law (UNIDROIT or the Institute) is an independent intergovernmental organization with its headquarters in Rome. UNIDROIT seeks to harmonize private and commercial law between states. UNIDROIT was established in 1926 as an organ of the League of Nations, the predecessor organization to the United Nations. The Institute remained in existence as an independent body after the League of Nations met its demise. After the United Nations was established in 1945, the UN created UNCITRAL to focus on issues of commercial law. For these reasons, both UNIDROIT and UNCITRAL have overlapping goals, although the two bodies differ in methods and in emphasis.

UNIDROIT is an independent organization so its work is less influenced by political issues and it tends to focus on technical matters. As a body of the UN, UNCITRAL is subject to political pressures and is particularly sensitive to the issues of developing nations. The principal drafters of UNIDROIT treaties in the past have mainly been Western European nations. Many states have been reluctant to adopt UNIDROIT treaties because they reflect the legal traditions of Western Europe but not traditions elsewhere. In recent years, UNIDROIT has shifted its work to nonbinding instruments such as model laws and general principles that are addressed directly to judges, arbitrators, and private parties. UNIDROIT's most influential recent work has been the Principles of International Commercial Contracts (the Principles) (1994), which are applicable to all commercial contracts and are not limited to contracts for the international sale of goods like the CISG. Unlike the CISG, the Principles were not drafted as an international treaty. Rather, the Principles are intended as a type of restatement of the law that can serve as a source of ideas for drafting domestic legislation, international conventions, or international commercial contracts. The Principles are offered as an interpretive tool that can supplement gaps in existing international or domestic law or in existing commercial agreements. On a more controversial level, the Principles are also intended to be a distillation or even a source for the *lex mercatoria*, the supranational law of commerce that has ancient roots and that continues to be a possible source of international commercial law.

Membership in UNIDROIT currently consists of 59 members with some overlap with the membership of UNCITRAL. The United States joined UNIDROIT in 1964.

3. The International Chamber of Commerce

Founded in 1919, the International Chamber of Commerce (ICC) is a private nonprofit organization. The members of the ICC are national chambers of commerce, trade and business associations, and companies from about 130 countries. Unlike UNCITRAL and UNIDROIT, the ICC is a nongovernmental agency whose goal is to represent the interests of private business and industry. A second goal of the ICC is to create uniform rules and standards for international business. As the ICC is a private body, it operates mainly through the promulgation of nonbinding rules that private parties can adopt by contract. Among the ICC's most influential contributions are Incoterms and the Uniform Customs and Practice for Documentary Credits (UCP). Both of these sets of rules are widely adopted by private parties to govern their transactions in the sale, transport, and financing of goods. We will examine Incoterms and the UCP in some detail.

The ICC also provides specialized services to facilitate international commerce. One of the ICC's services is its court of arbitration, which, since its establishment in 1922, has handled more than 15,000 commercial arbitrations. In 2012 alone, 759 cases were filed (up from 593 in 2006), involving 2,036 parties from 137 countries, more than any other organization. We will be examining the process of commercial arbitration in later sections of this book.

Besides UNCITRAL, UNIDROIT, and the ICC, the Hague Conference and the International Maritime Committee (known under its French title, Comité Maritime

International) have also played an important role in unifying or codifying international commercial law. On a regional level, the Council of the European Union and the European Parliament, institutions within the European Union, are the most important regional law-making institutions. EU institutions have direct law-making powers and can create supranational laws that, upon enactment, are immediately effective as a superseding international law within its membership.

F. Major Categories of International Business Law

A distinguishing feature of the modern era since the end of the Second World War is that private international transactions are often governed in whole or in part by a source of law that is other than the law of one of the countries involved in the international movement of goods, services, technology, or capital. This is quite a departure from the approach in the nineteenth century when legal theorists posited that all IBTs were necessarily governed by national, not international, laws (with the possible exception of the ancient *lex mercatoria*).

The modern law that applies to IBTs is a blend of domestic private law and the business law aspects of public international law. We can classify the law of international business transactions into four categories.

1. Public International Law

As we have previously noted, the traditional field of public international law concerned the law that governed relations between states. Under the traditional view, only states were subjects of international law and only states had rights and obligations. Any rights or obligations in individuals or other entities were deemed to be derivative from their relationship to the state. Public international law also traditionally concerned political issues, diplomatic activity, and public rights such as the determination of statehood, the right of peoples to self-determination, the use of force, and the recognition of governments.

Today, public international law is no longer confined to relations between states but also applies to intergovernmental international organizations and even to individuals, although to a more limited extent. *See* Restatement of the Law of Foreign Relations (Third) §101 (1987). Moreover, the field of public international law not only encompasses public rights but also is a significant source of law governing commercial activity that occurs between private parties. The applicability of international treaties to private business transactions and private rights signals a shift in modern public international law. In the latter half of the twentieth century, the dramatic rise of international commerce and transactions of all kinds crossing national boundaries led nations to focus their attention on international commercial activity. Today, public international law in the form of treaties between states is an important source of law for IBTs. One example of a treaty that is an important source of law for IBTs is the CISG applicable to certain international contracts for the sale of goods. As of May 1, 2014, 80 countries, including the United States, China, Japan, and most European countries, were signatories to the CISG. The CISG can apply directly to a sales contract between private parties.

Aside from treaties, customary international law is the other traditional major source of public international law. Customary international law holds that states in and by their conduct can consent to the creation of binding international legal rules among themselves. Whereas treaties are evidence of an explicit consent between nations to be bound by contract, customary international law can be understood as a form of implied consent to be bound. The practice of states alone was not sufficient to become law; the practice had to be accompanied by a sense of legal obligation in order to become customary international law. As we have previously discussed, the ancient *lex mercatoria* was one type of international law that was applied in national courts up until the nineteenth century, and some vestiges of the traditional *lex mercatoria* may continue to have some application today. Aside from the law merchant, however, in the area of IBTs, customary international law does not play a significant role.

2. Regional Supranational Law

Within a regional economic organization such as the European Community (EC) (the economic pillar of the EU), there are instances in which a supranational law in the form of a treaty or regulation will apply directly to its member countries and will supersede national law in the case of conflict. Thus, a business transaction with a connection to Germany may be subject in part or in whole to an EC *law* or *regulation* that overrides German law. In other cases in the EU, a *directive* will require a member country to ensure that its laws conform to EU law and policy.[10]

3. Uniform Codes and Other Harmonizing Measures

An important and perhaps unique source of law applicable to IBTs are the codes created by intergovernmental and by private and nongovernmental bodies for the purposes of promoting harmonization. These rules codify international commercial custom and usage and define trade terms. Unlike treaties, which are legally binding instruments creating legal duties and obligations, the codes themselves have no inherent legal force but become legally effective when they are incorporated by contract by the parties. A prominent example of a widely adopted code are Incoterms (from International Commercial Terms) promulgated by the International Chamber of Commerce. Incoterms provide a set of terms that define rights and duties for exporters and forwarders involved in the international shipment of goods. Concepts such as CIF (cost, insurance, and freight) and FOB (free on board) are given a uniform definition by Incoterms that the parties can adopt by contract. Use of Incoterms avoids the problem that these terms could have different meanings to a seller from the United States and a buyer from England. Another example is the Uniform Customs and Practice for Documentary Credits (UCP) also promulgated by the International Chamber of Commerce. The UCP governs letters of credit and is widely adopted by banks throughout the world. The UCP applies to the account party's application to its bank to open the credit, the credit itself, the relationship between the beneficiary and the advising and confirming banks, and the relationships of the banks among themselves. Each of the relevant contracts incorporates the provisions of the UCP by reference, creating a network of contracts subject to a uniform set of rules and definitions.

The role that these codifications play in providing a source of law for IBTs appears to have no direct analogy in domestic law. The harmonizing measures promulgated by the ICC and other nongovernmental organizations are not intended to be model laws that may be adopted by legislatures or restatements of the law that are an attempt to influence the development of the law by courts or legislatures. Rather, they are intended for incorporation by contract by private parties to directly govern their transactions. These

---

10. See p. 42 *infra.*

codifications appear to be unique in international law—although they are related to the ancient *lex mercatoria* as they attempt to codify and set out in precise terms some of the customs and usages of international commerce. Unlike the *lex mercatoria*, however, these codifications do not purport to be a type of customary international law that is binding on domestic courts; rather, these codifications are binding because of incorporation by contract by the parties. Together with other sources of international commercial law, these codifications may constitute a new *lex mercatoria* for the modern age.

4. *Domestic Law*

Domestic law, including private international law, continues to be an important source of law for many IBTs. In an IBT between parties in different nations, the domestic law of one of the states will apply to the transaction in the absence of a superseding treaty or the explicit adoption of a uniform code by the parties. Conflicts and choice of law as well as recognition and enforcement of judgments in an international context continue to be governed by the principles of private international law. Domestic law may be the substantive law applicable to an IBT because it is chosen under domestic conflicts of law rules, that is, private international law, or because the parties have agreed to have the transaction governed by domestic law. Even where a transaction is governed by one of the nondomestic sources of law for international business transactions discussed in this section, some aspects of the transaction may nevertheless be governed by domestic law. For example, the CISG explicitly excludes some contract issues, such as validity, from the scope of its coverage; these issues will be governed by domestic law. Whenever there is an issue that falls into a "gap" in the application of law to an IBT that is otherwise governed by a nondomestic source of law, domestic law can serve to fill the gap.

PROBLEM 1-6

To test your understanding of these concepts and to emphasize that a single IBT can be subject to many different sources and types of law, can you explain how a single IBT, such as an international transaction for the sale of goods involving a sales contract, export compliance, and import clearance issues, can involve:

(1a)   a private international law analysis?
(1b)   a public international law that deals with private law issues?
(2a)   a domestic law that deals with private law issues?
(2b)   a domestic law that deals with public law issues?

G.   Relationship of Sources of International Law to Domestic Law

The previous discussion indicated that the law governing IBTs is drawn from a number of sources. Among the most important sources now is public international law. What is the relationship between public international law and domestic U.S. law governing IBTs?

As a historical matter, international law was part of the law of England and, as such, it was also part of the law of the U.S. colonies. With independence, international law became part of the law of the United States. From the beginning, international law was incorporated into the law of the United States without the need for any action by the President or Congress, and U.S. courts, both state and federal, have applied it and given it effect. The Supremacy Clause of the U.S. Constitution states that treaties of the United States, as well as the Constitution and laws of the United States, are to be "the supreme Law of the Land." *See* U.S. CONST. art. VI. With respect to customary international law, the U.S. Supreme Court has stated that it is "a part of our law." *See The Paquete Habana,* 175 U.S. 677, 700 (1900). This equates customary international law to the law of treaties and other international agreements as part of the law of the United States.[11]

Both treaties and customary international law are regarded as a type of federal law, equivalent in rank to the laws of the United States and supreme over the laws of the states. It was long ago established in U.S. jurisprudence that where there is a conflict between international law and state law, the former prevails. *See Ware v. Hylton,* 3 U.S. (3 Dall.) 199, 236–237 (1796). Where there is conflict between a treaty and a federal statute, the one that is later in time controls. *See Whitney v. Robertson,* 124 U.S. 190, 194 (1888). The treaties that have the benefit of the Supremacy Clause and Article VI need not necessarily be treaties made pursuant to Article II of the Constitution, which are those made by the President with the advice and consent of two-thirds of the Senate. There are two other common types of international agreements that are also given the same effect as treaties entered into pursuant to Article II of the Constitution: statutory agreements or congressional-executive agreements where the President enters into international agreements pursuant to ordinary congressional legislation authorizing the President to act and executive agreements concluded by the President alone.

While international law is a type of federal law, there is an important distinction between treaties and other types of federal law. In *Foster v. Neilson,* 27 U.S. 253 (1829), Chief Justice Marshall drew a distinction between self-executing and non-self-executing treaties that is now followed by many other countries. A self-executing treaty has a direct effect within the United States as soon as the treaty enters into force without the need for implementing domestic legislation. A non-self-executing treaty requires implementing legislation passed by Congress before the treaty is given effect. In the case of a non-self-executing treaty, it is the domestic implementing legislation that has legal effect within the United States, not the treaty itself. Examples of non-self-executing treaties are the many WTO agreements that contemplate implementing domestic legislation. Customary international law, where applicable, is given direct effect in U.S. courts. *See The Paquete Habana,* 175 U.S. at 700.

How does one determine whether a treaty is self-executing? One common approach by courts in the United States is to examine the intent of the states that are party to the treaty. The court examines the provisions of the treaty to determine whether they are aimed directly at the courts and not at the Congress requiring legislation. *See Foster, supra,* 27 U.S. at 314; *see also Cheung v. United States,* 213 F.3d 82, 95 (2d Cir. 2000). A few years later, Justice Marshall, who held that the treaty at issue in *Foster* was non-self-executing, held that the very same article at issue in a Spanish language version of the treaty was self-executing, indicating the broad interpretive discretion of the courts. *See United States v. Percheman,* 32 U.S. 51, 53 (1833).

In the area of IBTs, self-executing treaties and domestic legislation enacted for the purpose of implementing non-self-executing treaties may be sources of law applicable to a particular transaction. In some cases, the different aspects of the same transaction may be subject to different sources of law. For example, a sales contract may be subject

---

11. Some scholars, however, dispute the current relevance of customary international law unless it has been explicitly incorporated into U.S. law. *See, e.g.,* J. Patrick Kelly, *The Twilight of Customary International Law,* 40 Va. J. Int'l L. 449 (2000).

to the CISG but the letter of credit procured by the parties to finance the sale may be subject to the Uniform Customs and Practice for Documentary Credits. The carriage of the goods by sea may be subject to a federal statute such as the Carriage of Goods by Sea Act. Even where certain aspects of a transaction appear to fall under one set of legal rules such as letters of credit under the UCP, where questions arise that are not treated in the UCP, such as fraud, gaps in the UCP may be filled by resort to domestic law, such as the Uniform Commercial Code. For now, it is important to understand that the emerging law of IBTs is often a hybrid of many different sources of law. We have identified the primary ones in this section, but the process of determining which law governs a particular aspect of an IBT can be complex and any transaction may be subject to different sources of law.

PROBLEM 1-7

A successful Ohio law firm uses a standard form for its domestic sales contracts. The form has a choice of law clause choosing Ohio law. The law firm has been retained by a client that wishes to sell sophisticated equipment to be adapted for use in Argentina. The law firm has represented the client in the past in its domestic transactions quite successfully through the use of its standard contracts. The law firm is considering adopting the standard sales contract to the international sale and retaining the choice of law clause stipulating Ohio law. The law firm believes that rather than subjecting the transaction to the various sources of law governing IBTs, the law firm would simply retain its choice of law clause and avoid the complexities of applying unfamiliar sources of law. The lawyers in the firm are familiar with Ohio law and would save the client the expense involved in having the firm's lawyers research Argentine law or international law applicable to the contract. Do you see any problems with this approach? Consider the following:

(1) Assume that Argentine law does not have the same types of implied warranties that are contained under the Ohio Uniform Commercial Code such as an implied warranty of fitness. How does this affect your answer?

(2) Both the United States and Argentina are parties to the Convention on Contracts for the International Sale of Goods. The CISG allows parties to opt out in favor of another law, including domestic law. Assume that the choice of law clause in the law firm's standard contract is sufficient to opt out of the CISG. How would you advise the Ohio law firm in light of the following discussion of whether a lawyer involved in an international contract needs to be aware of the CISG:

> The duty of competence set forth in Model Rule 1.1 clearly requires of a lawyer "the legal knowledge, skill, thoroughness and preparation reasonably necessary for the representation." Any lawyer involved in the negotiation or litigation of a contract for which the parties have their places of business in different countries has a duty to determine [whether the Convention applies.] If the lawyer determines that the [CISG] applies to the transaction, he or she then has a duty to understand fully the rules of the [CISG] and the application of those rules to the transaction. If the representation is in the context of negotiations, the lawyer is also responsible for determining and advising the client whether exercising the Article 6 possibility of "opting out" of the CISG rules would be to the benefit of the client. If the representation is in the context of litigation, the lawyer clearly has an obligation to know (1) whether the Convention applies to the transaction in question, and (2) if it does, the impact on his or her client of application of the Convention rules.

Ronald A. Brand, *Professional Responsibility in a Transnational Transactions Practice*, 17 J.L. & Com. 301, 335-336 (1998).

PROBLEM 1-8

A, an Illinois company, has entered into a contract to sell goods to B, a German company. Both the United States and Germany are contracting parties to the CISG. Article 1 of the CISG provides that "this Convention applies to contracts of sale of goods between parties whose places are in different States when the States are Contracting States." Article 6 of the CISG further provides, "The parties may exclude the application of this Convention or derogate from or vary the effect of any of its provisions." Suppose that the contract has a choice of law clause that provides, "This contract is to be governed exclusively by the laws of Illinois." A brings a lawsuit in an Illinois state court on the contract.

(1) Should the Illinois court apply Illinois state law, German law, the CISG, or some other law? *See Asante Technologies, Inc. v. PMC-Sierra, Inc.*, 164 F. Supp. 2d 1142, 1150 (N.D. Cal. 2001) (a choice of law provision selecting British Columbia law did not, without more, "evince a clear intent to opt out of the CISG. Defendant's choice of applicable law adopts the law of British Columbia, and it is undisputed that the CISG *is* the law of British Columbia"). *See also Ajax Tool Works, Inc. v. Can-Eng Manufacturing Ltd.*, 2003 WL 223187, at *3 (N.D. Ill. 2003) ("The parties' contract states that the 'agreement shall be governed by the laws of the Province of Ontario, Canada.' Obviously, this clause does not exclude the CISG."); *St. Paul Guardian Ins. Co. v. Neuromed Medical Systems & Support, GmbH*, 2002 WL 465312, at *3 (S.D.N.Y. 2002) (the CISG applies "[w]here parties, as here, designate a choice of law clause in their contract — selecting the law of a Contracting State without expressly excluding application of the CISG. To hold otherwise would undermine the objectives of the Convention which Germany has agreed to uphold.").

(2) How would you draft the choice of law clause to exclude the CISG?

(3) Is the CISG a self-executing treaty that has direct effect within U.S. courts or must the Illinois court look to domestic implementing legislation?

VI.   *International Economic Law: The Public Law Institutions and Rules That Facilitate and Regulate International Business*

Governments play a large role in both facilitating and regulating international business. Governments levy taxes (called tariffs) on imports, and they have the ability to influence trade, encouraging some and cutting off other transactions. Governments also have the ability to regulate international transactions just as they do domestic business through competition laws, securities laws, environmental laws, labor laws, taxation, and social legislation.

Theoretically, the doctrines of sovereignty and the existence of the nation-state system of world order would allow any state to impose whatever tax or regulation on international business it deemed necessary. This, of course, would be chaotic and damaging to world business. Fortunately, in the last 60 years an imposing structure of international rules and intergovernmental organizations has been created to impose some order on the way governments regulate international business. Without this framework, international business as we know it today would be literally impossible.

The legal mechanism used to create this framework of international institutions and rules is the international agreement or treaty, which was previously considered in our discussion of public international law. This legal method is a primary way of creating public international law, and this body of law is a specialized branch of public international law known as *international trade law* and also known as *international economic law.*

International economic law (IEL) consists, therefore, of the framework of intergovernmental organizations and international rules that govern international economic relations. IEL is created through bilateral, regional, and multilateral treaties. Such treaties cover all four of the channels of international business: trade in goods, trade in services, technology transfer, and foreign investment. Once the rules have been formulated internationally through the treaty-making process, the responsibility of participating governments is to transform these international obligations into domestic legislation and to apply them faithfully. Thus, the international business lawyer will deal with these rules more on the level of domestic law than as international law. Nevertheless, their international law source must be understood.

International trade law or international economic law is beyond the scope of this book, which concerns the law of IBTs. However, in each of the chapters of this book, IEL concepts will be introduced since they are an integral part of the legal practice relating to IBTs. In this chapter, we introduce the principal institutions and sources of IEL that the international business lawyer must learn to deal with.

PROBLEM 1-9

Medtech manufactures medical devices in its factory in Columbus, Georgia. It is a small, but very successful closely held corporation (no public stock outstanding) that has developed a market for its products in the Southern, Eastern, and Midwestern United States. Jane Bell, the dynamic and ambitious CEO and founder, now is thinking of expanding the business internationally. She has the following questions:

(1) Europe is a natural extension of the market for Medtech's products. However, there are many different countries all with different languages and cultures. Bell is concerned that these many cultural differences will be reflected in many different legal systems, including differing customs rates, export requirements, and the use of many different currencies. These differences could make doing business in Europe complex and costly. How difficult would it be to develop a European market for Medtech products?

(2) What about starting closer to home? Should Medtech expand to Canada? Mexico? Other countries in Latin America?

(3) How easy would it be to expand to Japan, China, Vietnam, Indonesia, and other Asian markets? How would developing a common strategy for Asia compare with developing a common approach for Europe?

(4) What about developing countries in Africa?

(5) Where can she get some help about what export markets would be best for Medtech's products? What if Medtech ran into difficulty in the form of an unfair or arbitrary action by a foreign government that prevented foreign sales, like an unruly customs agency that held up the distribution of Medtech products?

(6) Suppose that she goes to the trouble of developing a foreign market and Medtech products are successful. Can the foreign government raise taxes or otherwise shut down her operations?

(7) What about foreign competition for her products in the United States? Can anything be done if foreign competitors are "dumping" their products in the

United States, that is, selling their products at prices below cost in order to obtain a market access at the expense of Medtech?

In considering this problem, review the following materials in Sections A through I below.

A.   The World Trade Organization

The World Trade Organization (WTO), established in 1995, is a multilateral trade organization consisting of 159 members, including all of the major economies of the world. The WTO is the most powerful and influential organization in the world that deals with international trade in goods, services, and technology (intellectual property), three of the four major channels of trade. For historical reasons, the WTO does not regulate foreign direct investment, the fourth channel.[12] As this book concentrates private international business transactions in these channels, we will examine the WTO only by way of background, but it is important for every lawyer dealing in private transactions to understand a few basic facts about the WTO.

As international trade and business would be impossible if each nation were left to its own devices in erecting barriers to trade and business, the WTO operates as a forum to assist nations in reducing barriers to international trade. This is done through formal negotiations (called "rounds") under the WTO and its predecessor, the General Agreement on Tariffs and Trade (GATT). The WTO also serves as a forum in which nations can discuss, negotiate, and resolve trade disputes. The WTO is a successor to the GATT, which was founded in 1947 after the Second World War. The GATT was designed to allow nations to negotiate lower tariffs, which are customs duties or taxes imposed at the border before goods can be cleared for importation and entry into the internal market of the importing country. The GATT has been remarkably successful in lowering tariff rates, which are now at historical lows and stand in stark contrast to the draconian and prohibitively high rates of the 1930s when national protectionism was at or near a peak. This high protectionism was one of the causes of the Second World War and GATT 1947 was a direct response to the desire of nations to prevent the causes of another world war. In 1995, the WTO replaced the GATT 1947, which was a treaty limited to the trade in goods, with a comprehensive legal structure to serve as a mechanism to reduce barriers in all forms of trade.

The WTO administers four major multilateral agreements, which are mandatory for each WTO member upon accession to the WTO. Three of these four major treaties deal with three channels of trade: trade in goods, trade in services, and trade in technology. The WTO administers the GATT, which was renamed and reissued with amendments as GATT 1994 with the birth of the WTO. As we have already noted, the GATT is designed to reduce tariffs imposed at the border on imported goods by all modern trading states. Each GATT member, including the United States, agrees to "bind" its tariffs to ceilings under the GATT, i.e., not to impose tariffs above its agreed upon GATT rates. This is done through negotiations with all other GATT/WTO members. For example, the United States imposes tariffs (as we shall see in Chapter Two) that are subject to ceilings under the GATT. The United States agreed to these "bindings" in its GATT Schedule, which the United States submitted to the WTO. Every WTO member has submitted similar commitments to "bind" their tariffs, although tariff rates may differ among individual nations as each nation sets its own tariff schedule in negotiations with all other WTO members.

---

12. See pp. 397-399 *infra.*

GATS

The WTO also administers a general agreement that regulates trade in services, the General Agreement on Trade in Services (GATS). Under the GATS, nations can voluntarily agree to open up their services sectors to foreign competition. For example, Country A might agree to open its legal services sector to foreign competition, which might include allowing persons of foreign nationality to pass a qualification examination and to obtain a lawyer's license. The same might be true for services in accounting, insurance, banking, and retailing and distribution. Market access commitments under the GATS are purely voluntary but a nation that refuses to open its services sectors to foreign suppliers will find that it in turn is denied access to services sectors in the market of its foreign trading partners. Thus, every WTO member has institutional incentives to liberalize trade in services. This process is ongoing.

TRIPs

A third major agreement administered by the WTO is the Agreement on Trade Related Aspects of Intellectual Property Rights (TRIPs). The major goal of TRIPs is to achieve the harmonization in all WTO countries of intellectual rights such as patents, trademarks, and copyrights through the setting of minimum international standards in these areas to which all nations must adhere. For example, the United States, Germany, China, Japan, and all other WTO members have an obligation to enact intellectual property laws that meet the minimum standards set forth in TRIPs. Overall, TRIPs has been very successful in achieving harmonization, although enforcement of these laws can still create problems.

For historical reasons, the WTO never reached a general agreement on foreign direct investment, the fourth major channel of international trade. FDI is subject to some regulation under the WTO, but only in very limited ways.[13]

The WTO also administers a fourth major agreement, the Agreement on the Understanding of Rules and Procedures Governing the Settlement of Disputes (DSU). This dispute settlement mechanism includes the use of panels, which operate like a trial court of international trade, and an appellate body, which operates as a high court of international trade. Since 1995, the WTO dispute settlement mechanism has handled over 400 cases, which makes the WTO the single busiest international dispute settlement tribunal. WTO decisions are not legally binding on WTO members but there is institutional pressure to adhere to the decisions and most WTO dispute settlement decisions are given effect by WTO members.

The highest governing body in the WTO is the Ministerial Conference, which is a meeting of the trade ministers of all WTO members held every two years. The second highest body is the General Council, a permanent standing body, which consists of a trade delegation of each WTO member. Decisions in the Ministerial Conference and in the General Council are made by consensus, which is different from unanimity. Consensus means that no single member objects; thus, the minority will normally go along with the majority unless it has a serious objection. In return, the majority will not ramrod or impose decisions on the minority. As you might imagine, decision by consensus takes a great deal of time. In rare cases, when a consensus cannot be reached, a decision can, under some circumstances, be made by majority vote.

The WTO contains two foundation principles of international trade law that predate the WTO and that are found in many other regional and bilateral investment and trade agreements: the Most-Favored Nation (MFN) Principle and the National Treatment (NT) Principle. The MFN principle means that each nation will treat all other trading nations equally and will not extend special privileges or benefits to one nation. For example, if Country A, a WTO member, extends a trade privilege or benefit to Country B

---

13. See Chapter Six at pp. 397-399.

(whether or not B is a WTO member), Country A must immediately and unconditionally extend the same privilege or benefit to every other WTO country. The MFN principle universalizes trade benefits and serves as a major inducement to join the WTO. Under the NT Principle, a WTO member cannot discriminate in favor of domestic goods and against foreign goods. For example, Country A cannot impose a sales tax only on imports but exempt like domestic goods from the same tax. Both MFN and NT are principles of non-discrimination and are foundational to international business and trade. We will encounter these principles in Chapter Six on foreign investment and other parts of this book.

Finally, it is important to emphasize that many of the U.S. regulations and laws that we will examine in this book are implementations at the domestic level of obligations created at the multilateral level by the WTO. The WTO serves as a background to many of the laws we consider in this book, but our purpose in this section is merely to present an overview of the WTO. For extensive treatment of WTO, see Chow and Schoenbaum, *International Trade Law: Cases, Materials, and Problems* (Aspen 2d ed. 2012).

B. Preferential Trade Agreements

Since the 1940s, multilateralism has been the hallmark of international trade negotiations. Led by the GATT, successive "rounds" of successful multilateral trade negotiations helped to create the complex interlocking economic relations that today bind virtually all nations into the global economy. In the early twenty-first century, however, there appeared signs that this wave of multilateralism may have run its course, and future new multilateral agreements may be few and far between. The current deadlock in the Doha Development Agenda is a sign of resistance to further significant multilateral gains. Even if the Doha Round is successfully concluded, the results are expected to be minimal compared to the spectacular changes wrought by the Uruguay Round.

In the first decade of the twenty-first century there occurred an important shift toward the negotiation of bilateral and regional preferential trade agreements. As a result in virtually every area of the world there is a new architecture of such agreements, which seem to be the favored way of satisfying political constituencies. There are two basic types of such preferential trade agreements, customs unions and free trade agreements (FTAs).

Customs unions not only liberalize trade internally, they adopt a single external tariff and trade structure. All goods (and other trade channels) are allowed to move freely within the customs union without the payment of tariffs. For goods from nonmembers of the union, the single tariff means that it makes no difference whether goods are imported into any country of the customs union; the same tariff is imposed. The primary example of such a customs union is the European Union (also a political union), which has expanded in size to 28 members. Another important customs union is the South African Customs Union (SACU), which consists of South Africa, Botswana, Swaziland, Lesotho, and Namibia.

Free trade areas also eliminate all tariffs and other trade barriers for all members of the FTA, but each member is allowed to set its own trade policy with respect to external trade. Unlike a customs union, which sets a single tariff for all goods imported from nonmembers, each member of an FTA is allowed to set its own tariffs on goods from nonmembers. FTAs have sprouted all over the world. In Africa we find the Economic Community of West African States (ECOWAS) and the Common Market for Eastern and Southern

Africa (COMESA). In South America there is the Market of the South (Mercosur). In North America there is the North American Free Trade Agreement (NAFTA); in Asia we find the ten-member Association of Southeast Asian Nations (ASEAN). Japan and China have also concluded several free trade agreements and there is discussion in Asia of a giant "ASEAN plus six" free trade agreement encompassing ASEAN, Japan, China, South Korea, India, Australia, and New Zealand.

The United States is particularly active in creating free trade agreements with countries all over the world. An official U.S. government web site lists 20 countries with which the United States has an operating free trade agreement.[14] Information and the text of each agreement may be found on this site as well.

The United States seeks to expand this web of free trade agreements and to submit virtually all international trade to special free trade rules. To this end the United States has opened negotiations with Japan and 11 other Asian nations with a view to conclude a Trans-Pacific Partnership (TPP) Agreement covering virtually all U.S. trade with Asia (excluding China). The United States has also opened negotiations with the European Union to create a Transatlantic Trade and Investment Partnership (TTIP) Agreement. Both of these negotiations involve complex and difficult issues; it remains to be seen whether this ambitious trade policy will bear fruit and be accepted by the Congress of the United States.

As this movement toward preferential trade agreements plays itself out, it will be interesting to see how such agreements fit into the existing multilateral structure of world trade.

C. The North American Free Trade Agreement

The North American Free Trade Agreement (NAFTA) is the most important example of its kind. There are scores of such free trade agreements functioning in the world today. FTAs exist in every region of the world and every member of the WTO is a party to at least one. They are both bilateral and multilateral. The United States has free trade agreements with Israel, Jordan, Singapore, Chile, and South Korea in addition to NAFTA, and more are on the way. FTAs are political as well as economic instruments. Politically, they tie states together. In economic terms, FTAs both create and divert trade. They create trade between members, but part of this trade is diverted away from third-party states. In pure economic terms, FTAs are mixed blessings.

NAFTA is a prototypical example of an FTA that is extremely important to North American business entities, but almost as important to non-NAFTA countries that do business with Mexico, the United States, and Canada.

NAFTA encompasses all trade between Mexico, the United States, and Canada. As of 2003, virtually all customs duties (tariffs) have been eliminated on products moving between the three countries considered to have "NAFTA content" (more on the definition of this in Chapter Two). However, all three members retain complete control over their tariffs and commercial policies toward non-NAFTA states. This is the essence of an FTA: The parties do not give up their economic independence. They can also apply their unfair trade practice laws (antidumping and countervailing duty) against their NAFTA partners.

---

14. See *Free Trade Agreements*, OFF. OF THE U.S. TRADE REPRESENTATIVE, *http://www.ustr.gov/ trade-agreements/free-trade-agreements*.

1.   NAFTA Objectives

NAFTA became effective on January 1, 1994. NAFTA creates free movement of goods and fosters cross-border trade in services and investment flows. NAFTA also covers to some extent other economic issues such as labor, protection of the environment (through side agreements), intellectual property, and competition law. NAFTA's objectives are set forth below:

United States Department of Commerce,
A Guide to Customs Procedures (2004)
Description of the NAFTA

Objectives

The objectives of this Agreement are to:

- Eliminate barriers to trade in, and facilitate the cross-border movement of, goods and services between the territories of the Parties;
- Promote conditions of fair competition in the free trade area;
- Increase substantially investment opportunities in the territories of the Parties;
- Provide adequate and effective protection and enforcement of intellectual property rights in each Party's territory;
- Create effective procedures for the implementation and application of this Agreement, for its joint administration and for the resolution of disputes;
- Establish a framework for further trilateral, regional and multilateral cooperation to expand and enhance the benefits of this Agreement.

2.   NAFTA Administration and Dispute Settlement

We will cover many of the technicalities of NAFTA in subsequent chapters of this book; our objective here is simply to present an overview of this important agreement.[15] One of NAFTA's major objectives is to establish market access for goods and National Treatment. Market access means that goods that travel across the borders of NAFTA countries travel duty free. For example, goods imported into the United States from Canada and Mexico are in general subject to zero tariffs (although some automotive and apparel goods are given special treatment). This is considered to be "WTO plus" treatment since such favorable treatment is beyond what is available under the WTO.[16] To prevent other non-NAFTA members from shipping goods to Mexico and doing some simple assembly operations in order to ship the goods duty free into the United States, NAFTA has complex rules of origin. In the example just given, if Brazil were to ship parts of goods to Mexico and then assemble the parts and ship them as finished goods to the United States, U.S. Customs might consider the goods to be of Brazilian origin, even though the goods enter the United States from Mexico. The goods would then be subjected to ordinary U.S. tariffs as applied to Brazilian goods.

NAFTA covers not only trade in goods, but also services trade, technology trade, and investment trade. All forms of trade are subject to the principle of National Treatment, discussed above at pp. 36-37. Recall that the NT Principle prohibits members from

---

15. For the text of NAFTA and a detailed discussion, see *http://www.ustr.gov/webfm_send/2647.*

16. The WTO contains an exception to the Most Favored-Nation Principle for free trade agreements in Article XIV of the General Agreement on Tariffs and Trade, which permits countries in NAFTA to extend trade preferences to each other without having to extend the same preferences to all other WTO countries.

discriminating against foreign trade in favor of domestic trade. Under NAFTA, the United States, Mexico, and Canada are prohibited from discriminating against trade in goods, services, intellectual property, and investment from other NAFTA countries in favor of local trade in the same sector. All NAFTA members must treat trade from other NAFTA members on an equal basis with domestic trade.

NAFTA has special rules that apply to trade in energy and petrochemicals, agriculture and food safety, telecommunications, financial services, monopolies and state enterprises as well as competition policy. NAFTA also contains rules relating to government procurement, i.e., the purchase by NAFTA governments of goods and services from private vendors of each of the NAFTA countries. NAFTA also has special institutional rules: requirements of special customs procedures that apply to NAFTA products; requirements related to publication, notification, and administration of laws; and standardization of national measures that apply to trade to minimize their impact. NAFTA also contains special "safeguard" provisions that allow a NAFTA country to ignore or limit its NAFTA obligations in the case of a trade emergency. NAFTA also contains a general exceptions clause that deals with exceptions for safety, national security, culture and protection of the environment, and natural resources. NAFTA countries are excused from their NAFTA obligations under circumstances where these exceptions apply.

One of NAFTA's most important features is the NAFTA Free Trade Commission consisting of the trade ministers of the three countries, which established a special dispute settlement mechanism for the trade topics covered by NAFTA.

NAFTA establishes three different procedures to settle disputes:

- Chapter 19 allows exporters and domestic industries to appeal the results of national trade remedy investigations to an independent and objective bi-national panel. This process is an alternative to judicial review of such decisions in domestic courts. This dispute settlement procedure is administered by the NAFTA Secretariat.
- Chapter 20 offers a three-step process for resolving disputes concerning the implementation or interpretation of NAFTA. The first step is consultation among the disputing parties; the second is referral of the dispute to the NAFTA Free Trade Commission; the third step is referral to binding arbitration by a special panel.
- Chapter 11 on Investment allows a NAFTA investor to proceed to arbitration with a NAFTA state concerning an investment dispute. This matter is considered in Chapter Six of this book.

D.   The European Union

The European Union (EU) is a political, economic, and (partial) monetary union of 28 member states that have signed a succession of important international treaties delegating significant sovereign powers to pan-European institutions. The founding Maastricht Treaty on European Union (1993) originally created the EU as a tripartite structure as follows: "Pillar" One contained the European Community Treaties, the European Economic Community Rome Treaty (1957) as amended (the European Community Treaty or EC Treaty) and the EURATOM Treaty (1957). A third treaty community, the European Coal and Steel Community Treaty of 1951, expired in 2002, and its functions were allocated to the EC Treaty regime. "Pillar" Two (Articles 11–28 of the Maastricht Treaty) contained provisions establishing a common foreign and security policy. "Pillar" Three (Articles 29–45 of the Maastricht Treaty) contained provisions on policy and judicial cooperation in criminal matters. The Maastricht Treaty was significantly amended several times, notably by the Treaty of Amsterdam (entered into force 1999) and the Treaty of Nice (entered into force 2003). After a proposed new EU Treaty Constitution failed to achieve ratification in France and the Netherlands, EU leaders signed the Treaty of Lisbon, which entered into force on December 1, 2009. The Treaty of Lisbon now gives the EU a single international legal personality, abolishing the "three pillar" structure, and strengthens EU institutions and decision-making processes. *See http://europa.eu/lisbon_treaty*. The Treaty of Lisbon significantly amends and changes the name of the EC Treaty to the Treaty on the Functioning of the European Union.

The historical beginnings of the EU go back to the end of the Second World War when Europe was considering how to recover from devastation and to prevent future European wars. The first important initiative was taken in 1950 by Robert Schuman, the French foreign minister, and Jean Monnet, a French official, who proposed what became the European Coal and Steel Community of 1951, the first European Community. This was followed by two additional European Communities created by treaty in 1957, the European Economic Community and EURATOM. The institutions of these three Communities were combined by a Merger Treaty in 1967.

The founding member states of the EC (Belgium, France, Germany, Italy, Luxembourg, and the Netherlands) were soon joined by additional states, and beginning in 1972 with the addition of the United Kingdom, Denmark, and Ireland, the EC and later the EU periodically enlarged to its present membership of 28, with many additional states applying for admission.

The EU has created important supranational institutions that participate in the creation and administration of EU law, a new legal order that is separate from and superior to the national laws of the member states. These institutions are as follows:

- The Council of the European Union (formerly the Council of Ministers) is with the European Parliament the co-legislature of the EU. This Council is actually a disparate group consisting of the appropriate ministerial representatives of the member states who are concerned with whatever topic is on the agenda for decision. With respect to most matters (the most important exception being foreign and security policy), voting is by "Qualified Majority," which is a complex weighted voting system that allocates votes to member states on the basis of population (as well as political clout). Thus, a legislative proposal may pass although a significant number of states vote "no." The legislative competence of the Council is limited by the fact that draft legislation must be initiated by the European Commission.
- The European Commission is the executive branch of the EU with responsibilities to administer and to enforce the laws. The Commission also formulates initial legislative proposals for further action by the Parliament and the Council. Each member state is allocated one Commissioner (until 2014 when the number of Commissioners is set to be cut to two-thirds of the number of states), and each is in charge of a substantive portfolio of EU policy. These policy functions are carried out by 36 Directorates. A Secretary-General provides overall coordination and presides over the Commission's weekly meetings. The Commission employs about 25,000 permanent staff headquartered in Brussels. The Commission exercises important powers in the area of external relations of the EU and oversees the implementation of the EU budget.

- The European Parliament (EP), which shares legislative competence with the Council, consists of representatives directly elected by the peoples of the EU, and its 751 seats are allocated to the member states on the basis of populations. Plenary sessions of the EP are held both in Strasbourg and in Brussels, and the Secretariat is based in Luxembourg. The EP participates in the European Community legislative process, has approval power over the members (collectively) of the Commission, and participates in the EU budget approval process. The EP is also a deliberative body, and any citizen of the EU is entitled to address a petition to the EP on any matter pertinent to EU affairs.
- The European judicial system consists of a General Court (formerly the Court of First Instance) and a Court of Justice of the European Union. Among the important functions these courts have is the exclusive power to interpret EU treaties and the secondary laws. The courts exercise judicial review of EU laws and have the power to require compliance with EU treaties and law by member states.

In addition to the extensive series of treaties, EU law consists of regulations, directives, and decisions published in the Official Journal (OJ), available at *http://www.europa.eu.int*. Regulations have direct effect in the legal orders of the member states. Directives issued to member states require them to enact substantive laws on the matters concerned within a specified time. Decisions are binding on the parties to whom they are addressed.

The EU is managed politically by the European Council (a different body than the Council of the EU described above), a body consisting of the heads of the member states, which meets periodically at least four times a year. As a result of the Treaty of Lisbon, the EU has a full-time President, who serves a two and one-half year term, and a High Representative for Foreign Policy and Security.

In economic terms the EU is much like a sovereign state. The EU is a customs union with one external tariff and commercial policy and free movement of goods, services, money, and people within its borders. A business established in the EU has the right to establish branches and subsidiaries in any member state.

E. Free Trade in Asia

Asia is a vast area that varies greatly in terms of nations, cultures, and peoples. In South Asia the principal nation is India, a developing country but with pockets of very advanced technology and industry. In East and Northeast Asia, Japan and China dominate; however, each is at a different stage of political and economic development. In Southeast Asia, the largest state is Indonesia, which has severe political and economic problems. Singapore is a tiny enclave of stability and relative prosperity—it has recently concluded free trade agreements with Japan, South Korea, and the United States.

In addition to having great disparity in levels of economic development, Asia is also marked by areas of political instability and long-term unresolved political problems such as the North and South Korea predicament and China's claim to sovereignty over Taiwan. These economic and political issues have impeded the formation of any significant economic, political, and security architecture and multilateral institutions. This may change, but for now only two significant organizational groupings are relevant: the Association of Southeast Asian Nations (ASEAN) and the Asia Pacific Economic Cooperation forum (APEC), which also includes the United States and countries from outside of Asia that border on the Pacific Ocean.

1. ASEAN

ASEAN was established on August 8, 1967, in Bangkok and now consists of ten countries: Brunei Darussalam, Cambodia, Indonesia, Laos, Malaysia, Myanmar, Republic of the Philippines, Singapore, Thailand, and Viet Nam. As of 2014, the ASEAN region has a population of about 620 million, a total of 4.5 million square kilometers, a combined gross domestic product of $2.2 trillion, and a total trade with the United States of $229 billion ($198 billion in goods and $30 billion in services in 2012). The objectives of ASEAN are to promote economic growth and regional peace and stability.

One of ASEAN's first initiatives was the Preferential Trading Arrangement of 1977, which created tariff preferences among member nations in order to improve what were insignificant levels of intra-ASEAN trade that were between 12 and 15 percent in the late 1960s and early 1970s. In 1992, the Fourth ASEAN Summit in Singapore adopted plans for an ASEAN Free Trade Area or AFTA, which would eventually eliminate tariff and non-tariff barriers among member countries. Other ASEAN initiatives include plans to create trans-ASEAN networks for air, land, and sea transportation; telecommunications; and energy. ASEAN cooperation has led to some significant increases in trade. Within three years of the launching of AFTA, exports among ASEAN countries grew from $43.26 billion in 1993 to almost $80 billion in 1996, an average yearly growth rate of 28.3 percent. Intraregional ASEAN trade grew during the same period to almost 25 percent of total trade. As of 2012, total ASEAN trade exceeded $2.4 trillion, of which $600 billion, or about 25 percent, was intraregional ASEAN trade. On November 20, 2007, the ten ASEAN nations signed the ASEAN Charter, which founds a cooperative economic and political community loosely based on the EU model. *See http://www.aseansec.org.*

ASEAN has concluded free trade agreements with both China and Japan.

2. APEC

APEC is an informal cooperation forum of nations that border the Pacific Ocean rim. APEC was established in 1989 and currently has 21 member economies: Australia; Brunei Darussalam; Canada; Chile; People's Republic of China; Hong Kong, China; Indonesia; Japan; Republic of Korea; Malaysia; Mexico; New Zealand; Papua New Guinea; Peru; Republic of the Philippines; Russia; Singapore; Chinese Taipei (Taiwan); Thailand; the United States; and Viet Nam. As a trading group, APEC now accounts for about half of the world's exports and imports. APEC meetings allow leaders from member countries to discuss major issues in the APEC region in an informal setting. APEC meetings, such as that hosted by the United States in 1989 on Blake Island, Washington, provide a forum for leaders to meet on a regular basis as a group to discuss APEC's goals of free trade and investment and to discuss current issues and resolve disputes. Although these meetings are informal, they have resulted in significant market liberalization of APEC markets. APEC has also played a significant role in promoting the adoption of economic policies to stimulate growth and attract investment and has also addressed social issues such as environmental and labor standards, education, and disease prevention and control.

F. Free Trade in the Americas

In 1994, with great fanfare, the United States and 33 other Western Hemisphere nations announced negotiations that were to culminate in a Free Trade Area of the Americas

(FTAA). These countries resolved to unify the two existing Western Hemisphere trade blocks—NAFTA and MERCOSUR (Mercado Común del Sur) into one vast free trade area. Periodic meetings and negotiations were held regularly until 2005, the year that the FTAA was to have been completed. But since 2005, negotiations have been suspended. A third draft of the FTAA was concluded by negotiators, but no action on this matter is presently scheduled.

The goal of the FTAA was to create a free trade zone in the Western Hemisphere that will be consistent with WTO rules but will be "WTO plus"—will go beyond WTO rules with respect to trade. But international politics and the global financial crisis of 2009 intervened to put a halt to this idea. Instead, the United States has entered into individual free trade agreements with Latin American and Caribbean countries. As of 2014, in addition to NAFTA with Mexico and Canada, the United States has agreements with ten countries in the Americas: Chile, Colombia, Costa Rica, Dominican Republic, El Salvador, Guatemala, Honduras, Nicaragua, Panama, and Peru. The free trade area composed of the United States and six Central American countries plus the Dominican Republic is known as CAFTA-DR. It now appears that free trade in the Americas will only be achieved in a step-by-step fashion.

G.   Developing Countries

Importing from or to and investing in so-called developing countries involves special considerations. However, a threshold question is: What is the definition of a developing country?

There is no universally accepted definition of this important term, but the classification scheme developed by the World Bank is widely used. The World Bank classifies countries in terms of per capita income. A low-income developing country is one with a per capita income of $1,045 or less. Nations with per capita income of $1,046 to $4,125 are classified as lower-middle developing countries. Nations having per capita income from $4,126 to $12,745 are upper-middle developing countries. Nations with per capita income greater than $12,746 are high-income countries eligible for membership in organizations of the industrialized countries such as the Paris-based Organization of Economic Cooperation and Development. *See* Country and Lending Groups, WORLD BANK, *http:// data.worldbank.org/about/country-and-lending-groups.*

It is apparent that the term "developing country" encompasses most of the countries of the world and most of the membership of the WTO. However, the term includes widely different countries located in many different areas of the world. An umbrella organization that deals with the economic interests of developing countries is the Geneva-based United Nations Conference on Trade and Development (UNCTAD). As an arm of the United Nations Economic and Social Council (ECOSOC), UNCTAD undertakes a wide variety of activities to further the interests of developing countries.

In trade, developing countries benefit from what is known as the Generalized System of Preferences (GSP). This was intended to implement Part IV of the GATT, which called for preferential tariff rates for products manufactured in developing countries. Both the United States and the EU have implemented comprehensive GSP programs. Both the U.S. and EU GSP programs generally called for tariff free treatment of goods from developing countries. However, the GSP programs have had limited impact on trade from developing countries. Political considerations are at play in selecting countries that benefit from GSP programs and highly complex rules for obtaining GSP treatment have hampered developing country exporters. As Constantine Michalopoulos, a senior official at the World Bank, has stated, "the GSP turned out to be less than it has been touted to be at its inception. It was important for some products, for some countries, for some of the time. But it [has not] served to strengthen the integration of developing countries into the world trading system."[17]

An industry that has capitalized on the GSP and the U.S. African Growth and Opportunity Act (AGOA) is South Africa's auto industry. As a result of the AGOA, the auto industry has become South Africa's largest export sector; in 2001, the first year of the program, the industry's exports rose by 387 percent to $359 million. In 2011, exports grew again to $7.1 billion and accounted for 11.8 percent of total South African exports.

H. The Organization for Economic Cooperation and Development

The Organization for Economic Cooperation and Development (OECD), based in Paris, is a grouping of 34 industrialized countries: Australia, Austria, Belgium, Canada, Chile, Czech Republic, Denmark, Estonia, Finland, France, Germany, Greece, Hungary, Iceland, Ireland, Israel, Italy, Japan, Korea, Luxembourg, Mexico, the Netherlands, New Zealand, Norway, Poland, Portugal, Slovak Republic, Slovenia, Spain, Sweden, Switzerland, Turkey, United Kingdom, and the United States. The OECD produces internationally agreed upon instruments, decisions, and recommendations to promote international rules where multilateral agreement is necessary. These are produced by dialogue, peer review, pressure, and consensus.

I. Trade Institutions and Policy in the United States

In the United States, international economic and trade policy is controlled by the Congress, which has the constitutional power over foreign commerce (U.S. CONST. art. I, §8, cl. 3). However, the President and the executive branch of the U.S. government exercise practical control through congressional delegation of power and because the President has the constitutional authority to negotiate with foreign nations (U.S. CONST. art. II). The U.S. Court of International Trade (CIT) has exclusive jurisdiction to hear civil actions arising out of import transactions, and the CIT exercises judicial review of final agency decisions concerning U.S. trade laws. Decisions of the CIT can be appealed to the U.S. Court of Appeals for the Federal Circuit.

Authority over international trade and investment is divided among several agencies of the U.S. government.

(1) The U.S. Customs and Border Patrol, a part of the Department of Homeland Security, has primary authority over imports into the United States.
(2) The U.S. Department of Commerce is the primary agency for both export promotion and the regulation of exports under U.S. law. One of its departments, the International Trade Administration (ITA), provides help to individual businesses that desire to develop export markets anywhere in the world. The

---

17. Mitsuo Matsushita, Thomas J. Schoenbaum, and Petros Mavroidis, *The World Trade Organization: Law, Practice and Policy* 773–775 (2d ed. 2006).

Commercial Law Development Program fosters the opening of new export markets in developing countries. The Office of Export Licensing administers export licensing requirements.

(3) U.S. trade laws involving import competition are administered by both the ITA and an independent agency, the International Trade Commission (ITC), which consists of six persons appointed by the President for nine-year terms. The U.S. import competition trade laws are conceptually divided into the regulation of fair and unfair trade. Fair-trade imports that cause or threaten to cause serious injury to U.S. industries may be regulated by decision of the ITC, which issues §201 escape clause (19 U.S.C. §2251) and §406 market disruption (19 U.S.C. §2436) import relief determinations to the President. Private entities may petition the ITC for import relief.

     The ITC also has major responsibility for administration of U.S. trade laws involving unfair trade practices and shares that responsibility with the Department of Commerce. The ITC administers §337 proceedings (19 U.S.C.A. §1337) involving imports that infringe U.S. intellectual property laws. The ITC also decides whether U.S. industry is materially injured by unfairly priced or subsidized imports. The ITA, part of the Commerce Department, decides questions of the existence of dumping (i.e., artificially low-priced imports to gain market share) or subsidies (i.e., payments by foreign government to exporters) in these antidumping or countervailing duty cases. If dumping exists and if there is a material injury to U.S. industry, the ITC can order the imposition of an antidumping duty on the imported product, that is, a duty to offset the margin of dumping and equalize the prices for the product imported into the United States with the price in its home market. A private business can petition for import relief under these unfair trade practice laws.

(4) The Office of the United States Trade Representative (USTR) is in the Executive Office of the President of the United States, and the USTR is appointed by the President with the advice and consent of the U.S. Senate. The USTR offers policy advice and handles trade negotiations with foreign nations. The USTR receives complaints from U.S. businesses concerning breaches of international trade agreements or unjustifiable, unreasonable, or discriminating foreign practices. Under §301 of the Trade Act of 1974 (19 U.S.C. §2411), the USTR can trigger a dispute settlement proceeding against a foreign entity on behalf of U.S. businesses at the WTO or in NAFTA and can authorize retaliatory trade actions.

NOTES AND QUESTIONS

1. This great body of international economic law is the result of states following their perceived interests and negotiating trade arrangements and mutual trade concessions over the last half century. This law provides the framework in which international business must operate. In most cases, IEL will facilitate IBTs, by removing or lowering tariffs and other import barriers and by providing a procedure to obtain redress for foreign practices that impede trade. However, IEL rules can have a negative impact on international business, particularly if the rules are ignored. For example, an export transaction may be affected by export controls or an antidumping or countervailing duty complaint

in the importing nation. IEL usually does not directly affect private transactions, but the international business lawyer ignores it at his or her peril.

2. How can a U.S. company obtain help from the USTR? If a U.S. company enlists the help of the USTR in a dispute with a foreign company, what types of actions can the USTR undertake? Are there any negative consequences? Companies from other countries can also call on their governments for help.

2 _International Sale of Goods_

This chapter and the next two (Chapters Three and Four) should be considered as one unit as all three concern the international sale of goods. The following two chapters (Chapters Five and Six) can also be considered as one unit because they focus on the next steps in IBTs beyond the sales transaction. Chapters Five and Six focus on the progressive involvement and integration of a U.S. corporation in its overseas business expansion through agency/distributorships, contract manufacturing, and foreign direct investment.

We begin this chapter with an overview of the entire international sale of goods transaction, the most basic and most common form of IBTs. We begin with an examination of the documentary sales transaction, which continues to be the preferred method used by most parties today. The documentary sales transaction actually involves at least three different contracts: (1) the sales contract, (2) the letter of credit for payment, and (3) the bill of lading and contract of affreightment for the transport of the goods. The sales contract and letter of credit are introduced in this chapter but are treated in detail in Chapters Three and Four, respectively. In this chapter, after the overview materials, we provide a brief treatment of the bill of lading, contract of affreightment, and insurance issues.

In the final part of this chapter, we examine international trade law matters relating to the export and import issues in an international sales transaction. These are the trade issues that most directly affect the legal practitioner on a micro level.

I. Overview of the International Sales Transaction

To understand the international sale of goods, we first examine the basic expectations and risks of the seller and the buyer in any sales transaction. We focus on a pattern that is becoming increasingly common in the modern age: a buyer and seller who are strangers without a prior course of dealing and who may not trust the other.

A. Expectations of the Parties

In a typical sale, the buyer wishes to receive the bargained-for goods and the seller wishes to receive payment as expeditiously as possible. This can occur with minimal risks in a face-to-face transaction where the seller delivers the goods to the buyer; the buyer inspects the goods immediately to determine whether they conform to the contract; and the buyer makes payment to the seller. But such face-to-face transactions are rare today when sellers and buyers are separated by great distances and many never meet face to face even after many years of doing business together.

Once we introduce the separation of time and distance that is common in the modern age into the sales transaction, we can better understand the risks to the parties. The buyer will wish to first inspect the goods and make payment only after the buyer is satisfied that the goods conform to the contract. The buyer does not wish to first pay for goods that are unsuitable for the buyer's purposes. At this point, the buyer has already parted with its payment and is now in possession of goods for which the buyer has no use. The seller wishes to receive payment as expeditiously as possible and does not wish to endure an extended waiting period while the buyer inspects the goods. If the buyer has the right to inspect the goods, the seller is also subject to the risk that the buyer will reject the goods as nonconforming and refuse payment. At this point, the seller has already parted with the goods that are now in the possession of the buyer. The seller now has to deal with the recovery or disposition of goods that may be located a great distance away and with a buyer who refuses to make payment.

In the context of a domestic sale within the United States, these risks are often manageable. For both parties, a great deal of information is easily accessible from public sources about many businesses in the United States. The buyer can also inquire into the seller's reputation for honesty and dependability. Even where there is a disagreement, the parties may be able to resolve their differences if they are both easily accessible for meetings in person, by telephone, or by electronic means.

In a domestic sale in the United States, the legal issues should also be manageable. If the transaction crosses state lines, there will be a choice of law issue, but the laws governing contracts are not likely to differ significantly from state to state. Many states have adopted the Uniform Commercial Code to govern contracts. The court systems of the 50 states vary to some degree but these differences are minor. In many instances, after having established a level of trust and familiarity through a series of transactions, the parties may decide to operate on an open-account basis. Under this arrangement, the seller ships the goods to buyer, the buyer accepts the goods, and the seller's credit department sends an invoice to the buyer usually with credit terms (e.g., payment in 30 or 60 days).

B. The International Context

When we move from a domestic to an international context, the expectations of the parties generally remain the same but the risks can increase significantly. When the sale involves a seller in the United States and a buyer in Germany, China, or Brazil, the distances are far greater, making communications more difficult even in this modern age of information technology. There can be differences in time zones that delay communications and differences in language that may create additional hurdles. While English is the dominant business language in the world today, the level of English proficiency of a foreign party can vary from case to case. Even in the best of circumstances, there can continue to be misunderstandings when one of the parties must operate in a foreign language.

In an international sale, the buyer will have greater difficulty in ascertaining the reputation and trustworthiness of the seller. Representatives from the buyer may have first encountered the seller's goods only briefly at an international trade show or through the Internet. Whereas a buyer from Ohio can visit a seller's factory in California, the time and expense of a visit may preclude a buyer from China or Germany from visiting the same factory. The seller will also have greater difficulty in checking the creditworthiness of the buyer. If the buyer is a large corporation from an industrialized country such as Germany, the seller may be able to obtain reliable financial information about the buyer with some ease. But if the buyer is from a developing country such as China, Viet Nam, or a newly industrialized nation such as South Korea or Taiwan, reliable information may be difficult to obtain. Detailed financial information about business enterprises in China, for example, is not available publicly and there may be no reliable government sources of information about creditworthiness or business reputation.

While the expectations of the parties may not change in an international transaction, the risks of nonperformance are far greater for both the seller and the buyer. As in the domestic context, the buyer may wish to inspect the goods before payment and the seller will want payment as expeditiously as possible. If the buyer has the right to inspect the goods before payment, the risk to the seller of rejection of the goods by the buyer is compounded by what may be the thousands of miles that the goods have traveled only to be left at a foreign port and unclaimed by the buyer. For the buyer, the risk of making a payment before inspection of the goods is compounded by difficulties of time and distance in communicating with the seller that the goods are unsuitable and by the obstacles created by national boundaries and different legal systems in seeking the return of the funds or damages. What were relatively minor legal issues in the domestic context also become far more significant in the international context. Choice of law and forum issues in the international context can be quite significant. In a sales transaction to China, whether U.S. law or Chinese law governs the transaction can be a substantial and contentious issue between the parties. In addition, whether disputes are decided in a U.S. court or a Chinese court can be a critical issue as the two legal systems are divided by fundamental differences, including a significant language difference, which can add major costs in time and expenses. There is also the time and expense for the party that must appear in the foreign forum.

The response of the international trading community to the expectations and risks of the parties involved in the international sale described above has taken the following forms. First, to deal with the expectations of the parties, the international trading community has created a special lexicon of commercial terms that assigns duties and obligations in the sale. Terms such as FOB, CIF, negotiable bill of lading, nonnegotiable bill of lading, letter of credit, and confirmed letter of credit have specialized meanings that define, for example, whether the buyer has the right to inspect the goods before payment, when payment is to be made, and how payment is to be made. These terms are contained in the International Chamber of Commerce's International Commercial Terms and the Uniform Customs and Practice for Documentary Credits, both of which can be adopted by the parties by contract, and in other sources. We examine some of the most frequently used terms in the materials that follow.

The second type of response deals with the risks of nonperformance. As we noted earlier, these risks are lowest when the parties meet in a face-to-face transaction. Where the parties are separated by large distances and international boundaries, this arrangement appears to be impossible. But what if the parties were able to substitute a surrogate for the goods in the form of documents that are the equivalent of the goods themselves because the documents represent title to and control of the goods? While the transport of goods for delivery over long distances can involve weeks or months, the delivery of a set of documents can be done in a matter of a day or two except perhaps to the most remote locations. Under this arrangement, called the documentary sale, delivery of the documents constitutes a symbolic delivery of the goods and payment is then to occur upon delivery of the documents. The seller delivers a set of predetermined documents to the buyer and the buyer inspects the documents and then makes payment to the seller. Having obtained the documents, the buyer now has legal control of the goods and can obtain physical possession of the goods at the port of importation from the carrier by presenting the documents to the carrier. But what if the seller does not trust the buyer to make payment after delivery of the documents any more than after the buyer receives delivery of the goods in a non-documentary sale? In this case, the seller will insist that the buyer engage a bank in the buyer's home jurisdiction that will pay the seller upon the seller's delivery of the documents to the bank; the bank then either seeks reimbursement from the buyer in exchange for the documents or debits the buyer's account with the bank and forwards the documents to the buyer. Now with the documents in hand, the buyer goes to the port to obtain possession of the goods.

The documentary sale described above actually consists of at least three contracts: (1) the sales contract between the seller and buyer for the goods, (2) the letter of credit between the buyer's bank and the seller for payment, and (3) the bill of lading between the seller and the carrier, which serves as a contract for the transportation of the goods. In a documentary sale the parties need not use a letter of credit because the seller can submit the documents directly to the buyer for payment. However, if the seller does not wish to bear the risk that the buyer will not pay against the documents, the seller can demand that the buyer engage a bank to issue a letter of credit. We will proceed through the documentary sale that uses a letter of credit as the payment device, but remember that it is possible to have a documentary sale without the use of letters of credit.

NOTE ON TRADE FINANCING

In domestic business transactions, because a buyer's creditworthiness is usually not in question and because of the ease of debt collection, sellers typically finance sales of their products through open-account arrangements without formalities. In international sales trade financing is typically more formal, and a document known as a bill of exchange plays a key role.

A bill of exchange, which is also known as a "draft," is a written, dated, and signed commercial instrument involving an unconditional order by a drawer that directs a drawee to pay a certain sum of money to a named payee either on demand or by a specified future date. The former is known as a "sight bill" and the latter is termed a "time bill." The key to understanding a bill of exchange is to note that it is made possible when the drawee has an underlying obligation to pay money to the drawer. Where the drawee is holding the drawer's money on account, the drawee will be some form of bank, and the bill of exchange is known as a check. Where the drawee owes money to the drawer as a result of a loan, the bill is called a "note."[1] Where the drawer has sold goods to the drawee, who owes the sale price, the bill is called a "trade acceptance."

The trade acceptance is an important document in the financing of international trade. With regard to the international sale of goods, the seller will be both the drawer and the payee. A bill of exchange (draft) in connection with the transaction will order the buyer — the drawee — to pay a specified sum of money (the price of the goods). This bill is presented to the buyer (usually together with the invoice, bill of lading, and other documents). The buyer accepts the bill by signing it on its face and returning it to the seller or its agent. The bill can then function as a trade acceptance.

Many trade acceptances are time bills where the obligation to pay comes due in the future. For example, in the case of a 90-day time bill trade acceptance, the seller who has extended credit to the buyer in order to finance the sale can negotiate (sell) the bill in the commercial credit market. The buyer of the bill, who is a holder of the trade acceptance, which is a negotiable instrument, takes it free of most defenses involving the

---

1. A promissory note between two parties is a document whereby the maker (promisor) promises to pay the payee. A bill of exchange that is a note is a three-party document whereby the maker of the note orders a third party to pay.

underlying contract. The seller can thereby sell the trade acceptance more readily than it could assign an account receivable.

The law applicable to bills of exchange is beyond the scope of this book. In general national laws apply, which in the United States is the Uniform Commercial Code. The United Nations Commission on International Trade Law (UNCITRAL) has promulgated the United Nations Convention on International Bills of Exchange and International Promissory Notes, 28 I.L.M. 170 (1989), which has been approved by the United Nations General Assembly, but which is not yet in force.

Many countries, including the United States, maintain government-sponsored banks to aid domestic companies in exporting their products. The Export-Import Bank of the U.S., under the authority of 12 U.S.C. §635 *et seq.* (2012), has been providing financing to foreign buyers who buy U.S. products since its inception in 1934. The U.S. Ex-Im Bank works closely with the U.S. Overseas Private Investment Corporation (OPIC), which operates under the authority of 22 U.S.C. §§2191–2200b (2012). While OPIC supports U.S. foreign direct investment, particularly in developing countries, the Ex-Im Bank supports U.S. exports by providing financing that is comparable with other countries' export credit agencies. Although Ex-Im Bank is backed by the full faith and credit of the United States, its mandate is to be financially self-sustaining and to operate on a break-even basis over the long term. Ex-Im Bank's mandate is to fill market gaps that the private sector is unwilling or unable to meet; and to provide competitive financing to "level the playing field" for U.S. exporters in the face of foreign competition. In fiscal year 2012, Ex-Im Bank supplied more than $35.8 billion in export financing, supporting over $50 billion worth of U.S. exports.[2] Export credit financing benefits from an OECD Arrangement on Export Credits (1978)[3] as well as an exemption from the subsidy rules of the World Trade Organization.[4]

Critics charge that Ex-Im Bank is an egregious example of corporate welfare.[5] Defenders state that Ex-Im Bank saves American jobs and offers crucial help to exporters. Supporters further state that the United States cannot "unilaterally disarm" from export financing, which is carried out by over 90 other countries.

We now give a brief overview and provide samples of the three principal contracts involved in a documentary sale of goods.

1.   *The Sales Contract*

The international sales contract, like any other contract, is usually formed through negotiations leading to an offer by the buyer and an acceptance by the seller. In many cases, the first contact is initiated by the buyer who sends a letter requesting information on the price of goods. The letter may seek a pro forma invoice from the seller that includes the price of the goods, shipping arrangements, and insurance. The buyer then sends the seller a purchase order. Most sellers provide that all purchase orders are subject to an order acknowledgment.

---

2. Export-Import Bank of the U.S. Annual Report 2013, cover letter from Fred P. Hochberg, Chairman and President.

3. For the text of the Arrangement, see *The Export Credit Arrangement*, OECD, *http://www.oecd.org/trade/exportcredits/theexportcreditsarrangementtext.htm.*

4. See item (k) of the Illustrative List of Export Subsidies of the WTO Agreement on Subsidies and Countervailing Duties (1995).

5. *See* Charles Lane, *Grounding the Bank of Boeing,* Wash. Post, June 26, 2014, p. A15.

FORM 2-1
Letter of Inquiry

Mr. Paulo Netto, General Manager
GLOBO Products, S.A.
76 Rua Rui Barbosa
Rio de Janeiro, Brazil

By Fax   June 1, 2016

Dear Mr. Netto:

We enjoyed visiting your display at the Rio de Janeiro Trade Fair on April 20th of this year. Thank you for taking the time to come to our reception at the Hotel Central. We, too, are excited about possible business development opportunities for Value Industries in Brazil. Our Vice President for Business Development, Ms. Samantha Williams, will be in Rio de Janeiro in September and will be in contact with you to arrange for a factory visit to discuss business possibilities.

We now wish to order Christmas ornaments. Please send us a pro forma invoice in triplicate covering:

Item #15   50,000 Christmas Lights in Red, Green, and Yellow
Item #21   5,000 White Angel Ornaments
Item #13   5,000 Candy Cane Ornaments
Item #4   5,000 Sparkling Red Bells
Item #8   10,000 Super Deluxe 18″ Christmas Wreaths

Please include your best price, including packaging, FOB Rio de Janeiro, C&F Newark, New Jersey, and CIF Newark. We look forward to your prompt response.

Sincerely,

Henry Williams
Sales Director, North America
Value Industries, Inc.
Worthington, Ohio

FORM 2-2
Pro Forma Invoice

GLOBO Products, S.A.
76 Rua Rui Barbosa
Rio de Janeiro, Brazil

To: Mr. Henry Williams
    Sales Director
    Value Industries, Inc.   June 15, 2016
    Pro Forma Invoice No. 522

Description	Price per Unit (USD)	Total Price
50,000 Christmas Lights in Red, Green, and Yellow	$.55	$27,500
5,000 White Angel Ornaments	$1.95	$9,750
5,000 Candy Cane Ornaments	$1.25	$6,250
5,000 Sparkling Red Bells	$1.55	$7,750
10,000 Super Deluxe 18″ Christmas Wreaths	$9.85	$98,500
Total Price FOB Rio de Janeiro		$149,750
Ocean Freight to Newark, New Jersey		$5,500
Total Price C&F Newark		$155,250
Insurance at 110%		$935
Total Price CIF Newark		$156,185

   The prices quoted above are firm for 60 days. Payment terms are an irrevocable letter of credit issued by a U.S. Bank and confirmed by the Banco do Brasil, Rio de Janeiro Branch. Shipment will occur in approximately 15 days from receipt of your order and advice of credit. All purchase orders subject to written acknowledgment from us.

Yours Truly,

Paulo Netto
General Manager

FORM 2-3
Purchase Order

GLOBO Products, S.A.
76 Rua Rui Barbosa
Rio de Janeiro, Brazil

<u>By Fax</u>

July 1, 2016

Dear Mr. Netto:

Please supply us in accordance with your Pro Forma Invoice No. 522 dated June 15, 2016 with the following items:

Item #15	50,000 Christmas Lights in Red, Green, and Yellow @ $.55 USD per unit
Item #21	5,000 White Angel Ornaments @ $1.95
Item #13	5,000 Candy Cane Ornaments @ $1.25
Item #4	5,000 Sparkling Red Bells @ $1.55
Item #8	10,000 Super Deluxe 18" Christmas Wreaths @ $9.85

Total Price CIF Newark, New Jersey $156,185

Delivery Date: Prior to September 1, 2016

We have instructed Mid-America Bank to open a confirmed irrevocable letter of credit per your pro forma invoice and to ask the Banco do Brasil, Rio de Janeiro Branch, for its confirmation. We look forward to your early acknowledgment by mail.

Sincerely,

Henry Williams
Sales Director, North America
Value Industries, Inc.
Worthington, Ohio

NOTES AND QUESTIONS

1. Why would the buyer ask for various alternatives on shipping costs from the seller? Do you think that the seller would be able to make these arrangements at any cost savings to the buyer?

2. Why is it usually the policy of the seller to require an order acknowledgment in any sales transaction? How does this policy protect the seller?

3. When is a contract formed between the parties through an offer and an acceptance? Which document represents the offer and which the acceptance?

2. *Letter of Credit*

The method of payment for this sale is the letter of credit, mentioned in both the pro forma invoice and the purchase order. We give a quick overview of the letter of credit in this chapter so that you can see its role in the overall sales transaction. We return to a more detailed examination of the letter of credit in Chapter Four.

The letter of credit allows the seller to obtain payment from the buyer's bank upon the presentation of certain documents, usually including a bill of lading, which provides evidence that the goods have been shipped. To obtain a letter of credit, the buyer usually goes to its bank in the foreign nation and asks the bank to issue a credit in favor of the seller. The buyer may give the bank a copy of the pro forma invoice that the bank can use as a basis for detailing the contents of the credit. The buyer can either deposit funds for the amount of the credit with the bank or the buyer may have other accounts containing funds with the bank. In some cases, the bank may be willing to lend the funds to the buyer for the credit and then seek reimbursement from the buyer. By requiring a letter of credit from the buyer, the seller is able to obtain an assessment of the buyer's creditworthiness by a financial institution in the buyer's home location.

To obtain payment under the letter of credit, the seller must submit to the buyer's bank a set of required documents detailed in the credit, which usually includes a bill of lading, a commercial invoice, and an insurance certificate. The seller obtains a bill of lading from the carrier after the seller delivers the goods to the carrier. The seller (or manufacturer) provides a commercial invoice that details the quantity and nature of the goods that have been delivered to the carrier. The insurance certificate indicates that the goods have been insured during transit. The seller must usually comply exactly with the requirements of the terms of the credit as failure to submit a required document or the submission of a defective document will result in a refusal to pay by the bank. Once the buyer's bank receives the documents as required by the terms of the credit, the bank must pay the seller.

We have so far examined the unconfirmed letter of credit, which requires the seller to submit the documents directly to the buyer's bank. In the case of a confirmed letter of credit, another bank, usually a bank located in the seller's nation, will add its confirmation that it will pay the seller under the letter of credit when presented with the proper documents by the seller. This bank is the confirming bank, sometimes also called the seller's bank. The seller might insist on a confirmed letter of credit because the seller might not trust the buyer's bank any more than the seller trusts the buyer. In an unconfirmed credit, the seller must submit the documents to the buyer's bank usually situated in the same foreign location as the buyer. If the buyer's bank refuses to pay, then the seller, which has already parted with the goods, can sue the buyer's bank but this may be an impracticable option given the distance, time, and expense involved in a foreign litigation. To address these concerns, the seller may insist on the additional obligation of a local bank, as the confirming bank, in the seller's location to pay the seller on presentation of the documents. Once the confirming bank pays the seller, the confirming bank will then forward the documents to the buyer's bank for reimbursement. The seller is usually in a better position to assess the reputation of the confirming bank and the seller has more effective means of recourse if the confirming bank refuses to pay.

NOTES AND QUESTIONS

1. The distinction between the sales contract and the letter of credit is sometimes summed up by saying that the former is a contract for the sale of goods while the latter is a contract for the sale of documents. Can you explain what this means?

2. The international trading community has established the independence rule requiring payment on the letter of credit regardless of nonperformance of the underlying sales contract. Why? In answering this question, think about the following: Suppose that instead of this rule, we had a rule that banks paid at their peril on the letter of credit (i.e., the banks cannot obtain reimbursement from the buyer) if there were some defect in the performance of the sales contract. What would be the effect of such a rule on the international banking community and how would it affect the international sales transaction?

FORM 2-4
Commercial Letter of Credit

Banco do Brasil
18 Setor Bancario Sul
Rio de Janeiro, Brazil
Mr. Paulo Netto

July 5, 2016

GLOBO Products, S.A.
76 Rua Rui Barbosa
Rio de Janeiro, Brazil

Dear Mr. Netto:

We have been instructed by the Mid-America Bank of Worthington, Ohio, USA that it has opened an irrevocable credit in your favor in the amount of USD $156,185 available by your sight drafts on the Mid-America Bank accompanied by:

1. Full Original Set On Board Negotiable Bills of Lading in triplicate endorsed to the Banco do Brasil, Rio de Janeiro Branch.
2. Insurance Policy covering marine risk at 110% of value.
3. Commercial invoice in triplicate issued by Globo Products covering:

   50,000 Christmas Lights in Red, Green, and Yellow
   5,000 White Angel Ornaments
   5,000 Candy Cane Ornaments
   5,000 Sparkling Red Bells
   10,000 Super Deluxe 18″ Christmas Wreaths

All documents must indicate Letter of Credit No. 7151-C. All drafts must be marked "drawn under Letter of Credit No. 7151-C confirmed by the Banco do Brasil, Rio de Janeiro Branch." Drafts must be presented to us by no later than July 31, 2016.

This credit is subject to the Uniform Customs and Practice for Documentary Credits (UCP 600) 2007 version, International Chamber of Commerce Publication No. 600.

We confirm the credit and hereby undertake to purchase all drafts drawn as specified above and accompanied by the documents so specified.

Sincerely,

Cesar Calmon
General Manager, International
Credit Dept.

3. *The Bill of Lading and the Contract of Affreightment*

The third contract usually involved in the documentary sale is the contract of affreightment or carriage for the shipment of the goods from the seller to the buyer. Once the sales contract has been executed and the seller has received notification that the letter of credit has been established, the seller must now procure or manufacture the goods and ship them to the buyer. Most sellers (shippers) will engage a freight forwarder, a specialist in this field, to make the arrangements for transporting the goods from the factory to the port of shipment. When the goods are loaded on board the carrier, the carrier will then issue a bill of lading to cover the goods. The bill of lading usually serves two functions.

First, the bill is a contract of carriage between the shipper (the seller) and the carrier under which the carrier (usually an ocean vessel) promises to transport the goods to a certain destination in exchange for a fee paid by the seller to the carrier. The carrier undertakes the responsibility from the moment it takes receipt of the goods to deliver the goods to the port of discharge or a named place of delivery. The liability of the carrier for any damage to the goods if the carriage is to or from the United States is governed by the federal Carriage of Goods by Sea Act (COGSA), Pub. L. No. 74-521, 49 Stat. 1207-13 (1936) (currently omitted from the U.S. Code but codified at 46 U.S.C.A. §30701 hist. n. (West 2007)), which limits the liability of the carrier to $500 per package unless the shipper declares otherwise in the bill of lading. *See id.* at §30701 hist. n. §4(5). We discuss the legal aspects of the bill of lading as a contract of affreightment in detail later in this chapter at pp. 89-92. For now, we focus below and in the following cases on the second aspect of the bill of lading as a document of title.

Second, the bill of lading also determines to whom the carrier should deliver the goods and can serve either as a document of title or as a receipt, i.e., a record of the agreement by the carrier to deliver to a certain named consignee. If the bill of lading is *nonnegotiable* (also known as a straight or white bill of lading for the color of paper on which it is printed), the carrier is to deliver the goods to the person named as the consignee in the bill or to an agent or person designated by the consignee. The consignee need not submit the original of the nonnegotiable bill of lading to the carrier to obtain delivery of the goods. A copy, fax, or electronic version is sufficient. Thus, the nonnegotiable bill has no legal significance other than as a written record of the agreement of the parties. If the bill is *negotiable* (also known as a yellow bill of lading), then the carrier must deliver the goods only to the person in possession of the original negotiable bill properly endorsed. (Several sets of originals are usually issued.) The carrier must first obtain surrender of the negotiable bill of lading before delivering the goods. A negotiable bill of lading thus represents title to and control of the goods themselves because whoever has possession of a properly endorsed bill has a legal right to obtain possession of the goods. Most shippers use standard form contracts for bills of lading and fill in the information required. You can determine whether a bill is negotiable or nonnegotiable by examining the space reserved for naming the consignee. If the bill names a specific person, then the bill is nonnegotiable. If the bill is filled out "To Order of Shipper," then the bill is a negotiable bill and anyone to whom the bill has been properly endorsed by the shipper has a right to possession of the goods. In a documentary sales transaction, a negotiable bill must be used. The carrier issues the bill of lading to the seller after the goods have been loaded on board. The seller, in turn, endorses the bill of lading to the issuing bank and submits the other required documents for payment. Once the bank pays the seller, the bank then forwards the documents to the buyer for reimbursement. The bank endorses the bill of lading to the buyer who then submits the bill to the carrier and receives custody of the goods. This transaction is the simplest and most straightforward sale of goods, but note that a negotiable bill of lading allows the buyer to sell the goods before actually receiving physical custody of the goods. This is done through the sale, transfer, and endorsement of the bill of lading. The negotiable nature of the bill of lading allows the right to claim the goods to be transferred from person to person quite easily by signing the bill. In our example above, a negotiable bill allows a buyer (such as a wholesale distributor) who has received the negotiable bill of lading from the seller by express mail to sell the goods while the goods are still en route on board a vessel by simply endorsing the bill (in exchange for payment) to an end use buyer. The end use buyer now has title to the goods and can demand delivery directly from the carrier by surrendering the negotiable bill of lading to the captain of the vessel at the dock when the vessel arrives.

The bill of lading will contain a description of the goods but the description refers in general to what is loaded in containers (e.g., "Christmas ornaments and decorations") and is not specific enough to indicate whether the goods will meet the buyer's expectations. The commercial invoice issued by the seller, however, should provide detailed information about the goods because the invoice repeats the bulk of the buyer's purchase order. Read in combination, the bill of lading and the commercial invoice provide a reliable indication of whether the goods loaded on board the carrier are what the buyer expects to receive under the sales contract.

In the United States, bills of lading issued in interstate commerce and in export (but not import) transactions are subject to the Federal Bill of Lading Act (also known as the Pomerene Act), 49 U.S.C. §§80101–80116 (2006). This Act categorizes all bills as either negotiable or nonnegotiable (straight) bills of lading. When issuing a bill, the carrier is required to specify on its face which category of bill is involved. The Federal Bill of Lading Act protects the good faith purchaser of a bill. The person negotiating or transferring a bill also warrants that the bill is genuine and that the goods covered by the bill are merchantable and fit for a particular purpose. The issuer of a bill—a carrier—is liable for misleading statements about the goods and has a duty to deliver the goods to the consignee or the holder of the bill. *See Elgie & Co. v. S.S. "S.A. Nederburg,"* 599 F.2d 1177, 1179–1181 (2d Cir. 1979). In this way, the law reinforces the integrity of commercial transactions.

FORM 2-5

BILL OF LADING For Multimodal Transport or Port to Port Shipment

SHIPPER: GLOBO Products, S.A.	HAPAG-LLOYD REFERENCE HL-B-07915	
Consignee	(5) BOOKING NO. B-1592	(5A) BILL OF LADING NO B-256
	(6) EXPORT REFERENCES	
To order of Shipper		
Notify Address (Carrier not responsible for failure to notify, see clause 20 (1) hereof:	(7) FORWARDING AGENT, F.M.C. NO.	
	F.L. Monteiro & Co. 50 Rua General Jadim Rio de Janeiro Phone: (55) (21) 291-1224	
	(8) POINT AND COUNTRY OF ORIGIN Rio de Janeiro, Brazil	
(4) NOTIFY PARTY (COMPLETE NAME AND ADDRESS) Value Industries, Inc. Worthington, OH	(9) ALSO NOTIFY – ROUTING & INSTRUCTIONS Notify on arrival in Rio de Janeiro Port Mrs. J. Monteiro for further instructions	
(12) PRE-CARRIAGE BY* Container Trucks	(13) PLACE OF RECEIPT BY PRE-CARRIER* Rio de Janeiro	Phone: 136-735-0311 Trucks to deliver to Pier 15 Docks receipts required
(14) VESSEL VOY FLAG M/V Reefer Sun II	(15) PORT OF LOADING Rio de Janeiro	(10) LOADING PIER/TERMINAL Pier 15	(10A) ORIGINALS(S) TO BE RELEASED AT
(16) PORT OF DISCHARGE Newark, N.J.	(17) PLACE OF DELIVERY BY ON-CARRIER*	(11) TYPE OF MOVE (IF MIXED, USED BLOCK 20 AS APPROPRIATE)

PARTICULARS FURNISHED BY SHIPPER

MKS. & NOS. / CONTAINER NOS. (18)	NO. OF PKGS. (19)	HM	DESCRIPTION OF PACKAGES AND GOODS (20)	GROSS WEIGHT (21)	MEASUREMENT (22)
Value Industries, Inc. Order No. 52 Made in Brazil			Container 56A–TRU 1,424 Cartons Christmas Decorations Import License No. 14776 Letter of Credit No. 7151-C **CLEAN ON BOARD** **NO TRANSSHIPMENT ALLOWED**	5,252 lbs.	1,950 C.F.

(23) Declared Value $ _____ If shipper enters a value, carriers "package" limitation of liability does not apply and the ad valorem rate will be charged.

(23A) RATE OF EXCHANGE

(24) **FREIGHT PAYABLE AT/BY**

IP	RATED AS	PER	RATE	PREPAID	COLLECT	LOCAL CURRENCY
	TOTAL CHARGES					

☐ If this box is checked, goods have been loaded, stowed and counted by Shipper. Carrier has NOT done so and is not responsible for accuracy of count, condition or nature of goods described in PARTICULARS FURNISHED BY SHIPPER

THE RECEIPT, CUSTODY, CARRIAGE, AND DELIVERY OF THE GOODS ARE SUBJECT TO THE TERMS APPEARING ON THE FACE AND BACK HEREOF AND TO CARRIER'S APPLICABLE TARIFF

In witness whereof three (3) original bills of lading all of the same tenor and date one of which being accomplished the others to stand void, have been issued by the originating carrier for and on behalf of itself other participating carriers, the vessel and new master and owners or charterers.

Dated ....

At ....

.... (Originating Carrier)

By ....

BILL OF LADING NO   DATE   *APPLICABLE ONLY WHEN USED FOR MULTIMODAL TRANSPORTATION

NOTES AND QUESTIONS

1. The legal characteristics of the bill of lading arise from the provisions of the Federal Bill of Lading Act (Pomerene Act), 49 U.S.C. §§80101–80116 (2006), contained in the Documents Supplement. Consider the application of this Act: Does it apply to bills of lading in international trade? *See* §80102. What makes a bill of lading negotiable? *See* §80103. How is a bill of lading negotiated? *See* §80104. Does the person to whom a bill of lading is negotiated acquire title to the goods described in the bill? *See* §80105. What possible liabilities does the carrier have under the Pomerene Act? *See* §§80111–80113.

2. In a documentary sale, involving payment against documents, a negotiable bill of lading must be used. What does the buyer or bank receive in exchange for payment of a negotiable bill of lading? Does the buyer or bank receive the same in exchange for payment against a nonnegotiable bill of lading? If you were a buyer or bank would you pay against a nonnegotiable bill of lading?

3. If the buyer is a wholesaler or a distributor, the documentary sale can be very useful because it allows the buyer to sell the goods while they are still in transit. Can you explain how? For this to happen, a negotiable bill of lading is essential. Why?

4. Traditionally, bills of lading are issued in paper form, and this is still true today for security reasons. However, electronic bills of lading are gradually replacing paper bills. *See* Emmanuel T. Laryea, *Payment for Paperless Trade: Are There Viable Alternatives to the Documentary Credit?*, 33 Law & Pol'y Int'l Bus. 3 (2001). Parties who wish to use an electronic bill of lading in international trade typically employ the Rules for Electronic Bills of Lading of the Comité Maritime International (CMI). These Rules are reprinted in the Documents Supplement. The Rules may apply by contract between parties who choose to use them (Art. 1). How is confidentiality and prevention of fraud handled under these Rules? The shipper who agrees to the Rules may wish to negotiate the bill of lading to a third party while the goods are being transported. How can this be done under the rules? *See* Article 10. Currently, most electronic bills of lading are nonnegotiable waybills. In this case no document need be surrendered to procure release of the goods. When an electronic bill is negotiable, it must be printed before it can be used to procure the goods, and experience holds that this provides more opportunity for fraud than is the case with an original, signed paper document. It remains to be seen whether a system can be devised to overcome this problem so that fully electronic bills can become commonplace. *See* Susan Beecher, *Can the Electronic Bill of Lading Be Paperless?*, 40 Int'l Law. 627 (2006).

4. *Overview of the Entire Documentary Sale Transaction*

Now that we have examined all of the basic steps of the documentary sale, see if you can follow all of the steps in the transaction involving a confirmed letter of credit:

Let's review each step:

(1) Seller manufactures the goods and delivers them to Carrier;
(2) Carrier loads the goods and issues a bill of lading to Seller;

FIGURE 2-1

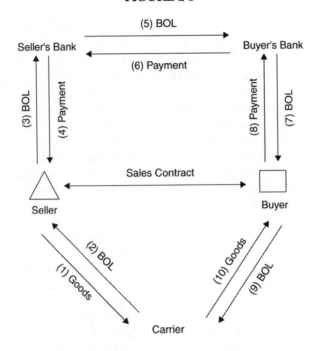

(3) Seller presents the bill of lading, a commercial invoice, and certificate of insurance to Seller's Bank, which acts as a confirming bank;

(4) Seller's Bank examines the bill of lading and other documents to determine whether they conform to the letter of credit; Seller's bank decides that the documents are conforming and makes payment to Seller;

(5) Seller's Bank forwards the documents to Buyer's Bank, which is the issuing bank;

(6) Buyer's Bank examines the documents to determine whether they conform to the terms of the letter of credit; Buyer's Bank decides that the documents are conforming and reimburses Seller's Bank for payment under the letter of credit;

(7) Buyer's Bank forwards the documents to Buyer;

(8) Buyer's Bank debits Buyer's account or Buyer makes payment to Buyer's Bank;

(9) Buyer presents bill of lading to Carrier; and

(10) Carrier delivers goods to Buyer.

The documentary sale has allowed the parties to address some of the risks involved in the international sales transaction where the parties are strangers to each other and there is not an established level of trust and familiarity. What was a set of risks and unknowns for the seller and buyer has now been broken down into a smaller set of discrete risks, and the task of assessing the risk has been placed on the party that is in the best position to make the assessment. For example, while the seller may not be in a position to make an assessment of the creditworthiness of the buyer, the buyer's bank or the issuing bank for the letter of credit should be in a good position to assess whether the buyer is a good commercial risk. By requiring payment under a letter of credit, the seller now has also the creditworthiness of the buyer's bank to rely on in addition to that of the buyer. If the seller does not trust buyer's bank, the seller can demand a confirmed letter of credit, which requires the seller's bank to make an additional assessment of the creditworthiness of the buyer's bank. The seller's bank is a member of the international banking community and should be able to make an accurate assessment of the reputation of the buyer's bank.

The seller is able to obtain expeditious payment because the seller should have all of the documents usually required by a letter of credit after it has delivered the goods to the carrier at the port of shipment. The seller can then submit the documents to the confirming bank for immediate payment and receive payment while the goods are still en route to the buyer. The buyer's interests are protected by the documents submitted by the seller for payment, which usually include the bill of lading, a commercial invoice, and a certificate of insurance. These documents indicate that the goods have been safely loaded aboard a carrier bound for the buyer; that the goods loaded fit the description in the commercial invoice, which is identical to the description in the sales contract; and that a policy of insurance protects the buyer against damage to the goods during the carriage. Because payment is made before the buyer inspects the goods, the buyer will sometimes require a certificate of inspection as one of the documents that must be submitted for payment under the letter of credit. The buyer will engage some third party to inspect the goods and provide a certification that they conform to the contract.

Although the documentary sale has been designed to manage risks in an international sale, there are still many ways in which things can go wrong. Here are some of the more common ways:

(1) The seller ships conforming goods but obtains documents from the carrier that do not comply with the requirements of the letter of credit;
(2) The seller ships nonconforming or defective goods and then submits forged documents to the confirming bank for payment;
(3) The carrier damages the goods during loading or transport or the goods are stolen;
(4) War, fire, or other supervening events prevent the seller from producing the goods or the carrier from completing the transport of the goods altogether or in a timely fashion;
(5) The buyer receives conforming documents but when the buyer receives the goods, the buyer discovers that the goods do not conform to the sales contract.

We will be exploring these situations in the materials that follow.

NOTES AND QUESTIONS

1. In the transaction above, the buyer must pay against documents presented by the seller. Suppose the buyer pays the seller, obtains the bill of lading, and retrieves the goods from the carrier. Upon inspecting the goods, however, the buyer finds that the goods are nonconforming. What remedies are available to the buyer? What disadvantages does the buyer confront in this situation? Can you think of a method for the buyer to protect itself from receiving nonconforming goods? What type of document might the buyer require from the seller for payment that might reduce this risk?

2. In a documentary sale involving letters of credit as the method of payment, banks will insist on a negotiable bill of lading, which serves as security to protect the bank's interest in the goods. Can you explain how? Can you explain why a nonnegotiable bill fails to protect the bank's interests in the goods?

NOTE ON INTERNATIONAL E-TRADE

Contracts formed by electronic means through the Internet, so-called B2B E-Trade contracts, are now common in international business. In 2005 the United Nations General Assembly addressed the matter, building on discussion by many experts from many countries, by adopting the United Nations Convention on the Use of Electronic Communications in International Contracts, Official Records of the General Assembly, Sixtieth Session, Doc. A/60/515 (Nov. 23, 2005). As of this writing, this Convention has entered into force for only five countries (Congo, Honduras, Russia, Singapore, and the Dominican Republic), but has been signed by 15 other countries, which are in various stages of ratifying the convention. The UN Convention provisions accord with the provisions of the U.S. Electronic Signatures in Global and National Commerce Act, 15 U.S.C. §§7001–7031 (2012); as well as the European Union E-Commerce Directive, 2000/31/EC, 2000 O.J. (L 178) 1.

PROBLEM 2-1

Suppose the first contact Value Industries has with Globo Products, S.A. is a visit to Globo's Internet web site where a great array of products is advertised for sale together with prices and terms. Suppose further that Henry Williams, the Sales Director of Value Industries, places an order for 50,000 Christmas lights at the price advertised online by Globo Products. How does the fact that the parties communicate by e-mail affect the formation of the contract? Consult the provisions of the UN Convention on Electronic Communications contained in the Documents Supplement and answer the following questions:

(1) What is the scope of application of the convention? Suppose Brazil but not the United States is a party—does the convention apply to Value Industries' communications? *See* Article 1. Note that the convention only applies to B2B transactions. Consumer transactions are excluded. *See* Article 2.

(2) What rules determine the location of the parties' places of business? Suppose Value Industries were to use an electronic e-mail address indicating residence in Greece because the sales director has a vacation home on a Greek island. Is the place of business in Greece? *See* Article 6.

(3) Can electronic communications alone be a valid means of concluding an international contract? *See* Article 8.

(4) Can electronic communications conclude a contract by means of one or more automated message systems? *See* Article 12.

(5) If the Globo Products Internet web site contains comprehensive information on available products and prices as well as specific terms of sale, is this an offer? *See* Article 11.

(6) Is an electronic signature sufficient to conclude a contract? *See* Article 9(3). United States domestic law is substantially the same. *See* 15 U.S.C. §7021.

(7) Do the provisions of older international conventions relating to international transactions, such as the UN Convention on Contracts for the International Sale of Goods (CISG) that predate the Internet age apply to B2B international E-trade contracts? *See* Article 20.

(8) Note that the convention does not contain specific rules as to the time and place of contract formation. Choice of law is also not covered. Article 10 addresses

only the matter of time and place of dispatch and receipt. Suppose Value Industries' communication to Globo is sent at 9:05 A.M. (U.S. Eastern Standard Time) on November 15, 2010 but because of a firewall problem Globo does not receive the communication at that time. After a telephone conversation to set matters straight, Globo sorts out the problem and receives the communication on December 5. If Globo raised its prices as of December 1, can Value Industries claim the benefit of the lower prices in effect on November 15?

(9)   Suppose in its communication Value Industries mistakenly places an order for 500,000 Christmas lights when it meant to order 50,000. Suppose further that an automated message arrives from Globo accepting this offer before anyone realizes the mistake. Can Value Industries correct this error? *See* Article 14.

C.   Commercial Terms Under the ICC Incoterms

There are numerous steps in the sales transaction, many of which are mechanical and routine: arranging for the shipment of the goods from the seller's factory to the carrier, clearing the goods for export and import, and packaging the goods. The steps may be routine but the parties need to have a clear understanding of who is to perform each task. Avoiding confusion and misunderstandings in the allocation of responsibilities for these mechanical tasks is essential, but parties to an international contract are unaware of the trading practices in their different states. To deal with these problems, the International Chamber of Commerce first published in 1936 a set of rules and definitions to guide the interpretation of commonly used commercial terms, called Incoterms ("Incoterms" comes from international commercial terms), which parties can adopt by contract. Once adopted, the terms acquire legal force by contract and displace any inconsistent terms in domestic law. Amendments and additions were later added to Incoterms in 1953, 1967, 1976, 1990, 2000, and 2011.

The scope of application of Incoterms is specific and limited. Incoterms apply only to matters concerning the duties and obligations of sellers and buyers to a contract of sale relating to the delivery of tangible goods sold. As we have noted earlier, in a documentary sale involving letters of credit, there are at least three contracts: the contract of sale, the carriage contract, and the letter of credit. Incoterms are directly relevant only to the first of these contracts and only in certain respects. In particular, avoid the common misunderstanding that Incoterms apply also to the carriage contract between the shipper and the carrier for the transport of the goods. In addition, Incoterms do not apply to all of the other rights and obligations under a sales contract that are not directly related to the delivery of the goods. Matters such as formation of the contract, warranties, breach, and remedies are all outside the scope of Incoterms. Many of these other matters are covered by a substantive contract law. In all instances where Incoterms have been adopted by the parties, they will apply hand in hand with a substantive contract law such as the CISG, another international convention, or a domestic contract law of one of the parties.

One important area in which commercial terms have traditionally applied is to the issue of risk of loss for the goods. In the documentary sale discussed in the previous section, an important issue between the buyer and the seller is who bears the risk of loss if the goods become damaged or destroyed before the buyer can take possession and title. How is this risk allocated? The basic approach is that the risk of loss remains with the seller until it has satisfied its delivery obligations to the buyer. But when is the delivery obligation satisfied? Let us begin with a contract for the sale of goods under which the seller is to deliver the goods to the buyer at the buyer's place of business. In these circumstances, the risk of loss (and title) does not pass from the seller to the buyer until the seller delivers physical possession of the goods into the custody of the buyer. If the goods are lost or damaged while being shipped by sea by the seller, the seller must bear the risk of loss and must still meet its obligations under the contract by providing substitute goods or by paying damages.

In most international sales today, the parties generally do not provide that the seller must deliver physical possession of the goods to the buyer at the buyer's place of business. Rather, a common arrangement is for the seller to make shipping arrangements from the seller's place of business on behalf of the buyer and charge the buyer. As the dominant mode of transport today is ocean carriage, i.e., transport by a carrier or ship overseas or inland waterways, the discussion below examines arrangements for ocean transport. In ocean carriage, the seller arranges for a carrier on behalf of the buyer and loads the goods on board the ship. Under this arrangement, when does the seller satisfy its delivery obligations transferring the risk of loss (and title) to the buyer? In the absence of an explicit agreement between the parties, it was understood as a matter of commercial practice and then codified under Incoterms that the risk of loss passed from the seller to the buyer when the goods were delivered by the seller into the custody of the carrier. Prior to Incoterms 2010, the term of art used to describe delivery of goods by the seller into the custody of the buyer was when the goods "passed the ship's rail." If you can picture the goods being hoisted from the dock by a lift, the risk passed from the seller to the buyer at the moment that the goods came under the custody of the carrier, that is, when they passed the ship's rail. Prior to this point, the seller assumed the risk of loss and thus the seller would be not be relieved from the sales contract if, for example, the goods were damaged in transit from its factory to the carrier. After the goods passed the ship's rail, however, the buyer assumed the risk of loss—which is why most buyers will procure insurance for the goods from this point forward. Incoterms 2010 is the first version of Incoterms that no longer uses the term "pass the ship's rail." Incoterms 2010 now states that the risk of loss passes from the seller to the buyer when the seller delivers the goods "on board the vessel" nominated by the buyer at the port of shipment. Although the terms have changed, the basic concept is the same: The risk of loss passes from the seller to the buyer when the seller satisfies its delivery obligation by delivering the goods into the custody of the carrier. While the term of art "passing the ship's rail" is no longer used in Incoterms 2010, you should be aware of it as you will see it in older cases and documents using earlier versions of Incoterms.

While the procedure of passing the ship's rail or on board the vessel might have described traditional delivery procedures, in modern maritime practice, goods are often delivered by the seller to a point on land where they are stored in a container in a warehouse for subsequent transport by sea or by a combined means of multimodal transport (sea, air, or land). As a result, Incoterms have been revised to reflect modern practice. The 1980 revision added the term "free carrier" (FCA) to deal with the frequent case where the reception point in maritime commerce was no longer the traditional passing of the ship's rail in a free on board (FOB) transaction but a point on land prior to the loading of the goods on the vessel. The 1990 revision also added clauses to permit the seller's obligation to provide proof of delivery through electronic data interchange (EDI) messages in place of the traditional paper documentation, provided that the parties agreed to communicate electronically. Note, however, in a documentary sale the bill of lading allows the buyer to obtain possession of the goods while in transit and the buyer surrenders the bill of lading in exchange for the goods from the carrier. Actual delivery of the paper document to the carrier makes the bill of lading difficult to replace by electronic communications. The 2010 revision of Incoterms reduces the number of terms from 13 to 11 in an effort to simplify and also reflects a modern trend in Europe to use Incoterms not only for international sales, where it was traditionally used, but also for what are considered to be domestic sales within the 28 states of the European Union, which forms a customs territory. No doubt Incoterms will continue to be periodically revised to reflect changes in international trade.

Incoterms are not intended as a law of contracts. Incoterms are intended only to clarify which party has to perform the various tasks necessary for the delivery of goods under the contract of sale. However, as Incoterms do create obligations on the part of the parties to perform certain tasks, these obligations can result in certain legal rights and obligations that arise under a background substantive contract law such as the CISG. Moreover, while Incoterms apply only to the sales contract, the adoption of certain terms in Incoterms may necessarily limit the parties with respect to the other contracts. For example, a seller having agreed to a sale CFR (cost and freight) or CIF (cost, insurance, and freight) cannot use a mode of transportation other than carriage by sea as the seller must present a bill of lading or other maritime document to the buyer, which is simply not possible if other modes of transportation are used. In addition, the documents required for payment under a letter of credit will depend on the mode of transportation used.

No matter which specific terms are chosen under Incoterms, the parties have certain uniform obligations. The seller must provide conforming goods and a commercial invoice and assist the buyer in arranging for the shipment of the goods. The buyer must make payment and, in some cases, notify the seller of the details of the shipping arrangement, such as the name of the carrier or port of destination. The 2010 version of Incoterms sorts all of the terms into two groups: one for any mode or modes of transport and one for sea and inland waterway transport.

In the first group (any mode of transport), under the first term (EXW), the seller has only the obligation to make the goods available to the buyer at the seller's premises or another named place (i.e., works, factory, or warehouse). This group also includes an obligation on the part of the seller to deliver to a carrier nominated by the buyer (FCA), an additional obligation (beyond delivery) on the seller to pay for the costs of carriage to the carrier (CPT), and another additional obligation (beyond delivery) of the seller to pay for the costs of carriage and insurance for the goods covering the transport of the good until they are delivered to the carrier (CIP). Under the D terms (DAT, DAP, DDP), the seller has to bear all costs and risks needed to deliver the goods to the buyer's disposal at the place of destination and must also clear the goods for export, where applicable.

In the second group dealing with sea and waterway transport (FAS, FOB, CFR, CIF), the seller must deliver the goods to a carrier named by the buyer. Under some terms, the seller must pay only for the costs of carriage to the carrier at the seller's port and has no obligation to pay for the cost of ocean carriage or transport from the seller's port to the buyer's port (FAS, FOB). Other terms require the seller to pay for the cost of ocean carriage to the buyer's port (CFR) as well as an additional obligation to procure insurance for the goods (CIF).

Under all of these terms, the risk of loss for the goods as well as the obligation for bearing the costs relating to the goods passes from the seller to the buyer once the seller has completed its delivery obligation.

The following chart summarizes all of these terms:

INCOTERMS 2010
Rules for Any Mode or Modes of Transport

EXW: Ex Works (. . . named place of delivery)
FCA: Free Carrier (. . . named place of delivery)
CPT: Carriage Paid To (. . . named place of destination)
CIP: Carriage and Insurance Paid To (. . . named place of destination)
DAT: Delivered at Terminal (. . . named terminal at port or place of destination)
DAP: Delivered at Place (. . . named place of destination)
DDP: Delivered Duty Paid (. . . named place of destination)

Rules for Sea and Inland Waterway Transport

FAS: Free Alongside Ship (. . . named port of shipment)
FOB: Free on Board (. . . named port of shipment)
CFR: Cost and Freight (. . . named port of destination)
CIF: Cost, Insurance, and Freight (. . . named port of destination)

PROBLEM 2-2

A U.S. seller and a UK buyer enter into a contract for the sale of books "FOB seller's factory, Rose Hill, New York. This contract incorporates Incoterms 2010." In accordance with its usual practice, the seller arranges for transport of the goods inland to New York City where the goods are to be loaded aboard the carrier nominated by the buyer and bound for England. However, the carrier nominated by the buyer does not arrive at New York before the goods. The seller arranges for storage of the books in a transit warehouse at a New York port and immediately notifies the buyer that the goods have been stored pending notification of a substitute carrier by the buyer. One week later, the buyer's instructions naming the substitute carrier are received by the seller, but in the meantime, the books are destroyed by a fire in the storage facility. The seller argues that it has satisfied its delivery obligations and that the risk of loss passed to the buyer. The seller seeks payment for the cost of transporting the goods from the factory to the port in New York, the cost of storage, and payment of the purchase price. The buyer responds that it owes nothing to the seller; the risk of loss remained with the seller because under an FOB sale, the seller assumed the risk of loss until the books were delivered by "placing them on board the vessel nominated by the buyer at . . . the named port of shipment" (A4), which never occurred. The buyer argues that because the seller cannot deliver the books, there is a total failure of consideration for the contract and the buyer does not have to pay the purchase price. In addition, the buyer argues that the seller should have insured the books against risk of loss. Does the buyer have to pay for the books, inland passage, and storage? See Incoterms on the FOB term below, especially at introductory paragraph, A3, B3, A4, B4, A5, B5, A6, B6, A7, and B7.

INCOTERMS 2010 ICC RULES FOR USE OF DOMESTIC AND INTERNATIONAL TRADE TERMS

FOB FREE ON BOARD (. . . named port of shipment)

This rule is to be used only for sea or inland waterway transport.

"Free on board" means that the seller delivers the goods on board the vessel nominated by the buyer at the named port of shipment or procures [sells] the goods already so delivered. The risk of loss of or damage to the goods passes when the goods are on board the vessel, and the buyer bears all costs from that moment onwards.

A   THE SELLER'S OBLIGATIONS

A1   General Obligations of the Seller

The seller must provide the goods and the commercial invoice in conformity with the contract of sale and any other evidence of conformity that may be required by the contract.

Any document referred to in A1-A10 may be an equivalent electronic record or procedure if agreed between the parties or customary.

A2   Licenses, Authorizations, Security Clearances and Other Formalities

Where applicable, the seller must obtain, at its own risk and expense, any export licence or other official authorization and carry out all customs formalities necessary for the export of the goods.

A3   Contracts of Carriage and Insurance

(a) Contract of carriage

The seller has no obligation to the buyer to make a contract of carriage.

(b) Contract of insurance

The seller has no obligation to the buyer to make a contract of insurance.

A4   Delivery

The seller must deliver the goods either by placing them on board the vessel nominated by the buyer at the loading point, if any, indicated by the buyer at the named port of shipment or by procuring the goods so delivered. In either case, the seller must deliver the goods on the agreed date or within the agreed period and in the manner customary at the port.

If no specific loading point has been indicated by the buyer, the seller may select the point within the named port of shipment that best suits its purpose.

B   THE BUYER'S OBLIGATIONS

B1   General Obligations of the Buyer

The buyer must pay the price of the goods as provided in the contract of sale.

Any document referred to in B1-B10 may be an equivalent electronic record or procedure if agreed between the parties or customary.

B2   Licenses, Authorizations, Security Clearances and Other Formalities

Where applicable, it is up to the buyer to obtain, at its own risk and expense, any import licence or other official authorization and carry out all customs formalities for the import of the goods and for their transport through any country.

B3   Contracts of Carriage

(a) Contract of carriage

The buyer must contract, at its own expense for the carriage of the goods from the named port of shipment.

(b) Contract of insurance

The buyer has no obligation to the seller to make a contract of insurance.

B4   Taking Delivery

The buyer must take delivery of the goods when they have been delivered as envisaged in A4.

A5   Transfer of Risks

The seller bears all risks of loss of or damage to the goods until they have been delivered in accordance with A4 with the exception of loss or damage in the circumstances described in B5.

A6   Allocation of Costs

The seller must pay

(a) all costs relating to the goods until they have been delivered in accordance with A4, other than those payable by the buyer as envisaged in B6; and

(b) where applicable, the costs of customs formalities necessary for export, as well as all duties, taxes and other charges payable upon export.

B5   Transfer of Risks

The buyer bears all risks of loss of or damage to the goods from the time they have been delivered as envisaged in A4.

If

(a) the buyer fails to notify the nomination of a vessel in accordance with B7; or

(b) the vessel nominated by the buyer fails to arrive on time to enable the seller to comply with A4, is unable to take the goods, or closes for cargo earlier than the time notified in accordance with B7;

then, the buyer bears all risks of loss of or damage to the goods:

(i) from the agreed date, or in the absence of an agreed date,

(ii) from the date notified by the seller under A7 within the agreed period, or, if no such date has been notified,

(iii) from the expiry date of any agreed period for delivery,
  •   provided that the goods have been clearly identified as the contract goods.

B6   Allocation of Costs

The buyer must pay

(a) all costs relating to the goods from the time they have been delivered as envisaged in A4, except, where applicable, the costs of customs formalities necessary for export, as well as all duties, taxes and other charges payable upon export as referred to in A6(b);

(b) any additional costs incurred, either because:

(i) the buyer has failed to give appropriate notice in accordance with B7, or

(ii) the vessel nominated by the buyer fails to arrive on time, is unable to take the goods, or closes for cargo earlier than the time notified in accordance with B7,
  •   provided that the goods have been clearly identified as the contract goods; and

(c) where applicable, all duties, taxes and other charges, as well as the costs of carrying out customs formalities payable upon import of the goods and the costs for their transport through any country.

A7 Notices to the Buyer

The seller must, at the buyer's risk and expense, give the buyer sufficient notice either that the goods have been delivered in accordance with A4 or that the vessel has failed to take the goods within the time agreed.

A8 Delivery Document

The seller must provide the buyer, at the seller's expense, with the usual proof that the goods have been delivered in accordance with A4.

Unless such proof is a transport document, the seller must provide assistance to the buyer, at the buyer's request, risk and expense, in obtaining a transport document.

B7 Notices to the Seller

The buyer must give the seller sufficient notice of the vessel name, loading point and, where necessary, the selected delivery time within the agreed period.

B8 Proof of Delivery

The buyer must accept the proof of delivery provided as envisaged in A8.

* * *   * * *

A10 Assistance with Information and Related Costs

The seller must, where applicable, in a timely manner, provide to or render assistance in obtaining for the buyer, at the buyer's request, risk and expense, any documents and information, including security-related information, that the buyer needs for the import of the goods and/or for their transport to the final destination.

The seller must reimburse the buyer for all costs and charges incurred by the buyer in providing or rendering assistance in obtaining documents and information as envisaged in B10.

B10 Assistance with Information and Related Costs

The buyer must, in a timely manner, advise the seller of any security information requirements so that the seller may comply with A10. The buyer must reimburse the seller for all costs and charges incurred by the seller in providing or rendering assistance in obtaining documents and information as envisaged in A10.

The buyer must, where applicable, in a timely manner, provide to or render assistance in obtaining for the seller, at the seller's request, risk and expense, any documents and information, including security-related information, that the seller needs for the transport and export of the goods and for their transport through any country.

PROBLEM 2-3

A French seller and a U.S. buyer agree on the sale of a quantity of luxury handbags "CIF Los Angeles with payment against documents. This contract is subject to Incoterms 2010." The seller loads the goods on board the carrier at Marseilles, a southern port city in France. To save on costs, the seller asks the carrier for a straight or nonnegotiable bill of lading made out in the name of the U.S. buyer. The seller forwards the bill of lading and other documents to the buyer and asks for payment against documents. The buyer argues that the seller must submit a negotiable bill of lading under a CIF transaction.

(1) Must the seller submit a negotiable bill of lading to the buyer?
(2) Who must arrange and pay for the contract of carriage?
(3) Who must arrange and pay for insurance for the goods?
(4) Suppose that no one pays for insurance and that the goods are damaged or lost during the ocean carriage. Did the risk of loss for the goods pass from the seller to the buyer?

To answer these questions, see Incoterms on the CIF term below, especially at introductory paragraph, A3, B3, A5, B5, A8, and B8.

CIF COST INSURANCE AND FREIGHT (. . . named port of destination)

This rule is to be used only for sea or inland waterway transport.

"Cost, insurance and freight" means that the seller delivers the goods on board the vessel or procures the goods already so delivered. The risk of loss of or damage to the goods passes when the goods are on board the vessel. The seller must contract for and pay the costs and freight necessary to bring the goods to the named port of destination.

The seller also contracts for insurance cover against the buyer's risk of loss or damage to the goods during the carriage.

A THE SELLER'S OBLIGATIONS

A1 General Obligations of the Seller

The seller must provide the goods and the commercial invoice in conformity with the contract of sale and any other evidence of conformity which may be required by the contract.

Any document referred to in A1-A10 may be an equivalent electronic record or procedure if agreed between the parties or customary.

A2 Licenses, Authorizations, Security Clearances and Other Formalities

Where applicable, the seller must obtain, at its own risk and expense, any export license or other official authorization and carry out all customs formalities necessary for the export of the goods.

A3 Contracts of Carriage and Insurance

(a) Contract of carriage

The seller must contract or procure a contract for the carriage of the goods from the agreed point of delivery, if any, at the place of delivery to the named port of destination or, if agreed, any point at that port. The contract of carriage must be made on usual terms at the seller's expense and provide for carriage by the usual route in a vessel of the type normally used for the transport of the type of goods sold.

B THE BUYER'S OBLIGATIONS

B1 General Obligations of the Buyer

The buyer must pay the price of the goods as provided in the contract of sale.

Any document referred to in B1-B10 may be an equivalent electronic record or procedure if agreed between the parties or customary.

B2 Licenses, Authorizations, Security Clearances and Formalities

Where applicable, it is up to the buyer to obtain, at its own risk and expense, any import licence or other official authorization and carry out all customs formalities for the import of the goods and for their transport through any country.

B3 Contracts of Carriage and Insurance

(a) Contract of carriage
The buyer has no obligation to the seller to make a contract of carriage.

(b) Contract of insurance
The buyer has no obligation to the seller to make a contract of insurance. However, the buyer must provide the seller, upon request, with any information necessary for the seller to procure any additional insurance requested by the buyer as envisaged in A3 b).

(b) Contract of insurance

The seller must obtain, at its own expense, cargo insurance complying at least with the minimum cover provided by Clauses (C) of the Institute Cargo Clauses (LMA/IUA) or any similar clauses. The insurance shall be contracted with underwriters or an insurance company of good repute and entitle the buyer, or any other person having an insurable interest in the goods, to claim directly from the insurer.

When required by the buyer, the seller shall, subject to the buyer providing any necessary information requested by the seller, provide at the buyer's expense any additional cover, if procurable, such as cover as provided by Clauses (A) or (B) of the Institute Cargo Clauses (LMA/IUA) or any similar clauses and/or cover complying with the Institute War Clauses and/or Institute Strikes Clauses (LMA/IUA) or any similar clauses.

The insurance shall cover, at a minimum, the price provided in the contract plus 10% (i.e., 110%) and shall be in the currency of the contract.

The insurance shall cover the goods from the point of delivery set out in A4 and A5 to at least the named port of destination.

The seller must provide the buyer with the insurance policy or other evidence of insurance cover.

Moreover, the seller must provide the buyer, at the buyer's request, risk, and expense (if any), with information that the buyer needs to procure any additional insurance.

A4   Delivery

The seller must deliver the goods either by placing them on board the vessel or by procuring the goods so delivered. In either case, the seller must deliver the goods on the agreed date or within the agreed period and in the manner customary at the port.

A5   Transfer of Risks

The seller bears all risks of loss of or damage to the goods until they have been delivered in accordance with A4, with the exception of loss or damage in the circumstances described in B5.

B4   Taking Delivery

The buyer must take delivery of the goods when they have been delivered as envisaged in A4 and receive them from the carrier at the named port of destination.

B5   Transfer of Risks

The buyer bears all risks of loss of or damage to the goods from the time they have been delivered as envisaged in A4.

If the buyer fails to give notice in accordance with B7, then it bears all risks of loss of or damage to the goods from the agreed date or the expiry date of the agreed period for shipment, provided that the goods have been clearly identified as the contract goods.

A6   Allocation of Costs

The seller must pay

(a) all costs relating to the goods until they have been delivered in accordance with A4, other than those payable by the buyer as envisaged in B6;

(b) the freight and all other costs resulting from A3 a), including the costs of loading the goods on board and any charges for unloading at the agreed port of discharge that were for the seller's account under the contract of carriage;

(c) the costs of insurance resulting from A3 b); and

(d) where applicable, the costs of customs formalities necessary for export, as well as all duties, taxes and other charges payable upon export, and the costs for their transport through any country that were for the seller's account under the contract of carriage.

B6   Allocation of Costs

The buyer must, subject to the provisions of A3 a), pay

(a) all costs relating to the goods from the time they have been delivered as envisaged in A4, except, where applicable, the costs of customs formalities necessary for export, as well as all duties, taxes and other charges payable upon export as referred to in A6 d);

(b) all costs and charges relating to the goods while in transit until their arrival at the port of destination, unless such costs and charges were for the seller's account under the contract of carriage;

(c) unloading costs including lighterage and wharfage charges, unless such costs and charges were for the seller's account under the contract of carriage;

(d) any additional costs incurred if it fails to give notice in accordance with B7, from the agreed date or the expiry date of the agreed period for shipment, provided that the goods have been clearly identified as the contract goods;

(e) where applicable, all duties, taxes and other charges, as well as the costs of carrying out customs formalities payable upon import of the goods and the costs for their transport through any country, unless included within the costs of the contract of carriage; and

(f) the costs of any additional insurance procured at the buyer's request under A3 b) and B3 b).

A7   Notices to the Buyer

The seller must give the buyer any notice needed in order to allow the buyer to take measures that are normally necessary to enable the buyer to take the goods.

B7   Notices to the Seller

The buyer must, whenever it is entitled to determine the time for shipping the goods and/or the point of receiving the goods within the named port of destination, give the seller sufficient notice thereof.

A8   Delivery Document

The seller must, at his own expense, provide the buyer without delay with the usual transport document for the agreed port of destination.

B8   Proof of Delivery

The buyer must accept the transport document provided as envisaged in A8 if it is in conformity with the contract.

This transport document must cover the contract goods, be dated within the period agreed for shipment, enable the buyer to claim the goods from the carrier at the port of destination and, unless otherwise agreed, enable the buyer to sell the goods in transit by the transfer of the document to a subsequent buyer or by notification to the carrier.

 Bill of lading.

When such a transport document is issued in negotiable form and in several originals, a full set of originals must be presented to the buyer.

A9 Checking — Packaging — Marking

The seller must pay the costs of those checking operations (such as checking quality, measuring, weighing, counting) that are necessary for the purpose of delivering the goods in accordance with A4, as well as the costs of any pre-shipment inspection mandated by the authority of the country of export.

The seller must, at its own expense, package the goods, unless it is usual for the particular trade to transport the type of goods sold unpackaged. The seller may package the goods in the manner appropriate for their transport, unless the buyer has notified the seller of specific packaging requirements before the contract of sale is concluded. Packaging is to be marked appropriately.

A10 Assistance with Information and Related Costs

The seller must, where applicable, in a timely manner, provide to or render assistance in obtaining for the buyer, at the buyer's request, risk and expense, any documents and information, including security-related information, that the buyer needs for the import of the goods and/or for their transport to the final destination.

The seller must reimburse the buyer for all costs and charges incurred by the buyer in providing or rendering assistance in obtaining documents and information as envisaged in B10.

B9 Inspection of Goods

The buyer must pay the costs of any pre-shipment inspection, except when such inspection is mandated by the authorities of the country of export.

B10 Assistance with Information and Related Costs

The buyer must, in a timely manner, advise the seller of any security information requirements so that the seller may comply with A10.

The buyer must reimburse the seller for all costs and charges incurred by the seller in providing or rendering assistance in obtaining documents and information as envisaged in A10.

The buyer must, where applicable, in a timely manner, provide to or render assistance in obtaining for the seller, at the seller's request, risk and expense, any documents and information, including security-related information, that the seller needs for the transport and export of the goods and for their transport through any country.

D. Interpretation of Commercial Terms

While Incoterms and other attempts at harmonization have alleviated many of the difficulties involved in the interpretation of international commercial terms and international commercial law, none of the modern instruments of harmonization was intended
by their drafters to answer all questions that may arise in the course of an international
contract. Rather, these instruments were viewed as needing supplementation from time
to time from the traditional sources of international commercial law, such as cases from
domestic legal systems.

    Biddell Brothers below involved a CIF contract where the parties did not explicitly pro-
vide for payment against documents. In such a situation, must the buyer pay against the
bill of lading or can the buyer wait until actual delivery and after the buyer inspects the
goods?

PROBLEM 2-4

    A U.S. seller and an Egyptian buyer meet at an agricultural trade fair. The seller
deals in Grade A, extra-fine grain and the buyer is a wholesale distributor of grain for the
African continent. The buyer informs the seller that the buyer must be able to sell the
grain while it is in transit from the United States. After several days of negotiations, the
parties agree to a sales contract, which provides in part:

> Seller is to arrange and prepay inland transportation to port of shipment and freight from
> port of shipment to the port of destination in Cairo. Purchase price includes freight. Payment
> in net cash upon delivery.

    The seller arranges for the carriage and loads the goods aboard the carrier, which
issues a bill of lading to the seller. The seller forwards the bill of lading to the buyer and
asks for payment. While the carrier is en route, however, heavy storms cause damage to
the carrier's deck and cargo. The buyer now has the bill of lading but takes the position that as the contract did not explicitly call for payment against documents, it has the
option of either paying against the bill of lading or paying against delivery of the goods
after inspection. The buyer argues that the term "[p]ayment in net cash against delivery"
refers to delivery of the goods. The buyer wishes to inspect the grain to make sure that it is
suitable for its customers and to also ensure that the goods did not suffer damage during
transit, especially as no one procured insurance. The seller argues that the buyer must
pay against documents and that the reference to "[p]ayment against delivery" refers to
delivery of the documents. Must the buyer pay? Did anyone have an obligation to procure
insurance? Read *Biddell Brothers* below.

Biddell Brothers v. E. Clemens Horst Company
In the Court of Appeals
[1911] 1 King's Bench 934

    Appeal from the judgment of HAMILTON J. in an action tried by him without a jury.
    The action was brought to recover damages for alleged breaches of two contracts,
dated respectively October 13, 1904, and December 21, 1904.

The first contract, which was made at Sunderland between the defendants, of San Francisco and London, parties of the first part, and Vaux & Sons, Limited, of the city of Sunderland, parties of the second part, provided that "the parties of the first part agree to sell to the parties of the second part one hundred (100) bales, equal to or better than choice brewing Pacific Coast hops of each of the crops of the years 1905 to 1912 inclusive.

"The said hops to be shipped to Sunderland.

"The parties of the second part shall pay for the said hops at the rate of ninety (90) shillings sterling per 112 lbs., c.i.f. to London, Liverpool, or Hull (tare 5 lbs. Per bale).

"Terms net cash.

"It is agreed that this contract is severable as to each bale.

"The sellers may consider entire unfulfilled portion of this contract violated by the buyers in case of refusal by them to pay for any hops delivered and accepted hereunder or if this contract or any part of it is otherwise violated by the buyers.

"Time of shipment to place of delivery, or delivery at place of delivery, during the months (inclusive) of October to March following the harvest of each year's crop.

"If for any reason the parties of the second part shall be dissatisfied with or object to all or any part of any lot of hops delivered hereunder, the parties of the first part may, within thirty days after receipt of written notice thereof, ship or deliver other choice hops in place of those objected to."

The second contract was between the same parties, and in the same terms, except that it provided for the sale by the defendants to Vaux & Sons, Limited, of fifty bales of British Columbian hops equal to or better than choice Pacific Coast hops of each of the crops of the years 1906 to 1912 inclusive; c.i.f. to London.

Upon August 11, 1908, Vaux & Sons, Limited, assigned for value to the plaintiffs all their rights and benefits under the two contracts, and express notice thereof in writing was given by the plaintiffs to the defendants.

Correspondence passed between the parties as to the shipment of the 150 bales of the 1909 crop, and on January 29, 1910, the defendants wrote to the plaintiffs stating that they were ready to make shipment of the 150 bales of the 1909 crop of the contracted quality, and that "for the invoice price less freight we will value on your good selves at sight with negotiable bills of lading and insurance certificates attached to draft, and if you wish we will also attach certificates of quality of the Merchants' Exchange, San Francisco, or other competent authority to cover the shipment." On February 1 the plaintiffs replied that they were prepared to take delivery on the terms of the contracts, and that it was "in accordance with the universal practice of the trade and the custom adopted by you in your dealings with other purchasers of your hops, and it has also been your custom with our assignors to submit samples, and the samples having been accepted to give delivery in bulk in accordance with the samples; but if you decline to adopt the usual and undoubtedly most convenient course, we can only pay for the hops against delivery and examination of each bale. We cannot fall in with your suggestion of accepting the certificate of quality of the Merchants' Exchange, San Francisco." On February 5 the defendants' solicitors wrote to the plaintiffs' solicitors that the refusal of the plaintiffs to pay for the hops except upon terms which were not in accordance with the contracts was a clear breach of the contracts by the plaintiffs, and, that being so, the defendants would not now ship to the plaintiffs the 150 bales of the 1909 crop, and they reserved all their rights in respect of the breach of contract by the plaintiffs.

Upon March 11, 1910, the plaintiffs issued the writ in this action claiming damages for breach of contract in refusing to ship or deliver the 150 bales of hops. The defence, after stating that the defendants raised no defence with reference to the assignment of the agreements, alleged that, by reason of the plaintiffs' violation of the entire unfulfilled portion of the agreements in refusing to pay for the hops in accordance with the terms of the agreements, the defendants were entitled to refuse to further perform the agreements, and they counterclaimed against the plaintiffs for damages for breach of contract in refusing to take and pay for the 150 bales of hops.

Hamilton J. gave judgment for the defendants.

VAUGHAN WILLIAMS, LORD JUSTICE: The judgment of the learned judge is [not] based primarily upon any authorities upon the meaning of the terms "cost freight and insurance," but is based upon the proposition that the terms c.i.f. "are now settled and, I hope I may add, well understood." Those are the words of the learned judge, and he goes on to say that it is not and cannot be contended but "that the seller under a c.i.f. contract has first of all to arrange to put on board a ship at the port of shipment goods of the description contained in the contract; secondly to arrange for a contract of affreightment under which they will be delivered at the destination contemplated in the contract; thirdly to arrange for an insurance upon the usual terms current in the trade, available for the benefit of the buyer; to make out an invoice; and, finally, he has to tender to the buyer those documents so that the buyer may know what freight he has to pay in order to obtain delivery of the goods, if they are intact, or so that he may recover for the loss of them if they have gone to the bottom."

There is no evidence in the present case of any law merchant or custom which reads such words as "payment to be made against shipping documents," or words to that effect, into the contract. As to the construction of the contract, I certainly think it very difficult to construe this c.i.f. contract as containing an implied condition for payment of "cash against documents."

The appeal, therefore, must be allowed, and judgment entered for the plaintiffs.

FARWELL, LORD JUSTICE: I will assume that as a matter of usage the seller is bound to tender the bill of lading to the buyer when it arrives, and, if the buyer accepts it, he must, of course, pay for the goods on such acceptance, because the delivery of the bill of lading is a symbolical delivery of the goods, and, if the goods are accepted, the right of antecedent (though not of subsequent) inspection before payment is thereby waived, just as it would be in the case of acceptance of the goods themselves without inspection. But I fail to follow the consequence said by the learned judge to ensue. The duty on A to tender to B a document before he can require payment does not impose on B a duty to accept such document as equivalent to goods, if he has a right to inspect such goods before accepting and paying for them. B has the option of choosing between two alternative rights: he may accept symbolical delivery or actual delivery, but in the absence of express contract it is at his option, not at the seller's. In the great majority of cases, it suits both buyer and seller better to give and accept symbolical delivery by the bill of lading, and the existence and exercise of this option explain why in cases where the c.i.f. contract does not contain the words "cash against documents," or the like, the contract is in fact often so carried out. But this is no evidence of usage for the buyer to accept in all cases, or, in other words, to waive the option. If the goods were lost at sea, the option would at once cease because inspection would have been rendered impossible, and the buyer would be bound to pay against documents.

The basis of my judgment is that the buyer has a common law right (now embodied in the Sale of Goods Act) to have inspected goods against payment, and this cannot be taken away from him without some contract expressed or implied, and here I can find neither.

In my opinion the appeal should be allowed and judgment entered for the plaintiffs.

KENNEDY, LORD JUSTICE: [T]he plaintiffs' assertion of the right under a cost freight and insurance contract to withhold payment until delivery of the goods themselves, and until after an opportunity of examining them, cannot possibly be effectuated except in one of two ways. Landing and delivery can rightfully be given by the shipowner only to the holder of the bill of lading. Therefore, if the plaintiffs' contention is right, one of two things must happen. Either the seller must surrender to the purchaser the bill of lading, where under the delivery can be obtained, without receiving payment, which, as the bill of lading carries with it an absolute power of disposition, is, in the absence of a special agreement in the contract of sale, so unreasonable as to be absurd; or, alternatively, the vendor must himself retain the bill of lading, himself land and take delivery of the goods, and himself store the goods on quay (if the rules of the port permit), or warehouse the goods, for such time as may elapse before the purchaser has an opportunity of examining them. But this involves a manifest violation of the express terms of the contract "90s. per 112 lbs. Cost freight and insurance." The parties have in terms agreed that for the buyer's benefit the price shall include freight and insurance, and for his benefit nothing beyond freight and insurance. But, if the plaintiffs' contention were to prevail, the vendor must be saddled with the further payment of those charges at the port of discharge which would be added to the freight and insurance premium which alone he has by the terms of the contract undertaken to defray.

Finally, let me test the soundness of the plaintiffs' contention that according to the true meaning of this contract their obligation to pay arises only when delivery of the goods has been tendered to them after they have had an opportunity of examination, in this way. Suppose the goods to have been shipped, the bill of lading taken, and the insurance for the benefit of the buyer duly effected by the seller, as expressly stipulated in the contract. Suppose the goods then during the ocean transit to have been lost by the perils of the sea. The vendor tenders the bill of lading, with the insurance policy and the other shipping documents (if any) to the purchaser, to whom from the moment of shipment the property has passed, and at whose risk, covered by the insurance, the goods were at the time of loss. Is it, I ask myself, arguable that the purchaser could be heard to say,

"I will not pay because I cannot have delivery of and an examination of the goods"? But it is just this which is necessarily involved in the contention of these plaintiffs. The seller's answer, and I think conclusive answer, is, "You have the bill of lading and the policy of insurance."

In my judgment, the judgment of Hamilton J. was right, and this appeal, so far as relates to the plaintiffs' claim, should be dismissed.

Disposition: Appeal allowed.

The judgment of the court of appeals in *Biddell Brothers* was appealed by the defendants E. Clemens Horst Company with the following result below.

E. Clemens Horst Company v. Biddell Brothers
House of Lords
[1912] A.C. 18

EARL LOREBURN, LORD CHANCELLOR: My Lords, in this case there has been a remarkable divergence of judicial opinion. For my part I think it is reasonably clear that this appeal ought to be allowed; and the remarkable judgment of Kennedy L.J., illuminating, as it does, the whole field of controversy, relieves me from the necessity of saying much upon the subject.

Now s. 28 of the Sale of Goods Act says in effect that payment is to be against delivery. Accordingly we have supplied by the general law an answer to the question when this cash is to be paid. But when is there delivery of goods which are on board ship? That may be quite a different thing from delivery of goods on shore. The answer is that delivery of the bill of lading when the goods are at sea can be treated as delivery of the goods themselves, this law being so old that I think it is quite unnecessary to refer to authority for it.

Now in this contract there is no time fixed at which the seller is entitled to tender the bill of lading. He therefore may do so at any reasonable time; and it is wrong to say that he must defer the tender of the bill of lading until the ship has arrived; and it is still more wrong to say that he must defer the tender of the bill of lading until after the goods have been landed, inspected, and accepted.

Accordingly, Hamilton J.'s order ought to be restored so far as the claim is concerned. Order of the Court of Appeal reversed.

NOTES AND QUESTIONS

1. In reversing the court of appeal, the Lord Chancellor states: "[D]elivery of the bill of lading when the goods are at sea can be treated as delivery of the goods themselves, this law being so old that I think it is quite unnecessary to refer to authority for it." As the early decisions indicated, there did not appear to be any clear English authority on this issue. If so, what "law" is he referring to?

2. To test your understanding of *Biddell Brothers*, suppose that the parties had agreed on the use of a nonnegotiable or straight bill of lading but were otherwise silent on payment. Under this arrangement, when is payment to be made? Does the buyer have the right of inspection?

3. The position set forth by Lord Justice Kennedy and upheld by the House of Lords that a CIF transaction implies payment against documents is now the standard position. Section 2-320(4) of the Uniform Commercial Code (2003) provides:

> Under the term C.I.F. or C&F., unless otherwise agreed the buyer must make payment against tender of the required documents and the seller may not tender nor the buyer demand delivery of the goods in substitution for the documents.

Review Incoterms 2010 CIF B(1) and A(8). Can you explain how the Incoterms definition of CIF also requires payment against documents?

E. Documents of Title

The negotiable bill of lading is crucial to a documentary sales transaction. Delivery of the bill of lading passes title to the goods and is equivalent to delivery of the goods. Are there other documents that can also serve as a document of title, such as a delivery order, that is, an order from the seller directed at the carrier to deliver the goods to the buyer? This raises the more basic question: What is the essential legal requirement that makes a document a document of title?

PROBLEM 2-5

A UK seller and a Pakistani buyer enter into a contract for the sale of wheat. The contract provides for "Sale of wheat CIF Pakistan at a port to be designated by buyer; payment against documents; seller can submit either a bill of lading or a delivery order." The seller loads the shipment aboard the carrier in exchange for a negotiable bill of lading. The seller gives the buyer a delivery order made out to the ship's master with instructions to the master to deliver the wheat to the buyer. The seller also gives the buyer an insurance policy insuring the goods against marine risk at 110 percent of value. While the ship is on its way to Pakistan, there is a brief military skirmish involving Pakistani and Indian ships and the carrier is damaged and the wheat is lost. The seller demands payment from the buyer, but the buyer refuses to pay on the grounds that the contract was one for payment against the delivery of goods, despite the use of the CIF term, and as the goods were lost, there was a total failure of consideration. Must the buyer pay? Does it make a difference whether the freight was prepaid or collect? See *The Julia* below. On the insurance issue, see Incoterms CIF, A3.

Comptoir d'Achat et de Vente du Boerenbond Belge S/A v. Luis de Ridder Limitada (The Julia)

House of Lords
[1949] A.C. 293

[On April 24, 1940, Luis de Ridder, an Argentinian grain exporting firm (seller), contracted to sell 500 tons of rye for about $5,000 to Comptoir d'Achat et de Vente du Boerenbond Belge (buyer), CIF Antwerp with payment against documents. The 500 tons of rye were part of a 1,120-ton shipment of rye that the seller had already loaded on board the Julia on April 18 prior to contracting with the buyer. The master of the Julia had given the seller a negotiable bill of lading covering the entire load of rye made out to the order of the seller's agent in Belgium, Belgian Grain and Produce Company (Belgian Grain).

Under the contract with the buyer, the seller was entitled to present either a delivery order or a bill of lading to the buyer. After the Julia set sail, the seller instructed Belgian Grain to present the buyer with a provisional invoice and a delivery order. The provisional invoice was for the amount of $5,000 covering the cost of the goods and insurance. The delivery order was addressed to the seller's cargo superintendent in Belgium, F. Van Bree, S.A. (Van Bree), with instructions to release the goods to the buyer upon presentation of the delivery order. The delivery order also stated that the buyer had a share in the insurance policy purchased by the seller covering the entire shipment of rye on board the Julia. The share given to the buyer was 2 percent over the invoice value of the rye purchased by the buyer. Before the delivery order was transmitted to the buyer, it was signed and endorsed by Van Bree promising to honor the delivery order in favor of the bearer. The buyer accepted both the provisional invoice and the delivery order and paid $5,000 to Belgian Grain. The same day, the seller presented two insurance certificates referenced in the delivery order to Van Bree (one certificate was for marine risks and the other was for war risks). The certificates provided that they represented the original policy of insurance with its coverage of the full shipment and conveyed all of the rights of the original policy holder (the seller) and could be exchanged for a duly stamped policy if and when required. The certificates also provided that they were invalid unless countersigned by

Belgian Grain. The record does not indicate whether they were ever signed. From the record, it appears that these certificates were never delivered to the buyer.

To obtain delivery of the goods, the buyer followed a rather complicated procedure that the parties had been using for 8 to 11 years and would have used in this case if the Julia had actually arrived in Antwerp. After the ship arrived, the buyer would give the delivery order with a check for the freight charges to its own agent, Carga S.A. (Carga), who served as the buyer's cargo superintendent at Antwerp. Carga would then hand the check to Belgian Grain for the freight charges and present the delivery order at the same time. Belgian Grain would then make an inscription at the bottom of the delivery order acknowledging receipt of the freight charges and would return the order so annotated to Carga. Next, Carga would hand the delivery order to Van Bree, seller's cargo superintendent, which retained the delivery order and issued a release addressed to themselves authorizing the delivery to Carga. Before Van Bree could obtain possession of the goods from the ship, however, the ship's master had to issue a captain's release. The master would issue the release only upon proof that the freight had been paid to the agents of the ship. Once the ship's captain was satisfied that the freight charges had been paid, he would issue a release instructing his crew aboard the ship to release them to Van Bree. In turn, Van Bree would release them to Carga, which would deliver the goods to the buyer.

Before the Julia could arrive at Antwerp, however, the Germans invaded Belgium and occupied Antwerp. The ship was diverted to Lisbon where the rye was sold at a considerably lower price than the price paid by the buyer. The seller offered to give the buyer the amount realized on this sale, but the buyer sought a refund of the entire purchase price. After the war, the buyer sought arbitration before an umpire and claimed that the nondelivery of the rye at Antwerp constituted a total failure of consideration under the contract and that the buyer was entitled to recover the purchase price. The umpire found that the contract was a genuine CIF contract and that the seller had delivered the documents to the buyer as required under the contract and was entitled to payment. The umpire's award was upheld by the court of first instance and by the court of appeals from which the sellers have appealed.]

Lord Porter: In the present case it is true, no doubt, to say that some steps had been taken towards the performance of this contract, e.g., the goods had been shipped, an invoice sent, the customary so-called delivery order had been transmitted and that delivery order amongst its provisions contained a declaration by the sellers' agents, Belgian Grain and Produce Co. Ld., that they gave a share of the present delivery order to $4,973 in a certificate of insurance. But the taking of steps towards performance is not necessarily a part performance of a contract. The question is whether the purchaser has got what he is entitled to in return for the price. That practice seems to me rather to show that the payment was not made for the documents but as an advance payment for a contract afterwards to be performed.

No doubt the contract could have been so performed as to make it subject to the ordinary principles which apply to a c.i.f. contract. The tender of a bill of lading or even of a delivery order upon the ship, at any rate if attorned to by the master, and a policy or a certificate of insurance delivered to or even held for them might well put it in that category. But the type of delivery order tendered in the present case was a preliminary step only. A complicated procedure had to be followed before the goods would be released. The buyers had to hand the sum due for freight to their agents; those agents would then pay the freight and present the delivery order to the Belgian Grain and Produce Co. Ld., who would sign a note on it acknowledging receipt of the freight; the agents thereupon would hand the delivery order to Van Bree who would retain it and issue a "laissez suivre" or release to themselves authorizing delivery to the agents. But before physical delivery of the goods could take place Van Bree must have received a "Captain's laissez suivre" authorizing delivery to them. "It was thus," as the umpire says, "the effective document upon which Van Bree obtained physical possession of the goods; it was issued to Van Bree and was never physically in the buyers' hands." Similarly, "the insurance certificates," as the umpire also finds, "were received by Van Bree from the Belgian Grain and Produce Co. Ld., and would not have passed through the hands of, or even have been seen by, the buyers." He further finds that Van Bree "were at no time and in no respect agents of the buyers and that the sellers did not, by delivering the certificates to Van Bree, constructively deliver them to the buyers nor did Van Bree at any time hold the certificates (whether countersigned by the Belgian Grain and Produce Co. Ld. or not) at the disposal of the buyers." In these circumstances the fact that the sellers twice collected the insurance money for a total loss and handed it to the buyers does not lead very far. It was a convenient method of settling accounts between the parties and, despite the extra two per cent., is in substance no more than a repayment of the money given for the goods.

The vital question in the present case, as I see it, is whether the buyers paid for the documents as representing the goods or for the delivery of the goods themselves. But the whole circumstances have to be looked at and where, as, in my opinion, is the case here, no further security beyond that contained in the original contract passed to the buyers as a result of payment, where the property and possession both remained in the sellers until delivery in Antwerp, where the sellers were to pay for deficiency in bill of lading weight, guaranteed condition on arrival and made themselves responsible for all averages, the true view, I think, is that it is not a c.i.f. contract even in a modified form but a contract to deliver at Antwerp. If this be the true view there was plainly a frustration of the adventure—indeed the sellers admit so much in their pleadings—and no part performance and the consideration had wholly failed. The buyers are accordingly entitled to recover the money which they have paid. I would allow the appeal and pronounce for the alternative award with costs in your Lordships' House and in the courts below.

LORD SIMONDS: My Lords, there is, in my opinion, no finding of fact by the umpire which would justify your Lordships in holding that the delivery order which was handed to the buyers had any commercial value in the ordinary sense. That it was not a document of title by itself entitling the buyers to delivery of the goods was expressly found. It is a matter of conjecture whether in these circumstances it had any commercial value, and your Lordships cannot found on conjecture. The case is, however, put not only on the general commercial value of such a document but upon the special value which is said to have accrued to the buyers from its terms. This is the view which was taken by the learned Master of the Rolls, whose words I have already cited. At this stage I would remind your Lordships that "when one is considering the law of failure of consideration and of the quasi-contractual right to recover money on that ground, it is, generally speaking, not the promise which is referred to as the consideration, but the performance of the promise." To this I would add that the receipt by the promisee of something which the promisor did not promise will not prevent a total failure of consideration. The value consideration which the Master of the Rolls thought the buyers received was a personal undertaking and guarantee by Van Bree, the local agents at Antwerp of the sellers, which was to be found in their indorsement of the delivery note. I cannot accept this view. It is, I think, reasonably clear that the words I have cited give rise to no independent contractual rights against Van Bree. There is nothing in the umpire's award to suggest that Van Bree were acting in any other capacity than as agents for the sellers. If they were in fact acting or purporting to act as principals in respect of their indorsement of the delivery note, then, if, as I assume to be the case in the absence of evidence to the contrary, Belgian law is the same as English law, the buyers acquired against them no enforceable rights; for, so far as they at least were concerned, there was no consideration for their engagement. But, as I have said, in my view Van Bree were acting throughout as agents, and, seen in its true perspective, their undertaking indorsed on the delivery order was not "a part of what they [the buyers] contracted to pay for," but a part of the machinery by which the sellers were to carry out their bargain. What the buyers bought was 500 tons of rye, not an indorsement on a piece of paper which brought them not a step nearer their rye until the ship arrived at Antwerp. I come, then, to the conclusion that the sellers performed neither all nor, in any material sense, a part of what they were required to do under the contract and the buyers obtained no part of that which they had contracted to buy. There was therefore failure of consideration.

LORD NORMAND: It is agreed that the delivery order was not the equivalent of the goods in the sense that its possession conferred on the holder the right of property in the goods valid against all the world. But the consideration for the price is nothing less than that right, unless there are special terms in the contract. If the delivery order had some value otherwise than as the equivalent of the goods the fact has not been proved, and if proved it would be without relevance. If, as is I think plain on the facts found, the delivery order is merely a cogwheel in the machinery for enabling the sellers to transfer the property, it cannot be treated as to any extent consideration for the price, for the consideration for the price is not what the seller does in order to effect the transfer but the actual transfer of the property itself. It is not therefore necessary to consider whether Van Bree intended to bind themselves personally by their signature to any of the undertakings contained in the delivery order. But I can find no evidence of such an intention and I can find no consideration moving from the buyers to Van Bree.

These subsidiary arguments by themselves therefore avail nothing, and the sellers must rely on their contention that the contract by its special terms provides that between the sellers and the buyers the delivery order shall be treated as equivalent to the goods. The sellers laid weight on the description of the price as a c.i.f. price and on the description of the business as c.i.f. business. They also founded on the clause dealing with payment which, they said, treated the delivery order as the equivalent of the bill of lading and the price as paid for it. I think, however, that the explanation of the description c.i.f. in relation to the price and the business carried on by these two parties is that the contract stipulates for a price the components of which were cost, insurance and freight, and that the printed form of the contract used was one which was suitable for an orthodox c.i.f. transaction though also for other transactions not conforming to the c.i.f. model. The use of the label c.i.f. was therefore not significant and I agree with Asquith L.J., that the question is not whether the label was appropriate but what was the effect of the terms of the contract when it was not intended or possible to perform it as an orthodox c.i.f. contract is performed. The stipulation that the price or part of it was to be paid in exchange for a bill of lading and policy or in exchange for a delivery order and certificate does not carry with it the implication that in relation to the rights of the parties inter se the delivery order is to have the effect of a bill of lading, and I can see no reason for reading into the words "in exchange for" anything more than their literal meaning or to read "payment . . . in exchange for . . . delivery order" as meaning "payment for the delivery order." But I think that if the words "delivery order" had had to be construed without the aid of the previous course of dealing, it would have been held to mean a document addressed to and accepted by one in physical possession of the goods. The sellers would then have been bound to tender a document which was in fact the legal equivalent of the goods. The effect of the course of dealing was to release the sellers from that obligation and to entitle them to payment on tender of a document which contains no more than a personal obligation. I do not find evidence in the contract that the parties have undertaken to treat this document as a document of title as between themselves. I would therefore allow the appeal, with costs, both here and in the courts below.

Appeal allowed.

NOTES AND QUESTIONS

1. Did the House of Lords find that this was a contract for payment against documents or a contract for payment against delivery of the goods?

2. If the lordships had found that this was a true CIF contract, would the buyer have recovered the purchase price?

3. In *The Julia*, what was the legally effective document that gave possession to the goods? Was this document ever delivered to the buyer?

4. Why was it the practice of the London and Belgium grain merchants to require the seller to hire a sales agent (Belgian Grain) as well as a cargo superintendent (Van Bree)?

5. *Background of the London Merchants' Trade Practices in* The Julia. For a number of years, the parties had engaged in a rather complex arrangement for the sale of rye under the rules of the London Corn Trade Association. This arrangement helped to create flexibility in the sales transaction for both the London merchants and the Belgium buyers and the industry had developed a sophisticated system of agents and superintendents to support this practice. The seller is able to load a large bulk shipment of rye on board the carrier destined for Antwerp without first having obtained any purchase orders. After the goods are loaded, the carrier issues a negotiable bill of lading that is made out to the seller's agent, Belgian Grain, in Antwerp. The seller also takes out two insurance policies for the entire shipment of rye to protect itself against damage or loss of the rye due to marine or war risks while en route to Antwerp. The seller can then sell all or a portion of the rye while the vessel is en route to Belgium. Once the seller and a buyer agree on a sale, the seller will issue a delivery order to its agent in Antwerp. The bill of lading covers the entire shipment of rye so the seller cannot instruct its Antwerp agent to endorse the bill of lading to the buyer unless the buyer purchases the entire shipment. As the seller ships a very large shipment in order to economize on costs, it is unlikely that any single buyer will purchase the entire shipment but rather each shipment may be subject to several orders from several different buyers, each purchasing a portion of the shipment. The seller will issue delivery orders addressed to its cargo superintendent to distribute a portion of the rye to each buyer. If all of the rye is not purchased by buyers while en route to Antwerp, the seller's Antwerp agent would pay the carrier for the freight charges and the seller's cargo superintendent would take possession of the rye by presenting the bill of lading to the carrier. The cargo superintendent would then deliver the rye to the agent who would then sell the rye on behalf of the seller.

As with the bill of lading, the insurance policies purchased by the seller also covered the entire shipment against loss during the carriage. The seller cannot endorse the policies and deliver them to the buyer unless the buyer purchased the entire shipment, which, as we noted, was not likely given the large size of the shipments. Instead, the practice used by the London Corn Trade Association was to have the seller make a note on the delivery order that the buyer was the beneficiary of a "share" of the two insurance policies covering marine and war risk for the portion purchased by the buyer; then the seller gave two "certificates of insurance," signed by the seller's insurance brokers, to the seller's cargo superintendent in Antwerp. The certificates purported to represent all of the rights in the original insurance policies with full coverage of the entire shipment and purported to convey all of these rights to the transferee. The combination of the notation on the delivery order specifying the buyer's share in the insurance policies and the delivery of the certificates representing the policies was thought to be sufficient to transfer a valid interest in the policies to the buyer to cover the portion of the rye purchased by the buyer against marine and war risk. Note in *The Julia* that Lord Porter doubted whether any valid interests in the insurance policies had been actually transferred to the buyer. Why?

Once the seller and buyer conclude a sale, the seller will instruct its Antwerp agent to issue a provisional invoice and a delivery order with the insurance annotation to the buyer. Against delivery of these documents, the buyer makes payment to the seller's agent. When the goods arrive, the buyer then instructs its local cargo superintendent to present an additional check for the freight charges and the delivery order to the seller's agent for its endorsement. The cargo was shipped freight collect with payment for the freight charges due before discharge of the goods. This arrangement saved the seller the expense of advancing the freight charges and placed the burden of paying these charges on the buyer as the ship would not discharge the goods until the freight was paid. From the buyer's viewpoint, however, the buyer did not wish to pay the freight while the ship was still en route. The insurance certificates endorsed to the buyer covered only the loss of the cargo, not the freight charges. If the buyer paid the freight charges while the carrier was en route and the carrier was lost due to no negligence of the ship's master, the buyer would suffer the loss of the freight charges. To deal with this risk, the buyer paid the freight charges after the arrival of the ship. Once the seller's agent received the freight charges, it then signed a note at the bottom of the delivery order acknowledging receipt of the freight and handed the delivery order back to the buyer's cargo superintendent who, in turn, handed it to the seller's superintendent. As the seller's Antwerp agent was a sales agent and distributor for the seller and not qualified to handle cargo, the seller had to engage another entity—F. Van Bree, S.A. in *The Julia*—specifically for the purpose of receiving and moving cargo from the carrier. The delivery order, however, did not entitle the seller's cargo superintendent to possession of the goods because the ship's master would only release the goods when he was satisfied that the freight had been paid. When the master was satisfied that the freight charges were paid, he would issue the captain's release (*laissez suivre*), which was addressed to the ship's crew and authorized the delivery of the cargo. Without the captain's release, the crew would not unload any cargo. Only this document, issued after the ship's master was satisfied that the costs of affreightment had been paid, would authorize the delivery of the goods to the seller's cargo superintendent who was under instructions to hand the goods to the buyer's cargo agent who would then hand over the goods to the buyer.

6. *Documents of Title.* In *The Julia,* the seller argued that the contract was a modified CIF transaction but still retained the essential CIF characteristic of payment against documents. In this case, the parties had agreed to acceptance of a delivery order instead of documents. Lord Porter rejected the argument that the transaction was a modified CIF transaction. He argued that, under a CIF transaction, the buyer must be given a document containing the right to the goods. Porter argued that the buyer was never given this right and so it was impossible to characterize this as a CIF transaction. Can you explain Porter's argument? Also review the opinion of Lord Normand, who argued that calling a transaction CIF does not make it so unless documents of title are used.

7. *Part Performance of the Contract as Consideration.* The seller also argued that handing over the delivery order, even if it was not a document of title, was part performance

of the contract and that there could not have been the total failure of consideration as alleged by the buyer. Lord Simonds rejected the notion that the delivery order constituted consideration because it created an obligation on the part of Van Bree to deliver the goods. Under Simonds' view, the buyer acquired no enforceable rights against Van Bree as a result of the delivery order. Van Bree was merely the agent of the seller and the arrangement was merely a mechanism by which the seller was to perform its obligations under the contract. The delivery order to Van Bree did not create any additional rights in the buyer.

8. *Freedom of Contract.* In *The Julia,* the lordships held that the delivery order was not a document of title and passed neither title nor possession of the goods to the buyer. As a consequence, the buyer is, in essence, making an advance payment of the purchase price against the delivery of the goods to occur later and assuming the risk if the goods are lost at sea. In an orthodox CIF transaction, the risk of loss shifts to the buyer once the goods are safely loaded aboard the ship, but the buyer is protected because it has a document of title, the negotiable bill of lading, and also a policy of insurance. But why should courts prevent sophisticated commercial parties from entering into such an arrangement? Perhaps the seller is willing to give the buyer a lower price because the buyer is willing to bear additional risks. Review Lord Normand's opinion. Is Normand restricting the freedom of contract of the parties?

9. The merchants in London and Antwerp had been using the complex arrangement described in note 5 above for a number of years for the sale of rye. These were sophisticated merchants and business people. Why would the Belgian buyers pay against delivery orders that did not pass title or possession?

PROBLEM 2-6

An international dealer in agricultural goods comes to your law office and asks for advice in light of *The Julia.* How would you set up a payment against documents transaction so the dealer can load the goods in bulk on board a carrier and sell the goods while in transit to several buyers and receive payment against documents? Please advise.

F.   Contracts of Affreightment, Bills of Lading, and Insurance

1.   *The Contract of Affreightment and the Bill of Lading*

In an international sales transaction, one of the parties will arrange the transportation of the goods. This will be done by concluding a contract—known as a *contract of affreightment*—for the transportation of the goods to a named destination. Typically, this duty falls to the seller; it is easier for the seller to arrange everything and charge the buyer. Thus, most export transactions are CIF in form. The seller will arrange this transport through an intermediary, a broker, or a freight forwarder. With regard to a contract of affreightment, the party shipping the goods (usually the seller) is called the "shipper"; the party transporting the goods is the "carrier."

The bill of lading, which we have already discussed as a document of title at pp. 60-61, also usually serves as the contract of affreightment. On the reverse side of the bill of lading on p. 62 are standard terms that govern the rights and obligations of the parties concerning the shipment of the goods. In some cases, the courts will look beyond the bill of lading to find the contract. *See EIMSHIP USA, Inc. v. Atl. Fish Market,* 417 F.2d 72,

76 (1st Cir. 2005) (oral statements included as part of contract of affreightment), but in most cases, the bill of lading is considered to be the contract of affreightment. Recall that the bill of lading also functions as a document of title (if it is negotiable) or as a receipt (if it is nonnegotiable). Our earlier discussion focused on the function of the bill of lading as a document of title. This discussion below focuses on the bill of lading as a contract of affreightment but assumes that you are already familiar with the bill of lading's function as a document of title. As a contract of affreightment, the bill of lading serves a crucial role beyond its role as a document of title. One of the most significant issues to be considered by the parties in a contract of affreightment is liability by the carrier for damage to the cargo (i.e., the goods). Although the bill of lading will set forth the rights and liabilities of the carrier, its key role as a contract of affreightment is that it serves as a nexus to trigger the application of a liability regime in all four modes of carriage (further discussed below) to be applied to the carrier for damage to the goods. Thus, the rights and liabilities set out in a bill of lading need to be consistent with the legal regime that they trigger. For example, in the United States, the existence of a contract of affreightment, usually the bill of lading, will trigger the application of the Carriage of Goods by Sea Act (COGSA) governing the liability of an ocean carrier. *See* COGSA, 46 U.S.C.A. §30701 hist. n., §12 ("This chapter shall apply to all contracts of carriage of goods by sea to or from ports of the United States"). As a result, any clauses concerning the carrier's rights, responsibilities, and liability in the bill of lading must be consistent with COGSA.

Ocean carriage is the dominant mode of shipment in modern global trade, but there are a total of four possible modes of transport: air, rail, road, and water. Each one involves a bill of lading that can be negotiable or nonnegotiable (which is sometimes referred to as a waybill) but note that it is the function of the bill of lading as a contract of carriage (not as a document of title) that triggers the application of each liability regime. In international business today, often more than one mode must be used, especially if door-to-door delivery is sought. This is known as multimodal transport. The most frequent device used in shipping goods in multimodal transport is the container, a metal box that can be loaded onto a ship as well as carried by rail or truck. Although multimodal transport is common especially in international trade, no international regime presently governs multimodal transport.

In international trade, transport by ship is frequently employed. In general, there are two types of ship transport: common carriage and private carriage. A common carrier is one that holds itself out to the general public as engaged in the business of marine transport for compensation. In private carriage, a ship will be leased in whole or in part by special arrangement. The contract of private carriage is known as a charter party. This distinction, which was important at common law, is blurred today and disregarded in most modes of carriage. Only in water transport does the distinction still hold: COGSA, the U.S. liability regime, does not apply to charter parties by statute. However, although parties to a charter have contractual freedom to negotiate their respective rights and duties, in practice the parties to a charter agree to a *Clause Paramount* in the charter party that incorporates COGSA or an international regime, such as Hague-Visby (further discussed below) by reference. *See, e.g., Steel Coils, Inc. v. Captain Nicholas I M/V*, 197 F. Supp. 2d 560, 562 n.1 (E.D. La. 2002). Thus, private carriage of goods by water is usually governed in substantial part by statutory liability schemes.

The U.S. Shipping Act of 1984 recognizes two distinct types of ocean common carriers: A Non-Vessel Operating Common Carrier (NVOCC) is "a common carrier that does not operate vessels by which the ocean transportation is provided, and is a shipper in its relationship with an ocean common carrier." 46 U.S.C. §40102(16) (2012). A second more traditional common carrier is a Vessel Operating Common Carrier (VOCC). Both types of common carrier are regulated by the U.S. Federal Maritime Commission. *See* 46 C.F.R. §515.11 (2013). In a typical shipping transaction the actual shipper (frequently through a broker) will arrange for the shipment of the goods through an NVOCC. The NVOCC will subcontract with a steamship line (a VOCC) to do the actual transport of the goods. The VOCC will issue a "true" bill of lading to the NVOCC covering the goods shipped. The steamship line's bill of lading will name the NVOCC as "shipper" and the NVOCC's destination agent as the "consignee." The NOVCC will then issue its own "house" bill of lading to its customer, showing the actual shipper and consignee. When the goods arrive at the destination, the actual consignee must surrender the original "house" bill of lading to the NVOCC's destination agent, who then surrenders the steamship line's original bill of lading to the VOCC's agent. The goods are delivered to the NVOCC's agent who in turn delivers them to the consignee (the buyer).

The NVOCC functions as a key intermediary that performs two kinds of valuable services: (1) consolidation of container shipments, which is essential to facilitate small shipments (the smallest size container contains 27 cubic meters of space, usually more than is needed for an export shipper); and (2) the negotiation of value discounts with steamship companies, passing some of the savings on to the actual shipper.

Under U.S. common law, distinctly different legal consequences attached to common carriage and private carriage. In general, the common carrier was chargeable with some exceptions as an insurer of the goods (*see New Jersey Steam Navigation Co. v. Merchant's Bank of Boston*, 47 U.S. (6 How.) 344, 381 (1848)) whereas the ship owner engaged in private carriage was only liable for loss or damage to the extent this was proximately caused by a breach of an obligation contained in a contract of carriage. *See, e.g., Commercial Molasses Corp. v. New York Tank Barge Corp.*, 314 U.S. 104, 109 (1941).

The law of international carriage of goods today has departed significantly from Anglo-American common law standards. All four modes of transport are now governed by a patchwork of international conventional liability regimes as well as statutes developed beginning in the late nineteenth century; under these regimes, the distinction between common and private carriage is much less important than before. The current liability system suffers from two main defects: (1) different liability systems are in effect for different modes of transport although goods today are frequently shipped using multimodal transport; and (2) despite best efforts, liability standards differ—sometimes greatly—from nation to nation. Four principal international liability regimes exist, one for each mode: air, water, rail, and road. As water transport is by far the most important, we briefly describe the other regimes and then focus on water transport:

Air Transport. The carriage of goods by air carriers is governed principally by the Convention for the Unification of Certain Rules for International Carriage by Air (the Montreal Convention), which entered into force in 2003. (Text available at *http://www.jus.uio.no/lm/air.carriage.unification.convention.montreal.1999/doc.*) Under the Montreal Convention, liability for lost or damaged cargo is limited to 17 SDRs (Special Drawing Rights)[6] per kilogram unless the shipper declares actual value and agrees to pay additional freight (the consideration for transporting the goods). *See* Art. 22(3). Liability for delay is similarly limited to 4,150 SDRs. *See* Art. 22(1). Carrier defenses to liability include inherent defect of the cargo, defective packaging, act of war, and act of public authorities. *See* Art. 18. The United States is a party to the Montreal Convention.

---

6. The Special Drawing Right is a weighted basket of the U.S. dollar, the British pound sterling, the euro, and the Japanese yen. The value of the SDR fluctuates on a daily basis.

Rail Transport. The major international regime governing carriage of goods by rail is the International Convention Concerning the Carriage of Goods by Rail (known as CIM, its French acronym) and the 1999 Protocol known by its French acronym COTIV.[7] This conventional scheme is applied primarily in Europe. The United States is not a party to the CIM.

Road Transport. The major international regime is the Convention of the International Carriage of Goods by Road, known by its French acronym CMR.[8] The United States is not a party to the CMR. In a later section, at p. 96, we will discuss the U.S. legal regime for rail and road transport, the Carmack Amendment, 49 U.S.C. §11706 (2006).

Water Transport. Carriage of goods by sea continues to be the dominant mode of transport in the world. The most widely adopted international liability scheme for carriage of goods by sea is the Hague-Visby Rules, the complex development of which is summarized below. The application of the Hague-Visby Rules is triggered by a contract of carriage of goods by sea, i.e. the bill of lading. *See* Hague-Visby Rules, Article II ("every contract of carriage of goods by sea the carrier, in relation to the loading, handling, stowage, carriage, custody, care and discharge of such goods, shall be subject to the responsibilities and liabilities and entitled to the rights and immunities hereinafter set forth") available at the web link below. The contract of carriage, i.e., the bill of lading, triggers the regime below governing the carrier's liability for loss or damage to the cargo. Note the structure of the Rules: The responsibilities and liabilities of the carrier are set forth in Article III and then explicit exemptions to liability for the carrier are set forth in Article IV. The United States is not a party to the Hague-Visby Rules but the United States applies a very similar regime, based upon a predecessor convention of Hague-Visby, as we shall discuss below. The provisions of Hague-Visby below are substantially similar to corresponding U.S. provisions contained in COGSA, the U.S. regime.

Hague-Visby Rules

http://www.jus.uio.no/lm/sea.carriage.hague.visby.rules.1968/doc.html

ARTICLE I [DEFINITIONS]

In these Rules the following words are employed, with the meanings set out below:

(a) "Carrier" includes the owner or the charterer who enters into a contract of carriage with a shipper.
(b) "Contract of carriage" applies only to contracts of carriage covered by a bill of lading or any similar document of title, in so far as such document relates to the carriage of goods by sea, including any bill of lading or any similar document as aforesaid issued under or pursuant to a charter party from the moment at which such bill of lading or similar document of title regulates the relations between a carrier and a holder of the same. . . .
(e) "Carriage of goods" covers the period from the time when the goods are loaded on to the time they are discharged from the ship.

---

7. *http://www.jus.uio.no/lm/cim.rail.carriage.contract.uniform.rules.19xx/doc.html.*
8. *http://www.jus.uio.no/lm/un.cmr.road.carriage.contract.convention.1956.amended.protocol.1978/doc.html.*

ARTICLE III [RESPONSIBILITIES AND LIABILITIES]

1. The carrier shall be bound before and at the beginning of the voyage to exercise due diligence to:
   (a) Make the ship seaworthy;
   (b) Properly man, equip and supply the ship;
   (c) Make the holds, refrigerating and cool chambers, and all other parts of the ship in which goods are carried, fit and safe for their reception, carriage and preservation.

2. Subject to the provisions of Article IV, the carrier shall properly and carefully load, handle, stow, carry, keep, care for, and discharge the goods carried.

3. After receiving the goods into his charge the carrier or the master or agent of the carrier shall, on demand of the shipper, issue to the shipper a bill of lading showing among other things:
   (a) the leading marks necessary for identification of the goods as the same are furnished in writing by the shipper before the loading of such goods start, provided such marks are stamped or otherwise shown clearly upon the goods if uncovered, or on the cases or coverings in which such goods are contained, in such a manner as should ordinarily remain legible until the end of the voyage;
   (b) either the number of packages or pieces, or the quantity, or weight, as the case may be, as furnished in writing by the shipper;
   (c) the apparent order and condition of the goods. Provided that no carrier, master or agent of the carrier shall be bound to state or show in the bill of lading any marks, number, quantity, or weight which he has reasonable ground for suspecting not accurately to represent the goods actually received or which he has had no reasonable means of checking.

4. Such a bill of lading shall be *prima facie* evidence of the receipt by the carrier of the goods as therein described in accordance with paragraphs 3(a), (b), and (c).

ARTICLE IV [RIGHTS AND IMMUNITIES]

1. Neither the carrier nor the ship shall be liable for loss or damage arising or resulting from unseaworthiness unless caused by want of due diligence on the part of the carrier to make the ship seaworthy, and to secure that the ship is properly manned, equipped and supplied, and to make the holds, refrigerating and cool chambers and all other parts of the ship in which goods are carried fit and safe for their reception, carriage and preservation in accordance with the provisions of paragraph 1 of Article III. Whenever loss or damage has resulted from unseaworthiness, the burden of proving the exercise of due diligence shall be on the carrier or other person claiming exemption under this article.

2. Neither the carrier nor the ship shall be responsible for loss or damage arising or resulting from:
   (a) Act, neglect, or default of the master, mariner, pilot, or the servants of the carrier in the navigation or in the management of the ship.
   (b) Fire, unless caused by the actual fault or privity of the carrier.
   (c) Perils, dangers and accidents of the sea or other navigable waters.
   (d) Act of God.
   (e) Act of war.

(f) Act of public enemies.

(g) Arrest or restraint of princes, rulers or people, or seizure under legal process.

(h) Quarantine restrictions.

(i) Act or omission of the shipper or owner of the goods, his agent or representative.

(j) Strikes or lockouts or stoppage or restraint of labour from whatever cause, whether partial or general.

(k) Riots and civil commotions.

(l) Saving or attempting to save life or property at sea.

(m) Wastage in bulk or weight or any other loss or damage arising from inherent defect, quality or vice of the goods.

(n) Insufficiency of packing.

(o) Insufficiency or inadequacy of marks.

(p) Latent defects not discoverable by due diligence.

(q) Any other cause arising without the actual fault or privity of the carrier, or without the fault or neglect of the agents or servants of the carrier, but the burden of proof shall be on the person claiming the benefit of this exception to show that neither the actual fault or privity of the carrier nor the fault or neglect of the agents or servants of the carrier contributed to the loss or damage.

3. The shipper shall not be responsible for loss or damage sustained by the carrier or the ship arising or resulting from any cause without the act, fault or neglect of the shipper, his agents or his servants.

4. Any deviation in saving or attempting to save life or property at sea or any reasonable deviation shall not be deemed to be an infringement or breach of these Rules or of the contract of carriage, and the carrier shall not be liable for any loss or damage resulting therefrom.

5. (a) Unless the nature and value of such goods have been declared by the shipper before shipment and inserted in the bill of lading, neither the carrier nor the ship shall in any event be or become liable for any loss or damage to or in connection with the goods in an amount exceeding 666.67 units of account per package or unit or units of account per kilo of gross weight of the goods lost or damaged, whichever is the higher.

The United States does not follow the Hague-Visby Rules but follows a predecessor convention, the Hague Rules adopted in 1921 by the International Law Association at its Hague meeting. The Hague Rules are substantially the same as Hague-Visby except for the limit of liability provision further discussed below. The U.S. version of the Hague Rules is called the Carriage of Goods by Sea Act (COGSA) enacted in 1936. COGSA is reprinted in the Documents Supplement and may be compared to the Hague-Visby Rules.

As this discussion indicates, COGSA, the current U.S. law dates from 1936 and is rather outdated. Virtually all nations except the United States have modernized their laws on carriage of goods in recent years. But the Congress has not only rejected all attempts to update COGSA but also, during the recodification of Title 46 (Shipping) of the U.S. Code, COGSA was omitted in what was apparently an oversight. As a result, COGSA is now an uncodified statute that remains in force without a place in the U.S. Code.

In 2008 the United Nations Commission on International Trade Law promulgated and opened for ratification a new Convention on Contracts for the International Carriage of Goods Wholly or Partially by Sea (Rotterdam Rules).[9] We reprint this Convention in the Documents Supplement although it is not yet in force. The Rotterdam Rules are widely expected to replace Hague-Visby in the coming years. This Convention is under consideration by the U.S. Congress as a possible basis for changes to or replacement of COGSA. Compare the Rotterdam Rules to COGSA. Do you think the U.S. Congress will accept the Rotterdam Rules?

2. COGSA: A Thumbnail Sketch

Over 90 percent of international trade moves by sea, and COGSA, the U.S. legal regime, applies in most cases to the contract of affreightment when the United States is involved in the transaction. Thus, it is imperative to understand COGSA. Before considering the cases, it is useful to list in summary form the COGSA requirements. (See the text of COGSA in the Documents Supplement.)

(1) COGSA applies mandatorily to all contracts for carriage of goods by sea from or to U.S. ports in foreign trade (section 12). 46 U.S.C. §30701 hist. n. §12. The mandatory period of COGSA application is from the time the goods are loaded on to the time they are discharged from the ship. *Id.* §1.

(2) COGSA does not apply to charter parties ("private carriage") or to special contracts to ship goods outside the ordinary course of trade. *Id.* §§5–6.

(3) Although COGSA only applies "tackle to tackle," it is common to insert a "carrier's period of responsibility clause" in a bill of lading that makes the carrier liable (by contract) under COGSA standards for the entire time the goods are in the carrier's custody. In the absence of such a clause, the Harter Act, 46 U.S.C. §§190–196, passed in 1893, applies to this period.

(4) Although COGSA does not mandatorily apply to "private carriage" of goods (charter parties and special contract carriage), a "clause paramount" is commonly inserted in such contracts so that COGSA applies by contract.

(5) A bill of lading commonly contains a "Himalaya Clause" that extends COGSA by contract to third parties who contract with the carrier to load, transport, unload or care for the cargo. This term comes from the English case *Adler v. Dickinson (The Himalaya),* [1954] 2 Lloyd's Rep. 267, 1 Q.B. 158 (CA).

(6) The carrier is prohibited from contracting away its liability for negligence or in any way lessening its liability under COGSA. 46 U.S.C. §30701 hist. n. §3(8).

(7) The carrier's duty is to issue a bill of lading to the shipper and (1) to exercise due diligence before and at the beginning of the voyage to supply a seaworthy ship and crew; (2) to carefully load, carry, stow, unload and discharge the cargo. *Id.* §3.

(8) The carrier enjoys 17 different statutory defenses to liability under COGSA. *Id.* §4.

(9) The shipper is liable for negligence and for damages due to dangerous cargo. *Id.* §§4(3), 6.

(10) The carrier may incur additional liability for an unreasonable deviation from the voyage. *Id.* §4(4).

(11) The carrier's liability is limited to $500 per package or, in the case of goods not shipped in packages, per customary freight unit, unless the shipper before

---

9. *See http://www.uncitral.org/uncitral/en/uncitral_texts/transport_goods/2008rotterdam_rules.html.*

shipment declares the actual value of the cargo or the shipper and the carrier agree on a maximum amount of liability. *Id.* §4(5). The term "customary freight unit" refers not to the physical shipping unit but rather is the unit "customarily used as the basis for the calculation of the freight to be charged." *See The Mormacoak,* 451 F.2d 24, 25 (2d Cir. 1971).

(12) To establish liability the shipper has the burden of proof and persuasion to make a prima facie case by showing that the goods were in good condition when turned over to the carrier and were damaged when discharged by the carrier. The carrier may rebut such a claim by showing that the cause of the damage was one of the 17 different "uncontrollable causes of loss" or, if the damage was caused by unseaworthiness, that it exercised due diligence. 46 U.S.C. §30701 hist. n. §4. If there are concurrent causes of the loss the carrier has the burden of showing what proportion of the damage was due to an excepted cause. If it carries this burden the carrier is not liable.

(13) A claim for damages must be filed by the shipper within one year of the delivery of the goods or within one year of the date when the goods should have been delivered. The shipper should give notice in writing that the goods are damaged at discharge by the carrier, or, if the damage is not immediately apparent, within three days of discharge.

We now turn to several cases involving lost or damaged cargo. In considering *Norfolk* and the *"K" Line* cases below, note that COGSA, like Hague-Visby, applies from "tackle to tackle"—from the point that the goods start to be loaded on board the ship (the goods on the seller's dock are hooked by the "tackle") to the point they are completely discharged from the ship (the goods are released by the "tackle" onto the buyer's dock). This covers the carrier's liability for the ocean portion of the voyage. As many shipments today are from door to door and involve more than one mode of transport, once the ship docks, the goods are then unloaded from the ship and reloaded onto a rail or truck (or both). Once the ocean portion of the transport is concluded, a different liability regime will apply to the inland transport portion. In European countries, it might be the CIM (rail) or CMR (road) conventions, but as the United States is not a party to either convention, in the United States liability for rail and road transport is governed by the Carmack Amendment, 49 U.S.C. §11706 (2006). Unlike COGSA, which limits liability of the carrier to $500 per package, the default position of the Carmack Amendment is to impose full-value liability on the carrier for lost or damaged cargo. 49 U.S.C. §11706(a) ("The liability imposed under this subsection is for the actual loss or injury to the property . . . " applicable to rail carriers); *see also* 49 U.S.C. §14706 (applicable to motor carriers). If the shipper agrees to make a reduced declaration of the value of the goods, the carrier will in turn charge the shipper a lower rate of freight and limit liability. The shipper will then obtain insurance for the goods. There is also an exception from full-value liability for household goods, express mail, and packaging services. *See* 49 U.S.C. §14706(f)(1).

As noted above, COGSA normally applies only to the ocean part of the transport; in addition, COGSA only applies to "carriers," i.e., parties to the bill of lading who have signed the bill such as the carrier or the owner (e.g., a parent company) of the carrier. *See Sabah Shipyard Sdn. Bhd. v. M/V Harbel Tapper,* 178 F.3d 400, 404–406 (5th Cir. 1999). Thus, COGSA normally applies the $500 per package liability limitation only to (1) the ocean portion of the voyage, i.e., from the time the goods are loaded on board the ship to the time that they are unloaded and (2) "carriers," i.e., parties to the bill of lading. However, it is possible to extend the application of COGSA to cover the entire transport of the goods, including the inland portion by rail or truck, by inserting a responsibility clause in the bill of lading explicitly extending COGSA inland (see point (3) above on COGSA). It is also possible to extend the coverage of COGSA to third parties through the use of a "Himalaya Clause" (see (5) above on COGSA). The Himalaya Clause extends COGSA protection to third parties who contract with the carrier to load, unload, and care for the cargo as well as truckers and railway lines, which deliver the goods inland to the point of final destination. Such parties would not normally be protected because they are not "carriers," i.e., parties to the ocean bill of lading. Armed with a Himalaya Clause and a responsibility clause extending COGSA inland throughout the entire transport of the goods, the carrier and its agents can be protected by COGSA's $500 per package limitation on liability.

We emphasize that to extend COGSA inland and to third parties who are not parties to the original bill of lading *two* clauses must be in the bill of lading: (1) a responsibility clause explicitly extending COGSA to the inland portion of the transport beyond ocean carriage and (2) a Himalaya Clause explicitly extending COGSA to third parties who are not parties to the bill of lading. The Himalaya Clause by itself only extends COGSA to third parties. A second clause must be added extending COGSA inland. In many cases, this second clause is part of the Himalaya Clause, but it might also be a separate clause.

With this discussion in mind, read the *Norfolk* case below, which deals with the following issue. Suppose that a shipper (the seller) enters into a contract of affreightment (bill of lading) with a foreign freight forwarding company that owns no ships but that arranges for transport of the goods from door to door in an international sale from Australia to the United States. (This company acts in the role of an NVOCC, see pp. 90-91.) The freight forwarding company issues a "house bill of lading" to the seller; the company in turn enters in a subcontract of affreightment with a carrier (a VOCC, see pp. 90-91), which issues to the freight forwarding company a bill of lading with a Himalaya Clause and a clause extending COGSA inland and to third parties (not parties to the bill of lading). The shipper (seller) has no knowledge of the subcontract. Will the shipper be bound by COGSA's limitation on liability contained in the subcontract if the cargo is damaged by one of the subcontractors, in this case a railway line, while transporting the goods in the United States?

Norfolk Southern Railway Co. v. Kirby
United States Supreme Court, 2004
543 U.S. 14

Justice O'CONNOR delivered the opinion of the Court.

This is a maritime case about a train wreck. A shipment of machinery from Australia was destined for Huntsville, Alabama. The intercontinental journey was uneventful, and the machinery reached the United States unharmed. But the train carrying the machinery on its final, inland leg derailed, causing extensive damage. The machinery's owner sued the railroad. The railroad seeks shelter in two liability limitations contained in contracts that upstream carriers negotiated for the machinery's delivery.

I

This controversy arises from two bills of lading (essentially, contracts) for the transportation of goods from Australia to Alabama. A bill of lading records that a carrier has received goods from the party that wishes to ship them, states the terms of carriage, and serves as evidence of the contract for carriage. See 2 T. Schoenbaum, Admiralty and Maritime Law 58–60 (3d ed. 2001) (hereinafter Schoenbaum); Carriage of Goods by Sea Act (COGSA), 49 Stat. 1208, 46 U.S.C. App. §1303. Respondent James N. Kirby, Pty Ltd. (Kirby), an Australian manufacturing company, sold 10 containers of machinery to the General Motors plant located outside Huntsville, Alabama. Kirby hired International Cargo Control (ICC), an Australian freight forwarding company, to arrange for delivery by "through" (*i.e.,* end-to-end) transportation. (A freight forwarding company arranges for, coordinates, and facilitates cargo transport, but does not itself transport cargo.) To formalize their contract for carriage, ICC issued a bill of lading to Kirby (ICC bill). The bill designates Sydney, Australia, as the port of loading, Savannah, Georgia, as the port of discharge, and Huntsville as the ultimate destination for delivery.

In negotiating the ICC bill, Kirby had the opportunity to declare the full value of the machinery and to have ICC assume liability for that value. Instead, and as is common in the industry, Kirby accepted a contractual liability limitation for ICC below the machinery's true value, resulting, presumably, in lower shipping rates. The ICC bill sets various liability limitations for the journey from Sydney to Huntsville. For the sea leg, the ICC bill invokes the default liability rule set forth in the COGSA of [$500 per package].

For the land leg, in turn, the bill limits the carrier's liability to a higher amount.[10] So that other downstream parties expected to take part in the contract's execution could benefit from the liability limitations, the bill also contains a so-called "Himalaya Clause." Meanwhile, Kirby separately insured the cargo for its true value with its co-respondent in this case, Allianz Australia Insurance Ltd. Having been hired by Kirby, and because it does not itself actually transport cargo, ICC then hired Hamburg Süd, a German ocean shipping company, to transport the containers. To formalize their contract for carriage, Hamburg Süd issued its own bill of lading to ICC (Hamburg Süd bill). That bill designates Sydney as the port of loading, Savannah as the port of discharge, and Huntsville as the ultimate destination for delivery. It adopts COGSA's default rule in limiting the liability of Hamburg Süd, the bill's designated carrier, to $500 per package. See 46 U.S.C. App. §1304. It also contains a clause extending that liability limitation beyond the "tackles"—that is, to potential damage on land as well as on sea. Finally, it too contains a Himalaya Clause extending the benefit of its liability limitation to "all agents . . . (including inland) carriers . . . and all independent contractors whatsoever." App. 63, cl. 5(b).

Acting through a subsidiary, Hamburg Süd hired petitioner Norfolk Southern Railway Company (Norfolk) to transport the machinery from the Savannah port to Huntsville. The Norfolk train carrying the machinery derailed en route, causing an alleged $1.5 million in damages. Kirby's insurance company reimbursed Kirby for the loss. Kirby and its insurer then sued Norfolk in the United States District Court for the Northern District of Georgia, asserting diversity jurisdiction and alleging tort and contract claims. In its

---

10. The bill provides that "the Freight Forwarder shall in no event be or become liable for any loss of or damage to the goods in an amount exceeding the equivalent of 666.67 SDR per package or unit or 2 SDR per kilogramme of gross weight of the goods lost or damaged, whichever is the higher, unless the nature and value of the goods shall have been declared by the Consignor." App. to Pet. for Cert. 57a, cl. 8.3. An SDR, or Special Drawing Right, is a unit of account created by the International Monetary Fund and calculated daily on the basis of a basket of currencies. In any case, because we conclude that Norfolk is also protected by the $500 per package limit in the second bill of lading at issue here, see Part III-B, *infra,* and thus cannot be liable for more than $5,000 for the 10 containers, each holding one machine, the precise liability under the ICC bill of lading does not matter.

answer, Norfolk argued, among other things, that Kirby's potential recovery could not exceed the amounts set forth in the liability limitations contained in the bills of lading for the machinery's carriage.

The District Court granted Norfolk's motion for partial summary judgment, holding that Norfolk's liability was limited to $500 per container. Upon a joint motion from Norfolk and Kirby, the District Court certified its decision for interlocutory review.

A divided panel of the Eleventh Circuit reversed. It held that Norfolk could not claim protection under the Himalaya Clause in the first contract, the ICC bill. It construed the language of the clause to exclude parties, like Norfolk, that had not been in privity with ICC when ICC issued the bill. 300 F.3d 1300, 1308–1309 (2002). The majority also suggested that "a special degree of linguistic specificity is required to extend the benefits of a Himalaya clause to an inland carrier." *Id.* at 1310. As for the Hamburg Süd bill, the court held that Kirby could be bound by the bill's liability limitation "only if ICC was acting as Kirby's agent when it received Hamburg Süd's bill." *Id.* at 1305. And, applying basic agency law principles, the Court of Appeals concluded that ICC had not been acting as Kirby's agent when it received the bill. *Ibid.* Based on its opinion that Norfolk was not entitled to benefit from the liability limitation in either bill of lading, the Eleventh Circuit reversed the District Court's grant of summary judgment for the railroad. We granted certiorari to decide whether Norfolk could take shelter in the liability limitations of either bill and now reverse.

II

[As a preliminary issue, the Court found that the bills of lading were maritime contracts governed by federal admiralty law under Art. III, §2, cl. 1 of the Constitution. While a small portion of the transport was to occur on land, the bills of lading had a substantial connection to maritime commerce because the primary objective of the bills was the transportation of goods by sea from Australia to the United States. The international nature of the bills of lading also demanded the application of a uniform federal law.]

III

A

[Turning first to the ICC bill of lading, the Court found that nothing in its previous decision relied upon by the Eleventh Circuit, *Robert C. Herd v. Krawill Machinery Corp.*, 359 U.S. 297 (1950), required any linguistic specificity or privity of contract between the shipper and the subcontractor, in this case Norfolk, but that the contract should be interpreted under ordinary principles of contract interpretation. As the Himalaya Clause in the ICC bill of lading extended COGSA to "*any* servant, agent, or other person (including any independent contractor) whose services have been used in order to perform the contract," the clause extended COGSA protection to Norfolk.]

B

The question arising from the Hamburg Süd bill of lading is more difficult. It requires us to set an efficient default rule for certain shipping contracts, a task that has been a challenge for courts for centuries. ICC and Hamburg Süd agreed that Hamburg Süd would transport the machinery from Sydney to Huntsville, and agreed to the COGSA "package limitation" on the liability of Hamburg Süd, its agents, and its independent contractors. The second question presented is whether that liability limitation, which ICC negotiated, prevents Kirby from suing Norfolk (Hamburg Süd's independent contractor) for more. As we have explained, the liability limitation in the ICC bill, the first contract, sets liability for a land accident higher than this bill does. Because Norfolk's liability will be lower if it is protected by the Hamburg Süd bill too, we must reach this second question in order to give Norfolk the full relief for which it petitioned.

To interpret the Hamburg Süd bill, we turn to a rule drawn from our precedent about common carriage: When an intermediary contracts with a carrier to transport goods, the cargo owner's recovery against the carrier is limited by the liability limitation to which the intermediary and carrier agreed. The intermediary is certainly not automatically empowered to be the cargo owner's agent in every sense. That would be unsustainable. But when it comes to liability limitations for negligence resulting in damage, an intermediary can negotiate reliable and enforceable agreements with the carriers it engages.

We derive this rule from our decision about common carriage in *Great Northern R. Co. v. O'Connor*, 232 U.S. 508 (1914). In *Great Northern*, an owner hired a transfer company to arrange for the shipment of her goods. Without the owner's express authority, the transfer company arranged for rail transport at a tariff rate that limited the railroad's liability to less than the true value of the goods. The goods were lost en route, and the owner sued the railroad. The Court held that the railroad must be able to rely on the liability limitation in its tariff agreement with the transfer company. The railroad "had the right to assume that the Transfer Company could agree upon the terms of the shipment"; it could not be expected to know if the transfer company had any outstanding, conflicting obligation to another party. *Id.* at 514. The owner's remedy, if necessary, was against the transfer company. *Id.* at 515.

Respondents object to our reading of *Great Northern*, and argue that this Court should fashion the federal rule of decision from general agency law principles. Like the Eleventh Circuit, respondents reason that Kirby cannot be bound by the bill of lading that ICC negotiated with Hamburg Süd unless ICC was then acting as Kirby's agent.

We think reliance on agency law is misplaced here. It is undeniable that the traditional indicia of agency, a fiduciary relationship and effective control by the principal, did not exist between Kirby and ICC. But that is of no moment. The principle derived from *Great Northern* does not require treating ICC as Kirby's agent in the classic sense. It only requires treating ICC as Kirby's agent for a *single, limited* purpose: when ICC contracts with subsequent carriers for limitation on liability. In holding that an intermediary binds a cargo owner to the liability limitations it negotiates with downstream carriers, we do not infringe on traditional agency principles. We merely ensure the reliability of downstream contracts for liability limitations. In *Great Northern*, because the intermediary had been "entrusted with goods to be shipped by railway, and, nothing to the contrary appearing, the carrier had the right to assume that [the intermediary] could agree upon the terms of the shipment." 232 U.S. 514. Likewise, here we hold that intermediaries, entrusted with goods, are "agents" only in their ability to contract for liability limitations with carriers downstream.

Respondents also contend that any decision binding Kirby to the Hamburg Süd bill's liability limitation will be disastrous for the international shipping industry. Various participants in the industry have weighed in as *amici* on both sides in this case, and we must make a close call. It would be idle to pretend that the industry can easily be characterized, or that efficient default rules can easily be discerned. In the final balance, however, we disagree with respondents for three reasons.

First, we believe that a limited agency rule tracks industry practices. In intercontinental ocean shipping, carriers may not know if they are dealing with an intermediary, rather than with a cargo owner. Even if knowingly dealing with an intermediary, they may not know how many other intermediaries came before, or what obligations may be outstanding among them. If the Eleventh Circuit's rule were the law, carriers would have to seek out more information before contracting, so as to assure themselves that their contractual liability limitations provide true protection. That task of information gathering might be very costly or even impossible, given that goods often change hands many times in the course of intermodal transportation. See 1 Schoenbaum 589.

Second, if liability limitations negotiated with cargo owners were reliable while limitations negotiated with intermediaries were not, carriers would likely want to charge the latter higher rates. A rule prompting downstream carriers to distinguish between cargo owners and intermediary shippers might interfere with statutory and decisional law promoting nondiscrimination in common carriage.

Finally, as in *Great Northern*, our decision produces an equitable result. Kirby retains the option to sue ICC, the carrier, for any loss that exceeds the liability limitation to which they agreed. And indeed, Kirby *has* sued ICC in an Australian court for damages arising from the Norfolk derailment. It seems logical that ICC—the only party that definitely knew about and was party to both of the bills of lading at issue here—should bear responsibility for any gap between the liability limitations in the bills. Meanwhile, Norfolk enjoys the benefit of the Hamburg Süd bill's liability limitation.

IV

The judgment of the United States Court of Appeals for the Eleventh Circuit is reversed, and the case is remanded for further proceedings.

In *Norfolk*, the Supreme Court held that the Himalaya Clause and the responsibility clause extending COGSA inland to cover the rail transport in a single through bill of lading limited the railway's liability to $500 per package. This meant that COGSA displaced the liability regime for inland transportation that would have otherwise applied, the Carmack Amendment, 49 U.S.C. §11706 (2006), discussed at p. 96, which would have imposed full value liability. An issue that *Norfolk* did not explicitly consider is whether a single through bill of lading containing a Himalaya Clause and a clause extending COGSA inland issued by the carrier at the point of origin of the transport in a foreign country is sufficient to displace Carmack for the inland portion through the United States. Or is it necessary that when the goods are loaded on board the railway in the United States after the ocean voyage for the railway to issue a second bill of lading (with a second Himalaya clause and a responsibility clause extending COGSA inland) in order to displace Carmack? The federal courts of appeals were split on this issue. *Cf. Attadis USA, Inc. v. Sea Star Line*, 458 F.3d 1288, 1291–1294 (11th Cir. 2006) (following the majority view that a single through bill of lading displaces Carmack in favor of COGSA) *with Sampo Japan Ins. v. Union Pacific*, 456 F.3d 54, 60–75 (2d Cir. 2006) (applying the minority and holding a single through bill of lading does not displace Carmack because a mere contract (the bill of lading) cannot oust an applicable federal statute, the Carmack Amendment, and imposing full value liability on the carrier of $479,000 instead of a mere $16,000, the $500 per package applicable COGSA damages). As *Norfolk* did not explicitly consider this issue, in the *"K" Line* case below, the Supreme Court resolved this conflict among the circuit courts.

Kawasaki Kisen Kaisha Ltd. v. Regal-Beloit Corp.
(The "K" Line Case)
United States Supreme Court, 2010
561 U.S. 89

Justice KENNEDY delivered the opinion of the Court.

These cases concern through bills of lading covering cargo for the entire course of shipment, beginning in a foreign, overseas country and continuing to a final, inland destination in the United States. The voyage here included ocean transit followed by transfer to a rail carrier in this country. The Court addressed similar factual circumstances in *Norfolk Southern R. Co. v. James N. Kirby, Pty Ltd.*, 43 U.S. 14 (2004). In that case the terms of a through bill of lading were controlled by federal maritime law and by a federal statute known as the Carriage of Goods by Sea Act (COGSA) hist. note following 46 U.S.C. §30701. *Kirby* held that bill of lading provisions permissible under COGSA can be invoked by a domestic rail carrier despite contrary state law.

The instant cases present a question neither raised nor addressed in *Kirby*. It is whether the terms of a through bill of lading issued abroad by an ocean carrier can apply to the domestic part of the import's journey by a rail carrier, despite prohibitions or limitations in another federal statute. That statute is known as the Carmack Amendment and it governs the terms of bills of lading issued by domestic rail carriers. 49 U.S.C. §11706(a).

I

Respondents Regal-Beloit Corporation, Victory Fireworks, Inc., PICC Property & Casualty Company Ltd., and Royal & Sun Alliance Insurance Company Ltd. are cargo owners or insurance firms that paid losses to cargo owners and succeeded to their rights, all referred to as "cargo owners." To ship their goods from China to inland destinations in the Midwestern United States, the cargo owners delivered the goods in China to petitioners in No. 08-1553, Kawasaki Kisen Kaisha, Ltd., and its agent, "K" Line America, Inc., both referred to as "K" Line. All agree the relevant contract terms governing the shipment are contained in four through bills of lading "K" Line issued to the cargo owners. The bills of lading covered the entire course of shipment.

The bills required "K" Line to arrange delivery of the goods from China to their final destination in the United States, by any mode of transportation of "K" Line's choosing. A bill of lading "records that a carrier has received goods from the party that wishes to ship them, states the terms of carriage, and serves as evidence of the contract for carriage." *Kirby*, 543 U.S., at 18–19. A through bill of lading covers both the ocean and inland portions of the transport in a single document. Id., at 25–26.

"K" Line's through bills contain five relevant provisions. First, they include a so-called "Himalaya Clause," which extends the bills' defenses and limitations on liability to parties that sign subcontracts to perform services contemplated by the bills. Second, the bills permit "K" Line "to subcontract on any terms whatsoever" for the completion of the journey. Third, the bills provide that COGSA's terms govern the entire journey. Fourth, the bills require that any dispute will be governed by Japanese law. Fifth, the bills state that any action relating to the carriage must be brought in "Tokyo District Court in Japan." The forum selection provision in the last clause gives rise to the dispute here.

"K" Line, pursuant to the bills of lading, arranged for the entire journey. It subcontracted with petitioner in No. 08-1554, Union Pacific Railroad Company, for rail shipment in the United States. The goods were shipped in a "K" Line vessel to a port in Long Beach, California, and then transferred to Union Pacific for rail carriage to the final destinations.

In March and April 2005, the cargo owners brought four different container shipments to "K" Line vessels in Chinese ports. All parties seem to assume that "K" Line safely transported the cargo across the Pacific Ocean to California. The containers were then loaded onto a Union Pacific train and that train, or some other train operated by Union Pacific, derailed in Tyrone, Oklahoma, allegedly destroying the cargo.

The cargo owners filed four separate lawsuits in the Superior Court of California, County of Los Angeles. The suit named "K" Line and Union Pacific as defendants. Union Pacific removed the suits to the United States District Court for the Central District of California. Union Pacific and "K" Line then moved to dismiss based on the parties' Tokyo forum-selection clause. The District Court granted the motion to dismiss. It decided that the forum-selection clause was reasonable and applied to Union Pacific pursuant to the Himalaya Clause in "K" Line's bills of lading.

The United States Court of Appeals for the Ninth Circuit reversed and remanded. The court concluded that the Carmack Amendment applied to the inland portion of an international shipment under a through bill of lading and thus trumped the parties' forum-selection clause. The court noted that this view was consistent with the position taken by the Court of Appeals for the Second Circuit (*Sompo Japan Ins. Co. of Am. v. Union Pacific R. Co.*, 456 F.3d 54 (2006)), but inconsistent with the views of the Courts of Appeal for the Fourth, Sixth, Seventh, and Eleventh Circuits. This Court granted certiorari to address whether Carmack applies to the inland segment of an overseas import shipment under a through bill of lading.

II

A

Before turning to Carmack, a brief description of COGSA is in order; for "K" Line's and Union Pacific's primary contention is that COGSA, not Carmack, controls. COGSA governs the terms of bills of lading issued by ocean carriers engaged in international trade. It requires each carrier to issue to the cargo owner a bill that contains certain terms. Although COGSA imposes some limitations on the parties' authority to adjust liability, it does not limit the parties' ability to adopt forum-selection clauses. See *Vimar Seguros y Reaseguros, S.A. v. M/V Sky Reefer*, 515 U.S. 528, 537–39 (1995). By its terms, COGSA only applies to shipments from United States ports to ports of foreign countries and vice versa. The statute, however, allows parties "the option of extending [certain COGSA terms] by contract" to cover "the entire period in which [the goods] would be under [a carrier's] responsibility, including [a] period of . . . inland transport." *Kirby*, 543 U.S., at 29. Ocean carriers . . . are regulated by the Federal Maritime Commission, which is responsible for oversight over "common carriage of goods by water in . . . foreign commerce." 46 U.S.C. §40101(1).

B

The next statute to consider is the Carmack Amendment, which governs the terms of bills of lading issued by domestic rail carriers. It . . . provides in relevant part:

(a) A rail carrier providing transportation or service subject to the jurisdiction of the [Surface Transportation Board (STB)] under this part shall issue a receipt or bill of lading for property it receives for transportation . . . . That rail carrier and any other carrier that delivers the property and is providing transportation or service subject to the jurisdiction of the [STB] . . . are liable to the person entitled to recover under the receipt or bill of lading. The liability imposed under this subsection is for the actual loss or injury to the property caused by—

(1) The receiving rail carrier;

(2) The delivering rail carrier; or

(3) Another rail carrier over whose line or route the property is transported in the United States or from a place in the United States to a place in an adjacent foreign country when transported under a through bill of lading.

Failure to issue a receipt or bill of lading does not affect the liability of a rail carrier. 49 U.S.C. §11706. See also §14706(a) (motor carriers).

The Carmack Amendment thus requires a rail carrier that "receives [property] for transportation . . . to issue a bill of lading." The provision "this part" refers to is the STB's jurisdiction over rail transportation within the United States. The STB is the successor to the Interstate Commerce Commission (ICC). The STB has "exclusive" jurisdiction to regulate "transportation by rail carriers" between places in the United States as well as between a place "in the United States and a place in a foreign country." Regulated rail carriers must provide transportation subject to STB jurisdiction "on reasonable request," at reasonable rates. [49 U.S.C. §§10501, 11101, 10701, 10707.]

In cases where it applies, Carmack imposes upon "receiving rail carrier[s]" and "delivering rail carrier[s]" liability for damage caused during the rail route under the bill of lading, regardless of which carrier caused the damage. §11706(a). Carmack's purpose is to relieve cargo owners "of the burden of searching out a particular negligent carrier from among the often numerous carriers handling an interstate shipment of goods" [citation omitted]. To help achieve this goal, Carmack constrains carriers' ability to limit liability by contract. §11706(c).

Carmack also limits the parties' ability to choose the venue of their suit: [The Court cites provisions of Carmack that require civil actions to be filed against the originating rail carrier in the judicial district in which the point of origin is located; against the delivering rail carrier in the judicial district in which the principal place of business of the claimant is located or in the judicial district in which the point of destination is located; or against the carrier alleged to have caused the damage in the judicial district in which the loss or damage is alleged to have occurred.].

For purposes of these cases, it can be assumed that, if Carmack's terms apply to the bills of lading here, the cargo owners would have a substantial argument that the Tokyo forum-selection clause in the bills is preempted by Carmack's venue provisions.

III

In *Kirby*, an ocean shipping company issued a through bill of lading, agreeing to deliver cargo from Australia to Alabama. Like the through bills of lading in the present cases, the *Kirby* bill extended COGSA's terms to the inland segment under a Himalaya Clause. There, as here, the property was damaged by a domestic rail carrier during the inland rail portion.

Much of what the Court said in *Kirby* applies to the present cases. "K" Line issued the through bills of lading under COGSA, in maritime commerce. Congress considered such international through bills and decided to permit parties to extend COGSA's terms to the inland domestic segment of the journey. The cargo owners and "K" Line did exactly that in these cases, agreeing in the through bills to require that any suit be brought in Tokyo.

IV

argues

The cargo owners argue that the Carmack Amendment, which has its own venue provisions and was not discussed in *Kirby*, requires a different result. In particular, they argue that Carmack applies to the domestic inland segment of the carriage here, so the Tokyo forum-selection clause is inapplicable. For the reasons set forth below, this contention must be rejected. Instructed by the text, history, and purposes of Carmack, the Court now holds that the amendment does not apply to a shipment originating overseas under a single bill of lading.

A

The text of the statute charts the analytic course. Carmack divides the realm of rail carriers into three parts: (1) receiving rail carriers; (2) delivering rail carriers; and (3) connecting rail carriers. A "receiving rail carrier" is one that "provid[es] transportation or service . . . for property it receives for transportation under this part." §11706(a)(1). The provision "this part" refers to is the SBT's jurisdiction over rail transportation in the United States. See sec. 10501. A "delivering rail carrier" "delivers the property and is providing transportation or service subject to the jurisdiction of the [STB] under this part." §11706(a)(2). A connecting rail carrier is "another rail carrier over whose line or route the property is transported in the United States or from a place in the United States to a place in an adjacent foreign country when transported under a through bill of lading." §11706(a)(3).

A rail carrier's obligation to issue a Carmack-compliant bill of lading is determined by Carmack's first sentence:

> "A rail carrier providing transportation or service subject to the jurisdiction of the [SBT] under this part shall issue a receipt or bill of lading for property it receives for transportation under this part." §11706(a).

This critical first sentence requires a Cormack-compliant bill of lading if two conditions are satisfied. First, the rail carrier must "provide transportation or service subject to the jurisdiction of the [STB]." Second, that carrier must "receive" the property "for transportation under this part," where "this part" is the STB's jurisdiction over domestic rail transport. Carmack thus requires the receiving rail carrier—but not the delivering or connecting rail carrier—to issue a bill of lading. As explained below, ascertaining the shipment's point of origin is critical to deciding whether the shipment includes a receiving rail carrier.

The conclusion that Carmack's bill of lading requirement only applies to the receiving rail carrier is dictated by the text and is consistent with this Court's precedent. *See St. Louis, I.M. & S.R. Co. v. Starbird*, 243 U.S. 592, 604 (1917) (explaining that Carmack "requires the receiving carrier to issue a through bill of lading"). A receiving rail carrier is the initial rail carrier, which "receives" the property for domestic rail transportation at the journey's point of origin. §11706(a). If Carmack's bill of lading requirement did not refer to the initial carrier, but rather to any rail carrier that in the colloquial sense "received" the property from another rail carrier, then every carrier during the shipment would have to issue its own separate bill. This would be altogether contrary to Carmack's purpose of making the receiving and delivering carriers liable under a single, initial bill of lading for damage caused by any carrier within a single course of shipment.

The Carmack Amendment's second sentence establishes when Carmack liability applies:

> "[The receiving rail carrier referred to in the first sentence] and any other carrier that delivers the property and is providing transportation or service subject to the jurisdiction of the [STB] under this part are liable to the person entitled to recover under the receipt or bill of lading." §11506(a).

Thus, the receiving and delivering carriers are subject to liability only when damage is done to this "property," that is to say, to property for which Carmack's first sentence requires the receiving rail carrier to issue a bill of lading. *Ibid.* Put another way, Carmack applies only to transport of property for which Carmack requires a receiving carrier to issue a bill of lading, regardless of whether that carrier erroneously fails to issue such a bill. *See ibid.* ("Failure to issue a receipt or bill of lading does not affect the liability of a rail carrier"). The language in some of the Court of Appeals' decisions, which were rejected by the Court of Appeals in the opinion now under review, could be read to imply that Carmack applies only if a rail carrier actually issued a separate bill of lading. This may have led to some confusion. The decisive question is not whether the rail carrier in fact issued a Carmack bill but rather whether that carrier was required to issue a bill by Carmack's first sentence.

The above principles establish that for Carmack's provisions to apply the journey must begin with a receiving rail carrier, which would have to issue a Carmack-compliant bill of lading. It follows that Carmack does not apply if the property is received at an overseas location under a through bill of lading that covers the transport into an inland location in the United States. In such a case, there is no receiving rail carrier that "receives" the property "for [domestic rail] transportation," §11706(a), and thus no carrier that must issue a Carmack-compliant bill of lading. The initial carrier in that instance receives the property at the shipment's point of origin for overseas multimodal import transport, not for domestic rail transport. (Today's decision need not address the instance where the goods are received at a point in the United States for export. Nor is it necessary to decide if Carmack applies to goods initially received in Canada or Mexico, for import into the United States).

B

[In section B of this part of the opinion, the Court concludes that the statutory history of Carmack supports the conclusion that it does not apply to a shipment originating overseas under a through bill of lading.]

C

Where the text permits, congressional enactments should be construed to be consistent with one another. And the interpretation of Carmack the Court now adopts attains the most consistency between Carmack and COGSA. First, applying Carmack to the inland segment of an international carriage originating overseas under a through bill would undermine Carmack's purposes. Carmack is premised on the view that the shipment has a single bill of lading and any damage during the journey is the responsibility of both the receiving and the delivering carrier. Yet under the Court of Appeals' interpretation of Carmack, there would often be no venue in which to sue the receiving carrier.

Applying two different bill of lading regimes to the same through shipment would undermine COGSA and international, container-based multimodal transport. As *Kirby* explained, "[t]he international transportation industry clearly has moved into a new era—the age of multimodalism, door-to-door transport, based on efficient use of all available modes of transportation by air, water and land." 543 U.S., at 25, quoting 1 T. Schoenbaum, *Admiralty and Maritime Law* 589 (4th ed. 2004). If Carmack applied to an inland segment of a shipment from overseas under a through bill, then one set of liability and venue rules would apply when cargo is damaged at sea (COGSA) and another almost always would apply when the damage occurs on land (Carmack). Rather than making claims by cargo owners easier to resolve, a court would have to decide where the damage occurred to determine which law applied. As a practical matter, this requirement often could not be met; for damage to the content of containers can occur when the contents are damaged by rough handling, seepage, or theft, at some unknown point. Indeed, adopting the Court of Appeals' approach would seem to require rail carriers to open containers at the port to check if damage has been done during the sea voyage. This disruption would undermine international, container-based transport.

Applying Carmack's provisions to international import shipping transport would also undermine the "purpose of COGSA, to facilitate efficient contracting in contracts for carriage by sea." *Kirby* at 29. These cases provide an apt illustration. The sophisticated cargo owners here agreed to maritime bills of lading that applied to the inland segment through the Himalaya Clause and authorized "K" Line to subcontract for that inland segment "on any terms whatsoever." The cargo owners thus made the decision to select "K" Line as a single company for their through transportation needs, rather than contracting for rail services themselves. The through bills provided the liability and venue rules for the foreseeable event that the cargo was damaged during carriage. Indeed, the cargo owners obtained separate insurance to protect against any excess loss. The forum-selection clause the parties agreed upon is "an indispensable element in international trade, commerce, and contracting" because it allows parties to "agree in advance on a forum acceptable" to them. *The Bremen v. Zapata Off-Shore Co.*, 407 U.S. 1, 13–14 (1972). A clause of this kind is enforced unless it imposes a venue "so gravely difficult and inconvenient that [the plaintiff] will for all practical purposes be deprived of his day in court." Id. at 18. The parties sensibly agreed that because their bills were governed by Japanese law, Tokyo would be the best venue for any kind of suit relating to the cargo.

V

"K" Line received the goods in China, under through bills for shipment into the United States. "K" Line was thus not a receiving carrier under Carmack and was not required to issue bills of lading under that Amendment. Union Pacific is also not a receiving carrier for this carriage and was thus not required to issue Carmack-compliant bills. Because the journey included no receiving rail carrier that had to issue bills of lading under Carmack, Carmack does not apply. The parties' agreement to litigate these cases in Tokyo is binding. The cargo owners must abide by the contracts they have made.

The judgment of the Court of Appeals for the Ninth Circuit is reversed, and the cases are remanded for further proceedings consistent with this opinion.

NOTES AND QUESTIONS

1. *COGSA versus Carmack.* Do you agree with the Court's analysis of the applicability of Carmack? The Court's opinion holds that a single through bill of lading involving multimodal transport with a Clause Paramount (contractually extending COGSA to the overland portions of the carriage) and a Himalaya Clause (contractually extending COGSA to the overland carrier-subcontractor) trumps Carmack, rendering it totally inapplicable in favor of COGSA. Justice Sotomayor's dissenting opinion, joined by Justices Stevens and Ginsburg, states that the Court misread the text of the statute as well as the legislative history and legislative policy. The matter is important because, as we have seen, in most cases Carmack provides greater protection and recovery to the shipper: Carmack, 49 U.S.C. §11706(b) (2006), provides that the extent of liability is the value established by written declaration of the shipper or by written agreement between the carrier and the shipper. To consider Justice Sotomayor's argument in dissent, read carefully the text of the statutory language, the Carmack Amendment for rail carriers, 49 U.S.C. §11706:

(a) A rail carrier providing transportation or service subject to the jurisdiction of the Board under this part shall issue a receipt or bill of lading for property it receives for transportation under this part. That rail carrier and any other rail carrier that delivers the property and is providing transportation or service subject to the jurisdiction of the Board under this part are liable to the persons entitled to recover under the receipt or bill of lading. The liability imposed under this subsection is for the actual loss or injury to the property caused by—
  (1) The receiving rail carrier;
  (2) The delivering rail carrier; or
  (3) Another rail carrier over whose line or route the property is transported in the United States or from a place in the United States to a place in an adjacent foreign country when transported under a through bill of lading.

Justice Sotomayor argues that the first sentence in this scheme concerns the circumstances under which a receiving rail carrier must issue a bill of lading (although another part of the statute makes clear that liability will ensue even if a bill is not issued); the second sentence sets out the "expansive scope" of rail carrier liability; and the third sentence establishes liability. Sotomayor further states that "Carmack plainly applies to the inland leg of a multimodal shipment traveling on a through bill of lading." She then charges that the *Court's* opinion "rests on the erroneous belief that the receiving carrier must receive the goods at the point of origin" of the carriage.

Justice Sotomayor further argues:

[M]y reading of the statute would not outlaw through shipments under a single bill of lading. To the contrary, an overseas ocean carrier like "K" Line can still issue a through bill of lading governing the entire international trip to an American destination. That bill of lading reflects the ocean carrier's agreement with and obligations to the original shipper of the cargo. As the ocean carrier has no independent Carmack obligation of its own, the ocean carrier and the shipper are free to select whatever liability terms they wish to govern their relationship during the entire shipment. Carmack simply requires an American "receiving rail carrier" like Union Pacific to issue a bill of lading to the party from whom it received the goods for shipment—here, "K" Line. As to that bill of lading, Carmack provides the legal regime and defines the relationship between the contracting parties. The issuance of this second bill of lading, however, in no way undermines the efficiency of the through bill of lading between the ocean carrier and the original shipper, nor does it require that those parties bind themselves to apply Carmack to the inland leg.

Which side is correct, the Court or Justice Sotomayor?

2. *Multimodal Export Transactions.* The Court's opinion in the *"K" Line* case settles the application of COGSA versus Carmack with respect to overseas *import* transactions. But the Court leaves open two key questions: Carmack's possible application to export transactions and to import transactions from Canada and Mexico. How should these questions be decided? A split of authority on export transactions seems to be developing. *Cf. Royal & Sun Alliance, PLC v. Service Transfer, Inc.*, 2012 WL 6028991, 2013 AMC 345 (S.D.N.Y. 2012) (COGSA applies) and *American Home Assurance Co. v. Panalpina Inc.*, 2011 WL 666388, 2011 AMC 733 (S.D.N.Y. 2011) (Carmack applies to inland segment). The Sixth Circuit in a case involving a multimodal export transaction came down in favor of *both* sides of the argument. In *CNA Ins. Co. v. Hyundai Merchant Marine Co., Ltd.*, 747 F.3d 339 (6th Cir. 2014), the court ruled, on the one hand, that "the Carmack Amendment does not apply to the road or rail leg of an international overseas export shipment under a single through bill of lading." On the other hand, the court upheld a jury verdict awarding the shipper $664,679.88 (full value of the damaged shipment of Corning glass), which was the amount due under Carmack, instead of the COGSA total damages of $10,000, on the basis that there was an additional long-term service contract between the shipper and the carrier providing liability for full value. *Id.* at 737–743.

What is the consequence of differing legal regimes applying to export and import transportation contracts?

3. *Outmoded Legal Regimes.* Is the problem that modern shipping methods are governed by ancient legal formulations? COGSA dates from 1936, while the Carmack Amendment dates fundamentally from 1906. Michael Sturley, *Maritime Cases About Train Wrecks: Applying Maritime Law to the Inland Damage of Ocean Cargo*, 40 J. Mar. L. & Com. 1, 40 (2009), states that "[b]ecause the current problem arises from the existence of outmoded legal regimes that did not anticipate the growth of multimodal shipments, the obvious solution would be to adopt a new legal regime expressly addressing modern commercial realities." The latest international reform effort, the Rotterdam Rules, adopts a "network" approach to multimodal liability similar to that advocated by Justice Sotomayor. *See* Rotterdam Rules, Article 26. But this provision would not affect the holding of the *"K" Line* case because the United States is not a party to international rail or road conventions.

4. *Choice of Law.* The opinion of the Court in the *"K" Line* case seems to accept the validity of the choice of law clause in the bill of lading selecting Japanese law. Can this be squared with COGSA, which requires that "every bill of lading . . . which is evidence of a contract for the carriage of goods by sea to or from the ports of the United States, in foreign trade, shall have effect subject to the provisions of this chapter"?

5. *Forum Selection.* The Court in *"K" Line* enforced the parties' forum selection clause. The Supreme Court's opinion in *Vimar Seguros y Reaseguros, S.A. v. M/V Sky Reefer*, 515 U.S. 528, 541 (1995), cited as authority for the enforcement of forum selection clauses in bills of lading in the Court's *"K" Line* opinion, was also authored by Justice Kennedy. The *Sky Reefer* case was somewhat of a surprise when it was handed down; the Courts of Appeal had uniformly invalidated forum selection clauses in bills of lading on the grounds of section 3(8) of COGSA and that "there could be no assurance that [the foreign court] would apply [COGSA] in the same way as would an American tribunal." *Indussa Corp.*

v. S.S. Ranborg, 377 F.2d 200, 203–204 (2d Cir. 1967). The Supreme Court in *Sky Reefer* discounted this problem and upheld the validity of a forum selection clause requiring arbitration in Japan. The Court stated that the worry about foreign forums disregarding COGSA rules was "premature." *Vimar Seguros y Reaseguros, S.A. v. M/V Sky Reefer,* 515 U.S. 528, 541 (1995). Since *Sky Reefer,* U.S. courts routinely uphold foreign arbitration clauses in bills of lading. *See, e.g., Ambraco, Inc. v. Bossclip B.V.,* 570 F.3d 233, 238–242 (5th Cir. 2009). As a result, most COGSA disputes are handled by foreign arbitration or in foreign venues, much to the chagrin of American lawyers. If the Rotterdam Rules come into force and are accepted by the United States, what would happen to the *Sky Reefer* ruling? *See* Articles 66, 67, and 75.

PROBLEM 2-7

A U.S. seller enters into a common carriage for the M/V Reefer Sun II to ship a large quantity of high-definition plasma flat-screen televisions packed into five shipping containers from the port of New Orleans to its final destination in a Mediterranean country. The shipment calls for the M/V Reefer Sun II to arrive in Italy where the standard containers will be unloaded on to trucks and transported inland to a second port on the other side of the peninsula where they will be reloaded on board a second carrier, the M/V Appollonia, for their final destination. The M/V Reefer Sun II issued a single through bill of lading covering all phases of the voyage, including inland transport through Italy, until the goods are loaded on board the second carrier. At this point, the M/V Appollonia will issue a second bill of lading to cover the voyage to the final port of destination. A clause in the through bill of lading states: "Himalaya Clause: All exceptions, defenses, immunities, limitations of liability, privileges and conditions applicable by COGSA to the carrier shall be extended to the benefit of all persons performing services on behalf of the carrier."

After the M/V Reefer Sun II arrives in Italy at the first port, the following events occur:

(1) The Italian stevedores hired by the carrier to unload the cargo damage the first container containing 20 package units, causing $1 million in damage.
(2) When the M/V Reefer Sun II arrives, not all of the trucks are at the port of call due to an oversight by the U.S. seller. The second container is loaded on to a truck for transshipment; the third, fourth, and fifth containers are placed in a dock warehouse where they await the arrival of additional trucks. While in the warehouse, a fire destroys the third container, resulting in a total loss of the cargo worth $4 million.
(3) The fourth container is loaded on a truck to transport the goods to the M/V Appollonia. While in transit, the truck is hijacked and all of the goods are stolen. According to the Italian police, the driver has a criminal record of previous hackings and had tipped off the hijackers on the route of the truck. For the purposes of this part of this problem only, assume that the bill of lading issued by the M/V Reefer Sun II also had a responsibility clause (in addition to the Himalaya Clause) extending COGSA for the entire transport, including all inland portions. The bill of lading issued by the M/V Reefer Sun II has an exceptions clause on the front page in bold letters: "The carrier and all entities or persons performing services on behalf of the carrier is not liable for

any hijackings or armed robberies by acts of public enemies, thieves, pirates, or assailing thieves."

(4)   The second and fifth containers are transshipped by truck to the second port where they arrive in the late afternoon. The containers are loaded on board the second vessel, the M/V Appollonia, which issues a bill of lading with a Clause Paramount providing that the bill of lading is subject to COGSA. The M/V Appollonia is scheduled for departure the next morning, but overnight both containers are broken into aboard the vessel and all of the goods are stolen, resulting in a loss of $4 million.

What is the liability, if any, of the stevedores, the warehouse company, the trucking company, and the M/V Appollonia? Review the discussion of the Himalaya Clause and the responsibility clause extending COGSA to inland transport at pp. 96-97. Also review the discussion of the effect of a Clause Paramount in the bill of lading issued by the M/V Appollonia (see p. 95. Consider also *Anvil Knitwear* and *Steel Coils* below and the accompanying notes.

Anvil Knitwear v. Crowley American Transport, Inc.
United States District Court, Southern District of New York, 2001
2001 AMC 2382, 2001 WL 856607

BUCHWALD, District Judge:

Plaintiff Anvil Knitwear, Inc. ("Anvil" or "plaintiff") brings this action against defendants Crowley American Transport, Inc. ("Crowley") and *M/V Ambassador*, her engines, boilers, etc., *in rem* (collectively "defendants") for damages resulting from the hijacking and theft of cartons of Anvil's cotton tee-shirts while in the custody of Crowley's agents. Defendants have moved pursuant to Fed. R. Civ. P. 56 for summary judgment. For the reasons discussed below, defendants' motion is granted and the case is dismissed.

BACKGROUND

Anvil is a manufacturer, importer, and distributor of clothing and does business importing clothing from Central America for sale in the United States. Beginning in January, 1995, Anvil and Crowley entered into a series of one-year contracts by which Crowley agreed to transport shipments of Anvil garments. Over the course of this time, Crowley transported "hundreds" of shipments from Central America to the United States for Anvil.

In May, 1999, Anvil contracted with Crowley to transport shipments of tee-shirts from a manufacturing plant in Santa Barbara, Honduras, C.A., to its United States' plant in South Carolina. The Service Contract, #99-05-00, provided for the transportation of a minimum of 1,300 containers per year at a fixed rate.

Pursuant to this contract, Crowley issued a bill of lading ("Bill") on June 18, 1999, covering the 786 cartons of cotton tee-shirts that were packed into container CMCZ833842. Anvil claims that the goods were valued at approximately $137,000. The Bill covered the transportation of the cartons from Santa Barbara, Honduras, to the load port, Puerto Cortes, Honduras, the ocean transportation via the Ambassador, and the ultimate delivery in South Carolina. The Bill stated that the Carriage of Goods by Sea Act of the United

States, 46 U.S.C. App. §1300 et seq. ("COGSA"), would govern the contract throughout the entire time Anvil's goods were in Crowley's possession.

In another section, entitled "Exceptions Clause," the Bill carved out a long list of events for which Crowley could not be held liable. In relevant part, the clause stated:

"18. Exceptions Clause. Carrier shall not be liable for any loss, damage, delay or failure in performance hereunder occurring at any time, including before loading on or after discharge from the vessel or during any voyage, arising or resulting from the happening and/or threat and/or aftereffects of one or more of the following: act of God, act of war, force majeure, quarantine restrictions, embargo, acts of public enemies, *thieves, pirates, assailing thieves* . . . (emphasis added)."

Furthermore, the Bill stated, on its front face, at the center of the page:

"IMPORTANT: CARRIER HAS MADE IT CLEAR IN THE EXCEPTIONS CLAUSE (CLAUSE 18 ON THE BACK OF THIS BILL OF LADING) THAT IT HAS NO LIABILITY FOR HIJACKINGS AND ARMED ROBBERIES."

The same Bill language appeared on each of the hundreds of bills of lading issued by Crowley to Anvil for shipments since 1995.

Crowley's local agent, Transportes Hispanos, picked up Anvil's cartons on or about June 16, 1999, from Anvil's vendor, M.J. Honduras, S.A. Shortly after departing from the vendor's plant, the truck carrying the shipment was hijacked and the goods were stolen. Both parties have stipulated to the fact that the Transportes Hispanos driver, Mr. Ramon Enrique Rosales, was not in any way involved with the hijacking.

Anvil had obtained cargo insurance for the shipment that covered hijackings and armed robberies. The cargo underwriter paid Anvil's claim and has sought compensation from Crowley.

DISCUSSION

Anvil's central argument in opposition to summary judgment is that the "Exceptions Clause" on the back of the Bill and the hijacking liability disclaimer (collectively "hijacking disclaimer") on the back are void because they violate COGSA. Specifically, Anvil contends that because the hijacking disclaimer does not fall into one of the statutory categories of waivable liability specified in COGSA section 1304(2)(a)–(p), it violates COGSA's general prohibition against carriers waiving liability for negligence. See COGSA section 1303(8).

In response, defendants argue that hijacking is sufficiently similar to several of COGSA section 1304(2)'s exceptions that it should be deemed to fall into one or constitute a penumbral exception. Although the exceptions are numerous, common to all are "Uncontrollable causes of loss." Among them, Crowley points to COGSA section 1304(2)(f), "Act[s] of public enemies" as a particularly strong candidate to support its hijacking disclaimer. Especially in light of the fact that COGSA section 1304(2) exceptions are focused on shipping, not land transport, Crowley contends, it is appropriate to analogize for similar terrestrial hazards.

If COGSA section 1304(2)'s exceptions were common law rules, Crowley's argument might be persuasive. However, construing section 1304(2) properly as part of a statutory scheme, we cannot stray from the statute's evident intent and historical interpretation. It is settled law that COGSA section 1304(2)(f)'s "Act[s] of public enemies" applies solely to "an actual state of war between the government of a foreign nation and the carrier's government. At most, the public enemy exception extends to pirates on the high seas or rebels in insurrection against their own government, not thieves, rioters and robbers."

Fesco, Inc. v. Shone, 205 F.3d 1322 (2d Cir. 2000). Furthermore, we cannot attempt to read a penumbral exception into COGSA section 1304(2), beyond that specified in COGSA section 1304(2)(q), which relieves a carrier from liability for:

> (q) Any other cause arising without the actual fault and privity of the carrier and without the fault or neglect of the agents or servants of the carrier, but the burden of proof shall be on the person claiming the benefit of this exception to show that neither the actual fault or privity of the carrier nor the fault or neglect of the agents or servants of the carrier contributed to the loss or damage.

We can analyze COGSA's effect on the hijacking disclaimer in two ways. If the hijacking is read broadly, i.e., to disclaim liability regardless of Crowley's negligence, it clearly runs afoul of COGSA section 1303(8)'s prohibition against liability limitation. Alternatively, we could choose to construe the hijacking disclaimer consistently with COGSA section 1303(8) and section 1304(2)(q). Under this approach we would reconcile the disclaimer and COGSA provisions simply by limiting the hijacking disclaimer to situations where there was no proof of Crowley's negligence. The bottom line is: negligence is the applicable liability standard and the burden lies with Crowley to prove its due care.

Anvil has failed to produce any evidence that Crowley was negligent. The court afforded both parties ample time for discovery to enable them to undertake a full investigation into the events surrounding the hijacking, including depositions in Central America.

Anvil has made no showing whatsoever of concrete evidence from which a reasonable juror could return a verdict in its favor. Weighing the stipulation that Crowley's agent was uninvolved in the hijacking and Anvil's ample opportunity to search for other possible negligence against Anvil's naked and unsupported pleading that "the above named vessel and defendant breached, failed and violated their duties and obligations as common carriers and were otherwise at fault," we find there is no triable issue of fact concerning defendants' diligence. Accordingly, we find that defendants have met their burden of proving they exercised due diligence under COGSA section 1304(2)(q) and are not liable for the loss of Anvil's goods in the hijacking. □ w ὴ S.

PROBLEM 2-8

Suppose that in Problem 2-7 above the additional following events occur. When the M/V Appollonia arrives at the port of final destination and the fifth (and final) container is unpacked, there is evidence of damage to the container, resulting in $2 million in damages to the goods. The U.S. seller has a clean bill of lading issued by the first carrier, the M/V Reefer Sun II. The cargo inspector hired by the seller to inspect the cargo as it was unloaded from the M/V Reefer Sun II in Italy issued a report indicating "clean unblemished exteriors" on all of the containers. The containers were then transported by the truckers to the M/V Appollonia, which also issued a clean bill of lading that is in the custody of the seller. Who is liable for the damage and what, if any, limitations on liability exist?

Suppose instead that the M/V Appollonia issued an "unclean" bill describing several dents in the containers when it received them for shipment. Is anyone liable and for how much? See *Steel Coils* below and the accompanying notes.

Steel Coils, Inc. v. M/V Lake Marion
United States Court of Appeals, Fifth Circuit, 2003
331 F.3d 422, *cert. denied*, 540 U.S. 949 (2003)

HIGGINBOTHAM, Circuit Judge.

I.

The plaintiff, Steel Coils, Inc., is an importer of steel products with its principal office in Deerfield, Illinois. It ordered flat-rolled steel from a steel mill in Russia. Itochu, which then owned ninety percent of the stock of Steel Coils, purchased the steel and entered into a voyage charter with Western Bulk for the M/V LAKE MARION to import the steel to the United States.[11] Western Bulk had time chartered the vessel from Lake Marion, Inc.[12] As Lake Marion, Inc.'s manager, Bay Ocean employed the master and crew of the vessel.

The LAKE MARION took on the steel coils at the Latvian port of Riga between February 26 and March 2, 1997. The steel had traveled to port by rail from the Severstal steel mill 400 miles north of Moscow. At Riga, the hot rolled coils were stored outside, while the cold rolled and galvanized coils were encased in protective steel wrappers and stored in a warehouse at the port.

After departing Riga, the vessel stopped at another Latvian port, Ventspils, where it took on more steel coils. The ship departed Ventspils on March 7, 1997 and arrived at Camden, New Jersey, on March 28, 1997. After Camden, the ship stopped at New Orleans and Houston. Steel Coils alleged that the coils unloaded at New Orleans and Houston were damaged by saltwater, which required Steel Coils to have the cargo cleaned and recoated.

II.

Steel Coils filed suit under COGSA against the M/V LAKE MARION *in rem* and against Lake Marion, Inc., Bay Ocean Management, and Western Bulk Carriers *in personam*, requesting $550,000 in damages, with a separate claim of negligence against Bay Ocean. The vessel interests and Western Bulk filed cross-claims against each other for indemnification, and Western Bulk filed a third party complaint for indemnification against Itochu.

After a bench trial, the district court held the defendants jointly and severally liable to Steel Coils for $262,000, and Bay Ocean liable for an additional $243,358.94. The court further found that Western Bulk was entitled to indemnity from Lake Marion, Inc. for any amount it pays to Steel Coils.

---

11. "A voyage charter is a contract for the hire of a vessel for one or a series of voyages. . . ." *Citrus Mktg. Bd. of Israel v. J. Lauritzen A/S*, 943 F.2d 220, 221 n. 3 (2d Cir. 1991) (internal quotation marks omitted).

12. "A time charter is a contract to use a vessel for a particular period of time, although the vessel owner retains possession and control." *Id.* at 221 n. 2 (internal quotation marks omitted).

III.

Defendants M/V LAKE MARION, Lake Marion, Inc., and Bay Ocean contend that the district court improperly shifted the burden to them to prove that the steel cargo was not in good condition prior to loading or was in undamaged condition at discharge, that it erred in finding that they failed to exercise due diligence to ensure that the vessel was seaworthy at the commencement of the voyage, and that it was wrong in disregarding their defenses to COGSA liability of peril of the sea and latent defect.

IV.

COGSA provides a complex burden-shifting procedure. Initially, the plaintiff must establish a prima facie case by demonstrating that the cargo was loaded in an undamaged condition and discharged in a damaged condition. For the purpose of determining the condition of the goods at the time of receipt by the carrier, the bill of lading serves as prima facie evidence that the goods were loaded in the condition therein described. If the plaintiff presents a prima facie case, the burden shifts to the defendants to prove that they exercised due diligence to prevent the damage or that the damage was caused by one of the exceptions set forth in section 1304(2) of COGSA, including "[p]erils, dangers, and accidents of the sea or other navigable waters" and "[l]atent defects not discoverable by due diligence." If the defendants show that the loss was caused by one of these exceptions, the burden returns to the shipper to establish that the defendants' negligence contributed to the damage. Finally, if the shipper is able to establish that the defendants' negligence was a contributory cause of the damage, the burden switches back to the defendants to segregate the portion of the damage due to the excepted cause from that portion resulting from the carrier's own negligence.

A.

The vessel interests first assert that the district court reversed the burden of proof, requiring them to demonstrate that the goods were loaded in a damaged condition or were unloaded in an undamaged condition instead of requiring Steel Coils to prove that the coils were loaded undamaged and discharged damaged. These defendants mischaracterize the district court's decision. The district court properly explained that under COGSA a plaintiff must establish a prima facie case by "proving that the cargo for which the bills of lading were issued was loaded in an undamaged condition, and discharged in a damaged condition." Applying this law the trial court determined that Steel Coils demonstrated its prima facie case by proving that "the cargo was delivered to the LAKE MARION in good order and condition" and "was unloaded at the ports of New Orleans and Houston in a damaged condition."

The district court cited specific evidence proffered by Steel Coils to support these conclusions. In determining that the coils were loaded in good condition, it examined "mates receipts, bills of lading containing comments on the condition of the cargo, and a cargo survey taken at the load port in Riga that contained commentary about and photographs of the cargo." It explained that although some of these documents contained notations regarding "atmospheric rust on the hot rolled coils and damage to the wrapping of the cold rolled and galvanized coils," the evidence showed that "these conditions did not damage the coils" and were not the result of exposure to seawater prior to embarkation.

We conclude that the district court in this case did not clearly err in finding that the hot rolled coils were in good condition prior to loading. That the rust noted on the coils was atmospheric and nondamaging in nature, and that the moisture on the coils also did not affect their good condition is supported by the evidence.

As for the cold rolled and galvanized coils, the vessel interests argue that the bill of lading notation that the condition of these coils was unknown fatally undermined Steel Coils's attempt to prove a prima facie case of good condition. For this argument they rely on *Caemint Food, Inc. v. Lloyd Brasileiro Companhia de Navegação*, in which the Second Circuit reasoned:

> Although a clean bill of lading normally constitutes prima facie evidence that cargo was in good condition at the time of shipment . . . it does not have this probative force where . . . the shipper seeks to recover for damage to goods shipped in packages that would have prevented the carrier from observing the damaged condition had it existed when the goods were loaded.[13]

Caemint held that a plaintiff could not recover for corned beef it claimed was ruined during the voyage because it could not present evidence as to the condition of the corned beef, which was inside metal containers, before shipment.

We have similarly stated that "[w]here because of the perishable or intrinsic nature of the commodity, the internal condition is not adequately revealed by external appearances, cargo may have a considerable burden of going further to prove actual condition."[14] That is not the case here. Captain Sparks testified that although the wrappers of the cold rolled and galvanized coils loaded at Riga were wet due to condensation, there was no evidence of "drip-down" or "run-down" of moisture to the coils and no mention in the bills of lading of "white rust or white oxidation marks," which are normal preshipment clauses indicating possible rust damage to the coils. He concluded that "[t]he amount of moisture on those coils must have been negligible" and "[t]here was no damage to those coils."

The evidence at trial showed that, had the cold rolled or galvanized coils been damaged by rust, their outer wrappers would have revealed it. Because the wrappers had no indication of rust, and the moisture on the outside of the wrappers was not dripping down into the coils, it was not clearly erroneous for the district court to conclude that the cold rolled and galvanized coils were in an undamaged state prior to loading.

The vessel interests further assert clear error in the finding that the steel coils were damaged upon unloading. The contention is that seawater could not have entered through the hatches because the top-stowed cargo unloaded at Camden had no seawater damage, and that perhaps the steel coils rusted on the way from the ship to their ultimate inland destinations.

The vessel interests' arguments are belied by a wealth of evidence relied upon by the district court that at unloading the cargo was damaged by seawater rust. For instance, the McLarens Toplis survey conducted in New Orleans noted "rust stains to coils to varying extents," and "[r]andom tests on the rust stained areas with a solution of silver nitrate proved positive" with respect to chlorides, "indicating water ingress." The McLarens Toplis survey in Houston similarly stated that "[t]he cargo was examined and found to be extremely rusty," and that "[e]xtensive silver nitrate tests were conducted with strong

13. 647 F.2d 347, 352 (2d Cir. 1981).
14. *United States v. Lykes Bros. S.S. Co.*, 511 F.2d 218, 223 (5th Cir. 1975).

positive results. It is our opinion [that] the . . . cargo came into contact with sea water, most likely through the poorly maintained hatch covers. . . ."

The vessel interests have not cited any evidence in the record that disputes these conclusions. Their argument that the district court "simply accepted plaintiff's survey reports and testimony *en masse* as setting forth the proper measure of damages, and that the damage was proven at discharge" implicitly acknowledges that substantial evidence in the record supports the district court's conclusions as to the damage evident at unloading.

B.

Facing a prima facie case, a defendant may escape liability if it shows that it exercised "due diligence . . . to make the ship seaworthy, and to secure that the ship is properly manned, equipped, and supplied, and to make the holds . . . and all other parts of the ship in which goods are carried fit and safe for their reception, carriage, and preservation."[15] The vessel interests urge that even if Steel Coils carried its initial burden, they exercised due diligence in making the vessel seaworthy and thus should have escaped liability.

In making its determination that the defendants did not exercise due diligence, the district court correctly noted that seaworthiness is defined as "reasonable fitness to perform or do the work at hand,"[16] and explained that, under COGSA, the carrier's duty to exercise due diligence in making the vessel seaworthy is nondelegable. It concluded that the ship was not reasonably fit to perform the work at hand—shipping steel coils—because the hatches were not maintained in good condition and had not been tested for watertightness before embarkation, which had resulted in an ingress of seawater during the voyage, and because the holds, which had previously carried a cargo of rock salt, had not been washed out with fresh water before the steel was loaded.

That the hatches were insufficiently maintained is further supported by the observations of the Seaspan Marine Consultants surveyor who inspected the hatches after the vessel docked in Camden. He noted that the rubber gaskets of the hatch panels had deep grooves in them, were worn out in several places, were heavily rusted and bent or waved in certain areas, and that parts of the gaskets were missing or cut in some places.

The vessel interests also argue that they were not responsible for conducting a watertightness test on the hatch covers prior to embarkation because pursuant to the voyage charter Itochu was supposed to "make an inspection of holds and test watertightness of hatches." This argument ignores the COGSA carrier's nondelegable duty to ensure that the vessel is reasonably fit to carry steel cargo.

In *Jamaica Nutrition Holdings, Ltd. v. United Shipping Co., Ltd.*, we rejected a similar argument.[17] There the trial court had found the defendant carrier liable for failing to adequately clean out the pipes of the vessel before loading its cargo of soybean oil. The ship's previous cargo had been molasses. Prior to loading the oil, a surveyor had visually inspected the ship's pipes and tanks and determined that they were suitable for carrying the oil. After the ship reached its destination, another surveyor examined the oil and found it contaminated with molasses. Based on this evidence, the district court concluded

---

15. 46 U.S.C. §[30701 hist. n. §4].
16. *See Farrell Lines, Inc. v. Jones,* 530 F.2d 10 n.2 (5th Cir. 1976).
17. 643 F.2d 376 (5th Cir. 1981).

that the defendant's failure to clean adequately the vessel's tanks, pipes, and pumps rendered the vessel unseaworthy.

On appeal, the defendant argued it should escape liability because the voyage charter party provided: "Vessel to clean tanks, lines and pumps *to Charterer's surveyor's satisfaction.*" It contended that because the charterer's surveyor had inspected the vessel's tanks and found them suitable, the carrier's obligation to the shipper was fulfilled. However, we concluded otherwise, reasoning:

> COGSA, whether applicable by its own force or by virtue of the clause paramount, imposed a nondelegable duty on [the carrier] to exercise due diligence to make the vessel fit for carriage of the cargo shipment. This duty was not abrogated by its covenant also to clean the vessel to the charterer's satisfaction. By permitting molasses residue to remain in the system, [the carrier] violated its duty.[18]

Because the duty to exercise due diligence to ensure the seaworthiness of a vessel is nondelegable, the district court here did not reversibly err in concluding that the vessel interests failed to exercise due diligence in part because they did not test the watertightness of the hatches.

C.

The vessel interests contend that even if the district court's finding on due diligence can be sustained, the coils became damaged due to causes for which COGSA liability is excepted.

1. peril at sea ?

Under §1304(2) of COGSA, "[n]either the carrier nor the ship shall be responsible for loss or damage arising or resulting from . . . [p]erils, dangers, and accidents of the sea or other navigable waters." At trial the defendants argued that a storm encountered by the M/V LAKE MARION on its transatlantic voyage constituted a "peril of the sea" and caused the saltwater to enter the holds. The ship's captain testified that he encountered very rough weather during the journey, with strong winds that occasionally reached Beaufort Scale Force 10 and, at their peak, reached force 11 to 12 for approximately two hours on March 26.

The trial judge rejected the peril of the sea defense for two reasons. First, such weather conditions were foreseeable in the North Atlantic during the late winter months. Second, no damage to the vessel resulted from the voyage, and the only conditions noted in the surveys at the discharge ports indicated preexisting damage as a result of prolonged neglect.

We sustain the district court's refusal to find the rough weather encountered by the M/V LAKE MARION to have been a peril of the sea given the ship's lack of injury. We cannot conclude on this record that the noted storm, even with its force 12 winds, constituted a peril "of an extraordinary nature or aris[ing] from irresistible force or overwhelming power" which could not "be guarded against by the ordinary exertions of human skill and prudence."[19]

---

18. *Id.* at 379.
19. *J. Gerber & Co.*, 437 F.2d at 588.

2. Latent Defect?

The vessel interests also urge another exception to COGSA liability. COGSA exempts any damage caused by "[l]atent defects not discoverable by due diligence."[20] Defendants argued at trial that a crack found in Hold No. 1 while the vessel was docked in New Orleans, which ruined 123 coils in that hold, was a latent defect that could not have been discovered through due diligence. The trial judge rejected the contention that the fracture was a latent defect.

"A true latent defect is a flaw in the metal and is not caused by the use of the metallic object" or by "gradual deterioration."[21] Such a defect "is one that could not be discovered by any known and customary test."[22] The ship owner has the burden to demonstrate that the defect was not discoverable.

The vessel interests posit that since a latent defect is one not discoverable in the ordinary course of surveys or inspections, and the M/V LAKE MARION's holds were inspected during the loading process, the crack was by definition a latent defect. However, Marine surveyor Captain Rasaretnam inspected the crack and determined that it was old, and had existed in some form since crews installed a doubling plate at the fracture site. The district court concluded that the crack was an extension of an old crack, and at least part of it had been present since the doubling plate had been put in place. Moreover, Captain Sparks hypothesized that the crack was caused by gradual deterioration, not by a defect in the metal. We cannot conclude that the district court clearly erred in finding that the fracture was old and in rejecting the latent defect defense.

V.

In addition to its COGSA claims, Steel Coils asserted a general maritime negligence claim against Lake Marion, Inc.'s managing agent, Bay Ocean. The claim is that Bay Ocean, as vessel manager, hired the crew and was responsible for maintaining the vessel's condition, and that it was negligent in maintaining and testing the hatch covers, failing to repair the crack in Hold No. 1, and in washing the holds with seawater. Bay Ocean contended at trial that Steel Coils could not assert a negligence claim against it outside of COGSA.

The district court disagreed, holding Bay Ocean liable in tort for its negligence separate from the COGSA claim, and finding Bay Ocean liable for the entire amount requested by Steel Coils because Bay Ocean was not entitled to claim the $500-per-package limitation on liability found in COGSA. These are conclusions of law and we conduct a *de novo* review.

"One of COGSA's most important provisions limits a [vessel or] carrier's liability to five hundred dollars . . . per package unless a higher value is declared by the shipper."[23] The term "carrier" includes "the owner or the charterer who enters into a contract of carriage with a shipper."[24] We have held that as long as an entity is a party to the con-

---

20. 46 U.S.C. App. §1304(2)(p).

21. *Waterman S.S. v. U.S. Smelting Ref. & Mining Co.*, 155 F.2d 687, 691 (5th Cir. 1946).

22. *Id.*

23. *Mannesman Demag Corp. v. M/V Concert Express*, 225 F.3d 587, 589 (5th Cir. 2000); *see* 46 U.S.C. App. §1304(5).

24. §1301(a).

tract of carriage, it is a carrier. In *Sabah Shipyard Sdn. Bhd. v. M/V Harbel Tapper,*[25] we stated, "[t]o determine whether a party is a COGSA carrier, we have followed COGSA's plain language, focusing on whether the party entered into a contract of carriage with a shipper. . . . [A] party is considered a carrier under COGSA if that party 'executed a contract of carriage.'"[26]

It is undisputed that Bay Ocean is not explicitly named in the applicable contract of carriage, the voyage charter between Western Bulk and Itochu.

Bay Ocean argues that even if it is nothing more than an agent of the carrier it may avoid liability altogether on Steel Coils's separate negligence claim because COGSA is the exclusive remedy for suits for damage to cargo. However, in a similar case, *Citrus Marketing Board of Israel v. J. Lauritzen A/S,*[27] the Second Circuit held that a plaintiff may sue a ship's manager in tort for damage to cargo and that COGSA does not govern such an action. The *Citrus Marketing* court rejected the manager's argument and the district court's holding that COGSA controlled the claim, explaining that COGSA only applied to disputes between shippers and carriers.[28] It explained, however, that a Himalaya Clause, which extends a carrier's rights under COGSA to agents of the carrier, might apply to save the manager from liability and remanded that issue for the district court to consider at trial.

Bay Ocean charges that the district court's ruling that Bay Ocean cannot take advantage of the $500-per-package limitation "ignores the reality of maritime commerce," because it is common for one-vessel corporations such as Lake Marion, Inc., who have no employees, to act solely through their managing agents. It also argues that this result will "allow shippers to circumvent not only the package limitation, but all of COGSA, when contracting with a vessel with a separate managing agent." However, Bay Ocean chose to separate itself from Lake Marion by binding only Lake Marion to the time charter. In doing so Bay Ocean chose that only Lake Marion would become a carrier for purposes of COGSA.[29]

We agree with the Second Circuit that a noncarrier can be held liable in tort outside of COGSA. Steel Coils's negligence action against Bay Ocean was not subject to the COGSA package limitation.

VI.

For these reasons, we affirm the district court's judgment.

NOTES AND QUESTIONS

1. State the allocation of burdens of proof under COGSA. A feature of this law is that there is a list of causes of loss for which the carrier is not liable. The two most important exceptions to carrier liability are losses caused by perils of the seas and losses caused by negligent navigation of the ship. What is the purpose of these exclusions?

---

25. 178 F.3d 400 (5th Cir. 1999).
26. *Id.* at 405.
27. 943 F.2d 220 (2d Cir. 1991).
28. *Id.* at 222.
29. Bay Ocean also ignores the availability of a Himalaya Clause.

2. In *Steel Coils*, the principal case above, there were four defendants. How many of these defendants were entitled to claim the COGSA $500 per package limitation and why? The plaintiff Steel Coils recovered a total judgment of $505,358.64 in the district court. What is the effect of the $500 per package or customary freight unit limitation on the plaintiff's ability to collect the full amount of this judgment? Which of the defendants is Steel Coils likely to pursue to satisfy the judgment?

3. Marine Insurance

Marine cargo insurance covers physical damage and loss of goods while in transit by land, sea, or air. Whenever goods are lost or damaged and the owner of the goods suffers a loss, fails to realize an expected profit, or incurs liability from the loss or damage, the owner is deemed to have an insurable interest in the goods. Litigation concerning a marine insurance contract (but not other types of insurance contracts) is deemed to invoke federal admiralty jurisdiction under 28 U.S.C. §1333 (2006).

American National Fire Insurance Co. v. Mirasco, Inc.
United States District Court, Southern District of New York, 2003
249 F. Supp. 2d 303

SWEET, District Judge.

[American National Fire Insurance Co. (American National) and Great American Insurance Co. (Great American) (collectively the Insurers) and Mirasco, Inc. (Mirasco), have cross-moved for summary judgment on issues regarding coverage under an ocean marine transportation policy.]

DECREE 465

On November 22, 1997, the Egyptian Government issued Decree 465, which, according to a translation provided by the Insurers, provided in part:

B) packets in which products must be firmly closed and healthy authorized. Moreover, the following information must be written, in a fixed unerasable material, on a card put inside the packet and also written outside it in [A]rabic (it might be written in two languages if [A]rabic is one):

>   its Certificate of Origin

>   product name and trade mark if exist[ing]

>   Importers' name and address

>   the authority which supervised the slay to [I]slamic sharia should be accredited by the trade office in the Certificate of Origin

>   slaughter house name

>   slay date.

As a result of Decree 465's labeling requirements, Mirasco marked all shipments with "Mirasco Misr" ("Misr"), one of Mirasco's largest customers, as the importer, even though a portion of the shipments was set aside for other customers. Misr would receive the product, clear it and turn over to Mirasco's other customers their portion of the shipment. Misr is a proprietorship organized under the laws of the nation of Egypt and maintains its principal place of business in Alexandria, Egypt. The Insurers claim, and Mirasco disputes, that Misr is controlled by Mirasco and used to facilitate clearing the cargo through Egyptian customs in light of Decree 465.

<h3 style="text-align:center">DECREE #6</h3>

In October 1998, the Egyptian authorities rejected a shipment of beef livers imported by Hady Enterprises and produced by one of Mirasco's suppliers, Iowa Beef Products ("IBP"), due to purported labeling irregularities in violation of Decree 465.

On January 3, 1999, the Egyptian government issued Decree #6 (the "Decree"). The Decree became effective on January 14, 1999, when it was officially published. According to a translation provided by the Insurers, the Decree stated that "[a]n embargo is placed on trade with the American company I.B.P. Corp in the United States of America as well as with any company with which it is associated." The Decree did not apply to cargo shipped by Mirasco's other suppliers, Excel Corporation ("Excel") or Monfort, Inc. ("Monfort").

Mirasco asserts, and the Insurers contest, that the Decree did not apply under Egyptian law to any IBP cargo that was shipped prior to January 14, 1999.

In an e-mail dated May 19, 1999, one of the Insurer's agents, Pam Kobin, the Divisional Assistant Vice-President for Specialty Claims of Great American's Cincinnati, Ohio office, stated that the decree "was not an embargo [of a ship] but it certainly was a prohibition." Although Mirasco asserts otherwise, Kobin has attested that she was not the one responsible for denying Mirasco's claim but that the decision was made by personnel of the New York Ocean Marine Business Unit.

<h3 style="text-align:center">THE BEEF LIVER SHIPMENT ON THE M/V SPERO</h3>

On December 31, 1998, stevedores hired and paid for by Mirasco completed the loading of the M/V Spero in Houston, Texas. The cargo consisted of 219,072 cartons of beef liver, including 132,535 cartons of IBP products (60.5 percent of the shipment), for which Mirasco had paid $1,081,500; 60,502 cartons of Excel products (27.6 percent of the shipment), for which Mirasco had paid $562,570.21; and 26,035 cartons of Monfort products (11.9 percent of the shipment), for which Mirasco had paid $285,450. The brands were not strictly segregated into different holds or hatches; instead, while Mirasco attempted not to break up lots of the same product, lots from different brands were stored together. The cartons of frozen beef liver were hard frozen and in apparently sound condition at the time of loading aboard the M/V Spero. In addition, the shipment was packed and labeled solely for Misr, but was to be sold to five customers, including Misr, upon the shipment's importation into Egypt.

After loading the cargo aboard M/V Spero in Houston, Mirasco obtained fifteen (15) bills of lading for carriage of the cargo to Alexandria, Egypt. Eight (8) bills of lading covered the IBP cargo, and seven (7) bills of lading covered the Monfort and Excel cargo.

The M/V Spero arrived in Alexandria on January 23, 1999. Yossif El Menoufy ("El Menoufy"), a representative of Sea Horse International ("Sea Horse"), which had been hired by the Insurers to investigate and report on the shipment, was present when the M/V Spero arrived and observed the later inspection of the Spero.

As discussed above, Decree #6 had gone into effect after the M/V Spero's departure but prior to the M/V Spero's arrival. Thus Mirasco then unsuccessfully attempted to convince the Egyptian authorities that the IBP cargo of the M/V Spero should be exempted from the Decree because the shipment sailed prior to the issuance thereof.

THE RETURN OF THE SHIPMENT

The M/V Spero sailed from Alexandria on March 26, 1999, with all cargo still aboard. The cargo was otherwise found in sound condition except for 387 cartons that thawed during the return trip due to stowage too close to heated fuel tanks. These cartons were destroyed, and the Insurers paid for them in the amount of $6,164 after the commencement of this lawsuit.

Mirasco marketed the rest of the rejected cargo to traders and buyers. The cargo was sold in the United States in May, June and July of 1999. Because the market had been steadily falling since August of 1998, the prices received by Mirasco for the M/V Spero cargo ranged as low as $0.115 per pound although the cargo had been purchased back in the fall of 1998 for as much as $0.34 per pound.

THERE IS NO DISPUTE OF MATERIAL FACT THAT THE EGYPTIAN AUTHORITIES REJECTED THE CARGO

The Insurers argue that the cargo was not rejected by the Egyptian authorities pursuant to the terms of the Policy. This question requires an analysis of the term "rejection" as used in the Policy.

As an initial matter, the Insurers do not appear to contest that the 60.5 percent of the shipment that was IBP brand was rejected and/or condemned as those words are defined under the policy because of Decree #6 and based on the fact that the inspectors never even sampled the IBP products. Indeed, the Insurers provided return freight as provided for by Clause D of the Rejection Coverage even though Mirasco did not present any Notices of Rejection or any other formal papers attesting to the fact that the cargo was rejected due to Decree #6.

This fact therefore contradicts the Insurers' contentions that "rejection" under the Policy is defined by custom and usage by the Egyptian government as requiring a Final Rejection Certificate after sampling and testing and adverse lab results, and an unsuccessful appeal. The Insurers did not require any such documents and appeal before sending return freight on the goods it claimed were embargoed. Indeed, this restrictive definition would mean that coverage would not exist if a governmental authority arbitrarily (1) refused to sample and/or test the cargo; (2) declined to permit and/or decide an appeal; or (3) did not issue "final rejection certificates." As Mirasco points out, such restrictive definition would undermine the purpose of rejection insurance, which is a type of political risks insurance that insures against the arbitrary acts of a government, including arbitrary rejection or detention or miscarriage of administrative determination.

The Insurers' unsupported allegations that the customs documents and [Misr's] testimony cannot be trusted or should not be construed to support a finding of rejection are insufficient to raise a material issue of fact. Similarly, the fact that Mirasco was originally given the opportunity to discharge 10 percent of the cargo per day to segregate the mislabeled cargo does not mean the cargo was not rejected, as discharge does not mean that the goods were accepted for import.

As a result, there is no genuine dispute of material fact that the M/V Spero cargo was rejected by the Egyptian authorities as that term is defined in the Policy.

SUMMARY JUDGMENT MAY BE GRANTED TO THE INSURERS IN PART BASED ON THE EXCLUSIONS

The Insurers contend that even if the cargo was rejected as that term is defined in the Policy, Mirasco is not entitled to coverage because of exclusions to the Rejection Coverage, including an exclusion (1) for loss of market as to all goods, (2) for recovery for anything but return freight due to an embargo announced after a shipment has set sail, as against the IBP cargo, and (3) of mislabeling as against the Excel and Monfort cargoes. Each will be addressed in turn.

A. THE LOSS OF MARKET EXCLUSION DOES NOT APPLY

The Insurers point out that Mirasco was able to sell its cargo once it returned to the United States, albeit for drastically lower prices than they would have received in Egypt due to the collapse of the market for beef livers. As a result, they claim that the Policy's loss of market exclusion applies. Mirasco replies that what occurred in this case was loss of market value, rather than loss of market.

Both parties rely on the same case arising in the Tenth Circuit Court of Appeals, *Boyd Motors, Inc. v. Employers Ins. of Wausau*, 880 F.2d 270 (10th Cir. 1989). *Boyd* involved an action to recover under a commercial inland marine policy, which included a "loss of market" exclusion, due to diminished value of automobiles damaged by hail. *Id.* at 271. The plaintiff had already received reimbursement for the cost of repairing the automobiles, and sought in this action an additional $40,609.48 based on its claim that the vehicles were worth less after the damage. *Id.* The district court had held that "the diminution [in] value which occurs after an accident, despite repairs, clearly is defined as loss in market." *Id.* at 273. The Tenth Circuit disagreed, stating that the above situation involved loss of market value, rather than loss of market, and that recovery was not precluded by the exclusion. In reaching this conclusion, the court discussed the two concepts of loss of market and loss of market value:

> "[M]arket" refers collectively to matters external to any particular product item, namely those conditions that determine the degree to which supply of that commodity exceeds or falls short of demand, whereas "market value" is a function of the qualities (*e.g.*, age, state of repair) inherent in the individual item itself, and refers to that price that that specific article with those qualities would command in a given market. Thus, . . . a market is lost when, for example, due to delay in distribution, changes in consumer habits, etc., a certain type of product is no longer in demand with its intended purchasers, while what is involved in the present case, in which particular merchandise in Boyd's inventory has allegedly suffered depreciation due to physical alteration (damage and restoration), is a loss of market value.

Id. at 273.

The discussion of "loss of market" above suggests that the loss must occur in the original market for which the goods are intended.

There is no evidence that Mirasco lost its customers in Egypt who had already agreed to purchase a good portion of the beef livers on the M/V Spero. As a result, and in the absence of any legal showing to the contrary from the Insurers, the loss of market exclusion does not apply and the Insurers' motion for summary judgment on this ground is denied.

B. THE IBP CARGO WAS REJECTED AS A RESULT OF AN "EMBARGO," AND THUS MIRASCO IS ENTITLED ONLY TO RETURN FREIGHT

The Policy explicitly provides that no claim may attach under Rejection Coverage "[i]n the event of any embargo or prohibition being declared or in being by importing country," except that return freight is provided where the embargo is announced or enforced after shipments have sailed. Rejection Coverage, Clause D. Decree #6 was announced after the beef liver shipment had sailed. Therefore, if Decree #6 is an "embargo or prohibition" under the Policy, the Insurers are only responsible for paying the return freight of $400,000, which they have already paid.

There is nothing in Clause D to suggest that the term "embargo" is ambiguous. Therefore, the Court will look to the ordinary meaning of the term. According to the United States Supreme Court, "the ordinary meaning of 'embargo' . . . is a governmentally imposed quantitative restriction—of zero—on the importation of merchandise." *K-mart Corp. v. Cartier*, 485 U.S. 176, 185 (1988).

K mart provided examples of other embargoes imposed by the United States, and referred not only to the embargo on Cuba, 22 U.S.C. §2370(a), but also to a number of "embargoes" imposed against general types of products. *Id.* at 184, 108 S. Ct. at 957 (*citing* 21 U.S.C. §381 (embargo against adulterated, misbranded or unapproved foods, drugs and cosmetics)); 15 U.S.C. §1397 (embargo against motor vehicles that do not conform to federal safety standards); 19 U.S.C. §1305 (embargo against obscene pictures, lottery tickets and articles for causing unlawful abortion); 15 U.S.C. §1241–44 (embargo on switchblade knives); and 19 C.F.R. §12.60 (1987) (embargo on fur-seal or sea-otter skins)).

It is true that the above examples involve embargoes against specific products or groups of products, rather than against products of a particular manufacturer. The definition of "embargo" should nonetheless cover this situation, as Egypt has imposed in Decree #6 "a quantitative restriction of zero" on the importation of IBP products.

As a result, the ban on all IBP products in Decree #6 constitutes an embargo or prohibition pursuant to Clause D, and the embargo or prohibition was the cause of the rejection of the goods. As a result, Mirasco is only entitled to the return freight for the IBP products, which constitute 60.5 percent of the claim. Because the Insurers have already provided such return freight, they are entitled to judgment on their claims with regard to the IBP products, and Mirasco's cross-motion for summary judgment is denied inasmuch as it relates to the IBP products.

C. THE EXCEL AND MONFORT CARGO

As an initial matter, there is no dispute that some percentage of the Excel and Monfort Cargo was rejected solely for mislabeling and thus falls under the exclusion in Clause C, Part 5. What is disputed, however, is exactly how much of the cargo falls under this exclusion. Mirasco contends that the correct percentage is represented by the settlements it reached with Excel and Monfort. The Insurers, relying on Mirasco's initial claims for complete remuneration from Excel and Monfort, assert that all of the Excel and Monfort cargo was mislabeled. Given this dispute, it can only be concluded at this time that at least as much of the cargo was mislabeled as was represented in the Excel and Monfort settlements—and potentially more.

What remains is the portion of the cargo that was purportedly rejected for either health and sanitary discrepancies alone or for mislabeling and health and sanitary violations. In seeking summary judgment against these claims, the Insurers assert that Mirasco chose to ship back the cargo after discovering it was rejected on the ground of noncovered events—Decree #6 and mislabeling—and therefore that any rejection on the basis of health was not the proximate cause of Mirasco's losses.

The Insurers have failed to establish that there is a dispute of material fact with regard to whether Mirasco's losses were proximately caused, at least in part, by events covered by the Policy. As a result, the Insurers' motion for summary judgment is denied. Mirasco's motion for summary judgment is denied because an issue of fact remains as to what portion of the Excel and Monfort cargo, if any, was rejected on grounds covered by the Policy.

SUE AND LABOR CLAUSE

For the first time in their reply papers, the Insurers have raised the defense that Mirasco failed to comply with Clause 34 of the Policy, the "sue and labor" clause, which states:

> In case of any imminent or actual loss or misfortune, it shall be lawful and necessary to and for The Insured, his or their factors, servants and assigns, to sue, labor and travel for, in and about the defense; safeguard and recovery of the said goods and merchandise, or any part thereof, without prejudice to this insurance. . . .

"When a policy contains a sue and labor clause, an insurer may be able to argue that the insured has forfeited its coverage if it does not sue and labor to minimize the covered loss." *International Commodities Export Corp. v. American Home Assurance Co.*, 701 F. Supp. 448, 452 (S.D.N.Y. 1988).

The Insurers claim that Mirasco should have unloaded the cargo at the permitted 10 percent-per-day rate and segregated the mislabeled Excel and Monfort goods from the correctly labeled goods. Thus, they argue, the correctly labeled goods could have been sold. There is no factual basis for the claim, however, that the goods could have been sold if they were, in fact, discharged and segregated.

Indeed, Mirasco contends that it did not begin unloading because it was awaiting the lab results from the inspectors and because of the general attitude of the Egyptian authorities, leading Mirasco to believe that even if it did segregate the correctly labeled cargo, the Egyptian authorities would find another reason to reject it. In addition, Mirasco contends (and the Insurers dispute) that the Insurers, through Sea Horse, ordered Mirasco to ship the cargo back to the United States and thus was obligated to follow that directive.

[The insurers'] motion for summary judgment is denied.

NOTES AND QUESTIONS

1. Marine cargo insurance covers the physical damage and loss of goods while they are in transit. Marine cargo insurance is usually purchased through a broker. The policy of insurance works on the basis of the principles of (1) indemnity; (2) insurable interest; and (3) utmost good faith. Indemnity means that to compensate for the loss or damage to the goods, the value is agreed between the assured and the insurer and this is the basis for any payment due the assured. Insurable interest means that payment will be made only to the party having title or the risk of loss. Utmost good faith means that the parties to the insurance contract owe each other full disclosure of all material facts. *See generally* Thomas J. Schoenbaum, *Key Divergences Between English and American Law of Marine Insurance* (1999).

There are a variety of insurance products that can be purchased to safeguard an international sale of goods. The most comprehensive is "all risks" insurance for which, of course, a higher premium must be paid. In the event of loss or damage, the owner of the goods, usually the buyer, is paid the insured value, and the insurer is subrogated to any claim against the carrier. The insurer can proceed against the carrier, standing in the shoes of the insured.

2. The law of marine insurance is remarkably uniform over much of the world. This is because of the influence of London underwriters that still dominate the market and the remarkable codification of English law, the Marine Insurance Act of 1906, Edw. 7, Ch. 41. Versions of this law have been enacted in most countries. Because of the high risks of the insurance industry and the possibility of fraud, English law long ago established the basic principle of the duty of absolute good faith on the part of the parties to the insurance contract.

3. Standard forms of cargo insurance are provided by the Institute Cargo Clauses of the Institute of London Underwriters. These Institute Clauses provide three alternative sets of forms—A, B, and C—which define the risks covered and the losses for which cover is excluded. Clause A provides the most extensive, "all risks" cover. Clause B is intermediate, and Clause C provides the least cover—only loss or damage reasonably attributable to fire, explosion, collision, jettison or general average, that is, intentional loss of cargo when necessary to save the ship. It must be emphasized that there are many exclusions even for "all risks" cover. The importer may want to insist on additional cover, for example, the Institute War Clauses or the Strikes, Riots, and Civil Commotions Clause. What was the cover in the principal case? When is such cover a good idea? Who decides on the extent of cover?

4. The law of marine insurance has never been codified in the United States. However, the basic substantive law of marine insurance is federal maritime law, which is derived from English law. In the absence of a controlling federal admiralty law principle, courts must apply applicable state law. *See Wilburn Boat Co. v. Fireman's Fund Ins. Co.*, 348 U.S. 310, *reh'g denied*, 349 U.S. 907 (1955).

5. *North American Foreign Trading Corp. v. Mitsui Sumitomo Insurance USA, Inc.*, 499 F. Supp. 2d 361 (S.D.N.Y. 2007), involved a claimed breach of a marine insurance policy. The plaintiff, North American, sued Mitsui to recover a loss incurred when some consumer electronics goods mysteriously disappeared from a warehouse in the southern city of Shenzhen, China. The All-risks, Open Cargo Policy issued by Mitsui contained an endorsement providing warehouse cover. The missing goods were never found and no explanation was advanced for their disappearance. Mitsui denied coverage on the ground that "the involved loss was not due to any insured peril under the policy." *Id.* at 372. The federal district court applied New York law because the policy was issued

there and because North American was a New York corporation. Under New York law the parties to an insurance contract owe each other a duty of absolute good faith (the federal admiralty law rule), but the court ruled that under state law this doctrine extends only to what is reasonable under the circumstances. The court also ruled that New York law requires ambiguities in an insurance contract to be construed against the insurer. Applying these principles, the court ruled in favor of North American:

> To prove that an all-risk policy covers its claim, the insured has the burden of demonstrating (1) the existence of an all-risk policy, (2) an insurable interest, and (3) the fortuitous loss of the covered property. The insured need not prove the cause of the loss. Absent an exclusion for mysterious disappearance, all-risk policies cover the mysterious disappearance or fortuitous loss of the goods insured. Under an all-risk policy, the insurer has the burden of putting forward evidence establishing that an exception to coverage applies.

499 F. Supp. 2d at 374. Was the court correct in applying New York law? Do you agree with the ruling?

PROBLEM 2-9

Medtech exports medical equipment to its Russian subsidiary company. Medtech procures an "all risks" cargo insurance policy. At the time the premium is paid, Medtech is aware of unrest in St. Petersburg, the port of destination, but this information was not disclosed to the insurer, American Northern Insurance Co. (ANI). When the cargo arrived, it was confiscated by the port authorities on a pretext and sold. ANI has since discovered Medtech's nondisclosure. Can ANI refuse to cover the loss and, if so, on what grounds? What law applies to this controversy? Even if Medtech was acting in good faith, does an "all risks" policy cover this type of loss?

II.   *The International Sales Contract and International Trade Law Considerations*

In addition to the private law aspects that must be dealt with in an international sales transaction, there are public law questions. Although these complex issues merit detailed treatment in a separate course, we briefly cover the salient points here. For detailed coverage of these public law issues, see Chow and Schoenbaum, *International Trade Law: Problems, Cases, and Materials* (Aspen 2d ed. 2012).

An international sale of goods is both an export from the country of the seller and an import into the country of the buyer. Thus, in the country of the seller, applicable laws concerning exports are relevant and must be observed. Most countries encourage exports since they improve their international balance of payments, create jobs, and cause an inflow of foreign exchange. Accordingly, in most cases, export regulations are not a concern. However, if politically sensitive products, such as goods that can be used for military purposes, are the subject of the transaction, export controls can come into play. Moreover, some countries, most notably the United States, have additional laws that concern exports based on political and foreign policy concerns. The United States also enforces antiboycott laws and regulations against foreign corrupt practices and economic espionage that may apply to exports. In the problems and readings below, we focus first on U.S. regulation of exports. In a following section, we turn to the more complex issue of U.S. regulation of imported goods.

A. Export Trade Matters

PROBLEM 2-10

Apex is a company located in northern Virginia and incorporated in Delaware. Apex has developed an extensive line of software products with business applications ranging from automated systems recovery of lost data to computer models that predict severe weather occurrences. Some of these products are used by the United States Coast Guard. Apex is investigating opportunities to sell its products internationally through foreign distributors located in various countries.

A distributor located in a Middle Eastern country says that to market in that country Apex will have to provide assurances that it does not presently do business with the state of Israel. Apex, in fact, has never sold its products in Israel and is considering writing a letter to the distributor to explain this.

Certain distributors located in the European Union tell Apex that sales will be easy to make if no restrictions are placed on the possible resale of the software so that the purchasers are not necessarily the ultimate customers for the products.

Advise Apex as to the legal problems that may arise with regard to its export plans.

PROBLEM 2-11

Universal Electronics (UE) is a large diversified U.S. company with interests in financial services and heavy industry. UE has just been approached by the Cuban government and has been offered a multi-billion-dollar contract to sell oil refinery services to Cuba. Concerned about accepting such a contract, UE has suggested to the Cuban government that it hire its affiliate, Universal Electronics-Indonesia, to perform the contract. UE has no ownership interest in UE-Indonesia but several of the directors of the board of UE-Indonesia are also directors of UE.

In discussing the transaction, an executive of UE living in the United States calls a director of UE-Indonesia living in Indonesia and discusses several UE trade secrets and proprietary know-how of UE, the U.S. company.

What legal issues are involved?

PROBLEM 2-12

Microtel, a leading U.S. computer manufacturer and software developer, has just hired a senior vice president from its arch rival, Zurich Systems, based in Switzerland. The senior executive has been intimately involved in Zurich's product development and marketing strategies for its bold new operating system for the European Union. Microtel is elated because it also wishes to sell its products in the EU. Should Microtel have any concerns?

For Problems 2-10 through 2-12, consult the following discussion.

U.S. Regulation of Exports: The Export Administration Act,
The Office of Foreign Assets Control, Antiboycott Laws,
The Economic Espionage Act, and The Foreign
Corrupt Practices Act

The United States government, like other governments, seeks to encourage exports of goods (and other forms of trade such as technology (intellectual property)); nevertheless, U.S. law also extensively regulates exports and exporting. The purpose of this note is to present an overview of U.S. export regulations with a focus on the export of goods.

The U.S. Department of Commerce maintains an extensive network of regional offices designed to help businesses seeking to export their products. These U.S. Export Assistance Centers can be accessed by visiting the web site *http://www.sba.gov.* These offices provide advice on exporting, and loans to finance exports may be available to small businesses.

1. U.S. EXPORT CLEARANCE PROCEDURES

Before a business exports goods from the United States, the exporter must first submit a "Shipper's Export Declaration" (SED) to the U.S. government. *See* 15 C.F.R. pt. 30 (2014). The purpose of this requirement is twofold: SEDs (1) are the means by which the United States compiles statistics on exports; and (2) allow the U.S. government to enforce the various export control laws. The exporter must first register and obtain an export identification number (EIN); and a SED must be filed for each export over $2,500 in value. These filings may be done electronically on the Automated Export System (AES) web site of the U.S. Census Bureau (AESDirect, *http://www.census.gov/foreign-trade/aes/index/html*). Errors in the preparation of an SED can result in monetary penalties of up to $10,000 per transaction.

2. U.S. EXPORT CONTROL LAWS

U.S. export controls can be divided in two categories: (1) property-based controls that focus on the good or technology that is being exported, and (2) person-based controls that limit the country or persons to whom a good can be exported. We consider these two regimes in turn.

(A) PROPERTY-BASED CONTROLS

U.S. Export controls that focus on the goods or technology being exported are authorized under several important acts.

The Export Administration Act (EAA) of 1979 (current version at 50 U.S.C. app. §§2401–2420 (2006)), as extended and continued in effect by executive orders under the International Emergency Economic Powers Act, 50 U.S.C. §1701 *et seq.* (2006). The EAA is the foundation for export controls that relate to exports of goods and technology administered by the Bureau of Industry and Security (BIS) (web site: *http://www.bis.gov*) of the U.S. Department of Commerce through the Export Administration Regulations (EAR). 15 C.F.R. pts. 732–774 (2014). Certain specialized areas of the EAR are administered by other U.S. agencies, the Department of Energy and the Nuclear Regulatory Commission.

The EAR controls industrial and consumer goods, particularly those which may have "dual use": both civilian and military application. To identify EAR controlled goods, the exporter must consult the Commodity Control List (CCL) maintained by BIS. The CCL controls the following categories of goods: nuclear; certain materials, chemicals, microorganisms and toxins; materials processing technology; electronics; computers; telecommunications; information security; sensors and lasers; navigation and avionics equipment and technology; marine equipment and technology; and aerospace and propulsion technology. These goods and technology may not be exported without obtaining an export license issued by the U.S. Department of Commerce. Exports not on the CCL fall under EAR99 and generally may be exported without a license. Licensing guidance may be found in the EAR, at 15 C.F.R. pt. 732 (2014). The EAR controls exports of goods and technology as well as exports to certain countries (see below) and persons (see also below) on the Specially Designated Nationals (SDNs) and Blocked Persons List.

The jurisdictional reach of the EAR controls is very broad. The property-based controls apply to exports of goods or technology (intellectual property) from the United States to any country (with certain exceptions to Canada) as well as to *re-exports* of U.S. origin products from one foreign country to another. The controls include "deemed exports"— transfer of goods or technology to foreign nationals in the United States. For example, giving access to a proprietary technology or know-how to a foreign national living in the United States (even if the disclosure is oral only such as through the verbal disclosure of a trade secret) is a deemed export (whereas an oral disclosure via telephone to a foreign national in a foreign country is a direct export). Even foreign-produced goods and technology that has entered U.S. customs territory come under the jurisdiction of EAR and can be exported from the United States only by complying with the EAR.

The re-export prohibition means that the EAR prohibits not only direct exports from the United States, but also no person may re-export goods or technology received from the United States to any third country unless specifically authorized to do so. For example, if a U.S. exporter obtains a license and exports a product to France, the French importer cannot re-export the product to a third country without first complying with the EAR. Moreover, a U.S. exporter may not transfer goods or technology from the United States if it knows that the items will be re-exported directly or indirectly in whole or in part. Thus, by reason of the re-export rules, companies and individuals around the world, whether U.S. or foreign, are subject to the EAR to the extent they deal with goods or technology that are subject to the rules.

(B) PERSON-BASED CONTROLS

Person- and country-based export controls are administered principally by the U.S. Department of the Treasury, Office of Foreign Assets Control (OFAC) under the authority of the Trading with the Enemy Act, 50 U.S.C. app. §1 *et seq.* and the International Emergency Economic Powers Act, 50 U.S.C. §1701 *et seq.* Various additional sanctions laws apply financial and trade sanctions to various foreign countries. Trade and investment embargoes are maintained against persons on the Specially Designated Nationals List as well as against various countries: Belarus, Ivory Coast, Cuba, Iran, Somalia, Sudan, Yemen, Libya, Lebanon, Zimbabwe, Myanmar, North Korea, Syria, and Iraq. Trade restrictions are also applied under various programs: counter narcotics trafficking; counter terrorism; rough diamond trade controls; non-proliferation trade controls; and the western Balkans stabilization program. (For information, see *http://treasury.gov/offices/enforcement/*

ofac/programs.) OFAC also is responsible for blocking U.S. controlled assets of various foreign governments and persons on the control list.

The jurisdictional reach of these sanctions programs includes all individuals subject to U.S. jurisdiction as well as U.S. companies, their foreign branches, and U.S. companies that are subsidiaries of foreign companies. They apply to U.S. citizens and residents living and working abroad; thus, a U.S. citizen who is the director of a foreign company would be barred from voting to approve any transaction with an embargoed person or country. Certain of the sanctions programs, such as those involving North Korea, Iran, and Cuba, jurisdictionally reach foreign business entities that are owned or "controlled" by U.S. companies or individuals. Ownership arises when a foreign entity is majority-owned or wholly-owned by a cover U.S. person. The term "control" is not otherwise defined, but "control" can arise where a U.S. company has the authority to control the management or board of directors of a foreign company or can otherwise exercise managerial control over the foreign company. The persons- and country-based controls contain prohibitions against evasion, which prevent, for example, a covered person from restructuring a transaction with a targeted country (such as by assigning performance of a contract to a non-covered foreign affiliate or individual) to avoid U.S. jurisdiction. Moreover, the OFAC sanctions are construed to prohibit U.S. persons from *facilitating* in any way any transaction that would be prohibited to U.S. persons. Any exporter uncertain about the application of the export control laws to its products or technology may request a "commodity jurisdiction" (CJ) determination from BIS.

The U.S. Department of State, Office of Defense Trade Controls (ODTC), administers controls on defense articles and munitions through the International Traffic in Arms Regulations (ITAR). *See* 22 C.F.R. pt. 121 (2014). All U.S. manufacturers, exporters and brokers of regulated items must register with ODTC.

(C) EXPORT CONTROL REFORM

In August 2009, President Obama announced a broad-based review of U.S. export control laws, launching the Export Control Reform Initiative, which is being carried out in three phases: Phases I and II will clarify and reconcile the various definitions, regulations and programs, and policies, while Phase III will introduce a single control list, licensing agency, and a unified information and technology system and enforcement and coordination center.

3. ANTIBOYCOTT LAWS

The United States maintains two antiboycott laws that seek to counteract the participation of U.S. citizens and companies in other nations' economic boycotts and embargoes. These laws are (1) a 1977 amendment to the Export Administration Act and (2) the Ribicoff Amendment to the 1976 Tax Reform Act (TRA). Although both of these laws are stated in general terms, the primary application of these antiboycott laws is to counter the Arab League boycott of Israel.

The EAA antiboycott law is administered by the U.S. Department of Commerce, Office of Antiboycott Compliance. The jurisdiction of this law includes all U.S. persons in interstate or foreign commerce as well as foreign residents of the United States. Included are foreign affiliates "controlled-in-fact by U.S. companies, and U.S. citizens residing abroad (except when they are employed by non-U.S. persons)."

Conduct that is prohibited includes:

- Agreements to refuse or actual refusal to do business with or in Israel or with blacklisted companies;
- Agreements to discriminate or actual discrimination against other persons based on race, religion, sex, national origin or nationality;
- Agreements to furnish or actual furnishing of information about business relationships with or in Israel or with blacklisted companies;
- Agreements to furnish or actual furnishing of information about the race, religion, sex, or national origin of another person;
- Implementing letters of credit containing prohibited boycott terms or conditions.

The EAR requires U.S. persons to report quarterly requests they have received to take any action to comply with or to further any foreign boycott. Violations are subject to a full range of administrative, civil, and criminal penalties. Acts of omission (failing to report requests to violate the EAR antiboycott or solicitations of information that violate the law) are considered to be violations. The maximum civil fine is $10,000 per violation. If a single letter provided five pieces of prohibited information, the U.S. person could be fined a maximum of $50,000.

The second antiboycott law, TRA, section 999 of the Internal Revenue Code, imposes tax penalties and requires taxpayers to report "operations" relating to boycotting countries and requests received to further boycotts. TRA violations may cause the loss of foreign tax credits by U.S. taxpayers.

4. THE ECONOMIC ESPIONAGE ACT

The Economic Espionage Act (EEA) of 1996, 18 U.S.C. §§1831–1839, was enacted to counteract the theft of trade secrets from U.S. companies by foreign governments and competitors, including U.S. companies and individuals. Given the growing importance of trade secrets and their theft in international business, the United States decided to enact a federal law, the EEA, instead of relying on state trade secret law. Section 1832 of the EEA makes it a federal crime for any person to "convert a trade secret, that is related to or included in a product that is produced for or placed in interstate or foreign commerce, to the economic benefit of anyone other than the owner thereof, and intending or knowing that the offense will injure any owner of that trade secret" and provide an economic benefit to another person. 18 U.S.C. §1832. We want to emphasize that the EEA applies to theft of trade secrets by U.S. and foreign companies and persons and not just by foreign governments and their agents. As a result, the EEA can be used to protect a business from theft of trade secrets by its competitors. The EEA provides authority to enjoin violations as well as significant criminal and civil penalties. The EEA applies to U.S. and foreign persons in the United States as well as to conduct outside the United States by U.S. persons or organizations.

5. THE FOREIGN CORRUPT PRACTICES ACT

The Foreign Corrupt Practices Act (FCPA), 15 U.S.C. §§78dd–78oo, is one of the most important export-related laws that reach conduct of U.S. companies in foreign countries. The FCPA prohibits U.S. companies and other covered entities from paying bribes to foreign officials to obtain or retain business. The FCPA reaches any act of bribery committed by a U.S. company in any country of the world. For example, if a U.S. company makes a bribe to a foreign official in a country in Asia, Africa, or South America to order to obtain business (such as a contract to sell goods to the government), such an act may be subject to liability under the FCPA. Issues under the FCPA are so important that we devote an entire section to FCPA in Chapter Six. While FCPA issues can arise in an international sale, these issues usually arise in the foreign direct investment context covered in Chapter Six.

NOTES AND QUESTIONS

1. One of the most important tasks for the seller-exporter in the United States is to determine whether the transaction is subject to the Export Administration Regulations and whether the items being exported are subject to the Commerce Control List (CCL) or the Export Control Classification Number (ECCN). If the items are classified under the CCL or the ECCN, the exporter may be required to submit a license application and obtain an export license for the products before they can be lawfully exported. The burden is upon the exporter to see that it fully complies with the EAR. For a detailed treatment of these issues, see Chow and Schoenbaum, *International Trade Law: Problems, Cases, and Materials* 653–662 (Aspen 2d ed. 2012).

2. After the 9/11 attacks on the United States, broad anti-terrorist legislation was enacted by the U.S. Congress, including the USA Patriot Act, Pub. L. No. 107-56, 115 Stat. 272 (2001). Title III of this Act, which deals with money laundering, requires the reporting of certain types of international payments.

B. Import Trade Matters

The importer in an international sales transaction must deal with the customs laws and regulations of the importing country and normally a tax — a tariff — must be paid. A tariff is a border tax levied on imported goods. Typically, it is paid by the importer, normally the buyer in an international sale of goods transaction. As the tariff or tax increases the price of the import, most importers consider the issue of tariffs to be very significant in buying goods and importing them. In our discussion below, we focus on an importer in the United States and the imposition of tariffs by the U.S. Customs authorities, but a similar analysis would be applied to any importing country.

In the United States, the tariff imposed on the import is determined by a three-step process: (1) classification, (2) valuation, and (3) rules of origin. Classification in the United States requires identifying the eight-digit tariff line in the U.S. tariff schedule applicable to the imported good. We shall see that while some classifications are straightforward, others can be difficult. To assist importers (who must submit paperwork that makes the initial classification subject to correction by U.S. Customs), the U.S. Customs authorities have issued a set of rules of interpretation. We take these up below in our materials on classification.

The second issue is valuation. Most tariffs in the United States are ad valorem tariffs, i.e., tariffs that are expressed as a percentage of the value of the imported item. This means that valuation of the product is extremely important since the higher the valuation, the higher the tax that must be paid. The United States and many other countries follow agreed upon rules on valuation. In the United States, the basic approach is to use "transaction value," i.e., the price actually paid for the import, as the basis to which the ad valorem is applied. We will further examine this issue in the readings below.

The third issue is the origin of the goods. Even after the goods have been classified and a valuation has been determined, the tariff rate — the ad valorem — cannot be determined until the country of origin of the goods has been identified. This is because the United States, like most countries, applies a different tariff rate to the same goods depending upon the source of the goods, i.e., the country that is exporting the goods. For example, the United States will in most cases apply a rate agreed upon with other countries in tariff negotiations through the World Trade Organization. This agreed upon rate will be applied to all goods imported from other WTO members. In technical terms, the applicable tariff will be "bound" — a ceiling amount will be fixed under Article II of the General Agreement on Tariffs and Trade, a major agreement of the WTO. However, if the goods come from a country that is not a member of the WTO or from a country with which the United States has unfriendly political relations, the United States might impose a much higher rate on the goods. By contrast, the United States has entered into free trade agreements with many countries so if the import comes from such a country, the import might enter the United States duty free, i.e., subject to a tariff of zero. To make this determination, it is necessary to determine the country of origin of the goods. Specific rules apply to this determination because in the modern world, many goods receive raw materials imported from other countries and are manufactured and processed in more than one country so there could be several candidates for the country of origin.

While tariffs are the most common type of import restriction, another type of important regulation is the quota, a numerical limit on the number of imports (e.g., no more than 10,000 tons of sugar can be imported in any year). There are also other customs procedures, charges, and formalities that the importer must satisfy. Countries also impose product standards and health and safety measures for food and agricultural products. Fortunately, most of these issues are addressed and harmonized by international rules contained in agreements administered by the World Trade Organization. Most tariffs are "bound" under the GATT. Quotas are generally prohibited under GATT Article XI. Arbitrary customs procedures and formalities are illegal under GATT Articles II and XI. Product standards and health and safety measures are disciplined by the WTO.

For now that is all we need to know about import matters as we present some problems and additional materials for you to work through the U.S. approach to imposing tariffs on imports. Remember that this approach is quite similar to many other WTO members, such as the EU. At the conclusion of this chapter, we will discuss briefly other international trade issues that relate to imports.

PROBLEM 2-13

Acme Tools is in the business of manufacturing and selling a complete line of hand tools for home use. Acme, based in Chicago, markets its products through various hardware stores in the Midwestern United States. Because of high demand, Acme finds it necessary from time to time to purchase hand tools from other suppliers to fill its orders. At present, Acme needs to purchase 1,000 screwdrivers and 1,000 electric power drills to fill pending orders from its U.S. customers.

Acme has the option of purchasing from suppliers in Peru, Israel, Belgium, Mexico, and the United States. The prices quoted are as follows (all FOB):

For screwdrivers:

Peru	$110
Israel	$115
Belgium	$120
Mexico	$118
United States	$120

For power drills:

Peru	$450
Israel	$550
Belgium	$400
Mexico	$500
United States	$560

Acme must handle all aspects of the importation of the tools if it chooses to purchase them outside the United States. Where is the best source of the tools in question? What other information might you need?

PROBLEM 2-14

Everlast Tools, an Indiana company, is the importer of record of a large shipment of hand tools made in China. The tools arrive in large crates with the notation "Made in China," but the tools themselves are unmarked. After clearing the goods with Customs, Everlast unpacks the crates and sends one shipment of tools to several specialty tool manufacturers, which break down, reshape, and rebuild the tools as specialty tools for sale to selected industrial consumers. When Everlast ships the tools to the manufacturers, the tools are shipped in containers marked "hand tools" and Everlast then separately sends an invoice marked "product of China" to each of the manufacturers. The manufacturers sell the reconfigured tools in packages marked "Proudly Made in the United States."

Everlast also incorporates some of the imported tools into a toolbox kit that contains other commonly used hand tools for everyday use. The toolbox is sold as a single unit and marked "Everlast Home Toolbox. Everlast Tools, Indiana, USA." The Chinese tools meet all industry standards and are the equal, if not superior, of Everlast tools made in its Indiana plant. Have any laws been violated?

PROBLEM 2-15

Nihon Kaisha (NK) is a Japanese company whose business is the manufacture of automobiles. NK has decided to set up a manufacturing facility in Mexico that will turn out substantial numbers of its best-selling line of cars. NK intends to import auto parts from Japan into Mexico (which has a low tariff rate for auto parts), assemble the automobiles in Mexico, and then take advantage of NAFTA by exporting the finished cars from Mexico into the United States and Canada duty free. Is this possible? If so, how?

NK also plans to establish a factory in France, import parts, and assemble the cars in France in order to sell its cars in the 28 countries that are members of the EU. Is this a good plan? What is the difference between the plan for NAFTA and the plan for the EU?

PROBLEM 2-16

National Semiconductor of Taiwan (NST) is considering Mexico or Peru as a location for its new factory, which will build laptop computers for export to the United States. NST will supply the plasma display ($200), the microprocessor ($250), and the motherboard ($150) to the factory, but the keyboard ($25), other electronic components ($200), and the costs of labor, production, and assembly ($175) will be supplied by its factory abroad. Assume that NST's products will be subject to rules of origin, including tests for regional value content. Should NST locate the factory in Mexico or Peru? Assume that the duty on laptop computers is 12 percent ad valorem.

For Problems 2-13 through 2-16, consult the reading below and the accompanying notes.

U.S. Regulation of Imported Goods: Classification, Valuation, Rules of Origin, Marking, Free Trade Areas and Customs Unions, and Other Import Restrictions

As we have already noted, in order to assess a tariff, three determinations must be made: (1) the classification of the imported article; (2) the valuation of the article; and (3) the country of origin of the article. We examine each of these issues in detail below.

1. CLASSIFICATION

The United States and all other countries of the WTO have voluntarily adopted a system of classification of imports that conform to the International Convention on the Harmonized Commodity Description and Coding System of 1988 (the Harmonized Convention). The Convention was drafted under the auspices of the World Customs Organization (WCO), which works closely with the WTO. The Harmonized Convention consists of 97 Chapters covering all goods. It is possible to classify any import under this system. Chapters are classified with a two-digit number. The higher the classification the more complex and industrial the product and the lower the classification, the more simple and close to nature will be the product. Within each Chapter, product classifications are subdivided into four-digit "subheadings." All WCO members (whose membership overlaps with that of the WTO) have agreed to adopt the Harmonized Convention up to the six-digit level. This means that for every WTO country, any import will be subject to an identical classification up to the six-digit level. This is a remarkable achievement of harmonization. The United States imposes the tariff at the eight-digit level. So countries have agreed on a high level of harmonization while preserving the freedom for individual countries to make their own final tariff assessments.

The United States has adopted the Harmonized Convention into U.S. law in a statute known as the Harmonized Tariff Schedule of the United States (HTSUS). Note carefully that the Harmonized Convention is a classification system only and does not have the force of law. Once the Harmonized Convention was adopted into U.S. law through the HTSUS, of course, the HTSUS acquired the force of law. However, it is the HTSUS that is the binding U.S. law, not the Harmonized Convention itself. We have included an excerpt from the 2002 version of the HTSUS below. The HTSUS is published and periodically updated by the United States International Trade Commission (USITC) pursuant to section 1207 of the Omnibus Trade and Competitiveness Act of 1988 (Public Law No. 100-418, 19 U.S.C. §3007 (2012)). On July 1, 2013, the USITC published a new version of the HTSUS with minor changes reflecting actions by the President and the Congress. All the information in the 2002 excerpt from the HTSUS is the same except for the rate of duty in column 1 applicable to Heading/Subheading 8205.59.20.[30]

Using the excerpt from the HTSUS, we start with Chapter 82, which applies to tools, implements, cutlery, spoons and forks of base metal. Heading 8205 applies to hand tools and the six-digit Subheading 8205.40 applies to screw drivers. Recall that this classification is the same in every WTO country as all have agreed to use identical classifications up to the six-digit level. The United States imposes the tariff at the eight-digit level. This is technically known as the "tariff line," which in this case is 8205.40.00 for "screw drivers and parts thereof." You will note that the United States also has a ten-digit line — 8205.40.00.00 — that is used for gathering information. The ten-digit level is unimportant for determining the tariff.

Once we have determined the tariff line — the eight digit number under the HTSUS — we have concluded (for now) the issue of classification and we then turn our attention to the issue of valuation or the rate of duty. In the excerpt, you will note that under the heading "rates of duty" to the right hand side of the excerpt, there are two columns: Column 1 refers to "general" and "special" rates. In Column 1, you will see the term "general," which was previously known as the Most Favored Nation (MFN) rates. This is the rate that is applied to imports from other WTO countries or contracting parties to the General Agreement on Tariffs and Trade (GATT), the predecessor to the WTO. MFN is a bit of a misnomer since it implies preferential treatment but, in reality, the general rate is the rate that is given to most developed countries of the WTO. For this reason, the United States now uses the term "Normal Trade Relations" (NTR) to describe the countries that receive the "general" rate. The Column 1 "special" rates are for countries with which the United States has a free trade agreement (FTA). These countries are designated by their abbreviations in the Column 1 "special" column with the abbreviations defined in the footnote * at the bottom of the schedule. These rates are lower than the "general" rate and are often zero so the imports enter the United States duty free. Column 2 contains the old Smoot-Hawley tariff rates that applied to imports during the 1930s in the period leading up to the Second World War and before tariffs were lowered through successive rounds of negotiations in the GATT/WTO. You can see from these rates that this was an era of high protectionism as these rates were prohibitively high and intended to prevent trade. Today, the United States applies these rates only to some pariah nations, such as Cuba or North Korea, which are subject to additional trade sanctions some of which we have already discussed in the previous section on exports. The Column 2 rates are also commonly known as the statutory rates.

---

30. Authors' Note: Instead of "27.5%" this line now reads: "Free." How does this affect Acme's planned purchase of power drills?

Harmonized Tariff Schedule of the United States (2002)*

Heading/ Subheading	Stat. Suffix	Article Description	Unit of Quantity	Rates of Duty		
				General	Special	2
8205		Handtools (including glass cutters) not elsewhere specified or included; blow torches and similar self-contained torches; vises, clamps and the like, other than accessories for and parts of machine tools; anvils; portable forges; hand- or pedal-operated grinding wheels with frameworks; base parts thereof:				
8205.10.00	00	Drilling, threading or tapping tools, and parts thereof	X	6.2%	Free (A, CA, E, IL, J, MX) 3.1% (JO)	45%
8205.20		Hammers and sledge hammers, and parts thereof:				
8205.20.30	00	With heads not over 1.5 kg each	doz	6.2%	Free (A, CA, E, IL, J, MX) 3.1% (JO)	45%
8205.20.60	00	With heads over 1.5 kg each	doz	Free		20%
8205.30		Planes, chisels, gouges and similar cutting tools for working wood, and parts thereof:				
8205.30.30	00	With cutting part containing by weight over 0.2 percent of chromium, molybdenum, or tungsten or over 0.1 percent of vanadium	X	5.7%	Free (A, CA, E, IL, J, MX) 2.8% (JO)	60%
8205.30.60	00	Other (including parts)	X	5%	Free (A, CA, E, IL, J, MX)	45%
8205.40.00	00	Screwdrivers, and parts thereof	X	6.2%	Free (A, CA, E, IL, J, MX) 3.1% (JO)	45%
8205.51		Other handtools (including glass cutters) and parts thereof: Household tools, and parts thereof: Of iron or steel:				

(Continued)

				Rates of Duty		
Heading/ Subheading	Stat. Suffix	Article Description	Unit of Quantity	General	Special	2
8205.51.15	00	Carving and butcher steels, with or without handles	No	Free		8¢ each +45%
8205.51.30		Other (including parts)		3.7%	Free (A, CA, E, IL, J, MX)	40%
	30	Kitchen and table implements	No			
	60	Other (including parts)	X			
8205.51.45	00	Of copper	X	Free		40%
8205.51.60	60	Of aluminum	Kg	2.2¢/kg +5%	Free (A, CA, E, IL, J, MX) 1.1¢/kg + 2.5% (JO)	19¢/kg +40%
8205.51.75	00	Other	X	3.75%	Free (A, CA, E, IL, J, MX)	40%
8205.59		Other				
8205.59.10	00	Pipe tools, and parts thereof	X	7.2%	Free (A, CA, E, IL, J, MX) 3.6% (JO)	45%
8205.59.20	00	Power-actuated handtools, and parts thereof:	X	27.5%	Free (A, CA, E, IL, J, MX)	45%
8205.59.30	00	Crowbars, track tools and wedges, and Parts thereof	kg	Free	Free (A, CA, E, IL, J, MX)	3¢/kg

*In the Special column there are the following preferences: A = GSP beneficiaries; CA = Canada; E= Caribbean Basin Economic Recovery Act beneficiaries; IL = Israel; J = Andean Trade Preferences Act beneficiaries; MX = Mexico; JO = Jordan. New preference programs will add African Growth and Opportunity Act beneficiaries; Singapore; and Chile. More will certainly follow.

2. VALUATION

Once we have completed classification, we need to get to the issue of valuation. For now we can see that for each classification, there are three possible rates of duty—the Column 1 "general" and "special" rates and the Column 2 statutory rate. We will not be able to make a final determination which rate of duty to apply until we are able to determine the country of origin, step 3 discussed below.

For now, we can see that each of the three possible rates of duty are all expressed as ad valorem tariffs, i.e., a percentage of the value of the imported article. How do we determine the value of the import, which will serve as the basis to which the applicable rate of duty will be applied? Most WTO members have adopted the WTO Valuation Code, formally known as adopted as the Agreement on Implementation of Article VII of the General Agreement on Tariffs and Trade 1994 negotiated as part of the Uruguay Round of Multilateral Trade Negotiations. Under the WTO Valuation Code, the touchstone test is "transaction value" defined as the price actually paid or payable for the goods at the time of exportation. Transaction value can be determined in most cases by examining the invoice price, i.e., the bill paid by the importer. Some adjustments of the transaction value upwards or downwards are allowed: for example, the cost of packing, selling commissions, and assists (parts and other materials provided to the foreign seller by the buyer free of charge or at a reduced price) can be added to transaction value. Similarly, some costs such as warehousing the goods and then shipping them to the port of the seller can be deducted from transaction value if included in the invoice price. The United States uses FOB prices, not CIF prices, so the cost of the contract of carriage and insurance for the goods are not included in transaction value. Where it is not possible to use transaction value for various reasons (for example the sale is not an arms-length transaction because the seller and buyer are affiliated entities), then the United States uses the following alternate methods in order of preference: transaction value of identical merchandise (19 C.F.R. §152.104), transaction value of similar merchandise (19 C.F.R. §152.104), deductive value (19 C.F.R. §152.05), and computed value (19 C.F.R. §152.106). *See* 19 C.F.R. §152.107 (2014).

3. RULES OF ORIGIN

Once classification and valuation have been made, the last step is determining the country of origin of the goods through the application of rules of origin. As we noted above, for each import article in the excerpt from the HTSUS, there are three applicable ad valorem rates of duty: Column 1 "general" and "special" rates and the Column 2 Smoot-Hawley rates. Determining the country of origin will decide which of these rates will apply to the imported article. Rules of origin are important in modern global trade because one article (or good) will often have connections to more than one country. Manufacturing has become split into multiple stages: For example, it is common for a good to have raw materials or other inputs from Country A, to be processed in Country B, and to be finished in Country C. Multiple connections involving even more countries are possible. Since each country might be subject to a different tariff rate, it becomes important to determine which Country (A, B, or C) is the country of origin of the goods.

(A) SUBJECTIVE TESTS

In the United States, the primary test used by Customs authorities and the courts is the "substantial transformation" test. The substantial transformation test will be applied in all cases unless a special statutory test contained in a free trade agreement displaces it (see further below). The substantial transformation test is called a "subjective" test because the courts will apply a three-prong test in which there is room for discretion by the courts. Under U.S. law, a product has been substantially transformed when it is transformed into a new and different article having a distinctive (1) name, (2) character, or (3) use. Under the U.S. approach, the country where the *last* substantial transformation takes place is the country of origin. In our example above, the courts will examine the manufacturing states in Country A, B, or C and decide the country in which the last substantial transformation occurred and that will determine whether Country A, B, or C is the country of origin. Let us assume that Customs or a court decides that Country B is the country of origin. At this point, the final step is to see whether Country B falls into Column 1 "general" or "special" or in some rare cases into Column 2. At this point, we now have the ad valorem rate to be applied to the product already classified and valued. The tariff can now be assessed.

(B) OBJECTIVE TESTS AND FREE TRADE AREAS (NAFTA)

The subjective test discussed above has come into some criticism as it appears to be vague and allows the courts too much discretion in making country of origin determinations. With the proliferation of free trade areas, it became even more important to create more rigorous and technical rules of origin. Article XXIV of the General Agreement on Tariffs and Trade, the principal global trade agreement administered by the WTO, permits states to create free trade areas and customs unions (CUs), associations of countries that enjoy trade preferences exceeding those provided to nonmember states. Free trade areas and CUs share a common feature in that all goods from member states pass within the territory duty free. However, free trade areas and CUs have some significant differences in how their members deal with goods from nonmembers. NAFTA is a preeminent example of a free trade area between Mexico, Canada, and the United States. While members of NAFTA have eliminated duties on most goods traveling across national boundaries of each of its members, each member is free to maintain its own separate tariff system on imports from nonmember countries; that is, the United States, Mexico, and Canada each has its own tariff system and levies its own set of duties on goods from nonmembers. By contrast, the EU is a customs union that maintains a common external tariff on goods imported from all nonmember countries. Once the goods lawfully enter any country in the EU, they are allowed to freely circulate within the EU without the payment of any additional duties. Since the EU has a common external tariff applied by all EU countries, it makes no difference whether goods enter France, Germany, Italy, or any other EU member state; the goods are subject to one uniform tariff no matter where they enter and then they are free to circulate within the EU duty free. By contrast, as each country in a free trade area enjoys its own authority to set its tariffs, it becomes possible for a nonmember to select the member with the lowest tariffs as a point of entry and then to export the goods duty free to other members of the free trade area. Suppose that Mexico has lower tariffs for certain goods than the United States. The nonmember could ship to Mexico, pay a lower tariff, conduct some simple processing operations, and then ship the goods to the United States duty free, saving the difference between the United States duty and the Mexican duty. To prevent this type of strategic behavior, a free trade area, such as NAFTA, will have rules of origin that determine whether the processed product will be treated as a product originating in the free trade area and thus receive duty-free treatment or whether the product will be treated as a non-originating product and sub-ject to the individual external tariffs of each member country. In our previous example, the United States may determine that although the goods are traveling from Mexico they are really of non-NAFTA origin as they originally came from a nonmember state and will subject those goods to the regular U.S. tariff. (This would mean that the non-originating goods were subject to two tariffs, one when they entered Mexico and a second tariff when they entered the United States, not what the exporter intended.) In some circumstances, however, the rules of origin will provide that the goods from the nonmember state are deemed to originate in a free trade area member state and enjoy duty-free status within the free trade area. The drafters of NAFTA and its predecessor the United States–Canada Free Trade Agreement (CFTA) believed that the substantial transformation test was too subjective to use in NAFTA country of origin determinations so NAFTA devised its own set of rules of origin, which are considered to be objective tests. NAFTA uses a tariff shift test and a regional value content test. In some cases, one or both will apply to the same imported article.

(i) Tariff Shift

The NAFTA tariff shift test is classification specific; that is, for each group or groups of classifications under the HTSUS, a specific NAFTA tariff shift will apply. Thus, there are hundreds or thousands of NAFTA tariff shift rules applicable to NAFTA imports under the HTSUS. The basic approach of the tariff shift test is that an article enters a NAFTA country under one HTSUS tariff classification and then leaves the country under a dif-ferent HTSUS tariff classification. Suppose that a product from Japan enters Mexico and then undergoes processing in Mexico and now seeks entry into the United States as a duty free product. U.S. Customs authorities will apply a tariff shift test. Using the applicable NAFTA tariff shift rule for the classification of the product, U.S. Customs will first deter-mine the classification under the HTSUS of the product when it entered Mexico and then determine the classification of the product when it leaves Mexico for entry into the United States. If the tariff classification has changed — if it has "shifted" — then the prod-uct is deemed to be a product of Mexico and can enter the U.S. duty free. Conversely, if no tariff shift has occurred then the product is subject to U.S. tariffs applicable to imports from Japan. Note that it is U.S. Customs that applies the tariff shift under the HTSUS. The actual classification or actions of the Mexican Customs authorities is not relevant in making this determination.

Let us take a look at a real example under a NAFTA tariff shift rule. Let us suppose that carbon steel seamless pipes are being imported into the United States from Mexico and the importer seeks duty free treatment. HTSUS subheading 7304.39.00 applies to carbon steel seamless standard pipes. The NAFTA rule of origin that applies to 7304.39.00 requires: "A change to subheadings 7304.10 through 7304.39 from any other chapter." HTSUS subheadings 7304.10 through 7304.39 cover all types of carbon steel seamless pipe. This tariff shift rule indicates that if carbon steel stainless pipe imported from Mexico into the United States is to receive duty free treatment, the pipe itself must have been manufactured in Mexico using raw materials that themselves are classified outside of Chapter 73 of the HTSUS, which covers all types of fabricated articles of iron and steel. Suppose that the raw materials imported into Mexico are steel billets and steel bars clas-sified under Chapter 72 of the HTSUS, which covers basic iron and steel mill products. Suppose further that the steel billets and steel bars imported into Mexico are manufac-tured and then processed into steel stainless pipe. Notice that there has now been a tariff shift. The raw materials entered Mexico classified under Chapter 72 of the HTSUS but have emerged from Mexico in the form of a product classified under Chapter 73, namely 7304.39.00 for stainless steel pipe. Now the NAFTA shift rule has been met because there has been a change to 7304.39.00 from "any other chapter" as required by the NAFTA tariff shift rule. The steel seamless pipe is deemed to be an originating product from Mexico, a NAFTA country, and so can enter the United States duty free. NAFTA has substituted the tariff shift test for the substantial transformation test described above.

(ii) Regional Value Content

The drafters of NAFTA believed that requiring only a tariff shift test might set too low a bar for duty free treatment so they have included an additional test, a regional value content (RVC) test that is sometimes applied in addition to the tariff shift test. The basic concept behind that regional value content requirement is that a certain percentage of the value of the product must be attributable to a NAFTA country in addition to any applicable tariff shift test. This requirement is to avoid the use of minor processing operations in Mexico, which have relatively low labor costs, which might satisfy the tariff shift test, as a means to ship goods duty free to the United States. The drafters of NAFTA were especially concerned about automobiles and textiles (clothing) undergoing minor processing operations in Mexico before being shipped to the United States.

NAFTA uses two methods to determine RVC, the transaction value method and the net cost method. The importer can choose either one. Under the transaction value method, 60 percent or more of the transaction value of the product must be attributable to a NAFTA country — in our examples, Mexico. Recall that the transaction value is the price at which the product is actually sold in an arms-length transaction by the seller to a buyer. The formula used to determine RVC using the transaction value method is:

$$RVC = \frac{TV - VNM}{TV} \times 100$$

where RVC is the Regional Value Content
TV is Transaction Value
VNM is the value of non-originating materials used by the producer in the production of the good.

When the transaction value method is not available (i.e., the transaction was not at arms-length) or when this method will not result in the needed 60 percent RVC, an alternative method, the net cost method, can be used. Net cost refers to all of the costs of producing the product, including labor, materials and overhead (although not profit) less the costs of sales promotion, royalties, shipping and packing, and non-allowable interest charges. Since profit is excluded from the net cost method, the required minimum content is lower than that for the transaction value method, which is based on the invoice price and thus includes the profit for the seller. Under the net cost method, 50 percent of the net cost of the product must be attributable to a NAFTA country. The formula for the net cost method is:

$$RVC = \frac{NC - VNM}{NC} \times 100$$

where RVC is the Regional Value Content
NC is the Net Cost
VNM is the value of non-originating materials used by the producer in the production of the good.

With these various methods in mind, let us take the following example of hibachis (a type of grill) made in Mexico from parts shipped to Mexico from other countries. Let us assume that the steel shell of the hibachi is imported into Mexico from Japan and valued at $4.00, the legs are from Canada with a value of $2.00 and the steel grill is produced in the United States with a value of $3.00. The transaction value (the price sold by the Mexican manufacturer to a U.S. buyer) of the hibachi is $12.00 Note that some of the parts are from NAFTA countries (the legs from Canada and the steel grill from the United States) but one part is from Japan, a non-NAFTA country. This means that the finished hibachi may have to meet a minimum regional content value from NAFTA countries in order to be deemed to be a NAFTA originating good. The NAFTA rule of origin that applies to hibachis is:

A change to subheadings 7321.12 through 7321.83 from any other heading; or
A change to subheadings 7321.12 through 7321.83 from subheading 7321.90 [parts of hibachis], whether or not there is also a change from any other heading, provided there is a regional value content of not less than:

(1)   *Sixty percent where the transaction value method is used, or*
(2)   *Fifty percent where the net cost method is used.*

The first sentence of this NAFTA rule of origin is a pure tariff shift test. Subheadings 7321.12 through 7321.83 refer to hibachis and other grills. If an importer from Mexico imported basic iron and steel mill products classified under Chapter 72 and manufactured and processed them into a steel shell, steel legs and a steel grill, and then assembled them into a hibachi then the tariff shift test will be met and the hibachi comes into the United States duty free. If the hibachi is made from basic steel products, there is a sufficient value-added process in Mexico that the product is deemed to originate in Mexico. However, in this example, the hibachi was not manufactured in Mexico from raw steel products but from parts of hibachis. So the first sentence of the NAFTA tariff shift rule does not apply and we will need to use the second part, which applies to hibachis made from parts. Since a hibachi assembled from parts involves less of a value-added process in Mexico, this type of hibachi must satisfy both a tariff shift test— a shift from 7321.90 (parts of hibachis) —and a regional value content test. Since the product satisfies the tariff shift that the hibachi is made from parts, we need to determine whether the product satisfies the RVC using the transaction value method:

$$RVC = \frac{NC - VNM}{TV} \times 100\% = \frac{\$12 - \$4}{\$12} \times 100 = \frac{\$8}{\$12} \times 100\% = 66.7\%$$

Since the RVC is 66.7 percent and exceeds the required 60 percent required by the transaction value method, the hibachi can enter the United States duty free.

While these are general rules that apply to most products, special rules apply to automobiles and automotive parts subjecting them to a more rigorous NAFTA shift rules. The purpose of these more rigorous tests is to protect the U.S. auto industry from foreign manufacturers setting up assembly plants in Mexico, shipping auto parts to Mexico, assembling the parts into automobiles and shipping them duty free into the United States.

(C) GSP AND OTHER FTAS

In addition to NAFTA, the United States has entered into many other free trade agreements. Among these agreements are those that are created pursuant to the United States' program known as the Generalized System of Preferences (which has its origin in the WTO), which is designed to benefit certain designated beneficiary developing countries by allowing imports from such countries to enter the United States duty free. Currently, there are 123 countries benefitting under the Generalized System of Preferences (GSP). The GSP also has rules of origin to prevent multinational companies from shipping products to GSP countries, performing some simple assembly operations, and then importing them duty free into the United States. Unlike NAFTA, the GSP programs do not apply a tariff shift test. Rather, to determine the country of origin under the GSP program, courts first apply the "substantial transformation" test set forth above in order to determine whether the product originates from the GSP beneficiary developing country. Once the substantial transformation test has been met, the GSP program also imposes a regional value content requirement as follows:

> *The duty free treatment provided under this subchapter shall apply to any eligible article which is the growth, product, or manufacture of a beneficiary developing country if*
>
> (1) *that article is imported directly from a beneficiary developing country into the customs territory of the United States; and*
> (2) *the sum of*
>
> > (a) *the cost or value of the materials produced in the beneficiary developing country or any two or more such countries that are members of the same association of countries and are treated as one country under section 2467(2) of this title, plus*
> > (b) *the direct costs of processing operations performed in such beneficiary developing country or such member countries, is not less than 35 percent of the appraised value of such article at the time it is entered.*

Note that unlike NAFTA that has RVC requirements of 60 percent for the transaction value method and 50 percent for the net cost method, the test under the GSP programs is 35 percent regional value content. This is intended as a benefit for developing countries.

Other preference programs that apply rules of origin, including the regional value content of 35 percent, similar to the U.S. GSP program are

- The Caribbean Basin Initiative ("CBI") established under the Caribbean Basin Economic Recovery Act, 19 U.S.C. §§2701–2707 (2006). The CBI is limited to countries in the Caribbean Sea and in Central America.
- The Andean Trade Preference Act ("ATPA"), 19 U.S.C. §§3201–3206 (2006), which creates a preferential duty program for the four members of the Andean Pact: Bolivia, Ecuador, Colombia, and Peru.
- The African Growth and Opportunity Act ("AGOA") enacted in 2000, 19 U.S.C. §§2466a, 2466b, 3701–3706, 3721–3724, 3731–3741 (2006), provides preferential duty treatment relating to articles not subject to GSP preferences to forty-eight sub-Saharan countries in Africa. The AGOA primarily covers textiles (clothing), which are permitted to enter the United States free of duty subject to certain restrictions.

4. COUNTRY OF ORIGIN MARKING

Another requirement that must be satisfied in order to import goods into the United States is country of origin marking. Unlike the other topics we have just considered (classification, valuation, and rules of origin), country of origin marking is not related to the assessment of the tariff. Nevertheless, the United States requires that each imported article to be marked with the name of the country of manufacture in a conspicuous place as legibly, indelibly, and as permanently as the nature of the article allows in order to notify the ultimate purchaser of the product's country of manufacture. Note that markings do not need to be placed when the products are transferred to an intermediate stage of process but only when sold to the ultimate purchaser. The United States believes that consumers have the right to know the country of origin, not for tariff purposes, but for consumer protection purposes as the country of origin influences some consumers in their purchasing decisions. What might be confusing is that similar tests rules of origin are used for country of origin marking purposes as are used for determining the country of origin to assess the tariff. Although the tests might be similar, their purposes are different. For example, suppose that products are shipped into the United States from China where they are substantially transformed by the U.S. manufacturer into a new article with a distinctive name, character, or use. At this point, the U.S. company can mark the product as "Made in the United States." This might influence some consumers to purchase the product. NAFTA also uses a tariff shift for country of origin marking. If the imported product undergoes a tariff shift when processing operations are performed in the NAFTA country then the NAFTA country becomes the country of origin and the product must be so marked. However, while these NAFTA country of origin marking rules are similar to the tariff shift test for country of origin purposes in determining tariffs, the rules are separate and distinct.

5. OTHER IMPORT RESTRICTIONS

The United States imposes other restrictions on imports. Again these restrictions are not related to the assessment of the tariff, but they are important and are also enforced by the U.S. Customs authorities on behalf of various other federal agencies at the port of entry:

- Food and agricultural imports are subject to regulation by the Food and Drug Administration (FDA), the Department of Agriculture, and the Department of Health and Human Services.
- Drugs are subject to regulations by the FDA and the Department of Health and Human Services.
- Household appliances are subject to energy and labeling standards imposed by the Department of Energy.
- Electronic products are subject to radiation performance standards set by the FDA and the Federal Communications Commission.
- Toxic substance imports are regulated by Customs and the Environmental Protection Agency.
- Hazardous substances are regulated by the FDA and Consumer Products Safety Commission and the Department of Transportation.

NOTES AND QUESTIONS

1. *WTO Tariff Rates.* As a matter of international law, all states that are members of the World Trade Organization or that are parties to bilateral or regional economic

arrangements have an obligation not to charge a tariff or to take any import measure that is different from their agreed ("bound") import schedules. The remedy for any violation of these international norms is a dispute settlement proceeding conducted by the WTO. *See, e.g.,* Appellate Body Report, *Argentina—Measures Affecting Imports of Footwear, Textiles, Apparel and Other Items,* WT/DS56/AB/R (Mar. 27, 1998) (Argentina held to have violated its obligations by charging more than the agreed bound tariff).

2. *Bonded Facilities and Foreign Trade Zones.* A bonded facility is a duty-free customs area used for storage, repacking, clearing, or sorting of imported merchandise. Duty must be paid only when the goods are withdrawn and put into the stream of commerce. A foreign trade zone is a specifically designated area where goods can be landed without the payment of duty. It may be possible to perform assembly or processing operations in this zone.

3. *Temporary Importation Under Bond.* Placing goods in an approved warehouse and posting bond equal to twice the estimated duty allows a delay in paying a duty for up to one year. This is particularly useful for goods that will be re-exported because it avoids the delay of the duty drawback process.

4. *Drawbacks and Refunds of Duties.* What happens if goods are imported and then exported as a whole or after processing? In this case, the importer/exporter can apply for and receive a duty drawback, which is usually 99 percent of the duty originally paid. *See, e.g., Texport Oil Co. v. United States,* 1 F. Supp. 2d 1393 (Ct. Int'l Trade 1998) (company entitled to drawback on exports of petroleum products). NAFTA, however, eliminates most drawbacks on goods circulating between the United States, Canada, and Mexico. *See Merck & Co., Inc. v. United States,* 499 F.3d 1348, 1356 (Fed. Cir. 2007).

5. In this book, we concentrate on U.S. Customs rules. However, every country or economic area has its own distinctive rules. For example, the 28-member European Union enforces EU-wide customs and allows free circulation of goods within the EU itself. *See* Edwin A. Vermulst, *EC Customs Classification Rules: Should Ice Cream Melt?,* 15 Mich. J. Int'l L. 1241 (1994).

The importer, typically the buyer in an international sale of goods, is normally responsible for handling all aspects of compliance with the customs laws of the importing country. Of primary concern to importers is determining the amount of customs duties that are due on imported goods. In the United States, contested issues arise more often in import cases than in export cases. Litigation and controversy centers around the following issues: (1) classification, (2) valuation, (3) rules of origin, and (4) marking. We explore each of these issues in the sections below.

While the importer makes the initial determinations of each of these issues in the paperwork submitted to import the products with U.S. Customs, duties are ultimately determined by the U.S. Customs Service. An importer can contest a customs determination through resort to two specialized federal courts, the Court of International Trade, which is a trial court, and the U.S. Court of Appeals for the Federal Circuit.

1. Classification Issues

The first issue in a tariff determination is the classification of the item under a regime such as the Harmonized Tariff Schedule of the United States, which establishes tariff rates for every import.

North American Processing Co. v. United States
United States Court of Appeals, Federal Circuit, 2001
236 F.3d 695

LOURIE, Circuit Judge.

The imported goods at issue in this case are bovine fat trimmings containing thirty-five percent chemical lean[31] and sixty-five percent fat, which were imported by North American on October 14, 1992. Customs originally classified the entry under subheading 1502.00.00 as "[f]ats of bovine animals . . . ," dutiable at a rate of 0.95/kg. Subheading 1502.00.00 reads as follows:

> 1502.00.00 Fats of bovine animals, sheep or goats, raw or rendered, whether or not pressed or solvent-extracted

HTSUS, subheading 1502.00.00. Customs later reliquidated the merchandise on February 23, 1993, and classified it under subheading 0202.30.60 as "[m]eat of bovine animals . . .," dutiable at a rate of 4.4/kg. Subheading 0202.30.60 reads as follows:

> 0202 Meat of bovine animals, frozen: . . .
> 0202.30 Boneless:
> 0202.30.60 Other
> HTSUS, heading 0202.

[North American filed a protest with Customs, which was denied. North American challenged the denial with the Court of International Trade, which agreed with Customs. North American then appealed to the court of appeals, which issued the opinion below.]

DISCUSSION

Determining whether imported merchandise has been properly classified under an appropriate tariff provision is ultimately an issue of statutory interpretation and thus a question of law. Resolution of that issue entails a two-step process: (1) ascertaining the proper meaning of specific terms in the tariff provision; and (2) determining whether the merchandise at issue comes within the description of such terms as properly construed. The first step is a question of law over which this court exercises complete and independent review. The second step is a question of fact that this court reviews for clear error. Furthermore, Customs' classification determinations are presumed to be correct. 28 U.S.C. §2639(a)(1) (1994).

Applied in numerical order, the GRIs [General Rules of Interpretation] of the HTSUS and the Additional United States Rules of Interpretation govern the proper classification of merchandise entering the United States. According to GRI 1, "classification shall be determined according to the terms of the headings and any relevant section or chapter notes." Thus, "a court first construes the language of the heading, and any section or chapter notes in question, to determine whether the product at issue is classifiable under

---

31. "Chemical lean" indicates the results of an analysis where the fat content of a sample of the imported merchandise is determined by chemical assay under standard laboratory conditions.

the heading." *Baxter,* 182 F.3d at 1337. Absent contrary legislative intent, HTSUS terms are to be construed according to their common and commercial meaning. A court may rely upon its own understanding of the terms used, lexicographic and scientific authorities, dictionaries, and other reliable information. *Id.*

We agree with the government that the merchandise is properly classified under subheading 0202.30.60. The Explanatory Notes to chapter 2 expressly state that "[a]nimal fat presented separately is excluded . . . , but fat presented in the carcass *or adhering to meat* is treated as forming part of the meat." HTSUS, ch. 2 Explanatory Notes (emphasis added). Although the Explanatory Notes are not legally binding or dispositive, they may be consulted for guidance and are generally indicative of the proper interpretation of the various HTSUS provisions. *E.g., Carl Zeiss,* 195 F.3d at 1378 n. 1 (citing H.R. Conf. Rep. No. 100-576, at 549 (1988), *reprinted in* 1998 U.S.C.C.A.N. 1547, 1582). Therefore, it is clear that Congress intended that the presence of fat in a mixture containing lean and fat components does not preclude its classification as "meat." In the present case, the subject merchandise is comprised of fat which adheres to a lean component, and is not separately presented. It thus fits within that classification. Moreover, USDA regulations define "meat" as "[t]he part of the muscle of any cattle, sheep, swine, or goats . . . *with or without the accompanying and overlying fat. . . .*" 9 C.F.R. §301.2 (2000) (emphasis added). While USDA regulations are not dispositive of whether a Customs classification ruling is correct, we find them to be persuasive regarding this issue. *See Carl Zeiss,* 195 F.3d at 1379 (permitting courts to consult any reliable information source to determine the proper classification of merchandise). Accordingly, we find that the imported merchandise at issue is properly classified as "meat" under subheading 0202.30.60.

We also agree with the government that the imported merchandise may not be classified as "fats" under subheading 1502.00.00. The government presented undisputed testimony at trial that the USDA considers trimmings that contain less than twelve percent lean to be properly classified as fat. Therefore, because the subject merchandise contains a lean component that comprises far more than twelve percent of the total mixture, it may not be classified as "fats." The dictionary definition of the term "fat" further supports this conclusion. "Fat" is defined as

> [the] part of the tissues of an animal that consists chiefly of cells distended with greasy or oily matter . . . [;] the oily or greasy substance that makes up the bulk of the cell contents of adipose tissue and occurs in smaller quantities in many other parts of animals and in plants. . . .

Webster's Third New International Dictionary 827 (1981). Accordingly, we conclude that subheading 1502.00.00 is inapplicable to the merchandise at issue.

[W]e AFFIRM.

JVC Co. of America v. United States
United States Court of Appeals, Federal Circuit, 2000
234 F.3d 1348

LOURIE, Circuit Judge.

The imported goods at issue in this case are video camera recorders, otherwise known as camcorders, which were imported by JVC in 1992. The parties agree that JVC's camcorders are "electrical machine[s] or apparatus possessing two independent functions generally used in conjunction with one another; a television camera and a video tape recorder." Customs classified the camcorders under subheading 8525.30.00, under the broader heading of 8525 of the HTSUS, as "television cameras," dutiable at a rate of 4.2 *ad valorem.* Heading 8525 and subheading 8525.30.00 read as follows:

> 8525   Transmission apparatus for radiotelephony, radiotelegraphy, radio-broadcasting or television, whether or not incorporating reception apparatus or sound recording or reproducing apparatus; television cameras:
>
> 8525.30.00   Television cameras

JVC timely protested Customs' classification and paid all of the liquidated duties that were due. JVC then challenged Customs' classification in the Court of International Trade, arguing that its camcorders should have been classified under subheading 8543.80.90. Heading 8543 and subheadings 8543.80 and 8543.80.90 read as follows:

> 8543   Electrical machines and apparatus, having individual functions, not specified or included elsewhere in this chapter; parts thereof:
>
> 8543.80   Other machines and apparatus:
>
> 8543.80.90   Other

HTSUS, heading 8543. JVC alternatively argued that its camcorders should have been classified under subheading 8479.89.90. Heading 8479 and subheadings 8479.89 and 8479.89.90 read as follows:

> 8479   Machines and mechanical appliances having individual functions, not specified or included elsewhere in this chapter; parts thereof:
>
> Other machines and mechanical appliances:
>
> 8479.89   Other
>
> 8479.89.80   Other

Merchandise classified under subheadings 8543.80.90 and 8479.89.90 are dutiable at the respective rates of 3.9% and 3.7% *ad valorem.*

[Customs classified JVC's camcorders under subheading 8525.30.00 as "television cameras." The ruling was challenged in the Court of International Trade where both parties cross-moved for summary judgment. The Court of International Trade upheld the ruling by Customs and JVC timely appealed.]

DISCUSSION

Determining the meaning of a tariff term in the HTSUS is an issue of statutory interpretation and thus a question of law. In this case, because the structure and use of the imported camcorders are not in dispute, and Customs has not promulgated any regulations interpreting the tariff terms at issue, our analysis of whether the imported merchandise has been properly classified turns on the determination of the proper meaning and scope of the relevant tariff classifications.

Applied in numerical order, the GRIs of the HTSUS and the Additional United States Rules of Interpretation govern the proper classification of merchandise entering the United States. Under GRI 3(a), when goods are *prima facie* classifiable under two or more headings, the court should determine which heading is the most specific, comparing only the language of the headings and not the language of the subheadings. Only after determining that a product is classifiable under a particular heading should the court look to the subheadings to find the proper classification.

As an initial matter, we agree with the government that the merchandise is *prima facie* classifiable under heading 8525. As an *eo nominee* provision, heading 8525 includes all forms of the named article, *i.e.,* "television cameras." The Explanatory Notes to heading 8525 expressly state that "[t]his heading covers television cameras. . . . Cameras for underwater work and portable cameras with or without a built-in video recorder are also classified here." Explanatory Notes, §XVI, 85.25(c), at 1375 (1986). Although the Explanatory Notes are not legally binding or dispositive, they may be consulted for guidance and are generally indicative of the proper interpretation of the various HTSUS provisions. In addition, according to the McGraw-Hill Encyclopedia of Science & Technology, "[a] television camera may fall within one of several categories: studio, *portable,* or telecine." 18 McGraw-Hill Encyclopedia of Sci. & Tech. 212 (8th ed. 1997) (emphasis added). This reference further states that:

> Television cameras intended for . . . portable use are usually one piece, with all elements of the camera system contained in one assembly. *Such cameras may be combined with a detachable or built-in videocassette recorder to form a camcorder* (Fig. 2). . . . Portable cameras . . . usually combine all of the basic elements into one package and may be used for a multitude of purposes. . . . The units often have built-in microphones, videocassette recorders, and batteries for completely self-contained operation (Fig. 2). These compact and lightweight camcorders can be easily handled by one person.

Id. at 212, 216 (emphasis added). While JVC argues that this authority distinguishes television cameras from camcorders, we agree with the government that this reference source supports the view that a camcorder is a type of television camera—one with a built-in videocassette recorder.

Having thus concluded that camcorders are *prima facie* classifiable under heading 8525 of the HTSUS, the only remaining issue is whether camcorders should nonetheless be classified under some alternative heading. JVC contends that its camcorders are described under headings 8543 and 8479, and therefore should be classified under either subheading 8543.80.90 or 8479.89.90. We disagree for the following reasons. First, as we noted earlier, the Explanatory Notes to heading 8525 explicitly state that "[t]his heading covers television cameras. . . . Cameras for underwater work and portable cameras with or without a built-in video recorder are also classified here." Explanatory Notes, Section XVI, 85.25(c), at 1375 (1986); *see also Carl Zeiss,* 195 F.3d at 1378 n. 1 (explaining that although the Explanatory Notes are not legally binding or dispositive, they may be consulted for guidance and are generally indicative of the proper interpretation of the various HTSUS provisions). Moreover, while heading 8543 ("Electrical machines and apparatus, having individual functions, not specified or included elsewhere") and heading 8479 ("Machines and mechanical appliances having individual functions, not specified or included elsewhere") may arguably describe camcorders, they should not be classified under these headings because heading 8525 ("television cameras") is more specific.

[W]e AFFIRM.

Better Home Plastics Corp. v. United States
United States Court of Appeals, Federal Circuit, 1997
119 F.3d 969

RICH, Circuit Judge.

The shower curtain sets in question comprise an outer textile curtain, an inner plastic magnetic liner, and plastic hooks. The outer textile curtain typically has a decorative pattern, and being semi-transparent, it permits the color of the plastic liner to show through. The inner plastic liner prevents water from escaping the shower and prevents the fabric curtain from being soiled with mildew or soap. The liner is opaque, and thereby also contributes to the decorative and privacy-maintaining functions of the set. The hooks attach the liner and the curtain to the overhead curtain rod found at the entrance to most domestic showers. The sets are at the low end of the shower curtain market: plaintiff, Better Home Plastics, sells the sets to discount stores for $5-$6 per set; they are resold to consumers for $9-$12 per set.

The General Rules of Interpretation (GRI) of the Harmonized Tariff Schedule of the United States (HTSUS) help determine which subheading should govern the duty to be assessed on imports of these sets. According to GRI 3(a), when "goods are, *prima facie*, classifiable under two or more headings," the court must choose the heading providing the most specific description. This is the so-called relative specificity test. GRI 3(a) provides an exception to the applicability of this test, however, when "two or more headings each refer . . . to only part of the items in a set." Pursuant to GRI 3(b), goods not classifiable under GRI 3(a) are classified by the "component which gives them their essential character." This is the so-called essential character test. GRI 3(c) provides a default rule for goods not classifiable after resort to either GRI 3(a) or (b). GRI 3(c) directs that such goods be classified "under the heading which occurs last in numerical order among those which equally merit consideration."

Two subheadings of the HTSUS are in issue. The sets might be classified on the basis of the textile curtain, pursuant to subheading 6303.92.000 of the HTSUS, resulting in a duty of 12.8%. Alternatively, they might be classified on the basis of the plastic liner, pursuant to subheading 3924.90.1010 of the HTSUS, resulting in a duty of 3.36%.

[Customs classified the sets on the basis of the textile curtain. Plaintiff challenged the ruling in the Court of International Trade, which held that sets should have been classified based on the plastic liner. The United States appealed the decision to the court of appeals.]

ANALYSIS

On appeal, there is extensive argument about presumptions and deference that can be quickly addressed. Acknowledging the procedural importance of presumptions, the Court of International Trade is nonetheless charged with the duty to "reach the correct decision." *Rollerblade*, 112 F.3d at 484 (quoting 28 U.S.C. §2643(b)). On appeal, we review the findings of that court—not those of Customs—for clear error; while we decide questions of law *de novo*.

We turn, then, to the merits of the arguments presented. The United States argues that the Court of International Trade erred in its application of the essential character test because, according to the United States, the fabric curtain provides the essential character of the sets. In the alternative, the United States argues that the essential character cannot be determined and the default rule of GRI 3(c) should apply. We disagree with both arguments.

The Court of International Trade carefully considered all of the facts, and, after a reasoned balancing of all the facts, concluded that Better Home Plastics offered sufficient evidence and argument to overcome the presumption of correctness. The court concluded that the indispensable function of keeping water inside the shower along with the protective, privacy and decorative functions of the plastic liner, and the relatively low cost of the sets *all combined* to support the decision that the plastic liner provided the essential character of the sets. Contrary to the argument offered by the United States, we are not persuaded that the court erred in looking to analogous areas of law concerning "indispensability" for guidance in analyzing "essential character." The court's decision did not rely solely, or even hinge, on the indispensability of the water-retaining function. The decision was substantially based on the importance of the other functions as well as the cost of the entire set. Therefore, we see no error in the court's ultimate conclusion of essential character in this case. As a result, we also see no error in this case in the court's refusal to reject the essential character test in favor of the default rule of GRI 3(c).

[W]e affirm.

NOTES AND QUESTIONS

1. Should the courts on judicial review accord deference to rulings of the U.S. Customs Service?

2. The three principal cases set forth above illustrate the basic rules of interpretation applied to determine the classification of a product. Make a list of these rules.

PROBLEM 2-17

Importer A imports several models of battery-operated toothbrushes. These have (1) one to four interchangeable plastic toothbrush heads, (2) a detachable plastic handle containing a battery-operated motor, and (3) a stand that incorporates a battery recharger.

The classification alternatives are:

9603   Brooms, brushes (including brushes constituting parts of machines, appliances or vehicles) . . .
9603.21.00   Toothbrushes (duty rate 1 percent *ad valorem*)
or
8509   Electromechanical domestic appliances, with self-contained motor
Other appliances (duty rate 4.2 percent 8509.80.00 *ad valorem*)

Importer A argues that the proper classification is 9603.21 on the ground that it is more specific under GRI 3(a) than 8509.80. However, in order for 9603.21 to apply the mechanical toothbrush must first satisfy 9603, the category heading. Importer A argues that a mechanical toothbrush falls within the phrase in heading 9603 "brushes (including brushes constituting parts of machines, appliances or vehicles)." However, if the mechanical toothbrush satisfies 9603, what prevents a street sweeper or a vacuum cleaner from also from falling within this heading? How would you interpret 9603 to avoid this result and what is the applicable rate of duty? *See Bausch & Lomb, Inc. v. United States*, 148 F.3d 1363 (Fed. Cir. 1998).

2. *Valuation Issues*

After classification, the next step is valuation of the product. Most tariffs are expressed as a percentage of the value of the product. Thus, accurate valuation of the product is essential to determine the amount of the duty (tax) owned.

Century Importers, Inc. v. United States
United States Court of Appeals, Federal Circuit, 2000
205 F.3d 1308

RADER, Circuit Judge.

Century is a wholly owned importing subsidiary of the Miller Brewing Company of Milwaukee, Wisconsin (Miller). On January 14, 1993, Miller entered an agreement (the Beer Agreement) with Molson Breweries of Toronto, Ontario, Canada (Molson), which covered the importation, sale, advertising, and distribution of beer. Exhibit 9(j) of the Beer Agreement, titled "Calculation and Payment of Transfer Prices," set the formula for calculating the price of Molson's beer. This price—the "transfer price"—included production, overhead, packaging, and shipping costs. Exhibit 9(j) also included tariffs, levies, taxes, and duties under "packaging costs" to be invoiced separately. The parties to the agreement treated these tariffs and duties as Molson's costs, which Molson would invoice separately to Miller. Because these tariff and duty costs appeared on a separate invoice, the parties did not count the duties in the price of the beer.

When Molson and Miller began to negotiate the Beer Agreement, the duty for beer imported from Canada was a specific (i.e., volume-based) rate under one cent per liter. During the negotiations, however, as a result of a trade dispute, the United States replaced the specific duty rate for beer imported from the Province of Ontario with a rate based upon value. This ad valorem rate was fifty percent of the value of the imported product. Molson and Miller agreed, in a side letter headed "Import Duties" accompanying the Beer Agreement, that Molson would "pay or reimburse" Miller and its affiliates for the cost of these duties.

When Century later imported Molson beer, Customs assessed fifty per cent ad valorem duties based on the price stated on the invoices or bills. The invoices did not contain any statements about subsequent duty reimbursements. Customs assessed the duty based on the sales invoice price. Century paid the duty to Customs. Later Miller billed Molson for the duties, and Molson reimbursed Miller (and Century) the billed amount.

Century brought an action in the Court of International Trade seeking a refund of part of the duties it paid, contending that Customs, in calculating the duties on the imported beer, should have deducted the reimbursed duties from the invoice price. In essence, Century argued that Molson had in reality reduced the price of its beer by agreeing to reimburse Miller for the duties. Molson had recovered, Century argued, only the invoice price minus the reimbursed duties. Therefore, Century contends that this reduction in the invoice reflects the value of the transaction.

Customs contends that it calculated the duty on the basis of 19 U.S.C. §1401a(b)(1) which sets the "transaction value," the basis for the duty calculation, at "the price actually paid or payable for the merchandise." Customs contended that the price "actually paid" for the beer was the invoice price. According to Customs, Molson's reimbursement was a rebate. Customs treated this alleged rebate according to the statutory formula: A "rebate of, or decrease in, the price actually paid . . . after the date of the importation . . . shall be disregarded in determining the transaction value." §1401a(b)(4)(B). Customs acknowledges that the transaction value would not include customs duties "if identified separately from the price actually paid." 19 U.S.C. §1401a(b)(3)(B). Customs notes, however, that neither Molson nor Century separately identified at importation the customs duties later reimbursed by Molson.

Century and Customs cross-moved for summary judgment. The Court of International Trade granted Century's motion, holding that the invoice price included a component for duties which Customs should have deducted before it assessed duties. Further, the trial court reasoned that repayment of duties to the importer after importation is not a "rebate in price" within the meaning of the statute. Therefore, the Court of International Trade held that Molson's failure to identify separately the reimbursement agreement was a ministerial error which the parties could later correct. The Government now appeals the decision of the Court of International Trade.

Title 19 authorizes Customs to determine the value of imported merchandise. See 19 U.S.C. §1500(a) (1999). According to title 19, Customs appraises imports "on the basis of . . . (A) The transaction value provided for under subsection (b) of this section." §1401a(a)(1). Transaction value is the "price actually paid or payable for the merchandise." §1401a(b)(1). Two further provisions inform the meaning of the "price actually paid or payable." Title 19 uses that phrase again in excluding rebates from the transaction value: "any rebate of, or other decrease in, the price actually paid or payable that is made or otherwise effected between the buyer and seller after the date of the importation shall be disregarded in determining the transaction value." §1401a(b)(4)(B). Again, title 19 uses the phrase in excluding from transaction value several items when identified separately from the price: "the transaction value does not include any of the following, if identified separately from the price actually paid or payable [or] (B) [t]he customs duties currently payable on the imported merchandise by reason of its importation." §1401a(b)(3)(B).

These provisions show that title 19 makes the transaction value a touchstone for valuation of imports. Transaction value or "the price actually paid or payable" is "the total payment made, or to be made, for imported merchandise by the buyer to the seller." §1401a(b)(4)(A). From this touchstone, title 19 authorizes deductions "for transportation, insurance, and related services incident to the international shipment of the merchandise." Those deductions are not at issue in this case. Title 19 also enumerates other costs that Customs must exclude from transaction value, but only if they were identified separately from the price actually paid or payable. These costs include "the customs duties and other Federal taxes currently payable on the imported merchandise." §1401a(b)(3)(B). According to title 19, the transaction value, the touchstone of duty calculation, does not include customs duties payable upon importation, if identified separately from the price actually paid.

Applying the statutory formula to this case, §1401a(b)(3) explicitly excludes customs duties from the transaction value if identified separately to Customs. Therefore, because the record shows that the parties did not identify these duties separately, Customs has no authorization to deduct them from the price calculation. Beyond this straightforward application of the statute to this case, title 19 supplies further confirmation for Customs' refusal to deduct the duties from the transactional value. Because Molson reimbursed the duties after the date of importation, that post-importation action was in fact a rebate. *See* Black's Law Dictionary 1266 (6th ed. 1990). Section 1401a(b)(4)(B) directs Customs to disregard rebates after the date of importation. Thus Customs properly appraised the merchandise at the invoiced unit prices.

In the declaration of its Import Specialist, Customs acknowledges that it might well have reached a different appraisal if it had been informed of the duty rebates at the time of importation. The Court of International Trade considered this omitted notice a simple error in the preparation of the entry papers and thus considered it remediable under 19 U.S.C. §1520I(1) (1994), which states:

> [A] clerical error, mistake of fact, or other inadvertence . . . not amounting to an error in the construction of a law, adverse to the importer and manifest from the record or established

by documentary evidence, in any entry, liquidation, or other customs transaction, [may give rise to a refund] when the error, mistake, or inadvertence is brought to the attention of the Customs Service within one year after the date of liquidation.

The Court of International Trade read §1520 to give Miller a year to correct its failure to identify the "duty paid" invoice at the time of importation. To the contrary, §1520 does not apply to this case.

Century's repeated failure to mark its documents "duty paid" falls outside the allowance for correction under §1520I(1). Section 1520 extends a correction chance to "a clerical error, mistake of fact, or *other inadvertence*." (Emphasis supplied.) A correctable inadvertence under §1520I(1) is easy to recognize because it is commensurate with, as the statute states, a "clerical error" or a "mistake of fact." Century's course of conduct with respect to the entries that occurred both before and after the entries at issue is relevant in demonstrating that its error is one of law. The repetition of "inadvertence" may indicate an advertent misunderstanding of the law. In this case, Century's repeated failures to provide notice of the duty arrangements over a period of at least four months do not qualify as inadvertent clerical errors or as inadvertent mistakes of fact. Century might well have known that it was not marking its import documents "duty paid," but not have known it was operating under a misapprehension of the law. To use an alternative label, Century acted negligently. Century's failure to provide notice falls outside the scope of inadvertence correctable under 19 U.S.C. §1520I(1).

Correction is not possible if the error is one in the construction of law. Mistakes of law occur where the facts are known but their legal consequences are not, or are believed to be different than they really are. Thus, misunderstanding or ignorance of the law does not qualify as a correctable inadvertence under §1520.

This court therefore vacates the grant of summary judgment to Century and reverses the denial of summary judgment to the United States.

NOTES AND QUESTIONS

1. Why was Century so careless in filling out the proper paperwork to get an accurate assessment of duties, which seems to be a simple, straightforward task? Who do you think discovered the error, Century or Molson?

2. As noted on p. 141, the transaction value method cannot be used in all cases such as in transactions between affiliated parties. At that point, alternative methods are used in order of preference. See p. 141 above.

3. If the U.S. importer and the foreign exporter are related companies, charge-backs and commissions paid by the importer to the exporter may be included in the transaction value of the goods. *See VWP of America v. United States*, 259 F. Supp. 2d 1289 (Ct. Int'l Trade 2003).

PROBLEM 2-18

A U.S. importer B imports glassware from its parent company in Italy. The parent company bills B an extra charge of 1.25 percent above the invoice price per month as interest. U.S. Customs has issued guidelines that it will not include interest as part of dutiable value where, among other conditions, the parties have their financing arrangement in writing. B and its parent company have a written agreement under which B is to pay accrued interest charges on a quarterly basis and the principal on the invoices within 90 days of billing. In practice, however, B has been paying interest charges every 6 to 12 months and also frequently pays the outstanding invoices up to 22 days after the expiration of the 90-day period. B says that the parties have contractually modified the agreement by their practices and by oral agreement. Should the interest charges be treated as dutiable value? Why would the parties have such an arrangement? *See Luigi Bormioli Corp., Inc. v. United States*, 304 F.3d 1362 (Fed. Cir. 2002).

3.   Rules of Origin

The country of origin of a product can be very important in determining the duty owed. How does Customs determine the country of origin? This is not always a straightforward inquiry, as the following case illustrates.

Zuniga v. United States
United States Court of Appeals, Federal Circuit, 1993
996 F.2d 1203

ARCHER, Circuit Judge.

[Refractarios Monterrey, S.A. (Refractarios) produced kiln furniture in Mexico using raw materials from the United States. Customs classified the kiln products as refractory articles under the Tariff Schedule of the United States 531.39 (the current U.S. tariff law is the Harmonized Tariff Schedule of the United States) subject to a 7.5 percent duty. Refractarios and F.F. Zuniga, the importer of record, sought to have the products enter the United States duty free under the General System of Preferences (GSP) under which Mexico is a beneficiary developing country. Under the GSP rules of origin, products could enter the United States duty free only if the sum of the cost or value of the materials and production in Mexico were at least 35 percent of the appraised value of the product. In order to reach this 35 percent level, however, the parties had to be able to include the value of raw materials from the United States as originating materials from Mexico. Refractarios and Zuniga argued that the raw materials were "substantially transformed" into a new and different article of commerce in the manufacturing process and could be considered to be of Mexican origin. Customs refused to find the products to be of Mexican origin and denied duty-free status to the kiln products. The CIT agreed with Customs and the parties appealed to the court of appeals.]

Before United States starting materials can be regarded as "materials produced" in Mexico, "[t]here must first be a substantial transformation of the [United States] material into a new and different article of commerce which becomes 'materials produced,' and these materials produced in [Mexico] must then be substantially transformed into a new and different article of commerce." *Azteca*, 890 F.2d at 1151. A substantial transformation occurs "when an article emerges from a manufacturing process with a name, character, or use which differs from [that] of the original material subjected to the process." *Torrington Co. v. United States*, 764 F.2d 1563, 1568 (Fed. Cir. 1985). Thus Refractarios must show first that the dry components processed into kiln furniture were, at an intermediate stage in the process, "substantially transformed . . . into a new and different article of commerce." 19 C.F.R. §10.177(a)(2). The determinative issue in this case is whether the casting slip is such a new and different article of commerce.

In this case, the trial court found that making the casting slip required only a simple addition of water and dispersing agents to the dry ingredients and that the slip did not lose the identifying characteristics of the dry components. It concluded that the "casting slip remained clearly recognizable as a simple blend of its dry ingredients, and was not substantially transformed." Although Refractarios contests these findings, it does not point to any evidence to the contrary. Instead, Refractarios merely argues that the process is more than a mere dilution and that performing it requires a considerable degree of experience. Because Refractarios points to no evidence that distinguishes the character of the casting slip from the dry components, we are not persuaded that the trial court clearly erred in finding no substantial transformation.

In addition to being substantially transformed, the intermediate product must also be an "article of commerce." *See* 19 C.F.R. §10.177(a)(2). In *Torrington,* this court said:

> By emphasizing that the article must be "of commerce," the Customs regulation imposes the requirement that the "new and different" product be commercially recognizable as a different article, i.e., that the "new and different" article be readily susceptible of trade, and be an item that persons might well wish to buy and acquire for their own purposes of consumption or production.
>
> [A]n "article of commerce"—for the purposes of the pertinent Customs regulation—is one that is ready to be put into a stream of commerce, but need not have actually been bought-and-sold, or actually traded, in the past.

Torrington, 764 F.2d at 1570. The trial court held that Refractarios' casting slip is not an article of commerce and that it is not "readily susceptible of trade." Refractarios contends however that it demonstrated that the casting slip is an article of commerce based on (1) testimony of a competitor's employee, that the competitor would buy the slip if it were economically feasible; (2) evidence that other casting slip is sold in the market; and (3) testimony by Mr. Turk, former president and chief executive officer of Refractarios, that he had once been asked to sell casting slip (though no actual sales were ever made). These same contentions were made at trial and were specifically considered and rejected by the trial court. Employees of Refractarios' competitor testified without contradiction that the confidential formula of Refractarios' kiln furniture could be ascertained if its casting slip was sold. Moreover, in their view the slip could not be sold at prices that would be economical for a competitor to purchase. Because of the potential disclosure of confidential information and the uncompetitive price at which the slip would have to be sold, the trial court concluded that Refractarios' casting slip is not "susceptible of trade." As to the sale of other slip, unrebutted testimony demonstrated that it is not comparable to Refractarios' casting slip in kind or quality. It is comprised of different ingredients and cannot be used in the making of kiln furniture. Rather, it is a lower quality product that is sold to hobbyists. By the same token, the evidence indicates that kiln furniture casting slip is not suitable for hobbyists because it contains excessive ingredients and the products made from it have an unattractive rough texture.

Accordingly, we affirm the judgment of the Court of International Trade that Refractarios is not entitled to duty free importation of the kiln furniture at issue.

Affirmed.

NOTES AND QUESTIONS

1. *Zuniga* was decided prior to NAFTA. If the case arose today, there would not be an origin issue as all of the originating materials and the production costs of the product are attributable to NAFTA countries (the United States and Mexico) and the kiln furniture

would pass duty free from Mexico into the United States. A determination using rules of origin and the substantial transformation test discussed in *Zuniga*, however, continues to be applicable to goods coming from other beneficiary developing countries under the GSP or to goods from other free trade zones.

2. With the tremendous proliferation of preferential trade agreements all over the world, origin determination has become an issue of paramount importance. How clear are the rules? What is the definition of "substantial transformation"? Is this test easy to apply?

3. There is a WTO Agreement on Rules of Origin (1994), but this is essentially an agreement to agree in the future, and little progress has been made on harmonization of rules of origin.

4. Two categories of problems arise in this area: (1) the proliferation and difficulty of applying the many rules of origin of domestic law and (2) lack of international standardization. Is this an argument for more trade agreements on a global scale?

PROBLEM 2-19

Fish are caught by a Spanish-flag vessel in the exclusive economic zone (EEZ), a band 200 miles offshore that is subject to Canadian sovereignty. Assume that the Spanish vessel has received permission from Canadian authorities to fish in the EEZ. The fish are beheaded, detailed, eviscerated, and cut into fillets on the Spanish vessel, then transported to South Korea where they are treated with preservatives and flavoring and then packaged into cans before being imported into the United States. What country is the origin of the fish? Is it Canada, Spain, or South Korea? In a situation like this involving multiple jurisdictions, each with a connection to the product, U.S. Customs will, if all else fails, use a default rule that is easy to apply. *See* 19 C.F.R. §102.11(d).

4. Marking

The United States (and many other countries) require that foreign products be marked with their country of origin. While marking is not relevant to the amount of the tariff imposed, it serves other purposes and is often an important issue for importers as the following case demonstrates.

Bestfoods v. United States
United States Court of Appeals, Federal Circuit, 2001
260 F.3d 1320

ARCHER, Circuit Judge.

[Bestfoods makes Skippy Peanut Butter in Arkansas using peanut slurry, a gritty peanut-based paste. Most of the paste is from the United States but 10 to 40 percent of the peanut slurry is made in Canada. In 1993, Bestfoods sought a ruling from Customs that it was not required to indicate under the federal marking statute, 19 U.S.C. §1304(a), that its peanut butter was partially of Canadian origin. The federal marking statute requires "article[s] of foreign origin imported into the United States [to] be marked in a conspicuous manner to indicate to an ultimate purchaser the English name of the country of origin of the article." 19 U.S.C. §1304(a) (1994). However, 19 C.F.R. §102.13 (2000), a subsection of the federal marking statute, contained a de minimis rule that excepts from the marking requirement products that contain foreign materials that make up less than 7 percent of the overall value of the good (or 10 percent of the value for a good of Chapter 22, Harmonized System). Under 19 C.F.R. §102.13(b), however, the de minimis exception is not applicable to most agricultural products. Bestfoods argued that the exclusion of agricultural products, such as its peanut butter, from the de minimis exception was arbitrary and capricious and, therefore, invalid. The Court of International Trade agreed with Bestfoods and entered judgment invalidating 19 C.F.R. §102.13(b), effectively extending the de minimis rule of 19 C.F.R. §102.13 to agricultural products such as Bestfoods' peanut butter. *Bestfoods v. United States*, 110 F. Supp. 2d 965 (Ct. Int'l Trade 2000). The United States appealed the decision to the court of appeals, which issued the opinion below.]

We review the Court of International Trade's consideration of Customs' regulations, a pure question of law, de novo. The federal marking statute expressly delegates to the Secretary of the Treasury the authority to promulgate regulations implementing the marking statute, in general, and as it specifically applies to goods imported from a NAFTA country. In reviewing the regulations promulgated pursuant to this grant of authority, we must defer to the administrative agency and, under the APA standard of judicial review, we must uphold these regulations unless they are "arbitrary, capricious, an abuse of discretion, or otherwise not in accordance with law." 5 U.S.C. §706 (1994).

The regulation at issue, 19 C.F.R. §102.13(b), is not arbitrary, capricious, an abuse of discretion, or otherwise not in accordance with law. Neither the federal marking statute, 19 U.S.C. §1304(a), nor the NAFTA marking rules requires a de minimis exception for agricultural products. Indeed, the federal marking statute does not provide specifically for any such de minimis exceptions. In general, it requires that "every article of foreign origin be marked." 19 U.S.C. §1304(a). The marking statute then sets out certain circumstances where a foreign product need not be marked. For example, no marking is required when the article cannot be marked (§1304(a)(3)(A)) or the article was produced more than 20 years before its import (§1304(a)(3)(I)) or where marking of the article in question would be economically prohibitive (§1304(a)(3)(K)). In view of the broad statutory language requiring marking of all articles, except for the listed exceptions, we cannot conclude that Customs was required to allow further exceptions from the marking requirement.

As the United States points out, Customs' treatment of agricultural products under the NAFTA marking rules codifies its past practice of strictly enforcing the marking statute with respect to such articles. For example, in 1985, Customs determined that orange juice manufacturers were required to mark their products to identify every source of foreign concentrate included in their juice. C.S.D. 85-47, 19 Cust. B. & Dec. No. 593 (1985); *Nat'l Juice Prods. Ass'n v. United States*, 628 F. Supp. 978 (Ct. Int'l Trade 1986) (affirming Customs' decision on appeal).[32]

In addition, withholding the de minimis exception from agricultural products tends to harmonize the country of origin rules for marking purposes with the country of origin rules for preferential tariff treatment under the NAFTA. The country of origin rules for preferential tariff treatment, while providing a de minimis exception for components comprising less than 7 percent of the value of the overall good, withhold this treatment from agricultural products. These rules withhold de minimis treatment from various

---

32. Customs subsequently relaxed this requirement, following a showing by the juice manufacturers that the marking was economically prohibitive. Treas. Dec. 89-66 (1989), reprinted in 54 Fed. Reg. 29,540 (July 13, 1989).

other products as well. Customs' action in establishing a de minimis rule, for purposes of the NAFTA marking rules, that closely tracks the de minimis rule for preferential tariff treatment under the NAFTA is not arbitrary.

We also reject Bestfoods' arguments that the regulations at issue are based on inappropriate health and safety concerns and lead to absurd results. Pointing to published comments concerning the regulation at issue, Bestfoods contends that Customs improperly withheld the de minimis exception from agricultural products out of a misplaced concern for consumer safety. Bestfoods argues that it is not the role of Customs to address food safety issues and, therefore, this was an inappropriate justification for Customs' regulation. We do not agree. Customs has the discretion to promulgate regulations to implement the federal marking statute, 19 U.S.C. §1304(a), as further directed by the NAFTA marking rules, for products from NAFTA countries. As noted above, the purpose of marking products under the marking statute is to inform consumers of the origin of foreign goods. It was surely within Customs' discretion to determine that consumers might be more concerned about foreign materials in agricultural products, including foods. Thus, Customs' reference to "health and food safety concerns" does not necessarily indicate that Customs has improperly taken on a role assigned to other federal agencies that are directly responsible for ensuring food safety. Rather, Customs was merely exercising its discretion to craft rules that would best inform consumers.

We similarly reject Bestfoods' arguments that the regulation leads to absurd results. Bestfoods points out that under the marking regulations consumers are not informed about any quantity of foreign ingredients, if such ingredients are substantially transformed (so as to undergo a shift in tariff classification) during manufacturing of the final product. Further, Bestfoods argues that potentially toxic foreign non-agricultural additives are subject to the de minimis exceptions, and the foreign origins of such additives need not be indicated if less than 7 percent. Again, we do not find Bestfoods' contentions persuasive. Although the marking regulations will not always indicate to consumers the foreign origin of certain components, we cannot conclude that it was arbitrary or capricious for Customs to consider substantially-transformed ingredients to be products of the country of manufacture, even if the raw materials come from some foreign location. Indeed, this was exactly the conclusion that the NAFTA Marking Rules required. As for Bestfoods' contention concerning non-agricultural additives, it is simply incorrect. The de minimis exception is withheld for foreign material incorporated into any agricultural product identified in §102.13(b), no matter whether the incorporated foreign material is an agricultural product or non-agricultural food additive.

We conclude that the regulations, when properly interpreted, do not lead to any absurd results.

Reversed.

NOTES AND QUESTIONS

1. Why was Bestfoods so concerned about marking its label to indicate that its peanut butter included Canadian peanuts? Are Canadian peanuts inferior to U.S. peanuts?

2. Origin marking requirements are a battleground between importers and domestic producers. A basic requirement of the WTO is the principle of national treatment prohibiting discrimination against foreign products in favor of domestic products. As a result, nations are not allowed to impose restrictions and conditions on imported products that do not also apply to domestic products. An exception, however, is made under

GATT Article IX for marks of origin. Should this be changed? Is origin marking necessary? Helpful?

3. Does origin marking really influence consumers to "buy American"?

4. Formerly, a domestic manufacturer could request the U.S. Customs Service to issue an interpretive "letter ruling" on whether foreign origin marking was required. This practice was overturned in *Norcal/Crosetti Foods, Inc. v. United States*, 963 F.2d 356 (Fed. Cir. 1992). Now a petition under 19 U.S.C. §1516 must be filed with the Customs Service, invoking an administrative procedure. *See* 19 C.F.R. §175. Failure to mark allows the assessment of additional duties.

PROBLEM 2-20

The State of Hawaii is particularly vulnerable to penetration by imported products because of its isolation and location, creating a need for many products not available locally. In order to satisfy the demands of domestic producers, the Hawaii legislature has enacted a law: All retail stores that sell eggs produced outside the United States must display a sign in a conspicuous place in their shops in capital letters at least 3 inches high stating, "WE SELL FOREIGN EGGS." A local supermarket that imports eggs from Australia objects to this new law. If federal law requires that the foreign origin of the eggs must be marked on the package anyway, why should there be an issue with this sign? Is this lawful? *See Hawaii v. Ho*, 41 Haw. 565 (1957).

NOTE ON INTERNATIONAL TRADE LAW AND THE IMPORT/EXPORT SALES TRANSACTION

As we explained in Chapter One, this book concerns IBTs, and our treatment of international trade law will only be introductory. Nevertheless, we wish to emphasize that in the "real world" international trade law is important. We have explored the principal effects of trade law concepts on import/export transactions, that is, the international sale of goods. Now we summarize and present the "big picture."

International trade laws exist on both the national and the international levels. The public international law of international trade operates to inject a necessary discipline into national laws that otherwise would be free to differ and conflict, impeding trade. Thus, the international law of trade consists of internationally agreed upon rules of conduct that must be observed by individual states. Not all national trade laws come within the discipline of the international rules, but most important concerns are addressed.

International trade law rules are agreed upon by states on a global level through the World Trade Organization and on a regional or bilateral basis through free trade and other international economic agreements. In the preceding section, the impacts of some of these rules were explored.

As this chapter indicates, the primary impact of international trade rules for the exporter/importer is the tariff that applies to the particular transaction. International rules subject tariffs to discipline and also ban quantitative restrictions (quotas) and other restrictions on imports. International agreements under the WTO also discipline other measures that can be used to impeded trade such as import licensing, product standards and technical requirements, and pre-shipment inspection.

The law of international trade also concerns:

- Rules on treatment that must be accorded to imported products once they clear customs and border formalities. "National treatment" is required that generally prohibits any measure or internal tax that puts imports at a competitive disadvantage with respect to domestic products.
- Rules on how imports can be subject to extra duties if they are unfairly traded. These concern the ability of states to levy antidumping and countervailing duties.
- Rules on "safeguards"—the ability of a state to limit fairly traded imports that are causing a serious adverse impact on a domestic industry.

The law of international trade also has processes for the periodic review, revision, and renegotiation of tariffs and trade matters. The WTO contains an important dispute settlement system as well. For complete treatment of international trade law issues, see Chow and Schoenbaum, *International Trade Law: Problems, Cases, and Materials* (Aspen 2d ed. 2012).

3 *The Sales Contract*

In the preceding chapter, we provided an overview of the entire international sales transaction. In this chapter and the next, we focus on two of the most important topics in the international sale: the sales contract and the letter of credit. We begin our study of sales contracts with some preliminary choice of law issues and examine the sales contract under the United Nations Convention on Contracts for the International Sale of Goods.

I. *Choice of Law*

We start with the basic issues: What law governs an international sales contract and how is the choice of law determined?

Kristinus v. H. Stern Com. e Ind. S.A.
United States District Court, Southern District of New York, 1979
463 F. Supp. 1263

LASKER, District Judge.

While visiting Rio de Janeiro in December, 1974, Rainer Kristinus, a Pennsylvania resident, purchased three gems from H. Stern Com. e Ind. S.A. (H. Stern) for $30,467.43. According to Kristinus, a flyer advertising H. Stern's wares had been slipped under the door of his hotel room in Brazil. The flyer contained the following statement (in English) in red type:

"Every sale carries Stern's one-year guarantee for refund, credit or exchange either here or in your own country. H. Stern Jewelers New York, (681 Fifth Avenue) are at your disposal for help and service."

Kristinus asserts that when he purchased the gems, a vice-president of H. Stern assured him that he would be able to return them for a complete refund in New York.

In January, 1975, Kristinus tendered the gems to H. Stern Jewelers, Inc. in New York City and requested a refund. His request was denied, and this suit for specific performance of the alleged oral promise to refund the purchase price followed.

H. Stern moves to dismiss the complaint on the ground that the alleged oral promise is unenforceable under the laws of Brazil, which H. Stern contends govern the transaction in question.

The provisions of Brazilian law on which H. Stern relies are Articles 141 and 142 of the Brazilian Civil Code, which provide:

"Article 141. Except in cases specifically provided for to the contrary, evidence which is solely by [oral] testimony is only admitted as to Contracts whose value does not exceed Cr$10,000.00 (ten thousand cruzeiros).

Sole Paragraph. Whatever the amount of the Contract, evidence by testimony is admissible as a subsidiary to or complement of evidence in writing.

Article 142. There cannot be admitted as witnesses:

IV. The person interested in the object of the litigation, as well as the ancestor and the descendant, or collateral relative, through the third degree of one of the parties, whether by blood or by affiliation."[1]

The question presented at this juncture is not whether H. Stern has properly stated Brazilian law, but whether a New York court would apply that law or the law of the state of New York in the circumstances of this case. We conclude that a New York court would apply the law of New York, and accordingly we deny H. Stern's motion to dismiss.

In deciding choice of law questions, the rule in New York is that "the law of the jurisdiction having the greatest interest in the litigation will be applied and that the facts or contacts which obtain significance in defining State interests are those which relate to the purpose of the particular law in conflict." *Miller v. Miller*, 22 N.Y.2d 12, 15–16 (1968). In short, New York courts balance New York's interest in having New York law apply against a foreign state's interest in having foreign law apply.

An examination of the provisions of the Brazilian Civil Code on which H. Stern relies suggests that those provisions promote two interests. First, they protect the integrity of the judicial process in Brazil against the taints of perjured and biased testimony, by 1) requiring that testimony regarding a contract be corroborated by written evidence (Article 141), and 2) barring testimony from interested parties (Article 142). This interest is not implicated in the present case, since the integrity of the Brazilian judicial process is not threatened in a suit in the United States District Court for the Southern District of New York.

Second, Article 141 protects persons who transact business in Brazil from unfounded contractual claims by requiring that such claims, to be enforceable, be supported by a writing. This interest of Brazil does have a bearing on this case, since presumably Brazil seeks to provide this protection to anyone who transacts business there, regardless of where suit on the transaction is brought. The question, then, is whether this interest is greater than any interest that New York may have in applying its own law (which we assume, for the purposes of this motion, would permit enforcement of the contract alleged by Kristinus) to the transaction involved here.

Although Kristinus is not a New York resident, New York may nonetheless assert an interest on his behalf. New York's contacts with this case are 1) that H. Stern transacts business in New York through its franchisee and agent, H. Stern Jewelers, Inc., and 2) that the alleged promise that Kristinus seeks to enforce was to refund the purchase price of the gems in New York through that franchisee. New York has some interest in ensuring that persons who transact business within its borders (and thus subject themselves to some extent at least to the authority of the state) honor obligations, including contracts made elsewhere. Usually, of course, this interest must bow to the paramount interest of the state or country where the contract is made in regulating the conduct of those within its territory. When the contract is to be performed in New York, however, New York's interest is heightened, since its ability to regulate business affairs and the rights and obligations of

---

1. H. Stern's expert on Brazilian law states that the statement in the flyer that Kristinus received in Brazil would not "be sufficient under Brazilian law to constitute a written contract or even a writing sufficient to enable plaintiff, or his wife, to testify as to the Contract." Affidavit of Paul Griffith Garland, Exhibit B to Defendant's Notice of Motion, P. 4.

those within its territory is then directly implicated. In such circumstances, we conclude that a New York court would decline to apply foreign law where, as here, that law would foreclose enforcement of a contract valid under New York law. In short, a New York court would not permit H. Stern of Brazil to contract in Brazil to refund Kristinus' purchase price in New York, and then rely on the laws of Brazil to avoid its obligation under the contract. Accordingly, New York law should be applied.

H. Stern's motion to dismiss is denied.

NOTES AND QUESTIONS

1. The choice of law materials in this section concern the law applicable to an international sales contract. Choice of law on general issues, of course, is also important in dispute resolution and needs to be considered in conjunction with choice of forum, jurisdiction, and other related issues, which we cover in Chapter Eight on dispute resolution.

2. In *Kristinus*, the plaintiff, a Pennsylvania resident, brought suit against a Brazilian defendant in a federal district court in New York City. The federal court, exercising diversity jurisdiction, applied the choice of law approach of the New York state courts under the rule established by *Erie Railroad Co. v. Tompkins*, 304 U.S. 64 (1938), and *Klaxon Co. v. Stentor Electric Manufacturing Co.*, 313 U.S. 487 (1941). In making a choice between New York and Brazilian law, the court is involved in an application of the rules of private international law, as we have discussed in Chapter One. If the case were brought in Brazil, then the Brazilian courts would apply their own choice of law rules. Brazil follows a civil law system based on the continental law traditions of its European settlers. Suppose that Brazil follows the continental law rule that the validity of a contract is governed by the law of the place where it was formed. Under this approach, the Brazilian court might chose Brazilian law to govern the case. What problems of perception might arise if it appeared that, depending on where the case was brought, a Brazilian court would apply the law of Brazil and a New York court would apply the law of New York to govern the case?

3. Section 1-105 of the Uniform Commercial Code (UCC) provides that

> Except as provided hereafter in this section, when a transaction bears a reasonable relation to this state and also to another state or nation the parties may agree that the law either of this state or of such other state or nation shall govern their rights and duties. Failing such agreement this Act applies to transactions bearing an appropriate relation to this state.

This last clause has been called the "Imperial Clause" because it allows the application by a U.S. court of U.S. law in any case where the court in its judgment deems the transaction to have an appropriate connection to the state. What issues for the international trading community might arise from this type of choice of law approach?

4. Approaches to choice of law analysis differ among nations, and in the United States, the analysis can differ among the 50 states, all of which have their own choice of law rules. These different approaches can lead to an unfortunate lack of predictability in results. In an effort to promote uniformity in choice of law analysis and the rules of private international law, a number of attempts have been made in the United States and Europe to promote a uniform approach. The Restatement Conflicts of Law (Second) (1971) provides in relevant part for the following choice of law approach in the case of contracts:

§188.   *Law Governing in Absence of Effective Choice by the Parties*

(1)   The rights and duties of the parties with respect to an issue in the contract are determined by local law of the state which, with respect to that issue, has the most significant relationship to the transaction and the parties.

(2)   In the absence of an effective choice of law by the parties (see §187), the contacts to be taken into account to determine the law applicable to an issue include:

    (a)   the place of contracting,

    (b)   the place of negotiation of the contract,

    (c)   the place of performance,

    (d)   the location of the subject matter of the contract, and

    (e)   the domicile, residence, nationality, place of incorporation and place of business of the parties.

These contacts are to be evaluated according to their relative importance with respect to the particular issue.

The Restatement creates a heavy burden on courts as it requires the above analysis to be made with regard to each issue concerning the contract. The Convention on the Law Applicable to Contractual Obligations (1980), which is applicable within certain states of the European Union, provides in Article 4(1) that the contract is to be governed by the law of the country "with which it is most closely connected." This approach is similar to the Restatement approach focusing on the state with "the most significant relationship" to the contract. How predictable do you think the Restatement and the EU approach would be in deciding international choice of law cases such as *Kristinus*?

5. In *Kristinus*, the court weighed the interests of Brazil against the interests of the state of New York and applied New York law. *See also J. Zeevi & Sons, Ltd. v. Grindlays Bank*, 333 N.E.2d 168 (N.Y. 1975), *cert. denied*, 423 U.S. 866 (1975) (refusing to apply Uganda national exchange law that would cancel a letter of credit opened in favor of Israeli companies and payable in New York). The use of state choice of law rules in international cases continues to be commonplace even though one might argue that the interests of foreign states ought to be a federal rather than a state matter and that a federal approach would promote uniformity in the international choice of law context. *See* Chow, *Limiting Erie in a New Age of International Law: Toward a Federal Common Law of International Choice of Law*, 74 Iowa L. Rev. 165 (1988).

6. The discussion above indicates the following areas of concern in an international choice of law situation: (1) the perception that nation-states may sometimes assert nationalistic interests in choosing their own law instead of foreign law, (2) the lack of predictability in results in applying the rules of private international law, and (3) the intrusion of the states in an area that may implicate federal interests. These concerns are addressed to some extent by the promulgation of the Convention for the International Sale of Goods, the subject of the remainder of this chapter. How does the CISG address each of the concerns set forth above?

II.   The United Nations Convention on Contracts for the International Sale of Goods

The United Nations Convention on Contracts for the International Sale of Goods (CISG), S. Treaty Doc. No. 9, 98th Cong., 1st Sess. 22 (1983), 19 I.L.M. 671, reprinted at 15 U.S.C.

App. 52 (1997), is a multilateral convention drafted and promulgated under the auspices of the United Nations Commission on International Trade Law (UNCITRAL) to which 73 nations, including the United States, are contracting parties. The CISG opened for signature April 11, 1980 and entered into force on January 1, 1988. The CISG is a self-executing treaty that applies directly within its contracting states without the need for domestic implementing legislation.

The CISG was one of the most important instruments of harmonization in the area of international commercial law in the twentieth century. The goal of the CISG is to promote uniformity in the treatment of contracts in the light of international commercial usage and practice. We will be exploring the meaning of this statement in the materials that follow. We will not examine the substantive provisions of the Uniform Commercial Code (UCC) in detail, although we highlight some significant differences between the CISG and the UCC and examine the relationship between the two laws. We leave a detailed consideration of the UCC, however, to other courses in the law school curriculum. Our focus is on the CISG.

When the CISG applies, it displaces domestic law. In the case of the United States, the CISG often displaces the UCC in international sales contracts. The CISG only applies to *international* sales contracts so the UCC and other domestic laws are not disturbed in their internal application. But where the contract is international and the CISG applies, a growing number of nations, including most of the major trading powers, have agreed to displace their domestic law in favor of a uniform substantive international contract law. This is a remarkable achievement.

Parties to the CISG

Albania	Czech Republic	Japan	Russian
Argentina	Denmark	Kyrgyzstan	Federation
Armenia	Dominican	Latvia	Saint Vincent and
Australia	Republic	Lebanon	Grenadines
Austria	Ecuador	Lesotho	San Marion
Bahrain	Egypt	Liberia	Serbia
Belarus	El Salvador	Lithuania	Singapore
Belgium	Estonia	Luxembourg	Slovakia
Benin	Finland	Macedonia	Slovenia
Brazil	France	Mauritania	South Korea
Bosnia and	Gabon	Mexico	Spain
Herzegovina	Georgia	Moldova	Sweden
Bulgaria	Germany	Mongolia	Switzerland
Burundi	Greece	Montenegro	Syria
Canada	Guinea	Netherlands	Turkey
Chile	Honduras	New Zealand	Uganda
China	Hungary	Norway	Ukraine
Colombia	Iceland	Paraguay	United States
Croatia	Iraq	Peru	Uruguay
Cuba	Israel	Poland	Uzbekistan
Cyprus	Italy	Romania	Zambia

For an article-by-article commentary on the CISG, see Stefan Kroll, Loukas A. Mistelis, and Maria del Pilar Perales Viscacillas (eds.), *The United Nations Convention on Contracts for the International Sale of Goods* (Oxford: Hart Publishing, 2011).

A. Basic Features of the CISG

The CISG is not a mandatory public law but a supplementary private one; the parties can exclude the application of the CISG, vary the effect of its provisions, and the terms of the contract will override any conflicting terms in the convention. In other words, the CISG, like domestic contract law, plays a supporting role in resolving questions that the parties have not themselves already agreed on.

The CISG is not a comprehensive treatment of contract law, and there are important areas that are excluded from its coverage. The CISG governs two basic aspects of the contract: Part I governs the formation of the contract and Part II governs the obligations of the parties to the contract. Contracting states can exclude either part by a specific declaration under Article 92. Important issues such as validity of the contract, third-party rights, and property rights in the goods are not governed by the CISG. The result is that these important excluded issues must be governed by another substantive law, usually the domestic law of one of the parties. Where the parties have not explicitly agreed on a domestic law to govern issues that are excluded from the CISG, the court must engage in a choice of law analysis. Thus, although the CISG is an important tool of harmonization, it does not avoid the need for the use of private international law analysis or the use of domestic law or both in any given case. Both of these matters will continue to play a major role in international contracts for the sale of goods in addition to the CISG.

B. Historical Origins

Although the CISG came into effect in 1988, its origins can be traced to the work of the International Institute for the Unification of Private Law (UNIDROIT, discussed in Chapter One at pp. 26-27) that was launched in the 1930s. UNIDROIT drafted two conventions, a Uniform Law for the International Sale of Goods and a Uniform Law on the Formation of Contracts for the International Sale of Goods, which were finalized at a diplomatic conference held at the Hague, Netherlands, in 1964. When it became clear that widespread adoption of the Hague conventions was impossible because of their Western European orientation, UNCITRAL began drafting a more universally acceptable convention, culminating in the CISG. Many of the provisions adopted in the CISG, however, reflect those of the Hague conventions and the legislative history of the Hague conventions continues to be useful in shedding light on the interpretation of the CISG.

C. Cases on the CISG

States that have implemented the CISG and other UNCITRAL uniform laws have been requested to designate national correspondents whose role is to send decisions applying the CISG (and other uniform laws) to the UNCITRAL secretariat. The correspondents have also been asked to prepare one-page abstracts of such cases. UNCITRAL has established a clearinghouse in its Vienna office that publishes abstracts of cases decided under the CISG and its other uniform laws. The cases are published under the acronym CLOUT (Case Law on UNCITRAL Texts) and are available at *http://www.uncitral.org* under "Case Law (CLOUT)."

Professor Michael J. Bonnell, University of Rome, has developed a comprehensive collection of CISG decisions that are compiled in a two-volume loose-leaf service that is widely considered to be authoritative: *UNILEX: International Case Law & Bibliography on CISG* (Transnational Publishers, New York). This is available at *http://www.unilex.info/*.

The decisions have been abstracted in English in Volume I with full texts of the decisions available in their original languages in Volume II. In the materials that follow, we will use materials from both CLOUT and UNILEX.

NOTE ON THE UNIDROIT PRINCIPLES

The UNIDROIT Principles of International Commercial Contracts are the result of 20 years of work, culminating in their adoption by UNIDROIT in May 1994. Unlike the CISG, the Principles are not a binding legal instrument; rather, the Principles are a type of international restatement of contracts, but, as set forth in the preamble, the Principles can have legal effect in the following circumstances, when: (1) the parties expressly agree that the contract shall be governed by them, (2) the parties agree that the contract shall be governed by general principles of international commercial law such as the *lex mercatoria*, (3) domestic law is unable to provide a solution, and (4) international instruments need supplementation or interpretation. By all accounts, the UNIDROIT Principles are an outstanding achievement and they are highly influential.

In general, the UNIDROIT Principles and the CISG complement each other and are not in conflict. The CISG applies only to sales contracts whereas the Principles apply to all international commercial contracts. In an IBT, the parties may not only need to contract for the sale of goods but may also need to engage in contracts related to agency, distribution, marketing, personnel issues, and other services. It is possible that in some transactions, some of the contracts are governed by the CISG while others are subject to the Principles. In addition, even where the CISG applies, the Principles may be used to supplement the CISG under Article 7, which provides that in interpreting the CISG, regard shall be given to its "international character and to the need to promote uniformity in its application." The Principles, as a distillation of international practice, may be used as a source of interpretation to promote uniformity. As the focus of this chapter is on the international sales contract most of our attention will be on the CISG, but we introduce the UNIDROIT Principles where appropriate.

D.   Sphere of Application of the CISG: Articles 1–6

Articles 1–6 of the CISG define its sphere of application. The most important provisions delimiting the scope of application of the CISG are contained in the first article:

Article 1

(1) This Convention applies to contracts of sale of goods between parties whose places of business are in different States:
   (a) when the States are Contracting States; or
   (b) when the rules of private international law lead to the application of the law of a Contracting State.
(2) The fact that the parties have their places of business in different States is to be disregarded whenever this fact does not appear either from the contract or from any dealings between, or from information disclosed by, the parties at any time before or at the conclusion of the contract.
(3) Neither the nationality of the parties nor the civil or commercial character of the parties or of the contract is to be taken into consideration in determining the application of this Convention.

1.   Article 1(1)(a) and the Test of Internationality

The CISG applies only to contracts for the sale of goods that are international. Of the three elements of its subject matter, the CISG defines only one: internationality. The test of whether a contract is international under Article 1(1)(a) is whether the parties have their places of business in different contracting states.

> *Illustration 1a.* In a contract for the sale of goods, seller has its place of business in country A and buyer has its place of business in country B. Both country A and country B are parties to the CISG. Unless the parties expressly exclude the application of the CISG, or an enumerated exception under the CISG applies, an action to resolve a dispute under the sales contract that is brought either in country A or country B is governed by the CISG under Article 1(1)(a).

In cases involving the United States, U.S. courts refuse to apply Article 1(1)(a) if the other state is not a party to the CISG. *See Princesse D'Isenbourg et Cie. Ltd. v. Kinder Caviar, Inc.*, No. 3:09-29-DCR, 2011 Dist. LEXIS 17281 (E.D. Ky. Feb. 22, 2011) (refusing to apply CISG in contract between a U.S. seller and a buyer from the UK, which is not a party to the CISG).

Suppose that the action were brought in a third nation, country C, a contracting state. What law should country C apply? Country C need look no further than Article 1(1)(a) for the answer: The CISG governs the contract so long as the parties have their places of business in two contracting states and the parties have not expressly excluded the CISG. The more difficult question occurs when country C is a non-contracting state. In many, if not most cases, country C would apply the CISG because the practical result should be the same whether country C recognizes the effect of subparagraph (1)(a) or if C applies a choice of law analysis. If country C recognizes subparagraph (1)(a), it applies the CISG; if C applies its own choice of law rules that result in a choice of either the law of country A or the law of country B, then the CISG applies as the CISG is part of the domestic law of both countries.

The most difficult situation occurs when country C's choice of law analysis results in the choice of country C's domestic law (e.g., suppose that delivery of the goods was to occur in C). What law should C apply in this case, the CISG or country C's domestic law? Even in this case, country C should apply the CISG unless the application of the CISG violates a basic public policy of the forum. The entry into the CISG by countries A and B is a type of implicit choice of law, and country C should give effect to the choice of law by parties; otherwise, country C would nullify the effect of Article 1(1)(a).

In this age of the multinational enterprise with multiple places of business around the world, it is not always easy to determine whether the parties have their places of business in different states as required by Article 1(1)(a). Consider the following problem.

PROBLEM 3-1

Microtel is a multinational enterprise engaged in the manufacture and sale of computer equipment with offices in five continents and headquarters in the United States. Microtel's wholly-owned foreign subsidiary in the United Kingdom manufactures microprocessors and enters into a contract to sell microprocessors to a Ugandan company. All of the early negotiations concerning the contract occur between in-house lawyers from the UK subsidiary and several executives of the Ugandan company. During these negotiations, the in-house lawyers for the UK subsidiary repeatedly asked for and received instructions from management in the U.S. headquarters. When the negotiations reached a critical stage, two senior executives from the U.S. headquarters traveled to Uganda, rented a suite of rooms in a hotel for a week, and worked out the final details of the contract. Most of the final negotiations with the Ugandans occurred in the hotel suite with the two senior U.S. executives as active participants. When the final details were worked out, the CEO of Microtel, the U.S. headquarters, traveled to Uganda and signed the contract in a ceremony held in the hotel suite. Is this contract governed by the CISG? *See* Article 1(1)(a) and (2); *see also* Article 10(a).

2. Article 1(1)(b)

If the CISG applies by virtue of Article 1(1)(a), it is unnecessary to apply the choice of law approach of Article 1(1)(b). If subparagraph (1)(a) is not applicable, then the CISG may apply as a result of subparagraph (1)(b):

> *Illustration 1b.* In a contract for the sale of goods, the seller is from country A, a contracting state to the CISG, and the buyer is from a non-contracting state. As country B is a non-contracting state, the CISG cannot apply by virtue of Article 1(1)(a). In a dispute brought in the courts of either country A or country B, the court must then make a choice of law decision applying the forum's choice of law rules. If the court chooses the law of country B, then the domestic law of country B will govern the contract. If the court chooses the law of country A, then under Article 1(1)(b) the CISG governs the contract as the CISG is part of the law of country A.

Article 95 of the CISG allows a party to make a reservation at the time of ratification that it will not be bound by Article 1(1)(b). The United States has made such a reservation. In fact, the United States and several other nations had attempted to have subparagraph (1)(b) deleted from the working drafts of the CISG, but this attempt was defeated. The compromise that was reached was the opt-out mechanism of Article 95. In explaining its position to exclude subparagraph (1)(b), the United States offered this rationale:

> [S]ubparagraph 1(b) would displace our own domestic law more frequently than foreign law. By its terms, subparagraph 1(b) would be relevant only in sales between parties in the United States (a Contracting State) and a *non*-Contracting State. Under subparagraph 1(b), when private international law points to the law of a foreign *non*-Contracting State the Convention will not displace that foreign law, since subparagraph 1(b) makes the Convention applicable only when "the rules of private international law lead to the application of the law of a *Contracting* State." Consequently, when those rules point to United States law, subparagraph 1(b) would normally operate to displace United States law (the Uniform Commercial Code) and would not displace the law of foreign *non*-Contracting States.

United States Department of State, *Legal Analysis of the UN Convention on Contracts for the International Sale of Goods*, Treaty Doc. No. 9809, 98th Cong., 1st Sess., Appendix B at 1380 (1983). The following case involves an application of Article 1(1)(b) and the U.S. reservation under Article 95.

Prime Start Ltd. v. Maher Forest Products Ltd.
United States District Court, Western District of Washington, 2006
442 F. Supp. 2d 1113

COUGHENOUR, District Judge.

This case is a contract dispute involving an approximately $1 million purchase of Western Red Cedar siding for use at a construction site in Moscow, Russia. Plaintiff Prime

Start, Ltd. is a British Virgin Islands corporation that supplies construction materials to clients around the world. Plaintiff entered into a contract with Defendant Maher Forest Products, Ltd. ("Maher"), a Washington corporation, for custom-manufactured wood products to be used by Plaintiff's client in Russia. Defendant Pacific Lumber Inspection Bureau ("PLIB") is a Washington corporation that contracted with Plaintiff to provide services related to quality control of the goods supplied by Defendant Maher.

Plaintiff's complaint alleges that both Defendants Maher and PLIB breached their contracts with Plaintiff. Defendant Maher allegedly supplied nonconforming goods, while Defendant PLIB allegedly failed to inspect the goods according to the terms of the parties' agreement, thus allowing delivery of nonconforming goods to the job site in Russia.

APPLICABLE LAW

The parties did not include choice-of-law clauses as terms to the contracts at issue here. Plaintiff alleges that the United Nations Convention on Contracts for the International Sale of Goods ("CISG"), 15 U.S.C. App., applies to the instant dispute. By its own terms, the CISG

applies to contracts of sale of goods between parties whose places of business are in different states:

   (a) When the States are Contracting States; or
   (b) When the rules of private international law lead to the application of the law of a Contracting State.

C.I.S.G., art. 1(1).

Here, Plaintiff is a British Virgin Islands corporation, while both Defendants are Washington corporations. The United States ratified the CISG in 1986. However, neither the British Virgin Islands nor the United Kingdom are signatories to the CISG. Thus, only one side of the contracts at issue here and only one side of this litigation involves parties of signatory States—Defendants Maher and PLIB. Because *all* contracting parties in this dispute are not businesses in States that are parties to the Convention, Article 1(1)(a) cannot provide a basis for application of the CISG.

Plaintiff argues that the fact that not all parties are from signatory States is irrelevant, invoking Article 1(1)(b). Plaintiff asserts that application of private international law would lead to the application of Canadian, United States, or Russian law, and because all three of *these* are Contracting States, *see* C.I.S.G., 15 U.S.C. App. (Parties to the Convention), the CISG applies *regardless* of Plaintiff's status as a corporation of the British Virgin Islands—a Non-Contracting State. The Court disagrees.

When the United States ratified the CISG, it invoked the option found in Article 95 of the Convention, which provides: "Any State may declare at the time of the deposit of its instrument of ratification, acceptance, approval or accession that it will not be bound by subparagraph (1)(b) of article 1 of this Convention." C.I.S.G., art. 95. The United States did exactly this, thus directly precluding the reasoning Plaintiff attempts to apply. As a matter of law, Plaintiff cannot circumvent the requirement of Article 1(1)(a) by relying on Article 1(1)(b). Instead, "the *only* circumstance in which the CISG could apply is if all the parties to the contract were from Contracting States." *Impuls I.D. Internacional, S.L. v. Psion-Teklogix Inc.*, 234 F. Supp. 2d 1267, 1272 (S.D. Fla. 2002) (emphasis added); *see also Chateau des Charmes Wines Ltd. v. Sabate USA Inc.*, 328 F.3d 528, 530 (9th Cir. 2003) (stating the precondition that CISG applies " 'when the States are Contracting States' ").

Because not all parties are from countries that signed the CISG, the CISG cannot apply to this dispute, even if a traditional choice-of-law analysis leads to the application of the law of the United States (or one of its states) or any other signatory State. Accordingly, some body of law other than the CISG will govern this dispute. [After finding that the CISG did not apply, the federal court, sitting in diversity jurisdiction, went on to consider a choice of law analysis under Washington state law as required by *Klaxon Co. v. Stentor Elec. Mfg. Co.*, 313 U.S. 487 (1941). The court found that Washington contract law, the UCC, applied to this contract. This case arose on motion for summary judgment, and the court denied the motion after finding that genuine issues of material fact were in dispute.]

NOTES AND QUESTIONS

1. In *Prime Start*, assume that the United States did not declare a reservation under Article 95 to Article 1(1)(b). In this event, then it would have been possible for the CISG to apply to the case under Article 1(1)(b) even though only the defendants, two Washington companies, were from a contracting state (the United States) whereas Prime Start, the plaintiff, a British Virgin Islands company, was from a non-contracting state, the United Kingdom. Can you go through the analysis and explain why? Under this analysis of Article 1(1)(b), could a court choose U.S. law, the UCC, to govern the case? Consider the effect of the U.S. Article 95 reservation to Article 1(1)(b). What possible laws are applicable to the case now? Does this explain why the United States declared a reservation under Article 95? The American Bar Association supported the reservation on the grounds that the use of Article 1(1)(b) might be disadvantageous to U.S. commercial lawyers and their clients. How does the Article 95 reservation "even the playing field" for the United States?

2. Article 1(1)(b) increases the application of the CISG because the CISG will apply even when one of the parties is from a non-contracting state if a private international law analysis chooses the law of the contracting state. Reservations such as that made by the United States result in fewer applications of the CISG because any contracts between the United States and a non-contracting state will now be governed by the domestic law of either the United States or the other state. In making a reservation under Article 95, has the United States put its own interests ahead of the interests of promoting harmonization through the broadest possible application of the CISG?

3. Return to *Kristinus, supra*, p. 165. That case was decided in 1979 before the CISG became effective on January 1, 1988. Suppose that the CISG were in effect when the case was decided and that both the United States and Brazil were contracting parties. (As of this writing both the United States and Brazil are contracting parties.) Would the CISG apply to govern the case? To determine the answer to this question, several questions need to be answered. First, was there a contract for the *international* sale of goods? The sale and purchase occurred in Brazil. Would that fact remove that case from the scope of CISG Article 1(1)(a)? *See also* CISG Article 10(b). Also, does this case fall within Article 1(2)? Second, do any other exclusions apply? *See* CISG Article 2(a). Brazil acceded to the CISG in 2013 and it entered into force for Brazil on April 1, 2014.

4. Under the CISG, when only one party is from a contracting state and the state has excluded subparagraph (1)(b) through a declaration under Article 95, then the domestic law of one of the states will apply. We now come to a more complex issue: What law applies when a contracting state has excluded Article 1(1)(b) but the dispute, between

the contracting state and a non-contracting state, is brought in a third contracting state? What effect will the third state give to the Article 95 declaration? The following problem requires you to work through the analysis of these issues.

PROBLEM 3-2

A U.S. computer company has a foreign subsidiary in Germany that services the European Union markets. The U.S. company makes a contract with a UK corporation for the sale of memory chip sets. The U.S. company buys the chip sets and then supplies them to its German subsidiary, among its other foreign subsidiaries. Suppose a dispute has arisen and the U.S. company decides to bring an action against the UK supplier in a German court. The United States and Germany are contracting parties to the CISG but the UK is not (as of this writing). The United States has made an Article 95 declaration excluding the application of Article 1(1)(b). Germany has not made an Article 95 declaration but has made the following statement:

> The Government of the Federal Republic of Germany holds the view that parties to the Convention that have made a declaration under Article 95 of the Convention are not considered Contracting States within the meaning of subparagraph 1(b) of Article 1 of the Convention. Accordingly, there is no obligation to apply—and the Federal Republic of Germany assumes no obligation to apply—this provision when the rules of private international law lead to the application of the law of a Party that has made a declaration to the effect that it will not be bound by subparagraph 1(b) of Article 1 of the Convention. Subject to this observation the Government of the Federal Republic of Germany makes no declaration under Article 95 of the Convention.

UN Depositary Notification C.N. 365.1989, Treaties -3, dated March 16, 1990. What possible laws can the German court apply to this transaction? Why would Germany take this position? A leading commentator believes that the German position is the correct interpretation of Article 1(1)(b). *See* John O. Honnold, *Uniform Law for International Sales Under the 1980 United Nations Convention* 43 (3d ed. 1999).

3.   Other Issues Relating to Scope

Articles 1–3 identify the transactions that are subject to the CISG, while Articles 4 and 5 define the issues that are governed by the CISG. We have already examined the scope of Article 1. The following problems and cases require you to work through the exclusions in Articles 2–5 and the opt-out provisions of Article 6.

PROBLEM 3-3

Acindar Argentine Steel (Acindar), located in Buenos Aires, Argentina, enters into a joint venture with Akron Steel (Akron), located in Ohio, for the manufacture, distribution, and sale of steel in Argentina and South America. Under the joint venture contract entered into between Acindar and Akron Steel, the new joint venture company, Akron-Acindar Steel, promised to use "its best efforts in light of market conditions" to purchase up to $2 million in steel in the first two years of the contract and serve as Akron Steel's Argentina distributor. In return, Akron Steel promised to purchase chromium from the joint venture, which would comprise 35 percent of the ingredients used by Akron Steel to manufacture the steel that would be sold to the joint venture. During the first year, the joint venture submits a purchase order with Akron for $350,000 in steel, which Akron fills. Later, Akron Steel argues that the joint venture has breached its good faith purchasing obligations under the joint venture contract and has also failed to secure various Argentine government approvals as required by the contract. Is this issue governed by the CISG? What about the $350,000 purchase of steel? *See American Meter, infra*; CISG Article 3.

PROBLEM 3-4

Suppose that in Problem 3-3 above the joint venture agreement allows the parties to enter into corollary agreements necessary to support the operations of the joint venture. The following separate agreements were entered into by the joint venture with Akron Steel and annexed to the joint venture agreement as appendices:

(1) Indemnification Agreement: The joint venture promised to hold Akron harmless for any death or injury caused by the use of Akron's products in Argentina;

(2) Technology Transfer Agreement: Within two years after the entry into the joint venture agreement, Akron Steel will then sell a ten-year license to the patents in the steel manufacturing process plus all supporting computer software and know-how needed to implement the patents to the joint venture, which would begin to manufacture steel directly in Argentina; Akron promised to indemnify the joint venture in the event that any third party asserted superior rights in the patent or software;

(3) Stock Sale Agreement: Within seven years after the entry into the joint venture agreement, Acindar will sell 100 percent of the common stock in its steel manufacturing subsidiary to Akron Steel (including several buildings with western-style housing for Akron's managers and a small fleet of automobiles made by a German-Argentine joint venture for use by the managers); the name of the subsidiary will be changed to Akron Steel (Argentina), S.A., the joint venture will terminate, and Akron Steel will thereafter operate Akron Steel (Argentina), S.A. as a wholly-owned subsidiary. A separate clause in the contract provides that the sale of stock is expressly made subject to the CISG by the parties; and

(4) Utilities Agreement: Once the Akron Steel wholly-owned subsidiary is established in Argentina, Acindar will sell electricity to the subsidiary.

[margin handwritten note: patent license]

Which of the agreements set forth above (or parts of such agreements) are governed by the CISG? *See* CISG Articles 2, 3, 4, 5, and 6; the *American Meter* case; CLOUT Cases 131 and 122 below.

Amco Ukrservice & Prompriladamco v. American Meter Co.
United States District Court, Eastern District of Pennsylvania, 2004
312 F. Supp. 2d 681

DALZELL, District Judge.

Plaintiffs Amco Ukrservice and Prompriladamco are Ukrainian corporations seeking over $200 million in damages for the breach of two joint venture agreements that, they contend, obligated defendant American Meter Company to provide them with all of the gas meters and related piping they could sell in republics of the former Soviet Union.

After extensive discovery, American Meter and Prompriladamco filed the cross-motions for summary judgment now before us. American Meter asserts that it is entitled to judgment against both plaintiffs as a matter of law because the joint venture agreements are unenforceable under both the United Nations Convention on Contracts for the International Sale of Goods ("CISG") and Ukrainian commercial law. Prompriladamco claims that its agreement is enforceable, that there is no genuine issue of material fact as to whether American Meter is in breach of that agreement, and that the only remaining issue is the extent of the damages it has sustained.

Upon consideration of this complex web of law, we conclude that American Meter is not entitled to summary judgment because the CISG does not apply to the joint venture agreements.

I. Factual and Procedural History

The origins of this action lie in the collapse of the Soviet Union and the newly-independent Ukraine's fitful transition to a market economy. American Meter began to explore the possibility of selling its products in the former Soviet Union in the early 1990s, and in 1992 it named Prendergast as Director of Operations of C.I.S. [Commonwealth of Independent States] Projects. Sometime in 1996, a Ukrainian-born American citizen named Simon Friedman approached Prendergast about the possibility of marketing American Meter products in Ukraine.

Ukraine was a potentially appealing market for American Meter at that time. During and immediately after the Soviet era, Ukrainian utilities had not charged consumers for their actual consumption of natural gas but instead had allocated charges on the basis of total deliveries to a given area. That system penalized consumers for their neighbors' wastefulness and saddled them with the cost of leakage losses. In 1997, the Ukrainian government enacted legislation requiring utilities to shift toward a usage-based billing system. Prendergast's early prediction was that implementation of the legislation would require the installation of gas meters in millions of homes and apartment buildings.

After some investigation, Prendergast and his superiors at American Meter concluded they could best penetrate the Ukrainian market by forming a joint venture with a local manufacturer. To this end, American Meter Vice-President Andrew Watson authorized Friedman on June 24, 1997 to engage in discussions and negotiations with Ukrainian organizations, and the corporation also hired a former vice-president, Peter Russo, to consult on the project. Prendergast, Russo, and Friedman began to identify potential joint venture partners, and by late 1997, they had selected Promprilad, a Ukrainian manufacturer of commercial and industrial meters based in Ivano-Frankivsk, the industrial capital of western Ukraine. On December 11, 1997, Prendergast (representing American Meter), Friedman (representing his firm, Joseph Friedman & Sons, International, Inc.), and representatives of Promprilad and American-Ukrainian Business Consultants, L.P. ("AUBC") met in Kyiv (the current preferred transliteration of "Kiev") and entered into the first of the agreements at issue here.

The agreement provided for the establishment of a joint venture company, to be called Prompriladamco, in which the four signatories would become shareholders.

Prompriladamco would work in conjunction with its principals to develop the market for American Meter products in the former Soviet Union and, most important for the purposes of this action, the agreement committed American Meter to the following obligations:

9.   AMCO shall grant Joint Venture Promprylad Amco exclusive rights to manufacture and install Meters within the former Soviet Union . . .

10.   AMCO shall grant Joint Venture Promprylad Amco exclusive rights to distribute the products manufactured by Promprylad Amco and all products manufactured by AMCO in the former Soviet Union . . .

13.   AMCO will deliver components and parts for Meters taking into account 90% assembly.

14.   Promprylad Amco (at the first stage) shall perform 10% of the work required to assemble the Meters using components and parts delivered by AMCO.

15.   AMCO will deliver the components and parts for Meters by lots in containers, payments for the delivery being subject to at least a 90-day grace period.

16.   The number of the components and parts for Meters to be delivered to Ukraine shall be based on demand in the former Soviet Union.

17.   Orders for the components and parts for Meters, with the quantities and prices according to paragraph 16 above shall be an integral part of this Agreement.

After executing the agreement, the parties incorporated Prompriladamco in Ukraine, and Friedman became its Chief Executive Officer. The new corporation set out to obtain Ukrainian regulatory approval for American Meter products, which required bringing Ukrainian officials to the United States to inspect American Meter's manufacturing process, and it sponsored a legislative measure that would give those products a competitive advantage in the Ukrainian market.

On April 20, 1998, Friedman and a representative of AUBC executed a second joint venture agreement for the purpose of marketing the gas piping products of Perfection Corporation, a wholly-owned subsidiary of American Meter. Again, the parties agreed to create and fund a corporation, this one to be called Amco Ukrservice, and American Meter committed itself to deliver, on credit, a level of goods based on demand in the former Soviet Union. The parties duly formed Amco Ukrservice, and Friedman became its Chief Executive Officer.

By early summer, Prompriladamco and Amco Ukrservice had begun submitting product orders to American Meter. In late June or early July, however, American Meter President Harry Skilton effectively terminated the joint ventures by stopping a shipment of goods that was on its way to Ukraine and by refusing to extend credit to either Prompriladamco or Amco Ukrservice. *See* Skilton Dep. at 123–24 (admitting that, as a result of his decisions, the project "died a natural death from then on out."). Finally, at a meeting on October 27, 1998, American Meter Vice-President Alex Tyshovnytsky informed Friedman that the corporation had decided to withdraw from Ukraine "due to unstable business conditions and eroding investment confidence in that country." Letter from Tyshovnytsky to Friedman of 10/29/98.

On May 23, 2000, Prompriladamco and Amco Ukrservice filed parallel complaints claiming that American Meter had breached the relevant joint venture agreement by refusing to deliver the meters and parts that the plaintiffs could sell in the former Soviet Union. Prompriladamco's complaint alleges that the breach caused it to lose $143,179,913 in profits between 1998 and 2003, and Amco Ukrservice claims lost profits of $88,812,000 for the same period. We consolidated the actions on August 18, 2000.

II. American Meter's Motion for Summary Judgment

American Meter argues that summary judgment is warranted here because the joint venture agreements are invalid under the CISG and Ukrainian law. It also contends that it is entitled to summary judgment because the plaintiffs' claims for damages are based on nothing but "rank speculation." We consider each of these arguments in turn.

A. THE CISG

The United States and Ukraine are both signatories to the CISG, which applies to contracts for the sale of goods where the parties have places of business in different nations, the nations are CISG signatories, and the contract does not contain a choice of law provision. American Meter argues that the CISG governs the plaintiffs' claims because, at bottom, they seek damages for its refusal to sell them goods and that, under the CISG, the supply provisions of the agreements are invalid because they lack sufficient price and quantity terms. Apart from a handful of exclusions that have no relevance here, the CISG does not define what constitutes a contract for the sale of goods. *See* CISG art. 2, reprinted in 15 U.S.C.A. App., at 335 (West 1998). This lacuna has given rise to the problem of the Convention's applicability to distributorship agreements, which typically create a framework for future sales of goods but do not lay down precise price and quantity terms.

In the few cases examining this issue, courts both here and in Germany have concluded that the CISG does not apply to such contracts. In *Helen Kaminski PTY. Ltd. v. Marketing Australian Prods.*, 1997 U.S. Dist. LEXIS 10630, 1997 WL 414137 (S.D.N.Y. 1997), the court held that the CISG did not govern the parties' distributorship agreement, but it suggested in dictum that the CISG would apply to a term in the contract that addressed specified goods. *Id.* at 3. Three years later, Judge DuBois of this Court followed *Helen Kaminski* and held that the CISG did not govern an exclusive distributorship agreement, an agreement granting the plaintiff a 25% interest in the defendant, or a sales commission agreement. *Viva Vino Import Corp. v. Farnese Vini S.r.l.*, 2000 U.S. Dist. LEXIS 12347, No. 99-6384, 2000 WL 1224903, at 1–2 (E.D. Pa. 2000). Two German appellate cases have similarly concluded that the CISG does not apply to distributorship agreements, which they termed "framework agreements," but does govern sales contracts that the parties enter pursuant to those agreements. *See OLG Düsseldorf,* UNILEX, No. 6 U 152/95 (1996); *OLG Koblenz,* UNILEX, No. 2 U 1230/91 (1993).

American Meter argues that this line of cases is inapplicable here because the plaintiffs do not claim damages for breach of what it terms the "relationship" provisions of the joint venture agreements,[2] but instead seek to enforce an obligation to sell goods. In other words, American Meter claims that the supply and credit provisions are severable and governed by the CISG, even if the Convention has no bearing on the remainder of the two agreements.

There are a number of difficulties with this argument, both in its characterization of the plaintiffs' claims and its construction of the CISG. To begin with, Prompriladamco and Amco Ukrservice are not seeking damages for American Meter's refusal to fill particular orders. Instead, they are claiming that American Meter materially breached the joint venture agreements when it refused to sell its products on credit, and as the *ad damnum*

---

2. In this category, American Meter would place terms dealing with such matters as quality control, the use of registered trademarks, and the parties' advertising and marketing obligations.

clauses of their complaints make clear, they seek damages for their projected lost profits between 1998 and 2003.

American Meter's construction of the CISG is equally problematic. It is premised on an artificial and untenable distinction between the "relationship" and supply provisions of a distributorship agreement—after all, what could be more central to the parties' relationship than the products the buyer is expected to distribute? American Meter's rhetorical view would also render it difficult for parties to create a general framework for their future sales without triggering the CISG's invalidating provisions. Such a construction of the Convention would be particularly destabilizing, not to mention unjust, in the context of the joint venture agreements at issue here. On American Meter's reading of the CISG, it could have invoked ordinary breach of contract principles if the plaintiffs had failed to exercise their best efforts to promote demand for its products, all the while reserving the right to escape its obligation to supply those products by invoking Article 14's price and quantity requirements. The CISG's provisions on contract formation do not compel such an expectation-defeating result.

We therefore join the other courts that have examined this issue and conclude that, although the CISG may have governed discrete contracts for the sale of goods that the parties had entered pursuant to the joint venture agreements, it does not apply to the agreements themselves. [The court went on to find that Pennsylvania law, not Ukrainian law, governed the joint venture agreements and denied Prompriladamco's motion for summary judgment on the liability issue on the ground that there is a genuine issue of material fact as to whether Prendergast, the American Meter official who signed the Prompriladamco joint venture agreement, had authority to make the commitments on behalf of American Meter. This portion of the opinion is contained in Chapter Eight at pp. 634-638.]

UNCITRAL CLOUT Case 131
Germany: Landgericht München I (February 8, 1995)

The German defendant ordered a computer programme from the French plaintiff. The programme was delivered and installed. The parties also intended to conclude a second contract concerning the use of the programme, but the negotiations on that contract failed. The defendant then refused to pay the purchase price of the programme, which was delivered and installed.

The court held that the CISG was applicable as the parties had their place of business in different CISG Contracting States and as the CISG applies to standard software. The court further found also that the parties had agreed on all particulars of the sale of the programme and therefore had concluded a sales contract.

It was held that the defendant could not rely on a possible lack of conformity of the software programme, since it had not effectively given notice of the defect but had only asked for assistance in addressing the problems identified. As a result, the court ordered the defendant to pay the purchase price and interest at the rate of 5%.

UNCITRAL CLOUT Case 122
Germany: Oberlandesgericht Köln (August 26, 1994)

The plaintiff, a Swiss market research institute, had elaborated and delivered a market analysis, which had been ordered by the defendant, a German company. The defendant refused to pay the price alleging that the report did not comply with the conditions agreed upon by the parties.

The court held that the CISG was not applicable, since the underlying contract was neither a contract for the sale of goods (article 1(1) CISG) nor a contract for the production of goods (article 3(1) CISG). Noting that the sale of goods is characterized by the transfer of property in an object, the court found that, although a report is fixed on a piece of paper, the main concern of the parties is not the handing over of the paper but the transfer of the right to use the ideas written down on such paper. Therefore, the court held that the agreement to prepare a market analysis is not a sale of goods within the meaning of articles 1 or 3 CISG.

NOTES AND QUESTIONS

1. For a recent case reiterating the general position of the courts that the CISG does not apply to distribution agreements, see *Gruppo Essenziero Italiano, S.p.A v. Aromi D'Italia, Inc.*, Civil No. CCB–08–65, 2011 WL 3207555 (D. Md. July 27, 2011).

2. One reason why the CISG is an effective law and enjoys the strong allegiance of a large contingent of contracting states is that it is limited in its scope of application to areas that states felt were amenable to international legislation and it does not (1) govern areas that states might view as difficult to legislate or (2) intrude in areas viewed as important to their sovereign interests. As an example of the former, the CISG excludes sales by auction under Article 2(b), which present some unique problems with respect to contract formation as the seller may not know who the buyer is until the sale is concluded. Sales on execution are excluded under Article 2(c) as these transactions are fundamentally different from other transactions because of the inability of the parties to negotiate the contract. As an example of the latter concern with avoiding conflict with state interests, Article 2(a) provides that certain consumer purchases are excluded from the CISG. A number of states have developed national legislation and case law designed to protect consumers, and the drafters of the CISG agreed that the convention should not supersede these rules. Ships and vessels are excluded under Article 2(e) as such vessels are often subject to registration requirements under national legislation. Under Article 4, the CISG does not displace domestic rules on the validity of the contract or prejudice the rights of third parties. Thus, the ability of states to prohibit certain types of contracts as against public policy is not compromised by the CISG. Article 5 excludes issues of the liability of the seller for death or injury caused by the goods to any person on the grounds that these issues are more appropriately treated under domestic legislation.

3. Article 2(d) excludes stocks, other securities, and negotiable instruments from the CISG, illustrating that the CISG is concerned with physical, tangible things and not intangible rights. The exclusion of "negotiable instruments" refers to instruments calling for the payment of money and does not refer to documents that allow the bearer to control goods, such as the negotiable bill of lading. *See* Honnold, *supra*, at 54.

4. Article 6 provides:

> The parties may exclude the application of this Convention or, subject to Article 12, derogate from or vary the effect of any of its provisions.

Article 6 reflects the supplementary nature of the CISG by allowing the parties to opt out of the convention. The parties are also allowed to change the effect of any of the convention's provisions, recognizing the primacy of the contract. Thus, the parties can vary the effect of Parts II and III of the CISG regarding the formation of the contract and rights and obligations of the parties. If the parties can opt out of the convention, can they also opt in by altering the effect of Articles 1–5 so that the CISG governs contracts that would otherwise be outside of its scope? In considering this question, note that Articles 1–5 strike a balance between domestic and international law: Contracting states have agreed to allow the CISG to displace domestic law for certain transactions and issues while preserving others for domestic control. Article 6 now introduces a third interest: the intent of the contracting parties and the primacy of the contract. Can this third interest change this balance by making an additional displacement of domestic law? The only explicit limit that Article 6 imposes on the parties' right to vary the convention is the recognition of the privilege of a contracting state under Articles 12 and 96 to maintain its domestic law requiring a writing. Does this mean that other than this limitation, the parties can vary any other provisions, even those affecting the balance struck between domestic law and the CISG, that is, Articles 1–5? We believe that the answer is "yes" but a qualified one and one that depends on a case-by-case analysis. Would it depend on whether the contract attempts to opt in an area that (1) is difficult to legislate or (2) is considered to be an area of state sovereignty? Now consider CISG Article 1. Should parties be able to opt in by varying the effect of Article 1? What is the underlying purpose of Article 1?

4.   Interpreting the CISG: Articles 7–13

Articles 7–13 concern the interpretation of the CISG. While the CISG is a major step forward in harmonization, there will continue to be a need for choice of law analysis and the application of domestic law to international contracts for the sale of goods. We have already seen the continuing need for private international law analysis under Article 1(1)(b) but Article 7 provides another reason. The reason for this need is that the scope of the CISG is limited; it covers (1) the formation of contracts and (2) the rights and obligations of the parties. There are many issues that fall within a gap in the CISG or an exclusion that is outside the scope of coverage of the CISG.

It is important to distinguish between a gap, which can be filled without any choice of law, and an exclusion, which requires a choice of law determination. A gap refers to an issue that is governed by the CISG but on which the CISG is silent, whereas an exclusion refers to an issue that is not governed by the CISG but which must be governed by some other substantive law.

> *Illustration 7a.* Article 78 of the CISG provides that a party that fails to pay a money obligation on time must pay interest. However, nothing in the CISG specifies the interest rate or how it is to be determined. The issue of interest is a subject that is clearly governed by the CISG but the rate of interest is not specified. The interest rate issue falls into a gap or is an interstitial issue.

> *Illustration 7b.* Article 4 of the CISG provides that only the rights and obligations of the seller and buyer are covered by the CISG; third-party rights are excluded. Article 4 also provides that matters concerning the validity of the contract and the effect that the contract may have on the property in the goods sold are also excluded from the CISG. Article 5 provides that the Convention does not apply to liability for death or personal injury caused by the goods sold. All of these issues are not governed by the CISG. These are excluded from the CISG scope of coverage.

The treatment of gaps and exclusions is quite different under the CISG. Article 7 provides that gaps should be settled in conformity with the general principles on which the CISG is based or in the absence of such principles through the application of domestic law after a choice of law analysis. Under this prescription, a gap, such as that involved in Illustration 7a, should be filled first through the use of principles upon which the CISG is based before a resort to a private international choice of law analysis, which will result in the choice of a domestic national law. Where are these general principles? A number of commentators believe that the general principles must be found within the CISG itself either by extracting these principles from specific articles of the CISG or by applying existing articles by analogy to a specific case. As an example of a general principle, one need look no further than Article 7(1): The CISG should be interpreted so as "to promote the observance of good faith in international trade." An additional norm is a reasonableness standard: Under Article 8(2) and (3), statements, conduct, and the intent of parties are to be interpreted according to the understanding of a reasonable person. The requirements of good faith and reasonableness underlie numerous other articles of the CISG. *See* Henry Mather, *Choice of Law for International Sales Issues Not Resolved by the CISG*, 20 J.L. & Com. 155, 157–158 (2001). In Illustration 7a above concerning the determination of interest rates, Professor Mather suggests that Article 74 requiring full compensation in the case of breach leads to a conclusion that the rate should be the average prime lending rate in the aggrieved party's country. *See id.* at 158. Additional important general principles derived from the specific provisions of the CISG and applicable by analogy are the primacy of the contract and freedom of contract (Article 6), a general rule that international sales contracts should not be subject to writing requirements and other formal requirements (Article 11), and a general presumption that the parties have formed a binding contract (Articles 16, 18(1), 19(2), and 21). *See id.* at 158. Only if an appeal to general principles fails to find a basis for resolving the gap should the court then resort to private international law and domestic law.

The treatment of the exclusions in Illustration 7b is quite different. Here these are issues that are not governed by the CISG—in other words, these are matters normally covered by a substantive contract law that are completely outside the scope of the CISG. As a result, these matters will be governed by a different substantive contract law to be determined by a private international choice of law analysis (absent a choice of law clause in the contract). Under Article 7, exclusions are to be treated by a direct appeal to domestic law and there is no need to first attempt to find general principles of international law.

NOTES AND QUESTIONS

1. Aside from the general rules of interpretation set forth under Article 7 above, the policy orientation of the CISG against the use of excessive formalities in the contract may also provide a useful interpretive guide for those who come to a study of the CISG from a common law tradition. Various provisions under the CISG demonstrate a policy decision by the drafters to avoid the formalities associated with the Anglo-American approach to contract law as typified by American common law and the Uniform Commercial Code. Some examples of such formalities are the statute of frauds, the parol evidence rule, and rules requiring consideration for enforceable promises. The following materials will highlight some of the major differences between the approach to formalities in the CISG and the UCC.

2. The parol evidence rule has been used in the United States to bar examination of any contemporaneous oral agreement or prior agreement (whether oral or in writing)

that contradicts a subsequent writing intended by the parties as the final expression of their agreement. *See* UCC §2-202 (2003). The typical approach to the parol evidence rule under U.S. law is outlined by the court in *Prime Start Ltd. v. Maher Forest Products, Ltd.*, 442 F. Supp. 2d 1113, 1121 (W.D. Wash. 2006):

> Where terms are *not* stated in the parties' writing, parol evidence of "consistent additional terms" may be considered "unless the court finds the writing to have been intended also as a complete and exclusive statement of the terms of the agreement." [U.C.C. §2-202.] Thus, additional terms that do not contradict the writing may be part of the contract, creating a partly-written and partly-oral contract for sale. Furthermore, "[w]hether the parties intended the written contract to be the sole agreement is a question of fact." *Morgan v. Stokely-Van Camp, Inc.*, 34 Wash. App. 801, 663 P.2d 1384, 1389 (1983).

Should a parol evidence rule, such as that stated by the court in *Prime Start*, apply to contracts under the CISG? The CISG does not address whether it contains a parol evidence rule. However, CISG Article 8(3) provides that in interpreting the contract "due consideration is to be given to all relevant circumstances of the case." *See also* Articles 11, 12, and 13. U.S. courts differ on whether the rule applies to contracts governed by the CISG. *See Cedar Petrochemicals, Inc. v. Dongbu Hannong Chem. Co.*, No. 06 Civ. 2972, 2011 Dist. LEXIS 110716, at *13-14 (S.D.N.Y. Sept. 28, 2011) (CISG requires consideration of extrinsic evidence); *but see Beijing Metals & Minerals Imp./Exp. Corp. v. Am. Bus. Ctr., Inc.*, 993 F.2d 1178, 1182 n.9 (5th Cir. 1993) (Texas parol evidence rule applies whether the contract was governed by Texas law or by the CISG). Which decision do you think is correct? Which approach is easier to apply?

3. On the basis of the discussion of formalities so far, under the CISG, is "consideration" in the Anglo-American common law sense required to form an effective contract? See also the discussion in Sections 5.A and B below on pp. 190-191.

PROBLEM 3-5

A U.S. seller and a Mexican buyer meet at a trade fair and enter into negotiations for the sale of power tools. The seller and the buyer have discussions at the fair and then exchange various e-mail messages and phone calls. During one phone call, the Mexican buyer says, "Can you send me 450 power drills and 500 power saws CIF Mexico for $19,600?" The seller says, "I can do it for $22,000." The buyer says, "You sure drive a hard bargain. Throw in extra parts for the drills and we have a deal." The seller sends the buyer an e-mail stating, "As you requested, we have included extra spare drill parts and will ship via truck tomorrow." The buyer calls the seller and leaves a message on the seller's voice mail, "Hey, got your e-mail. Sounds good." The seller then ships the tools to Mexico whereupon the buyer refuses to accept delivery. The seller sues the buyer for breach of contract. The buyer moves to dismiss on the ground that no contract ever existed because of failure to satisfy the statute of frauds contained in UCC §2-201, which provides in relevant part that "a contract for the sale of goods for the price of $500 or more is not enforceable by way of action or defense unless there is some writing sufficient to indicate that a contract for sale has been made between the parties and signed by the party against whom enforcement is sought." What result? *See* CISG Articles 1(1)(a) and 11; *see also GPL Treatment* below.

UNCITRAL CLOUT Case 137
GPL Treatment, Ltd. v. Louisiana-Pacific Corp.
Oregon Supreme Court, 1996
113 Or. App. 633, 894 P.2d 470, *aff'd*, 323 Or. 116, 914 P.2d 682

Plaintiffs, three Canadian manufacturers and sellers of raw shakes (long wooden shingles), sued a U.S. corporation to recover damages for breach of alleged contracts for the sale and purchase of truckloads of cedar shakes. Defendant denied entering into these contracts. Defendant moved *in limine* for dismissal on the ground that plaintiffs failed to satisfy the writing requirement of the "statute of frauds" of the Uniform Commercial Code (UCC) as enacted in Oregon. The trial court denied the motion. During the trial, the plaintiffs attempted to raise the issue of whether the CISG, rather than the UCC, governed, but the trial court ruled that plaintiffs' attempt was untimely and that they had waived reliance on that theory. The jury returned a verdict awarding lost profits to the plaintiffs and the trial court entered judgment on the verdict.

Defendant appealed to an intermediate appellate court on the ground, inter alia, that the trial court had erred when it denied defendant's motion *in limine*. A majority of the three-judge appellate court found that plaintiffs had satisfied the UCC statute of frauds. The dissenting judge disagreed with the majority's analysis of the UCC as applied to the facts in the case. In a final footnote, the dissenting judge also stated that he would have addressed the issue of whether the trial court abused its discretion in its ruling on the applicability of the CISG.

On appeal to the Oregon Supreme Court, the decisions of the trial and intermediate courts were affirmed. The majority, concurring, and dissenting opinions do not address the issue of whether the CISG governed or whether the trial court abused its discretion.

NOTES AND QUESTIONS

Plaintiffs were able to prevail on the statute of frauds issue in *GPL Treatment*. Suppose that the court had found that the contract did not satisfy the statute of frauds and had dismissed the plaintiffs' case. In that case, would the failure of the plaintiffs' lawyers to timely raise the applicability of the CISG constitute malpractice? Recall our earlier discussion of the responsibility of the lawyer to be knowledgeable about the CISG. See Chapter One, *supra*, p. 32.

———————————

Article 12 of the CISG provides that a contracting state can preserve its writing requirement by making a declaration under Article 96 that Article 11 does not apply in any case where one of the parties has a place of business in that state. *GPL Treatment* above involved a contract dispute between companies based in two contracting states to the CISG (Canada and the United States) that accepted the CISG without preserving the writing requirement by making a declaration under CISG Article 96. But what happens if a dispute arises over an oral contract where the seller has a place of business in a state that has not made an Article 96 declaration while the buyer is located in a state that has made such a declaration? The court addressed this issue in the following case.

Forestal Guarani S.A. v. Daros International Inc.
United States Court of Appeals, Third Circuit, 2010
613 F.3d 395

FISHER, Circuit Judge.

Forestal Guarani S.A. is an Argentina-based manufacturer of various lumber products, including wooden finger-joints. Daros International, Inc., is a New Jersey-based import-export corporation. In 1999, Forestal and Daros entered into an oral agreement whereby Daros agreed to sell Forestal's wooden finger-joints to third parties in the United States. Pursuant to that agreement, Forestal sent Daros finger-joints worth $1,857,766.06. Daros paid Forestal a total of $1,458,212.35. Forestal demanded the balance due but Daros declined to pay. In April 2002, Forestal sued Daros in the Superior Court of New Jersey, asserting a breach-of-contract claim based on Daros' refusal to pay. Daros thereafter removed the case to the United States District Court for the District of New Jersey.

In June 2005, Daros moved for summary judgment, arguing that the parties lacked a written agreement in violation of the United Nations Convention on Contracts for the International Sale of Goods. [T]he District Court granted Daros' summary judgment motion, concluding that the CISG governed the parties' dispute and barred Forestal's claim because the parties' agreement was not in writing. Forestal has timely appealed the District Court's ruling.

The parties do not dispute that the CISG governs their dispute. While Daros does not deny that it had a contract with Forestal, the thrust of Daros' argument is that the parties do not have a written contract and that, under the CISG, the absence of a writing precludes Forestal's claim. While conceding that the CISG applies generally, Forestal contests the District Court's ruling on the ground that the lack of a writing, in its view, is inconsequential in light of the parties' course of dealing, as evidenced by Forestal's delivery of finger-joints to Daros and Daros' remittance of payments to Forestal, as well as an accountant's report and invoices Forestal claims show that Daros owes it money.

[T]he CISG dispenses with certain formalities associated with proving the existence of a contract. Specifically, Article 11 instructs that "[a] contract of sale need not be concluded in or evidenced by writing and is not subject to any other requirement as to form. It may be proved by any means, including witnesses." *Id.*, Art. 11. Similarly, Article 29 permits a contract modification to be proved even if it is not in writing. *Id.*, Art. 29. And Part II of the CISG, titled "Formation of the Contract," outlines requirements governing offer and acceptance but does not impose a writing requirement.

Article 11's elimination of formal writing requirements does not apply in all instances in which the CISG governs. Article 96 of the CISG carves out an exception to Article 11, Article 29 and Part II. It says that

> [a] Contracting State whose legislation requires contracts of sale to be concluded in or evidenced by writing may at any time make a declaration in accordance with article 12 that any provision of article 11, article 29, or Part II of this Convention, that allows a contract of sale or its modification or termination by agreement or any offer, acceptance, or other indication of intention to be made in any form other than in writing, does not apply where any party has his place of business in that State.

Id., Art. 96.

Article 12, to which Article 96 refers, states that

[a]ny provision of article 11, article 29 or Part II of this Convention that allows a contract of sale . . . to be made in any form other than in writing does not apply where any party has his place of business in a Contracting State which has made a declaration under article 96 of this Convention. The parties may not derogate from or vary the effect of this article.

Id., Art. 12.

The United States has not made an Article 96 declaration, so Article 11 governs contract formation in cases involving a United States-based litigant and a litigant based in another non-declaring signatory state. Argentina, however, has made a declaration under Article 96, thereby opting out of Article 11, Article 29 and Part II.

Our research has turned up almost no case law from courts in the United States informing how to address a case, such as this one, in which one state has made an Article 96 declaration and the other has not. Courts in foreign jurisdictions and commentators alike are divided over how to proceed in such a scenario. According to one school of thought, a court must at the outset conduct a choice-of-law analysis based on private international law principles to determine which state's law governs contract formation, and then apply that law to a party's claim. Our study of the available sources on the subject establishes this position as the clear majority view. In contrast, under what appears to be the minority view, a court should simply require the existence of a writing without reference to either state's law, though it is unclear what form such a writing would have to take to be considered sufficient.

Although none of the supporters of what we perceive as the majority view have explained their reasoning in any detail, we conclude that the majority has it right. Our conclusion is compelled by the CISG's plain language. The CISG says that "[q]uestions concerning matters governed by this Convention which are not expressly settled in it are to be settled in conformity with the general principles on which it is based or, in the absence of such principles, in conformity with the law applicable by virtue of the rules of private international law [i.e., choice of law]." 15 U.S.C. App., Art. 7(2). Because Argentina has opted out of Articles 11 and 29 as well as Part II of the CISG, the CISG does not "expressly settle" the question whether a breach-of-contract claim is sustainable in the absence of a written contract. So Article 7(2) tells us to consider the CISG's "general principles" to fill in the gap. We have already outlined some of the general principles undergirding the CISG, but we fail to see how they inform the question whether Forestal's contract claim may proceed. Indeed, given the inapplicability in this case of any of the CISG's provisions relaxing or eliminating writing requirements, we do not believe that we can answer the question presented here based on a pure application of those principles alone. Given that neither the CISG nor its founding principles explicitly or implicitly settle our inquiry, Article 7(2)'s reference to "the rules of private international law" is triggered. In other words, we have to consider the choice-of-law rules of the forum state, in this case New Jersey, to determine whether New Jersey or Argentine form requirements govern Forestal's claim.

In making a choice-of-law determination in a breach-of-contract case, New Jersey courts ask which forum has the most significant relationship with the parties and the contract. To that end, the New Jersey Supreme Court has adopted the principles set forth in §188 and §6 of the Restatement (Second) of Conflicts of Laws. [The court lists the factors set out in section 188 on p. 168 above.]

We ordinarily decline to consider issues not decided by a district court, choosing instead to allow that court to consider them in the first instance. This case bolsters the rationale behind our reluctance to wade into matters that the parties have not joined and that a district court has not addressed, as the record here sheds practically no light on many, if not most, of the choice-of-law considerations listed above.

It is true that we can affirm a district court's ruling on any ground supported by the record. There is no dispute here that Forestal's contract with Daros was verbal at best, so we could feasibly skip a choice-of-law analysis and apply both New Jersey and Argentine law to Forestal's claim to test its viability. New Jersey's statute of frauds provides that "a contract for the sale of goods for the price of $500 or more is not enforceable by way of action or defense unless there is some writing sufficient to indicate that a contract for sale has been made between the parties and signed by the party against whom enforcement is sought. . . ." N.J. Stat. Ann. §12A:2-201(1). While Forestal's claim might fail under that provision, the statute also makes several exceptions to the general rule. The parties have not briefed, and the record in this case prevents us from concluding definitively, whether any such exception is applicable here. As for Argentine law, we may safely assume that it requires some sort of writing, as Article 96 of the CISG permits a country to opt out of Article 11 only if its domestic law "requires contracts of sale to be concluded in or evidenced by writing. . . ." 15 U.S.C. App., Art. 96. We have looked at the Argentine Civil Code; it contains several provisions governing contract formation and ways of proving a contract. Forestal's offer of proof may or may not suffice under those provisions. In the end, we think it unwise either to venture into this choice-of-law thicket — the outcome of which is determinative of this case — or to engage in a largely speculative exercise about the viability of Forestal's claim under either jurisdiction's law without the benefit of either any briefing whatsoever by the parties or any analysis by the District Court on this point. Because these issues deserve a full airing, we conclude that remand is a better course of action.

For the foregoing reasons, we will vacate the District Court's grant of summary judgment for Daros and remand for further proceedings. On remand, the District Court may determine, based on New Jersey's choice-of-law rules, whether New Jersey or Argentine law governs and then apply that forum's law to this case.

5.   Part II of the CISG: Formation of the Contract

Part II of the CISG, Formation of the Contract, is subject to the rules of Part I (Articles 1–13) on the interpretation of the contract but is independent of Part III dealing with the obligations and rights of the parties (Articles 25–88). The structure of the CISG reflects its historical antecedents, the Uniform Law on the Formation of Contracts for the International Sale of Goods and the Uniform Law for the International Sale of Goods, both of which were finalized under the auspices of UNIDROIT at the Hague in 1964. The CISG reflected UNCITRAL's decision to promulgate a single convention but allows contracting parties to make a declaration under Article 92 excluding Part II on formation or Part III on the obligations and rights of the parties.

Articles 14–17 of Part II deal with the offer, including the minimum prerequisites for an effective offer (Article 14), withdrawal (Article 15), revocation (Article 16), and termination of an offer (Article 17). Articles 18–22 deal with the acceptance, including the form of the acceptance (Article 18), the effect of an acceptance that varies the terms of the offer (Article 19), time allowed for acceptance (Articles 20–21), and withdrawal of the acceptance (Article 22). Articles 23 and 24 deal with the time when a contract is concluded. For a common law lawyer trained to expect a comprehensive and detailed code such as the UCC, the CISG, which follows a civil law model, may appear to be brief and general in nature. In addition, the CISG does not contain some provisions usually found in a common law code: There is no statute of frauds, no provision for the modification of contracts, and no consideration is required for a contract. The following materials will provide an overview of the articles relating to contract formation.

A. THE OFFER

Article 14 sets forth the basic criteria for an offer. The CISG recognizes that many sales transactions today can occur in a casual and rapid way rather than through the formal model of negotiation, an offer, and an acceptance. For an effective offer, the key issue is whether the offeror intended to be bound by the offer. This issue is affected by two corollary issues: the number of people to whom the offer is addressed and the definiteness of the proposal.

Illustration 14a. A German seller sends out a sales catalog for hand-held electronic organizers to persons on a mailing list that the seller has obtained from a consumer research company that identifies American buyers who have purchased high-end electronic goods within the past two years. The catalog lists the organizers at $55 each. An American buyer sends in an order for 50 organizers. No contract has been made as there was no offer. The offer has not been addressed to specific persons.

Illustration 14b. The German seller tells the American buyer, "We will give you a nice discount if you order a large quantity of the organizers." The buyer responds by sending in an order for 100 organizers at $50 each. The proposal is addressed to a specific person but unless the parties have a prior course of dealing that would indicate the quantity and price referred to by the seller (see Article 9), no contract has been made as the offer was insufficiently definite as to quantity and price.

B. ACCEPTANCE, WITHDRAWAL, AND REVOCATION OF AN OFFER

Article 15 provides that the seller has the power to withdraw an offer at any time before the offer reaches the offeree, even if it purports to be irrevocable.

Illustration 15a. The German seller sends the American buyer a letter by next-day delivery with an offer to sell 150 organizers at $50 each, offer good for 10 days. Later the same day, the seller telephones the buyer and says, "I hereby withdraw the offer sent to you by my letter." The buyer receives the letter the next day and writes back, "I accept your offer as it is good for 10 days." No contract has been made as the offer was withdrawn before it reached the buyer. As the offer never reached the buyer prior to the withdrawal and the buyer was never aware of the offer, the buyer cannot suffer any harm by its withdrawal.

Article 15 empowers the seller to withdraw an offer before it reaches the buyer. In contrast, Article 16 deals with the power of the seller to revoke an offer after it has reached the buyer and has become an effective offer. Article 16(2)(a) and (2)(b) provide that certain offers are irrevocable even though they are not supported by consideration. This is a departure from the traditional common law approach in the United States that a promise is not irrevocable unless the offeree has given a payment, some other thing, or performed an act in consideration for the promise to hold the offer open. For example, under the common law approach, a seller who makes an offer to a buyer and who promises to hold the offer open for 15 days is free to revoke the offer at any time. The offer is revocable despite the explicit statement that it is irrevocable unless there is some consideration given such as a payment by the buyer to the seller. If the buyer gives the seller a payment to hold the offer open, then the offer is irrevocable for the 15 days (under the common law, this becomes an option contract).

Illustration 16a. The seller telephones the buyer and offers to sell the buyer 50 live chickens for $45, offer good for 15 days. The next day the seller calls the buyer and revokes the offer. Under Article 16(2)(a), the seller cannot revoke the offer and it remains irrevocable for the period fixed as open for acceptance.

The common law rule requiring consideration has been limited by some important exceptions. One is the famous mailbox rule established by the celebrated case of *Adams v. Lindsell*, 1 B. & Ald. 681 (1818), which provides that if the offeror has impliedly authorized the offeree to respond by mail, the power of the offeror to revoke an offer without consideration is cut off once the offeree dispatches a letter. Article 16(1) of the CISG has adopted a significant aspect of the mailbox rule. How is the CISG mailbox rule different from the common law rule?

In addition, section 2-206 of the Uniform Commercial Code has modified the common law by providing that an offeree is authorized to use any reasonable medium (e.g., letter, e-mail, telephone) for communicating acceptance.[3] Some offers are irrevocable even if not supported by consideration:

Uniform Commercial Code §2-205. Firm Offers

An offer by a merchant to buy or sell goods in a signed record that by its terms gives assurance that it will be held open is not revocable, for lack of consideration, during the time stated or if no time is stated for a reasonable time, but in no event may the period of irrevocability exceed three months. Any such term of assurance in a form supplied by the offeree must be separately signed by the offeror.

PROBLEM 3-6

A German seller telephones an American buyer and says, "I will sell you 150 hand-held organizers at $50 each. This offer is open for ten days; all acceptances must be in writing."

(1) The next day, the seller telephones the buyer and says, "Sorry, I have to withdraw the offer as I am having inventory problems." The buyer replies, "I hereby accept your offer. As you telephoned me yesterday with this offer, the offer received by me became effective and by its own terms the offer was irrevocable for a period of ten days. The acceptance was within the ten days you held the offer open so a contract has been formed." Was the seller's second phone call an attempted withdrawal or revocation? *See* Articles 15 and 16. Was the buyer's oral acceptance effective or must the buyer respond in writing? *See* Article 11. Neither Germany nor the United States has made a declaration under Articles 12 and 96. *See also* Article 6.

---

3. Section 2-206 (2004) provides:

§2-206. Offer and Acceptance in Formation of Contract.

(1) Unless otherwise unambiguously indicated by the language or circumstances
   (a) an offer to make a contract shall be construed as inviting acceptance in any manner and by any medium reasonable in the circumstances;
   (b) an order or other offer to buy goods for prompt or current shipment shall be construed as inviting acceptance either by a prompt promise to ship or by the prompt or current shipment of conforming or non-conforming goods, but such a shipment of non-conforming goods does not constitute an acceptance if the seller seasonably notifies the buyer that the shipment is offered only as an accommodation to the buyer.

(2) Where the beginning of a requested performance is a reasonable mode of acceptance an offeror who is not notified of acceptance within a reasonable time may treat the offer as having lapsed before acceptance.

See also Restatement (Second) of Contracts §30 ("Unless otherwise indicated by the language or the circumstances, an offer invites acceptance in any manner and by any medium reasonable in the circumstances") & 60 (same) (1981).

(2) Suppose that after receiving the initial telephone call in which the seller makes the offer, the buyer calls back the same day and says, "Sorry, the price is too high so I can't accept your offer." The next day, the buyer calls the seller and says, "I talked it over with the finance department and it's a go. We accept the offer and I am having a written acceptance delivered to you within the hour." The seller says, "Sorry, but you already rejected the offer yesterday so no deal." The buyer says, "You promised to hold the offer open for ten days and my written acceptance will be received by you within this period." Is there a contract? *See* Article 17.

PROBLEM 3-7

An English seller meets an American buyer at a trade fair in London. During their conversation, the seller offers to sell the buyer a specified quantity of tea at a specified price. The buyer is interested but needs to review the offer with headquarters in Atlanta. The seller ends the discussion by saying, "Okay, but if you want the tea, you need to let me know in three business days. Hope to hear from you. Call me." The next day, the buyer sends a letter by express mail accepting the offer but before it reaches the seller, the seller calls and says, "I take back the offer." The buyer immediately replies, "I've already dispatched an acceptance by mail but I now also add my oral acceptance of your offer." The United Kingdom is not a contracting state to the CISG.

(1) What is the result under the common law?
(2) What is the result under UCC §2-205? What about UCC §2-206?
(3) What is the result under the CISG? *See* Article 16.

C. ACCEPTANCE

The first four articles of Part II deal with the offer; the last six articles deal with the acceptance. Of these, Articles 18 and 19 are the most basic and important. Article 18 provides that there are two elements to an acceptance: assent to the offer and communicating that assent to the offeror. *See* Article 18(1) and (2). Once the assent of the offeree reaches the offeror, acceptance of the offer becomes effective and a contract is formed. *See* Article 18(2). While this might seem straightforward enough, there can be a number of complications. The offeror might withdraw or revoke the offer before the offeree can communicate the acceptance to the offeror or the offeree may exceed the time limits on the offer set by the offeror. Article 18 deals with the issue of communication of the assent to the offeror. We further examine the application of Article 18 in Problem 3-8.

Article 19 deals with an assent that contains alterations or modifications of the terms of the offer. A reply to an offer may contain additional terms that add to or are inconsistent with the terms of the offer. Such a situation is commonplace in today's commercial marketplace that is marked by high-speed communications and rapid transactions that often involve the use of preprinted and standard offer sheets, orders, and sales acknowledgment forms. The front of the offer form will contain blank spaces regarding quantity, delivery, and price that one party will fill in while the back of the form may contain a dense collection of standard clauses on issues such as liability, warranties, dispute resolution, and remedies. The seller's forms will be drafted to protect the seller's rights and the buyer's forms will be drafted to protect the buyer's rights. No problem arises if an offer on a preprinted form is rejected by the offeree. A problem can arise when the offeree purports to accept an offer on a preprinted form with a reply on a preprinted form of its own that contains additions or modifications specifically added by the offeree or that contains different or additional standard terms on the back of the form. To be sure, the use of different forms or exchanges containing conflicting or discrepant terms is in most instances not a problem in ordinary commercial life. Business is routinely conducted by sellers and buyers using different forms containing different terms and no issue arises because the seller supplies the goods and the buyer pays for them without incident. Only when there is some problem that arises in the performance of the contract will the parties need to resolve the problem of which of the conflicting or discrepant terms were incorporated into the contract. This problem has been known to generations of lawyers and law students as the so-called battle of the forms.

The approach of Article 19 to the battle of the forms problem reflects the pre–Uniform Commercial Code practice of the common law. Article 19(1) provides that a reply to an offer must be a precise "mirror image" of the offer; there can be no deviations in the terms of the response to an offer if that response is to operate as an acceptance. If the reply contains additional terms, the reply is treated as a rejection and a counteroffer. Article 19(2) qualifies this rule by providing that the alterations or additions must "materially alter the terms of the offer" to constitute a rejection and counteroffer. Otherwise, the new terms become part of the contract unless the offeror objects without undue delay. Article 19(3) provides some examples of terms that are "material" such as terms relating to price, payment, quality and quantity of the goods, delivery, liability, and dispute settlement.

Illustration 19a. A German seller sends an offer on a preprinted form to an American buyer for the sale of screws at a specific price for a specified quantity. The American buyer uses its own order form in sending back a reply that purports to accept the seller's offer. Standard clauses on the back of the buyer's form subject the contract to the jurisdiction of U.S. courts and contain other material alterations. On the advice of counsel, the buyer draws the seller's attention to the choice of forum clause. The seller does not respond and no goods are shipped. No contract has been made as the acceptance contains terms that materially alter the offer. The buyer's reply is a rejection and a counteroffer under Article 19(1) that the seller has failed to accept.

Illustration 19b. A Chinese seller sends an offer on a preprinted form to an American buyer for the sale of Republican Period (1912-1949) Chinese furniture and art. The back of the form contains a clause providing for shipment in "commercial furniture crates designed for the safe shipment of art objects and antiques." The buyer sends back a reply purporting to accept the seller's offer. On the front of the buyer's form, the buyer has added a clause providing, "All furniture and art to be separately packaged and shipped in separate crates." The seller receives the form, reads the buyer's clause, and does not object. A contract has been formed as the buyer's clause does not materially alter the terms of the offer. The buyer's clause is part of the contract.

If the reply contains any terms that are not identical to the terms of the offer, even if they are non-material, the offeror has the power to avoid making a contract by objecting to the discrepancy under Article 19(2). As the offeror has objected to the discrepancy, the offeree's reply is treated as a rejection and counteroffer under Article 19(1) and as the offeror has not accepted the counteroffer, no contract is formed.

Illustration 19c. Under the same facts in Illustration 19b, the seller immediately objects to the buyer's reply with the following notice, "We cannot agree to separately package and ship furniture and art without a modest increase in price." Although the buyer's clause is not a material alteration under Article 19(3), the result of the seller's timely objection to the buyer's modification is that the buyer's response is treated as a rejection and a counteroffer and no contract is formed under Article 19(1).

In Illustration 19a, if the seller ships the goods and the buyer pays the price, a contract may be formed by the conduct of the parties under Article 18(3). If so, what are the terms of the contract? Is the German seller subject to the jurisdiction of U.S. courts? Under Article 19(1), the buyer's reply is treated as a rejection and counteroffer. As the buyer has specifically called the seller's attention to the forum selection clause, the seller cannot claim surprise. Under the approach of the "last shot theory," a corollary to the mirror image approach, when the seller shipped the goods, the act constituted an acceptance of the buyer's counteroffer. *See* Article 18(3). The parties formed a contract by their conduct and the contract was governed by the terms of the only valid offer that existed between the parties, that is, the buyer's counteroffer with the clause subjecting the contract to the jurisdiction of U.S. courts. We further examine the application of Article 19 in Problem 3-9.

In Illustration 19a, the buyer has specifically called the seller's attention to the forum selection clause. What happens if the buyer does not specifically call the seller's attention to the forum selection clause printed on the back of the form? Is the seller still bound under the "last shot approach"? In this situation, it might seem unfair to hold the seller to a standard clause printed on the back of the buyer's form when neither the seller nor the buyer paid any attention to the boilerplate clauses on the backs of each other's forms. Under these circumstances, the resolution of the dispute as to the terms of the contract might be resolved in light of CISG Article 8 where the surrounding circumstances and the course of dealing between the parties provide an indication of the parties' intent to be bound by the discrepant clause. Similarly, in Illustration 19a, what happens if the buyer's reply does not contain the forum selection clause (or other terms that materially alter the offer) printed in the form itself but only makes ambiguous references to these terms and invites the seller to view the material alterations on a source external to the printed form, such as the seller's web site? In that case, a court might find that the buyer has not made a rejection and counteroffer but has accepted the seller's offer because CISG Article 8(1) requires that the seller know or should have known that the buyer intended to have the material alterations apply to the contract. *Cf. CSS Antenna, Inc. v. Amphenol-Tuchel Electronics, GmbH*, 764 F. Supp. 2d 745, 751–754 (D. Md. 2011) (finding no rejection and counteroffer under similar circumstances without further proof under CISG Article 8 that offeror knew or should have known that offeree's reply intended to have general conditions available on offeree's web site to apply to contract).

PROBLEM 3-8

On September 1, an American buyer sends the following telex to a French seller, "I will buy from you 500 four-ounce bottles of your perfume at $35 per bottle. As this offer is $5 over the wholesale price per bottle, I am sure that you will accept. If we do not hear otherwise from you by September 5, we will expect delivery by September 10."

(1) The seller does not respond by September 5. Is there a contract? *See* Article 18(1).

(2) The seller ships the bottles on September 2. On September 3, the buyer calls the seller and says, "I revoke my offer." The bottles arrive on September 10. The buyer refuses to accept the shipment on the grounds that the offer was revoked before an indication of assent—the shipment—by the seller reached the buyer. Is the buyer in breach? *See* Article 18(2) and (3).

(3) Suppose that the buyer had put in the telex, "Any disputes under this agreement shall be settled by arbitration in the United States. Payment by confirmed irrevocable letter of credit." On September 6, the seller notifies the buyer by e-mail, "Okay, we can do

the shipment. I will draw up a written confirmation and send it to you with the shipment." The buyer establishes the letter of credit and the shipment arrives, but the seller's written confirmation mentions nothing about arbitration. Is there a contract? Is the arbitration part of the contract? *See* Article 18(3) and the *Chilewich* case below.

Filanto, S.p.A. v. Chilewich International Corp.
United States District Court, Southern District of New York, 1992
789 F. Supp. 1229

BRIEANT, Chief Judge.

By motion fully submitted on December 11, 1991, defendant Chilewich International Corp. moves to stay this action pending arbitration in Moscow. Plaintiff Filanto has moved to enjoin arbitration or to order arbitration in this federal district.

Plaintiff Filanto is an Italian corporation engaged in the manufacture and sale of footwear. Defendant Chilewich is an export-import firm incorporated in the state of New York with its principal place of business in White Plains. On February 28, 1989, Chilewich's agent in the United Kingdom, Byerly Johnson, Ltd., signed a contract with Raznoexport, the Soviet Foreign Economic Association, which obligated Byerly Johnson to supply footwear to Raznoexport. Section 10 of this contract—the "Russian Contract"—is an arbitration clause, which reads in pertinent part as follows:

"All disputes or differences which may arise out of or in connection with the present Contract are to be settled, jurisdiction of ordinary courts being excluded, by the Arbitration at the USSR Chamber of Commerce and Industry, Moscow, in accordance with the Regulations of the said Arbitration." [sic]

The next document in this case, and the focal point of the parties' dispute regarding whether an arbitration agreement exists, is a Memorandum Agreement dated March 13, 1990. This Memorandum Agreement, number 9003002, is a standard merchant's memo prepared by Chilewich for signature by both parties confirming that Filanto will deliver 100,000 pairs of boots to Chilewich at the Italian/Yugoslav border on September 15, 1990, with the balance of 150,000 pairs to be delivered on November 1, 1990. Chilewich's obligations were to open a Letter of Credit in Filanto's favor prior to the September 15 delivery, and another letter prior to the November delivery. This Memorandum includes the following provision:

"It is understood between Buyer and Seller that USSR Contract No. 32-03/93085 [the Russian Contract] is hereby incorporated in this contract as far as practicable, and specifically that any arbitration shall be in accordance with that Contract."

Chilewich signed this Memorandum Agreement, and sent it to Filanto. Filanto at that time did not sign or return the document. Nevertheless, on May 7, 1990, Chilewich opened a Letter of Credit in Filanto's favor in the sum of $2,595,600.00. The Letter of Credit itself mentions the Russian Contract, but only insofar as concerns packing and labeling.

Then, on August 7, 1990, Filanto returned the Memorandum Agreement, sued on here, that Chilewich had signed and sent to it in March; though Filanto had signed the Memorandum Agreement, it once again appended a covering letter, purporting to exclude all but three sections of the Russian Contract.

According to the Complaint, what ultimately happened was that Chilewich bought and paid for 60,000 pairs of boots in January 1991, but never purchased the 90,000 pairs of boots that comprise the balance of Chilewich's original order. It is Chilewich's failure to do so that forms the basis of this lawsuit, commenced by Filanto on May 14, 1991.

Against this background based almost entirely on documents, defendant Chilewich on July 24, 1991 moved to stay this action pending arbitration, while plaintiff Filanto on August 22, 1992 moved to enjoin arbitration, or, alternatively, for an order directing that arbitration be held in the Southern District of New York rather than Moscow, because of unsettled political conditions in Russia.

JURISDICTION/APPLICABLE LAW

This Court finds [as a] basis for subject matter jurisdiction chapter 2 of the Federal Arbitration Act, which comprises the Convention on the Recognition and Enforcement of Foreign Arbitral Awards. The United States, Italy and the USSR are all signatories to this Convention, and its implementing legislation makes clear that the Arbitration Convention governs disputes regarding arbitration agreements between parties to international commercial transactions. The Arbitration Convention specifically requires courts to recognize any "agreement in writing under which the parties undertake to submit to arbitration." The term "agreement in writing" is defined as "an arbitral clause in a contract or an arbitration agreement, signed by the parties or contained in an exchange of letters or telegrams."

This Court concludes that the question of whether these parties agreed to arbitrate their disputes is governed by the Arbitration Convention and its implementing legislation. In this case, [t]he central disputed issue [under the Arbitration Convention] is whether the correspondence between the parties, viewed in light of their business relationship, constitutes an "agreement in writing."

[A]s plaintiff correctly notes, the "federal law of contracts" to be applied in this case is found in the United Nations Convention on Contracts for the International Sale of Goods (the "Sale of Goods Convention"). This Convention, ratified by the Senate in 1986, is a self-executing agreement which entered into force between the United States and other signatories, including Italy, on January 1, 1988. Since the contract alleged in this case most certainly was formed, if at all, after January 1, 1988, and since both the United States and Italy are signatories to the Convention, the Court will interpret the "agreement in writing" requirement of the Arbitration Convention in light of, and with reference to, the substantive international law of contracts embodied in the Sale of Goods Convention.

Not surprisingly, the parties offer varying interpretations of the numerous letters and documents exchanged between them. The Court will briefly summarize their respective contentions.

Defendant Chilewich contends that the Memorandum Agreement dated March 13 which it signed and sent to Filanto was an offer. It then argues that Filanto's retention of the letter, along with its subsequent acceptance of Chilewich's performance under the Agreement—the furnishing of the May 11 letter of credit—estops it from denying its acceptance of the contract. Although phrased as an estoppel argument, this contention is better viewed as an acceptance by conduct argument, e.g., that in light of the parties' course of dealing, Filanto had a duty timely to inform Chilewich that it objected to the incorporation by reference of all the terms of the Russian contract. Under this view, the return of the Memorandum Agreement, signed by Filanto, on August 7, 1990, along with the covering letter purporting to exclude parts of the Russian Contract, was ineffective as a matter of law as a rejection of the March 13 offer, because this occurred some five months after Filanto received the Memorandum Agreement and two months after Chilewich furnished the Letter of Credit. Instead, in Chilewich's view, this action was a proposal for modification of the March 13 Agreement. Chilewich rejected this proposal, by its letter of August 7 to Byerly Johnson, and the August 29 fax by Johnson to Italian Trading SRL, which communication Filanto acknowledges receiving. Accordingly, Filanto under this interpretation is bound by the written terms of the March 13 Memorandum Agreement; since that agreement incorporates by reference the Russian Contract containing the arbitration provision, Filanto is bound to arbitrate.

Plaintiff Filanto's interpretation of the evidence is rather different. While Filanto apparently agrees that the March 13 Memorandum Agreement was indeed an offer, it characterizes its August 7 return of the signed Memorandum Agreement with the covering letter as a counteroffer. While defendant contends that under Uniform Commercial Code §2-207 this action would be viewed as an acceptance with a proposal for a material modification, the Uniform Commercial Code, as previously noted, does not apply to this case, because the State Department undertook to fix something that was not broken by helping to create the Sale of Goods Convention which varies from the Uniform Commercial Code in many significant ways. Instead, under this analysis, Article 19(1) of the Sale of Goods Convention would apply. That section, as the Commentary to the Sale of Goods Convention notes, reverses the rule of Uniform Commercial Code §2-207, and reverts to the common law rule that "A reply to an offer which purports to be an acceptance but contains additions, limitations or other modifications is a rejection of the offer and constitutes a counter-offer." Although the Convention, like the Uniform Commercial Code, does state that non-material terms do become part of the contract unless objected to, Sale of Goods Convention Article 19(2), the Convention treats inclusion (or deletion) of an arbitration provision as "material," Sale of Goods Convention Article 19(3). The August 7 letter, therefore, was a counteroffer which, according to Filanto, Chilewich accepted by its letter dated September 27, 1990. Though that letter refers to and acknowledges the "contractual obligations" between the parties, it is doubtful whether it can be characterized as an acceptance.

More generally, both parties seem to have lost sight of the narrow scope of the inquiry required by the Arbitration Convention. All that this Court need do is to determine if a sufficient "agreement in writing" to arbitrate disputes exists between these parties.

Since the issue of whether and how a contract between these parties was formed is obviously related to the issue of whether Chilewich breached any contractual obligations, the Court will direct its analysis to whether there was objective conduct evidencing an intent to be bound with respect to the arbitration provision. The Court is satisfied on this record that there *was* indeed an agreement to arbitrate between these parties.

There is simply no satisfactory explanation as to why Filanto failed to object to the incorporation by reference of the Russian Contract in a timely fashion. As noted above, Chilewich had in the meantime commenced its performance under the Agreement, and the Letter of Credit it furnished Filanto on May 11 *itself* mentioned the Russian Contract. An offeree who, knowing that the offeror has commenced performance, fails to notify the offeror of its objection to the terms of the contract within a reasonable time will, under certain circumstances, be deemed to have assented to those terms. The Sale of Goods Convention itself recognizes this rule: Article 18(1) provides that "A statement made by or other conduct of the offeree indicating assent to an offer is an acceptance." Although mere "silence or inactivity" does not constitute acceptance, Sale of Goods Convention

Article 18(1), the Court may consider previous relations between the parties in assessing whether a party's conduct constituted acceptance, Sale of Goods Convention Article 8(3). In this case, in light of the extensive course of prior dealing between these parties, Filanto was certainly under a duty to alert Chilewich in timely fashion to its objections to the terms of the March 13 Memorandum Agreement—particularly since Chilewich had repeatedly referred it to the Russian Contract and Filanto had had a copy of that document for some time.

REMEDY

Having determined that the parties should arbitrate their disputes in accordance with their agreement, the Court must address the question of remedy. As this action is governed by the Convention and its implementing legislation, the Court has specific authority to order the parties to proceed to arbitration in Moscow. Defendant has not sought this remedy, since it would likewise be the defendant in the arbitration. However, it would be clearly inequitable to permit the party contending that there is an arbitration agreement to avoid arbitration. In the interests of justice, the Court will compel the parties to arbitrate in Moscow.

So ordered.

NOTES AND QUESTIONS

1. Suppose that in *Chilewich*, Filanto had replied on March 15 by express mail to Chilewich's March 13 memorandum agreement and that the reply contained the same contents as the August 7 reply that was actually sent in the case. Under these facts, would the arbitration clause be a part of the contract? *See* Article 19(3).

2. A good foil to the *Chilewich* case is *CSS Antenna, Inc. v. Amphenol-Tuchel Electronics (ATE), GmbH*, 764 F. Supp. 2d 745 (D. Md. 2011), which involved a breach of contract action filed by CSS, a Maryland-based electronics company, and ATE, a German-based electronic company with a sales office in Canton, Michigan. After initial negotiations, CSS and ATE conducted business through a series of contracts by means of a purchase order, purchase confirmation arrangement. CSS would send a purchase order to ATE's Michigan office. In response, ATE would then send a purchase order confirmation form to CSS. CSS would subsequently accept the goods shipped and pay the price. When a dispute arose and CSS sued ATE in Maryland district court, it came to light that the purchase order confirmation forms sent to CSS contained a forum selection clause stating that the sole venue of any dispute was "the supplier's [ATE's] place of business." The court first interpreted this arrangement under the CISG as an offer (the purchase order) followed by a counteroffer (the purchase order confirmation) under CISG Article 19(3) since the latter contained "General Conditions," one of which was the forum selection clause. 764 F. Supp. 2d at 751–755. Thus, a contract was formed under CISG Article 18(1) by conduct when CSS accepted the goods and paid the price. *Id.*

The court distinguished two cases holding that a forum selection clause contained in a seller's confirmation order did not become a part of the contract on the grounds that in those cases the parties had formed oral contracts prior to the exchange of purchase orders and confirmations, so these instruments were separate from the basis of the parties' agreement. *See Chateau des Charmes Wines, Ltd. v. Sabate USA, Inc.*, 328 F.3d 528 (9th

Cir. 2003), and *Solae, LLC v. Hershey Canada, Inc.*, 557 F. Supp. 2d 452 (D. Del. 2008). Under these circumstances, the purchase order/purchase confirmations were proposed modifications to existing contracts and there was no meeting of the minds to modify the existing contracts. *See* CISG Article 29(1).

But the court in *CSS* case treated as a separate issue the question whether the language in ATE's purchase confirmation form was sufficient to put CSS on notice that ATE intended the General Conditions on the form to apply. To decide this issue, the court applied Article 8 of the CISG. The court declared that "statements made by and other conduct of a party are to be interpreted according to his intent where the other party knew or could not have been unaware of what that intent was." 764 F. Supp. 2d at 753 (Article 8(1).) "Statements made by a party are interpreted according to the understanding of a reasonable person, and '[i]n determining the intent of a party or the understanding a reasonable person would have had, due consideration is given to all relevant circumstances of the case, including the negotiations, any practices the parties have established between themselves, usages and any subsequent conduct of the parties.' (CISG Article 8(2)-(3))." *Id.* The court then ruled that "[b]ased on the facts currently on the record, the court cannot conclude that CSS knew or should have known that ATE intended the General Conditions to apply to their contract." *Id.*

3. The UCC also provides that an offeree can accept an offer by prompt shipment of the goods, but there is a difference between the UCC and the CISG. Under Article 18(3) if an offeree ships the goods, the acceptance is effective, without notice to the offeror, the moment the act is performed if it occurs within the time fixed by the offeror or, if no time is fixed, within a reasonable time. Under UCC §2-206(2), set forth in footnote 3 above, an additional act must be performed. What is this additional act?

PROBLEM 3-9

A Czech buyer contacts an American seller for the purchase of replacement parts for heavy industrial production equipment in the buyer's factory. As part of the negotiations, the seller sent a team of engineers and business officials to the Czech Republic for several weeks to get an understanding of the intended uses of the parts by the buyer. After several weeks of negotiations, the buyer sends the seller a purchase order for the parts for a total price of $1 million with delivery in the Czech Republic by October 10 and payment against documents by confirmed irrevocable letter of credit. The purchase order is a single one-page printed form. On the front of the page in large bold letters is a printed clause stating, "Seller will be responsible for damages caused by any defects in the replacement parts, including consequential damages."

The seller replies with a standard order acknowledgment form confirming the quantity of parts, price, delivery, and payment terms. The seller's form is also a short one-page form. On the front of the seller's form is a handwritten clause in large bold letters stating, "Seller will repair or replace any defective parts, but Seller is in no event liable for any other damages including consequential damages."

The seller ships the parts, which arrive in the Czech Republic by October 10. The buyer pays the price against documents while the parts are en route to the Czech Republic. By November 1, the parts have been installed in the buyer's factory but a malfunction in the parts causes serious damage to the buyer's production facilities, requiring total replacement of all of the production equipment. The buyer also misses several big production orders and is facing several irate customers who are threatening to sue.

The buyer brings an action against the seller in the Czech Republic for recovery of the purchase price of $1 million plus $10 million in damages. Assume that, under Czech law, consequential damages are an available remedy. The seller argues that the buyer is limited to replacement costs. What is the result under the CISG? *See* Article 19(1), (2), and (3) and Article 18(3).

NOTES AND QUESTIONS

1. Suppose that in Problem 3-9 the seller's counsel, an experienced U.S. commercial lawyer, was able to convince the Czech buyer to opt out of the CISG and have the dispute governed by U.S. law. How would the issues in Problem 3-9 be resolved using the UCC? Work through the analysis using UCC §2-207 set forth in note 2 below. Is the seller better off under the CISG or the UCC?

2. UCC §2-207, the battle of the forms provision, provides:

§2-207. *Additional Terms in Acceptance and Confirmation*

(1) A definite and seasonable expression of acceptance or a written confirmation which is sent within a reasonable time operates as an acceptance even though it states terms additional to or different from those offered or agreed upon, unless acceptance is expressly made conditional on assent to the additional or different terms.

(2) The additional terms are to be construed as proposals for addition to the contract. Between merchants such terms become part of the contract unless:

    (a)   the offer expressly limits acceptance to the terms of the offer;
    (b)   they materially alter it; or
    (c)   notification of objection to them has already been given or is given within reasonable time after notice of them is received.

(3) Conduct by both parties which recognizes the existence of a contract is sufficient to establish a contract for sale although the writings of the parties do not otherwise establish a contract. In such case the terms of the particular contract consist of those terms on which the writings of the parties agree, together with any supplementary terms incorporated under any other provisions of this Act.

UCC §2-207 rejects the common law mirror image rule in favor of an approach that would specifically recognize the creation of a contract even though the offeror and the offeree exchanged less than identical terms so long as the parties intended a contract to exist. While the common law approach operated upon a presumption that no contract exists unless the exchanges of the offeror and offeree were identical, the UCC reversed this presumption by providing that even though the exchanges were not identical, the contract is formed. Any additional terms, if material (e.g., a limitation on liability), do not become part of the contract. *See* UCC §2-207(2)(b). Non-material additional terms in the acceptance are incorporated into the contract unless the offer expressly limits acceptance to its terms or the offeror objects in a timely fashion. *See* UCC §2-207(2)(a) and (c). The effect of an objection to a non-material additional term in the acceptance is also treated differently in the CISG and the UCC. While CISG Article 19(2) gives the offeror the power to reject any reply that is not identical to the offer and avoid the making of a contract under Article 19(1), the effect of an objection to a non-material additional term under §2-207 is that the contract exists but the additional term falls out. The drafters of the UCC wanted to create a legal framework in which parties could not welsh on a contract due to technical differences in the terms of the offer and acceptance so long as the parties otherwise intended a contract to be formed. As a result, the drafters rejected the common law mirror image rule embodied in Article 19(1), adopting instead an approach that explicitly recognized a contract despite differences in terms.

The American Law Institute has proposed a revised Article 2, which contains two sections (§§2-206 and 2-207) designed to simplify the battle of the forms analysis. However, as of this writing, no state has adopted revised Article 2 and its future adoption is doubtful.

3. The UNIDROIT Principles of International Commercial Contracts provides in relevant part:

Article 2.1.22

(Battle of Forms)

> Where both parties use standard terms and reach agreement except on those terms, a contract is concluded on the basis of the agreed terms and of any standard terms which are common in substance unless one party clearly indicates in advance, or later and without undue delay informs the other party, that it does not intend to be bound by such a contract.

The UNIDROIT Principles also reject the mirror image approach of the CISG. Similar to the proposed revised UCC provisions, the Principles will result in the formation of a contract on the basis of the agreed terms and any standard terms that are similar in substance. Moreover, any additional terms that are different in substance from the original terms that concern the same issue cancel each other out. The difference between the approaches of UNIDROIT and CISG is that the former may lead to the formation of a contract in a greater number of cases.

How would Problem 3-9 be resolved under the Principles? In order to answer this question, you need to also consider UNIDROIT Article 2.1.21: "In case of conflict between a standard term and a term which is not a standard term the latter prevails."

D. FORMATION OF THE COMPLEX SALES CONTRACT UNDER THE CISG

So far, we have considered contracts for simple sales transactions. The buyer wishes to purchase a specific quantity of goods and the seller is willing to sell them for a specific price. Once the parties exchange goods and payment, the transaction has concluded and the parties go their separate ways. The sale of shoes, perfume, and furniture are some examples of these straightforward transactions and these types of contracts fall neatly within the framework of the CISG.

At the other end of the spectrum, there are complex sales transactions that are subject to many issues and variations. Questions of exact price and quantity may be difficult to determine. Performance may take place over several months or years requiring a continuing business relationship between the parties. The buyer may be unsure of what quantity and combination of goods and services will be necessary to achieve the desired result. The seller wants to sell to the buyer but is unsure of what the price will be and cannot determine the price until well into the negotiations or until the project itself is underway. What types of contracts are these and how would such contracts fare under the CISG?

PROBLEM 3-10

The Telecommunications Bureau of Argentina (TBA) is negotiating to purchase a telecommunications system from General Telecom (GT), a multinational enterprise with its headquarters in Chicago. The TBA needs a system that brings telephone, Internet, and television access to an entire region of Argentina. The preliminary negotiations take several months and involve numerous visits by GT's executives to Argentina. After studying Argentina's situation, GT tells TBA that there are three options that would deliver (a) basic, (b) sophisticated, or (c) state-of-the-art telecommunications service. Each option requires extended training programs for maintenance and upgrade of the systems. GT's engineers and finance managers have estimates for each of the options, but these estimates are rough figures only. There is no "market price" for the installation of entire telecommunications systems as each situation is different. The total cost of any system will vary as the project is actually implemented over a five-year period due to the inevitable unexpected developments and problems on the ground during installation. The TBA says that it is sure that it will purchase a system from GT over its rival Western Electronics. The TBA has now asked GT to send a senior management team to Buenos Aires for a two-week stay at a hotel to make presentations and to engage in negotiations.

GT is worried that negotiations have already gone on for several months. GT's management would like to sign a binding contract with the TBA as soon as possible. GT is nervous that all of these negotiations may finally lead to nowhere. GT has heard rumors that TBA is using the negotiations with GT as leverage to get a better deal from Western Electronics. Can a binding contract be structured now with the three options with final prices to be determined during the five-year period it will take to install the system? What issues exist under the CISG? *See* Article 14(1) and the case involving Pratt & Whitney below. What about using the UCC?

United Technologies International Pratt & Whitney Commercial Engine Business v. Malev Hungarian Airlines

The Supreme Court of the Republic of Hungary GF. I. 31 349/1992/9
Translated in 13 J.L. & Com. 31–47 (1993)

[In the fall of 1990, Pratt & Whitney Commercial Engine Business (PW) began negotiating with Malev Hungarian Airlines (MHA) on the sale of replacement engines for MHA's Soviet-made aircraft and the purchase of new aircraft engines, the PW 4000 series. Concerned that the negotiations had already lasted several months, PW asked MHA to sign a nonbinding letter of intent. In the letter, the parties agreed that the signing of a final agreement would depend on MHA's acceptance of a support offer (a service contract) for the new PW 4000 engines that would be part of new aircraft to be purchased by MHA. PW also attempted at various times to make the sale of replacement engines conditional upon MHA's purchase of new engines. At the time, MHA was also separately negotiating with two aircraft companies to purchase two or three airplanes and was choosing from among different aircraft companies. Under the practice of the industry, a buyer would not select an engine until it chose the aircraft that it would purchase. Subsequently, PW submitted two purchase-support offers dated December 14, 1990 to MHA, one for each of type of plane, which replaced an earlier November 9 purchase-support offer. According to the offers, depending on which plane MHA chose, MHA would then purchase a different PW engine that would come installed in the aircraft. For example, if MHA decided to purchase the Boeing 767, MHA would purchase a PW 4056, which had a base price of $5.84 million (MHA could also select the PW 4060 engine or two replacement engines for the Boeing but no base price was included for these other engines); if MHA decided to purchase the Airbus 310-300 aircraft, MHA would purchase a PW 4152, which had a base price of $5.55 million, or the PW 4156 for $5.84 million and two spare engines. The Airbus was slightly different from the Boeing in that while the Boeing could receive the installation of the engines without any further modification, the Airbus had to be further modified and additional parts such as a gondola had to be installed. As a result, the Airbus was to receive a "jet engine system" as opposed to a simple engine as in the case of the Boeing planes. (The offer for the Airbus engines, however, did not include a price for the engine system, but just for the engine.) Under these types of arrangements, MHA would pay the aircraft manufacturer for the cost of a complete plane and the aircraft manufacturer would then pay PW for the cost of the engine. The support offers from PW also offered financing to MHA.

Both of the purchase-support offers contained a place where MHA was to sign, but rather than signing the offers, MHA composed a letter on December 21, 1990 stating that it had selected the PW 4000 engine for the new fleet of aircraft. MHA also mentioned in the letter that it was looking forward to cooperating with PW on the replacement engines as well. The letter further mentioned that it was wholly based on the conditions contained in the December 14, 1990 purchase-support offers. In February 1991, PW sent a letter adding a $65,000 advertising budget and stated that PW would come to Budapest to continue discussions on the replacement engines and to finalize the contract for the new PW 4000 engines. MHA then chose the Boeing aircraft but notified PW that it would not choose the PW engines. PW countered that MHA had committed to purchase the Boeing aircraft and the PW 4000 engines and asked MHA to immediately notify Boeing about its selection and to make a public announcement.

When MHA refused to do so, PW brought suit in Hungary. As both Hungary and the United States are contracting parties to the CISG, the contract was governed by the CISG. PW claimed that the purchase-support offers of December 14, 1990 constituted offers within the meaning of Article 14 of the CISG because they clearly stated the product, the quantity, and data on which the price could be determined precisely. According to PW, the offers were definite because the parties could determine, based on the aircraft type, the number of engines and the price. Further, MHA's declaration of December 21, 1990 operated as an acceptance of PW's offer. MHA argued that the December 14, 1990 offers were not definite within the meaning of CISG Article 14. The price and quantity of the engines all depended on the type of plane that MHA was to purchase and could not be determined through the December 14, 1990 offers alone. Once MHA chose a certain type of aircraft, then the type of engine and the cost of the engine could be determined with precision. Here neither the quantity nor the price could be determined through the December 14, 1990 offers alone. MHA also argued that in its February 11, 1991 letter, PW referred to the finalization of the contract and did not transfer a $1 million U.S. payment as a dollar premium for signing. This was a contractual premium given to the buyer in case the buyer signed the contract within the deadline.

The lower court found that a contract had been established under the CISG. The court found that the December 1990 offers were sufficiently definite because once MHA selected the aircraft the quantity and price of the engines could be determined concretely. MHA's December 21, 1990 declaration was the acceptance of the offer. The court treated the February 11 letter as a later addition or modification of the contract. On appeal, MHA's argument was that the December 14, 1990 purchase support offers were not definite offers but still part of the process of negotiations. The court of appeals agreed with MHA and reversed. The court of appeals noted that in the case of the Airbus as the engines were to be built into the planes, MHA was really buying a "jet engine system" and not merely the base engine. The jet engine system included additional parts—in the case of the Airbus the jet engine system included the engine, other parts, and the gondola as well. The court found that if the offers were to be definite under CISG Article 14, the offers had to include the price of all of the products, engines, and jet engine systems. In the case of the Boeing, the engine only was needed as Boeing planes included all of the other parts that otherwise had to be supplied for the Airbus. PW then appealed to the Hungarian Supreme Court, which rendered the decision below.]

It clearly follows from the above, that none of Plaintiff's offers, neither the one for the Boeing aircraft's engines, nor the one for the Airbus aircraft's jet engine systems, complied with the requirements stipulated in Paragraph 1, Section 14 of the Agreement, for it did not indicate the price of the services or it could not have been determined.

Plaintiff's parallel and alternative contractual offers should be interpreted, according to the noticeable intention of the offer's wording and following common sense, so, that Plaintiff wished to provide an opportunity to Defendant to select one of the engine types defined in the offer at the time of the acceptance of the offer.

For according to the wording of Section Y of the offers:

- Defendant, following the acceptance of the proposal, immediately notifies the aircraft manufacturer about the selection of one of the numerically defined engines (jet engine systems) for use on the wide bodied aircrafts;
- Plaintiff sells the selected engine (jet engine system) to Defendant according to a separate agreement made with the aircraft manufacturer;
- Thereby (that is, with the acceptance of the proposal) Defendant sends a final and unconditional purchase order to Plaintiff for the delivery of the spare engines of the determined type.

In addition to grammatical interpretation, the assumption of Plaintiff granting "power" to Defendant, made by the court of first instance, essentially entitling Defendant to make its selection until some undetermined point of time or even during performance from the services offered alternatively, goes against economic reasoning as well. For the legal consequences of this would be that Plaintiff should manufacture the quantity, stipulated in the contract, of all four types—two engines and two jet engine systems—and prepared with its services wait for Defendant to exercise its right to make its selection with no deadline.

It follows from this all that Plaintiff provided was an opportunity to choose a certain type of engine or jet engine system at the time of the acceptance of its offer.

Plaintiff's offers were alternative, therefore Defendant should have determined which engine or jet engine system, listed in the offers, it chose. There was no declaration made, on behalf of Defendant, in which Defendant would have indicated the subject of the service, the concrete type of the engine or jet engine system, listed in the offers, as an essential condition of the contract. Defendant's declaration, that it had chosen the PW 4000 series engine, expresses merely Defendant's intention to close the contract, which is insufficient for the establishment of the contract.

Therefore, the court of first instance was mistaken when it found that with Defendant's December 21, 1990 declaration the contract was established with the "power" —or, more precisely stipulation—according to which Defendant was entitled to select from the indicated four types (PW 4056 or PW 4060 engine and spare engine, PW 4152 or PW 4156 jet engine system and spare engine) with a unilateral declaration later, after the contract had been closed. The opportunity to choose after closing the contract does not follow from the offer. If perhaps such a further condition would have been intended by Defendant, then this should have been regarded as a new offer on its behalf.

Lacking an appropriately explicit offer from Plaintiff and not having a clear indication as to the subject of the service in Defendant's declaration of acceptance, no sales contract has been established between the Parties.

NOTES AND QUESTIONS

1. Pratt & Whitney and the prospective buyer signed a letter of intent, which is often used in contracts involving complex negotiations. The letter indicates the good faith commitment of the parties to enter into a binding agreement so that each party has some assurance that the other party is serious and that the negotiations are not a waste of time. The letter of intent is not legally binding so either or both parties can walk away from the transaction with impunity. The parties may not want a binding commitment because while they would like to consummate a deal, they realize that they might not be able to agree on the details.

2. Why did the Hungarian Supreme Court find that there was no contract in the principal case? Does the *Pratt & Whitney* case stand for the proposition that offers that contain open price and open quantity terms are not "offers" within the meaning of Article 14(1) and that an acceptance of such "offers" will not form a contract?

3. Does this also mean that the CISG refuses to recognize open price and open quantity contracts? Consider the following: The key issue under Article 14(1) is whether the offeror intends to be bound by an acceptance of the offer. Offerors do not usually intend to be bound by offers that are indefinite as to price and quantity. Rather, offerors usually intend to be bound when a proposal is addressed to specific persons containing definite terms on price and quantity. Thus, a final or definite price and quantity function as an indication of the intent of the offeror to be bound by an acceptance. The key issue is the intent of the offeror to be bound and the reasonable expectation of the offeree that an answer of "yes" creates a binding contract. Usually, this requires a final price and final quantity but there are instances when a long-term or complex contract is involved and the parties intend to be bound when there is a provisional price and quantity that may need to be adjusted as the contract is being performed.

4. Suppose that Pratt & Whitney and the buyer had inserted the following clause into their contract: "The parties hereby exercise their power under CISG Article 6 to derogate from the requirements of CISG Article 14(1) providing a proposal must be sufficiently definite as to quantity and price in order to constitute an offer. The parties hereby declare their intention to be bound by this open price and open quantity contract." Would such a statement be effective to create a binding contract without details as to a final price and quantity? Is it a sufficient response to this query to simply note that Article 14(1) provides that a proposal that is not sufficiently definite is not an offer and so thus a response of "I accept" cannot conclude a contract because there was no offer to accept?

In considering this question, note the following points. First, recall that the CISG is not concerned with the validity of the contract but only with contract formation and the rights and obligations of the parties. Issues of validity are governed by another source of substantive law, which would most likely be domestic law. To suggest that a proposal without concrete terms on quantity and price cannot be a valid offer under Article 14(1) is raising the issue of the validity of the contract, which is not within the scope of the CISG. Open price and quantity contracts are valid under both the common law and the Uniform Commercial Code. Second, the creation of a contract through the model of a formal offer and an acceptance under Article 14(1) is not the only way that a binding contract can be created under the CISG. Article 18(3) provides that a binding contract can be created by the conduct of the parties. Consider also Article 55, which provides in part:

> Where a contract has been validly concluded but does not expressly or implicitly fix or make provision for determining the price, the parties are considered to have impliedly made reference to the price generally charged at the time of the conclusion of the contract for such goods sold under comparable circumstances in the trade concerned.

After considering these materials, what is your answer?

6.   Performance of the Contract

Once a contract is formed, the parties must then carry out their obligations under the contract: The seller must deliver conforming goods and the buyer must pay the purchase price. The materials below focus on three elements: delivery, conformity of the goods, and payment.

A. DELIVERY BY SELLER

While delivery may seem straightforward enough where the parties are involved in a face-to-face, cash-for-goods transaction where the seller can hand over the goods to the buyer, these types of transactions are very rare in any context today, but especially so in the context of an international sale. When the seller and buyer are in different countries, what does the seller have to do to satisfy its delivery obligation?

PROBLEM 3-11

The buyer, a manufacturer of auto parts in Cleveland, Ohio, calls the seller, a supplier of machine parts, in Toronto, Canada, and says, "I saw your web site and you've got just what we need. Can you sell me 6,000 widgets for $15,000?"

(1) The seller responds, "Sorry, my costs have gone up recently. I can't do it for any less than $16,500." The buyer then says, "Okay, let's do it." What must the seller do to satisfy its obligation to deliver the goods? *See* Articles 30 and 31. When must the seller deliver the goods? *See* Article 33.

(2) Suppose instead that the seller responds, "I can do it for $17,000 inland freight by truck. I'll have the trucker's bills of lading waiting for you in my office." What must the seller do to satisfy its delivery obligations with respect to the goods and the documents under these circumstances? *See* Articles 31 and 34. Suppose that during the course of transport the truck is involved in a traffic accident and the goods are damaged. Who bears the risk of loss? *See* Article 67. Were there any obligations concerning insurance? *See* Article 32(3).

NOTES AND QUESTIONS

1. Recall that the CISG is a supplementary law that is meant to interpret the contract, which remains primary. In Problem 3-11, the parties could have explicitly agreed on place of delivery, insurance, and risk of loss. In contracts that are formed through casual contacts, however, it is not unusual for the parties to omit some or all of these terms. The CISG serves to supply these obligations in the absence of an agreement by the parties.

2. While the parties can set out in detail the delivery obligations of the seller, this can be time consuming and misunderstandings about the meaning of terms can also arise between the parties. In Chapter Two, we introduced the ICC Incoterms, which are standard terms for delivery obligations that the parties can incorporate by contract. Incoterms help to define the terms of the contract and the use of Incoterms is entirely consistent with the CISG. Incoterms offer a short-cut through the incorporation of a set of agreed on definitions that reflect international commercial practice. Once the contract is formed, it is then governed by the CISG. In Problem 3-11, the parties could have supplemented the CISG through an explicit agreement incorporating Incoterms. The parties could have agreed, for example, on a contract "CIF Cleveland (Incoterms 2000)." Article 32 details the seller's obligations where the seller is bound to arrange for carriage of the goods, leaving it up to the parties to decide whether to place the burden for arranging carriage on the seller. The incorporation of the CIF term now explicitly places the obligation on the seller to arrange for transport of the goods, and Article 32 is now applicable and the seller must comply with its requirements. If the parties had not agreed on Incoterms or otherwise specified that the seller was to arrange for the carriage contract, then Article 32 is not applicable unless such an obligation can be inferred from the circumstances. In the case of casual contracts, such as that involved in Problem 3-11, the parties may not refer to Incoterms and the CISG will be applied in the absence of such details in the contract.

B. CONFORMING GOODS

A seller has an obligation to deliver the goods that conform to the contract, that is, of the same quality, quantity, and condition as expressed in the contract. There are often cases, however, where the contract may be silent or does not expressly resolve an issue relating to the conformity of the goods. Domestic U.S. law has dealt with these obligations of the seller through three types of warranties: an express warranty (UCC §2-313), an implied warranty of merchantability (UCC §2-314), and an implied warranty of fitness (UCC §2-315). In the *Prime Start* case, *supra*, the court explained the warranties under the UCC as follows:

> Express warranties may arise from, among other things, (1) "any description of the goods that is made part of the bargain," which creates an "express warranty that the goods will conform to that description," or (2) a "sample or model which is made part of the basis of the bargain," which creates an "express warranty that the whole of the goods shall conform to the sample or model." [U.C.C. §2-313(1).] The words "warrant" or "guarantee" are not required, nor must there be a specific intention to make a warranty for one to be created. [U.C.C. §2-313(2).]
>
> [I]mplied warranties are "obligation[s] which the law imposes without regard to any supposed agreement of the parties." *Fossum v. Timber Structures, Inc.*, 54 Wash. 2d 317, [339,] 341 P.2d 157, 170 (1959). For example, the implied warranty of "merchantability" requires, among other things, that goods "pass without objection in the trade under the contract description" and are "run, within the variations permitted by the agreement, of even kind, quality and quantity within each unit and among all units involved." [U.C.C. §2-314.] The implied warranty of "fitness for a particular purpose" governs cases where a buyer relies on a seller's "skill or judgment to select or furnish suitable goods." [U.C.C. §2-315.]

442 F. Supp. 2d at 1129–1130. Under U.S. law, perhaps the most significant difference between express and implied warranties is that the latter can be disclaimed under UCC §2-316(2) while the former cannot. How does the CISG approach differ from the U.S. approach? The approach of the CISG is to combine all of the seller's obligations concerning the conformity of the goods into Article 35.

PROBLEM 3-12

A South Korean manufacturer of plasma flat-screen high-definition televisions contracts to sell a large quantity of televisions to a U.S. wholesale distributor. The contract called for Model H-1. The seller has a surplus of H-2s, which exceed the performance standards of the H-1 and actually have a higher retail market value. The seller ships the H-2 instead. Has the seller met its obligations under Article 35?

PROBLEM 3-13

In Problem 3-12 above, the seller ships the H-1 sets.

(1) Due to differences in the U.S. satellite system, the TV cannot display a picture at the high-definition level but only at the level of ordinary television. The buyer refuses to accept the goods. Has the seller met its obligation under Article 35(2)(b) and (c)?

(2) The goods are packaged in shipping crates that are used for ordinary TVs and are damaged en route to the United States. The contract is silent on the type of packaging that needs to be used. Has the seller met its obligation under Article 35(2)(d) and *Medical Marketing* below?

(3) When the TVs arrive in a U.S. port, Customs officials will not allow the TVs entry into the United States because their electrical wiring systems do not meet U.S. safety standards. Is it the seller's responsibility to know about U.S. electrical safety standards or is it the buyer's responsibility? *See* Article 35(2) and *Medical Marketing* below. What if the seller had a sales office in the United States?

(4) Assume that the contract calls for delivery to the buyer in the port of Los Angeles. Before the seller ships the goods, the buyer engages a South Korean company to check the TVs for use in the United States. The South Korean company reports that the goods satisfy U.S. safety standards but upon their arrival in the United States the goods are refused entry by U.S. Customs. The seller argues that the buyer has waived the right to assert any nonconformity. The buyer argues that as delivery is to occur in the United States, the buyer has the right to defer examination until the goods have arrived and to assert the nonconformity upon inspection of the goods in the United States. What is the result? *See* Articles 36, 38, and 39. Suppose the seller knew that the TVs did not satisfy U.S. safety standards? *See* Article 40; *see also Medical Marketing* and *BP Oil* below.

Medical Marketing International, Inc. v. Internazionale Medico Scientifica, S.r.l.
United States District Court, Eastern District of Louisiana, 1999
1999 WL 311945

Duval, District Judge.

Before the court is an Application for Order Confirming Arbitral Award and Entry of Judgment, filed by plaintiff, Medical Marketing International, Inc. ("MMI"). Having considered the memoranda of plaintiff, and the memorandum in opposition filed by defendant, Internazionale Medico Scientifica, S.r.l. ("IMS"), the court grants the motion.

FACTUAL BACKGROUND

Plaintiff MMI is a Louisiana marketing corporation with its principal place of business in Baton Rouge, Louisiana. Defendant IMS is an Italian corporation that manufactures radiology materials with its principal place of business in Bologna, Italy. On January 25, 1993, MMI and IMS entered into a Business Licensing Agreement in which IMS granted exclusive sales rights for Giotto Mammography H.F. Units to MMI.

In 1996, the Food and Drug Administration ("FDA") seized the equipment for non-compliance with administrative procedures, and a dispute arose over who bore the obligation of ensuring that the Giotto equipment complied with the United States Governmental Safety Regulations, specifically the Good Manufacturing Practices (GMP) for Medical Device Regulations. MMI formally demanded mediation on October 28, 1996, pursuant to Article 13 of the agreement. Mediation was unsuccessful, and the parties entered into arbitration, also pursuant to Article 13, whereby each party chose one arbitrator and a third was agreed upon by both.

An arbitration hearing was held on July 13–15, July 28, and November 17, 1998. The hearing was formally closed on November 30, 1998. The arbitrators rendered their decision on December 21, 1998, awarding MMI damages in the amount of $357,009.00 and legal interest on that amount from October 28, 1996. IMS moved for reconsideration on December 30, 1998, and this request was denied by the arbitrators on January 7, 1999. Plaintiff now moves for an order from this court confirming the arbitral award and entering judgment in favor of the plaintiff.

ANALYSIS

IMS has alleged that the arbitrators' decision violates public policy of the international global market and that the arbitrators exhibited "manifest disregard of international sales law." Specifically, IMS argues that the arbitrators misapplied the United Nations Convention on Contracts for the International Sale of Goods, commonly referred to as CISG, and that they refused to follow a German Supreme Court Case interpreting CISG.

MMI does not dispute that CISG applies to the case at hand. Under CISG, the finder of fact has a duty to regard the "international character" of the convention and to promote uniformity in its application. CISG Article 7. The Convention also provides that in an international contract for goods, goods conform to the contract if they are fit for the purpose for which goods of the same description would ordinarily be used or are fit for any particular purpose expressly or impliedly made known to the seller and relied upon by the buyer. CISG Article 35(2). To avoid a contract based on the nonconformity of goods, the buyer must allege and prove that the seller's breach was "fundamental" in nature. CISG Article 49. A breach is fundamental when it results in such detriment to the party that he or she is substantially deprived of what he or she is entitled to expect under the contract, unless the party in breach did not foresee such a result. CISG Article 25.

At the arbitration, IMS argued that MMI was not entitled to avoid its contract with IMS based on nonconformity under Article 49, because IMS's breach was not "fundamental." IMS argued that CISG did not require that it furnish MMI with equipment that complied with the United States GMP regulations. To support this proposition, IMS cited a German Supreme Court case, which held that under CISG Article 35, a seller is generally not obligated to supply goods that conform to public laws and regulations enforced at the buyer's place of business. *Entscheidungen des Bundesgerichtshofs in Zivilsachen* (BGHZ) 129, 75 (1995). In that case, the court held that this general rule carries with it exceptions in three limited circumstances: (1) if the public laws and regulations of the buyer's state are identical to those enforced in the seller's state; (2) if the buyer informed the seller about those regulations; or (3) if due to "special circumstances," such as the existence of a seller's branch office in the buyer's state, the seller knew or should have known about the regulations at issue.

The arbitration panel decided that under the third exception, the general rule did not apply to this case. The arbitrators held that IMS was, or should have been, aware of the GMP regulations prior to entering into the 1993 agreement, and explained their reasoning at length. IMS now argues that the arbitration panel refused to apply CISG and the law as articulated by the German Supreme Court. It is clear from the arbitrators' written findings, however, that they carefully considered that decision and found that this case fit the exception and not the rule as articulated in that decision. The arbitrators' decision was neither contrary to public policy nor in manifest disregard of international sales law. This court therefore finds that the arbitration panel did not "exceed its powers" in violation of the FAA. Accordingly,

It is ordered that the Application for Order Confirming Arbitral Award is hereby Granted.

BP Oil International, Ltd. v. Empresa Estatal Petroleos de Ecuador
United States Court of Appeals, Fifth Circuit, 2003
332 F.3d 333

SMITH, Circuit Judge.

Empresa Estatal Petroleos de Ecuador ("PetroEcuador") contracted with BP Oil International, Ltd. ("BP"), for the purchase and transport of gasoline from Texas to Ecuador. PetroEcuador refused to accept delivery, so BP sold the gasoline at a loss. BP appeals a summary judgment dismissing PetroEcuador and Saybolt, Inc. ("Saybolt"), the company responsible for testing the gasoline at the port of departure. We affirm in part, reverse in part, and remand.

I.

PetroEcuador sent BP an invitation to bid for supplying 140,000 barrels of unleaded gasoline deliverable "CFR" to Ecuador. "CFR," which stands for "Cost and Freight," is one of thirteen International Commercial Terms ("Incoterms") designed to "provide a set of international rules for the interpretation of the most commonly used trade terms in foreign trade." Incoterms are recognized through their incorporation into the Convention on Contracts for the International Sale of Goods ("CISG").

BP responded favorably to the invitation, and PetroEcuador confirmed the sale on its contract form. The final agreement required that the oil be sent "CFR La Libertad-Ecuador." The contract further specifies that the gasoline have a gum content of less than three milligrams per one hundred milliliters, to be determined at the port of departure. PetroEcuador appointed Saybolt, a company specializing in quality control services, to ensure this requirement was met.

To fulfill the contract, BP purchased gasoline from Shell Oil Company and, following testing by Saybolt, loaded it on board the M/T TIBER at Shell's Deer Park, Texas, refinery. The TIBER sailed to La Libertad, Ecuador, where the gasoline was again tested for gum content. On learning that the gum content now exceeded the contractual limit, PetroEcuador refused to accept delivery. Eventually, BP resold the gasoline to Shell at a loss of approximately two million dollars.

BP sued PetroEcuador for breach of contract and wrongful draw of a letter of guarantee. After PetroEcuador filed a notice of intent to apply foreign law pursuant to Fed. R. Civ. P. 44.1, the district court applied Texas choice of law rules and determined that Ecuadorian law governed. BP argued that the term "CFR" demonstrated the parties' intent to pass the risk of loss to PetroEcuador once the goods were delivered on board the TIBER. The district court disagreed and held that under Ecuadorian law, the seller must deliver conforming goods to the agreed destination, in this case Ecuador. The court granted summary judgment for PetroEcuador.

BP also brought negligence and breach of contract claims against Saybolt, alleging that the company had improperly tested the gasoline. Saybolt moved for summary judgment, asserting a limitation of liability defense and waiver of claims based on the terms of its service contract with BP. The court granted Saybolt's motion, holding that BP could not sue in tort, that BP was bound by the waiver provision, and that Saybolt did not take any action causing harm to BP. Pursuant to Fed. R. Civ. P. 54(b), the court entered final judgment in favor of PetroEcuador and Saybolt.

[The court of appeals held that the CISG, not Ecuadorian domestic law, governed the contract, then turned to a discussion of the CISG.]

The CISG incorporates Incoterms through article 9(2), which provides:

> The parties are considered, unless otherwise agreed, to have impliedly made applicable to their contract or its formation a usage of which the parties knew or ought to have known and which in international trade is widely known to, and regularly observed by, parties to contracts of the type involved in the particular trade concerned.

CISG art. 9(2). Even if the usage of Incoterms is not global, the fact that they are well known in international trade means that they are incorporated through article 9(2).

PetroEcuador's invitation to bid for the procurement of 140,000 barrels of gasoline proposed "CFR" delivery. The final agreement, drafted by PetroEcuador, again specified that the gasoline be sent "CFR La Libertad-Ecuador" and that the cargo's gum content be tested pre-shipment. Shipments designated "CFR" require the seller to pay the costs and freight to transport the goods to the delivery port, but pass title and risk of loss to the buyer once the goods "pass the ship's rail" at the port of shipment. The goods should be tested for conformity before the risk of loss passes to the buyer. In the event of subsequent damage or loss, the buyer generally must seek a remedy against the carrier or insurer.

In light of the parties' unambiguous use of the Incoterm "CFR," BP fulfilled its contractual obligations if the gasoline met the contract's qualitative specifications when it passed the ship's rail and risk transferred to PetroEcuador. CISG art. 36(1). Indeed, Saybolt's testing confirmed that the gasoline's gum content was adequate before departure from Texas. Nevertheless, in its opposition to BP's motion for summary judgment, PetroEcuador contends that BP purchased the gasoline from Shell on an "as is" basis and thereafter failed to add sufficient gum inhibitor as a way to "cut corners." In other words, the cargo contained a hidden defect.

Having appointed Saybolt to test the gasoline, PetroEcuador "ought to have discovered" the defect before the cargo left Texas. CISG art. 39(1). Permitting PetroEcuador now to distance itself from Saybolt's test would negate the parties' selection of CFR delivery and would undermine the key role that reliance plays in international sales agreements. Nevertheless, BP could have breached the agreement if it provided goods that it "knew or could not have been unaware" were defective when they "passed over the ship's rail" and risk shifted to PetroEcuador. CISG art. 40.

Therefore, there is a fact issue as to whether BP knowingly provided gasoline with an excessive gum content. The district court should permit the parties to conduct discovery as to this issue only.

IV.

BP raises negligence and breach of contract claims against Saybolt, alleging that the company improperly tested the gasoline's gum content before shipment. These claims amount to indemnification for BP's losses suffered on account of PetroEcuador's refusal to accept delivery. Our conclusion that PetroEcuador is liable so long as BP did not knowingly provide deficient gasoline renders these claims moot. Summary judgment was therefore proper, though we need not review the district court's reasoning.

If PetroEcuador improperly refused CFR delivery, it is liable to BP for any consequential damages. In its claims against Saybolt, BP pleaded "in the alternative"; counsel also acknowledged, at oral argument, that beyond those damages stemming from PetroEcuador's refusal to accept delivery, BP has no collateral claims against Saybolt. If Saybolt negligently misrepresented the gasoline's gum content, PetroEcuador (not BP) becomes the party with a potential claim.

Even if PetroEcuador is not liable because BP knowingly presented gasoline with an inadequate gum content, BP's claims drop out. BP alleges that Saybolt "negligently misrepresented the quality" of the gasoline before its loading in Texas; it also claims that Saybolt's improper testing was "a proximate cause of the gasoline to be refused by PetroEcuador and/or the gum content to increase which caused BP to suffer pecuniary loss." BP's claims depend on the fact that Saybolt misrepresented the quality of the gasoline. It goes without saying, however, that if BP knew that the gasoline was deficient, it could not have relied on Saybolt's report to its detriment.

The judgment dismissing PetroEcuador is reversed and remanded for proceedings consistent with this opinion. The judgment dismissing Saybolt is affirmed.

NOTES AND QUESTIONS

In *BP Oil*, the Fifth Circuit held that, under CISG Article 9(2), Incoterms applied to the contract because the parties "impliedly made applicable to their contract or its formation a usage of which the parties knew or ought to have known." The court then noted that even if the use of Incoterms "is not global, the fact that they are well known in international trade means that they are incorporated through article 9(2)." *See BP Oil*, 332 F.3d at 337–338. Is the effect of the court's decision to incorporate Incoterms into all CISG contracts?

C. PAYMENT BY BUYER

The buyer's obligation is to pay against delivery but if the transaction is not a face-to-face one, questions arise as to under what conditions, when, and where payment is to be made.

PROBLEM 3-14

A wholesale distributor in Mexico City sends a fax to a grain dealer in Indiana with the following message, "I need 1,000 bushels of corn. Can you get them to me by June 15th?" The seller responds with a reply by fax, "Yes, we accept your offer. We can make delivery on or before June 15th in Mexico City at the market price of $3 per bushel." The buyer responds, "Sorry, but our fax was one of several inquiries sent out and not an offer. We have already concluded a contract with another dealer so we cannot agree to accept delivery." The seller responds, "Our lawyers have advised us that when we accepted your offer a valid contract was formed. We intend to hold you to the contract." Is there a valid contract and must buyer pay for the goods? *See* Article 14(1).

PROBLEM 3-15

Suppose that under the same facts above the Mexican distributor states in the fax, "I am in urgent need of 1,000 bushels of corn at market price." The seller immediately ships 1,000 bushels and the next day sends a fax, "We have shipped 1,000 bushels of corn at the low price of $6 per bushel." Must the buyer pay for the goods and at what price? *See* Article 18(3), Article 55, and the case below.

Unilex, D. 1995-1
France: Cour de Cassation (April 1, 1995)

A French buyer ordered electronic components from a German seller. The order specified that the final purchase price, previously indicated by the seller, would have to be revised taking into account a possible decrease in market prices, and that the goods would be delivered at certain dates, upon confirmation by the seller. The seller replied, specifying that the purchase price would have to be revised according to both the increase and decrease in market prices. Later, the buyer cancelled the order involving some other components. The seller objected to such partial cancellation, alleging that it had already dispatched the goods concerned for delivery. Upon delivery the buyer rejected the goods in excess and requested the seller to take back the said goods. The seller refused to take back the goods rejected by the buyer and demanded payment.

As to the buyer's argument that the offer was not sufficiently definite (Art. 14(1) CISG), the appellate court held that the revision of price according to the market trends indicated in the buyer's original offer did make the price determinable.

Upon the buyer's appeal, the Supreme Court affirmed the appellate court decision.

PROBLEM 3-16

A Kentucky farmer sells a large quantity of paddlefish caviar to a buyer in the Ukraine. The contract called for carriage of the goods by sea and a negotiable bill of lading. As for the price, the parties had orally agreed to a price of $250,000 but did not agree on currency or a place of payment. Both parties assumed that they would work out these details eventually but the caviar is now en route. The seller is reluctant to part with the bill of lading until several payment issues are resolved. The buyer insists that payment is to be made in the Ukraine in local currency after it receives a formal written request for payment from the seller. The seller wants payment in U.S. dollars in the United States. Where does the buyer need to make payment and in what currency? *See* Articles 57 and 58.

Should the seller consider a confirmed letter of credit in this case? How would a confirmed letter of credit help the seller resolve the payment issues?

The buyer also insists on inspection of the goods before payment, saying that it is not sure that the paddlefish roe will be suited to local tastes. Does the buyer have the right to inspect the goods before payment? *See* Article 58.

D. EXCUSED PERFORMANCE

In the course of a contract, any number of unexpected difficulties can arise that prevent its performance: war, civil strife, government prohibitions, the closing of a well-known transportation route such as the Suez Canal, strikes, fire, and economic conditions. The situations themselves can be the subject of endless variations but the legal issue remains the same: Under what conditions will the performance of the contract by one of the parties be excused? If nonperformance is excused, then the nonperforming party is not liable to the disappointed party for breach of contract. Domestic courts deal with this issue through the various doctrines of frustration, impossibility, and force majeure.

(1) Article 79

Under the CISG, excused performance is governed by Article 79, which applies when the parties have not themselves allocated the risk of nonperformance due to unforeseen circumstances. If the parties have a force majeure clause in their contract of sale, then the clause, if it applies, will supersede Article 79.

Article 79 provides as follows:

Article 79

(1) A party is not liable for a failure to perform any of his obligations if he proves that the failure was due to an impediment beyond his control and that he could not reasonably be expected to have taken the impediment into account at the time of the conclusion of the contract or to have avoided or overcome it or its consequences.

Article 79(1) consists of three elements: (1) The failure to perform must be due to an impediment beyond the control of the nonperforming party; (2) the nonperforming party could not reasonably be expected to take the impediment into account; and (3) the nonperforming party could not overcome the impediment.

Illustration 79a. In a contract for the sale of widgets, the seller's operating costs unexpectedly go up and the seller will suffer serious financial hardship if it performs the contract. The seller is not excused under Article 79. An "impediment" to performance connotes a barrier that prevents performance, not an event that makes performance more difficult or costly.

Illustration 79b. In a contract for the sale of widgets, the seller's factory is destroyed by a fire caused by faulty wiring. The city had inspected the factory in the prior month and had given the seller a warning that the factory's electrical wiring did not satisfy city fire code standards. The seller is not excused. In this case, the destruction of the factory by fire is an impediment under Article 79 but it is one that the seller should have taken into account under the circumstances of the case.

Illustration 79c. In a contract for the sale of widgets, the seller's factory is destroyed by a fire even though the seller's factory had just passed a city fire inspection and had no history of fire problems. The contract calls for the sale of widgets but did not specify that the widgets were to be produced in the seller's factory. The seller is not excused. Although the seller's non-performance is caused by an impediment that the seller could not reasonably be expected to take into account, the seller can overcome the impediment by purchasing substitute widgets on the market and delivering them to the buyer.

If a party fulfills all of the conditions under Article 79, the party is excused from performance. However, the exemption provided by Article 79 to a nonperforming party is a narrow one. Assuming that the nonperforming party is exempt, Article 79(5) provides "[n]othing in this Article prevents either party from exercising any right other than to claim damages." The most important consequence of this limitation is that the disappointed party's ability to avoid the contract is not impaired. (Avoidance is governed by Articles 25, 49, 64, 72, and 73, which we take up in the following section on remedies.) Suppose that the seller is excused from performance under Article 79; the buyer cannot sue the seller for damages but the buyer can avoid the contract and does not have to pay the contract price. The buyer is also entitled to restitution (Article 81(2)) of whatever the buyer may have paid to the seller. The same holds true if the nonperforming party is the buyer: The seller cannot sue the buyer for damages but the seller does not have to deliver the goods.

PROBLEM 3-17

An Ecuadorian seller enters into a sales contract with a U.S. buyer for goods. The contract does not specify the route but states, "delivery to occur in Miami by the most economically available route." The seller arranges for the contract of carriage to set sail through the Panama Canal to reach Miami. The buyer knows that the route through the Panama Canal is the usual and customary shipping route for merchants in Ecuador and all of its immediately adjacent neighboring countries. While the carrier is en route to the Panama Canal, however, a military coup breaks out in the region and the Panama Canal is closed. The alternative route is to sail around the southern tip of South America and then up to Miami but the trip will take an additional two months and will add 75 percent to the cost of carriage.

(1) Two weeks after the ship returns to Ecuador, the seller informs the buyer that its performance is prevented by an impediment under Article 79. Has the seller fulfilled its obligations under Article 79(4)?

(2) The contract is for the sale of Ecuadorian fruit. If the seller takes the trip around the southern tip of South America, the goods will perish. But upon return of the ship to port, the seller can ship the goods via air but this would cost 20 times more than ocean transport and may force the seller into bankruptcy. What is the result under Article 79(1)? Does it make a difference whether the contract is construed as a contract for goods from Ecuador to Miami or as a contract for goods from Ecuador to Miami via the Panama Canal?

(3) The contract is for the sale of Ecuadorian-made shoes. What is the result under Article 79(1)? See *Tsakiroglou* below.

Tsakiroglou & Co. Ltd. v. Noblee Thorl G.m.b.H.
House of Lords
[1962] A.C. 93

[In an arbitration between Tsakiroglou & Co. Ltd., sellers, and Noblee Thorl G.m.b.H., buyers, the arbitrators awarded the buyers the sum of £5,625 against the sellers as damages for breach of contract. Diplock J. upheld the award and his decision was affirmed by the court of appeal. The sellers (appellants) appealed the decision of the court of appeal to the House of Lords.]

VISCOUNT SIMONDS.

[Under the contract, the sellers] agreed to sell to the respondents 300 tons of Sudanese groundnuts at £50 per 1,000 kilos including bags c.i.f. Hamburg, shipment during November/December, 1956. No goods were shipped by the sellers.

All groundnuts exported from the Sudan to Europe are shipped from Port Sudan, which is the only suitable port. At the date of the contract (October 4, 1956), the usual and normal route for the shipment of Sudanese groundnuts from Port Sudan to Hamburg was via the Suez Canal. Both parties then contemplated that shipment would be made by that route. It would have been unusual and rare for any substantial parcel of Sudanese groundnuts from Port Sudan to Europe to be shipped via the Cape of Good Hope. Before the closure of the Suez Canal the appellants acquired 300 tons of Sudanese groundnuts in shell which were held to their order in warehouses at Port Sudan as from November 1, 1956. They also, before the closure, booked space for 300 tons of nuts in one or [the] other of four vessels scheduled to call at Port Sudan between November 10 and December 26, 1956. The shipping company cancelled these bookings on November 4, 1956. British and French armed forces began military operations against Egypt on October 29, 1956. The Suez Canal was blocked on November 2 and remained closed for effective purposes until at least April 9, 1957. But the appellants could have transported the goods from Port Sudan to Hamburg via the Cape of Good Hope during November and December, 1956.

The distance from Port Sudan to Hamburg via the Suez Canal is about 4,386 miles, and via the Cape about 11,137 miles. The freight ruling at the time of the contract for the shipment of groundnuts from Port Sudan to Hamburg via the Canal was about £7 10s. per ton. After the closure of the Canal the Port Sudan United Kingdom Conference imposed the following surcharges for goods supplied on vessels proceeding via the Cape, namely, as from November 10, 1956, 25 per cent., and as from December 13, 1956, 100 per cent. The market price of Sudanese nuts in shell shipped from Port Sudan c.i.f. Hamburg was £68 15s. per ton between January 1 and 13, 1957. [The sellers] did not ship any nuts. They claimed that they were entitled to consider the contract as cancelled.

I come then to the main issue and, as usual, I find two questions interlocked: (1) What does the contract mean? In other words, is there an implied term that the goods shall be carried by a particular route? (2) Is the contract frustrated?

It is convenient to examine the first question first, though the answer may be inconclusive. It is put in the forefront of the appellants' case that the contract was a contract for the shipment of goods via Suez. This contention can only prevail if a term is implied, for the contract does not say so. To say that that is nevertheless its meaning is to say in other words that the term must be implied. For this I see no ground. It has been rejected by the learned trial judge and each of the members of the Court of Appeal; and in two other cases, *Carapanayoti & Co. Ltd. v. E.T. Green Ltd.*[4] and *Gaon (Albert D.) & Co. v. Societe Interprofessionelle des Oleagineux Fluides Alimentaires*,[5] where the same question arose, it was rejected by McNair J. and Ashworth J. respectively. A variant of this contention was that there should be read into the contract by implication the words "by the usual and customary route" and that, as the only usual and customary route at the date of the contract

4. [1959] 1 Q.B. 131.
5. [1960] 2 Q.B. 318.

was via Suez, the contractual obligation was to carry the goods via Suez. Though this contention has been viewed somewhat differently, I see as little ground for the implication for it seems to me that there are precisely the same grounds for rejecting the one as the other. Both of them assume that sellers and buyers alike intended and would have agreed that, if the route via Suez became impossible, the goods should not be shipped at all. Inasmuch as the buyers presumably wanted the goods and might well have resold them, the assumption appears wholly unjustified. Freight charges may go up or down. If the parties do not specifically protect themselves against change, the loss must lie where it falls.

I turn now to what was the main argument for the appellants: that the contract was frustrated by the closure of the Canal from November 2, 1956, till April 1957. Were it not for the decision of McNair J. in *Green*'s case I should not have thought this contention arguable and I must say with the greatest respect to that learned judge that I cannot think he has given full weight to the decisions old and new of this House upon the doctrine of frustration. He correctly held that "where a contract, expressly or by necessary implication, provides that performance, or a particular part of the performance, is to be carried out in a customary manner, the performance must be carried out in a manner which is customary at the time when the performance is called for." But he concluded that the continued availability of the Suez route was a fundamental assumption at the time when the contract was made and that to impose upon the sellers the obligation to ship by an emergency route via the Cape would be to impose upon them a fundamentally different obligation which neither party could at the time when the contract was performed have dreamed that the sellers would be required to perform. Your Lordships will observe how similar this line of argument is to that which supports the implication of a term that the route should be via Suez and no other. I can see no justification for it. We are concerned with a c.i.f. contract for the sale of goods, not a contract of affreightment, though part of the sellers' obligation will be to procure a contract of affreightment. There is no evidence that the buyers attached any importance to the route. They were content that the nuts should be shipped at any date in November or December. There was no evidence, and I suppose could not be, that the nuts would deteriorate as the result of a longer voyage and a double crossing of the Equator, nor any evidence that the market was seasonable. In a word, there was no evidence that the buyers cared by what route or, within reasonable limits, when the nuts arrived. What, then, of the sellers? I recall the well-known passage in the speech of Lord Atkinson where he states the obligations of the vendor of goods under a c.i.f. contract, and ask which of these obligations is "fundamentally" altered by a change of route. Clearly the contract of affreightment will be different and so may be the terms of insurance. In both these respects the sellers may be put to greater cost: Their profit may be reduced or even disappear. But it hardly needs reasserting that an increase of expense is not a ground of frustration.

Nothing else remains to justify the view that the nature of the contract was "fundamentally" altered . . . [or] "radically different." Whatever expression is used, the doctrine of frustration must be applied within very narrow limits. In my opinion this case falls far short of satisfying the necessary conditions. In my opinion the appeal should be dismissed with costs.

(2) Performance Delegated to a Third Party

In some cases, a party, usually the seller, will subcontract with a third party to perform the contract. What happens when the seller's failure to perform is due to the nonperformance of the third party? Article 79(2) addresses this situation:

Article 79

> (2) If the party's failure is due to the failure of a third person whom he has engaged to perform the whole or a part of the contract, that party is exempt from liability only if:
>
>   (a)   he is exempt under the preceding paragraph; and
>
>   (b)   the person whom he has so engaged would be so exempt if the provisions of that paragraph were applied to him.

Article 79(2) contemplates a two-step analysis under subparagraphs (2)(a) and (b). Under subparagraph (2)(a), the issue is whether the failure of the third party is an impediment to performance by the seller of its contract with the buyer within the meaning of Article 79(1).

> *Illustration 79d.* In a contract for the sale of hand tools, the seller, a manufacturer of tools, subcontracts the manufacture to T, a third-party manufacturer. The seller is already working at near capacity and the production of tools for the buyer would require higher costs in overtime pay. T's factory is destroyed by a fire. The seller is not exempt under Article 79(2). Under subparagraph (2)(a), T's failure is not an "impediment" to the seller's performance within the meaning of Article 79(1). The seller can produce the tools at a higher cost.

The key to Article 79(2) is subparagraph (2)(b): Would the third party be exempt from liability to the seller under Article 79(1)?

> *Illustration 79e.* The seller, a distributor, enters into a contract to sell specialty farm equipment to the buyer. The seller subcontracts the manufacture of the equipment to T, a well-known manufacturer with a good reputation for reliability. In this case, however, T makes several errors in the manufacturing process and is unable to deliver the equipment on time. The seller is unable to procure substitute equipment. The seller argues that under Article 79(2)(a) it is exempt because its nonperformance is due to "an impediment" beyond its control under Article 79(1), namely, the failure of T to deliver the equipment. The seller is not excused for nonperformance of the contract with the buyer. The seller is excused from nonperformance of its contract with the buyer only if under Article 79(2)(b), T is excused from nonperformance of its contract with the seller. Here T is not excused as T made errors in the manufacturing process.

PROBLEM 3-18

A U.S. buyer enters into a contract with an Italian seller for the purchase of silk dresses to be delivered in the United States in time for the peak summer season. The Italian seller subcontracts the production of the dresses to a third party, a manufacturer in Pakistan. The production by the third party is disrupted by several government decrees imposing curfews that shorten the workday. The government decrees are mandatory laws and failure to comply would result in government sanctions. The third party is unable to deliver the dresses to the seller who, in turn, cannot deliver the dresses to the U.S. buyer on time. It is now too late to find a substitute manufacturer. The seller pleads excuse under Article 79(2). What is the result? See the following case.

Unilex, D. 1996-3.4
Germany: Schiedsgericht der Handelskammer-Hamburg

A German buyer concluded two separate but substantially identical framework agreements with two Hong Kong companies (sellers), concerning delivery of goods produced in the People's Republic of China. Further to the agreements the buyer placed several orders on behalf of its customers. Price and time of delivery varied each time, taking into account that the buyer needed the goods at short notice. Payment had to take place within 90 days of delivery but in individual cases the buyer paid in advance on delivery.

In the course of the business relationship the buyer ordered 10,000 units of product from one of the sellers. The latter asked for advance payment; later on it informed the buyer that its own Chinese supplier was undergoing serious financial and personal difficulties, and refused to deliver the goods unless the buyer paid all outstanding debts. The buyer refused. The seller brought an action before the Arbitral Court. The buyer declared the sales contract avoided and asked for damages deriving from breach of the individual sales contract in dispute and breach of the framework agreement.

In the opinion of the court, the buyer was entitled to avoid the sales contract pursuant to Arts. 49(1)(b) and 47(1) CISG because the seller refused to deliver without receiving payment for all outstanding debts deriving from past deliveries to the buyer. Such a request was inconsistent with a term in the sales contract providing for advance cash payment by the buyer, which by its nature implied that delivery should not be conditioned on payment of any amount due under previous contracts.

Moreover, the seller was not exempted for non-performance under Art. 79 CISG. According to Art. 79 CISG, a party is not liable for failure to perform its obligation if it provides that the failure was due to an impediment beyond its control and that it could not reasonably be expected to have taken it into account. As a rule, difficulties in delivery due to the seller's financial problems, or to financial problems of the seller's supplier (even when connected to the act of public authority in the supplier's country) are not to be considered an impediment beyond the seller's control but belong to the seller's area of risk.

NOTES AND QUESTIONS

1. Suppose that in Problem 3-18, the Pakistani government issued a decree prohibiting the export of products to the United States or Italy under pain of serious civil and criminal sanctions. What is the result under Article 79(2)?

2. In any situation where the seller (S) delegates performance of the contract to a third party (T), there are four different possibilities concerning liability of T to S and of S to buyer (B):

(1)   T is not exempt from liability to S; S is not exempt from liability to B;
(2)   T is not exempt from liability to S; S is exempt from liability to B;
(3)   T is exempt from liability to S; S is not exempt from liability to B;
(4)   T is exempt from liability to S; S is exempt from liability to B.

Which of these scenarios are permitted under Article 79? Can you go through each one of the scenarios permitted by Article 79 and give a policy reason why it is permitted? If any of these scenarios are not permitted, can you give a policy rationale justifying the exclusion?

7.   Remedies

The CISG specifies extensive remedies for both buyers and sellers in international sales transactions. We will consider each in turn. This will be followed by a consideration of remedies in the case of an anticipatory breach or an installment contract, for which the CISG gives similar options to a buyer and to a seller.

The CISG's basic approach to remedies is that buyers and sellers in commerce have a cooperative relationship that the parties will seek to preserve and maintain. For example, when faced with a dissatisfied buyer, sellers often do not need to be coerced into repairing a defective performance but rather are usually anxious to "make things right." Buyers also have an interest in maintaining relationships with dependable sellers and will rarely allow a single mishap to result in the termination of the relationship. Given that both parties have a stake in preserving the business relationship, the CISG remedial system provides many mechanisms that serve as tools of cooperation that can be used to remedy, repair, or cure a defective performance rather than as weapons that can be used by an aggrieved party to punish a breaching party. Of course, there will be failures in performance that will require drastic remedies that will likely result in the termination of the business relationship. In these cases, the CISG's remedial system allows for a set of remedies to put the aggrieved party in as good a position as if the breaching party fully performed.

A. REMEDIES OF THE SELLER

Articles 61–65 govern the seller's remedies for breach by the buyer. Article 61 provides an overview of the remedial system and the relationship of each of the provisions to each other. The heart of the remedial system for the seller is contained in Articles 62–64. The seller is allowed to compel performance (Article 62), to extend the time for performance by the buyer (Article 63), to avoid the contract (Article 64), and to sue for damages under Articles 74–77. Article 65 deals with the right of the seller under some circumstances to provide specifications for the goods. The following case is an illustration of how Articles 62–64, 74–77 might displace the relevant UCC provisions in a contract dispute brought in U.S. courts.

Dingxi Longhai Dairy, Ltd. v. Becwood Technology Group, LLC
United States Court of Appeals, Eighth Circuit, 2011
635 F.3d 1106

Loken, Melloy, and Shepard, Circuit Judges.
Per Curiam.
[Dingxi Longhai Dairy (Dingxi) agreed to ship 612 metric tons of Inulin, a dietary fiber extract, in four shipments from the port of Tianjin-Xingang, China, to Londonderry, New Hampshire, under a contract with Becwood Technology Group, a Minnesota distributor. Becwood received and paid for the first shipment but refused payment for the second because of mold on the exterior of the packaging. Dingxi then recalled the third and fourth shipments and filed suit against Becwood for breach of contract. The district court dismissed Dingxi's breach of contract claims for shipments three and four and Dongxi filed a timely appeal. The Court of Appeals first found that the contract was governed by the CISG and then ruled as follows.]

For its breach of contract claim, Dongxi's complaint alleged that it timely delivered all four shipments "FOB to Tianjin-Xingang Port, China," as specified in the signed purchase order; that Becwood failed to pay for the last three shipments; and that Dongxi was therefore entitled to recover $1,415,086 "together with interest, costs, expenses, and reasonable attorney's fees." Under the UCC, this would be a section 2-709 "Action for the Price" of the goods by the seller. Under the CISG, it was a claim by the seller for breach of contract subject to the remedy provisions in Articles 61–65 and 74–77. See CISG Article 61(1).

We can agree that it is highly unlikely — though not inconceivable — that an aggrieved seller in this situation would recover the full contract price for shipments three and four. But Becwood's Rule 12(b)(6) motion to dismiss the breach of contract claim was nevertheless ill-conceived.

***

Dingxi recalled shipments three and four before they reached the buyer. That fact will likely preclude recovery of the full contract price. But if Dongxi proves that Becwood breached the contract as to shipments three and four, it is almost certain to be entitled to some monetary relief. Accordingly the district court erred in granting Becwood's Rule 12(b)(6) motion to dismiss.

Reversed.

PROBLEM 3-19

A seller in Japan receives an order from a French company for 16,000 uni-ball, fine-point pens. Since this model comes in several colors, the seller e-mails the French company asking for guidance on which colors to supply. There is no response. The Japanese company then e-mails the buyer that the order will be filled with 16,000 black-ink models. The e-mail concludes, "Kindly inform us whether this specification meets your requirements. We plan to ship to you in 14 days."

There is no response and two weeks later the pens are shipped by air freight.

The day after the pens are received in France by the buyer, the seller receives a nastily worded e-mail that says the shipment does not conform to the contract, that the buyer will not pay the agreed price, and that all of the pens will be returned at the seller's expense only if the seller forwards payment for shipment fees in advance. The buyer explains that the pens are "nonconforming" because in France only blue-ink pens are marketed because "black after all is the color of death." The seller contends that the pens conform to the contract and that the buyer must accept delivery.

What should the seller do? Consider Articles 62, 63, and 64 of the CISG. Which party is in the right concerning whether the pens are nonconforming and whether the buyer must accept delivery? Consider Article 65.

NOTES AND QUESTIONS

1. Articles 62–64 provide three options to the seller. Go through and discuss each of these options and what purpose they are designed to serve. Which should the seller choose? How realistic or practicable is the first option of compelling performance by the buyer under Article 62? Are there are any limitations on the power of the court to compel specific performance under the CISG? Consider Article 28.

2. Suppose that in this case the seller is allowed to compel performance by the buyer in a French court. Would you recommend this option?

3. Suppose the seller has in hand an irrevocable letter of credit authorized by the buyer and issued by a Paris bank. How would this affect the seller's situation? What does this suggest about the utility of letters of credit, which we consider in the next chapter, in the international sale of goods?

4. Suppose that the price has not been paid and that the sale was made on open account. Should the seller declare the contract avoided under Article 64? Article 64 provides that an aggrieved seller can declare a contract avoided where (1) the buyer has

committed a fundamental breach and (2) the buyer has not paid the price or accepted delivery of the goods within the additional time period fixed by the seller. What constitutes a fundamental breach and what is the effect of an avoidance? Consider Article 25, 26, and 81 of the CISG.

5. Can the seller in Problem 3-19 avoid the contract?

6. The articles governing damages under the CISG are Articles 74–76. What is the basic general principle of damages that is set forth in Article 74 and what is the relationship of Article 74 to Articles 75 and 76? What is the difference between the methods of determining damages under Articles 75 and 76? Consider these questions in light of the following problems.

PROBLEM 3-20

A Japanese seller has contracted with an English buyer to manufacture 3,000 lawn mower engines for $150,000. After the Japanese seller has shipped the engines by ocean carrier, the buyer runs into financial problems and apologizes profusely but says it cannot go through with the order. The seller avoids the contract under Article 64 and sues for damages. Similar engines sell in England for $60 each and the seller has found another buyer who is willing to buy the entire shipment for $120,000. What should the seller do? Consider CISG Articles 74–76.

PROBLEM 3-21

Suppose that in Problem 3-20 the buyer cancels before the seller begins production of the motors. Due to limitations in production capacity, the seller had turned down an order for 2,500 lawn mower engines from a French buyer to accept the English order. The French buyer found a South Korean manufacturer to make the motors. The English buyer says, "Sorry, but you never told me that you were turning down the French offer to accept ours. Anyway, these are the breaks of the business. As you didn't manufacture the goods, you have suffered no damages. So please accept our most heartfelt apologies." Can the seller recover anything for the French order?

B.   REMEDIES OF THE BUYER

The remedies available to the buyer under Articles 46–49 mirror the remedies available to the seller under Articles 62–64. We start with Article 45, which provides a general overview of the remedies available to the buyer and the relationship of each of the remedies to each other. Like the seller, the buyer has the right to compel performance (Article 46), to fix an additional time for the seller to perform (Article 47), and to avoid the contract and sue for damages (Article 49). Mirroring Article 64, Article 49 allows the buyer to avoid the contract where the seller has committed a fundamental breach or has failed to deliver the goods within the additional time period fixed by the buyer. Article 48 provides for a restricted right on the part of the seller to cure defects in performance even after delivery of the goods. Articles 50–52 deal with three special situations: the buyer's right to reduce the price, the applicability of remedies to only part of the goods, and deliveries that are early or excessive in quantity. Articles 74–76, which we reviewed in connection with our discussion of the seller's right against a breaching buyer, apply equally to govern the rights of an aggrieved buyer to damages against a breaching seller.

PROBLEM 3-22

A seller in Japan agrees to deliver 1,000 special high-speed photomax printers of the latest design to a buyer in the United Kingdom. The delivery date is April 25, and the UK buyer inserts a clause into the contract that "time is of the essence" since the buyer has a resale contract with a major retail marketer-customer.

On April 15, the Japanese seller telephones the UK buyer and apologizes profusely—a major subcontractor is in financial difficulty, and the delivery of the printers will be delayed.

The UK buyer calls his customer and is told that the customer needs the machines without fail on April 27 for a promotion already announced.

What options does the UK buyer have under the CISG?

Suppose, alternatively, that the UK buyer's customer is agreeable to waiting until May 15 for the delivery. What then? Consider CISG Articles 46, 47, and 49 and apply them to this problem. What about damages under Articles 74–76?

PROBLEM 3-23

A U.S. buyer contracts with a Japanese seller for the sale of laptop computers. The contract calls for one battery and one spare battery for each laptop. The computers arrive with only one battery instead of two. The buyer immediately informs the seller of this deficiency and sends the seller an e-mail in April, which states, "We must have the additional spare battery for all of the computers by no later than May 31, 2009. We will not accept delivery after that date." Under Article 47, the buyer "may fix an additional period of time of reasonable length for performance by the seller of his obligations." Article 49(1)(b) allows the buyer to declare the contract avoided if the seller does not deliver within the additional period fixed under Article 47. The buyer can sell the laptops with one battery without difficulty on the market as most other laptops sold on the market have only one battery. The seller cannot deliver the spare batteries in time. Under Article 49, can the buyer avoid the contract?

PROBLEM 3-24

A seller in Japan fills an order from a German customer for 2,000 room air conditioners. By an oversight, the electric plugs on the air conditioners are small gauge, North American models. When notified, the Japanese seller offers to send a representative to the buyer's place of business to swap out the incorrect plugs for the correct ones. Consider Article 48.

Should the buyer accept this offer?

Does the buyer have the right to refuse this offer?

In considering the second question, note that the exercise of the seller's right to cure under Article 48(1) is explicitly made subject to the buyer's right to avoid the contract under Article 49. Suppose that after the seller offers to cure the buyer quickly avoids the contract by declaring a fundamental breach under Article 49. Has the seller committed a fundamental breach within the meaning of Article 25, which requires that all circumstances be considered?

PROBLEM 3-25

A seller in Japan has an order for 3,000 punch presses from a Canadian buyer for $60,000. Demand for the punch presses soars unexpectedly in Japan, and the seller runs short. He ships 2,000 to Canada and e-mails the Canadian buyer apologies that he can supply no more.

What is the buyer's remedy under Articles 50 and 51?

C. ANTICIPATORY BREACH AND INSTALLMENT CONTRACTS

So far, we have considered the remedies available to a buyer and seller when one party fails to perform at the time the performance is due. Suppose, however, that *before* the time that performance is due, it appears or becomes certain that one of the parties will be unable to perform either the entire contract or one portion or installment of the contract. This, of course, is the problem of anticipatory breach. What remedies are available to the aggrieved party in these cases? Consider Articles 71, 72, and 73 in solving the problems below.

PROBLEM 3-26

A Japanese seller has a contract to sell 1,000 computers to a customer in Germany. Two weeks before the shipment date, the buyer e-mails the seller that, due to circumstances beyond his control, he must cancel the order. What remedies are available to the seller?

PROBLEM 3-27

A Japanese buyer has an installment contract with a Canadian seller for delivery of 1,000 cubic tons of wood chips on the first of each month. On April 1, there is no delivery. The buyer is concerned, but wants to continue the arrangement, which has been conducted faithfully for over two years. What should the buyer do in this situation?

NOTES AND QUESTIONS

1. Articles 71 and 72 offer two different approaches that would be available to our seller in Problem 3-26. What is the purpose of Article 71? Between Articles 71 and 72, which is the most drastic remedy and which article contains the higher standard?

2. Must an aggrieved party elect between Articles 71 and 72? Does the exercise by the aggrieved party of its rights under Article 71 preclude the later exercise of rights under Article 72?

3. Compare the approach under Article 51 that we examined in Problem 3-25 and the approach under Article 73. Both of these articles share a common approach. What is this approach? Both of these articles can also be considered tools of cooperation consistent with the general approach of the CISG. Why?

4   *Letters of Credit*

In this chapter, we turn to a detailed consideration of the letter of credit, the third of the three contracts involved in a typical documentary sale of goods together with the sales contract, which we covered in Chapter Three, and the contract of carriage, which we discussed in Chapter Two. This chapter is the last in the unit of Chapters Two, Three, and Four that considers the international sales transaction.

The letter of credit has a long history in the law merchant and is international in its origins, traceable to practices in the twelfth century. European merchants used credits in the form of drafts or bills of exchange to make payments in the international sale of goods. The bill was a request or order for payment that through mercantile usage became well established and accepted as a method of payment. The use of the bills allowed merchants to avoid the risky practice of carrying large amounts of gold or silver and to solve the problem of the unavailability of large amounts of currency to make large and frequent payments. *See* John F. Dolan, *Letters of Credit* ¶3.02 (2007).

In international commerce today, the role of the letter of credit in the documentary sale is to provide a mechanism for payment. This type of credit is referred to as the documentary credit and it is the subject of the first part of this chapter. We then turn the standby letter of credit, which is used to guarantee the performance of some obligation.

I.   Sources of Letter of Credit Law

Unlike in the case of contracts for the sale of goods, there is no comprehensive multilateral treaty that serves as a source of law for letters of credit. The principal sources of law for the international letter of credit that we will be considering below are the Uniform Customs and Practice for Documentary Credits (UCP), issued by the International Chamber of Commerce on July 1, 2007 (the ICC is discussed in Chapter One at p. 28), and Article 5 of the Uniform Commercial Code (2003). The UCP was first published in 1933 and revised in 1951, 1962, 1974, 1983, 1993, and 2007. The most recent version of the UCP was published in ICC publication no. 600 and is generally known as UCP 600. (The 1993 version is known as UCP 500.) The UCP 600 is less technical and more streamlined than its predecessor and is intended to be more accessible to non-specialists. The UCP 600 embodies international practices and becomes effective when incorporated by the parties in the letter of credit. Standby letters of credit have additional sources of law that we shall consider in a later section.

Article 1 of the UCP 600 provides that the UCP "are rules that apply to any documentary credit (including, to the extent to which they may be applicable, any standby letter of credit) when the text of the credit expressly indicates that it is subject to these rules. They are binding on all parties thereto unless expressly modified or excluded by the credit." UCC §5-103(c) provides, with some exceptions, that "the effect of this article may be varied by agreement or by a provision stated or incorporated by reference in an undertaking." Thus, the UCC explicitly recognizes that parties to a letter of credit that is otherwise governed by the UCC may exclude the UCC in favor of the UCP. As the UCP is designed for use in international letters of credit, most U.S. credits that are not international in character are governed by the UCC. Even where the UCP applies there is an important area in which the UCP is completely silent that must be decided by domestic law: the issue of fraud as a defense to payment of the letter of credit. (On other issues that fall within an exclusion in the UCP, resort must also be had to a domestic law.) The UCP drafters took the position that the fraud issue, developed by common law courts that share the same language and commercial culture, was best left to domestic law as international regimes do not have the same advantages. UCC Article 5 has an extensive fraud provision and jurisprudence. Our focus in these materials shall be on the UCP 600 except on the issue of fraud, where we examine the UCC.

II.   Letter of Credit Basics

In a typical letter of credit transaction that is part of a documentary sale, the letter of credit is a separate undertaking between the buyer of goods and its bank that the bank will pay the seller against the presentation of certain documents. The letter of credit is an undertaking (i.e., a contract) by the issuing bank to honor drafts [see below (8)] drawn on it if the draft is accompanied by specified documents. You should now review Figure 2-1 on p. 64 in Chapter Two.

We now set forth some letter of credit basics, consistent with both the UCP 600 and the UCC. The terms explained below are used throughout the UCP 600 so it is important that you master them. The discussion below applies primarily to the documentary credit but also to the standby letter of credit where appropriate. As the latter serves different purposes, we postpone detailed coverage of standby letters of credit until later in this chapter. You need to review these materials carefully to answer the problems that follow at the end of this section.

(1) *Applicant and Beneficiary.* The party establishing the credit is the *applicant* and the party entitled to payment under the credit is the *beneficiary* of the credit. In a documentary credit, the buyer is usually the applicant and the seller is the beneficiary.

(2) *Issuing Bank.* The applicant's bank is the *issuing bank*, which undertakes to honor the letter of credit against the presentation of a specified set of documents. The issuing bank will receive reimbursement (plus a fee) for the amount of the credit from the applicant. In the documentary credit, the seller will usually present a bill of lading, commercial invoice, insurance certificate, packing list, and other documents required by the letter of credit to the issuing bank. The absolute obligation of the issuing bank to pay against the documents provides the seller with the assurance of payment. If the issuing bank pays, then it is protected from liability and is entitled to get reimbursement of the credit from the buyer-applicant. If the issuing bank refuses to honor a demand for payment that complies with the terms of the credit, then the issuing bank may be liable to the presenter of the draft for wrongful dishonor. If the issuing bank makes an improper payment, that is, pays the letter of credit against nonconforming documents in violation of the terms of the letter of credit, then the issuing bank loses its right to receive reimbursement from the buyer-applicant.

(3) *Revocable and Irrevocable Credits.* Letters of credit can be *revocable*, or capable of termination at any time by the applicant, or *irrevocable*. Under an irrevocable letter of credit, the credit will be subject to expiration if not exercised within a stated period. An irrevocable credit is required in most modern commercial transactions.

(4) *Straight and Negotiation Credits.* A letter of credit can be a straight or a negotiation credit. If the issuing bank issues a straight letter of credit, the credit is an undertaking from the bank that runs only to the named beneficiary and not to any other endorser or purchaser of the draft and documents from the beneficiary. If the credit is a negotiation credit, the undertaking from the bank runs to the beneficiary and to any nominated (authorized) bank that negotiates or purchases the credit. The negotiation credit may authorize any bank or a single bank to negotiate. The distinction between straight and negotiation credits has important consequences for payment, which we further discuss in (8) below.

(5) *Advising Bank.* The issuing bank may engage another bank, usually one within the beneficiary's locality, to notify the beneficiary of the establishment and terms of the credit. An advising bank has an obligation to make reasonable efforts to check the authenticity of the credit that it advises but has no obligation to make payment under the credit.

(6) *Confirming Bank.* An issuing bank will sometimes engage a second bank to serve as a *confirming bank*. The use of a confirming bank is usually due to the insistence of the seller-beneficiary of the credit and the confirming bank is usually situated in the beneficiary's locality and may be an institution with which the beneficiary is familiar. The confirming bank independently assumes all of the obligations of the issuing bank by adding its own undertaking, in addition to the undertaking by the issuing bank, that it will pay the seller upon presentation of documents. Now the seller has a letter of credit that is backed by the credit of two banks. If the confirming bank has properly paid the credit against conforming documents, then the issuing bank must reimburse the confirming bank. If the issuing bank refuses to reimburse the confirming bank, then the issuing bank is liable for wrongful dishonor. If the confirming bank has made a wrongful payment (e.g., against discrepant documents), however, the confirming bank loses the right to receive reimbursement from the issuing bank.

(7) *Nominated Bank.* An issuing bank may authorize another bank to pay under the letter of credit. The bank so authorized is the *nominated bank*. Unless the nominated bank is also a confirming bank, the nominated bank undertakes no obligation to pay under the letter of credit but may choose to do so for a fee.

(8) *Settlement.* There are four different methods of settlement: payment, acceptance, negotiation, or deferred payment. The first three methods all involve the use of a draft (or a bill of exchange), which the beneficiary will submit along with any required documents. The draft is an unconditional order in writing addressed from one person to another requiring the person to whom it is addressed to make payment on demand or on some future date to or to the order of a specific person or to bearer. The beneficiary stands in the position of the *drawer*, the bank (or sometimes the applicant) is the *drawee*, and the beneficiary is also the *payee*.

  (a) *Payment Credit.* A payment credit requires the bank to honor the draft immediately. The beneficiary submits a *sight draft* payable instantly (on sight). Articles 14(b) and 15(a) of the UCP 600 allow the bank five banking days to pay the credit. The drawee of the draft is usually the issuing bank or a nominated bank.

  (b) *Acceptance Credit.* An acceptance credit is payable within a stipulated period, such as 60 days. The beneficiary submits a *time draft*, which requires payment by the date specified in the draft. When the bank accepts the draft, the acceptance becomes a banker's acceptance, which entails the obligation of the bank to pay the draft at maturity. After the drawer presents the draft, the bank will usually stamp the time draft as accepted with a signature of a bank official and will return it to the drawer.

(c) *Payment Under a Straight Credit.* Under a straight letter of credit, the beneficiary submits a draft to the issuing bank. The issuing bank must purchase the draft (i.e., pay the face amount) from the beneficiary if the documents comply with the terms of the credit.

(d) *Payment Under a Negotiation Credit.* Under a negotiation credit, the beneficiary submits a draft to a nominated bank, that is, a bank authorized by the issuing bank to pay the draft. The draft will usually be drawn on the issuing bank (not the nominated bank) and will be made payable to the beneficiary, that is, the draft is addressed to the issuing bank ordering the issuing bank to pay the beneficiary. The nominated bank will purchase the draft (by paying the face amount of the draft or, in some cases, a discounted amount) from the beneficiary who endorses it to the nominated bank. The endorsement of the draft by the beneficiary to the nominated bank means that the nominated bank is now the beneficiary of the draft and is entitled to demand payment from the issuing bank in place of the original beneficiary. The nominated bank will then forward the draft and documents to the issuing bank. Under a negotiation credit, the issuing bank must purchase the drafts from the nominated bank.

(e) *Differences Between Payment Under a Straight and Negotiation Credit.* Under a negotiation credit, the issuing bank is required to purchase the drafts from the beneficiary or from the nominated bank. Under a straight letter of credit, the issuing bank is required to purchase the drafts only from the named beneficiary under the credit and no other party. Suppose that under a straight letter of credit, the beneficiary decides to submit a draft to its own local bank and not to the issuing bank. The beneficiary submits a draft to its local bank but the draft is drawn on or addressed to the issuing bank and the draft demands payment from the issuing bank to the beneficiary. Because the draft itself is a negotiable instrument, any bank is permitted to purchase or negotiate the draft from the beneficiary and have the beneficiary endorse the draft to the negotiating bank (note that under a straight letter of credit, there is no nominated bank; that is why we must refer to the local bank as the negotiating bank). The local bank may decide to negotiate or purchase the draft to earn a fee or may purchase the draft at a discount from its face amount. The negotiating bank then forwards the draft and documents to the issuing bank. Under a straight letter of credit, the issuing bank is under no obligation to purchase the draft from the negotiating bank but may do so (for a fee), whereas in a negotiation credit the issuing bank must purchase the draft from the nominated bank.

(f) *Presentation Under a Straight and Negotiation Credit.* The difference between a straight and negotiation credit can be important in determining whether a timely presentation of the documents has been made under the credit. All credits are subject to an expiration date so the submission of documents for payment must occur before the credit expires. Under a negotiation credit, the submission by the beneficiary of the draft and documents to the nominated bank before the expiration of the credit satisfies the presentation requirements of the credit because the submission triggers the issuing bank's engagement to honor the draft. Where the credit is a straight credit and the beneficiary chooses to negotiate the draft with a negotiating bank, presentation, which must occur before the expiration of the credit, does not occur until the negotiating bank presents the documents to the issuing bank. In these cases, the beneficiary must be careful to ensure that there is enough time for the drafts to reach the issuing bank before the expiration of the credit.

(9) *Transfer and Assignment of Credit.* If the credit expressly so provides, it may be transferred. A *transfer* of the credit means that the transferee acquires the right to perform all or some of the obligations of the credit, to receive all or a portion of the payments due under the credit, and to enforce the right of payment under the credit. An *assignment* of the credit means that the assignee acquires only the right to receive all or some portion of the payment under the credit after all of the conditions for payment under the credit have been satisfied by the assignor or another party who is entitled to satisfy the conditions for payment under the credit such as a purchaser of the draft from the assignor. Unlike a transferee, the assignee does not have the right to enforce payment against a party obligated to pay such as an issuing bank or confirming bank. However, unlike a transfer, an assignment does not have to be expressly authorized by the terms of the credit. A transferable credit creates a flexible financing device in international commerce. A seller who obtains a transferable credit can fill the buyer's purchase by subcontracting the manufacture of the goods to a third party. Suppose that under a contract for the sale of goods CIF buyer's port, the buyer has its issuing bank open a transferable letter of credit in favor of the seller in the amount of $100,000. The seller can engage a third party to manufacture the goods for $80,000. The seller then transfers the credit to the third party who presents a draft for $80,000, an invoice, a bill of lading, and other documents required by the letter of credit to the issuing bank. Meanwhile, the seller has submitted a draft for $100,000 to the issuing bank. If the issuing bank finds the documents to be in order, the issuing bank will pay the seller's draft for $100,000 to the order of seller's account and then charge that account $80,000 to pay the draft drawn by the third party. The issuing bank then charges the buyer's account in the amount of $100,000 and forwards the bill of lading and other documents to the buyer. The seller earns a profit of $20,000 just by subcontracting the work to a third party.

(10) *Back-to-Back Credits.* In the case of the transferable credit, the buyer will have knowledge of the seller's subcontracting arrangements because the issuing bank receives documents from the third-party subcontractor and will forward them to the buyer. (These documents include a bill of lading that the buyer will need to obtain the goods.) The seller may wish to keep the identity of the buyer and third-party supplier confidential in order to avoid the possibility that they will deal directly with each other in the future. The seller may also wish to use the payment from the buyer to pay several third-party suppliers. Finally, the seller may wish to use the letter of credit as a financing device to pay for the goods acquired from third parties. For these reasons, the seller will set up a back-to-back credit by using the credit established by the buyer as the basis for a second letter of credit. This can be done as follows. Suppose that in our example discussed in (9) above, the seller takes the letter of credit opened in its favor by the buyer to a local bank in the seller's country. The seller then assigns the right to receive the proceeds under the prime letter of credit to the seller's bank, which gives the bank a security interest in the credit. On the strength of the assignment of the prime letter of credit by the seller, the seller's bank now issues a second letter of credit in the amount of $80,000 naming the third-party supplier as the beneficiary. For the back-to-back credit to work properly, however, the documents required by the second letter of credit must be tailored to meet the requirements under the first letter of credit so that once the third-party supplier provides the

documents required for payment under the second letter of credit, the seller's bank is now assured that it has all of the documents that will trigger payment under the prime letter of credit. There will be some differences, however, between the documents required for payment under the second and the prime letter of credit, and the seller's bank must be careful to assure that these differences can be reconciled. For instance, the draft submitted by the third-party supplier will most likely be drawn on the seller's bank and will name the third party as the beneficiary. On the other hand, it is likely that the prime letter of credit will require a draft drawn by the seller on the issuing bank. If a negotiable bill of lading is required, the bill supplied by the third party will not satisfy the prime letter of credit (which requires a bill of lading naming the seller, not the third party, as the shipper), but the bill will allow the seller to unload the goods and reload them on a different carrier that will issue a new bill of lading to the seller that will satisfy the requirements of the prime letter of credit. In other cases, there is only one shipment (i.e., the seller and the third party are in the same location). In this situation, the seller can ask the carrier to "switch" the bill, that is, reissue the original bill of lading with the same information but substituting the name of seller for the name of the third-party supplier as the shipper. As back-to-back credits are now common, an experienced bank should be able to structure the transaction so that it can obtain the proper documents for payment under the prime letter of credit. Once this is worked out, the back-to-back credit transaction would proceed as follows: The third-party supplier presents a draft, bill of lading, and other documents to the seller's bank, which will pay $80,000, the amount of the back-to-back credit, to the supplier; the seller's bank then forwards a draft drawn by the seller, a substituted bill of lading, and other documents to the issuing bank and receives payment in the amount of $100,000 under the prime letter of credit. The seller's bank will then credit the seller's account in the amount of $20,000 minus a fee. Through the back-to-back credit, a seller can obtain funds for the manufacture of the goods from a supplier (or many different suppliers) without using any funds of its own.

PROBLEM 4-1

In the sample letter of credit in Chapter Two at p. 59, the Banco do Brasil notifies the seller that: "We have been instructed by the Mid-America Bank of Worthington, Ohio, USA that it has opened an irrevocable credit in your favor in the amount of USD $156,185 available by your sight drafts on the Mid-America Bank accompanied by [a list of documents]. We confirm the credit and hereby undertake to purchase all drafts drawn as specified above." Is this a revocable or irrevocable credit? Confirmed or unconfirmed? Straight or negotiation credit? Hint: You can determine whether it is a straight or negotiation credit by examining the bank on which the credit is to be drawn. See 8(c)–(e) above.

PROBLEM 4-2

At the request of the seller, the buyer in a CIF contract for the sale of goods obtains a straight letter of credit from its issuing bank requiring payment against documents. The issuing bank then asks a local bank in the seller's foreign jurisdiction to be an advising bank on the credit. The seller loads the goods, receives a bill of lading from the carrier, and presents the bill of lading, other documents, and a draft drawn on the issuing bank to the advising bank.

(1) Does the advising bank have an obligation to pay on the letter of credit? *See* UCP 600 Article 9(a); see also (5) in the discussion of the letter of credit basics above.

(2) If the advising bank does not have an obligation to pay on the letter of credit, can the advising bank purchase the draft if it wishes to do so and obtain reimbursement from the issuing bank? See (4) and 8(c)–(e) above. Would you counsel the advising bank to purchase the draft? If so, what measures would you advise the bank to first undertake?

PROBLEM 4-3

In a confirmed letter of credit transaction, the seller ships the goods and obtains the necessary documents for payment under the letter of credit. Rather than presenting the documents to the confirming bank, which is experiencing some unexpected financial difficulties, the seller forwards the documents directly to the issuing bank in the buyer's country. The issuing bank refuses to pay on the grounds that the seller must first submit the documents to the confirming bank. What is the result? *See* UCP 600 Article 7; see also (6) above.

PROBLEM 4-4

In a documentary sale, an issuing bank establishes an unconfirmed letter of credit in favor of the seller. On July 30, 2016, the seller goes to its local bank and submits a draft and documents. The local bank purchases the drafts and documents from the seller and then forwards them to the buyer's bank. The documents arrive on August 2. The buyer's bank refuses to honor the letter of credit on the grounds that it has expired. What is the result under each of the following scenarios?

(1) The language of the credit provides: "We hereby engage with drawers, endorsers, and bona fide purchasers of drafts drawn under the terms of this credit that the drafts shall be paid. All drafts must be presented not later than August 1, 2016." *See* UCP 600 Article 6(a) and 6(d); see also (4) and (8)(f) above.

(2) The language of the credit provides: "We hereby undertake to honor the beneficiary's drafts if submitted not later than August 1, 2016." *See* UCP 600 Article 6(a) and 6(d); see also (4) and (8)(f) above.

PROBLEM 4-5

A is the beneficiary of a negotiation credit. The issuing bank has nominated National Bank, a large and well-known bank in A's locality, to be the negotiating bank. A comes to your law office with the following questions:

(1) "Who is the drawer, who is the drawee, and who is the beneficiary of the draft that I need to submit to the local bank for payment?" See (8) above.

(2) "I don't like dealing with National Bank. Can I submit the draft to my own bank for negotiation?" *See* UCP 600 Article 7(c).

(3) "Must the nominated bank pay the draft or can it lawfully refuse to do so?" *See* UCP 600 Article 12(a); see also (7) above.

(4) "Are there any circumstances in which a nominated bank under a negotiation credit is obligated to negotiate the credit?"

PROBLEM 4-6

The seller, the beneficiary under a confirmed letter of credit, assigns the letter of credit to the confirming bank to establish a back-to-back credit for the purpose of paying T, a third-party manufacturer of goods that the seller has contracted to sell to the buyer. The seller uses the back-to-back credit because the seller does not want the buyer or T to know each other's identities. The prime letter of credit provides for payment against a draft drawn on the issuing bank, a negotiable bill of lading, and a commercial invoice. T produces the goods and has them loaded on board the carrier for shipment to the buyer. T gives the confirming bank (1) a bill of lading naming T as the shipper consigned to order, (2) a draft drawn on the confirming bank naming T as the payee, (3) and a commercial invoice from T to the seller detailing the quantity of the goods and the price. The confirming bank pays T under the back-to-back credit and asks you the following question: "Can we simply forward these documents to the issuing bank for payment under the prime letter of credit? If not, why not? How would you suggest that we get the documents that we need?" See (10) above.

III. Basic Principles of Letter of Credit Law

In this section, we turn to two of the most basic principles of letter of credit law: (1) the independence principle stating that the letter of credit is independent from the underlying sales contract and (2) the strict compliance principle requiring that documents submitted for payment must conform to the terms of the credit.

A.   The Independence Principle

UCP 600 Article 4(a) provides:

> A credit by its nature is a separate transaction from the sale or other contract on which it may be based. Banks are in no way concerned with or bound by such contract, even if any reference whatsoever to it is included in the credit. Consequently, the undertaking of a bank to honor, to negotiate or to fulfill any other obligation under the credit is not subject to claims or defenses by the applicant resulting from its relationships with the issuing bank or the beneficiary.

UCP 600 Article 5 provides:

> Banks deal with documents and not with goods, services or performance to which the documents may relate.

PROBLEM 4-7

A Kuwaiti buyer entered into a contract with a U.S. seller for the purchase of medical devices in three shipments at $100,000 each. The sales contract called for the seller to sterilize the medical devices so that they are safe for human implantation and to provide with each shipment a certification that each device in the shipment has been sterilized. The contract also included the following provision:

> Payment is to be made by documentary credit subject to UCP 600. Buyer shall open a credit in favor of seller at the Kuwaiti National Bank (KNB) in the amount of $300,000. KNB shall make payment to seller upon the presentation of a bill of lading, commercial invoice, packing list, insurance certificate, and a written certification by seller that the delivered devices have been sterilized and are safe for human implantation. Seller acknowledges the importance of the sterilization procedure and that failure to perform this procedure shall be treated as a breach of the contract. Seller further acknowledges that in the case that it fails to test the devices buyer shall have the right to test the devices and deduct the costs of the tests from the purchase price of the goods.

The seller makes the first shipment to the buyer and includes the certification specified in the contract. The buyer learns from industry sources that the seller's tests may have been conducted by untrained staff. The buyer conducts its own tests and finds that the devices are marginally unsuitable. The buyer then has the devices sterilized at its own expense.

Meanwhile, the seller has sent the second shipment and has forwarded the documents to KNB for both shipments for payment under the letter of credit. The buyer sends KNB written instructions directing KNB to pay on the first shipment minus a set-off for the costs of the tests and sterilization procedure and to refuse payment on the second shipment unless the seller retests the devices with trained staff.

(1) Must KNB pay the entire amount of the credit for the first two shipments ($200,000) or can KNB make the first payment minus a set-off for the costs of testing and sterilization and refuse payment for the second shipment?

(2) The buyer's concern is that it will receive medical devices that are not suitable for use. The certificate of inspection by the seller did not adequately address this concern. How would you advise the buyer to structure the letter of credit transaction to alleviate these concerns? Will your suggestion ensure that the devices are safe to use?

(3) Can the buyer simply revoke the credit? *See* UCP 600 Article 3.

(4) If KNB must pay and has failed to do so, KNB is liable for wrongful dishonor. What damages can the seller recover? Can the seller recover damages against the bank for the third shipment, which has not yet been sent?

In addition to UCP 600 Articles 4(a) and 5 set forth above, consider *Urquhart* and *Maurice O'Meara* below.

Urquhart Lindsay and Company, Ltd. v. Eastern Bank, Ltd.
King's Bench Division
[1922] 1 King's Bench 318

The plaintiffs were manufacturers of machinery, and the defendants were bankers with various branches in the East, including Calcutta. In December, 1919, the plaintiffs agreed to manufacture for the Benjamin Jute Mills Co., Ltd., who were customers of the defendants, a quantity of machinery for delivery f.o.b. Glasgow to the amount of 64,942£.

This contract contained the following terms: (1.) that in the event of any increase taking place in wages or cost of materials or transit rates or any further reduction taking place in working hours, the plaintiffs' prices would be correspondingly increased; and

(2.) that the Benjamin Jute Co., Ltd., should open in this country a confirmed irrevocable banker's credit to the extent of 70,000 pounds.

On February 14, 1920, the defendants wrote to the plaintiffs the following letter:

"4 Crosby Square, London.

TO MESSRS. URQUHART LINDSAY & CO., DUNDEE.

DEAR SIRS,

Confirmed + Irreversible

We beg to advise you that under instructions received from our Calcutta branch we are prepared to pay you the amounts of your bills on B.N. Elias, managing agent, the Benjamin Jute Mills Co., Ltd., Calcutta, to the extent of, but not exceeding 70,000 pounds in all (say seventy thousand pounds). The bills are to be accompanied by the following complete documents covering shipments of machinery to Calcutta, are to be drawn payable 30 days after sight, and are to be received by us for payment on or before April 14, 1921:

- Signed Invoices in duplicate.
- Complete sets of bills of lading made out 'to order' indorsed in blank and marked by the shipping company 'freight paid.'
- Policies of insurance against marine or war risks.

This is to be considered a confirmed and irrevocable credit, and the bills should bear a clause to the effect that they are drawn under credit No. 102 dated Calcutta, January 15, 1920.

Kindly acknowledge receipt.

Yours faithfully,
M. HARKNESS, Manager"

The plaintiffs thereupon bought raw material and in 1920 began to manufacture the goods. They made two shipments under the contract in February and March, 1921, and tendered to the defendants bills of exchange together with shipping documents, which the defendants duly paid. On February 18, 1921, the defendants wrote to the plaintiffs, in reference to their former letter of February 14, 1920, a further letter advising them that they had heard from Calcutta that should it be necessary for the plaintiffs to include in their invoice for extra cost of labor, this extra amount must be referred to the buyers, before they (the defendants) would be at liberty to pay the same. The defendants then refused to meet the bills of exchange presented by the plaintiffs on the third shipment, and only did so, under protest on May 9, 1921, when the confirmed credit had expired.

The plaintiffs meantime on April 12, 1921, issued a writ in the action, and in their points of claim, dated June 29, 1921, alleged that the defendants' letter of February 18, 1921, was a breach of the contract contained in their letter of February 14, 1920, and that they (plaintiffs) had suffered damage, and lost the profit which they would otherwise have made, and that there was no available market for the goods.

The defendants in their points of defense (July 30, 1921) alleged that it was a term or condition in the contract between the plaintiffs and the Benjamin Jute Mills Co., Ltd., that the plaintiffs should not draw bills of exchange for more than shippers' current prices in December, 1919, and in particular that they should not include in such bills any increased cost over the price in 1919 on which the agreed credit of 70,000£. was calculated. They contended that the plaintiffs had acted in breach of this term or condition; and further that the damage (if any) was too remote and was not recoverable.

ROWLATT, J.

In my view the defendants committed a breach of their contract with the plaintiffs when they refused to pay the amount of the invoices as presented. [The defendants] contended that the letter of credit must be taken to incorporate the contract between the plaintiffs and their buyers; and that according to the true meaning of that contract the amount of any increase claimed in respect of an alleged advance in manufacturing costs was not to be included in any invoice to be presented under the letter of credit, but was to be the subject of subsequent independent adjustment. The answer to this is that the defendants undertook to pay the amount of invoices for machinery without qualification, the basis of this form of banking facility being that the buyer is taken for the purposes of all questions between himself and his banker or between his banker and the seller to be content to accept the invoices of the seller as correct. It seems to me that so far from the letter of credit being qualified by the contract of sale, the latter must accommodate itself to the letter of credit. The buyer having authorized his banker to undertake to pay the amount of the invoice as presented, it follows that any adjustment must be made by way of refund by the seller, and not by way of retention by the buyer.

There being thus in my view a breach of contract, the question arises what damages the plaintiffs can recover. The point is a new one, and not free from difficulty. It is, of course, elementary that as a general rule the amount of damages for non-payment of money is only the amount of the money itself. If, for instance, the defendants had merely undertaken to pay the price of goods as and when shipped, nothing being said about the undertaking being irrevocable within limits of time and amount, such undertaking would become binding only in respect of each shipment upon its being made, the successive shipments being the separable considerations for the separable undertakings referring to them respectively; and the engagement could be revoked at any time as to future shipments. In such a case the damages in case of a refusal to pay for any shipment made before revocation would be merely the amount owing in respect of the shipment. In the present case, however, the credit was irrevocable; and the effect of that was that the bank really agreed to buy the contemplated series of bills and documents representing the contemplated shipments just as the buyer agreed to take and pay for by this means the goods themselves. Now, if a buyer under a contract of this sort declines to pay for an installment of the goods, the seller can cancel and claim damages upon the footing of an anticipatory breach of the contract of sale as a whole. These damages are not for non-payment of money. It is true that non-payment of money was what the buyer was guilty of; but such non-payment is evidence of a repudiation of the contract to accept and pay for the remainder of the goods; and the damages are in respect of such repudiation. I confess I cannot see why the refusal of the bank to take and pay for the bills with the documents representing the goods is not in the same way a repudiation of their contract to take the bills to be presented in future under the letter of credit; nor, if that is so, why the damages are not the same.

The damages to which the plaintiffs are entitled are the difference between on the one hand the value of the materials left on their hands and the cost of such as they would have further provided, and, on the other hand, what they would have been entitled to receive for the manufactured machinery from the buyers, the whole being limited to the amount they could in fact have tendered before the expiry of the letter of credit.

NOTES AND QUESTIONS

1. The February 14 letter from the bank advising the sellers of the credit provides that the sellers will be paid under the credit if the sellers submit a commercial invoice, a bill of lading, and an insurance policy. The buyers argued, however, that the sellers could not lawfully draw on the credit if the sellers increased their prices beyond those that existed for the goods as of December 1919. Is there anything in the February 14 letter that gives the buyers this right? If not, what was the source of the buyers' right to refuse payment? Note that in most cases banks feel compelled to pay on letters of credit if all of the terms of the credit have been met by the beneficiary. In this case, the buyers were likely valuable customers of the bank and the bank decided to consult the buyers before payment.

2. The buyers argued that the letter of credit had incorporated the terms of the sales contract under which the buyers were entitled to a price for the goods set as of December 1919. The result of incorporating the sales contract into the letter of credit is that the letter of credit will not be paid if there is some nonperformance of the sales contract. This result would abrogate the independence principle. What was the court's response to this argument?

3. The buyers wanted to protect themselves against an increase in price for the goods by having the bank pay under the letter of credit for the third shipment only up to the price of the goods as of December 1919 and not the full amount of the bills of exchange, which included an added charge for increased labor costs. The buyers were not very skillful in protecting their interests. If you were advising the buyers, what would you suggest to the buyers to protect against increases in the price of the goods due to increased costs of the sellers?

Maurice O'Meara Co. v. National Park Bank of New York
Court of Appeals of New York, 1925
239 N.Y. 386, 146 N.E. 636

McLaughlin, J.

This action was brought to recover damages alleged to have been sustained by the plaintiff's assignor, Ronconi & Millar, by defendant's refusal to pay three sight drafts against a confirmed irrevocable letter of credit. The letter of credit was in the following form:

"The National Park Bank of New York.
Our Credit No. 14956

October 28, 1920.

Messrs. Ronconi & Millar, 49 Chambers Street, New York City, N.Y.—Dear Sirs: In accordance with instructions received from the Sun-Herald Corporation of this city, we open a confirmed or irrevocable credit in your favor for account of themselves, in amount of $224,853.30, covering the shipment of 1,322 2/3 tons of newsprint paper in 72 1/2" and 36 1/2" rolls to test 11-12, 32 lbs. at 8 1/2 cents per pound net weight—delivery to be made in December, 1920, and January 1921.

Drafts under this credit are to be drawn at sight on this bank, and are to be accompanied by the following documents of a character which must meet with our approval:

Commercial invoice in triplicate.

Weight returns.

Negotiable dock delivery order actually carrying with it control of the goods.   B/L

This is a confirmed or irrevocable credit, and will remain in force to and including February 15, 1921, subject to the conditions mentioned herein.

When drawing drafts under this credit, or referring to it, please quote our number as above.

Very truly yours,

R. Stuart, Assistant Cashier.

(R. C.)"

The complaint alleged the issuance of the letter of credit; the tender of three drafts, the first on the 17th of December, 1920, for $46,301.71, the second on January 7, 1921, for $41,416.34, and the third on January 13, 1921, for $32,968.35. Accompanying the first draft were the following documents:

1. Commercial invoice of the said firm of Ronconi & Millar in triplicate, covering three hundred (300) thirty-six and one-half (36 1/2) inch rolls of newsprint paper and three hundred (300) seventy-two and one-half (72 1/2) inch rolls of newsprint paper, aggregating a net weight of five hundred and forty-four thousand seven hundred and twenty-six pounds (544,726), to test eleven (11), twelve (12), thirty-two (32) pounds.

2. Affidavit of Elwin Walker, verified December 16, 1920, to which were annexed samples of newsprint paper, which the said affidavit stated to be representative of the shipment covered by the accompanying invoices and to test twelve (12) points, thirty-two (32) pounds.

3. Full weight returns in triplicate.

4. Negotiable dock delivery order on the Swedish American Line, directing delivery to the order of the National Park Bank of three hundred (300) rolls of newsprint paper seventy-two and one-half (72 1/2) inches long and three hundred (300) half rolls of newsprint paper."

The documents accompanying the second draft were similar to those accompanying the first, except as to the number of rolls, weight of paper, omission of the affidavit of Walker, but with a statement: "Paper equal to original sample in test 11/12-32 pounds;" and a negotiable dock delivery order on the Seager Steamship Company, Inc. The complaint also alleged defendant's refusal to pay, a statement of the amount of loss upon the resale of the paper due to a fall in the market price, expenses for lighterage, cartage, storage, and insurance amounting to $3,045.02, an assignment of the cause of action by Ronconi & Millar to the plaintiff, and a demand for judgment.

The answer denied, upon information and belief, many of the allegations of the complaint, and set up (a) as an affirmative defense, that plaintiff's assignor was required by the letter of credit to furnish to the defendant "evidence reasonably satisfactory" to it that the paper shipped to the Sun-Herald Corporation was of a bursting or tensile strength of 11 to 12 points at a weight of paper of 32 pounds; that neither the plaintiff nor its assignor, at the time the drafts were presented, or at any time thereafter, furnished such evidence; (b) as a partial defense, that, when the draft for $46,301.71 was presented, the defendant notified the plaintiff there had not been presented "evidence reasonably satisfactory" to it, showing that the newsprint paper referred to in the documents accompanying said drafts was of the tensile or bursting strength specified in the letter of credit; that thereupon an agreement was entered into between plaintiff and defendant that the latter should cause a test to be made of the paper represented by the documents then presented, and, if such test showed that the paper was up to the specifications of the letter of credit, defendant would make payment of the draft; (c) for a third separate and distinct defense that the paper tendered was not, in fact, of the tensile or bursting strength specified in the letter of credit; (d) for a fourth separate and distinct defense that on or about January 15, 1921, and after the respective drafts referred to in the complaint had been presented to defendant for payment and payment refused, and at a time when the paper was owned and possessed by plaintiff or Ronconi & Millar, the Sun-Herald Corporation, in accordance with whose instructions and for whose account the letter of credit was issued, offered to the plaintiff that it would accept the newsprint paper referred to and pay for the same at a price of 8 1/2 cents per pound, provided the plaintiff or its assignor would promptly and reasonably satisfy the Sun-Herald Corporation that the newsprint paper tested as much as 11 points to 32 pounds as specified in the letter of credit, and was of the sizes specified therein; that the plaintiff refused to accept said offer; and (e) as a fifth separate and partial defense, all of the allegations of the fourth defense were repeated.

After issue had been joined the plaintiff moved, upon the pleadings and affidavits, pursuant to rule 113 of the Rules of Civil Practice, to strike out the answer and for summary judgment.

The claim for damages for the nonpayment of the third draft was, apparently, abandoned at or prior to the time the motion was made. It is unnecessary, therefore, to further consider that and it will not be again referred to in the discussion as to the first two drafts.

The motion for summary judgment was denied and the defendant appealed to the Appellate Division, where the order denying the same was unanimously affirmed, leave to appeal to this court granted, and the following question certified: Should the motion of the plaintiff for summary judgment herein have been granted?

I am of the opinion that the order of the Appellate Division and the Special Term should be reversed and the motion granted. The facts set out in defendant's answer and in the affidavits used by it in opposition to the motion are not a defense to the action.

The bank issued to plaintiff's assignor an irrevocable letter of credit, a contract solely between the bank and plaintiff's assignor, in and by which the bank agreed to pay sight drafts to a certain amount on presentation to it of the documents specified in the letter of credit. This contract was in no way involved in or connected with, other than the presentation of the documents, the contract for the purchase and sale of the paper mentioned. That was a contract between buyer and seller, which in no way concerned the bank. The bank's obligation was to pay sight drafts when presented if accompanied by genuine documents specified in the letter of credit. If the paper when delivered did not correspond to what had been purchased, either in weight, kind or quality, then the purchaser had his remedy against the seller for damages. Whether the paper was what the purchaser contracted to purchase did not concern the bank and in no way affected its liability. It was under no obligation to ascertain, either by a personal examination or otherwise, whether the paper conformed to the contract between the buyer and seller. The bank was concerned only in the drafts and the documents accompanying them. This was the extent of its interest. If the drafts, when presented, were accompanied by the proper documents, then it was absolutely bound to make the payment under the letter of credit, irrespective of whether it knew, or had reason to believe, that the paper was not of the tensile strength contracted for. This view, I think, is the one generally entertained with reference to a bank's liability under an irrevocable letter of credit of the character of the one here under consideration. *Could it have?*

The defendant had no right to insist that a test of the tensile strength of the paper be made before paying the drafts; nor did it even have a right to inspect the paper before payment, to determine whether it in fact corresponded to the description contained in the documents. The letter of credit did not so provide. All that the letter of credit provided was that documents be presented which described the paper shipped as of a certain size, weight, and tensile strength. To hold otherwise is to read into the letter of credit something which is not there, and this the court ought not to do, since it would impose upon a bank a duty which in many cases would defeat the primary purpose of such letters of credit. This primary purpose is an assurance to the seller of merchandise of prompt payment against documents.

It has never been held, so far as I am able to discover, that a bank has the right or is under an obligation to see that the description of the merchandise contained in the documents presented is correct. The documents presented were sufficient. The only reason stated by defendant in its letter of December 18, 1920, for refusing to pay the draft, was that—

> "There has arisen a reasonable doubt regarding the quality of the newsprint paper. Until such time as we can have a test made by an impartial and unprejudiced expert we shall be obliged to defer payment."

This being the sole objection, the only inference to be drawn therefrom is that otherwise the documents presented conformed to the requirements of the letter of credit. All other objections were thereby waived.

Some criticism is made as to the statement contained in the documents when the second draft was presented. The criticism, really, is directed towards the expressions "in test 11/12, 32 lbs." and "paper equal to original sample in test 11/12, 32 pounds." It is claimed that these expressions are not equivalent to "rolls to test 11-12, 32 lbs." I think they are. I do not see how any one could have been misled by them or misunderstood them. The general rule is that an obligation to present documents is complied with if any of the documents attached to the draft contain the required description. The purpose, obviously, was to enable defendant to know that dock delivery orders had been issued for the paper.

The orders appealed from should therefore be reversed and the motion granted, with costs in all courts. The question certified is answered in the affirmative.

CARDOZO, J. (dissenting).

I am unable to concur in the opinion of the court.

I assume that no duty is owing from the bank to its depositor which requires it to investigate the quality of the merchandise. I dissent from the view that, if it chooses to investigate and discovers thereby that the merchandise tendered is not in truth the merchandise which the documents describe, it may be forced by the delinquent seller to make payment of the price irrespective of its knowledge.

I think we lose sight of the true nature of the transaction when we view the bank as acting upon the credit of its customer to the exclusion of all else. It acts not merely upon the credit of its customer, but upon the credit also of the merchandise which is to be tendered as security. *Security Interest.* The letter of credit is explicit in its provision that documents sufficient to give control of the goods shall be lodged with the bank when drafts are presented. I cannot accept the statement of the majority opinion that the bank was not concerned with any question as to the character of the paper. If that is so, the bales tendered might have been rags instead of paper, and still the bank would have been helpless, though it had knowledge of the truth, if the documents tendered by the seller were sufficient on their face. A different question would be here if the defects had no relation to the description in the documents. In such circumstances it would be proper to say that a departure from the terms of the contract between the vendor and the vendee was of no moment to the bank. That is not the case before us. If the paper was of the quality stated in the defendant's answer the documents were false.

I think the conclusion is inevitable that a bank which pays a draft upon a bill of lading misrepresenting the character of the merchandise may recover the payment when the misrepresentation is discovered, or at the very least, the difference between the value of the thing described and the value of the thing received. If payment might have been recovered the moment after it was made, the seller cannot coerce payment if the truth is earlier revealed.

I think the defendant's answer and the affidavits submitted in support of it are sufficient to permit a finding that the plaintiff's assignors misrepresented the nature of the shipment. The misrepresentation does not cease to be a defense, partial if not complete, though it was innocently made.

The order should be affirmed and the question answered "No."

NOTES AND QUESTIONS

1. In *Oliver v. Dubai Bank Kenya Ltd*, [2007] EWHC (Comm) 2165 (Eng.), 2007 WL 2573907, the letter of credit provided as follows:

The credit is available by payment against presentation to us of the following documents:

1. Draft for the default amount.
2. Certificate from the beneficiary stating that Colonial Homes (Europe) Limited failed to perform its obligation as per agreement dated 30th May 2006 between (1) Philip Thomas Oliver (2) Colonial Homes (Europe) Limited.
3. Authenticated SWIFT msg[1] and tested telex addressed to beneficiary's bank through advising bank issued by us, i.e. Dubai Bank of Kenya Limited [the issuer] confirming the beneficiary's fulfillment of their commitments towards the Colonial Homes (Europe) Limited.

Id. ¶2. The court refused to disregard the third condition and held that this condition must be satisfied before the beneficiary can receive payment under the letter of credit. This holding is arguably inconsistent with the independence principle. Why? *See* UCP 600 Article 14(h).

2. The independence principle holds that breach or nonperformance of the sales contract alone is no defense to payment under the letter of credit. The documents that must be submitted for payment under the letter of credit are linked to the performance of the sales contract because they evidence that conforming goods have been shipped but the documents themselves (not the performance of the sales contract that they evidence) trigger the duty to pay under the credit. Once conforming documents have been presented by the seller to the confirming or issuing bank, the bank must pay regardless of nonperformance

---

1. "SWIFT" refers to the Society for Worldwide Interstate Financial Telecommunications, an organization established by banks to facilitate electronic communications.

of the sales contract. In turn, the buyer-applicant must reimburse the bank. The remedy of the buyer is to sue the seller for breach of the underlying sales contract and not to withhold payment under the letter of credit. The independence principle is considered to be the "paramount principle . . . in which letters of credit are completely independent of the underlying sales contract on which they are based." *Success Universal Ltd. v. CWJ Int'l Trading Co.*, No. 95 Civ. 1210 (DLC), 1966 WL 535541, at *4 (S.D.N.Y. Sept. 20, 1996).

3. The independence principle serves at least two important functions in international commerce. First, the seller is provided an assured method of payment. So long as the seller presents conforming documents, the seller will receive prompt payment. The seller does not need to worry that the bank will become embroiled with complex and time-consuming issues relating to the performance of the underlying contract. *See CVD Equipment Corp. v. Taiwan Industrial Glass Corp.*, No. 10 Civ. 573 (JPO), 2014 WL 641420, at *4–6 (S.D.N.Y. Feb. 19, 2014). Second, bankers act as "document merchants." The role of the bank is a simple and mechanistic one of dealing only with the documents. Limiting banks to an examination of documents helps to assure that letters of credit will be paid expeditiously and at minimal expense and gives the letter of credit its utility in financial transactions. *See id.* at *4.

4. Judge Cardozo's dissent brings up the need to set limits on the independence principle when faced with an undeserving beneficiary who may have misrepresented the quality of the goods in the documents submitted to the bank. Judge Cardozo's argument foreshadows the landmark case of *Sztejn v. J. Henry Schroder Banking Co.*, 31 N.Y.S.2d 631 (Sup. Ct. 1941), which established the fraud exception to the independence principle, which we take up in detail in Section C below. The fraud exception, however, is more narrow than the approach advocated by Judge Cardozo, which does not distinguish between the unscrupulous seller out to intentionally defraud the buyer and the well-meaning seller who may have interpreted the contract differently from the buyer. For example, suppose that in *O'Meara* the seller truly believed that the paper met the tensile strength requirements under the contract and that a genuine commercial dispute arose when the buyer did not agree with the seller's interpretation of the contract. Under Judge Cardozo's view, if the bank had investigated the goods and agreed with the buyer that they did not conform to the documents, should the bank withhold payment? In other words, should a bank withhold payment where there is a genuine contract dispute between the buyer and the seller?

B.   Strict Compliance

Banks must pay against documents that comply with the requirements of the letter of credit. What constitutes compliance? UCP 600 Article 14 provides in relevant part:

Standard for Examination of Documents

(a) A nominated bank acting on its nomination, a confirming bank, if any, and the issuing bank must examine a presentation to determine, on the basis of the documents alone, whether or not the documents appear on their face to constitute a complying presentation.

PROBLEM 4-8

A U.S. buyer purchases computer chips from Sine-Tech, a manufacturer in Taiwan, under a contract calling for payment by letter of credit. The buyer's bank advises the Taiwanese manufacturer of the credit as follows:

Payment against the letter of credit will be made upon the submission of a commercial invoice, full set original on board bills of lading in triplicate, certificate of insurance, and inspection certificate. All documents to refer to Altima III Central Processing Units at 1250 Megahertz and 2048 Random Access Memory Chips shipped from Sine-Tech. All documents must strictly conform with the terms of this credit in light of standard international banking practices.

The buyer's senior vice president for sales stops by Sine-Tech while on a business trip to Asia and is able to inspect the shipment of chips. The vice president signs the inspection certificate and writes a handwritten note on the certificate: "Samples fit our contract specifications precisely. Note to bank: Please pay seller without delay."

Sine-Tech subsequently ships the chips and submits the documents, including the inspection certificate signed by the buyer's vice president, to its own bank in Taiwan. The seller's bank then forwards the documents to the buyer's bank in the United States along with a sight draft. The bill of lading refers to:

Altima III CPUs @ 1250 MHz and 2048 RAM memory chips shipped from Sino-Tech.

The examiner in the credit department of the buyer's bank looks at the documents and writes a memo to the head of the credit department: "I have two master's degrees in computer science and I know for a fact that the terms that are being used in the documents (e.g., CPU, MHz, RAM) are well-known technical equivalents that completely match the terms under the letter of credit. The documents are conforming and we should pay." Is he right? Are there any other compliance issues?

Is it safe for the bank to pay the credit on the basis of the vice president's endorsement of the inspection certificate and does that constitute a waiver of discrepancies by the applicant under UCP 600 Article 16(b)?

In addition to Articles 14 and 16, see also *Rayner* and *Hanil Bank* below.

J.H. Rayner and Company, Ltd. v. Hambro's Bank, Ltd.
Court of Appeal
[1943] 1 King's Bench 37

Appeal from ATKINSON J.

On March 29, 1940, the defendants, Hambro's Bank, Ltd., received a cable from correspondents in Denmark, which was not then in enemy occupation, requesting them to open an irrevocable sight credit expiring June 1, 1940, in favour of J.H. Rayner & Co., the plaintiffs. The material words of this cable were: ". . . account Aarhus Oliefabrik for about £16,975 against invoice full set straight clean bills of lading to Aarhus Oliefabrik dated Madras during April, 1940, covering about 1400 tons Coromandel groundnuts in bags at £12 2s. 6d. per ton f.o.b. Madras shipment motorship *Stensby* to Aarhus." On April 1, the defendants issued a letter of credit to the plaintiffs in these terms.

"Confirmed credit No. 14597.

We beg to inform you that a confirmed credit has been opened with us in favour of yourselves for an amount of up to about £16,975 account of Aarhus Oliefabrik available by drafts on this bank at sight to be accompanied by the following documents—invoice, clean on board bills of lading in complete set issued to order Aarhus Oliefabrik, dated Madras during

April, 1940, covering a shipment of about 1400 tons Coromandel groundnuts in bags at £12 2s. 6d. per ton f.o.b. Madras per m.s. *Stensby* to Aarhus.

This credit is valid until June 1, 1940. All drafts drawn here against must contain the clause 'Drawn under confirmed credit No. 14597.' We undertake to honour drafts on presentation, if drawn in conformity with the terms of this credit."

On April 15, the plaintiffs presented to the defendant bank a draft, accompanied by an invoice of the same date for "17,724 bags Coromandel groundnuts. Bill of lading dated 2.4.40" and three bills of lading, differing only as to the number of bags, which totalled 17,724, in each of which the goods were described in these terms: In the margin were the marks

"O.T.C. C.R.S. Aarhus,"

and in the body of the bill

". . . bags machine-shelled groundnut kernels, each bag said to weigh 177 lb. net. Country of origin, British India. Country of final destination, Denmark. Goods are Danish property."

Those documents having been presented to the defendants, they refused to accept the draft, on the ground that the terms of the letter of credit called for an invoice and bill of lading both covering a shipment of "Coromandel groundnuts" whereas the bills of lading presented described the goods as "machine shelled groundnut kernels. Country of origin, British India." The plaintiffs thereupon brought this action, alleging that the defendants' refusal to honour their draft was wrongful, and a breach of the undertaking in the letter of credit. At the trial before Atkinson J. evidence was given and accepted by him that "machine-shelled groundnut kernels" were the same commodity as "Coromandel groundnuts" and would be universally understood to be so in the trade in London, and, further, that the marginal mark "C.R.S." was short for "Coros" or "Coromandels" and would be so understood in the trade. Atkinson J. gave judgment for the plaintiffs, and the defendants appealed.

MACKINNON L.J.

The legal result of a banker issuing a letter of credit has been considered in various cases to which I do not think it is necessary to refer, but two passages which have been mentioned by Goddard L.J. seem to me to sum up the position in general terms with the greatest accuracy. In *English, Scottish and Australian Bank, Ltd. v. Bank of South Africa*,[2] Bailhache J. said:

"It is elementary to say that a person who ships in reliance on a letter of credit must do so in exact compliance with its terms. It is also elementary to say that a bank is not bound or indeed entitled to honour drafts presented to it under a letter of credit unless those drafts with the accompanying documents are in strict accord with the credit as opened."

Lord Sumner in *Equitable Trust Co. of New York v. Dawson Partners, Ltd.*,[3] said:

"It is both common ground and common sense that in such a transaction the accepting bank can only claim indemnity if the conditions on which it is authorized to accept are in the

---

2. (1922) 13 Ll. L. Rep. 21, 24.
3. (1927) 27 Ll. Rep. 49, 52.

matter of the accompanying documents strictly observed. There is no room for documents which are almost the same, or which will do just as well. Business could not proceed securely on any other lines. The bank's branch abroad, which knows nothing officially of the details of the transaction thus financed, cannot take upon itself to decide what will do well enough and what will not. If it does as it is told, it is safe; if it declines to do anything else, it is safe; if it departs from the conditions laid down, it acts at its own risk."

The defendant bank were told by their Danish principals to issue a letter of credit under which they were to accept documents—an invoice and bills of lading—covering "Coromandel groundnuts in bags." They were offered bills of lading covering "machine-shelled groundnut kernels." The country of origin was stated to be British India. The words in that bill of lading clearly are not the same as those required by the letter of credit. The whole case of the plaintiffs is, in the words of Lord Sumner, that "they are almost the same, or they will do just as well." The bank, if they had accepted that proposition, would have done so at their own risk. I think on pure principle that the bank were entitled to refuse to accept this sight draft on the ground that the documents tendered, the bill of lading in particular, did not comply precisely with the terms of the letter of credit which they had issued.

Atkinson J., however, in his judgment says

"A sale of Coromandel groundnuts is universally understood to be a sale of machine-shelled kernels that is, dry decorticated, and there is a standard form of contract, No. 37, used in the trade. The marking C.R.S. is short for 'Coros,' which is itself an abbreviation for 'Coromandels.' If a bag of kernels is marked 'C.R.S.,' it means that it is a bag of Coromandel groundnuts."

That is stating the effect of evidence given by persons who deal in groundnuts in Mincing Lane, and when Atkinson J. says that it is "universally understood," he means that these gentlemen from Mincing Lane have told him:

"We dealers in Mincing Lane all understand these things. We understand that 'Coromandel groundnuts' are machine shelled groundnut kernels, and we understand when we see 'C.R.S.' that that means 'Coromandels.'"

It is suggested that as a consequence the bank, when this bill of lading for machine-shelled groundnut kernels with C.R.S. in the margin was brought to them, ought to be affected with this special knowledge of those witnesses who deal in these things on contracts in Mincing Lane. I think that is a perfectly impossible suggestion. To begin with, this case does not concern any transaction in Mincing Lane. It is a transaction with Denmark, and for aught I know and for aught the evidence proved, the people in Denmark know nothing about this business usage of Mincing Lane. Moreover, quite apart from that special application of the relevant considerations, it is quite impossible to suggest that a banker is to be affected with knowledge of the customs and customary terms of every one of the thousands of trades for whose dealings he may issue letters of credit. A homely illustration is suggested by the books in front of me. If a banker were ordered to issue a letter of credit with respect to the shipment of so many copies of the "1942 Annual Practice" and were handed a bill of lading for so many copies of the "1942 White Book," it would be entirely beside the mark to call a lawyer to say that all lawyers know that the "1942 White Book" means the "1942 Annual Practice." It would be quite impossible for business to be carried on, and for bankers to be in any way protected in such matters, if it were said that they must be affected by a knowledge of all the details of the way in which particular traders carry on their business. For these reasons, I think that this appeal succeeds, that the judgment in favour of the plaintiffs must be set aside, and judgment entered for the defendants with costs, here and below.

GODDARD L.J.

I agree. It seems to me that Atkinson J. has based his judgment on the consideration that the bank was affected in some way by this custom of the trade, and, secondly, that he has considered whether what the bank required was reasonable or unreasonable. I protest against the view that a bank is to be deemed affected by knowledge of the trade of its various customers, but, quite apart from that, even if the bank did know of this trade practice by which "Coromandel groundnuts" can be described as "machine-shelled groundnut kernels," I do not think that would be conclusive of the case.

There are three parties concerned in a banker's credit—the person who requests the bank to establish the credit, the bank which establishes it, and the beneficiary who can draw on it. The person who requests the bank to establish the credit can impose what terms he likes. If he says to the bank: "I want a bill of lading in a particular form," he is entitled to it. If the bank accepts the mandate which its customer gives it, it must do so on the terms which he imposes. The bank, as between itself and the beneficiary, can impose extra terms if it likes. For instance, in this case, the bank imposes a term: "All drafts drawn here against must contain the clause: 'Drawn under confirmed credit No. 14597.'" The bank can say to the beneficiary: "These are the terms on which the bank will pay," and if it has only been authorized by its customer to pay on certain terms it must see that those terms are included in the notification which it gives to the beneficiary, and it must not pay on any other terms. If it does pay on any other terms, it runs the risk of its customer refusing to reimburse it. It does not matter whether the terms imposed by the person who requires the bank to open the credit seem reasonable or unreasonable. The bank is not concerned with that. If it accepts the mandate to open the credit, it must do exactly what its customer requires it to do. If the customer says: "I require a bill of lading for Coromandel groundnuts," the bank is not justified, in my judgment, in paying against a bill of lading for anything except Coromandel groundnuts, and it is no answer to say: "You know perfectly well that 'machine-shelled groundnut kernels are the same as Coromandel groundnuts.'" For all the bank knows, its customer may have a particular reason for wanting "Coromandel groundnuts" in the bill of lading. At any rate, that is the instruction which the customer has given to the bank, and if the bank wants to be reimbursed and remunerated by its customer, it must show that it has performed his mandate.

In my opinion, in this case, whether the bank knew or did not know that there was this trade practice to treat "Coromandel groundnuts" and "machine-shelled groundnut kernels" as interchangeable terms, is nothing to the point. They were told to establish a credit, and to pay against a bill of lading describing particular goods, and the beneficiary under that credit presented a bill of lading which was not what they had promised to pay against. Therefore, it seems to me, whether it is reasonable or unreasonable for their principals to say that they want a bill of lading for "Coromandel groundnuts," or whether the bank had or had not knowledge of some of the trade practices which are referred to, is not the question. The question is "What was the promise which the bank made to the beneficiary under the credit, and did the beneficiary avail himself of that promise?" In my opinion, in the present case, he did not, and, therefore, I think that the bank was justified in refusing to pay. The other matters are, in my opinion, quite irrelevant, though the judge seems to have paid particular attention to them. I agree that this appeal should be allowed.

Hanil Bank v. PT. Bank Negara Indonesia
United States District Court, Southern District of New York, 2000
No. 96 Civ. 3201, 41 U.C.C. Rep. Serv. 2d 618

KEENAN, District Judge.

Before the Court are cross-motions for summary judgment, pursuant to Fed. R. Civ. P. 56. For the reasons discussed below, the Court grants Defendant's motion for summary judgment and denies Plaintiff's motion for summary judgment.

THE PARTIES

Plaintiff Hanil Bank ("Hanil") was, at all times relevant to this action, a banking corporation organized under the laws of the Republic of Korea, with an agency in New York, New York.

Defendant PT. Bank Negara Indonesia (Pesero) ("BNI") is a banking corporation organized under the laws of Indonesia, with an agency located in New York, New York.

BACKGROUND

On July 27, 1995, PT. Kodeco Electronics Indonesia ("Kodeco") applied to BNI to issue a letter of credit (the "L/C") for the benefit of "Sung Jun Electronics Co., Ltd." ("Sung Jun"). On July 28, 1995, BNI issued the L/C, No.IM1MHT0272.95, in the amount of $170,955.00 but misspelled the name of the beneficiary as "Sung Jin Electronics Co. Ltd." The beneficiary did not request amendment of the L/C to change the name of the beneficiary. On August 2, 1995 Sung Jun negotiated the L/C to Hanil. Hanil purchased the L/C and the documents submitted by Sung Jun thereunder from Sung Jun for $157,493.00, the face amount of the draft, less Hanil's commission. On August 2, 1995, Hanil submitted the documents, a draft, a commercial invoice, bill of lading, insurance policy, a packing list, and a fax advice, to BNI for payment. On August 16, 1995, BNI rejected the documents tendered by Hanil and refused to pay under the L/C. BNI alleges that it compared the documents with the L/C and identified four discrepancies, and based upon those discrepancies, refused the documents and demand for payment. The alleged discrepancies are as follows:

(1) The Name of the Beneficiary: The L/C identifies the beneficiary as Sung Jin Electronics Co. Ltd. instead of Sung Jun Electronics Co. Ltd.
(2) The Packing List: BNI claims that the packing list did not show the contents of each carton as required by the L/C.
(3) "Export Quality": BNI claims that the packing list also fails to specify that the goods were of "export quality."
(4) The Bill of Lading: BNI claims that Hanil supplied a "Freight Bill of Lading" instead of the required "Ocean Bill of Lading."

BNI alleges that before it issued its notice of refusal on August 16, 1995, it contacted Kodeco to ask whether it would accept the discrepancies and approve the requested payment, but Kodeco declined to do so. BNI further alleges that it continued to ask Kodeco to waive the discrepancies after August 16, but that Kodeco continued to refuse to waive the discrepancies. BNI then returned the entire original package of documents back to Hanil on September 4, 1995.

Hanil contends that BNI decided to reject the documents presented by Hanil after consulting with, and on the instructions of, Kodeco. In support of this contention, Hanil points to a letter from BNI to Hanil, dated October 4, 1995, which stated that "we are acting at the request and on the instruction of the applicant, i.e., PT. Kodeco Electronics Indonesia. We will, anyhow make a final attempt to have the applicant reconsider their determination and to accept the discrepancies and give as the approval [sic] for payment of the documents." BNI denies the contention that it acted on the instructions of Kodeco when BNI refused to pay because of the alleged discrepancies.

Plaintiff brought suit in New York State court on April 19, 1996, asserting claims for breach of contract, breach of the Uniform Customs and Practice for Documentary Credits (1993 Revision) International Chamber of Commerce Publication No. 500 (the "UCP"), unjust enrichment, and breach of an implied covenant of good faith and fair dealing, and seeking $157,493 in damages, plus interest. Defendant then removed the case to this Court. Both parties now move for summary judgment.

SUMMARY JUDGMENT STANDARDS

In this case, both parties argue that summary judgment is appropriate because there is no genuine issue of material fact. Hanil argues that the documents it presented to BNI complied with the terms of the L/C and that, as a result, Hanil is entitled to judgment enforcing the L/C. BNI, however, contends that each of the four discrepancies it identified justified rejection of Hanil's presentation under the L/C and the refusal to pay and that the Complaint should therefore be dismissed.

LETTERS OF CREDIT AND THE UCP

The principles of letter of credit law are embodied in the Uniform Customs and Practice for Documentary Credits (1993 Revision) International Chamber of Commerce Publication No. 500 (the "UCP"). The UCP is a compilation of internationally accepted commercial practices. Although it is not law, the UCP commonly governs letters of credit by virtue of its incorporation into most letters of credit. In this case, the L/C provides that it is governed by the UCP and both parties agree that the provisions of the UCP govern the L/C in this case. The New York Uniform Commercial Code (the "U.C.C.") provides that if a letter of credit is subject in whole or part to the UCP, as in this case, the U.C.C. does not apply.

A fundamental tenet of letter of credit law is that the obligation of the issuing bank to honor a draft on a credit is independent of the performance of the underlying contract. "The duty of the issuing bank to pay upon the submission of documents which appear on their face to conform to the terms and conditions of the letter of credit is absolute, absent proof of intentional fraud." *E & H Partners*, 39 F. Supp. 2d at 280. Because the credit engagement is concerned only with documents, "[t]he essential requirements of a letter of credit must be strictly complied with by the party entitled to draw against the letter of credit, which means that the papers, documents and shipping description must be as stated in the letter." *Marino Indus.*, 686 F.2d at 114. "There is no room for documents which are almost the same, or which will do just as well." *Alaska Textile*, 982 F.2d at 816. Even under the strict compliance rule, however, "some variations might be so insignificant as not to relieve the issuing or confirming bank of its obligation to pay," for example, if there were a case where "the name intended is unmistakably clear despite what is obviously a typographical error, as might be the case if, for example, 'Smith' were misspelled 'Smithh.'" *Beyene*, 762 F.2d at 6. The Court will now consider the alleged discrepancies in this case.

THE NAME OF THE BENEFICIARY

As set out above, the name of the beneficiary in this case was Sung Jun. Kodeco's application to BNI for the issuance of the L/C requested that the L/C be issued to Sung Jun. BNI, however, issued the L/C identifying the beneficiary as Sung Jin. BNI argues that under *Beyene v. Irving Trust Co.*, 762 F.2d 4 (2d Cir. 1985) and *Mutual Export Corp. v. Westpac Banking Corp.*, 983 F.2d 420 (2d Cir. 1993), this discrepancy was a proper basis to reject the letter of credit presentation. Hanil argues, however, that the strict compliance rule does not permit an issuing bank to dishonor a letter of credit based on a discrepancy such as the misspelling in this case which could not have misled or prejudiced the issuing bank. For the reasons discussed below, the Court agrees with BNI.

In *Beyene*, Plaintiffs brought suit seeking damages for the alleged wrongful refusal of the defendant trust company, Irving Trust Co. ("Irving"), to honor a letter of credit. The district court granted Irving's motion for summary judgment because the bill of lading presented to Irving misspelled the name of the person to whom notice was to be given of the arrival of the goods, listing the name of the party as Mohammed Soran instead of Mohammed Sofan. As a result, the district court found that the bill of lading failed to comply with the terms of the letter of credit and that Irving was under no obligation to honor the letter of credit. The Second Circuit agreed, finding that "the misspelling in the bill of lading of Sofan's name as 'Soran' was a material discrepancy that entitled Irving to refuse to honor the letter of credit" and stating that "this is not a case where the name intended is unmistakably clear despite what is obviously a typographical error, as might be the case if, for example, 'Smith' were misspelled 'Smithh.'" 762 F.2d at 6. The Second Circuit also noted that it was not claimed that in the Middle East, where the letter of credit was issued, that "Soran" would be obviously recognized as a misspelling of the surname "Sofan." The Court finds the misspelling in the present case to be similar to the misspelling in *Beyene* and notes that Hanil likewise does not claim that Sung "Jin" would be obviously recognized as a misspelling of Sung "Jun."

Plaintiff argues that *Beyene* is distinguishable from the present case because in *Beyene* the beneficiary made the error, while in the present case, the issuing bank made the error. However, the Second Circuit has made it clear that under letter of credit law, "[t]he beneficiary must inspect the letter of credit and is responsible for any negligent failure to discover that the credit does not achieve the desired commercial ends." *Mutual Export*, 983 F.2d at 423. Thus, in *Mutual Export*, even though the issuing bank had issued a letter of credit with an incorrect termination date, the Second Circuit reversed the district court's finding that the letter of credit should be reformed to reflect the appropriate date, and held that the beneficiary was responsible for failure to discover the error. The *Mutual Export* court explained that this rule is important because

> [t]he beneficiary is in the best position to determine whether a letter of credit meets the needs of the underlying commercial transaction and to request any necessary changes . . . "[i]t is more efficient to require the beneficiary to conduct that review of the credit before the fact of performance than after it, and the beneficiary that performs without seeing or examining the credit should bear the costs." . . .

Pursuant to *Beyene* and *Mutual Export*, this Court concludes that BNI properly rejected payment on the ground that the documents improperly identified the beneficiary of the letter of credit. Although Hanil contends that BNI should have known that the intended beneficiary was Sung Jun, not Sung Jin, based on the application letter in BNI's own file, the Second Circuit has stated that in considering whether to pay, "the bank looks solely at the letter and the documentation the beneficiary presents to determine whether the documentation meets the requirements in the letter." *See Marino Indus.*, 686 F.2d at 115.

Although Plaintiff argues that *Bank of Montreal v. Federal Nat'l Bank & Trust Co.*, 662 F. Supp. 6 (W.D. Okla. 1984), allowed recovery when the error was greater than the misspelling of a single letter, in *Bank of Montreal*, the letter of credit contained two, internally inconsistent, statements of the name of one of the entities whose indebtedness was secured. The letter of credit referred to "Blow Out Products, Ltd." in its first paragraph and to "Blow Out Prevention, Ltd." in its second paragraph. Based on this inconsistency on the face of the letter of credit itself, the court found that the letter of credit was ambiguous and resolved the ambiguity against the issuer. There is no internal inconsistency or ambiguity in the L/C at issue in the present case, however.

Having found that BNI properly refused payment based on the improper identification of the beneficiary of the L/C, the Court need not address the three remaining alleged discrepancies.

Finally, as to Hanil's argument that BNI dishonored the L/C at the instruction of Kodeco and thereby violated its duty of good faith and fair dealing, the Court again disagrees. As noted above, the issuing bank's obligation under the letter of credit is independent of the underlying commercial transaction. Thus, BNI had an obligation to independently review Hanil's submissions to determine if there were any discrepancies. However, under the UCP, BNI is permitted to approach the payor of the letter of credit, in this case Kodeco, for a waiver of any discrepancies with or without the beneficiary's approval. See UCP, Art. 14(c). In this case there is no evidence that BNI communicated with Kodeco other than to ask whether Kodeco would accept the discrepancies and approve the requested payment. As a result, the Court finds that Hanil has not set forth facts showing there is a genuine issue as to whether BNI breached its duty of good faith and fair dealing by dishonoring the L/C. Summary judgment for BNI is therefore appropriate.

For the reasons discussed above, the Court grants BNI's motion for summary judgment and denies Hanil's motion for summary judgment.

NOTES AND QUESTIONS

1. *Hanil* followed *Beyene v. Irving Trust Co.*, 762 F.2d 4 (2d Cir. 1985), in finding that unless the name of the intended beneficiary is unmistakably clear despite an obvious typographical error, any difference in the name constitutes noncompliance. In *Voest-Alpine Trading USA Corp. v. Bank of China*, 167 F. Supp. 2d 940 (S.D. Tex. 2000), *aff'd*, 288 F.3d 262 (5th Cir. 2002), the district court held that although documents naming the beneficiary "Voest-Alpine USA Trading Corp." did not conform to the letter of credit requiring documents identifying the beneficiary as "Voest-Alpine Trading USA Corp.," the discrepancy did not justify dishonor. Looking at other documents and the transaction as a whole, the court concluded that the documents did not appear to come from a beneficiary other than that named in the credit. On appeal, the Fifth Circuit held that the issuing bank had waived its right to reject payment of the letter of credit because the bank did not give a proper notice of refusal within the period required by the UCP but did not address the

discrepancy issue. *See Voest-Alpine*, 288 F.3d at 266. In general, typographical errors occur with some regularity in letter of credit transactions and in documents presented under credits, especially when foreign names are involved that use combinations of the alphabet that are not found in the English language. "[L]eading figures in the U.S. LC community support the *Voest-Alpine* approach and regard as too narrow the approach taken in *Hanil* and its forerunner, *Beyene v. Irving Trust Co.* The LC community has no interest in inviting reformation of LCs, but it does wish the courts to take a more practice oriented view with respect to typographical errors." James G. Barnes and James E. Byrne, *Letters of Credit: 2000 Cases*, 56 Bus. Law 1805 (2001). For a review of recent letter of credit cases, see James G. Barnes and James E. Byrne, *Letters of Credit*, 67 Bus. Law 1281 (2012).

2. In *Rayner*, the sellers emphasized that it was universally understood in the trade that "Coromandel groundnuts" are machine-shelled groundnut kernels and that "C.R.S." means "Coromandels." On this basis, the sellers argued that documents referring to "machine-shelled groundnut kernels" and "C.R.S." are conforming documents. The court of appeals rejected this argument and emphasized that bankers cannot be charged with knowledge of the customs of merchants in particular trades. The purpose of the strict compliance principle is to reduce the bank's task to the mechanical one of comparing the documents on their face with the terms of the credit. A mechanical examination would relieve the burden on banks of being charged with extraneous knowledge or having to engage in research of unfamiliar topics. But what about terms that are now generally if not universally known in all trades and channels of commerce such as "C.O.D." for "cash on delivery"? Should banks be charged with knowledge of such widely accepted terms?

3. *Rayner* is the landmark case establishing the principle of strict compliance. The leading case for a less stringent standard is *Banco Espanol de Credito v. State Street Bank and Trust Co.*, 385 F.2d 230 (1st Cir. 1967). The letter of credit required an inspection certificate to specify that "the goods were in conformity with the order." The inspector submitted a certificate that the goods were in conformity but added a statement that the certificate was delivered "under reserves," which nullified the statement required by the credit. The First Circuit Court of Appeals held that the certificate complied with the letter of credit. *See* 385 F.2d at 237. The official comment to UCC §5-108 provides that *State Street Bank* applied a "substantial compliance" standard but that this standard is rejected in favor of the standard of strict compliance. UCC §5-108(a) provides: "[A]n issuer shall honor a presentation that appears on its face strictly to comply with the terms and conditions of the letter of credit." The Official Comment further provides:

> Strict compliance does not mean slavish conformity to the terms of the letter of credit. For example, standard practice (what issuers do) may recognize certain presentations as complying that an unschooled layman would find as discrepant. By adopting standard practice as a way of measuring strict compliance, this article indorses the conclusion of the court in *New Braunfels Nat'l Bank v. Odiorne*, 780 S.W.2d 313 (Tex. Ct. App. 1989) (beneficiary could collect when draft requested payment on "Letter of Credit No. 86-122-5" and letter of credit specified "Letter of Credit No. 86-122-S" holding strict compliance does not demand oppressive perfectionism). The section also indorses the result in *Tosco Corp. v. Federal Deposit Insurance Corp.*, 723 F.2d 1242 (6th Cir. 1983). The letter of credit in that case called for "drafts Drawn under Bank of Clarksville Letter of Credit Number 105." The draft presented stated "drawn under Bagenk of Clarksville, Clarksville, Tennessee letter of Credit No. 105." The court correctly found that despite the change of upper case "L" to a lower case "l" and the use of the word "No." instead of "Number," and despite the addition of the words "Clarksville, Tennessee" the presentation conformed. Similarly a document addressed by a foreign person to General Motors as "Jeneral Motors" would strictly conform in the absence of other defects.

UCC §5-108, Official Comment note 1. While minor spelling discrepancies can be disregarded, courts usually insist that documents, such as the bill of lading (involved in *Rayner*) must strictly comply with the letter of credit. *See CVD Equipment Corp. v. Taiwan Glass Indus. Corp.*, No. 10 Civ. 573, 2011 WL 1210199, at *3–4 (S.D.N.Y. Mar. 31, 2011) (submission of received bill of lading showing that goods were delivered to freight forwarder was nonconforming because letter of credit called for a clean on board bill of lading showing that goods were loaded on board the vessel).

PROBLEM 4-9

On February 17, the National Bank of Cleveland (NBC) received drafts and documents from a Danish seller for payment under a letter of credit issued by NBC. Upon examining the documents, NBC noticed that the bills of lading were not marked "clean on board" as required by the terms of the credit. NBC notified the seller by fax on February 19 of the discrepancy, informing the seller that it could not pay on the letter of credit due to the discrepancy and that it was holding the documents to the disposal of the seller. Later the same day, NBC's documents examiners notice an additional discrepancy: The commercial invoice was not issued in the name of the seller as required by the credit but was in the name of a third party. On February 20, NBC notified the seller of this additional discrepancy. Is the notice by NBC effective as to both discrepancies under UCP 600 Article 16(d) because both were given within the five banking day notice period? What is the purpose of the notice requirement of Article 16(d)? *See also* UCP 600 Article 16(c).

PROBLEM 4-10

Mid-America Bank (MAB) receives drafts and documents from a Swiss seller for payment under a letter of credit. MAB examines the documents and notices no discrepancies and sends the following e-mail to the buyer-applicant of the credit: "We have examined the documents and have found that they are conforming. We are forwarding the documents for your review for discrepancies." Upon examining the documents, the buyer tells MAB that the seller did not submit an inspection certificate as required by the credit. MAB thereafter sends a fax within the five banking day period of UCP 600 Article 16(d) to the seller stating that it will not pay as the documents are discrepant and that it is holding the documents to the disposal of the seller. Is this notice effective under UCP 600 Article 16(d)? *See also* UCP 600 Article 16(b).

NOTE ON ELECTRONIC COMMUNICATIONS

Electronic communications have become a significant part of letter of credit practice, but, at least for the present, there are a number of limitations on the use of an electronic system to fully replicate the traditional documentary credit transaction that relied on paper documents.

The most significant hurdle in accommodating the letter of credit transaction within electronic commerce is related to the bill of lading. As we have previously noted, in a documentary sale of goods using letters of credit, the negotiable bill of lading serves the vital function of being a document of title entitling the bearer to physical possession of the goods. In a typical documentary sale, the seller will present a paper bill of lading (and other documents) to the buyer's bank, which will pay against presentation and then transfer the bill properly endorsed to the buyer who will then present the bill of lading to the carrier to recover possession of the goods. Traditionally, of course, the bill of lading has been a paper document, which is physically transferred from one party to another, and it is the physical transfer of the paper document, accompanied by a proper endorsement, which creates legal rights in the person to whom the bill is transferred. The electronic letter of credit will only work successfully if somehow the characteristics of the physical transfer normally associated with such a transaction, in particular the physical transfer of the bill of lading, can be successfully replicated in electronic form. So far, these attempts have met with only limited success. The best known and most successful to date of all of these electronic systems is Bolero (Bills of Lading Electronic Registry Organization), which maintains a central registry of ownership of title operated by a company called Bolero International Limited, founded in part by SWIFT, the Society for Worldwide Interstate Financial Telecommunications, a not-for-profit organization established in Belgium by banks for the purpose of facilitating the flow of financial transactions information. Under Bolero, an electronic bill of lading is registered with Bolero International Limited and transfer is then effected by the registered holder (party A) sending a message to the central title registry indicating that the Bolero bill of lading has been transferred to a new holder (party B) who is now the official registered holder.

One of the major problems with Bolero is that the system will work effectively only if all parties to the transaction subscribe to the Bolero framework and are members of the Bolero Association. Consider the limitations of Bolero where the carrier, a Bolero member, faces competing claims for goods from a holder of a Bolero bill of lading and a person who claims to be the rightful owner of the goods but who is not a Bolero member. Under the traditional system, a long history of accumulated mercantile and legal convention provides that the carrier would be fully protected if it delivered the goods to the holder of the paper bill of lading and the holder of the bill would have the unquestioned right to the delivery of the goods. In the situation just described, however, it is far from clear that the accumulated conventions of the traditional system would apply to the electronic transaction and protect the carrier. This example illustrates the technological limitations of attempting to fully replicate the physical bill of lading in electronic form. In addition to the problems of technological limitations, the future of the Bolero system or any form of electronic bill also depends on the further development of a mature legal regime that confers incidents on the electronic bill that are identical to that of the paper bill.

While there are limitations to the use of electronic communications to fully replicate the documentary sale, two areas in which electronic communications have become quite commonplace is in bank-to-bank communications and in the initiation by beneficiaries of the letter of credit application process. Most bank-to-bank communications about letter of credit transactions occur via the dedicated network operated by SWIFT, which provides for a specific format for all messages, message types, and message space. Thus, an issuing bank will often notify an advising or confirming bank about a letter of credit established by the buyer in favor of the seller via electronic communications. In addition, the initial establishment of the letter of credit by the buyer can also be done through electronic commerce. However, while electronic communications are frequently used to initiate the letter of credit application and to communicate its terms, most seller-beneficiaries usually want a "hard copy" or a letter of credit in the traditional form of a paper document that commits the bank to paying upon certain conditions. Where the initiation of the letter of credit has been done electronically, the issuing or confirming bank will need to convert the SWIFT electronic message creating the letter of credit into a paper form. One issue that has arisen in the age of electronic communications is the risk of errors in the transmission of messages or the conversion of electronic messages into paper documents. The following problem explores these issues.

PROBLEM 4-11

A New York tea merchant contracts to buy a large quantity of English tea from a London seller. The buyer asks its New York bank to open a confirmed letter of credit in favor of the seller. The Merchants' Bank of New York uses the dedicated SWIFT network to contact the London Commercial Bank and asks it to add its confirmation and advise the London seller that a confirmed letter of credit has been issued in favor of the seller by the New York buyer. The electronic message calls for "Payment against documents for English Green Tea in bulk. Details to follow by mail."

As the London seller insists on a hard copy of the letter of credit, the New York bank sends the confirming bank the following message, "To save time, please print out our electronic letter of credit and forward to the seller." However, as the London bank is printing out the electronic letter, a glitch occurs in the computer software program that converts the message in the SWIFT electronic format to a word processing format. The glitch results in the deletion of the word "Green" so the hard copy of the letter of credit printed out by the London bank refers to "Payment against documents for English Tea in Bulk." As this problem had never occurred before, the London bank simply forwards the documents to the London seller. The seller subsequently submits documents for English tea to the London bank and receives payment under the letter of credit. The London bank forwards the documents to the New York bank, which notifies the London bank, "We cannot reimburse you as documents refer to 'English Tea' instead of 'English Green Tea' as per our SWIFT instructions on the letter of credit. We hold these documents at your disposal."

The London bank discovers the computer software problem but argues that the operative document is not the electronic message but as per the instructions from the New York bank the printed-out hard copy, which requires documents relating to "English Tea." The operative document called for documents relating to English Tea and such documents were submitted that strictly complied with the terms of the credit as fixed by the hard copy. The London bank argues that its payment was therefore proper and that the New York bank must now reimburse or the London bank will sue for wrongful dishonor. The New York bank argues that the operative letter of credit is contained in the SWIFT electronic message that required documents for English Green Tea and that as the documents for English Tea are nonconforming the New York bank has no obligation to reimburse the London bank. Who is right? *See* UCP 600 Article 11 and Article 35.

C.   The Fraud Exception to the Independence Principle and Enjoining the Letter of Credit

1.   *The Problem of Fraud*

While the purpose of the independence principle is to provide the seller an assured method of payment, courts soon realized that an overly rigid extension of the independence rule could result in the unjust enrichment of an undeserving and fraudulent beneficiary and undermine the very commercial utility that the independence principle was designed to promote. The problem arises as follows:

Illustration 4-1. A seller contracts to sell new bristles (or brushes) to a buyer. Instead of shipping new bristles, the seller ships worthless discarded materials and submits fraudulent documents such as a commercial invoice and bills of lading covering new bristles to the issuing bank for payment under a letter of credit. The buyer discovers the fraud before the issuing bank pays under the letter of credit. A strict application of the independence principle, one which does not allow the bank to look behind the documents, might result in the bank paying the letter to an unscrupulous beneficiary in an obvious fraud situation.

These were essentially the facts in the landmark pre-Uniform Commercial Code case of *Sztejn v. J. Henry Schroder Banking Co.*, 31 N.Y.S.2d 631 (Sup. Ct. 1941), which established the fraud exception that was foreshadowed by Judge Cardozo's dissent in *O'Meara v. National Park Bank, supra.* As the court in *Sztejn* recognized, an overly rigid application of the independence principle to require payment to an unscrupulous seller-beneficiary who intentionally provides forged documents for the purpose of defrauding the buyer would undermine the legitimate purposes of the letter of credit. For this reason, the court established an exception to the independence principle for fraud; that is, in some cases the nonperformance of the underlying contract due to fraud will constitute grounds for nonpayment of the letter of credit.

In *Sztejn,* the Schroder bank issued a commercial letter of credit for its customer, Charles Sztejn, in favor of the beneficiary, Transea Traders, Ltd., a company doing business in India. The letter of credit was to finance the sale of 50 cases of bristles and could be drawn upon the presentation of an invoice and a bill of lading. The sellers presented documents to their bank in India, Chartered Bank, which acted as a collection agent by forwarding the documents to the Schroder bank for payment. Before payment, the buyers learned that the sellers had instead shipped cow hair and other worthless material to simulate genuine merchandise and that the documents presented by the sellers were fraudulent. The buyers brought suit against the Schroder bank to declare the letter of credit void and to enjoin payment. In holding for the buyers, the court stated:

It is well established that a letter of credit is independent of the primary contract of sale between the buyer and the seller. The issuing bank agrees to pay upon presentation of documents, not goods. This rule is necessary to preserve the efficiency of the letter of credit as an instrument for the financing of trade. One of the chief purposes of the letter of credit is to furnish the seller with a ready means of obtaining prompt payment for his merchandise. It would be a most unfortunate interference with business transactions if a bank before honoring drafts drawn upon it was obliged or even allowed to go behind the documents, at the request of the buyer and enter into controversies between the buyer and the seller regarding the quality of the merchandise shipped. Of course, the application of this doctrine presupposes that the documents accompanying the draft are genuine and conform in terms to the requirements of the letter of credit. [A] different situation is presented in the instant action. This is not a controversy between the buyer and seller concerning a mere breach of warranty regarding the quality of the merchandise. [T]he seller has intentionally failed to ship any goods ordered by the buyer. In such a situation, where the seller's fraud has been called to the bank's attention before the drafts and documents have been presented for payment, the principle of the independence of the bank's obligation under the letter of credit should not be extended to protect the unscrupulous seller. It is true that even though the documents are forged or fraudulent, if the issuing bank has already paid the draft before receiving notice of the seller's fraud, it will be protected if it exercised reasonable diligence before making such payment. However, in the instant action Schroder has received notice of Transea's active fraud before it accepted or paid the draft. The Chartered Bank, which under the allegations of the complaint stands in no better position than Transea, should not be heard to complain because Schroder is not forced to pay the draft accompanied by documents covering a transaction which it has reason to believe is fraudulent. The distinction between a breach of warranty and active fraud on the part of the seller is supported by authority and reason. As one court has stated: "Obviously, when the issuer of a letter of credit knows that a document, although correct in form, is, in point of fact, false or illegal, he cannot be called upon to recognize such a document as complying with the terms of a letter of credit." *Old Colony Trust Co. v. Lawyer's Title & Trust Co.*, 297 F. 152, 158 (2d Cir. 1924). On this motion only the complaint is before me and I am bound by its allegation that the Chartered Bank is not a holder in due course but is a mere agent for collection for the account of the seller charged with fraud. Therefore the Chartered Bank's motion to dismiss the complaint must be denied.

Sztejn, 31 N.Y.S.2d at 633–636. As set forth in *Sztejn* the fraud exception is rather narrow. The issuing bank had discovered the fraud before payment and only the fraudulent party and no innocent third party, such as a confirming bank or a negotiating bank, had relied on the letter of credit (see the last two sentences of the quotation from *Sztejn*). Because *Sztejn* was rather limited in scope, many unresolved questions relating to the fraud exception were left unanswered as we shall see shortly in the principal cases below.

2.   Sources of Law

What is the law governing fraud in international letters of credit? As we noted earlier, the UCP 600 is silent on the issue of fraud as the drafters of the UCP 600 believed that fraud should be left to domestic law. The doctrine of fraud that was established by *Sztejn* has been codified in §5-109 of the Uniform Commercial Code and extensive case law has arisen concerning the interpretation of this provision and its predecessors. Many of the fraud cases involving a U.S. party under an international letter of credit will be governed by the UCC.

For reasons that will become apparent in the discussion below, the issue of fraud usually arises in the context of the buyer-applicant of the letter of credit seeking to enjoin the issuing bank from paying against fraudulent documents submitted by the seller-beneficiary. The UCC treats the issue of fraud and enjoining letters of credit together in the following article:

§5-109. *Fraud and Forgery.*

(a) If a presentation is made that appears on its face strictly to comply with the terms and conditions of the letter of credit, but a required document is forged or materially fraudulent, or honor of the presentation would facilitate a material fraud by the beneficiary on the issuer or applicant:

(1) the issuer shall honor the presentation, if honor is demanded by (i) a nominated person who has given value in good faith and without notice of forgery or material fraud, (ii) a confirmer who has honored its confirmation in good faith, (iii) a holder in due course of a draft drawn under the letter of credit which was taken after acceptance by the issuer or nominated person, or (iv) an assignee of the issuer's or nominated person's deferred obligation that was taken for value and without notice of forgery or material fraud after the obligation was incurred by the issuer or nominated person; and

(2) the issuer, acting in good faith, may honor or dishonor the presentation in any other case.

(b) If an applicant claims that a required document is forged or materially fraudulent or that honor of the presentation would facilitate a material fraud by the beneficiary on the issuer or applicant, a court of competent jurisdiction may temporarily or permanently enjoin the issuer from honoring a presentation or grant similar relief against the issuer or other persons only if the court finds that:

(1) the relief is not prohibited under the law applicable to an accepted draft or deferred obligation incurred by the issuer;

(2) a beneficiary, issuer, or nominated person who may be adversely affected is adequately protected against loss that it may suffer because the relief is granted;

(3) all of the conditions to entitle a person to the relief under the law of this State have been met; and

(4) on the basis of the information submitted to the court, the applicant is more likely than not to succeed under its claim of forgery or material fraud and the person demanding honor does not qualify for protection under subsection (a)(1).

Section 5-109(a) divides cases involving fraud into two categories: (1) cases where the honor is demanded by certain third parties who have given value in good faith and without notice of the fraud and (2) all other cases. In the first category, the issuing bank *must* honor the presentation even if forgery or a material fraud exists within the meaning of §5-109(a). In all other cases, the bank *may*, acting in good faith, choose to honor or dishonor. What is the purpose of making this distinction? We now turn to this issue.

3.   Different Types of Innocent Parties

In fraud cases, the UCC will, if possible, impose the loss on the wrongdoer. However, that is not always possible as the wrongdoer may have disappeared or be unavailable as a defendant for other reasons. At this juncture, it may become necessary to impose the loss on an innocent party, but as between innocent parties not all are treated equally. The rationale for requiring honor in the case of certain third parties is that where there are two innocent parties subject to the fraud—the buyer-applicant and a third party who has given value in good faith—it is the buyer-applicant who has voluntarily chosen to deal with the fraudulent party (the seller-beneficiary) and who has brought the third party into contact with the fraudulent party.

> *Illustration 4-2.* A buyer enters into a sales contract with an unscrupulous seller and at the behest of the seller asks its issuing bank to open a confirmed letter of credit engaging a local bank in the seller's jurisdiction to add its confirmation. The seller submits fraudulent documents to the confirming bank, which pays the seller without notice of the fraud. The confirming bank forwards the documents to the issuing bank, which in the meanwhile has been alerted to the fraud by the buyer-applicant. In this case, both the buyer and the confirming bank are innocent parties to the fraud. This issue that arises is which party should bear the loss caused by the seller's fraud.

Of the two innocent parties in our illustration, the confirming bank and the buyer-applicant, the UCC drafters decided that it is the buyer-applicant who should bear the higher risk. Under §5-109(a)(1)(ii), the issuing bank must reimburse the confirming bank and the buyer-applicant must, in turn, reimburse the issuing bank. As a result, the loss is imposed on the buyer. The buyer's remedy is to sue the seller for fraud. If the buyer recovers, then the loss is imposed on the wrongdoer, but if not, then the buyer-applicant must bear the loss.

Section 5-109(a)(1) does not protect *all* innocent third parties who give value but only certain third parties, that is, nominated persons (§5-109(a)(1)(i)), a confirmer (§5-109(a)(1)(ii)), a holder in due course of a draft drawn under a letter of credit that was taken *after* acceptance by the issuer (§5-109(a)(1)(iii)), or an assignee of the issuer or nominated person's deferred obligation (§5-109(a)(1)(iv)). What all of these innocent third parties have in common is that they were brought into contact directly or indirectly with the wrongdoer by the applicant of the credit. Where there is an innocent third party that is not brought into contact directly or indirectly by the applicant, then that third party would *not* be protected. For example, suppose that the fraudulent seller sells or negotiates the drafts to a third-party financial institution. Even if the third party takes without notice of the fraud and pays value, this third party is not protected under §5-109(a)(1). This third party voluntarily chose to deal with the seller or wrongdoer in the stream of commerce, presumably in order to make a profit. In this case, the drafters of the UCC decided that the loss will stay where it falls, that is, on the third party whose only remedy is to sue the wrongdoer. However, if the third party takes up the drafts *after* the drafts were accepted by the issuer or a nominated person (§5-109(a)(1)(iii)), then that third party is protected as that party should be able to rely on the credit of solvent banks and the banks (and the third party indirectly) were brought into contact with the wrongdoer by the applicant in having the letter of credit issued by the issuing bank.

4. Fraud Cases Not Involving Innocent Third Parties

Under §5-109(a)(2) where honor is demanded in all other cases that do not involve third parties falling within §5-109(a)(1), the bank is protected if it chooses in good faith either to honor or dishonor.

> *Illustration 4-3.* In a contract for the sale of goods financed by a letter of credit authorized by the buyer, the seller submits fraudulent documents to the issuing bank. Before payment, the buyer learns of the fraud and asks the bank to withhold payment. The bank may at its option honor or dishonor the demand for payment from the seller.

In most cases, banks will choose to honor as this is the less burdensome course of action and involves fewer risks. If the bank chooses to honor the letter of credit in the face of allegations of fraud by the buyer, the bank is protected and entitled to receive reimbursement of the letter of credit from the buyer-applicant so long as the bank acts in good faith. The bank also has the option of dishonor but this course of action may involve considerably more risk and expense to the bank. If the bank chooses to dishonor and the seller-beneficiary then brings a lawsuit against the bank for wrongful dishonor, the bank must defend its dishonor in the litigation by proving forgery or material fraud as set forth in UCC §5-109(a). In many cases, the facts surrounding the fraud are not within the bank's knowledge so proving fraud may be difficult and time consuming. In addition, because fraud is treated as an affirmative defense, the bank has the burden of proof that fraud existed and will lose the lawsuit if it cannot sustain its burden. Faced with the option of simply honoring the demand for payment and receiving reimbursement from the buyer-applicant and facing a claim of wrongful dishonor and a lawsuit, most banks will presumably choose to honor in the face of allegations of fraud.

Faced with a fraudulent seller and a bank that intends to pay on the credit, the buyer-applicant's recourse under §5-109(b) is to sue for an injunction against the bank prohibiting payment. The bank is, of course, protected against any claims of wrongful dishonor by the seller-beneficiary if it is prevented from payment by an injunction issued by a competent court. If the applicant fails to obtain an injunction and the bank pays despite allegations of fraud, the applicant will have recourse against the bank only in the rare cases where the applicant can prove that the bank did not act in good faith, that is, intended to perpetuate a fraud on the applicant.

PROBLEM 4-12

Maxwell & Associates, a car distributor based in Columbus, Ohio, enters into negotiations with Chincotti, an Italian automobile manufacturer, for rights to become the sole U.S. distributor of a new high-end sports car. Maxwell believes that the sports car will do well in its market, which encompasses most of the Midwestern United States. Chincotti is in the process of rebranding its image from a staid manufacturer of family sedans to a progressive manufacturer of sleek luxury cars. Chincotti tells Maxwell that in order to receive the exclusive rights to sell Chincotti sports cars, Maxwell must first buy a large shipment of its sedans. Maxwell agrees to the deal and authorizes a Columbus bank to establish a letter of credit, subject to the UCP, in the amount of $20 million in favor of Chincotti for the purchase of 500 sedans. Maxwell then discovers that Chincotti has already given the exclusive U.S. rights to the sports car to a competitor in Indiana. In the meantime, Chincotti has presented conforming documents to the Columbus bank for payment under the letter of credit. Maxwell seeks to enjoin the Columbus bank from paying on the letter of credit on the basis of fraud. In its defense, Chincotti argues:

(1) The parties' agreement to have the letter of credit governed by the UCP results in the complete exclusion of the UCC, including its fraud provision, §5-109. The UCP's silence on the issue of fraud means that in cases where the parties have opted for the UCP and excluded the UCC, the fraud defense is not available at all.

(2) Even if the fraud doctrine applies to this case, the use of fraud as a defense to payment under the letter of credit fails for two reasons: (a) The fraud doctrine, as established in *Sztejn* and codified in the UCC, requires fraud in the letter of credit transaction; fraud in the underlying sales transaction is not sufficient unless the fraud is also manifested in the letter of credit transaction, that is, in a required document. In *Sztejn*, the seller presented fraudulent documents. Here the documents are genuine as they are for the 500 sedans and strictly conform to the requirements of the letter of credit. In cases where there is fraud in the underlying transaction that does not manifest itself in the letter of credit transaction itself, the independence principle insulates the letter of credit from the fraud defense. Maxwell's recourse is to pay the letter of credit and to sue Chincotti directly for breach of contract; and (b) Chincotti's actions did not amount to fraud. This was a simple breach of contract.

How should these issues be decided? *See* UCC §5-109 and *Mid-America Tire* below.

Mid-America Tire, Inc. v. PTZ Trading Ltd.

Supreme Court of Ohio, 2002
95 Ohio St. 3d 367, 768 N.E.2d 619

Resnick, J.

Parties and Participants

Given the multilateral nature of the negotiations and arrangements in this case, it is beneficial to provide a working list of the various parties and key participants and their relationships to one another and the transactions at hand.

The American parties and participants are as follows:

(1) Plaintiff-appellant and cross-appellee, Mid-America Tire, Inc. ("Mid-America"), is an Ohio corporation doing business as a tire wholesaler. Mid-America provided the financing for the purchase of the tires in this case and was the named applicant by whose order and for whose account the LC was issued.

(2) Arthur Hine is the president of Mid-America and signatory to the LC application.

(3) Plaintiff-appellant and cross-appellee, Jenco Marketing, Inc. ("Jenco"), is a Tennessee corporation doing business as a tire wholesaler. Jenco formed a joint venture with Mid-America to purchase the tires at issue.

(4) Fred Alvin "F.A." Jenkins is the owner of Jenco and also acted as Mid-America's agent in the underlying negotiations.

(5) Paul Chappell is an independent tire broker who resides in Irvine, California. Chappell works as an independent contractor for Tire Network, Inc., a company owned by his wife, and acted throughout most of the negotiations as an agent for Jenco.

(6) First National Bank of Chicago ("First National"), on behalf of NBD Bank Michigan, is the issuer of the LC in this case. First National was a defendant below, but is not a party to this appeal.

The European parties and participants are as follows:

(1) Defendant-appellee and cross-appellant, PTZ Trading Ltd. ("PTZ"), is an off-shore import and export company established in Guernsey, Channel Islands. PTZ is the seller in the underlying transaction and the beneficiary under the LC.

(2) Gary Corby is an independent tire broker operating as Corby International, a trading name of Corby Tyres (Wholesale) Ltd., in Wales, United Kingdom. Corby was the initiator of the underlying negotiations. The trial court's findings with regard to Corby's status as PTZ's agent form the subject of PTZ's cross-appeal.

(3) John Evans is the owner of Transcontinental Tyre Company located in Wolverhampton, England, and PTZ's admitted agent in the underlying negotiations.

(4) Aloysius Sievers is a German tire broker to whom PTZ owed money from a previous transaction unconnected to this case. Sievers, also an admitted agent for PTZ, procured and shipped the subject tires on behalf of PTZ, and signed and presented the draft for payment under the LC.

(5) Patrick Doumerc is the son of the proprietor of Doumerc SA, a French company that is authorized to sell Michelin overstock or surplus tires worldwide. Doumerc is the person from whom Sievers procured the mud and snow tires for sale to Jenco and Mid-America.

(6) Barclays Bank PLC in St. Peter Port, Guernsey, is the bank to which Sievers presented the invoice and shipping documents for payment under the supporting LC. Barclays Bank was a defendant below, but is not a party to this appeal.

EVENTS LEADING TO THE ISSUANCE OF THE LC

In October 1998, Corby approached Evans about obtaining large quantities of Michelin winter tires. Evans contacted Sievers, to whom PTZ owed money. Evans knew that Sievers had a relationship with a sole distributor of Michelin surplus tires out of France. Eventually, an arrangement was worked out under which Sievers would buy the tires from Doumerc's warehouse in France and Evans would sell them on behalf of PTZ through Corby to an American purchaser.

Meanwhile, Corby contacted Chappell in California and asked whether he was interested in importing Michelin tires on the gray market for sale in the United States. "Gray imports" are tires that are imported without the knowledge or approval of a manufacturer into a market that the manufacturer serves, at a greatly reduced price. Corby told Chappell that he had a large client who negotiated an arrangement directly with Michelin to handle all of its overstock blem tires from France and who could offer 50,000 to 70,000 Michelin tires per quarter at 40 to 60 percent below the United States market price on an exclusive and ongoing basis. Chappell contacted Jenkins in Tennessee, who called Hine in Ohio, and it was arranged that Jenco and Mid-America would pursue the deal through Chappell.

On October 28, 1998, Corby faxed Chappell a list of Michelin mud and snow tires that were immediately available for shipment and Chappell forwarded the list to Jenkins. The list was arranged in columns for quantity, size, pattern, and other designations applicable to the European market with which Chappell and Jenkins were unfamiliar. In particular, many of the tires on the list bore the designation "DA/2C." Chappell and Jenkins understood that DA meant "defective appearance," a European marking for a blem, but they were not familiar with the "/2C" portion of the designation. When they asked for clarification, Corby told Chappell that "DA/2C" means the same thing as "DA," but since all of the listed tires are not warehoused at a single location, "/2C" is used merely to indicate that those blemished tires are located in a different warehouse.

Chappell also asked Corby whether he could procure and offer summer or "highway" tires, along with the winter tires. Chappell, Jenkins, and Hine had no interest in purchasing strictly snow tires, as it was already too late in the season to market them profitably. However, they would have an interest in buying both winter and highway tires and marketing them together as a package deal.

Corby told Chappell that 50,000 to 70,000 highway tires would be made available on a quarterly basis at 40 to 60 percent below the United States market price. However, when Chappell received another list of available tires from Corby on November 11, 1998, he complained to Corby that this list contained no summer tires and nowhere near 50,000 units. Corby responded that Michelin was anxious to get rid of these tires first, as the market for snow tires in Europe was coming to a close, that a list of summer highway tires would be made available over the next few weeks, and that Chappell and appellants would not have an opportunity to procure the highway tires unless they first agreed to purchase the snow tires. Corby explained that Michelin does not list available summer tires in the mid-month of a quarter. Instead, it waits for these tires to accumulate in a warehouse and then puts out the list at the end of the month. Thus, a list of summer tires would be available over the next few weeks.

[On November 13, 20, and 23, Corby sent various faxes with information about Michelin summer or highway tires in the 50,000-70,000 quantity range but none of the faxes contained complete information on the availability or prices of the summer tires. On numerous occasions in December and January 1999 Corby continued to press Chappell and Jenkins on issuing a letter of credit for the winter tires, sometimes making repeated daily phone calls to Chappell.]

THE ISSUANCE OF THE LC

By the end of January 1999, Jenkins and Hine were convinced that they had to open the LC for the winter tires as a show of good faith towards the quarterly acquisition of summer tires and that, upon doing so, PTZ would honor its end of the bargain.

Effective February 1, 1999, and expiring in Guernsey, Channel Islands, on April 2, 1999, First National issued an irrevocable credit at Hine's request in favor of PTZ and for the account of Mid-America in the amount of $517,260.33. The LC provided, among other things:

"COVERING SHIPMENT OF:

"14,851 MICHELIN TYPES AT USD 34.83 PER TIRE IN ACCORDANCE WITH SELLER'S PROFORMA INVOICE 927-98 DATED 11-19-98

"SHIPPING TERMS: EXWORKS ANY EUROPEAN LOCATION

"THE CREDIT IS SUBJECT TO THE UNIFORM CUSTOMS AND PRACTICE FOR DOCUMENTARY CREDITS (1993 REVISION), INTERNATIONAL CHAMBER OF COMMERCE -PUBLICATION 500."

EVENTS FOLLOWING THE ISSUANCE OF THE LC

[Following the issuance of the letter of credit Corby and Evans wanted to make shipping arrangements for the winter tires in order to receive payment under the letter of credit but Chappell and Jenkins continued to insist on a complete list for the summer tires. Chappell and Jenkins had to authorize Corby and Evans to ship the winter tires or else Corby and Evans would be unable to ship them and receive payment under the letter of credit. Corby again sent several incomplete lists and Chappell and Jenkins became increasingly frustrated until they decided to withdraw their offer on March 1, 1999. Between March 1 and March 5, 1999, Chappell and Jenkins discovered that it was Doumerc, not PTZ, who all along had the direct and exclusive relationship with Michelin to sell its overstock and blemished tires. Chappell also discovered that Corby had misrepresented the "DA/2C" designation. The "/2C" designated meant that the Department of Transportation serial numbers had been buffed off from these units so the tires could not be legally imported or sold in the United States. Chappell and Jenkins made plans to travel to France to meet Doumerc to inspect the Michelin tires but while trying to phone Doumerc, Sievers answered the phone. Sievers, to whom PTZ owed money, did not care what Doumerc had agreed to and said that "I have a letter of credit and I am shipping the tires." Mid-America then instituted an action to enjoin payment under the letter of credit. The trial court issued a temporary restraining order on March 16, 1999 and a preliminary injunction. On October 8, 1999, after a trial, the trial court issued a permanent injunction enjoining payment on the letter of credit. On appeal, the court of appeals reversed, holding that the UCP 500, not the Ohio Revised Code 1305.08(B) dealing with fraud,[4] governed the transaction and that under the UCP there was no exception for fraud to the independence principle. The court of appeals also held under former UCC §5-114, which provided for an exception to the independence principle where "there is fraud in the transaction," the fraud must be in the letter of credit transaction — that is, the letter of credit documents must be forged —

---

4. Authors' Note: Ohio Revised Code Chapter 1305 is Ohio's version of Article 5 of the Uniform Commercial Code. R.C. 1305.08(B) provides:

If an applicant claims that a required document is forged or materially fraudulent or that honor of the presentation would facilitate a material fraud by the beneficiary on the issuer or applicant, a court of competent jurisdiction may temporarily or permanently enjoin the issuer from honoring a presentation.

This provision is substantially equivalent to UCC §5-109(b).

but not in the underlying transaction involving the sales contract. The Supreme Court of Ohio found that the appeal presented the following issues:]

ISSUES FOR REVIEW

The issue generally presented by both appeals is whether the trial court abused its discretion in granting a permanent injunction against LC honor under the facts and circumstances of this case.

The specific questions that arise under the appeal brought by Mid-America and Jenco are as follows:

[1] With regard to the availability and scope of a fraud exception to the independence principle, is the LC in this case governed by the UCP or R.C. 1305.08(B)?

[2] Under the governing law, is there any fraud exception to the independence principle beyond the situation involving the beneficiary's presentation of forged or fraudulent documents? In particular, does the governing law recognize an exception for fraud in the inducement of the underlying contract and the supporting LC?

[3] Are the trial court's factual findings sufficient to support the application of a recognized exception to the independence principle?

GOVERNING LAW

R.C. Chapter 1305 is Ohio's version of Article 5 of the Uniform Commercial Code ("UCC"). It was enacted in its current form, effective July 1, 1998, to reflect the 1995 revision of Article 5, and is applicable to any LC that is issued on or after its effective date.

The court of appeals found essentially that the UCP's silence on the issue of fraud precludes the applicant from obtaining relief under R.C. 1305.08(B). We disagree.

In adopting the UCP, "the International Chamber of Commerce undertook to fill in operational details for documentary letter of credit transactions by stating a consensus view of the customs and practice for documentary credits." Because "the UCP 'is by definition a recording of practice rather than a statement of legal rules,' [it] does not purport to offer rules which govern the issuance of an injunction against honor of a draft." Thus, the UCP's silence on the issue of fraud "should not be construed as *preventing* relief under the 'fraud in the transaction' doctrine, where applicable law permits it."

In fact, the overwhelming weight of authority is to the effect that Article 5's fraud exception continues to apply in credit transactions made subject to the UCP. These courts hold, in one form or another, that the UCP's failure to include a rule governing injunctive relief for fraud does not prevent the applicant from obtaining such relief under Article 5. Stated variously, these courts recognize that there is no inherent conflict between the UCP's statement of the independence principle and Article 5's remedy against honor where fraud is charged. Instead, this is merely a situation where Article 5 covers a subject not covered by the UCP.

We hold, therefore, that when a letter of credit expressly incorporates the terms of the UCP, but the UCP does not contain any rule covering the issue in controversy, the UCP will not replace the relevant provisions of R.C. Chapter 1305.

Accordingly, the rights and obligations of the parties in this case are governed by R.C. 1305.08(B), and the judgment of the court of appeals is reversed as to this issue.

ESTABLISHING FRAUD UNDER R.C. 1305.08(B)

Having determined the applicability of R.C. 1305.08(B), we must now consider its boundaries. In this regard, we have been asked to decide whether an issuer may be enjoined from honoring a presentation on the basis of beneficiary's fraud in the underlying transaction and to characterize the fraudulent activity justifying such relief.

FRAUD IN THE UNDERLYING TRANSACTION

May the issuer be enjoined from honoring a presentation under R.C. 1305.08(B) on the basis of the beneficiary's fraudulent activity in the underlying transaction? The short answer is yes, since R.C. 1305.08(B) authorizes injunctive relief where "honor of the presentation would facilitate a material fraud by the beneficiary on the applicant." To fully appreciate the import of this language, however, it is necessary to review some of the history leading to its adoption.

As originally drafted in 1955, UCC 5-114 provided that a court of appropriate jurisdiction may enjoin honor only if there was forgery or fraud in a required document. In 1957, the drafters added language providing that the court may enjoin such honor where "a required document is forged or fraudulent *or there is fraud in the transaction*." (Emphasis added.) UCC 5-114(2).

One of the major disputes surrounding former UCC 5-114(2) centered on whether the "transaction" meant only the credit transaction per se or encompassed the underlying transaction as well.

R.C. 1305.08(B) (UCC 5-109(b)) now provides that a court of competent jurisdiction may grant injunctive relief where "honor of the presentation would facilitate a material fraud by the beneficiary on the issuer or applicant." In so doing, R.C. 1305.08(B) refocuses the court's attention away from the particular transaction in which the fraud occurred and toward the level of fraud committed. It clarifies that the beneficiary's fraud in either transaction will suffice to enjoin the issuer from honoring a presentation, provided the fraud is material.

We hold, therefore, that material fraud committed by the beneficiary in either the letter of credit transaction or the underlying sales transaction is sufficient to warrant injunctive relief under R.C. 1305.08(B). Accordingly, the judgment of the court of appeals is reversed as to this issue.

MEASURE OF FRAUD

Another controversy that surrounded the "fraud in the transaction" language of UCC 5-114(2) involved the degree or quantity of fraud necessary to warrant injunctive relief. However, UCC 5-109(b) (R.C. 1305.08(B) clarifies that only "material fraud" by the beneficiary will justify an injunction against honor.

As another court adhering to this standard explained, the applicant must show that the letter of credit was, in fact, being used by the beneficiary "as a vehicle for fraud," or in other words, that the beneficiary's conduct, if rewarded by payment, "would deprive the [applicant] of any benefit of the underlying contract and transform the letter of credit into a means for perpetrating fraud." *GATX Leasing Corp.*, 657 S.W.2d at 183.

Thus, we hold that "material fraud" under R.C. 1305.08(B) means fraud that has so vitiated the entire transaction that the legitimate purposes of the independence of the issuer's obligation can no longer be served.

The court of appeals did establish its so-called "vitiation exception," but construed the exception so narrowly as to preclude relief where the beneficiary's fraudulent conduct occurs solely in the underlying transaction. As a consequence, the court of appeals declined to address the issues of agency and fraud in the underlying contract, holding instead that the trial court should not even have taken evidence on these issues.

Accordingly, the judgment of the court of appeals is reversed on this issue as well.

PTZ's Actions

The trial court found the following facts to have been established by clear and convincing evidence:

"12. The Court finds, specifically, that the representation that PTZ had a direct relationship with Michelin Tire, the representation that PTZ was the exclusive distributor for surplus Michelin Tires, the representation that a substantial quantity of between fifty and seventy thousand tires would be available quarterly on an exclusive basis to Jenco and Mid America Tire, Inc. at 40 to 60 percent of the U.S. market price were all material statements inducing Plaintiffs to issue the underlying letter of credit and were in fact false and made with knowledge of their falsity."

Whether or not this court would have made the same factual findings is irrelevant. This court does not resolve questions of fact. We are constrained to accept these facts as established because the trial court sat as factfinder in this case and because the record contains ample evidence to support them.

Given these facts, we are compelled to conclude that PTZ's actions in this case are sufficiently egregious to warrant injunctive relief under the "material fraud" standard of R.C. 1305.08(B). Keenly aware that appellants would not agree to purchase the winter tires without the summer tires, PTZ made, participated in, and/or failed to correct a series of materially fraudulent promises and representations regarding the more lucrative summer tires in order to induce appellants to commit to purchasing the winter tires and to open an LC in PTZ's favor to secure payment. Dangling the prospect of the summer tires just beyond appellants' reach, PTZ sought first the issuance of the LC, and then shipping instructions, in an effort to cash in on the winter deal before appellants could discover the truth about the "DA/2C" tires and PTZ's lack of ability and intention ever to provide summer tires at the price and quantity represented.

Under these facts, it can truly be said that the LC in this case was being used by PTZ as a vehicle for fraud and that PTZ's actions effectively deprived appellants of any benefit in the underlying arrangement. PTZ's demand for payment under these circumstances has absolutely no basis in fact, and it would be pointless and unjust to permit PTZ to draw the money. PTZ's conduct has so vitiated the entire transaction that the only purpose served by invoking the independence principle in this case would be to transform the LC into a fraudulent seller's Holy Grail, which once obtained would provide cover for fraudulent business practices in the name of commercial expedience.

Based on all of the foregoing, the judgment of the court of appeals is hereby reversed, and the permanent injunction as granted by the trial court is reinstated.

NOTES AND QUESTIONS

1. As the Ohio Supreme Court noted, a prior version of UCC §5-109—the former §5-114—referred to "fraud in the transaction" giving rise to a long debate on whether the "transaction" was limited to the letter of credit transaction or also encompassed the underlying sales transaction. *American Bell International, Inc. v. Islamic Republic of Iran*, 474 F. Supp. 420 (S.D.N.Y. 1979), which we include in the materials on standby letters of credit in the following section, gives an indication of the many authorities arrayed on both sides of this issue under former §5-114. Proponents of either view could point to *Sztejn* for support as there was fraud in both transactions in that case: The seller committed fraud in the letter of credit transaction by submitting forged documents to the bank and also committed fraud in the sales contract by shipping worthless merchandise and rubbish instead of the contracted-for goods. If the "transaction" in former UCC §5-114 referred only to the letter of credit transaction, then it would appear that the UCC codification of fraud as a defense to payment under the credit is unnecessary as fraud is an equitable defense that should have been available to the issuing bank in any event with or without codification in the Uniform Commercial Code. Moreover, a narrow fraud doctrine that is limited to fraud in the letter of credit transaction would not constitute an exception to the independence principle. Can you see why?

2. What clarification does UCC §5-109 provide on whether fraud must be in the letter of credit or underlying sales transaction?

3. *Mid-America Tire* also, in our view, correctly states the relationship between the UCP 600 and the UCC. Where the parties have opted for the UCP, the UCC may still apply on issues where the UCP is silent. Fraud is one major area where the UCP is silent and thus the parties must look to another source of substantive law, but it is not the only issue that is not covered by the UCP. The Ohio Supreme Court appears to have assumed that Ohio law would govern these other issues as well but that may not always be the case. Can you see why? If you were advising a U.S. buyer on how to ensure that the UCC would govern in all areas in which the UCP is silent, what measures would you suggest?

4. Courts continue to apply UCC §5-109 in international letter of credit cases. *See, e.g., Banco Nacional de Mexico S.A. v. Societe Generale*, 820 N.Y.S.2d 588 (N.Y. App. Div. 2006) (refusing to accept French issuing bank's argument that Mexican confirming bank should be enjoined from paying on letter of credit on the basis of fraud under UCC §5-109).

5. *Enjoining the Standby Letter of Credit*

We turn now to the standby letter of credit. As most of the U.S. cases involving standby letters of credit occur in the context of an attempt to enjoin payment under the credit based on fraud under UCC §5-109 (and its predecessor), we treat the standby letter along with the materials that we have already introduced on these topics.

A. THE STANDBY LETTER OF CREDIT

Unlike the commercial letter of credit, which is a method used by the buyer to pay the seller under a contract for the sale of goods, the standby letter of credit is generally used to secure the performance by the seller of its obligations under the sales contract for the benefit of the buyer. In the cases that we examine below, the sales contract is typically a long-term contract for equipment and consulting services. The buyer is relying on the seller to perform a contract that will take several years to complete so the buyer is at risk that the seller will be unable or unwilling to complete the contract. Not only has the

FIGURE 4-1

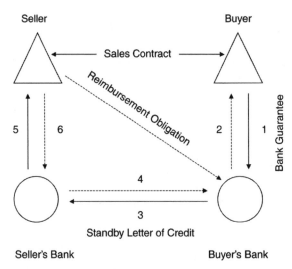

buyer lost a great deal of time in relying on the seller and now must find a substitute seller but the subject matter of the contract may involve an essential service or product that the buyer needs urgently. In order to protect itself from the risk of nonperformance by the seller, the buyer requires the following arrangement to secure performance: The seller must establish a standby letter of credit in favor of the buyer that is payable upon the submission of a pro forma declaration by the buyer that the seller has failed to perform the contract. The seller goes to its own bank, usually located in the seller's jurisdiction, to issue the standby letter of credit in favor of the buyer. However, the buyer might not trust the seller's bank so the buyer may insist upon obtaining an obligation from its own bank to pay upon presentation of documents. The buyer's bank stands in a position analogous to that of a confirming bank in a documentary letter of credit. Once the buyer's bank pays the buyer, the bank then forwards the documents to the seller's bank for payment under the standby letter of credit. To distinguish the obligation of the buyer's bank from that of the standby letter of credit, we refer to the commitment of the buyer's bank as a bank guarantee.

Payment under the standby letter of credit occurs as follows:

(1) Buyer submits a pro forma declaration and a demand for payment (such as a sight draft) to Buyer's Bank;
(2) Buyer's Bank pays Buyer upon the Bank Guarantee;
(3) Buyer's Bank forwards the documents and a demand for reimbursement to Seller's bank;
(4) Seller's Bank reimburses Buyer's Bank under the Standby Letter of Credit;
(5) Seller's Bank forwards the documents to Seller;
(6) Seller reimburses Seller's Bank.

Compare payment under the commercial letter of credit on p. 64 where the payment obligations run in the reverse direction. There are several other notable differences between the standby letter of credit and the commercial letter of credit.

First, while the commercial letter of credit is payable upon performance of the sales contract, the standby letter is payable upon some nonperformance. For this reason, the standby letter has been called the "psychological opposite" of the commercial credit. *See* Henry Harfield, *The Increasing Domestic Use of the Letter of Credit*, 4 U.C.C. L.J. 251, 258 (1972). Whereas the applicant-buyer of the commercial letter of credit wishes to see the credit paid as this would represent successful completion of the transaction, the applicant-seller of the standby letter does not wish for the standby letter to be paid for this would signal some failure of the transaction. The seller under the standby letter of credit is also more likely to oppose payment by way of injunctive relief.

Second, in a commercial letter of credit, the documents submitted for payment will often include documents issued by third parties, such as the negotiable bill of lading. These documents provide some indicia that the goods have been shipped and that the underlying contract has been performed. A standby letter of credit will typically call for the submission only of a pro forma declaration by the buyer that the seller has breached the underlying contract. As the independence principle applies to standby and commercial letters of credit alike, the bank is under no duty to investigate the underlying facts to determine whether in fact the seller has breached. Rather, as the strict compliance principle applies to the standby letter of credit as well, the bank is required only to determine whether the declaration complies on its face with the terms of the credit. For this reason, the documentary requirement in a standby letter of credit does not provide much of a safeguard against an undeserving beneficiary. At the most, the requirement of a pro forma declaration may prevent an obvious forgery.

Third, issuers are exposed to greater risks in the case of standby letters because the documents required for payment are not documents of title. In the case of a commercial letter of credit, in the event that the banks are unable to receive reimbursement for payment under the credit, the banks can recover possession of the goods through presentation of the negotiable bill of lading and then sell the goods to recoup their losses. Banks that pay under a standby letter of credit or a bank guarantee do not have a security interest in the goods to protect their interest. Banks must rely solely on the credit of the applicant (or in the case of a confirming bank on the credit of the issuing bank) and for this reason, banks have an incentive to conduct a full credit evaluation of the customer.

B.   SOURCES OF LAW FOR THE STANDBY LETTER OF CREDIT

As we previously noted, standby letters of credit are also subject to UCC Article 5 and the UCP 600 to the extent applicable. In addition, there are several other possible sources of law: The United Nations Convention on Independent Guarantees and Standby Letters of Credit (G.A. Res. 50/48, U.N. Doc. A/RES/50/48 (Jan. 26, 1996)); the Uniform Rules for Demand Guarantees (URDG) (I.C.C. Pub. No. 758E, 2010); and the International Standby Practices (ISP98) (I.C.C. Pub. No. 590, 1998).

The United States is a signatory to the UN Convention on Independent Guarantees and Standby Letters of Credit, but it does not have legally binding effect because the United States has not yet ratified the convention. *See http://www.uncitral.org/uncitral/en/ uncitral_texts/payments/1995Convention_guarantees_status.html.* The UN Convention is in force only for a handful of contracting states. Like many other UN conventions in the area of private law, the parties are allowed to opt out of the convention in favor of some other source of law.

The URDG was promulgated by the International Chamber of Commerce to provide guidance on all forms of bank guarantees, which include standby letters of credit. The ICC decided that special rules were needed for standby letters of credit and promulgated the ISP in 1998. At present, the ICC intends the UCP 600 to apply primarily to commercial letters of credit and to standby letters of credit to the extent applicable, the URDG to apply to all forms of bank guarantees, and the ISP to apply specifically to standby letters of credit. As we have earlier noted, the ICC rules and practices are not laws but become legally effective through incorporation by contract. The three separate sets of ICC rules are available for incorporation by parties to govern the three principal forms of primary obligor or independent issuer undertakings that are in current use in the banking industry.

NOTES AND QUESTIONS

1. While the standby letter of credit is used to guarantee some performance by the seller, it should be distinguished from a similar device such as a surety contract or performance bond, which serves a similar function but involves higher costs and is usually payable only after a factual determination of default rather than upon an examination of documents. In the case of a surety contract guaranteeing performance by the seller, the surety usually undertakes to complete the performance of the seller (by hiring a third party to complete the seller's contract) but the surety will first need to make a factual determination whether the seller has defaulted. Performance bonds also require a factual investigation into the nonperformance of the contract before payment, which can involve a lengthy investigation. The advantage of the standby letter is that it is inexpensive and efficient as payment is based on an examination of the documents alone, not on a breach of the underlying sales contract.

2. While the standby letter of credit may have the advantage of efficiency, it also carries higher risk for the issuer and the seller than a performance bond or surety contract. The standby letter of credit is often referred to as a "suicide" credit because the buyer often has to do nothing more than submit a declaration that the seller has breached the contract. Establishing a surety contract or performance bond would entail higher costs for the parties but would afford the seller greater protection against the possibility of a baseless demand for payment by the beneficiary. The risks associated with the standby or suicide letter of credit, however, have not diminished their popularity. Why are sellers willing to assume such risks?

The following is an example of an actual standby letter of credit. The credit is similar to the credit described in Figure 4-1 except that it does not involve a guarantee by a local bank:

"TO: THE PRESIDENT OF INDIA
India
BY ORDER OF: ELECTRONICS SYSTEMS DIVISION OF DYNAMICS CORPORATION OF AMERICA
For account of same
GENTLEMEN:
WE HEREBY ESTABLISH OUR IRREVOCABLE CREDIT IN YOUR FAVOR, FOR THE ACCOUNT INDICATED ABOVE, FOR A SUM OR SUMS NOT EXCEEDING IN ALL FOUR HUNDRED TEN THOUSAND FOUR HUNDRED SEVENTY TWO AND 60/100 US DOLLARS (US$410,472.60)- AVAILABLE BY YOUR DRAFT(S) AT sight,
DRAWN ON: us
Which must be accompanied by:
1. Your signed certification as follows: The President of India being one of the parties to the Agreement dated March 14, 1971 signed and exchanged between The President of India and the Dynamics Corporation of America for the license to manufacture, purchase and supply of radio equipment as per Schedule I thereof for the total contract value of $1,368,242.00, does hereby certify in the exercise of reasonable discretion and in good faith that the Dynamics Corporation of America has failed to carry out certain obligations of theirs under the said Order/Agreement."

Dynamics Corporation of America v. Citizens and Southern National Bank, 356 F. Supp. 991, 994 (N.D. Ga. 1973).

The buyer-beneficiary in *Dynamics* and in the cases set forth below were foreign sovereign governments and the sums involved in the underlying contracts and letters of credit were very large. What does this suggest to you about the bargaining power of the parties and why sellers would agree to accept the risks of a standby letter of credit?

PROBLEM 4-13

World Telecom (WT), a U.S.-based multinational enterprise, enters into a contract with the National Television and Radio Ministry (NTRM) of a South American country to supply consulting services and telecommunications equipment. Under the terms of the contract, WT would receive $80 million over three years during the performance of the contract. As required by the contract, NTRM paid WT an advance payment of $10 million. The contract also provided that NTRM would be entitled to return of the $10 million plus an additional $40 million representing NTRM's damages if WT failed to perform the contract. The $50 million in total payments to NTRM were secured by a standby letter of credit issued by Chase Manhattan Bank in New York City naming NTRM as the beneficiary. The terms of the standby letter of credit called for the submission of a declaration by the director of the NTRM that "World Telecom has breached its contract with NTRM." Three months later, a radical group overthrows the reigning government and has now established a new Revolutionary People's Government. Chase Manhattan Bank notifies WT that it has received a declaration from the director of the People's Telecommunications Ministry, the renamed NTRM, that "World Telecom has breached its contract with the People's Telecommunications Ministry" and a sight draft for $50 million.

WT argues:

(1) The beneficiary of the standby letter of credit is NTRM. Only NTRM is allowed to draw on the letter of credit because it is non-assignable and non-transferable. As events have occurred that have caused NTRM to cease to exist, the letter of credit is terminated as a matter of force majeure or impossibility.

(2) The documents fail to satisfy the terms of the credit under the strict compliance principle as the credit calls for documents from NTRM and the submitted documents are from the People's Telecommunications Ministry.

(3) If the People's Telecommunications Ministry were to resubmit a declaration and demand for payment under the NTRM name, this would be a document that is "forged or materially fraudulent" within the meaning of UCC §5-109(a) and would be sufficient to constitute a fraud that prevents payment under the letter of credit.

How should each of these claims be resolved? See *American Bell* and *Harris* below.

American Bell International, Inc. v. Islamic Republic of Iran

United States District Court, Southern District of New York, 1979
474 F. Supp. 420

MacMahon, District Judge.

Plaintiff American Bell International Inc. ("Bell") moves for a preliminary injunction pursuant to Rule 65(a), Fed. R. Civ. P. enjoining defendant Manufacturers Hanover

Trust Company ("Manufacturers") from making any payment under its Letter of Credit No. SC 170027 to defendants the Islamic Republic of Iran or Bank Iranshahr.

The action arises from the recent revolution in Iran and its impact upon contracts made with the ousted Imperial Government of Iran and upon banking arrangements incident to such contracts. Bell, a wholly-owned subsidiary of American Telephone & Telegraph Co. ("AT & T"), made a contract on July 23, 1978 (the "Contract") with the Imperial Government of Iran Ministry of War ("Imperial Government") to provide consulting services and equipment to the Imperial Government as part of a program to improve Iran's international communications system.

The Contract provides a complex mechanism for payment to Bell totaling approximately $280,000,000, including a down payment of $38,800,000. The Imperial Government had the right to demand return of the down payment at any time. The amount so callable, however, was to be reduced by 20% of the amounts invoiced by Bell to which the Imperial Government did not object. Bell's liability for return of the down payment was reduced by application of this mechanism as the Contract was performed, with the result that approximately $30,200,000 of the down payment now remains callable.

In order to secure the return of the down payment on demand, Bell was required to establish an unconditional and irrevocable Letter of Guaranty, to be issued by Bank Iranshahr in the amount of $38,800,000 in favor of the Imperial Government. The Contract provides that it is to be governed by the laws of Iran and that all disputes arising under it are to be resolved by the Iranian courts.

Bell obtained a Letter of Guaranty from Bank Iranshahr. In turn, as required by Bank Iranshahr, Bell obtained a standby Letter of Credit, No. SC 170027, issued by Manufacturers in favor of Bank Iranshahr in the amount of $38,800,000 to secure reimbursement to Bank Iranshahr should it be required to pay the Imperial Government under its Letter of Guaranty.

The standby Letter of Credit provided for payment by Manufacturers to Bank Iranshahr upon receipt of:

> "Your (Bank Iranshahr's) dated statement purportedly signed by an officer indicating name and title or your Tested Telex Reading: (A) 'Referring Manufacturers Hanover Trust Co. Credit No. SC170027, the amount of our claim $ _____ represents funds due us as we have received a written request from the Imperial Government of Iran Ministry of War to pay them the sum of _____ under our Guarantee No. _____ issued for the account of American Bell International Inc. covering advance payment under Contract No. 138 dated July 23, 1978 and such payment has been made by us.'"

In the application for the Letter of Credit, Bell agreed — guaranteed by AT&T — immediately to reimburse Manufacturers for all amounts paid by Manufacturers to Bank Iranshahr pursuant to the Letter of Credit.

Bell commenced performance of its Contract with the Imperial Government. It provided certain services and equipment to update Iran's communications system and submitted a number of invoices, some of which were paid.

In late 1978 and early 1979, Iran was wreaked with revolutionary turmoil culminating in the overthrow of the Iranian government and its replacement by the Islamic Republic. In the wake of this upheaval, Bell was left with substantial unpaid invoices and claims under the Contract and ceased its performance in January 1979. Bell claims that the Contract was breached by the Imperial Government, as well as repudiated by the Islamic Republic, in that it is owed substantial sums for services rendered under the Contract and its termination provisions.

On July 25 and 29, 1979, Manufacturers received demands by Tested Telex from Bank Iranshahr for payment of $30,220,724 under the Letter of Credit, the remaining balance of the down payment. Asserting that the demand did not conform with the Letter of Credit, Manufacturers declined payment and so informed Bank Iranshahr. Informed of this, Bell responded by filing this action and an application by way of order to show cause for a temporary restraining order bringing on this motion for a preliminary injunction. Following argument, we granted a temporary restraining order on July 29 enjoining Manufacturers from making any payment to Bank Iranshahr until forty-eight hours after Manufacturers notified Bell of the receipt of a conforming demand, and this order has been extended pending decision of this motion.

On August 1, 1979, Manufacturers notified Bell that it had received a conforming demand from Bank Iranshahr. At the request of the parties, the court held an evidentiary hearing on August 3 on this motion for a preliminary injunction.

CRITERIA FOR PRELIMINARY INJUNCTIONS

The current criteria in this circuit for determining whether to grant the extraordinary remedy of a preliminary injunction are:

"(T)here must be a showing of possible irreparable injury And either (1) probable success on the merits or (2) sufficiently serious questions going to the merits to make them a fair ground for litigation And a balance of hardships tipping decidedly toward the party requesting the preliminary relief."

We are not persuaded that the plaintiff has met the criteria and therefore deny the motion.

A. IRREPARABLE INJURY

Plaintiff has failed to show that irreparable injury may possibly ensue if a preliminary injunction is denied. Bell does not even claim, much less show, that it lacks an adequate remedy at law if Manufacturers makes a payment to Bank Iranshahr in violation of the Letter of Credit. It is too clear for argument that a suit for money damages could be based on any such violation, and surely Manufacturers would be able to pay any money judgment against it.

Bell falls back on a contention that it is without any effective remedy unless it can restrain payment. This contention is based on the fact that it agreed to be bound by the laws of Iran and to submit resolution of any disputes under the Contract to the courts of Iran. Bell claims that it now has no meaningful access to those courts.

There is credible evidence that the Islamic Republic is xenophobic and anti-American and that it has no regard for consulting service contracts such as the one here. Although Bell has made no effort to invoke the aid of the Iranian courts, we think the current situation in Iran, as shown by the evidence, warrants the conclusion that an attempt by Bell to resort to those courts would be futile. However, Bell has not demonstrated that it is without adequate remedy in this court against the Iranian defendants under the Sovereign Immunity Act which it invokes in this very case.

Accordingly, we conclude that Bell has failed to demonstrate irreparable injury.

B. PROBABLE SUCCESS ON THE MERITS

Even assuming that plaintiff has shown possible irreparable injury, it has failed to show probable success on the merits.

In order to succeed on the merits, Bell must prove, by a preponderance of the evidence, that either (1) a demand for payment of the Manufacturers Letter of Credit conforming to the terms of that Letter has not yet been made or (2) a demand, even though in conformity, should not be honored because of fraud in the transaction. It is not probable, in the sense of a greater than 50% likelihood, that Bell will be able to prove either nonconformity or fraud.

As to nonconformity, the August 1 demand by Bank Iranshahr is identical to the terms of the Manufacturers Letter of Credit in every respect except one: it names as payee the "Government of Iran Ministry of Defense, Successor to the Imperial Government of Iran Ministry of War" rather than the "Imperial Government of Iran Ministry of War." It is, of course, a bedrock principle of letter of credit law that a demand must strictly comply with the letter in order to justify payment. Nevertheless, we deem it less than probable that a court, upon a full trial, would find nonconformity in the instant case.

At the outset, we notice, and the parties agree, that the United States now recognizes the present Government of Iran as the legal successor to the Imperial Government of Iran. That recognition is binding on American Courts. Though we may decide for ourselves the consequences of such recognition upon the litigants in this case, we point out that American courts have traditionally viewed contract rights as vesting not in any particular government but in the state of which that government is an agent.

Accordingly, the Government of Iran is the successor to the Imperial Government under the Letter of Guaranty. As legal successor, the Government of Iran may properly demand payment even though the terms of the Letter of Guaranty only provide for payment to the Government of Iran's predecessor and a demand for payment under the Letter of Credit reciting that payment has been made by Bank Iranshahr to the new government is sufficient.

Finally, an opposite answer to the narrow question of conformity would not only elevate form over substance, but would render financial arrangements and undertakings worldwide wholly subject to the vicissitudes of political power. A nonviolent, unanimous transformation of the form of government, or, as this case shows, the mere change of the name of a government agency, would be enough to warrant an issuer's refusal to honor a demand. We cannot suppose such uncertainty and opportunity for chicanery to be the purpose of the requirement of strict conformity.

If conformity is established, as here, the issuer of an irrevocable, unconditional letter of credit, such as Manufacturers normally has an absolute duty to transfer the requisite funds. This duty is wholly independent of the underlying contractual relationship that gives rise to the letter of credit. Nevertheless, both the Uniform Commercial Code of New York, which the parties concede governs here, and the courts state that payment is enjoinable where a germane document is forged or fraudulent or there is "fraud in the transaction." Bell does not contend that any documents are fraudulent by virtue of misstatements or omissions. Instead, it argues there is "fraud in the transaction."

The parties disagree over the scope to be given as a matter of law to the term "transaction." Manufacturers, citing voluminous authorities, argues that the term refers only to the Letter of Credit transaction, not to the underlying commercial transaction or to the totality of dealings among the banks, the Iranian government and Bell. On this view of the law, Bell must fail to establish a probability of success, for it does not claim that the Imperial Government or Bank Iranshahr induced Manufacturers to extend the Letter by lies or half-truths, that the Letter contained any false representations by the Imperial Government or Bank Iranshahr, or that they intended misdeeds with it. Nor does Bell claim that the demand contains any misstatements.

Bell argues, citing equally voluminous authorities, that the term "transaction" refers to the totality of circumstances. On this view, Bell has some chance of success on the merits, for a court can consider Bell's allegations that the Government of Iran's behavior in connection with the consulting contract suffices to make its demand on the Letter of Guaranty fraudulent and that the ensuing demand on the Letter of Credit by Bank Iranshahr is tainted with the fraud.

There is some question whether these divergent understandings of the law are wholly incompatible since it would seem impossible to keep the Letter of Credit transaction conceptually distinct. A demand which facially conforms to the Letter of Credit and which contains no misstatements may, nevertheless, be considered fraudulent if made with the goal of mulcting the party who caused the Letter of Credit to be issued. Be that as it may, we need not decide this thorny issue of law. For, even on the construction most favorable to Bell, we find that success on the merits is not probable. Many of the facts alleged, even if proven, would not constitute fraud. As to others, the proof is insufficient to indicate a probability of success on the merits.

Bell sets forth five contentions which, in its view, support the issuance of an injunction. Bell asserts that (1) both the old and new Governments failed to approve invoices for services fully performed; (2) both failed to fund contracted-for independent Letters of Credit in Bell's favor; (3) the new Government has taken steps to renounce altogether its obligations under the Contract; (4) the new Government has made it impossible to assert contract rights in Iranian courts; and (5) the new Government has caused Bank Iranshahr to demand payment on the Manufacturers Letter of Credit, thus asserting rights in a transaction it has otherwise repudiated.

As to contention (4), it is not immediately apparent how denial of Bell's opportunity to assert rights under the Contract makes a demand on an independent letter of credit fraudulent.

Contentions (1), (2), (3) and the latter part of (5) all state essentially the same proposition that the Government of Iran is currently repudiating all its contractual obligations with American companies, including those with Bell. Again, the evidence on this point is uncompelling.

Bell points to (1) an intragovernmental order of July 2, 1979 ordering the termination of Iran's contract with Bell, and (2) hearsay discussions between Bell's president and Iranian officials to the effect that Iran would not pay on the Contract until it had determined whether the services under it had benefited the country. Manufacturers, for its part, points to a public statement in the Wall Street Journal of July 16, 1979, under the name of the present Iranian Government, to the effect that Iran intends to honor all legitimate contracts. Taken together, this evidence does not suggest that Iran has finally and irrevocably decided to repudiate the Bell contract. It suggests equally that Iran is still considering the question whether to perform that contract.

Even if we accept the proposition that the evidence does show repudiation, plaintiff is still far from demonstrating the kind of evil intent necessary to support a claim of fraud. Surely, plaintiff cannot contend that every party who breaches or repudiates his contract is for that reason culpable of fraud. The law of contract damages is adequate to repay the economic harm caused by repudiation, and the law presumes that one who repudiates has done so because of a calculation that such damages are cheaper than performance. Absent any showing that Iran would refuse to pay damages upon a contract action here or in Iran, much less a showing that Bell has even attempted to obtain such a remedy, the evidence is ambivalent as to whether the purported repudiation results from nonfraudulent economic calculation or from fraudulent intent to mulct Bell.

Plaintiff contends that the alleged repudiation, viewed in connection with its demand for payment on the Letter of Credit, supplies the basis from which only one inference fraud can be drawn. Again, we remain unpersuaded.

Plaintiff's argument requires us to presume bad faith on the part of the Iranian government. It requires us further to hold that that government may not rely on the plain terms of the consulting contract and the Letter of Credit arrangements with Bank Iranshahr and Manufacturers providing for immediate repayment of the down payment upon demand, without regard to cause. On the evidence before us, fraud is no more inferable than an economically rational decision by the government to recoup its down payment, as it is entitled to do under the consulting contract and still dispute its liabilities under that Contract.

While fraud in the transaction is doubtless a possibility, plaintiff has not shown it to be a probability.

C. SERIOUS QUESTIONS AND BALANCE OF HARDSHIPS

If plaintiff fails to demonstrate probable success, he may still obtain relief by showing, in addition to the possibility of irreparable injury, both (1) sufficiently serious questions going to the merits to make them a fair ground for litigation, and (2) a balance of hardships tipping decidedly toward plaintiff. Both Bell and Manufacturers appear to concede the existence of serious questions, and the complexity and novelty of this matter lead us to find they exist. Nevertheless, we hold that plaintiff is not entitled to relief because the balance of hardships does not tip decidedly toward Bell, if indeed it tips that way at all.

To be sure, Bell faces substantial hardships upon denial of its motion. Should Manufacturers pay the demand, Bell will immediately become liable to Manufacturers for $30.2 million, with no assurance of recouping those funds from Iran for the services performed. While counsel represented in graphic detail the other losses Bell faces at the hands of the current Iranian government, these would flow regardless of whether we ordered the relief sought. The hardship imposed from a denial of relief is limited to the admittedly substantial sum of $30.2 million.

But Manufacturers would face at least as great a loss, and perhaps a greater one, were we to grant relief. Upon Manufacturers' failure to pay, Bank Iranshahr could initiate a suit on the Letter of Credit and attach $30.2 million of Manufacturers' assets in Iran. In addition, it could seek to hold Manufacturers liable for consequential damages beyond that sum resulting from the failure to make timely payment. Finally, there is no guarantee that Bank Iranshahr or the government, in retaliation for Manufacturers' recalcitrance, will not nationalize additional Manufacturers' assets in Iran in amounts which counsel, at oral argument, represented to be far in excess of the amount in controversy here.

Apart from a greater monetary exposure flowing from an adverse decision, Manufacturers faces a loss of credibility in the international banking community that could result from its failure to make good on a letter of credit.

CONCLUSION

Finally, apart from questions of relative hardship and the specific criteria [for a preliminary injunction], general considerations of equity counsel us to deny the motion for injunctive relief. Bell, a sophisticated multinational enterprise well advised by competent counsel, entered into these arrangements with its corporate eyes open. It knowingly and voluntarily signed a contract allowing the Iranian government to recoup its down payment on demand, without regard to cause. It caused Manufacturers to enter into an arrangement whereby Manufacturers became obligated to pay Bank Iranshahr the unamortized down payment balance upon receipt of conforming documents, again without regard to cause.

Both of these arrangements redounded tangibly to the benefit of Bell. The Contract with Iran, with its prospect of designing and installing from scratch a nationwide and international communications system, was certain to bring to Bell both monetary profit and prestige and good will in the global communications industry. The agreement to indemnify Manufacturers on its Letter of Credit provided the means by which these benefits could be achieved.

One who reaps the rewards of commercial arrangements must also accept their burdens. One such burden in this case, voluntarily accepted by Bell, was the risk that demand might be made without cause on the funds constituting the down payment. To be sure, the sequence of events that led up to that demand may well have been unforeseeable when the contracts were signed. To this extent, both Bell and Manufacturers have been made the unwitting and innocent victims of tumultuous events beyond their control. But, as between two innocents, the party who undertakes by contract the risk of political uncertainty and governmental caprice must bear the consequences when the risk comes home to roost.

Accordingly, plaintiff's motion for a preliminary injunction is denied.

Harris Corporation v. National Iranian Radio & Television
United States Court of Appeals, Eleventh Circuit, 1982
691 F.2d 1344

HILL, Circuit Judge.

I. THE FACTS

On February 22, 1978, the Broadcast Products Division of Harris Corporation entered into a contract with NIRT ("the contract") to manufacture and deliver 144 FM broadcast transmitters to Teheran, Iran, and to provide related training and technical services for a total price of $6,740,352. Harris received an advance payment of $1,331,470.40, which was to be amortized over the life of the contract by deducting a percentage of the payment due upon shipment of the equipment or receipt of the services and training from the balance of the advance.

Pursuant to the contract, Harris obtained a performance guarantee in favor of NIRT from Bank Melli, an agency of the State of Iran. The guarantee provides that Melli is to pay NIRT any amount up to $674,035.20 upon Melli's receipt of NIRT's written declaration that Harris has failed to comply with the terms and conditions of the contract. The contract between Harris and NIRT makes the guarantee an integral part of the contract and provides that NIRT must release the guarantee upon termination of the contract due to force majeure. Before Melli issued the guarantee it required that Harris obtain a letter of credit in Melli's favor. Continental Bank issued this standby, which provides that Continental is to reimburse Melli to the extent that Melli pays on the guarantee it issued. Harris, in turn, must indemnify Continental Bank to the extent that Continental pays Melli.

From August 1978 through February 1979, Harris shipped to Iran 138 of the 144 transmitters (together with related equipment for 144 transmitters) and also conducted a 24-week training program in the United States for NIRT personnel. In February 1979, the Islamic Republic of Iran overthrew the Imperial Government of Iran. After the overthrow, one shipment of goods which Harris sent could not be delivered safely in Iran. Harris notified NIRT, by telex dated February 27, that those goods were taken to Antwerp, Belgium, and Sharjah, United Arab Emirates.

Frank R. Blaha, the Director of Customer Products and Systems Operations of the Broadcast Products Division of Harris Corporation, met with NIRT officials in Teheran in early May, 1979, to help them obtain the goods in Antwerp, to discuss amendments to the contract, and to discuss a revised delivery schedule made necessary by Iranian events. Harris, offering Blaha's affidavit, contends that all parties at those meetings acknowledged the existence of force majeure as defined in the contract.

Blaha worked in May to obtain the Antwerp goods for NIRT, then returned to Teheran to continue discussions with NIRT officials. At these discussions, NIRT agreed to delay shipment of the final six transmitters until the fall of 1979 due to the conditions in Iran.

Negotiations on contract modifications continued during the summer and fall of 1979. On August 18, 1979, Harris formally advised NIRT of the additional costs it had incurred with respect to the goods that had been reshipped from Antwerp, and Harris requested payment for the additional amount in accordance with the contract's force majeure clause and with a letter from NIRT authorizing Harris to reship the goods.

On November 4, 1979, Iranian militants took 52 hostages at the United States Embassy in Teheran. Harris received no further communications from NIRT after the seizure of the hostages.

Harris completed the remaining six transmitters in November 1979 and inventoried them for future delivery. Harris, supported by Blaha's affidavits, has argued that disruptive conditions created by the Iranian revolution initially prevented shipment of the final six transmitters. Subsequently, Harris contends, it was unable to ship the materials as a result of the Iranian Assets Control Regulations effective November 14, 1979. In particular, Harris points out, the Treasury voided all general licenses to ship to Iran and required sellers to obtain special license[s] on a case-by-case basis before exporting goods. An affidavit submitted by Blaha states that Harris's counsel was advised by the Office of Foreign Assets Control that special licenses would be issued only in emergency situations or for humanitarian reasons and would not be issued for the transmitters. This request is not documented, and Harris did not inform NIRT of its inability to ship. On April 7, 1980, Treasury Regulation 535.207 became effective and prohibited the shipment of nonessential items to Iran.

On June 3, 1980, Continental Bank received a telex from Melli reporting that NIRT had presented Melli with a written declaration that Harris had failed to comply with the terms of the contract and stating that NIRT had demanded that Melli extend or pay the guarantee. Melli demanded that it be authorized to extend the guarantee and that Continental Bank extend its corresponding letter of credit to Melli, or else Melli would pay the guarantee and demand immediate payment from Continental.

In response to the demand by Melli, Harris sought and obtained the preliminary injunction at issue in this case. On July 11, 1980, Harris filed a verified complaint against NIRT and Melli in the United States District Court for the Middle District of Florida, seeking to enjoin payment and receipt of payment on the guarantee and receipt of payment on the letter of credit. The complaint also sought a declaratory judgment that the contract underlying the guarantee and the letter of credit had been terminated by force majeure. The court granted a temporary restraining order on June 13, 1980, pending a hearing on Harris's motion for a preliminary injunction.

On June 16, 1980, a copy of the TRO was mailed to Melli's counsel and on the following day was hand-delivered to Melli's branch office in Manhattan. On June 20, 1980, three days after receipt of the June 13th TRO at its Manhattan branch office, and despite the restraint against payment contained in the TRO, Melli telexed Continental Bank that it had paid the full amount of the guarantee "after receipt of a demand for payment from the National Iranian Radio and Television stating that there has been a default by Harris Corporation, Broadcast Products Division[,] to comply with the terms and conditions of contract F-601-1." The telex also demanded that Continental pay Melli by crediting Melli's London office with the amount of the letter of credit. After a hearing on August 15, 1980, the district court issued the preliminary injunction at issue here.

IV. The Preliminary Injunction

A. THE FRAMEWORK FOR REVIEW

The appellants contend that the district court erred in entering the preliminary injunction against payment or receipt of payment on the NIRT-Melli guarantee letter of credit and against receipt of payment on the Melli-Continental letter of credit. The four prerequisites for the injunction are: (1) a substantial likelihood that the plaintiff will prevail on the merits; (2) a substantial threat that the plaintiff will suffer irreparable injury if the injunction is not granted; (3) threatened injury to the plaintiff must outweigh the threatened harm that the injunction may cause to the defendant; and (4) granting the preliminary injunction must not disserve the public interest.

B. SUBSTANTIAL LIKELIHOOD OF SUCCESS ON THE MERITS

The merits of this case involve letter of credit law. Harris asserts that the existence of force majeure terminated its obligations under the contract with NIRT, making illegitimate NIRT's subsequent attempt to draw upon the performance guarantee issued by Melli. The appellants respond by relying upon a fundamental principle of letter of credit law: The letter of credit is independent of the underlying contract. Harris advanced two ways to overcome this barrier to enjoining a letter of credit transaction.

[Harris argued that the independence of the standby letter of credit from the underlying contract was abrogated because the parties expressly incorporated the letter of credit into the contract. Since force majeure terminated the underlying sales contract, the standby letter of credit was also terminated. The court decided not to consider this argument but instead relied on Harris's fraud defense.]

The second avenue pursued by Harris is the doctrine of "fraud in the transaction." Under this doctrine, a court may enjoin payment on a letter of credit, despite the independence principle, where there is shown to be fraud by the beneficiary of the letter of credit. Unfortunately, one unsettled point in the law is what constitutes fraud in the transaction, i.e., what degree of defective performance by the beneficiary justifies enjoining a letter of credit transaction in violation of the independence principle?

Contending that a narrow definition of fraud is appropriate, the appellants assert that an injunction should issue only upon a showing of facts indicating egregious misconduct. They argue that fraud in the transaction should be restricted to the type of chicanery present in the landmark case of *Sztejn v. Henry Schroder Banking Corp.* where a seller sent fifty crates of "cowhair, other worthless material, and rubbish with intent to simulate genuine merchandise and defraud [the buyer]."

The appellants further contend that Harris does not and cannot allege conduct on the part of NIRT or Melli that would justify a finding of fraud under *Sztejn.* The egregious conduct, they assert, was by Harris. They state that it was Harris which failed to ship the remaining goods, unreasonably refused to extend the letter of credit obtained from Continental, and deliberately abandoned and destroyed the underlying contract. In contrast, they point out that they informed Continental that they would have been satisfied if the letter of credit had been extended long enough for Harris to complete performance. According to the view of NIRT and Melli, all that Harris has — taking its assertions as true — is an impossibility defense to an action on the underlying contract.

Appellants' arguments are not persuasive in the context of this case. *Sztejn* does not offer much direct guidance because it involved fraud by the beneficiary seller in the letter of credit transaction in the form of false documentation covering up egregiously fraudulent performance of the underlying transaction. That does not mean that the fraud exception should be restricted to allegations involving fraud in the underlying transaction, nor does it mean that the exception should be restricted to protecting the buyer in the framework of the traditional letter of credit. The fraud exception is flexible and it may be invoked on behalf of a customer seeking to prevent a beneficiary from fraudulently utilizing a standby (guarantee) letter of credit.

Thus, the independent contracts rule does not make a fraudulent demand completely irrelevant to a bank's obligation to honor a standby. The differences between the allegations in this case and those in *Sztejn* merely require us to focus on the conduct of the buyer rather than the seller as we evaluate the beneficiary's conduct in light of the terms of the particular documents involved in the demand.

In order to collect upon the guarantee letter of credit, NIRT was required to declare that Harris had failed to comply with the terms and conditions of the contract. Harris contends that NIRT intentionally misrepresented the quality of Harris's performance; Harris thus asserts fraud as it has been defined traditionally.

We find that the evidence adduced by Harris is sufficient to support a conclusion that it has a substantial likelihood of prevailing on the merits. The facts suggest that the contract in this case broke down through no fault of Harris's but rather as a result of problems stemming from the Iranian revolution. NIRT apparently admitted as much during its negotiations with Harris over how to carry out the remainder of the contract. Nonetheless, NIRT sought to call the performance guarantee. Its attempt to do so necessarily involved its representation that Harris had defaulted under the contract. Yet the contract explicitly provides that it can be terminated due to force majeure. Moreover, NIRT's demand was made in a situation that was subtly suggestive of fraud. Since NIRT and Bank Melli had both become government enterprises, the demand was in some sense by Iran upon itself and may have been an effort by Iran to harvest undeserved bounty from Continental Bank. Under these circumstances, it was within the district court's discretion to find that, at a full hearing, Harris might well be able to prove that NIRT's demand was a fraudulent attempt to obtain the benefit of payment on the letter of credit in addition to the benefit of Harris's substantial performance.

C. IRREPARABLE INJURY

The district court did not abuse its discretion in finding a substantial likelihood of irreparable injury to Harris absent an injunction. Harris has sufficiently demonstrated that its ability to pursue a legal remedy against NIRT and Melli (*i.e.*, to recover the proceeds of the standby) has been precluded. It is clear that the Islamic regime now governing Iran has shown a deep hostility toward the United States and its citizens, thus making effective access to the Iranian courts unlikely. Similarly, the cooperative response of agencies of Iran to orders of a United States court would be unlikely where the court's order would impose a financial obligation on the agencies.

D. THE BALANCE OF HARMS

Neither appellant argues that the preliminary injunction has caused or will cause it any harm. Since there would otherwise be a likelihood that Harris would suffer irreparable injury, the balance of harms weighs heavily in Harris's favor.

E. THE PUBLIC INTEREST

In a Statement of Interest filed with the district court on July 16, 1982, the United States indicated that new amendments to the Iranian Assets Control Regulations governing letter of credit claims still permit American litigants to proceed in United States Courts and to obtain preliminary injunctive relief. The supplementary information explaining the changes provides a good indication that preliminary injunctions such as the one entered here are in the public interest:

> Iran filed more than 200 claims with the Iran-U.S. Claims Tribunal (the "Tribunal") based on standby letters of credit issued for the account of United States parties. United States nationals have filed with the Tribunal a large number of claims related to, or based on, many of the same standby letters of credit at issue in Iran's claims. Other United States nationals have litigation pending in United States courts concerning some of these same letters of credit.
>
> The purpose of the amendment is to preserve the status quo by continuing to allow U.S. account parties to obtain preliminary injunctions or other temporary relief to prevent payment on standby letters of credit, while prohibiting, for the time being, final judicial action permanently enjoining, nullifying or otherwise permanently disposing of such letters of credit.
>
> Preservation of the status quo will provide an opportunity for negotiations with Iran regarding the status and disposition of these various letter of credit claims. Preservation of the status quo for a period of time also permits possible resolution in the context of the Tribunal of the matters pending before it. The amendment will expire by its terms on December 31, 1982.

Melli has charged, however, that the entry of a preliminary injunction here would threaten the function of letters of credit in commercial transactions. Admittedly, that has given us pause, for it would be improper to impose relief contrary to the intentions of parties that have contracted to carry out their business in a certain manner. Some might contend that the use of the fraud exception in a case such as this damages commercial law and that Harris could have chosen to shift the risks represented in this case. Under the circumstances, however, we disagree. First, the risk of a fraudulent demand of the type which Harris has demonstrated a likelihood of showing is not one which it should be expected to bear in light of the manner in which the documents in this transaction were structured. Second, to argue that Harris could have protected itself further by inserting special conditions in the letters of credit and should be confined to that protection is to ignore the realities of the drafting of commercial documents. Third, unlike the first line of argument presented by Harris, the issuance of a preliminary injunction based on a showing of fraud does not create unfortunate consequences for a bank that honors letters of credit in good faith; it is up to the customer to seek and obtain an injunction before a bank would be prohibited from paying on a letter of credit. Finally, foreign situations like the one before us are exceptional. For these reasons, the district court's holding is not contrary to the public interest in maintaining the market integrity and commercial utility of guarantee letters of credit.

V. CONCLUSION

[T]he requirements for preliminary injunctive relief have been met. Accordingly, the decision of the district court is affirmed.

NOTES AND QUESTIONS

1. The situations in *American Bell* and *Harris* were similar but the seller was able to sustain an allegation of fraud only in *Harris.* What events occurred in the intervening time between these two cases that might have had an influence on the courts involved?

2. Review these cases and examine the approach taken by the sellers in each case in asserting its allegations of fraud. The sellers took very different approaches in each of these cases. In *American Bell,* the approach was unsuccessful whereas the approach in *Harris* was successful in surviving the defendant's motion to dismiss. How would you characterize the differences in approach taken by the sellers in alleging fraud in these two cases? What lessons can you draw from these two cases?

3. Both *American Bell* and *Harris* were decided under former UCC §5-114, a prior version of UCC §5-109. The current standard of fraud under §5-109(a) requires that "a document is forged or materially fraudulent, or honor of the presentation would facilitate a material fraud by the beneficiary on the issuer or applicant." Fraud under §5-109(a) continues to be a defense to payment in standby letter of credit cases. *See Archer Daniels Midland Co. and ADM Rice v. JP Morgan Chase Bank*, No. 11 Civ. 0988 (JSR) (S.D.N.Y. Mar. 8, 2011) (court enjoined payment under standby letter of credit to entities of the Iraqi government on grounds that documents submitted showing that rice failed to meet quality standards were fraudulent).

PROBLEM 4-14

A representative of a multinational computer company comes to your law office and tells you that it has entered into a major contract with a foreign sovereign government to provide computer equipment, software, and consulting services. The foreign sovereign has asked the company for a standby letter of credit payable in the amount of $80 million dollars in the event that the company fails to fulfill its contract obligations. The client has made it clear that it wishes to go through with the contract and does not want to be talked out of the standby letter of credit. Rather, the company asks for your advice on how to structure the standby letter of credit transaction to control and minimize its risks. What is your advice?

5

Non-Establishment Forms of International Business: Agency and Distributorships, Technology Transfer, Contract Manufacturing, and Franchising

In Chapters Two through Four, we examined the basic sales transaction of goods across national boundaries. The direct export-import sales transaction remains the simplest IBT and is the method by which many business entities first enter the international business arena. Export-import transactions have become common because in the modern age of electronic communications, information about products and services may reach large numbers of potential international customers. However, passively waiting for buyers to visit a web site, to respond to advertising, or to visit annual trade fairs may not be sufficient to satisfy the aspirations of some sellers. A seller may wish to take more active steps and be more aggressive in penetrating a certain targeted market. What steps are available to the seller beyond the international sale? This is the subject of this chapter and the next.

Beyond the Sales Transaction

This chapter and the next chapter are interrelated and can be seen as a progression for the seller, a U.S. company, from actions that are the least integrated in the foreign operations of its business to the most integrated. In this chapter, we discuss "non-establishment" forms of doing business abroad, whereas the next chapter involves "establishment" forms of doing business. In non-establishment forms, the seller hires an agent, distributor, or contract manufacturer (i.e., a third party authorized by the U.S. seller to manufacture the seller's products for sale abroad) in a foreign market. These non-establishment forms allow the U.S. company to achieve greater control than possible through direct selling but less control than if the U.S. company actually acquired partial or total ownership of a business entity in the foreign market that will manufacture the seller's products. The movement from various forms of non-establishment to establishment forms of doing business abroad marks a progression in the amount of control, integration, and commitment for the U.S. company. This is a theme that will underline all of the topics that we cover in this chapter and the next.

While this progression is a useful concept in an academic setting such as this textbook, it is one that is also openly acknowledged in the real world. Many U.S. companies and foreign parties enter into agency arrangements or distributorships with the explicit understanding that a successful relationship may lead to contract manufacturing. The parties may further provide that if the contract manufacturing relationship is successful, the parties will further deepen their business relationship by forming a joint venture. Alternatively, the U.S. company may wish to acquire a foreign manufacturer or set up its own wholly-owned foreign subsidiary. Many U.S. companies find this progression useful as it allows them to "test the waters" with small steps along the way and does not involve one huge leap into the unknown.

This leap or last step—forming a joint venture, foreign subsidiary, or acquiring a foreign company—is what is generally known as foreign direct investment (FDI) and allows the U.S. corporation the greatest control in the foreign market, but also involves the greatest risk and commitment. FDI is such an important decision that many U.S. companies regard it as a fundamental turning point in the life of any corporation. However, while the risks and commitment are much greater in FDI than in the topics covered in this chapter, FDI can and should be understood as a progression from the present topics.

Of course, FDI is not appropriate for some U.S. companies at all or may not be appropriate at certain points in their corporate lives. What are the initial steps that a seller can take in moving beyond the simple sales transaction but short of establishing a business abroad? We now turn to these topics.

Non-Establishment Forms of Business Abroad

There are two methods that we will examine in this chapter. First, the seller can engage a person or business entity in the foreign market to serve as its sales representative. Having a representative in the foreign market will allow the seller to have on-the-ground knowledge and expertise as well as someone who will actively market its products and seek out customers. Second, if the sales representative proves to be successful, the seller may wish to take the additional step of contract manufacturing, i.e., licensing a foreign entity to manufacture its products in the foreign market. By having its products manufactured by a local manufacturer under authorization in the foreign market, the seller can save on the costs of transportation and storage. In addition, as products sold in a foreign market require different packaging and may require certain physical alterations, the use of a local manufacturer with expertise in these areas may also create greater efficiencies.

Contract manufacturing is a form of licensing under which the seller authorizes a third party to use its intellectual property in order to manufacture its products. In the area of the trade in services, franchising is another form of licensing under which the owner will allow a third party to use its intellectual property to provide services or a combination of services and products. In the case of both contract manufacturing for products and franchising for services (or services and products), the transfer of technology (intellectual property) is a critical issue. There is often tension between the owner-licensor and the licensee in access to proprietary technology. The licensee typically wishes to have greater access, whereas the owner wishes to allow sufficient access but at the same time protect its intellectual property. How these intellectual property issues are handled in the various agreements are among the most important topics that we consider in this chapter.

I. *Agency and Distributorships*

Suppose that a seller in Ohio with little knowledge about Germany has been able to generate business through trade fairs and direct sales to several customers in Germany. The seller is confident that other companies in Germany would be interested in purchasing its products and wishes to adopt a more aggressive strategy to generate higher sales in Germany. One of the most difficult problems that sellers often encounter is how to establish a distribution network in a foreign market. Sellers, like the one in our hypothetical, that have limited their activities to direct exports may have little contact with the foreign market except for the few customers with whom the seller has developed a business relationship. To compensate for its lack of knowledge about Germany, the seller can engage a German party in the target market to sell its products. This is the first step in developing a distribution network in Germany. If the seller is a small company, the seller may choose to retain a representative that handles many different products for different customers. A large company may establish its own foreign agent or distributor. In most cases, it is more likely that the U.S. seller will hire some local entity for the distribution of its products.

In choosing a local entity to distribute its products, the seller generally has two options. The seller can engage (1) an independent foreign agent or (2) an independent foreign distributor. While the seller usually has the option to choose either of these forms, in some cases, especially in developing countries, the seller may not have a choice of the form of distribution as the form may be mandated by local law.

An independent foreign agent is an entity in a foreign country that solicits orders for the goods but does not take title to the goods. As the agent does not take title to the goods, the agent does not bear the risk that the local buyer will not pay. Rather, this risk remains with the seller. The agent will obtain sales orders on behalf of the seller in the foreign country and forward those orders to the seller. The seller completes the transaction by selling directly to the buyer so there is no need to store the goods in the foreign country. The buyer usually pays the seller directly and some portion of the sales price will be given to the agent as a commission in addition to a regular salary. The foreign agent usually does not have the power to bind the seller, but as a principal-agent relationship exists between the seller and the agent, whether the agent can bind the principal may depend on the law of the foreign jurisdiction. In some cases, the foreign agent may have the implied power to do so and in all cases the seller may expressly confer such power upon the agent.

An independent foreign distributor, unlike an agent, buys the goods from the seller for resale in the foreign country. As the foreign distributor takes title to the goods, the distributor assumes the risk of being unable to resell the goods. The distributor must also usually arrange for a place of storage for the goods. As the seller has already sold the goods to the distributor, buyers of the products are buying directly from the distributor. Unlike the uncertainty on this issue in the case of the foreign agent, a distributor usually has no power to bind the seller. The distributor is essentially buying the products from the seller for resale in the foreign nation and the relationship between the seller and the distributor is that of principal and independent contractor or principal to principal. It is possible for the distributor to also act as an agent for goods not already obtained from the seller. It is also possible for the seller to explicitly confer a power on the distributor to bind the seller. A foreign distributor must usually make a greater financial commitment than a foreign agent. While an agent may be a small company or even an individual, a distributor is usually a larger company with more resources.

A.   Control

As the role of the agent is to find a buyer and not to set the terms of the sale, the agency relationship allows the seller-principal to control the price of the goods and the parties to whom the products are sold. By contrast, an independent distributor takes title to the goods for resale and so the seller may lose control over the sales price and the customers to whom the products are sold. The seller can attempt to limit the powers of the independent distributor by contract but as this will be an attempt to inhibit inherent features of the distributor relationship, the seller may encounter resistance in contract negotiations with the distributor. Local laws may also restrict the ability of the seller to limit the freedom of the distributor.

Another element of control concerns the ability to appoint subagents or sub-distributors without the prior consent of the seller. An agent normally does not have the power to appoint a subagent but a distributor, as a principal in its own right, can enter into its own arrangements with third parties for distribution unless the contract provides otherwise.

While the seller will usually wish for greater control over the agent/distributor, there are some downsides. In general, the greater the degree of control, the more likely the seller will be subject to liability under the laws of the foreign nation. If the agent is an actual employee of the seller, then the seller will be able to exert the greatest possible degree of control allowed by law. However, if the seller actually hires the agent as an employee, then the seller may become subject to the labor and tax laws of the foreign nation. As further discussed below, the termination of agents or distributors is always an important issue to consider, but the termination of an employee, as opposed to an independent contractor, is usually subject to stricter requirements. For example, local labor laws might restrict the seller from terminating an employee without first satisfying requirements such as review by a labor bureau. Some national labor laws might require the seller-employer to contribute to social welfare, insurance, and health care funds for employees. None of these requirements would generally apply to an independent contractor such as an agent or distributor.

An additional consideration is that where the agent/distributor is an employee, the sale of the product by the employee might subject the seller to the income tax laws of the foreign nation. The sale of the product by a local employee might be deemed to be income earned in the foreign nation by the seller. Local tax laws are less likely to apply in the case of an independent agent/distributor as the seller's connection with the foreign nation is more tenuous; but, in this matter, the seller would be well advised to review all tax issues with local foreign counsel as laws vary from jurisdiction to jurisdiction.

One other consideration concerns the seller's liability for the actions of the sales representative. Where the representative is an employee of the seller, the actions of the employee may not only be imputed to the seller for purposes of tort or contract liability, but the presence of the employee in the foreign nation may be a basis for the assertion by the foreign courts of territorial jurisdiction over the seller in a lawsuit. The costs in time and resources of defending a lawsuit in a foreign nation are a substantial burden that most sellers wish to avoid and should be a major consideration in choosing the form of sales representation in the foreign nation. It is less likely that the seller will be liable for the actions of an independent agent and even less so in the case of an independent distributor but the precise determination of these issues is also a matter of local law that the seller should review with local counsel.

A final issue concerning control relates to the conduct of the agent/distributor that may implicate the seller in illegal activity. Foreign agents and distributors have been known to make bribes to government officials in order to obtain business, engage in tax evasion, and use company funds for personal purposes. In many developing countries without strong legal systems, illegal or questionable activities by business enterprises are common practices and often go ignored or unpunished, but there is always the possibility for the seller of being implicated in illegal acts in the foreign nation. For a U.S. seller, there is also the specter of the Foreign Corrupt Practices Act (FCPA), Pub. L. No. 95-213, 91 Stat. 1494 (1977) (codified at 15 U.S.C. §§78dd-1 to -3 and amending scattered subsections of §78), *amended by* Foreign Corrupt Practices Act Amendments of 1988, Pub. L. No. 100-418, 102 Stat. 1415 (1988) (amending sections throughout the U.S.C.), which would expose the seller to criminal or civil liability for making or causing improper payments to foreign government officials. The seller should carefully screen potential candidates and should include an explicit provision in the agency/distributorship agreement that prohibits any act that violates the laws of the host nation. We consider the FCPA in detail in Chapter Six on foreign direct investment, but the issue of illegal bribes is a common problem in the case of agents and distributors.

B. Competition Law Issues

The agent/distributor will wish to have exclusive rights for a particular territory and an exclusive arrangement may even be required by local law. As the agent/distributor will expend a considerable amount of time and resources in selling the products, it should not be surprising that the agent/distributor will seek to obtain exclusive rights to the territory.

Exclusive agreements involving a distributor, as opposed to an agent, may create antitrust or competition law issues. The distributorship involves an agreement between two independent business entities; if the agreement provides for exclusive territorial rights, the agreement may be considered to be an undertaking to divide markets that runs afoul of local antitrust laws. Outside of the United States, the European Union has the most advanced antitrust laws in the world, so the seller must be aware of the possible antitrust implications of doing business in the EU. The EU has specific competition law rules that deal with exclusive distribution agreements that differ from those in the United States. The EU considers the territories of all of its member nations to be a single territory for competition purposes and so arrangements that might not appear on their face to be anticompetitive from a U.S. perspective might violate EU law. For example, a prohibition against selling outside of an EU country, such as Germany, may not be permitted because it restricts competition within all of the EU territories as a whole. As antitrust issues are important considerations in using distributorships in the EU, we consider this topic in detail in the materials that follow.

A similar competition law issue may arise if the distributor is prohibited from selling competing or similar products. Such an arrangement may create issues both under the extraterritorial application of U.S. antitrust law (as the arrangement may prevent other U.S. companies from entering the foreign market) and under local competition laws.

C. Termination Issues

How and when an agency or distributorship may be terminated can be very important to both the seller and the agent/distributor. For this reason, it is essential for the seller to be familiar with the laws governing the termination in the host nation. A number of nations, especially developing countries, are concerned about attempts by foreign sellers to exploit the local agent/distributor. Some sellers may use an agent/distributor to establish a distribution network of local customers. Once the seller becomes familiar with the customers and is able to establish direct contacts with the customers, the seller can terminate the agency/distributorship relationship and sell directly to the customers. Many nations consider this type of conduct to be unfair and have enacted laws to protect the agent/distributor.

The seller must bear in mind that the termination of the agency/distributorship relationship is rarely a happy event except in those cases where the parties proceed to form a business partnership, such as a joint venture. In most cases, the termination signals a permanent end to the business relationship between the parties, a business failure in the relationship, and disappointment on the part of the seller or both parties. The agent/distributor might seek to vindicate its rights under the protection afforded by local law if it feels that the seller has acted unfairly. For these reasons, the seller must consider the choice of the agent/distributor carefully and provide for a detailed treatment of the termination issues in the agreement before the relationship is established. While the parties may not wish to consider termination issues during the flush of goodwill and optimism that usually accompanies the establishment of an agency/distributorship, these issues need to be carefully considered at the outset because the relationship between parties usually deteriorates significantly by the time of termination, making negotiations far more difficult.

In the bulk of national laws governing termination, a distinction is usually drawn between termination with cause and termination without cause. The distinction is important because the most onerous penalties for the seller-principal usually accompany termination without cause. The laws themselves may define just cause, but regardless of whether such definitions exist, the seller should list in the agreement the reasons that justify termination for cause and provide the agent/distributor with numerous opportunities to cure defects in performance. The agreement should also provide for other contingencies that automatically terminate the agreement, such as insolvency of the agent/distributor, nationalization of the property of the agent/distributor by the host nation, or other events that will terminate the agreement by way of force majeure. The most difficult termination issue involves whether the agent/distributor's failure to reach stated sales quotas or minimum performance goals will constitute just cause for termination. In some countries, such a failure may not constitute just cause. Even where such failure may constitute just cause, the seller would be well advised to be scrupulously fair in its treatment of the agent/distributor in nations that have restrictive laws protecting agents/distributors.

In the event of a termination that is deemed to be without cause, the agent/distributor may have extensive rights against the seller. The agent/distributor is usually entitled to a monetary settlement, which is calculated as a percentage of the seller's gross sales during the entire period of the agreement or as a multiple of the agent/distributor's earnings during the term of the agreement. The seller may be required to pay the agent/distributor for any goods still in its possession, for the cost of any goodwill created by the agent/distributor with customers in connection with the seller's product, and for any advertising and promotional expenses incurred by the agent/distributor. Where there is a dispute about the rights of the agent/distributor, the seller may need to have its claims decided in a local court. The court may enjoin the seller from terminating the agency/distribution agreement and prevent the seller from engaging another sales representative until the dispute is resolved. The foreign nation may also deny any import privileges for the seller for any additional products until the agent/distributor has been fully compensated and all termination issues have been finally resolved.

D. Intellectual Property Issues

It is imperative that the seller protect its intellectual property rights in the products or services that are the subject of the agency/distributorship. Before entering into any agency/distribution agreement, the seller must first comply with the laws of the host nation to obtain local protection for its trademarks, patents, copyrights, and other forms of intellectual property. We examine the procedures for obtaining local protection of intellectual property in greater detail later in this chapter. For now we can simply note that many nations require the intellectual property owner to register its trademarks, patents, and copyrights under local law. The seller must ensure that all of these protections for its intellectual property are in place before doing business in the foreign nation.

In this chapter and in Chapter Six on foreign direct investment, we focus on planning and preventive measures the seller can undertake to protect its intellectual property rights. Most of our attention will be on what procedures the seller or intellectual property owner must follow under international and national laws to obtain recognition of its patents, trademarks, and copyrights. We also examine contractual provisions the seller should include in the various agreements with the agent/distributor, licensee, or franchisee. We return to intellectual property in Chapter Seven where our focus shifts to what can be done after an infringement has already occurred, which concerns the growing problem of commercial piracy. In other words, Chapter Seven focuses on enforcement while Chapters Five and Six focus on prophylactic measures.

The agreement between the seller and the agent/distributor must establish that the seller is the sole and exclusive owner of the intellectual property rights in the product (or services) and that the agent/distributor only has the right to obtain sales orders or to sell the products under the authority of the seller. The agreement should provide that the agent/distributor will not make any claims to the intellectual property in the products and must not copy, alter, develop, or use any of the intellectual property rights in the products for its own purposes. The agent/distributor should also agree to notify the seller of any violations of its intellectual property rights in the territory and to assist the seller in enforcing its rights.

The seller will also likely disclose other confidential business information that may not qualify as intellectual property under applicable law. Such information can usually be protected only by contract that imposes confidentiality obligations upon the agent/distributor and its employees. Many agreements provide that the confidential obligations survive the termination of the business relationship for a period of years or indefinitely. Examples of confidential business information include the seller's corporate structure, financial information about the seller, the seller's marketing plans and business strategies, lists of customers, and information about the seller's personnel. The agreement should provide that the agent/distributor will share confidential information with its own employees only on a need-to-know basis.

E. Other Considerations

While the discussion above has drawn a number of distinctions between agents and distributors, in many cases it may not be clear whether the party is an agent or a distributor under foreign law. Many foreign nations use these terms interchangeably or without precision. In some countries, laws regulating agency agreements have been extended by analogy to distribution agreements and laws regulating distributorships have been extended to agency agreements. Foreign laws may regulate both agency/distributorships far more extensively than laws in the United States. It is usually advisable that the seller have local counsel examine foreign laws closely and that the agreement between the parties is drafted to make as clear as possible what type of relationship is being created. In general, language associated with an independent contractor should be used in connection with a distributor.

The parties must reduce their agreement to writing prior to entering into a business relationship. While this may seem evident, the parties often do not have a written agreement at all, have an agreement that is not drafted by an experienced lawyer, or orally agree on a business relationship and leave it to their lawyers to draft the agreement later. Any agency or distribution agreement requires an understanding of U.S. law, the law of the distributor or agent's country, and any applicable international law, including regional international law that applies to agency/distributorships as in the case of the European Union. As with the sales contract, choice of law issues can also arise.

PROBLEM 5-1

Worthington Superabrasives manufactures high-technology industrial diamonds and other abrasives under the trademark "Superabrasives" for use in drills and other industrial tools. The products manufactured by Worthington are considered to be technologically superior to standard abrasives and have a much higher capacity for drilling through tough substances. In fact, Worthington's products do not even compete with ordinary abrasives, but only against other newly developed technologies. Worthington has secured a U.S. patent for its products. Worthington, based in Ohio, has had only limited success in selling its products directly in Germany for several years and is seeking a sales representative in Germany for its products. Worthington is considering the use of an independent agent or distributor. Worthington's general counsel has a number of questions for your law firm.

For the purposes of answering these questions, review the introductory materials on agents and distributors set forth above. You are also to assume that general principles of German law on issues such as jurisdiction and liability are similar to U.S. law.

(1) Worthington would like to pay the sales representative on a salary and commission basis rather than a salary.

(2) If a person using tools that contain products manufactured by Worthington is injured in Germany, which form of business arrangement will more likely lead to jurisdiction over Worthington in a lawsuit filed in Germany?

(3) In a personal injury lawsuit in Germany, which form of business arrangement will more likely lead to a finding of liability on the part of the company?

(4) Worthington wishes to maintain price controls over the products sold so that its pricing structure in Germany is similar to its pricing structure in other European markets. Which business relationship will allow Worthington to maintain stricter control over pricing?

(5) Worthington also wishes to maintain strict control over customer lists. Worthington wants its products to be used by high-end, qualified customers and does not wish for its products to be used in low-end manufacturing. Which business relationship will allow the company to maintain stricter control over the customers who buy its products?

Which form of business arrangement, independent agent or distributor, would you recommend to Worthington?

PROBLEM 5-2

One of the sales representatives that is being considered by Worthington is an upstart, aggressive German company with strong connections to suppliers of industrial products to the German government. The German company has asked to be paid in sales commissions and has asked that Worthington make all payments to its account in a Luxembourg bank. The German company says that it has kept the account for years to service all of its operations in Europe. Advise Worthington.

PROBLEM 5-3

Worthington has entered into the distribution agreement below with Berens, a German company that manufactures and distributes industrial abrasives in Germany and several other European nations. The products manufactured and sold by Berens are standard abrasives so Berens is thrilled to have access to Worthington's technologically superior products. Several issues have arisen:

(1) As part of its promotional activities, Berens intends to take out a number of advertisements in newspapers and industrial journals stating that "Berens is proud to offer a new line of industrial abrasives under the brand name 'Superabrasives' that will meet the world's highest standards for your industrial uses. Contact Wolfgang Schmidt for a demonstration of our exciting new products and to place your order." Should Worthington take issue with this advertisement? See Articles 4 and 6 of the distribution agreement. If you were advising Worthington, what language would you suggest for the Berens advertisement?

(2) Berens has given some of the Worthington industrial diamonds that it purchased but was unable to sell to its research and development laboratory, which has discovered that through a process of polishing and refining, the diamonds can be transformed into diamonds that are suitable for use in expensive watches and clocks. Berens now seeks to obtain a German patent on the refining process. Berens claims that the process could have been developed using any industrial diamonds. Worthington does not compete in any diamond industries related to uses for watches or clocks. Have any of Worthington's rights under the agreement been breached? See Article 4. What remedies are available to Worthington under the agreement? Can Worthington assert any rights to the patent for the refining process or prevent Berens from obtaining the patent?

Distribution Agreement

This Agreement is made by and between:

Worthington Superabrasives (hereinafter "MANUFACTURER/SELLER"), a corporation formed under the laws of the State of Ohio, United States of America

- and -

Berens, GmbH (hereinafter "DISTRIBUTOR"), a corporation formed under the laws of the Federal Republic of Germany.

WITNESSED:

WHEREAS:

I. MANUFACTURER/SELLER is engaged in the business of manufacturing industrial diamonds and other abrasives (the "Products") and selling the Products in the United States; is the owner of the trademark "Superabrasives" in the United States, the Federal Republic of Germany, and other countries around the world; is also the owner of German patent No. 6820-1564 for the Products and the owner of patents for the Products in the United States and other countries around the world;

II. DISTRIBUTOR has the means and experience to market and distribute the products in the Federal Republic of Germany; and

III. MANUFACTURER/SELLER and DISTRIBUTOR have reached an agreement as hereinafter set forth.

In consideration of the mutual covenants and agreements herein contained, the Parties hereto, intending to be legally bound hereby, covenant and agree as follows:

Article 1.   Appointment

MANUFACTURER/SELLER hereby appoints DISTRIBUTOR and DISTRIBUTOR hereby accepts appointment as exclusive distributor of the Products (as detailed in Exhibit A hereto) in the Federal Republic of Germany (the "TERRITORY") subject to the terms and conditions of this Agreement.

Article 2.   Independent Contractor Status

DISTRIBUTOR is an independent contractor, and this Agreement does not constitute DISTRIBUTOR the agent or legal representative of MANUFACTURER/SELLER for any purpose whatsoever. DISTRIBUTOR is not granted any right or authority to assume or to create an obligation or responsibility, expressed or implied, on behalf of or in the name of MANUFACTURER/SELLER or to bind MANUFACTURER/SELLER in any manner.

Article 3.   Performance by DISTRIBUTOR

3.1   DISTRIBUTOR agrees to use its best good-faith efforts to achieve the highest possible sales volume in the Territory with a goal of purchasing no less than $100,000 of the Products from the MANUFACTURER/SELLER in each one-year period of this Agreement.

3.2   DISTRIBUTOR hereby agrees not to sell, develop, or manufacture any product that competes with the Products or to distribute any of the products by a competitor of the MANUFACTURER/SELLER that competes with the Products as set forth in Exhibit A attached hereto. This agreement shall not apply to any products that the DISTRIBUTOR may offer for sale as of the date of execution of this agreement.

Article 4.   Intellectual Property and Other Proprietary Rights of the MANUFACTURER/SELLER

4.1   DISTRIBUTOR hereby acknowledges that any patents, trademarks, copyrights, trade secrets, know-how, or any other forms of intellectual property (collectively "Intellectual Property") in the Products are the sole and exclusive property of the MANUFACTURER/SELLER. Any use by DISTRIBUTOR of the Intellectual Property in the Products for promotional, advertising, or any other purposes must be in furtherance of the purposes of this Agreement. DISTRIBUTOR shall not make, assert, or cause any third parties to make or assert any claim to the Intellectual Property of the MANUFACTURER/SELLER. DISTRIBUTOR further acknowledges that it shall not provide access to such intellectual property to any third parties without the prior written authorization of the MANUFACTURER/SELLER.

4.2   DISTRIBUTOR shall immediately notify MANUFACTURER/SELLER of any violations or infringements upon MANUFACTURER/SELLER's Intellectual Property rights in the Products within the Territory and shall assist MANUFACTURER/SELLER in the protection and enforcement of its Intellectual Property within the Territory. However, in no event shall DISTRIBUTOR seek to enforce the Intellectual Property rights in the Products in its own name but shall act at all times on behalf of MANUFACTURER/SELLER. All expenses incurred in connection with the protection of the Intellectual Property within the Territory shall be borne by MANUFACTURER/SELLER.

4.3   DISTRIBUTOR further acknowledges that it shall be given access to other valuable and confidential information of the MANUFACTURER/SELLER including, but not limited to, confidential business and financial information, marketing plans, developmental designs and information, processes, procedures, addresses, telephone numbers, customers lists, information about personnel, and other confidential information and data relating to the business of MANUFACTURER/SELLER (hereinafter "Proprietary Information"). DISTRIBUTOR further acknowledges that MANUFACTURER/SELLER has valid reasons to protect such Proprietary Information and DISTRIBUTOR hereby agrees to take the following steps: (1) keep all Proprietary Information confidential and secret by not disclosing such information to any third parties without the prior written authorization of MANUFACTURER/SELLER; (2) use such Proprietary Information only in accordance with the purposes of this Agreement; (3) provide such Proprietary Information only to employees of the DISTRIBUTOR who have the need to know such information; and (4) take all steps to protect the confidentiality of such Proprietary Information in accordance with the laws of the Federal Republic of Germany. The obligations set forth in this Article shall survive the termination of this Agreement indefinitely.

Article 5.   Purchase Price and Payment

5.1   Each order for the Products shall be placed by DISTRIBUTOR by a written purchase order at the offices of the MANUFACTURER/SELLER or at such other place as the MANUFACTURER/SELLER may designate by notice to the DISTRIBUTOR. The order shall become effective upon the DISTRIBUTOR's receipt of an order acknowledgment from MANUFACTURER/SELLER.

5.2   Unless otherwise agreed to by the parties in writing, prices for all products shall be C&F Hamburg (as per Incoterms 2010) and the Products shall be shipped by ocean freight on board a vessel to be nominated by Berens. The prices for the Products shall be the wholesale prices established by the MANUFACTURER/SELLER in the price list attached as set forth in Exhibit A attached hereto plus cost and freight. Each order shall be placed at least ninety days in advance of delivery to DISTRIBUTOR.

5.3   Unless otherwise agreed by the parties in writing, MANUFACTURER/SELLER shall invoice DISTRIBUTOR within thirty days after delivery of the products to DISTRIBUTOR. DISTRIBUTOR shall pay by bill of exchange within thirty business days from the date of the invoice.

Article 6.   Marketing

6.1   DISTRIBUTOR shall use its best efforts to actively promote the sale of the Products in the Territory. Best efforts include the use of appropriate advertising levels to support the sale of the Products according to the change of market conditions.

Marketing Plan

6.2   DISTRIBUTOR hereby agrees to submit to MANUFACTURER/SELLER a marketing plan within thirty days from the date of execution of this agreement and, on a quarterly basis, which shall include such information as sales projections, marketing strategies, marketing objectives, and achievement of those objectives.

6.3   All expenses incurred in advertising and promoting the Products in the Territory shall be the responsibility of the DISTRIBUTOR. The marketing and advertising spending plan shall be developed by DISTRIBUTOR. MANUFACTURER/SELLER shall be given an opportunity to review the plan and to provide comments.

Article 7.   Service and Marketing Assistance

7.1   MANUFACTURER/SELLER shall provide to DISTRIBUTOR at no cost, operation, instruction, and service manuals that DISTRIBUTOR shall provide to customers.

7.2   MANUFACTURER/SELLER agrees to sell DISTRIBUTOR replacement or spare parts for the Products in accordance with the prices set forth in Exhibit A attached hereto. The sale of spare parts shall occur in accordance with the terms and conditions set forth in Article 5.

Article 8.   Warranties and Liability

8.1   MANUFACTURER/SELLER hereby warrants that the Products sold by MANUFACTURER/SELLER to DISTRIBUTOR shall be free from any defects in materials and workmanship for a period of twelve months from the date of shipment by DISTRIBUTOR to its customer. This warranty shall not apply to any defects caused by normal wear and tear, improper or unreasonable use, or improper installation.

8.2   MANUFACTURER/SELLER's sole obligation under the warranty set forth in this section is expressly limited to providing replacement or repair of defective Products or parts thereof.

8.3   The warranty in this Article is expressly in lieu of any other express or implied warranty, including any implied warranty of merchantability or fitness for any particular purpose, with respect to any of the Products sold by MANUFACTURER/SELLER under this Agreement.

Article 9.   Compliance with Laws and Regulations

DISTRIBUTOR shall at all times in the conduct of the distribution and sale of the Products strictly comply with all laws and regulations in force in the Territory pertaining to the Products distributed hereunder. DISTRIBUTOR shall also comply with all laws and regulations in force in the Territory pertaining to the proper and lawful conduct of business activity, including laws applicable to improper and illegal payments to government officials for the purpose of obtaining or retaining business. DISTRIBUTOR also acknowledges that it is familiar with the United States Foreign Corrupt Practices Act (FCPA) and that it shall not perform or cause to be performed any act that would result in any liability of the MANUFACTURER/SELLER under the FCPA. DISTRIBUTOR shall be solely responsible for any penalties occasioned by the act or failure to act of DISTRIBUTOR.

Article 10.   Term and Termination

10.1   Subject to the termination provisions herein, the Term of this Agreement shall begin on the date of execution set forth below; and shall continue thereafter for successive periods of three years unless and until either party shall give the other not less than ninety (90) days written notice prior to the next expiration date of its decision not to renew. At the end of the first three-year period, the parties shall enter in good faith in discussions concerning the formation of a joint venture in the Federal Republic of Germany for the production and sale of the Products.

(a) In the event that a Party hereto defaults in the observance or performance of any of its obligations hereunder the other Party shall have the right to terminate this Agreement on thirty (30) days' prior written notice, provided, however, that such notice shall be without effect if such default is remedied within the thirty (30) days' notice period. Defaults in the observance or performance of any obligations under this Agreement shall constitute grounds for termination with cause.

(b) If DISTRIBUTOR fails to make timely payment of any amounts due to MANUFACTURER/SELLER hereunder, MANUFACTURER/SELLER may notify DISTRIBUTOR in writing, of its intention to terminate this Agreement, and if payment in full is not received within thirty (30) days after the giving of such notice, MANUFACTURE/SELLER may terminate this Agreement immediately.

(c) If either Party shall cease to do business or be adjudicated as bankrupt or insolvent or shall file or consent to a bankruptcy petition, or a receiver or trustee is appointed for either Party then the other Party shall be entitled to terminate this Agreement at any time with written notice.

(d) Upon termination of this Agreement for any cause whatsoever, all amounts owing hereunder between the Parties hereto shall become immediately due and payable.

(e) Upon termination of this Agreement for any reason, MANUFACTURER/SELLER shall be entitled to repurchase and take possession of any Products previously purchased by DISTRIBUTOR that are not committed under a prior business arrangement for sale to customers of the DISTRIBUTOR. The parties shall negotiate a price for the repurchase of such products but in no case shall the repurchase price exceed the price paid by the DISTRIBUTOR. DISTRIBUTOR shall also return any instruction manuals, brochures, installation manuals, or any other written materials provided by MANUFACTURER/SELLER to DISTRIBUTOR in connection with the performance of this Agreement.

(f) Upon termination of this Agreement for any reason other than the non-renewal of the Agreement by MANUFACTURER/SELLER without cause, DISTRIBUTOR shall not demonstrate, promote, sell, distribute, or service any products that are similar to or compete with the Products for a period of one year. The MANUFACTURER/SELLER shall have the sole right to determine which products are similar to or compete with the Products.

10.2   Within the first 21 days of the first quarter of each year MANUFACTURER/SELLER shall pay to DISTRIBUTOR an amount equal to 5% of the gross annual purchases for the prior year of the products by DISTRIBUTOR from MANUFACTURER/SELLER. This payment shall be considered an advance payment of any claims to compensation by DISTRIBUTOR in the event of termination by MANUFACTURER/SELLER of the business relationship between the parties. DISTRIBUTOR hereby acknowledges that it shall not receive and that it shall not seek any additional compensation from MANUFACTURER/SELLER in the event of termination by MANUFACTURER/SELLER.

Article 11. General

11.1   Force Majeure: If a Party is prevented, interrupted, or delayed in the performance of its obligations hereunder by riots, wars, acts of war, acts of God, fires, floods, accidents, strikes, labor disputes, embargoes, governmental orders or regulations, delays of carriers, lack of transportation facilities, inability to obtain raw materials, curtailment of or failure in obtaining fuel or electrical power, or by any other similar or dissimilar occurrence, the said Party shall be excused from the performance of its obligations to the extent that it is so prevented, interrupted and/or delayed; provided, that the Party so affected shall use its best efforts to avoid or remove such causes of nonperformance and shall continue performance immediately whenever such causes are removed.

11.2   Governing Law: The Parties agree that this Agreement and their respective rights and obligations hereunder shall be governed by and construed in accordance with the laws of the State of Ohio, United States of America.

11.3   Dispute Resolution: In the event of any controversy or claim arising out of or relating to this contract, the parties shall attempt to reach a solution satisfactory through consultation. If they do not reach settlement within 60 days, then either party may, upon notice to the other party and the International Centre for Dispute Resolution, demand mediation under the International Mediation Rules of the International Centre for Dispute Resolution. If settlement is not reached within 60 days, any unresolved controversy or claim shall be settled by arbitration under the UNCITRAL Arbitration Rules. The appointed authority shall be the International Centre for Dispute Resolution.

11.4   Assignment: No Party may assign this Agreement or any rights granted hereunder without the prior written consent of the other Party.

11.5   Language: The English language version of this Agreement shall be the authoritative text for all purposes.

---

1. Local and Regional Legal Requirements

The distribution agreement set forth above is subject to various sources of both private and public law. It is subject to the substantive private law of contracts and any specific laws relating to agency and distributorships of the United States and Germany. We have included the German Commercial Code in the materials below as an example of a private law governing agency and distribution agreements in a foreign nation. German contract law and general civil law provisions may also apply to this contract. In addition to German law, the law of the European Union may also apply to the agreement. While German law will apply to the private law issues (e.g., contract), European Union law in the form of the Treaty on the Functioning of the European Union and related regulations will apply to the mandatory public law issues of competition law regulation. Under the hierarchy of sources of law, EU law applies directly to activity in Germany and will supersede German law in case of a conflict.

A. GERMAN LAW

The distribution agreement set forth above is subject to regulation under the German Commercial Code, which contains a number of provisions designed to protect the appointed agent. The provisions of the German Commercial Code apply to agents as opposed to independent distributors. The concept of an independent distributor is relatively recent under German law and there are currently no distinct rules that apply to independent distributors. However, German courts have held that certain provisions of the law of agency set forth below, including §§86, 86a, 88, 89, 89a, 90, and 90a, apply to independent distributors by analogy. *See* Ingo Koller, Wulf-Henning Roth, and Winfried Morck, *Handelsgesetzbuch: Kommentar* (Beck Juristischer Verlag 2007).

PROBLEM 5-4

Two years after the execution of the distribution agreement set forth above, Worthington becomes dissatisfied with Berens' performance. Berens has purchased $100,000 worth of products from Worthington during this period and has been able to earn a profit during this period from its resale of the products to consumers in Germany. Berens' purchases of products from Worthington for resale in Germany are much higher than Worthington's previous direct sales to Germany but having examined Berens' customer lists, having attended sales meetings with Berens' customers, and doing some additional research, Worthington believes that it could easily double Berens' sales if Worthington were able to market these products directly to customers in Germany. Worthington now wants to terminate the agreement with Berens but has several questions:

(1) Can Worthington sell into Germany on its own? See Article 1 of the distribution agreement. If Worthington does so, what rights will Berens have?

(2) Can Worthington terminate for cause? See Article 3.1. How much notice must Worthington give Berens? See Article 10; *see also* German Commercial Code §§89 and 89a. Suppose instead that Berens had been selling competing products made by a Swiss company. Could Worthington terminate for cause? How much notice would Worthington have to give Berens?

(3) What is the advantage to Worthington of terminating for cause as opposed to terminating without cause? *See* German Commercial Code §89b(3).

(4) If Worthington terminates because of unsatisfactory performance, is Berens entitled to compensation after termination? See Article 10.2; *see also* German Commercial Code §89b(4). If Berens is entitled to compensation, what is the maximum amount that Berens can receive?

(5) Should Worthington even be concerned about compensation after termination? Assume that Ohio law is silent on this issue. See Article 11.2. *But cf.* German Civil Code Article 6 and note 2 in the Notes and Questions on pp. 306-307, below.

(6) After Worthington terminates the distributorship, Berens begins selling industrial abrasives that are of ordinary capacity as opposed to the super-hard abrasives sold by Worthington. Can Worthington prohibit Berens from selling these products? See Article 10.1(f); *see also* German Commercial Code §90a.

German Statutes Relating to Agency Agreements

COMMERCIAL CODE SECTION 84

(1) A commercial agent is anyone who, as an independent person pursuing a trade, is regularly entrusted to negotiate business transactions for another (the "principal") or to conclude business transactions in his name. A person is independent if he is essentially free to arrange his activity and specify his hours of work.

(2) Anyone who, without being independent within the meaning of subsection (1), is regularly entrusted to solicit business transactions for a principal or to conclude business transactions in his name is deemed an employee.

COMMERCIAL CODE SECTION 89

(1) Where the contractual relationship is for an indefinite duration, it can be terminated in the first year of the agreement on one month's notice, in the second year of the agreement on two months' notice and in the third to fifth years on three months' notice. Where another termination notice period is agreed to, it must be at least one month; termination can only be as of the close of a calendar month. After a contractual duration of five years, the contract may be terminated on six months' notice. Notice shall only take effect at the end of a calendar month, unless otherwise agreed.

(2) The notice periods according to subsection (1) sentences 1 and 2 may be extended by agreement; the notice period may not be shorter for the principal than for the agent. Where a shorter period is agreed for the principal, then the notice period agreed for the agent shall apply instead.

(3) Where a contractual relationship concluded for a definite duration is continued by both parties after expiration of the agreed duration it shall be deemed to be extended indefinitely. For determining the notice periods under subsection (1), sentences 1 and 2, the cumulative duration of the relationship shall be controlling.

COMMERCIAL CODE SECTION 89A

(1) The contractual relationship can be terminated without notice by either party for good cause. This right cannot be excluded or limited.

(2) Where termination results from conduct of the other party, this party is obligated to compensate for damages resulting from the termination of the contractual relationship.

COMMERCIAL CODE SECTION 89B

(1) The commercial agent can, after expiration of the contractual relationship, demand from the principal reasonable compensation if and in so far as

1. the principal obtained substantial advantages, after expiration of the contractual period, from the business relations with new customers solicited by the commercial agent;
2. the commercial agent lost, by reason of termination of the contractual relationship, rights to commissions relating to concluded business transactions or business transactions to be concluded in the future with those customers he had solicited, which he would have had the contractual relationship continued; and
3. the payment of compensation is equitable, in consideration of all circumstances.

Where the commercial agent has so significantly expanded business with a customer that this commercially corresponds to solicitation of a new customer, it shall be considered to be the solicitation of a new customer.

(2) Compensation may amount to no more than the average of the annual commission or other annual compensation over the last five years of the activity of the commercial agent; in the event that the contractual relationship has lasted less than five years, the average during the period of activity is applicable.

(3) The right does not exist if:

1. the commercial agent has terminated the contractual relationship, unless conduct of the principal provided reasonable cause therefore or the commercial agent cannot be reasonably expected to continue because of age or ill health, or
2. the principal terminated the contractual relationship for serious cause based upon the fault of the commercial agent, or
3. based on an agreement between the principal and the commercial agent, a third party succeeds the commercial agent in the contractual relationship; the agreement may not be concluded before the termination of the contractual relationship.

(4) The right to compensation cannot be excluded in advance. It must be asserted within one year following termination of the contractual relationship.

COMMERCIAL CODE SECTION 90A

(1) An agreement by which a commercial agent is restricted in his commercial activity following termination of the contractual relationship (agreement prohibiting competition) must be in writing and the document containing the conditions agreed to signed by the principal must be provided to the commercial agent. The agreement can be made for no longer than two years following the termination of the contractual relationship; it may only relate to the region or group of customers allocated to the commercial agent, and only to the objects regarding which the commercial agent is to strive to solicit or conclude business transactions for the principal. The principal is obligated to pay reasonable compensation to the commercial agent for the duration of the prohibition of competition. . . .

(3) Where the commercial agent terminates the contractual relationship for cause based on the fault of the principal, he can, in writing within one month following the termination, declare himself unrestricted by the prohibition of competition.

(4) Agreements differing from these provisions to the detriment of the commercial agent cannot be made.

COMMERCIAL CODE SECTION 92C

(1) Where it is intended that the commercial agent will not perform his activities for the principal under the contract within the territory of the European Community or other Contracting State of the Agreement on the European Economic Area, then all provisions of this Part can be altered by agreement.

CIVIL CODE ARTICLE 6

The application of any foreign law is excluded if its application could obviously not be reconciled with basic principles of German Law. In particular the application is excluded, if this could not be reconciled with the basic constitutional rights.

B. THE EUROPEAN UNION

The lawyer who is negotiating and drafting the elements of a non-establishment form of international business arrangement for a client must keep in mind the necessity to comply with applicable antitrust and competition laws. In this section we introduce the competition law of the European Union, which has developed what many experts believe is the most restrictive body of such laws in the world.

The EU competition laws stem from Articles 101 and 102 of the Treaty of the Functioning of the European Union (TFEU) (ex Articles 81 and 82 of the Treaty Establishing the European Community (TEC)). The TEC was renamed as the TFEU by the Treaty of Lisbon, which entered into force on December 1, 2009. These articles are reproduced below. TFEU Article 101, which is analogous to §1 of the U.S. Sherman Act, 15 U.S.C. §§1–7, prohibits agreements, decisions by associations, and concerted practices, that have as their object or effect the prevention, restriction, or distortion of competition that may affect trade between member states. TFEU Article 102, like §2 of the U.S. Sherman Act, addresses issues of monopolization and abuse of dominant position. We cover matters associated with Article 101 in this chapter, while Article 102 is more appropriately addressed in Chapter Six on Foreign Direct Investment.

Article 101(1) itself provides a non-exhaustive list of types of agreements that fall within its prohibition. Article 101(2) provides that any agreement or decision in breach of Article 101(1) is automatically void. Article 101(1) contains three elements: (1) some form of collusive conduct; (2) which may affect trade between member states; and (3) which may have as its object or effect the prevention, restriction, or distortion of competition within the common market. Collusive conduct under Article 101(1) can refer to undertakings, agreements, and even concerted practices without agreement. *Imperial Chemical Industries Ltd. v. Commission of the European Communities*, [1972] ECR 619.

An agreement within the scope of Article 101 may be either vertical or horizontal (or both). Vertical agreements are those between undertakings at different levels of trade or industry, such as between a producer and a distributor. Horizontal agreements are between undertakings on the same level of trade, for instance, between two manufacturers or two wholesalers who compete with each other. Vertical agreements usually pose less threat to competition, but they may nevertheless fall within Article 101(1).

The business necessity and economically beneficial effects of vertical as well as some horizontal agreements are reflected in the provisions of Article 101(3), the exemption section. Article 101(3) specifies both positive and negative reasons for exemption. Two positive reasons are (1) that the agreement contributes to the improvement of the production or distribution of goods or to the promotion of technical or economic progress; and (2) allows consumers to receive a fair share of the resulting benefit. Two negative conditions are that the agreement (1) imposes no restrictions on competition that are not indispensable to obtaining the benefit; and (2) does not create the possibility for the undertaking involved to eliminate competition with respect to a substantial part of the products in question.

The EU approach to restrictive agreements that have an effect on competition differs importantly from U.S. antitrust law. Whereas in the United States there is no exemption mechanism, and §1 of the Sherman Act incorporates a "rule of reason" approach whereby an agreement's pro- and anticompetitive effects are balanced against each other, in the EU, the pro- and anticompetitive effects may be weighed only within the framework of Article 101(3).[1]

Until 2004, the European Commission (EC) had exclusive competence to grant exemptions under Article 101(3) after prior notification. Now, however, under the provisions of Regulation 1/2003, effective May 1, 2004, the application of Article 101(3) has been decentralized. Prior notification of such agreements is no longer necessary, and it is up to private companies and their lawyers to determine whether their vertical and horizontal agreements are exempt. Regulation 1 devolves enforcement powers to national competition authorities and national courts. To facilitate this process, Article 101(3) is made directly effective in member state law. Member state authorities are forbidden from invoking national law to prohibit an agreement that may affect trade between member states that is not prohibited by Community competition law.

National courts also have exclusive competence to entertain lawsuits involving private damage actions by victims of infringements of Articles 101 and 102. Although private damage actions are not yet commonplace in the EU, the European Court of Justice has ruled that private damage actions are a significant aid to public enforcement to ensure the full effectiveness of the EU competition law scheme. *See Courage Ltd. v. Crehan*, [2001] ECR I-6297.

How should a business decide whether a specific agreement, decision, or practice that falls within the scope of Article 101(1) is exempt? Prior to 2004 the Commission issued negative clearances (i.e., official determinations of exemption) and comfort letters, but this process is now ended, although the Commission will still offer informal guidance to firms on novel questions and in cases of high economic importance. *See* Commission Notice—Guidelines on the Effect on Trade Concept Contained in Articles 101 and 102 of the Treaty, 2004 O.J. (C 101). In most cases for guidance on the application of Article 101(3), firms and their attorneys now must rely upon the jurisprudence under this article and especially the block exemption regulations issued with respect to the following types of restrictions:

- Commission Regulation 330/2010 on the Application of Article 101(3) of the TFEU to Categories of Vertical Agreements and Concerted Practices, 2010 O.J. (L 102), replacing Commission Regulation 2790/1999, 1999 O.J. (L 336/21), which expired on May 31, 2010.[2]
- Commission Regulation 1218/2010 of December 14, 2010 on the Application of Article 101(3) of the TFEU to Certain Categories of Specialisation Agreements, 2010 O.J. (L 335).
- Commission Regulation 461/210 of May 27, 2010 on the Application of Article 101(3) of the TFEU to Categories of Vertical Agreements and Concerted Practices in the Motor Vehicle Sector, 2010 O.J. (L 129).

---

1. The EU does apply a de minimis principle, however, whereby any Article 101(1) prohibited agreement will not be caught if it does not have an appreciable effect on competition. For horizontal agreements the aggregate market share must not exceed 10 percent; for vertical agreements the share must not exceed 15 percent.

2. See p. 304, *infra*.

- Commission Regulation 316/2014 of March 21, 2014 on the Application of Article 101(3) of the TFEU to Categories of Technology Transfer Agreements, 2014 O.J. (L 93).

The Commission issues guidelines on each of these block exemptions that are available at *http://europa.eu/*.

PROBLEM 5-5

Worthington Superabrasives is considering a renewal of the distribution agreement with some amendments but is concerned about whether any of the existing provisions or proposed amendments might run afoul of competition law issues under European Union law. In answering the following questions, assume that Berens has annual total revenues of EUR 50 million and has a 25 percent market share and that Worthington has a 25 percent market share in Germany. Worthington has the following questions:

(1) Is the distribution agreement, as written, subject to the prohibition contained in Article 101(1) of the TFEU set forth below? If so, the agreement is void under Article 101(2) unless there is an applicable exemption under Article 101(3). Does the agreement fall within the exemption contained in Article 2 of Commission Regulation No. 330/2010 on the Application of Article 101(3) of the Treaty to Categories of Vertical Agreements and Concerted Practices set forth below on p. 304? Are competing undertakings involved? See Problem 5-1 on p. 290. Why is this important? *See* Article 2(4) of Commission Regulation No. 330/2010. What about Article 3 of the Commission Regulation?

(2) Worthington wishes to add a provision that requires Berens to sell its products at no less than 90 percent of the sales price of the product in the United States. Is this lawful? *See* Article 4(a) of Commission Regulation No. 330/2010.

(3) Worthington seeks to add a provision that restricts Berens from actively soliciting orders to sell the products in France and Italy. Worthington wishes to sell directly to customers in those two countries. Would such a provision be lawful? *See* Article 4(b)(i) of Commission Regulation No. 330/2010.

(4) Does the non-competition clause contained in Article 10.1(f) of the distribution agreement violate EU law? What about the nondisclosure clause in Article 4.3 of the distribution agreement? On both questions, see Article 5(1) of Commission Regulation 330/2010.

PROBLEM 5-6

Suppose that Worthington would like to include several new clauses in the distribution agreement for the purpose of controlling Internet sales by Berens. Worthington would like to include clauses that:

(1) set reasonable standards relating to service, warranties, and refunds for the Internet offer on the distributor's home page;

(2) specify that the distributor must sell the products in a traditional bricks and mortar establishment in addition to selling over the Internet;

(3) require the distributor to bar out-of-area potential customers from accessing or viewing its web site;

(4) impose a limit on Internet sales in proportion to overall sales;

(5) require the distributor to terminate a sale to a customer upon receiving credit card information that the customer is located outside a certain defined area; and

(6) require the distributor to charge a higher price for products sold online.

Are any of these clauses in violation of Commission Regulation No. 330/240? *See* Article 4 of the Regulation.

Treaty on the Functioning of the European Union

ARTICLE 101 (EX ARTICLE 81 TEC)[3]

1. The following shall be prohibited as incompatible with the internal market: all agreements between undertakings, decisions by associations of undertakings and concerted practices which may affect trade between Member States and which have as their object or effect the prevention, restriction or distortion of competition within the internal market, and in particular those which:

(a) directly or indirectly fix purchase or selling prices or any other trading conditions;
(b) limit or control production, markets, technical development, or investment;
(c) share markets or sources of supply;
(d) apply dissimilar conditions to equivalent transactions with other trading parties, thereby placing them at a competitive disadvantage;
(e) make the conclusion of contracts subject to acceptance by the other parties of supplementary obligations which, by their nature or according to commercial usage, have no connection with the subject of such contracts.

2. Any agreements or decisions prohibited pursuant to this Article shall be automatically void.

3. The provisions of paragraph 1 may, however, be declared inapplicable in the case of:

- any agreement or category of agreements between undertakings;
- any decision or category of decisions by associations of undertakings;
- any concerted practice or category of concerted practices, which contributes to improving the production or distribution of goods or to promoting technical or economic progress, while allowing consumers a fair share of the resulting benefit and which does not:

(a) impose on the undertakings concerned restrictions which are not indispensable to the attainment of these objectives;
(b) afford such undertakings the possibility of eliminating competition in respect of a substantial part of the products in question.

---

3. Treaty on the Functioning of the European Union, 2012 O.J. (C 326) 47.

Commission Regulation (EC) No. 330/2010 on the Application of Article 101(3)[4] of the Treaty to Categories of Vertical Agreements and Concerted Practices[5]

ARTICLE 2

Exemption

1. Pursuant to Article 101(3) of the Treaty and subject to the provisions of this Regulation, it is hereby declared that Article 101(1) of the Treaty shall not apply to vertical agreements.

This exemption shall apply to the extent that such agreements contain vertical restraints.

2. The exemption provided for in paragraph 1 shall apply to vertical agreements entered into between an association of undertakings and its members, or between such an association and its suppliers, only if all its members are retailers of goods and if no individual member of the association, together with its connected undertakings, has a total annual turnover exceeding EUR 50 million. Vertical agreements entered into by such associations shall be covered by this Regulation without prejudice to the application of Article 101 of the Treaty to horizontal agreements concluded between the members of the association or decisions adopted by the association.

***

4. The exemption provided for in paragraph 1 shall not apply to vertical agreements entered into between <u>competing undertakings</u>.[6] However, it shall apply where competing undertakings enter into a non-reciprocal vertical agreement and:

(a) the supplier is a manufacturer and a distributor of goods, while the buyer is a distributor and not a competing undertaking at the manufacturing level; or

(b) the supplier is a provider of services at several levels of trade, while the buyer provides its goods or services at the retail level and does not provide competing services at the level of trade where it purchases the contract services.

5. This Regulation shall not apply to vertical agreements the subject matter of which falls within the scope of any other block exemption regulation, unless otherwise provided for in such a regulation.

---

4. Article 81(3) of the Treaty Establishing the European Community was renumbered as Article 101(3) of the Treaty of the Functioning of the European Union when the Treaty of Lisbon became effective on December 9, 2009.

5. Commission Regulation 330/2010, on the Application of Article 101(3) of the TFEU to Categories of Vertical Agreements and Concerted Practices, 2010 O.J. (L 102), available at *http://eur-lex.europa.eu/LexUriServ/LexUriServ.do?uri=OJ:L:2010:102:0001:0007:EN:PDF* (amending Commission Regulation 2790/1999, [1999] O.J. L 336/21, which expires May 31, 2010; the amended regulation became effective June 1, 2010).

6. Article 1 of Commission Regulation 330/2010 provides, in relevant part, that "(c) 'competing undertaking' means an actual or potential competitor; 'actual competitor' means an undertaking that is active on the same relevant market; 'potential competitor' means an undertaking that, in the absence of the vertical agreement, would, on realistic grounds and not just as a mere theoretical possibility, in case of a small but permanent increase in relative prices be likely to undertake, within a short period of time, the necessary additional investments or other necessary switching costs to enter the relevant market."

ARTICLE 3

Market Share Threshold

1. The exemption provided for in Article 2 shall apply on condition that the market share held by the supplier does not exceed 30 percent of the relevant market on which it sells the contract goods or services and the market share held by the buyer does not exceed 30 percent of the relevant market on which it purchases the contract goods or services.
***

ARTICLE 4

Restrictions That Remove the Benefit of the Block Exemption — Hardcore Restrictions

The exemption provided for in Article 2 shall not apply to vertical agreements which, directly or indirectly, in isolation or in combination with other factors under the control of the parties, have as their object:

(a) the restriction of the buyer's ability to determine its sale price, without prejudice to the possibility of the supplier to impose a maximum sale price or recommend a sale price, provided that they do not amount to a fixed or minimum sale price as a result of pressure from, or incentives offered by, any of the parties;

(b) the restriction of the territory into which, or of the customers to whom, a buyer party to the agreement, without prejudice to a restriction on its place of establishment, may sell the contract goods or services, except:

    i. the restriction of active sales into the exclusive territory or to an exclusive customer group reserved to the supplier or allocated by the supplier to another buyer, where such a restriction does not limit sales by the customers of the buyer,

    ii. the restriction of sales to end users by a buyer operating at the wholesale level of trade,

    iii. the restriction of sales by the members of a selective distribution system to unauthorised distributors within the territory reserved by the supplier to operate that system, and

    iv. the restriction of the buyer's ability to sell components, supplied for the purposes of incorporation, to customers who would use them to manufacture the same type of goods as those produced by the supplier;

(c) the restriction of active or passive sales to end users by members of a selective distribution system operating at the retail level of trade, without prejudice to the possibility of prohibiting a member of the system from operating out of an unauthorized place of establishment;

(d) the restriction of cross-supplies between distributors within a selective distribution system, including between distributors operating at different level of trade;

(e) the restriction, agreed between a supplier of components and a buyer who incorporates those components, of the supplier's ability to sell the components as spare parts to end-users or to repairers or other service providers not entrusted by the buyer with the repair or servicing of its goods.

ARTICLE 5

Excluded Restrictions

1. The exemption provided for in Article 2 shall not apply to any of the following obligations contained in vertical agreements:

(a) any direct or indirect non-compete obligation, the duration of which is indefinite or exceeds five years;
(b) any direct or indirect obligation causing the buyer, after termination of the agreement, not to manufacture, purchase, sell or resell goods or services;
(c) any direct or indirect obligation causing the members of a selective distribution system not to sell the brands of particular competing suppliers.

For the purposes of point (a) of the first subparagraph, a non-compete obligation which is tacitly renewable beyond a period of five years shall be deemed to have been concluded for an indefinite duration.

NOTES AND QUESTIONS

1. Article 2 of the Commission Regulation 330/2010 makes clear that it only applies to certain types of agreements. Does an exclusive territorial agreement between a U.S. distributor and a German distributor (i.e., a "horizontal" agreement) fall within this exemption? What is the difference between this type of agreement and the ones that are covered and what is the rationale for this distinction?

2. Article 8 of the distribution agreement deals with one of the most important issues in any distributorship agreement: warranties and the waiver of express and implied warranties. Article 8 was clearly drafted with UCC §§2-313 to 2-315 in mind. Will the UCC govern this agreement or is the agreement governed by the Convention on Contracts for the International Sale of Goods, as both Germany and the United States are parties to the CISG? Under existing authority, the CISG does not apply to this agreement as it is a distribution agreement and not a contract for the sale of goods. *See Gruppo Essenziero Italiano, S.p.A v. Aromi D'Italia, Inc.*, Civil No. CCB-08-65, 2011 WL 3207555, at *3-4 (D. Md. July 27, 2011). Although the agreement has a choice of law provision choosing Ohio law, that provision may not be effective to exclude the CISG as the CISG is a part of Ohio law. Moreover, a court might find that German law applies to the agreement despite the choice of law clause. *See Southern International Sales Co., Inc. v. Potter & Brumfield Division of AMF Inc.*, 410 F. Supp. 1339 (S.D.N.Y. 1976) (refusing to apply Indiana law to distributorship despite a choice of law clause on the grounds that contacts with Puerto Rico justified an application of Puerto Rican law that included protections for distributors not present under Indiana law). What if there were no express choice of law provision or the choice of law provision was not effective to exclude the CISG? If the CISG did apply to this agreement, then Articles 35 and 36 of the CISG covering warranties would apply to the agreement. The language of CISG Article 35 is similar to that of UCC §§2-313 to 2-315, except that the CISG does not draw an explicit distinction between implied and express warranties. Despite these similarities, however, in a situation where the CISG warranty provisions do apply, a U.S. lawyer cannot rely on foreign courts to interpret the CISG using the U.S. jurisprudence that has been developed under the UCC. However, foreign courts would seek to promote uniformity in the application of the CISG. If a U.S. lawyer is really intent

on having the UCC warranty provisions apply to the distribution agreement, do you think that the choice of law provision presently contained in Article 11.2 of the agreement is sufficient to ensure this result?

3. Under German law, the purpose of providing compensation to an agent or distributor when the principal terminates the contractual relationship is neither to compensate the agent for any damage suffered as a result of the termination nor to compensate him for the loss of a right or protected position as in the case of a terminated employee. It is also not the intent of German law to discourage principals from exploiting agents who establish successful distribution networks only to have the principal discharge the agent and take over once the principal has been able to achieve a foothold in the marketplace. Rather, compensation serves a remunerative purpose. The award of compensation recognizes that the principal will likely receive further orders from customers solicited by the agent, for which the agent would have otherwise received commissions. *See* German Commercial Code §89B(1) reprinted *supra*, at p. 298. The agent will now lose these commissions since a prerequisite of a right to a commission is that the principal accepted the order during the existence of the agency relationship. *See id.* §89B(2). As a result, it is considered unfair for the agent not to receive any compensation. Since allowing the agent to collect commissions after the termination of the agency would continue the principal-agent relationship for an indefinite period, would create burdens in the administration of claims, and would likely lead to disputes, it was decided under German law to award the agent a lump sum in the form of compensation to resolve all of the agent's claims to future commissions.

4. Tax issues are another important consideration in distributorships. Worthington Superabrasives would not wish to have its sales revenue subject to double taxation under German and U.S. tax law. To avoid this problem, the United States has entered into treaties with a number of foreign nations to avoid the problem of double taxation. Under the Convention for the Avoidance of Double Taxation with Respect to Taxes on Income, U.S.-F.R.G., July 22, 1954, 5 U.S.T. 2768, a U.S. entity would be subject to German taxation only if the entity had a permanent establishment in Germany, and an agent or distributor is not deemed to be a permanent establishment.

II. *Technology Transfer and Licensing*

Suppose that Worthington decides that the market in Germany and Europe for its products offers so much potential that it needs to move beyond the distributorship into other forms of doing business that will allow additional penetration into these markets. The agency/distributorship form has a number of limitations for Worthington or any principal.

First, in many cases the agent/distributor is engaged in other businesses. In the problems that we considered in the previous section, the U.S. principal chose a German company that was engaged in the production and sale of a similar product although at a lower level of technology. In most cases, a principal will seek to find an agent/distributor that is engaged in the same industry as the agent/distributor will need to have knowledge about the product in order to promote and sell it to customers. The agent/distributor may also need to provide technical and support services to customers using the product in the foreign market. In many cases, the agent/distributor may sell its own products or similar products that compete with the products of the foreign principal. The distribution agreement included a non-competition clause to deal with this issue. However, if the distributor is engaged in a number of other business activities, the sale of the principal's products may not receive the priority or attention that would satisfy the principal.

A second limitation is created by the manufacture of the product in the United States and the need to ship the product from Worthington's manufacturing plant to Germany. To get an idea of the costs in time and resources, let's review the entire transaction. Suppose that a customer in Germany places an order for certain industrial abrasives with Berens. Worthington does not have an inventory of the products ordered but must manufacture the products. It may be that it is too inefficient and costly to keep large stockpiles of industrial diamonds or it may be the case that the customer has a specific need for a certain product that is not in Worthington's inventory. Worthington now must manufacture the product, ship the product to Germany where Berens must pay any customs duties on the importation of the products, and place the products in a warehouse owned or leased by Berens for storage. The product is then delivered by Berens to the customer at the end of a lengthy process. Like most sellers, Berens will likely pass these costs on to its customers by raising the price for the products. The costs in time and additional expenses can create competitive pressures for Berens and Worthington. In the previous problems we have assumed that Worthington has a product with leading-edge technology. But let us now suppose that a German competitor is able to invent a product that is of equivalent or similar technological capability. In this case, Worthington and Berens are now at a disadvantage as the German competitor is not burdened with the same costs that Worthington must face in doing business in the German market. Not only is the German market in jeopardy for Worthington, but Worthington's other European markets will also come under competitive pressure. Even if there is no current competitor offering a similar product, is it a sound business strategy and planning for Worthington to simply assume that, in a highly competitive industry, no competitor will come along with a similar product of an equivalent level of technology? How many businesses can you think of that are always able to maintain a significant gap in technology between themselves and their competitors? What can Worthington do to meet this concern and new challenge?

Beyond the Agency/Distributorship to Technology Transfer

One response is for Worthington to establish a manufacturing subsidiary in Germany, but suppose that Worthington is not yet convinced that the potential revenues in the German or European markets justify the significant commitment that is involved in a foreign direct investment. As we shall see in the next chapter, a foreign direct investment is a major undertaking and represents a fundamental policy decision for Worthington. For now, Worthington has decided that it will be able to meet some of the concerns and challenges discussed above by contract manufacturing or by *licensing* Berens to manufacture Worthington Superabrasives in Germany. Licensing is a form of technology transfer.

A.   What Is Technology Transfer and Why Is It Important?

We have now come to the topic of technology transfer. We will explore this topic in this section, and in the next section we take up the topic of the international legal framework for the transfer and protection of intellectual property (IP) rights.

What do we mean by technology transfer? By technology, we are referring to information that is often protected by intellectual property rights such as patents, trademarks, copyrights, trade secrets, and other forms that are given statutory protection by both domestic and international law. In addition, by technology we also mean know-how or valuable business information that may or may not receive statutory protection or recognition as intellectual property. Examples of know-how that may not qualify as intellectual property are confidential financial information and marketing and business strategies. Support services for recognized intellectual property rights might also qualify as know-how. While this information may be commercially valuable and many others would be willing to pay substantial sums for this knowledge, it does not fall into any of the recognized categories of intellectual property. Commercially valuable information that does not qualify as intellectual property is usually protected by contract or by keeping the information secret.

All of these intellectual property rights are what we mean by technology in this context. Technology transfer refers to the process by which an owner of technology gives access to its technology to another. Access can consist of the transfer of complete ownership through a sale or assignment of the technology or the transfer of a more limited right such as a right to use of the technology through a licensing agreement.

1. *Technology Transfer in International Business*

Two very different forms of international technology transfer may be usefully distinguished. Smaller firms with valuable technology may wish to enter into a technology licensing agreement as a mechanism to enter a foreign market quickly with no investment and with an immediate financial return. In such a case, technology licensing is a distribution technique, and the license is a vertical one between the firm holding the technology and the other firm who wishes to use the technology and market the resulting products. A second form of licensing is a horizontal license, which is made by a firm with certain technology in order to induce another firm with complementary or related technology to enter into a cross-licensing arrangement so that both firms gain access to the other's technology. Horizontal licensing is often used even between competitors so that a range of technologies can be applied to develop new products on the cutting edge of the market. For example, two competing computer software companies may enter into a cross-licensing arrangement to develop a new product. Horizontal licensing in this case is an alternative to a joint venture; cross-licensing may be easier and cheaper than entering into and operating an international joint venture.

Before we turn to a more technical review of the international and domestic frameworks protecting intellectual property rights, we want to emphasize the importance of technology transfer in modern international business transactions. In the modern world, knowledge and information of all kinds have become increasingly important to international commerce. Some of the world's most valuable business property today consists of intellectual property and other forms of knowledge. Our hypothetical company, Worthington Superabrasives, possesses a technological advantage over its competitors and its most important asset is its advanced technology. The German distributor seeks to promote Worthington's products because they are technologically superior to the products of Worthington's competitors in Germany. Even where a company does not have a clear technological advantage over its competitors, a company's intellectual property in the form of patents, trademarks, and copyrights is among its most valuable properties. Think of patents for pharmaceuticals owned by Pfizer, Merck, and Eli Lilly; patents and copyrights for computer software owned by IBM, Microsoft, and

Cisco Systems; and trademarks owned by Coca-Cola, Johnson & Johnson, and Procter & Gamble. The Coca-Cola trademark is among the most valuable commercial properties in the world, worth hundreds of billions of dollars at the very least. One indication of the value of intellectual property rights is the dramatic surge in copyright piracy and trademark counterfeiting around the world. We explore these topics in a subsequent chapter, but for present purposes we simply note that theft of intellectual property by pirates has become a major business problem for IP owners. This theft reflects the value of IP in the modern world.

As the discussion above suggests, the bulk of the world's most valuable IP is owned by MNEs. The creation or development of almost all commercially valuable IP rights requires the investment of a significant amount of resources in research and development and in marketing. In most cases, only MNEs have these types of resources. For every pharmaceutical that is successfully brought to market, hundreds of millions of dollars are spent in research and development. The costs for developing a successful business software program can also involve similar sums. In the case of trademarks, MNEs spend millions of dollars annually in advertising and marketing the trademark in order to create goodwill, brand image, and identity with consumers.

The licensing of these valuable intellectual property rights is a complex issue and one with many risks and pitfalls. In most cases, the licensee wishes to acquire the latest possible technology and to obtain as much access as possible to the technology and supporting information. The IP owner seeks to provide sufficient access for the purposes of the licensing agreement but also seeks to protect its rights. As its technology is often the most valuable business property owned by the business entity, the entity is taking a number of risks in providing access to a third party. Among these risks are that the licensee will make improper use of the IP, use the technology to become a competitor of the licensor, or allow the IP to get into the hands of a counterfeiter or pirate. For this reason, IP owners often refuse to allow access to their core technology but will license only their nonessential technology. The licensee, of course, seeks access to the core technology. We examine the complex issues involving a licensing agreement in the following section.

2. Intellectual Property and World Economic Development

Not only is IP more valuable than ever in international business, but intellectual property and technology of all kinds play a central role in international economic development and implicate larger political issues. As the twenty-first century gets underway, most developing countries have shifted the focus of their national energies on closing the gap between the developing and developed world. It is a national priority for many developing countries to modernize and industrialize their economies and achieve a higher standard of living for their citizens. These goals will also allow many developing countries to eventually compete in international business and trade as opposed to being outsiders who must depend on the largesse of developed countries. A critical tool for modernization and industrialization is advanced technology, most of which is now owned and created by a few advanced industrialized nations. The leading nation in the creation and export of advanced technology and IP is the United States. Developed nations feel constant pressure to share the fruits of their advanced technology with developing nations. Of course, access by developing nations to technology is a political issue and is not usually a direct concern in an IBT. But the topic is of considerable concern in the area of international trade law and within the World Trade Organization. We touch upon these issues in our discussion of the public law international regulatory issues in Chapter Seven on protecting intellectual property. For a full treatment of the international trade law issues involving IP, see Chow and Schoenbaum, *International Trade Law: Problems, Cases, and Materials* (Aspen 2d ed. 2012), especially Chapter Thirteen.

3. Intellectual Property and Related Topics

The materials in the next section concern a topic that anyone interested in setting up a licensing agreement must consider: the international and national legal frameworks that have been established for the acquisition, recognition, and protection of IP rights.

However, before we examine the international IP system, we wish to place these materials in the larger context of topics that we have already covered and those yet to come. First, although the materials below concern international IP laws, technology transfers may also be subject to national export controls where the technology is sensitive and may pose national security concerns, which is frequently the case when advanced technology is involved. We examined this topic in Chapter Two on export trade law matters. You should keep these export controls in mind as you work through the materials below. Second, the materials on the international IP system below focus on laws creating substantive rights and the procedures that must be followed to acquire those rights. In Chapter Seven, we focus on a separate set of international and national laws targeted at the enforcement of those rights when they have been breached. The enforcement regime has a very different set of laws relating to intellectual property. We treat the topic of enforcement separately as it has grown in complexity and detail corresponding to the rise in the theft of intellectual property. Finally, our treatment of international IP is necessarily limited to its role in business. For a comprehensive treatment of all issues of international IP, including political, social, and cultural issues, see Chow and Lee, *International Intellectual Property: Problems, Cases, and Materials* (West 2d ed. 2012).

After reviewing the international intellectual property system, we turn to specific issues in the drafting of a patent licensing agreement and a business format franchise agreement.

NOTES AND QUESTIONS

1. One of the authors once heard the CEO of one of the world's largest MNEs in the consumer products industry claim that his company's people, not its brands or capital, were the key to the company's success. "Take away all of our brands, our capital, and our resources," he said, "but leave our people and we can rebuild our business in one generation." What do you think of this statement? Do you think that the current employees of Coca-Cola or Procter & Gamble, stripped of their brands and capital, can rebuild their businesses in one generation?

2. Developing countries are most eager to obtain technology that results in production processes that maximize the use of labor and natural resources to make products that are competitive in the world marketplace. They are less interested in technology that requires significant capital investment unless the IP owner is also willing to make a significant portion of the capital investment in the form of foreign direct investment. One issue for the IP owner is whether developing countries eager for advanced technology have the capability to absorb it. Suppose, for example, that a developing country with a weak system of education and poorly educated labor force sought to license the patent technology from Worthington Superabrasives. What issues might there be? Why would a country without the capability to absorb advanced technology seek it?

B. The International Intellectual Property Legal System

The international IP legal system can be divided into two categories: individual national legal systems and international treaties, including regional treaties such as those for the European Union and North America. In general, most substantive laws that directly create, recognize, and protect IP rights are those that belong to domestic legal systems. International treaties generally serve two purposes: They establish legal standards that its members must implement through domestic legislation, and they establish certain principles and procedures regarding the treatment of foreign intellectual property rights. With some exceptions, however, international treaties do not directly create intellectual property rights.

As a general matter, IP rights are territorial in nature and are independent creatures of the domestic law of the nation that has created or recognized those rights. For example, when an IP owner obtains a trademark from the U.S. Patent and Trademark Office, it is a U.S. trademark effective within the territory of the United States only and, in the absence of a treaty, has no legal effect in any other country. When the same IP owner obtains a German or Chinese trademark, it is a German trademark or a Chinese trademark with rights created by German and Chinese law and is a different and independent legal entity from the U.S. trademark. In the absence of an international treaty, an IP owner must comply with the procedures for obtaining intellectual property rights of every country in which the owner seeks intellectual property protection. For MNEs, this would mean complying with the application procedures in every country in which the MNE seeks to do business. A particular product or brand of goods is likely to have trademarks in many different languages. In the case of the trademark owner discussed previously, the owner will likely have to apply for a German language trademark and a Chinese language trademark that will be different from the U.S. trademark. Even where the foreign trademark is identical in language and appearance to a U.S. trademark, for example, where a U.S. trademark owner also owns a trademark in England or Australia, these are legally discrete trademarks. The same principle of territoriality also holds for patents and copyrights, so an IP owner could have a U.S., German, and Chinese patent or copyright for the same product and so on. Some MNEs hold hundreds, or even thousands, of foreign patents, trademarks, and copyrights.

On the international level, most treaties serve two purposes. One purpose is to harmonize legal standards by creating minimum legal standards of IP rights for all of its members. Prior to the establishment of the World Trade Organization in 1995, two of the most important instruments of harmonization were the International Convention for the Protection of Industrial Property (the Paris Convention), Mar. 20, 1883, 828 U.N.T.S. 11851 (revised most recently in Stockholm in 1967), which applies to patents and trademarks; and the Berne Convention for the Protection of Literary and Artistic Works (the Berne Convention), Sept. 9, 1886, 1161 U.N.T.S. 18338 (revised most recently in Paris in 1971), which applies to copyrights. Both of these treaties will be discussed below in connection with a more detailed treatment of patents, trademarks, and copyrights, but for now it is important to note that they established minimum substantive legal standards for some intellectual property rights for their members (although the Paris Convention established few rights for patents). Most member states do not regard these treaties as having direct legal effect within their territories, but each member gave effect to the Paris and Berne Conventions by enacting domestic legislation that embodied their requirements. Both treaties are administered by the World Intellectual Property Organization, a specialized agency of the United Nations.

After the establishment of the WTO, the most important intellectual property treaty is now the Agreement on Trade-Related Aspects of Intellectual Property Rights (TRIPs) (available at *http://www.wto.org/english/docs_e/legal_e/27-trips_01_e.htm*), which is one of the essential disciplines to which all WTO members must submit. TRIPs incorporates the major provisions of the Paris and Berne Conventions. In the area of patent and trademark, TRIPs goes beyond the Paris Convention by providing that patent and trademark protection must be provided by all WTO members. (The Paris Convention does not require patent and trademark protection but sets forth the type of rights and protections required if a Paris member decided to provide patent and trademark rights.) TRIPs is also the first international treaty to set forth the minimal substantive standards for all seven major categories of rights: copyright, trademarks, geographical indications, industrial designs, patents, integrated circuit designs, and trade secrets. In addition, TRIPs is also the first international treaty to recognize the importance of effective enforcement of laws and explicitly incorporates enforcement obligations.

A second major purpose served by international treaties is to provide a procedural mechanism that allows IP owners to enjoy protections and benefits across national boundaries and that simplifies and facilitates the process of obtaining intellectual property rights within national legal systems. On a regional level, the European Union has created procedures under the European Patent Convention, first signed in 1973, whereby a single application decided by a single European patent authority can result in a basket of national patents (or trademarks) that has the same effect as a national patent or trademark in each participating country. The North American Free Trade Agreement, which was signed in 1993 and went into effect on January 1, 1994, incorporates the major provisions of TRIPs and goes beyond TRIPs in some areas (such as enforcement). We shall examine these procedural protections in further detail in connection with our discussion of patents, trademarks, and copyrights.

1.   Patents

Under U.S. law, patents are granted to inventions or processes that are novel, useful, and non-obvious. *See* 35 U.S.C. §101 (2006). On March 16, 2013, U.S. patent law was changed to adopt what is called the "first inventor to file" system of patent registration. Under this system, the first inventor to file for a patent is the eligible party to receive the patent. Up to this date, the United States maintained a pure "first to invent" system, while all other nations maintain a "first to file" system. The change in U.S. law was accomplished under the America Invents Act, codified at 35 U.S.C. §§100–102; this was done to better harmonize U.S. law with the rest of the world, which employs a "first to file" standard. The term of a U.S. patent remains 20 years from the date of filing, the minimum term required under TRIPs. Although the terms used to describe the requirements for patents may vary from nation to nation, the three requirements set forth under U.S. law for patents or their equivalents are found in TRIPs and most patent laws in nations around the world. This does not mean, however, that every product or process that receives patent protection in one country will receive similar protection in another country. The promulgation of TRIPs and its wide acceptance by developing countries has now resulted in greater harmonization of all patent eligibility issues, but there are still variations among nations in the application of their own laws and implementation of TRIPs; therefore, you should not assume that patentability standards are uniform even among TRIPs members.

Examples of products that receive patents are machines, pharmaceuticals, biotechnology advancements, and chemical compounds. A patent issued by the U.S. Patent and Trademark Office (PTO) gives the patent owner a monopoly for 20 years that will allow the patent owner to exclude others from making, using, or selling the invention without the patentee's permission. The patentee can enforce these rights against an infringer in U.S. courts and obtain damages and injunctive relief. In addition, the patentee can also prevent the importation into the United States of foreign-made goods that violate the patent by obtaining an exclusion order from the International Trade Commission under §337 of the Tariff Act of 1930. *See* 19 U.S.C. §1337(d) (2006). These orders are enforced by the U.S. Customs Office.

There are two basic systems for the granting of patents in the world: the examination system (followed by the United States) and the registration system (followed by most other countries). The difference between the two systems is that the examination system requires a determination of the validity of the patent prior to granting it whereas the registration system does not. Under the examination system, the patent-granting authority will examine the prior art and the statutory criteria to determine whether the patent application qualifies for patent protection. The patent authority will also provide public notice of the application in order to permit an opposition to the patent. A patent granted under the examination system is more likely to survive a subsequent challenge to its validity. In most cases, the challenge arises in the context of an infringement action. The patent owner files an action against an alleged infringer and the infringer asserts as a defense that the patent is invalid. Although the United States follows the examination system, many U.S. patents are subsequently held to be invalid, leading to criticism that the United States Patent and Trademark Office is not sufficiently rigorous in its examination of patent applications.

Under the registration system, a patent is issued when the application, with accompanying documents and fees, is registered. The issuance of the patent occurs without a determination of its validity. The validity of the patent is determined when and if there is a challenge to the patent. The merits of the registration system are its low costs and speed of the issuance process. The examination system typically involves a much longer period before a patent is issued, a much higher demand on the resources of the patent authority, and higher costs to the applicant in the form of attorney's fees and processing costs.

International Patent Treaties

The major international treaties governing patents are the Paris Convention discussed previously and the Patent Cooperation Treaty (PCT) of June 19, 1970. Article 2 of TRIPs expressly incorporates Articles 1–12 and Article 19 of the Paris Convention (the bulk of the substantive provisions). As a result, the Paris Convention now applies among all of its members, which number 173 countries (including the United States), and its main obligations also apply among all members of the WTO, which now numbers 153 member countries with an additional 30 observing countries, many of which are not signatories to the Paris Convention.

The two most important rights created by the Paris Convention are the right of national treatment and the right of priority. Article 2 of the Paris Convention sets forth the right of national treatment, which holds that a nation cannot discriminate against foreigners in connection with patents or trademarks but must provide them with treatment equal to that received by domestic owners. For example, a French citizen who registers a patent or trademark in Germany must receive all of the rights that a German owner would receive and also cannot be subjected to additional burdens. If Germany were to require the French citizen to pay higher fees for the processing of its German patent, such a requirement would violate the national treatment principle.

The second principle established by the Paris Convention is the right of priority. Under Article 4 of the Paris Convention, an applicant who files a patent application in a Paris country will receive priority for any additional patent applications it wishes to file for the same invention in other Paris countries for a 12-month period. The right of priority entitles the applicant to a Paris priority date as the filing date of the first application in all other Paris countries in which the first applicant files other applications within the 12-month period. Competing applications filed after the Paris priority date will be deemed to be later in time and will be defeated in a priority dispute. The same holds true for trademarks except that the priority period is six months.

While the Paris Convention sets forth important procedural rights, it does not affect the basic principle of territoriality of patent rights and thus does not obviate the necessity for the inventor to file a patent application in every country in which the inventor seeks to obtain patent protection. A second major treaty administered by the World Intellectual Property Organization (WIPO), the Patent Cooperation Treaty (PCT) (available at *http:// www.wipo.int/treaties/en*) consisting of 141 parties (including the United States), provides procedures to facilitate international patent filings. Under the PCT, an applicant can file a single international application that has the effect of a national application in each of the PCT's member countries that are designated in the application. The application can be filed with the national patent authorities of the United States, Japan, Sweden, the European Patent Office at Munich, or any of the other designated international search authorities. The countries in which the applicant seeks patent protection are called the "designated states." Under the 2004 amended regulations to the PCT, the application now automatically selects all states of the PCT as designated states, a change from the former procedure in which the applicant had to designate states. The patent search authority will then conduct a novelty search and forward the results of the non-binding search along with a copy of the patent application to the national patent authorities of each of the designated states. The applicant can also arrange for a preliminary examination report in which the search authority will issue a non-binding opinion on whether the application has met the general patentability requirements of novelty, utility, and non-obviousness (or their equivalents). The applicant can then decide whether it wishes to amend, withdraw, or proceed with the application process in each of the designated states. The major advantage of the PCT is that the applicant is afforded an additional 18 months on top of the 12-month period under the Paris Convention in which to decide whether to proceed with a national application. In other words, an applicant under the PCT obtains a total period of up to 30 months (while maintaining Paris priority) in which to decide whether to file national patent applications for the invention.

The PCT does not create a truly international patent system. While the PCT facilitates the novelty search, offers a preliminary examination, and reduces the paperwork involved, the final decision on whether to grant the patent continues to be made by each national patent office. While no international patent system now exists, the European Patent Convention (EPC) of October 5, 1973, offers a regional patent system. The EPC provides a procedure whereby an applicant can file a single application in a single language, have it subjected to a single examination procedure carried out by the European Patent Office (EPO) located in Munich, Germany, and the Hague, Netherlands, and obtain a patent that has the effect of a national patent in all of the EPC countries designated by the applicant. No national patent authorities participate in the patent approval process. The European patent has a term of 20 years from the date of filing and confers upon its holder the same rights as a national patent. The effect of a European patent under the EPC is that the application obtains a basket of national patents in each of the EPC countries. The EPC does not replace national patent systems in Europe. Each nation continues to have its own patent system and its own substantive laws that may conflict with the EPC and an applicant can choose to apply for a single national patent as opposed to a European patent. Foreign applicants filing in Europe can apply for a European patent under the Patent Cooperation Treaty by designating all of the member countries of the EPC as "designated states" and the EPO as the international search authority. Under the PCT, the patent application then becomes a European patent application.

The proposed European Community Patent Convention, if and when it comes into effect, will go beyond the EPC in creating a truly unitary, supranational European patent. While patents under the EPC have the same effect as a national patent within each of the EPC member countries and the scope of the rights conferred and remedies available may vary from country to country depending on its substantive law, the European Community Patent Convention will create a unitary European patent that will have the same effect in every country regardless of the country's national law. Due to internal legal and political issues, it is unclear when the European Community Patent Convention will be implemented.

Although it may come, the day seems to be far off in the future when the world will have a truly international patent system in which a single patent application will be decided by a single authority resulting in a single unitary international patent, not a basket of national patents, that will have the same effect in every country in the world. There are many advocates for this approach, but there are also many unresolved issues. The most important issue is one of national sovereignty since many nations would be unwilling to cede the authority to decide for themselves whether to issue a patent. Another issue is language. A single language would have to be used for the system and the most likely candidate is English, the most used business and scientific language. What cultural, legal, and political issues can you foresee in the adoption of English as the universal language for an international patent system?

2.   *Trademarks*

Under the U.S. trademark law, the Lanham Act, a trademark is any word, name, symbol, or device or any combination thereof that is capable of distinguishing goods from those of another. *See* 15 U.S.C. §1127 (2006). While novelty is the hallmark of a patent, distinctiveness is the hallmark of a trademark. A trademark must be capable of distinguishing the goods or services of one origin from another. A generic term or a descriptive one may not be eligible for trademark protection because such a term may lack distinctiveness. Trademarks may be a word or words or a design or logo. In some cases, sounds and colors can also qualify as a trademark. Many countries draw distinctions among trademarks applied to goods; "service marks" applied to services; "collective marks" applied by a group or organization; "certificate marks" designating a certain quality, standard, or origin; and "trade names" that designate the name of a business or entity. All of these different categories are treated as trademarks. The United States follows a "first to use" rule in establishing priority rights (i.e., ownership) to trademarks whereas some other countries use a "first to file" approach.

Traditionally, a trademark served an origin and a guarantee function: The trademark indicated the source of origin of the goods as being produced by a certain manufacturer and also indicated the quality of the product. For instance, all goods with the same trademark indicated that the product was from the same company and that the goods were of a certain quality. The guarantee function of a trademark did not have to be an indication of high quality; it is an indication of similar quality; that is, all goods bearing the same trademark were also of a similar quality whether the quality was that of a luxury brand, a mid-tier brand, or an economy brand. The origin and guarantee functions allow consumers to act more efficiently in making decisions about goods or services that they purchase.

Today, trademarks also serve a marketing and advertising role. Most of the world's most commercially valuable trademarks are owned by MNEs, which routinely invest millions or hundreds of millions of dollars annually in advertising and promotion, creating a significant amount of prestige and goodwill associated with their trademarks. In the case of some of the world's most successful trademarks, the marketing function and goodwill of the trademark may now be more important than the trademark's traditional origin and guarantee functions. Think of "Nike" for example. When the "Nike" brand name is used, is it always used to sell athletic apparel or does it stand for a certain type of lifestyle, image, or attitude that transcends the goods to which the brand name is applied? The success of MNEs in creating highly valuable trademarks is one reason for the surge in worldwide trademark counterfeiting and infringement.

In many countries, trademarks must be used in connection with some commercial activity and cannot exist independently of such activity. Accordingly, in many countries, a trademark cannot be obtained by mere adoption but only through use or intended use. So long as the trademark continues to be used, it can remain valid indefinitely, unlike patents and copyrights, which have limited duration.

In the United States, unlike patents, which are exclusively governed by federal law, trademarks are a creature of both state and federal law. Unlike the case of patents, which enjoy the protection of the Patent Clause, there is nothing specific in the Constitution relating to trademarks, and common law remains the source of substantive trademark rights. Based on the Interstate Commerce Clause, Congress passed the Lanham Act in 1946, 15 U.S.C. §§1051–1072, 1091–1096, 1111–1127, 1141–1141n (2006), but the Act neither created new trademark rights nor codified common law rights. Rather the Lanham Act provides a framework in which common law trademark can be enforced at the federal level. Under the Lanham Act, the U.S. Patent and Trademark Office (PTO) keeps a register of trademarks. The proper registration of a trademark with the PTO allows the trademark owner to assert remedies in federal courts, which are empowered to issue injunctions or award monetary relief. In addition, §526 of the Tariff Act of 1930, 19 U.S.C. §1526 (2006), allows the U.S. Customs Service to seize goods entering the United States that bear a counterfeit or infringing version of a registered U.S. trademark. We examine the remedies available to a trademark owner in enforcing its rights against counterfeiters and infringers in further detail in Chapter Seven.

International Trademark Treaties

The Paris Convention discussed earlier in connection with patents also applies to trademarks. Article 2 of TRIPs incorporates all of the major substantive provisions of the Paris Convention concerning trademarks. The principle of national treatment and the right of priority (six months in the case of trademarks) discussed in connection with patents under the Paris Convention apply as well to trademarks.

The 1957 Nice Agreement Concerning the International Classification of Goods and Services for the Purposes of the Registration of Marks (to which the United States became a party in 1984) provides a single classification system for the registration of trademarks. As trademarks are always used in connection with goods (or services), the applicant for registration needs to identify the class of goods to which the trademark applies. For example, an applicant seeking registration for the trademark must identify the products (e.g., clothing, eyeglasses, handbags, etc.) to which the trademark will be used, and the trademark, once registered, will receive legal protection only if used in connection with these goods. In some countries, the use of a registered trademark with a different class of goods is illegal and can lead to the cancellation of the mark. In some countries, it is possible that the same sign or mark that is applied to two or more different classes of goods might result in multiple trademarks for multiple owners (e.g., "Grand Luxe" for automobiles and chocolates). Prior to the Nice Agreement, different countries had different classification systems for goods and some countries had no classification systems at all. The Nice Agreement brought unification and order to the field by providing a single classification scheme.

The Madrid Agreement Concerning the International Registration of Marks (1891) (the "Madrid Agreement") and Protocol Relating to the Madrid Agreement Concerning the International Registration of Marks (1989) (the "Madrid Protocol") establish a system for the international registration of trademarks. Although drafted as a codicil to the Madrid Agreement, the Madrid Protocol has greater participation perhaps due to the United States' joining of the Madrid Protocol (but not the Madrid Agreement). Under the Madrid Protocol, any person or entity based in a member country can file a single application that will allow the applicant to obtain trademark protection and the equivalent of national registration in all of the Madrid Protocol's other member countries (78 countries as of this writing). The applicant is allowed to file an application for the international registration of the mark with the World Intellectual Property Organization (WIPO), located in Geneva, Switzerland, at any time after it has registered or filed an application in its home country for that mark as applied to the same goods or services. Once WIPO registers the trademark in its international registry, the international registration is given the same effect in all member states as a national registration. An international registration is valid for ten years from the date of issue of the applicant's home country registration. *See* Madrid Protocol, Article 6(1). The registration can be renewed indefinitely for additional ten-year periods by the payment of fees. *See id.* at Article 7. The United States joined the Madrid Protocol on August 2, 2003.

On a regional level, the Council of the European Community adopted Council Regulation No. 40/94 on December 23, 1993, which establishes a unitary European Community trademark that is uniformly valid in the entire territory of the European Union independent of any existing national laws and regulations. The EU trademark does not displace national trademarks in the EU, so an applicant can choose, if it wishes, to apply instead for a national registration in each country in which it seeks a trademark. The European Community trademark may be obtained through the filing of a single application and registration proceeding through the Office for Harmonization in the International Market in Alicante, Spain. The term of the trademark is ten years and can be renewed indefinitely. In North America, the United States is a party with several Latin American countries to the General Inter-American Convention of 1920, which is closely modeled after the Paris Convention.

3.   Copyright

Under the U.S. Copyright Act of 1976, copyright protection is available for all original works fixed in a tangible medium of expression. As novelty is to patent and distinctiveness is to trademarks, originality is to copyright. The requirement of originality, however, is met so long as the author created the work independently and did not copy it from any other source. The author has fixed the work in a tangible medium of expression when the work is permanently embodied in a copy or a phonorecord. A U.S. copyright is valid for the life of the author and extends for 70 years after the death of the author.

Categories of copyrightable material recognized under U.S. law include: (1) literary works; (2) musical works, including any accompanying words; (3) dramatic works, including any accompanying music; (4) pantomimes and choreographic works; (5) pictorial, graphic, and sculptural works; (6) motion pictures and other audiovisual works; (7) sound recordings; and (8) architectural works. *See* 17 U.S.C.A. §102. The owner of a U.S. copyright has the exclusive rights "to do and authorize" (1) reproduction, (2) adaptation, (3) public distribution, (4) public performance, and (5) public display of the copyrighted matter. *See* 17 U.S.C. §106 (2006). The basic right of copyright ownership is the right to prevent unauthorized copying without permission. There is a limited exception for educators, librarians, critics, and news reporters who are allowed limited copying for educational and archival purposes under the common law "fair use doctrine" now codified in the 1976 Copyright Act, which created Title 17 of the U.S.C.

In order to obtain a U.S. copyright for a U.S. work, no formal procedures are necessary and it is not even necessary to publish the work. Copyright exists in the work so long as it is original and fixed in a tangible medium of expression. A U.S. copyright owner has the right to exclude copies of copyrighted materials from entering the United States without the permission of the copyright owner under §602(a) of the Copyright Act of 1976. *See* 17 U.S.C. §602(a) (2006).

International Copyright Treaties

Aside from TRIPs, the most important international treaty concerning copyright is the Berne Convention. The basic features of the Berne Convention are the national treatment principle and the requirement of minimum substantive standards of protection. Among the rights established by the Berne Convention are a minimum term of protection of the life of the author plus 50 years, rights of the copyright owner pertaining to translation, reproduction, public broadcasting, adaptation, arrangement, and other alterations. The Berne Convention also prohibits the requirement of any formalities such as registration for the enjoyment of copyright. The United States joined the Berne Convention in 1989. TRIPs incorporates Articles 1–21 of the Berne Convention, its major substantive provisions.

Under the national treatment provision (Article 5) of the Berne Convention, a work that receives copyright protection in a signatory country is entitled to receive the same copyright protection in every other signatory country that nationals of the signatory country receive. The effect of this provision is that an author of a work receives a basket of national copyrights. For example, a U.S. author who creates or publishes a work in the United States automatically receives a copyright in all Berne countries, i.e., the U.S. author receives a German copyright under German law, a Chinese copyright under Chinese law, a Brazilian copyright under Brazilian law, and so on.

One area in which the Berne Convention has differed from U.S. law is in the area of moral rights. U.S. copyright law has traditionally viewed copyright as consisting of economic rights, that is, the rights to profit from and exploit the copyrighted work. In addition to economic rights, European nations have traditionally also associated copyright with a set of moral rights, which are essentially rights that are personal to the author. Moral rights include the right to be known as the author of the work; the right to prevent others from distorting, mutilating, or modifying the work; the right to prevent others from using the work in such a derogatory way that it may prejudice the author's good name and professional standing; and the right to withdraw the work. Article 6*bis* of the Berne Convention guarantees the recognition of moral rights—this being one of the reasons the United States resisted accession to the Berne Convention for many years. Article

6*bis* of the Berne Convention also provides that moral rights, as opposed to economic rights, are nonassignable. As a result, an author retains moral rights even after the transfer of his or her economic rights. Why would U.S. corporations object to moral rights?

Although Article 9 of TRIPs incorporates the bulk of the substantive provisions of the Berne Convention, it expressly excludes Article 6*bis* relating to moral rights. Does the United States have a current legal obligation to recognize moral rights?

During its long history, the Berne Convention has been extended to recognize new technologies in the form of radio, cinematography, and television, but the emergence of new computer and Internet technologies has raised new issues about copyright protection that appear to be more difficult to accommodate than technological challenges in the past. One issue concerned whether computer software was eligible for copyright protection as computer software has both an expressive function associated with copyright and a utilitarian function associated with patent. Rather than permit each nation to decide on the scope of protection for computer software, Article 10 of TRIPs expressly provides that computer programs shall be protected by copyright. Other types of *sui generis* forms of intellectual property protection have been recently created for semiconductor chip designs and, in Europe, for the content of certain types of electronic databases that are not eligible for copyright protection.

4. Know-How and Trade Secrets

Know-how is knowledge that has commercial value. Know-how may be entitled to protection as a patent, trade secret, or other form of intellectual property. Where know-how does not qualify as intellectual property, it is protected primarily through contract and tort. Contracts can impose confidentiality obligations on the recipient of the know-how. Tort law includes the law of unfair competition, which would prevent third parties from misappropriating valuable commercial information. In some cases, even where know-how qualifies for intellectual property protection, the owner may opt to forgo such protection because of a desire to prolong the commercial exploitation of the know-how. For example, an owner may decide to apply for a patent to protect its know-how but the patent expires after 20 years and the know-how then enters the public domain. Rather than risk losing the know-how, some owners may simply protect the know-how by keeping it closely guarded.

In the United States, know-how may qualify for patent protection or for protection as a trade secret. Until 1996, the regulation of trade secrets was governed solely by state law. Over 40 states and the District of Columbia have adopted the definition of a trade secret of the Uniform Trade Secrets Act of 1979, which provides:

> "Trade Secret" means information, including a formula, pattern, compilation, program device, method, technique, or process that (i) derives independent economic value, actual or potential, from not being generally known to, and not being readily ascertainable by proper means by, other persons who can obtain economic value from its disclosure or use; and (ii) is the subject of efforts that are reasonable under the circumstances to maintain its secrecy.

Uniform Trade Secrets Act §1(4) (1985). In 1996, the United States passed the Economic Espionage Act of 1996 (EEA), 18 U.S.C. §§1831–1839 (2006), which creates federal criminal penalties for the misappropriation of trade secrets for the benefit of foreign governments, private companies, and individuals. The EEA reflects Congress's concern that the theft of trade secrets has become a serious national security and business problem that must made subject to federal law. Trade secrets are defined as "all forms and all types of financial, business, scientific, technical, economic or engineering information whether tangible or intangible if the information derives independent economic value, actual or potential, from not being generally known to, and not being readily ascertainable through proper means by, the public." 18 U.S.C. §1839(3). The EEA applies to all products "produced for or placed in interstate or foreign commerce," 18 U.S.C. §1832(a), and to foreign crimes committed by citizens and resident aliens of the United States as well as to acts in furtherance of such offense committed by any persons within the United States. *See id.*

International Treaties

TRIPs is the first international treaty that recognizes trade secrets. Article 39 of TRIPs provides that its members shall provide procedures to protect "undisclosed information" from being acquired by others in "a manner contrary to honest commercial practices," so long as such information is secret, has commercial value, and has been subject to reasonable steps by the person in control of the information to keep it secret.

NOTES AND QUESTIONS

1. The goal of countries such as the United States is the standardization and harmonization of all substantive intellectual property laws and procedures. TRIPs represents a major achievement toward these goals. Harmonization, of course, implies that one set of standards is to be adopted on a global basis. In the area of intellectual property, what or whose standards are these? Who might object to these goals and why?

2. As an example of the types of changes brought about by TRIPs, consider that some countries have historically imposed local working requirements as a condition for obtaining a local patent. The idea behind this requirement was to prevent a patent owner from abusing the patent. For example, an inventor in Country A would first have to obtain a patent in Country B before introducing its product into Country B in order to prevent infringement and counterfeiting in Country B. But some nations found that the inventor in Country A would simply manufacture the patented product in Country A, export the product to Country B, and not use the patent locally in Country B. As a result, many countries required as a condition of granting or maintaining the patent that the patent owner had to use the patent in the foreign nation by establishing a foreign subsidiary that used the patent or by licensing the patent to a local manufacturer. Why do some countries object to granting patents to owners who intend to manufacture the product in their home nation and then simply export the patented products to the foreign nation? Why is a patent that is locally worked viewed as creating a mutually beneficial economic relationship? The relevant article of TRIPs applicable to local working requirements is set forth below.

Article 27

Patentable Subject Matter

[P]atents shall be available for any inventions, whether products or processes, in all fields of technology, provided that they are new, involve an inventive step and are capable of industrial application. [P]atents shall be available and patent rights enjoyable without discrimination as to the place of invention, the field of technology, and whether the products are imported or locally produced.

What is the TRIPs position on local working requirements and who stands to benefit? As between developing and developed countries, which countries would favor local working requirements? Which countries would object to them?

3. Only a handful of people in the world know the formula for Coca-Cola, one of the world's most valuable pieces of know-how. Coca-Cola made the decision not to obtain a U.S. patent for the formula, which would expire after 20 years. Why do pharmaceutical companies apply for patent protection for their drugs, which confers a monopoly for 20 years, which many consider to be a rather short period considering that these companies invest hundreds of millions of dollars in developing some of these drugs? Why don't pharmaceutical companies follow the example of Coca-Cola and protect their know-how by keeping it closely guarded in perpetuity and forgo patent protection?

III. Selected Issues in Licensing: The Patent License Agreement

Suppose that, for some of the reasons we discussed earlier, Worthington has decided to move forward with a contract manufacturing agreement that will permit Berens to manufacture the products in Germany and serve as a base for the German market. Worthington has a U.S. patent for its products. Set forth below is a patent license agreement. Assume for the purposes of the problems that Worthington and Berens both have a 25 percent share of the relevant market. Further, a market survey indicates that consumers consider the Worthington Superabrasive to be a technologically superior product to ordinary industrial abrasives and worthy of a price premium.

PROBLEM 5-7

Worthington has a U.S. patent for its products but in order to do business in Germany, Worthington must obtain a German patent by filing an application in Germany and a trademark registration for its mark "Superabrasives." Berens has proposed the following: Rather than having Worthington apply for a German patent and then license it to Berens as would be the normal procedure that Worthington would follow, Berens can file the patent application and trademark registration for the Worthington products in its own name in Germany and then assign the patent and trademark to Worthington at the end of the contract manufacturing period. Berens will assume all of the paperwork and costs of the filing procedures and will save Worthington substantially on legal fees and other costs. The duty to assign can be explicitly included in the contract manufacturing agreement. Such a clause is enforceable under applicable law by damages and specific performance. Based on the general principles discussed in Section II on the value of intellectual property, what advice do you have for Worthington?

PROBLEM 5-8

Suppose that, after the patent agreement goes into effect, Worthington sets up a factory on its own in Germany and begins to use the patent in manufacturing and selling products under the "Superabrasives" trademark. Berens now brings an action in German court, seeking to enforce its patent and trademark rights against Worthington. In its defense, Worthington moves to dismiss the action on the grounds that, under a patent and trademark license agreement, the licensee cannot sue the licensor for breach of patent and trademark rights. Review Articles 2 and 3 of the patent agreement. What types of rights were granted to Berens? Can Berens prevent Worthington using the patent and trademark rights and, if so, on what basis?

PROBLEM 5-9

Advise Worthington on whether the patent license agreement below violates any competition laws in the EU. Compare Article 2 of the patent agreement with Article 1 and Article 2 of EC Regulation No. 316/2014 on pp. 330-331 below. What about market share thresholds under Article 3 of the EC Regulation? To answer this question, you need to determine whether Worthington and Berens are competing undertakings (see Problem 5-1 on p. 290) and their market share, see Problem 5-5 at p. 302. What if Worthington and Berens were competing undertakings and each had a 20 percent market share?

Worthington is also considering whether to sell its products directly (by establishing a branch office) or indirectly through other licenses in other EU countries. To protect these other markets, Worthington inserted a provision in Article 2(a) of the patent licensing agreement that prevents Berens from making any sales of the products in France and the UK or any other countries where Worthington enters into an exclusive licensing agreement with a licensee or sells the products through a branch office. Sellers and buyers sometimes distinguish between "active" sales, i.e., sales that are solicited by the seller, and "passive" sales, i.e., sales that occur because the seller responds to an unsolicited offer from a buyer. What types of sales are prohibited by Article 2(a) of the patent licensing agreement? Is this permitted? On the restriction of sales, see Article 4(2)(b) of EC Regulation No. 316/2014 set forth below.

PROBLEM 5-10

Worthington is also concerned about protecting its intellectual property. In particular, Worthington does not want to get into a dispute with Berens over who owns the patent rights for the products. The agreement licenses the German patent rights to Berens, but Worthington knows that it is common for licensees to make some changes and improvements to the patented product as the product is adapted for the local market or as a result of the licensee's using the patent in the manufacturing process. As the patent covers only the technology described in the patent application, any improvements by the licensee will be outside the scope of the existing patent. Often, disputes arise over who owns the improvements to the original patent. Many licensors take the position that they own the basic technology covered by the patent and that without access to the patent in the first place, the licensee would have been unable to create any improvements. Licensees, on the other hand, often take the position that as they have invested the resources in making the improvements, they should be the owner of the improvements, not the licensor. In order to avoid such disputes, Worthington has added a "grant back clause" in the license agreement that makes clear that it is the owner of any improvements by Berens. *See* Article

12 of the patent license agreement. Is the grant back clause lawful? *See* Article 5(1)(a) EC Regulation No. 316/2014. Can Worthington simply prohibit Berens from making any improvements at all on the licensed technology? *See* Article 5(2) of the EC Regulation.

Patent License Agreement

THIS AGREEMENT is made this 1st day of January 2010 between Worthington Superabrasives, a corporation organized and existing under the laws of the State of Ohio, having a place of business at 59 Scots Brook Road, Worthington, Ohio, United States of America (Licensor), and Berens, GmbH, a company duly incorporated under the Laws of the Federal Republic of Germany whose Registered Office is at 35 Wilheimstrasse, Munich, Federal Republic of Germany (Licensee).

WHEREAS:

(1) Licensor is the owner of German Patent No. 6,820-1564 on certain industrial abrasives and of patents and patent applications in other countries relating thereto;

(2) Licensor is the owner of the trademark SUPERABRASIVES in the Federal Republic of Germany and the trademark SUPERABRASIVES in other countries; and

(3) Licensee is interested in the manufacture and sale of industrial abrasives in the Federal Republic of Germany (the Territory), and in that connection seeks to avail itself of said German Patent No. 6,820-1564.

Now, THEREFORE, in consideration of the covenants and agreements herein contained, it is agreed as follows:

ARTICLE 1
DEFINITIONS

(1) The "Products" shall mean and include any industrial abrasive that is manufactured, used, or sold making use of German Patent No. 6,820-1564 in the Territory.

(2) "Sales" will mean: the sale, rental, lease, or other transfer of the Products by Licensee to parties other than its subsidiaries and affiliates; the sale, rental, lease, or other transfer of the Products by a subsidiary or affiliate of Licensee to a third party for use or consumption; the use or consumption of the Products by Licensee in its own business; and the use or consumption of the Products by a subsidiary or affiliates of Licensee in its own business.

(3) The "selling price" will mean the price paid to Licensee by the party to whom the Products are transferred. Licensee shall establish the selling price in consultation with Licensor.

(4) "License Year" will mean each twelve (12) month calendar period commencing with January 1 and beginning with the year 2010 and continuing during the existence in force of the exclusive licenses.

ARTICLE 2
GRANTS

(1) Licensor hereby agrees to grant to Licensee exclusive licenses to manufacture, use, and sell in the Territory industrial abrasives as described in and covered by German

Patent No. 6,820-1564 subject to any and all provisions and conditions of this Agreement. This grant is subject to the following conditions:

(a) Licensee shall not manufacture, use, or sell the Products in France, the United Kingdom, or any other country within the European Union in which Licensor enters into an exclusive licensing agreement for the Products with another licensee.

(b) Licensee shall not sell the Products to users in the Territory who are known to resell the Products in France, the United Kingdom, or any other country within the European Union in which Licensor enters into an exclusive licensing agreement for the Products with another licensee.

(c) Licensee shall not advertise or promote the Products in France, the United Kingdom, or any other country within the European Union in which Licensor enters into an exclusive licensing agreement for the Products with another licensee.

(d) Licensee shall not solicit any orders from France, the United Kingdom, or any other countries within the European Union in which Licensor enters into an exclusive licensing agreement for the Products and shall not sell any Products on the basis of any orders, solicited or unsolicited, to customers in any of these countries.

(2) Licensor hereby agrees to grant to Licensee the right to use, and will appoint Licensee a Registered User or Licensee of the registered German trademark SUPER-ABRASIVES within the Territory. Licensee shall place the trademark SUPERABRASIVES in a prominent location on all Products that are sold under this Agreement.

ARTICLE 3
OWNERSHIP OF INTELLECTUAL PROPERTY RIGHTS

(1) Licensee hereby acknowledges that Licensor is the sole and exclusive owner of German Patent No. 6,820-1564, the registered German trademark SUPERABRASIVES, know-how, and other proprietary business information ("intellectual property") to which Licensee shall have access.

(2) Licensee shall make use of all intellectual property only for the purposes of this Agreement.

(3) Licensee shall not assert or assist any third parties in asserting a claim to the intellectual property of the Licensor. If Licensee shall make or assist any third parties in making a claim to the intellectual property of the Licensor, Licensor shall be entitled to terminate this Agreement upon thirty (30) days' written notice.

ARTICLE 4
NONCOMPETITION

During the term of this Agreement, Licensee shall not manufacture, sell, promote, or distribute any products that compete directly or indirectly with the Products. This obligation does not apply to any products that the Licensee was manufacturing, selling, promoting or distributing at the time that this Agreement was signed. A list of products that compete directly or indirectly with the Products is included in Appendix A attached hereto. If the Licensee is in violation of this Article, the Licensor shall have the right to grant licenses to other licensees within the Territory and the Licensor shall also have the right to manufacture and sell the Product within the Territory.

ARTICLE 5
SUPPLY OF KNOW-HOW, TECHNICAL ASSISTANCE, AND ENGINEERING DEVELOPMENT

(1) From time to time as Licensor shall deem reasonably necessary for the performance of this Agreement, Licensor shall provide any know-how, technical information, and knowledge that will assist Licensee in the manufacture, operation, installation, repair, maintenance, and sale of the Products. Licensee shall pay any out-of-pocket costs in connection with any training, meetings, and travel incurred in connection with this technical assistance.

(2) Licensor and Licensee may enter into separate written agreements from time to time as both parties deem appropriate for the separate development of special engineering projects or research and development concerning the Products.

ARTICLE 6
CONFIDENTIALITY

(1) Licensee acknowledges that it shall be given access to valuable commercial information in the form of patents, trademarks, know-how, and other proprietary business information. Licensee shall undertake all measures in conformity with German law to keep such valuable commercial information confidential by limiting access to such information only to employees who must have access to this information in order to perform this Agreement.

(2) Licensee shall be bound by this confidentiality obligation after the termination of this Agreement. If this Agreement were to terminate, Licensee shall immediately return to Licensor any brochures, pamphlets, instructional manuals, computer disks, or any other physical or written materials relating to the Products and any other proprietary business information received by Licensee from Licensor in connection with this Agreement.

ARTICLE 7
ROYALTIES

(1) Licensee, in consideration of the grant of the licenses hereunder, will pay to Licensor the sum of fifty thousand United States dollars (US $50,000) (in the manner provided in paragraph (5) below) within one month of the date hereof, less any taxes assessed against Licensor on said payment which Licensee may be required by law to deduct. In the absence of any clearly defined legal restrictions, Licensor will have the right to determine how any taxes will be paid.

(2) During the continuance of these licenses, Licensee will pay to Licensor on all sales by it of the Products a royalty of ten percent (10%) of the selling price for each Product manufactured by or on behalf of Licensee and sold by Licensee, its affiliates, and subsidiaries.

(3) Royalties are to be paid in quarterly installments (less taxes as aforesaid) within thirty (30) days after the close of each quarter of the License Year. Any payment (less taxes as aforesaid) (hereinafter referred to as a Deficiency Payment) required to be made by Licensee to ensure that the aggregate royalties paid in respect of any License Year are equal to the minimum royalty for that License Year will become due and payable by Licensee with the quarterly installment of royalties due and payable for the quarter ending on December 31 of that License Year.

Each of these installment or Deficiency Payments will be converted to U.S. dollars by reference to the official exchange rates between the Euro and U.S. dollar prevailing at the close of the last day of the quarter for which the payment is due and will be paid at Licensor's office in Worthington, Ohio, USA, or at such other places as Licensor may specify from time to time, in U.S. dollars and through a New York bank designated by Licensor.

(4) Each Royalty payment shall be accompanied by a statement of the number of Products sold, the date of sale, and the selling price.

(5) For as long as royalties are due under this Agreement, Licensee will keep true and accurate records adequate to permit royalties due to Licensor to be computed and verified, which records will be open, at all reasonable times during business hours, for inspection by a chartered accountant or, alternatively, another independent accountant acceptable to Licensee duly authorized in writing by Licensor to the extent necessary for the determination of the accuracy of the reports made hereunder. Licensor's accountants will have the right to make copies of the relevant records. If in any of these audits there is an error in the reports or payments by Licensee to Licensor of five percent (5%) or more in the royalty paid or payable to Licensor, Licensee will forthwith reimburse Licensor the cost of that audit and all other costs of the collection of the unpaid royalty, including, but not limited to, reasonable attorney's fees and court fees. Upon request by Licensor, Licensee will have the independent accountant that is auditing its books for the benefit of its shareholders provide Licensor with an auditor's certificate as to the accuracy of the royalty statements and payments made hereunder for the two (2) years immediately preceding such a request.

ARTICLE 8
BEST EFFORTS

Licensee agrees to be diligent and to use its best endeavors to manufacture, promote, and develop the sale of and the market for the Products within the Territory. Licensee shall provide Licensor with a promotional and marketing plan for the Products on a semi-annual basis for comment.

ARTICLE 9
MANUFACTURE AND MARKETING

(1) Licensee agrees to manufacture the Products in accordance with the designs, specifications, drawings, and other information supplied or approved by Licensor, in accordance with standards set by Licensor. Licensor will not unreasonably withhold approval of improvements suggested by Licensee.

(2) Licensor will have the right to inspect the production facilities and processes used by Licensee in manufacturing the Products and to test the finished Products sold under any trademark of Licensor.

(3) Licensee agrees to mark the Products and the packages or containers in which the Products are sold and shipped in a manner which conforms with the patent and trademark law of the Territory with respect to notice or other matters relating to patent and trademark ownership license and infringement.

(4) Licensee agrees to use the trademark SUPERABRASIVES or other trademark selected by Licensor on all the Products within the Territory in accordance with the provisions of paragraph (3) under "Trademarks" of this Agreement.

ARTICLE 10
TERM

(1) This Agreement shall have a term of ten (10) years. The licenses granted pursuant to Article 2 "Grants" of this Agreement shall be in effect for the term of this Agreement and shall terminate at the end of the term of this Agreement or upon the earlier termination of this Agreement. If for any reason, German Patent No. 6,820-1564 shall terminate before the expiration of the 10-year term of this Agreement, this Agreement and the licenses granted hereunder shall automatically terminate.

(2) At the conclusion of five (5) years, the parties shall enter into good faith negotiations for a joint venture partnership for the manufacture and sale of the Products and other products or services within the Federal Republic of Germany.

(3) If Licensee defaults in making royalty payments in pursuance to the provisions of paragraph (3) under "Royalties" or commits any other material breach of the terms of this Agreement, Licensor, at its option (to be exercised within thirty (30) days of knowledge of occurrence of said breach), can give written notice of its intention to terminate to Licensee, specifying the default or breach and a termination date not earlier than thirty (30) days from the date of the mailing of that notice, in the case of default in making royalty payments, and not earlier than ninety (90) days from the date of mailing of that notice for any other breach.

If Licensee fails to repair the default or breach prior to the specified date of termination, the licenses hereunder will then terminate. No failure by Licensor to exercise the option hereunder upon any occurrence therefore will be a waiver of Licensor's right to exercise the option respecting a subsequent default or breach.

(4) In the event either party commits any act of bankruptcy, becomes insolvent, enters into any arrangement with creditors, or goes into liquidation (other than for purposes of amalgamation or reconstruction), the other party will be entitled to terminate this Agreement forthwith by notice in writing without prejudice to the rights and remedies of either party against the other accrued prior thereto.

(5) The licenses under this Agreement cannot be terminated because either Licensor or Licensee undergoes reorganization, provided that the obligations under this Agreement are fulfilled.

(6) Subject to the royalty provisions of this Agreement, Licensor, for a period of one hundred and twenty (120) days upon termination of the licenses hereunder for cause by Licensor, can sell all Products in inventory and finish and sell all thereof in the process of manufacture. Upon termination for reasons other than cause by Licensor, the period will be one (1) year.

ARTICLE 11
INFRINGEMENT AND WARRANTY

If any infringement or threatened infringement of any patents and trademarks licensed hereunder comes to the notice of Licensee, it will forthwith notify Licensor giving particulars thereof. Licensee shall provide all reasonable aid and assistance to Licensor in enforcing the patent and trademark rights of the Licensor. Licensor shall be responsible for all costs in connection with the enforcement and protection of its patent and trademark rights in Germany.

ARTICLE 12
GRANT BACK OF IMPROVEMENTS

(1) Licensor agrees to promptly notify Licensee of any improvements or inventions relating to the Products developed or in the process of development by Licensor. Licensee will have the right to use those improvements. In the event that Licensor secures patents on any of these improvements within the Territory, Licensee will have the right, at its option, to include those patents within the terms of the present Agreement. Only one (1) royalty per Product will be due regardless of the number of patents involved in a Product.

(2) Licensee agrees to promptly notify Licensor of any improvements or inventions relating to the Products developed or in the process of development by Licensee, and of any such inventions or improvements which may be acquired by or come under the control of Licensee, its officers, or employees. Licensor shall be entitled to seek patents for such improvements in any country in the world. Licensee will execute or cause to be executed, delivered, or filed, as Licensor may direct, all papers, documents, and assignments as Licensor, at its sole expense, prepares in order to vest effectively in Licensor full right, title, and interest in and to the applications and patents resulting therefrom.

ARTICLE 13
TRADEMARKS

(1) Licensor agrees to register and maintain, at its expense, in the Territory any Licensor trademarks relating to the Products in use during the continuance of this Agreement if so requested by Licensee from time to time.

(2) Licensee agrees to use the trademark SUPERABRASIVES or other trademark selected by Licensor on all the Products within the Territory. This marking will be conspicuous on all manufactured products, advertising media brochures, and other technical data transmitted to customers regarding the Products. Licensee will be entitled, at its own discretion, to use in addition its own name, provided that the ownership by Licensor of the trademark SUPERABRASIVES or other trademarks is made distinct. Upon termination of the licenses under this Agreement, Licensee will cease to use the word SUPERABRASIVES or other Licensor mark as soon as reasonably practicable for it to do so.

(3) The term of use of any trademark licensed in connection with this Agreement will be coincident with the life of this Agreement.

ARTICLE 14
MISCELLANEOUS

(1) The terms and provisions of this Agreement will be construed in accordance with the laws of the United States.

(2) Any dispute or difference arising between the parties hereto will be resolved by consultation between the parties. If such consultation cannot resolve the dispute, such dispute shall be submitted to arbitration in Columbus, Ohio.

(3) Licensee covenants that at any time hereafter, it will not contest, nor assist others in contesting: (a) the validity of the patents and patent applications which are the subjects of this Agreement, (b) the title of Licensor thereto, nor (c) the novelty, utility, or patentability of any subject matter of any of the patents. The patents, throughout their respective terms and for all purposes, will be deemed in force and valid unless declared invalid by a court of last resort or by any court from the decision of which an appeal is not taken within the time provided by law.

ARTICLE 15
TRANSFER

This Agreement and the rights hereunder cannot be assigned by any party without the prior written consent of the other party except to an assignee of the entire business of the transferring party. This Agreement has been drawn up in triplicate and all copies duly signed by all parties, as witness the signatures of the parties the date and year first above written.

Commission Regulation (EU) No. 316/2014 of 21 March 2014 on the Application of Article 101(3) of the Treaty to Categories of Technology Transfer Agreements[7]

ARTICLE 1
DEFINITIONS

1. For the purposes of this Regulation, the following definitions shall apply:

(a) "agreement" means an agreement, a decision of an association of undertakings or a concerted practice;

(b) "technology transfer agreement" means:

    (i) a technology rights licensing agreement entered into between two undertakings for the purpose of the production of contract products by the licensee and/or its sub-contractor(s),

    (ii) an assignment of technology rights between two undertakings for the purpose of the production of contract products where part of the risk associated with the exploitation of the technology remains with the assignor;

* * *

---

7. Available at http://eur-lex.europa.eu/legal-content/EN/TXT/PDF/?uri=CELEX:32014R0316&from=EN.

(j) "competing undertakings" means undertakings which compete on the relevant market, that is to say:

   (i) competing undertakings on the relevant market where the technology rights are licensed, that is to say, undertakings which license out competing technology rights (actual competitors on the relevant market),

   (ii) competing undertakings on the relevant market where the contract products are sold, that is to say, undertakings which, in the absence of the technology transfer agreement, would both be active on the relevant market(s) on which the contract products are sold (actual competitors on the relevant market) or which, in the absence of the technology transfer agreement, would, on realistic grounds and not just as a mere theoretical possibility, in response to a small and permanent increase in relative prices, be likely to undertake, within a short period of time, the necessary additional investments or other necessary switching costs to enter the relevant market(s) (potential competitors in the relevant market)[.]

ARTICLE 2
EXEMPTION

1. Pursuant to Article 101(3) of the Treaty and subject to the provisions of this Regulation, Article 101(1) of the Treaty shall not apply to technology transfer agreements.

2. The exemption provided for in paragraph 1 shall apply to the extent that such agreements contain restrictions of competition falling within the scope of Article 101(1) of the Treaty. The exemption shall apply for as long as the licensed technology rights have not expired, lapsed or been declared invalid or, in the case of know-how, for as long as the know-how remains secret., However, where know-how becomes publicly known as a result of action by the licensee, the exemption shall apply for the duration of the agreement.

3. The exemption provided for in paragraph 1 shall also apply to provisions, in technology transfer agreements, which relate to the purchase of products by the licensee or which relate to the licensing or assignment of other intellectual property rights or know-how to the licensee, if, and to the extent that, those provisions are directly related to the production or sale of the contract products.

ARTICLE 3
MARKET-SHARE THRESHOLDS

1. Where the undertakings party to the agreement are competing undertakings, the exemption provided for in Article 2 shall apply on condition that the combined market share of the parties does not exceed 20 percent on the relevant market(s).

2. Where the undertakings party to the agreement are not competing undertakings, the exemption provided for in Article 2 shall apply on condition that the market share of each of the parties does not exceed 30 percent on the relevant market(s).

ARTICLE 4
HARDCORE RESTRICTIONS

1. Where the undertakings party to the agreement are competing undertakings, the exemption provided for in Article 2 shall not apply to agreements which, directly or

indirectly, in isolation or in combination with other factors under the control of the parties, have as their object any of the following:

(a) the restriction of a party's ability to determine its prices when selling products to third parties;

(b) the limitation of output, except limitations on the output of contract products imposed on the licensee in a non-reciprocal agreement or imposed on only one of the licensees in a reciprocal agreement;

(c) the allocation of markets or customers except:

  (i) the obligation on the licensor and/or the licensee, in a non-reciprocal agreement, not to produce with the licensed technology rights within the exclusive territory reserved for the other party and/or not to sell actively and/or passively into the exclusive territory or to the exclusive customer group reserved for the other party,

  (ii) the restriction, in a non-reciprocal agreement, of active sales by the licensee into the exclusive territory or to the exclusive customer group allocated by the licensor to another licensee provided the latter was not a competing undertaking of the licensor at the time of the conclusion of its own license,

  (iii) the obligation on the licensee to produce the contract products only for its own use provided that the licensee is not restricted in selling the contract products actively and passively as spare parts for its own products,

  (iv) the obligation on the licensee, in a non-reciprocal agreement, to produce the contract products only for a particular customer, where the license was granted in order to create an alternative source of supply for that customer[.]

(d) the restriction of the licensee's ability to exploit its own technology rights or the restriction of the ability of any of the parties to the agreement to carry out research and development, unless such latter restriction is indispensable to prevent the disclosure of the licensed know-how to third parties.

2. Where the undertakings party to the agreement are not competing undertakings, the exemption provided for in Article 2 shall not apply to agreements which, directly or indirectly, in isolation or in combination with other factors under the control of the parties, have as their object:

(a) the restriction of a party's ability to determine its prices when selling products to third parties, without prejudice to the possibility of imposing a maximum sale price or recommending a sale price, provided that it does not amount to a fixed or minimum sale price as a result of pressure from, or incentives offered by, any of the parties;

(b) the restriction of the territory into which, or of the customers to whom, the licensee may passively sell the contract products, except:

  (i) the restriction of passive sales into an exclusive territory or to an exclusive customer group reserved for the licensor,

  (ii) the obligation to produce the contract products only for its own use provided that the licensee is not restricted in selling the contract products actively and passively as spare parts for its own products,

  (iii) the obligation to produce the contract products only for a particular customer, where the license was granted in order to create an alternative source of supply for that customer,

      (iv) the restriction of sales to end-users by a licensee operating at the wholesale level of trade,

      (v) the restriction of sales to unauthorized distributors by the members of a selective distribution system;

   (c) the restriction of active or passive sales to end-users by a licensee which is a member of a selective distribution system and which operates at the retail level, without prejudice to the possibility of prohibiting a member of the system from operating out of an unauthorized place of establishment.

3. Where the undertakings party to the agreement are not competing undertakings at the time of the conclusion of the agreement but become competing undertakings afterwards, paragraph 2 and not paragraph 1 shall apply for the full life of the agreement unless the agreement is subsequently amended in any material respect. Such an amendment includes the conclusion of a new technology transfer agreement between the parties concerning competing technology rights.

ARTICLE 5
EXCLUDED RESTRICTIONS

1. The exemption provided for in Article 2 shall not apply to any of the following obligations contained in technology transfer agreements:

   (a) any direct or indirect obligation on the licensee to grant an exclusive license or to assign rights, in whole or in part, to the licensor or to a third party designated by the licensor in respect of its own improvements to, or its own new applications of, the licensed technology;

   (b) any direct or indirect obligation on licensee party not to challenge the validity of intellectual property rights which the other party holds in the Union, without prejudice to the possibility of providing for termination of the technology transfer agreement in the event that the licensee challenges the validity of any of the licensed technology rights.

2. Where the undertakings party to the agreement are not competing undertakings, the exemption provided for in Article 2 shall not apply to any direct or indirect obligation limiting the licensee's ability to exploit its own technology rights or limiting the ability of any of the parties to the agreement to carry out research and development, unless such latter restriction is indispensable to prevent the disclosure of the licensed know-how to third parties.

NOTES AND QUESTIONS

1. Violations of Article 4 (hardcore restrictions) and Article 5 (excluded restrictions) have distinctly different effects on the entire agreement. Can you explain how? *Cf.* Article 4(1) and Article 5(1).

2. Commission Regulation No. 316/2014 is another example of a block exemption to the prohibitions contained in Article 101(1) of the Treaty on the Functioning of the European Union. We have already seen an example of a block exemption issued by the

commission, namely, the Commission Regulation No. 330/2010 that applies to vertical agreements, including distributorships. EU Commission Regulation No. 316/2014 applies specifically to technology transfer agreements, including patent and know-how licenses and some types of mixed licenses. Both block exemptions take the approach that everything that is not prohibited is allowed. Both regulations are also distinctly practical in examining the market power of the undertakings involved, although each sets different market thresholds and tests of economic power. The basic concept is that technology licensing agreements and distribution agreements often improve economic efficiency but can be anticompetitive if the undertakings involved exert too much market power. Although the block exemption is a type of general exception, Article 6 of EU Commission Regulation No. 316/2014 allows the commission to withdraw the benefit of the exemption for a technology transfer agreement where the commission finds that the agreement results in certain specified anticompetitive effects.

3. Problem 5-10 above dealt with the common issue of disputes over ownership of improvements made to the patent by the licensee and the use of so-called grant back clauses that assigns the improvement to the licensor. But what if the licensee produces (or purchases from a third party) a technical breakthrough that the licensee claims is not an improvement at all but an entirely new invention and intellectual property right that is independent of the technology licensed by the agreement? The licensor/patentee might disagree and may charge the licensee with patent infringement. How is this type of dispute resolved? The licensor/patentee may have to bring an infringement lawsuit against the licensee to determine whether the new technology is within the scope of the technology licensed by the agreement. By longstanding precedent, the burden of persuasion is on the licensor/patentee. *See Agawam Co. v. Jordan*, 74 U.S. (7 Wall.) 583, 609 (1869). But what happens if the licensee in such a case brings a declaratory judgment action against the licensor/patentee to resolve the issue? In 2014, the Supreme Court ruled that, since declaratory judgment actions are purely procedural, the burden of proof/persuasion stays with the licensor/patentee. *See Medtronic, Inc. v. Mirowski Family Ventures, LLC*, 134 S. Ct. 843 (2014). The unanimous Supreme Court reversed the Federal Circuit, which had ruled that the burden of proof/persuasion shifts in a declaratory judgment action to the licensee. Justice Breyer's opinion stated that it is in the public interest that patents be kept "within their legitimate scope"; and that a patentee should not be able to "exact royalties for the use of an idea that is beyond the scope of the patent monopoly granted." 134 S. Ct. at 851–852.

IV. *Business Format Franchising*

In both of the topics we have considered so far in this chapter, selling overseas through an agent/distributor or by contract manufacturing, the U.S. company is able to establish deeper penetration of the foreign market. In both cases, the U.S. company does not establish a business entity overseas but works through a third party that is authorized to sell or manufacture its products. While these two methods may allow greater penetration by the product of the foreign market, there are limitations to how effective these methods will be in establishing the identity and business reputation of the U.S. company overseas. In the distribution agreement that we considered earlier in this chapter, the distributor is an independent contractor and is required to avoid creating any confusion on the part of consumers that the distributor owns the products or is authorized to act on behalf of the U.S. company. One intended purpose of this approach is to create a separation between the distributor and the U.S. company in the minds of consumers. Similar provisions also exist in the patent licensing agreement. The limitation created by this approach is that while the U.S. company's product may achieve a greater penetration of the foreign market, the U.S. corporation is unable to achieve a broader international recognition of its trade name, business reputation, and identity in the foreign market.

Suppose that our U.S. company wishes not only to sell its products overseas but also to achieve international recognition for its trademarks, trade name, business identity, and reputation. We are, of course, now inching ever closer to the topic of foreign direct investment, the subject of the next chapter, as one clear way of achieving this goal is to invest capital and establish a business entity overseas in the form of a wholly- or partially-owned foreign subsidiary. But this method is the subject of the next chapter, and the question we wish to consider now is how a U.S. corporation can expand its international reputation without the investment of capital overseas, but by using a non-establishment form of overseas expansion consistent with the other topics covered in this chapter. For these purposes, the U.S. corporation should consider the last topic in this chapter: the business format franchise — a non-establishment form of doing business that moves the progression of penetrating foreign markets even closer to the final step of FDI.

In a business format franchise, the franchisee operates its business under the franchisor's trade name and under the franchisor's business identity. The franchisee is identified as part of a select group of dealers and is generally required to assume a standard appearance and to follow standardized methods of operation. A wide variety of products and services can be offered through this format. Note that the advantage of the franchise is that the franchisor is able to achieve international trademark and trade name recognition within a short time without the outlay of capital and the franchisee is able to obtain status as an independent business and the use of valuable trademarks, trade names, business methods, and knowledge, all under the guidance of an experienced company. Because of its advantages, the franchising concept has now become a major factor in both the United States and the global economy. According to the U.S. Department of Commerce:

> Franchising is one of the most creative of the various marketing techniques that have emerged in this century. Today, the key to a successful franchise operation is a strong system. It is the system that provides the appearance that all outlets belong to a chain; it is the system that all franchisees can follow; it is the system that provides the know-how to franchisees to keep one step ahead of the competition; and it is the system that will continue to provide abundant opportunities to all that want to fulfill the dream of owning one's own business.

U.S. Department of Commerce, *Franchising in the Economy 1984–1986* (1986). While the patent licensing agreement primarily concerns the licensing of patents, the franchise agreement concerns primarily the licensing of trademarks and trade names as these are essential to establish business identity and reputation.

In the United States, both federal and state laws govern the franchise relationship. The Federal Trade Commission has promulgated legislation setting forth disclosure requirements and prohibitions. *See* FTC Disclosure Requirements and Prohibitions Concerning Franchising, 16 C.F.R. pt. 436 (2009). Other examples of federal legislation are the Automobile Dealers' Day in Court Act, 15 U.S.C. §§1221–1225 (2006), and the Petroleum Marketing Practices Act, 15 U.S.C. §2801 *et seq.* (2006). Many states also have statutes governing the franchise relationship. *See, e.g.,* Business Opportunity Purchaser's

Protection Act, O.R.C. §§1334.01–1334.99. On an international level, some nations do not have specific laws governing franchise agreements but apply general principles of contract law. Others, such as Canada, have laws governing issues such as misrepresentation in the franchise prospectus and providing the franchisee with a period in which the agreement can be canceled without penalty. *See, e.g.,* Arthur Wishart Act (Franchise Disclosure), S.O. 2000, c. 3, s. 6 (Can.) Other laws, such as EU competition laws, may also apply, as we shall see in the materials below.

NOTES AND QUESTIONS

1. Authorizing an independent entity to sell the franchisor's product, as in a distributorship, or licensing a franchisee to manufacture the franchisor's product, as in contract manufacturing, can also be considered franchising, although in a more limited form. Our focus in this section is on the business format franchise.

2. Business format franchise agreements usually impose requirements on the uniformity of the product, decor of the restaurant, and services. Think of the case of successful fast-food franchises such as McDonald's. Why?

3. Culture, not usually an issue in international patent licensing, can present some significant issues in international franchise agreements. Again, think of successful international franchises such as Pizza Hut or Friday's. Why?

PROBLEM 5-11

Hamburger Heaven (HH), an Ohio corporation, is a fast-food restaurant specializing in wholesome, hearty American food. HH's menu consists mostly of hamburgers and chicken. HH owns several U.S. service marks and trademarks for its foods, each using alliterative sounds, for example, "Harry's Heartland Hamburger," "Betty's Buckeye Breakfast," and "Charlie's Cleveland Club." HH is considering overseas franchises in Germany, including in some old historical cities near some famous landmarks to attract the tourist crowd, and would like to maintain the same business approach. HH also has a distinctive decorative scheme that includes the use of an outdoor sign featuring a 25-foot-tall representation of Brutus Buckeye, the Ohio State University mascot. (Brutus wears a football jersey and has a very large buckeye, a nut that is the state symbol, for a head.)

(1) Review the discussion in Section II.B above on the international intellectual property system and the subsection on trademarks (Section II.B.2). What must HH do to protect its trademarks in Europe? Are there any preliminary issues relating to language that need to be resolved before submitting the marks for registration?

(2) HH has asked you to review the franchise agreement below, which HH uses for its franchises in the United States. HH asks whether the agreement is suitable for an international franchisee. In particular, HH asks you whether any additional issues in the case of an international franchise might require changes to Article 2 (Development and Opening of Restaurant), Article 3 (Training and Operating Assistance), and Article 4 (Restaurant Image and Operating Standards). What other provisions need to be adapted for an international franchise?

Franchise Agreement

THIS AGREEMENT is made and entered into this _____ day of _____, 2010, by and between Hamburger Heaven, an Ohio corporation, with its principal office at 2436 Heartland Drive, Toledo, Ohio (the Company), and _____, a corporation, whose principal address is _____ (the Franchisee). The parties hereby agree as follows:

ARTICLE 1
GRANT AND RENEWAL OF FRANCHISE

(1) *Grant of Franchise.* Subject to the provisions of this Agreement, the Company hereby grants to the Franchisee a franchise to operate a Company Restaurant at premises identified, or to be identified, in Exhibit 1 or a substitute premises hereafter approved by the Company (the Restaurant), and to use the Names and Marks in the operation thereof, for a term of ten (10) years commencing on the date of this Agreement (the Franchise). Termination or expiration of this Agreement shall constitute a termination or expiration of the Franchise.

(2) *Exclusive Territory.* The Company agrees that during the term of the Franchise, provided that the Franchisee is in substantial compliance with this Agreement, the Company will not operate or grant a franchise for the operation of a Company Restaurant within the area described in Exhibit 2 as Franchisee's exclusive territory.

ARTICLE 2
DEVELOPMENT AND OPENING OF RESTAURANT

(1) *Lease or Purchase of Premises of Restaurant.* Franchisee, contemporaneously with the execution of this Agreement, will lease or purchase the premises of the Restaurant identified in Exhibit 1, provided that if a premises has not then been selected or approved by the Company, the Franchisee agrees to lease or purchase suitable premises, reasonably acceptable to the Company, within ninety (90) days after the execution of this Agreement. The Company will reasonably assist Franchisee in site evaluation and lease or purchase negotiations. If Franchisee fails to lease or purchase suitable premises within ninety (90) days after execution of this Agreement, the Company shall have the right to terminate this Agreement, effective upon delivery of written notice of termination to Franchisee.

(2) *Required Lease Provisions.* The lease for the premises of the Restaurant shall provide that upon termination or expiration of the Franchise for any reason, other than a termination by Franchisee for cause, the Company shall have the right to assume the Franchisee's status and replace the Franchisee as lessee.

(3) *Development of Restaurant.* The Company will furnish to the Franchisee standard basic plans and specifications for a Company Restaurant, including requirements for dimensions, exterior design, interior layout, building materials, equipment, signs, and color scheme.

(4) *Equipment, Fixtures, and Signs.* The Franchisee agrees to use in the operation of the Restaurant only those brands and models of equipment, fixtures, and signs that the Company has approved for Company Restaurants. The Franchisee further agrees to place or display at the premises of the Restaurant (interior and exterior) only such signs, emblems, lettering, logos, and display materials that are from time to time approved in

writing by the Company. The Franchisee may purchase or lease approved brands and models of equipment, fixtures, and signs from any supplier. If the Franchisee proposes to purchase or lease any brand and/or model of equipment, fixture, or sign which is not then approved by the Company, the Franchisee shall first notify the Company and obtain the Company's written consent.

(5) *Restaurant Opening.* The Franchisee agrees to open the Restaurant for business and commence the conduct of its business within fifteen (15) days after the Company's determination that it is in suitable condition.

ARTICLE 3
TRAINING AND OPERATING ASSISTANCE

(1) *Training.* Prior to the opening of the Restaurant, the Company shall train the Franchisee and the manager of the Restaurant in the operation of a Company Restaurant.

(2) *Completion of Training/Termination.* The Franchisee shall complete training in the operation of a Company Restaurant to the satisfaction of the Company. If the Company reasonably determines that the Franchisee is unable to satisfactorily complete such training, this Agreement shall terminate.

ARTICLE 4
RESTAURANT IMAGE AND OPERATING STANDARDS

(1) *Condition and Appearance of Restaurant.* The Franchisee agrees to maintain the condition and appearance of the Restaurant consistent with the image of a Company Restaurant as an attractive, modern, sanitary, convenient, and efficiently operated restaurant selling high-quality products and service.

(2) *Alterations to Restaurant.* The Franchisee shall make no material alterations to the leasehold improvements or appearance of the Restaurant, nor shall the Franchisee make any material replacements of or alterations to the equipment, fixtures, or signs of the Restaurant without prior written approval by the Company.

(3) *Authorized Products and Services.* The presentation of a uniform image to the public and the furnishing of uniform products and services is an essential element of a successful franchise system. The Franchisee therefore agrees that the Restaurant will offer all hamburgers, sandwiches, chicken, beverages, ice cream flavors and dishes, and all other products and services that the Company from time to time authorizes for Company Restaurants. The Franchisee further agrees that the Restaurant, without prior written approval by the Company, will not offer any other products or services, nor shall the Restaurant or the premises which it occupies be used for any purpose other than the operation of a Company Restaurant.

(4) *Food and Beverage Products, Supplies, and Materials.* The reputation and goodwill of the Company Restaurant is based upon, and can be maintained and enhanced only by, the sale of high-quality products and the rendering of fast, efficient, and high-quality service. The Franchisee therefore agrees that all food and beverage products, cooking materials, containers, packaging materials, other paper and plastic products, glassware, utensils, uniforms, menus, forms, cleaning and sanitation materials, and other supplies and materials used in the operation of the Restaurant shall conform to the specifications and quality standards established by the Company and shall be purchased from suppliers

approved by the Company. If the Franchisee proposes to use in the operation of the Restaurant any product, supply, or material not theretofore approved by the Company, the Franchisee shall submit to the Company sufficient specifications, photographs, and/or other information or samples for examination and/or testing and for a determination by the Company of whether such product, supply, or material, and/or such supplier, meets the Company's specifications and standards. . . .

(6) *Standards of Service.* The Restaurant shall at all times give prompt, courteous, and efficient service to its customers. The Restaurant shall in all dealings with its customers, suppliers, and the public adhere to the highest standards of honesty, integrity, fair dealing, and ethical conduct.

(7) *Specifications, Standards, and Procedures.* The Franchisee agrees to comply with all mandatory specifications, standards, and operating procedures relating to the operation of a Company Restaurant.

(8) *Compliance With Laws and Good Business Practices.* The Franchisee shall secure and maintain in force all required licenses, permits, and certificates relating to the operation of the Restaurant and shall operate the Restaurant in full compliance with all applicable laws, ordinances, and regulations. The Franchisee agrees to refrain from any business or advertising practice which may be injurious to the business of the Company and the goodwill associated with the Names and Marks and other Company Restaurants.

(9) *Prices to Be Determined by Franchisee.* The Company may from time to time advise or offer guidance to the Franchisee relative to menu prices for Company Restaurants. The Franchisee shall not be obligated to accept any such advice or guidance and shall have the sole right to determine the prices and charges to be charged by the Restaurant.

(10) *Insurance.* The Franchisee shall at all times during the term of the Franchise maintain in force at his sole expense comprehensive public and product liability insurance against claims for bodily and personal injury, death, and property damage caused by or occurring in conjunction with the operation of the Restaurant. Such insurance coverage shall be maintained under one or more policies of insurance containing minimum liability protection of two million dollars ($2,000,000) for bodily and personal injury and death and two hundred thousand dollars ($200,000) for property damage. All such liability insurance policies shall name the Company as an additional insured and shall provide that the Company shall receive ten (10) days prior written notice of termination, expiration, or cancellation of any such policy.

ARTICLE 5
OPERATING MANUAL

The Company will loan to the Franchisee during the term of the Franchise one or more copies of an operating manual for Company Restaurants containing mandatory and suggested specifications, standards, and operating procedures. The operating manual contains proprietary information of the Company and the Franchisee agrees to keep the operating manual confidential at all times during and after the term of the Franchise.

ARTICLE 6
TRADE SECRETS OF COMPANY

The Franchisee acknowledges that its knowledge of the operation of a Company Restaurant will be derived from information disclosed by the Company and that certain pieces of such information, including but not limited to that contained in the operating manual, is proprietary, confidential, and a trade secret of the Company. The Franchisee agrees that it will maintain the absolute confidentiality of all such information during and after the term of the Franchise, and that it will not use any such information in any other business or in any manner not specifically authorized or approved in writing by the Company.

ARTICLE 7
ADVERTISING AND PROMOTION

(1) *By Company.* The Company will develop, prepare, and furnish to the Franchisee fliers, posters, ad formats, and other direct mail, point of sale, and media advertising materials for Company Restaurants and will implement advertising and promotion programs in such form and media as it determines to be most effective and economical. The Franchisee agrees to pay to the Company as its share of the cost of the development and preparation of such advertising . . . four percent (4%) of the net revenues of the Restaurant, payable monthly with the royalty and service fee hereinafter described.

(2) *By Franchisee.* The Company shall have the right to require the Franchisee to submit for prior approval by the Company any or all advertising and promotional materials prepared by the Franchisee, and the Franchisee shall not use any disapproved advertising or promotional materials.

***

ARTICLE 9
NAMES AND MARKS

(1) *Ownership of Names and Marks.* The Franchisee acknowledges that the Company is the owner of all Names and Marks licensed to the Franchisee by this Agreement, that the Franchisee's right to use the Names and Marks is derived solely from this Agreement, is limited to the operation of the Restaurant in compliance with this Agreement at the location and premises identified in Exhibit 1. The Franchisee agrees that all usage of the Names and Marks by the Franchisee and any goodwill established thereby shall inure to the exclusive benefit of the Company. The Franchisee further agrees that after the termination or expiration of the Franchise, it will not directly or indirectly at any time or in any manner identify himself, any restaurant, or any other business as a Company Restaurant, a former Company Restaurant, or as a franchisee of or otherwise associated with the Company.

(2) *Limitations on Franchisee's Use of Names and Marks.* The Franchisee agrees to use the Names and Marks as the sole service mark and trade name identification of the Restaurant. The Franchisee shall not use any Name or Mark as part of any corporate name or with any prefix, suffix, or other modifying words, terms, designs, or symbols (other than logos licensed to the Franchisee hereunder), or in any modified form, nor may the Franchisee use any Name or Mark in connection with the sale of any unauthorized product or service, or in any other manner not explicitly authorized in writing by the Company.

ARTICLE 10
INITIAL FRANCHISE FEE

The Franchisee shall pay to the Company a nonrecurring and nonrefundable initial franchise fee for the Franchise in the amount of one hundred thousand dollars ($100,000), payable upon the execution of this Agreement.

ARTICLE 11
ROYALTY AND SERVICE FEE

(1) *Amount and Payment of Royalty and Service Fee.* The Franchisee agrees to pay to the Company a royalty and service fee of four percent (4%) of the net revenues of the Restaurant, payable by the fifteenth (15th) day of each month on net revenues for the preceding month.

***

ARTICLE 13
TERMINATION OF FRANCHISE

(1) *By Franchisee.* If the Franchisee is in substantial compliance with this Agreement and the Company breaches this Agreement and fails to cure such breach within thirty (30) days after written notice thereof is delivered to the Company, the Franchisee may terminate this Agreement effective ten (10) days after delivery to the Company of notice thereof.

(2) *By Company.* The Company may terminate this Agreement effective upon delivery of notice of termination to the Franchisee, if the Franchisee or the Restaurant:

(a) Makes an assignment for the benefit of creditors or an admission of its inability to pay its obligations as they become due;

(b) Files a voluntary petition in bankruptcy or any pleading seeking any reorganization, liquidation, or dissolution under any law or is adjudicated bankrupt or insolvent, or a receiver is appointed for a substantial part of the assets of the Franchisee or the Restaurant;

(c) Abandons, surrenders, or transfers control of the operation of the Restaurant, or fails to actively operate the Restaurant, unless precluded from doing so by damage to the premises of the Restaurant, war or civil disturbance, natural disaster, labor dispute, or other event beyond the Franchisee's reasonable control;

(d) Suffers cancellation of, fails to renew or extend the lease for, or otherwise fails to maintain possession of the premises of the Restaurant;

(e) Submits to the Company on two (2) or more separate occasions a monthly report, financial statement, tax return or schedule, or other information or supporting records that understates the net revenues of the Restaurant for any period by more than three percent (3%);

(f) Consistently fails or refuses to submit when due monthly reports, quarterly and annual financial statements, tax returns, schedules, or other information or supporting records; to pay when due the royalty and service fees, advertising contributions, amounts due for any products purchased from the Company, or other payments due to the Company; or otherwise repeatedly fails or refuses to comply with this Agreement;

(g) Operates the Restaurant in a manner that presents a health or safety hazard to its customers, employees, or the public;

(h) Makes an unauthorized assignment of the Franchise or ownership of the Franchisee;

(i) Fails or refuses to pay any amount owed to the Company for royalty and service fees, advertising contributions, products purchased from the Company, or any amounts otherwise due to the Company, or fails or refuses to comply with any mandatory specification, standard, or operating procedure prescribed by the Company and does not correct such failure or refusal within seven (7) days after written notice thereof; or

(j) Fails to comply with any other provision of this Agreement or any other mandatory specification, standard, or operating procedure prescribed by the Company, and does not correct such failure within thirty (30) days after written notice of such failure to comply is delivered to the Franchisee.

ARTICLE 14
FRANCHISEE'S OBLIGATION UPON TERMINATION OR EXPIRATION

(1) *Payment of Amounts Owed to Company.* The Franchisee agrees to pay to the Company within fifteen (15) days after the effective date of termination or expiration of the Franchise such royalty and service fees, advertising contributions, amounts owed for products purchased by the Franchisee from the Company, and all other amounts owed to the Company which are then unpaid.

(2) *Return of Manuals.* The Franchisee further agrees that upon termination or expiration of the Franchise, it will immediately return to the Company all copies of the operating manual for Company Restaurants that have been loaned to it by the Company.

(3) *Company Has Right to Purchase Restaurant.* If this Agreement is terminated prior to its expiration by the Company in accordance with the provisions of this Agreement, or by the Franchisee without cause, the Company shall have the right to purchase from the Franchisee the assets of the Restaurant (including the premises of the Restaurant if owned by the Franchisee) and to an assignment of the Franchisee's lease for the premises of the Restaurant.

(4) *Covenant Not to Compete.* If this Agreement is terminated prior to its expiration by the Company in accordance with the provisions of this Agreement, or by the Franchisee without cause, the Franchisee agrees that for a period of two (2) years it will not have any interest as an owner, partner, director, officer, employee, consultant, representative, or agent, or in any other capacity, in any restaurant serving hamburgers, sandwiches, chicken, or ice cream and located within the metropolitan area wherein the Restaurant is located.

ARTICLE 15
ASSIGNMENT, TRANSFER, AND ENCUMBRANCE

The Franchise is personal to the Franchisee, and neither the Franchise nor any part of the ownership of the Franchise may voluntarily, involuntarily, directly, or indirectly be assigned, subdivided, sub-franchised, or otherwise transferred by the Franchisee or its owners without the prior written approval of the Company.

PROBLEM 5-12

Based on the agreement set forth above, Hamburger Heaven has entered into a franchise with Schmidt, a German franchisee. The franchisee has opened up a restaurant called "Schmidt's Hamburger Heaven." The franchisee also wishes to conduct an extensive advertising campaign in the German television and print media. Schmidt would also like to add a few menu items such as "Schmidt's Bavarian Burger," "Schmidt's Bratwurst Blast," and a few kinds of German beer because such items are more suited to local tastes. Finally, Schmidt would like to move his restaurant five miles to a location near a new shopping center development.

(1) Under the franchise agreement, is the franchisee allowed to use his own name in the trade name of the restaurant? See Article 9 of the franchise agreement.
(2) Can Schmidt add the menu items? See Articles 4 and 9. Suppose that Hamburger Heaven's own marketing research shows that these items will be popular with German consumers. What advice would you have for Hamburger Heaven on these items?
(3) Can Schmidt proceed with his advertising campaign? Who controls the advertising for the franchise and why? See Article 7.
(4) Can Schmidt move his restaurant? See Article 1. Suppose that Hamburger Heaven opposes the move. Why might Hamburger Heaven do so?
(5) Are the restrictions established by Articles 1, 7, and 9 consistent with European Community law? Evaluate each of these restrictions in light of the *Pronuptia* case below.

Pronuptia de Paris GmbH v. Pronuptia de Paris
European Court of Justice[8]
[1986] ECR 353 (Jan. 28, 1986)

[Mrs. Schillgalis is a franchisee carrying on business under the name Pronuptia de Paris in Hamburg. The franchisor is Pronuptia de Paris GmbH, a German subsidiary of the French company of the same name. The French parent company distributes wedding dresses and other articles of clothing worn at weddings under the trademark "Pronuptia de Paris." In Germany, these products are sold in shops operated directly by the Germany subsidiary or under franchise contracts. Mrs. Schillgalis claimed that she did not owe royalties under the franchise agreement to the German subsidiary because the franchise agreement was in violation of EC competition law, namely, Article 85(1) now renamed Article 101(1) TFEU (see p. 303). After litigating the case in German courts, the issue, as

<hr/>

8. Authors' Note: The Court of Justice of the European Union, with its seat in Luxembourg, was created by the Treaty of Rome and given responsibility for its interpretation and application. Among its other powers, the Court is authorized by Article 177 to render preliminary decisions on questions of European Community law when so requested by a court of a member state as in *Pronuptia.*

it concerned EC competition law, was referred to the European Court of Justice, which rendered the opinion below. The ECJ first set forth the issue as follows:]

"Is Article 85(1) of the EEC Treaty [now renamed Article 101(1) TFEU] applicable to franchise agreements such as the contracts between the parties, which have as their object the establishment of a special distribution system whereby the franchisor provides to the franchisee, in addition to goods, certain trade names, trade-marks, merchandising material and services?"

Pronuptia de Paris GmbH, Frankfurt am Main, the franchisor, argues that a system of franchise agreements makes it possible to combine the advantages offered by a form of distribution which presents a uniform image to the public (such as a system of subsidiaries) with the distribution of goods by independent retailers who themselves bear the risks associated with selling. The system is made up of a network of vertical agreements intended to ensure uniform presentation to the public and reinforces the franchisor's competitive power at the horizontal level, that is to say, with regard to other forms of distribution. It makes it possible for an undertaking which would not otherwise have the necessary financial resources to establish a distribution network beyond the confines of its own region, a network which enables small undertakings to participate as franchisees while retaining their independence. In view of those advantages Article 85(1) does not apply where the franchise agreements do not include restrictions on the liberty of the contracting parties which go beyond those which are the necessary concomitants of the franchise system. Exclusive delivery and supply obligations, in so far as they are intended to ensure a standard selection of goods, uniform advertising and shop lay-out and a prohibition on selling goods supplied under the contract in other shops, are inherent in the very nature of the franchise contract and are outside the scope of Article 85(1).

[Mrs. Schillgalis argued that Article 85(1) did apply to the franchise agreement and that therefore the agreement was void and no royalties were owed. She argued that the franchise agreements divided markets by giving exclusive territorial rights to franchisees and created significant restrictions on competition in violation of Article 85(1).] The most significant characteristic of the contracts in question is the territorial protection given to the franchisee. They cannot be compared with agency agreements, since franchisees, unlike agents, act in their own name and on their own account and bear all trading risks. The system of franchise agreements at issue gives rise to significant restrictions of competition, having regard to the fact that Pronuptia is, as it itself asserts, the world's leading French supplier of wedding dresses and accessories.

[The ECJ first turned to restrictions necessary to protect the franchisor's intellectual property rights, reputation, and goodwill.]

In a system of distribution franchises of that kind an undertaking which has established itself as a distributor in a given market and thus developed certain business methods grants independent traders, for a fee, the right to establish themselves in other markets using its business name and the business methods which have made it successful. Rather than a method of distribution, it is a way for an undertaking to derive financial benefit from its expertise without investing its own capital. Moreover, the system gives traders who do not have the necessary experience access to methods which they could not have learned without considerable effort and allows them to benefit from the reputation of the franchisor's business name. Franchise agreements for the distribution system, which do not involve the use of a single business name, involve the application of uniform business methods or the payment of royalties in return for the benefits granted. Such a system, which allows the franchisor to profit from his success, does not in itself interfere with competition. In order for the system to work two conditions must be met.

First, the franchisor must be able to communicate his know-how to the franchisees and provide them with the necessary assistance in order to enable them to apply his methods, without running the risk that that know-how and assistance might benefit competitors, even indirectly. It follows that provisions that are essential in order to avoid that risk do not constitute restrictions on competition for the purpose of Article 85(1). That is also true of a clause prohibiting the franchisee, during the period of validity of the contract and for a reasonable period after its expiry, from opening a shop of the same or a similar nature in an area where he may compete with a member of the network. The same may be said of the franchisee's obligation not to transfer his shop to another party without the prior approval of the franchisor; that provision is intended to prevent competitors from indirectly benefiting from the know-how and assistance provided.

Secondly, the franchisor must be able to take the measures necessary for maintaining the identity and reputation of the network bearing his business name or symbol. It follows that provisions which establish the means of control necessary for that purpose do not constitute restrictions on competition for the purposes of Article 85(1).

The same is true of the franchisee's obligation to apply the business methods developed by the franchisor and to use the know-how provided.

That is also the case with regard to the franchisee's obligation to sell the goods covered by the contract only in premises laid out and decorated according to the franchisor's instructions, which is intended to ensure uniform presentation in conformity with certain requirements. The same requirements apply to the location of the shop, the choice of which is also likely to affect the network's reputation. It is thus understandable that the franchisee cannot transfer his shop to another location without the franchisor's approval.

The prohibition of the assignment by the franchisee of his right and obligations under the contract without the franchisor's approval protects the latter's right freely to choose the franchisees, on whose business qualifications the establishment and maintenance of the network's reputation depend.

By means of the control exerted by the franchisor on the selection of goods offered by the franchisee, the public is able to obtain goods of the same quality from each franchisee. It may in certain cases—for instance, the distribution of fashion articles—be impractical to lay down objective quality specifications. Because of the large number of franchisees it may also be too expensive to ensure that such specifications are observed. In such circumstances a provision requiring the franchisee to sell only products supplied by the franchisor or by suppliers selected by him may be considered necessary for the protection of the network's reputation. Such a provision may not however have the effect of preventing the franchisee from obtaining those products from other franchisees.

Finally, since advertising helps to define the image of the network's name or symbol in the eyes of the public, a provision requiring the franchisee to obtain the franchisor's approval for all advertising is also essential for the maintenance of the network's identity, so long as that provision concerns only the nature of the advertising.

[The ECJ next turned to territorial restrictions in the franchise agreement.]

It must be emphasized on the other hand that, far from being necessary for the protection of the know-how provided or the maintenance of the network's identity and reputation, certain provisions restrict competition between the members of the network. That is true of provisions that share markets between the franchisor and franchisees or between franchisees.

In that regard, the attention of the national court should be drawn to the provision which obliges the franchisee to sell goods covered by the contract only in the premises specified therein. That provision prohibits the franchisee from opening a second shop.

Its real effect becomes clear if it is examined in conjunction with the franchisor's under-taking to ensure that the franchisee has the exclusive use of his business name or symbol in a given territory. In order to comply with that undertaking the franchisor must not only refrain from establishing himself within that territory but also require other franchisees to give an undertaking not to open a second shop outside their own territory. A combination of provisions of that kind results in a sharing of markets between the franchisor and the franchisees or between franchisees and thus restricts competition within the network.

Finally, it must be added that franchise agreements for the distribution of goods which contain provisions sharing markets between the franchisor and the franchisees or between the franchisees themselves are in any event liable to affect trade between Member States, even if they are entered into by undertakings established in the same Member State, in so far as they prevent franchises from establishing themselves in another Member State.

In view of the foregoing, the answer to the question must be that:

Provisions that are strictly necessary in order to ensure that the know-how and assis-tance provided by the franchisor do not benefit competitors do not constitute restrictions of competition for the purposes of Article 85(1). Provisions which establish the control strictly necessary for maintaining the identity and reputation of the network identified by the common name or symbol do not constitute restrictions of competition for the purposes of Article 85(1).

Provisions that share markets between the franchisor and the franchisees or between franchisees constitute restrictions of competition for the purposes of Article 85(1). Franchise agreements for the distribution of goods which contain provisions sharing mar-kets between the franchisor and the franchisees or between franchisees are capable of affecting trade between Member States.

NOTES AND QUESTIONS

1. In *Pronuptia*, the European Court of Justice (ECJ) reasoned that franchise systems provided valuable economic benefits to the parties involved and to the customers of the systems. As a result, franchise systems should be permitted and should not be considered to be anticompetitive within the meaning of Article 85(1) (now Article 101(1) of the Treaty on the Functioning of the European Union). The ECJ distinguished between two types of restrictions: those necessary to maintain a franchise system and those restrictions that are not. The restrictions protecting know-how and other intellectual property rights of the franchisor and those restrictions necessary to maintain the common identity and reputation of the franchise network are deemed to be necessary and thus outside the prohibitions of Article 85(1) (now Article 101(1) of the TFEU). Mutually exclusive ter-ritorial restrictions, however, are not considered by the ECJ to be absolutely necessary to maintain a franchise system and run afoul of the restriction against market sharing. These restrictions, unless they fall within an exemption under Article 85(3) (now Article 101(3) of the TFEU), would render the entire franchise agreement void. The ECJ agreed with the German appeals court that the 1967 block exemption for exclusive purchasing agree-ments did not apply to the franchise agreement in the case and therefore did not exempt the agreement from the scope of Article 85(1).

2. After *Pronuptia* was decided, the EC issued Regulation No. 4087/88 in 1989 that was specifically directed at distribution and service franchises. The 1989 block exemption

exempted the types of territorial restrictions involved in *Pronuptia*, that is, (1) an exclusive right to the franchisee to operate a franchise in a particular territory from the contract premises and (2) a prohibition against the sale of competing goods and services by the franchisee. EC Regulation No. 4087/88 was superseded by EC Regulation No. 2790/1999, which expired on May 31, 2010 and was itself superseded by Commission Regulation 330/2010 (see pp. 304-306), which became effective on June 1, 2010. Commission Regulation 330/2010 includes most distribution and service franchises within its scope and will permit the types of exclusive territory restrictions that were recognized by its predecessors and that were involved in *Pronuptia*.

6   *Foreign Direct Investment*

I.   *Introduction*

A.   The Decision to Invest: Medtech Reaches a Crossroads

Suppose that you are fortunate enough to have a client, Medtech, whose founders have developed very innovative medical technology and equipment. Medtech has its corporate offices and manufacturing facilities in the United States, and business is booming. Medtech equipment has an impressive domestic market share and, with a minimum of effort, foreign sales orders are also coming in. Every year for the past five years, Medtech's foreign sales have increased by an average of over 20 percent. Despite appearances, however, all is not well.

For the past five years, Medtech has been servicing what it considers to be its most important foreign markets—Europe, Asia, and South America—through the use of foreign distributors and contract manufacturers. Because its products are so successful, Medtech has already secured a significant and growing share in these markets. However, there has been a recent slowdown and Medtech's management is concerned. After healthy double-digit growth in market share in its three major markets abroad for the first three years, growth has begun to slow down considerably in the past two years. Medtech's growth in its foreign markets averaged 25 percent during the first three years of its expansion abroad but dipped to 15 percent during the fourth year and was just 10 percent last year. First- and second-quarter receipts from the current fiscal year indicate that growth will likely be in single digits. Medtech's management believes that this slowdown is due to increasing competition in its foreign markets by Medtech's domestic competitors and by foreign competitors. Another factor appears to be the growing number of counterfeits of Medtech's products in its foreign markets, especially in Asia (but Medtech's executives will delay consideration on this issue as it is the topic of Chapter Seven).

Medtech is generally considered to be a "star" in the medical technology field in the United States. But Medtech executives know that they must take steps now to anticipate future market developments because it has become clear that foreign growth cannot be sustained using its current strategies. Although Medtech is still doing very well, its executives, using the foresight that made Medtech successful in the first place, are now very concerned about Medtech's future and there is a growing feeling within the company that it has reached a critical point in its corporate life.

At a corporate retreat for senior management, several new strategies were discussed. One strategy that was proposed was to abandon its foreign markets and to concentrate just on the U.S. market. Medtech has reached the same point at which many companies that sell overseas through the use of distributors and contract manufacturers also find themselves: Use of non-establishment forms of doing business abroad has limits in expanding business abroad and may not be a viable strategy against aggressive local competition. However, the suggestion to abandon foreign markets was quickly rejected. All of Medtech's domestic competitors have foreign operations and Medtech believes that it cannot survive if it concentrates just on the U.S. market. While Medtech is about the same size as some of its competitors, Medtech's executives realize that a few domestic competitors are likely to double in size within the next decade through foreign expansion. The larger companies will be able to put intense competitive pressure on the smaller companies because those with greater resources will have an advantage in research and development and pricing. Medtech also realizes that although there are several competitors in the field now, not all of these companies will survive as the industry grows and consolidates. Although a market leader now, Medtech realizes that its position could completely change in several years and is also well aware that some of today's "stars" will disappear in this period due to the intensively competitive global marketplace. Another set of strategies concerns geographical expansion into the Middle East and Africa. These strategies struck a responsive chord and a subcommittee was established to study this prospect further and to report to senior management. However, Medtech executives soon turned to a discussion of the more basic topic that was on everyone's mind: whether it will continue its plan of using non-establishment forms of doing business abroad under directions from its U.S. headquarters or whether it will set up a foreign subsidiary or joint venture company to manufacture medical equipment in an important foreign market. Medtech has thoroughly studied the probable costs and revenues likely to result from each alternative. Its analysis depends on estimates and suppositions, but Medtech is ready to make a calculated leap into the unknown: foreign direct investment (FDI).

A useful definition refers to FDI as an "investment that is made to acquire a lasting interest in an enterprise operating in an economy other than that of an investor, the investor's purpose being to have an effective choice in the management of the enterprise."[1] FDI is usually a fundamental policy decision for a domestic business entity that may affect its identity for the future. Why?

FDI usually entails a major long-term commitment of capital and other resources. MNEs might need to invest hundreds of millions, or even billions, of dollars to establish successful FDI projects. Not only can the capital expenditures be significant, but successful FDI projects usually involve a significant commitment of time by senior management and some of the company's key personnel will need to move overseas with their families for an extended stay. The costs of extended assignments abroad for employees and their families and the collateral labor issues of managing foreign local employees are often significant. In addition, while the termination of a distributorship or licensing agreement due to business failure may involve costs, the legal issues tend to be relatively straightforward. Unwinding a foreign business establishment and repatriating all employees can present complex legal issues that will take years to resolve. Withdrawing an FDI is also often perceived as a significant business failure. The costs and the level of commitment required for an FDI suggest that the decision to make an FDI is a watershed event in a company's life.

As Medtech expands into foreign markets through FDI, the character of the company will also change. If its foreign expansion resumes its double-digit growth as a result of FDI, then in a few years Medtech will need to establish independent management headquarters in its major overseas markets. The more successful Medtech's foreign expansion abroad becomes, the more likely Medtech's identity will be transformed. The U.S. market,

---

1. International Monetary Fund, *Balance of Payments Manual*, ¶408 (1980).

once its most important market, may become only one of several important markets, and its U.S. headquarters, once the center of the entire company, may become a national or regional office on par with similar offices in other regions. Although the CEO might still be based in the U.S. office, the CEO might be a European who has earned the top position by successfully running Medtech's European operations. In other words, once Medtech decides to plunge into the world of FDI, it has started on a path that may one day lead to a change in its identity from a U.S. company to a multinational corporation.

As you can see, the decision to make an FDI is an important one for Medtech and the stakes are high. What leads a U.S. business concern to make a foreign direct investment in a particular foreign market?

1. Market Penetration

The business concern may decide that the non-establishment forms of doing business abroad do not result in a sufficient degree of market penetration for a number of reasons. We have already seen that direct sales to a foreign market are often limited by the seller's lack of knowledge of the foreign market and a lack of a local distribution network. In the case of licensing of patents and trademarks, considered in the last chapter, the licensor is sharing the foreign market with the licensee. The licensor receives royalties, commissions, or a percentage of sales from the licensee while the licensee keeps the revenues that it earns from the sales of the product. A U.S. business entity that is attracted by the size and potential of a foreign market may not be satisfied with the limited returns available through licensing fees and may wish to enter the market directly. Before the U.S. business concern can enter a foreign market, however, the concern needs to make sure that the target country has a supply chain logistics system that will enable the delivery of the goods or services to the end user consumer. This will require a reliable transportation and communications system. If manufacturing will occur in the target country, the country must also have sufficient infrastructures necessary to support a manufacturing facility, such as a steady and adequate supply of power and water.

2. Management and Control

An additional consideration is the desire to exercise greater management and control over the foreign market. A local distributor, sales agent, or licensee may not have the capability, resources, or desire to manage an aggressive penetration of the foreign market. Many agents, distributors, and licensees will have other products, including their own, that they are seeking to promote and may not wish to devote the bulk of their time and resources to the one product sold under authority of the U.S. business entity. The U.S. business entity may wish to develop a marketing strategy and long-term business plan for the foreign market and surrounding countries. A major component of any long-term business plan is an advertising strategy in television, the print media, and electronic media. Even where a local entity has the capability and resources to develop some market penetration, the U.S. business entity is unlikely to entrust the marketing of its proprietary trademarks and brands to any independent third-party agents, distributors, or licensees. In order to exercise significant management and control over market penetration, the U.S. business entity may decide that it needs to have a presence in the foreign market.

3. Intellectual Property

The U.S. business concern may also be reluctant to license its patents, trademarks, copyrights, and other intellectual property to foreign entities. For many U.S. business concerns, the commercial value of their brands and the goodwill associated with those brands constitute their most valuable business assets. This is increasingly true in a global marketplace where consumer demand for well-known brands and leading-edge technology continues to be on the rise. How those brand names are presented and marketed on a global basis are of vital importance to the U.S. business concern, which is in the best position to market its brands and technology while maintaining consistency with the product's image on a worldwide basis.

The U.S. business concern may also wish to directly control and protect its intellectual property and forgo licensing to a third party altogether. As we noted previously, providing access to one's own proprietary technology to a third party always creates some risks of breaches of security, improper use, infringement, and piracy. No matter how well drafted the licensing agreement, effective enforcement of these agreements can be difficult and time consuming. Some companies deal with these risks by licensing only their secondary technologies. Many licensees, especially in developing nations, complain that companies never license their most advanced and valuable intellectual property. But licensing only secondary technology also presents limitations for the U.S. business concern as it will not be able to market its leading-edge products. These considerations have led some U.S. business owners to take a total or partial ownership interest in the foreign business entity that is given access to its proprietary technology. By being the owner of the foreign business entity, the U.S. business concern is in a better position to exercise greater control and to protect its most valuable technology. The U.S. business concern can send over its own business managers and lawyers to manage its intellectual property portfolio.

4. *Research and Development Abroad*

A concern closely related to the previous topic, intellectual property, is research and development abroad. A U.S. business concern that is manufacturing and selling products in a foreign market may soon find it necessary to establish research and development capabilities to service that market and other markets in the region. For many U.S. business concerns, the first stage of a foreign investment enterprise (FIE) involves establishing basic capabilities and reapplying the techniques and results of research and development from the U.S. market to the foreign market. For example, a particular advertising campaign that worked successfully in the United States may be adapted to the foreign market. After this initial stage, the FIE may move beyond reapplication to create and implement innovations particular to the foreign market. The FIE may begin to develop advertising specifically for the foreign market and make adjustments to the products to suit the needs of the foreign consumer. For example, one well-known consumer products company found that certain European consumers were less fond of high-sudsing laundry detergents than their U.S. counterparts and created a low-sudsing formula more suited to local tastes. Where the product is a high-technology product such as cellular phones, switching devices, or electronic products, the U.S. concern may need to make technical adjustments to the products to meet the different technical requirements of a foreign system. Many foreign countries also have their own national quality standards and approval procedures for new products and technologies. These requirements would suggest that establishing a local research and development facility may be more efficient than relying on global research and development in the United States and then adapting the technology to comply with local standards.

Where the U.S. business begins to achieve significant market penetration and its business abroad begins to mature, the research and development facilities abroad will need to focus on innovations for the particular foreign markets rather than reapply or adapt global research and development results. This further allows the FIE to meet the particular needs of the foreign market. At some point, the foreign research and development facility may become a platform for meeting the needs of the entire region. For example, a research and development facility established in Germany, Brazil, or China may become the platform for supporting all of the European, South American, or Southeast Asian markets. At the end of this cycle, the FIE moves from a business dependent on the U.S. domestic business's centers for research and development support to a regional business center with research and development capabilities of its own that support other regional and national markets.

Research and development often involves the company's cutting-edge and core technologies, and there will be a great need to protect the company's intellectual property rights. To accomplish these long-term objectives, the U.S. business concern will find it necessary to establish a wholly- or partially-owned FIE engaged specifically in research and development for the foreign markets. Research and development of core technologies is of such strategic importance that most U.S. business concerns will insist on total or substantial control through ownership of the foreign facility, which can be accomplished by establishing an FIE. Independent, regional research and development facilities dedicated to foreign markets are a hallmark of a mature international business. Of course, before an MNE can establish a research and development facility in a foreign country, the MNE needs to evaluate whether the country has an adequate number of engineers, scientists, lawyers, accountants, and business managers to staff such a facility.

5. Global Competition

The final impetus for the expansion into FDI is increasing global competition. As companies are under increasing pressure to find new markets and to increase revenues and as new technologies reduce the barriers of time and distance, many business concerns find that FDI is no longer optional, but rather a necessary long-term strategy. Competition for foreign markets is becoming increasingly fierce and, particularly in developing countries, early entry can create a sizeable advantage. Early entry by Coca-Cola into the China market, for example, has created a significant advantage that competitors are finding difficult to overcome. Many developing countries also provide preferential treatment in the form of tax incentives, currency exchange, rebates of fees, and land incentives to foreign investors that enter the market early. As markets mature, these preferential incentives are gradually reduced and later entrants may find themselves faced with higher barriers to entry.

B. Mergers and Acquisitions (M&A)

Our discussion so far has focused on the reasons why Medtech might decide to take the plunge into FDI by establishing a new business entity abroad (called a "Greenfield" investment) in the form of a subsidiary, branch, or joint venture. Another alternative for a successful business enterprise such as Medtech is to acquire an existing foreign company. Cross-border M&A is now becoming commonplace, particularly among developed nations. The M&A alternative has several advantages: (1) foreign market penetration is immediate because the foreign target company will have an established network of customers and goodwill and (2) economies of scale and the resulting synergisms can redound to the firm's benefit in both foreign and home markets. However, a foreign acquisition may be impeded by a variety of defensive strategies and legal restrictions. For example, the German Takeover Law[2] not only requires full disclosure by the bidder, the bid must remain open for at least four weeks and the bidder must offer to acquire all of the target shares. For many reasons, therefore, a hostile bid should probably be avoided, and even a friendly acquisition may encounter hostile minority shareholders.

Cross-border M&A may also face a hurdle in the form of national security review of the transaction. A foreign acquisition of a U.S. company, for example, triggers a national security review under the provisions of the Exon-Florio Amendment to the Defense Production Act, 50 U.S.C. app. §2170 (2006). This law allows the President of the United States to suspend or prohibit any foreign acquisition, merger, or takeover of a U.S. corporation if the action is deemed to threaten national security. The President has delegated this review authority to a Committee on Foreign Investment in the United States (CFIUS). CFIUS is made up of key presidential aides and Cabinet officials, who have 45 days to conduct a review and to make a recommendation to the President, who has in turn 15 days to decide whether to take blocking action. 50 U.S.C. app. §§2170(b)(2)(C), 2170(d)(2) (2011).

Most developed nations have similar national security review laws. For example, national laws in Spain, the United Kingdom, France, and Germany allow public interest and national security review of acquisitions. Such review is also allowed under EU law. Council Regulation (EC) No. 139/2004, art. 21, 2004 O.J. (L 24) 1; Council Directive 2005/56/EC, art. 4, 2005 O.J. (L 310) 1. Finally, an acquisition might trigger review under competition laws because the resulting entity might be deemed to be so economically powerful or dominant that it will be harmful to competitors. We shall see this type of issue arise within the EU in the materials below and the many hurdles involved in obtaining approval.

Assuming such obstacles can be overcome and a company such as Medtech finds a willing and appropriate takeover target, the next step will be to negotiate a stock purchase agreement whereby the shares of the foreign company are purchased directly by Medtech from the foreign shareholders. After the transaction is completed, the foreign company will become a foreign subsidiary of the purchasing (parent) company. There may be business and legal reasons (such as taxation or fear of unknown liabilities) to cast the transaction in the form of an asset acquisition. In this case it is advisable for the acquiring company to form a foreign subsidiary, possibly a holding company, in the jurisdiction of the target, which will then serve as the corporate vehicle to purchase the target's specified assets. After the transaction, the acquiring company will become a wholly-owned foreign subsidiary of the parent company, now invested with the target's assets. A third alternative is a "triangular merger" whereby the acquiring company creates a wholly-owned foreign subsidiary whose only assets are the stock of the parent-acquiring company. The foreign subsidiary and the target then enter into a stock swap agreement transferring the shares of the parent-acquiring company to the shareholders of the target in exchange for their shares in the target. After the shares of the target are acquired, a merger can be effected under local law between the two foreign companies.

The choice of these various techniques depends on tax considerations and the business and legal environment in the country of the target.

---

2. Gesetz zur Regelung von öffentlichen Angeboten zum Erwerb von Wertpapieren und von Unternehmensübernahmen (WpÜG), Law of 20 December 2001, Federal Gazette I (2001) p. 3822. An English translation can be found in Peltzer and Voight, Wertpapierwerbs-und Übernahmegesetz/ German Securities Acquisition and Takeover Act, German-English Text (2002).

II. Global Trends in Foreign Direct Investment

A. Recent Growth

Growth in FDI has been one of the defining features of the world economy and global-ization over the past 25 years. FDI has grown at an unprecedented rate in the past two and a half decades until a slowdown caused by the global recession of 2007. FDI has since rebounded from the recession as the figures in the paragraph below indicate. As we noted in Chapter One, the growth in FDI can be traced to increased liberalization in laws and practices pertaining to foreign trade and investment, technological change, and growing competition.[3] An additional factor is political reform leading to the open-ing up of heretofore closed markets in major destinations of FDI such as China and parts of Eastern Europe.[4] The 1990s also witnessed the removal of domestic barriers through widespread regulatory reform.

The growth of FDI in the past three decades has been exceptional. In 2000, the total dollar value of world FDI inflows reached $1.3 trillion up from just over $200 billion in 1993, a growth of over 600 percent in less than a decade. After a slight downturn in the early 2000s, world FDI inflows peaked in 2007 at $1.97 trillion, but declined again in 2008 and 2009 due to the global recession. FDI inflows increased again from 2009 to 2011 before fal-tering in 2012. The 2013 UNCTAD World Investment Report forecast an increase in global FDI inflows from 2013 to at least 2015. In 1990, total FDI stock represented only about 9 percent of world GDP, but this portion had nearly tripled by 2005 (25 percent) and almost quadrupled by 2012 (32 percent). The tremendous growth in FDI has been propelled and dominated by MNEs. Today, there are about 65,000 MNEs with about 850,000 foreign affiliates in countries around the world. In 2012, foreign subsidiaries totaled 71 million employees as compared to fewer than 22 million in 1990; their sales of about $19 billion were double the world's exports in 2001 as compared to 1990 when sales and exports were approximately equal. The stock of FDIs increased from $1.7 trillion to $6.6 trillion in the same period and reached $14.9 trillion in 2008, and $20.4 trillion in 2012.[5]

The vast majority of world investment still takes place among the advanced indus-trialized countries of the OECD (and a few other developed economies), though their share is decreasing.[6] More than 75 percent of world FDI outflows originate in developed economies and they receive nearly 44 percent of FDI inflows as well. Developing coun-tries' share of inflows has gone from 18 percent in 2000 to 56 percent in 2012. Asian countries have the largest share of these non-OECD inflows with nearly 58 percent, while the Americas have almost 35 percent and Africa has 7 percent. This trend indicates the growing importance of FDI in developing countries. Eighteen MNEs located in devel-oping economies are on the Forbes 2014 list of the world's 100 largest publicly traded companies, including the Industrial and Commercial Bank of China, Petrobras-Petróleo Brasil, Saudi Basic Industries, China Mobile (Hong Kong), and Gazprom (Russia).[7]

---

3. See pp. 16-18, *supra.*

4. See pp. 13-14, *supra.*

5. The data in this paragraph are from the UNCTAD Handbook of Statistics 2013; UNCTAD World Investment Report 2013; UNCTAD World Investment Report 2010.

6. See pp. 17-18, *supra.*

7. The data in this paragraph are from the OECD Stat Extracts, available at *http://stats.oecd.org/index.aspx?r=169006,* the UNCTAD World Investment Report 2013, and the Forbes Global 2000, available at *http://www.forbes.com/global2000/.*

FDI has become strongly oriented toward the services sector. In 2011, 40 percent of global outflows involved the services sector with banks and other financial institutions accounting for the bulk of these investments. FDI in electricity, gas and water, as well as transportation and telecommunications enjoyed the largest percentage increases, reflecting the widespread privatization and deregulation of the public utilities on a worldwide basis in the past decade. Information on OECD outflows in 2007 shows the continued importance of the services sector, which accounted for approximately two-thirds of these outflows.[8]

B.   Role of FDI in Economic Development

For all recipient countries, FDI means an infusion of capital and technology transfer, but these benefits are most important to developing countries as FDI represents the fastest route to economic growth. FDI is usually the best source of finance for domestic capital needs. Other types of private capital inflows are portfolio equity from foreign investors who purchase domestic stocks for investment purposes and debt flows, which involve lending by private entities such as investment banks and financial companies. Portfolio equity tends to be more volatile than FDI as investors may liquidate or shift their investments in accordance with market performance or portfolio needs. Debt requires payments of principal and interest that restrict short-term economic growth. Compared to these other forms of private capital flows, FDI is more stable and long term.

While the benefits of FDI in creating a capital base for the recipient nation may stimulate economic growth, the role of FDI in technology transfer may be even more important for long-term economic development. In general, FDI is the most effective form of technology transfer. Some of the technologies available through FDI are simply not available through other channels, including licensing. Technology transfer, including the sharing of managerial knowledge and skills, can lead to increased productivity by the recipient nation, which in turn leads to greater competitiveness in the world market for exports of goods and services. This results in economic growth and development and higher standards of living for the recipient country. While the effects of technology transfer and the spillover on productivity and economic development are still being debated and studied and though there continue to be many strident opponents of globalization, most studies conclude that technology transfer has a positive impact on productivity and economic growth. However, the impact of FDI varies from country to country and from industry to industry. Some countries, such as China, have enjoyed spectacular success in exploiting FDI, while other similarly situated countries, such as Brazil, have enjoyed only modest success up to the present. Capturing the benefits of FDI appears to require, among other things, that the host country reach a certain level of development so that there is not too large of a "technology gap" between the MNE and the local firms.

NOTES AND QUESTIONS

1. FDI is generally a more effective means of technology transfer than licensing for two reasons: The level of technology acquired is higher and the absorption and assimilation

---

8. The data in this paragraph are from the UNCTAD World Investment Report 2013. *See also* OECD Stat Extracts, available at *http://stats.oecd.org/index.aspx?r=169006.*

of the technology by the recipient nation is more effective. Can you explain why the level of technology acquired is higher? As for the second reason, why does FDI result in a more effective absorption of technology than licensing? In considering this question, note that a great deal of FDI in developing countries occurs through joint ventures in which an MNE partners with a local company; but even where the MNE sets up a wholly-owned subsidiary, the technology transfer can be far more easily absorbed than in licensing. Why?

2. One of the major problems for developing countries is that they may not have the capacity to absorb or fully exploit the advanced technology that they are seeking. How does technology transfer through FDI address this concern?

PROBLEM 6-1

Based on the readings so far in this chapter, consider the following:

An MNE that produces and sells daily-use products such as shampoos, soaps, skin cream, and laundry detergent is considering FDI in a developing country but is concerned about whether the country has reached a minimum level of development adequate for FDI. The MNE's products are world famous and involve many patents, trademarks, and trade secrets. About 80 percent of the country's population is concentrated in two regions: the north and south. The rest of the population lives in large rain forests located in the middle of the country. The plan calls for the building of a manufacturing facility and a corporate headquarters in the southern region with a distribution center in the north that will together serve markets throughout the north and south with plans to establish smaller distribution centers in the middle regions to reach the remaining population. The headquarters will house some of the MNE's senior and mid-level employees and their families who will spend up to five years abroad setting up the business and operating the facility. A major responsibility of the expatriate employees will be to train their replacements from the local workforce. After five years, the plan is to repatriate all of the MNE's employees who will be replaced on a permanent basis with local employees. The MNE is concerned about whether the target country has reached a stage of development that permits FDI. The MNE asks that you make a list of the minimum "hard" (e.g., physical structures) and "soft" (e.g., social structures and institutions) infrastructures that must be in place before the MNE can proceed with its plans.

III. International Investment Law

There is no truly comprehensive multilateral treaty or uniform international law on investment. As we shall see, efforts to create such a general treaty regulating FDI within the World Trade Organization failed, so all efforts to regulate FDI have occurred at the regional and bilateral level. In this part, we review the bilateral and regional frameworks governing FDI and in a later section, we review the WTO or multilateral approach to FDI, which is quite limited. Within the past two to three decades, great strides have been made to establish on the bilateral and multilateral levels an international law framework that governs foreign direct investment as well as to provide forums for the resolution of international investment disputes. The current international legal framework governing investment (like other areas of IBT) is a patchwork consisting of various types of treaties:

(1) bilateral investment treaties,
(2) regional economic treaties such as the North American Free Trade Agreement and the Treaty on the Functioning of the European Union,
(3) sector-specific treaties such as the Energy Charter Treaty,
(4) ad hoc tribunals such as the Iran-U.S. Claims Tribunal, and
(5) multilateral treaties dealing with some aspects of FDI such as the Convention on the Settlement of Investment Disputes Between States and Nationals of Other States.

In Section A below, we explore the older, traditional international law reflected in cases decided by the International Court of Justice (ICJ). This traditional international law approach has been replaced by the modern patchwork summarized above. As we shall see, the ICJ was not a very effective mechanism for protecting foreign direct investment. One of the obstacles to the use of the ICJ to protect foreign investment is that only states have standing to appear before the ICJ. Private parties, such as multinational corporations, cannot appear directly but must have their interests represented by their governments. This limitation, along with others described below, severely hampered the ICJ's effectiveness as an arbiter of private investment disputes. The shortcomings of the ICJ led to the development of the modern law of international investment, as described in Sections B through D below.

Section B covers the modern law as reflected by multilateral and bilateral investment treaties; Section C turns to an important regional treaty, NAFTA; and Section D covers the limited impact of the WTO on foreign direct investment.

A. The Traditional Framework for Protecting FDI: The International Court of Justice

We now turn to the traditional international law approach to FDI that existed until the middle of the twentieth century when dissatisfaction with the system led to the development of the modern patchwork approach. A basic issue in FDI concerns the availability of an effective forum to resolve investment disputes between the foreign investor, often a multinational corporation, and the host country of the investment. Traditionally, one of the most important concerns of the foreign investor is that the host country might unexpectedly seize or expropriate the foreign investor's business assets in the country of investment. When these events occurred, resort to the courts of the country in which the expropriation occurred was usually futile. Foreign investors, enlisting the aid of their governments as plaintiffs, attempted to resolve these disputes in the International Court of Justice, a specialized agency of the United Nations. We summarize three famous cases that arose in the post-War ICJ. In each case, the ICJ refused to consider the expropriation claim, citing a different hurdle. This refusal frustrated foreign investors and exposed the limitations of the ICJ as a forum in which investment disputes can be effectively resolved and spurred the efforts at modern reform. As you read our summary of these cases below, keep in mind: What was each of these hurdles?

Anglo-Iranian Oil Co. Case (U.K. v. Iran)
1952 I.C.J. 93 (July 22)

The Anglo-Iranian (AI) Oil Company, Ltd., which was incorporated in the United Kingdom (and which is now known as BP), held a huge investment stake in Iran, much of it in money supplied by the British government. The legal foundation for AI's business was a Concession Agreement signed in April 1933, giving AI the exclusive right to mine oil in Iran for 60 years in consideration for substantial royalties paid to the Iranian government. The dispute arose when, in March 1953, the Iranian Parliament enacted a law nationalizing the oil industry and creating the state-owned National Iranian Oil Company. AI invoked an arbitration clause in the 1933 Agreement, but Iran rejected arbitration. The British government then intervened by suing Iran in the International Court of Justice to recover damages and lost profits. The ICJ, invoking its powers under Article 41 of the Statute of the International Court of Justice, granted interim relief, which Iran ignored. Iran also denied that the ICJ had jurisdiction under Article 36(2) of the Statute. The issue revolved around Iran's 1930 Declaration granting the ICJ jurisdiction in any dispute "arising after the satisfaction of the present Declaration with regard to situations or facts relating directly or indirectly to the application of treaties or conventions accepted by [Iran] and subsequent to the ratification of this Declaration." The British government argued that the ICJ had jurisdiction because, although the Concession Agreement was not a treaty, the Declaration referred to "situations or facts" arising subsequently to the Declaration. Thus the ICJ had jurisdiction because the UK and Iran (Persia) had concluded a 1928 treaty which provided that British nationals in Iran would be treated in conformity with international law.

The ICJ ruled 9 to 5, however, that "subsequently" in the Declaration referred to "treaties or conventions"; thus, the ICJ did not have jurisdiction because the Concession Agreement was not a treaty but only a private contract subject to Iranian domestic law not international law. Iran won the case because Iran never effectively consented to the jurisdiction of the ICJ in the 1930 Declaration or otherwise; this ruling meant that Iran won a victory as the ICJ did not have to decide the expropriation issue but this victory was a principal factor in the successful coup mounted by the U.S. CIA against Iran in 1953, which continues to poison relations between Iran and the United States and the West.

Case Concerning Barcelona Traction, Light and Power Company (The Barcelona Traction Case) (Belgium v. Spain), Second Phase
1970 I.C.J. 3 (Feb. 5)

This case involved Barcelona Traction (BT), a holding company incorporated in Toronto, Canada, in 1911, to produce and distribute electric power in Catalonia, Spain. Most of the shares of Barcelona Traction were held by Belgian nationals, both natural and juristic persons. BT became heavily indebted by issuing bonds to mainly Spanish interests. On petition of one of the creditors, BT was adjudged bankrupt in a Spanish court and its assets were seized and put into receivership. BT was then reorganized and new shares were issued mainly to Spanish interests. After several years of negotiation over the rights of the former shareholders of BT, Belgium filed suit against Spain in the ICJ, alleging a "creeping nationalization" of the company by Spain and demanding some $90 million in reparations. The basis of Belgian's complaint in the ICJ was the 1927 Treaty of Conciliation between Belgium and Spain. Spain objected to the ICJ's jurisdiction on the ground that Belgium had no standing to sue; it was not the seat of incorporation of BT or the site of its business operations, and international law does not recognize the right of a state to represent shareholders of a foreign company. The ICJ explained that, while some legal interests are so important that all states have a legal interest in their enforcement (such rights are *erga omnes*), company investment rights do not fit in this category so

Belgium cannot diplomatically represent the interest of BT, and international law does not recognize the existence of shareholder rights independent of the rights of the company. The ICJ ruled that "international law authorizes the national state of the company alone [Canada] to make a claim." 1970 I.C.J. 3, ¶88. The ICJ also famously commented that legal questions concerning investment "created an intense conflict of systems and interests." *Id.* ¶¶89–90.

Case Concerning Elettronica Sicula S.p.A.
(The ELSI Case) (U.S. v. Italy)
1989 I.C.J. 15 (July 20)

Elettronica Sicula, S.p.A. (ELSI) was an Italian company engaged in manufacturing sophisticated electronic equipment in Palermo, Italy. ELSI was a wholly-owned subsidiary of Raytheon Manufacturing Company, a major U.S. electronics company. In 1968, after 15 years of putting capital and technology into ELSI, Raytheon decided to shut down ELSI as an unprofitable failure. Raytheon accordingly adopted a business termination plan and sent notices to its employees. Shortly after letters were sent out terminating its employees, the mayor of Palermo, citing an 1865 law and "grave public necessity" took over control of the plant. Raytheon appealed the mayor's order, but the new directors of ELSI voted to declare bankruptcy and a court-appointed trustee took over the plant and its properties. For six years, Raytheon pursued relief without success in Italian courts for recovery of its assets or compensation; Raytheon eventually enlisted the aid of the U.S. State Department. In 1974, the State Department submitted a diplomatic note to Italy espousing Raytheon's claims but it took Italy four years to respond, denying the claim. After almost a decade of diplomatic exchanges, the United States and Italy agreed to submit the case to the ICJ. The United States's international claim was for "creeping nationalization" in violation of the Italy-United States Friendship, Commerce and Navigation Treaty and its Protocol. In 1989, the ICJ Chamber ruled that the questions of expropriation and "taking" raised by the United States could not be resolved by the tribunal because it was not possible to determine whether the loss was caused by the acts of the Italian government or by ELSI's own imprudent financial decisions. 1989 I.C.J. 15, ¶119. The 1989 decision of the ICJ was issued 21 years after the events giving rise to the dispute. Why is this a concern?

NOTES AND QUESTIONS

1. Why did the ICJ avoid reaching the merits of the disputes in each of these three cases? Were the issues involved in these cases politically sensitive? Why? Read note 3 below. Given the cases discussed above, if you were a foreign investor, how confident would you be in using the ICJ to resolve an investment dispute? How long does it take to resolve a case through diplomatic channels and the ICJ? Is this a concern?

2. *The Case of Ahmadou Sadio Diallo.* The ICJ again considered the international law of diplomatic protection with regard to investment in the case of Ahmadou Sadio Diallo, *Republic of Guinea v. Democratic Republic of the Congo (DRC)*, 46 I.L.M. 712 (2007). The case involved the arrest, detention, and expulsion of Diallo, who was a citizen of Guinea as well as the director and a principal shareholder in two companies, Africacom-Zaire and Africontainers, both incorporated under Congolese law. The incident occurred as

Diallo was engaged in legal proceedings to recover monies owed to the two companies. The ICJ affirmed that under customary international law, a state can exercise diplomatic protection on behalf of its nationals with regard to an injury caused by the commission of an internationally wrongful act. *Republic of Guinea*, 46 I.L.M. 712 at ¶48. Accordingly, the ICJ ruled that Guinea could exercise diplomatic protection with regard to Diallo's direct rights as a shareholder (and *associe*) of the two companies. *Id.* ¶64. However, the ICJ rejected the argument that Guinea could exercise diplomatic protection with respect to the two corporations. *Id.* ¶87. The Court distinguished the *ELSI* case (in which the United States asserted claims on behalf of a U.S. company) on the basis that the *ELSI* case did not involve customary international law, but was based on a Friendship, Commerce, and Navigation Treaty. *Id.* ¶88. The Court indicated that because of bilateral and multilateral investment treaties "the role of diplomatic protection [has] somewhat faded." *Id.*

3. *State Responsibility to Foreign Investors.*

(a) *Hull Formula.* The traditional U.S. view of the law of state responsibility toward foreign investors is that no government is entitled to expropriate private property, for whatever purpose, without payment of prompt, effective, and adequate compensation. This is known as the "Hull formula," as it was relied on by U.S. Secretary of State Cordell Hull, who was embroiled in controversies with Mexico in the 1930s over a series of agrarian expropriations. This principle was articulated as well by the Permanent Court of International Justice in the *Chorzów Factory* cases,[9] which involved the taking of a nitrogen factory by the government of Poland. The World Court declared the taking unlawful and stated that "reparation must, as far as possible, wipe out all the consequences of the illegal act and reestablish the situation which would have existed if that act had not been committed." *Factory at Chorzów*, 1928 P.C.I.J. (ser. A) No. 17, at 47 (Sept. 13, 1927).

(b) *The Calvo Doctrine.* The Hull formula was criticized and disputed by many developing countries and socialist countries in the twentieth century. It was contended that a sovereign nation has a right to nationalize property and to assert control over its natural resources. Many constitutions, especially in Latin America, recognize that property has a social welfare function. Therefore, compensation need not be prior or prompt, and the amount may be determined by the law of the expropriating state, which may take into account the equities of the situation. This is known as the "Calvo doctrine" after the Argentine jurist who expounded these views. *See* Donald R. Shea, *The Calvo Clause* (1955).

(c) *Current Law.* What is the current law on expropriation? Consider the formulation of the Restatement (Third) of the Foreign Relations Law of the United States (1987):

Section 712. State Responsibility for Economic Injury to Nationals of Other States

A state is responsible under international law for injury resulting from:

(1)   a taking by the state of the property of a national of another state that

   (a)   is not for a public purpose, or
   (b)   is discriminatory, or
   (c)   is not accompanied by provision for just compensation.

For compensation to be just under this subsection, it must, in the absence of exceptional circumstances, be in an amount equivalent to the value of the property taken and

---

9. Certain German Interests in Polish Upper Silesia (Merits), 1926 P.C.I.J. (ser. A) No. 7 (May 25); Factory at Chorzów (Jurisdiction), 1927 P.C.I.J. (ser. A) No. 9 (July 26); Factory at Chorzów, 1928 P.C.I.J. (ser. A) No. 17 (Sept. 13); Factory at Chorzów, 1929 P.C.I.J. (ser. A) No. 19 (May 25).

be paid at the time of taking, or within a reasonable time thereafter with interest from the date of taking, and in a form economically usable by the foreign national.

B.   Multilateral and Bilateral Treaties

The limitations of the ICJ as an arbiter of disputes involving foreign direct investment created the need to develop a more effective forum: the International Centre for the Settlement of Investment Disputes (ICSID). As you read the material below, keep in mind how the ICSID addresses the limitations of the ICJ as an arbiter of FDI disputes.

Modern International Investment Law: Bilateral Investment Treaties, Free Trade Agreements and Customs Unions, and the Convention on the Settlement of Disputes Between States and Nationals of Other States (the ICSID Convention)

The awkward statement by the International Court of Justice in the Barcelona Traction case that investment law is full of "intense conflicts" and the handling of investment cases by that court convinced international lawyers to create upon new foundations for international investment law. These new foundations have been constructed in the last 50 years profoundly changing this area of law. Modern investment law rests on three bases: (1) bilateral investment treaties; (2) free trade agreements and other trade agreements; and (3) the law and jurisprudence of the International Center for Investment Disputes.

1. BILATERAL INVESTMENT TREATIES

The primary source of international investment law today is bilateral investment treaties (BITs). Standards for investment were first developed for bilateral treaties we now call BITs in 1959,[10] and the first historical BIT was the Treaty for the Promotion and Protection of Investments, with Protocol and Exchange of Notes, Ger.-Pak., Nov. 25, 1959, 457 U.N.T.S. 23. From this small beginning grew the formidable network of BITs now in force all over the world. More than 2,500 BITs are now in force with the primary object to protect foreign investment and investors. At this writing 48 BITs are in force for the United States.[11] One of the antecedents of the BIT was the Treaty of Friendship, Commerce and Navigation (TFCN), long a staple of international law concerning trade and investment. But largely because of the growth of BITs, the United States has not entered into a TFCN since 1968, although more than 40 are still in force for the United States.[12] From time to time efforts have been made to regulate investment on an international level (rather than on a bilateral level) by concluding a multilateral agreement that focused on standards

---

10. Hermann Abs and Hartley (Lord) Shawcross, *Draft Convention on Investments Abroad*, 1960 J. Pub. L. 115.
11. *See* the State Department web site, *http://www.state.gov.*
12. *See* John F. Coyle, *The Treaty of Friendship, Commerce and Navigation in the Modern Era*, 51 Colum. J. Transnat'l L. 302 (2013).

for the admission and protection of FDI. But these efforts have come to naught. OECD efforts—the OECD draft Convention on the Protection of Foreign Property (1967) and the OECD-sponsored Multilateral Agreement on Investment (1995)—both collapsed; the WTO Trade-Related Agreement on Investment (TRIMs) of 1994, which is limited to trade matters (domestic content and export requirements), is the only significant multilateral agreement on investment and, in a later section at pp. 397-399, we will examine why all efforts within the WTO to create a multilateral agreement on investment have failed. Investment law today is a largely self-contained regime, although scholars have made significant attempts to relate investment law to general international law[13] and international human rights law.[14]

Despite the multiplicity of BITs, they are remarkably similar in scope. At this point read and study the 2012 U.S. Model Bilateral Investment Treaty (reprinted in the Documents Supplement), which is used by the U.S. State Department and the U.S. Trade Representative as the basis for negotiating BITs. A BIT is a legally binding agreement that provides significant legal protections for investors and investments in a partner country. BITs are traditionally negotiated with developing countries. Note that BITs have six core benefits for investors:

- Investors and investments are accorded National (NT) and Most-Favored Nation (MFN) treatment, i.e., all foreign investments must receive treatment as least as favorable as local investments (NT) and all foreign investments from any country must be treated equally (MFN).
- Clear limits are established on expropriation of investments and payment of prompt, adequate, and effective compensation is required when expropriation occurs.
- The transferability of investment-related funds into and out of the host country without delay and using a market exchange rate is assured.
- Performance requirements such as local content targets and export quotas as a condition for the establishment and conduct of the business are not permitted.
- Investors are granted the right to engage managerial personnel of their choosing.
- Investment disputes are subject to international arbitration.

Admission of the investment. All BITs provide for admission of FDI in accordance with the party's rules and regulations, but according to national and most-favored nation treatment standards (with certain exceptions, such as for telecommunications, financial institutions, and energy concerns, among other sectors that, due to national security concerns, receive special treatment).

Fair and equitable treatment. A typical BIT spells out in detail what is meant by fair and equitable treatment and minimum standards of treatment. These include "full protection and security"—providing police and security protection—and applicable customary law standards for the protection of aliens. For example, in the case of *Asian Agricultural*

---

13. Campbell McLachlan QC, *Investment Treaties and General International Law*, 57 Int'l & Comp. L.Q. 361 (2008).

14. Susan L. Karamanian, *Human Rights Dimensions of Investment Law, Hierarchy in International Law: The Place of Human Rights* ch. 9, Erika De Wet and Jure Vidmar (eds.) (Oxford: Oxford University Press, 2011).

Products, Ltd. v. Republic of Sri Lanka, Award of 27 June 1990, ¶¶85-86, 30 I.L.M. 577 (1991), the tribunal ruled:

> [F]aced with the impossibility of obtaining conclusive evidence about what effectively caused the destruction of the farm premises during the period in which the entire area was out of bounds under the exclusive control of the government security force, the Tribunal considers the State's responsibility established under international law.

Expropriation and compensation. Article 6 of the Model BIT lays down strict requirements governing expropriation and compensation. What are these standards? Not only direct but also "indirect" expropriation is covered so that so-called creeping expropriations and certain regulatory expropriations are also covered.

Environment and labor. Note the protections in the Model BIT for the environment and workers' rights. These are not typical in all U.S. BITs with other countries.

Dispute settlement. BITs typically provide for compulsory arbitration to settle investment disputes. Most BITs allow the private investor to sue the host state in an independent arbitral tribunal rather than relegating the investor to the domestic laws and procedures of the host nation or depending on the government of the investor to bring suit against the government of the host nation in an international forum, such as the ICJ.

BITs provide, therefore, an excellent general framework to promote international investment, and the growth of FDI has been directly influenced by the network of BITs in force around the world. The conclusion of BITs may not be adequate for certain specialized economic sectors, however; the energy sector, for example, requires special attention due to challenges of climate change, energy security, protection of the environment, and economic growth. The Energy Charter Treaty (ECT) of 1994[15] is the existing multilateral treaty for the energy sector. However, the ECT is largely European-centered; key countries are not parties. There are many calls for the negotiation of a multilateral energy investment treaty,[16] but no action has resulted from these initiatives.

2. Free Trade Agreements (NAFTA) and Customs Unions (EU)

FTAs such as the North American Free Trade Agreement and Customs Unions such as the European Union also contain protections for FDI. For example, NAFTA members — Mexico, the United States, and Canada — have agreed to include in NAFTA commitments on market access, the National Treatment and Most-Favored Nation Principles, Fair and Equitable Treatment, obligations with respect to labor and the environment, protections against expropriation, and a dispute resolution mechanism. The EU also has many protections for FDI both on a regional level and on a national level. In the EU, one main concern is limiting the ability of EU members to restrict the free flow of FDI across national borders. We mention NAFTA and the EU only briefly here because both are so important to FDI that we single out these two areas for detailed treatment in separate sections in a later part of this chapter.

---

15. *See, e.g.*, Energy Charter Treaty, Dec. 17, 1994, 2080 U.N.T.S. 100, 34 I.L.M. 360 (1995).
16. Edna Sussman, *A Multilateral Energy Sector Investment Treaty: Is It Time for a Call for Adoption?*, 44 Int'l Law. 939 (2010).

3. The ICSID Convention

In the 1960s the World Bank, seeking to spur investment in developing countries, came up with a plan to create a system to settle disputes not only between states, but also between private investors and governments hosting their investments. The result of this initiative was the conclusion of the Convention on the Settlement of Investment Disputes Between States and Nationals of Other States.[17] This Convention, generally known as the ICSID Convention, established the International Centre for Settlement of Investment Disputes (also ICSID) as a part of the World Bank. The ICSID Convention is reprinted in the Documents Supplement. A major advantage of ICSID is that private investors are allowed to directly bring an arbitration action against the host government. This is considered to be an improvement over the ICJ, where cases had to be brought by one state against another state. Make sure that you see this distinction and why it is advantageous to private investors.

- Note the establishment of ICSID institutions and the ICSID secretariat. *See* ICSID Convention, Articles 1–24.
- What is the jurisdiction of the Centre? *See* ICSID Convention Articles 25–27. Article 25 extends the jurisdiction of the Centre to "any legal dispute arising directly out of an investment." But the term "investment" is not defined in the ICSID Convention. Thus, if jurisdiction of the Centre is contested, the first phase of the proceedings will be to decide the jurisdiction issue. (Article 41(1) provides that the arbitral tribunal is the judge of its own competence.) A typical recent case discussing jurisdiction is *Philip Morris Brands Sàrl v. Oriental Republic of Uruguay*, ICSID Case No. ARB/10/7, Decision on Jurisdiction (July 2, 2013), available at *https://icsid.worldbank.org*. In this case Uruguay promulgated three public health measures regulating the sale and packaging of cigarettes. The claimants, Swiss subsidiaries of the Phillip Morris Corporation, alleged that the measures diminished the value of its investment and violated provisions of the Switzerland/Uruguay BIT. The arbitral tribunal examined the "investment" jurisdictional issue under the multi-pronged *Salini* test, stated by the arbitral tribunal in *Salini Costruttori S.p.A. v. Kingdom of Morocco*, ICSID No. ARB/00/4, Decision on Jurisdiction, ¶52 (July 23, 2001), 6 ICSID Rep. 400 (2004), 42 I.L.M. 609 (2003). The *Salini* test states that an investment involves: (1) an economic contribution; (2) a certain duration; (3) assumption of risks; (4) contribution to the economic development of the host nation; and (5) the realization of profit and economic returns. In the *Philip Morris case* the tribunal focused on the issue of whether the investment contributed to the economic development of the host state. In the face of Uruguay's argument that, since 5,000 people die in Uruguay from smoking-related illnesses and the direct health costs of smoking diseases surpass $150 million each year, the cigarette companies' investments have harmed and continue to harm Uruguay's economic development, the tribunal rejected delving into an ex post facto analysis of what constitutes economic development and ruled that an investment may or may not be useful for a country without losing its character as an investment.

---

17. 17 U.S.T. 1270, 575 U.N.T.S. 159, entered into force 14 October 1966.

- Note that consent to arbitrate in writing is required, but once given this cannot be withdrawn. *See* ICSID Convention, 17 U.S.T. 1270, arts. 25–26. Such consent can be contained in a BIT or other agreement.

- The arbitrability of an investment claim is controlled by the agreement between the parties and the BIT. Most BITs require recourse to domestic administrative and judicial remedies as a first recourse, but this requirement may be deemed to have been waived by the arbitral tribunal. *See BG Group PLC v. Republic of Argentina,* 134 S. Ct. 1198 (2014). In this case the Supreme Court decided the question: What deference should the courts give arbitral tribunal decisions relating to the local litigation requirement? Should a reviewing court decide the question de novo, or should a court defer to the decision of the arbitrators? The Supreme Court decided (Chief Justice Roberts and Justice Kennedy dissenting) that the contractual nature of arbitration presumes that the parties intend the arbitral tribunal to decide disputes about the meaning and preconditions for the use of arbitration. Thus, the court's review of jurisdictional prerequisites must be highly deferential. Only if the arbitrators' decision strays from the interpretation and application of the agreement to arbitrate and dispenses its own brand of justice will a court intervene. *BG Group PLC,* 134 S. Ct. at 1213. Thus, the Supreme Court ruled that the arbitrators' decision that the foreign investor in Argentina was, under the circumstances, excused from having to comply with the local litigation requirement could not be disturbed by the court.

- What substantive law is applicable? *See* ICSID Convention, art. 42. If a BIT is in force between the host state and the state of the investor, are the standards in the BIT applicable?

- Note that, although there is no appeal of an ICSID arbitration award, Article 52 provides that either party to an arbitration proceeding may request annulment of an award by an application in writing addressed to the Secretary-General. The request for annulment is handled by an ad hoc committee of three persons. The grounds for annulment are narrow: (1) that the Tribunal was not properly constituted; (2) that the Tribunal has manifestly exceeded its powers; (3) that there was corruption on the part of a member of the Tribunal; (4) that there has been a serious departure from a fundamental rule of procedure; or (5) that the award has failed to state the reasons on which it is based.

NOTES AND QUESTIONS

1. *A New Era of Investment Protection.* The international community has clearly bypassed the ICJ as a forum for dealing with investment disputes in favor of a range of alternative forums that are more hospitable to investors. Not only has ICSID been used, but also more particular regimes have been created, such as the Iran-U.S. Claims Tribunal, which was created in 1980 to deal with expropriation and other commercial claims growing out of the Islamic Revolution in Iran. The United Nations Compensation Commission was established by the Security Council in 1991 to deal with claims growing out of the invasion of Kuwait by Iraq. The Energy Charter Treaty of 1994 provides a forum for energy investor claims against states. Clearly, we are in a new era as far as protection of international investor rights is concerned.

2. *Investment Guaranty Programs.* In addition to establishing ICSID, the World Bank also established the Multilateral Investment Guarantee Agency (MIGA), which is

designed to enhance the flow of capital to developing countries by providing insurance against the risks associated with investing in such countries. Investors can purchase insurance against the inconvertibility of local currency, expropriation, breach of contract, war and civil disturbance, even terrorist acts and political sabotage. Today, private companies, such as Lloyd's of London, also offer political risk insurance to investors as well as export credit insurance, which protects against a private buyer's failure to pay for goods or services. In addition, individual governments have established their own programs. In the United States, insurance against a wide variety of international investment and commercial risks is offered by the Overseas Private Investment Corporation (OPIC). The MIGA, discussed above, is designed to complement national and private investment schemes.

3. *Creeping Expropriation.* This term is used for unreasonable interference with an investment that is not a physical taking. How is "creeping expropriation" to be distinguished from economic regulation of property or property taxation? The Restatement (Third) of Foreign Relations Law of the United States §712 cmt. g (1987) defines "creeping expropriation" as subjecting

> alien property to taxation, regulation, or other action that is confiscatory, or that prevents, unreasonably interferes with, or unduly delays, effective enjoyment of an alien's property or its removal from the territory [of] a state. A state is not responsible for loss of property or for other economic disadvantage resulting from bona fide general taxation, regulation, forfeiture for crime, or other action of the kind that is commonly accepted as within the police power of states, if it is not discriminatory and is not designed to cause the alien to abandon the property to the state or sell it at a distress price.

4. *Prompt, Adequate, and Effective Compensation.* What is the measure of adequate compensation? There are at least three common methods of business valuation. First, the present "going concern" value of a business can be measured by estimating future earnings based on the past and present earnings. Second, the replacement value of the assets of the business can be determined. Third, the book value (original cost) of the assets may be used. Which is best?

Would payment of the fair market value mean payment in convertible currency without restriction as to repatriation? Would bonds be acceptable if they bear interest at an economically reasonable rate?

PROBLEM 6-2

In 2016, the Province of Tucuman in Argentina decided to privatize its water and sewerage facilities. Accordingly, Tucuman signed a concession contract with Puritech Corporation, an Ohio utility company. The concession contract committed Puritech to make investments for the improvement and expansion of the water and sewage system and for its operation.

Argentina is a party to a bilateral investment treaty signed in 1994 with the United States. Both Argentina and the United States are also parties to the ICSID Convention. The BIT commits contracting parties to "fair and equitable treatment" to investors and protection against expropriation or nationalizing measures. Argentina was not a party to the concession contract.

Puritech has recently filed with ICSID a request for arbitration against the Argentine Republic under the ICSID Convention. Puritech alleges that between 1995 and 1999 it was subjected to a steady stream of decrees and laws passed by the government of Tucuman designed to undermine the concession contract. Tucuman authorities made public verbal attacks on Puritech and encouraged customers not to pay their bills and otherwise interfered with the operation of the water and sewerage system. It claims $63 million in damages.

A provision of the concession contract states that the resolution of all contract disputes concerning both the interpretation and the application of the contract are to be submitted to the exclusive jurisdiction of the administrative courts of Tucuman. Puritech has never brought any challenge to the acts of the government of Tucuman in the administrative courts. Argentina argues that the forum selection clause deprives ICSID of jurisdiction and also argues that it was not a party to the concession agreement. What is the result? Consult *Lanco* below.

Lanco International, Inc. v. Argentine Republic
December 8, 1998
40 I.L.M. 457 (2001)
ICSID Case No. ARB/97/6

FACTUAL BACKGROUND

[Lanco International, Inc. owns 18.3 percent of the shares in an Argentine corporation formed for the purpose of bidding to build and operate a port terminal in Buenos Aires. The bid was successful and a concession agreement was signed between the Argentine Ministry of Economy, Public Works, and Services and the Grantee Argentine corporation on June 6, 1994. Article 12 of the concession agreement provided as follows:

> For all purposes derived from the agreement and the BID CONDITIONS, the parties agree to the jurisdiction of the Federal Contentious-Administrative Tribunals of the Federal Capital of the ARGENTINE REPUBLIC.

A dispute has arisen and Lanco argues that the dispute should be resolved by ICSID arbitration under Article VII(3)(i) of the Treaty Concerning the Reciprocal Encouragement and Protection of Investment by nationals and companies of one party in the territory of the other party (the Argentina-U.S. Treaty). Argentina argues that the forum selection clause in the concession agreement deprives ICSID of jurisdiction and that as a shareholder in the Argentine corporation that won the bid, Lanco is not a party to the concession agreement and has no standing to bring an arbitration action. The ICSID Tribunal, in the opinion below, examined and resolved these jurisdictional issues.]

A. APPLICABILITY OF THE BILATERAL TREATY BETWEEN THE UNITED STATES OF AMERICA AND THE ARGENTINE REPUBLIC CONCERNING THE RECIPROCAL ENCOURAGEMENT AND PROTECTION OF INVESTMENT

To determine whether the ARGENTINA-U.S. Treaty applies, this Tribunal must analyze (a) whether LANCO's involvement in the Argentine Republic can be characterized as an investment; (b) whether there is an investment dispute, as defined in Article VII *ab initio*; and (c) whether the conditions established in Article VII for access to ICSID arbitration have been met.

**(A) THE EXISTENCE OF AN INVESTMENT FOR THE PURPOSES OF
THE ARGENTINA-U.S. TREATY**

This Tribunal must analyze the definition of the term "investment" in the ARGENTINA-U.S. Treaty, set forth in its Article I(1) as follows:

> (a) "investment" means every kind of investment in the territory of one Party owned or controlled directly or indirectly by nationals or companies of the other Party, such as equity, debt, and service and investment contracts; and includes without limitation:
>> (i) tangible and intangible property, including rights, such as mortgages, liens and pledges;
>> (ii) a company or shares of stock or other interests in a company or interests in the assets thereof;
>> (iii) a claim to money or a claim to performance having economic value and directly related to an investment;
>> (iv) intellectual property which includes, *inter alia*, rights relating to:
>>> literary and artistic works, including sound recordings,
>>> inventions in all fields of human endeavor,
>>> industrial designs,
>>> semiconductor mask works,
>>> trade secrets, know-how, and confidential business information, and
>>> trademarks, service marks, and trade names; and
>> (v) any right conferred by law or contract, and any licenses and permits pursuant to law.

[A]s regards shareholder equity, the ARGENTINA-U.S. Treaty says nothing indicating that the investor in the capital stock has to have control over the administration of the company, or a majority share; thus the fact that LANCO holds an equity share of 18.3% in the capital stock of the Grantee allows one to conclude that it is an investor in the meaning of Article I of the ARGENTINA-U.S. Treaty.

[A]s LANCO is [also] a party to this agreement as awardee and guarantor, LANCO is liable to the Argentine State not only because of its direct equity ownership in the Grantee company, but also by reason of its direct liability to the Grantee and to all of its co-awardees in their liability to the State, in the event of a default by any of them. From this liability, it can be concluded that LANCO is a party to the Concession Agreement, in its own name and right, and in its capacity as a foreign investor; and for the purposes of Article VII(1) of the ARGENTINA-U.S. Treaty, it can be considered that the Concession Agreement is in effect an investment agreement.

**(B) THE EXISTENCE OF AN INVESTMENT DISPUTE FOR THE PURPOSES
OF ARTICLE VII(1) OF THE ARGENTINA-U.S. TREATY**

The ARGENTINA-U.S. Treaty requires the existence of an investment dispute in order for its dispute-settlement provisions to be applicable.

Article VII of the ARGENTINA-U.S. Treaty provides:

> For the purposes of this Article, an investment dispute is a dispute between a Party and a national or a company of the other Party arising out of or relating to:
>   (a) an investment agreement between that Party and such national or company;
>   (b) an investment authorization granted by that Party's foreign investment authority (if any such authorization exists) to such national or company; or
>   (c) an alleged breach of any right conferred or created by this Treaty with respect to an investment.

Article I of the ARGENTINA-U.S. Treaty does not require, as the Argentine Republic alleges, that the investment agreement refer to an exclusively foreign investment. Nor can this Tribunal agree with the definition offered by the Argentine Republic of an investment agreement, according to which "a concession agreement that does not contain specific clauses referring to foreign investments is not an investment contract in the terms and scope of the BIT, not even under the assumption that the Concession Agreement had been entered into by a State Party and a national or company of the other Party controlled 100% by foreigners" (Respondent's Rejoinder of November 9, 1998, page 2) (Translation).

It should be recalled here that the Bid Conditions do provide for foreign companies to come forth as bidders, as arises from the reference it makes to the legislation regulating foreign investment; thus, Article 8 of the Bid Conditions specifically indicates:

> This bidding is national and international in character. It shall be governed by the laws of the Argentine Republic and the provisions of these Bid Conditions, its Circulars, the accepted Bid, and the Agreement signed with the awardee. . . . With respect to foreign investments, the Laws . . . shall apply along with their regulatory decrees.

[T]he Argentine Republic having included the awardees in their own name and right (in our case, LANCO) to ensure the sound completion of the project, the Argentine Republic should bear in mind that the ARGENTINA-U.S. Treaty applies to its relationship with LANCO.

(C) COMPLIANCE WITH THE REQUIREMENTS OF ARTICLE VII
OF THE ARGENTINA-U.S. TREATY

Article VII establishes:

> 2. In the event of an investment dispute, the parties to the dispute should initially seek a resolution through consultation and negotiation. If the dispute cannot be settled amicably, the national or company concerned may choose to submit the dispute for resolution:
>   (a) to the courts or administrative tribunals of the Party that is a party to the dispute; or
>   (b) in accordance with any applicable, previously agreed dispute-settlement procedures; or
>   (c) in accordance with the terms of paragraph 3.
> 3. (a) Provided that the national or company concerned has not submitted the dispute for resolution under paragraph 2(a) or (b) and that six months have elapsed from the date on which the dispute arose, the national or company concerned may choose to consent in writing to the submission of the dispute for settlement by binding arbitration:

(i) to the International Centre for Settlement of Investment Disputes ("Centre") established by the Convention on the Settlement of Investment Disputes between States and Nationals of other States, done at Washington, March 18, 1965 ("ICSID Convention"), provided that the Party is a party to such Convention; or

(ii) to the Additional Facility of the Centre, if the Centre is not available; or

(iii) in accordance with the Arbitration Rules of the United Nations Commission on International Trade Law (UNCITRAL); or

(iv) to any other arbitration institution, or in accordance with any other arbitration rules, as may be mutually agreed between the parties to the dispute.

(b) Once the national or company concerned has so consented, either party to the dispute may initiate arbitration in accordance with the choice so specified in the consent.

4. Each Party hereby consents to the submission of any investment dispute for settlement by binding arbitration in accordance with the choice specified in the written consent of the national or company under paragraph 3. Such consent, together with the written consent of the national or company when given under paragraph 3 shall satisfy the requirement for:

(a) written consent of the parties to the dispute for purposes of Chapter II of the ICSID Convention (Jurisdiction of the Centre) and for purposes of the Additional Facility Rules; and

(b) an "agreement in writing" for purposes of Article II of the United Nations Convention on the Recognition and Enforcement of Foreign Arbitral Awards, done at New York, June 10, 1958 ("New York Convention").

(1) Article VII(2): Dispute-Settlement Mechanisms at the Option of the Investor

[Under Article VII(2)(b) of the BIT the parties are to resolve a dispute in accordance with "any previously agreed dispute-settlement procedures." Under Article VII(3)(a) if the parties have not submitted the dispute to agreed on dispute settlement procedures and six months have elapsed from the time the dispute arose, the parties can submit the dispute to ICSID arbitration. Argentina argued, however, that when Article VII(2)(b) refers to "previously agreed dispute-settlement procedures," it is referring to agreements entered into prior to the BIT. Agreements entered into after the BIT, such as the concession agreement in this case, fall outside the scope of Article VII(2)(b) altogether. As a result, the provision in the concession agreement providing for settlement of disputes in the courts of Argentina is controlling and provides the exclusive method for resolving all disputes between the parties. The ICSID panel therefore had no jurisdiction over this case. The Tribunal turns to consider this argument below.]

This Tribunal shares the view of the Claimant that the expression "previously agreed" means prior to the moment that the dispute arises, consistent with Article VII(2) *ab initio* where it specifies: "In the event of an investment dispute . . . the national or company concerned may choose" among dispute-settlement procedures.

This Tribunal understands that the stipulation of Article 12 of the Concession Agreement, according to which the parties shall submit to the jurisdiction of the Federal Contentious-Administrative Tribunals of the City of Buenos Aires, cannot be considered a previously agreed dispute-settlement procedure. The Parties could have foreseen submission to domestic or international arbitration, but the choice of a national forum could only lead to the jurisdiction of the contentious-administrative tribunals, since administrative jurisdiction cannot be selected by mutual agreement. In this regard, the Parties could not have selected the jurisdiction of the Federal Contentious-Administrative Tribunals of the City of Buenos Aires because it would hardly be possible to select the jurisdiction of courts whose own jurisdictions are, by law, not subject to agreement or waiver, whether territorially, objectively, or functionally. As the contentious-administrative jurisdiction cannot be selected or waived, submission to the contentious-administrative tribunals cannot be understood as a previously agreed dispute-settlement procedure.

Nor can this Tribunal agree with the interpretation of the Argentine Republic, according to which Article VII(2)(b) makes reference to agreements entered into between the Parties prior to the entry into force of the ARGENTINA-U.S. Treaty, and consequently agreements concluded after the entry into force of the ARGENTINA-U.S. Treaty are not subsumed by this Article, and therefore are not an option for the investor, but rather prevail.

The Argentine Republic forgets that Article XIV of the ARGENTINA-U.S. Treaty clearly establishes that it "shall apply to investments existing at the time of entry into force as well as to investments made or acquired thereafter." Therefore, it applies to all investments, and their respective agreements, whether prior or subsequent to entry into force of the Treaty.

(2) Article VII(3): Submission to Binding International Arbitration

According to Article VII(3)(a):

> Provided that the national or company concerned has not submitted the dispute for resolution under paragraph 2(a) or (b) and that six months have elapsed from the date on which the dispute arose, the national or company concerned may choose to consent in writing to the submission of the dispute for settlement by binding arbitration:
>   (i) to the International Centre for the Settlement of Investment Disputes ("Centre") established by the Convention on the Settlement of Investment Disputes between States and Nationals of other States, done at Washington, March 18, 1965 ("ICSID Convention"), provided that the Party is a party to such Convention.

The investor has not submitted the dispute to the Federal Contentious-Administrative Tribunals of the Argentine Republic nor to any other previously agreed dispute-settlement system. In addition, aside from the efforts to reach agreement, more than six months have elapsed since the letter sent on March 18, 1997, by the President of LANCO to the Minister of Economy and Public Works and Services setting forth the dispute that had arisen, such that the letter of September 17, 1997, sent by LANCO's attorney to the Minister expresses the written consent of the national for the purposes of the ARGENTINA-U.S. Treaty to submit to the arbitration provided for at Article VII(3)(i).

B. THE REQUIREMENTS OF ARTICLE 25 OF THE ICSID CONVENTION

The Tribunal shall now proceed to consider its jurisdiction to decide the dispute in the instant case. The general rule that determines the jurisdiction of ICSID, and consequently that of this Tribunal, is established in Article 25 of the ICSID Convention[, which] enumerates several requirements to determine ICSID's jurisdiction, among which the fundamental and central consideration is the consent given by the parties to the dispute to submit their dispute to ICSID. This consent must be in writing, and once given it may not be withdrawn unilaterally.

(A) CONSENT TO JURISDICTION

In the case before us the consent of the Argentine Republic arises from the ARGENTINA-U.S. Treaty, in which the Argentine Republic has made a generic offer for submission to ICSID arbitration.

In effect, Article VII(3) provides: "Once the national or company concerned has so consented, either party to the dispute may initiate arbitration in accordance with the choice so specified in the consent." And Article VII(4) provides: "Each Party hereby consents to the submission of any investment dispute for settlement by binding arbitration in accordance with the choice specified in the written consent of the national or company under paragraph 3. Such consent, together with the written consent of the national or company when given under paragraph 3 shall satisfy the requirement for: (a) written consent of the parties to the dispute for purposes of Chapter II of the ICSID Convention (Jurisdiction of the Centre) and for purposes of the Additional Facility Rules."

The investor's consent, as noted, has been given by the investor LANCO and it has been so expressed unequivocally, such that this will, together with that of the Argentine Republic expressed in the ARGENTINA-U.S. Treaty, creates the consent necessary for conferring jurisdiction on ICSID, and therefore on this Tribunal.

The written consent by the Argentine Republic is set forth in the ARGENTINA-U.S. Treaty; as concerns the investor, as indicated supra, such consent was set forth in its letter of September 17, 1997, and in the request for arbitration, which was filed with ICSID on October 1, 1997.

(B) PERSONAL JURISDICTION

The requirement of Article 25 in terms of the nature of the parties is not at issue, since on the one hand we have the Argentine State, and on the other a corporation constituted under laws of the State of Illinois, in the United States, both the United States and the Argentine Republic being parties to the ICSID Convention.

(C) SUBJECT-MATTER JURISDICTION

Article 25 establishes that the dispute must be legal in nature and arise directly from an investment. In the instant case, LANCO understands that the Argentine Republic has breached its obligations established in the ARGENTINA-U.S. Treaty; it thus seeks to have the Tribunal rule on the following points: (i) the Argentine Republic has breached the obligations it assumed in Article II(2)(c) of the ARGENTINA-U.S. Treaty with respect to investments, and (ii) those assumed in Article II(2)(a) to the effect that it must accord fair and equitable treatment to investments; in addition, (iii) its breach constitutes a deprivation of a right conferred on the Claimant by the Concession Agreement, and therefore under Article IV(1) it should receive compensation; and (iv) finally, its breach also constitutes conduct equivalent to an expropriation, because it is responsible for the damages incurred by the Claimant. All of these are points indicative of a legal dispute.

PRELIMINARY DECISION

In view of the foregoing, from the documents and arguments made by the Parties, this Arbitral Tribunal must decide, as a preliminary matter—and its decision shall be included in its final award—that it has jurisdiction to examine the merits of the dispute that has arisen, pursuant to the provisions of the Convention on the Settlement of Investment Disputes between States and Nationals of Other States, done at Washington, D.C. on March 18, 1965.

NOTES AND QUESTIONS

1. In the *Lanco* case, the U.S. investor was part of a consortium that had been granted the right to operate a port terminal in Argentina. The investor claimed that Argentina had damaged its investment by giving more favorable treatment to a competitor operating another terminal in the same port. What substantive investment requirements or principle does this allegedly violate?

2. What were the two objections to jurisdiction raised by Argentina? How were they resolved?

Wena Hotels, Ltd. v. Arab Republic of Egypt
May 25, 1999
41 I.L.M. 881 (2002)
ICSID Case No. ARB/98/4

I. The Proceedings

The present arbitration was initiated on July 10, 1998 when Claimant, Wena Hotels Limited ("Wena"), filed a request for arbitration with the Secretary-General of the International Centre for Settlement of Investment Disputes ("ICSID"). The request was filed against Respondent, the Arab Republic of Egypt ("Egypt"), and asserted that "as a result of Egypt's expropriation of and failure to protect Wena's investment in Egypt, Wena has suffered enormous losses leading to the almost total collapse of its business."[18] Wena requested the following relief:

(a) a declaration that Egypt has breached its obligations to Wena by expropriating Wena's investments without providing prompt, adequate and effective compensation, and by failing to accord Wena's investment in Egypt fair and equitable treatment and full protections and security;

(b) an order that Egypt pay Wena damages in respect of the loss it has suffered through Egypt's conduct described above, in an amount to be quantified precisely during this proceeding but, in any event, no less than USD 62,820,000; and

(c) an order that Egypt pay Wena's costs occasioned by this arbitration including the arbitrators' fees and administrative costs fixed by ICSID, the expenses of the arbitration, the fees and expenses of any experts, and the legal costs incurred by the parties (including fees of counsel).

In accordance with Article 36 of the ICSID Convention and Rule 6(1) of the ICSID Institution Rules, the Acting Secretary-General of ICSID registered the request for arbitration on July 31, 1998, and invited the parties to constitute an Arbitral Tribunal.

---

18. Claimant's Request for Arbitration, at 1 (submitted on July 10, 1998) ("Request").

The Tribunal was constituted on December 18, 1998 and held its first session, at the Permanent Court of Arbitration in The Hague, on February 11, 1999. During this first session, Egypt objected to the request for arbitration filed by Wena and raised objections as to the Tribunal's jurisdiction to hear the dispute.

For the reasons discussed below, the Tribunal has concluded that Respondent's objections should be denied and jurisdiction exercised over the dispute.

II. THE FACTS

This dispute arose out of agreements to develop and manage two hotels in Luxor and Cairo, Egypt.

On August 8, 1989, Wena and the Egyptian Hotels Company ("EHC"), "a company of the Egyptian Public Sector affiliated to the General Public Sector Authority for Tourism"[19] entered into a 21 year, 6 month "Lease and Development Agreement" for the Luxor Hotel in Luxor Egypt. Pursuant to the Agreement, Wena was to "operate and manage the 'Hotel' exclusively for [its] account through the original or extended period of the 'Lease,' to develop and raise the operating efficiency and standard of the 'Hotel' to an upgraded four star hotel according to the specifications of the Egyptian Ministry of Tourism or upgrade [sic] it to a five star hotel if [Wena] so elects. . . ." Wena also agreed to make certain "additions to and expansion of the 'Hotel,'" including "at least forty additional guest rooms, a coffee shop, fast food shops, a children's swimming pool, a recreation center" and other improvements.

On January 28, 1990, Wena and EHC entered into a similar, 25-year agreement for the El Nile Hotel in Cairo, Egypt. Wena also entered into an October 1, 1989 Training Agreement with EHC and the Egyptian Ministry of Tourism "to train in the United Kingdom . . . Egyptian Nationals in the skills of hotel management. . . ."[20]

Shortly after entering into the agreements, disputes arose between EHC and Wena concerning their respective obligations. Wena claims that it "found the condition of the Hotels to be far below that stipulated in the lease [and] withheld part of the rent, as the lease permitted."[21] In turn, Egypt claims that Wena "failed to pay rent due to EHC on May 15 and August 15, 1990, and EHC in turn liquidated the performance security posted by Claimant."[22]

According to Egypt, Wena subsequently instituted arbitration proceedings in Egypt against EHC. The Tribunal has not seen copies of the resulting arbitration decision; however, Wena, so far, has not contested Egypt's summary of the award as requiring Wena "to pay rental due," but denying "EHC's request to revoke the Luxor Lease."[23]

On April 1, 1991, large crowds attacked the Luxor and Nile Hotels and the staff and guests were forcibly evicted. Both parties agree that EHC participated in these attacks and subsequently took control of the hotels. As Egypt notes, "it has been recognized by the

---

19. As explained during oral argument, the Egyptian government holds all of the shares of EHC, but the company is considered a separate legal entity.

20. An Agreement between His Excellency Fouad Sultan Minister of Tourism for the Egyptian Government jointly with Mr. Kamal Kandil of the Egyptian Hotels Company and Wena Hotels Limited (October 1, 1989).

21. Request, at 8.

22. Respondent's Memorial on its Objections to Jurisdiction, at 4 (submitted March 4, 1999) ("Memorial").

23. *Id.*

authorities in Egypt that the repossession by EHC of the Luxor and Nile Hotels and EHC's eviction of the Claimant from the Hotels on April 1, 1991 was wrong."[24] The Tribunal expects that both parties will present additional information about these attacks—and Egypt's role, if any—as part of their submissions on the merits.

In January 1992, the Chief Prosecutor of Egypt ruled that the attack on the Nile Hotel was illegal and, on February 25, 1992, the hotel was returned to Wena's control. Similarly, on April 28, 1992, the Chief Prosecutor of Egypt ruled that the attack on the Luxor Hotel was illegal and Wena resumed control of the hotel sometime thereafter.

On November 24, 1993 EHC requested that a receiver be appointed for the Luxor Hotel because of Wena's alleged failure to pay rent. Soon thereafter, on December 2, 1993, Wena initiated arbitration in Egypt against EHC for damages from the Nile Hotel invasion. Similar arbitration was initiated by Wena regarding the Luxor Hotel.

On April 10, 1994, an arbitration award of LE 1.5 million for damages from the invasion of the Nile Hotel was issued in favor of Wena. However, the award also required Wena to surrender the Nile Hotel to EHC's control. On June 21, 1995, Wena was evicted from the Nile Hotel.

The Luxor Hotel arbitration panel also found in favor of Wena, awarding the company, in a September 29, 1994 decision, nearly LE 18 million for damages from the invasion. However, this award subsequently was nullified by the Cairo Appeal Court on December 20, 1995. On August 14, 1997, Wena was evicted from the Luxor Hotel and, according to Egypt, the hotel was turned over to a court-appointed receiver requested by EHC. Again, the Tribunal expects that both parties will present additional information about Wena's eviction from the two hotels, and Egypt's responsibility, if any, for the evictions.

In addition to the disputes regarding the two hotels, Wena also has alleged a "campaign of continual harassment of Wena," including the following allegations: "in 1991 the Minister of Tourism made defamatory statements about Wena that were reproduced in the media; in 1992 Egypt revoked the Nile Hotel's operating license without reason; in 1995 Egypt imposed an enormous, but fictitious, tax demand on Wena; in 1996 Egypt removed the Luxor Hotel's police book, effectively rendering it unable to accept guests; and, last but not least, in 1997 Egypt imposed a three-year prison sentence and a LE 2000,000 bail bond on the Managing Director of Wena based on trumped-up charges."[25] With the exception of the 1997 conviction of Mr. Nael El-Farargy, the Managing Director of Wena, the parties have discussed none of these allegations in detail before the Tribunal. The Tribunal looks forward to the parties' elaboration on these issues.

IV. Objection 1: "The Respondent Has Not Agreed to Arbitrate with the Claimant as It Is, by Virtue of Ownership, to Be Treated as an Egyptian Company"

The Arab Republic of Egypt's principal objection is that, "although the claimant is an English company, it is, by virtue of Mr. El-Farargy's ownership and his Egyptian nationality, to be treated as an Egyptian company pursuant to Article 8(1)" [of the Agreement between the Arab Republic of Egypt and the United Kingdom of Great Britain and Northern Ireland for the Protection and Promotion of Investments, June 11, 1975

---

24. *Id.* at 9.
25. Request, at 16.

(IPPA)]. Accordingly, "as the respondent has not consented under the IPPA, to arbitrate with companies, such as the claimant, that are to be treated as Egyptian there under, it therefore follows from the IPPA's express terms that the respondent has not consented to the present arbitration."[26]

A. ARTICLE 8(1) OF THE IPPA AND ARTICLE 25 OF THE ICSID CONVENTION

Consent of the parties is the "cornerstone of the jurisdiction of the Centre."[27] In its deliberations, the Tribunal gave considerable attention to the instrument in which Egypt expressed its consent to ICSID arbitration—Article 8(1) of the IPPA between Egypt and the United Kingdom. The first sentence of this article contains a general consent to arbitration between a contracting State to the IPPA and a juridical person of the other contracting State to the IPPA, the situation in this case:

> Each Contracting Party hereby consents to submit to the International Centre for the [sic] Settlement of Investment Disputes . . . any legal dispute arising between that Contracting Party and a national or party of the other Contracting Party concerning an investment of the latter in the territory of the former.

Of considerable importance to this arbitration, however, is the second sentence of Article 8(1), which states that:

> Such a company of one Contracting Party in which before such a dispute arises a majority of shares are owned by nationals or companies of the other Contracting Party shall in accordance with Article 25(2)(b) of the Convention be treated for the purposes of the Convention as a company of the other Contracting Party.

Article 25(2)(b) of the ICSID Convention, which the second sentence expressly references, provides that, for purposes of jurisdiction under Article 25(1) of the Convention, "National of another Contracting State" means:

> (b) any juridical person which had the nationality of the Contracting State other than the State party to the dispute on the date on which the parties consented to submit such dispute to conciliation or arbitration and any juridical person that had the nationality of the Contracting State party to the dispute on that date and which, because of foreign control, the parties have agreed should be treated as a national of another Contracting State for the purposes of this Convention.

B. THE PARTIES' INTERPRETATION OF ARTICLE 8(1)

Egypt contends that the second sentence of Article 8(1) of the IPPA "reverses the nationality of a company incorporated in the United Kingdom but majority owned by Egyptian nationals."[28] Thus, "a company such as the Claimant, in which the majority of shares are held by an Egyptian national, is to be treated as an Egyptian company, not a

---

26. Respondent's Reply on Jurisdiction, at 2 (submitted on April 8, 1999) ("Reply").
27. Report of the Executive Directors on the Settlement of Investment Disputes between States and Nationals of Other States, ICSID Document No. 2 (March 18, 1965).
28. Memorial, at 12.

United Kingdom company."[29] Because the first sentence of Article 8(1), quoted above, requires diversity of nationality between the "Contracting Party" and the "national or party of the other Contracting Party," Egypt argues that the second sentence of Article 8(1) has the effect of "excluding jurisdiction in cases, such as this one, where a company is majority-owned by shareholders having the nationality of the State with which the company has a dispute."[30]

In contrast, Wena argues that "Egypt has completely misconstrued the meaning of Article 8(1): [I]t is a provision allowing companies incorporated in a state to sue that state where local companies are under foreign control; it does not prevent companies incorporated in that state from suing the other state."[31] In other words, "Wena's construction of this provision is that it applies not in every case, but only to a company which has the 'nationality of the Contracting State party to the dispute,' in accordance with Article 25(2)(b) of the ICSID Convention . . . to which the second sentence of Article 8(1) cross-refers."[32] Thus, according to Wena, the "second sentence of Article 8(1) . . . does not apply to Wena, a company which does not have the nationality of Egypt, the Contracting State party to this dispute."[33]

C.   THE TRIBUNAL'S ANALYSIS

[T]he Tribunal agrees with Wena's interpretation that the purpose of the sentence is to expand jurisdiction in cases where a company incorporated in the host State is controlled by nationals of the non-host State, "in accordance with Article 25(2)(b) of the [ICSID] Convention."

The literature rather convincingly demonstrates that Article 25(2)(b) of the ICSID Convention—and provisions like Article 8 of the United Kingdom's model bilateral investment treaty—are meant to expand ICSID jurisdiction by "permitting parties to a dispute to stipulate that a subsidiary of a 'national of another contracting state' which is incorporated in the host state (and therefore arguably a 'local national') will be treated as itself a 'national of another contracting state.'"[34] In the absence of any direct evidence of the intent of the Arab Republic of Egypt and the United Kingdom in negotiating Article 8(1), the Tribunal was strongly convinced by this common academic interpretation.

The purpose of Article 25(2)(b) is "to account for the rather common situation in which a host government insists that foreign investors channel their investment through a locally incorporated company. In the absence of this qualification to the general rule, such a company could not resort to ICSID facilities. . . ."[35] As every commentator cited by the parties explains, Article 25(2)(b) was specifically "designed to accommodate this problem by creating an exception to the diversity of nationality requirement."[36] Thus, the article acts to expand the Convention's normal jurisdiction—allowing a "juridical person

---

29. *Id.* at 11.
30. Reply, at 7.
31. Response, at 25.
32. Claimant's Rejoinder on Jurisdiction (submitted on April 22, 1999), at 21–22.
33. *Id.* at 22.
34. Aron Broches, *Bilateral Investment Protection Treaties and Arbitration of Investment Disputes,* in *The Art of Arbitration* edited by Jan C. Schultz (1982) [Annex W38, at 70].
35. Georges R. Delaume, *ICSID Arbitration: Practical Considerations,* Journal of International Arbitration, vol. 1 (1984) [Annex W33, at 112].
36. Christoph Schreuer, *Commentary on the ICSID Convention,* 12 ICSID Review—FILJ (1997) [Annex ARE24, at 94].

incorporated in the host State [to] be regarded as the national of another Contracting state if 'because of foreign control,' the parties have agreed that it should be treated as such for the purposes of the Convention."[37]

VI.   OBJECTION: "THERE IS NO LEGAL DISPUTE BETWEEN THE CLAIMANT AND THE RESPONDENT"

Egypt's [other] objection is that there is no "legal dispute" between Wena and Egypt. Specifically, Egypt contends that Wena has attempted to "make a succession of disputes arising out of a series of private relations into something larger than the sum of its parts—a dispute with Respondent. . . ."[38] According to Egypt, Wena's disputes actually are with the Egyptian Hotel Company ("EHC"), with whom Wena entered its original lease agreements and whose employees allegedly attacked the two hotels. As Egypt concluded, "Claimant has not demonstrated, and cannot, that there is any dispute between it and the Respondent."[39]

Wena, of course, disagrees. During the second session, Wena's counsel argued that Claimant actually has two separate disputes. One dispute, Wena acknowledges, is with EHC for violating its agreements with Wena. As the parties agree, this dispute with EHC has been the subject of at least four domestic arbitrations in Egypt. However, Wena also contends that it has a separate dispute with Respondent for "expropriating Wena's investments without providing prompt, adequate and effective compensation, and by failing to accord Wena's investments in Egypt fair and equitable treatment and full protection and security."[40]

From a jurisdictional perspective, the Tribunal believes that Wena has satisfied [its] burden. Wena has raised allegations against Egypt—of assisting in, or at least failing to prevent, the expropriation of Wena's assets—which, if proven, clearly satisfy the requirement of a "legal dispute" under Article 25(1) of the ICSID Convention. In addition, Wena has presented at least some evidence that suggests Egypt's possible culpability.[41]

VIII.   CONCLUSION

In sum, the Tribunal concludes that it has jurisdiction under the IPPA and the ICSID Convention for this matter to proceed to the merits of this case.

NOTES AND QUESTIONS

1. In *Wena Hotels*, is the Egyptian government legally responsible for the actions of the mob of private persons who attacked the hotels? What if it can be proven that the Egyptian government did not instigate the attack?

---

37. Georges R. Delaume, *ICSID Arbitration: Practical Considerations*, Journal of International Arbitration, vol. 1 (1984) [Annex W33, at 112].

38. Memorial, at 26.

39. *Id.* at 20.

40. Request, at 18.

41. *See, e.g.*, "British tourists are beaten and thrown out of Egypt hotels," Daily Telegraph (April 4, 1991) [Annex W7].

2. In a subsequent arbitration on the merits of the case, the tribunal held that Egypt had violated its duties of "fair and equitable treatment" and "full protection and security" as required by Article 2(2) of the IPPA. Compensation was awarded as measured by the standard: "the market value of the expropriated property immediately before the expropriation." *See* 41 I.L.M. 892 (2002).

LG&E Energy Corp., et al. v. Argentine Republic
October 3, 2006
46 I.L.M. 40 (2007)
ICSID Case No. ARB/02/1

[The Claimants, LG&E Energy Corp., LG&E Capital Corp., and LG&E International Inc. (collectively LG&E), were three United States corporations that had acquired equity interests in several Argentine gas distribution companies. The companies benefited from favorable guarantees granting the companies (but not the investors individually) long-term licenses for the transportation and distribution of gas, including stable tariff charges and inflation protection. Those guarantees were abrogated in 2001, when the Argentine government, faced with a severe economic crisis, enacted an Emergency Law modifying public service contracts, abolishing all clauses calling for tariff adjustments in U.S. dollars, and eliminating all indexing mechanisms. All public service contracts were renegotiated and no compensation was granted for the contract changes. The Tribunal examined the Claimants' claims that these measures violated certain provisions of the BIT in effect between the United States and the Argentine Republic and certain principles of public international law.]

DECISION ON LIABILITY
ARTICLE II(2)(a): FAIR AND EQUITABLE TREATMENT

[The Tribunal found that Argentina denied fair and equitable treatment to LG&E's investments. By withdrawing its pledged guarantees of LG&E's investments, Argentina failed to provide a stable legal and business environment and, in contravention of the principle of good faith established by international law, denied the investors' expectations when making its investments in reliance on the protections guaranteed by Argentina. The Tribunal further explained these findings as follows:]

133. Emerging from the economic crisis of the late 1980s, Argentina created an economic recovery plan mainly dependent upon foreign capital. Argentina prepared with the investment banks an attractive framework of laws and regulations that addressed the specific concerns of foreign investors with respect to the country risks involved in Argentina. In light of these risks, Claimants relied upon certain key guarantees in the Gas Law and implementing regulations, such as calculation of the tariffs in U.S. dollars before their conversion into pesos, the semi-annual PPI [(Producer Price Index)] adjustments, tariffs set to provide sufficient revenues to cover all the costs and a reasonable rate of return, and compensation in the event that the Government altered the tariff scheme. Having created specific expectations among investors, Argentina was bound by its obligations concerning the investment guarantees vis-à-vis public utility licensees, and in particular, the gas-distribution licensees. The abrogation of these specific guarantees violates the stability and predictability underlying the standard of fair and equitable treatment.

134. Specifically, it was unfair and inequitable to pass a law discarding the guarantee in Decree No. 1738/92 that the tariffs would be calculated in U.S. dollars and then converted into pesos. As pointed out by Claimants, this was not merely an economic and monetary policy of the Argentine Government which materialized through the Convertibility Law. Rather, it was a guarantee laid down in the tariff system. This guarantee was very important to investors to protect their investment, which was made in dollars, from a subsequent devaluation of the peso.

135. Argentina also acted unfairly and inequitably in the manner in which it abrogated the guarantees of the Gas Law and its implementing regulations, adversely affecting the gas-distribution sector but not affecting other sectors of the economy. For example, certain contracts, such as those in the export industry, were excluded from the forced conversion to pesos regulation, or the conversion was performed at a more favorable rate to the individual or company.

136. Argentina acted unfairly and inequitably when it prematurely abandoned the PPI tariff adjustments and essentially froze tariffs prior to the onset of the public disorder and threats to its essential security in December 2001, and when it refused to resume adjustments when conditions had normalized in April 2003, forcing instead the licensees to renegotiate. History has shown that the PPI adjustments that initially were supposed to be postponed have been abandoned completely and are now being "negotiated" away.

137. Argentina also has acted unfairly and inequitably in forcing the licensees to renegotiate public service contracts, and waive the right to pursue claims against the Government, or risk rescission of the contracts. Even though the Gas Law provided for the renegotiation of public service contracts, in practice there was no real renegotiation, but rather the imposition of a process.

138. Likewise, the Government's Resolution No. 38/02 issued on 9 March 2002, which ordered ENARGAS to discontinue all tariff reviews and to refrain from adjusting tariffs or prices in any way, also breaches the fair and equitable treatment standard.

STATE OF NECESSITY

201. Respondent contends in the alternative that, if Argentina would have breached its Treaty obligations, the state political, economic and social crisis that befell Argentina allowed it to take action contrary to the obligations it had assumed with respect to the gas-distribution licensees. Thus, even if the measures adopted by the State in order to overcome the economic crisis suffered during the years 1998 through 2003 resulted in a violation of the rights guaranteed under the Treaty to foreign investments, such measures were implemented under a state of necessity and therefore, Argentina is excused from liability during this period.

202. Respondent pleads its defense as a "state of necessity" defense, available under Argentine law, Treaty in Articles XI and IV(3), as well as customary international law.

204. Article XI of the Bilateral Treaty provides:

This Treaty shall not preclude the application by either Party of measures necessary for the maintenance of public order, the fulfillment of its obligations with respect to the maintenance or restoration of international peace or security, or the protection of its own essential security interests.

[The Tribunal next turned to whether a state of necessity existed under the Treaty and then, in a later section, whether a state of necessity existed under public international law.]

226. In the judgment of the Tribunal, from 1 December 2001 until 26 April 2003, Argentina was in a period of crisis during which it was necessary to enact measures to maintain public order and protect its essential security interests.

228. It is to be pointed out that there is a factual emergency that began on 1 December 2001 and ended on 26 April 2003, on account of the reasons detailed below, as well as a legislative emergency, that begins and ends with the enactment and abrogation of the Emergency Law, respectively. It should be borne in mind that Argentina declared its state of necessity and has extended such state until the present. Indeed, the country has issued a record number of decrees since 1901, accounting for the fact that the emergency periods in Argentina have been longer than the non-emergency periods. Emergency periods should be only strictly exceptional and should be applied exclusively when faced with extraordinary circumstances. Hence, in order to allege state of necessity as a State defense, it will be necessary to prove the existence of serious public disorders. Based on the evidence available, the Tribunal has determined that the situation ended at the time President Kirchner was elected.

229. Thus, Argentina is excused under Article XI from liability for any breaches of the Treaty between 1 December 2001 and 26 April 2003. The reasons are the following:

230. These dates coincide, on the one hand, with the Government's announcement of the measure freezing funds, which prohibited bank account owners from withdrawing more than one thousand pesos monthly and, on the other hand, with the election of President Kirchner. The Tribunal marks these dates as the beginning and end of the period of extreme crisis in view of the notorious events that occurred during this period.

231. Evidence has been put before the Tribunal that the conditions as of December 2001 constituted the highest degree of public disorder and threatened Argentina's essential security interests. This was not merely a period of "economic problems" or "business cycle fluctuation" as Claimants described. Extremely severe crises in the economic, political and social sectors reached their apex and converged in December 2001, threatening total collapse of the Government and the Argentine State.

232. All of the major economic indicators reached catastrophic proportions in December 2001. An accelerated deterioration of Argentina's Gross Domestic Product (GDP) began in December 2001, falling 10 to 15 percent faster than the previous year. Private consumption dramatically dropped in the fourth quarter of 2001, accompanied by a severe drop in domestic prices. Argentina experienced at this time widespread decline in the prices and in the value of assets located in Argentina. The Merval Index, which measures the share value of the main companies of Argentina listed on the Buenos Aires Stock Exchange, experienced a dramatic decline of 60 percent by the end of December 2001. By mid-2001, Argentina's country risk premium was the highest premium worldwide, rendering Argentina unable to borrow on the international markets, and reflecting the severity of the economic crisis.

233. At this time, capital outflow was a critical problem for the Government. In the fourth quarter of 2001, the Central Bank of Argentina lost US$ 11 billion in liquid reserves, amounting to 40 percent. The banking system lost 25 percent of its total deposits.

234. While unemployment, poverty and indigency rates gradually increased from the beginning of 1998, they reached intolerable levels by December 2001. Unemployment reached almost 25 percent, and almost half of the Argentine population was living below poverty. The entire healthcare system teetered on the brink of collapse. Prices of pharmaceuticals soared as the country plunged deeper into the deflationary period, becoming unavailable for low-income people. Hospitals suffered a severe shortage of basic supplies. Investments in infrastructure and equipment for public hospitals declined as never before. These conditions prompted the Government to declare the nationwide health

emergency to ensure the population's access to basic health care goods and services. At the time, one quarter of the population could not afford the minimum amount of food required to ensure their subsistence. Given the level of poverty and lack of access to healthcare and proper nutrition, disease followed. Facing increased pressure to provide social services and security to the masses of indigent and poor people, the Government was forced to decrease its per capita spending on social services by 74 percent.

235. By December 2001, there was widespread fear among the population that the Government would default on its debt and seize bank deposits to prevent the bankruptcy of the banking system. Faced with a possible run on banks, the Government issued on 1 December 2001 Decree of Necessity and Emergency No. 1570/01. The law triggered widespread social discontent. Widespread violent demonstrations and protests brought the economy to a halt, including effectively shutting down transportation systems. Looting and rioting followed in which tens of people were killed as the conditions in the country approached anarchy. A curfew was imposed to curb lootings.

236. By 20 December 2001, President De la Rúa resigned. His presidency was followed by a succession of presidents over the next days, until Mr. Eduardo Duhalde took office on 1 January 2002, charged with the mandate to bring the country back to normal conditions.

237. All of these devastating conditions—economic, political, social—in the aggregate triggered the protections afforded under Article XI of the Treaty to maintain order and control the civil unrest.

[The Tribunal next considered whether the actions of Argentina were justified under international law as reflected in Article 25 of the United Nations International Law Commission's Draft Articles on State Responsibility.[42]]

246. In international law, a state of necessity is marked by certain characteristics that must be present in order for a State to invoke this defense. As articulated by Roberto Ago, one of the mentors of the Draft Articles on State Responsibility, a state of necessity is identified by those conditions in which a State is threatened by a serious danger to its existence, to its political or economic survival, to the possibility of maintaining its essential services in operation, to the preservation of its internal peace, or to the survival of part

---

42. Article 25 of the Draft Articles on Responsibility of States for Internationally Wrongful Acts provides:

1. Necessity may not be invoked by a State as a ground for precluding the wrongfulness of an act not in conformity with an international obligation of that State unless the act:
    a. Is the only way for the State to safeguard an essential interest against a grave and imminent peril; and
    b. Does not seriously impair an essential interest of the State or States towards which the obligation exists, or of the international community as a whole.
2. In any case, necessity may not be invoked by a State as a ground for precluding wrongfulness if:
    a. The international obligation in question excludes the possibility of invoking necessity; or
    b. The State has contributed to the situation of necessity.

The ILC's Draft Articles, after some debate regarding the original prepared under the auspices of the Society of Nations in 1930, was abandoned and then resumed by the General Assembly in 1963. Its definitive version, due mainly to the works of Mssrs. Roberto Ago, Willem Riphagen and Gaetano Arangio-Ruiz, was approved in 1981 and subject to a revision in 1998, which was approved in 2001, during the 85th plenary session of the United Nations' General Assembly. (Session dated 12 December 2001, during the fifty-sixth session, Agenda item 162 of the Program, A/RES/56/83).

of its territory. In other words, the State must be dealing with interests that are essential or particularly important.

247. The United Nations Organization has understood that the invocation of a state of necessity depends on the concurrent existence of three circumstances, namely: a danger to the survival of the State, and not for its interests, is necessary; that danger must not have been created by the acting State; finally, the danger should be serious and imminent, so that there are no other means of avoiding it.

250. Taking each element in turn, Article 25 requires first that the act must be the only means available to the State in order to protect an interest. According to S.P. Jagota, a member of the Commission, such requirement implies that it has not been possible for the State to "avoid by any other means, even a much more onerous one that could have been adopted and maintained the respect of international obligations. The State must have exhausted all possible legal means before being forced to act as it does."[43] Any act that goes beyond the limits of what is strictly necessary "may not be considered as no longer being, as such, a wrongful act, even if justification of the necessity may have been admitted."[44]

251. The interest subject to protection also must be essential for the State. What qualifies as an "essential" interest is not limited to those interests referring to the State's existence. As evidence demonstrates, economic, financial or those interests related to the protection of the State against any danger seriously compromising its internal or external situation, are also considered essential interests. Roberto Ago has stated that essential interests include those related to "different matters such as the economy, ecology or other."[45] Julio Barboza affirmed that the threat to an essential interest would be identified by considering, among other things, "a serious threat against the existence of the State, against its political or economic survival, against the maintenance of its essential services and operational possibilities, or against the conservation of internal peace or its territory's ecology."[46]

253. The interest must be threatened by a serious and imminent danger. The threat, according to Roberto Ago, "must be 'extremely grave' and 'imminent.'"[47] In this respect, James Crawford has opined that the danger must be established objectively and not only deemed possible.[48] It must be imminent in the sense that it will soon occur.

255. The international obligation at issue must allow invocation of the state of necessity. The inclusion of an article authorizing the state of necessity in a Bilateral Investment Treaty constitutes the acceptance, in the relations between States, of the possibility that one of them may invoke the state of necessity.

257. [The Tribunal concluded that the essential interests of Argentina were threatened by the circumstances enumerated in ¶¶231–235 above.] Finally, as addressed above, Article XI of the Treaty exempts Argentina of responsibility for measures enacted during the state of necessity.

258. While this analysis concerning Article 25 of the Draft Articles on State Responsibility alone does not establish Argentina's defense, it supports the Tribunal's

---

43. United Nations, Report A/CN.4/SER.A/1980, pp. 155 and 175.
44. *Ibidem.*
45. United Nations, Report A/CN.4/SER.A/1980, p. 174.
46. *Ibidem.*
47. United Nations, Report A/CN.4/318/ADD.5-7. p. 20.
48. Crawford, James, *Second Report on State Responsibility op. cit.*, p. 31. In fact, this is so reflected in Principle 15 of the Rio Declaration on Environment and Development, adopted by the United Nations' Conference on Environment and Development in 1992.

analysis with regard to the meaning of Article XI's requirement that the measures implemented by Argentina had to have been necessary either for the maintenance of public order or the protection of its own essential security interests.

[The Tribunal concluded that a state of necessity existed in this case from December 1, 2001 through April 26, 2003 and that all measures taken into effect by Argentina were justified under the BIT and international law. Argentina was not required to provide any compensation to the Claimants for damages suffered as a result of these measures during this period. However, after the state of necessity ended on April 26, 2003, Argentina should have either reestablished its obligations to the Claimants or paid them compensation caused by measures adopted before and after the state of necessity.]

NOTES AND QUESTIONS

1. Many parts of the *LG&E* opinion were non-controversial. The decision to allow the "state of necessity" defense as an excuse for non-payment of financial obligations is the most controversial part of the Tribunal's *LG&E* opinion. In a prior case, *CMS Gas Transmission Co. v. Republic of Argentina*, 44 I.L.M. 1205 (ICSID Case No. ARB/01/8, 2005), involving similar facts, the Tribunal rejected the necessity defense as a defense to non-payment. After prevailing in the *LG&E* case, Argentina filed with ICSID a request that the CSM decision be annulled. A special three-person, ad hoc Committee was empanelled to handle this request, ruling as follows (Decision of the Ad Hoc Committee, 25 September 2007). The Committee concluded that although the Tribunal did not, as it should have, engage in a separate analysis of the test of necessity under international law (Article 25 of the ILC Draft Articles on Responsibility of States for Internationally Wrongful Acts) and Article XI of the BIT, the Tribunal's reasoning could be interpreted to mean that the same measures, which could not be considered necessary under international law, were also not necessary under Article XI. *See id.* ¶125. On a second issue, however, the Committee found that the Tribunal had made a manifest error. Even though a state of necessity may exist under both Article 25 codifying international law and Article XI of the BIT, the use of either article to justify as a defense the measures taken by Argentina in response to the state of necessity had to be separately analyzed under each article. The Committee elaborated as follows:

129. Article XI [necessity under the BIT] is a threshold requirement: if it applies, the substantive obligations under the Treaty do not apply. Article 25 [necessity under international law] is an excuse which is only relevant once it has been decided that there has otherwise been a breach of those substantive obligations.

130. Furthermore Article XI and Article 25 are substantively different. The first covers measures necessary for the maintenance of public order or the protection of each Party's own essential security interests. The second subordinates the state of necessity to four conditions. It requires for instance that the action taken "does not seriously impair an essential interest of the State or States towards which the obligation exists, or of the international community as a whole," a condition which is foreign to Article XI. In other terms the requirements under Article XI are not the same as those under customary international law as codified by Article 25. On that point, the Tribunal made a manifest error of law.

Despite these errors, the Ad Hoc Committee rejected Argentina's claim for annulment. The Ad Hoc Committee ruled that the award could stand because there was no manifest excess of powers and the CMS Tribunal had applied Article XI of the BIT, albeit "cryptically and defectively." Id. ¶136

Do you agree with the committee on the distinction between the necessity standard under international law and necessity in situations of financial crisis?

2. The issue of "necessity" as a justification for a state's refusal or suspension of payment obligations on sovereign bonds has arisen in actions by private investors who filed suit in German courts. In 2007, the German Constitutional Court (the Bundesverfassungsgericht) rejected the "necessity" defense by Argentina. The Court ruled that "currently no rule of general international law can be ascertained entitling a state vis-à-vis individuals to suspend the performance of obligations for payment arising under private law by invoking necessity based on inability to pay." Bundesverfassungsgericht [BverfG], Decision of May 8, 2007, available at *http://www.bverfg.de/entscheidungen/ms20070508_ 2bvm000103.html.* However, Judge Lübbe-Wolf filed a dissent stating that although "necessity" cannot be established as current rule of treaty law or customary international law, economic necessity can be recognized as a "general principle of law" between nations that can also be applied in cases vis-à-vis private individuals. *Id.* Thus, "necessity" as a defense in international investment cases continues to be unsettled and to raise conflicting answers in courts and in international tribunals.

NOTE ON ENFORCEMENT OF ICSID AWARDS

The ICSID Convention provides that ICSID awards are final and have binding force. Article 53(1) of the Convention provides that ICSID awards "shall be binding on all parties and shall not be subject to any appeal or to any other remedy except those provided for in this Convention." The Convention's remedies referenced in Article 53(1) are limited to annulment, revision, and interpretation of an award and must be obtained through the Convention not national laws. *See* ICSID Convention, Articles 50–52.

Article 54(1) of the Convention imposes upon State Parties the obligation to "recognize an award rendered pursuant to this Convention as binding and enforce the pecuniary obligations imposed by that award within its territories as if it were a final judgment of a court of that State." Thus, ICSID awards cannot be set aside by resort to national courts.

The obligation to enforce ICSID awards is transposed into U.S. law by 22 U.S.C. §1650a(a), which provides:

> The pecuniary obligations imposed by such an award shall be enforced and shall be given the same full faith and credit as if the award were a final judgment of a court of general jurisdiction of one of the several states. The Federal Arbitration Act (9 U.S.C. §1 et seq.) shall not apply to enforcement of awards rendered pursuant to the Convention.

In Chapter Eight of this book, we cover international arbitration under the New York Convention and the Federal Arbitration Act (FAA), 9 U.S.C. §1 *et seq.* (2012), which, we will see, governs generally the recognition and enforcement of foreign arbitration awards and provides several defenses to recognition and enforcement. But note that the FAA does *not* apply in the case of ICSID awards. As a result, the enforcement rate of ICSID awards is very high. *See* Loukas Mistelis and Crina Baliag, *Recognition and Enforcement of Arbitral Awards and Settlement in International Arbitration: Corporate Attitudes and Practice,* 19 Am. Rev. Int'l Arb. 320, 321 (2008). For example, in the *CMS Gas Transmission Co. Case* discussed above in note 1, the investors sought to confirm and enforce the ICS Award under Article 54 of the ICSID Convention in the federal district court for the Southern District of New York. Argentina pleaded sovereign immunity to the confirmation of the award based upon the U.S. Foreign Sovereign Immunity Act (FSIA), 28 U.S.C. §§1602-1611 (2012). The court, however, rejected Argentina's claim of immunity on two separate grounds. First, the court ruled that Argentina had waived its immunity by becoming a Party to the ICSID Convention and therefore the implied waiver exception of the FSIA, 28 U.S.C. §1605(a)(1), applied. Second, the court also ruled that the arbitral award exception to the FSIA, 28 U.S.C. §1605(a)(6), applied because ICSID arbitration awards fall squarely within this immunity exception. *See Blue Ridge Invs., LLC v. Republic of Argentina*, 902 F. Supp. 2d 367, 375-376 (S.D.N.Y. 2012), *aff'd*, 735 F.3d 72 (2d Cir. 2013). Thus, although the FSIA lays down a general rule of foreign sovereign immunity from the jurisdiction of U.S. courts, arbitral awards may be recognized and enforced by the courts under the implied waiver and the arbitral award exceptions to the FSIA.

C. An Example of a Regional Trade Agreement: NAFTA

In Chapter One, we provided a brief overview of the North American Free Trade Agreement (NAFTA) and its objectives at pp. 39-40, which we suggest that you review now. In this section, we focus on NAFTA Chapter 11, which provides a special regime to facilitate investment. The key provisions of Chapter 11 are as follows:

Article 1102: National Treatment

1. Each Party shall accord to investors of another Party treatment no less favorable than that it accords, in like circumstances, to its own investors with respect to the establishment, acquisition, expansion, management, conduct, operation, and sale or other disposition of investments.

2. Each Party shall accord to investments of investors of another Party treatment no less favorable than that it accords, in like circumstances, to investments of its own investors with respect to the establishment, acquisition, expansion, management, conduct, operation, and sale or other disposition of investments.

3. The treatment accorded by a Party under paragraphs 1 and 2 means, with respect to a state or province, treatment no less favorable than the most favorable treatment accorded, in like circumstances, by that state or province to investors, and to investments of investors, of the Party of which it forms a part.

Article 1103: Most-Favored-Nation Treatment

1. Each Party shall accord to investors of another Party treatment no less favorable than that it accords, in like circumstances, to investors of any other Party or of a non-Party with respect to the establishment, acquisition, expansion, management, conduct, operation, and sale or other disposition of investments.

2. Each Party shall accord to investments of investors of another Party treatment no less favorable than that it accords, in like circumstances, to investments of investors of any other Party or of a non-Party with respect to the establishment, acquisition, expansion, management, conduct, operation, and sale or other disposition of investments.

Article 1104: Standard of Treatment

Each Party shall accord to investors of another Party and to investments of investors of another Party the better of the treatment required by Articles 1102 and 1103.

Article 1105: Minimum Standard of Treatment

1. Each Party shall accord to investments of investors of another Party treatment in accordance with international law, including fair and equitable treatment and full protection and security.

2. Without prejudice to paragraph 1 . . . , each Party shall accord to investors of another Party, and to investments of investors of another Party, non-discriminatory treatment with respect to measures it adopts or maintains relating to losses suffered by investments in its territory owing to armed conflict or civil strife.

Article 1106: Performance Requirements

1. No Party may impose or enforce any of the following requirements, or enforce any commitment or undertaking, in connection with the establishment, acquisition, expansion, management, conduct or operation of an investment of an investor of a Party or of a non-Party in its territory:

(a) to export a given level or percentage of goods or services;

(b) to achieve a given level or percentage of domestic content;

(c) to purchase, use or accord a preference to goods produced or services provided in its territory, or to purchase goods or services from persons in its territory;

(d) to relate in any way the volume or value of imports to the volume or value of exports or to the amount of foreign exchange inflows associated with such investment;

(e) to restrict sales of goods or services in its territory that such investment produces or provides by relating such sales in any way to the volume or value of its exports or foreign exchange earnings;

(f) to transfer technology, a production process or other proprietary knowledge to a person in its territory, except when the requirement is imposed or the commitment or undertaking is enforced by a court, administrative tribunal or competition authority to remedy an alleged violation of competition laws or to act in a manner not inconsistent with other provisions of this Agreement; or

(g) to act as the exclusive supplier of the goods it produces or services it provides to a specific region or world market.

2. A measure that requires an investment to use a technology to meet generally applicable health, safety or environmental requirements shall not be construed to be inconsistent with paragraph 1(f). For greater certainty, Articles 1102 and 1103 apply to the measure.

3. No Party may condition the receipt or continued receipt of an advantage, in connection with an investment in its territory of an investor of a Party or of a non-Party, on compliance with any of the following requirements:

(a) to achieve a given level or percentage of domestic content;

(b) to purchase, use or accord a preference to goods produced in its territory, or to purchase goods from producers in its territory;

(c) to relate in any way the volume or value of imports to the volume or value of exports or to the amount of foreign exchange inflows associated with such investment; or

(d) to restrict sales of goods or services in its territory that such investment produces or provides by relating such sales in any way to the volume or value of its exports or foreign exchange earnings.

4. Nothing in paragraph 3 shall be construed to prevent a Party from conditioning the receipt or continued receipt of an advantage, in connection with an investment in its territory of an investor of a Party or of a non-Party, on compliance with a requirement to locate production, provide a service, train or employ workers, construct or expand particular facilities, or carry out research and development, in its territory.

5. Paragraphs 1 and 3 do not apply to any requirement other than the requirements set out in those paragraphs.

6. Provided that such measures are not applied in an arbitrary or unjustifiable manner, or do not constitute a disguised restriction on international trade or investment, nothing in paragraph 1(b) or (c) or 3(a) or (b) shall be construed to prevent any Party from adopting or maintaining measures, including environmental measures:

(a) necessary to secure compliance with laws and regulations that are not inconsistent with the provisions of this Agreement;

(b) necessary to protect human, animal or plant life or health; or

(c) necessary for the conservation of living or non-living exhaustible natural resources.

Article 1110: Expropriation and Compensation

1. No Party may directly or indirectly nationalize or expropriate an investment of an investor of another Party in its territory or take a measure tantamount to nationalization or expropriation of such an investment ("expropriation"), except:

(a) for a public purpose;

(b) on a non-discriminatory basis;

(c) in accordance with due process of law and Article 1105(1); and

(d) on payment of compensation in accordance with paragraphs 2 through 6.

2. Compensation shall be equivalent to the fair market value of the expropriated investment immediately before the expropriation took place ("date of expropriation"), and shall not reflect any change in value occurring because the intended expropriation had become known earlier. Valuation criteria shall include going concern value, asset value including declared tax value of tangible property, and other criteria, as appropriate, to determine fair market value.

3. Compensation shall be paid without delay and be fully realizable. . . .

Article 1114: Environmental Measures

1. Nothing in this Chapter shall be construed to prevent a Party from adopting, maintaining or enforcing any measure otherwise consistent with this Chapter that it considers appropriate to ensure that investment activity in its territory is undertaken in a manner sensitive to environmental concerns.

———————————

Chapter 11 of NAFTA provides for a choice by the investor between arbitration under UNCITRAL rules or under ICSID in investment disputes. Since 1978, ICSID has operated a so-called additional facility that is open to arbitrations where either of the host countries are parties to ICSID. The United States is a party to ICSID, but Mexico and Canada are not.

The following case deals with the particular aspects of the investment law of NAFTA.

Marvin Feldman v. Mexico
December 16, 2002
42 I.L.M. 625 (2003)
ICSID Case No. ARB(AF)99/1

[Corporación de Exportaciones Mexicanas, S.A. de V.C. (CEMSA), a corporation organized under the laws of Mexico and controlled by the Claimant Marvin Feldman, a U.S. citizen and its sole investor, was engaged in the purchase and export of American branded cigarettes produced under license in Mexico to the United States. CEMSA purchased cigarettes from retailers in Mexico such as Wal-Mart and Sam's Club because cigarette producers and their wholly-owned distributors refused to sell to CEMSA or other exporters. Mexico imposed a tax on the production and sale of cigarettes in Mexico (139.5 percent from 1990 through 1994 and 85 percent from 1995 through 1997) under the Impuesto Especial Sobre Producción y Servicios (IESP) but provided a rebate on those cigarettes when they were exported, which resulted in an effective tax rate of 0 percent on all exported cigarettes. The tax was collected and rebated by the Mexican Ministry of Finance and Public Credit (Secretaria de Hacienda y Crédito Público or SHCP). CEMSA began exporting cigarettes in 1990 and received rebates on its cigarettes by SHCP. According to the Claimant, in 1991, one of the producers of cigarettes in Mexico, Carlos Slim, protested against CEMSA's exports with Mexican authorities and influenced the authorities to pass a law in 1991 that denied the tax rebates to resellers of cigarettes such as CEMSA. The Claimant subsequently challenged the 1991 law in Mexican courts on the grounds that it violated the constitutional principle of the "equity of taxpayers" by excluding exports by resellers from the possibility of obtaining the 0 percent tax rate. After the lawsuit was filed, the Mexican Congress amended the IEPS law effective January 1, 1992, to allow the IEPS rebates to all cigarette exporters, and CEMSA was able to export cigarettes with rebates that year. However, in January 1993, the Mexican authorities shut down the Claimant's cigarette export business for a second time because the Claimant could not produce tax invoices in accordance with legal requirements. Under the IEPS tax law, the tax on cigarettes must be stated "separately and expressly in their invoices." However, only producers of cigarettes had access to such itemized invoices. As CEMSA purchased its cigarettes from retailers such as Wal-Mart and Sam's Club, CEMSA did not receive invoices that separately stated the tax. As a result, CEMSA could not comply with the IEPS tax law.

In August 1993, the Supreme Court of Mexico ruled on CEMSA's lawsuit brought in 1991 and held that the IEPS measures allowing rebates only to producers and their distributors violated constitutional law.

From 1993 to 1995, Mexican authorities recognized that as a taxpayer CEMSA was entitled to receive a 0 percent tax rate on cigarette exports but continued to demand that the Claimant meet the tax invoice requirements. CEMSA also claimed that from 1995 to 1996 it received oral assurances from Mexican authorities that they would permit CEMSA to export cigarettes in large quantities and receive rebates. In 1996–1997, CEMSA continued to receive rebates and by late 1997, CEMSA accounted for almost 15 percent of Mexico's cigarette exports.

On December 1, 1997, however, the SHCP terminated rebates to CEMSA and refused to pay rebates of U.S. $2.35 million on exports made by CEMSA in October and November 1997. On December 1, 1997, the IEPS law was amended again to bar tax rebates to cigarette resellers such as CEMSA, limiting rebates to the "first sale" in Mexico. As CEMSA purchased its cigarettes from retailers who had already completed the first sale in Mexico, CEMSA was not entitled to any rebates under the "first sale" rule. In addition, the amendments also imposed an obligation on exporters of certain goods, including cigarettes, of registering with Mexican authorities in order to apply for the 0 percent tax rate on exports. CEMSA was refused registration as a cigarette exporter.

On July 14, 1998, SHCP began an audit of CEMSA and demanded that CEMSA repay the approximately $25 million that it received during the 21-month period from January 1996 to September 1997. CEMSA challenged this assessment in the Mexican courts, and that challenge was still pending at the time of the ICSID arbitration.

CEMSA was not the only reseller and exporter of cigarettes in Mexico. Two other firms, Mercados I and Mercados II, both owned by Mexican nationals, also purchased cigarettes from Mexican volume retailers such as Wal-Mart for export. These Mexican firms were allowed to obtain tax rebates for the exports during the same period that such rebates were denied to CEMSA even though these other exporters were also resellers and also lacked tax invoices.

The Claimant thereafter challenged Mexico's refusal to rebate excise taxes on cigarettes exported by CEMSA in an arbitral proceeding before ICSID on the grounds that the actions of the Mexican government amounted to a nationalization and expropriation of Claimant's investment in violation of NAFTA Article 1110 and violated the national treatment principle embodied in NAFTA Article 1102.

In the first part of the opinion below, the ICSID panel examines whether an expropriation has occurred, and in the second part, the panel examines whether the national treatment principle has been violated.]

[Expropriation: NAFTA Article 1110]

Expropriation under Chapter 11 is governed by NAFTA Article 1110, although NAFTA lacks a precise definition of expropriation. That provision reads in pertinent part as follows:

> 1. No Party may directly or indirectly nationalize or expropriate an investment of an investor of another Party in its territory or take a measure tantamount to nationalization or expropriation of such an investment ("expropriation"), except:
> (a) for a public purpose;
> (b) on a non-discriminatory basis;
> (c) in accordance with due process of law and article 1105(1); and
> (d) on payment of compensation in accordance with paragraphs 2 through 6.

The key issue, in general and in the instant case, is whether the Respondent's actions constitute an expropriation.

This Tribunal's rationale for declining to find a violation of Article 1110 [is as follows:]

MANY BUSINESS PROBLEMS ARE NOT EXPROPRIATIONS

First, the Tribunal is aware that not every business problem experienced by a foreign investor is an indirect or creeping expropriation under Article 1110, or a denial of due process or fair and equitable treatment under Article 1110(1)(c). Governments, in their exercise of regulatory power, frequently change their laws and regulations in response to changing economic circumstances or changing political, economic or social considerations. Those changes may well make certain activities less profitable or even uneconomic to continue.

Here, it is undeniable that the Claimant has experienced great difficulties in dealing with SHCP officials, and in some respects has been treated in a less than reasonable manner, but that treatment under the circumstances of this case does not rise to the level of a violation of international law under Article 1110. Unfortunately, tax authorities in most countries do not always act in a consistent and predictable way. The IEPS law on its face (although not necessarily as applied) is undeniably a measure of general taxation. As in most tax regimes, the tax laws are used as instruments of public policy as well as fiscal policy, and certain taxpayers are inevitably favored, with others less favored or even disadvantaged.

Gray Market Exports and International Law

Second, NAFTA and principles of customary international law do not, in the view of the Tribunal, require a state to permit cigarette exports by unauthorized resellers (gray market exports). A prohibition to this effect may rely on objective reasons. Such reasons include discouragement of smuggling (of cigarettes purportedly exported back into Mexico), which may deprive a government of substantial amounts of tax revenue, maintenance of high cigarette taxes to discourage smoking (as in Canada) and, as a Mexican government official has suggested, assisting producers in complying with trademark licensing obligations under private agreements (*see* statement of Ismael Gomez Gordillo, App. 6045–6054). It is undeniable, as both parties in this proceeding have recognized, that smuggling of cigarettes is a serious problem not only for Mexico but for many other nations.

Continuing Requirements of Article 4(III) of IEPS Law

Third, in the present case, a *per se* government ban on reseller exports of cigarettes (or other products) from Mexico was not in force during the entire 1990–1997 period. The Respondent's efforts to impose such a ban legislatively in 1990 were held unconstitutional by the Supreme Court in a 1993 *Amparo* decision. In a narrow interpretation of that decision — that it required both producers and resellers be offered the zero percent tax rate for exports, but no more — it was legally possible for the Claimant to export cigarettes at the 0 percent rate if the Claimant could meet the other requirements of the IEPS law. However, the Claimant was effectively prevented from benefiting from the 0 percent rate, and therefore from exporting cigarettes, unless he could also obtain a rebate of the taxes reflected (but not separately stated) in the price that the Claimant paid to large retailers — Walmart and Sam's — for his cigarettes. This problem resulted from the fact that Mexican cigarette producers — particularly Cigatam, the Mexican licensee of the Marlboro brand — refused to sell to him because they wanted to maintain an export monopoly or perhaps for other reasons, a refusal which was apparently within their right under Mexican law. In economic terms, it would have been impossible for the Claimant to pay the price of the cigarettes in Mexico, including the 85 percent excise tax required under the IEPS law, and then sell the cigarettes in any foreign country. (Once the foreign nation added its own excise taxes upon importation, the Mexican cigarettes with both tax amounts included would have been priced far out of the market.)

In his efforts to obtain the rebates, the Claimant was stymied by a long-standing requirement of the IEPS law, the requirement in Article 4(III) that when seeking rebates he, as non-taxpayer, present invoices showing that the IEPS tax had been separately transferred to the taxpayer. The Claimant could not obtain the information from the retailers who supplied his cigarettes (since they did not know the tax amounts themselves), and the producers of the cigarettes were unwilling to provide the information.

[A] finding of expropriation here depends in significant part on whether under the circumstances the Article 4 invoice requirements are inconsistent with the Claimant's rights under NAFTA Article 1110. On the basis of the evidence presented to the Tribunal, the Tribunal is not persuaded that they are. The Article 4 invoice requirements have been part of the IEPS law at least since 1987, that is, for at least three years before CEMSA was first registered as an export company in 1991. Since the operation of its export business depended substantially on the terms of the IEPS law, the Claimant was or should have been aware at all relevant times that the separate invoice requirement existed, as there has been no *de jure* change in it at any time relevant to this dispute. Equally important, the Tribunal is reluctant to find an expropriation based largely on the failure of Mexican government officials to comply with an agreement in which those officials allegedly waived an explicit requirement of a tax law, even though there is some evidence, albeit contested by the Respondent, that the requirement was *de facto* ignored at some times both for the Claimant and for other cigarette resellers, including but not limited to members of the [so-called] Poblano group. This, however, is not in the view of the Tribunal evidence of expropriatory action and will be dealt with below in the section on national treatment.

National Treatment (NAFTA Article 1102)

[CEMSA also argued that it was denied national treatment under NAFTA.] In the present case, there are only a handful of relevant investors, one foreign (the Claimant) and one domestic (the Poblano-Guemes Group), each engaged in the business of purchasing Mexican cigarettes and marketing those cigarettes abroad. These investors cannot purchase the cigarettes from Mexican cigarette producers because the producers (and their wholly owned distributors) refuse to sell to them. Therefore, the Claimant or the Poblano Group firms must purchase their cigarettes from volume retailers, Walmart and Sam's Club. Since Walmart and Sam's Club are retailers and not IEPS taxpayers, they do not have available to them the precise amounts of the IEPS taxes included in the price paid first by the retailers in the transaction with the producers or distributors, and then by the Claimant and other reseller/exporters. Accordingly, neither the Claimant nor the Poblano Group companies can comply with the requirement of the IEPS law, Article 4(III), which makes it a condition of obtaining tax rebates upon export that the applicant be a taxpayer who possesses invoices showing the tax amount stated separately.

[Although the Poblano Group did not comply with the IEPS law, Article 4(III), its members were able to obtain tax rebates during 1996–1997 and 1998–2000. In addition, in order to receive tax rebates, an exporter had to register under Mexican law as an export trading company. CEMSA was denied registration as an export trading company, while members of the Poblano group were able to register. CEMSA also argued that while Mexico recouped rebates given to CEMSA, no similar effort was made to recoup rebates given to the members of the Poblano group.]

ANALYSIS BY THE TRIBUNAL

The national treatment/non-discrimination provision is a fundamental obligation of Chapter 11. Despite its deceptively simple language, the interpretative hurdles for Article 1102 are several. They include (a) which domestic investors, if any, are in "like circumstances" with the foreign investor; (b) whether there has been discrimination against foreign investors, either *de jure* or *de facto*, [and] (c) the extent to which differential treatment must be demonstrated to be a *result of* the foreign investor's nationality.

IN LIKE CIRCUMSTANCES

In this instance, the disputing parties agree that CEMSA is in "like circumstances" with Mexican owned resellers of cigarettes for export, including the two members of the Poblano Group, Mercados Regionales and Mercados Extranjeros.

Accordingly, the Tribunal holds that the companies which are in like circumstances, domestic and foreign, are the trading companies, those in the business of purchasing Mexican cigarettes for export, which for purposes of this case are CEMSA and the corporate members of the Poblano Group.

EXISTENCE OF DISCRIMINATION

The limited facts made available to the Tribunal demonstrate on balance to a majority of the Tribunal that CEMSA has been treated in a less favorable manner than domestically owned reseller/exporters of cigarettes, a *de facto* discrimination by SHCP, which is inconsistent with Mexico's obligations under Article 1102. The only confirmed cigarette exporters on the limited record before the tribunal are CEMSA, owned by U.S. citizen Marvin Roy Feldman Karpa, and the Mexican corporate members of the Poblano Group, Mercados I and Mercados II. According to the available evidence, CEMSA was denied the rebates for October–November 1997 and subsequently; SHCP also demanded that CEMSA repay rebate amounts initially allowed from June 1996 through September 1997. Thus, CEMSA was denied IEPS rebates during periods when members of the Poblano Group were receiving them.

The evidence also shows that CEMSA was denied registration as an export trading company, apparently in part because this action was filed, and in part as a result of the ongoing audit of the rebates for exports during 1996 and 1997, even though three other cigarette export trading companies had been granted registration. An unsigned memorandum which reasonably could have been generated only in SHCP indicates that registration was being denied on the basis of the audit of the Claimant's rebate payments. There is no evidence that any domestic reseller/exporter has been denied export privileges in this manner. Moreover, there appears to have been differential treatment between CEMSA and Mr. Poblano with regard to registration issues as well. According to the Claimant's witness, Mr. Carvajal, taxpayer CEMSA filed its application for export registration status on June 30, 1998; information was still being requested in writing seven months later. For taxpayer Mr. Poblano, information was requested by SHCP orally within 14 days of the date of Poblano's application, and any questions were apparently resolved.

DISCRIMINATION AS A RESULT OF NATIONALITY

It is clear that the concept of national treatment as embodied in NAFTA and similar agreements is designed to prevent discrimination on the basis of nationality, or "by reason of nationality." (U.S. Statement of Administrative Action, Article 1102.) However, it is not self-evident, as the Respondent argues, that any departure from national treatment must be *explicitly* shown to be a result of the investor's nationality. There is no such language in Article 1102. Rather, Article 1102 by its terms suggests that it is sufficient to show less favorable treatment for the foreign investor than for domestic investors in like circumstances.

However, in this case there is evidence of a nexus between the discrimination and the Claimant's status as a foreign investor. In the first place, there does not appear to be any rational justification in the record for SHCP's less favorable *de facto* treatment of CEMSA other than the obvious fact that CEMSA was owned by a very outspoken foreigner, who had, prior to the initiation of the audit, filed a NAFTA Chapter 11 claim against the Government of Mexico. Certainly, the action of filing a request for arbitration under

Chapter 11 could only have been taken by a person who was a citizen of the United States or Canada (rather than Mexico), i.e., as a result of his (foreign) nationality. While a tax audit in itself is not, of course, evidence of a denial of national treatment, the fact that the audit was initiated shortly after the Notice of Arbitration (first Feldman affidavit, paras. 85–86) and the existence of the unsigned memo at SHCP noting the filing of the Chapter 11 claim in the context of the Claimant's export registration efforts, at minimum raise a very strong suspicion that the events were related, given that no similar audit action was taken against domestic reseller/exporter taxpayers at the time.

On the basis of this analysis, a majority of the Tribunal concludes that Mexico has violated the Claimant's rights to non-discrimination under Article 1102 of NAFTA.

DECISION

For these reasons, the Tribunal:

Finds that the Respondent has not violated the Claimant's rights or acted inconsistently with the Respondent's obligations under NAFTA Article 1110;

Finds that the Respondent has acted inconsistently with the Claimant's rights and the Respondent's obligations under NAFTA Article 1102;

Orders the Respondent to pay immediately to the Claimant the sum of 9,464,627.50 Mexican pesos as principal, plus interest generated at the time of signature of this award, in the amount of 7,496,428.47 Mexican pesos, which interest shall accrue until the date the payment is effectively made. [The Tribunal found that the Claimant proved only that it was entitled to rebates due in the period of October–December 1997.]

NOTES AND QUESTIONS

1. Are you convinced by the tribunal's analysis and rejection of the Claimant's "creeping expropriation" argument?

2. Is the tribunal correct in its interpretation of discrimination based on national treatment? Does the discrimination point make it easy to find some discrimination in every case?

3. Because of the controversy over NAFTA investment decisions, Canada and Mexico have allowed review of awards in annulment proceedings to be conducted by principal courts at the seat of arbitration. For an argument against such review, see Charles H. Brower II, *Investor-State Disputes Under NAFTA: The Empire Strikes Back*, 40 Colum. J. Transnat'l L. 43 (2001).

The problem with allowing judicial review is that different courts apply different standards of review in investment arbitrations. For example, in the *Feldman* case, the award was challenged in Ontario, Canada, the seat of arbitration. The Ontario Court of Appeals upheld the award, ruling that courts should show a high degree of deference to NAFTA arbitrations and that Mexico had not shown any basis on which to interfere with the award. *Mexico v. Karpa*, [2005] O.J. 16 (Ontario C.A., Jan. 11, 2005). But in *Mexico v. Metalclad*, 2001 B.C.S.C. 664, available at *http://www.courts.gov.bc.ca*, the Supreme Court of British Columbia partially set aside a NAFTA award. Does judicial review of investment awards in different forums raise substantial problems? What should be done? For a proposal to create an Appellate Body that would have the authority to review investment awards, see Barton Legum, *Options to Establish an Appellate Mechanism for Investment Disputes*, in *Appeals Mechanism in International Investment Disputes* 231 (Karl P. Sauvant, ed., 2008).

4. In 2000 United Parcel Service (UPS) and its Canadian subsidiary filed an arbitration claim under NAFTA Chapter 11 asking for damages of at least $160 million plus interest and costs. UPS alleged that Canadian Post Corporation, a Crown corporation wholly owned by the Canadian government, was abusing its monopoly power. The Arbitral Tribunal, however, rejected the UPS claim on the merits, one arbitrator dissenting. *United Parcel Service v. Canada*, 46 I.L.M. 922 (2007). As a threshold matter, the Tribunal ruled that there is no rule of customary international law that prohibits or regulates anticompetitive behavior, and consequently, under NAFTA Article 1502(3), the Government of Canada was responsible for Canada Post's conduct only insofar as Canada Post was exercising delegated government authority. This narrow construction allowed the Tribunal to focus on a few salient points. First, the majority ruled that NAFTA Article 1102 was not violated by certain special payments, preferences, and exemptions with regard to the customs clearance process because Canada Post was not in "like circumstances" with UPS; the customs process concerning international mail (delegated to Canada Post) was found to be significantly different than the UPS process of handling and clearing express consignments. Second, the subsidization of Canadian periodicals through Canada's "Publication Assistance Program" was found to come within the scope of NAFTA Article 2106, which exempts "any measure adopted or maintained with respect to cultural industries." Does this case draw a necessary line in the sand to discourage future cases litigating the provision of public services and desirable public initiatives? If there is no customary international law rule on competition, should there be? Does this decision narrow the scope of NAFTA Article 1105?

5. In *Methanex Corporation v. United States*, 44 I.L.M. 1345 (2005), Methanex, a Canadian producer of methanol, claimed compensation under NAFTA Articles 1102, 1005, and 1110 because the State of California had enacted regulations banning gasoline produced with methyl tertiary-butyl ether (MTBE), an oxygenate containing methanol. Methanex asserted that the effect of this ban was to protect the U.S. ethanol industry, its main competitor. The Arbitral Tribunal dismissed this claim, finding that Methanex had not carried the burden that California was favoring the U.S. ethanol industry, since the measure was justified for environmental reasons. The Tribunal further determined that under the "like circumstances" provision of Article 1102, the California ban had the same impact on U.S. producers of methanol as on Methanex.

6. *Chemtura Corp. v. Government of Canada, Ad Hoc NAFTA Arbitration Under UNCITRAL Rules, Award* (U.S. v. Can.), available at *http://www.italaw.com/cases/249*, involved a claim by Chemtura that Canada violated its obligations under NAFTA Articles 1105 (minimum standard of treatment) and 1110 (expropriation) when Canada cancelled the registration of the pesticide lindane. Chemtura argued that Canada's review procedures were unfair and arbitrary. After first determining that it had jurisdiction, *id.* ¶¶99–105, the tribunal ruled that the ban on the pesticide was not arbitrary and was based upon widely accepted data, *id.* ¶¶124–163, and did not violate most-favored nation treatment, *id.* ¶¶226–237. The tribunal found that there was no expropriation, since the revoking of registration was not a substantial deprivation of Chemtura's business because sales of lindane were a relatively small part of Chemtura's business, *id.* ¶¶ 257–265.

PROBLEM 6-3

New Life Corp. is a U.S. company that manufactures biotechnology products. New Life has a Canadian subsidiary company that manufactures and markets a variety of such products, including a genetically modified potato plant that is engineered to produce a poison to kill the plant's chief predator insects. Canada has recently enacted a law that makes the sale of this plant illegal on the basis of evidence that the plant may have a deleterious effect on certain beneficial insects, such as the monarch butterfly. Is this a violation of NAFTA Chapter 11?

D.   Investment and the World Trade Organization

The World Trade Organization has comprehensive treaties dealing with three of the four channels of trade: The General Agreement on Tariffs and Trade (GATT) deals with merchandise trade, the Agreement on Trade Related Intellectual Property Rights (TRIPs) deals with technology trade, and the General Agreement on Trade in Services (GATS) deals with services trade. However, the WTO lacks a comprehensive agreement on investment trade. The reasons for this gap are historical and political. In the 1990s, a serious effort was made to negotiate a Multilateral Agreement on Investment (MAI), but the MAI failed to win support. Developed countries made a strategic error when they assigned the task of negotiating the MAI to the Organization of Economic Cooperation and Development (OECD), a group of developed and mostly Western states, with its headquarters in Paris. Many developing countries do not trust the OECD, which is viewed as a rich nations' club. Developing countries were permitted to be observers in the negotiations of the MAI, but could not participate directly. The goal was to have the OECD negotiate an ambitious and wide-ranging treaty and then to have the MAI adopted as one of the agreements of the WTO. It became clear, however, that developing countries, now a majority of the states in the WTO, and many nongovernmental organizations (NGOs) concerned with human rights and the environment had no interest in supporting the MAI. The MAI was criticized for reflecting the interests of developed countries and for ignoring the interests of developing countries. In particular, many critics believed that the MAI would facilitate economic domination and exploitation of developing countries by developed countries. Many NGOs also feared that the MAI would allow multinational companies to exploit workers in low wage countries and to damage the environment by locating their most dangerous operations in developing countries, which have lower environmental law standards or which fail to enforce them. The unprecedented opposition to the MAI, composed of developing countries and NGOs, doomed the MAI to failure and no efforts to have it adopted in the WTO were ever made. Although some attempts were made in recent years to resuscitate the negotiation of a comprehensive agreement on foreign investment within the WTO, there are too many controversial issues concerning FDI on which developed and developing nations strongly disagree for meaningful progress to occur. In addition, there now appears to be little impetus for further negotiations as the attention of many states within the WTO has shifted to other areas, such as intellectual property trade and agricultural trade.

There are two current WTO agreements that directly relate to foreign direct investment. The most important is the WTO Agreement on Trade-Related Investment Measures (TRIMs). TRIMs Article 2 declares that "no Member [of the WTO] shall apply any TRIM [trade-related investment measure] that is inconsistent with Article III[49] or Article XI[50] of

---

49. Article III of the GATT sets forth the national treatment principle, which prohibits WTO members from discriminating against imported goods in favor of domestically produced goods.

50. Article XI of the GATT sets forth a general rule, although subject to many exceptions, which prohibits countries from imposing quantitative restrictions (quotas) on imports.

GATT 1994." An Annex to the TRIMs Agreement contains the following "Illustrative List" of forbidden TRIMs:

Illustrative List

1. TRIMs that are inconsistent with the obligation of national treatment provided for in paragraph 4 of Article III of GATT 1994 include those which are mandatory or enforceable under domestic law or under administrative rulings, or compliance with which is necessary to obtain an advantage, and which require:

(a) the purchase or use by an enterprise of products of domestic origin or from any domestic source, whether specified in terms of particular products, in terms of volume or value of products, or in terms of a proportion of volume or value of its local production; or

(b) that an enterprise's purchases or use of imported products be limited to an amount related to the volume or value of local products that it exports.

2. TRIMs that are inconsistent with the obligation of general elimination of quantitative restrictions provided for in paragraph 1 of Article XI of GATT 1994 include those which are mandatory or enforceable under domestic law or under administrative rulings, or compliance with which is necessary to obtain an advantage, and which restrict:

(a) the importation by an enterprise of products used in or related to its local production, generally or to an amount related to the volume or value of local production that it exports;

(b) the importation by an enterprise of products used in or related to its local production by restricting its access to foreign exchange to an amount related to the foreign exchange inflows attributable to the enterprise; or

(c) the exportation or sale for export by an enterprise of products, whether specified in terms of particular products, in terms of volume or value of products, or in terms of a proportion of volume or value of its local production.

Note that the effect of TRIMs on FDI is rather limited because TRIMs applies only to the purchase of goods by foreign investment enterprises. TRIMs is designed primarily to prevent host countries from forcing foreign investment enterprises to purchase local goods used in manufacturing (e.g., raw materials and other inputs) in place of imports.

The second WTO agreement that directly relates to foreign investment, although again only in a limited way, is the General Agreement on Trade in Services (GATS). Under GATS, countries that voluntarily agree to open up a services sector to trade through the establishment of a foreign subsidiary have made a commitment to permit foreign direct investment in that sector. For example, suppose that Country A commits to opening up the insurance services sector and commits to allow foreign insurance companies to provide the service in Country A through a branch established in Country A. (This is known as a mode of service called "commercial presence" under GATS Article I:2. The other modes of service do not involve FDI.) If Country A has made such a commitment, and has not qualified the commitment as permitted by GATS, then Country A has, in effect, made a commitment under the WTO to permit foreign direct investment in the insurance services sector. Note that countries decide voluntarily whether to open up a services sector to foreign competition and whether to permit trade in services through the mode of a commercial presence, i.e., a foreign entity established in the host country. This aspect of GATS directly affects FDI.

Other than these provisions of TRIMs and GATS, the WTO does not regulate FDI. The regulation of FDI has been left to a growing patchwork of regional, national, and domestic laws. Given the current impasse between developed and developing nations and other pressing issues within the WTO, it does not appear likely that the WTO will complete a general agreement on investment on par with the other general agreements relating to goods, technology, and services.

NOTES AND QUESTIONS

1. How does TRIMs compare with NAFTA or the U.S.-Argentina BIT as a general investment treaty? NAFTA is an example of a comprehensive agreement on investment trade, although only applicable at a regional level. NAFTA has provisions on Most-Favored Nation Treatment (Article 1103), minimum standard of treatment of foreign investments, such as fair and equitable treatment (Article 1105), and expropriation and compensation (Article 1110). How many of these types of provisions are contained in TRIMs? Is TRIMs meant to be a comprehensive agreement and play a role on the multinational level similar to the role that NAFTA plays on a regional level? What is the role of TRIMs?

2. At the 2001 WTO Ministerial Conference in Doha, Qatar, it was agreed to begin negotiations on a comprehensive WTO Agreement on Investment in 2003. At the 2003 WTO Ministerial Conference in Cancún, Mexico, however, there was no agreement, and the conference failed because of sharp disagreements between developing and developed countries. Should a comprehensive investment agreement be concluded at a future WTO meeting? This does not appear likely. Is it a shortcoming of the WTO that while there are comprehensive agreements for the trade in goods, services, and technology, it lacks a comprehensive agreement on the trade in investment? For a closer examination of the MAI, its history, and the obstacles to reaching a general agreement on investment trade within the WTO, see Chapter Twelve of Chow and Schoenbaum, *International Trade Law: Problems, Cases, and Materials* 319–326 (Aspen 2d ed. 2012).

IV. Limits on Corporate Conduct in International Investment: The Foreign Corrupt Practices Act

In Part V, we will turn to the transactional aspects of establishing a foreign investment enterprise and the many collateral issues involved. One of these issues is so common and of such importance, however, that it is the subject of this entire section: the demand for bribes, payments, gifts, and other favors from government officials in the foreign host nation. The corrupt payment issue is one that involves serious legal consequences, and U.S. companies must be fully prepared to deal with this issue. Recent accounts indicate that government corruption involving foreign companies exists in every corner of the world ranging from advanced developed countries such as those in the European Union to developing countries such as Brazil and China. Some of these accounts tell lurid tales of avarice and personal indiscretions on the part of both foreign government officials and U.S. companies. Some examples of the types of payments and machinations involved are detailed in the three principal cases below.

While companies need to be vigilant about government corruption in every host nation, the problem of corruption appears to be especially serious in developing countries for several reasons. In many cases, a strict government regulatory regime empowers a few local government officials, who are largely unaccountable to the general populace, with the discretion to control the fate of wealthy MNEs. A local government official in a developing country who earns a salary equivalent to several hundred dollars per month may be in a position to decide whether to approve a foreign investment project involving tens of millions of dollars—or more—by one of the world's leading companies. This type of power structure leads to demands of exchanges of money for the exercise of power. In addition, many developing countries appear to be resigned to accept that some corruption on the part of government officials is unavoidable and must be tolerated. As many developing countries have weak legal systems, corrupt government officials are often able to act without fear of punishment. The vesting of significant power in low-paid officials in combination with a weak legal regime and a culture that tolerates "squeeze" among government officials in many developing countries has combined to create a business environment where demands for payments, gifts, and favors are all too common. Each of the three principal cases below involves a developing country.

Of course, not every U.S. company that pays bribes does so because it feels pressured or compelled by the host nation to do so. Rather, some companies and individuals like an environment of corruption and seek out opportunities to make bribes and gifts and to lure government officials into improper situations to secure an advantage. An atmosphere of corruption allows a company with an inferior product to make a bribe and overcome a competitor's superior product and the effect of market forces. The fruits of an improper payment may also result in personal gain and professional advantage for the individual business officials in the company making the payment. On the other hand, corruption can harm the company and its shareholders. In developing countries, government corruption harms the public by diverting public funds. These are some reasons why governments have become increasingly concerned about corruption in international business. What are the limits on corporate conduct concerning improper payments, gifts, and favors? An answer to this question must begin with an examination of the Foreign Corrupt Practices Act (FCPA), 15 U.S.C. §78 *et seq.*

We begin our examination of these issues with the following problems. To solve these problems, consider the discussion of the FCPA in Section A below and the notes and questions following. You will also need to carefully review §§78m(b), 78dd-1, 78dd-2, and 78dd-3 of the FCPA.

One final note: As FCPA issues often arise in the context of foreign investment, we have chosen to study it in the context of FDI. However, the FCPA can also apply to the sales contract, agency/distributorships, and licensing.

PROBLEM 6-4

Medtech is a publicly traded company located in Atlanta, Georgia. Medtech wishes to establish a foreign subsidiary to manufacture and sell its products in a developing country but has been warned by a local business consultant that it is customary to pay "substantial" fees for a business license. In addition, Medtech has been told that it is expected for new companies to make an additional payment of a "closing fee" of $1 million to the minister of trade. The consultant says, "Don't worry, this is all part of the business and legal culture here—everybody knows that it is legal and no one ever gets into trouble. It's been done in the open for years and the ministry has even said that the practice will be codified in a new law. All of your foreign competitors are making payments and you don't want to lose out to them, do you? I'll handle everything for you and you won't need to concern yourself with details. Just send payments to me when I ask for them. Also, if you are worried about your shareholders, you can file these payments under 'Closing Costs.' In fact,

I'll be in the U.S. on another matter next week and I can come and pick up the first payment from you at your head office." What issues are involved? *See* 15 U.S.C. §§78m and 78dd-1.

PROBLEM 6-5

Medtech is one of several companies that has applied to establish a $30 million joint venture in Chile. Before Medtech submitted its joint venture project application, several officials from Medtech's U.S. headquarters flew to Chile and invited various officials of the national bureau on foreign investment, which will decide whether to approve Medtech's application for the project, out for an evening's get together in order to get acquainted with Medtech's business and its plans for Chile and South America. The government officials were first treated to a World Cup soccer match between Chile and Germany, then a lavish champagne dinner at an expensive restaurant, and, finally, an extravagant evening at an exclusive nightclub, all paid for by Medtech. The whole evening cost more than a year's salary of the chief of the investment bureau. As the evening concluded, the chief of the investment bureau asked Medtech where he can find a scholarship for his daughter to attend a prestigious university in California. A Medtech official later sends the following e-mail message to Medtech's finance department in Atlanta: "Can you look into the scholarship? There must be a way, so let's find it." What are the legal issues involved? *See* 15 U.S.C. §78dd-1(c)(2).

PROBLEM 6-6

Medtech has been approached by Sino-Med, a privately owned medical company in China, to be its joint venture partner for the Chinese market. The president of Sino-Med has mentioned that it is customary for a foreign investor such as Medtech to give him $250,000 cash in "lucky money" as a gesture of goodwill and mutual friendship. Is this unlawful under the FCPA or any other relevant laws? What if 60 percent of the shares of Sino-Med were owned by the Supervision Bureau of Pharmaceuticals, a local regulatory agency? Would you advise Medtech to make the payment? *See* 15 U.S.C. §§78dd-1(a)(1)-(2) and 78dd-1(f)(1).

A. Overview of the FCPA

The Foreign Corrupt Practices Act was enacted in 1977 to deal with the rising problem of foreign corrupt payments. We do not examine the history of the FCPA in detail here as *United States v. Kay*, one of the principal cases below, offers an excellent summary of its legislative history. Rather, we offer an overview of its major substantive provisions.

The FCPA provides for two sets of obligations contained in its antibribery provisions and books and records provisions. The antibribery provisions proscribe the making of improper payments to foreign government officials and certain other persons. The books and records provision applies only to entities qualified as issuers under the Securities and Exchange Act of 1934 and requires that such issuers keep accurate records that do not disguise improper payments as something innocuous. As the antibribery provisions are the centerpiece of the FCPA, we focus on these provisions below.

The antibribery provisions of the FCPA, 15 U.S.C. §§78dd-1, 78dd-2, and 78dd-3, prohibit:

(1) Issuers, domestic concerns, and any person
(2) from making use of interstate commerce
(3) corruptly
(4) in furtherance of an offer or payment of anything of value
(5) to a foreign official, foreign political party, or candidate for political office
(6) for the purpose of influencing any act of that foreign official in violation of the duty of that official or to secure any improper advantage in order to obtain or retain business.

Enforcement of the FCPA is divided between two federal agencies: The Securities and Exchange Commission has civil and administrative authority over issuers, and the Justice Department has civil and criminal authority over all covered persons. A criminal violation of the antibribery provisions by a corporation can result in a statutory fine of up to $2 million. *See* 15 U.S.C. §78ff(c). Officers, directors, shareholders, employees, or agents may also be subject to fines of up to $10,000 and five years' imprisonment. *See id.* There is no private cause of action under the FCPA.

Each of the six elements of a violation of the FCPA is further discussed below.

1. *Persons Subject to the FCPA*

"Issuers"—who are subject to both the antibribery and books and records provisions—include any U.S. or foreign corporation that has a class of securities registered, or that is required to file reports, under the Securities and Exchange Act of 1934. In other words, the FCPA applies to any U.S. or foreign corporation with publicly traded securities in the United States.

"Domestic concerns" refer to any individual who is a citizen, national, or resident of the United States and any corporation and other business entity organized under the laws of the United States or having its principal place of business in the United States. The term "domestic concern" does not cover foreign subsidiaries of U.S. companies. Company officials such as officers, directors, employees, or agents of issuers and domestic concerns are also covered by the FCPA.

"Any person" covers both enterprises and individuals. Foreign entities that do not have publicly traded securities are included within this term as well as foreign nationals so long as they commit an act within the territory of the United States.

An issuer, domestic concern, or any covered person cannot circumvent the FCPA by having the payment made through an intermediary, such as a sales agent, distributor, or business consultant. It is unlawful for a covered person to make a payment to any person "while knowing that all or a portion of the payment will be offered, given or promised, directly or indirectly, to any foreign official, foreign political party or official thereof." 15 U.S.C. §78dd(3).

2. *Nexus with Interstate Commerce*

As the FCPA is a federal statute, there must be a nexus with interstate commerce to justify federal jurisdiction. However, this requirement is easily met. Any connection with interstate commerce, such as a single phone call, a single e-mail, or the posting of a letter will satisfy this requirement.

3.   Corrupt Intent

The FCPA has a scienter or *mens rea* requirement that the covered person made the payment with an evil motive, intent, or purpose in order to (1) wrongfully influence the recipient to abuse his or her official position or to influence someone else to do so (2) for the purpose of wrongfully directing business to the payor or to wrongfully obtain favorable legislation or regulations. *See United States v. Liebo*, 923 F.2d 1308, 1312 (8th Cir. 1991). Corrupt intent is also discussed in *Schreiber* and *Kozeny*, two of the principal cases below.

4.   Proscribed Payments

The FCPA covers acts "in furtherance of any offer, payment, promise to pay, or authorization of the payment of any money, gift, promise to give, or authorization of the giving of anything of value." 15 U.S.C. §78dd-1(a). Not only are payments prohibited, but any acts "in furtherance" of payments are also proscribed. In addition, any person who participates in or even authorizes such a payment can be held liable. A U.S. company that plans to make a corrupt payment and takes some concrete steps toward the making of such a payment may also be held liable under the FCPA even though the payment is never made.

The FCPA contains an exception, commonly called the "grease payment" exception, when the payment is a facilitating payment to secure the performance of a routine government action. *See* 15 U.S.C. §78dd-1(b). In addition, the FCPA contains an affirmative defense for payments that are lawful under the written laws of the foreign official's country or are for "bona fide expenditures" such as travel and lodging incurred by a foreign government official for the purpose of promoting the payor's products or services. *See* U.S.C. §78dd(c)(1)–(2).

5.   Persons to Whom Payments Are Made

The FCPA does not apply to payments made to private persons but covers only payments made to foreign officials, foreign political parties, party officials, or candidates for political office. An officer or employee of a foreign government or any instrumentality thereof acting in an official capacity will qualify as a foreign official. In a transition economy such as China, where it is difficult to distinguish between private and public sectors, the issue of persons to whom payments are prohibited can be difficult to determine.

6.   Purpose of the Payment

To violate the FCPA, the payment must be made in order to assist the payor in obtaining, retaining, or directing business to any person. This is the so-called business purpose test. Note that under the FCPA the recipient of the payment must be a foreign government official, party official, or candidate for political office but the business gained does not have to be with the foreign government. The scope of the business purpose test is the subject of *United States v. Kay*, one of the principal cases below.

NOTE ON THE OECD BRIBERY CONVENTION
AND OTHER INTERNATIONAL TREATIES

On December 17, 1997, 28 of the 29 members of the Organization for Economic Cooperation and Development, including the United States, signed the OECD Convention on Combating Bribery of Foreign Public Officials in International Business Transactions.

This represented a victory for the United States, which had long been a proponent of promulgating international legal standards proscribing bribery. The Convention was ratified in 1998 by ten countries and entered into force on February 15, 1999. As of this writing, 41 countries have ratified the Convention, including all OECD Member countries. All ratifying states have complied with the Convention by enacting legislation prohibiting transnational bribery. The United Kingdom has enacted the Bribery Act, 2010, c. 23 (effective July 1, 2011), which is viewed as expansive and as far reaching as the FCPA. The elements of the transnational bribery offense are slightly narrower but otherwise track those of the FCPA. In 1998, the United States enacted changes to the FCPA that have expanded the jurisdictional scope of the Act as it applies to foreign persons.

The OECD Convention requires that contracting states enact domestic criminal laws that prohibit the making of payments directly or through an intermediary to a foreign government official for the purpose of inducing that official to act or refrain from acting in an official capacity in order to retain or obtain business or obtain some other improper advantage. Unlike the FCPA, the Convention does not apply to payments to political parties, party officials, or candidates for political office. When it was enacted, the Convention was broader than the FCPA because it also proscribed payments to secure an "improper advantage." The FCPA has since been amended to incorporate this language. The effect of this new language on the business purpose test is discussed in *United States v. Kay* below.

On October 31, 2003, the General Assembly of the United Nations approved the United Nations Convention Against Corruption. The UN Convention goes beyond the FCPA and the OECD Convention in that it also proscribes commercial bribery, trading in influence, and "laundering" of the proceeds of corruption. The UN Convention also breaks new ground in providing for asset recovery. This feature was of particular importance to developing countries as they often suffer the most harm when public funds are diverted for personal gain. The UN Convention entered into force on December 14, 2005 (90 days after deposit of the thirtieth instrument of ratification) and has been ratified, approved, or acceded to by 171 countries, including the United States.

The United States has also signed the 1996 Inter-American Convention Against Corruption, 35 I.L.M. 724 (1996), and the Council of Europe's 1999 Criminal Law Convention on Corruption.

NOTES AND QUESTIONS

1. Prior to the OECD Convention on Transnational Bribery, it appears that the United States was the only nation in the world that had laws prohibiting payments to *foreign* government officials. Some U.S. businesses complained that the FCPA created a competitive disadvantage, as paying bribes to government officials is a common part of doing business in many host countries. Businesses from other countries were not prohibited from making bribes in the host country and some nations even allowed tax deductions for bribes. What national interests of the United States are furthered by prohibiting improper payments to government officials in a foreign country that outweigh any business disadvantages? Why is controlling corruption in international business transactions in the best interests of U.S. businesses even if it creates a possible short-term competitive disadvantage? Why would a "level playing field" help U.S. businesses?

2. The FCPA prohibits bribery of foreign *officials*. Commercial bribery in the form of payments or kickbacks given to foreign private entities is not covered by the FCPA or any other U.S. laws. Commercial bribes, while not prohibited by the FCPA, may be illegal

under the domestic laws of some foreign countries. Why does the United States draw a distinction between official and commercial bribery?

3. Most U.S. companies are quite vigilant about the FCPA. Should they be as concerned with local laws against commercial bribery in the host nation, especially if, as is often the case, the host nation, because of a weak legal system, does not regularly enforce such laws?

4. What is the rationale for the FCPA exception for "grease payments" in 15 U.S.C. §78dd-1(b)? See *United States v. Kay* below.

5. The FCPA also provides for an affirmative defense for certain other types of payments as discussed in Section A above. *See* 15 U.S.C. §78dd-1(c). From the standpoint of the payor, the difference between an exception, as for grease payments, and an affirmative defense can be significant because of burden of proof issues. Why?

6. Are foreign companies or individuals subject to the FCPA? If so, under what conditions and how can the United States justify its regulation of foreign entities? *See* 15 U.S.C. §§78dd-1 and 78dd-3.

B. Basic Issues Under the FCPA

The cases below touch on three important topics under the FCPA discussed above: (1) the scope of the requirement under the FCPA that the payment must be for the purpose of obtaining or retaining business; (2) the payment must be made "corruptly"; and (3) the affirmative defense that the payment was lawful under foreign law.

PROBLEM 6-7

Hyde Chemical Industries, a Delaware corporation, has established a wholly-owned subsidiary in the Congo Republic (CR). Under the CR's foreign investment laws, foreign invested companies are eligible to receive one of three designations: Level 1 for state-of-the-art technology, Level 2 for advanced technology, and Level 3 for high technology. Each designation carries a number of benefits. A Level 1 designation exempts the company from the CR's onerous environmental laws for a period of 20 years. Under the CR's laws, any foreign invested company can apply to the government for a review for a fee of $500,000. Most companies that pay for the review obtain a technology designation. In 2003, Hyde donated $5 million to CR's environmental protection bureau in order to allow the bureau to purchase and install a new computer system. In 2004, Hyde applied for a review and received a Level 1 designation. Later that year, the Justice Department charged Hyde with a violation of the FCPA. In its defense, Hyde argued that the donation was not for the purpose of obtaining new business. Hyde's plant was already established and Hyde had no intention of establishing any new businesses in the CR or in expanding its present operations. Does Hyde have a good argument? Consult *United States v. Kay* below. What other arguments would you suggest for Hyde? See *Schreiber* below following *Kay*.

United States v. Kay
United States Court of Appeals, Fifth Circuit, 2004
359 F.3d 738

WIENER, Circuit Judge.

Plaintiff-appellant, the United States of America ("government"), appeals the district court's grant of the motion of defendants-appellees David Kay and Douglas Murphy ("defendants") to dismiss the Superseding Indictment ("indictment") that charged them with bribery of foreign officials in violation of the Foreign Corrupt Practices Act ("FCPA"). In their dismissal motion, defendants contended that the indictment failed to state an offense against them. The principal dispute in this case is whether, if proved beyond a reasonable doubt, the conduct that the indictment ascribed to defendants in connection with the alleged bribery of Haitian officials to understate customs duties and sales taxes on rice shipped to Haiti to assist American Rice, Inc. in obtaining or retaining business was sufficient to constitute an offense under the FCPA. Underlying this question of sufficiency of the contents of the indictment is the preliminary task of ascertaining the scope of the FCPA, which in turn requires us to construe the statute.

The district court concluded that, as a matter of law, an indictment alleging illicit payments to foreign officials for the purpose of avoiding substantial portions of customs duties and sales taxes to obtain or retain business are not the kind of bribes that the FCPA criminalizes. We disagree with this assessment of the scope of the FCPA and hold that such bribes could (but do not necessarily) come within the ambit of the statute. Concluding in the end that the indictment in this case is sufficient to state an offense under the FCPA, we remand the instant case for further proceedings consistent with this opinion.

I. FACTS AND PROCEEDINGS

American Rice, Inc. ("ARI") is a Houston-based company that exports rice to foreign countries, including Haiti. Rice Corporation of Haiti ("RCH"), a wholly-owned subsidiary of ARI, was incorporated in Haiti to represent ARI's interests and deal with third parties there. As an aspect of Haiti's standard importation procedure, its customs officials assess duties based on the quantity and value of rice imported into the country. Haiti also requires businesses that deliver rice there to remit an advance deposit against Haitian sales taxes, based on the value of that rice, for which deposit a credit is eventually allowed on Haitian sales tax returns when filed.

In 2001, a grand jury charged Kay with violating the FCPA and subsequently returned the indictment, which charges both Kay and Murphy with 12 counts of FCPA violations. As is readily apparent on its face, the indictment contains detailed factual allegations about (1) the timing and purposes of Congress's enactment of the FCPA, (2) ARI and its status as an "issuer" under the FCPA, (3) RCH and its status as a wholly owned subsidiary and "service corporation" of ARI, representing ARI's interest in Haiti, and (4) defendants' citizenship, their positions as officers of ARI, and their status as "issuers" and "domestic concerns" under the FCPA. The indictment also spells out in detail how Kay and Murphy allegedly orchestrated the bribing of Haitian customs officials to accept false bills of lading and other documentation that intentionally understated by one-third the quantity of rice shipped to Haiti, thereby significantly reducing ARI's customs duties and sales taxes. In this regard, the indictment alleges the details of the bribery scheme's machinations, including the preparation of duplicate documentation, the calculation of bribes as a percentage of the value of the rice not reported, the surreptitious payment of monthly retainers to Haitian officials, and the defendants' purported authorization of withdrawals of funds from ARI's bank accounts with which to pay the Haitian officials, either directly or through intermediaries all to produce substantially reduced Haitian customs and tax costs to ARI.

Although it recites in great detail the discrete facts that the government intends to prove to satisfy each other element of an FCPA violation, the indictment recites no particularized facts that, if proved, would satisfy the "assist" aspect of the business nexus element of the statute, i.e., the nexus between the illicit tax savings produced by the bribery and the assistance such savings provided or were intended to provide in obtaining or retaining business for ARI and RCH. In other words, the indictment recites no facts that could demonstrate an actual or intended cause-and-effect nexus between reduced taxes and obtaining identified business or retaining identified business opportunities.

In granting defendants' motion to dismiss the indictment for failure to state an offense, the district court held that, as a matter of law, bribes paid to obtain favorable tax treatment are not payments made to "obtain or retain business" within the intendment of the FCPA, and thus are not within the scope of that statute's proscription of foreign bribery. The government timely filed a notice of appeal.

II. ANALYSIS

A. STANDARD OF REVIEW

We review de novo questions of statutory interpretation, as well as "whether an indictment sufficiently alleges the elements of an offense." Because an offense under the FCPA requires that the alleged bribery be committed for the purpose of inducing foreign officials to commit unlawful acts, the results of which will assist in obtaining or retaining business in their country, the questions before us in this appeal are (1) whether bribes to obtain illegal but favorable tax and customs treatment can ever come within the scope of the statute, and (2) if so, whether, in combination, there are minimally sufficient facts alleged in the indictment to inform the defendants regarding the nexus between, on the one hand, Haitian taxes avoided through bribery, and, on the other hand, assistance in getting or keeping some business or business opportunity in Haiti.

B. WORDS OF THE FCPA

None contend that the FCPA criminalizes every payment to a foreign official: It criminalizes only those payments that are intended to (1) influence a foreign official to act or make a decision in his official capacity, or (2) induce such an official to perform or refrain from performing some act in violation of his duty, or (3) secure some wrongful advantage to the payor. And even then, the FCPA criminalizes these kinds of payments only if the result they are intended to produce their quid pro quo will assist (or is intended to assist) the payor in efforts to get or keep some business for or with "any person." Thus, the first question of statutory interpretation presented in this appeal is whether payments made to foreign officials to obtain unlawfully reduced customs duties or sales tax liabilities can ever fall within the scope of the FCPA, i.e., whether the illicit payments made to obtain a reduction of revenue liabilities can ever constitute the kind of bribery that is proscribed by the FCPA.

The principal thrust of the defendants' argument is that the business nexus element, i.e., the "assist . . . in obtaining or retaining business" element, narrowly limits the statute's applicability to those payments that are intended to obtain a foreign official's approval of a bid for a new government contract or the renewal of an existing government contract. In contrast, the government insists that, in addition to payments to officials that lead directly to getting or renewing business contracts, the statute covers payments that indirectly advance ("assist") the payor's goal of obtaining or retaining foreign business with or for some person. The government reasons that paying reduced customs duties and sales taxes on imports, as is purported to have occurred in this case, is the type of "improper advantage" that always will assist in obtaining or retaining business in a foreign country, and thus is always covered by the FCPA.

C. FCPA LEGISLATIVE HISTORY

As the statutory language itself is amenable to more than one reasonable interpretation, it is ambiguous as a matter of law. We turn therefore to legislative history in our effort to ascertain Congress's true intentions.

1. 1977 Legislative History

Congress enacted the FCPA in 1977, in response to recently discovered but widespread bribery of foreign officials by United States business interests. Congress resolved to interdict such bribery, not just because it is morally and economically suspect, but also because it was causing foreign policy problems for the United States.[51] In particular, these concerns arose from revelations that United States defense contractors and oil companies had made large payments to high government officials in Japan, the Netherlands, and Italy. Congress also discovered that more than 400 corporations had made questionable or illegal payments in excess of $300 million to foreign officials for a wide range of favorable actions on behalf of the companies.

In deciding to criminalize this type of commercial bribery, the House and Senate each proposed similarly far-reaching, but non-identical, legislation. In its bill, the House intended "broadly [to] prohibit[] transactions that are corruptly intended to induce the recipient to use his or her influence to affect any act or decision of a foreign official. . . ." Thus, the House bill contained no limiting "business nexus" element. Reflecting a somewhat narrower purpose, the Senate expressed its desire to ban payments made for the purpose of inducing foreign officials to act "so as to direct business to any person, maintain an established business opportunity with any person, divert any business opportunity from any person or influence the enactment or promulgation of legislation or regulations of that government or instrumentality." In the end, Congress adopted the Senate's proposal to prohibit only those payments designed to induce a foreign official to act in a way that is intended to facilitate ("assist") in obtaining or retaining of business.

Congress expressly emphasized that it did not intend to prohibit "so-called grease or facilitating payments,"[52] such as "payments for expediting shipments through customs or placing a transatlantic telephone call, securing required permits, or obtaining adequate police protection, transactions which may involve even the proper performance of duties."[53] Instead of making an express textual exception for these types of non-covered payments, the respective committees of the two chambers sought to distinguish permis-

---

51. The House Committee stated that such bribes were "counter to the moral expectations and values of the American public," "eroded public confidence in the integrity of the free market system," "embarrassed friendly governments, lowered the esteem for the United States among the citizens of foreign nations, and lended credence to the suspicions sown by foreign opponents of the United States that American enterprises exert a corrupting influence on the political processes of their nations." H.R. Rep. No. 95-640, at 4–5 (1977); S. Rep. No. 95-114, at 3–4 (1977), reprinted in 1977 U.S.C.C.A.N. 4098, 4100–01.

52. H.R. Rep. No. 95-640, at 4; S. Rep. No. 95-114, at 10.

53. S. Rep. No. 95-114, at 10.

sible grease payments from prohibited bribery by only prohibiting payments that induce an official to act "corruptly," i.e., actions requiring him "to misuse his official position" and his discretionary authority,[54] not those "essentially ministerial" actions that "merely move a particular matter toward an eventual act or decision or which do not involve any discretionary action."[55]

In short, Congress sought to prohibit the type of bribery that (1) prompts officials to misuse their discretionary authority and (2) disrupts market efficiency and United States foreign relations, at the same time recognizing that smaller payments intended to expedite ministerial actions should remain outside of the scope of the statute. The Conference Report explanation, on which the district court relied to find a narrow statutory scope, truly offers little insight into the FCPA's precise scope, however; it merely parrots the statutory language itself by stating that the purpose of a payment must be to induce official action "so as to assist an issuer in obtaining, retaining or directing business to any person."

To divine the categories of bribery Congress did and did not intend to prohibit, we must look to the Senate's proposal, because the final statutory language was drawn from it, and from the SEC Report on which the Senate's legislative proposal was based. In distinguishing among the types of illegal payments that United States entities were making at the time, the SEC Report identified four principal categories: (1) payments "made in an effort to procure special and unjustified favors or advantages in the enactment or administration of the tax or other laws" of a foreign country; (2) payments "made with the intent to assist the company in obtaining or retaining government contracts"; (3) payments "to persuade low-level government officials to perform functions or services which they are obliged to perform as part of their governmental responsibilities, but which they may refuse or delay unless compensated" ("grease"), and (4) political contributions. The SEC thus exhibited concern about a wide range of questionable payments (explicitly including the kind at issue here) that were resulting in millions of dollars being recorded falsely in corporate books and records.

As noted, the Senate Report explained that the statute should apply to payments intended "to direct business to any person, maintain an established business opportunity with any person, divert any business opportunity from any person or influence the enactment or promulgation of legislation or regulations of that government or instrumentality."[56] We observe initially that the Senate only loosely addressed the categories of conduct highlighted by the SEC Report. Although the Senate's proposal picked up the SEC's concern with a business nexus, it did not expressly cover bribery influencing the administration of tax laws or seeking favorable tax treatment. It is clear, however, that even though the Senate was particularly concerned with bribery intended to secure new business, it was also mindful of bribes that influence legislative or regulatory actions, and those that maintain established business opportunities, a category of economic activity separate from, and much more capacious than, simply "directing business" to someone.

The statute's ultimate language of "obtaining or retaining" mirrors identical language in the SEC Report. But, whereas the SEC Report highlights payments that go toward "obtaining or retaining government contracts," the FCPA, incorporating the Senate Report's language, prohibits payments that assist in obtaining or retaining business, not

---

54. H.R. Rep. No. 95-640, at 7–8; S. Rep. No. 95-114, at 10.

55. H.R. Rep. No. 95-640, at 8. Similarly, when the House defined "foreign official" it excluded those individuals "whose duties are essentially ministerial or clerical." *Id.*

56. S. Rep. No. 95-114, at 17.

just government contracts. Had the Senate and ultimately Congress wanted to carry over the exact, narrower scope of the SEC Report, they would have adopted the same language. We surmise that, in using the word "business" when it easily could have used the phraseology of SEC Report, Congress intended for the statute to apply to bribes beyond the narrow band of payments sufficient only to "obtain or retain government contracts." The Senate's express intention that the statute apply to corrupt payments that maintain business opportunities also supports this conclusion.

For purposes of deciding the instant appeal, the question nevertheless remains whether the Senate, and concomitantly Congress, intended this broader statutory scope to encompass the administration of tax, customs, and other laws and regulations affecting the revenue of foreign states. To reach this conclusion, we must ask whether Congress's remaining expressed desire to prohibit bribery aimed at getting assistance in retaining business or maintaining business opportunities was sufficiently broad to include bribes meant to affect the administration of revenue laws. When we do so, we conclude that the legislative intent was so broad.

Congress was obviously distraught not only about high profile bribes to high-ranking foreign officials, but also by the pervasiveness of foreign bribery by United States businesses and businessmen. Congress thus made the decision to clamp down on bribes intended to prompt foreign officials to misuse their discretionary authority for the benefit of a domestic entity's business in that country. This observation is not diminished by Congress's understanding and accepting that relatively small facilitating payments were, at the time, among the accepted costs of doing business in many foreign countries.

In addition, the concern of Congress with the immorality, inefficiency, and unethical character of bribery presumably does not vanish simply because the tainted payments are intended to secure a favorable decision less significant than winning a contract bid. Obviously, a commercial concern that bribes a foreign government official to award a construction, supply, or services contract violates the statute. Yet, there is little difference between this example and that of a corporation's lawfully obtaining a contract from an honest official or agency by submitting the lowest bid, and either before or after doing so bribing a different government official to reduce taxes and thereby ensure that the under-bid venture is nevertheless profitable. Avoiding or lowering taxes reduces operating costs and thus increases profit margins, thereby freeing up funds that the business is otherwise legally obligated to expend. And this, in turn, enables it to take any number of actions to the disadvantage of competitors. Bribing foreign officials to lower taxes and customs duties certainly can provide an unfair advantage over competitors and thereby be of assistance to the payor in obtaining or retaining business. This demonstrates that the question whether the defendants' alleged payments constitute a violation of the FCPA truly turns on whether these bribes were intended to lower ARI's cost of doing business in Haiti enough to have a sufficient nexus to garnering business there or to maintaining or increasing business operations that ARI already had there, so as to come within the scope of the business nexus element as Congress used it in the FCPA. Answering this fact question, then, implicates a matter of proof and thus evidence.

In short, the 1977 legislative history suggests that Congress intended for the FCPA to prohibit all other illicit payments that are intended to influence non-trivial official foreign action in an effort to aid in obtaining or retaining business for some person. The congressional target was bribery paid to engender assistance in improving the business opportunities of the payor or his beneficiary, irrespective of whether that assistance be direct or indirect, and irrespective of whether it be related to administering the law, awarding, extending, or renewing a contract, or executing or preserving an agreement. In light of our reading of the 1977 legislative history, the subsequent 1988 and 1998 legislative history is only important to our analysis to the extent it confirms or conflicts with our initial conclusions about the scope of the statute.

2. 1988 Legislative History

After the FCPA's enactment, United States business entities and executives experienced difficulty in discerning a clear line between prohibited bribes and permissible facilitating payments. As a result, Congress amended the FCPA in 1988, expressly to clarify its original intent in enacting the statute. In this effort to crystallize the scope of the FCPA's prohibitions on bribery, Congress chose to identify carefully two types of payments that are not proscribed by the statute. It expressly excepted payments made to procure "routine governmental action" (again, the grease exception),[57] and it incorporated an affirmative defense for payments that are legal in the country in which they are offered or that constitute bona fide expenditures directly relating to promotion of products or services, or to the execution or performance of a contract with a foreign government or agency.[58]

We agree with the position of the government that these 1988 amendments illustrate an intention by Congress to identify very limited exceptions to the kinds of bribes to which the FCPA does not apply. A brief review of the types of routine governmental actions enumerated by Congress shows how limited Congress wanted to make the grease exceptions. Routine governmental action, for instance, includes "obtaining permits, licenses, or other official documents to qualify a person to do business in a foreign country," and "scheduling inspections associated with contract performance or inspections related to transit of goods across country."[59] Therefore, routine governmental action does not include the issuance of every official document or every inspection, but only (1) documentation that qualifies a party to do business and (2) scheduling an inspection—very narrow categories of largely non-discretionary, ministerial activities performed by mid- or low-level foreign functionaries. In contrast, the FCPA uses broad, general language in prohibiting payments to procure assistance for the payor in obtaining or retaining business, instead of employing similarly detailed language, such as applying the statute only to payments that attempt to secure or renew particular government contracts. Indeed, Congress had the opportunity to adopt narrower language in 1977 from the SEC Report, but chose not to do so.

3. 1998 Legislative History

In 1998, Congress made its most recent adjustments to the FCPA when the Senate ratified and Congress implemented the Organization of Economic Cooperation and Development's Convention on Combating Bribery of Foreign Public Officials in International Business Transactions (the "Convention"). Article 1.1 of the Convention prohibits payments to a foreign public official to induce him to "act or refrain from acting in relation to the performance of official duties, in order to obtain or retain business *or other improper advantage* in the conduct of international business."[60] When Congress amended the language of the FCPA, however, rather than inserting "any improper advantage" immediately following "obtaining or retaining business" within the business nexus

---

57. 15 U.S.C. §§78dd-1(b) & (f)(3)(A).
58. 15 U.S.C. §78dd-1(c).
59. 15 U.S.C. §78dd-1(f)(3)(A).
60. Convention on Combating Bribery of Foreign Public Officials in International Business Transactions, Dec. 17, 1997, art. 1.1, S. Treaty Doc. No. 105-43, 37 I.L.M. 1, 4 (1998) (emphasis added).

requirement (as does the Convention), it chose to add the "improper advantage" provision to the original list of abuses of discretion in consideration for bribes that the statute proscribes. Thus, as amended, the statute now prohibits payments to foreign officials not just to buy any act or decision, and not just to induce the doing or omitting of an official function "to assist . . . in obtaining or retaining business for or with, or directing business to, any person,"[61] but also the making of a payment to such a foreign official to secure an "improper advantage" that will assist in obtaining or retaining business.[62]

The district court concluded, and defendants argue on appeal, that merely by adding the "improper advantage" language to the two existing kinds of prohibited acts acquired in consideration for bribes paid, Congress "again declined to amend the 'obtain or retain' business language in the FCPA."[63] In contrast, the government responds that Congress's choice to place the Convention language elsewhere merely shows that Congress already intended for the business nexus requirement to apply broadly, and thus declined to be redundant.

The Convention's broad prohibition of bribery of foreign officials likely includes the types of payments that comprise defendants' alleged conduct. The commentaries to the Convention explain that "'other improper advantage' refers to something to which the company concerned was not clearly entitled, for example, an operating permit for a factory which fails to meet the statutory requirements."[64] Unlawfully reducing the taxes and customs duties at issue here to a level substantially below that which ARI was legally obligated to pay surely constitutes "something [ARI] was not clearly entitled to," and was thus potentially an "improper advantage" under the Convention.

4. Summary

Given the foregoing analysis of the statute's legislative history, we cannot hold as a matter of law that Congress meant to limit the FCPA's applicability to cover only bribes that lead directly to the award or renewal of contracts. Instead, we hold that Congress intended for the FCPA to apply broadly to payments intended to assist the payor, either directly or indirectly, in obtaining or retaining business for some person, and that bribes paid to foreign tax officials to secure illegally reduced customs and tax liability constitute a type of payment that can fall within this broad coverage. [W]e conclude that bribes paid to foreign officials in consideration for unlawful evasion of customs duties and sales taxes could fall within the purview of the FCPA's proscription. We hasten to add, however, that this conduct does not automatically constitute a violation of the FCPA: It still must be shown that the bribery was intended to produce an effect here, through tax savings that would "assist in obtaining or retaining business."

III. Conclusion

We are satisfied that for purposes of the statutory provisions criminalizing payments designed to induce foreign officials unlawfully to perform their official duties in administering the laws and regulations of their country to produce a result intended to assist

---

61. *See* 15 U.S.C. §78dd-1(a)(1).
62. *Id.*
63. *Kay*, 200 F. Supp. 2d at 686.
64. Commentaries on the Convention on Combating Bribery of Foreign Public Officials in International Business Transactions, 37 I.L.M. at 8.

in obtaining or retaining business in that country an unjustified reduction in duties and taxes can, under appropriate circumstances, come within the scope of the statute.

Reversed and remanded.

Stichting Ter behartiging Van de Belangen Van Oudaandeelhouders in Het Kapitaal Van Saybolt International B.V. v. Schreiber

United States Court of Appeals, Second Circuit, 2003
327 F.3d 173

SACK, Circuit Judge.

The plaintiff, Stichting ter behartiging van de belangen van oudaandeelhouders in het kapitaal van Saybolt International B.V. (Foundation of the Shareholders' Committee Representing the Former Shareholders of Saybolt International B.V.), appeals from a decision of the United States District Court for the Southern District of New York (Jed S. Rakoff, Judge) granting the defendants' motion for summary judgment. *See Stichting Ter behartiging Van de Belangen Van Oudaandeelhouders in Het Kapitaal Van Saybolt International B.V. v. Schreiber,* 145 F. Supp. 2d 356 (S.D.N.Y. 2001) ("*Stichting*"). The plaintiff claims that the erroneous legal advice given by defendant Philippe E. Schreiber caused a United States-based corporation that was a subsidiary of a Dutch company to violate the Foreign Corrupt Practices Act, 15 U.S.C. §§78dd-1, *et seq.* ("FCPA"). The corporation pleaded guilty in a Massachusetts federal district court to violating the FCPA, and its former chief executive officer ("CEO") was convicted of violating the FCPA by a New Jersey federal district court jury.

In the case at bar, the district court concluded that the guilty plea and the conviction collaterally estop the plaintiff, as the corporation's assignee, from claiming that Schreiber caused the corporation to think that its acts would not violate the FCPA. We disagree with the district court's conclusion that the corporation's guilty plea is inconsistent with the plaintiff's theory of how Schreiber misled the corporation. We also disagree with the district court's conclusion that the corporation was in privity with its former CEO at the time of his trial and therefore is bound by the trial's outcome. We vacate the judgment and remand for further proceedings consistent with this opinion. In so doing, we do not question the validity of either the plea or the conviction.

BACKGROUND

This appeal is from the district court's grant of the defendants' motion for summary judgment. The facts we adduce here are undisputed except as otherwise noted.

THE BRIBE

In 1995, Saybolt International was a private Dutch limited-liability company whose various worldwide subsidiaries were engaged in "the business of performing quantitative and qualitative testing of bulk commodities such as oil, gasoline, and other petrochemicals, as well as grains [and] vegetable oils." Am. Compl. P 20. Saybolt International owned Saybolt North America, Inc., a Delaware corporation with principal offices in Parsippany,

New Jersey. All directors and officers of Saybolt North America were also directors or officers of Saybolt International. One such person was David H. Mead, who served as chief executive officer of Saybolt North America and as an officer and director of Saybolt International. Mead also served as the de facto head of all operations under the control of Saybolt International in the Western Hemisphere.

Beginning in late 1994 or early 1995, Saybolt de Panama S.A. ("Saybolt de Panama"), a subsidiary of Saybolt International under Mead's supervision, sought to acquire property in Panama for the construction of a laboratory and office complex. Sometime in 1995, Mead was told that Saybolt de Panama had identified suitable property in the Panama Canal Zone but that the lease could be acquired only if the company would first pay a $50,000 bribe to a Panamanian government official.

Mead raised the issue of the bribe in a Saybolt North America board meeting held in New Jersey on November 9, 1995. Schreiber, a lawyer admitted to practice in New York State, was present at the meeting. In addition to serving as a director of Saybolt North America, Schreiber occasionally provided legal services to the corporation. At the meeting, Schreiber advised those present that Saybolt North America could not pay the proposed bribe to the Panamanian official without subjecting the corporation and its officers and directors to potential liability. Then and in the weeks that followed, however, Schreiber allegedly led Mead and others to believe that "the bribe payment could legally be made under U.S. law by [their] Dutch affiliate," Saybolt International. Am. Compl. P 13. Allegedly on this basis, on December 17, 1995, an employee of Saybolt North America traveled by commercial airline from New Jersey to Panama for purposes of arranging the bribe. On December 21, 1995, Saybolt International wired $50,000 from the Netherlands to a bank account controlled by Saybolt de Panama. The Saybolt North America employee then directed an employee of Saybolt de Panama to deliver the $50,000 to an individual acting as an intermediary for the Panamanian official.

THE CRIMINAL PROCEEDINGS

On November 20, 1996, United States officials investigating possible environmental crimes by Saybolt North America executed a search warrant at its offices in New Jersey. The search uncovered evidence of the Panama bribe.

Shortly thereafter, on May 12, 1997, Core Laboratories, N.V. ("Core") purchased Saybolt International and its controlling interest in Saybolt North America. Pursuant to the purchase agreement, Saybolt International's former shareholders placed $6 million in escrow to cover any criminal liability that might arise from the company's activities in Panama. In exchange, Core assigned the former shareholders all causes of action for any legal malpractice related to the Panama incident.

United States prosecutors decided to bring separate criminal proceedings against Saybolt North America and its officers. Mead was arrested in January 1998, at which point he stopped actively working for the various Saybolt entities, which were by then part of Core. On April 20, 1998, a federal grand jury in the District of New Jersey returned an indictment charging Mead with, inter alia, violating the FCPA, 15 U.S.C. §78dd-2(a)(3), and conspiring to violate the FCPA, 18 U.S.C. §371.

At about that time, the United States Attorney for the District of Massachusetts and the United States Attorney for the District of New Jersey jointly issued an information charging Saybolt North America with substantially the same offenses charged in Mead's indictment: violating, and conspiring to violate, the FCPA. On August 18, 1998, officers of Core caused Saybolt North America to enter into a plea agreement in which Saybolt

North America promised to "cooperate truthfully and completely with the United States . . . in any trial or other proceedings arising out of this investigation of [Saybolt North America] and any of [its] present and former officers and employees." On December 3, 1998, Saybolt North America pleaded guilty to the charges in the information before the United States District Court for the District of Massachusetts. In the plea colloquy, the court instructed John D. Denson, the Core officer representing Saybolt North America, as follows:

> You understand that before the corporation or corporations can be found guilty of [violating the FCPA], the government would have to prove beyond a reasonable doubt that an agent of the corporation, acting for the corporation and so situated with respect to the management of the corporation[] that the act or acts can properly be considered the acts of the corporation itself, has to have entered into a corrupt, that is, a bribe-like transaction in the international commerce of the United States. It has to be not just that there was a mistake, that this agent or agents of the corporations knew what they were doing.
>
> Do you understand that?

Denson answered "Yes, sir." The court then entered judgment against the corporation.

Unlike his former employer, Mead decided to fight the charges against him. His case went to trial before the United States District Court for the District of New Jersey (Anne E. Thompson, Judge) in early October 1998. At trial, Mead presented evidence that, Mead contended, suggested that Schreiber led Mead to believe that "the bribe payment could legally be made," Am. Compl. P 13, if the bribe of the Panamanian official were paid by a non-United States entity. The court instructed the jury that "if the evidence shows you that the defendant actually believed that the transaction was legal, he cannot be convicted." Mead Trial Tr. at 6.131. The jury convicted Mead on both charges, and the district court sentenced him to four months' imprisonment and a $20,000 fine.

THE MALPRACTICE SUIT

Saybolt International's former shareholders assigned their legal malpractice causes of action to the plaintiff, which brought this diversity action in the United States District Court for the Southern District of New York on November 18, 1999. In its amended complaint, the plaintiff alleged that Schreiber, and through him Walter, Conston, Alexander & Green, P.C., defendant-third-party-plaintiff, a law firm with which Schreiber was affiliated, committed legal malpractice by failing to advise Saybolt North America that "the bribe payment as proposed to be paid by a Dutch company to Panamanian officials would violate the FCPA." Am. Compl. P110. Without Schreiber's malpractice, the amended complaint alleged, "the bribe payment would not have been made, even at the cost of the entire Panama deal." Am. Compl. P 111. The plaintiff further alleged that by committing such malpractice, Schreiber also breached his lawyer's fiduciary duty to Saybolt North America and breached his contract to provide competent professional services. Finally, the plaintiff alleged that Schreiber's malpractice cost the former Saybolt International shareholders $4.2 million, mostly in criminal fines.

In a June 12, 2001, Memorandum Order, the district court granted the defendants' motion for summary judgment on all claims. *Stichting*, 145 F. Supp. 2d at 359. The court noted that the plaintiff alleged that Schreiber's erroneous advice led Saybolt North America to act without the knowledge that its conduct violated United States law. *Id.* at 357. The court then held that this allegation necessarily contradicts Saybolt North America's guilty plea to the charges that it violated the FCPA:

To enter such a plea Saybolt [North America] had to affirm, as it did, that it undertook the misconduct in question with knowledge of the corruptness of its acts. Since, if it had in fact relied on Schreiber's allegedly erroneous and misleading advice, Saybolt [North America] would not have believed at the time that its misconduct was unlawful or corrupt, it could never have made this admission at its allocution or, indeed, entered its guilty plea at all.

Id. On this basis, the district court concluded that under the doctrine of collateral estoppel, Saybolt North America's guilty plea forecloses the plaintiff's theory of causation. "Since Saybolt did . . . plead guilty and admit its criminal intent, it is bound by those admissions, and therefore cannot now contend either that it relied on Schreiber's alleged advice or that that advice, even if erroneous, . . . proximately caused whatever damages . . . were incurred by Saybolt." *Id.* at 357–58.

The district court also held that Mead's criminal convictions are an independent basis for entering judgment against the plaintiff. *Id.* at 358. The court observed that the plaintiff's theory of how Schreiber misled Saybolt North America had been "squarely put before, and rejected by, the jury that convicted Mead." *Id.* The court then held that "Mead was indicted and convicted for criminal activity he undertook for [the corporation's] benefit in his capacity as chief executive officer . . . , and his intent is therefore directly imputable" to the corporation. *Id.* at 358–59. On this basis, the district court concluded that the plaintiff is collaterally estopped from relitigating the issue of Saybolt North America's reliance on Schreiber's legal advice. *Id.*

The plaintiff appealed.

DISCUSSION

II. THE GUILTY PLEA

As indicated, the district court held that Saybolt North America's guilty plea constituted an admission that the corporation acted with knowledge that its conduct was "unlawful or corrupt." *Stichting*, 145 F. Supp. 2d at 357. For this reason, the district court concluded that the plaintiff is collaterally estopped from arguing that Schreiber led Saybolt North America to believe that its acts would not violate the FCPA. The plaintiff challenges this conclusion on appeal. We agree with the plaintiff.

A. THE ELEMENTS OF THE CRIME

[The court sets forth the six elements of the crime discussed at p. 402, above.]

As the district court described it, the plaintiff's claim in its civil suit is that its lawyer, Schreiber, "advised Saybolt [North America] that a bribe payment by a foreign affiliate might be legal but also failed to advise Saybolt [North America] that any involvement by Saybolt [North America] or its officers in arranging the affiliate's payment could result in criminal liability." *Stichting*, 145 F. Supp. 2d at 357. "[I]f Saybolt [North America] had in good faith relied on Schreiber's advice, Saybolt [North America] would have believed that its arranging the bribe through a foreign affiliate was permissible." *Id.*

By pleading guilty, Saybolt North America admitted the six elements of the FCPA crime. But by pleading guilty, Saybolt North America did not admit that at the time of the criminal act it knew that the act of arranging, rather than paying, such a bribe was criminal. Knowledge by a defendant that it is violating the FCPA—that it is committing all the elements of an FCPA violation—is not itself an element of the FCPA crime. Federal statutes in which the defendant's knowledge that he or she is violating the statute is an element of the violation are rare; the FCPA is plainly not such a statute. Saybolt North America did not, therefore, by pleading guilty, preclude an assertion in a subsequent civil action—the case at bar—that it did not know it was violating the FCPA at the time of the violation.

The plaintiff is thus not collaterally estopped by Saybolt North America's criminal plea from arguing in this civil suit that, even though Saybolt North America admittedly did commit a violation of the FCPA, it did not know that it was committing a violation of the FCPA at the time; that it did not know it was committing such a violation because Schreiber negligently told it that it was not committing a violation by causing a foreign entity to pay the bribe; and that it suffered damages as a result of the negligent advice.

We therefore conclude that the case should be remanded to the district court to permit the plaintiff to attempt to establish what the district court identified as its claim: that the defendant advised Saybolt North America that a bribe payment by a foreign affiliate might be legal, but failed to advise Saybolt North America that any involvement by Saybolt North America or its officers in arranging the affiliate's payment could result in criminal liability, i.e., as stated in the Complaint, that "Schreiber erroneously advised [Saybolt North America] that the bribe payment could legally be made under U.S. law by a Dutch affiliate," Am. Compl. P 13; and that, as stated by the district court, Saybolt North America "in good faith relied on Schreiber's advice" that "arranging the bribe through a foreign affiliate was permissible," *Stichting*, 145 F. Supp. 2d at 357.

B. THE "CORRUPTLY" ELEMENT

To be sure, by pleading guilty, Saybolt North America admitted that it acted "corruptly" in its actions related to the Panamanian bribe. The defendants see in this admission a collateral bar to the plaintiff's assertion that Saybolt North America did not know that it was violating the FCPA at the relevant time and, indeed, was misled into believing that it was acting legally. The district court apparently agreed. *See Stichting*, 145 F. Supp. 2d at 357. We do not. We conclude that an admission that an act was done "corruptly" in this context is not equivalent to an admission that the person committing it knew that it violated the particular law at the time the act was performed.

It is difficult to determine the meaning of the word "corruptly" simply by reading it in context. We therefore look outside the text of the statute to determine its intended meaning.

The Senate Report for the FCPA explains the statute's use of the term "corruptly" as follows:

> The word "corruptly" is used [in the FCPA] in order to make clear that the offer, payment, promise, or gift, must be intended to induce the recipient to misuse his official position in order to wrongfully direct business to the payor or his client, or to obtain preferential legislation or a favorable regulation. The word "corruptly" connotes an evil motive or purpose, an intent to wrongfully influence the recipient.

S. Rep. No. 95-114, at 10 (1977), reprinted in 1977 U.S.C.C.A.N. 4098, 4108.

The Senate's explanation of the term "corruptly" tracks closely our interpretation of that term in 18 U.S.C. §201(b). We have repeatedly held in that context that "a fundamental component of a 'corrupt' act is a breach of some official duty owed to the government or the public at large." *United States v. Rooney*, 37 F.3d 847, 852 (2d Cir. 1994). Our case law defining the term "corruptly" in federal bribery statutes thus parallels the Senate

Report's explanation of the term as denoting an evil motive or purpose and an intent to induce an official to misuse his position.

We thus conclude that the word "corruptly" in the FCPA signifies, in addition to the element of "general intent" present in most criminal statutes, a bad or wrongful purpose and an intent to influence a foreign official to misuse his official position. But there is nothing in that word or any thing else in the FCPA that indicates that the government must establish that the defendant in fact knew that his or her conduct violated the FCPA to be guilty of such a violation.

Finally in this connection, we note that had Saybolt North America gone to trial, it would have been allowed to present evidence that it relied on Schreiber's advice that the benefit sought from the Panamanian official would not require the official to misuse his position or breach his duties—i.e., that it did not act corruptly—precisely because "corruptly" is an element of the offense. Saybolt North America also would have been allowed a jury instruction on this allegation. By pleading guilty, Saybolt North America effectively admitted that it could not factually support such a theory of reliance.

But Saybolt North America would not properly have been entitled to a jury instruction on an allegation that Schreiber led it to believe that its acts did not violate the FCPA. A defense of reliance on advice of counsel is available only to the extent that it might show that a defendant lacked the requisite specific intent and specific intent to violate the FCPA is not an element of an FCPA violation. Thus, Saybolt North America's guilty plea does not constitute an admission that it could not factually support the theory of reliance on counsel that is the basis of the plaintiff's malpractice action.

C. CONCLUSION

We conclude that the question whether Saybolt North America acted with knowledge that its conduct violated the FCPA was not answered by its guilty plea, and thus that the plea does not collaterally estop the plaintiff from litigating the issue in its claim against Schreiber and the law firm with which he was affiliated. *See N.L.R.B. v. Thalbo Corp.*, 171 F.3d 102, 109 (2d Cir. 1999) (collateral estoppel applies only to issues "actually decided" in the previous proceeding).

III. THE CONVICTION OF MEAD

[The court went on to hold that the conviction of Mead, the former CEO of Saybolt North America, did not bar the plaintiff from relitigating the issue of malpractice against Schreiber. Mead had argued at his trial that he relied on the advice of Schreiber that the payments were lawful. The trial court had instructed the jury to convict only if the jury found that Mead knew that the transactions were illegal. The district court then found that because the jury convicted Mead, it must have concluded that Mead knew that the transactions were illegal and was not misled by Schreiber. The district court then held that plaintiff was collaterally estopped to challenge this finding. However, as neither the plaintiff nor Saybolt North America was a party to Mead's trial, the plaintiff would be barred by collateral estoppel only if at the time of Mead's trial, Mead was in privity with Saybolt North America. The court of appeals found that no such privity existed as Mead was released from his duties for all of the Saybolt entities before the trial and Saybolt North America, by then Mead's former employer, did not exercise any degree of actual control over his defense. As no privity existed between Mead and Saybolt North America, plaintiff was not barred by collateral estoppel in pursuing its claims against Schreiber.]

CONCLUSION

For the foregoing reasons, the judgment of the district court is vacated, and the case remanded for further proceedings consistent with this opinion.

PROBLEM 6-8

Jones, the vice president for global investment of Titan Steel, a U.S.-based company, has traveled to Country E for the purpose of seeking approval to establish a foreign subsidiary. Jones is invited to the isolated mountaintop mansion of General Sosa, the country's leader, for a lavish private dinner. At the dinner, General Sosa asks Jones for a payment of $5 million to Sosa's private account as a gesture of goodwill. Jones offers a polite but non-committal reply. Later at the dinner, also attended by a group of tough-looking soldiers, the General offers a toast, "To good health and a long life, worth more than all the money in the world. My guards will give you a ride to the airport tomorrow." Later when Jones returns to his hotel, he immediately wires $5 million to General Sosa's private account. The payment is discovered one year later by the U.S. Justice Department through an informant. Jones argues that he cannot be prosecuted under the laws of Country E because the statute of limitations on bribes is six months. Country E's laws also require a paper record of the payment and all records in the hotel and the General's bank have been lost. When Jones arrives back in the United States, he receives a letter from General Sosa pardoning Jones from all crimes, if any, committed during his stay. Jones argues that he has an affirmative defense under the FCPA because he is not subject to criminal liability in Country E. Is he right? Does Jones have any other defense? Consult the case below.

United States v. Kozeny
United States District Court, Southern District of New York, 2008
582 F. Supp. 2d 535

SCHEINDLIN, District Judge.

This prosecution relates to alleged violations of the Foreign Corrupt Practices Act ("FCPA") by defendant Frederic Bourke, Jr. and others in connection with the privatization of the State Oil Company of the Azerbaijan Republic ("SOCAR"). Bourke has requested that the Court make determinations as to the content of applicable law in Azerbaijan and instruct the jury on certain defenses that might be available under the law of Azerbaijan.

I. BACKGROUND

In the mid-1990s, Azerbaijan began a program of privatization. The program gave the President of Azerbaijan, Heydar Aliyev, discretionary authority as to whether and when to privatize SOCAR. Bourke and others allegedly violated the FCPA by making payments to Azeri officials to encourage the privatization of SOCAR and to permit them to participate in that privatization. Bourke argues that the alleged payments were legal under Azeri law and thus under the FCPA (which provides an affirmative defense for payments that are legal under relevant foreign law).

The Government and Bourke have submitted expert reports. The Government's expert is William E. Butler, John Edward Fowler Distinguished Professor of Law at the Dickinson School of Law, Pennsylvania State University, and Emeritus Professor of Comparative Law at the University of London. Bourke's expert, Paul B. Stephan, is the Lewis F. Powell, Jr. Professor of Law at the University of Virginia. On September 11, 2008, the Court held a hearing in which the experts testified as to their interpretations of the relevant law. Azerbaijan, a sovereign nation in the Caspian Sea region that borders Russia, was formerly integrated as a Republic of the Soviet Union. Azerbaijan declared independence in 1991. The current criminal code of Azerbaijan took effect in 2000.

II. Legal Standard

[The court sets forth the elements of an offense under the FCPA. An affirmative defense under FCPA, 15 U.S.C. §78dd-2(c)(1), is that the payment was lawful under the written laws of a foreign nation. Such a payment cannot be prosecuted under the FCPA.]

III. Discussion

During the relevant period, Article 170 of the Azerbaijan Criminal Code ("ACC") provided that "[t]he receiving by an official . . . of a bribe in any form whatsoever for the fulfillment or the failure to fulfill any action in the interest of the person giving the bribe which the official should have or might perform with the use of his employment position . . . shall be punished by deprivation of freedom. . . ." Professor Stephan asserts that during the same period, Article 171 of the ACC provided that "[g]iving a bribe shall be punished by deprivation of freedom for a term of from three to eight years. . . . A person who has given a bribe shall be free from criminal responsibility if with respect to him there was extortion of the bribe or if that person after giving the bribe voluntarily made a report of the occurrence." Professor Butler believes that a more accurate translation of the last clause is "[a] person who has given a bribe shall be relieved from criminal responsibility if extortion of the bribe occurred with respect to him or if this person after giving the bribe voluntarily stated what happened."[65]

The Supreme Court of the U.S.S.R. interpreted Article 171 in a Resolution published in 1990. It defines extortion as "a demand by an official for a bribe under the threat of carrying out actions that could do damage to the legal interests of the briber. . . ." The Resolution further explains that "a voluntary declaration of having committed the crime absolves from criminal responsibility not only the bribe giver but his accomplices." Finally, the Resolution provides that "[t]he absolution of a bribe-giver from criminal responsibility because of extortion of the bribe or the voluntary declaration of the giving of the bribe . . . does not signify an absence in the actions of such persons of the elements of an offense. For that reason, they cannot be considered victims and are not entitled to claim restitution of the items of value given as bribes."

As a threshold matter, I must determine the meaning of "relieved (or free) from criminal responsibility." Bourke contends that if an individual is relieved of criminal responsibility, his action was "lawful" and he may thus avail himself of the FCPA's affirmative defense. I disagree.

---

65. The word appears to be "osvobozhdenie," which is generally translated as "liberation," but can also mean "relieved."

For purposes of the FCPA's affirmative defense, the focus is on the payment, not the payer. A person cannot be guilty of violating the FCPA if the payment was lawful under foreign law. But there is no immunity from prosecution under the FCPA if a person could not have been prosecuted in the foreign country due to a technicality (e.g., time-barred) or because a provision in the foreign law "relieves" a person of criminal responsibility. An individual may be prosecuted under the FCPA for a payment that violates foreign law even if the individual is relieved of criminal responsibility for his actions by a provision of the foreign law.

As Professor Butler observes, the structure of the reporting exception to liability in Article 171 illustrates that the initial payment of a bribe was certainly not lawful. The ACC relieves the payer of a bribe from criminal liability if the bribe is properly reported not because such an action retroactively erases the stain of criminality, but because the state has a strong interest in prosecuting the government official who received the bribe. By waiving liability for reporting payers, the state increases the likelihood that it will learn of the bribery. But at the moment that an individual pays a bribe, the individual has violated Article 171. At that time, the payment was clearly not "lawful under the written laws" of Azerbaijan. If the individual later reports the bribe, she can no longer be prosecuted for that payment. But it is inaccurate to suggest that the payment itself suddenly became "lawful"—on the contrary, the payment was unlawful, though the payer is relieved of responsibility for it. This is why the Resolution provides that the payer cannot receive restitution. Further, if the payment were retroactively lawful, the official who received the payment could not be prosecuted for receiving it. This cannot be correct because the purpose of the reporting exception is to enable the government to pursue the official. Thus, the relief from liability in Article 171 operates to excuse the payer, not the payment.

The exception for extortion contained in the same sentence must operate in the same manner. A payment to an Azeri official that is made under threat to the payer's legal interests is still an illegal payment, though the payer cannot be prosecuted for the payment.

This conclusion does not preclude Bourke from arguing that he cannot be guilty of violating the FCPA by making a payment to an official who extorted the payment because he lacked the requisite corrupt intent to make a bribe. The legislative history of the FCPA makes clear that "true extortion situations would not be covered by this provision." Thus, while the FCPA would apply to a situation in which a "payment [is] demanded on the part of a government official as a price for gaining entry into a market or to obtain a contract," it would not apply to one in which payment is made to an official "to keep an oil rig from being dynamited," an example of "true extortion." The reason is that in the former situation, the bribe payer cannot argue that he lacked the intent to bribe the official because he made the "conscious decision" to pay the official. In other words, in the first example, the payer could have turned his back and walked away—in the latter example, he could not.

If Bourke provides an evidentiary foundation for the claim that he was the victim of "true extortion," I will instruct the jury on what constitutes a situation of "true extortion" such that Bourke would not be found to have possessed the "corrupt" intent required for a violation under the FCPA. In any event, the jury will be instructed regarding the "corrupt" intent that the Government must prove he possessed beyond a reasonable doubt he possessed. Such instruction will define "corrupt" intent as "having an improper motive or purpose" and will explain that the payment must have been intended to "induce the recipient to misuse his official position" in discharging an official act. The charge will also emphasize that the proper focus is on Bourke's intent and that the Government is not required to show that "the official accepted the bribe," that the "official [ ] had the power or authority to perform the act [ ] sought" or that the "defendant intended to influence an official act which was lawful."

IV. CONCLUSION

For the reasons stated above, the Court will not instruct the jury on the exceptions to criminal liability in Article 171. The Court will, in any case, instruct the jury on the requisite elements of the crime of bribery under the FCPA, including the element of "corrupt" intent.

So ordered.

[The court's jury instructions were affirmed and the conviction was affirmed on appeal. *See United States v. Kozeny*, 667 F.3d 122 (2d Cir. 2011).]

NOTES AND QUESTIONS

1. After *Schreiber* was decided, the case went back to the trial court, which held that under New York law, the attorney malpractice claim, which was the basis of the FCPA claim, could not be assigned to the shareholders' committee and the case was dismissed. *Stichting Ter Behartiging Van de Belangen Van Oudaandeelhouders in Het Kapitaal Van Saybolt International B.V. v. Schreiber*, 279 F. Supp. 2d 337, 339–340 (S.D.N.Y. 2003). The dismissal was appealed to the Second Circuit, which certified two questions to the highest state court in New York. Before the state court could issue a ruling, the case was settled by the parties. The history of this case illustrates the problems that clients must consider when an attempted assignment is made. First, is the claim assignable? Second, what is the law applicable to the claim?

2. In recent years, the Justice Department has become more aggressive in pursuing actions under the FCPA. This might be related to the general heightened concern with national security interests and terrorism in light of the events of September 11, 2001. How so?

3. The Justice Department provides an opinion procedure under which a company may request an opinion regarding whether the proposed conduct violates the antibribery provisions of the FCPA. The request must describe an actual—not a hypothetical—transaction and must be based on full and true disclosure of all relevant facts. *See* 28 C.F.R. Part 80 (1995). The Department of Justice must provide an opinion within 30 days after a complete request is submitted. So far, this procedure, available since 1992, has been rarely used. In *Schreiber*, why didn't Mead use this procedure instead of getting an opinion from Schreiber?

4. There has recently been an increased emphasis on enforcement of the FCPA. For discussion, see *Symposium: The FCPA at 35 and Its Impact on Global Business*, 73 Ohio St. L.J. 833–1352 (2012). For an overview of the FCPA, see Mike Koehler, *The Foreign Corrupt Practices Act in a New Era* (2014). For special issues involving the FCPA and China, see Chow, *China Under the Foreign Corrupt Practices Act*, 2012 Wis. L. Rev. 574 (2012).

NOTE ON THE U.S. FOREIGN INVESTMENT AND NATIONAL SECURITY ACT OF 2007

In the age of terrorism, there is heightened concern in the United States over foreign direct investment. For many years national security concerns regarding foreign direct investment in the United States were managed by an executive body, the U.S. Committee on Foreign Investment in the United States (CFIUS). In 2007, Congress enacted the Foreign Investment and National Security Act (FINSA), 50 U.S.C. app. §2170 (2006), which codifies and reforms the activities of CFIUS. Foreign direct investors in the U.S. market must consider whether their investment will be scrutinized under FINSA. The purpose of FINSA is to determine if foreign acquisitions, mergers, or takeovers of U.S companies trigger national security concerns.

Under FINSA, the CFIUS is now a statutory body with power to review and to block or modify foreign acquisitions of U.S. companies. Foreign investors may obtain a "safe harbor" from CFIUS by voluntarily filing a notification to CFIUS. This notification begins a 90-day process during which the U.S. government has an opportunity to review the proposed transaction and to address any national security concerns. A transaction approved during this period cannot later be prohibited or altered unless there was a material misstatement in the notification.

The FINSA review process allows the U.S. government to prohibit or to require changes in any foreign direct investment that would result in the foreign control of any "critical infrastructure." 50 U.S.C. app. §2170(a)(6) (2006). FINSA defines "critical infrastructure" broadly to include "systems or assets, whether physical or virtual, so vital to the United States that the incapacity or destruction of such assets would have a debilitating impact on national security." This provision expands the types of transactions subject to CFIUS review. An additional feature of the statutory CFIUS is what is called "evergreen" review, that is, if the initial CFIUS review results in a mitigation agreement, the conduct of the foreign investment can be monitored, and if there is a material breach of the mitigation agreement at some later time, the President may reopen the review. FINSA decisions are implemented by the President and are not subject to judicial review.

National security review of foreign direct investment is not peculiar to the United States. Many nations have similar review procedures, and some nations ban foreign direct investment in certain industries. But the United States has a greater stake in foreign direct investment than any other country. Affiliates of foreign companies employ over five million people in the United States, about a third of whom work in manufacturing industries. The average annual wage paid by foreign affiliates is about $65,000 per worker, a third higher than the national average wage. Foreign affiliates also account for about one-fifth of U.S. exports. FDI into the United States is over $1 billion annually and totals over $2 trillion.

Is the significantly more stringent CFIUS law really necessary or does it simply encourage other nations to put up barriers to FDI?

V. The Transactional Aspects of FDI: Establishment in the European Union, China, and Brazil

A. Introduction

Despite the growing importance of international investment law, the lawyer's most crucial role is to handle the *transactional* aspects of an investment decision. These will vary with each business deal and will be vastly different in differing countries and areas of the world. Legal counsel will, therefore, require a familiarity with the legal system and laws of the country that is the target of the investment, as well as a good understanding of the political, economic, and cultural conditions of that country. Obviously, no one person possesses this knowledge with respect to every country in the world. Thus, an association with local counsel will be crucial in most cases.

In every foreign direct investment, several categories of issues arise. Consider the example of Medtech, the medical technology company described at the outset of this chapter. First, Medtech must decide where to establish its investment. Second, it must decide whether to establish a joint venture, a wholly-owned foreign subsidiary, or to purchase the stock or assets of an existing company. Third, the requisite legal form must be decided—this will normally be a stock company, but in exceptional cases may be a branch office or a partnership. Fourth, relevant government approvals must be secured; these may involve approvals from competition law authorities or government investment agencies. Fifth, a list of the required different contracts should be compiled and each must be negotiated and carefully drafted in meetings with other parties to the venture. Sixth, careful attention should be given to financial planning, present and future financing, and tax matters. Seventh, government regulatory standards that must be met should be studied, particularly those dealing with environmental protection, labor rights, consumer issues, land use, and construction matters. Finally, a plan should be prepared for the dissolution or liquidation of the project if and when the decision is made to terminate the venture.

The following materials that focus on foreign investment in three countries and regions—the European Union, China (Asia), and Brazil (Latin America)—are designed to provide an analysis of the aforementioned set of issues in very different settings, each a very important one for international business. We have selected the European Union for its obvious importance as an economic power. The materials on the EU also illustrate the issues of an investment in advanced industrialized countries and in the most important customs union in the world. We have also selected China and Brazil as they are developing countries and are the world's largest and second largest recipients, respectively, of FDI among developing countries in the world. The United States is also the largest foreign investor in Brazil and, in the view of many, the most important foreign investor in China. Both countries also play prominent and leading roles in their regions. China has begun to dominate Asia and Brazil has a leading role in South America. It is no coincidence that China hosted the Summer Olympics in 2008 and that Brazil will host the Summer Olympics in 2016. These events are symbolic of the rise of these two countries and their stature in their regions.

China and Brazil also offer important contrasts. Although the countries are in many ways in similar stages of economic development as first emerging economies, they take very different approaches to FDI. Both China and Brazil also differ from the EU in their approach as to whether FDI requires a special legal regime that is distinct from the general legal rules regulating business activity:

- European Union member nations have few special national legal rules regulating FDI but instead generally subject FDI to the same rules governing domestic investment. Some states have filing and disclosure requirements. Any laws of each member that attempt to regulate FDI are subject to the superseding laws of the EU.
- China has a special mandatory legal regime for FDI and subjects FDI to extensive regulation.
- Brazil has an optional FDI regime based on an incentive system of sticks and carrots.

There are, of course, fundamental differences in the political, economic, and legal systems of these regions and countries. An examination of all of these differences is beyond the scope of this book, but one major difference is that the EU has a developed legal system and is governed by the rule of law whereas China and Brazil cannot be said to be subject to the rule of law, at least not in the sense that this term is commonly used in the United States. Any foreign investor who enters China or Brazil must keep this caution firmly in mind. An example of the types of major problems that exist in China and Brazil traceable to a weak legal system is commercial piracy, the focus of Chapter Seven, but other problems, such as government corruption that is often tolerated and unpunished, examined in Part IV, are also serious and common. In addition, while it is possible to assume that laws in the EU will be applied and enforced by courts on a consistent and pre-dictable basis and that judgments of courts will be regularly enforced, the same cannot be assumed in China or Brazil. These cautions about the weakness of the legal system apply in varying degrees to all foreign investment in developing countries and our materials on China and Brazil are intended as examples of such issues. Moreover, while China and Brazil, as developing countries, share some similarities, there are also some fundamental differences between them. China is a socialist country under an authoritarian one-party rule, and its markets are still under extensive state control although there are now signif-icant free-market elements. China also shares traditions that are very different from the Western traditions of countries like the United States. On the other hand, after a period of authoritarian rule under a military government from 1964 to 1985, Brazil now operates under a democratic system of government with free markets. Although Brazil is an ethnic melting pot, it was also under European rule for a long period and shares some traditions associated with its European settlers, including a civil law legal system. Each country faces different challenges, some unique but also representative of challenges faced by other developing countries in Asia and South America. We will point out how China and Brazil can serve as examples for other countries in their regions in the materials below.

Note that while the area with the strongest legal system, the EU, has relatively few special laws governing FDI, China, the country with arguably the least developed legal system, has the most comprehensive legal regime governing FDI, with Brazil somewhere in between. What explains this?

While we do not wish to minimize the differences of doing business in these three areas, there are, of course, also some common issues. We offer a brief conceptual outline of investment issues.

CONCEPTUAL OUTLINE AND CHECKLIST OF FOREIGN DIRECT INVESTMENT ISSUES

1. In what country will the investment be made?

This will be determined primarily by business considerations, but legal provisions will also be important.

   A.   Is there a treaty on friendship, commerce, and navigation and/or a bilat-eral investment treaty that creates a legal right to establishment and legal protections?
   B.   Is there an applicable free trade agreement, such as NAFTA, that grants the right of establishment as well as national treatment and protects the investor against arbitrary and discriminatory conduct and against expropriation?

C. Investment in a free trade area or a customs union may give the investor access to the entire multi-country market. For example, a U.S. investor in Mexico or Canada may obtain free movement of products to be sold in all three NAFTA countries. Even a non-NAFTA investor in a NAFTA country may obtain free-movement access by complying with NAFTA rule of origin requirements so as to obtain a NAFTA Certificate of Origin. Another example is that an investor in the European Union may obtain the right under the Treaty Establishing the European Community to free movement of goods, services, and capital and the right of further establishment throughout the EU.

2. Will the investment be made by (1) establishing a joint venture, (2) establishing a wholly-owned subsidiary, or (3) acquiring an existing company?

In most cases, this necessitates the formation of a foreign stock company. There may be a choice of form — for example, in Germany there is a form called the Aktiengesellschaft (AG) for ordinary companies and the Gesellschaft mit beschränkter Haftung (GmbH) form for closely held companies.

Acquiring a substantial equity interest in an existing foreign company may be suitable in a particular case. This can be done through a purchase of assets, a purchase of stock, or an exchange of a foreign company's stock for the stock of a U.S. company. In all but the latter case, the investor is best advised to incorporate a local (foreign) company to effect the acquisition. Tax considerations will be paramount here.

3. What host-country government approvals are necessary?

A. Even in OECD countries relatively open to investment, certain disclosure and reporting forms must be filed with government agencies. In some cases, advance approval may be required. For example, the Investment Canada Act restricts acquisitions in certain sectors such as natural resources, transportation, financial, and cultural industries.

B. In the United States, foreign investors must contend with reporting requirements under such federal statutes as the International Investment Survey Act, 22 U.S.C. §§3101–3108 (2006); the Agricultural Foreign Investment Disclosure Act, 7 U.S.C. §§3501–3508 (2006); and the Foreign Investment in Real Property Tax Act, 26 U.S.C. §§897, 6039C (2006). In addition, the so-called Exon-Florio Amendment, 19 U.S.C. §2901 (2006), authorizes the President to investigate mergers, acquisitions, and takeovers of U.S. companies by foreign parties and to suspend or prohibit investment that could impair "national security."

4. What steps must be taken to secure and protect intellectual property rights?

5. What immigration permits and visas are necessary to allow personnel from the investor's country to live and work in the host country?

6. What competition law disclosures, permits, or approvals are required? For example, in the EU under Council Regulation 139/2004, 2004 O.J. (L 24) 1, joint ventures, mergers, and acquisitions over a certain size (250 million euros) must be notified and cleared by the EU Commission.

7. What environmental and labor laws must be observed?

8. If financing is to come in whole or in part from the host country, what are the securities laws aspects of the deal?

9. Will tax treaties ameliorate the tax aspects of the venture?

B.   Foreign Investment in the European Union

We now turn to FDI in the European Union, which is the largest and most important customs union in the world (for a discussion of customs unions, see p. 142, and for a background discussion of the EU, see pp. 40-42). The free movement of goods, services, capital, and people is a fundamental feature at the forefront of doing business in any EU nation. As you work through these materials, keep in mind that the lessons learned in the context of the EU can also be applied to the customs unions that are being developed around the world or, with some qualifications, to free trade areas, such as NAFTA.

The EU today is the result of over 50 years of negotiations and a series of landmark treaties and international understandings. Beginning as an international union of the coal and steel industries in six European countries (Belgium, France, Germany, Italy, the Netherlands, and Luxembourg), the Europeans then agreed to form a customs union (a free trade area with a common external tariff), the European Economic Community, under the Treaty of Rome (the EC Treaty), in 1957. In 1986, the decision was taken to form the Common Market, a single economic area. In the 1990s, a series of treaties created the EU itself, a political, social, and monetary union. Periodic enlargements have expanded the number of participating states to 28. At the start of the new millennium, an attempt was made to create a "Constitution for Europe" but it was abandoned when France and the Netherlands failed to ratify it. Many of the proposed changes in the failed constitution, however, were implemented by the Treaty of Lisbon, which went into effect on December 1, 2009. The Treaty of Lisbon gives the EU a full-time President, who serves a renewable term of two and one-half years, and increases the powers of the European Parliament.

A salient characteristic of EU-U.S. economic relations is the extensive flow of foreign direct investment in both directions. Each is the most significant investment host for the other. The EU has a total population of over 505 million and an $18.5 trillion economy, which is 24 percent of the world GDP. It accounts for 14.7 percent of world exports and 15.4 percent of world imports of goods and 25 percent of world exports and 20.2 percent of world imports in services.[66] The EU is also effectively a single internal market so that goods, services, capital, and, to a great extent, people can move freely throughout the area. This presents opportunity for foreign as well as European companies. The EU and its member states have completed negotiations on friendship, commerce, and navigation treaties, bilateral investment treaties, and treaties on taxation with most of the states of the world, including the United States and Japan. Moreover, through its commitments to the World Trade Organization, the EU permits extensive trade and establishment in service sectors, including financial services, insurance, and telecommunications.

1.   Access to the Internal Market of the EU: The Four Freedoms

The key advantage for businesses operating in the EU is access to all 28 member countries as a single economic area. This is because the various legal instruments that created the EU mandate free movement of four elements—goods, services, capital, and persons (including legal persons such as corporations)—throughout the EU area. This

---

66. *See Trade Profiles: European Union,* WORLD TRADE ORG., *http://stat.wto.org/CountryProfile/ WSDBCountryPFView.aspx?Language=E&Country=E27.*

is known as the "four freedoms." For international business, this means that operating within the EU will give access to the entire EU as a single market.

PROBLEM 6-9

Logos Beauty Products is a privately held company based in Kansas City, Missouri, and incorporated in Delaware, which manufactures and sells world-famous soaps, cosmetics, shampoos, and facial toners. As Logos's U.S. manufacturing plants will reach capacity within three years, Logos has decided to expand by investing and establishing in the EU, which is potentially a significant and growing market for its products.

Before establishing an enterprise in the EU, Logos would like to test the EU market. Logos has a successful perfume, "Logos No. 3," that it would like to sell in France, which is one of the world's most important markets for perfumes and cosmetics. Assume that France has a law providing that all products called "perfumes" must have at least 5 percent active ingredients but the Logos perfume has only 3 percent active ingredients. The purpose of the law is to protect consumers, as companies can generally charge higher prices for perfumes than for other scented fragrances. France's neighbors, Belgium, Germany, and Italy, impose a 3 percent active ingredient limit. Logos shipped a large supply of its perfume to France where the shipment was refused entry by French Customs. French authorities have told Logos that it must either reformulate its product to meet French standards or it can label its product "scented water." In a recent case, a French manufacturer had to change its labeling for its product as it failed to meet the 5 percent minimum test.

Is the French rejection of the Logos product consistent with EU law? How would you advise Logos to sell its product in France? See *Cassis de Dijon* below and the accompanying notes.

Rewe-Zentral AG v. Bundesmonopolverwaltung für Branntwein (Cassis de Dijon Case)
European Court of Justice, 1979
Case 120/78, [1979] E.C.R. 649

[Germany had a law requiring that liqueurs must have a minimum alcohol content of 25 percent. German liqueurs all met this standard. However, liqueurs made in France commonly had a lower alcohol content. Cassis de Dijon was a French liqueur with an alcohol content of 15 to 20 percent and could not be legally sold in Germany. The German importer challenged this ban in a German court, which referred the case to the European Court of Justice to determine whether the German ban was contrary to EC law.]

8. In the absence of common rules relating to the production and marketing of alcohol, it is for the Member States to regulate all matters relating to the production and marketing of alcohol and alcoholic beverages on their own territory.

Obstacles to movement within the Community resulting from disparities between the national laws relating to the marketing of the products in question must be accepted insofar as those provisions may be recognized as being necessary in order to satisfy mandatory requirements relating in particular to the effectiveness of fiscal supervision, the protection of public health, the fairness of commercial transactions and the defence of the consumer.

9. The Government of the Federal Republic of Germany put forward various arguments which, in its view, justify the application of provisions relating to the minimum alcohol content of alcoholic beverages, adducing considerations relating on the one hand to the protection of public health and on the other to the protection of the consumer against unfair commercial practices.

10. As regards the protection of public health the German government states that the purpose of the fixing of minimum alcohol content by national legislation is to avoid the proliferation of alcoholic beverages on the national market, in particular alcoholic beverages with a low alcohol content, since, in its view, such products may more easily induce a tolerance towards alcohol than more highly alcoholic beverages.

11. Such considerations are not decisive since the consumer can obtain on the market an extremely wide range of weakly or moderately alcoholic products and furthermore a large proportion of alcoholic beverages with a high alcohol content freely sold on the German market is generally consumed in a diluted form.

12. The German government also claims that the fixing of a lower limit for the alcohol content of certain liqueurs is designed to protect the consumer against unfair practices on the part of producers and distributors of alcoholic beverages.

This argument is based on the consideration that the lowering of the alcohol content secures a competitive advantage in relation to beverages with a higher alcohol content, since alcohol constitutes by far the most expensive constituent of beverages by reason of the high rate of tax to which it is subject.

Furthermore, according to the German government, to allow alcoholic products into free circulation wherever, as regards their alcohol content, they comply with the rules laid down in the country of production would have the effect of imposing as a common standard within the Community the lowest alcohol content permitted in any of the Member States, and even of rendering any requirements in this field inoperative since a lower limit of this nature is foreign to the rules of several Member States.

13. As the Commission rightly observed, the fixing of limits to the alcohol content of beverages may lead to the standardization of products placed on the market and of their designations, in the interest of greater transparency of commercial transactions and offers for sale to the public.

However, this line of argument cannot be taken so far as to regard the mandatory fixing of minimum alcohol contents as being an essential guarantee of the fairness of commercial transactions, since it is a simple matter to ensure that suitable information is conveyed to the purchaser by requiring the display of an indication of origin and of the alcohol content on the packaging of the products.

14. It is clear from the foregoing that the requirements relating to the minimum alcohol content of alcoholic beverages do not serve a purpose which is in the general interest and such as to take precedence over the requirements of the free movement of goods, which constitutes one of the fundamental rules of the Community.

In practice, the principal effect of requirements of this nature is to promote alcoholic beverages having a high alcohol content by excluding from the national market products of other Member States which do not answer that description.

It therefore appears that the unilateral requirement imposed by the rules of a Member State of a minimum alcohol content for the purposes of the sales of alcoholic beverages constitutes an obstacle to trade which is incompatible with the provisions of Article [28] of the Treaty.

There is therefore no valid reason why, provided that they have been lawfully produced and marketed in one of the Member States, alcoholic beverages should not be introduced into any other Member State; the sale of such products may not be subject to a legal prohibition on the marketing of beverages with an alcohol content lower than the limits set by the national rules.

NOTES AND QUESTIONS

1. What was the public health reason given by Germany for requiring a minimum alcohol content of 25 percent for liqueurs? Do you find this reason persuasive? What other possible explanations might there be for such a requirement? How did the court rule on how Germany could meet its stated objective of protecting public health while still complying with Article 34 of the Treaty on the Functioning of the European Union (TFEU) (ex Article 28 of the Treaty Establishing the European Community (TEC))?

2. The ECJ ruling in the *Cassis de Dijon* case is the leading case interpreting Article 34 TFEU (ex Article 28 TEC) amended 2007; came into force 2008. This article provides as follows: "Quantitative restrictions on imports and all measures having equivalent effect shall be prohibited between Member States." Consolidated Versions of the Treaty on European Union and the Treaty on the Functioning of the European Union, May 9, 2008, 2008 O.J. (C 115) art. 34.

Article 35 TFEU (ex Article 29 TEC) establishes the same rule with respect to exports. Note that the German measure was not discriminatory, yet it was contrary to Article 34 TFEU (ex Article 28 TEC).

Article 36 TFEU (ex Article 30 TEC) contains an exception to Articles 34 TFEU (ex Article 28 TEC) and 35 TFEU (ex Article 29 TEC): Member states may justify a restriction on grounds of "public morality, public policy or public security; the protection of life or health of humans, animals or plants; the protection of national treasures possessing artistic, historic, or archaeological value; or the protection of industrial and commercial property. Such prohibitions or restrictions shall not, however, constitute a means of arbitrary discrimination or a disguised restriction on trade between Member States." *Id.* at Article 36 TFEU (ex Article 30 TEC). Why was this not applied in the *Cassis de Dijon* case?

3. What if it is found that one of the goals of Article 36 TFEU (ex Article 30 TEC) could be accomplished by a less restrictive means than a trade ban?

PROBLEM 6-10

As Logos is considering a strategy for penetrating all of the key markets of the EU, it needs an overall corporate structure for its European operations. Logos has identified ten key markets; it would ideally like to have a corporate presence in each market. Logos is currently exploring the following approach proposed by its local counsel in Kansas City: In each key market, Logos should set up subsidiaries that will be wholly owned by the Logos parent company in Kansas City. This is the same strategy proposed by Kansas counsel for expansion of Logos operations in the United States and it seems logical to Logos management to extend this approach in Europe. An issue that Logos has encountered, however, is that it has set aside a capital fund for investment in the EU and the minimum capital requirements of a number of EU nations will exhaust the capital fund set aside and will limit the number of subsidiaries that Logos can establish. Logos's Kansas counsel has advised Logos that it will have to abandon its plans to set up subsidiaries in all ten member countries (as there is not sufficient capital to do so) but should decide instead which two or three countries will be most strategically important and set up subsidiaries in those countries that can serve the rest of the EU market. Do you agree with this advice? What approach would you suggest? See *Centros* and the accompanying notes below.

Centros Ltd. v. Erhvervs-og Selskabsstyrelsen
European Court of Justice, 1999
Case C-212/97, [1999] E.C.R. 1-1459

[In this case, Mr. and Mrs. Bryde, who were Danish citizens living in Denmark, wanted to set up a company in Denmark. However, Danish Company Law required a minimum capital investment of DKK 200,000 (about $30,000) to set up a new company. The Brydes thus set up a company in the UK, where there was no minimum capital requirement, and established a "branch office" in Denmark. The company did no business in the UK, and a friend of the Brydes agreed that his home would be their registered office in the UK. The Brydes brought suit under EC law after the Danish Companies Board rejected the application for a branch office.]

21. Where it is the practice of a Member State, in certain circumstances, to refuse to register a branch of a company having its registered office in another Member State, the result is that companies formed in accordance with the law of that other Member State are prevented from exercising the freedom of establishment conferred on them by Articles 52 and 58 of the Treaty.

22. Consequently, that practice constitutes an obstacle to the exercise of the freedoms guaranteed by those provisions.

23. According to the Danish authorities, however, Mr. and Mrs. Bryde cannot rely on those provisions, since the sole purpose of the company formation which they have in mind is to circumvent the application of the national law governing formation of private limited companies and therefore constitutes abuse of the freedom of establishment. In their submission, the Kingdom of Denmark is therefore entitled to take steps to prevent such abuse by refusing to register the branch.

24. It is true that according to the case-law of the Court a Member State is entitled to take measures designed to prevent certain of its nationals from attempting, undercover of the rights created by the Treaty, improperly to circumvent their national legislation or to prevent individuals from improperly or fraudulently taking advantage of provisions of Community law. . . .

25. However, although, in such circumstances, the national courts may, case by case, take account—on the basis of objective evidence—of abuse or fraudulent conduct on the part of the persons concerned in order, where appropriate, to deny them the benefit of the provisions of Community law on which they seek to rely, they must nevertheless assess such conduct in the light of the objectives pursued by those provisions.

26. In the present case, the provisions of national law, application of which the parties concerned sought to avoid, are rules governing the formation of companies and not rules concerning the carrying on of certain trades, professions or businesses. The provisions of the Treaty on freedom of an establishment are intended specifically to enable companies formed in accordance with the law of a Member State and having their registered office, central administration or principal place of business within the Community to pursue activities in other Member States through an agency, branch or subsidiary.

27. That being so, the fact that a national of a Member State who wishes to set up a company chooses to form it in the Member State whose rules of company law seem to

him the least restrictive and to set up branches in other Member States cannot, in itself, constitute an abuse of the right of establishment. The right to form a company in accordance with the law of a Member State and to set up branches in other Member States is inherent in the exercise, in a single market of the freedom of establishment guaranteed by the Treaty.

29. In addition, the fact that a company does not conduct any business in the Member State in which it has its registered office and pursues its activities only in the Member State where its branch is established is not sufficient to prove the existence of abuse or fraudulent conduct which would entitle the latter Member State to deny that company the benefit of the provisions of Community law relating to the right of establishment.

30. Accordingly, the refusal of a Member State to register a branch of a company formed in accordance with the law of another Member State in which it has its registered office on the grounds that the branch is intended to enable the company to carry on all its economic activity in the host State, with the result that the secondary establishment escapes national rules on the provision for and the paying-up of a minimum capital, is incompatible with Articles 52 and 58 of the Treaty, in so far as it prevents any exercise of the right freely to set up a secondary establishment which Articles 52 and 58 are specifically intended to guarantee.

NOTES AND QUESTIONS

1. The *Centros* case referred to several articles of the TEC, now replaced by the TFEU. Article 49 TFEU (ex Article 52 TEC) provides in relevant part:

> [R]estrictions on the freedom of establishment of nationals of a Member State in the territory of another Member State shall be prohibited. Such prohibitions should also apply to restrictions on the setting-up of agencies, branches, or subsidiaries by nationals of any Member State established in the territory of any Member State.

Consolidated Versions of the Treaty on European Union and the Treaty on the Functioning of the European Union, May 9, 2008 O.Y. (C 115) art. 49.

Article 54 TFEU (ex Article 58 TEC) provides in relevant part that:

> [C]ompanies or firms formed in accordance with the law of a Member State and having their registered office, central administration or principal place of business within the Union shall, for the purposes of this Chapter, be treated in the same way as natural persons who are nationals of Member States.

Id. at art. 54 TFEU (ex Article 58 TEC).

2. In *Centros*, how was it possible to override Danish authorities? The ECJ was careful to point out that measures may be taken by national authorities to protect creditors and to combat fraud. However, such measures will be scrutinized against four requirements: They must (1) be applied in a non-discriminatory manner; (2) be justified by imperative requirements relating to the public interest; (3) be suitable for securing the attainment of their objective; and (4) not go beyond what is necessary.

3. Do the "four freedoms" create a "race to the bottom" because the lowest legal standards in any EU country became the de facto standard for the entire EU?

NOTE ON PROTECTION OF INTELLECTUAL
PROPERTY IN THE EU

Protection of intellectual property in the EU also benefits from the establishment of a single market. Through the EC Patent Convention concluded in 1975 and its implementing regulations, it is now possible to apply for and obtain patent protection throughout the EU area. Under EU trademark law (Council Regulation 207/2009, 2009 O.J. (L 78) 1 (EC)), an applicant may now register a mark for the EU as a whole. In the field of copyright, EU directives and regulations have harmonized the laws of member states concerning cable and satellite technology, computer software, e-commerce, and other matters. *See* Council Directive 2006/115/EC, 2006 O.J. (L 376) 28; Council Directive 93/83, 1993 O.J. (L 248) 15; Council Directive 96/9, 1996 O.J. (L 77) 20. For additional materials, see Chapter Five of this casebook, which deals with intellectual property in international business. For a comprehensive treatment of many issues of intellectual property in the EU, see Chow and Lee, *International Intellectual Property: Problems, Cases, and Materials* (West 2d ed. 2012).

2. Establishment in the EU

Once the decision is made to invest in the EU, many additional considerations will arise:

- Which EU member state is the best place to do business?
- Should the investment be a branch office or a corporate or other business entity?
- Should the investment be in the form of a joint venture? If so, a good business partner will have to be found. If not a joint venture, then a wholly-owned subsidiary company might be best.
- Should the investment be a new one ("Greenfield Investment"), or can an existing company be acquired as the core, at least, of the new business? If the decision is made to acquire an existing business, what form should the acquisition take — (1) a purchase of assets, (2) a purchase of stock, or (3) a merger? The latter would typically involve the formation of a shell company into which the acquired company can be merged under local law.

Keep these and other factors in mind as you read the following materials.

PROBLEM 6-11

Logos has narrowed its locations where it will establish its first foreign subsidiary in Europe to one of three countries, France, Germany, or England (the United Kingdom). Logos has asked your law firm to recommend which of these three jurisdictions it should choose. As previously mentioned, Logos is a privately held company and is not interested in a public ownership structure in Europe although Logos is open to forming a joint venture with a suitable partner. For example, Logos is considering as a potential partner an old-line UK company, Boats, PLC, with its headquarters in Newcastle Upon Tyne, and a line of beauty products and soaps that it markets throughout the UK through an established distribution network. Another potential partner is La Jeunesse, an up-and-coming Marseilles manufacturer, and RTK Kosemetik GmbH, a large, well-established Munich company. Logos is also open to the idea of acquiring a foreign company in France, Germany, or England. An acquisition will likely lead to the layoff of some workers of the acquired company.

Logos is owned by the Jackson family of Kansas City with the patriarch, James Sr., heading up a small group of his family members who form an inner management circle. James is known to be very shrewd but also somewhat eccentric. Although he "retired" many years ago and has no official title, he continues to run management meetings and is consulted on all important strategic decisions. One of James's most eccentric habits is that he often travels unannounced to the various subsidiaries of Logos around the United States and will stay for weeks at a time to review production and management. When some of these subsidiaries first complained to James Jr., the current CEO, James Jr. replied that he fully supports whatever his father wishes to do. James Sr. also cherishes the warm family-like atmosphere of his company and is viewed as a benevolent patriarch by Logos employees. He will often spend hours on the plant floor chatting with employees and will regularly treat a large group of employees and their families to a steak dinner. James has also always championed generous compensation and vacation packages for his employees who seem to be content and have had little interest in organizing a labor union or demanding a voice in management affairs.

The Jackson family would like to use the same flexible "approach" to management in Europe. In fact, James Sr. has already mentioned how much he is looking forward to spending time in his plants in Europe.

Where should the Jacksons establish their EU company? What about an acquisition?

What about setting up a European Company, which is a creature of EU law and not subject to the laws of any individual EU nation? Consult the three readings below, on business forms in the United Kingdom, France, and Germany and the accompanying notes.

An Overview of Company Establishment in Three European Legal Systems: The United Kingdom, France, and Germany

THE UNITED KINGDOM

Consisting of England, Wales, Scotland, and Northern Ireland, the UK is a common law jurisdiction where the language of the law is English. The UK provides a receptive home to many American companies. The UK is also a member of the European Union and so provides a gateway to doing business in all 28 EU countries. It must not be forgotten, however, that the UK comprises three legal systems: English law in England and Wales; Scots law in Scotland, and Northern Ireland legislation in Northern Ireland. Of course, the three jurisdictions share many laws in common, and English law is the most important of the three systems.

Forming a UK limited company is quite similar to forming a company in the United States. A limited UK company may be formed under the Companies Act 2006. Although a limited company may be formed under UK law, company law must observe relevant directives and regulations passed by the European Union. UK companies registered under the Companies Act 2006 must be incorporated in England and Wales, in Scotland, or in

Northern Ireland under equivalent statutory provisions so that the term "UK company" is technically incorrect. Incorporation in England is most common for multinational companies.

Two varieties of companies are recognized in the UK: public limited companies identified by the term PLC, and private limited companies, whose name must end with the term "limited" (Ltd.). Only PLCs may sell their shares to the public. Financial services to consumers are regulated by the Financial Control Authority, an independent nongovernmental body that is, nevertheless, responsible to the UK Parliament, under the Financial Services Act of 2012. Regulation of accounting practices and auditing of companies is handled by the Financial Reporting Council. English law requires extensive disclosure about the company and its business similar to that required in the United States. A company's constitution (equivalent to the articles of association and by-laws of a U.S. company) as well as the company's audited financial statements, the directors' report, the auditor's report, and, if the company has subsidiaries, the consolidated financial statement, must be available to the public.

The management of a UK company is up to the directors, who have duties to act with due care, in good faith, and avoiding conflicts of interest. A UK company has flexibility in setting up its management structure. A public company is required to have at least two directors while a private company must have at least one director. However, beyond such requirements, there is great flexibility. In general, the larger the company the more likely the executive functions will be undertaken by a small class of executive directors and senior management. Specific management authority can also be delegated to a managing director, who may be viewed as a third organ of the company in addition to the shareholders and the directors. The flexibility allowed in setting up a management structure can be attributed at least in part to the common law origins of the law in contrast to the stricter statutory requirements of civil law that governs in countries such as France and Germany. A main statutory duty is the "success duty," requiring directors to act so as to promote the success of the company. The success duty includes a requirement to act in the long-term interests of the company, taking into consideration the interests of employees and protection of the environment.

FRANCE

France is a country under the influence of Roman law, which holds that statutory rather than case law is the basis of the legal system. France has a Civil Code to govern all aspects of private conduct and a Commercial Code and other statutes that govern business practices.

French law recognizes several types of business entities. A sole proprietorship (*Enterprise individuelle*) may do business without incorporation. A general partnership may be formed as a *Société en Nom Collectif* (SNC). A closely held corporation in France is called a *Société à Responsabilité Limitée* (S.A.R.L.); this entity combines the features of a partnership and a stock company. A S.A.R.L. must have at least two directors and not more than 100. France also permits the organization of a hybrid entity, the *Société par Actions Simplifiée* (S.A.S.), which is a stock company that may be operated similar to a partnership. The main stock company in France is the *Société Anonyme* (S.A.), which is typically a public company. France also permits a *Société en Commandite par Actions*, a type of limited partnership that is allowed to issue negotiable stock shares, making it possible to separate control and investment.

Like a UK company, a French stock company must observe and implement EU directives and regulations.

Labor relations in France are extensively regulated by a national Labor Code, various applicable collective bargaining and union contracts, and by individual employment contracts. Every company has a work council, which consists of committees of workers. The work council must be consulted by company managers prior to taking any decision that affects the company's economic or legal structure. This means that the company must consult the work council on such matters as mergers and acquisitions, organization of subsidiaries, changes of control, and modifications of working conditions and labor redundancies. Failure to consult a work council can be punished as a criminal offense leading to imprisonment of management employees. French law protects employees from layoffs and reductions in working conditions. Dismissal of an employee must occur in accordance with strict legal guidelines. The employer will have to follow French law in terms of procedure, justification, and payment of dismissal indemnities. The employer must schedule a pre-dismissal meeting with the employee. After the meeting there is a compulsory waiting period before the dismissal can occur. In addition, the employer must base the dismissal on reasons concerning the employee or the economic conditions of the company. If more than one employee is to be dismissed, the procedure becomes much more cumbersome and in companies with more than 50 employees, the work council must be consulted on both the economic justification and a plan for redeployment of the dismissed employees.

GERMANY

Germany, like France, is a civil law country with a civil code, the *BGB*, a commercial code (HGB) and numerous important statutory laws. Company law in Germany is controlled by the *Aktiengesetz* (AktG), which establishes the framework for the organization and management of the primary type of German company, the *Aktiengesellschaft* or *AG*, and another type of company, the *Kommanditgesellschaft auf Aktien* (KGaA), a corporation with stock but with fully liable general partners. Germany also permits the organization of a closely held company called the *Gesellschaft mit beschränkter Haftung* (GmbH), many of which have only one shareholder and one director. Since 2008, German law allows the organization of the *Unternehemergesellschaft* (UG), which is colloquially known as the "mini GmbH" since it is similar to the GmbH, but may be operated with less capital and fewer formalities. Most German companies take the form of the AG, GmbH, or UG.

Corporate governance in Germany is in the hands of the board of directors. For the AG a two-tier management system is mandatory: The management board (*Vorstand*) is subject to the supervisory board (*Aufsichtsrat*). These two boards are strictly separate and no individual is allowed to serve on both. The management board cannot be given instructions by the shareholders; rather, the management board is subject to the control of the supervisory board, on which employees serve as members (see the note below on co-determination). An AG must involve workers in management decisions through a system known as "co-determination" (*Mitbestimmung*). This system requires that employees serve on the supervisory board that instructs the management board and that work councils be consulted about company decisions that affect layoffs and work conditions.

Employment and labor conditions are closely regulated in Germany. German workers are protected under the Employment Protection Act (*Kündigungsschutzgesetz*), under which employment contracts lasting over six months cannot be terminated unless this is deemed "socially justified." If the employment is being terminated not on personal grounds but on business grounds, the employer must show compelling economic, technical, or operational reasons for the termination, such as declining sales, profits, or an important change in the business of the company. Financial reasons, such as the need to cut costs through the reduction of overhead or payroll expenses, are not considered to directly justify termination. A business reason is deemed to be compelling when there is no means of preventing the dismissal, such as cuts in working time or in overtime are not available. For example, if an employee can be assigned to another position within the employer's business, the dismissal is not permitted. Typically, the employer must notify the Federal Employment Agency (*Bundesagentur für Arbeit*) in advance of dismissing an employee. The complex rules applicable to employment in Germany make it very difficult for companies to transfer or lay off workers.

NOTE ON EMPLOYEE CO-DETERMINATION IN MANAGEMENT ISSUES IN FRANCE AND GERMANY

Like some other European countries, both France and Germany recognize the right of workers to participate in management. Participation in management can occur at either the plant level or the enterprise level. Both France and Germany recognize worker participation at the plant level in the form of work councils, consisting of employees, which have a right of co-determination with shareholders on a number of issues such as the formal conditions of work, including work hours; time, place, and form of payment; and measures to prevent accidents. Work councils also have a right of co-determination on personnel issues that relate to layoffs, dismissals, and proposed organizational changes that may adversely affect workers.

Germany goes beyond France in recognizing co-determination rights at the enterprise level involving issues of the business management of the company itself. In Germany, workers participate in the management of the enterprise through representation on the supervisory board, a management body found in both the AG and the GmbH. Under Germany's various co-determination laws, workers have a potential voice in naming the managing directors, declaring dividends, and other strategic business decisions involving the enterprise. German unions have taken the position that they need to participate at the enterprise level on an equal level with shareholders. The Codetermination Act of 1976 greatly expanded the number of businesses that are potentially subject to the principle of parity co-determination. The 1976 Act mandates the formation of a supervisory board composed of 50 percent shareholders and 50 percent employees or their representatives for each business organization regularly employing more than 2,000 members. For this reason, many companies in Germany have adopted the GmbH form, which is more flexible and allows management to limit the role of the supervisory board and have reorganized subsidiaries with limited workforces to fall outside the scope of the 1976 Act. However, while there is some resistance to co-determination, German employers accept the principle in theory although they often disagree on whether workers should be entitled to "parity" in decision making and what constitutes "parity."

Unlike all other EU members, the United Kingdom refused to sign the Charter of the Fundamental Social Rights of Workers, commonly known as the Social Charter, promulgated in 1989 in the form of a non-legally binding declaration creating "moral obligations" to recognize certain workers' rights. One of the main factors that led the United Kingdom government to refuse to agree to the EU Social Charter is that it contained articles that established participation rights for workers. The UK has taken the position that worker participation in management issues should be a matter for industry to determine on a country-by-country basis. As a result, no legislation exists at the present in the UK that requires any degree of worker participation in the decision-making process of management.

NOTES AND QUESTIONS

1. Suppose, after carefully considering all options, the Logos Company has decided to set up a joint venture. An attraction of the joint venture for Logos is the expertise and experience of a European partner as well as the existing, ready-made distribution network. Joining forces with a European partner will also allow the new joint venture company to undertake to market and establish its brand name and products throughout the EU.

What steps, decisions, and legal documents are necessary to form and operate the joint venture? Consider the following:

- A letter of intent or memorandum of understanding
- The joint venture agreement
- A shareholders' agreement
- A nondisclosure agreement
- A trademark licensing agreement

2. A key document will be the joint venture agreement. This must be carefully considered, drafted, and tailored to the particular business operations. Some of the issues that must be addressed include:

- Objectives
- Nature of the company or companies to be formed
- Capital and financing
- Percentage ownership shares of the parties
- Transfers of shares
- Minority rights clauses, quorums for voting, dividend policy, and voting rights
- Management clauses covering membership on the board of directors and management policies and responsibilities
- Taxation
- General relationship issues (e.g., disclosure, representations, warranties, and non-competition promises)
- Dispute resolution and applicable law
- Deadlock and dissolution
- Duration and termination
- Due diligence and comfort-letter requirements
- Intellectual property rights

3. *Societas Europaea.* Under Council Regulation 2157/2001, 2001 O.J. (L 294) 1, it is now possible to establish in the EU incorporating as a European Company or Societas Europaea (SE). The advantage is that an SE is a creature of EU law, not member state

law, and its functioning will be largely determined by EU norms. An SE can be set up to function as a European holding company with subsidiaries as national law companies or subsidiary SE companies. Perhaps the greatest disadvantage is that an SE must comply with Council Directive 2001/86, 2001 O.J. (L 294) 22, which requires including workers of the company as members of the managing board.

If the Logos joint venture is successful in penetrating the entire EU market, it may be wise to form an SE or to employ the UK company as a holding company with subsidiary operating companies in various EU member states. An EU directive known as the Parent-Subsidiary Directive, Council Directive 90/435, 1990 O.J. (L 225) 6, eliminates withholding and double taxation and facilitates capital transfers between related corporations doing business in the EU.

What will be the tax consequences for Logos and its U.S. operations? Taxation is beyond the scope of this book, but generally speaking, while a U.S. corporation is taxed on its worldwide income, a foreign corporation is taxed on its taxable income effectively connected with a U.S. trade or business. *See* I.R.C. §11 (2006). Foreign source income may generally be shielded from U.S. tax through careful planning, but Logos will not be able to avoid taxation on intercompany export sales from its U.S. operations. Intercompany pricing is carefully regulated by the Internal Revenue Service. *See* I.R.C. §482 (2006).

4. *EU Company Law Harmonization.* Logos must be aware that, under Article 50(g) TFEU (ex Article 44(g) TEC), the EU has the authority to issue directives requiring the harmonization of the company law of the EU member states. This is an ongoing process. Several directives have been issued and implemented by the EU member states. Logos must realize that future directives from Brussels may have an impact on its European business operations.

3. EU Competition Law Affecting Foreign Direct Investment

As we saw in Section B.1 above, the EU protects the common market through the famous "four freedoms" that ensure the free movement of goods, capital, services, and persons throughout the EU. In addition, the EU prohibits anticompetitive conduct and practices that may also disrupt the common market. EU competition law is comprehensive and sophisticated and all foreign investors in the EU are well advised to be aware of its application. EU competition law can be categorized under three major headings:

(1) The prohibition in Article 101(1) TFEU (ex Article 81(1) TEC) against horizontal and vertical agreements and restrictive practices that may adversely affect trade between member states;
(2) The prohibition contained in Article 102 TFEU (ex Article 82 TEC) against "abuse of a dominant position";
(3) The EU merger policy contained in Council Regulation 139/2004, 2004 O.J. (L 24) 1, on the control of concentrations between undertakings.

We have already examined in Chapter Five horizontal and vertical agreements that constituted restrictive practices in connection with distribution agreements. In this chapter, we concentrate on the other two competition law requirements: abuse of a dominant position and the EU merger policy.

A. ABUSE OF A DOMINANT POSITION

Article 102 TFEU (ex Article 82 TEC) reads as follows:

Any abuse by one or more undertakings of a dominant position within the internal market or in a substantial part of it shall be prohibited as incompatible with the internal market in so far as it may affect trade between Member States.

Such abuse may, in particular, consist in:

(a) directly or indirectly imposing unfair purchase or selling prices or other unfair trading conditions;

(b) limiting production, markets or technical development to the prejudice of consumers;

(c) applying dissimilar conditions to equivalent transactions with other trading parties, thereby placing them at a competitive disadvantage;

(d) making the conclusion of contracts subject to acceptance by the other parties of supplementary obligations which, by their nature or according to commercial usage, have no connection with the subject of such contracts.

Article 102 TFEU (ex Article 82 TEC) is by its terms directly effective (self-executing) and forbids abuse of a dominant position in (a substantial part of) the EU/EC by one or more undertakings. It therefore covers monopolists, monopsonists, and joint abuse. Note carefully that dominance per se is not condemned, but rather abuse of dominance. The first element of proof, however, is dominance. A finding of dominance can be made only after defining the relevant market, as to the product or products, as to geographical area, and as to the temporal aspect of the market. We elaborate on each of these elements:

- *The Product Market.* The product market includes all the products that, by reason of their characteristics, price, and intended use, are regarded by consumers as substantially interchangeable. High cross-elasticity of demand (i.e., the substitutability of products by consumers) is an indication of a single product market. The definition of product market is important because the narrower the definition, the more likely the finding of dominance.
- *The Temporal Market.* The temporal market refers to the time during which market supply conditions are uniform. Demand for some products (such as Christmas cards) is seasonal. Assessing the temporality of the market means that the dominance can occur with respect to even a temporary or seasonal market. *See* Joined Cases 6 & 7/73, *Instituto Chemioterapico Italiano S.p.A v. Commission,* 1974 E.C.R. 223.
- *The Geographic Market.* The relevant geographic market is the area within the EU where the goods are regularly bought and sold. This can be one member state or even a substantial part of one member state. Case 322/81, *Banden Industrie Michelin v. Comm'n,* 1983 E.C.R. 3461. However, under the terms of Article 102 TFEU (ex Article 82 TEC), there must be an effect on the trade between member states.
- *Dominance.* Dominance is the power to behave to an appreciable extent independently of competitors, customers, and consumers. Some structural factors relevant to proof of dominance include:
  - Market share
  - Access to labor, finance, technology, and raw materials

- Degree of vertical integration
- Ownership of intellectual property
- The existence of barriers to market entry (lack of market contestability) Case 85/76, *Hoffman-La Roche & Co. v. Comm'n*, 1979 E.C.R. 464. Behavior may also be an indication of dominance. Some behavioral factors are the ability to charge monopolistic prices and predatory pricing. Case C-62/86, *AZKO Chemie BV v. Comm'n*, 1991 E.C.R. I-3439.
- *Abuse.* Note that Article 102 TFEU (ex Article 82 TEC) contains no examples of abuse and there is no possibility of exemption. Abuse can be either exploitive or anticompetitive. No causal connection need be shown between dominance and the abuse. Some examples of abuse include:
  - Excessive prices
  - Predatory pricing
  - Refusals to deal
  - Tactics excluding competitors
  - Acquisitions that strengthen an already dominant position.

In order to implement the merger control regulation, the EU Commission issued Regulation (EC) No. 802/2004 with Annexes comprising three forms to be used for merger notifications: Form CO; Short Form CO; and Form RS. On December 5, 2013, the Commission amended Regulation No. 802/2004, issuing Regulation (EC) No. 1269/2013, 2013 O.J. (L 336) 1. This new regulation introduces a simplified procedure designed to reduce the administrative burden of EU merger control. Effective January 1, 2014, the Commission set the market share limits that may benefit from the new simplified procedure. The simplified procedure (using Short Form CO for notification) is now available for (1) transactions where parties' combined market shares are below 20 percent for horizontal overlaps and below 30 percent for vertical relationships; (2) joint ventures that have no or de minimis actual or foreseen activities within the European Economic Area (a turnover test of less than EUR 100 million is used to determine this); and (3) horizontal mergers that lead to only small increments in market shares (where market shares are less than 50 percent).

PROBLEM 6-12

Medtech's subsidiary, Med-Foods USA, has established several joint ventures in Europe with local partners to produce and market a super chicken that can grow up to a massive ten pounds. Med-Foods has imposed the following conditions on all its European affiliates:

(1) Only chickens between six and eight pounds can be sold as whole chickens or chicken parts for consumption. Chickens above the weight limit can be used for processed foods;

(2) All European affiliates must buy ordinary feed from Med-Foods;

(3) All European affiliates must buy Med-Foods' special proprietary feed, which is protected as a trade secret, to be mixed with ordinary feed and given to the chickens once a week.

Since the chickens grow very quickly (one pound per week), there is only a small window in which to sell the chickens. Assume that there are no health and safety issues and no ethical concerns. Assume also that Med-Foods has a dominant position in Europe. Review each of these conditions. Are any of these an abuse of a dominant position? Consult

United Brands and *Microsoft* below. Now assume the position of Med-Foods. What arguments can be made for imposing these conditions above? Suppose Med-Foods has an EU trademark, "Super Chicken," for its bird. Will this help?

United Brands Company v. Commission of the European Communities
Case 27/76 (14 February 1978)
European Court of Justice

[In this case the ECJ examined three instances of abuse found by the Commission. United Brands (UBC) was found to have (1) prohibited its distributors from reselling bananas while still green; (2) cut off a Danish distributor (Olesen) that was promoting a rival brand; and (3) calibrated its selling prices differently in different member states.]

12. As far as the product market is concerned it is first of all necessary to ascertain whether, as the applicant maintains, bananas are an integral part of the fresh fruit market, because they are reasonably interchangeable by consumers with other kinds of fresh fruit such as apples, oranges, grapes, peaches, strawberries, etc. or whether the relevant market consists solely of the banana market which includes both branded bananas and unlabelled bananas and is a market sufficiently homogeneous and distinct from the market of other fresh fruit.

13. The applicant submits in support of its argument that bananas compete with other fresh fruit in the same shops, on the same shelves, at prices which can be compared, satisfying the same needs: consumption as a dessert or between meals.

14. The statistics produced show that consumer expenditure on the purchase of bananas is at its lowest between June and December when there is a plentiful supply of domestic fresh fruit on the market.

15. Studies carried out by the Food and Agriculture Organization (FAO) (especially in 1975) confirm that banana prices are relatively weak during the summer months and that the price of apples for example has a statistically appreciable impact on the consumption of bananas in the Federal Republic of Germany.

16. Again, according to these studies, some easing of prices is noticeable at the end of the year during the "orange season."

17. The seasonal peak periods when there is a plentiful supply of other fresh fruit exert an influence not only on the prices but also on the volume of sales of bananas and consequently on the volume of imports thereof.

18. The applicant concludes from these findings that bananas and other fresh fruit form only one market and that UBC's operations should have been examined in this context for the purpose of any application of Article 86 of the Treaty.

19. The Commission maintains that there is a demand for bananas which is distinct from the demand for other fresh fruit especially as the banana is a very important part of the diet of certain sections of the Community.

20. The specific qualities of the banana influence customer preference and induce him not to readily accept other fruits as a substitute.

21. The Commission draws the conclusion from the studies quoted by the applicant that the influence of the prices and availabilities of other types of fruit on the prices and availabilities of bananas on the relevant market is very ineffective and that these effects

are too brief and too spasmodic for such other fruit to be regarded as forming part of the same market as bananas or as a substitute therefor.

22. For the banana to be regarded as forming a market which is sufficiently differentiated from other fruit markets it must be possible for it to be singled out by such special features distinguishing it from other fruits that it is only to a limited extent interchangeable with them and is only exposed to their competition in a way that is hardly perceptible.

23. The ripening of bananas takes place the whole year round without any season having to be taken into account.

24. Throughout the year production exceeds demand and can satisfy it at any time.

25. Owing to this particular feature, the banana is a privileged fruit and its production and marketing can be adapted to the seasonal fluctuations of other fresh fruit which are known and can be computed.

26. There is no unavoidable seasonal substitution since the consumer can obtain this fruit all the year round.

27. Since the banana is a fruit which is always available in sufficient quantities the question whether it can be replaced by other fruits must be determined over the whole of the year for the purpose of ascertaining the degree of competition between it and other fresh fruit.

28. The studies of the banana market on the Court's file show that on the latter market there is no significant long term cross-elasticity any more than—as has been mentioned—there is any seasonal substitutability in general between the banana and all the seasonal fruits, as this only exists between the banana and two fruits (peaches and table grapes) in one of the countries (West Germany) of the relevant geographic market.

29. As far as concerns the two fruits available throughout the year (oranges and apples), the first are not interchangeable, and in the case of the second, there is only a relative degree of substitutability.

30. This small degree of substitutability is accounted for by the specific features of the banana and all the factors which influence consumer choice.

31. The banana has certain characteristics, appearance, taste, softness, seedlessness, easy handling, a constant level of production which enable it to satisfy the constant needs of an important section of the population consisting of the very young, the old and the sick.

32. As far as prices are concerned two FAO studies show that the banana is only affected by the prices—falling prices—of other fruits (and only of peaches and table grapes) during the summer months and mainly in July and then by an amount not exceeding 20%.

33. Although it cannot be denied that during these months and some weeks at the end of the year this product is exposed to competition from other fruits, the flexible way in which the volume of imports and their marketing on the relevant geographic market is adjusted means that the conditions of competition are extremely limited and that its price adapts without any serious difficulties to this situation where supplies of fruit are plentiful.

34. It follows from all these considerations that a very large number of consumers having a constant need for bananas are not noticeably or even appreciably enticed away from the consumption of this product by the arrival of other fresh fruit on the market and that even the personal peak periods only affect it for a limited period of time and to a very limited extent from the point of view of substitutability.

35. Consequently, the banana market is a market which is sufficiently distinct from the other fresh fruit markets.

157. [In response to the first practice:] To impose on the ripener the obligation not to resell bananas so long as he has not had them ripened and to cut down the operations of such a ripener to contacts only with retailers is a restriction of competition.

158. Although it is commendable and lawful to pursue a policy of quality, especially by choosing sellers according to objective criteria relating to the qualifications of the seller, his staff and his facilities, such a practice can only be justified if it does not raise obstacles, the effect of which goes beyond the objective to be attained.

159. In this case, although these conditions for selection have been laid down in a way which is objective and not discriminatory, the prohibition on resale imposed upon duly appointed Chiquita ripeners and the prohibition of the resale of unbranded bananas—even if the perishable nature of the banana in practice restricted the opportunities of reselling to the duration of a specific period of time—when without any doubt an abuse of the dominant position since they limit markets to the prejudice of consumers and affects trade between Member States, in particular by partitioning national markets.

160. Thus UBC's organization of the market confined the ripeners to the role of suppliers of the local market and prevented them from developing their capacity to trade vis-à-vis UBC, which moreover tightened its economic hold on them by supplying less goods than they ordered.

161. It follows from all these considerations that the clause at issue forbidding the sale of green bananas infringes Article 86 of the Treaty.

182. [In response to the second practice:] In view of these conflicting arguments it is advisable to assert positively from the outset that an undertaking in a dominant position for the purpose of marketing a product—which cashes in on the reputation of a brand name known to and valued by the consumers—cannot stop supplying a long standing customer who abides by regular commercial practice, if the orders placed by that customer are in no way out of the ordinary.

183. Such conduct is inconsistent with the objectives laid down in Article 86, especially in paragraphs (b) and (c), since the refusal to sell would limit markets to the prejudice of consumers and would amount to discrimination which might in the end eliminate a trading party from the relevant market.

184. It is therefore necessary to ascertain whether the discontinuance of supplies by UBC in October 1973 was justified.

185. The reason given is in the applicant's letter of 11 October 1973 in which it upbraided Olesen in no uncertain manner for having participated in an advertising campaign for one of its competitors.

189. Although it is true, as the applicant points out, that the fact that an undertaking is in a dominant position cannot disentitle it from protecting its own commercial interests if they are attacked, and that such an undertaking must be conceded the right to take such reasonable steps as it deems appropriate to protect its said interests, such behaviour cannot be countenanced if its actual purpose is to strengthen this dominant position and abuse it.

192. In fact UBC could not be unaware of that fact that by acting in this way it would discourage its other ripener/distributors from supporting the advertising of other brand names and that the deterrent effect of the sanction imposed upon one of them would make its position of strength on the relevant market that much more effective.

193. Such a course of conduct amounts therefore to a serious interference with the independence of small- and medium-sized firms in their commercial relations with the undertaking in a dominant position and this independence implies the right to give preference to competitors' goods.

194. In this case the adoption of such a course of conduct is designed to have a serious adverse effect on competition on the relevant banana market by only allowing firms dependant upon the dominant undertaking to stay in business.

227. [In response to the third practice:] Although the responsibility for establishing the single banana market does not lie with the applicant, it can only endeavour to take "what the market can bear" provided that it complies with the rules for the Regulation and coordination of the market laid down by the Treaty.

228. Once it can be grasped that differences in transport costs, taxation, customs duties, the wages of the labour force, the conditions of marketing, the differences in the parity of currencies, the density of competition may eventually culminate in different retail selling price levels according to the Member States, then it follows those differences are factors which UBC only has to take into account to a limited extent since it sells a product which is always the same and at the same place to ripener/distributors who—alone—bear the risks of the consumers' market.

229. The interplay of supply and demand should, owing to its nature, only be applied to each stage where it is really manifest.

230. The mechanisms of the market are adversely affected if the price is calculated by leaving out one stage of the market and taking into account the law of supply and demand as between the vendor and the ultimate consumer and not as between the vendor (UBC) and the purchaser (the ripener/distributors).

231. Thus, by reason of its dominant position UBC, fed with information by its local representatives, was in fact able to impose its selling price on the intermediate purchaser. This price and also the "weekly quota allocated" is only fixed and notified to the customer four days before the vessel carrying the bananas berths.

232. These discriminatory prices, which varied according to the circumstances of the Member States, were just so many obstacles to the free movement of goods and their effect was intensified by the clause forbidding the resale of bananas while still green and by reducing the deliveries of the quantities ordered.

233. A rigid partitioning of national markets was thus created at price levels, which were artificially different, placing certain distributor/ripeners at a competitive disadvantage, since compared with what it should have been competition had thereby been distorted.

234. Consequently the policy of differing prices enabling UBC to apply dissimilar conditions to equivalent transactions with other trading parties, thereby placing them at a competitive disadvantage, was an abuse of a dominant position.

Microsoft Corp. v. Commission of the European Communities
Case T-201/04 (17 September 2007)
Court of First Instance (Grand Chamber)

21. In the contested decision, the Commission finds that Microsoft infringed Art. 82 EC by twice abusing a dominant position.

22. The Commission first identifies three separate worldwide product markets and considers that Microsoft had a dominant position on two of them. It then finds that

Microsoft had engaged in two kinds of abusive conduct. As a result it imposes a fine and a number of remedies on Microsoft.

I — RELEVANT PRODUCT MARKETS AND GEOGRAPHIC MARKET

23. The contested decision identifies three separate product markets, namely the markets for, respectively, client PC operating systems (recitals 324–342 to the contested decision), work-group server operating systems (recitals 343–401 to the contested decision) and streaming media players (recitals 402–425 to the contested decision).

24. The first market defined in the contested decision is the market for client PC operating systems. Operating systems are defined as "system software" which controls the basic functions of the computer and enables the user to make use of the computer and run application software on it (recital 37 to the contested decision). Client PCs are defined as general-purpose computers designed for use by one person at a time and capable of being connected to a network (recital 45 to the contested decision).

25. As regards the second market, the contested decision defines work-group server operating systems as operating systems designed and marketed to deliver collectively "basic infrastructure services" to relatively small numbers of client PCs connected to small or medium-sized networks (recitals 53 and 345 to the contested decision).

26. The contested decision identifies, more particularly, three types of services. These are, first, the sharing of files stored on servers, secondly, the sharing of printers and, thirdly, the administration of groups and users, that is to say, the administration of the means whereby those concerned can access network services (recitals 53 and 345 to the contested decision). This last type of services is that of ensuring that users have access to and make use of the network resources in a secure manner, first, by authenticating users and secondly, by checking that they are authorised to perform a particular action (recital 54 to the contested decision). The contested decision states that, in order to provide for the efficient storing and checking of group and user administration information, work-group server operating systems rely extensively on "directory service" technologies (recital 55 to the contested decision). The directory service included in Microsoft's Windows 2000 Server operating system is called "Active Directory" (recital 149 to the contested decision).

28. The third market identified in the contested decision is the streaming media player market. Media players are defined as software products capable of reading audio and video content in digital form, that is to say, of decoding the corresponding data and translating them into instructions for the hardware (for example, loudspeakers or a display) (recital 60 to the contested decision). Streaming media players are capable of reading audio and video content "streamed" across the internet (recital 63 to the contested decision).

29. As regards the relevant geographic market, the Commission finds in the contested decision, as stated at [22] above, that it has a worldwide dimension for each of the three product markets (recital 427 to the contested decision).

II — DOMINANT POSITION

30. In the contested decision, the Commission finds that Microsoft has had a dominant position on the client PC operating systems market since at least 1996 and also

on the work-group server operating systems market since 2002 (recitals 429–541 to the contested decision).

31. As regards the client PC operating systems market, the Commission relies essentially on the following factors to arrive at that conclusion:

— Microsoft's market shares are over 90 per cent (recitals 430 to 435 to the contested decision);

— Microsoft's market power has "enjoyed an enduring stability and continuity" (recital 436 to the contested decision);

— There are significant barriers to market entry, owing to indirect network effects (recitals 448–464 to the contested decision);

— Those network effects derive, first, from the fact that users like platforms on which they can use a large number of applications and, secondly, from the fact that software designers write applications for the client PC operating systems that are the most popular among users (recitals 449 and 450 to the contested decision).

32. The Commission states at recital 472 to the contested decision that that dominant position presents "extraordinary features" in that Windows is not only a dominant product on the market for client PC operating systems but, in addition, is the "de facto standard" for those systems.

33. As regards the work-group server operating systems market, the Commission relies, in substance, on the following factors:

— Microsoft's market share is, at a conservative estimate, at least 60 per cent (recitals 473–499 to the contested decision);

— The position of Microsoft's three main competitors on that market is as follows: Novell, with its NetWare software, has 10 to 25 per cent; vendors of Linux products have a market share of 5 to 15 per cent; and vendors of UNIX products have a market share of 5 to 15 per cent (recitals 503, 507 and 512 to the contested decision);

— The work-group server operating systems market is characterised by the existence of significant entry barriers, owing in particular to network effects and to Microsoft's refusal to disclose interoperability information (recitals 515–525 to the contested decision);

— There are close commercial and technological links between the latter market and the client PC operating systems market (recitals 526–540 to the contested decision).

III — Abuse of a Dominant Position

A—Refusal to Supply and Authorise the Use of Interoperability Information

36. The first abusive conduct in which Microsoft is found to have engaged consists in its refusal to supply its competitors with "interoperability information" and to authorise the use of that information for the purpose of developing and distributing products competing with Microsoft's own products on the work-group server operating systems market,

between October 1998 and the date of notification of the contested decision (Art. 2(a) of the contested decision). That conduct is described at recitals 546–791 to the contested decision.

37. For the purposes of the contested decision, "interoperability information" is the: "complete and accurate specifications for all the protocols [implemented] in Windows work-group server operating systems and . . . used by Windows work-group servers to deliver file and print services and group and user administrative services, including the Windows domain controller services, Active Directory services and 'group Policy' services to Windows work-group networks" (Art. 1(1) of the contested decision).

38. "Windows work-group network" is defined as "any group of Windows client PCs and Windows work-group servers linked together via a computer network" (Art. 1(7) of the contested decision).

39. A "protocol" is defined as "a set of rules of interconnection and interaction between various instances of Windows work-group server operating systems and Windows client PC operating systems running on different computers in a Windows work-group network" (Art. 1(2) of the contested decision).

B—TYING OF THE WINDOWS CLIENT PC OPERATING SYSTEM AND WINDOWS MEDIA PLAYER

43. The second abusive conduct in which Microsoft is found to have engaged consists in the fact that from May 1999 to the date of notification of the contested decision Microsoft made the availability of the Windows client PC operating system conditional on the simultaneous acquisition of the Windows Media Player software (Art. 2(b) of the contested decision). That conduct is described at recitals 792–989 to the contested decision.

44. In the contested decision, the Commission considers that that conduct satisfies the conditions for a finding of a tying abuse for the purposes of Art. 82 EC (recitals 794–954 to the contested decision). First, it reiterates that Microsoft has a dominant position on the client PC operating systems market (recital 799 to the contested decision). Secondly, it considers that streaming media players and client PC operating systems constitute separate products (recitals 800–825 to the contested decision). Thirdly, it asserts that Microsoft does not give consumers the opportunity to buy Windows without Windows Media Player (recitals 826–834 to the contested decision). Fourthly, it contends that the tying in question restricts competition on the media players market (recitals 835–954 to the contested decision).

IV — FINE AND REMEDIES

46. In respect of the two abuses identified in the contested decision, a fine of €497,196,304 [(U.S. $645 million at the time)] is imposed (Art. 3 of the contested decision).

47. Furthermore, the first paragraph of Art. 4 of the contested decision requires that Microsoft bring an end to the infringement referred to in Art. 2, in accordance with Arts. 5 and 6 of that decision. Microsoft must also refrain from repeating any act or conduct that might have the same or equivalent object or effect to those abuses (second paragraph of Art. 4 of the contested decision).

48. By way of remedy for the abusive refusal referred to in Art. 2(a) of the contested decision, Art. 5 of that decision provides as follows:

(a)   Microsoft shall, within 120 days of the date of notification of [the contested decision], make the interoperability information available to any undertaking having an interest in developing and distributing work-group server operating system products and shall, on reasonable and non-discriminatory terms, allow the use of the interoperability information by such undertakings for the purpose of developing and distributing work-group server operating system products;

(b)   Microsoft shall ensure that the interoperability information made available is kept updated on an ongoing basis and in a timely manner;

(c)   Microsoft shall, within 120 days of the date of notification of [the contested decision], set up an evaluation mechanism that will give interested undertakings a workable possibility of informing themselves about the scope and terms of use of the interoperability information; as regards this evaluation mechanism, Microsoft . . . may impose reasonable and non-discriminatory conditions to ensure that access to the interoperability information is granted for evaluation purposes only; . . .

49. By way of remedy for the abusive tying referred to in Art. 2(b) of the contested decision, Art. 6 of that decision orders Microsoft to offer, within 90 days of the date of notification of that decision, a full-functioning version of the Windows client PC operating system which does not incorporate Windows Media Player, although Microsoft retains the right to offer a bundle of the Windows client PC operating system and Windows Media Player.

50. Lastly, Art. 7 of the contested decision provides:

Within 30 days of the date of notification of [the contested decision], Microsoft shall submit a proposal to the Commission for the establishment of a suitable mechanism assisting the Commission in monitoring [Microsoft's] compliance with [the contested decision]. That mechanism shall include a monitoring trustee who shall be independent from Microsoft.

In case the Commission considers [Microsoft's] proposed monitoring mechanism not suitable it retains the right to impose such a mechanism by way of a decision.

[The Court of First Instance (CFI) upheld all the main points of the Commission's decision as well as the fine levied against Microsoft. Microsoft's arguments on the definition of the relevant product markets were dismissed in that the Court found the evidence confirmed the Commission (para. 504). Microsoft's main argument to annul the contested decision was that the decision forced it to disclose its protocols for interoperability systems to its competitors and that these protocols were trade secrets protected by intellectual property laws. Microsoft argued that the remedy imposed by the contested decision forced Microsoft to license its trade secrets against its will and thus was a violation of Microsoft's intellectual property rights under European law. Microsoft further argued that it could not be forced to expose its trade secrets even in the face of a claim that failure to do so would result in a violation of EC competition law. The Court found that the issue was whether it was ever justified under EC competition law to order a competitor to license its trade secrets or whether intellectual property laws protected a competitor from being forced to license its trade secrets even in the face of a claim that a refusal to issue a license was a violation of EC competition law. The Court resolved this issue as follows:]

329. In *IMS Health*, the Court of Justice again ruled on the conditions in which a refusal by an undertaking holding a dominant position to grant to a third party a licence to use a product protected by an intellectual property right might constitute abusive conduct within the meaning of Art. 82 EC.

330. The Court of Justice first of all confirmed, at [34], with reference to *Volvo*, and *Magill*, that, according to settled case law, the exclusive right of reproduction formed

part of the rights of the owner of an intellectual property right, so that refusal to grant a licence, even if it is the act of an undertaking holding a dominant position, cannot in itself constitute abuse of that position. The Court of Justice also observed, at [35], that it was clear from that case law that exercise of an exclusive right by the owner might, in exceptional circumstances, involve abusive conduct. Next, after reciting the exceptional circumstances found to exist in *Magill*, the Court held, at [38], that it followed from that case law that, in order for the refusal by an undertaking which owns a copyright to give access to a product or service indispensable for carrying on a particular business to be treated as abusive, it was sufficient that three cumulative conditions be satisfied, namely, that that refusal prevents the emergence of a new product for which there is a potential consumer demand, that it is unjustified and that it is such as to exclude any competition on a secondary market.

331. It follows from the case law cited above that the refusal by an undertaking holding a dominant position to license a third party to use a product covered by an intellectual property right cannot in itself constitute an abuse of a dominant position within the meaning of Art. 82 EC. It is only in exceptional circumstances that the exercise of the exclusive right by the owner of the intellectual property right may give rise to such an abuse.

332. It also follows from that case law that the following circumstances, in particular, must be considered to be exceptional:

— In the first place, the refusal relates to a product or service indispensable to the exercise of a particular activity on a neighbouring market;
— In the second place, the refusal is of such a kind as to exclude any effective competition on that neighbouring market;
— In the third place, the refusal prevents the appearance of a new product for which there is potential consumer demand.

333. Once it is established that such circumstances are present, the refusal by the holder of a dominant position to grant a licence may infringe Art. 82 EC unless the refusal is objectively justified.

NOTES AND QUESTIONS

1. Why did United Brands prohibit its distributors from selling green bananas? How did this policy extend United Brands's market power?

2. The United States government and some state governments had also challenged Microsoft under U.S. antitrust law. In 2001, the parties reached a settlement. The solution adopted in the settlement of that case, which was approved by the United States District Court for the District of Columbia, was to require Microsoft to allow masking of access to Microsoft programs bundled with Windows, though consumers are free to turn them back on. *United States v. Microsoft Corp.*, 2002 WL 31654530 (D.D.C. Nov. 12, 2002). Is there any problem with inconsistent decisions by regulators in the United States and the EU? In 1998, the United States and the EU signed an agreement to share information and to cooperate on competition matters. *See* 37 I.L.M. 1070 (1998).

3. A key aspect of the *Microsoft* decision was that Microsoft improperly tied its Windows Media Player to its dominant Windows operating system. Is the media player a separate product or, as Microsoft contended, simply a functional part of its operating system product?

4. Microsoft decided not to appeal the CFI's decision. In 2004, Microsoft had already agreed with the Commission to market a slimmed-down version of its Windows software without the integrated Windows Media Player. In 2007, Microsoft further agreed that open software developers will be able to access and use Microsoft's interoperability information. Such developers will, upon payment of a one-time €10,000 fee, gain access to Microsoft's communication protocols, which specify how to exchange data between Windows and rival products. (The protocols are (were) trade secrets not patented.) Microsoft also agreed that competitors can license Microsoft patents by paying a royalty of only 0.4 percent of sales. Microsoft had originally demanded 7 percent for such rights.

5. On December 16, 2009, the EU Commission announced a comprehensive settlement agreement with Microsoft, which agreed to send updates to Windows computers in Europe so that when PC users log on, they will see a pop-up screen giving them the choice to use one or more of 12 web browsers that they can download and install. Purchasers of new PCs will see this screen when they start up for the first time. *See* Neelie Kroes, European Commissioner for Competition Policy, Your Internet, Your Choice: Microsoft Web Browsers Decision, Opening Remarks at Press Conference Brussels 16th December 2009 (transcript available at *http://europa.eu/rapid/pressReleasesAction.do?reference=SPEECH/09/582*).

B.   THE EC MERGER REGULATION

In the EU, as we have seen, a merger or acquisition (M&A) may attract the Commission's attention as an abuse of a dominant position. In addition, under the most recent EU merger regulation, Council Regulation (EC) No. 139/2004, M&A activity involving large business enterprises must notify the Commission in advance and submit to special standards and scrutiny. A foreign investor that seeks to acquire a European company must be aware of the EU merger regulation.

Prior notification (after the agreement but before implementation) is necessary where M&A is deemed to create a "concentration with a Community dimension." (Merger Regulation, Article 1.) Such concentration is deemed to exist if (a) the aggregate worldwide turnover of all the undertakings concerned is more than €5,000 million and (b) the aggregate Community-wide turnover of at least two of the undertakings concerned is more than €250 million. Even below these thresholds, M&A will be deemed to have a Community dimension where:

- The combined aggregate worldwide turnover of the undertakings is greater than €2,500 million;
- In at least three member states the combined turnover is over €100 million (and at least two of three have turnover of more than €25 million); and
- The Community-wide turnover of each of at least two of the undertakings is more than €100 million.

Upon receiving the notification, the Commission must publish the "notified concentration" and transmit the information to all member states. (Merger Regulation, Article 4.) The M&A in question cannot be carried out until the Commission finds that it is "compatible with the common market" (Article 7). The criteria for this finding applied by the Commission are economic in nature to determine whether the concentration "would significantly impede effective competition." The Commission (Article 8) has wide powers of investigation, as well as the authority (1) to require the undertakings to dissolve the concentration, or (2) to place various conditions on its completion. The Commission may also (Article 9) refer the matter to the authorities of a member state. The Commission must operate within certain time deadlines (generally 25 days, but this may be extended). Under the TFEU, judicial review of the Commission's decisions is vested in the CFI and the ECJ. Consider the following case.

Tetra Laval BV v. Commission of the European Communities
Case T-5/02, [2002] ECR II-4381
Court of First Instance

[This case involved a stock acquisition by Tetra Laval, a privately held company incorporated under French law, of Sidel, a public corporation also based in France and a leading producer of PET (polyethylene terephthalate) plastic containers for liquids. Tetra Laval is a world leader in the production of cartons for the packaging of milk, juice, and other drinks. The Commission refused to authorize the acquisition because it found that Tetra Laval would use its dominance in carton packaging to leverage itself into a dominant position in the PET bottle market. The parties sought an annulment of the Commission's decision.]

12. Tetra comprises, *inter alia*, the Tetra Pak company, which is mainly active in the area of liquid food carton packaging, where Tetra Pak is the world-wide market leader. Tetra also has more limited activities in the plastic packaging sector, mainly as a converter (which consists of manufacturing and supplying empty packaging to producers who then fill the packaging themselves), particularly of high density polyethylene (hereinafter HDPE) bottles.

13. Sidel is involved in the design and production of packaging equipment and systems, particularly stretch blow moulding machines (hereinafter SBM machines), which are used in the production of polyethylene terephthalate (hereinafter PET) plastic bottles. It is the world-wide leader for the production and supply of SBM machines. It is also active in barrier technology, used to make PET compatible with products which are sensitive to gas and light, as well as in the manufacture of filling machines for PET and, to a lesser extent, HDPE bottles.

28. The Commission considers that the competitive impact of [the notified transaction] will be primarily in the liquid food packaging industry, (liquid food meaning essentially liquid dairy products (LDPs), fruit juices and nectars (juices), fruit-flavoured still drinks (FFDs) and tea/coffee drinks, these four products together being referred to hereinafter as the sensitive products) and, in particular an impact on the sectoral segments in which the parties are primarily active, namely plastic, in particular PET packaging, and carton packaging.

1. PRELIMINARY OBSERVATIONS

142. It is common ground between the parties that the modified merger is conglomerate in type, that is, a merger of undertakings which, essentially, do not have a pre-existing competitive relationship, either as direct competitors or as suppliers and customers. Mergers of this type do not give rise to true horizontal overlaps between the activities of the parties to the merger or to a vertical relationship between the parties in the strict sense

of the term. Thus it cannot be presumed as a general rule that such mergers produce anti-competitive effects. However, they may have anti-competitive effects in certain cases.

2. The First Pillar: Leveraging

146. It should be observed, first, that the Regulation, particularly at Article 2(2) and (3), does not draw any distinction between, on the one hand, merger transactions having horizontal and vertical effects and, on the other hand, those having a conglomerate effect. It follows that, without distinction between those types of transactions, a merger can be prohibited only if the two conditions laid down in Article 2(3) are met. Consequently, a merger having a conglomerate effect must, like any other merger, be authorised by the Commission if it is not established that it creates or strengthens a dominant position in the common market or in a substantial part of it and that, as a result, effective competition will be significantly impeded.

147. However, the analysis of potentially anti-competitive conglomerate effects of a merger transaction raises a certain number of specific problems relating to the nature of such a transaction.

154. In this context, it is appropriate to distinguish, on the one hand, between a situation where a merger having conglomerate effects immediately changes the conditions of competition on the second market and results in the creation or strengthening of a dominant position on that market due to the dominant position already held on the first market and, on the other hand, a situation where the creation or strengthening of a dominant position on the second market does not immediately result from the merger, but will occur, in those circumstances, only after a certain time and will result from conduct engaged in by the merged entity on the first market where it already holds a dominant position. In this latter case, it is not the structure resulting from the merger transaction itself which creates or strengthens a dominant position within the meaning of Article 2(3) of the Regulation, but rather the future conduct in question.

159. Accordingly, when the Commission, in assessing the effects of such a merger, relies on foreseeable conduct which in itself is likely to constitute abuse of an existing dominant position, it is required to assess whether, despite the prohibition of such conduct, it is none the less likely that the entity resulting from the merger will act in such a manner or whether, on the contrary, the illegal nature of the conduct and/or the risk of detection will make such a strategy unlikely. While it is appropriate to take account, in its assessment, of incentives to engage in anti-competitive practices, such as those resulting in the present case for Tetra from the commercial advantages which may be foreseen on the PET equipment markets (recital 359), the Commission must also consider the extent to which those incentives would be reduced, or even eliminated, owing to the illegality of the conduct in question, the likelihood of its detection, action taken by the competent authorities, both at Community and national level, and the financial penalties which could ensue.

162. It follows from the foregoing that it is necessary to examine whether the Commission based its analysis of the likelihood of leveraging from the aseptic carton markets, and of the consequences of such leveraging by the merged entity, on sufficiently convincing evidence. In addition, since the anticipated dominant position would only emerge after a certain lapse of time, by 2005 according to the Commission, its analysis of the future position must, whilst allowing for a certain margin of discretion, be particularly plausible.

[The strong dominant position of Tetra on the aseptic carton markets, its dominant position on the global carton packaging market, the first mover advantage of the merged entity, and the financial strength of the parties were relevant elements to establish the possibility of leveraging. However, it was necessary for the Commission to prove also that the merged entity would have an incentive to engage in leveraging practices, taking into consideration the probable levels of growth in the PET market. There was a likelihood of a significant increase in the use of PET by 2005, and the incentive to leverage could not be excluded.]

(III) LEVERAGING METHODS

217. [T]he leveraging would be carried out by two types of measures: first, through pressure leading to tied sales or sales which bundle equipment and consumables for carton packaging jointly with PET packaging equipment. Second, measures could be adopted to offer incentives, such as predatory pricing, price wars and loyalty rebates.

218. However, the use, by an undertaking with a dominant position like Tetra's on the aseptic carton markets, of pressure in the form of tied sales or incentives such as predatory pricing or loyalty rebates that are not objectively justified, would usually constitute an abuse of that position. As this Court has already held, the possible recourse to such strategies cannot be presumed by the Commission, as it has done in the contested decision, in order to justify a decision prohibiting a merger transaction which has been notified to it in accordance with the Regulation. It follows that the leveraging practices which may be taken into consideration by the Court are limited to those which, at least probably, do not constitute an abuse of a dominant position on the aseptic carton markets.

219. It is, therefore, necessary merely to consider strategies for tied or bundled sales which are not in themselves forced, for loyalty rebates that are objectively justified on the carton markets, and for offers of reduced prices for carton or PET packaging equipment that are not predatory within the meaning of well-established case-law.

[After examination of the leveraging methods that could be used by Tetra Laval in light of the law and its deterrence effect, the commitments offered by the parties, and econometric analysis, the Court concluded that "the merged entity's possible means of leveraging would be quite limited." ¶224. The Commission did not prove the likelihood of foreseeable leveraging effects. "[I]n relying as it did on the consequences of leveraging by the merged entity in order to support its findings that a dominant position would be created by 2005 on the PET packaging equipment markets, the Commission committed a manifest error of assessment." ¶308.]

3. THE SECOND PILLAR: REDUCTION OF POTENTIAL COMPETITION ON THE CARTON MARKETS

310. The present case raises the question whether the Commission, when it wishes to prohibit a merger on the ground that it would strengthen an existing dominant position, in this case that of the acquiring party on the aseptic carton markets, may rely on the elimination or, as it stated at the hearing, at least the significant reduction, of potential but growing competition on a neighbouring market from the undertaking acquired, in this case Sidel, which holds a significant position on the PET markets.

312. The Court finds in that regard that when the Commission relies on the elimination or significant reduction of potential competition, even of competition which will

tend to grow, in order to justify the prohibition of a notified merger, the factors which it identifies to show the strengthening of a dominant position must be based on convincing evidence. The mere fact that the acquiring undertaking already holds a clear dominant position on the relevant market may constitute an important factor, as the contested decision finds, but does not in itself suffice to justify a finding that a reduction in the potential competition which that undertaking must face constitutes a strengthening of its position.

324. In maintaining that significant competitive pressure will be eliminated as a result of the modified merger, the Commission relies principally on the considerable growth it foresees in PET use for packaging sensitive products. However, the above analysis of the first pillar, concerning leveraging, shows that this growth, with the exception of growth in FFDs and tea/coffee drinks, will probably be much less marked than the Commission believes. As for FFDs and tea/coffee drinks, the contested decision itself recognises that their potential influence on the position of carton is more limited than that of other sensitive products in view of the fact that their segments are smaller in size. It is, therefore, not possible, on the basis of the evidence relied on in the contested decision, to determine, with the certainty required to justify the prohibition of a merger, whether the implementation of the modified merger would place Tetra in a situation where it could be more independent than in the past in relation to its competitors on the aseptic carton markets.

329. Turning to the allegedly diminished need for Tetra to innovate following implementation of the modified merger, both the contested decision and the explanations given in the Commission's written and oral pleadings show that, at present, competition on the various carton markets takes place principally through innovation. According to the Commission, Tetra's introduction in the past of new carton packages with more user-friendly features such as the carton top package with screw top closure (recital 398) shows that innovation is a practical necessity. According to Tetra's pleadings at the hearing, which were not disputed on this point by the Commission, these innovations were not due to pressure from the PET equipment markets, but rather to the demands of consumers of carton-packaged products. Even if the acquisition of Sidel were to reduce the pressure on innovation emanating from the indirect, but growing, competition from the PET equipment markets, at least as regards FFDs and tea/coffee drinks packaging, for which not insignificant growth is predicted by 2005, the contested decision does not state why demand from customers wishing to remain with carton would not continue in the future to be the driving force behind innovation, especially on the aseptic carton markets.

[T]he divestiture decision is annulled.

NOTES AND QUESTIONS

1. The European Court of Justice substantially affirmed the CFI's decision. The Court, however, overturned the CFI's requirement (from ¶159) that the Commission assess whether leveraging enabled by the merger would probably be deterred by Article 102 TFEU (ex Article 82 TEC). This was too speculative an endeavor. Cases C-12/03 P and C-13/03 P, 15 February 2005.

2. In what respect precisely, according to the CFI, did the Commission fail to prove competitive harm?

3. The Commission ultimately cleared the Sidel acquisition. *Commission of the European Communities v. Tetra Laval BV*, Case C-12/03 P (February 15, 2005).

4. There are some major differences concerning M&A between EU law and U.S. law. The U.S. Clayton Act, section 7, prohibits mergers and acquisitions where "the effect . . . may be substantially to lessen competition, or to tend to create a monopoly." 15 U.S.C. §18 (2006). The Hart-Scott-Rodino Antitrust Improvement Act, 15 U.S.C. §18a (2006), requires pre-merger notification to the Department of Justice and the U.S. Federal Trade Commission of large acquisitions. This pre-notification requirement applies to mergers involving foreign business entities as well if they affect U.S. commerce. However, the FTC and the Justice Department have no power to block a merger; they must ask for an injunction after filing suit in federal court. The United States and the EU also take a different approach to the substantive standards in M&A: EU authorities presume that anticompetitive effects will arise out of a concentration, while U.S. authorities believe competition will be maintained if there are no substantial barriers to market entry. The United States and the EC have a cooperative agreement to share information on antitrust and competition matters, European Communities-United States Agreement on the Application of Positive Comity Principles in the Enforcement of Competition Law, 37 I.L.M. 1070 (1998), but mergers are explicitly excluded from this cooperation.

NOTE ON THE EXTRATERRITORIAL APPLICATION OF EU COMPETITION LAW

For many years, the European Court of Justice used the "economic entity" theory to find jurisdiction over foreign companies. The economic entity theory asserts jurisdiction on the basis that a company doing business in the EU may be a part of the same economic enterprise as a foreign company even though they are legally separate entities. *See, e.g., ICI v. Commission*, [1972] E.C.R. 619.

A new basis for extraterritorial jurisdiction was announced, however, in the *Wood Pulp* case, *Ahlstrom v. Commission*, [1988] E.C.R. 5193. This case involved Kraft Export Association, a U.S. membership cartel of wood pulp producers benefiting from antitrust immunity under the U.S. Webb-Pomerene Act of 1918. The ECJ upheld the Commission's application of Article 101 TFEU (ex Article 81 TEC), stating: "The decisive factor [in this case] is . . . the place where [a price fixing undertaking] is implemented. The producers in this case implemented their pricing agreement within the common market. It is immaterial in that respect whether or not they had recourse to subsidiaries, agents, sub-agents, or branches within the Community in order to make their contacts within the Community." Compare this holding to the statement by the U.S. Supreme Court in *Hartford Fire Ins. Co. v. California*, 509 U.S. 764, 796 (1993), that "it is well established . . . that the Sherman Act applies to foreign conduct that was meant to produce and did in fact produce some substantial effect in the United States."

On the basis of the *Wood Pulp* case, the Commission asserted jurisdiction over U.S. companies, not only under Article 101 TFEU (ex Article 81 TEC), but also under the Merger Regulation, Council Regulation 4064/89, 1989 O.J. (L 395) 1, and Article 102 TFEU (ex Article 82 TEC). For example, in *Boeing/McDonnell Douglas v. Commission*, Case IV/M, 1997 O.J. (L 336) 16, the Merger Regulation was applied to prohibit Boeing from enforcing exclusive arrangements to sell aircraft to several airlines and from leveraging its relationships with suppliers to pressure the suppliers into giving Boeing preferential treatment and into refusing to deal with Boeing's competitors.

In 2004, the European Commission acted to block General Electric's $43 billion acquisition of Honeywell. The Commission's case, which is on appeal to the ECJ, is based on the theory that GE would be able to shut out competitors by bundling its aircraft engines with Honeywell's in-flight electronic systems. The Commission's decision blocking the General Electric-Honeywell merger was affirmed by the European Court of Justice as to the horizontal effects of the concentration, but was reversed as to the vertical and conglomerate effects. *General Electric v. Commission* (Case T-210/01), 14 Dec. 2005. However, the Court affirmed the Commission's decision to block the merger, causing an outcry in some quarters in the United States.

In May 2004, the Commission also objected to a proposed deal between Japan's Sony Corp. and Germany's Bertelsmann, AG, a 50-50 joint venture to be called Sony BMG, on the basis that the deal might "create or strengthen a collective dominant position in the world music market." The joint venture would hold about 25 percent of the global music market and would be the second ranking entity behind only Universal Music Group, a U.S. company. The deal was later approved only after the parties accepted conditions recommended by the Commission. The Commission continues to play an active role in regulating corporate acquisitions in the EU. For example, in 2014, the Commission raised objections to an acquisition by Teléfonica, a Spanish telecommunications giant, of KPN E-Plus, a German company, on the grounds that it would create a formidable rival to Deutsche Telekom and Vodafone Germany. As of this writing, the Commission's investigation is ongoing.

C.   Foreign Direct Investment in China

We move now to a consideration of FDI in China. Keep in mind as you review these materials that although many FDI issues in China are unique there are some issues common to FDI in other developing countries in Asia and elsewhere: different goals and expectations of the foreign investor and its local joint venture partner, conflicts in management styles and approaches and the need to resolve them, labor issues involving local employees, and the need to protect intellectual property rights in the FDI project from theft and misappropriation.

1.   China's Economic System

As China's economic and social system may be unfamiliar to you, we first introduce the Chinese economic system and the background environment for FDI.

**Daniel C.K. Chow, The Legal System of the
People's Republic of China in a Nutshell,
21–35 (3d ed. 2015)**

[1] CHINA'S ECONOMY, 1949–78

Although never subject to the type of overwhelming central control exercised by such countries as the Soviet Union, the economy of the PRC for most of the period since its founding until economic reforms begun in 1978 was a command economy. Under this system, the state owned all property and all enterprises were essentially administrative units of the state. The state received all revenues from industrial and agricultural enterprises, redistributed revenues in accordance with state goals, and subsidized or absorbed all losses. Production targets for all enterprises were set in accordance with a five-year economic plan promulgated by the State Council, the executive arm of the PRC government. The plans set forth production quotas for commodities, set prices for products, and allocated products for distribution. Although economic reforms have relaxed state control over the economy and China no longer sets production quotas for as many sectors of the economy, China still continues to use state sponsored economic plans. China is now in the midst of its Eleventh Five-Year Plan covering 2006-2010.

A. THE COLLECTIVIZATION OF AGRICULTURE

Early in its history, from 1953–54, the PRC implemented a system of collectivization of agriculture in which private ownership of farmland and crops was abolished. The state confiscated lands owned by landlords, many of who were killed in the process, and redistributed the lands to large collectives of workers who farmed the land communally. By the 1960s, the collectives were reorganized into massive communes with responsibility for meeting government quotas set forth in the state sponsored five-year economic plans.

All crops grown and harvested by agricultural communes were sold to the state at government fixed prices. Government units then distributed revenues to the individual workers of the communes in accordance with a set of guidelines that awarded workers a number of work points for their daily work. In many cases, workers would accumulate the same number of work points whether they worked industriously or not, creating little incentive for effective performance. Many of these communes were massive in size. For example, on the eve of reforms in 1978 that would dismantle the collective system of agriculture, Guangdong province's 9.2 million farm families were organized into approximately 2,000 communes, each containing 46,000 farm families.

B. INDUSTRY AND THE STATE ENTERPRISE SYSTEM

In the industrial sector, the foundation of China's pre-reform economy was the state-owned enterprise system. A state-owned enterprise (SOE) is owned by the state as opposed to any private entity, individual, or group of individuals. An SOE was expected to meet state production targets, to turn over all of its revenues to the state, and to have all of its losses subsidized or absorbed by the state. The state also controlled all of the enterprise's business and management functions including matters that fell within the business scope of the firm. While many governments, including the United States, regulate enterprise matters that affect the public interest, pre-reform China went far beyond this limited scope of government regulation and exerted control over all matters of the firm, including business strategies, marketing, distribution, and sales. Because the state also owned the enterprise, the state served both as regulator and entrepreneur in many cases.

SOEs were subject to the control and supervision of government departments at all levels. For example, a local chemicals factory would report to the local bureau of light industry, which would have supervisory authority over all enterprises engaged in the light industry sectors. Because of a massive and complex bureaucracy, however, complicated lines of authority resulted in a number of government bureaus exerting some control over the enterprise. For example, the planning departments at all levels of government determined how much capital investment was required for enterprises. The economic and trade committees determined the use of technology by enterprises in their operations. Labor and financial departments determined wages of employees. No single government bureau was completely responsible for all facets of the operations of the enterprise, but rather many entities had uncoordinated input into the management of the enterprise. This chaotic supervisory structure resulted in enterprises that were inefficiently managed and performed poorly. For most of the history of the PRC, SOEs have operated with chronic losses even during the period since economic reforms began in 1978 and even though the overall economy of the PRC has grown consistently during this same period.

Throughout most of the period since 1949, the state sector has played a major role in the PRC industrial economy. Prior to economic reform, the percentage of China's industrial output from SOEs stood at 83 percent. Since reforms in 1978, the state sector has experienced a diminishing role. By 1994, SOEs accounted for 38 percent of industrial output. Although the state sector rebounded to account for 48.3 percent of industrial output in 2000, its share of the total output of the economy has continued to shrink. By 2010, SOEs accounted for only about 25 percent. Despite the diminishing output of the state sector, SOEs continue to play a critical role in China's economy. All vital sectors of the economy, such as banking, telecommunications, steel production, oil and gas exploration and refining, electricity and water supply, and train and air transport continue to be controlled by SOEs. An ongoing challenge for China's rulers is that SOEs, while vital to the economy, continue to suffer chronic losses despite many attempts at reform. The continuing reform of the state sector remains one of China's most significant challenges in the years ahead.

C. SOCIAL WELFARE FUNCTIONS OF SOES

A primary reason for the inefficiency of SOEs is their social welfare role. Prior to reform, workers in SOEs found their professional, personal, and family lives to be inseparable and that all revolved around the work unit. Social services that are provided by the private sector or government social welfare agencies in the United States were all provided by the work unit in pre-reform China. SOEs not only provided employment, but also housing, schooling, medical care, and pension benefits. In a typical case, an SOE worker would live in a dormitory or housing provided by the SOE, work in the adjacent SOE factory or plant, send his children to the nearby school operated by the SOE, shop at the nearby markets owned by the SOE, visit the doctor at the nearby SOE hospital, watch movies at a theater operated by the SOE, and receive pension benefits supplied by the SOE upon retirement. Workers' personal lives became inseparable from their professional lives. For example, a worker was expected to seek permission from supervisors for marriage and other personal decisions. Seeking permission from the work unit supervisors was required because marriage meant that the new spouse and any children would create additional demands for employment, housing, and other services. The SOE work unit came to be viewed as a social net that provided its employees with a basic level of guaranteed social services. Typically, an SOE would not discharge workers for unsatisfactory work, and all workers received a common salary regardless of performance.

The role of the SOE as a provider of social welfare services meant that there was constant pressure to absorb more workers and their families. Some SOEs are the size of the world's largest multinational enterprises. For example, the Capital Iron and Steel Corporation in western Beijing at one time employed approximately 150,000 workers, more than most of the largest private companies in the world. Some SOEs have compounds that resemble small towns. The Wuhan Iron & Steel Corporation was considered to be a "company run society" and was known as "Red Steel Town." As many as one-third or more of SOE workers were redundant.

Given the social welfare role of SOEs, the main goals of such enterprises were not profits, efficiency, and productivity. When an enterprise lost money or faced bankruptcy, the state would intervene and grant it another subsidy or exemption because failure of the SOE would result in significant social costs. While this system served important social welfare goals, the inefficient and poorly managed state sector resulted in the bulk of China's economy operating at a loss, a situation that needed to be remedied if China was to step into the modern industrial age.

[2] CHINA'S REFORMS, 1978

With Mao's death marking the end of the Cultural Revolution in 1976, the Communist Party of China (CPC) turned its attention to rebuilding the nation's long neglected economy. Party elders were shocked and embarrassed by China's backwardness and poverty by comparison to some of its neighbors such as Hong Kong and Japan. In 1978, the CPC, under the leadership of Deng Xiaoping, announced that the focus of its work would shift from class struggle to economic development.

To implement this shift, the CPC endorsed the development of some free markets and a limited role for private enterprise within an overall framework of socialism, creating a mixed economic system. This shift represented a relaxation of the command economy approach of the PRC that had been in place for most of the period since 1949. Under China's reforms, the private sector is viewed as an adjunct or complement to the state sector, which remains prominent, despite its many problems. Some free markets and some private ownership of wealth will be developed, but the vital areas of the economy will continue to be state-owned and controlled. Consistent with Marxist-Leninist principles, the state will continue to own all real property and the means of production.

China's policy is to create a socialist market economy as distinguished from a market economy based upon liberal capitalism, such as that of the United States, which contemplates private ownership of property and the means of production. As long as China's political commitment to socialism remains firm, there will be limits on the private ownership of wealth and the state sector will continue to be a vital portion of the economy. For example, complete privatization of most state-owned enterprises will not be an option under the present approach. The state continues to own SOEs—in principle at least. In the view of China's rulers, the nation is undergoing economic, not political, reform.

A. REFORMS IN THE AGRICULTURAL SECTOR

The 1978 reforms met with immediate and dramatic success in the agricultural sector. While the collectivization of agriculture was trumpeted with great fanfare, the dismantling of the system was done quietly and unobtrusively. In addition to disbanding the communes, the reforms instituted a basic shift in responsibility within the production system. Under the new system, responsibility for meeting production quotas was shifted from the massive commune organizations down to the family household unit. Once households met the assigned government quotas, they were free to sell any excess product at market prices and to keep the proceeds. In another major shift, fixed government quotas were gradually replaced by contracts between the state and local collectives, composed of individual households. The collectives in turn contracted with household units. These seemingly minor changes created a basic change in incentives. Farming households now had incentive to maximize production because they were allowed to keep revenues above certain levels. Under the old system of assigning work points, hard work or indolence was rewarded in the same way. The new household responsibility system was immediately popular with farming households and agricultural production soared in the years after the reforms.

B. REFORMS IN THE STATE SECTOR

By contrast with reforms in the agricultural sector, effective reform of the state sector has been difficult to achieve and continues to be one of China's most significant challenges. Reforms have reflected two policy goals. First, China enacted legislation early in the reform era that granted SOEs independent legal status and the right to make their own managerial decisions. Subsequent legislation provided greater details about the types of decision-making authority that state-owned enterprises would enjoy, including greater independence to import and export, make investment and production decisions, hire and manage workers, and set prices and wages. This shift represented an attempt to protect SOEs from government intrusion into their business operations that would hamper their efficient operation.

Second, these reforms also attempted to wean SOEs from dependence upon state subsidies. For example, one fundamental change of the reform movement is that government funds are no longer given as free capital grants or investment subsidies, but are now treated as low-interest bank loans. SOEs are required to pay charges on their fixed assets and working capital. Equally important, SOEs are no longer eligible in principle to be rescued by state subsidies in the event of losses. In theory, SOEs are now in principle fully responsible for their own profits and losses. To create further incentives for enterprises to improve their economic performance, the reformers also enacted the Enterprise Bankruptcy Law (1986, revised 2006), requiring chronically mismanaged and inefficient enterprises to be closed down.

One of the obstacles faced by reformers in the state sector is coping with the broader social and political consequences of reform. As previously discussed, state-owned enterprises create a system of integrated social welfare institutions. Any reform of the enterprise system will affect the delivery of essential social services to industrial workers. Under this system, China cannot simply announce that SOEs will now be governed by principles of profit and loss and that unprofitable enterprises will be closed under the Bankruptcy Law. Closing an unprofitable enterprise will not only result in the loss of employment for workers, many of who will be unable to find new jobs, but will also result in a family catastrophe. The family loses housing, medical care, and schooling upon separation from the SOE. The costs of unemployment can be so severe that desperate workers use threats, demonstrations, and even violence against managers to avoid losing their jobs. Effective reform of the state sector involves creating alternative means for providing social services for the employable industrial worker as well as benefits for the unemployable and redundant workers for whom the state-owned enterprise has traditionally served as a caretaker. These are fundamental long-term reforms.

Some of China's reforms in the state sector have been bold. One reform involves restructuring state enterprises using international capitalist models of the corporate form. Recent legislation now allows for the "corporatization" of state-owned enterprises, which involves the reorganization of the SOE as a stock corporation, with the stock of some companies trading on public stock exchanges. The state maintains a controlling interest by owning a majority of the shares once the enterprise has been reorganized into a stock corporation. Other reforms include reorganizing and merging state-owned enterprises into mega-enterprise conglomerates. Not long ago, the very notion of state enterprises as corporations with stock openly traded on public stock exchanges and available for private ownership would have been regarded by China's leaders as repugnant to socialism. These new directions indicate China's willingness to experiment and its receptivity to western corporate and business law concepts.

Other sweeping changes are underway. In recent years China has been able to create a substantial private housing market and has now largely removed cost-free housing as a benefit of the SOE. The booming construction of high-rise apartment buildings in the teeming cities of Shanghai and Guangzhou serve as a testament to the new private housing industry. Efforts are under way to establish an independent social welfare system in order to decrease the social welfare role of SOEs so that they can be further subjected to the pressures of the competitive marketplace. Re-employment centers have been established to help retrain and find new jobs for workers who have been terminated from SOEs undergoing reform. Basic pension programs and general health care programs are all in the process of being established outside of the SOE system.

Despite more than two decades of reforms, however, effective changes have been difficult to achieve because of the complex and interrelated issues involved in reforming this fundamental sector of the economy, which continues to operate with chronic losses. New and even greater challenges may await this sector with China's entry into the WTO, as China will need to open protected areas of industry to international competition.

[3] CHINA'S ECONOMY SINCE 1978

Since economic reforms began in 1978, China has achieved unprecedented economic growth for an economy of its size. From 1978–97, China experienced an average annual GDP growth rate of 9.8 percent. Despite the economic retrenchment in Asia in 1999, China reported an average annual growth rate of 7.5 percent for 1999–2001 and a 7.6 percent growth rate in 2002. In 2007, China had the fourth largest economy in the world measured by GDP with $2.67 trillion and was behind only the United States, Japan, and Germany. China's growing economic power stands as a remarkable achievement for a nation that was mired in poverty and backwardness and caught in upheaval and turmoil for the bulk of the twentieth century.

GDP of Top Ten Countries (U.S. $ Billions)

Country	2004 GDP	Rank	2005 GDP	Rank	2006 GDP	Rank	2007 GDP	Rank	2013 GDP	Rank
USA	11,667.5	1	12,486.6	1	14,979.2	1	13,980.0	1	16,799.7	1
Japan	4,623.4	2	4,663.8	2	5,083.4	2	5,290.0	2	4,901.5	3
Germany	2,714.4	3	2,730.1	3	2,812.6	3	3,280.0	3	3,636.0	4
China	**1,649.3**	**7**	**1,772.7**	**6**	**2,588.0**	**4**	**3,010.0**	**4**	**9,181.4**	**2**
U.K.	2,140.9	4	2,227.6	4	2,292.1	5	2,570.0	5	2,535.8	6
France	2,002.6	5	2,054.9	5	2,108.3	6	2,520.0	6	2,737.4	5
Italy	1,672.3	6	1,709.7	7	1,728.5	7	2,090.0	7	2,072.0	9
Canada	979.8	9	1,034.5	8	1,057.3	9	1,360.0	9	1,825.1	11
Spain	991.4	8	1,019.0	9	1,069.5	8	1,410.0	8	1,358.7	13
Brazil	492.3	15	587.8	15	620.7	15	934.0	12	2,242.9	7

In foreign trade, China has been able to become a world leader in the span of just two decades. China's foreign trade rose from twenty-seventh in the world with $20.6 billion in 1978 to first in the world in 2012 at $2.05 trillion, an increase of almost 103-fold. China now has the largest foreign currency reserves in the world, with reserves rocketing from $167 million in 1978 to nearly $4 trillion in mid-2014.

A. THE ROLE OF FOREIGN INVESTMENT IN CHINA'S DEVELOPMENT

The pace of foreign investment in China has increased dramatically within the past two decades and has played a major role in the nation's rising economy. Ninety percent of China's foreign investment has occurred since 1992 when Deng Xiaoping's southern tour of China helped to propel his reform policies forward. Since 1992, China has been the world's second largest recipient of foreign capital behind the United States with foreign investment reaching $121 billion in 2012 up from $69 billion in 2005 and an average of just $11.7 billion during 1985–1995. Foreign direct investment in China (including Hong Kong) accounted for 27.9 percent of all FDI in developing countries in 2012.

Foreign investment enterprises, such as joint ventures and wholly foreign-owned enterprises, have now assumed a major role in China's economy. According to recent official statistics, foreign investment enterprises accounted for slightly more than one quarter of all of China's industrial output and for approximately 20 percent of all annual tax revenues in the industrial and commercial sector. Official Chinese sources report that in 2012, there were over 400,000 foreign invested enterprises that accounted for 77 percent of all inward FDI. In 2013, nearly 23,000 FIEs were approved. There are now approximately 200 multinational enterprises with foreign investments in China, including 17 of Japan's largest companies, and 9 out of 10 of Germany's largest companies. Some of the largest companies in the United States, such as Coca-Cola, General Motors, General Electric, McDonald's, Motorola, Boeing, and Procter & Gamble, all have sizeable business operations in China.

NOTES AND QUESTIONS

1. According to some estimates, China is on track to have the largest economy in the world early in the first decades of the twenty-first century. Japan currently has the third largest economy in the world and is deepening its economic integration with China, which began in the 1990s even though Japan and China were bitter enemies for long stretches during the twentieth century. India has recently emerged as a growing economic power with strength in innovation, technology, and services. These developments signal that Asia may, for the first time in modern history, assume a leadership role in the world. Do the developments in Asia pose a threat for U.S. business? An opportunity?

2. Prior to economic reforms in China, most state-owned enterprises were not primarily concerned with profits and losses. Why not? In most state-owned enterprises, there are many "redundant workers," that is, many more workers than are necessary to operate the SOE at full efficiency. In a typical SOE, up to a third or more of all workers are redundant. Why? Why would a worker in an SOE need to seek permission from the work unit for personal decisions such as marriage and children? Do marriage and children have an impact upon the SOE? How?

3. Are the economic reforms in China designed to transform China's economy from a command economy to a market economy and from a socialist system to a capitalist one and from a communist country into a democracy?

2. *China's FDI Legal Regime and Foreign Investment Business Vehicles*

Like many developing countries, China has specific laws that apply to FDI. Developing countries believe that while FDI is crucial to their economic development it also poses many risks for their growing economic systems. As a result, special attention in the form of separate legal rules must be applied. In China, FDI is considered a matter of national policy and is considered to play a vital role in the nation's continued economic development.

All FDI projects must be approved by PRC government authorities. FDI in China is a privilege, not a right, and a foreign investor has no recourse if government authorities refuse to approve an FDI project.

There are three standard business vehicles available for FDI: the equity joint venture, the contractual joint venture, and the wholly foreign-owned enterprise. As there are many similarities between the two joint venture forms, the materials below will focus on the equity joint venture. Although the contractual joint venture offers the parties more flexibility to determine their rights and obligations, most MNEs prefer the stability of the equity joint venture, and it is generally used when large sums of capital are invested.

A. THE JOINT VENTURE

A joint venture in China is a business entity formed by a combination of two or more business entities into a third separate entity. A joint venture should be distinguished from other business arrangements such as mergers or acquisitions. In a joint venture, both of the original partners continue to maintain their existence as separate legal entities while forming a third legal entity, the joint venture. For example, when Company A (a foreign company) and Company B (a PRC company) form a joint venture, Company C (a PRC company), the end result is three separate corporate entities: A, B, and C. In a merger, A and B combine to form a new Company C, but neither A nor B continues to exist after the merger. In an acquisition, A absorbs B, which ceases to exist as a separate legal entity and the sole surviving entity would be Company A.

The joint venture was the overwhelming investment vehicle of choice in the 1980s and continues to be popular. The advantage of this investment form is that it offers the foreign investor the opportunity to partner with a local entity that is familiar with the local environment and the labyrinth of local regulations and politics. A local partner is able to help obtain initial government approvals for the joint venture and to help navigate the constant complex of additional government approvals for taxation, customs, and other matters that are part of the daily existence of foreign investment enterprises (FIEs) in China. Finding a suitable local partner is usually the single most important decision for an MNE. The wrong partner can lead to conflict, turmoil, and, in some cases, the premature termination of the joint venture itself.

In general, PRC authorities view the joint venture as a temporary measure to introduce advanced technology and management skills into China. Although PRC law no longer imposes mandatory maximum limits on the duration of the joint venture, government authorities usually require the joint venture contract or articles of association to include a term limit of between 10 and 50 years. The local partner will be exposed to these benefits and at the termination of the joint venture, the foreign partner will depart the scene and the Chinese partner will have the opportunity to acquire the assets of the joint venture and to continue to operate the company as an ongoing concern.

B.   THE WHOLLY FOREIGN-OWNED ENTERPRISE

Unlike the joint venture, the wholly foreign-owned enterprise (WFOE) is a foreign investment vehicle that is owned entirely by the foreign investor and there is no participation by a Chinese entity. The advantage of a WFOE is that there is no possibility of a conflict with a local partner. In addition, the WFOE will provide the MNE with greater control over technology and intellectual property than will a joint venture as there will be no local partner who may misuse or misappropriate the technology of the foreign investor. The disadvantage of the WFOE is the absence of a local partner who may have many business contacts, deep knowledge of the industry, and who can serve as an intermediary with PRC government authorities. A local partner also creates an image that the joint venture is an entity with local participation and this may be politically and tactically advantageous. The WFOE, while technically a Chinese legal entity, is sometimes viewed as foreign by local authorities, which may result in less favorable treatment in some circumstances.

Recent trends indicate that the WFOE is becoming increasingly popular. In 1997, the number of WFOEs approved exceeded for the first time the number of equity joint ventures approved by PRC authorities. *See* 1997 Bulletin of the PRC Ministry of Foreign Trade and Economic Cooperation, at 12.

NOTES AND QUESTIONS

1. In the past, China has placed greater restrictions on the WFOE than on the joint venture. For example, PRC law banned the use of WFOEs in certain industries and restricted their use in other industries. Until recently, a WFOE was also required to import advanced technology and to export at least 50 percent of its products per year, restrictions that did not apply to joint ventures. China has since relaxed some of these restrictions as a result of its entry into the WTO, but as a practical matter approvals of WFOEs continue to be more difficult to obtain in some areas than approvals for joint ventures. Why would China favor joint ventures over WFOEs?

2. If China favors joint ventures over WFOEs, why permit the WFOE at all?

3. Suppose that you were advising an MNE on the best business form for a research and development center in China to support its manufacturing operations. Which form would you suggest and why?

NOTE ON A GAMBLE BY AN MNE THAT PAID OFF

During the initial stages of FDI in China in the 1980s and early 1990s, some MNEs, such as Procter & Gamble, made a strategic decision not to form a joint venture directly with a Chinese local entity. Rather, some MNEs formed an off-shore joint venture with large diversified companies in Hong Kong or Singapore and the new off-shore joint venture became the foreign investor that partnered with local entities in China. For example, in the 1980s, P&G formed a joint venture with Hutchinson-Whampoa, a large diversified multinational Hong Kong company involved in many businesses such as real estate, hotels, and telecommunications in Hong Kong and China. The new joint venture, based in Hong Kong, was called Procter & Gamble-Hutchinson (PGH). PGH, a Hong Kong company, then served as the foreign investor in a number of joint ventures with different partners in China. The reasoning behind such a strategic move is that companies like Hutchinson, with Hong Kong executives with facility in both Chinese and English as well as training and education in Western countries, would be able to advise P&G and other MNEs on the suitability of potential venture partners and locations in China as well as on doing business in China generally. By the late 1980s, Hutchinson had already established a long track record of investing in China well ahead of Western companies, many of which were just entering the China market. P&G felt that Hutchinson would be instrumental in helping to find a suitable location for the new joint venture and a suitable joint venture partner, which is probably the single most important factor in the success or failure of any joint venture. Many MNEs did not believe that they were in a good position to make a judgment about potential partners and did not trust the many business consultants who held themselves out as "old China hands" but who were little more than charlatans. Hutchinson, a sophisticated MNE in its own right, would be accustomed to Western business practices and would be in a good position to work with P&G's Western executives. At the same time, Hutchinson's Hong Kong executives had no language or cultural problems in dealing with China and, in addition, had strong ties with the PRC government and could help to open doors. With the help of Hutchinson, P&G was one of the earliest MNEs to enter the Chinese market and was able to secure a sizeable market share and competitive advantage over its global rivals such as Unilever, Colgate, and Johnson & Johnson.

When P&G entered China in 1988, China was just beginning to open up to the West and to shed the Mao suits and nondescript work uniforms in favor of more freedom in dress. In addition, China was just emerging from the culture of fervent self-sacrifice and asceticism that had marked its history since the founding of the PRC in 1949. P&G struck a responsive chord when it introduced high-quality shampoos into China in the late 1980s through the use of television commercials. Most shampoos in China at the time were coarse and hardly different from detergents used to wash clothes, as personal luxury was not viewed as a priority in China. The high quality and perfume of P&G's shampoos immediately differentiated them from local brands, but it was the image created by P&G or the "branding" of its products that was its real success. One of P&G's earliest and most effective television shampoo advertisements featured glamorous and stylishly dressed young Chinese airline flight attendants walking through airports with lustrous black hair. For many of China's female audience at the time, a job as a flight attendant represented a life of travel, adventure, and opportunity, and P&G's advertisement immediately struck a responsive chord. P&G's products quickly came to stand for Western sophistication and glamour and offered a bit of luxury into ordinary lives. The timing and message were right and P&G products were a resounding success with Chinese consumers. By the mid-1990s, P&G had become well-known as a rare success story in China and had built a business generating over $1 billion in annual revenues. P&G brands have been able to obtain a level of recognition and prestige in China that far exceeds their levels in the United States.

3. Establishing the Joint Venture

A. APPROVAL PROCESS

Establishing a joint venture in China usually involves three levels of approvals: (1) a preliminary approval by the government department supervising the local Chinese enterprise, (2) final approval by the PRC authorities with jurisdiction over foreign trade and economic planning, and (3) the issuance of a business license by the appropriate government entities with authority over the regulation of industry and commerce. Equity joint ventures are governed by the PRC Equity Joint Venture Law (1979, revised 1990 & 2001) and the PRC Equity Joint Venture Law Implementing Regulations (1983, amended 1986, 1987, 2001 & 2014).

Before the Chinese partner, usually a state-owned enterprise, can proceed with the project, it must obtain the preliminary approval of its supervisory department, a government bureau. All economic and industrial sectors are subject to the supervision of a particular supervisory authority and all entities operating with these sectors, including the joint venture that is later established, must report to the supervisory authority—although, by law, joint ventures are entitled to operate independently. To obtain this approval, the Chinese partner must submit a preliminary feasibility report that demonstrates the economic viability of the joint venture.

After the preliminary approvals have been obtained, final approvals must be obtained from the appropriate foreign trade and economic planning authorities. To obtain final approval, the applicant must submit the joint venture application, the joint venture contract, articles of association, and ancillary documents. PRC approval authorities will scrutinize all of the documents carefully. Approval authorities will examine these documents line by line and raise specific objections and suggest detailed changes. In most cases, it is advisable to submit drafts well in advance to the approval authorities for comment. Note that the approval process is, in reality, a process of negotiation with the approval authorities. Thus, there are three parties to any joint venture negotiation in China: the foreign investor, the local partner, and the approval authorities.

The appropriate authority for approval depends on the size of the investment in the joint venture. Local approval authorities at the municipal and provincial level have authority to approve joint ventures if the total investment (discussed in the next section) in the joint venture does not exceed $50 million in certain restricted industries or $300 million in permitted and encouraged industries. A list of encouraged, permitted, and restricted industries is set forth in the 1995 Tentative Provisions on Guiding the Direction of Foreign Investment and supplemented by the more comprehensive and detailed Foreign Investment Industrial Guidance Catalog first promulgated in 1995 and most recently revised in 2011. Approval of investments with total investment levels above the amounts set forth above must come from central level authorities in Beijing. Under Article 10 of the Equity Joint Venture Law Implementing Regulations, the approval authorities must make a decision within three months of submission of the application. Once approval is granted, the authorities will issue an approval certificate.

The last step in this process is the submission of the approval certificate to the appropriate Administration of Industry and Commerce, which will issue a business license. The scope of the business license will reflect the scope of business approved for the joint venture by the approval authorities as set forth in the joint venture contract. The issuance of the business license should be routine as long as there are no improprieties in the approval process, but the business license itself is essential as no enterprise can lawfully operate in China without one. With the approval certificate and business license in hand, the joint venture is now able to lawfully commence operations. For a detailed discussion of the approval process and other issues, see Chapter Ten (Foreign Investment) in Chow, *The Legal System of People's Republic of China in a Nutshell* (3d ed. 2015).

Based on the readings so far, consider the following:

PROBLEM 6-13

The whole process of negotiating the joint venture contract, articles of association and related documents, and obtaining the needed approvals and business license usually takes between 18 months and 2 years. Negotiating the joint venture documents will require the significant expenditure of senior management time in travel and meetings and other significant costs in the form of legal fees as law firms are often engaged to draft the legal documents and assist in the negotiations. MNEs are, of course, reluctant to invest such significant resources in this whole process if the application is eventually rejected by the approval authorities. How can an MNE address these concerns? What role can the local partner play?

B.   CAPITAL INVESTMENT

A basic issue for the foreign investor is deciding on the amount of capital to invest in the joint venture and the related issue of management structure as management control is usually determined by the ratio of capital investment of the parties. Under PRC laws, the initial capital investment in the joint venture is called its "registered capital." The concept of registered capital refers to the amount of capital needed (sometimes referred to as "basic construction funds") for the start-up costs of the company to become operational and is used mainly to meet the physical needs of the joint venture. It is referred to as "registered" capital because the initial amount of the capital contributed is recorded or registered with PRC authorities and cannot be reduced without official authorization. What are some of these basic start-up costs? Every business venture in China must start out with certain basic physical needs such as land, buildings, equipment, and access to utilities. In many cases, existing buildings and equipment must be refurbished or renovated to suit the needs of the joint venture. Other common start-up costs for the joint venture are payments to the MNE in order to license its patents, trademarks, and copyrights. The joint venture will also need to make payments to the local partner to obtain the assignment or license of its intellectual property rights. In most cases, registered capital is invested in fixed assets such as land and buildings, but some of the start-up costs such as required fees for access to electricity are not reflected in the acquisition of a permanent physical asset. Unlike the United States where businesses can be established with minimal start-up costs, PRC approval authorities will usually require a substantial investment of start-up capital as a condition of approval of the joint venture. The amount of registered capital must be approved by PRC approval authorities and is stated in the joint venture contract and articles of association. The amount of registered capital also represents the value of the investor's equity interest or ownership in the joint venture company.

Registered capital cannot take the form of debt but can consist of cash or physical assets. It is common for the foreign investor to contribute cash and for the local partner to contribute assets to satisfy a part or all of its capital requirements. The joint venture can assume debt to provide working capital used to pay for salaries, raw materials, and supplies. The joint venture's registered capital plus the amount of any debt is referred to, under PRC law, as its total investment. PRC laws prescribe specific limits on the debt to equity ratio in all FIEs.

C.   MANAGEMENT STRUCTURE

By law, the management structure of a joint venture consists of a board of directors, the highest authority within the company, a general manager, and one or more deputy general managers. The board of directors is jointly appointed by the foreign investor and the local partner as prescribed by law. The board appoints the general manager who runs the day-to-day affairs of the joint venture.

PROBLEM 6-14

Company B, an MNE with its headquarters in the United States, wishes to establish an 80 percent equity ownership interest in a PRC joint venture with Company A, a state-owned enterprise. The joint venture will have a total investment of $40 million, $10 million of which is debt used to finance working capital.

(1) How much registered capital must B contribute? See Equity Joint Venture Law Implementing Regulations (EJVLIR), Arts. 17 and 18 below.

(2) How much registered capital must the local partner contribute?

(3) How many members of a five-member board can B appoint? See EJVLIR, Art. 31 below.

(4) What percentage of profits or dividends from the joint venture must be paid to A? See Equity Joint Venture Law (EJVL), Art. 4 below.

(5) After the equity contributions are made, what legal document serves as the evidence of ownership by each of the joint venture partners? See the Joint Venture Contract (JV Contract) below, Article 6.9.

PROBLEM 6-15

A fundamental issue for a U.S. corporation in any joint venture in China, Brazil, or any other country in the world concerns ownership and management control. In considering the ownership ratio of the joint venture between A and B, B considered three options: 51/49, 60/40, and 80/20. Assume that the local partner A has enough capital to contribute its share under each of these options so that the total amount of registered capital of the joint venture under each of these options remains the same and will be sufficient to meet start-up costs but that each party's contribution will be more or less in accordance with the option chosen. Under each of these options, B will be a majority owner and will be entitled to appoint a majority of the board of directors of the joint venture. As the board is the highest authority within the joint venture, control of the board is, in theory, equivalent to control of the joint venture. One of B's priorities is management control of the joint venture.

(1) Why should B consider any ownership ratio other than the 51/49 option, which would give B majority control without the requirement of investing additional capital of its own? In answering this question, consider the following: Although B has control of the board and, in theory, can vote down any dissent by A under any of these options, board resolutions as a practical matter are invariably passed unanimously in joint venture companies operating in China (as well as in corporations everywhere). Why? In light of this practical reality, which of these options would you advise B to choose?

(2) The local partner A argues that if B controls the board then A should be allowed to appoint the general manager. A argues that this will save B in costs as well, as A will appoint one of its own employees. As the general manager is under the authority of the board, this should not compromise the control by B. Should B agree? In answering this question, consider the role of the board and the general manager described in Articles 12 and 13 of the JV Contract below and in Articles 30–39 of the EJVLIR. The board of directors is required to meet once a year under law and most boards in China meet no more than twice a year. What does this suggest on how much authority the board must delegate to the general manager?

PROBLEM 6-16

One of the most important issues for a joint venture, not just in China but anywhere in the world, has to do with how intellectual property rights are treated. As the joint venture is a new and distinct legal entity in China that is formed by Acme (the foreign investor) and its local partner, the joint venture at its inception owns no intellectual property rights at all. Rather Acme, the MNE, owns its trademarks and Seagull, the local partner, is the owner of its trademarks. As the new joint venture company will manufacture detergents and sell them in China using the trademarks of both Acme and Seagull, the joint venture must somehow acquire the rights to do so.

(1) How are these rights to use these trademarks acquired by the joint venture and who owns the trademarks in China? In answering this question, distinguish between the treatment of the trademarks owned by Seagull and Acme under Articles 10.1(a) and 10.1(b) of the JV contract, respectively. What bedrock principle concerning its intellectual property rights must Acme follow in dealing with the joint venture in China or anywhere in the world? We saw this same basic principle applied to the distribution agreement (Article 4.1 at pp. 292-295), the patent license agreement (Article 3 at p. 325), and the franchise agreement (Article 9 at p. 340).

(2) Note that Acme should insist that the Seagull trademarks are to be treated differently under Article 10.1(a) of the JV contract. The joint venture will manufacture and sell products under both the Acme trademark and the Seagull brands. Acme brands will be premium products designed for the high-end market, whereas Seagull brands will be economy brands offered at a lower price. Seagull, the local partner, will no longer manufacture any brands using the Seagull trademarks. The reason why Article 10.1(a) is so important is because without such a clause Seagull may be able to continue to produce some laundry detergent products or related products such as household cleansers and soaps using the Seagull trademarks. Under this scenario, the joint venture manufactures detergent sold under Acme's trademarks while Seagull continues to manufacture and sell detergent and related products under its own brands. Note that the local partner is given access to the advanced technology of the foreign investor used in the manufacture of detergent. This situation creates significant risks for the foreign investor and may also jeopardize the continuing working relationship between the parties. What are these risks and how does Article 10.1(a) address them? Does it make sense for the joint venture to buy all of Seagull's trademarks even if the joint venture never intends to use them?

(3) Why are these intellectual property issues with local partners also commonly found by MNEs in other developing countries? Are these issues also likely to exist to the same extent with a joint venture partner in a developed country?

PROBLEM 6-17

The local partner's capital contribution to the joint venture is also a common issue in joint ventures in developing countries. The problem arises because the local partner is often short on cash. For example, one of the basic issues that the parties must resolve relates to basic physical requirements: a site for the joint venture, buildings, equipment, and utilities. Although all land in China is owned by the state, business entities and individuals are allowed to acquire and transfer land use rights. Access to utilities must be authorized by state authorities in exchange for payments of fees.

(1) A is eager to locate the joint venture on a plot of land within its grounds used for its own operations. Why? See JV Contract, Art. 6.2; EJVLIR, Art. 22.

(2) How will the joint venture be supplied with electricity, water, steam, and other utilities? See JV Contract, Art. 9.

(3) Why would B agree to this arrangement for land and utilities?

(4) The arrangement proposed by the local partner A is popular in China although it involves locating the joint venture on a plot surrounded by other lands owned by A and accessible only by crossing roads owned by A. This arrangement also makes the joint venture dependent on the local partner for utilities. Do you see any long-term problems with this arrangement for B?

PROBLEM 6-18

After several years, Acme, the foreign investor in the joint venture governed by the JV Contract below, decides to expand into the manufacture and sale of shampoo and body soaps in China. Acme will need to inject additional capital into the existing joint venture to expand the present plant and to add new production lines.

(1) Can Acme expand its product lines using the existing joint venture? See JV Contract, Art. 5.2 below.

(2) If Acme uses the existing joint venture to manufacture shampoo and soap, what might be the consequences?

(3) Advise Acme on what procedures it should undertake internally and with PRC authorities to accomplish these goals. For internal procedures, see JV Contract, Art. 12.3, and EJVLIR, Art. 33. For steps that Acme must take with PRC authorities, see EJVL, Art. 3, and EJVLIR, Art. 21.

PRC Equity Joint Venture Law (2001)

ARTICLE 2

The Chinese government shall, according to the law, protect the investment of foreign parties, the profits due them and their other lawful rights and interests in an equity joint venture, pursuant to the agreements, contracts and articles of association approved by the Chinese government.

All activities of an equity joint venture shall comply with the provisions of the laws, decrees, and pertinent regulations of the People's Republic of China.

The State shall not nationalize or expropriate any equity joint venture. Under special circumstances, when public interests require, equity joint ventures may be expropriated by following legal procedures and appropriate compensation shall be made.

ARTICLE 3

The equity joint venture agreement, contract and articles of association concluded by the parties to the venture shall be submitted to the state's competent department for foreign economic relations and trade. When approved, the equity joint venture shall register with the state's competent department in charge of industry and commerce, and acquire a business license and start operations.

ARTICLE 4

An equity joint venture shall take the form of a limited liability company. The parties to the venture shall share the profits, risks, and losses in proportion to their contributions to the registered capital.

Equity Joint Venture Law Implementing Regulations
(2001, revised 2011, 2014)

ARTICLE 1

These regulations are formulated with a view to facilitating the implementation of the People's Republic of China, Sino-Foreign Equity Joint Venture Law (hereinafter, "Equity Joint Venture Law").

ARTICLE 2

Any Sino-Foreign equity joint venture enterprise (hereinafter, "EJV") established in China, subject to approval in accordance with the Equity Joint Venture Law is a Chinese legal person, and shall be governed and protected by Chinese laws.

ARTICLE 5

Within the scope specified by Chinese laws and regulations and the agreements, contracts, and articles of association of an EJV, the EJV is entitled to operate and manage the enterprise on its own. All relevant authorities shall provide support and assistance therein.

ARTICLE 17

The total investment of an EJV (including its loans) refers to the sum total of the funds for fundamental construction and working capital for production to be invested as required by the production scale specified in the contract and articles of association of the EJV.

ARTICLE 18

The registered capital of an EJV refers to the total capital registered with the relevant registration and administration authority for the purpose of establishing the EJV, and shall be the aggregate amount of contribution paid up by each party thereto.

ARTICLE 21

Any increase or decrease of the registered capital of an EJV shall be approved by the board meeting and submitted to the relevant Examination and Approval Authority for approval and be subject to going through the formalities for change of registration with the relevant Registration Administration Authority.

ARTICLE 22

A party to an EJV may make capital contribution in the form of currency, or alternatively may make capital contribution with valuated and priced buildings, factory buildings, machinery and equipment or other supplies, industrial property rights, know-how, or rights to use the premises (land use rights).

ARTICLE 30

A board of directors is the top governing body of the EJV, and makes all decisions on all major issues of the EJV.

ARTICLE 31

The number of board members shall be at least three. The distribution of the quota of directors shall be determined by the parties to an EJV through consultation and by reference to the ratio of their capital contribution.

ARTICLE 33

The resolutions on the following matters shall be subject to unanimous adoption by the directors who attend the board meeting:

(1) Amendment of the articles of association of the EJV;
(2) Suspension or dissolution of the EJV;
(3) Increase or decrease of the registered capital of the EJV; and
(4) Merger or division of the EJV.

The resolution on other matters may be made in accordance with the rules of procedure set forth in the articles of association of the EJV.

ARTICLE 35

An EJV has an operation and management body to be responsible for the daily operation and management of the enterprise. The operation and management body has one general manager and a certain number of deputy general managers. The deputy general managers shall assist the general manager in his/her work.

ARTICLE 36

The general manager executes the various resolutions of the board meetings, and organizes and leads the daily operation and management of the EJV. Within the scope of authority granted by the board, the general manager externally represents the EJV and internally appoints and dismisses the personnel under his/her management as well as exercises other authorities granted by the board.

ARTICLE 37

The general manager and deputy general manager shall be appointed by the board of the EJV.

Joint Venture Contract Between Beijing Seagull Detergent Group Corp. and Acme (China), Ltd.

This Joint Venture Contract ("Contract") is made on this day of December 10, 2009 between Beijing Seagull Detergent Group Corp. ("Party A"), a limited liability company established and existing under the laws of the People's Republic of China (PRC or "China"), and Acme (China), Ltd., a wholly foreign-owned investment company incorporated and existing under the laws of the PRC ("Party B").

ARTICLE 1 GENERAL PROVISIONS

1.1 PRELIMINARY STATEMENT

Party A is a limited liability company producing laundry detergents and other cleansing products in its factory in Beijing, China. Party B, a WFOE incorporated and existing under the laws of the PRC, is a wholly-owned subsidiary of Acme-Henderson, Ltd., which is a company incorporated and existing under the laws of Hong Kong, and also is an affiliated corporation of the Acme Company, an internationally well-known producer of detergents and other products ("Acme"). Henderson is a diversified Hong Kong company with interests in real estate, hotels, and telecommunications. The Parties wish to establish a joint venture company for the production of detergents and other cleansing products which will utilize Acme's advanced technology and the well recognized trademarks pertaining to detergents of both Parties, and the facilities, plant, equipment, assets and business to be contributed by Party A and Party B.

Therefore, after friendly consultations conducted in accordance with the principles of equality and mutual benefit, Party A and Party B have agreed to establish an equity joint venture enterprise for the production of detergents and other cleansing products in accordance with the Law of the People's Republic of China on Joint Ventures Using Chinese and Foreign Investment (the "Joint Venture Law"), the implementing regulations issued thereunder (the "Joint Venture Regulations"), other relevant laws and regulations of China, and the provisions of this Contract.

ARTICLE 2 PARTIES TO THE CONTRACT

2.1 PARTIES

The parties to the Contract are as follows:

1. Beijing Seagull Detergent Group Corp. (Party A), a limited liability company, established and existing under the laws of the PRC, registered with the Beijing

Municipal Administration of Industry and Commerce, Beijing, PRC (Business License No. 13638555-2-1) and with its legal address at Meng Jia Gou, Beijing, China.

The Legal Representative Person of Party A is:

Name: Yu Heyi
Position: General Manager
Nationality: People's Republic of China

2.   Acme (China), Ltd. (Party B), a company incorporated and existing under the laws of China, with its registered office at 15/F Yuehai Building, No 472, Huanshi East Road, Guangzhou, China (Business License No. 221).

The Legal Representative Person of Party B is:

Name: Dennis Smith
Position: Chairman
Nationality: United States

Party A and Party B are collectively referred to herein as the "Parties," and individually as a "Party."

ARTICLE 4 ESTABLISHMENT OF THE JOINT VENTURE COMPANY

4.1 ESTABLISHMENT OF THE JOINT VENTURE COMPANY

In accordance with the Joint Venture Law and relevant Chinese laws and regulations, the Parties hereby agree to establish the Company pursuant to the terms of this Contract.

4.2 NAME AND ADDRESS OF THE COMPANY

(a) The name of the Company shall be _____ in Chinese and Acme Seagull (Beijing), Ltd., in English. In the event that Party B ceases to own more than 50 percent of the registered capital of the Company, the Parties shall, unless ACME specifically agrees otherwise in writing, ensure that the name of the Company is changed to delete the words "Acme" in English and _____ in Chinese.

(b) The legal address of the Company shall be Meng Jia Guo, Beijing, China.

4.3 LIMITED LIABILITY COMPANY

The Company shall be a limited liability company. The liability of each Party to the Company shall be limited to the amount of its respective subscribed capital contributions required to be made pursuant to this Contract and neither Party shall have any liability to the Company in excess of such amount. Neither Party shall have any liability to any third party jointly or severally in respect of the debts or obligations of the Company. The Parties shall share the profits and bear risks and losses in accordance with the ratio of their respective capital contributions as set forth in Article 6.2.

4.4 LEGAL PERSON

The Company shall be a legal person under the laws of China.

ARTICLE 5 THE PURPOSE, SCOPE AND SCALE OF PRODUCTION AND BUSINESS

5.1 PURPOSE OF THE COMPANY

The purpose of the Parties to this Contract, in accordance with their desire to strengthen economic cooperation and technical exchange, and to adopt advanced and appropriate technology and scientific management methods, is:

(a) to utilize both Parties' advanced technology and the well recognized Trademarks of both Parties to produce and sell laundry detergent and other cleansing products as well as to produce related raw materials and packaging materials;

(b) to apply Acme's advanced technology and management expertise to upgrade existing Chinese manufacturing entities;

(c) to develop, manufacture and market high quality consumer products to meet the growing demands of consumers inside and outside China;

(d) to further improve living standards and spur faster development of China's consumer industry, so as to enable the Parties to achieve satisfactory economic benefits.

5.2 SCOPE OF BUSINESS OF THE COMPANY

The scope of business of the Company is:

(a) to produce and sell laundry detergents and other cleansing products used for laundry (collectively, the "JV Products"); and

(b) to produce related raw materials and packaging materials.

5.3 ESTIMATED SCALE OF PRODUCTION

The total productive capacity of the Plant with intended modifications should be _____ metric tons of JV Products in ten years.

The Parties agree that the Board of Directors will regularly review the operations and economic performance of the Company.

ARTICLE 6 TOTAL AMOUNT OF INVESTMENT AND REGISTERED CAPITAL

6.1 TOTAL INVESTMENT

The total amount of investment of the Company shall be US$ _____ (_____ Million United States Dollars).

6.2 REGISTERED CAPITAL

The total amount of the registered capital of the Company shall be US$ _____ (_____ Million United States Dollars).

Party A's contribution to the Company shall be the equivalent of US$ _____ (_____ Million United States Dollars) in the form of facilities, buildings and equipment, as set forth on Schedule 1, which is _____ % of the total registered capital of the Company.

Party B's contribution to the Company shall be US$ _____ (_____ Million United States Dollars) or the equivalent in RMB in the form of cash, which shall be % of the total registered capital.

6.3 USE OF REGISTERED CAPITAL

The cash contribution of Party B shall be used in part by the Company to obtain the ownership of Party A's Trademarks as set out in Article 10.1, and land use rights, to buy equipment and to renovate the Company's equipment and production facilities.

6.5 ADDITIONAL FINANCING

(a) In addition to the registered capital, the Company may borrow any necessary funds from domestic or international banks or other financial institutions on terms and conditions approved by the Board of Directors.

(b) In the event that pursuant to Article 6.6 below, the Board of Directors approves an increase in the registered capital of the Company and the Approval Authority grants its approval to such increase, but either Party is unable to contribute its pro-rata share, the other Party may contribute its and the aforesaid Party's pro-rata share (or a portion thereof), resulting in an increase of the contributing Party's share of the registered capital of the Company.

6.6 INCREASE OF REGISTERED CAPITAL

During the term of the Company, any increase in the registered capital of the Company shall require the unanimous approval of the Board of Directors and the approval of the Approval Authority.

6.7 TRANSFER OF REGISTERED CAPITAL

(a) Subject to the provisions of paragraphs (b) and (c) below, either Party may assign all or part of its registered capital contribution to the Company to any third party, provided it first obtains the unanimous approval of the Board of Directors and the approval of the Approval Authority.

(b) When a Party (the "Disposing Party") wishes to assign, sell or otherwise dispose of all or part of its registered capital contribution to a third party (a "Transfer"), it shall notify the other Party (the "Non-Disposing Party") in writing of its wish to make the Transfer, the capital contribution it wishes to transfer, the terms and conditions of the Transfer and the identity of the proposed transferee (the "Notice"). The Non-Disposing Party shall have a preemptive right to purchase the whole of such capital contribution on terms and conditions no less favorable than those specified in the Notice.

Notwithstanding the provisions of this Article 6.7 and subject to requisite Chinese government approvals, Party B may transfer all of its interest in the Company to another Acme Affiliate or Henderson Affiliate, and Party A hereby agrees to such transfer. Such transfer may be made in either case only if the nature of the Company will not be affected by the transfer. In the event of such a transfer as contemplated herein, Party B's trans-feree shall undertake all of the responsibilities and obligations of Party B hereunder.

6.8 ENCUMBRANCE OF REGISTERED CAPITAL

No Party shall mortgage or otherwise encumber all or any part of its contribution to the registered capital of the Company without the prior written consent of the other Party hereto.

6.9 INVESTMENT CERTIFICATES

After the Parties have made their capital contributions, the Joint Venture Company shall engage an accountant registered in China to verify the contributions. Upon the issuance of a verification report by such an accountant, the Joint Venture Company shall issue an investment certificate to each of the Parties as required by the Joint Venture Law.

ARTICLE 7 RESPONSIBILITIES OF THE PARTIES

7.1 RESPONSIBILITIES OF PARTY A

In addition to its other responsibilities under this Contract, Party A shall:

(a) be responsible for handling all matters relating to the establishment of the Company, including the submission of applications for approval of this Contract to the Approval Authority and any other governmental authority whose approval is required, registration of the Company and issuance of a business license, and assist in the opening of Renminbi and foreign exchange bank accounts;

(b) assist the Company, if requested to do so, in the submission of applications for, and the grant of, all necessary approvals, permits, certificates and licenses required in connection with safety, environmental matters, and other matters regulated by governmental authorities; enter into the Land Use Transfer Agreement pursuant to article 9.1(a); and handle all other necessary procedures in relation thereto to ensure that the Company has the right to use the Site in conformity with the scope of its operations for 50 years;

(c) assist the Company in contracting for and obtaining the electricity, water, and other necessary utilities required by the Company and conforming to the specifications and conditions set forth in the Feasibility Study on a continuous uninterrupted basis and in quantities sufficient to meet the full operational requirements of the Company;

(d) assist directors and foreign personnel of Party B and the Company to obtain all necessary entry visas, travel documents, and work permits;

(e) assist the Company with the smooth transfer of employees from Party A that are recruited by the Company, with handing over employee files, and with other employment-related matters and with the recruitment of other qualified Chinese management personnel, technical personnel, workers, and other needed personnel;

(f) assist the Company and Party B in applying for, and use its best efforts to assist the Company and Party B to obtain tax reductions and exemptions and any other investment incentives available to the Company and Party B, and assist the Company to liaise with the relevant tax authorities in order to assist the Company to obtain tax reductions or exemptions and access to cost effective raw material;

(g) generally assist the Company in its relations with local government authorities and Chinese domestic companies, including the customers of Party A;

(h) assist the Company to buy raw materials, and in sourcing, purchasing, or leasing local equipment, means of transportation, articles for office use, and communication facilities;

(i) assist the Company in processing import customs declarations for the machinery, equipment, vehicles, and telecommunications systems purchased within the amount of the Company's total capital and in going through customs declaration procedures for the importation into China of such other machinery, equipment, materials, supplies, and raw materials as are required by the Company (including applying for and procuring any approval documents for the import of the same) as well as assisting in arranging for the inland transportation of the same to the Company's Site;

(j) assist the Company in obtaining Renminbi and foreign exchange loans from financial institutions in China;

(k) assist the Company in qualifying for the status of "Technologically Advanced Enterprise," to ensure that the Company is charged the most favorable rates for land use and for utilities;

(l) be responsible for any damage to the environment prior to the date the Joint Venture begins operations and to indemnify the Company and Party B for any such damages in respect to environmental pollution, worker injuries and other related hazards; and

(m) handle other matters entrusted to it by the Company.

7.2 RESPONSIBILITIES OF PARTY B

In addition to its other responsibilities under this Contract, Party B shall:

(a) assist the Company, if requested, to procure from abroad equipment, supplies, and raw materials which are not otherwise available within China or which the Company considers should be imported;

(b) assist the Company as requested to recruit appropriate management and senior technical personnel and assist the Company in the provision of training for employees of the Company;

(c) procure that Acme, or its subsidiaries or other Affiliates, enters into (i) an agreement to license the use of the Trademarks to the Company in the form of Annex E2 hereto and (ii) an agreement to provide management and technical assistance to the Company in the form of Annex D hereto;

(d) provide technical assistance to the extent possible to upgrade the manufacturing process of Party A's own brand products manufactured in its existing factory;

(e) assist the Company to become familiar with international market conditions;

(f) assist the Company in obtaining foreign exchange loans from financial institutions outside China;

(g) provide technical assistance to the Company in relation to packaging and product quality of JV Products; and

(h) handle other matters entrusted to it by the Company.

ARTICLE 8 PURCHASE OF MATERIALS AND SUPPLIES

8.1 LOCALLY SOURCED MATERIALS

Party A shall ensure that all raw materials required by the Company are available through the existing channels of supply currently utilized by Party A for its detergent factory. The purchase of all such items from Chinese suppliers shall be paid for in RMB and, to the extent possible, at the equivalent price levels to those enjoyed by state-owned enterprises. Attached to this Contract as Schedule 2 is a list of raw materials required by the Company that are available locally in Beijing and their current stated prices in RMB.

8.2 IMPORTED MATERIALS

To the extent that the Company's specifications with respect to quality, quantity, price, and delivery terms and dates cannot be met from sources within China, the Company may procure such materials and supplies from abroad. For items purchased from abroad, the Company shall give preference to procurement from Party B or its Affiliates and suppliers recommended by Party B or its Affiliates if the quality, quantity, price and delivery terms are competitive.

ARTICLE 9 RIGHT TO USE SITE; UTILITIES

9.1 RIGHT TO USE THE SITE

(a) Party A shall enter into a Land Use Transfer Agreement substantially in the form attached hereto as Annex B which shall be valid for the Joint Venture Term, and grant to the Company the exclusive right to use the Site, as more particularly set forth on the Site Map attached as Annex C (inclusive of all necessary and sufficient easements over adjacent property to the nearest public roads to enable the Company fully and freely to access the Site and to conduct thereon the activities contemplated by this Contract, irrespective of whether or not such easements presently vest in the Site). The actual boundaries of the Site will be verified by an independent certified surveyor chosen by Party B. The Land Use Transfer Agreement shall guarantee that the Company shall have the exclusive right to use the Site for fifty years from the Establishment Date. The Land Use Transfer Agreement should be recorded with the Land Management Bureau. In the event of a dispute between the Parties on this issue either Party may submit the question to arbitration before the China International Economic Trade Arbitration Commission for resolution.

(b) The total fee payable by the Company to Party A for the exclusive right to use the Site shall be RMB _____ which amount shall be payable in one lump sum during _____.

(c) Party A warrants that the Site to be provided to the Company by Party A shall be as set forth in the Site Map attached as Annex C.

9.2 UTILITIES

Party A shall supply to the Company all water, electricity and steam required by the Company at the favorable prices and on the favorable terms and conditions to be agreed by the Parties. Payment for all such services shall be made in RMB. Attached to this Contract as Schedule 3 is a list of the utility services to be supplied by Party A and their current prices in RMB. The Parties shall ensure that the Company supplies to Party A all sewerage services and waste water treatment services required by Party A on terms to be agreed by the Parties.

ARTICLE 10 TRADEMARK ASSIGNMENT AND LICENSE; TECHNICAL ASSISTANCE

10.1 TRADEMARK ASSIGNMENT AND LICENSE

(a) Party A covenants that within _____ days after the Establishment Date, the Seagull Trademark Assignment Agreement shall be signed between the Company and Party A so as to ensure that the Company obtains the ownership and the exclusive right to use the Seagull Trademarks needed for marketing and sale of the JV Products. The Company shall pay to Party A a one time lump sum payment of RMB 45,000,000 (Forty-Five Million RMB) within ninety (90) days after the assignment of Seagull trademarks to the Company. In consideration of the payment referred to above, Party A agrees not to produce nor permit any other party to produce any laundry detergent products to compete with the Company.

(b) The Parties agree that within thirty (30) days after the Establishment Date, the ACME Trademark License Agreement shall be signed between the Company and ACME or its relevant Affiliate so as to ensure that the Company obtains the right to use the Trademarks needed for marketing and sale of the JV Products.

10.2 TECHNICAL ASSISTANCE

The Parties agree that within thirty (30) days after the Establishment Date, the Technical Assistance Agreement (Annex D) shall be signed between the Company and ACME so that the Company will receive management and technical assistance from ACME or its relevant Affiliate, including production techniques, product and equipment design, and training of personnel. Considering the technical assistance provided to the Company by both Parties and the Distribution Agreement (Annex A) between the Company and Acme (China) Ltd., both Parties agree that no technical assistance fee shall be charged to the Company.

ARTICLE 11 SALE OF JV PRODUCTS

11.1 GENERAL PRINCIPLES

In accordance with relevant Chinese regulations, the Company shall have the right to price and sell its products at its own discretion on the domestic market and shall develop other sales-related services.

11.2 DOMESTIC SALES

The Company shall appoint Party B as its exclusive agent to sell and distribute the products of the Company on the Chinese domestic market. Party B shall in addition to selling and distributing the JV Products, market the JV Products and provide ancillary services in relation thereto pursuant to the Distribution Agreement. The price charged to domestic purchasers of the Company's products shall be denominated in RMB. The sales prices of products sold on the domestic market shall be determined by the General Manager.

11.3 EXPORT SALES

JV Products sold by the Company in the export market shall also be handled by Party B. Export price decisions shall be made by the General Manager in the light of market conditions.

ARTICLE 12 BOARD OF DIRECTORS

12.1 ESTABLISHMENT

The Board of Directors of the Company shall be established on the Establishment Date. The first meeting of the Board of Directors shall be held after the Establishment Date.

12.2 COMPOSITION

The Board of Directors of the Company shall consist of _____ directors, as follows:

(a) _____ to be appointed by Party A, one of whom shall be appointed by Party A to be the vice Chairman of the Board for the first term; and

(b) _____ to be appointed by Party B, one of whom shall be appointed by Party B to be the Chairman of the Board for the first term.

The term of office of the Board of Directors shall be four (4) years and directors may serve consecutive terms if reappointed by the appointing party.

The first set of officers of the Company shall be appointed at the first Board of Directors' meeting. Each Party shall have the right, at any time, to remove or replace any director appointed by it by providing prior written notice to the other Party, the Company, and the other Directors.

12.3 AUTHORITY

The Board of Directors shall be the highest authority of the Company and shall decide all major issues of the Company. The following matters shall require the unanimous approval of the Board of Directors:

(a) The amendment of the Articles of Association of the Company;

(b) The termination or dissolution of the Company;

(c) The increase or assignment of the registered capital of the Company;

(d) The merger of the Company with any other economic organization.

Decisions with respect to all other matters shall be adopted if they receive the affirmative votes of a simple majority of the directors present and voting in person or by proxy, or in the case of a resolution in writing, by a simple majority of the directors.

12.4 LEGAL REPRESENTATIVE

The Chairman of the Board shall be the legal representative of the Company but may not bind the Company beyond the scope of the express authorization of the Board of Directors. If the Chairman of the Board is unable to perform his duties for any reason he may authorize the Vice Chairman to perform his duties. If the Vice Chairman is also unable to perform such duties, the Board of Directors shall authorize another director to perform such duties.

12.5 COMPENSATION AND EXPENSES

Directors shall serve the Company without compensation except when a director is also an officer or employee of the Company. Expenses incurred by directors in connection with attending meetings of the Board of Directors shall be deemed to be regular expenditures of the Company.

12.6 MEETINGS

The quorum for all Board of Directors' meetings shall be _____ of the directors present in person or by proxy. Meetings of the Board of Directors shall be held at least once a year to review the operations of the Company. Board meetings shall be convened and presided over by the Chairman of the Board.

12.7 MEETINGS BY TELEPHONE

The Board may, in lieu of meeting in person, conduct any meeting by means of telephone, provided that each Director present at the meeting is able to hear and speak to all other Directors present at all times.

In lieu of a meeting of the Board of Directors, a written resolution may be adopted by the Board of Directors if such resolution is sent to all members of the Board and signed and affirmatively adopted by the number of directors necessary to make such a decision as stipulated in Article 12.3 hereof.

12.8 FURTHER POWERS AND PROCEDURES

The detailed powers and procedures of the Board of Directors shall be as set forth in the Articles of Association.

ARTICLE 13 BUSINESS MANAGEMENT

13.1 BUSINESS MANAGEMENT

The day-to-day operation and management of the Company shall be under the direction of the General Manager of the Company, who shall be assisted by two (2) Deputy General Managers and such other officers as may be appointed by the Board of Directors as necessary. On important issues, the General Manager shall consult with the Deputy General Managers. The General Manager shall have the right to decide all such issues.

13.2 APPOINTMENT OF GENERAL MANAGER, THE DEPUTY
GENERAL MANAGERS AND OTHER OFFICERS

The General Manager shall be nominated by Party _____ and shall be appointed by the Board. Party A and Party B each shall nominate one Deputy General Manager and the Deputy General Managers shall be appointed by the Board. As requested by the General Manager, the Board shall appoint other senior officers to assist the General Manager in the performance of his duties. Any such senior officer shall report to and be under the direction of the General Manager.

13.3 TERM OF OFFICE

The General Manager and the Deputy General Managers shall, unless they become incapacitated, retire or are removed from office earlier by the Board of Directors, hold office for a term of four years each and are eligible for reappointment for further terms.

13.4 RESPONSIBILITIES OF GENERAL MANAGER AND
THE DEPUTY GENERAL MANAGERS

The General Manager shall have overall responsibility for the management and operations of the Company. The principal responsibilities of the General Manager shall be (a) to exercise his best efforts to achieve the business objectives of the Company set forth in the Feasibility Study; (b) to carry out the various decisions of the Board; and (c) to organize and manage the daily business of the Company. The responsibility of the Deputy General Managers shall be to assist the General Manager to carry out various decisions of the Board and to organize and manage the daily business of the Company as instructed by the General Manager. The powers and duties of the General Manager are set forth in the Articles of Association.

ARTICLE 14 PERSONNEL AND LABOR MANAGEMENT

14.1 PERSONNEL

(a) All matters relating to the selection, appointment, retirement, dismissal, wages, benefits, labor insurance, labor protection, labor discipline of the Company's employees, and so on shall be handled in accordance with the Regulations of the People's Republic of China on Labor Management in Chinese-Foreign Joint Ventures. The Company shall in principle have the right to recruit and dismiss its own employees freely in accordance with applicable Chinese laws and regulations. In the initial period, the Company shall give priority to employing current employees of Party A, provided that the Company will employ only those employees of Party A who have suitable qualifications determined pursuant to examination by the Company. Such employees shall be placed on a six (6) month probation period at the end of which the Company will, in its sole discretion, decide whether to offer the employee permanent employment. Any such employee who is not offered permanent employment with the Company will be the responsibility of Party A and shall be treated as those not employed by the Company pursuant to sub-paragraph (b) below.

(b) Party A shall be solely responsible for wages, salaries, benefits, pensions, termination payments, and any other remuneration of any Party A employees who are not employed by the Company, provided, however that the Company shall pay Party A a one-time payment of RMB 50,000 for any Party A employee who is not employed by the Company except as set forth below. Any such payment by the Company to Party A may only be used for the purposes described in the Redundancy Payment Policy.

(c) In the event that the Company does not offer permanent employment to a Party A employee offered probationary employment (the "Probationary Employee") pursuant to paragraph (a), the Company shall decide whether or not to offer probationary employment to another employee of Party A. If the Company does offer probationary employment to another employee of Party A, the Company shall not be required to make any payment in respect of the Probationary Employee. If the Company does not offer probationary employment to an employee of Party A in place of the Probationary Employee, the Company shall make a one-time payment of RMB 50,000 in respect of such Probationary Employee, and shall not be required to make any further offer of employment to an employee of Party A in the place of such Probationary Employee. Notwithstanding the above, the Company shall not be required to make any such payment in respect of an employee, or to accept another employee of Party A in place of an employee, who resigns voluntarily from the Company or is dismissed for disciplinary reasons.

(d) It is currently contemplated by the Parties, as set forth in the Feasibility Study, that the complement of salaried employees from Party A will not be less than _____ workers.

14.3 LABOR CONTRACTS

The Company shall enter into individual labor contracts between the Company and individual employees in the form agreed by the Parties. All local employees shall be paid in RMB. The Company shall only employ those who pass the physical examination based on the relevant Chinese regulations and Acme standards.

14.5 CONTRIBUTING FUNDS

The Company shall pay an amount equal to:

(a) two (2%) percent of the actual wages received by local Chinese employees of the Company into the Company's trade union fund for such trade union's use in accordance with the applicable laws of China on the management of trade union funds; and

(b) the percentage of the actual wages received by local Chinese employees of the Company required by applicable law to be paid into the insurance, welfare, pension, housing, and other statutory funds for the benefit of the employees and any other employee allowance required by applicable law.

The General Manager shall approve the disbursement of amounts from the funds referred to in Article 15.1, paragraph (b).

ARTICLE 15 FINANCIAL AFFAIRS AND ACCOUNTING

15.1 ACCOUNTING SYSTEM

(a) The chief financial officer of the Company, under the supervision of the General Manager, shall be responsible for the financial management of the Company.

(b) The standard bookkeeping currency of the Company shall be Renminbi. The accounting system and procedures to be adopted by the Company shall be drafted in accordance with the Accounting System of the People's Republic of China for Foreign Investment Enterprises and other relevant rules and regulations ("Accounting System"). The internationally used debit and credit method, as well as the accrual basis of accounting, shall be adopted as the methods and principles for keeping accounts.

15.2 AUDIT

(a) An independent auditor (the "Independent Auditor") registered in China who is capable of performing accounting work meeting both Chinese domestic accounting standards and international standards shall be engaged by the Company, as its auditor, to examine and verify the Annual Accounts, and submit its report to the Board of Directors and the General Manager. The Company shall submit to the Parties and to each director the audited Annual Accounts within 60 days after the end of the fiscal year, together with the audit report of the Independent Auditor.

15.6 DIVIDENDS DECLARATION

Considering the cash flow and financial position at the end of each fiscal year, the Board of Directors shall determine if dividends shall be distributed to the Parties in Renminbi in proportion to their respective shares in the registered capital. If the Board of Directors determines that dividends should be distributed to a Party or the Parties in foreign exchange, the Company shall convert Renminbi into the relevant foreign exchange at the official rate announced by the Bank of China on the date the distribution is made and payment shall be made in foreign exchange. Such dividends shall, unless the Board of Directors decides otherwise, be distributed once a year and the plan of dividends distribution shall be determined by the Board of Directors within sixty (60) days after the receipt of the audited Annual Accounts referred to in paragraph (a) of Article 15.2 above.

ARTICLE 16 TAXATION AND INSURANCE

16.1 INCOME TAX, CUSTOMS DUTIES AND OTHER TAXES
—REQUESTS FOR PREFERENTIAL TREATMENT

(a) The Company shall pay tax in accordance with the relevant laws and regulations of China and local regulations applicable in Beijing Municipality. Chinese and foreign employees shall pay individual income tax in accordance with applicable Chinese law and regulations.

(b) The Parties shall assist the Company to apply for the Company the benefits of all applicable tax exemptions, reductions, privileges, and preferences which are available.

16.2 INSURANCE

(a) Insurance will, as required by applicable Chinese law, be obtained in China and such policies will be denominated in RMB and/or foreign currencies, as appropriate.

(b) The Company shall maintain third party liability insurance and other relevant insurance coverage in order to protect the Company, its employees, agents, and other appropriate parties from claims.

ARTICLE 18 FAIR DEALING

18.2 NON-COMPETITION

Each Party agrees that it will not enter into any joint venture, contract manufacturing agreement, or other production arrangement (each, a "Transaction") in the Area of Beijing with any of the competitors of Party A or Party B or with any other company whose business is connected with the competitors unless such Party has first given a notice in writing (the "Notice") to the other Party setting forth the name, address, and ownership information of the third Party, (b) summarizing the terms on which the Party proposes to enter into the Transaction, and (c) offering the other Party the preferential right to participate in the Transaction on terms no less favorable than those offered to the third Party. If the other Party fails to commence good faith negotiations with such Party to enter into the Transaction within three (3) months after receiving the Notice, such Party may enter into the Transaction with the third Party on the terms set forth in the Notice no later than one year after the date of the Notice.

ARTICLE 19 JOINT VENTURE TERM

19.1 EFFECTIVE DATE

This Contract and its Annexes shall be submitted to the Approval Authority for approval and shall come into force on the day on which the Approval Authority issues its certificate of approval, provided that, in the event that this Contract is not approved within four (4) months of the date set forth on the first page of this Contract, both Parties will take the necessary steps to effectuate the termination of this Contract.

19.2 JOINT VENTURE TERM

The term of the Company (the "Joint Venture Term") shall be 50 years from the Establishment Date.

19.3 EXTENSION OF JOINT VENTURE TERM

At least two (2) years prior to the expiration of the Joint Venture Term, the Parties shall hold consultations to discuss the extension of the Joint Venture Term. If both Parties agree to extend the Joint Venture Term, an application for such extension shall be submitted to the Approval Authority for approval not less than six (6) months prior to the expiration of the Joint Venture Term.

ARTICLE 20 TERMINATION; DISPOSAL OF ASSETS ON DISSOLUTION

20.1 TERMINATION OR DISSOLUTION

The Company shall be dissolved and the Contract terminated in accordance with the Joint Venture Law, the Joint Venture Regulations and the Articles of Association of the Company (i) upon expiration of the Joint Venture Term (if not extended) or any extension thereof, or (ii) if any of the conditions or events set forth below shall occur and be continuing, in which case the Parties shall cause their representatives on the Board of Directors, upon written notice by any Party, to unanimously adopt a resolution to dissolve the Company:

(a) The Company sustains significant losses in three (3) consecutive years and, after consultations, the Parties are unable to agree on a method to improve the economic situation of the Company to the extent satisfactory to both Parties;

(b) The Company is unable to continue operations for six (6) months or more because of an Event of Force Majeure;

(c) The Seagull Trademark Exclusive Licensing Agreement, the Acme Trademark License Agreement or Technical Assistance Agreement, or the Foreign Exchange Services Agreement are not entered into within six (6) months after the Establishment Date or are terminated early;

(d) The Company is unable to continue operations because of the failure of any Party to perform its obligations under the Contract if, in the reasonable opinion of the non-breaching Party, such non-performance defeats the economic objectives of the Contract and of the establishment of the Company or creates a material risk of loss to such non-breaching Party or materially and adversely affects the value of its interest in the Company;

(e) Either Party fails to make its contributions in accordance with the provisions of Article 6 of this Contract, where such failure continues for a period of more than three months and is not waived by the other Party;

(f) A material portion of the assets or property of the Company or the interest of either Party in the Company is subject to expropriation or requisition or the Chinese or other personnel of the Company are subject to reassignment or withdrawal with the effect that the operations of the Company are, in the reasonable opinion of either of the Parties, adversely affected;

(g) Any law or regulation is imposed by the Chinese government which controls the export or sale for foreign exchange of the products of the Company, the effect of which will render the Company unable to carry out its normal operation; or

(h) The Parties mutually agree to dissolve the Company.

After the Board of Directors resolves to dissolve the Company, it shall apply to the Approval Authority for approval of such dissolution.

ARTICLE 23 LAWS APPLICABLE

23.1 APPLICABLE LAW

The formation, validity, interpretation, execution, amendment, settlement of disputes, and termination of this Contract shall be governed by the laws of the PRC. In the event that there is no relevant provision of Chinese law, international practices may be used as a reference.

ARTICLE 24 SETTLEMENT OF DISPUTES

24.1 ARBITRATION

(a) Any dispute arising from, out of or in connection with the Contract shall be settled through friendly consultations between the Parties. Such consultations shall begin immediately after one Party has delivered to the other Party a written request for such consultation. If within 30 days following the date on which such notice is given, the dispute cannot be settled through consultations, the dispute shall be submitted to arbitration in Beijing under the China International Economic Trade and Arbitration Commission ("CIETAC") upon the request of any Party with notice to the other Party.

(b) There shall be three (3) arbitrators. Each Party shall select one arbitrator within thirty (30) days after giving or receiving the demand for arbitration.

(c) The arbitration proceedings shall be conducted in English.

(d) Each Party shall cooperate with the other Party in making full disclosure of and providing complete access to all information and documents requested by the other Party in connection with such proceedings, subject only to any confidentiality obligations binding on such Party.

(e) The arbitral award shall be final and binding upon all Parties. The costs of the arbitration shall be as fixed by the arbitration tribunal.

ARTICLE 25 MISCELLANEOUS

25.4 LANGUAGE

This Agreement is written in English and Chinese and the two versions shall have equal weight and validity. In case of any inconsistency between the English version and Chinese version, the Parties shall enforce the version that is more consistent with their intent as evidenced by the context of the entire agreement. Where there is a discrepancy between the two interpretations, such a question may be submitted for arbitration as provided herein.

25.6 ANNEXES

The Annexes and Schedules attached hereto are hereby made an integral part of this Contract and are equally binding with these Articles 1 to 25. The Annexes and Schedules are as follows:

Annex A   Distribution Agreement
Annex B   Land Use Transfer Agreement
Annex C   Site Map
Annex D   Technical Assistance Agreement
Annex E1   Seagull Trademark Assignment Agreement
Annex E2   Acme Trademark License Agreement
Annex E3   Seagull Trademark Exclusive-Licensing Agreement

Annex F   Redundancy Payment Policy
Annex G   Foreign Exchange Services Agreement
Annex H   Service Agreement
Annex I   Supplemental Service Agreement
Schedule 1 Plant and Equipment to Be Contributed by Party A
Schedule 2 Raw Materials
Schedule 3 Utilities

NOTES AND QUESTIONS

1. In addition to the joint venture contract set forth, the parties must also agree to articles of association for the new company. The JV contract set forth the rights and obligations of the two parties to the venture whereas the articles of association set forth the basic organization of the joint venture itself. Annexes A–H and Schedules 1–3 described in Article 25.6 above give you an idea of the types of ancillary documents that must accompany the joint venture contract. All of these joint venture documents form part of the package that must be submitted to PRC authorities for approval.

2. Review Articles 1 and 2 of the JV contract. Who are the parties to the joint venture? Why did Acme set up the joint venture this way?

3. Local partners will generally attempt to transfer as large a number of its workers to the joint venture as possible. Why? How does the JV contract deal with this issue? See JV Contract, Art. 14.

The number of workers to be transferred from the local partner to the joint venture tends to be one of the most contentious issues in negotiations. This is an issue that is unrelated to the actual operations or business of the joint venture but will consume substantial energies of the foreign investor during the setup process and likely throughout the life of the joint venture. This is an example of peripheral issues in China and other developing countries that are generally not encountered in the United States but which require significant attention in running a business enterprise. In addition to a disagreement over the number of workers from the local partner needed to run the joint venture, there are also many issues relating to conflicts in the workplace caused by the collection of a diverse workforce usually consisting of many nationalities and backgrounds. An expatriate foreign manager from the United States or Hong Kong (still treated equivalent to a foreign nation) may have a salary that is ten times higher than the salary for a local manager who works at the next desk even though both have the same position and responsibility within the company. As China is viewed as a "hardship" assignment, expatriate workers often receive other amenities such as company-provided housing, subsidies for international schools for their children, and company-provided chauffeured automobiles. There are often perceived (as well as real) issues of superiority, arrogance, and condescension among foreign employees, including those from Hong Kong and Taiwan, toward local employees that result in tensions at the workplace. Some practices by MNEs did not help in alleviating these perceptions of superiority. In the 1990s at Procter & Gamble (China), Ltd., for example, P&G's Western executives lived in company-provided housing in Hong Kong and commuted to P&G's China headquarters in nearby Guangzhou (about 100 miles inland) during the week. A typical schedule would have the executive work at P&G's Hong Kong office on Monday, take a flight on Tuesday morning and arrive at P&G's China headquarters by noon, stay in a hotel, and work in the China offices until Thursday at about 3 p.m. when they would fly back to Hong Kong and work at the Hong Kong office on Friday. The policy was based on the view that it was too much of a "hardship" to live in Guangzhou on a full-time basis. As you can imagine, many of P&G's local employees viewed this arrangement as an example of Western condescension and arrogance (not to mention extravagance) as they had to live in the "hardship" environment of China every day of their lives. P&G eliminated this practice of commuting in the late 1990s, but as a cost-cutting measure.

Despite the many efforts of MNEs to combat perceptions of inequality, there is still a widespread perception that there is an unspoken hierarchy on issues of rank and salary with U.S. or European expatriates at the top, followed by overseas Chinese from Hong Kong, Singapore, and Taiwan in the second tier, and followed at the bottom by local PRC employees. There is also often a perceived "glass ceiling" for local workers who feel that they can never obtain a certain level of professional achievement and salary without a degree from a Western university and foreign citizenship. Many local employees in MNEs in China aspire to obtain the salaries, benefits, and perks given to Western expatriate managers but this is usually impossible under company policy as these arrangements are available only as temporary inducements to expatriates to work in China. The theory of many companies is that foreign expatriate managers are to remain in China only for a short period of time in order to train local employees to be their permanent replacements. The local employees would then be paid at local wages, which are high in comparison to other jobs in China, but only a small fraction of the cost of an expatriate manager. However, many companies, such as Procter & Gamble, found that they had to keep foreign expatriate managers in China far longer than expected and some on a permanent rotating basis. As a result, a perception arose of a permanent hierarchy and vast differentials in pay and benefits at the workplace for foreigners and locals. It is often said in China that the "dream" of many local workers is to study abroad, acquire foreign citizenship, and return to China as an expatriate to live among friends and relatives under conditions provided for expatriate managers.

The types of labor issues described above are also pervasive in other developing countries. Why? Why are these issues less likely to exist in a developed country?

4. Although foreign investors entered into joint ventures in great numbers during the first phase of foreign investment in China in the 1980s, many MNEs soon found that there were many conflicts with the local partner. There are many areas of conflict but we focus on two major areas in this note. First, in many cases, the parties had different goals and expectations. (A popular expression in China is "same bed, different dreams.") The foreign investor usually had a long-term horizon and during the initial years of operation often wanted to reinvest its profits into building the business. The local partner, however, often wanted profits to be paid out as soon as possible in the form of dividends as it was under pressure from local supervisory authorities to demonstrate profits and to pay taxes on those profits to local governments. A second major area of contention is that the local partner often saw the joint venture as a means to improve its own operations. The local partner often saw nothing wrong with using technology acquired from the foreign investor used for the joint venture to improve its own operations and upgrade its products. After all, this was one of the reasons why the local partner entered into the joint venture in the first place. If the two companies were in the same business (such as Acme and Seagull in our hypothetical case), the local partner was actually using the foreign investor's technology to make itself into a better competitor with the joint venture. This use of technology would usually incense the foreign investor who saw this as misappropriation of technology and, more important, a breach of trust. Many foreign investors found that managing conflicts with the local partner consumed significant time and resources that could have otherwise been devoted to operating the business. These and other issues have led many foreign investors to seek out the WFOE as an investment vehicle and are

some of the reasons for the increasing popularity of the WFOE in China. This experience in China mirrors that of many MNEs in other developing countries as well.

D.   Foreign Direct Investment in Brazil

We now turn to an examination of FDI in Brazil. A symbol of Brazil's leading role in the region is the recent decision to award the 2016 Summer Olympics to Rio de Janeiro, which will mark the first time that the Olympics will be held in South America. This event will be a watershed in the history of Brazil and South America. Brazil will make the most of this event to develop business and its economy and to advance its standing in the world.

Keep in mind when you review these materials that although there are some aspects of FDI in Brazil that are unique to that country, there are also some larger issues of strategic importance to the foreign investor involving the region as well as some issues that are common among other developing countries, including other countries in South America. What are some of these issues?

First, a foreign investor making an initial foray into FDI in a South American country will not only consider the issue of which country will serve as a good target of FDI in the present but will also ponder the obvious issue of which country can also act as a base for expanding business into other countries in the region. Even the largest MNEs are unlikely, at least initially, to enter two or more countries in South America simultaneously but will choose the country that offers them the best prospect for business success in the present as well as a strategic position for future expansion. Keep in mind whether Brazil can serve these purposes or whether another country will be a better option.

Second, like many other developing countries, Brazil has a long history of a shortage of foreign currency and problems related to its balance of payments obligations, that is, the obligation to repay loans or other monetary obligations using foreign currency. Like many developing countries, Brazil's currency, the real, could not be freely converted into a hard currency such as U.S. dollars until recently. As it had a shortage of hard currency, Brazil had to carefully regulate the exodus of hard currency because its limited stores of hard currency were needed for most types of international monetary obligations and transactions, including the repayment of loans, as few, if any, foreign creditors accepted reals. Note that while countries will regulate the exodus of foreign currency, like many other countries, Brazil allowed foreign investors to repatriate the foreign capital that they had brought into Brazil for the purpose of making a foreign direct investment and also authorized, under certain conditions, the exodus of foreign currency for the purpose of repatriating profits and for other types of payments. Without such an exception for the repatriation of foreign capital brought into countries that restrict the conversion of their currency and an allowance for the repatriation of profits in foreign currency, these countries would be able to attract few foreign investors. How, and under what conditions, capital, profits, and other payments can be repatriated in foreign currency, that is, U.S. dollars, is a fundamental issue for foreign investors in many developing countries.

As we have suggested, obtaining foreign currency is a common problem in developing countries. How common? Until just several years ago, China also had strict currency exchange controls but these have been relaxed as China now boasts the largest foreign currency reserves in the world. Similarly, Argentina subjected foreign currency to strict controls for four decades but lifted the controls in 1989, allowing foreign exchange to be freely sold and transferred in and out of the country. But while some developing countries eliminate their foreign currency controls once they have reached a stage of development where they are no longer burdened by chronic shortages of hard currency, many other developing countries in the world did not find themselves in this fortunate position. Other South American countries, such as Chile, continue to maintain foreign currency controls and, like Brazil, Chile also maintains a registration system under which foreign capital and loans brought into the country must be registered with central banking authorities. Keep in mind that foreign currency issues, which are of fundamental importance for foreign investors in Brazil, are common problems for foreign investors in developing countries and that the management of these issues in Brazil, explored in the problems below, offers lessons for dealing with the same problem in other countries in the world.

1.   Brazil's Approach to FDI

Brazil's approach to FDI differs from the approach that some developing nations have adopted, which is to create a specific legal regime regulating FDI and to designate certain government authorities to screen foreign investment. A useful comparison is that of Brazil with China. As we have seen, China's laws recognize a certain class of business entities called foreign investment enterprises that are specifically designed as vehicles for foreign capital. In addition, PRC law requires that all foreign investment enterprises must be approved by PRC authorities and continue to be subject to regular supervision in the form of regular reporting requirements. By contrast, Brazilian law has not created a special class of business vehicles for FDI but allows foreign investors to participate freely in the general group of business vehicles available to all investors in Brazil. No special permission or screening is required in Brazil for a foreign investor to buy or establish a Brazilian company. Rather, foreign investors follow the laws governing the establishment of business entities as if they were no different from domestic investors. In Brazil, FDI is chiefly regulated through the Profits Remittance Law and Brazilian tax laws, which operate together to create a system of sticks and carrots relating to the repatriation of capital and profits. Moreover, while China's FDI laws are mandatory, compliance with Brazil's Profit Remittance Law is optional as foreign investors are not required to register their capital with the Central Bank. As you review the materials in this section, keep in mind the different approaches taken by Brazil and China, two countries in a similar stage of economic development, and consider the merits and disadvantages of each approach from the perspective of the foreign investor.

The rationale for Brazil's approach is that screening FDI at the point of entry into the market involves the making of judgments by government agencies on what are meritorious FDI projects, which is a difficult task that government agencies may not be qualified to handle and often results in erroneous conclusions. In addition, the type of pervasive regulation of FDI typical of some developing countries can deter foreign investors who may find such regulation to be intrusive. Brazil's approach is to allow market forces and the foreign investor to decide what projects will be successful and to limit government oversight in all areas except for repatriation of capital and profits. Regulation of FDI will not occur at the point of entry and continue throughout the life of the foreign invested business entity as it does in some countries but at the other end of the process when the foreign investor seeks to repatriate capital or profits.

To be sure, the issue of repatriation of capital and profits is a crucial issue and if a nation were to regulate any one aspect of FDI, repatriation of capital and profits is the most logical choice. For example, once a U.S. company has established a successful business abroad, the U.S. foreign investor will seek to reap the benefits of its success by returning the profits earned to the United States. If capital and profits cannot be easily repatriated to the foreign investor's home country, then the investor (and its shareholders) will not be able to enjoy the full fruits of its success. How and under what conditions such repatriation occurs is of crucial importance to the foreign investor.

We include the main provisions from the Profits Remittance Law and summarize some of the key aspects of Brazilian tax law in the materials that follow, but we turn first to a closer examination of the policies behind those laws.

A. POLICY OBJECTIVES

The regulation of FDI in Brazil through the Profits Remittance Law and various tax laws is based on two basic policy goals: (1) the need to regulate and control the exodus of foreign hard currency that is used to repatriate foreign capital and to make payments such as dividends, interest, and royalties to a foreign investor located in a foreign nation, such as the United States; and (2) the need to ensure that foreign companies pay their share of taxes on any payments that are remitted to a foreign nation so that foreign investors do not exploit Brazil by earning unfairly high profits. At times, a third objective of providing a legal environment that can attract and retain FDI is in tension with these two policy goals. The recent history of FDI in Brazil indicates that the first two policies have been in conflict with the third objective and have at times, especially in the decades preceding the 1990s, discouraged FDI. After its adoption of a democratic form of government in the latter half of the 1980s, Brazil made a number of changes in the 1990s, which have indicated that the balance has been shifted in favor of fewer harsh controls and more liberal laws that are designed to implement the two policy objectives in favor of greater incentives for foreign investment.

B. SOME BACKGROUND ECONOMIC HISTORY AND CONSIDERATIONS

To understand the first policy goal, which is largely driven by a need to protect the Brazilian currency against devaluation and to prevent depletion of Brazil's store of foreign currency reserves, it is necessary to review Brazil's recent economic history during the latter half of the twentieth century. For much of this period, Brazil's currency, the real, came under severe inflationary pressure caused by a number of Brazilian fiscal policies that led to hyperinflation and a drastic depreciation of the value of the real. The depreciation within Brazil of the value of the real, in turn, created pressures on Brazil's Central Bank to devalue the Brazilian currency against a basket of hard currencies, including the U.S. dollar, on the foreign exchange market. The economic policy that led to severe internal inflation was primarily a longstanding policy of deficit spending by the Brazilian government. Deficit spending exists when a government spends beyond what it has the capacity to pay for with funds in the government treasury. Beginning in the 1950s, Brazil, which has also long viewed itself as being on the cusp of a first world country, embarked on an aggressive campaign of government spending to catch up to advanced industrialized countries. As government corruption and patronage were also common, the demands for government largesse were further increased by an endless amount of unnecessary spending for phantom projects in the form of "pork" that was required to garner legislative support among Brazil's many political parties for any type of government expenditure.

Brazil's deficit spending was not in itself the cause of the country's inflation woes. A common method used by governments to cover the deficit is to raise funds through the use of credit, such as by borrowing money to pay its debts through the issuance of government bonds, which are essentially debts owed by the government to the bondholder. The bondholder buys the bond at a discount from the face amount of the bond to the government. The bond is treated as a loan and the government pays interest on the bond to the borrower (which is interest on the loan) and then pays off the face amount of the bond at maturity, which represents the repayment of the principal of the loan usually plus some amount that was discounted when the bond was originally purchased. Bonds and other debt instruments raise short-term cash that the government can use to cover its expenses but do not address the long-term issues of how to eliminate the budget deficit through economic growth and, as a result, are usually used as part of an overall economic stimulus package. In Brazil's case, however, the government covered its deficit spending not by using credit (in the form of government bonds or otherwise) but by printing more money and encouraging the use of "near money" such as U.S. dollars, which only led to additional spending. As a fiscal policy, moreover, the issuance of more paper money to cover the deficit was a disastrous policy as it led directly to chronic hyperinflation. As there was an ever-increasing oversupply of Brazilian reals in the economy, it took more reals to buy the same goods and services as the value of each real was worth less, resulting in a severe depreciation of the currency. Other policies that led to hyperinflation included a decision by the Central Bank to cover all loans made by state banks, creating an incentive for local banks to issue ill-advised, worthless, and unrepayable loans as the banks knew that they were protected by the Central Bank. The issuance of unrepayable loans resulted in an even higher increase in the amount of money in circulation and also encouraged irresponsible spending, which also contributed to inflation. The depreciation of the real caused by chronic inflation also meant that the real was depreciating in value in the foreign exchange market against such currencies as the U.S. dollar. As the value of the real declined and was worth less in Brazil, the real was devalued in relation to other currencies such as the dollar and an ever higher number of reals were needed to be exchanged for each U.S. dollar.

By 1993, the inflationary pressures had reached critical levels. The annual inflation rate had reached 2,703 percent, threatening to destabilize the Brazilian economy. In 1994, the Brazilian government introduced the Real Plan to stabilize the currency and to bring inflation under control. A key feature of the Real Plan was to peg the real against the U.S. dollar based on a one-to-one exchange rate to keep domestic prices in check. The one-to-one exchange rate had the psychological effect of creating stabilization and confidence in the real for the Brazilian consumer as the consumer knew that the real would not be devalued. Pegging the real to a high exchange rate in relation to the U.S. dollar, however, did not curb the inflation that continued to create depreciation pressure on the real at home and devaluation pressure on the real in the foreign exchange market. To control some of the excessive spending at home, the Central Bank raised interest rates up to as high as 45 percent in order to increase the cost of borrowing money and to limit spending. The Central Bank also used its reserves of foreign hard currency in the form of U.S. dollars to buy up reals on the open market in order to decrease the amount of reals in circulation to support the value of the real at home and in the foreign exchange market. While these measures did check inflation in the 1990s, it came at a high cost as by some estimates the Central Bank used $60 billion in foreign currency reserves to buy reals on the open market and to prop up the value of its currency.

As these fiscal policies began to prop up the value of the real, it began to appreciate against other hard currencies. Appreciation of the real through government intervention rather than through the growth of the Brazilian economy had the unintended side effect of making Brazilian goods more expensive for foreign consumers as the consumer had to pay more in domestic currency to exchange for the same amount of reals. For example, goods sold from Brazil to the United States were expensive because the U.S. importer had to pay the same amount in U.S. dollars for the goods as they cost in reals, even though the goods did not have an equivalent value on the market, as the currency exchange did not reflect market forces but was due to the intervention of the Brazilian government. As you can imagine, the increase in the price of Brazilian goods led to a decline in global demand for the goods and to a decrease in total exports from Brazil in the 1990s to 0.86 percent of total global exports, the lowest figure in three decades. The high interest rates also had the effect of increasing the costs of doing business in Brazil. In the meantime, the use of such a large amount of foreign currency reserves to support the real in the foreign exchange market left Brazil dangerously low on foreign currency reserves. Having a sufficient amount of foreign hard currency was essential for Brazil's balance of payments obligations. As the real was not a freely convertible currency, Brazil had to use hard currencies, such as the U.S. dollar, in buying products from countries, in repaying credit, or in satisfying any other monetary obligations as few countries would accept the real. In addition, hyperinflation caused a constant and continuing depreciation of the real so it was quite risky to accept reals for payment even if one were able to go to the thriving black market in Brazil to exchange reals for hard currency. To deal with these pressures, Brazil borrowed $41 billion, $15.7 billion, and $30 billion in U.S. dollars from the International Monetary Fund in 1998, 2000, and 2001 to replenish its stores of hard currency and to restore confidence in the Brazilian economy. Brazil repaid all of its debts to the IMF in 2005. The result of these somewhat painful measures is that Brazil appears to have stabilized its economy and to have eliminated the hyperinflation of the preceding decades through the Real Plan, but at the cost of imposing a heavy burden on the country's economic growth and development. A comparison between Brazil and China, for example, shows the marked difference between their economic growth in the 1990s. Brazil's GDP grew from $465 billion in 1990 to $504 billion in 2001, an 8 percent increase, while China's GDP grew from $387 billion to $1.1 trillion during the same period, a 199 percent increase. Brazil's GDP grew substantially to reach $2.24 trillion in 2013, an increase of 337 percent since 2001, but this pace was again outmatched by China, whose GDP increased by 735 percent to $9.18 trillion in 2013.

C. THE ENACTMENT OF THE PROFITS REMITTANCE LAW

Against this background of inflationary pressure and pressure on the value of the real, the Profits Remittance Law was first enacted in 1962 and has been continuously amended up to the present. During the beginning of this period, the Brazilian government was of two minds about foreign direct investment. While the government wanted the benefits of FDI, it was also concerned that foreign investors would exploit Brazil by making unconscionably high profits and by contributing to Brazil's balance of payments problems. One way in which foreign investors would potentially harm Brazilian interests would be to bring in foreign capital in the form of foreign investment and then suddenly repatriate all of the original foreign capital as well as additional foreign currency in the form of capital appreciation and profits. As these funds would need to be taken out of Brazil in foreign currency, such a swift departure of foreign capital could intensify Brazil's problems by suddenly depleting Brazil's foreign currency reserves, further exacerbating Brazil's chronic balance of payment problems. Nationalistic pressure led to the enactment of the Profits Remittance Law, which contained a number of harsh provisions limiting the repatriation of foreign currency. For example, as originally enacted, Articles 31 and 32 placed an annual limitation on capital repatriation of 20 percent of registered capital and 10 percent of registered capital on profit remittances. Registered capital refers to the original amount of the foreign capital that was brought into Brazil by the foreign investor and that was recorded or registered with Brazilian authorities. In addition, the

Profits Remittance Law limited remittances for patent and trademark royalties and fees for technical assistance to 5 percent of gross sales for a maximum term of five years. These harsh restrictions have all been relaxed or eliminated as we shall examine in detail in a subsequent section.

The Profits Remittance Law worked in tandem with Brazil's tax and customs laws to control the outflow of foreign currency. A foreign investor had to submit proof that all taxes had been properly paid before any remittance in foreign currency could be lawfully permitted. If the foreign investor had the required documentary proof, the foreign investor could then apply to certain designated banks authorized to deal in foreign exchange for remittance in foreign currency to its home jurisdiction. To further discourage the remittance of large amounts of foreign capital, the tax laws imposed prohibitive taxes on certain types of payments. For example, prior to its repeal in 1991, existing Brazilian tax law provided that repatriated dividends that do not exceed 12 percent of registered capital were subject to a withholding tax of 15 percent, but dividends that exceeded 12 percent were subject to a prohibitive supplementary tax of between 40 and 60 percent. The requirement that proof of payment of all taxes before repatriation was also designed to ensure that foreign investors did not take advantage of Brazil by disguising profits as other types of payments and evading Brazilian taxes that were due on profits earned. This feature of the Profits Remittance Law requiring proof of tax payments still exists although much of the harsher tax obligations have also been relaxed.

2. The Business Climate in Brazil

PROBLEM 6-19

Acme, a U.S. company in the consumer products industry, is considering establishing or acquiring a subsidiary in Brazil. Acme manufactures and sells premium-brand shampoos, soaps, toothpaste, and other daily-use consumer products aimed at the upper echelon of the consumer market. Acme's CEO asks you to prepare a report on Brazil as a target market and has the following questions:

(1) What are the main strengths of Brazil such as demographics and consumer markets that would support establishing an Acme subsidiary there as opposed to another country in South America such as Chile, which is also being considered?

(2) What are the main problems with the consumer market for Acme's products? Can Acme adapt to these issues?

(3) Where should Acme locate the subsidiary in Brazil?

(4) Is Brazil a potential platform for the export of Acme products to other countries in South America?

(5) Acme wants to develop a line of organic body soaps and lotions, herbal teas, natural vitamin supplements, and biotechnology products (including pharmaceuticals) in Brazil and export these products to North America. Is this a good plan?

Consider the following reading and accompanying notes.

Brazil's Environment for Doing Business and for Foreign Direct Investment

Located in the southern cone of Latin America, the Federative Republic of Brazil is the fifth largest country in the world by area, comprising 8,514,215 square kilometers or 3,286,000 square miles, with the fifth largest population in the world at 202.7 million.

Brazil occupies nearly one-half of the entire South American continent, is larger than the continental United States, and is slightly smaller than all of the European countries put together. Brazil borders all South American countries except Chile and Ecuador. The coastline runs for more than 5,700 miles, most of it along the South Atlantic Ocean.

Brazil's environment offers a great deal of biological diversity and bio-resources. Brazil has diverse mix of climates, fauna, flora, and geological formations. Due to Brazil's biological resources, Brazil has been called an "El Dorado" for biotechnology companies. Brazil has the largest rainforest in the world, which covers 60 percent of Brazilian territory. The equator runs through the north of Brazil where the rain forest is located. The climate varies from equatorial in the north to subtropical in the south but temperatures can also reach below freezing in the south in the winter. Brazil was under rule by Portugal for more three centuries from 1500 to 1822. Brazil gained independence from Portugal in 1822 but many Portuguese influences continue to exist. For example, the national language of Brazil is Portuguese. In 1899, the Federal Republic of Brazil was established. Currently, Brazil consists of five major regions: the North, Northeast, Southeast, South, and Central West. The southeast region includes the states of São Paulo, and Rio de Janeiro. São Paulo is Brazil's largest city with an estimated population of 19.2 million. Rio de Janeiro is the second largest city with an estimated population of 16 million. In total, these regions contain 26 states, the Federal District, and 5,561 municipalities. The population of Brazil consists of many different ethnic groups with those of European, African, Asian, and Arab descent mixed with a native Brazilian population.

Brazil is a recently industrialized country. Prior to 1950, Brazil was mainly engaged in agriculture. In 1940, about 66 percent of Brazil's work force was in the agricultural sector with 9.4 percent in industrial sectors and 24.6 percent in services. From 1950–1970, Brazil experienced a major shift from agriculture to manufacturing and production and services, with the trend continuing into the 2000s. In 2011, 16 percent of the labor force was in the agricultural sector, 13.3 percent was in the manufacturing sector, and 71 percent was in the services sectors. Coinciding with Brazil's industrialization has been the migration of the bulk of the population from rural areas to urban centers located in the interior of the country. In 2010, 87 percent of the Brazilian population lived in urban centers, with an estimated 1.1 percent annual increase from 2010 to the present. Today, Brazil has over 16 metropolitan centers with a population exceeding 1 million people. The concentration of Brazil's population in urban centers has a discernible impact upon the business strategies of multinational companies doing business in Brazil. In 1970, only 20 percent of Brazil's top 500 companies had business operations in the interior of Brazil. By 2013, many of Brazil's top companies have set up operations in Brazil's interior.

ECONOMY

Brazil's economy has more than quadrupled in size over the past decade. Gross Domestic Product rose from about $500 billion in 2002 to more than $2.2 trillion in 2013, surpassing both Russia and Mexico's domestic product at that time. (For comparison, the EU ($17.4 trillion), Germany ($3.6 trillion), the United States ($16.8 trillion), and China ($9.2 trillion) remain far ahead.) While developing quickly and the largest in Latin America, Brazil's economy can be considered to be an emerging mid-tier economy, behind the largest economies in the world. More recently, Brazil's growth has slowed down as consumers and investors have begun to be concerned once again with Brazil's growing government debt and deficits. After a relatively high growth rate of 3.6 percent from 2001–2008, Brazil's growth has slowed to an average of 1.7 percent for 2011–2012 and is expected to be similarly subdued in 2014 and 2015. Among the concerns leading to slower growth are inadequate investments in infrastructure and low productivity (competitiveness). Concerns also persist about a bloated government bureaucracy, wasteful government spending, and inflation, problems with a long history in Brazil and other countries in the region, such as Argentina.

Table 1 offers an overview of the key economic indicators of Brazil, comparing them to Mexican and Chilean economic indicators. As the table indicates, Brazil is far ahead of both Mexico and Chile in GDP and in GDP growth rate, both positive factors. However, Mexico is ahead of Brazil in trading of both exports and imports, which can be traced to the positive effects of NAFTA. Some possible concerns in Brazil are indicators of inflation (8.1 percent) and a high interest rate (29.7 percent) that could make access to credit difficult, creating obstacles to investment.

TABLE 1
Economic Indicators for Brazil, Mexico, and Chile (2012)

Economic Indicator	Brazil	Mexico	Chile
GDP (US$ billions)	2,252.7	1,178.1	269.9
GDP % Growth Last 5 Years	2.2	1.4	4.4
Real Interest Rate	29.7	1.1	8.1
Inflation GDP Deflator (annual %)	8.1	5.5	6.1
Share of Sectors/GDP (%):			
Agriculture	5	4	4
Industry	26	36	36
Service	68	61	61
Exports (US$ billions)	282.4	387.5	90.9
Exports Growth Rate, 2008–2012 (%)	5.7	3.6	4.5
Exports of Goods and Services/GDP (%)	13	33	34
Imports of Goods and Services/GDP (%)	14	34	34
High Tech. Exports/Manufactured Exports	9.7	16.5	4.6
Present Value of External Debt (US$ billions)	440.5	354.9	No data
Total Debt Service (% of Exports of Goods and Services)	15.5	17.7	No data

GLOBAL COMPETITIVENESS

Every major industry is represented in the Brazilian economy. Brazil's main industries include: manufacturing industries, such as production of aluminum, cement, fuel, machinery, paper, plastics, and steel; consumer and food industries, consisting of manufacturing cleaning supplies, food production and hygiene, medicine and textile manufacturing; and the durable goods industries, consisting of manufacturing domestic appliances and vehicles (including automobiles). Financial services represent the principle services industry. Brazil is also a major world producer of bananas, coffee, corn, orange juice concentrate, rice, soybeans, alcohol, and sugarcane.

Brazil's source of competitiveness can be traced to four different assets: factor endowments, firm strategy and rivalry, related and supporting industry, and local demand conditions. Ranked by global competitiveness (see table below), Brazil can be considered to be a mid-tier emerging economy on par with Mexico, behind Korea and China, and well behind top-tier countries, such as the United States and Germany. It is important to note, however, that while about on par with Mexico on certain competitiveness factors, Brazil's economy is much larger than Mexico's and is the largest in Latin America.

TABLE 2
Global Competitiveness Index, Components Index (GCI), 2013

Country	GCI Rank	Basic Requirements Rank	Efficiency Enhancers Rank	Innovation and Sophistication Factors Index Rank
Switzerland	1	3	5	1
U.S.	5	36	1	6
Korea	25	20	23	20
Chile	34	30	29	45
Mexico	55	63	55	55
Brazil	56	79	44	46
Argentina	104	102	97	98
Germany	4	9	8	4
China	29	31	31	34

NATURAL RESOURCES

Brazil is rich in basic factors (natural resources, climate, location, and demographics), as well as rich in advanced factors (communication infrastructure, skilled labor, indigenous technology, and know-how). Brazil has been called an "El Dorado" for the biotechnology industry. Brazil accounts for 20 percent of the world's fresh water necessary for agriculture, is rich in minerals necessary for metals production, and has a population that is young and increasingly well-educated.

TRADE LIBERALIZATION AND DEREGULATION

The Brazilian government has traditionally exercised considerable control over private businesses through extensive and constantly changing regulations. In addition, large sectors of the economy were dominated by state-owned enterprises, not subject to free-market principles. In the past several decades, the government has been dedicated to economic reform and has moved to liberalize trade. The government has begun to deregulate industries such as energy, mining, telecommunications, and transportation, and has, in a major shift, moved to privatize state-owned enterprises. These efforts have resulted in a significant improvement in the quality of life for the Brazilian consumer. For example, in the 1980s, Brazilian consumers found 20,000 different items on supermarket shelves. In the auto industry, the number of models increased from 40 in the 1980s to about 400 in 2003. Today, multinational companies such as General Motors, Ford, Fiat, and Volkswagen all have a strong presence in Brazil. In 2010, 3.52 million new cars were sold in Brazil, an indication of the growing power of Brazil's middle class. Another fruit of deregulation and market-driven reforms is that the increasing competition in the engineering industry has led to the overseas expansion of Brazilian engineering companies. Brazilian engineering companies such as Odebrecht are operating in North America, Europe, and Latin America.

POLICIES SUPPORTING INDUSTRY

Brazil implemented an import substitution strategy as part of its overall industrialization plan. Brazil's import substitution strategy directs Brazilian firms to purchase inputs and raw materials domestically rather than importing the inputs or materials from foreign countries. This strategy has led to the creation of diversified supporting industries. For example, Brazil's auto industry has led to the creation of competitive domestic steel, glass, and rubber industries that supply the auto industry with parts. In agriculture, the import substitution policies have led to the development of competitive suppliers of seeds, agricultural equipment, fertilizers, and insecticides. These policies have made the Brazilian agribusiness industry competitive on a global scale.

CONSUMER DEMAND

Brazil's trade liberalization policies, discussed above, exposed consumers to higher quality products and today consumers have become sophisticated and demanding. Several leading Brazilian companies such as the media company TV Globo have created high quality products for Brazilian consumers and have expanded overseas. For example, TV Globo's programing is now sold in Latin America, North America, Europe, and Asia. TV Globo has risen to become the world's fourth largest television network.

FOREIGN DIRECT INVESTMENT

Foreign direct investment has played a major role in Brazil's transition to a leading industrialized country in South America. From 2009–2012, the country received U.S. $206.4 billion, behind only China and the British Virgin Islands among developing countries. The following factors have contributed to Brazil's attractiveness as a target of foreign direct investment.

- *Market Size.* Brazil has the world's fifth largest population. The size of the middle class is estimated to be over 60 million people. Total expenditure by Brazilian consumers for 2012 was U.S. $1.4 trillion, the largest in Latin America. By contrast, Mexico's total household consumer expenditure was $800 billion in the same year.
- *Liberalization of Regulation.* Brazil's reforms in the 1990s were designed to remove onerous regulatory restrictions on foreign direct investment. In general Brazil does not restrict foreign ownership of domestic enterprises. The reforms also made Brazil's regulatory environment more transparent and less bureaucratic and difficult to navigate. Brazilian legislation prohibits discrimination against foreign invested companies and the reduction of state-owned enterprises has opened up many new sectors for private competition and investment. Unlike

China, Brazil does not require foreign direct investment to take the form of special business entities. In some areas, however, such as media, some restrictions still apply. For example, a foreign investor is limited to ownership of a maximum of 30 percent of capital of a media company.

- *Low Labor Costs and Effective Resources.* Brazil has low wages and an increasingly well-educated productive workforce.
- *Lower Political Risks.* Since 1988, Brazil has been under the rule of a solid democratic regime after almost 30 years of a military dictatorship. Since the introduction of economic reforms to stabilize its currency in 1994, Brazil has achieved higher levels of economic stability with increasingly lower levels of inflation. Brazil's recent political stability and economic reforms make it less likely that events such as expropriation of foreign assets or defaults on monetary obligations will create significant risks for foreign investors.

Multinational companies have played an important role in driving Brazil's transformation from an agriculture-based economy to an economy based on industry and services. In the 1950s, after the Second World War, the United States became the largest foreign investor in Brazil. Multinational companies also played a key role in increasing Brazil's exports in the 1960s and early 1970s. By establishing operations in Brazil in concert with Brazil's import substitution program, multinational companies helped to diversify Brazil's industrial sectors and to accelerate its growth. For instance, by 2002, Brazil had 15 car manufacturers, making Brazil the world's fourth largest manufacturer of small-size vehicles. By the 1990s, foreign direct investment shifted to Brazil's services sector. At the same time, Brazil began to privatize the services sector opening up key areas such as telecommunications, energy generation, transportation, and financial services for foreign direct investment.

The United States continues to be the largest foreign investor in Brazil. In 1990, U.S. foreign direct investment in Brazil was $280 million; by 2000, FDI from the United States increased to $33.4 billion and then declined to $16.5 billion by 2002 due to the global economic recession. By 2013, FDI from the United States was $79.4 billion.

Table 3 indicates the recently increasing share of sales by multinational companies and the decreasing share of sales by state-owned enterprises. From 1978 to 2000 (the most recent data available), multinational companies increased their share from 35.4 percent to 45.6 percent. This development reflects the market-oriented reforms implemented in the 1990s. The reforms led the share of state-controlled companies to decline from 29.7 percent to about 18.7 percent.

TABLE 3[67]

Changing Shares of Sales by MNCs, State Companies, and Domestic Companies

	1978	1989	1995	2000
Multinational Corporations	35.4%	30.8%	33.3%	45.6%
Domestic Companies	34.9%	44.0%	43.6%	35.7%
State Companies	29.7%	25.2%	23.1%	18.7%

---

67. This table is from Raul Gouvea, Doing Business in Brazil: A Strategic Approach, 46 Thunderbird Int'l Bus. Rev. 165, 175 (2004).

Brazil's market-oriented reforms in the 1990s had a dramatic impact on Brazil's ability to attract foreign direct investment. In the 1990s, Brazil was ranked fifth among the world's largest recipients of foreign direct investment and was ranked eighth for its total stocks of foreign direct investment. Brazil increased its share of total world FDI by 0.7 percent in the early 1990s to about 4.8 percent by the end of 2012. By 2013, Brazil was ranked fourth among the world's largest recipients of foreign direct investment with capital inflows of $65 billion and ranked seventh with total stocks of $702 billion of foreign direct investment. This increase in FDI is marked by the entry into Brazil of 80 percent of the world's top 500 companies by 2013. By the late 1990s, Brazil began to set the services sector as a target for foreign direct investment. Table 4 shows the recent dramatic shift of foreign direct investment into the services sector. An investment in services is a hallmark of the stage of development of a country. In general, the more developed a country, the higher the level of services industries that will form a part of the economy.

TABLE 4
FDI in the Brazil, Main Economic Sectors, 1995–2009
(percentage of total FDI)

	1995	2000	2009
Agriculture & Mining	4.5%	2.5%	14.7%
Manufacturing	64.7%	28.0%	39.2%
Services	30.8%	69.5%	46.1%

FOREIGN TRADE

Brazil is a member of Mercosur (Common Market of the South), along with Argentina, Uruguay, Venezuela, Bolivia, and Paraguay; Chile, Peru, Ecuador, Guyana, Suriname, and Colombia are associate members, allowing them to have some of the benefits of Mercosur. Mercosur represents a total population of approximately 290 million people, living in an area of 5,364,000 square miles, more than half again the size of the continental United States. In 2012, the total GDP of the six principal members of Mercosur was approximately U.S. $3.2 trillion. Since Mercosur is a free trade area, goods trade duty free among all members of Mercosur. That is, goods imported into Brazil from another member of Mercosur come subject to zero tariffs. For goods from non-members of Mercosur, the members apply a Common External Tariff with an average rate of 15 percent. Brazil is also a member of the WTO but the WTO recognizes FTAs, such as Mercosur, as consistent with the WTO.

In recent years, Brazil has enjoyed a trade surplus as a result of several factors, including the devaluation of the real and high foreign demand for many of its products. The Brazilian trade balance in 2013 stood at exports of $244.8 billion and imports of $241.4 billion resulting in a trade surplus of $3.4 billion. Overall, Brazil's volume of trade is very small compared with that of the United States ($1.575 trillion exports and $2.273 trillion imports in 2013) or China ($2.21 trillion exports and $1.95 trillion imports in 2013). In 2013, Brazil's leading exports were iron ore, crude petroleum, soybeans, raw sugar, coffee, poultry, soybean meal, woodpulp, semi-finished iron products, refined petroleum, and aircraft. Brazil's principal imports were crude petroleum oil, electric engines and parts, automotive and tractor equipment, and drugs for human and veterinary medicine. Brazil's principal trading partners are the United States, Argentina and other Latin American countries, the members of the EU, Japan, Saudi Arabia, South Korea, and China.

INFRASTRUCTURE

Infrastructure in Brazil is of an uneven quality and sophistication. The quality of the infrastructure mirrors the country's regional income disparities. The most sophisticated and highest quality infrastructure is located in the most densely populated and high income areas of the Southeast and Southern regions. Transportation in Brazil relies mainly on road transport by truck, which accounts for 63 percent of freight transportation. However, only about 10 percent of Brazil's roads are paved and the cost of fuel is high. Road transport is generally inefficient compared with other forms, such as rail. However, due to inadequate investment in railways as a means of transportation, the last two or three decades has seen the decline of railways as a means of freight transport. Rail transport accounts for only about 21 percent of all freight transport. Airfreight transport is minor accounting for only 0.3 percent. Waterway transport accounts for 21 percent and pipeline transport accounts for 3.9 percent. The large majority of imports and exports use Brazil's 13 major seaports. However, the seaports are antiquated and inefficient. The current state of Brazil's seaports cause delays in clearing goods for import and export, causing losses estimated at $2.5 billion per year. The government is undertaking several initiatives to improve the quality of the seaports to increase port efficiency.

TELECOMMUNICATIONS

Telecommunications are well developed in Brazil, especially in urban centers. This has been achieved mainly as a result of aggressive privatization programs achieved in the 1990s. Nevertheless, certain regions are in need of improved telecommunications infrastructure, mainly in the North and Center-West regions. In 2000, Brazil had 909,000 public access phone lines compared to 740,000 in 1999. The ratio of conventional telephones per 100 inhabitants is proof that Brazil is getting closer to countries such as Chile and Argentina. Cellular technology has made phones more accessible to the average Brazilian. In 1994, Brazil had 755,000 cell phones, and by 2014 this number had increased to 273 million.

INTERNET

Brazil had more than 100 million people using the Internet in 2012. Brazil is the sixth largest country in the world measured by Internet users and the number is increasing every year. Brazil has a significant participation in the electronic commerce in South America. As of June 2014, a total of 3.4 million Brazilian addresses were registered on the web. Registrations have more than doubled in the last five years but with a population of over 200 million people, there is room for substantial growth.

ENERGY

Brazil relies mainly on hydroelectric power plants for its power (electricity). Lack of investment in other forms of energy generation led to a nationwide energy crisis in 2001. Brazil is currently attempting to diversity its energy sources and is adding gas-powered plants to service the country's energy needs. In 2011, gas accounted for 4.7 percent of the country's power. Ethanol, a sugar cane-derived fuel, is also receiving more attention. However, energy generation continues to be an issue and unless new investments are made, Brazil may continue to suffer energy shortages in the near future.

Changing Consumer Market

Brazil's consumer market is experiencing dynamic growth and changes. In 2002, Brazilian consumers spent a total of $298 billion, the largest in South America. Figure 1 indicates that the urban center of São Paulo is Brazil's largest urban center of economic activity, with an estimated 2010 gross product of $241.3 billion, followed by Rio de Janeiro with $103.4 billion.

One of the main issues that constrain further growth of Brazil's consumer market is the income inequality. Nevertheless, Brazil's small middle class appears to offer potential business opportunities. For example, in 2011, the number of non-cash transactions, driven mostly by the use of credit cards, was at 22 billion transactions behind only the United States and the EU. On the other hand, the small middle class means that only 30 million Brazilians, or about 17 percent of the population, have bank accounts, so retail banking services have been negatively affected by the small size of the middle class.

FIGURE 1   Brazil's Most Productive Municipalities, 2010 (US$ billions)

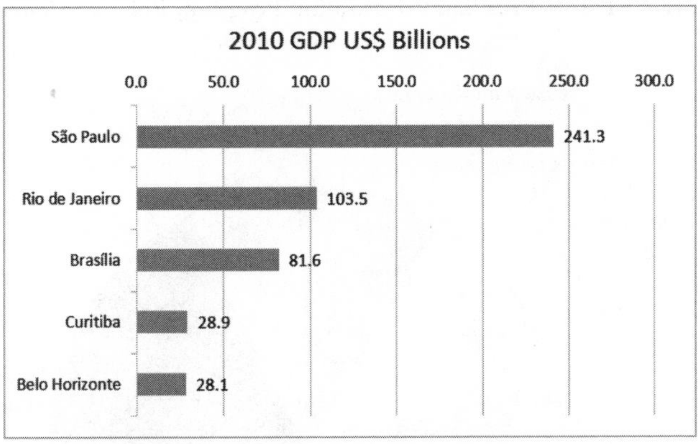

Urban Centers and Consumption

Income inequality in Brazil is a persistent problem as Brazil has a large populace of persons with low incomes. However, in the past decade tens of millions of Brazilians have emerged from poverty to join Brazil's burgeoning middle class. This rise was due in part to developments in the economy such as rapidly rising wages and employment and to government transfer payments from those in wealthier parts of the country to those in poorer parts. Like their middle-class counterparts in other countries around the world, the growing middle class is demanding more access to a larger variety of goods such as computers, mobile phones, and washing machines. The growing middle class is also demanding less government corruption, more transparency and social inclusion, less inflation, and more stable inflation and financial security.

Some companies are developing new strategies given the changing nature of the middle class. In the past, most companies have focused on so-called Class A and B of consumers, i.e., those with incomes ten times higher than minimum wages. Classes A and B traditionally accounted for 52 percent of Brazil's total consumer consumption. Class C, those with incomes between four and ten times higher than the minimum wage, accounted for 28 percent of consumption. Consumers in Classes D and E with incomes one to three times higher than the minimum wage accounted for 20 percent of total consumer consumption. However, since Class C has experienced a 37 percent growth from 1992 to 2000, companies have created new so-called B-brands specifically targeted at this growing group of consumers. These "B-Brands" have been able to take away market share from some multinational companies. For instance, Kellogg's share of the Brazilian cereal market has dropped from 72 percent to 47 percent as a result of the introduction of B-Brands. Nestle's share of the market for chocolate dropped from 62 percent to 52 percent as a result of B-Brands. It is estimated that B-Brands now account for 30 percent of the consumer products market in Brazil.

PRIVATIZATION

State-led industrialization of the economy occurred in Brazil between 1950 and 1980 but by the 1990s, it became clear that the inefficiencies of state-owned enterprises

FIGURE 2[68]   Brazilian Privatization Program, Relative Share of Total Revenues by Sectors

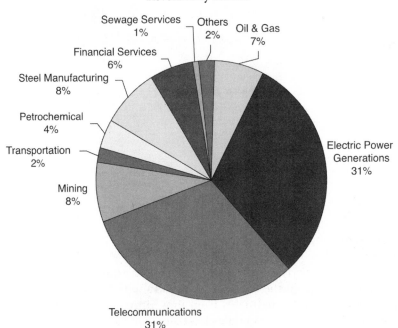

68. This figure is from Raul Gouvea, *Doing Business in Brazil: A Strategic Approach*, 46 Thunderbird Int'l Bus. Rev. 165, 182 (2004).

were creating barriers to further progress and economic development. As a result, Brazil embarked on an aggressive privatization program in the 1990s to wean industries from the protection of the state. Brazil implemented a privatization program at the same time that the country also engaged in deregulation of many parts of the economy, implementing market-oriented reforms designed to attract foreign direct investment. From 1990 to 2002, the Brazilian privatization program generated $105 billion in revenues obtained through the sales of state-owned enterprises to private companies. The first phase in the privatization program focused on manufacturing but later shifted to the services sectors of the economy. Figure 2 gives an overview of the relative share of the different sectors subject to privatization in the period from 1991 to 2002. Privatization continues to this day in Brazil, but at a slower pace than the peak period of the 1990s.

INTELLECTUAL PROPERTY RIGHTS

Like many developing countries, Brazil was late to adopt intellectual property rights. In the 1990s, Brazil began to adopt modern intellectual property laws. Today, the Brazilian National Institute of Industrial Property (INPI) oversees the administration of intellectual property rights in Brazil. Note that since Brazil is a member of the World Trade Organization, Brazil is bound by the Agreement on Trade Related Intellectual Property Rights (TRIPs) to implement intellectual property laws in accordance with the standards set forth in TRIPs. The following are some basic intellectual property rights of importance in foreign direct investment in Brazil:

(a) Trademarks: All trademarks should be registered with the INPI. Any trademark that is not registered may not receive protection. If a foreign investor has a well-known trademark, Brazil may provide additional protection for the well-known trademark consistent with the special protections given to well-known trademarks under TRIPs. Under Brazilian law, trademarks must be registered every ten years and failure to use the mark for five years subjects the mark to cancellation for lack of use.

(b) Patents: All patents must be registered with the INPI. Patents must be used within three years of their registration or they will be subject to cancellation.

(c) Franchising: All franchise agreements are subject to the oversight of the INPI. The INPI enforces Brazilian Law number 8955, which created the Franchise Law. The law governs the relationship between franchisees and franchisors.

Like many countries, Brazil has a software piracy problem. According to the Business Software Alliance, a software-industry trade group organized to combat software piracy, losses caused by software piracy in Brazil amounted to $2.8 billion in 2011. This represents an increase from $346 million in 2001.

SPECIFIC SECTORS FOR INVESTMENT

The Brazilian economy has a number of sectors recently subject to market access reforms that create attractive opportunities for foreign direct investment, including:

- *Oil and Gas.* This sector was opened up to private competition in 1998 and as a result, Petrobras, the Brazilian oil company, no longer has a monopoly. This sector is expected to grow at 15 percent for the next five years. Areas where foreign companies can compete are offshore petroleum services, offshore production equipment

. **Foreign Direct Investment**

and onshore exploration services, each of which offers a number of business opportunities for foreign companies. Petrobras has indicated that it will invest $224 billion in explorations and development through 2015. In 2012, oil rents (the difference between the price and cost of production) were 3 percent of GDP or in excess of $67 billion.

- *Banking and Financial Sector.* Brazil privatized the banking and financial services sector as part of its reforms in the 1990s. Aggressive moves by foreign banks now mean that among Brazil's top 15 banks, 6 are foreign banks from Europe and the United States: HSBC, ABN, Santander, Bank of Boston (Fleet Bank), and Citibank. In 1994, foreign banks accounted for 8.2 percent of the Brazilian banking industry. In 2009, foreign banks accounted for 38 percent of the Brazilian banking industry. Available data indicates that there has been a strong increase in the presence of foreign banks from the 1990s to 2014.
- *Auto Parts.* This is a fast growing sector, generating $56.9 billion in revenues for 2013 up from $11.7 billion in 2002. Foreign companies account for more than 70 percent of the domestic market share. The main markets are in gears and friction wheels, rubber products, ball axles, and rollers. On the production of automobiles, the following foreign companies account for over 97 percent of the domestic output of automobiles by units: Volkswagen, Fiat, General Motors, Ford Renault, Peugeot-Citroen, Hyundai, Toyota, Honda, Daimler, Nissan, and Mitsubishi.
- *Drugs and Pharmaceuticals.* In 2012, sales of drugs to Brazil generated over $25 billion in revenues with an annual growth rate of 15 percent. Brazil is the largest Latin American market for the drug and pharmaceutical industry. Foreign firms and their Brazilian affiliates supply 70 percent of the pharmaceutical market. Not only is there a large demand for name-brand drugs in Brazil, but the demand for generic drugs—drugs for which the patent has expired—is also growing. Estimates are that 24 percent of all drugs sold in Brazil are generic. Multinational drug companies are attracted to Brazil as a country where they can manufacture generic brand drugs.
- *Electrical Power Systems.* Brazil's dependence on hydroelectric power generation and the lack of investment in other sources of energy led to an energy crisis from 2001 to 2002. This creates opportunities for investment in other sources of power generation, such as thermal and gas. The Brazilian market for electric power is estimated to be at least $2 billion.
- *Telecommunications.* Privatization in this sector and market-oriented reforms have led to open competition in what is considered to be Latin America's largest telecommunication sector. In 2011, investment in this sector reached nearly $11 billion. There is still potential for further growth. For example, cellular phones increased exponentially from thousands of phones in 1992 to 273 million cellular phones in 2014. These numbers show a rapidly growing industry.
- *Computer Hardware and Information Technology.* Brazil is investing heavily in computers, software, and information technology and growth in these sectors are outpacing the rest of Latin America. In 1990, Brazil had only 1.6 million computers. As of 2012, approximately 50 percent of Brazilian households had computers. The number of Internet users increased from 700,000 in 1996 to approximately 100 million in 2012. Although Brazil is growing quickly, these numbers indicate that Brazil is still behind other developing countries in Internet use and this sector appears ready for further rapid growth.

- *Media.* Brazil opened the media industry to foreign direct investment in 2002. Some sources indicate that the value of the entertainment and media market in Brazil is $35.4 billion. The media industry reaches over 90 percent of Brazilian households. It is estimated that the expansion of digital television in Brazil will require massive resources with most of it to be supplied by multinational companies.
- *Retailing.* Brazilian consumers are becoming more sophisticated and demanding. One sign of this change is an increasing concentration of the industry into a few large players and the elimination of smaller firms. Retail industries have also benefitted from technological upgrades in the delivery of goods and services. The retailing industry has attracted large multinational companies such as Walmart and Carrefour. The Brazilian food retailing industry has attracted an increasing number of foreign competitors. Both Walmart and Carrefour (a French company) are among Brazil's top ten largest food retailers.

3.   *Brazilian Laws Relating to Foreign Direct Investment and Business Organizations*

The Brazilian legal system is modeled on the civil law system and may be compared to the French, Italian, and Spanish systems, all of which have exerted influence on the development of the Brazilian legal system. Brazil has a federal constitution that extensively regulates the legal system, defining the powers of the federal, state, and municipal administrations, the Brazilian legislature, and the courts. Business organizations, to which we turn below, are regulated by civil and commercial codes, both part of Brazil's federal law.

A.   BRAZILIAN BUSINESS ORGANIZATIONS

As noted earlier, Brazil does not create specialized business forms for foreign capital and investment. Rather, the foreign investor will choose one of the Brazil business organization forms. As these business forms were created for domestic use, however, the foreign investor may need to be creative and adapt them for use as vehicles for FDI. The question remains which form of business entity should the foreign investor use and how can the foreign investor adapt it to suit its purposes, such as establishing a joint venture with a local Brazilian company? An overview of these forms is set forth below.

PROBLEM 6-20

Pharma, Inc., is considering forming a joint venture with Medico do Brasil, a large state-owned pharmaceutical company. The joint venture is to be a separate legal entity formed and jointly owned by Pharma and Medico. Both joint venture partners also want to manage the new company as it enters into the pharmaceutical industry. Pharma will bring its technology and research and development capabilities and Medico will bring its knowledge of the Brazilian pharmaceutical industry and market to the joint venture. Pharma wants to structure the joint venture so that Pharma has a 60 percent ownership interest and Medico has a 40 percent ownership interest. All of Pharma's senior officials work at the company headquarters in Chicago and are all needed at headquarters to run Pharma's U.S. operations and to plan Pharma's international expansion. Pharma asks you to describe which business form you would recommend for the joint venture and how the joint venture should be set up to accomplish Pharma's ownership interests and other goals. Unlike China, Brazil has no special laws governing joint ventures between foreign companies and local Brazilian companies, so Pharma will have to be creative in using Brazil's existing business laws to achieve its goals. Will setting up a consortium with Medico work? Consider the reading below.

Overview of Business Entities Available for Use in Foreign Direct Investment in Brazil

Unlike China, Brazil allows foreign ownership of domestic business entities. As a result, foreign direct investment is not subject to a special legal regime but is subject to the same regime available to domestic investors. Brazil, like the EU, has one single regime for business entities, but unlike the EU, Brazil regulates FDI at the level of exit of the foreign direct investment in the form of repatriation of capital and profits. We will explore those issues in the next section. For now, we examine Brazil's business vehicles available for domestic and foreign investors alike.

A large variety of business organizations are available in Brazil. The most common is the sole proprietorship. While it is the most simple business vehicle and is used widely by small businesses, it also has the disadvantage that all of the proprietor's individual assets are subject to the debts of the company. Medium and larger companies tend to favor the limited liability company or a stock company.

1. LIMITED LIABILITY COMPANY (SOCIEDADE LIMITADA)

The limited liability company, popularly known as the *limitada*, is one of the most popular business vehicles in Brazil because of its flexibility. Many multinational companies such as Ford, Pfizer, and Walmart organize their subsidiaries as limited liability companies. The *limitada* is governed by Articles 1052 *et seq.* of the new Civil Code.

Ownership in a *limitada* is represented by quotas designated in the company's charter. A quota, unlike a share of stock, is not represented in a certificate that can be transferred by endorsement. A quota can be transferred only by amending the charter of the company and filing a copy of the amendment with the Commercial Registry. The amount of capital in the *limitada* must be set forth in the charter and must be paid in by two or more persons who may be either individuals or entities. The *limitada* has no minimum capital requirement. The quota holders are jointly and severally liable for the full amount of the company's legal capital until it has been paid in. Once the capital has been fully paid, individual quota holders will be liable for the company's debts only if the company is irregularly wound up or if the quota holder violates the charter or commits an unlawful act. A *limitada* is automatically dissolved if there are fewer than two quota holders. For this reason, at least three quota holders are commonly used unless the two quota holders are legal entities.

Quota holders are required to decide company matters by formal meeting. Annual financial statements, including a balance sheet and an inventory, are mandatory. All decisions must occur in writing and no decisions can be undertaken by informal understanding (as was possible before the enactment of the new Civil Code). All resolutions of the *limitada* are normally approved by majority vote although some specific matters such as a transformation of the *limitada* into a different type of company require a unanimous vote. A three-fourths vote is required on other matters such as appointment of quota holders, amendments to the charter, merger, amalgamation, and dissolution. Generally, the management of a *limitada* is entrusted to one or more of the quota holders as provided in the charter. Depending on how the charter is written, a majority or super majority of the quota holders will be required for approval of various actions (unless otherwise required by law such as a unanimous vote for certain actions). Or a particular quota holder might be empowered to make decisions by himself. Some of the quota holders can be managers while others are passive investors. The drafters of the charter have great freedom to structure these management issues for the *limitada*.

There are three principal advantages of the *limitada* over the stock corporation, discussed below, as a vehicle for foreign investors to establish subsidiaries or joint ventures. First, the *limitada* is less expensive to organize and maintain. Second, even though the *limitada* is characterized as a corporation under Brazilian law, the *limitada* can be either a partnership or a corporation for U.S. tax purposes. It is up to the taxpayer to elect which status to choose upon election with the Internal Revenue Service. Third, unlike the directors of a stock corporation, the mangers of a *limitada* do not have to be residents of Brazil. The principal disadvantage of a *limitada* is the lack of public participation. The *limitada* cannot issue stock or debentures. Artificial names or the names of the quota holders followed by "e companhia" or "e cia" can be used in organizing a *limitada*. If an artificial name is used, the name must suggest the company's business activity. Unless the company's name ends with *limitada* or *ltda*, quota holders have unlimited liability.

2. STOCK CORPORATION (SOCIEDADE ANÓNIMA)

The stock corporation (SA) resembles the United States corporation. The SA's capital is divided into shares of stock. The liability of each shareholder is limited to the price of the shares to which he has subscribed but has not paid in. The SA must have at least two shareholders. The subscribers may be Brazilian or foreign individuals or legal entities. Foreign subscribers who are not residents in Brazil must be represented by Brazilian citizens in order to receive subpoenas for legal process. At least 10 percent of the price of the shares subscribed must be paid in cash and deposited in a bank authorized by the Securities and Exchange Commission of Brazil (CVM).

The SA is regarded as a commercial entity and must file its charter with the Commercial Registry and publish its acts of incorporation and minutes of annual meetings in public records. All financial statements and balance sheets must also be published once a year.

SAs can be either closely held or publicly held. If the SA is publicly held, the SA must register its shares with the CVM. The SA has great flexibility in issuing a wide variety of shares, including registered, treasury, endorsable, as well as different classes of stock, such as preferred or common.

The SA is subject to the management of a board of directors, which is made up of at least two directors. The SA may also set up an administrative council, consisting of at least three members elected by the shareholders. An administrative council is optional unless the SA is a public corporation. The directors discharge most of the management functions of officers in a U.S. corporation while the administrative council performs the general policy making of a board of directors of a U.S. corporation. The board of directors is elected either by the shareholders or by the administrative council. The administrative council is always elected by the shareholders. All members of the board of directors and the administrative council must be residents of Brazil but do not have to be citizens of Brazil. This requirement can create problems for foreign controlled corporations in Brazil since, under previous law, members of the administrative council could be non-residents. If a corporation is not publicly held then it is possible to dispense with the administrative council, but if the SA is publicly held then the multinational company might have to move key personnel to Brazil or appoint straw members to the administrative council.

The SA is required by law to have an annual shareholder's meeting. At this meeting, the management's accounts and balance sheets are reviewed and a dividend distribution policy is adopted. In addition, the shareholders elect the management and audit committee for the following year.

Corporate charters usually require a minimum annual dividend. If there is no such provision, Brazilian law requires that a dividend of 50 percent of net profits less amounts set aside as reserves must be distributed to shareholders. Five percent of net profits must be placed in a legal reserve to secure the safety of the company's capital. The reserve can be used only to offset losses or to increase capital. If the reserve reaches 20 percent of the company's capital, the reserves do not need to be increased. If the reserves exceed the company's capital, then the excess will be subject to a 25 percent tax unless it is capitalized, i.e., distributed as a dividend.

3. BRANCH OFFICE

A foreign corporation can attempt to operate in Brazil by setting up a branch office, but few do as a branch requires a decree issued by the President of Brazil. Long delays in issuing such decrees are common and occasionally the President refuses to issue the decree. Setting up a branch office is significantly more time consuming and expensive than establishing a *limitada*. In addition, the branch office is subject to unfavorable tax treatment under Brazilian law. As a result, the branch office is not a popular vehicle for foreign investors.

4. JOINT VENTURES

Under Brazilian law, there is no specific business vehicle for a joint venture. Brazilian law also does not have any written provisions requiring the foreign investor to form a joint venture. Nevertheless, in certain industries, such as petrochemicals, engineering, and mining, the joint venture is considered to be a de facto requirement for foreign companies that wish to do business in Brazil. Foreign companies that wish to establish joint ventures in Brazil must find creative ways in using existing business vehicles to set up a joint venture. The most commonly used vehicles used to form joint ventures are the *limitada* or the stock corporation.

The advantage of using a *limitada* to form a joint venture is that the joint venture rules can be set out in the charter. The foreign company and its Brazilian joint venture partner each become quota holders in accordance with their respective ownership interests in the joint venture. Since the charter of the *limitada* cannot be changed without the authorization of each quota holder, the joint venture partners have some assurance that the term of the joint venture will be observed. However, if the terms of the charter are not respected, Brazil provides no remedy of specific performance of the charter. The joint venture partners might wish to include a liquated damages clause in light of this gap in remedies available for breach of the joint venture rules.

The second possibility is to form an SA or the stock corporation. The rules of the joint venture can be set forth in the shareholders' agreement concerning transfers and voting. Provided that such shareholders' agreements are registered on the books of the SA and noted on the share certificates, the agreements are specifically enforceable under Brazilian law. This would allow the joint venture partners to draft shareholder agreements to contain the specific rules of the joint venture. The agreement should contain some mechanism for breaking a deadlock should the shareholders disagree. In most cases, one of the shareholders will have a majority interest in the joint venture, which would give the shareholder the right to cast a majority vote so long as the shareholder agreement did not require a super majority. These specific issues concerning voting, whether a majority vote is sufficient on all issues, and the power of one shareholder to override the votes of the other should be set out in detail in the shareholder agreement.

5. Consortia

Under Brazilian law, companies can form consortia but the consortium is not recognized as a separate entity for tax purposes or for purposes of liability. Foreign companies are allowed to participate in consortia. Brazilian law permits a consortium to be formed by an agreement to which two or more companies agree to participate in a common project. Under Brazilian law, the consortium agreement must cover at a minimum the following:

(a) the name of the consortium;
(b) the objective;
(c) period of duration;
(d) location of the principal place of business;
(e) responsibilities and duties of each participant;
(f) rules for receipt of income and allocation of profits and losses;
(g) rules for operating the consortium, accounting system, representation of participants, and management fees, if any;
(h) number of votes to which each participant is entitled;
(i) the contribution of each participant to expenses.

The consortium agreement must be filed with the Commercial Registry, which issues a certificate of filing. The certificate must be published. Each participant in the consortium is responsible for its agreed upon share of the consortium's debt. There is no presumption of joint and several liability. The bankruptcy of one participant does not affect other participants in the consortium. In Brazil, the consortium is commonly used for large construction projects.

B. BRAZILIAN LAWS APPLICABLE TO FOREIGN DIRECT INVESTMENT

PROBLEM 6-21

Advanced Precision Tools (APT), a Delaware corporation in the industrial tool and machine industry, has been under pressure from its shareholders to increase earnings and dividend payouts. APT has decided on a strategy of global expansion to increase revenue. APT seeks to establish a manufacturing facility in Brazil. One option is to purchase the Brazilian subsidiary of a Canadian company, Worktools do Brasil, which has a capital investment of $50 million and has earned a steady stream of profits for the past ten years. Worktools Canada has mentioned in passing that the capital of Worktools do Brasil is not registered with the Central Bank of Brazil but that registration is not required by law. Worktools' asking price for its subsidiary is $75 million. Another option is for APT to establish its own subsidiary but this would require an investment of at least $75 million and will take several years in order to become operational. Which option would you recommend for APT? See Profits Remittance Law, Articles 1, 3, 5, and 9. See also the following accompanying notes discussing the Profits Remittance Law and the Brazilian tax laws. If you were advising Worktools Canada, the parent company of the Brazilian subsidiary, would you ask for payment in Canada in Canadian dollars or payment in Brazilian reals? Worktools Canada is really intent on selling its Brazilian subsidiary. What type of buyer should Worktools look for?

PROBLEM 6-22

Pharma, an Illinois company, has established a subsidiary in Brazil to manufacture various pharmaceuticals for sale in Brazil. Pharma has entered into a patent agreement with the subsidiary. Under the terms of the agreement, Pharma's Brazilian subsidiary is to make annual royalty payments to Pharma's Chicago bank account equal to 12 percent of the subsidiary's total annual receipts from the sale of the products in Brazil. The 12 percent annual receipts also coincidentally equal 12 percent of Pharma's registered capital in Brazil. Pharma has forwarded all of the documentation needed to register Pharma's U.S. patents to the Brazilian subsidiary, but so far no one in Brazil has followed the local procedures to verify that the U.S. patents are valid in the United States. How much of its annual royalty payments under the licensing agreements will Pharma receive after taxes? The key issue is whether the payments are considered to be royalties under the patent licensing agreement or whether they are considered to be the repatriation of profits and dividends earned on registered capital under Article 43 and subject to a special tax. This could have a significant impact on the amount of profits received by Pharma. See Profits Remittance Law, Articles 11, 12, 13, and 43 and note 2 on pp. 520-521 below.

Profits Remittance Law
Law No. 4.131 of September 3, 1962

(Annotated translation, as originally enacted and as amended by Law No. 4.390 and other enactments)[69]

ARTICLE 1

For the purposes of this Law, foreign capital shall mean assets, machinery and equipment entering Brazil without an initial outlay of foreign exchange, destined for

---

69. Subsequent amendments are placed in brackets.

the production of goods or services, as well as financial or monetary resources brought into the country for investment in economic activities, provided that, in either case, they belong to individuals or legal entities resident, domiciled, or headquartered abroad.

ARTICLE 2

Foreign capital invested in the country shall be accorded identical legal treatment with that granted to nation capital, under equal conditions, prohibiting any discrimination not provided for in this Law.

OF THE REGISTRATION OF CAPITAL, REMITTANCE AND REINVESTMENT

ARTICLE 3

A special service for the registration of foreign capital, regardless of its form of entry into the country, as well as for foreign financial operations, is hereby instituted in the Superintendency of Money and Credit,[70] which shall register:

(a) foreign capital entering the country in the form of a direct investment or a loan, whether in money or in physical assets;
(b) foreign remittances as a return of capital or as capital earnings, profits, dividends, interest, amortization, as well as royalties, payments for technical assistance, or any other type of payment that involves the transference of income out of the country;
(c) reinvestment of earnings from foreign capital;
(d) changes in the monetary value of the capital of companies, effectuated in accordance with the legislation in force.

Sole Paragraph. Registration of the reinvestments referred to in letter (c) above shall also be made for legal entities headquartered in Brazil when affiliated with foreign companies or controlled by a majority of shares belonging to individuals or legal entities resident or headquartered abroad.

ARTICLE 4

Registration of foreign capital shall be made in the currency of the country of origin and that of reinvested profits in national currency. Registration of foreign capital shall be made in the currency of the country of origin, and reinvestment of profits shall be made simultaneously in national currency and the currency of the country to which it could have been remitted, with the conversion being carried out at the exchange rate of the period during which it was proven that the reinvestment was actually made.

---

70. The Superintendency of Currency and Credit (SUMOC) was transformed into the Central Bank of Art. 8 of Law No. 4.595 of Dec. 31, 1964.

Sole Paragraph. If the capital is in the form of physical assets, the registration shall be made at their value in the country of origin or, in the absence of satisfactory substantiation, in accordance with the value carried on the books of the company receiving the capital or by valuation according to criteria to be determined in appropriate regulations.

ARTICLE 5

Registration of foreign investment shall be applied for within 30 (thirty) days from the date of its entry into the country and shall be free from payment of any charge or fee. Registration of reinvested profits shall be made within the same period, starting from the date of approval of the respective accounting entry by the proper department of the company.

Sole Paragraph. Foreign capital and respective reinvested profits already present in the country are also subject to registration, which shall be requested by its owners or the parties responsible for the companies in which they have been invested, within the period of 180 (one hundred and eighty) days from the date of publication of this law.

[§1 Foreign capital and respective reinvested profits already present in the country are also subject to registration, which shall be requested by its owners or those responsible for the firms in which they have been invested, within a period of 180 (one hundred and eighty) days from the date of publication of this law.]

[§2 The Council of the Superintendency of Currency and Credit shall determine that proof shall be required for concession of registration of capital dealt within the prior paragraph.]

ARTICLE 7

For the purposes of registration, reinvestment is considered to be those amounts which could have been legally remitted abroad as profits but, were instead reinvested into the same company that generated them, or were invested in another sector of the national economy.

[There shall be considered as reinvestment, for the purposes of this law, income derived from companies established in the country and attributed to residents and domiciliaries abroad and which was invested in the same companies from which it was derived or in another sector of the national economy.]

OF THE REMITTANCE OF INTEREST, ROYALTIES AND TECHNICAL ASSISTANCE PAYMENTS

ARTICLE 8

To the extent that remittance of interest on loans, credits and financing exceeds the interest rate noted in the respective contract and in the respective registration, it shall be considered as amortization of capital. SUMOC is entitled to contest and reject that part of the rate that exceeds the interest charged in the financial market from which the loan, credit or financing originated for operations made at the same time and in similar conditions.

ARTICLE 9

Individuals and legal entities wishing to make transfers abroad for profits, dividends, interest, amortization, royalties, technical, scientific or administrative assistance or the like, must submit the contracts and documents considered necessary to justify the remittance to the proper departments of SUMOC and the Income Tax Division.

Sole Paragraph. Remittances abroad depend upon registration of the company with SUMOC and upon proof of payment of any income tax owed.

[§1 Remittances abroad depend upon registration of the company with SUMOC and proof of payment of any income tax owed.]

ARTICLE 11

Transfers for the payment of royalties for patents of invention, industrial and commercial trademarks, or other similar rights, require proof from the interested party that the respective rights have not expired in the country of origin.

[Requests for registration of contracts for the purpose of financial transfers for payment of royalties owed for the use of patents, industrial and commercial trademarks or other similar types of property, shall be accompanied by a certificate proving the existence and effectiveness in Brazil of the respective privileges granted by the National Department of Industrial Property, as well as an appropriate document showing that they have not expired in the country of origin.]

ARTICLE 12

The total amounts due for royalties for the exploitation of patents of invention or for the use of industrial or commercial trademarks or for technical, scientific, administrative or similar assistance, that may be deducted on income tax returns for the purposes of Article 37 of Decree No. 47.373 of December 7, 1959, shall be limited to a maximum of 5% (five percent) of the gross receipts from the product manufactured or sold.

§1 The percentage coefficients permitted for the deductions referred to in this article shall be set and periodically revised by acts of the Finance Ministry, taking into consideration the types of production or activities, classified by groups, according to the degree to which they are essential.

§2 The deductions referred to in this article shall be permitted when the expenses for technical, scientific, administrative or similar assistance have been proven, provided that such services have been effectively rendered, and that a contract for the assignment or license of the use of the trademarks and patents of invention has been properly registered in the country in accordance with the prescriptions of the Code of Industrial Property.

§3 Expenses for technical, scientific, administrative or similar assistance may only be deducted during the first 5 (five) years of the functioning of the firm or the introduction of the special process of production, when its necessity has been demonstrated. This period may be extended up to 5 (five) more years by authorization of the Council of the Superintendency of Currency and Credit.

ARTICLE 13

The sums owed for royalties for the exploitation of patents of invention or for technical, scientific, administrative or similar assistance that do not satisfy the conditions or exceed the limits provided for in the prior article shall be considered as distributed profits and taxed in accordance with Arts. 43 and 44.

Sole Paragraph. The total of the amounts owed to individual or legal entities resident or headquartered abroad for the use of industrial or commercial trademarks shall also be taxable in accordance with Articles 43 and 44.

ARTICLE 28

Whenever a serious disequilibrium in the balance of payments occurs, or when there are serious reasons to foresee that such a situation is imminent, the Council of the Superintendency of Currency and Credit may impose restrictions for a limited period on imports and the remittance of profits on foreign capital, and for this purpose, it may grant the Bank of Brazil a total or partial monopoly on foreign exchange operations.

§1 In the case provided for in this article, remittances for the return of risk capital are prohibited and profit remittances are limited to 10% (ten percent) of registered capital, in accordance with Articles 3 and 4.

[In the case provided for in this article, remittances for the return of capital are prohibited and remittance of profits shall be limited to 10% (ten percent) per annum upon capital and reinvestments registered in the currency of origin in accordance with articles 3 and 4 of this Law.]

§2 Earnings that exceed 10% (ten percent) of capital shall be communicated to SUMOC, which, in the event the restriction referred to in this article is extended for more than one financial year, may authorize the remittance, in the next fiscal year, of the quantities relating to the excess when the profits earned then do not reach that limit.

[Earnings that exceed the percentage fixed by the Council of the Superintendency of Currency and Credit, in accordance with the prior paragraph, shall be communicated to the Superintendency, which, in the event that the restriction referred to in this article is extended for more than a year, may authorize the remittance in the following fiscal year of amounts that represent the excess when the profits realized in that year did not reach that limit.]

§3 In the same cases in this article, the Council of the Superintendency of Currency and Credit may limit the remittance of quantities for the payment of royalties and technical, administrative or similar assistance up to the maximum cumulative annual limit of 5% (five percent) of the gross receipts of the firm.

§4 Also, in the cases described in this article, the Council of SUMOC is authorized to issue instructions limiting exchange expenses for "International Travel."

§5 Restrictions shall not be imposed, however, on the remittance of interest and amortization quotas contained in duly registered foreign loan agreements.

ARTICLE 29

Whenever it becomes advisable to economize the use of foreign exchange reserves, the Executive is authorized to demand temporarily, via an instruction from the Council of the Superintendency of Currency and Credit, a financial charge of a strictly monetary character which shall be imposed upon the importation of merchandise and upon financial transfer up to a maximum limit of 10% (ten percent) on the value of imported products and up to 50% (fifty percent) on the value of any financial transfer including "International Travel."

ARTICLE 30

Amounts collected from the financial charge provided for in the preceding article shall constitute a cruzeiro monetary reserve to be maintained by the Superintendency of Currency and Credit in a separate account, and shall be utilized, whenever deemed opportune, exclusively for the purchase of gold and foreign exchange to reinforce the foreign exchange reserves and capabilities.

FISCAL PROVISIONS

ARTICLE 41

The following earnings shall be subject to income tax withholding in the terms of this Law:

(a) dividends from bearer shares payments attributed thereto;
(b) interest and any other earnings and benefits from bearer securities denominated participation "Shares" or "Founder's Shares";
(c) the profits, dividends, and any other benefits and interest from registered shares or any other securities in registered form from legal entities, received by individuals or legal entities resident, domiciled or headquartered abroad, or by the branches or subsidiaries of foreign firms.

ARTICLE 42

Legal entities with a predominance of foreign capital, or which are branches or subsidiaries of firms headquartered abroad, are subject to the rules and rates of income tax established in the legislation for this tax.

ARTICLE 43

The amount of net profits and dividends on investments in foreign currency distributed to individuals and legal entities domiciled abroad shall be subject to a supplementary income tax whenever the profits and dividends exceed 12% (twelve percent) of registered capital and reinvestment pursuant to articles 3 and 4 of this Law calculated on average distributions in a three year period starting from 1984.

(1) The additional tax referred to in this article shall be charged according to the following table: between 12 percent and 15 percent of profits on capital and reinvestment: 40% (forty percent); between 15 percent and 25 percent of profits: 50 percent (fifty percent); above 25 percent of profits: 60% (sixty percent).

(2) The foregoing shall not apply to dividends and reinvested earnings in the country in accordance with Article 7 of this Law.

(3) The additional tax will be collected by the payer and debited to the payee as discount during the subsequent distributions.]

NOTES AND QUESTIONS

1. *The Profits Remittance Law.* The fundamental feature of the Profits Remittance Law (PRL) is the registration of foreign capital, reinvestment, and payments such as dividends, profits, and royalties. Despite the language of the PRL in Article 5, registration is not mandatory. However, there are several features of the PRL that create strong incentives for registration:

(1) All registered capital can be repatriated in foreign currency in its entirety at any time without penalty or restriction.

(2) Payments of dividends, profits, interest, and royalties can be repatriated in foreign currency if they have been properly registered under the PRL and proof is submitted that all taxes due have been withheld or paid.

(3) Capital or payments that are not registered cannot be lawfully repatriated in foreign currency.

Repatriation in the form of hard currency is crucial to the foreign investor because Brazilian currency, which can be removed from Brazil without restrictions, is not a freely convertible currency. However, a thriving black market and various schemes have arisen to funnel unregistered foreign capital and payments in foreign currency out of Brazil to other countries. The real can be exchanged for U.S. dollars through various unauthorized vendors in the black market and ferreted out of Brazil. These schemes are commonly used by some foreign companies doing business in Brazil and some Brazilian officials appear to tolerate these schemes in exchange for payoffs. Should a U.S. company be concerned about using any of these black-market schemes since they are widespread and tolerated?

2. *Brazilian Tax Laws.* As the PRL works in tandem with Brazilian tax laws, we summarize several key current features of the tax laws below. Tax is payable at the following rates:

(1) 15 percent on all corporate income plus a surtax based on portions of income above a certain level;

(2) 15 percent on the remittance of interest payments on loans;

(3) 15 percent on the payment of royalties and technical assistance payments on all technology transfer contracts that exceed 5 percent of gross receipts from the product manufactured or sold;

(4) 0 percent on all dividends and profits earned from Brazilian sources as of January 1, 1996;

(5) 0 percent on all dividends and profits that are reinvested as registered capital; and

(6) 0 percent on the remittance of registered capital but if the registered capital
     that is remitted is larger than the original amount registered then the excess is
     treated as capital gains subject to a 15 percent withholding tax. Note that capital
     gains tax on capital appreciation is due only if the sale of the capital occurs in
     Brazil. Under current Brazilian tax laws, sale of registered capital in Brazil that
     occurs entirely overseas is not subject to the capital gains tax.

One of the recent changes in the Brazilian tax regime is the exemption of dividends
and profits earned after January 1, 1996, from withholding. Prior to this change, dividends were subject to the general withholding rate of 15 percent. This tax structure created incentives for the foreign investor to reinvest profits in registered capital, which were
then not subject to taxation, rather than pay out profits in the form of dividends, which
was a taxable event. Under the current tax structure, however, the foreign investor no
longer has a tax-driven incentive to reinvest profits as the payout of dividends is also tax
free. Of course, Brazil's tax laws, like many other regimes, are subject to periodic revisions
so the foreign investor would be best advised to consult experts on the latest changes in
the law.

    3. One of the original purposes of the PRL was to protect Brazil from the sudden
flight of foreign currency through repatriation that might endanger Brazil's foreign currency reserves. As previously discussed, some of the harshest limitations on the exodus
of foreign currency that set a ceiling on how much capital could be repatriated on an
annual basis have now been revoked. Under the current PRL, what mechanisms are available to protect Brazil against foreign currency flight? See Profits Remittance Law, Articles
28–30.

    4. To be successful, Brazil's legal regime governing FDI depends on the strict obser-
vance of the Profits Remittance Law and the tax laws. What problems do you see with the
current system? Does the current system invite corruption?

NOTE ON SOVEREIGN DEBT COLLECTION

Virtually all nation-states issue bonds to investors, in many cases to international
investors. This sovereign debt is usually repaid without incident. Occasionally, however,
a nation-state will get into financial difficulty and repudiate or "restructure" its sovereign
debt. Sometimes (rarely) this is done with the approval of the International Monetary
Fund, which oversees sovereign debt obligations and is a lender of last resort to nation-
states in financial trouble.

    In 2001, the government of Argentina defaulted on more than $82 billion worth
of sovereign bonds, the largest such default in history. In such a case, bondholders have
few options; there is no global bankruptcy process and individual bondholders, unlike
foreign direct investors, normally cannot force the defaulting government to pay. Thus,
sovereign default on bonds usually leads to a restructuring of the country's debt, and
creditors are forced to take a "haircut"— a heavy loss on the debt— while the country
pays something, usually pennies on the dollar, in order to regain access to global credit
markets. This scenario played itself out in the case of Argentina.

    In 2005 and 2010, the government of Argentina, trying to extricate from financial
crisis, reached agreement with about 93 percent of its creditors holding Argentine bonds
totaling about $100 billion. The government agreed to issue new bonds to creditors in
substitution for the bonds they were holding. The new bonds were, however, worth less

than 30 percent of the value of the original bonds. Argentina carried out this exchange and repudiated the original bonds as part of the deal. However, investors holding about $25 billion of the original bonds refused to agree to the deal, and many of the original bonds were bought for pennies on the dollar by a variety of mutual funds and hedge funds. Some of these investors holding the original bonds— termed by the government of Argentina as "vulture funds"—engaged in a variety of legal tactics in order to make Argentina pay on the original bonds.

NML Capital, a hedge fund that is the principal holder of the Argentine bonds, filed suit against Argentina in New York federal district court to recover on the original bonds. This lawsuit bore fruit as the court ruled in favor of the investors on the ground that the Argentine government had violated the "*pari passu*" clause in the original loan agreement, which promised "equal footing" treatment to all its creditors. Thus, when Argentina pays the next installment of its sovereign debt to its admitted creditors, it must also pay a total of $1.33 billion to the funds holding the original, repudiated bonds. Furthermore, anticipating that Argentina would not comply with a court order, the district court issued a broad injunction against Argentina and against intermediary banks that might facilitate Argentina's payment of creditors without honoring the claims of the holders of the original bonds. The district court also approved a broad discovery request by the bondholders, allowing post-judgment discovery to the extent that Argentina must disclose all assets, even if located outside the United States, and regardless of their location or use. The U.S. Court of Appeals for the Second Circuit largely affirmed the district court, remanding only for clarification of the injunctive relief against third-party intermediaries. *See NML Capital, Ltd. v. Republic of Argentina*, 727 F.3d 230 (2d Cir. 2013).

Do you think it wise or proper for the U.S. federal courts to become so involved in foreign sovereign debt matters?

There is no insolvency procedure for sovereign states under international law. The International Monetary Fund and others have proposed that such a procedure be instituted. Do you agree?

NML Capital has relentlessly pursued the enforcement of the New York judgment:

- In 2013, NML Capital sought enforcement of the New York judgment in Ghana by filing a temporary injunction under Ghanaian law attaching the Argentine frigate, Libertad, a three-masted naval ship that was docked in Accra. The ship's seizure sparked a decision by the International Tribunal for the Law of the Sea ordering Ghana to release the vessel. *ARA Libertad (Arg. v. Ghana)*, Case No. 20, Order of Dec. 15, 2012, 2000 ITLOS Rep. 332, available at *http://www.itlos.org*. The Ghanaian Supreme Court, while ruling that a decision of an international tribunal is not binding under Ghanaian law absent implementing legislation, nevertheless ordered the ship released as a matter of public policy. *Republic v. High Court Accra, ex parte Attorney General*, Civil Motion No. J5/10/2013 (Ghana 2013), available at *http://pca-cpa.org/showfile.asp?fil_id=2336*.
- NML Capital successfully attached a New York bank account owned by Argentina's Ministry of Science, Technology and Productive Innovation. The court allowed the attachment of sovereign funds under the commercial activity exception to the FSIA. *See NML Capital, Ltd. v. Republic of Argentina*, 680 F.3d 254 (2d Cir. 2012).

Although Argentina has settled with some of the holders of the original-issue bonds, creditors such as NML Capital are pursuing Argentine assets in courts around the world. For efforts in France and the United Kingdom, see Note, 108 Am. J. Int'l L. 73 (2014).

On June 16, 2014, the U.S. Supreme Court delivered a one-two punch against Argentina's attempts to evade paying its sovereign bonds. First, the Supreme Court denied certiorari (for the second time) in the NML Capital case discussed above. *Republic of Argentina v. NML Capital Ltd.*, *cert. denied*, 135 S. Ct. 2819 (2014). Second, the Court (opinion by Justice Scalia) upheld the lower court's broad, world-wide post-judgment discovery and execution order concerning Argentina's sovereign assets. *Republic of Argentina v. NML Capital, Ltd.*, 134 S. Ct. 2250 (2014).

7   *Protecting Intellectual Property Rights*

In the three principal forms of IBTs we considered in Chapters Five and Six—the agency/distributorship, licensing/contract manufacturing, and various forms of foreign direct investment (FDI)—intellectual property (IP) rights play an important role. This is a major difference between these IBTs and the international sales/export-import transaction that we analyzed in Chapters Two, Three, and Four where IP issues arise less frequently. Thus, the progression of IBTs from international sales to FDI generally requires providing greater access to intellectual property rights, which at the same time also creates greater risks to the foreign investor. In previous chapters, we have examined the types of legal procedures and precautionary steps under the international intellectual property system that a U.S. corporation must undertake in order to protect its IP, which include following the filing and registration requirements for its IP abroad. We also examined how a U.S. corporation should attempt to structure the licensing and FDI transactions through contract to protect its IP while at the same time providing appropriate access to those rights to third parties, which is now such an important part of international business. However, no matter how careful the planning of a transaction and thorough the precautions taken by a foreign investor, there is a limit to how effective prophylactic measures can be when there are pirates and profiteers who are intent upon the theft of IP. While the previous chapters discussed how to take the appropriate steps in the planning stages to protect IP from misuse and theft, the bulk of this chapter focuses on what happens after a theft has occurred and on the enforcement and protection of rights that have been breached. This brings us to the growing problem of commercial piracy, which refers to the unauthorized copying of copyrights, trademarks, patents, and trade secrets. Why is commercial piracy a growing problem for all IP owners?

The rise in commercial piracy can be directly traced to the growing importance and value of IP. We are now in an age where information, knowledge, and know-how, most of which are protected by IP, are increasingly integral to success in business and for the economic development of nations. As IP has become increasingly valuable, its theft by pirates has also become an increasingly lucrative criminal activity. In fact, as we detail below, commercial piracy has become, in many cases, one of the most significant business problems for IP owners, many of them MNEs. In this chapter, we will consider the problem of commercial piracy and the strategies and methods that IP owners, in most cases MNEs, can undertake to enforce their rights. After an overview of the problem, we will take a closer look at commercial piracy in the People's Republic of China (PRC). It is no coincidence that China, one of the largest recipients of foreign direct investment and one of the fastest growing economies in the world, also has one of the world's most serious commercial piracy problems. While in certain respects unique, commercial piracy in China also illustrates some of the common and daunting challenges for IP owners that exist in many other developing countries. While commercial piracy exists in all countries to some extent, some of the worst problems are in developing countries due to the lack of mature legal systems and differences in social values. Modern IP rights have been primarily developed by Western nations and reflect a Western legal culture. In contrast, many developing countries do not have a tradition of recognizing property rights in individuals to knowledge and information. While many developing countries may have adopted laws modeled on Western IP laws, the basic social institutions and values underlying many of these societies do not support a Western-style legal regime protecting IP. As a result, commercial piracy often pits MNEs and their home countries, advanced industrialized countries, against developing countries and their constituencies. This alignment of interests has resulted in a number of controversial issues. For example, one debate concerns whether public health needs justify the disregard of patents by some countries that are without the resources to pay for patented drugs that are needed to treat widespread deadly diseases such as AIDS. Is it commercial piracy for countries to disregard patents when doing so helps to make medicines available to treat major problems of public health that might otherwise lead to a social and political crisis? We will take a look at the "access to medicines" debate. Commercial piracy, moreover, is not the only type of piracy that we shall be examining. In this chapter, we shall also look at the current controversy concerning "biopiracy," which is a term used by some to describe the attempts by MNEs to obtain IP in forms of traditional knowledge indigenous to many developing countries rich in biological resources without sharing any profits with these countries. In the final section of this chapter, we explore the means available to IP owners to combat the import of "gray-market" goods, that is, genuine goods intended for sale in a foreign market but which are diverted for import into the United States.

I.   Overview of Commercial Piracy

Commercial piracy is a broad term that encompasses copyright piracy, trademark counterfeiting, and patent infringements. This section begins with an overview of the size and scope of all forms of commercial piracy and the following sections will examine each specific type of piracy in more detail.

A.   Rise in Commercial Piracy

In the past few decades, commercial piracy has increased dramatically around the world. In 1982, the U.S. International Trade Commission estimated that commercial piracy resulted in losses of U.S. $5.5 billion. A similar study by the ITC in 1988 estimated losses at over U.S. $60 billion. As of its most recent study, the Organization for Economic Cooperation and Development (OECD) estimates that global trade in counterfeit goods has surpassed U.S. $250 billion (almost 2 percent of world trade), causing losses of U.S. $150 billion to G20 countries, the leading industrialized nations of the world. *Joint Press Release, World Intellectual Property Organization, Counterfeiting and Piracy Endangers Global Economic Recovery Say Global Congress Leaders*, PR/2009/621 (Dec. 3, 2009). Based on data in the OECD study, one source states that by 2015, the total global value of counterfeit goods will surpass $1.2 trillion.[1] Beyond the direct losses, the indirect effects—loss of government tax revenue, the impact on welfare spending, the increased costs of crime enforcement, and the increase costs in health services—will cost the G20 countries an additional $125 billion.[2]

In subsequent sections of this chapter, we set forth some more detailed information on the size and scope of this problem. In this section, we discuss some of the causes for this trend. One way to understand the rise in commercial piracy is to view it as the illegal by-product of the development of legitimate commercial and economic activity. As lawful commercial activity has increased dramatically so has unlawful economic activity. For example, in some countries the growth of the market in legitimate products is mirrored by the growth of an underground economy selling pirated versions of the same products. In certain parts of Asia, it is well known that some sections of cities trade in genuine products through large department stores while other sections of town offer knock-offs and smuggled versions of the same products in open-air street markets, small stores, and stalls.

There are several specific factors that we wish to highlight:

(1) *Access to Materials and Technology.* The relatively free flow of products and information across national borders and the availability of inexpensive, high-quality copy technology have been major contributors to the rise in commercial piracy. In the area of copyright, the use of the Internet to download copyrighted materials and the availability of cheap computer technology means that individuals can make massive numbers of copies at a low cost. A common practice is to use handheld digital cameras to copy first-run movies during a showing in a movie theater and then to churn out massive numbers of DVDs that are then sold while the movie is still in its first run. Other techniques involve obtaining digital copies of movies in their original format, through some breach of internal security, from movie studios before the movies are publicly released. In the area of trademark counterfeiting, high-quality, low-cost technologies such as color copiers and printers have made it easier than ever to duplicate labels, packaging, and symbols with accuracy and speed.

(2) *Increasing Importance of Trademarks and Brands.* As competition becomes increasingly sharp on a global basis, companies are spending more on advertising, promotion, and marketing to further distinguish their trademarks or brands and to create a clearly identifiable image. The issue of creating a brand image or "branding" has become more important as competition becomes ever more acute and brand owners are looking for every possible avenue to distinguish themselves from their competitors. In many instances, as technology advances, the only difference between products is brand image as competitors offer products that are indistinguishable in quality. As a result, IP owners are spending hundreds of millions of dollars on advertising and other promotional activities (including sponsorship of sporting events, educational programs, and charitable events) to create differences between what are essentially similar products through the creation of an identifiable image and goodwill with consumers. As brands become more valuable and brand

1. *http://www.iccwbo.org/Data/Documents/Bascap/Global-Impacts-Study-Full-Report.*
2. *See id.*

image becomes a more valuable commercial good, the incentive to counterfeit these brands also increases. To some extent, the sharp increase in counterfeiting and piracy is a reflection of the success of IP owners in increasing the value of their brands.

(3) *Technology Transfer Through FDI.* The increase of FDI in countries around the world has led to an unprecedented rate of technology transfer and has created widespread access to all forms of intellectual property that were simply unavailable before. FDI also encourages the development of an infrastructure to support the absorption of advanced technology by the host countries. Offering advanced training for employees, sponsoring employees for education at universities abroad, and establishing research and development centers are some of the ways in which FDI helps host countries to increase their capabilities to absorb technology. One of the main benefits of licensing and foreign direct investment is the authorized transfer of technology to the recipient, but such transfers also carry the risk of the unauthorized use of the technology by the recipient or by third parties. It is no coincidence that in many cases as the level of technology transfer increases to a recipient country so does the level of the unauthorized use of that technology. As FDI is often the most effective form of technology transfer, some of the countries that are receiving large amounts of FDI also have some of the world's most serious commercial piracy problems. In many developing countries, the areas where goods are manufactured by authorized factories are also the same areas where the bulk of pirated and counterfeit goods are produced.

PROBLEM 7-1

Acme Company, a U.S.-based MNE engaged in the consumer products business, has entered into a joint venture in Argentina with a local company to manufacture and sell shampoo. As is consistent with Acme's global business practices, the Acme joint venture sources its bottles from a third-party supplier and its raw materials, such as enzymes and perfumes, from third parties and then combines these raw materials using its own special formula and manufacturing process to make its world-famous shampoo. Acme has discovered that within a week of the launch of a new product with all-new packaging, its heavily advertised and promoted two-in-one shampoo and conditioner, counterfeits in large quantities have appeared on the market. The counterfeits are of such high quality in both packaging and content that Acme must have the counterfeits tested in its laboratories to distinguish them from the real product. In fact, the counterfeits were so clever that at first Acme thought that the products were real but then discovered that they contained a layer of real Acme shampoo that occupied the top third of the bottle so Acme scientists started taking some of the shampoo from the bottom of the bottles, which contained only some minor blemishes and other imperfections. Acme's CEO is incensed and has called upon you—Acme's general counsel—to fix the problem. According to the CEO, the first order of business is for you to meet with the Buenos Aires authorities and ask them to locate and shut down the underground factories making these counterfeits. Do you agree with this approach? What would you suggest as a first step?

B. Categories of Commercial Piracy

1. Copyright Piracy

Copyright piracy refers to the unauthorized copying of a fixed content of a medium of expression such as books, films, musical recordings, and computer software that are contained in print, audio and videotapes, compact disks, and DVDs. Copyright piracy, the focus of this section, refers to the exact duplication of a copyrighted work as opposed to copyright infringement, which refers to the partial copying of a work. In many instances, copyright infringement may involve a legitimate business dispute between two business entities that is resolved in a civil litigation. Copyright piracy never involves a legitimate business dispute and may also be a criminal offense.

In the case of copyright piracy, there is not necessarily any attempt to convince the customer that the pirated product was manufactured and distributed by the original copyright owner. Many consumers knowingly purchase a product that is pirated because the consumer wants the content of the product and is not concerned that it is not manufactured by the copyright owner. As modern technology makes it possible to provide exact or high-quality duplicates of original material, the quality of the pirated product may not be a major concern to the consumer.

Studies by government and industry groups show that losses from copyright piracy on a global basis are in the tens of billions of dollars. Piracy losses are largest in the business software industry. The Business Software Alliance (BSA), an industry advocacy group, estimated that in 2011 the commercial value of global software theft was over $63 billion.[3] The Recording Industry Association of America (RIAA) meanwhile claims that music piracy causes $12.5 billion in losses to the U.S. economy annually,[4] while another study suggests that yearly losses to e-book piracy reach $3 billion.[5] Furthermore, the problem of piracy is greater in some regions than others. In the market for PC software, for example, while the United States had the largest commercial value of pirated software at $9.77 billion in 2011 it had one of the lowest piracy rates, at only 19 percent.[6] Of the 20 economies with the largest commercial value of pirated software, six had piracy rates below 30 percent: the United States, Germany, the United Kingdom, Japan, Canada, and Australia. China, on the other hand, had a piracy rate of 77 percent and the second largest market for pirated software at $8.90 billion. India, Thailand, and Indonesia also made the list, each with piracy rates higher than 60 percent. As a group, the piracy rate for developing countries was 68 percent in 2011, compared to just 24 percent in developed economies.

Some of the worst copyright piracy problems are in the area of business and entertainment software. As the following chart indicates, although world software piracy rates have fluctuated recently, it is still about 42 percent in a recent year.

---

3. *Global Software Piracy Study 2011*, BUSINESS SOFTWARE ALLIANCE, *http://globalstudy.bsa.org/2011*.

4. *Who Music Theft Hurts*, RECORDING INDUSTRY ASS'N AM., *http://www.riaa.com/physicalpiracy.php?content_selector=piracy_details_online*.

5. *Guardian for E-Books*, DIGIMARC, *http://www.digimarc.com/guardian/e-books*. It is worth pointing out that various studies estimating the economic impact of intellectual property piracy have recently come under scrutiny and criticism by the Government Accountability Office, whose experts "observed that it is difficult, if not impossible, to quantify the economy-wide impacts [of piracy]." U.S. Gov't Accountability Office, GAO-10-423, Intellectual Property: Observations on Efforts to Quantify the Economic Effects of Counterfeit and Pirated Goods (2010), available at *http://www.gao.gov/new.items/d10423.pdf*.

6. *Global Software Piracy Study 2011*, BUSINESS SOFTWARE ALLIANCE, *http://globalstudy.bsa.org/2011*.

FIGURE 7-1
World Piracy Rate[7]

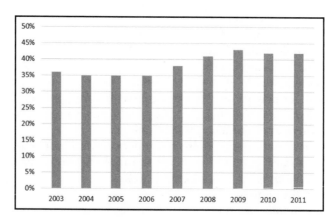

For 2011, Central and Eastern Europe is the region with the highest piracy rate (62%), followed by Latin America (61%), Asia Pacific (60%), Middle East/Africa (58%), Western Europe (32%), and North America (19%).

Measured by the amount of losses rather than by the piracy level, Asia/Pacific is by far the leading region in the world.

FIGURE 7-2
Dollar Losses by Region (U.S. $ billions)[8]

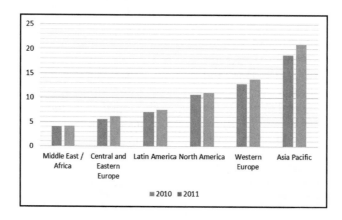

Most experts believe that the piracy level is a more reliable indicator of the seriousness of the problem than the amount of losses. For example, losses in the United States are the highest in the world at $9.8 billion but the piracy level for software in the United

---

7. Source: 2011 Business Software Alliance Global Software Piracy Study.
8. *Id.*

States is about 19 percent. U.S. losses are high because of the size of the U.S. economy. As a result, the piracy problem in the United States is considered mild by comparison to a country such as Georgia (formerly part of the Soviet Union) where nine of every ten software applications is pirated. In China, levels of copyright piracy are dropping but due to the expanding market total losses are mounting. In 2002, China had a piracy rate of 92 percent, the second highest of any country. While China decreased its piracy rate to 77 percent in 2011, a significant drop, losses reached $8.9 billion, an increase of more than $2 billion in the space of two years. China may be on course to surpass the United States ($9.8 billion) as the country with the largest losses due to copyright piracy. With one of the world's most serious copyright piracy problems (by losses) and a much greater trademark counterfeiting problem, discussed below, China stands alone as the nation with the most IP piracy in the world.

NOTES AND QUESTIONS

1. For all forms of commercial piracy, there appears to be a widespread perception on the part of some consumers that it is not a serious offense as the only "harm" involved is that wealthy multinational enterprises may earn fewer profits. The perception that the offense is harmless especially appears to apply to copyright piracy. Low-quality, counterfeit goods and pirated drugs might endanger the health and safety of consumers, but pirated software and music seem to harm no one. Pirated business and entertainment software, music, and movies flood some markets, particularly in Asia, where Western tourists eagerly flock to look for "bargains." Many consumers also eagerly buy certain types of counterfeit goods, such as copies of famous watches, handbags, and clothing. Some well-known public figures, including a former U.S. Trade Representative, have been reported in the media as having knowingly purchased counterfeit products while in China negotiating the conditions of China's entry into the WTO.[9] Some consumers seem to find buying pirated products at home or abroad to be fun, exciting, and harmless. Is there really nothing wrong with buying pirated goods? Is the only consequence of commercial piracy that wealthy MNEs make smaller profits?

2. Looking at Figure 7-3 below, how would you characterize the developmental stage of these countries? Is piracy being used as a tool of economic development?

3. Some have argued that commercial piracy of IP mostly owned by developed countries and their constituents benefits developing countries, many of which were colonized by developed countries and were set back in their development through years of exploitation and oppression. What these developing countries, many liberated from colonization only within the past several decades, need most is advanced technology to modernize and industrialize their economies. Can commercial piracy be viewed as free technology transfer and a form of justified retribution or compensation exacted by developing countries upon developed countries for past injustices?

---

9. *See* Andrew C. Mertha, *The Politics of Piracy* 1 (2005).

FIGURE 7-3[10]
25 Countries with the Highest Software Piracy Rates

Country	2011	2010
Zimbabwe	92%	91%
Georgia	91%	93%
Bangladesh	90%	90%
Libya	90%	88%
Moldova	90%	90%
Yemen	89%	90%
Venezuela	88%	88%
Armenia	88%	89%
Belarus	87%	88%
Azerbaijan	87%	88%
Indonesia	86%	87%
Pakistan	86%	84%
Iraq	86%	85%
Ukraine	84%	86%
Sri Lanka	84%	86%
Algeria	84%	83%
Paraguay	83%	83%
Cameroon	83%	82%
Nigeria	82%	82%
Zambia	82%	82%
Vietnam	81%	83%
Ivory Coast	81%	79%
El Salvador	80%	79%
Botswana	80%	79%
Guatemala	79%	80%

2. Trademark Counterfeiting

While copyright piracy is a serious problem that causes losses in the tens of billions of dollars, industry groups claim that trademark counterfeiting accounts for annual losses in the hundreds of billions of dollars worldwide. Copyright piracy is usually limited to software, movies, music, and books, but counterfeiting today can occur in an almost unlimited array of products from all different sectors. Counterfeiters not only target consumer products but also fake industrial products such as automobiles, aircraft engines, and airplane parts; agricultural products such as seed and fertilizers; foods such as baby formula; and drugs. The International Chamber of Commerce estimates that 5 to 7 percent of global commerce consists of counterfeit goods. The bulk of the total worldwide losses caused by commercial piracy can be attributed to trademark counterfeiting.

Counterfeiting refers to the unauthorized act by one party of producing and passing off exact duplicates of authentic products with trademarks owned by another party.

---

10. Source: 2011 Business Software Alliance Global Software Piracy Study.

In contrast to copyright piracy discussed in the previous section, counterfeiters often attempt to pass off the counterfeit as the genuine product through making copies that are often indistinguishable from the authentic product and that will often bear the registered or unregistered trademark of another party along with the company name, address, and trade dress of the lawful manufacturer or trademark owner. In many cases, the trademark or brand owner cannot distinguish between the counterfeit and genuine product without subjecting the product to detailed laboratory testing and analysis.

While many copyright pirates may make little or no attempt to convince the consumer that the product is genuine, consumer deception is a more serious issue in the case of trademark counterfeiting. However, not all consumers who buy counterfeits are deceived. Consumers tend to be willing to buy counterfeit goods where product quality is not a major issue. With "high involvement" products that consumers ingest or put on their skin or hair, most consumers do not tend to knowingly buy counterfeits. However, many consumers knowingly purchase counterfeits of "low involvement" products that are worn such as clothing, shoes, or watches or carried such as handbags or luggage. In these cases, consumers are less concerned with product quality and more concerned about the prestige of the brand.

Consumer health and safety, not usually an issue in the area of copyright piracy, can also be a problem in dealing with counterfeit goods. As many, although not all, counterfeit goods are of an inferior quality, they can cause harm to consumers. For example, counterfeit airplane and car parts and counterfeit consumer products, such as fake liquor and medicines, have resulted in injury or death to consumers.

A recent trend is that criminal organizations around the world have been drawn to commercial piracy—particularly counterfeiting—by high profits and the relatively low-risk nature of the crime. The participation of criminal organizations of considerable size and with considerable resources is necessary in order to coordinate the manufacture, export, import, distribution, and sale of counterfeit goods in international markets. Take the growing problem of counterfeit cigarettes that are being smuggled into the United States, which is estimated to exceed $1 billion annually. A single entity must be able to coordinate the supply of tobacco plants, the production of the counterfeit cigarettes in underground factories, the export of the cigarettes to the United States, the clearance of the counterfeits through U.S. Customs and Border Protection under false documentation (using names of importers acquired through identity theft making them untraceable), and the distribution of the product to weak links in the distribution chain of the brand owner. As most legitimate brand owners deal only with qualified large-scale distributors who will not deal in counterfeits, the counterfeiters must identify the "soft" spots in the distribution network, that is, those "sub-jobbers" or "sub-distributorships" who purchase goods from the qualified distributors but who are also willing to purchase counterfeits to mix in with the supply of genuine product. The sub-jobbers then sell the counterfeit product to small retail stores (no large retail store will buy from sub-jobbers). This type of organization must have the capability of coordinating all of these operations and must have a large number of "foot soldiers" in the United States and abroad to implement this business. At the first sign of trouble, these "foot soldiers" board a plane leaving the United States and disappear. According to Los Angeles Customs officials, the Asian criminal organizations involved in the trade in counterfeit cigarettes are every bit as well organized, ruthless, and violent as South American organizations involved in narcotics.

A comparison between the trade in narcotics and the trade in counterfeit cigarettes illustrates the attraction of counterfeiting to criminal organizations. At a profit margin of more than ten to one, the trade in counterfeit cigarettes is highly lucrative and rivals that for narcotics but with much lower costs and risks. While the trade in counterfeit cigarettes is most likely the most profitable, trade in counterfeit luxury items such as handbags and clothing and counterfeit and pirated software is also extremely lucrative. The maximum jail sentence for counterfeiting under the Trademark Counterfeiting Act of 1984, 18 U.S.C. §2320 (2006), further discussed on p. 551, is ten years in prison, but trafficking in narcotics will routinely result in much more severe jail sentences. In addition, there is the issue of priorities for law enforcement entities. The U.S. Customs and Border Patrol, part of the Department of Homeland Security, has stated that its first priority is detecting and preventing terrorism. The FBI places priority on targeting terrorism, violent crimes, and narcotics. With thousands of shipping containers arriving every day at the port of Los Angeles alone, it is not possible for Customs officials to do a detailed inspection of every container, which involves opening the container and inspecting its contents. Customs will target certain containers but only on the basis of specific intelligence, which is usually supplied by brand owners but is difficult to obtain. When Customs has seized containers with counterfeits, it often discovers that the name of the importer has been obtained through identity theft, making it impossible to trace those involved. Counterfeiters seem to have decided that as some containers will inevitably be seized, they simply consider the seized containers as a cost of doing business, given the large number of containers that do go through undetected. Tracing the seized containers involves setting up a "sting" operation that would allow a pass-through of the counterfeit goods into commerce through the use of federal agents assuming false identities to penetrate the criminal organizations. This usually involves months of work and a substantial commitment of resources from Customs, the FBI, and the U.S. Attorney.

Industry groups have provided some evidence that some organizations are selling counterfeit products to finance terrorist activities. However, it has been difficult to prove a systematic link between terrorist organizations and commercial piracy, although industry groups are continuing to try to make this connection.

The high profits involved combined with the low-risk nature of the crime have prompted some law enforcement officials to call counterfeiting the crime of the twenty-first century.

NOTES AND QUESTIONS

1. Not only are profits high, but costs in the trade in counterfeit cigarettes and other goods are also lower than costs in drug trafficking. Counterfeit goods can be moved undetected through normal channels of commerce in plain sight in trucks or trains, can be stored in common warehouses, and can be sold through normal retail channels in public stores. Why do these attributes result in lower costs than those in drug trafficking?

2. One of the problems with counterfeits that generally does not exist in the case of copyright piracy is harm to the reputation of the brand owner and its goodwill with consumers. Suppose a consumer inadvertently buys a counterfeit product and soon discovers it to be of inferior quality. How might this harm the reputation of the brand owner?

3. Consumers who later discover that they have been deceived into purchasing a counterfeit are often angry and wish to voice their complaints. Which person or what entity are these consumers most likely to contact in order to complain? How might this process affect the reputation of the brand owner?

3. Patent Infringements

Patent infringements in this context refer to the unauthorized copying of a registered patent. In many cases, patent infringements tend to be complex matters because determining whether a patent has been infringed can involve detailed scientific and technical analysis. In the United States, patent infringements are often legitimate business disputes that are highly esoteric and involve expert testimony. On a global scale, patent infringements are not usually grouped together with other forms of commercial piracy with the notable exception of pharmaceuticals where the unauthorized copying of patents is widespread. Because of the underground nature of drug piracy and the inconsistency of reporting violations, estimates of the extent of pirated pharmaceuticals and losses are inevitably inaccurate. *See* World Health Organization, FAQs, available at *http://www.who. int/medicines/services/counterfeit/faqs/12/en/index.html.* The illegal copying of drugs occurs more frequently in developing countries, although the problem is ubiquitous. *Id.* As you can well imagine, pharmaceutical companies and industry groups are seeking more effective enforcement of their rights. Companies point out that unauthorized copies do not allow them to recoup the exceptionally high cost of research and development, which is now estimated to be almost $1.5 billion for each new pharmaceutical product brought to market. *See* Pharm. Research & Mfrs. of Am., *2013 Biopharmaceutical Research Industry Profile* (2013), available at *http://www.phrma.org/industryprofile2013.* The pharmaceutical industry is particularly vulnerable to unauthorized copies because while it takes the expenditure of hundreds of millions of dollars to invent a new drug, the drug can in many cases be easily reverse engineered and a serviceable copy can be made at low cost. Unlike the area of counterfeit products where issues of liability tend to be clear, however, drug patents and the unauthorized copying of pharmaceuticals have a public health dimension that raises complex public policy issues on an international level. We return to a more detailed examination of this issue in a later section.

NOTES AND QUESTIONS

1. In setting forth the different types of commercial piracy, we do not mean to imply that they are mutually exclusive. To the contrary, one product may involve different types of commercial piracy. Can you give an example of a single product that (1) involves both copyright piracy and trademark counterfeiting, (2) involves both patent infringement and trademark counterfeiting, and (3) involves all three types of commercial piracy?

2. When faced with a pirated product that violates multiple rights, IP owners usually assert a trademark counterfeiting claim because of issues of proof. Why? How do you prove a claim of counterfeiting, copyright piracy, or patent infringement?

3. *Methods for Determining Levels of Piracy.* We have included a number of tables with statistics and other information on piracy. Most of this information is provided by MNEs who have formed industry groups to deal with piracy, such as the International Anti-Counterfeiting Coalition and the Business Software Alliance. These statistics are impressive, but what methods do MNEs use in arriving at some of these statistics on the level of piracy and the losses involved? MNEs calculate the level of commercial piracy using some variant of the following method: For example, in the area of trademark counterfeiting, MNEs first calculate the demand for their product by determining how much product overall there is in any given market. This can be done through market surveys. The MNE will hire a marketing company to do an on-site survey of how much of their products are available for sale in a given location through store visits. The MNE will then determine how much genuine product is shipped to the particular market through its own legitimate distribution channels. The difference between the amount of total product and the amount of legitimate product shipped by the MNE equals the amount of counterfeits on the market. For example, if there are 100,000 bottles of shampoo sold in a particular city and the MNE has shipped 80,000 units to that city, then 20,000 units are counterfeit. Owners of computer software use a similar method. The difference between

the number of applications supplied to a particular location, which represents demand, and the number of genuine applications shipped, which represents supply, equals the estimate of software applications pirated. What assumptions must these methods make about the amount and type of control exercised by MNEs over the distribution of their products? Do you find these assumptions to be sound?

4. *Methods of Determining Losses.* MNEs calculate losses from commercial piracy using a variant of the following method. Sometimes, MNEs appear to assume that the mere presence or availability on the market of a pirated product equals a lost sale of a genuine product at retail price. At other times, MNEs claim that a lost sale occurs for each pirated or counterfeit product that is purchased by a consumer. For example, if a consumer purchases a bottle of counterfeit shampoo, the manufacturer will consider that purchase to result in the loss of a purchase of a bottle of authentic shampoo at the retail price that would have otherwise occurred but for the counterfeit. Using the estimate of the amount of counterfeit and pirated products that exist in any given market under the methods set forth in note 3 *supra*, MNEs then claim that the amount of pirated products valued at the retail price of the genuine product represents their losses. For example, if 20 percent of the shampoo on the market in a given location is counterfeit, the MNE will then calculate that it has lost 20 percent of sales revenue of the genuine shampoo at retail prices. If the total sales for the location is $100,000 and 20 percent of the product on the market is counterfeit, then MNEs will claim that their losses for that market are $20,000. A similar method is used in the case of software applications by copyright owners. Assume that a genuine bottle of shampoo costs $8 and that a counterfeit costs $2.50. Assume also that a genuine software application costs $185 and that a pirated copy costs $15. Using these figures, which reflect the actual differences between real and pirated products in many markets, do you agree with the position of the MNEs that each purchase of a pirated product represents the loss of a sale of a genuine product? Why do MNEs make these claims?

5. *Is Some Counterfeiting Beneficial?* Some MNEs will privately admit that some piracy of their products is beneficial at the early stages of the product's introduction in a developing market. The reason is that in developing markets there is often the lack of a sophisticated distribution system. As in all cases, success in a market requires a strong distribution system in order to deliver the product to the end use consumer. To fully exploit a product that is in high demand requires providing convenient access to the product to the consumer. If consumers cannot find the product in a market, store, or retail outlet, the manufacturer will lose sales even if the product is in high demand. In many developing countries, the lack of transportation, roads, and a sophisticated logistics system results in a limited number of markets where legitimate and qualified distributors can deliver their products. Pirated products, however, do not rely on legitimate distributors but travel through underground channels using the same illegal distributors that also bring smuggled products to consumers who want them. Pirated products can reach a larger number of end use consumers in some developing markets, creating brand and name recognition for the IP owner. As the developing market matures and distribution systems are established, the legitimate product can further penetrate into these more remote areas and benefit from the brand recognition established by the pirated product. Are MNEs exaggerating the seriousness of the commercial piracy problem?

6. *Distribution Networks.* Established distribution systems are also important because counterfeits and pirated products tend to flourish where the legitimate products are not available. Where legitimate products are not available, consumers are more likely to be confused into thinking that a pirated product is a genuine one as there is no way for consumers to make a comparison. In addition, where there is strong consumer demand for a good, consumers are more likely to purchase counterfeits where no genuine goods are available.

In developing countries, there are often "soft spots" in the market where logistical problems prevent distribution of the genuine products and where pirated products fill consumer demand. Brand owners often place a priority on developing distribution channels in developing countries as one strategy for controlling the proliferation of counterfeits and pirated products. In some of the least developed countries, such as those in Eastern Europe and Asia that border China's western front, there is no market for some genuine products at all and, as a result, there is a flourishing market in cheap pirated goods of all kinds.

C. Counterfeiting and Commercial Piracy in China

In this section, we take a closer look at trademark counterfeiting and other forms of commercial piracy in China to get a sense of the complexity of the problem and the challenges facing government policy and lawmakers, enforcement authorities, and brand owners. We begin with an overview of counterfeiting in China and first read a statement issued when commercial piracy in China first gained attention in the early 2000s as a major global business problem.

Statement of Professor Daniel Chow before the U.S. Senate Government Oversight and Management Subcommittee, April 20, 2004

In terms of size, scope, and magnitude, trademark counterfeiting in China is considered by many to be the most serious counterfeiting problem in world history. A recent study by the PRC State Council Research and Development Center reported that in 2001 the PRC economy was flooded with between $19–$24 billion worth of counterfeit goods. (The PRC has not released more recent information.) Brand owners in China estimate that 15 to 20 percent of all well-known brands in China are counterfeit and estimate their losses to be in the tens of billions of dollars per year. Counterfeiting is estimated to now account for approximately 8 percent of China's gross domestic product.

China has also become the platform for the export of counterfeit products to other countries in Asia, Europe, and the United States. In 2003, China accounted for 66 percent or over $62 million of the $94 million of all counterfeit and infringing goods seized by the U.S. Customs Service at ports of entry into the United States. An ominous development is that beginning in 2004, exports of counterfeits from China to the United States and other parts of the world may begin to increase significantly for the foreseeable future.

There are several explanations for the unprecedented size and scope of counterfeiting in China:

(1) *Foreign Direct Investment and Advanced Technology.* In recent years, China's economy has enjoyed unprecedented growth for an economy of its size with growth rates of 9.8 percent from 1980–92 and at 9 percent more recently. According to some estimates, China is on track to have the world's largest economy in the first decades of the twenty-first century. This is a remarkable achievement for a nation that was mired in backwardness and poverty just several decades ago. This economic growth has been fueled in large part by foreign direct investment from multinational enterprises. In the 1990s, China emerged as the world's second largest recipient of foreign direct investment behind only the United States and

in 2002, China surpassed the United States to become the world's largest recipient of foreign direct investment with $50 billion of foreign capital inflows. FDI is the best means in the world today for the transfer of advanced technology, intellectual property, and other forms of valuable information. In many cases today the intellectual property component of a FDI in the form of patents, copyrights, and trademarks is the most important component of the foreign investment. For example, the value of the Coca-Cola trademark in China is worth many more times to that company than the millions of dollars in capital that it has invested in China. The same is true for the patents and copyrights owned by pharmaceutical companies and software companies doing business in China today. However, while MNEs are creating a transfer of technology through FDI that is being absorbed into China's legitimate economy through joint ventures and wholly foreign-owned enterprises, some of this intellectual property is also being diverted into China's illegitimate economy as pirates steal this technology to engage in counterfeiting and other forms of commercial piracy. It is no coincidence that China, the world's largest recipient of FDI, advanced technology, and intellectual property also has the world's most serious commercial piracy problem.

(2) *State Support of Counterfeiting and Local Protectionism.* No problem of this size and scope could exist without the direct or indirect involvement of the state. In China, the national government in Beijing appears to be sincere in its recognition of the importance of protecting intellectual property rights, but national level authorities are policy and law-making bodies whereas enforcement occurs on the ground at the local level. At this level, local governments are either directly or indirectly involved in supporting the trade in counterfeit goods. Counterfeiting has become so important that this illegal trade now supports entire local economies and a crackdown on counterfeiting would result in a shutdown of the local economy with all of the attendant costs of unemployment, dislocation, social turmoil, and chaos. Because the costs of a crackdown at the local level can be so severe, counterfeiting is heavily defended at local levels.

(3) *Ineffective Legal Enforcement and Lack of Deterrence.* China has a developing legal system that is weak in many respects by comparison to legal systems in advanced industrialized countries such as the United States. While China's intellectual property laws are now considered by most observers to be in compliance with the standards set by TRIPs, enforcement of these laws remains inadequate and fails to create sufficient deterrence to counterfeiting.

The combination of these factors — the world's largest influx of foreign direct investment and widespread access to advanced technology, direct or indirect government involvement and support of the counterfeit trade, and a weak legal system that does not create sufficient deterrence for counterfeiters in a very lucrative trade — has resulted in a counterfeiting and commercial piracy problem that is unprecedented in world history.

NOTES AND QUESTIONS

1. *Exports.* In 2013, U.S. Customs seized $1.18 billion[11] in counterfeit and pirated products at ports of entry in the United States that were exported from China, accounting

---

11. *See* U.S. Customs and Border Patrol, *http://www.cbp.gov/sites/default/files/documents/2013%20 IPR%20Stats.pdf.*

for 68 percent of the total illegal products seized. Since many counterfeits from China are transshipped to Hong Kong where they are exported, if exports from Hong Kong are included, then China accounts for 93 percent of the total illegal products seized. In 2012, the EU seized about EUR 900 million worth of counterfeit goods.[12] Of course, the amount of counterfeits seized can represent only a tiny fraction of what actually enters the U.S. market. Counterfeiters easily penetrate the U.S. market even though the United States has a sophisticated border control system. In other countries, particularly developing countries, customs authorities lack resources, and training and border controls are lax. Such countries provide easy targets for counterfeiters.

2. *Enforcement in China.* The discussion of the counterfeiting problem in China in the materials above indicates a daunting problem. What are brand owners in China to do? Most brand owners take matters into their own hands through aggressive action in pursing counterfeiters. Brand owners hire private investigation companies to track down counterfeiters. Once the counterfeiter is located, brand owners have the option of bringing a lawsuit in court or seeking redress through PRC administrative authorities. With information in hand, almost all brand owners choose to go to PRC administrative authorities, such as the Administration of Industry and Commerce (AIC), which has administrative authority (but no police powers) to enforce trademark rights and seek an enforcement action in the form of a raid and seizure. Compared with a court action, the procedure for obtaining a raid is much faster, simpler, and more straightforward. All most brand owners need to do is to have one of their representatives appear at the local AIC office and file a one-page written complaint. The experience of most brand owners in China is that the AICs are quite eager to conduct enforcement actions. In most cases, AIC officials will leave shortly with the brand owner, sometimes in as little as 15 minutes, after the filing of the complaint. The private investigator and the brand owner will then lead the AIC officials to the site of the suspected counterfeiter. Most brand owners will not reveal the location in advance but usually insist on leading the authorities to the suspect premises to avoid tip-offs. The AICs will then raid the site of the suspected counterfeiter with the brand owner present and have the power to seize all illegal product, equipment, and funds. The products are later donated to charity, auctioned off, or destroyed or sold after the counterfeit marks are obliterated and equipment is auctioned off to the public.

The AICs have authority to impose a fine and to order compensation to the brand owner. They also have the authority to award expenses incurred by the brand owner in the enforcement action. Where evidence of large sales of counterfeits is found, AICs also have discretion to transfer cases to judicial authorities for criminal prosecution.

Set forth in Figure 7-4 is a summary of the enforcement results of the AICs for a recent period. After reviewing the statistics in Figure 7-4, what issues do you see with current levels of enforcement against counterfeiting in China?

3. *Court-Ordered Damages.* In addition to having powers to award damages based on proof by the brand owner, PRC courts also have the power under Article 56 of the PRC Trademark Law to award statutory damages of up to RMB 500,000 or about $60,000 in cases where damages are difficult to prove. Thus, it appears that PRC courts have adequate powers to provide for adequate compensation. Why don't brand owners just sue counterfeiters in court and obtain full compensation, which, if large enough, should serve as a deterrent? Do counterfeiters appear in court?

---

12. *See Report on EU Customs Enforcement of Intellectual Property Rights*, EUROPEAN COMMISSION, *http://ec.europa.eu/taxation_customs/resources/documents/customs/customs_controls/counterfeit_piracy/ statistics/2013_ipr_statistics_en.pdf.*

FIGURE 7-4
AIC Trademark Enforcement Activity, 1999–2012

Year	Cases	Average Fine	Average Damages	Criminal Prosecutions
1999	16,938	$754	$40	21 total (1 in 806 cases)
2000	22,001	$794	$19	45 total (1 in 489 cases)
2001	22,813	$1150	$18	86 total (1 in 265 cases)
2002	23,539	$1136	$19	59 total (1 in 399 cases)
2003	26,488	$1142	$51	45 total (1 in 589 cases)
2004	40,171	$834	$26	96 total (1 in 418 cases)
2005	49,412	$1017	$40	91 total (1 in 209 cases)
2006	50,534	$1158	$53	252 total (1 in 200 cases)
2007	50,318	$1220	N/A	229 total (1 in 209 cases)
2008	56,634	$1212	N/A	137 total (1 in 413 cases)
2009	51,044	$1117	N/A	92 total (1 in 555 cases)
2010	56,034	$1164	N/A	175 total (1 in 320 cases)
2011	79,021	$1119	N/A	421 total (1 in 188 cases)
2012	66,227	$1206	N/A	576 total (1 in 115 cases)

Source: State Administration of Industry and Commerce Annual Statistics.

4. *Payments to Officials.* Another troublesome issue that brand owners have encountered in enforcement are demands by authorities for entertainment in the form of lavish banquets and the payment of "case fees." Such payments or gifts might be considered to be violation of the U.S. Foreign Corrupt Practices Act. Should U.S. corporations be concerned about payments of "case fees" to enforcement officials? For a discussion of this and related issues, see Chow, China Under the Foreign Corrupt Practices Act, 2012 Wis. L. Rev. 573 (2012).

5. *Costs of Enforcement.* The total annual costs of enforcement against counterfeiting for MNEs in China can be quite high. Many MNEs in China spend millions to tens of millions of dollars just on enforcement actions against counterfeiting annually. Other expenses include lobbying of the PRC government, and litigation in courts. Many MNEs believe that it is necessary to be vigilant with independent contractors such as private investigators, but some MNEs have taken the attitude that they don't need to know all the details. Is this advisable from a legal standpoint? Is this prudent from a business standpoint?

PROBLEM 7-2

An MNE has asked you to analyze the damage done to two of its brands in China based on the following two graphs (based on two actual cases involving real brands). In the graphs, the vertical axis represents the percentage of the market share for the product category. The vertical bar represents the total amount of all products, authentic and counterfeit, at any given time. The jagged line represents all genuine products in the market, which is determined according to the amount of actual shipments by the brand owner to its distributors to that market. If all products sold in the market are genuine, then the amount of products actually supplied by the brand owner should closely approximate the total amount of the product available. The horizontal axis is a time line beginning in August–September 2012 and ending in April–May 2015.

Beijing Case Study

Actual Shipmenent Versus Volume Share Data

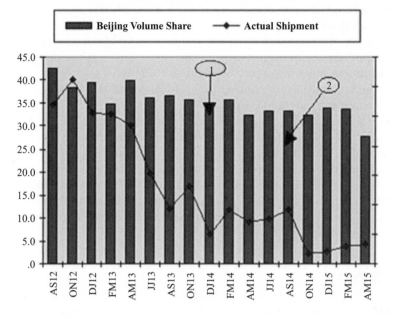

Guangdong Case Study

Actual shipment Versus Volume share Data

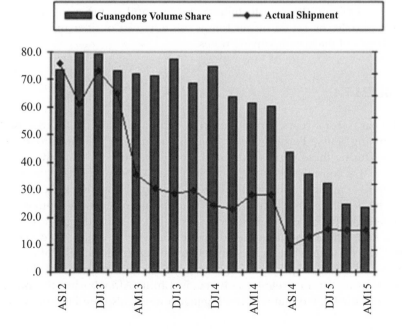

(1) What was the total market share of the product, real and counterfeit, in Beijing (first graph) in August–September 2012? What was the market share of the genuine product in August–September 2012? What was the total market share of the brand, both genuine and counterfeit, in April–May 2015? What was the total market share of the genuine product?

(2) What was the market share of the product, real and counterfeit, in Guangdong (second graph) in August–September 2012? What was the market share of the genuine product in August–September 2012? What was the total market share of the brand, real and counterfeit, in April–May 2015? What was the total market share of the genuine product?

(3) In the second case, counterfeits have greatly damaged the market position of the brand while in the first case, counterfeits have harmed the market less substantially. Assuming that in both cases the counterfeits were of low quality but that the first case involved a "low involvement" product whereas the second case involved a "high involvement" product (see p. 533), can you explain why?

(4) What must the brand owner in the second case study do to recover its market share? What lessons do you draw from this case on the harm from counterfeiting to brands?

PROBLEM 7-3

An MNE brand owner that has a manufacturing facility in north China finds that large quantities of counterfeits have recently appeared in parts of south China. Through the use of a private investigation agency, the brand owner has identified the counterfeiter and has located its factory. Aware of the difficulties of law enforcement in China, an intellectual property law expert in the United States has advised the brand owner to seek out the counterfeiter and to discuss the possibility of forming a joint venture together. The brand owner does not have a manufacturing facility in the south and has been seriously considering an expansion in that area so forming a joint venture can help achieve two goals at once: eliminate the counterfeiting problem and secure a manufacturing base in the south. Should the brand owner follow this advice? Consider the article below by Professor Chow and the accompanying notes.

PROBLEM 7-4

For the past several years, Mrs. Johnson, a flight attendant for a U.S.-based airline, has been holding "Purse Parties" at her home in an upscale neighborhood in a city in the Midwest. During these parties, attended mostly by professional women and wealthy homemakers, Mrs. Johnson gives the participants an opportunity to order counterfeits from catalogs of genuine handbags. She begins each party by telling the customers at the outset that the handbags are counterfeits so that no one is deceived about what they are buying. She says, "These are not genuine products but they are the highest quality fakes that we can find. There's nothing illegal about what we are doing. So everybody enjoy yourselves." The customers then pick genuine handbags from catalogs of products from famous brand owners. Mrs. Johnson will then buy counterfeit versions of their selections during her trips to visit her regular contacts in China. After buying the bags, she will carry them into the United States in her luggage and will also send the bags from China to some friends in New York where they enter the United States through N.Y. Customs. No one seems to be very concerned that the bags are counterfeit, and Mrs. Johnson promotes these parties as "harmless fun." Are any laws being violated? Who, if anyone, might be liable? What about Mrs. Johnson's "customers"? Do you think that Mrs. Johnson has a connection to organized crime in China? Consider the article below and the accompanying notes.

Daniel C.K. Chow, Organized Crime, Local Protectionism, and the Trade in Counterfeit Goods in China
14 China Econ. Rev. 473–484 (2003) (revised 2015)

This paper examines the role of organized crime and local protectionism in promoting and protecting the trade in counterfeit goods in the People's Republic of China ("PRC" or "China"). By "organized crime," this paper refers to a group of persons or entities acting in concert to engage in criminal conduct within an overall organizational structure and under the direction of an individual or group of individuals. "Local protectionism" refers to the role of local governments in protecting illegal activity by failing to fully enforce the law. Note that under the definitions set forth above some forms of local protectionism may also be considered forms of organized crime.

THE ROLE OF ORGANIZED CRIME AND LOCAL PROTECTIONISM

The illegal trade in counterfeit goods in China can be divided into two components: manufacture and distribution. Criminal organizations play a significant role in the manufacturing side whereas local governments are involved in the distribution side. Local governments also protect the illegal but useful economic activity of counterfeiters through the imposition of light fines and penalties, which do not serve as a deterrent to further counterfeiting by the same offender.

A. MANUFACTURE AND ORGANIZED CRIME

The manufacture of counterfeits appears to be concentrated in the southeastern region of China, mostly in Fujian and Guangdong Provinces. Fujian, located across the China Straits from Taiwan, is the ancestral home of many Taiwanese. Guangdong Province is adjacent to Hong Kong and the ancestral home of many Hong Kongese. Both Guangdong and Fujian Provinces were some of the first areas opened to foreign investment in China and were some of the first locations for sino-foreign joint ventures and wholly foreign-owned enterprises engaged in the manufacture of famous international brands of consumer products. Both of these areas were among the first areas in China to legally acquire foreign technology used in the production and manufacture of famous brands. Some of this technology and know-how has been acquired for illegal purposes. In a pattern that appears throughout other parts of China, an area where legitimate manufacturing is concentrated has given rise to illegal underground factories manufacturing counterfeits of the genuine products that are manufactured in nearby factories under the authority of the intellectual property owner.

Criminal organizations based in Hong Kong and Taiwan who have maintained connections with their ancestral homelands often provide the financing for the underground factories that manufacture illegal counterfeits in Guangdong and Fujian provinces. Anecdotal evidence indicates that these are the same criminal organizations that are involved in smuggling products into China, narcotics, prostitution, and pornography.

These criminal organizations promoting the counterfeit trade in China benefit from the jurisdictional and legal issues that are created by the international borders that separate Hong Kong and Taiwan from mainland China. As Hong Kong is an autonomous administrative unit of China, it continues to maintain its own police force, system of courts, and laws. As a result, police in China must work together with police in Hong Kong to pursue Hong Kong criminal organizations that support counterfeiting in Guangdong. The involvement of more than one set of enforcement authorities, laws, and legal systems create practical and logistical problems that impede law enforcement. In the case of Taiwan-based criminal organizations, the political problems that continue to divide China and Taiwan result in little or no law enforcement cooperation across the China Straits and Taiwan enforcement authorities have shown little interest in pursuing Taiwan persons or corporations for illegal activity on mainland China. Many Taiwan organizations feel that they can act with relative impunity in China.

1. Exports: Counterfeit Cigarettes

Recent investigations by U.S. tobacco companies have revealed that these criminal organizations are heavily involved in the export of counterfeit cigarettes made in China to the United States.

A carton of genuine premium cigarettes sells in the United States for between $50 to $60 in many states; a high quality carton of counterfeits produced in China can sell for as much as $50 to $60 in the U.S. while the cost of producing a counterfeit carton is $3.00. [A]t a recent meeting, U.S. Customs officials reported that every day containers of counterfeit cigarettes produced in China are unloaded from ships in Los Angeles port and enter the United States under false import documents as U.S. officials are unable to detect and seize all of these containers. Each container that is seized has a street value of up to $2 million yet the cost of producing the counterfeit product in the container to the manufacturer is about $80,000. In the same meeting, U.S. Customs officials estimated that as many as 8–10 containers pass through Los Angeles Customs undetected everyday. On the basis of the street value of each container at about $2 million, the trade in counterfeit cigarettes produced in China and exported to the United States through Los Angeles port alone likely exceeds $1 billion per year. Criminal organizations with entities active in the United States, China, and Hong Kong are known to be behind this highly successful trade.

B. DISTRIBUTION AND LOCAL PROTECTIONISM

The manufacture of counterfeit products is of little use if the products cannot be delivered to the end use consumer. For this reason, the distribution of counterfeit products to retail levels of commerce is crucial to the counterfeit trade in China as elsewhere in the world. Large, legitimate wholesale distributors deliver products to state-owned stores or foreign-owned chain stores. Counterfeits cannot enter retail markets through these regular channels.

In China, the distribution of counterfeit products occurs through a series of large open air or partially enclosed wholesale markets located in densely populated areas with convenient transportation access. These markets are often massive in size and can contain more than one thousand outlets, each a wholesale distributor, occupying a stall or a semi-finished storefront. In the author's experience there is no wholesale market in China that does not carry counterfeit and infringing goods for sale. Many wholesale dealers have counterfeit goods on open display while others will display genuine products but have counterfeits in a back room or under the counter and available for the asking. In the heart of Beijing, hundreds of small retail vendors swarm the Tianyi wholesale market everyday and use three wheel bicycles, lorries, and small trucks to furnish the street stalls, open air kiosks, and small retail stores with abundant supplies of counterfeit and infringing products.

These wholesale markets are established and regulated by the local Administration of Industry and Commerce (AIC), a branch of the local government responsible for promoting, regulating, and policing commercial activity. In a typical situation, AICs will invest their own funds in establishing the wholesale market and will collect rent from each of the individual wholesale distributors. In addition, AICs will issue business licenses for a fee to each individual proprietor. Once the business is in operation, AICs will also collect a management fee from each individual proprietor. In a large wholesale market such as Tianyi, the operating revenues to the local AIC can easily exceed $100,000 per year. As noted above, many if not most of these wholesale distributors deal in counterfeit goods. As AICs are also one of the primary government entities in China charged with the enforcement against counterfeiting, AICs are faced with a conflict of interest as they are charged with policing and enforcing the very markets in which AICs and the local government have a substantial investment and financial interest. Shutting down these wholesale markets would not only result in a direct loss of revenue to the AIC but would also have many repercussions as many retail businesses, hotels, restaurants, and nightclubs are all supported by the trade in counterfeit goods. In some cities, such as Yiwu discussed below, the entire local economy is connected to the trade in counterfeits.

[T]here are at least five major wholesale markets in China: Hanzhen Jie in Wuhan City, Hubei Province; Linyi Market in Linyi, Shandong Province; Nansantiao Market in Shijiazhuang in Hebei Province; China Small Commodities City in Yiwu City, Zhejiang Province; and Wuai Market in Shenyang, Liaoning Province. Together these markets serve the entire coastal region of China and its most populous urban areas including Guangzhou in the south, Shanghai in the east and Beijing and Tianjin in the northeast. A branch of the China Small Commodities City market of Yiwu located in Wulumuqi in Xinjiang Province serves as an export post for the Middle East and Eastern Europe. These markets (represented by circles) and their relationship to the manufacturing centers (shaded areas) are set forth in the map opposite.

Major Distributors and Manufacturers of Counterfeit Goods in China

1. The Zhejiang China Small Commodities City Group, Ltd.

A sense of the formidable size, scope, organization, and resources of these wholesale markets is provided by a review of the China Small Commodities City wholesale market in Yiwu, Zhejiang Province, one of the most highly organized and successful wholesale markets for counterfeit and infringing goods in China.

In 1982, the Yiwu Administration of Industry and Commerce ("AIC") established the Zhejiang China Small Commodities City Group, Ltd. (hereinafter "CSCG"), a wholesale market specializing in trading small commodities.[13] By its own estimates, the Yiwu City AIC invested US$10 million to establish this market, which immediately experienced rapid and sustained growth. Recognizing the potential for further growth and the potential for expanding into related businesses, the Yiwu City AIC and related government entities decided to privatize the management and operation of the wholesale markets by forming the CSCG as a limited liability stock company in 1993. Privatization extended to management only but not to ownership of the CSCG. A majority interest in the CSCG continues to be held by state and collective enterprises and a substantial minority interest is held by individuals.

---

13. The information in this section was gathered through the course of several weeks of investigation in Yiwu by the author working with a private investigation company.

a. Privatization.   Privatization has served a critical strategic purpose for the CSCG. Under previous practice so long as the markets were under the direct management of the AIC or other local government entities, all revenues derived from such operations had to be transferred to the national government treasury with some portion of the funds returned as a type of rebate to the local government. After privatization, the company became responsible for its own profits and losses and company revenues and profits can be distributed in any manner in accordance with management directives. An additional advantage of privatization is that the company can now branch out into other related businesses that are beyond the scope of the AIC's jurisdiction, which is limited to regulating markets. This allows the privatized company to form a conglomerate of different businesses and to benefit from the synergy that such a combination creates. Forming a conglomerate of different businesses was far more difficult to accomplish so long as the markets were directly under the management of the AIC with its circumscribed jurisdiction. Privatization has served the key function of allowing the shareholders of the company direct access to the substantial wealth generated by the company and has created the framework for aggressive expansion.

The CSCG is unique among the wholesale markets in China described in this paper in that it is the only distribution center to the author's knowledge to have privatized its operations.

b. Ties with Local Government.   Although ostensible efforts were made to sever direct connections between government entities and the business operations of the CSCG, there are still strong ties between the CSCG and local government. In practice, the process of privatization meant that many of the same government officials responsible for forming and operating the CSCG left their government posts and assumed leadership roles within the corporation as private citizens. The lines between government and private spheres, however, continue to be blurred. The CSCG Chairman is a former vice mayor of Yiwu who continues to maintain office space in the Yiwu city government building. The Director of the Yiwu City AIC was also at the same time the legal representative of the CSCG's largest corporate shareholder. The Director is said to have resigned from all CSCG offices and is currently a director of one of Yiwu's four municipal offices, but his name continues to be listed second on a list of the CSCG's top executives in the CSCG's internal documents. The Vice-Director of the Yiwu City Government Municipal offices uses a name card that also bears the logo and the name of the China Small Commodities City Group. It appears to be a common practice for Yiwu government officials to use name cards with the China Small Commodities City Group logo. In practice, the CSCG conducts its affairs as if it carries government authority. In the case of the CSCG, as in many other instances in China, the line between a private enterprise and government authority is blurred.

Given the historical and present links between the Yiwu government and the CSCG and the CSCG's importance to the local economy, it is reasonable to assume that there is a *de facto* partnership between the Yiwu government and the CSCG. This partnership is likely to be a significant cause of the CSCG's remarkable growth from US$470,000 in sales in 1982 to US$2.2 billion in 1996—a growth of 4,700 percent in 14 years. It is also reasonable to assume that the CSCG and the Yiwu City government are well aware of the size and magnitude of the traffic in counterfeit goods in the CSCG markets and elsewhere in Yiwu.

c. Shareholding and Corporate Structure.   With a total registered capital of US$14 million, the CSCG currently has six corporate shareholders, all state owned or collectively owned enterprises, which own 55.59 percent of all shares. The shareholders and their respective shareholder's interest in percentage terms and value in RMB are:

(1)   Zhejiang Yiwu China Small Commodities City Hengda Development Corp.
         Capital Contribution: RMB 43,211,300 (37%);
(2)   Yiwu City Financial Development Corp.
         Capital Contribution: RMB 6,600,000 (5.7%);
(3)   Zhejiang Province International Trust Investment Corp.
         Capital Contribution: RMB 5,500,000 (4.7%);
(4)   Zhejiang Province Financial Development Corp.
         Capital Contribution: RMB 5,500,000 (4.7%);
(5)   Zhongxin Trading Corp.
         Capital Contribution: RMB 2,200,000 (1.9%);
(6)   Shanghai Shenyin Bond Corp.
         Capital Contribution: RMB 2,200,000 (1.9%).

Individual shareholders own 41% of all total shares worth RMB 47,401,200[14] and employees of the CSCG own 2.5% of all total shares worth RMB 2,887,500.

The CSCG operates through a board of directors, with a president, and a CSCG parent holding company that has a president's office, and separate departments for marketing, development, finance and securities. The CSCG parent holding company operates through a series of 14 wholly-owned subsidiaries that have expanded into other businesses, most of which directly or indirectly support its trading operations through its wholesale markets, which seems to remain the CSCG's core business. These subsidiaries are as follows:

(1)   China Small Commodities Market ("CSCM") Management Company
(2)   CSCM Property Management Company
(3)   CSCM Information Internet Company
(4)   CSCM Hengda Development Company
(5)   CSCM Trading Development Company
(6)   Yindu Hotel Limited Liability Company
(7)   Shangcheng Hotel
(8)   Yiwu City Finance Development Company
(9)   CSCM Real Estate Company
(10)   CSCM Advertising Company
(11)   Shangcheng Urban Credit Cooperative
(12)   Yiwu City Property Right Exchange
(13)   CSCM Highway Construction Company, Ltd.
(14)   CSCM Exhibition Company

One CSCG subsidiary, the CSCM Management Company, actually engages in the trading of counterfeit goods and serves a major role in distribution of these products to the CSCG's branch markets. The CSCM internet company has set up a website advertising numerous small commodities for sale, creating worldwide access to goods sold in Yiwu

---

14. The current exchange rate is approximately 6 RMB = 1 U.S. dollar.

and attracting buyers worldwide. Notable among the other subsidiaries is the Yindu Hotel Limited Liability Company, which operates a four star hotel that is by far the best hotel in Yiwu and that is part of a complex also housing the corporate headquarters of the CSCG, which includes a nightclub and karaoke bar in the lower level of the hotel. The CSCG has also set up a trade development subsidiary that has been exploring the establishment of representative branches in countries abroad, although the recent economic downturn seems to have curtailed these expansion efforts for the time being.

d. The CSCG Yiwu Wholesale Markets. The CSCG manages the China Small Commodities City, which has been by far the largest wholesale market in the PRC for the past six successive years. In 1996, the last year for which statistics published by the Yiwu City AIC are available, the market reached a floor space of over 500,000 square meters and had over 24,000 booths. The CSCG rents these booths to individual proprietors who hold individual business licenses. Over 50,000 business people operate in this market and over 200,000 people visit the market each day to conduct business. Based upon the author's own experience, at least 90 percent of the products sold in the China Small Commodities City are either counterfeit or infringing products.

During a four year period in the 1990s, the wholesale market grew at a rate of over 100 percent annually and its average annual growth rate through the entire history of the market is 90 percent. From 1991 to 1996, total volume of business in the market grew 22 times from US$100 million in 1991 to US$2.2 billion in 1996. No official data are available after 1997, but even assuming a modest growth rate, total sales for the China Small Commodities City wholesale market should reach nearly US$3 billion in 2003. Revenues at this level would place the CSCG above most of the largest multinational enterprises doing business in China.

Given its rapid growth, the China Small Commodities City has quickly assumed a major role in supporting the entire local economy. In the 1990s, the tax revenues from the wholesale market operations have averaged 26 percent of the entire tax revenues for the city of Yiwu. The CSCG's total annual revenue from rental fees alone paid by the 30,000 wholesalers and 3,500 stores is about US$55 million. Total annual management fees paid by individual businesses to the local AIC are about US$6 million. Total local taxes paid by individual businesses in the CSCG wholesale markets to the Yiwu city government are approximately US$8 million. The CSCG appears to be involved in virtually every aspect of the local economy with over 50 pages of listings in the local 112 page phone book related to the CSCG. The remarkable growth of the CSCG's trade in counterfeit goods and the growth of other wholesale markets parallel the recent sharp rise in the amount of counterfeiting in the PRC.

e. Role of Yiwu in Distribution. Yiwu serves as a central distribution center for counterfeit goods to markets around the country. At the center of town, two large transportation companies occupy two open area transport areas, both the size of football fields. Around the perimeter of these areas are representative local transport offices from cities and towns all over China. Operating continuously day and night, trucks and lorries unload counterfeit products made in southern China in factories financed by criminal organizations in Hong Kong and Taiwan in one open transport area for storage and sale in Yiwu's wholesale markets. In the other open transport area, other trucks and lorries load counterfeit products already purchased from these wholesale markets for delivery to all parts of China.

15-Year Development of China Small Commodities
City Wholesale Market

	Number of Booths	Business Area (m² in 1,000s)	Business Volume (RMB, millions)	Business Volume Annual Growth (%)	Tax Volume (RMB, 1,000s)	Tax Volume Annual Growth (%)	% of Total Yiwu Tax Revenues
1982	750	4.252	3.92	—	160	—	0.64
1983	1,050	4.252	14.44	268	380	137	1.12
1984	1,874	4.252	23.21	61	640	68	1.02
1985	2,874	13.59	61.90	167	1,290	102	2.03
1986	5,500	13.59	100.29	62	2,840	120	5.24
1987	5,600	57	153.8	54	5,650	99	9.45
1988	6,130	57	265	72	9,360	66	11.09
1989	8,400	57	390	47	14,870	59	17.45
1990	10,500	57	606	55	19,760	33	24.1
1991	10,500	57	1,025	67	42,050	113	28
1992	13,910	103	2,054	99	42,350	0.7	31
1993	13,910	103	4,515.2	120	55,750	32	25.14
1994	22,731	269	10,212	126	52,100	0.7	24.69
1995	15,747	269	15,200	49	61,640	18	23.8
1996	24,069	500.1	18,468	21.5	—	—	—

By 1997, the CSCG stopped providing information about its business operations so despite the many attempts of the author it has now been proven impossible to obtain any data after that date.

f. Importance of the CSCG to the Local Economy. As this brief examination of the CSCG indicates, the trade in counterfeit goods has become an integral part of the Yiwu economy. Businesses that engage in the sale of counterfeit products pay taxes to the local government, which support public services for the local economy. This point is worth emphasizing because brand owners have argued that China suffers from a loss of tax revenues on counterfeit goods that otherwise would be paid by legitimate manufacturers on sales that are lost to counterfeiting. In Yiwu, local businesses operating within the CSCG markets negotiate a flat tax rate that becomes a substantial portion of the tax revenue of the city, thus helping to integrate the economic benefits of counterfeiting into the local economy. The myriad other businesses operated by the CSCG all depend directly or indirectly on the robust trade in counterfeit goods. The second point worth emphasizing is the close link between the CSCG, composed of former or current government officials, and the Yiwu government. This link suggests that the operations of the CSCG will be strongly defended at local levels.

Recent eyewitness accounts indicate that the counterfeiting trade continues to flourish in Yiwu although the local businesses are more cautious about openly displaying counterfeit and infringing goods.

NOTES AND QUESTIONS

1. Based on the discussion above, what do you think is the single most serious problem in the effective enforcement against counterfeiting in China? Is this an issue of intellectual property rights?

2. Review the bottom category of the chart on p. 550 on the percentage of total tax revenues paid by the CSCG, the corporate conglomerate that operates the wholesale market in counterfeit goods in Yiwu City, for the five-year period from 1991 to 1995. How important is the corporate group and the trade in counterfeit goods for the tax revenues of the city? What would happen if the trade in counterfeit goods were shut down?

3. In response to the serious problem of the smuggling of counterfeit goods into the United States by organized crime, Congress has made counterfeiting a predicate offense under the Racketeer Influenced and Corrupt Organizations Act (RICO), 18 U.S.C. §§1961–1968 (2006), the federal organized-crime statute. Congress has also passed the Trademark Counterfeiting Act of 1984, 18 U.S.C. §2320 (2006), which provides in relevant part that "[w]hoever intentionally traffics or attempts to traffic in goods or services and knowingly uses a counterfeit mark on or in connection with such goods or services shall, if an individual, be fined not more than $2,000,000 or imprisoned not more than 10 years, or both, and, if a person other than an individual, be fined not more than $5,000,000." *Id.* §2320(a). The term "traffic" here means to "transport, transfer, or otherwise dispose of, to another, as consideration for anything of value." *Id.* §2320(e)(2). Importing counterfeit merchandise under false documentation into the United States is a violation of 18 U.S.C. §545 (2006), the anti-smuggling statute, which provides in relevant part that "whoever knowingly and willfully smuggles, or clandestinely introduces or attempts to smuggle or clandestinely introduce into the United States any merchandise which should have been invoiced, or makes out or passes, or attempts to pass, through the customhouse any false, forged, or fraudulent invoice, or other document or paper [s]hall be fined under this title or imprisoned not more than 20 years, or both." In addition, other federal laws such as those relating to money laundering and the use of interstate commerce to transport smuggled and illegal goods may also be applicable.

Civil remedies are also available against counterfeiting under federal law. A plaintiff in a civil action against a counterfeiter is entitled to recover "(1) defendant's profits, (2) any damages sustained by the plaintiff, and (3) the costs of the action." 15 U.S.C. §1117(a) (2006). In cases where the act of counterfeiting is intentional, courts are required, in the absence of attenuating circumstances, to enter judgment for three times such profit or damages, whichever is higher, along with an award to the plaintiff of reasonable attorney's fees. 15 U.S.C. §1117(b). In addition, the plaintiff may elect, at any time before a final judgment is entered by the court, to recover statutory damages instead of actual damages and profits. 15 U.S.C. §1117(c). Statutory damages range from $500 to $100,000 where the actions were not willful and up to $1,000,000 where the counterfeiting was willful. *Id.* In addition to federal laws, the states may have their own criminal and civil laws that apply to counterfeiting.

NOTE ON RESPONSES BY MNEs AND FOREIGN GOVERNMENTS

A number of powerful MNEs in China have formed an industry lobbying group to influence the PRC government to address the counterfeiting and piracy problem. Originally named the "China Anti-Counterfeiting Coalition," the name of the group was changed, at the behest of the PRC government, to the less threatening, "Quality Brands Protection Committee" (QBPC). The QBPC engages in training sessions, best practices seminars, and other cooperative, non-confrontational activities with the PRC government.

The United States government works the PRC government on IP issues through various formal and informal channels. In the past, the United States has resorted to threats of trade sanctions against China under Special 301 of the U.S. Trade Act of 1974, 19 U.S.C. §§2416–2417 (2006). Under Special 301, the United States Trade Representative (USTR) evaluates foreign countries that do not protect U.S. intellectual property rights under four categories: priority foreign country (PFC); priority watch list; watch list; and special mention. If a country is designated as a PFC, the USTR is required to initiate a process that will result in mandatory trade sanctions. The other categories do not require mandatory action but put countries on notice that they are at risk of being designated as a PFC. In 2005, the United States designated Ukraine as a PFC and imposed trade sanctions worth $75 million in the form of higher tariffs and denied other trade benefits to Ukraine. In the recent past, the United States and China have undergone a period of tense diplomatic negotiations over China's protection of IP rights with periodic threats of trade sanctions by the United States and counter-threats of retaliation by China. In 2014, China was once again designated as a priority watch list country, but not as a PFC, which would mandate trade sanctions. Other countries on the priority watch list in 2014 include Algeria, Argentina, Chile, India, Indonesia, Pakistan, Russia, Thailand, and Venezuela. Recently, the United States has begun to use the WTO dispute settlement system as a forum in which to challenge China's protection of intellectual property rights, but with mixed results. *See China—Measures Affecting the Protection and Enforcement of Intellectual Property Rights*, WT/DS362/R, January 26, 2009 (adopted March 20, 2009).

PROBLEM 7-5

A popular current approach by MNEs in China is to get "tough" with counterfeiters. MNEs will often hire former military commandos, special forces agents, FBI agents, and police officers to head up their brand protection units within their China operations. Many brand protection units go on frequent raids accompanied by PRC officials and vow to smash counterfeiters. Persons within these brand protection units call themselves "soldiers," and will sometimes threaten and physically "rough up" any counterfeiters found on the premises as well as destroy equipment and property on the spot. Is getting "tough" a good approach? Are there any legal issues with such an approach? Since the problem in China is that there is a lot of enforcement but little deterrence, might such an approach actually backfire and lead to even more counterfeiting by inciting and provoking the counterfeiters? *See* Chow, *Anti-Counterfeiting Strategies of Multinationals in China*, 41 Geo. J. Int'l L. 749 (2010).

II.   *TRIPs and the Protection of Intellectual Property Rights*

In Chapter Five, we examined the international intellectual property system and the role of TRIPs in promulgating harmonized substantive legal standards on IP for all WTO members. In this section, we focus on the impact of TRIPs on the enforcement and protection of IP rights against commercial piracy and other types of infringements. Most of these obligations are contained in Part III of TRIPs, which will be the focus of this section.

In addition to the application of TRIPs to commercial piracy, we will also examine two of the WTO's most hotly debated current topics: the impact of TRIPs on access to medicines and biopiracy.

A.   Intellectual Property, TRIPs, and the WTO

One of the major triumphs of the Uruguay Round of negotiations that led to the establishment of the WTO was the inclusion of intellectual property rights within the world trade framework through TRIPs, one of the treaties administered by the new WTO established in 1995. As we noted in Chapter One, one of the weaknesses of the GATT system was that contracting states were allowed to pick and choose which treaty obligations to which they were bound. Some called this system "GATT à la carte," which permitted many free-riders, that is, those contracting states that enjoyed GATT trading benefits even though they refused to enact intellectual property laws that met international standards. As a result of the Uruguay Round, this problem has been addressed as membership in the WTO requires adherence to all of the WTO's major treaties, including TRIPs. The new framework meant that developing nations had to accept TRIPs standards as one of the requirements of admission to the WTO.

As TRIPs is generally considered to be a non-self-executing treaty, membership in the WTO obligates each member to enact domestic IP legislation that complies with the minimum standards established by TRIPs. When the WTO agreements took effect on January 1, 1995, all 146 WTO members had to ensure that their laws and practices complied with TRIPs; within one year for developed countries (by January 1, 1996) and within five years for developing countries (by January 1, 2000). Developing countries that had previously denied patent protection for pharmaceuticals were given an additional five years from January 1, 1996 (by January 1, 2006) to extend patent protection for pharmaceuticals as required by TRIPs. Least developed countries were given until January 1, 2006 to comply with TRIPs, which was later extended to July 1, 2013, and most recently extended a further eight years to July 1, 2021. Least developed countries were given until January 1, 2016 to extend patent protection for pharmaceuticals. As we shall see in the materials below, special provisions were needed for pharmaceuticals because they figure in one of the most controversial debates in the WTO: access to medicines.

The result of TRIPs is the eventual widespread promulgation of intellectual property laws on copyright, patent, trademark, and other IP rights based on standards established by the United States and a number of other developed countries that were the main proponents of including TRIPs within the WTO framework.

WTO members not only have obligations to enact comprehensive laws in all IP areas, but under Part III of TRIPs, they also have specific obligations to enact laws specifically directed against commercial piracy. TRIPs also imposes specific enforcement obligations on its members. However, while TRIPs has been effective in obtaining the widespread enactment of complying legislation, TRIPs has been less effective in securing enforcement of these laws. In most instances in the world today, the problem is not with the existence of IP laws but with their effective enforcement.

From a larger political perspective, the incorporation of TRIPs into the WTO framework was viewed at the time as a major triumph for advanced industrialized nations and a major shift in the way that intellectual property was viewed in international commerce. The Paris Convention that applies to patents, trademarks, and industrial property and the Berne Convention that applies to copyright (see Chapter Five at pp. 312, 314-315, 317, 319-320) as well as other major international treaties are administered by the World Intellectual Property Organization (WIPO), a specialized agency of the United Nations located in Geneva. These intellectual property treaties were administered in isolation from other issues concerning trade and commerce, and the WIPO is a largely toothless organization that has little, if any, enforcement power. Many developing nations had sought to keep intellectual property outside of the jurisdiction of the WTO and its predecessor, the GATT, as these organizations were viewed as a club for rich nations. The incorporation of intellectual property rights into the WTO now means that intellectual property has become a trade issue connected with other trade issues within the WTO framework and can no longer be viewed in isolation. For example, if a developing nation that is a WTO member is not enforcing laws against commercial piracy as required by TRIPs, a member that is harmed can challenge this non-compliance by bringing a complaint within the WTO dispute settlement system. Among the remedies available to the complaining member would be retaliation in any industrial sector, not limited to intellectual property rights. Returning to our example, a developing member nation that failed to provide adequate intellectual property rights protection as required by TRIPs might find, for example, that the complaining member is allowed to impose tariffs on agricultural goods imported from the offending nation. The mere threat of this type of remedy (as opposed to its actual implementation), not possible under the WIPO system, has created pressure on all nations to comply with WTO obligations, including TRIPs.

While TRIPs was initially viewed as a triumph for developed nations, TRIPs has more recently come under intense criticism. We will return to other lines of criticism of TRIPs in the biopiracy debate but for now consider the following line of argument. Some critics of TRIPs have argued that there is an explanation from culture that illuminates why problems of commercial piracy can be so difficult to control in developing countries. TRIPs standards are premised upon the values of free-market capitalism. Developing countries are being asked to transplant Western-style IP laws to societies with entirely differently cultural traditions and social institutions. It is one matter to ask a developing country to enact Western-style intellectual property laws but another matter to expect that country to give full effect to those laws if its underlying social institutions and traditions are in tension with those laws. Advanced capitalist democracies such as the United States have a powerful and independent judiciary, a sophisticated legal profession with lawyers and judges with expertise in IP, and powerful interests groups, all of which support an approach to IP rights that rewards individual creativity and entrepreneurship. All of these social institutions are necessary in addition to IP laws to support a rigorous enforcement of IP rights. However, many developing countries have historically adhered to a different set of social values, which emphasized communal ownership of knowledge and information. In traditional Asian societies, for example, copying the work of another was not seen as wrongful but as a way to spread knowledge and culture, which were viewed as the common heritage of the nation. One cannot simply ask a developing country to fully enforce its TRIPs-compliant IP laws without first developing the social and legal institutions that would support such enforcement. Just as advanced industrialized countries have put pressure on developing and non-Western countries to adopt Western-style IP laws, industrialized countries are now asking developing countries to fully enforce these laws and to implement the rule of law, which means also adopting the Western-style social and legal institutions that underlie free-market capitalism.

NOTES AND QUESTIONS

1. Are developing countries being coerced into rejecting their traditional culture and social institutions and replacing them with their Western counterparts as a price of meeting the standards of TRIPs?

2. Should alternative types of intellectual property laws that respect non-Western cultures be considered and adopted by the WTO?

B. Enforcement Obligations Under TRIPs Against Commercial Piracy

1. General Enforcement Obligations

Recognizing that the enactment of laws that meet international standards means little if those laws are not adequately enforced, Part III of TRIPs provides for specific enforcement obligations as follows.

Article 41

1. Members shall ensure that enforcement procedures as specified in this Part are available under their law so as to permit effective action against any act of infringement of intellectual property rights covered by this Agreement, including expeditious remedies to prevent infringements and remedies which constitute a deterrent to further infringements.

2. Procedures concerning the enforcement of intellectual property rights shall be fair and equitable. They shall not be unnecessarily complicated or costly, or entail unreasonable time-limits or unwarranted delays.

Article 45

Damages

1. The judicial authorities shall have the authority to order the infringer to pay the right holder damages adequate to compensate for the injury the right holder has suffered[.]

Article 51

Suspension of Release by Customs Authorities

Members shall adopt procedures to enable a right holder, who has valid grounds for suspecting that the importation of counterfeit trademark or pirated copyright goods may take place, to lodge an application in writing with competent authorities, administrative or judicial, for the suspension by the customs authorities of the release into free circulation of such goods.

Article 61

Members shall provide for criminal procedures and penalties to be applied at least in cases of willful trademark counterfeiting or copyright piracy on a commercial scale. Remedies available shall include imprisonment and/or monetary fines sufficient to provide a deterrent, consistently with the level of penalties applied for crimes of a corresponding gravity. In appropriate cases, remedies available shall also include the seizure, forfeiture and destruction of the infringing goods and of any materials and implements the predominant use of which has been in the commission of the offence. Members may provide for criminal procedures and penalties to be applied in other cases of infringement of intellectual property rights, in particular where they are committed wilfully and on a commercial scale.

Consistent with TRIPs, U.S. law contains simple procedures for trademark and copyright owners to obtain border enforcement measures against counterfeit and pirated copyright goods. These procedures are set forth in 19 C.F.R. Chap. 1, Part 133, Subparts C & D. Counterfeit goods are subject to seizure at ports of entry by U.S. Customs under 19 C.F.R. §133.21. Customs is also authorized to detain goods that infringe (but do not counterfeit) a registered U.S. trademark under 19 C.F.R. §133.22. While the trademark owner does not need to record its trademark with Customs in order for Customs to seize counterfeits, Customs will detain infringing (but not counterfeit) goods only if a registered U.S. trademark owner first records the trademark with Customs under the procedures set forth in §§133.1–133.4. (Note the trademark owner must first register the mark with the Patent and Trademark Office then record the registered mark with Customs.) A similar procedure exists for copyrights. U.S. Customs will detain goods that infringe a registered U.S. copyright where the owner has recorded the copyright with Customs under §133.31. Unlike in the case of trademarks, Customs does not distinguish between pirated copyright goods (identical copies) and infringing goods (partial copies). The copyright owner must first record the copyright in all cases. Once the suspect goods have been seized or detained, Customs regulations contain detailed procedures for the forfeiture and destruction of the goods or for their release to the importer (with possible indemnification) if the charges of piracy and infringement cannot be substantiated by the IP owner. U.S. Customs regulations do not contain similar procedures for the protection of U.S. patents against infringing imports. For reasons of history, patent holders are protected from unfair import competition under a different statutory scheme, §337 of the Tariff Act of 1930, 46 Stat. 687, which was codified as 19 U.S.C. §1337 (2006). Unlike the cases of trademarks and copyrights, which require only a simple recording procedure with Customs, a patent holder must obtain an exclusion order under §337 before the International Trade Commission, which requires bringing an action and the presentation of evidence at an adversary hearing before the ITC.

NOTES AND QUESTIONS

What happens if a WTO member believes that another member has failed to satisfy its TRIPs enforcement obligations? If a dispute arises concerning a nation's compliance with its TRIPs obligations, it is possible for the complaining nation to seek dispute settlement under the WTO Understanding on Dispute Settlement. The parties undergo a process much like that of civil litigation in which the dispute is first heard by a dispute settlement panel that has fact-finding powers. Review of the report issued by the panel is available through an appellate body with a scope of review that is limited to issues of law. A report can then be adopted by the Dispute Settlement Body (DSB) of the WTO. If the report finds that a measure is inconsistent with the requirements of a covered WTO agreement, the report will recommend that the member bring its measure into conformity with the concerned agreement and may suggest ways that the member concerned can implement the report's recommendations. If a member fails to comply with the recommendations of the DSB or otherwise bring an inconsistent measure into conformity, the complaining party can seek compensation; if compensation cannot be agreed upon, the complaining member can seek authorization for retaliation. For a detailed examination of the WTO dispute settlement process, see Chapter Two of Chow and Schoenbaum, *International Trade Law: Problems, Cases, and Materials* (Aspen 2d ed. 2012).

2. *Provisional Measures*

A major problem that IP owners face is that most counterfeiters and pirates destroy evidence and flee at the first sign of trouble. As a result, it is essential that IP owners preserve the element of surprise in enforcement actions. To address this concern, Part III of TRIPs requires that its members provide provisional (or temporary) measures that can be used against infringers.

A review of the procedures available to an IP owner under U.S. law illustrates how provisional measures can be used effectively against an infringer. Under Rule 65 of the Federal Rules of Civil Procedure, a plaintiff can appear ex parte before a federal court and apply for a seizure order for counterfeit, pirated, or infringing goods and a temporary restraining order (TRO) against a suspected offender. In the past, some IP owners have encountered some problems in obtaining a TRO as they are sometimes unable to obtain the name and identity of the suspected offender. To accommodate this issue, some federal courts will issue a "John Doe" TRO. If the court decides to grant the plaintiff's application, the plaintiff is then entitled to go to the premises of the suspected infringer accompanied by a federal marshal and serve a copy of the TRO and order on the defendant and seize the goods. (When a federal court issues a TRO and seizure order, a copy is usually sent to the U.S. Attorney's office, which then has the option to consider a criminal prosecution.) If the defendant is not present, the plaintiff can post the order or find other substitute means to provide legally effective notice. The order served by the plaintiff also notices a hearing before the expiration of the TRO at which the plaintiff can seek a preliminary injunction that would prevent the defendant from engaging in additional illegal activity until the case is finally resolved. Where true counterfeiting is involved, the entry of the TRO and the seizure of the goods is usually the final resolution of the case as issues of liability are rarely contested by the counterfeiters, if they appear in court at all. In other instances, the parties agree to settle the case without a trial and the court enters a consent decree. In some instances, the final resolution of the case may involve a permanent injunction, a court order that permanently bars the defendant from engaging in certain activities. The critical feature of these provisional remedies discussed above is that they allow a brand owner to immediately stop a counterfeiter from engaging in additional harmful conduct at the same time (or before) a complaint is filed in civil court. Many IP owners believe that pretrial relief that can be obtained ex parte is essential to preserve the element of surprise and to obtain effective civil action in the United States.

Many of these features available under U.S. provisional measures are now required by Article 50 of TRIPs, which provides in relevant part:

Article 50

1. The judicial authorities shall have the authority to order prompt and effective provisional measures:

(a) to prevent an infringement of any intellectual property right from occurring, and in particular to prevent the entry into the channels of commerce in their jurisdiction of goods, including imported goods immediately after customs clearance;

(b) to preserve relevant evidence in regard to the alleged infringement.

2. The judicial authorities shall have the authority to adopt provisional measures *inaudita altera parte* where appropriate, in particular where any delay is likely to cause irreparable harm to the right holder, or where there is a demonstrable risk of evidence being destroyed.

6. [P]rovisional measures taken on the basis of paragraphs 1 and 2 shall, upon request by the defendant, be revoked or otherwise cease to have effect, if proceedings leading to a decision on the merits of the case are not initiated within a reasonable period, to be determined by the judicial authority ordering the measures where a Member's law so permits or, in the absence of such a determination, not to exceed 20 working days or 31 calendar days, whichever is the longer.

7. Where the provisional measures are revoked or where they lapse due to any act or omission by the applicant, or where it is subsequently found that there has been no infringement or threat of infringement of an intellectual property right, the judicial authorities shall have the authority to order the applicant, upon request of the defendant, to provide the defendant appropriate compensation for any injury caused by these measures.

PROBLEM 7-6

As a new member of the WTO, a developing country has issued several new laws to meet its TRIPs obligations. One set of laws deals with civil enforcement procedures. The key features of the law are as follows:

(1) The plaintiff can obtain injunctive relief against an infringer by (a) filing a complaint against the infringer with a court and (b) serving a copy of the complaint and notice of the hearing on the infringer.
(2) At the hearing, the plaintiff must establish irreparable harm or the threat thereof. The defendant is allowed to offer a defense at the hearing.
(3) If the court decides to issue the injunction, the plaintiff must post a bond to indemnify the defendant.
(4) The preliminary injunction is continued for the duration of the trial at the end of which a permanent injunction can be issued if the defendant is found liable.

Go through each feature of this law and explain whether it is consistent with Article 50 of TRIPs. Is this law an effective measure against commercial piracy?

C. TRIPs and the Access to Medicines Debate

One area where TRIPs helped initially to address some of the concerns of MNEs about commercial piracy and counterfeiting is in the longstanding and heated debate over patents for pharmaceuticals. Prior to joining TRIPs, some developing countries, such as Thailand

and India, refused to offer patent protection for pharmaceuticals. These countries justified this decision on the grounds that public health needs required unrestricted access to
essential medicines. As all patents are territorial in nature, a U.S. patent for a drug would
have effect within the United States but would have no legal effect in Thailand. Rather, the
U.S. patent holder would have to apply for a patent under the laws of Thailand in order to
receive patent protection within that country. Thailand and other developing countries,
however, refused to enact patent legislation in order to allow copying of these drugs. As a
result, it was arguably not illegal prior to TRIPs to make inexpensive copies of a U.S. drug
in Thailand as it violated no applicable patent law. The effect of TRIPs, however, is that
all WTO members must now enact IP laws that meet the minimal substantive standards of
TRIPs, which include patent protection for pharmaceuticals. As a result, Thailand now has
a domestic patent law, and the U.S. patent holder can now receive patent protection for
its drug within Thailand. Assuming that the U.S. drug company obtains a Thai patent, if
unauthorized copies of the U.S. drug are produced in Thailand, these copies are now illegal. The U.S. drug maker can now seek assistance from the Thai authorities to shut down
the pirates and the Thai authorities would be subject to political pressure from the U.S.
government if they did not comply. The U.S. company could also seek to ban the entry
of parallel imports into Thailand, that is, less expensive but genuine versions of the drug
produced in another country and imported into Thailand.

Soon after the implementation of TRIPs, however, it came under intense criticism
for its effect on access to medicines on those in the world who need them the most. The
critics of TRIPs argued that (1) increased patent protection leads to higher drug prices,
which will cause drugs to be out of reach for many developing countries; (2) enforcement
of TRIPs will restrict local manufacturing capacity and remove a source of drugs on which
many in the developing world depend; (3) widespread patent protection will further discourage drug companies from undertaking research and development on diseases such
as malaria and tuberculosis, widespread in developing countries, because drugs developed to treat these diseases will not earn high profits; and (4) TRIPs compliance appears
to be only a minimum threshold as many developed countries are putting pressure on
developing countries to provide "TRIPs plus" protection by extending patent protection
beyond the required 20-year period.

Although TRIPs requires its members to provide patent protection, the drafters of
TRIPs did recognize that, in certain cases, host countries should be able to override a
patent without having to obtain the consent of the patent holder for reasons of public
health. This is the basic concept behind a compulsory license that is the subject of the
following article of TRIPs:

Article 31

Other Use Without Authorization of the Right Holder

Where the law of a Member allows for other use[15] of the subject matter of a patent without the authorization of the right holder, including use by the government or third parties
authorized by the government, the following provisions shall be respected:

(a) authorization of such use shall be considered on its individual merits;

(b) such use may only be permitted if, prior to such use, the proposed user has made
efforts to obtain authorization from the right holder on reasonable commercial terms and
conditions and that such efforts have not been successful within a reasonable period of time.

---

15. "Other use" refers to use other than that allowed under Article 30.

This requirement may be waived by a Member in the case of a national emergency or other circumstances of extreme urgency or in cases of public non-commercial use.

(c) the scope and duration of such use shall be limited to the purpose for which it was authorized[.]

(d) such use shall be non-exclusive;

(e) such use shall be non-assignable, except with that part of the enterprise or goodwill which enjoys such use;

(f) any such use shall be authorized predominantly for the supply of the domestic market of the Member authorizing such use;

(g) authorization for such use shall be liable . . . to be terminated if and when the circumstances which led to it cease to exist and are unlikely to recur.

(h) the right holder shall be paid adequate remuneration in the circumstances of each case, taking into account the economic value of the authorization[.]

Most critics of TRIPs, however, found this provision to be too restrictive and not useful as a tool to address the concerns that TRIPs denied meaningful access to medicines.

The controversy over access to medicines flared and galvanized world opinion against the interests of drug companies due to several well-publicized incidents in the 1990s. In one incident, a group of multinational drug companies brought suit in 1998 against the South African government, arguing that a law that permitted broad access to patented medicines violated TRIPs. Both the United States and the European Commission threatened trade sanctions to put pressure on the South African government to repeal the law. A storm of protest erupted in the United States as AIDS activists argued that the United States valued profits over people. These protests created public pressure and embarrassed government leaders in several well-known incidents to force a change to these policies. By the time the lawsuit came to trial in South Africa, the United States had reversed its policy, and the drug companies, which could no longer count on the support of their governments, dropped the case. In 2001, the United States brought a claim against Brazil with the WTO Dispute Settlement Body, challenging a Brazilian law that imposed a local working requirement on all Brazilian patent holders to manufacture drugs locally or be subject to a compulsory license after three years. As a result of this law, U.S. drug makers could no longer simply export their drugs protected by a Brazilian patent to Brazil but had to establish a factory in Brazil or the Brazilian government would issue a license for the Brazilian patent to local drug makers without the authorization of the U.S. companies (and owners of the patent in Brazil). The Brazilian law was the linchpin of a government AIDS program that had reduced AIDS mortality among the estimated 536,000 people infected with AIDS in Brazil by more than 50 percent between 1996 and 1999. The U.S. action came under fierce criticism from international nongovernmental organizations (NGOs) such as the World Health Organization, which were concerned that the U.S. action would have a negative effect on the efforts by other developing nations to institute government programs to combat AIDS. Faced with mounting international pressure, the United States eventually withdrew its complaint with the WTO.

By the time that the Fourth Ministerial Conference of the WTO was held in Doha in 2001, the access to medicines issue was a key item on the agenda. After much debate, the following declaration, based on a compromise between the United States and Brazil, was adopted by the Ministerial Conference:

Doha WTO Ministerial Conference 2001: TRIPs

WT/MIN(01)/DEC/2 (November 20, 2001)

1. We recognize the gravity of the public health problems afflicting many developing and least-developed countries, especially those resulting from HIV/AIDS, tuberculosis, malaria and other epidemics.

2. We stress the need for the WTO Agreement on Trade-Related Aspects of Intellectual Property Rights (TRIPs Agreement) to be part of the wider national and international action to address these problems.

3. We recognize that intellectual property protection is important for the development of new medicines. We also recognize the concerns about its effects on prices.

4. We agree that the TRIPs Agreement does not and should not prevent members from taking measures to protect public health. Accordingly, while reiterating our commitment to the TRIPs Agreement, we affirm that the Agreement can and should be interpreted and implemented in a manner supportive of WTO members' right to protect public health and, in particular, to promote access to medicines for all. In this connection, we reaffirm the right of WTO members to use, to the full, the provisions in the TRIPs Agreement, which provide flexibility for this purpose.

5. Accordingly and in the light of paragraph 4 above, while maintaining our commitments in the TRIPs Agreement, we recognize that these flexibilities include:

a. In applying the customary rules of interpretation of public international law, each provision of the TRIPs Agreement shall be read in the light of the object and purpose of the Agreement as expressed, in particular, in its objectives and principles.

b. Each member has the right to grant compulsory licences and the freedom to determine the grounds upon which such licences are granted.

c. Each member has the right to determine what constitutes a national emergency or other circumstances of extreme urgency, it being understood that public health crises, including those relating to HIV/AIDS, tuberculosis, malaria and other epidemics, can represent a national emergency or other circumstances of extreme urgency.

d. The effect of the provisions in the TRIPs Agreement that are relevant to the exhaustion of intellectual property rights is to leave each member free to establish its own regime for such exhaustion without challenge, subject to the MFN and national treatment provisions of Articles 3 and 4.

6. We recognize that WTO members with insufficient or no manufacturing capacities in the pharmaceutical sector could face difficulties in making effective use of compulsory licensing under the TRIPs Agreement. We instruct the Council for TRIPs to find an expeditious solution to this problem and to report to the General Council before the end of 2002.

7. We reaffirm the commitment of developed-country members to provide incentives to their enterprises and institutions to promote and encourage technology transfer to least-developed country members pursuant to Article 66.2. We also agree that the least-developed country members will not be obliged, with respect to pharmaceutical products, to implement or apply Sections 5 and 7 of Part II of the TRIPs Agreement or to enforce rights provided for under these Sections until 1 January 2016, without prejudice to the right of least-developed country members to seek other extensions of the transition periods as provided for in Article 66.1 of the TRIPs Agreement. We instruct the Council for TRIPs to take the necessary action to give effect to this pursuant to Article 66.1 of the TRIPs Agreement.

Paragraph 6 of the Doha Declaration on TRIPs recognized that the least developed countries in the world have a special problem in the area of access to medicines. Although such countries were given the authority under the Doha Declaration to grant a compulsory license to their domestic companies for the purpose of making inexpensive copies, granting a compulsory license is not much use if the domestic companies lacked the technical ability or resources to manufacture these medicines. Paragraph 6 above recognizes this situation and instructed the Council on TRIPs to address this problem resulting in the following:

Implementation of Paragraph 6 of the Doha Declaration on the TRIPs Agreement and Public Health

Decision of the WTO General Council, August 30, 2003 WT/L/540 (September 2, 2003)

The General Council . . .

[d]ecides as follows:
  1. For the purposes of this Decision:
    (a) "pharmaceutical product" means any patented product, or product manufactured through a patented process, of the pharmaceutical sector needed to address the public health problems as recognized in paragraph 1 of the Declaration. It is understood that active ingredients necessary for its manufacture and diagnostic kits needed for its use would be included;
    (b) "eligible importing Member" means any least-developed country Member, and any other Member that has made a notification to the Council for TRIPs of its intention to use the system as an importer, it being understood that a Member may notify at any time that it will use the system in whole or in a limited way, for example only in the case of a national emergency or other circumstances of extreme urgency or in cases of public non-commercial use. It is noted that some Members will not use the system set out in this Decision as importing Members[16] and that some other Members have stated that, if they use the system, it would be in no more than situations of national emergency or other circumstances of extreme urgency;
    (c) "exporting Member" means a Member using the system set out in this Decision to produce pharmaceutical products for, and export them to, an eligible importing Member.
  2. The obligations of an exporting Member under Article 31(f) of the TRIPs Agreement shall be waived with respect to the grant by it of a compulsory licence to the extent necessary for the purposes of production of a pharmaceutical product(s) and its export to an eligible importing Member(s) in accordance with the terms set out below in this paragraph:
    (a) the eligible importing Member(s) has made a notification to the Council for TRIPs, that:
      (i) specifies the names and expected quantities of the product(s) needed;
      (ii) confirms that the eligible importing Member in question, other than a least-developed country Member, has established that it has insufficient or no manufacturing capacities in the pharmaceutical sector for the product(s) in question in one of the ways set out in the Annex to this Decision; and
      (iii) confirms that, where a pharmaceutical product is patented in its territory, it has granted or intends to grant a compulsory licence in accordance with Article 31 of the TRIPs Agreement and the provisions of this Decision;
    (b) the compulsory licence issued by the exporting Member under this Decision shall contain the following conditions:
      (i) only the amount necessary to meet the needs of the eligible importing Member(s) may be manufactured under the licence and the entirety of this production shall be exported to the Member(s) which has notified its needs to the Council for TRIPs;
      (ii) products produced under the licence shall be clearly identified as being produced under the system set out in this Decision through specific labeling or

---

16. Australia, Austria, Belgium, Canada, Denmark, Finland, France, Germany, Greece, Iceland, Ireland, Italy, Japan, Luxembourg, the Netherlands, New Zealand, Norway, Portugal, Spain, Sweden, Switzerland, the United Kingdom, and the United States.

marking. Suppliers should distinguish such products through special packing and/or special colouring/shaping of the products themselves, provided that such distinction is feasible and does not have a significant impact on price; and

(iii) before shipment begins, the licensee shall post on a website the following information:

- the quantities being supplied to each destination as referred to in indent (i) above; and
- the distinguishing features of the product(s) referred to in indent (ii) above;

(f) the exporting Member shall notify the Council for TRIPs of the grant of the licence, including the conditions attached to it. The information provided shall include the name and address of the licensee, the product(s) for which the licence has been granted, the quantity(ies) for which it has been granted, the country(ies) to which the product(s) is (are) to be supplied and the duration of the licence. The notification shall also indicate the address of the website referred to in subparagraph (b)(iii) above[.]

5. Members shall ensure the availability of effective legal means prevent the importation into, and sale in, their territories of products produced under the system set out in this Decision and diverted to their markets inconsistently with its provisions, using the means already required to be available under the TRIPs Agreement. If any Member considers that such measures are proving insufficient for this purpose, the matter may be reviewed in the Council for TRIPs at the request of that Member.

11. This Decision, including the waivers granted in it, shall terminate for each Member on the date on which an amendment to the TRIPs Agreement replacing its provisions takes effect for that Member. The TRIPs Council shall initiate by the end of 2003 work on the preparation of such an amendment with a view to its adoption within six months.

NOTES AND QUESTIONS

1. The 2003 Implementation Decision will be in force until the WTO enacts an amendment to TRIPs to deal with access to medicines. A December 2005 amendment was to be approved by the WTO by 2007 but the deadline passed with no action. It has now been extended to December 2015—ten years after its proposal—with no indication that the amendment will be approved. How do you evaluate the Decision on access to medicines? The NGO Doctors Without Borders has criticized this Decision as creating "a burdensome drug-by-drug, country-by-country decision-making process, which does not take into account the fact that economies of scale are needed to attract interest from manufacturers of medicines." *http://www.doctorswithoutborders.org/ press/release*, 6 Dec. 2005. The European Union (Regulation 816/2006) and Canada (Access to Medicines Act, R.S.C. ch. P-4, sec. 21) have passed laws implementing the General Council Decision allowing compulsory licenses to be issued for the production of medicines for export to least developed countries. *See* George Tsai, *Canada's Access to Medicines Regime's Compulsory Licensing Scheme Under the WTO Doha Declaration*, 49 Va. J. Int'l L. 4 (2009). Actual use of this compulsory licensing authority has been sparse; why do you think this is the case?

2. Drug companies argue that patent protection under TRIPs is necessary to allow them to obtain a fair return in the commercial exploitation of the drug. It now takes on average almost $1.5 billion to develop a new drug (see p. 535, *supra*). A patent gives the drug company a monopoly for a limited period, that is, 20 years, in which to recoup its expenses and to earn a profit. After the patent period expires, generic versions are allowed to enter the market, which often drastically reduce the future sales of the original drug.

3. The Doha Declaration on TRIPs and the Implementation Decision, both set forth above, can be used by developing and least developed countries to obtain access to patented drugs owned by multinational drug companies at little or minimal cost. How do you think pharmaceutical companies will respond?

PROBLEM 7-7

For most of its history, Z, a populous developing country, has suffered from several infectious diseases caused by poor sanitation and diet. Although these diseases have a very low mortality rate, thousands of people die needlessly in the country each year as these diseases can be completely cured if antibiotics are used effectively. Others survive these diseases but are permanently affected. After Z joined the WTO, it issued a number of patent laws, but the health minister has recently issued a compulsory license to local manufacturers for a powerful antibiotic and has authorized the payment of a nominal fee to the patent owner, a Swiss pharmaceutical company. The local manufacturers not only produce enough for their own use but have also exported additional supplies to several neighboring countries and to the EU. Z has also begun importing inexpensive copies of the drug made by its neighbors in violation of the patent. The Swiss company claims that there is no national emergency and that the importation of the copies of its drug violates its patent obtained in Z.

(1) Are the actions of Z consistent with Article 31 of TRIPs pre-Doha?
(2) Are the actions of Z consistent with Article 31 in light of the Doha Declaration on TRIPs and Public Health and the Implementation Decision?

D.   TRIPs and the Biopiracy Debate

Another issue that was debated during the WTO Doha Ministerial Conference in 2001 was a practice that some developing countries have called "biopiracy." While commercial piracy generally pits MNEs and developed countries against developing countries and their constituencies, the array of interests is reversed in biopiracy. Developing countries claim to be owners of traditional knowledge and biological resources and accuse MNEs and developed countries of theft. Biopiracy is also accused of subverting the legitimate purposes of the patent system, which is to protect individual knowledge so that it can be brought out into the public domain for public good. The patenting of indigenous knowledge achieves the opposite effect: It is a legal mechanism through which the commonly shared knowledge and traditions of a community are converted into private property and exploited for the financial gain of a few.

Consider the following illustrations.

Illustration 7-1. An MNE pharmaceutical company is looking for a new treatment for heart disease and sends researchers to a South American country rich in biological diversity and where some indigenous tribes have a long life span and a low incidence of heart disease despite a diet consisting mainly of meat. After interviewing tribe members and being allowed to observe their dietary habits for several months, the researchers discover that one of the few vegetables that tribal members consume is a locally grown plant that helps to create a highly potent form of HDL (high-density lipoprotein) cholesterol that keeps the heart healthy and arteries unclogged. The few weeks spent with the tribe have saved the researchers years in research time and the pharmaceutical company millions of dollars in research and development expenses. Moreover, without tapping into the habits and knowledge of the tribe, the company may never have discovered as effective a heart disease medicine. The researchers return home, isolate and purify the genetic materials that give rise to the super HDL, patent the invention, and produce a highly successful drug that earns hundreds of millions of dollars in its first few years on the market. The indigenous tribe never receives any compensation.

Illustration 7-2. An MNE agricultural and food processing company is looking for a new variety of rice that has a low starch content and is disease resistant. Researchers from the MNE travel to Asia and work with local universities to find a variety of rice grown for hundreds of years in only two Asian countries that has some of these characteristics. The researchers return home and cross-breed the Asian rice with a U.S. variety and produce a new and superior breed of rice. The MNE obtains a patent for the new product, which is a major success in the United States and overseas. The company never shares any profits with the local universities or with the Asian countries. Nationwide outrage erupts when the Asian countries discover that the MNE has patented "their" national product and there is a backlash against intellectual property rights in Western products.

One response to the concerns raised by these illustrations might be to urge the owners of traditional knowledge to protect themselves by acquiring patents or other IP rights of their own. However, the problem is that forms of traditional knowledge do not usually qualify for patent protection under TRIPs standards. For example, U.S. patent law, consistent with TRIPs Article 27(1), requires three elements for a patent: novelty, utility, and non-obviousness. A product that is found in nature such as the plant in Illustration 7-1 is not eligible for patent protection because it does not satisfy the novelty requirement. The patentable invention in Illustration 7-1 is the isolated and purified genetic material, which is not found in nature, not the plant itself. Similarly, in Illustration 7-2, the patentable product is not the Asian rice but the cross-breed variety, a newly invented product not found in nature. What about the knowledge itself in Illustration 7-1? Here the knowledge has been publicly available for hundreds of years as part of the cultural heritage of the tribe and does not qualify as novel. Patent laws also require a single act of discovery and do not recognize common knowledge the origins of which are unknown. An applicant for a patent must also normally be an individual not a group. The dilemma is that traditional knowledge does not qualify for intellectual property protection under TRIPs standards. However, these standards, of course, were created by developed nations and did not take into consideration the possibility of rights in traditional knowledge and bioresources.

While TRIPs standards did not appear to accommodate forms of traditional knowledge, another international treaty, the 1992 Convention for Biological Diversity (CBD), June 5, 1992, 1760 U.N.T.S. 79, negotiated at a United Nations conference in Rio de Janeiro, provides a legal basis for recognizing ownership rights in traditional knowledge. Article 8(j) of the CBD requires its contracting parties "to respect, preserve, and maintain knowledge, innovations and practices of indigenous and local communities embodying traditional lifestyles relevant for the conservation and sustainable use of biological diversity and promote their wider application with the approval and involvement of the holders of such knowledge, innovations and practices and encourage the equitable sharing of the benefits arising from the utilization of such knowledge, innovations, and practices." Until the Doha Ministerial Conference, however, the CBD was overshadowed by TRIPs, which was far more influential and powerful. By the time of the Doha Conference, however, international controversy over the biopiracy issue sparked by several well-known international incidents had drawn the attention of the WTO. At the Doha Ministerial

Conference, a well-organized and effective lobbying effort by developing countries succeeded in gaining recognition of the problem of traditional knowledge by the conference. The Doha Conference stated as part of its ministerial declaration:

> We instruct the Council for TRIPs to examine, *inter alia*, the relationship between the TRIPs Agreement and the Convention on Biological Diversity, the protection of traditional knowledge and folklore, and other relevant new developments raised by Members. In undertaking this work, the TRIPs Council shall be guided by the objectives and principles set out in Articles 7 and 8 of the TRIPs Agreement and shall take fully into account the development dimension.

The TRIPs Council is currently working with the World Intellectual Property Organization and the CBD in addressing these issues, but progress is very slow. On April 12, 2011, several developing countries submitted a draft amendment to TRIPs, but the amendment has received no further action. For a fuller account of this debate, see *Poor People's Knowledge: Promoting Intellectual Property in Developing Countries* (J. Michael Finger and Philip Schuler, eds., 2004).

PROBLEM 7-8

Brazil is rich in rain forests and biological resources and has become a fertile ground for developing new drugs, organic consumer products, and herbal medicines. Brazil has grown increasingly concerned about "bioprospecting" by various aggressive multinational pharmaceutical companies that are actively exploring various local plant and animal species as sources of new medicines. Suppose that the legislature is considering a new national law recognizing *sui generis* intellectual property rights in traditional knowledge in its indigenous communities and also property rights in the nation's biological resources. Will this new law fully protect the interests of the country? What is required?

PROBLEM 7-9

You are a consultant to a group of developing countries and are being asked to explain what appears to be an inconsistency in the position of the United States on IP rights and international trade. The United States was a major driving force behind including intellectual property rights in the World Trade Organization through the implementation of TRIPs. Developing countries wanted to keep IP issues within the jurisdiction of WIPO but ultimately capitulated to demands of the United States and other developed countries. On the issue of biopiracy, however, the United States has taken the position that WIPO, not the WTO, is the proper forum to consider this issue. Why would the United States take this position? Is this hypocritical?

III.   Gray-Market Goods and Parallel Imports

As we have seen, IP owners have serious concerns about pirated and infringing products. While IP owners consider commercial piracy to be a far more serious problem, they are also concerned about the unauthorized distribution of their genuine goods or "gray-market goods." In this section, we turn to the issue of protection against imports of gray-market goods and parallel imports.

IP owners often seek to exclude the importation of gray-market goods. The exclusion of gray-market goods is governed by different rules depending upon whether the intellectual property rights involved concern trademark, copyright, or patent. In the discussion below, we focus on gray-market goods involving trademarks, which present the most common situation. We also discuss gray-market goods involving copyright, which are subject to a different set of rules, and make reference to gray-market goods involving patent rights.

A.   What Are Gray-Market Goods and Parallel Imports?

We have already been introduced to the concept of gray-market goods in an international context in *Feldman v. Mexico* in Chapter Six at pp. 389-395. We turn now to a consideration of gray-market trademarked goods in the United States.

Consider the following illustration.

Illustration 7-3. A consumer goes to a large discount department store to buy a new consumer electronics product. The consumer wants to buy a famous brand because of its reputation for quality. The consumer sees the branded product on two different shelves with two prices. The packaging of one set of goods has English language labeling that appears to have been later pasted on top of a foreign language printed on the package itself. This product sells for about 30 percent less and carries a store warranty rather than a manufacturer's warranty. Aware of the global problem of commercial piracy and concerned that the less expensive product may be a counterfeit, the customer asks a sales manager for an explanation. The manager assures the consumer that the product is not a counterfeit or pirated product but a genuine product produced abroad by the manufacturer and originally intended for a foreign market. The department store was able to take advantage of currency fluctuations and a strong dollar to buy the products in the foreign market at a discount and import them into the United States to pass the savings on to the consumer. The consumer is satisfied and buys the less expensive item. The consumer has just bought a "gray-market good." When the U.S. manufacturer finds out about the sale, the manufacturer seeks to prevent any further imports of the gray-market electronics goods into the United States.

Gray-market goods and parallel imports are terms that are often used interchangeably and there is probably no harm in this usage, but a gray-market good is not necessarily a parallel import. A true parallel import situation arises as follows.

Illustration 7-4. Because of less expensive labor costs abroad, a U.S. trademark owner licenses the right to manufacture products under the U.S. registered trademark to a foreign company. The company manufactures the goods abroad for import by the U.S. trademark owner into the U.S. market where the goods will be sold. The foreign manufacturer is also authorized to sell the products to foreign markets. A foreign distributor buys a quantity of goods manufactured by the foreign licensee for sale in foreign markets at a discount and finds a large U.S. discount department store that is willing to buy the goods for import into the United States. Now there are two channels of imports. There is one channel that is authorized by the U.S. trademark owner and a second, "parallel" channel that is not authorized by the U.S. trademark owner.

In Illustration 7-3, the U.S. trademark owner did not authorize any imports of its product but manufactured all products sold in the United States at its U.S. manufacturing facilities. This is a situation involving gray-market goods but not parallel imports because there is no authorized channel of imports at all.

Note that, unlike counterfeits and pirated goods, gray-market goods[17] are genuine products and the market for these goods is lawful. Gray-market goods are also allowed to enter the United States under some circumstances despite the wishes of the U.S. trademark owner.

Although some brand owners object to gray-market goods, note that these goods can often still represent a sale to the trademark owner. Illustrations 7-3 and 7-4 are such examples because in each case a foreign distributor has purchased the goods at the wholesale level overseas, taking advantage of currency fluctuations to buy the goods at a favorable exchange rate in order to import and sell the goods in the United States. These overseas transactions represent sales to the U.S. trademark owner.

NOTES AND QUESTIONS

1. Many consumers view gray-market goods to be a benefit as they offer consumers more choice and better prices. Why should the U.S. manufacturer be concerned if consumers are happy? Note that many manufacturers engage in price discrimination between markets, i.e., charging higher prices in those markets that can support them and lower prices in other markets. Why would gray-market goods undermine this approach?

2. If a gray-market good imported into the United States usually represents a sale abroad to the U.S. manufacturer, why would the U.S. company ever object to gray-market goods? Hint: Assume that you are the U.S. sales and marketing director of the U.S. manufacturer.

3. If gray-market goods are genuine and lawful, why should Customs ever want to exclude them?

4. Given that gray-market goods provide some benefits but that trademark owners also have some legitimate concerns, should Customs enforce a total ban or a partial ban on the imports of gray-market goods? The following materials address this issue.

B. Gray-Market Goods Under U.S. Law

In Illustration 7-3, we explained the concept of a gray-market trademarked good but the illustration did not explain how a gray market arises or how the gray-market goods were obtained by the U.S. department store. The gray market may have been created through a number of different scenarios that we set forth below. How the gray market is created is important because U.S. law treats gray-market goods differently depending on which of the following situations has given rise to the gray market.

In general, a gray market in goods arises from one of three prototypical situations. In each of the cases set forth below, A is a U.S. company that seeks to ban the importation of the gray-market goods and B is a foreign company that manufactures the gray-market goods.

---

17. In the materials that follow unless otherwise indicated, "gray-market goods" also includes parallel imports.

(1) *U.S. Owner of a Foreign Trademark.* A, a U.S. company, purchases the U.S. rights to a foreign trademark from B, a foreign company and trademark owner, and registers the mark as a U.S. trademark. For example, suppose that B has a famous brand of perfume that is protected by a foreign trademark. A purchases the U.S. trademark rights for the perfume from B, registers the mark as a U.S. trademark, and begins to manufacture and sell the perfume in the United States. After B sells the trademark rights to A, however, B begins to import the perfume into the United States, creating a gray market for the goods that compete with A's products. This has been called the "classic" gray-market goods case.

(2) *Affiliated Companies Under a Common Ownership.* A and B are related companies and have a parent-subsidiary relationship or are otherwise subject to a common ownership and control. There are two variants of this situation:

    (a) A is a U.S. subsidiary of B, the foreign parent company and the owner of the foreign trademark. B has incorporated A in the United States for the purpose of controlling and serving the U.S. market. B is the owner of the foreign trademark for the goods but A is the registered owner of the U.S. trademark for the goods. A manufactures and sells the goods on the U.S. market but the goods are also imported into the United States by B or by a third party who has purchased the goods overseas from B.

    (b) A is a U.S. parent company and has established B in a foreign country as a subsidiary, a foreign branch, or an unincorporated foreign department. The goods are manufactured abroad by B for import into the United States and also for sale abroad. The goods are purchased abroad by a third-party distributor who then imports them into the United States.

(3) *Licensed Manufacturing Abroad.* A, a U.S. company and trademark owner, licenses the manufacture of its products in a foreign country to B, a foreign company. B then imports the goods into the United States or sells the products to a third-party distributor who imports the goods into the United States.

Prior to 1922, the United States did not regulate gray-market goods at all and, as a result, they were permitted free entry into the United States. At that time, U.S. trademark law only protected trademark owners from the importation of infringing or counterfeit goods, and as gray-market goods bore a genuine trademark, they were permitted to be imported into the United States over the objections of U.S. trademark owners. In 1922, as the direct result of the storm of protest that arose in reaction to *A. Bourjois & Co. v. Katzel*, 275 F. 539 (2d Cir. 1921), *rev'd*, 260 U.S. 689 (1923), Congress enacted legislation that imposed a ban on the importation of gray-market goods. In *Katzel*, a U.S. citizen purchased the U.S. trademark rights from a French powder manufacturer. After the purchase was completed, the French manufacturer sold the powder to a U.S. druggist who began to import the product into the United States. The purchaser of the trademark sued the druggist, seeking injunctive relief to protect the value of its trademark. You should recognize that the situation in *Katzel* involved the first of the three prototypical situations set forth above giving rise to a gray market.

The Second Circuit found that the trademark owner could exclude the goods only if they infringed its trademark. Finding that the importation of genuine goods was not trademark infringement, the court allowed the imports. The decision incensed U.S. trademark owners who viewed the actions of the French company as an underhanded attempt to undermine the U.S. purchaser's investment. They appealed directly to Congress to enact legislation that would overturn the Second Circuit decision. Before the U.S. Supreme Court could hear the appeal from the Second Circuit, Congress enacted §526 of the Tariff Act of 1922 (Fordney-McCumber Act), 42 Stat. 858, as a last-minute legislative amendment. Section 526, which was subsequently adopted as §526 of the Tariff Act of 1930, 19 U.S.C. §1526 (2006), provided that a U.S. trademark owner had to give its prior consent before the importation into the United States of "any merchandise of foreign manufacture if such merchandise . . . bears a trademark owned by a citizen of, or by a corporation . . . created" within the United States. *Id.* §1526(a).

As §526 was enacted to overturn the result of the Second Circuit decision in *Katzel*, it is clear that §526 prohibited the importation of gray-market goods under the *Katzel* facts or in case (1) above. However, did Congress intend to create a total ban of all gray-market goods and not just those that arise as a result of case (1) or out of the *Katzel* facts? In other words, were gray-market goods that arose as a result of cases (2) and (3) above also included within the scope of the prohibition of §526?

As Congress acted swiftly and under pressure from trademark owners, §526 was hastily and poorly drafted and left these questions unanswered. Note that the language of §526 is sufficiently ambiguous that resort to the text of §526 alone cannot answer these questions. For example, take case (2)(a) above. In this case, A, the U.S. subsidiary of B, the foreign parent, is the owner of the registered U.S. trademark and is faced with gray-market importation. Whether or not A can prevent the importation under §526 depends on whether the trademark is "*owned by* a citizen" of the United States. In this case, A owns the U.S. trademark but as B, the foreign parent, owns A, it is possible to argue that B, not A, is actually the owner of the U.S. trademark. If B, the foreign parent, is deemed to be the owner of the U.S. trademark, then the gray-market goods do not bear a trademark owned by a citizen of the United States and thereby fall outside the prohibition of §526 and are permitted entry into the United States.

A similar ambiguity exists with respect to case (2)(b) above. In this case, A is the U.S. parent and B is a foreign subsidiary that manufactures the goods. Section 526 prohibits importation of merchandise of *foreign manufacture*. However, although B is located in a foreign country and the goods are manufactured abroad, B is a subsidiary owned by A, the U.S. parent company. As A is the owner of B, it is arguable that the goods manufactured by B are not goods of foreign manufacture and fall outside the prohibition of §526. As for case (3), licensing arrangements were not common when §526 was enacted and it was also unclear whether Congress intended to include case (3) within the scope of the prohibition set forth in §526.

As this discussion indicates, while it was clear that case (1) was included within the prohibition of §526, it was unclear from the text or legislative history of the statute whether cases (2) and (3) were included. In other words, it was unclear whether Congress intended to enact a total ban on the importation of gray-market goods (without the permission of the trademark owner) or only a partial ban. Left to enforce §526 and without clear answers to these questions, the U.S. Customs Service enacted a series of regulations that interpreted these ambiguities in §526 to result in a partial ban. As §526 on its face and at first glance appears to create a total ban and as Customs interpreted §526 to create a partial ban, Customs styled its regulations as creating "exceptions" to §526. At the time that the following principal case, *K Mart Corp. v. Cartier*, was decided, Customs regulations interpreted §526 to ban case (1) only and contained exceptions that took cases (2) and (3) outside the prohibition of §526. *K Mart* concerns the Supreme Court's review of whether the U.S. Customs regulations recognizing a partial ban were a reasonable interpretation of §526.

PROBLEM 7-10

A U.S. manufacturer licenses its foreign affiliate in Canada to produce a soft drink for the Canadian market. In addition to selling the product in the Canadian market, the Canadian affiliate also exports the soft drink into the United States. The U.S. manufacturer objects to the imports because the soft drink contains less carbonation than its U.S. soft drinks as Canadians are less fond of highly carbonated drinks than Americans. Can the U.S. company exclude the soft drink? For the purposes of this problem, assume that there are no food safety issues or regulations involved. Consider the issues in this problem in the following order: (1) the license, (2) the affiliation between the two companies, and (3) the differences in the products. See *K Mart* and *Lever Bros.* below and the current 19 C.F.R. §133.23 following *Lever Bros.* in the accompanying notes.

K Mart Corp. v. Cartier, Inc.
United States Supreme Court, 1988
486 U.S. 281

Justice KENNEDY announced the judgment of the Court and delivered the opinion of the Court with respect to Parts I, II-A, and II-C, and an opinion with respect to Part II-B, in which WHITE, J., joined.

A gray-market good is a foreign-manufactured good, bearing a valid United States trademark, that is imported without the consent of the United States trademark holder. These cases present the issue whether the Secretary of the Treasury's regulation permitting the importation of certain gray-market goods, 19 C.F.R. §133.21 (1987), is a reasonable agency interpretation of §526 of the Tariff Act of 1930 (1930 Tariff Act), 46 Stat. 741, as amended, 19 U.S.C. §1526.

I

A

The gray market arises in any of three general contexts. The prototypical gray-market victim (case 1) is a domestic firm that purchases from an independent foreign firm the rights to register and use the latter's trademark as a United States trademark and to sell its foreign-manufactured products here. Especially where the foreign firm has already registered the trademark in the United States or where the product has already earned a reputation for quality, the right to use that trademark can be very valuable. If the foreign manufacturer could import the trademarked goods and distribute them here, despite having sold the trademark to a domestic firm, the domestic firm would be forced into sharp intrabrand competition involving the very trademark it purchased. Similar intrabrand competition could arise if the foreign manufacturer markets its wares outside the United States, as is often the case, and a third party who purchases them abroad could legally import them. In either event, the parallel importation, if permitted to proceed, would create a gray market that could jeopardize the trademark holder's investment.

The second context (case 2) is a situation in which a domestic firm registers the United States trademark for goods that are manufactured abroad by an affiliated manufacturer. In its most common variation (case 2a), a foreign firm wishes to control distribution of its wares in this country by incorporating a subsidiary here. The subsidiary then registers under its own name (or the manufacturer assigns to the subsidiary's name) a United States trademark that is identical to its parent's foreign trademark. The parallel importation by a third party who buys the goods abroad (or conceivably even by the affiliated foreign manufacturer itself) creates a gray market. Two other variations on this theme occur when an American-based firm establishes abroad a manufacturing subsidiary corporation (case 2b) or its own unincorporated manufacturing division (case 2c) to produce its United States trademarked goods, and then imports them for domestic distribution. If the trademark holder or its foreign subsidiary sells the trademarked goods abroad, the parallel importation of the goods competes on the gray market with the holder's domestic sales.

In the third context (case 3), the domestic holder of a United States trademark *authorizes* an independent foreign manufacturer to use it. Usually the holder sells to the foreign manufacturer an exclusive right to use the trademark in a particular foreign location, but conditions the right on the foreign manufacturer's promise not to import its trademarked goods into the United States. Once again, if the foreign manufacturer or a third party imports into the United States, the foreign-manufactured goods will compete on the gray market with the holder's domestic goods.

B

Until 1922, the Federal Government did not regulate the importation of gray-market goods, not even to protect the investment of an independent purchaser of a foreign trademark, and not even in the extreme case where the independent foreign manufacturer breached its agreement to refrain from direct competition with the purchaser. That year, however, Congress was spurred to action by a Court of Appeals decision declining to enjoin the parallel importation of goods bearing a trademark that (as in case 1) a domestic company had purchased from an independent foreign manufacturer at a premium. *See A. Bourjois & Co.* v. *Katzel*, 275 F. 539 (2d Cir. 1921), *rev'd*, 260 U.S. 689, (1923).

In an immediate response to *Katzel*, Congress enacted §526 of the Tariff Act of 1922, 42 Stat. 975. That provision, later reenacted in identical form as §526 of the 1930 Tariff Act, 19 U.S.C. §1526, prohibits importing

> "into the United States any merchandise of foreign manufacture if such merchandise . . . bears a trademark owned by a citizen of, or by a corporation or association created or organized within, the United States, and registered in the Patent and Trademark Office by a person domiciled in the United States . . . , unless written consent of the owner of such trademark is produced at the time of making entry." 19 U.S.C. §1526(a).

The regulations implementing §526 for the past 50 years have not applied the prohibition to all gray-market goods. The Customs Service regulation now in force provides generally that "foreign-made articles bearing a trademark identical with one owned and recorded by a citizen of the United States or a corporation or association created or organized within the United States are subject to seizure and forfeiture as prohibited importations." 19 C.F.R. §133.21(b) (1987). But the regulation furnishes a "common-control" exception from the ban, permitting the entry of gray-market goods manufactured abroad by the trademark owner or its affiliate:

(c) *Restrictions not applicable.* The restrictions . . . do not apply to imported articles when:

(1) Both the foreign and the U.S. trademark or trade name are owned by the same person or business entity; [or]

(2) The foreign and domestic trademark or trade name owners are parent and subsidiary companies or are otherwise subject to common ownership or control. . . .

The Customs Service regulation further provides an "authorized-use" exception, which permits importation of gray-market goods where

"(3) the articles of foreign manufacture bear a recorded trademark or trade name applied under authorization of the U.S. owner. . . ." 19 C.F.R. §133.21(c) (1987).

Respondents, an association of United States trademark holders and two of its members, brought suit in Federal District Court in February 1984, seeking both a declaration that the Customs Service regulation, 19 C.F.R. §§133.21(c)(1)–(3) (1987), is invalid and an injunction against its enforcement. *Coalition to Preserve the Integrity of American Trademarks v. United States,* 598 F. Supp. 844 (D.D.C. 1984). They asserted that the common-control and authorized-use exceptions are inconsistent with §526 of the 1930 Tariff Act. Petitioners K mart [sic] and 47th Street Photo intervened as defendants.

The District Court upheld the Customs Service regulation, but the Court of Appeals reversed[,] holding that the Customs Service regulation was an unreasonable administrative interpretation of §526. We granted certiorari, 479 U.S. 1005 (1986), to resolve a conflict among the Courts of Appeals.

A majority of this Court now holds that the common-control exception of the Customs Service regulation, 19 C.F.R. §§133.21(c)(1)–(2) (1987), is consistent with §526. See *post,* at 309–310 (opinion of BRENNAN, J.). A different majority, however, holds that the authorized-use exception, 19 C.F.R. §133.21(c)(3) (1987), is inconsistent with §526. See *post,* at 328–329 (opinion of SCALIA, J.). We therefore affirm the Court of Appeals in part and reverse in part.

II

A

In determining whether a challenged regulation is valid, a reviewing court must first determine if the regulation is consistent with the language of the statute. "If the statute is clear and unambiguous 'that is the end of the matter, for the court, as well as the agency, must give effect to the unambiguously expressed intent of Congress.' The traditional deference courts pay to agency interpretation is not to be applied to alter the clearly expressed intent of Congress." *Board of Governors, FRS v. Dimension Financial Corp.,* 474 U.S. 361, 368 (1986).

Following this analysis, I conclude that subsections (c)(1) and (c)(2) of the Customs Service regulation, 19 C.F.R. §§133.21 (c)(1) and (c)(2) (1987), are permissible constructions designed to resolve statutory ambiguities. All Members of the Court are in agreement that the agency may interpret the statute to bar importation of gray-market goods in what we have denoted case 1 and to permit the imports under case 2a. As these writings state, "owned by" is sufficiently ambiguous, in the context of the statute, that it applies to situations involving a foreign parent, which is case 2a. This ambiguity arises from the inability to discern, from the statutory language, which of the two entities involved in case

2a can be said to "own" the United States trademark if, as in some instances, the domestic subsidiary is wholly owned by its foreign parent.

A further statutory ambiguity contained in the phrase "merchandise of foreign manufacture," suffices to sustain the regulations as they apply to cases 2b and 2c. This ambiguity parallels that of "owned by," which sustained case 2a, because it is possible to interpret "merchandise of foreign manufacture" to mean (1) goods manufactured in a foreign country, (2) goods manufactured by a foreign company, or (3) goods manufactured in a foreign country by a foreign company. Given the imprecision in the statute, the agency is entitled to choose any reasonable definition and to interpret the statute to say that goods manufactured by a foreign subsidiary or division of a domestic company are not goods "of foreign manufacture."

Subsection (c)(3), 19 C.F.R. §133.21(c)(3) (1987), of the regulation, however, cannot stand. The ambiguous statutory phrases that we have already discussed, "owned by" and "merchandise of foreign manufacture," are irrelevant to the proscription contained in subsection (3) of the regulation. This subsection of the regulation denies a domestic trademark holder the power to prohibit the importation of goods made by an independent foreign manufacturer where the domestic trademark holder has authorized the foreign manufacturer to use the trademark. Under no reasonable construction of the statutory language can goods made in a foreign country by an independent foreign manufacturer be removed from the purview of the statute.

We hold that the Customs Service regulation is consistent with §526 insofar as it exempts from the importation ban goods that are manufactured abroad by the "same person" who holds the United States trademark, 19 C.F.R. §133.21(c)(1) (1987), or by a person who is "subject to common . . . control" with the United States trademark holder, §133.21(c)(2). Because the authorized-use exception of the regulation, §133.21(c)(3), is in conflict with the plain language of the statute, that provision cannot stand.

It is so ordered.

Lever Brothers Co. v. United States
United States Court of Appeals, D.C. Circuit, 1993
981 F.2d 1330

SENTELLE, Circuit Judge.

Lever Brothers Company ("Lever US" or "Lever"), an American company, and its British affiliate, Lever Brothers Limited ("Lever UK"), both manufacture deodorant soap under the "Shield" trademark and hand dishwashing liquid under the "Sunlight" trademark. The trademarks are registered in each country. The products have evidently been formulated differently to suit local tastes and circumstances. The U.S. version lathers more, the soaps smell different, the colorants used in American "Shield" have been certified by the FDA whereas the colorants in British "Shield" have not, and the U.S. version contains a bacteriostat that enhances the deodorant properties of the soap. The British version of "Sunlight" dishwashing soap produces less suds, and the American version is formulated to work best in the "soft water" available in most American cities, whereas the British version is designed for "hard water" common in Britain.

The packaging of the U.S. and U.K. products is also somewhat different. The British "Shield" logo is written in script form and is packaged in foil wrapping and contains a wave motif, whereas the American "Shield" logo is written in block form, does not come in foil wrapping and contains a grid pattern. There is small print on the packages indicating where they were manufactured. The British "Sunlight" comes in a cylindrical bottle labeled "Sunlight Washing Up Liquid." The American "Sunlight" comes in a yellow, hourglass-shaped bottle labeled "Sunlight Dishwashing Liquid."

Lever asserts that the unauthorized influx of these foreign products has created substantial consumer confusion and deception in the United States about the nature and origin of this merchandise, and that it has received numerous consumer complaints from American consumers who unknowingly bought the British products and were disappointed.

Lever argues that the importation of the British products was in violation of section 42 of the Lanham Act, 15 U.S.C. §1124 which provides that with the exception of goods imported for personal use:

> No article of imported merchandise which shall copy or simulate the name of the [sic] any domestic manufacture, or manufacturer . . . or which shall copy or simulate a trademark registered in accordance with the provisions of this chapter . . . shall be admitted to entry at any customhouse of the United States.

Id. The United States Customs Service ("Customs"), however, was allowing importation of the British goods under the "affiliate exception" created by 19 C.F.R. §133.21(c)(2), which provides that foreign goods bearing United States trademarks are not forbidden when "the foreign and domestic trademark or trade name owners are parent and subsidiary companies or are otherwise subject to common ownership or control."[18]

In *Lever I*, we concluded that "the natural, virtually inevitable reading of section 42 is that it bars foreign goods bearing a trademark identical to the valid U.S. trademark but physically different," without regard to affiliation between the producing firms or the genuine character of the trademark abroad. 877 F.2d 101, 111 (D.C. Cir. 1989).

After reviewing the submissions of the parties, the District Court found that Customs' administrative practice was "at best inconsistent" and, in any event, had "never addressed the specific question of physically different goods that bear identical trademarks." *Lever Bros. Co. v. United States*, 796 F. Supp. 1, 5 (D.D.C. 1992). The District Court concluded that "section 42 . . . prohibits the importation of foreign goods that . . . are physically different, regardless of the validity of the foreign trademark or the existence of an affiliation between the U.S. and foreign markholders." *Id.* The court accordingly concluded that "neither the legislative history of the statute nor the administrative practice of the Customs Service clearly contradicts the plain meaning of section 42" and granted summary judgment against the government. *Id.* at 13.

Customs' main argument from the legislative history is that section 42 of the Lanham Act applies only to imports of goods bearing trademarks that "copy or simulate" a registered mark. Customs thus draws a distinction between "genuine" marks and marks that "copy or simulate." A mark applied by a foreign firm subject to ownership and control common to that of the domestic trademark owner is by definition "genuine," Customs urges, regardless of whether or not the goods are identical. Thus, any importation of goods manufactured by an affiliate of a U.S. trademark owner cannot "copy or simulate" a registered mark because those goods are *ipso facto* "genuine."

---

18. This case does not involve a dispute between corporate affiliates. Neither Lever US nor Lever UK has authorized the importation, which is being conducted by third parties. *See Lever Bros. Co. v. United States*, 877 F.2d 101, 103 (D.C. Cir. 1989) [hereinafter *Lever I*].

This argument is fatally flawed. It rests on the false premise that foreign trademarks applied to foreign goods are "genuine" in the United States. Trademarks applied to physically different foreign goods are not genuine from the viewpoint of the American consumer. As we stated in *Lever I*:

> On its face . . . section [42] appears to aim at deceit and consumer confusion; when identical trademarks have acquired different meanings in different countries, one who imports the foreign version to sell it under that trademark will (in the absence of some specially differentiating feature) cause the confusion Congress sought to avoid. The fact of affiliation between the producers in no way reduces the probability of that confusion; it is certainly not a constructive consent to importation.

877 F.2d at 111.

There is a larger, more fundamental and ultimately fatal weakness in Customs' position in this case. Section 42 on its face appears to forbid importation of goods that "copy or simulate" a United States trademark. Customs has the burden of adducing evidence from the legislative history of section 42 and its administrative practice of an exception for materially different goods whose similar foreign and domestic trademarks are owned by affiliated companies. At a minimum, this requires that the specific question be addressed in the legislative history and administrative practice. The bottom line, however, is that the issue of materially different goods was not addressed either in the legislative history or the administrative record. It is not enough to posit that silence implies authorization, when the authorization sought runs counter to the evident meaning of the governing statute. Therefore, we conclude that section 42 of the Lanham Act precludes the application of Customs' affiliate exception with respect to physically, materially different goods.

For the foregoing reasons, we affirm the District Court's ruling that section 42 of the Lanham Act, 15 U.S.C. §1124, bars the importation of physically different foreign goods bearing a trademark identical to a valid U.S. trademark, regardless of the trademark's genuine character abroad or affiliation between the producing firms.

So ordered.

NOTES AND QUESTIONS

1. Review the discussion of cases (1)–(3) on p. 569. After *K Mart*, which of these cases are within the ban of §526 and which are outside the ban of §526?

2. In *Lever Bros.*, plaintiff Lever US invoked §42 of the Lanham Act to exclude the gray-market goods and decided not to invoke §526 of the Tariff Act of 1930. Why?

3. After the decisions in *K Mart* and *Lever Bros.*, the Customs Service amended its regulations. The current regulation, 19 C.F.R. §133.23, provides:

> (a) *Restricted gray market articles defined.* "Restricted gray market articles" are foreign made articles bearing a genuine trademark or trade name identical with or substantially indistinguishable from one owned and recorded by a citizen of the United States or a corporation or association created or organized within the United States and imported without the authorization of the U.S. owner. "Restricted gray market goods" include goods bearing a genuine trademark or trade name which is:
>
> > (1) *Independent licensee.* Applied by a licensee (including a manufacturer) independent of the U.S. owner, or
> >
> > (2) *Foreign owner.* Applied under the authority of a foreign trademark or trade name owner other than the U.S. owner, a parent or subsidiary of the U.S.

owner, or a party otherwise subject to common ownership or control with the U.S. owner, from whom the U.S. owner acquired the domestic title, or to whom the U.S. owner sold the foreign titles(s); or

(3) "Lever-*Rule.*" Applied by the U.S. owner, a parent or subsidiary of the U.S. owner or a party otherwise subject to common ownership or control with the U.S. owner to goods that the Customs Service has determined to be physically and materially different from the articles authorized by the U.S. trademark owner for importation or sale in the U.S.

(b) *Labeling of physically and materially different goods.* Goods determined by the Customs Service to be physically and materially different [and] bearing a genuine mark applied under the authority of the U.S. owner, a parent or subsidiary of the U.S. owner, or a party otherwise subject to common ownership and control with the U.S. owner shall not be detained where the merchandise or its packaging bears a conspicuous and legible label designed to remain on the product until the first sale to a retail consumer in the United States stating that: "This product is not a product authorized by the United States trademark owner for importation and is physically and materially different from the authorized product."

(c) *Denial of Entry.* All restricted gray market goods imported into the United States shall be denied entry and subject to detention.

PROBLEM 7-11

Microtel licenses its wholly-owned subsidiary in England to manufacture its latest office software under the "Microtel" trademark. In a separate agreement, Microtel also licenses its copyright in the software to the subsidiary. Microtel discovers that the British subsidiary is selling software directly to distributors in the United States and has also sold the software to a French distributor, which has also been exporting the software to the United States.

(1) Can Microtel use trademark rights to exclude the software? Consider §526 of the Tariff Act of 1930 quoted and discussed in *K Mart, supra,* 19 C.F.R. §133.23, *supra,* and §42 of the Lanham Act, 15 U.S.C. §1124 quoted and discussed in *Lever Bros., supra.*

(2) Can Microtel exclude the software under copyright law? Consider the Copyright Act of 1976 as interpreted and applied by *Quality King* and *Kirtsaeng* below.

Quality King Distributors, Inc. v. L'anza Research International, Inc.

United States Supreme Court, 1998
523 U.S. 135

Justice STEVENS delivered the opinion of the Court.

Section 106(3) of the Copyright Act of 1976 (Act), 17 U.S.C. §106(3), gives the owner of a copyright the exclusive right to distribute copies of a copyrighted work. That exclusive right is expressly limited, however, by the provisions of §§107 through 120. Section 602(a) gives the copyright owner the right to prohibit the unauthorized importation of copies. The question presented by this case is whether the right granted by §602(a) is also limited by §§107 through 120. More narrowly, the question is whether the "first sale" doctrine endorsed in §109(a) is applicable to imported copies.

I

Respondent, L'anza Research International, Inc. (L'anza), is a California corporation engaged in the business of manufacturing and selling shampoos, conditioners, and other hair care products. L'anza has copyrighted the labels that are affixed to those products. In the United States, L'anza sells exclusively to domestic distributors who have agreed to resell within limited geographic areas and then only to authorized retailers such as barber shops, beauty salons, and professional hair care colleges. L'anza has found that the American "public is generally unwilling to pay the price charged for high quality products, such as L'anza's products, when they are sold along with the less expensive lower quality products that are generally carried by supermarkets and drug stores." L'anza promotes the domestic sales of its products with extensive advertising in various trade magazines and at point of sale, and by providing special training to authorized retailers.

L'anza also sells its products in foreign markets. In those markets, however, it does not engage in comparable advertising or promotion; its prices to foreign distributors are 35% to 40% lower than the prices charged to domestic distributors. In 1992 and 1993, L'anza's distributor in the United Kingdom arranged the sale of three shipments to a distributor in Malta; each shipment contained several tons of L'anza products with copyrighted labels affixed. The record does not establish whether the initial purchaser was the distributor in the United Kingdom or the distributor in Malta, or whether title passed when the goods were delivered to the carrier or when they arrived at their destination, but it is undisputed that the goods were manufactured by L'anza and first sold by L'anza to a foreign purchaser.

It is also undisputed that the goods found their way back to the United States without the permission of L'anza and were sold in California by unauthorized retailers who had purchased them at discounted prices from Quality King Distributors, Inc. (petitioner). There is some uncertainty about the identity of the actual importer, but for the purpose of our decision we assume that petitioner bought all three shipments from the Malta distributor, imported them, and then resold to retailers who were not in L'anza's authorized chain of distribution.

After determining the source of the unauthorized sales, L'anza brought suit against petitioner and several other defendants. The complaint alleged that the importation and subsequent distribution of those products bearing copyrighted labels violated L'anza's "exclusive rights under 17 U.S.C. §§106, 501 and 602 to reproduce and distribute the copyrighted material in the United States." App. 32. The District Court rejected petitioner's defense based on the "first sale" doctrine recognized by §109 and entered summary judgment in favor of L'anza. Based largely on its conclusion that §602 would be "meaningless" if §109 provided a defense in a case of this kind, the Court of Appeals affirmed.

II

This is an unusual copyright case because L'anza does not claim that anyone has made unauthorized copies of its copyrighted labels. Instead, L'anza is primarily interested in protecting the integrity of its method of marketing the products to which the labels are affixed. Although the labels themselves have only a limited creative component, our interpretation of the relevant statutory provisions would apply equally to a case involving more familiar copyrighted materials such as sound recordings or books. Indeed, we first endorsed the first sale doctrine in a case involving a claim by a publisher that the resale of its books at discounted prices infringed its copyright on the books. *Bobbs-Merrill Co. v. Straus*, 210 U.S. 339 (1908).

In that case, the publisher, Bobbs-Merrill, had inserted a notice in its books that any retail sale at a price under $1.00 would constitute an infringement of its copyright. The defendants, who owned Macy's department store, disregarded the notice and sold the books at a lower price without Bobbs-Merrill's consent. We held that the exclusive statutory right to "vend"[19] applied only to the first sale of the copyrighted work:

> What does the statute mean in granting "the sole right of vending the same"? Was it intended to create a right which would permit the holder of the copyright to fasten, by notice in a book or upon one of the articles mentioned within the statute, a restriction upon the subsequent alienation of the subject-matter of copyright after the owner had parted with the title to one who had acquired full dominion over it and had given a satisfactory price for it? It is not denied that one who has sold a copyrighted article, without restriction, has parted with all right to control the sale of it. The purchaser of a book, once sold by authority of the owner of the copyright, may sell it again, although he could not publish a new edition of it.
>
> In this case the stipulated facts show that the books sold by the appellant were sold at wholesale, and purchased by those who made no agreement as to the control of future sales of the book, and took upon themselves no obligation to enforce the notice printed in the book, undertaking to restrict retail sales to a price of one dollar per copy.

210 U.S. 339 at 349–350.

The statute in force when *Bobbs-Merrill* was decided provided that the copyright owner had the exclusive right to "vend" the copyrighted work. Congress subsequently codified our holding in *Bobbs-Merrill* that the exclusive right to "vend" was limited to first sales of the work. Under the 1976 Act, the comparable exclusive right granted in 17 U.S.C. §106(3) is the right "to distribute copies . . . by sale or other transfer of ownership." The comparable limitation on that right is provided not by judicial interpretation, but by an express statutory provision. Section 109(a) provides

> Notwithstanding the provisions of section 106(3), the owner of a particular copy or phonorecord lawfully made under this title, or any person authorized by such owner, is entitled, without the authority of the copyright owner, to sell or otherwise dispose of the possession of that copy or phonorecord. . . .

The *Bobbs-Merrill* opinion emphasized the critical distinction between statutory rights and contract rights. In this case, L'anza relies on the terms of its contracts with its domestic distributors to limit their sales to authorized retail outlets. Because the basic holding in *Bobbs-Merrill* is now codified in §109(a) of the Act, and because those domestic distributors are owners of the products that they purchased from L'anza (the labels of which were "lawfully made under this title"), L'anza does not, and could not, claim that the statute would enable L'anza to treat unauthorized resales by its domestic distributors as an infringement of its exclusive right to distribute copies of its labels. L'anza does claim, however, that contractual provisions are inadequate to protect it from the actions of foreign distributors who may resell L'anza's products to American vendors unable to buy from L'anza's domestic distributors, and that §602(a) of the Act, properly construed, prohibits

---

19. In 1908, when *Bobbs-Merrill* was decided, the copyright statute provided that copyright owners had "the sole liberty of printing, reprinting, publishing, completing, copying, executing, finishing, and *vending*" their copyrighted works. Copyright Act of 1891, §4952, 26 Stat. 1107 (emphasis added).

such unauthorized competition. To evaluate that submission, we must, of course, consider the text of §602(a).

III

The most relevant portion of §602(a) provides:

> Importation into the United States, without the authority of the owner of copyright under this title, of copies or phonorecords of a work that have been acquired outside the United States is an infringement of the exclusive right to distribute copies or phonorecords under section 106, actionable under section 501.

It is significant that this provision does not categorically prohibit the unauthorized importation of copyrighted materials. Instead, it provides that such importation is an infringement of the exclusive right to distribute copies "under section 106." Like the exclusive right to "vend" that was construed in *Bobbs-Merrill*, the exclusive right to distribute is a limited right. The introductory language in §106 expressly states that all of the exclusive rights granted by that section—including, of course, the distribution right granted by subsection (3)—are limited by the provisions of §§107 through 120. One of those limitations, as we have noted, is provided by the terms of §109(a), which expressly permit the owner of a lawfully made copy to sell that copy "notwithstanding the provisions of section 106(3)."

After the first sale of a copyrighted item "lawfully made under this title," any subsequent purchaser, whether from a domestic or from a foreign reseller, is obviously an "owner" of that item. Read literally, §109(a) unambiguously states that such an owner "is entitled, without the authority of the copyright owner, to sell" that item. Moreover, since §602(a) merely provides that unauthorized importation is an infringement of an exclusive right "under section 106," and since that limited right does not encompass resales by lawful owners, the literal text of §602(a) is simply inapplicable to both domestic and foreign owners of L'anza's products who decide to import them and resell them in the United States.

The judgment of the Court of Appeals is reversed.

Justice GINSBURG, concurring.

This case involves a "round trip" journey, travel of the copies in question from the United States to places abroad, then back again. I join the Court's opinion recognizing that we do not today resolve cases in which the allegedly infringing imports were manufactured abroad.

Kirtsaeng v. John Wiley & Sons, Inc.
United States Supreme Court, 2013
133 S. Ct. 1351

[In 1997, Supap Kirtsaeng, a citizen of Thailand, moved to the United States to study mathematics at Cornell University. While he was studying in the United States, he asked his relatives to purchase copies of English language textbooks at bookstores in Thailand where the books sold at low prices. Kirtsaeng's relatives then mailed the books to Kirtsaeng in the United States where Kirtsaeng sold them for a profit. Some of the books sold by Kirtsaeng were published by John Wiley & Sons (Wiley), Inc., which is a U.S. publisher of academic textbooks. Wiley also publishes English language editions of its textbooks in foreign countries, such as Thailand. Wiley includes a written statement in its foreign English language editions that the books are to be used only in a particular country or region outside of the United States and that importing or bringing the books into the United States is prohibited. Wiley sued Kirtsaeng in the United States District Court for the Southern District of New York. As a defense, Kirtsaeng asserted the "first sale doctrine" discussed in *Quality King*. He argued that the books were lawfully manufactured in Thailand and that he acquired them lawfully in Thailand. The first sale in Thailand exhausted Wiley's rights so Kirtsaeng was free to import the books into the United States. The District Court rejected Kirtsaeng's assertion of the first sale doctrine on the grounds that it did not apply to works manufactured abroad and assessed statutory damages of $600,000. The Second Circuit affirmed the District Court's ruling. Kirtsaeng appealed to the United States Supreme Court, which issued the opinion below.]

Justice BREYER delivered the opinion of the Court.

Section 106 of the Copyright Act grants "the owner of copyright under this title" certain "exclusive rights," including the right "to distribute copies . . . of the copyrighted work to the public by sale or other transfer of ownership." 16 U.S.C. §106(3). These rights are qualified, however, by the application of various limitations set forth in the next several sections of the Act, §§107 through 122. Those sections, typically entitled "Limitations on exclusive rights," include . . . the "first sale" doctrine (§109).

Section 109(a) sets forth the "first sale" doctrine as follows:

"Notwithstanding the provisions of section 106(3) [the section that grants the owner exclusive distribution rights], the owner of a particular copy or phonorecord *lawfully made under this title* . . . is entitled, without the authority of the copyright owner, to sell or otherwise dispose of the possession of that copy or phonorecord." (Emphasis added.)

Thus, even though §106(3) forbids distribution of a copy of, say, the copyrighted novel Herzog without the copyright owner's permission, §109(a) adds that, once a copy of Herzog has been lawfully sold (or its ownership otherwise lawfully transferred), the buyer of that *copy* and subsequent owners are free to dispose of it as they wish. In copyright jargon, the "first sale" has "exhausted" the copyright owner's §160(3) exclusive distribution right.

What, however, if the copy of Herzog was printed abroad and then initially sold with the copyright owner's permission? Does the "first sale" doctrine still apply? Is the buyer, like the buyer of a domestically manufactured copy, free to bring the copy into the United States and dispose of it as he or she wishes?

To put the matter technically, an "importation" provision, §602(a)(1), says that

"[i]mportation into the United States, without the authority of the owner of copyright under this title, of copies . . . of a work that have been acquired outside the United States is an infringement of the exclusive right to distribute copies . . . *under section 106*. . . ." 17 U.S.C. §602(a)(1) (2006 ed., Supp. V) (emphasis added).

Thus §602(a)(1) makes clear that importing a copy without permission violates the owner's exclusive distribution right. But in doing so, §602(a)(1) refers explicitly to the *§106(3)* exclusive distribution right. As we have just said, §106 is by its terms "[s]ubject to" the various doctrines and principles contained in §§107 through 122, including §109(a)'s "first sale" limitation. Do those same modifications apply—in particular, does the "first sale" modification apply—when considering whether §602(a)(1) prohibits importing a copy?

In *Quality King Distributors, Inc. v. L'anza Research Int'l, Inc.*, 523 U.S. 135, 145 (1998), we held that §602(a)(1)'s reference to §106(3)'s exclusive distribution right incorporates the later subsections' limitations, including, in particular, the "first sale" doctrine of §109. Thus, it might seem that, §602(a)(1) notwithstanding, one who buys a copy abroad can freely import that copy into the United States and dispose of it, just as he could had he bought the copy in the United States.

But *Quality King* considered an instance in which the copy, though purchased abroad, was initially manufactured in the United States (and then sent abroad and sold). This case is like *Quality King* but for one important fact. The copies at issue here were manufactured abroad. That fact is important because §109(a) says that the "first sale" doctrine applies to "a particular copy or phonorecord *lawfully made under this title.*" And we must decide here whether the five words, "lawfully made under this title," make a critical legal difference.

Putting section numbers to the side, we ask whether the "first sale" doctrine applies to protect a buyer or other lawful owner of a copy (of a copyrighted work) lawfully manufactured abroad. Can that buyer bring that copy into the United States (and sell it or give it away) without obtaining permission to do so from the copyright owner? Can, for example, someone who purchases, say at a used bookstore, a book printed abroad subsequently resell it without the copyright owner's permission?

In our view, the answers to these questions are, yes. We hold that the "first sale" doctrine applies to copies of a copyrighted work lawfully made abroad.

II

We must decide whether the words "lawfully made under this title" restrict the scope of §109(a)'s "first sale" doctrine geographically. The Second Circuit, the Ninth Circuit, Wiley, and the Solicitor General (as *amicus*) all read those words as imposing a form of *geographical* limitation. The Second Circuit held that they limit the "first sale" doctrine to particular copies "made in territories *in which the Copyright Act is law,*" which (the Circuit says) are copies "manufactured domestically," not "outside of the United States." 654 F.3d at 221–222 (emphasis added). Wiley agrees that those five words limit the "first sale" doctrine "to copies made in conformance with the [United States] Copyright Act *where the Copyright Act is applicable,*" which (Wiley says) means it does not apply to copies made "outside the United States" and at least not to "foreign production of a copy for distribution exclusively abroad." Similarly, the Solicitor General says that those five words limit the "first sale" doctrine's applicability to copies "'*made subject to* and in compliance with [the Copyright Act],'" which (the Solicitor General says) are copies "made in the United States" (emphasis added). And the Ninth Circuit has held that those words limit the "first sale" doctrine's applicability (1) to copies lawfully made in the United States, and (2) to copies lawfully made outside the United States but initially sold in the United States with the copyright owner's permission. *Denbicare U.S.A., Inc. v. Toys "R" Us, Inc.*, 84 F.3d 1143, 1149–1150 (1996).

Under any of these geographical interpretations, §109(a)'s "first sale" doctrine would not apply to the Wiley Asia books at issue here. And, despite an American copyright owner's permission to *make* copies abroad, one who *buys* a copy of any such book or other copyrighted work—whether at a retail store, over the Internet, or at a library sale—could not resell (or otherwise dispose of) that particular copy without further permission.

Kirtsaeng, however, reads the words "lawfully made under this title" as imposing a *non*-geographical limitation. He says that they mean made "in accordance with" or "in compliance with" the Copyright Act. In that case, §109(a)'s "first sale" doctrine would apply to copyrighted works as long as their manufacture met the requirements of American copyright law. In particular, the doctrine would apply where, as here, copies are manufactured abroad with the permission of the copyright owner. See §106 (referring to the owner's right to authorize).

In our view, §109(a)'s language, its context, and the common-law history of the "first sale" doctrine, taken together, favor a *non*-geographical interpretation. We also doubt that Congress would have intended to create the practical copyright-related harms with which a geographical interpretation would threaten ordinary scholarly, artistic, commercial, and consumer activities. We consequently conclude that Kirtsaeng's nongeographical reading is the better reading of the Act.

A

The language of §109(a) read literally favors Kirtsaeng's nongeographical interpretation, namely, that "lawfully made under this title" means made "in accordance with" or "in compliance with" the Copyright Act. The language of §109(a) says nothing about geography. The word "under" can mean "[i]n accordance with." 18 Oxford English Dictionary 950 (2d ed. 1989). See also Black's Law Dictionary 1525 (6th ed. 1990) ("according to"). And a nongeographical interpretation provides each word of the five-word phrase with a distinct purpose. The first two words of the phrase, "lawfully made," suggest an effort to distinguish those copies that were made lawfully from those that were not, and the last three words, "under this title," set forth the standard of "lawful[ness]." Thus, the nongeographical reading is simple, it promotes a traditional copyright objective (combatting piracy), and it makes word-by-word linguistic sense.

The geographical interpretation, however, bristles with linguistic difficulties. It gives the word "lawfully" little, if any, linguistic work to do. (How could a book be *un*lawfully "made under this title"?) It imports geography into a statutory provision that says nothing explicitly about it. And it is far more complex than may at first appear.

To read the clause geographically, Wiley, like the Second Circuit and the Solicitor General, must first emphasize the word "under." Indeed, Wiley reads "under this title" to mean "in conformance with the Copyright Act *where the Copyright Act is applicable.*" Brief for Respondent 15. Wiley must then take a second step, arguing that the Act "is applicable" only in the United States. *Ibid.* And the Solicitor General must do the same. See Brief for United States 6 ("A copy is '*lawfully* made under this title' if Title 17 governs the copy's creation *and* the copy is made in compliance with Title 17's requirements").

One difficulty is that neither "under" nor any other word in the phrase means "where." See, *e.g.,* 18 Oxford English Dictionary, *supra,* at 947–952 (definition of "under"). It might mean "subject to," see *post,* at 1376, but as this Court has repeatedly acknowledged, the word evades a uniform, consistent meaning.

A far more serious difficulty arises out of the uncertainty and complexity surrounding the second step's effort to read the necessary geographical limitation into the word "applicable" (or the equivalent). Where, precisely, is the Copyright Act "applicable"? The Act does not instantly *protect* an American copyright holder from unauthorized piracy taking place abroad. But that fact does not mean the Act is *inapplicable* to copies made abroad. As a matter of ordinary English, one can say that a statute imposing, say, a tariff upon "any rhododendron grown in Nepal" applies to *all* Nepalese rhododendrons. And, similarly, one can say that the American Copyright Act is *applicable* to *all* pirated copies, including those printed overseas. Indeed, the Act itself makes clear that (in the Solicitor General's language) foreign-printed pirated copies are "subject to" the Act. §602(a)(2) (2006 ed., Supp. V) (referring to importation of copies "the making of which either constituted an infringement of copyright, or which would have constituted an infringement of copyright if this title had been applicable"). Brief for United States 5. See also *post,* at 1376 (suggesting that "made under" may be read as "subject to").

In sum, we believe that geographical interpretations create more linguistic problems than they resolve. And considerations of simplicity and coherence tip the purely linguistic balance in Kirtsaeng's, nongeographical, favor.

***

For these reasons we conclude that the considerations supporting Kirtsaeng's nongeographical interpretation of the words "lawfully made under this title" are the more persuasive. The judgment of the Court of Appeals is reversed, and the case is remanded for further proceedings consistent with this opinion.

It is so ordered.

NOTES AND QUESTIONS

1. *Kirtsaeng* resolved a split among the circuits. The Ninth Circuit found that the first sale doctrine allowed the copyright owner to bar the importation of copies manufactured abroad. *See Omega SA v. Costco Wholesale Corporation,* 541 F.3d 982 (9th Cir. 2008). *Costco* was affirmed 4-4 by the Supreme Court with Justice Kagan abstaining because she worked on the case as attorney general. *See* 131 S. Ct. 565 (2010). This meant that the Supreme Court decision had no precedential value but the Ninth Circuit decision stood. In the lower court decision in *Kirtsaeng,* the Second Circuit ruled that the first sale doctrine did not apply to copies manufactured abroad creating a split among the circuits, see *John Wiley & Sons, Inc. v. Kirtsaeng,* 654 F.3d 210 (2d Cir. 2011). This split was resolved by the Supreme Court's decision in *Kirtsaeng* set forth above.

2. L'anza used a copyright theory to attempt to exclude its shampoo. Why didn't L'anza attempt to use a trademark theory and exclude the items as a restricted gray-market good? Review §526 of the Tariff Act of 1930 and 19 C.F.R. §133.23. Why didn't L'anza attempt to exclude the goods under §42 of the Lanham Act, 15 U.S.C. §1124?

3. The discussion in this section concerns rights of a United States IP owner to exclude gray-market goods on the basis of trademarks and copyrights registered in the United States. A different regime applies to patent rights: The United States follows a principle of national exhaustion with regard to patents, i.e., only those patented products first sold in the United States and then shipped abroad (in a second sale) can be imported into the United States without the permission of the U.S. patent owner. *See Jazz Photo Corp. v. International Trade Commission,* 264 F.3d 1094, 1108–1109 (1st Cir. 2001). Patented goods first sold abroad can be barred from importation by the U.S. patent owner. *See id.* Further, a U.S. patent owner cannot use the simplified customs procedures

set forth above for trademarks and copyrights but must proceed under §337 of the U.S. Tariff Act, 19 U.S.C. §1337 (2006), which requires a hearing before the International Trade Commission. The rules we have examined apply only to the United States. Each country has its own set of rules. For a discussion of the approach in the European Union, see Chow and Lee, *International Intellectual Property: Problems, Cases, and Materials*, 742–776 (West 2d ed. 2012).

8 *Dispute Resolution*

I. *Introduction*

A party entering into an international business relationship may not wish to think about the possibility that something might go awry, and an amicable business venture might turn into a dispute. But it is inevitable that disputes arise in international business transactions, and it is best to be prepared. The time for dealing with the possibility of a dispute is usually at the outset of the relationship, not after the dispute erupts. Provisions for dealing with a dispute should be a feature of any international contract but not every one will have the foresight to plan ahead. Despite the many advantages of agreeing upon a dispute resolution procedure during business negotiations, many international disputes continue to arise without any prior planning.

When lawyers think about dispute resolution, they usually assume litigation will occur. In international business, this is usually not the case. Alternative methods of dispute settlement—arbitration, mediation, and conciliation—are more frequently employed rather than the courts. But these alternative methods must be chosen by agreement of the parties; otherwise, litigation may be the only option.

International dispute resolution is a vast topic, and entire casebooks are devoted to it. Our focus below, of course, is not on the entire field of international dispute resolution but the more specialized topic of the resolution of international business disputes. All of the cases that we have chosen in this chapter involve disputes in an international business context.

As the topic is a complex one, we begin this chapter by providing an overview of the issues involved in an international business dispute and how these issues might differ from its domestic counterpart. We introduce some of the main issues in the overview below, and we will return to them in detail during the course of the chapter. Of course, the variations on the issues in an international business dispute are potentially infinite. But there are some main issues and recurring themes, and the emphasis in this chapter is on advance planning to prevent problems from arising.

Overview of International Business Dispute Resolution Issues

In the discussion below, we will assume that there is a business dispute between a U.S. company and a foreign business entity. We will also assume that you represent the U.S. company either as a plaintiff or as a defendant. The business dispute can involve any of the forms of IBTs that we have considered in Chapters Three through Six: contracts, agency/distributorships, technology transfer, and foreign direct investment.

In this overview and in this chapter, we will focus on the use by the U.S. company of the U.S. legal system in international business disputes. We do not attempt to examine in any detail how disputes will be resolved in a foreign legal system as each system is different and unique.

Preliminary Issues

Suppose a business dispute has arisen and that the parties have not planned ahead by agreeing upon a dispute resolution procedure by contract. The parties are unable to settle the dispute informally and amicably. Although the U.S. company fully realizes that the bringing of a lawsuit will likely terminate the business relationship with the foreign entity, it is now reluctantly considering that possibility.

Choice of Forum

A threshold question is: In which forum should the lawsuit be brought? One aspect of an international business dispute is that there may be any number of forums in which an action can be brought. An IBT can involve many different countries and each is a potential forum in which a lawsuit can be brought. However, although there may be many options, in many cases where the U.S. company is acting as a plaintiff the preference is to bring the action in a federal or state court in the United States. The reasons are clear: familiarity with the legal system and applicable law, a world-class legal system with sophisticated judges, the ability to conduct all proceedings in English, convenience, and costs. At the same time, compelling a foreign defendant to appear in a U.S. court could create a strong strategic advantage. The lawsuit may be inconvenient and expensive for the foreign defendant, creating additional pressures on the defendant that may add to the plaintiff's bargaining power. By contrast, where the litigation occurs in a foreign country, the interests are reversed. It is now the U.S. company that may have to suffer all of the disadvantages that come with proceeding in a distant location, under a different legal system, and in a foreign language.

In some cases, securing a forum in the home nation is such an advantage that there may be a race to the courthouse by the parties. Even where the plaintiff has already filed a lawsuit in a foreign court, the defendant may, instead of appearing in the foreign court, file an action in its home nation against the plaintiff. A race can sometimes lead to situations in which there are multiple proceedings going forward simultaneously in courts of different countries. When such situations occur, one issue that U.S. courts must decide is whether to defer to foreign courts by dismissing or staying the U.S. action. These issues involve the doctrines of international comity and *forum non conveniens*. Other issues involve whether a U.S. or foreign court might wish to enter an "antisuit" injunction, that is, an order prohibiting a party from suing in a foreign jurisdiction. As you can imagine, this can lead to tensions between international legal systems and can even lead to political conflict. We will cover all of these issues in this chapter.

Where the U.S. company is a defendant in a lawsuit, the interests may be quite different. In this case, the corporation might prefer for the litigation to proceed in a foreign jurisdiction, especially if the foreign forum is in a developing country with a weak legal system. Relegating the lawsuit to a country with a weak legal system may result in damage awards that may be lower than those in the United States and it may be difficult for the foreign plaintiff to enforce the judgment due to weaknesses in the legal system. In a number of cases, a U.S. company that is sued in the United States will attempt to have the case dismissed in order to compel the foreign plaintiff to sue in a foreign court. We will return to a number of cases in Chapter Nine on corporate social responsibility where a U.S. company is a defendant in an action for wrongful conduct brought by a foreign plaintiff. While a U.S. company may prefer a U.S. forum in many cases where it is the plaintiff and may prefer a foreign court in some cases where it is the defendant, in both cases the U.S. company usually has a clear preference for a forum in which the dispute should be resolved. Rarely will the U.S. company be indifferent between forums. The choice of forum, one of the first issues that need to be decided by the parties, is also usually a key consideration in international business dispute resolution.

Choice of Law

Let us assume that our hypothetical U.S. company is a plaintiff in a business dispute and has chosen its forum by filing an action in federal district court against the defendant. A second threshold issue that will arise concerns what law governs the transaction. Again assuming that the parties have not agreed to a choice of law by contract, the U.S. court will need to engage in a choice of law analysis in order to determine the applicable law. In an international business dispute, there are often at least three possible sources of law: the domestic laws of either the plaintiff's nation (here the United States), the law of the defendant's home nation, and an international law usually embodied in a treaty. If the transaction is one that has connections with many different countries, the choice of law analysis may be even more complex as the domestic laws of each nation with which the IBT has a connection are potentially applicable to different aspects of the litigation. Note that the choice of law issue becomes much more complex in an international as opposed to a domestic U.S. setting where the choice usually involves the laws of different states, which do not differ in fundamental ways. In an international context, however, the choice of law among the competing alternatives may involve differences that are far greater than those in a domestic U.S. context.

The choice of law determination, which we introduced as private international law in Chapter One, will need to be done by the court using a statute or treaty if one is applicable or by judicially created doctrines of choice of law. As you can imagine, this analysis can be complex and burdensome.

Jurisdiction

As we noted, most parties in an international business dispute will have a clear preference for the forum in which the dispute is to be resolved as the decision will often create strong advantages for one party while simultaneously creating disadvantages for the other. We have already noted that a U.S. company that is a plaintiff will often prefer to file a lawsuit in a business dispute in the United States. However, whether the plaintiff will be able to effectively choose a forum depends on whether the tribunal can assert jurisdiction over the defendant. Of course, there are many different types of jurisdictions but in an international business dispute involving foreign defendants, the most important issue is often whether the court can assert territorial jurisdiction over the defendant. Whether a U.S. court can assert jurisdiction over a foreign defendant depends on whether the defendant has the minimum contacts with the United States in accordance with a long line of classic U.S. cases, including *International Shoe Co. v. State of Washington*, 326 U.S. 310 (1945), and its progeny. We will examine how this jurisdictional analysis is made in an international business context.

In the era of the multinational enterprise with entities and affiliations around the globe, a related jurisdictional issue that also often arises is whether the activities of one corporate entity, such as a subsidiary, which meet the tests for territorial jurisdiction can serve as the basis of jurisdiction over a related entity, such as a holding company or the parent corporation. Special judicial doctrines have been created to determine when the assertion of jurisdiction over affiliated entities is appropriate.

Sovereign Immunity and the Act of State Doctrine

So far, we have examined issues that may be familiar to you from a course on civil procedure or civil litigation. Most of these issues, choice of forum, choice of law, and jurisdiction, are similar to issues that arise in domestic litigation and dispute settlement although the issues might be more complex in an international setting. In the area of territorial jurisdiction, for example, the same basic concepts developed in a domestic context can be applied without much modification to an international setting. In an international business dispute, however, a U.S. company will encounter another set of jurisdictional issues that it will rarely find in a domestic setting: sovereign immunity and related issues.

Unlike the issue of territorial jurisdiction, which concerns the power of the court over the defendant, sovereign immunity is related to the court's subject matter jurisdiction. Even where a court has territorial jurisdiction over a foreign sovereign defendant, the court may be deprived of subject matter jurisdiction to hear the dispute.

As multinational enterprises dominate international business today, it is not unusual for a transaction to involve foreign sovereign parties, either foreign government entities that are acting in a commercial capacity or state-owned companies that involve a mix of both public and private interests. One reason is that MNEs now routinely engage in transactions involving tens or even hundreds of millions of dollars or more. MNEs are also intimately involved in providing products and services that are of vital importance for the economic development of whole nations. Government entities, especially in developing countries, often need to be involved directly or indirectly when the sums and stakes are this large. For example, think of cases in which an MNE is engaged to mine the production of gas and oil, to install an entire telecommunications system, or to build a port or a terminal. All of these projects not only involve significant sums but also implicate significant public interests of a nation. As a result, a U.S. company may find itself dealing directly with a government or state-owned entity in the business transaction. In other cases, even when only foreign private parties are ostensibly involved, foreign governments may be lurking not too far behind.

In such cases, there are special concerns, including the potential immunity of such entities from jurisdiction in U.S. courts under the Foreign Sovereign Immunities Act of 1976 (FSIA), 28 U.S.C. §§1602–1611 (2006). A threshold issue in such cases is whether a particular entity is qualified for immunity under the FSIA. If the entity is so qualified, then it is immune from the jurisdiction of U.S. courts unless one of the exceptions to the FSIA applies to the case.

In addition to FSIA issues, disputes involving foreign sovereigns might implicate broader political issues not usually found when purely private parties are involved. For example, suppose that our hypothetical U.S. company has entered into a transaction with a foreign sovereign government and a business dispute erupts. Suppose further that the U.S. company sues the foreign government in a U.S. court and the court decides to exercise jurisdiction under some exception to sovereign immunity. Such a lawsuit by a private party against a foreign government might have an adverse impact on the foreign relations of the United States. Even though U.S. courts might have jurisdiction over the foreign sovereign, the courts might decline to exercise such jurisdiction on policy grounds as they do not wish to interfere with the foreign relations of the United States, a subject matter that is within the exclusive competence of the executive branch. Such cases also implicate issues of institutional competence and doctrines of judicial deference to the executive branch. To deal with these issues, the U.S. Supreme Court in *Banco Nacional de Cuba v. Sabbatino*, 376 U.S. 398 (1964), set forth the modern act of state doctrine, which precludes U.S. courts from examining the acts of foreign sovereigns within their own territories. As the result of the application of the act of state doctrine is that a court will decline to adjudicate an issue implicating the foreign relations of the United States, the doctrine is often asserted as a defense in a lawsuit by the defendant.

Resolving Preliminary Issues by Agreement

The discussion of the types of issues involved in an international business dispute has proceeded so far based on the assumption that the parties have not agreed on a resolution of any of these issues by contract. When this is the case, the only option to resolving these issues may be by way of litigation. For example, when the parties have not agreed to a choice of forum or choice of law, then what often occurs is that the U.S. company will bring a case in a U.S. court and the defendant will appear for the purpose of contesting the jurisdiction of the court and the choice of law issues. As you can imagine, this can be time consuming and costly. Issues of choice of forum, choice of law, and jurisdiction can often be complex, even when they are uncontested, but when the parties battle over these issues, a great deal of time and expense will be consumed in resolving these issues—and these are only preliminary issues and are not generally issues related to the merits of the dispute. Litigation is obviously a less than optimal way of resolving these issues so parties now will often reach an agreement on these issues before a dispute arises by agreeing to a forum selection clause, choice of law clause, and consent to jurisdiction in the contract that structures the international business transaction in question. While U.S. courts will usually uphold these agreements, interesting issues concerning the enforceability of such clauses do occasionally arise. We examine some of these issues in the cases below.

Dispute Resolution Other Than by Litigation

While parties may agree on preliminary issues to a business dispute and reduce the time and expense involved in settling these issues in court, litigation through the court system can still be a time-consuming process because of all of the formalities that must be followed in any court-based process of litigation. In addition, litigation is often inflexible as it is based on a formal model that is heavily governed by rules and procedures. An additional disadvantage is that as litigation is also adversarial in nature, the business relationship between the parties may be unable to survive after a lawsuit even if the dispute itself is a minor business problem. Adversarial litigation over a small dispute might poison or destroy a more valuable long-term business relationship between the parties.

As a result, some parties today may wish to forgo litigation altogether by agreeing at the outset on forms of alternative dispute resolution (ADR) as a way of handling difficulties. ADR can be chosen by agreement at any time, even after a dispute has arisen, but it is best to choose it at the outset. ADR refers to certain informal methods of dispute settlement. Of course, negotiation is always an option, and many disputes, especially minor ones, are settled this way. Negotiation does not require the assistance of a third party. Mediation, however, requires an impartial third party who seeks to reconcile the parties' positions and to suggest solutions. The level of active involvement of the mediator will depend on the situation and the parties' wishes, but in any case the mediator has no power to impose a binding decision. Conciliation and arbitration are two additional methods of ADR. Conciliation is more formal than mediation; the conciliator hears evidence, perhaps conducts an investigation, makes findings of fact and law, and gives a proposed solution. Unlike arbitration, however, the conciliator's decision is not binding, so many attorneys think it is a waste of time and money. UNCITRAL has developed and published conciliation rules. The final method is arbitration, which, in the context of international business, usually refers to a private and voluntary dispute resolution process that is final and binding upon the parties.

Some of the advantages of choosing arbitration for an international business dispute are the following:

- *Saving Time.* Each case stands on its own so there is no backlog of cases. In addition, an appeal from an award is possible only on very narrow grounds so the entire process is relatively quick.
- *Saving Money.* Arbitration is usually much cheaper than litigation.
- *Flexibility.* The parties and the arbitrators have discretion to depart from rigid rules of court procedure.
- *Expertise.* The parties may choose specialist arbitrators who have an understanding of both the industry and the nature of the dispute. Arbitrators may be chosen for their ability to work on a professional level in a foreign language.
- *Neutrality.* Arbitrators may be more neutral than judges from certain jurisdictions who may favor national parties.
- *Confidentiality.* Arbitrations may be kept confidential.
- *Enforceability.* Arbitral awards are enforceable in more than 130 countries because of the New York Arbitration Convention (discussed below).
- *Availability of Institutional Help.* Many arbitration institutions around the world are available to provide administrative assistance and formal supervision of the arbitration process.
- *Mitigation of Hostilities.* Arbitration is generally more conducive to maintaining friendly relations and preserving the option for future cooperation than litigation, which is often adversarial and hostile.

We have already seen the choice of arbitration before the International Center for the Settlement of Investment Disputes as a dispute resolution method concerning foreign direct investment issues in Chapter Six. In this chapter, we offer a broad treatment of arbitration as it is now the preferred method of dispute resolution in international business. Although agreements to arbitrate disputes are now generally enforceable, there can still be some interesting issues that arise.

Other Issues

The discussion above has reviewed some of the major issues in an international business dispute that we will cover in this chapter but there are also many ancillary issues as well. Among those that we will cover in this chapter are:

- enforcement of U.S. court judgments abroad and enforcement of foreign judgments in the United States
- enforcement of arbitral awards
- evidence
- discovery
- service of process

We now turn to a closer examination of the issues introduced in this context through the problems, cases, and materials below.

II. *Arbitration*

A. Choosing Arbitration

Arbitration is now the normal way to address and resolve international business disputes. Arbitration allows parties engaged in international business to avoid a possible hostile local judicial forum and to resolve differences before a more neutral tribunal. The U.S. courts recognize a strong federal interest in arbitration and will respect parties' written promises to arbitrate even if this means referring the dispute to a tribunal outside the United States and the application of foreign law. The principal centers of international arbitration are the International Chamber of Commerce in Paris, the London Court of Arbitration, and the Stockholm Chamber of Commerce.

The United States and 148 other nations have acceded to the Convention on the Recognition and Enforcement of Foreign Arbitral Awards, June 10, 1958, 21 U.S.T. 2517, 330 U.N.T.S. 3, commonly called the New York Convention. National law, however, gives arbitration its legally binding character. In the United States, the relevant law is the Federal Arbitration Act (FAA), 9 U.S.C. §§1-16, 201-208, 301-307. The FAA contains three chapters that establish rules for recognizing and enforcing arbitration agreements in both the domestic and the international context. FAA Chapter 1, 9 U.S.C. §§1-16 (2006), which is commonly referred to as the "Domestic FAA," authorizes enforcement of arbitration agreements in domestic and foreign commerce. FAA Chapter 2, 9 U.S.C. §§201-208 (2006), enacted in 1970, implements the New York Convention and is referred to as the

"Convention Act." FAA Chapter 3, 9 U.S.C. §§301–307 (2006), enacted in 1990, implements another arbitration convention, the Inter-American Convention on International
Commercial Arbitration, Jan. 30, 1975, 14 I.L.M. 336. Chapter 3 is commonly referred to
as the "Panama Convention Act."

A trilogy of international commercial arbitration cases in the U.S. Supreme Court
has established the strong federal policy in favor of arbitration. In *Scherk v. Alberto-Culver
Co.*, 417 U.S. 506 (1974), which involved a suit by the American purchaser of securities
from a German seller, the Court upheld a choice of law/forum clause in the agreement between the parties as an "almost indispensable precondition" for the "orderli-
ness and predictability essential to any international business transaction." *Id.* at 516.
In *Mitsubishi Motors Corp. v. Soler Chrysler-Plymouth, Inc.*, 473 U.S. 614 (1985), the Court
held that a claim under the U.S. antitrust laws could be arbitrated in Japan as agreed
by the parties. In *Vimar Seguros y Reaseguros, S.A. v. M/V Sky Reefer*, 515 U.S. 528 (1995),
the Court enforced an arbitration clause in a bill of lading relating to the carriage of
goods by sea.

The relationship between the New York Convention and the U.S. FAA is analyzed in
the following article.

Susan Karamanian, The Road to the Tribunal and Beyond: International Commercial Arbitration and United States Courts
34 Geo. Wash. Int'l L. Rev. 17, 19–21 (2002)

The New York Convention is republished as a note following section 201 of [the FAA
Chapter 2, also known as] the Convention Act. The Convention's requirements as to the
arbitral award and arbitration agreement are as follows:

The Arbitral Award. The Convention applies to an arbitral award "made in the territory of a State other than the State where the recognition and enforcement of such
awards are sought" and an award "not considered as domestic awards in the State where
their recognition and enforcement are sought." The need for the two award categories
became apparent during the Convention's drafting sessions. In some civil law countries,
whether an award is foreign or domestic does not depend on the territory where an award
is made but on the parties' nationalities, the subject of the dispute, the rules of arbitral
procedure, or the applicable law. Eight European nations argued that the arbitral award
should include a "non-domestic" concept to recognize awards other than those considered domestic "in the country in which they are relied upon." Eventually, the non-domestic concept was narrowed to apply only to the place where recognition and enforcement
of the award is sought. The common law countries and certain Eastern European countries, however, were bound to the concept of a foreign award based on territory; thus,
article I included both the territorial and non-domestic concepts of the foreign arbitral
award.

Enforcement of the Award. The Convention's article III requires a Contracting State
to recognize as binding an arbitral award under article I. The award must be enforced
under the procedural rules of the territory where the award is relied upon, under the
Convention's conditions, and the enforcement conditions must not be substantially more
onerous than the conditions for enforcing a domestic award. A Contracting State may
"declare that it will apply the Convention to the recognition and enforcement of awards
made only in the territory of another Contracting State." The United States made such a
reciprocity declaration.

The Arbitration Agreement. Article II addresses the arbitration agreement. Paragraph 1 of article II states as follows:

> Each Contracting State shall recognize an agreement in writing under which the parties undertake to submit to arbitration all or any differences which have arisen or which may arise between them in respect of a defined legal relationship, whether contractual or not, concerning a subject matter capable of settlement by arbitration.

A Contracting State can elect to apply the Convention only to differences arising out of commercial legal relationships. In acceding to the Convention, the United States adopted the commercial declaration. The "agreement in writing" under the Convention "shall include an arbitral clause in a contract or an arbitration agreement, signed by the parties or contained in an exchange of letters or telegrams." A court of a Contracting State, at a party's request, shall order arbitration "unless the agreement is null and void, inoperative or incapable of being performed." Notably, the Convention did not impose article 1's territorial or non-domestic restrictions on the agreement to arbitrate. Also, the Reciprocity Declaration arguably applies only to the arbitration award and not to the arbitration agreement.

Section 202 of the Convention Act. In the Convention Act, the Congress set forth in a single provision, section 202, a definition of both the arbitration agreement and the arbitration award enforceable under the Convention. Section 202 provides, in part, as follows:

> An arbitration agreement or arbitral award arising out of a legal relationship, whether contractual or not, which is considered as commercial, including a transaction, contract, or agreement described in section 2 of this title, falls under the Convention. An agreement or award arising out of such a relationship which is entirely between citizens of the United States shall be deemed not to fall under the Convention unless that relationship involves property located abroad, envisages performance or enforcement abroad, or has some other reasonable relation with one or more foreign states.

In simple terms, section 202 covers any commercial arbitration agreement or award "unless it is between two United States citizens, involves property located in the United States, and has no reasonable relationship with one or more foreign states." Relying on section 202, an arbitral award made in the United States under U.S. law when only one of the parties is domiciled or has its principal place of business outside of the United States has been enforced under the Convention. Section 202 covers an agreement to arbitrate between two non-U.S. citizens, even though the arbitration occurred in the United States. Similarly, courts have held that section 202 is the basis for confirming an award made in the United States involving two U.S. firms when the goods at issue were to be manufactured in the United States but distributed abroad.

The Convention Act and the Federal Courts. Three sections of the Convention Act attempt to steer claims involving the Convention into the federal courts. Section 201 provides that the Convention "shall be enforced in United States courts" in accordance with the Convention Act. Under section 203, an action or proceeding falling under the Convention "shall be deemed to arise under the laws and treaties of the United States." In contrast to the Domestic FAA, under the Convention Act, U.S. district courts have original jurisdiction over an action or proceeding falling under the Convention, regardless of the amount in controversy. Section 205 provides a liberal right to remove a case whose subject matter "relates to an arbitration or award falling under the Convention" from a state court to a U.S. district court. Unlike the general removal statute, removal under the Convention Act may occur "any time before the trial [of the action or proceeding]." Removal is to the U.S. district court for the district and division where the action or proceeding pends. The procedure for removal of causes of action otherwise provided by law applies, except the removal grounds need not appear on the complaint's face but need only be shown in the removal petition.

Venue of cases falling under section 203 rests in any court that would have venue "save for the arbitration agreement" or if the agreement designates a place of arbitration within the United States, then in the court for the district and division which embrace the arbitration site.

Authorization to Compel Arbitration. Section 206 of the Convention Act gives broad authority to the district court to compel arbitration. While the Domestic FAA authorizes a district court to order arbitration in the district where it sits, the district court can, under section 206, order parties to arbitrate under their agreement, which may be outside the United States. Furthermore, the district court can appoint arbitrators per the parties' agreement. But in spite of this, section 206 applies only if the arbitration agreement identifies a place for the arbitration. The district court cannot select an arbitral forum when the agreement to arbitrate fails to do so, nor can a court order the parties to arbitrate in a location they did not designate.

Recognition and Enforcement of an Arbitral Award. Additionally, as with the Domestic FAA, the Convention Act authorizes a district court to confirm an arbitration award. A party has three years after the making of an award to seek confirmation. The district court shall confirm the award unless it finds a ground for refusal or deferral of recognition or enforcement as provided in the Convention. Under article V(1) of the Convention, recognition and enforcement of an award "may be refused" if the party against whom it is invoked furnishes proof that:

(1) the parties to the agreement to arbitrate were under some incapacity under the law applicable to them or the agreement to arbitrate "is not valid under the law to which the parties subjected it or, failing any indication thereon, under the law of the country where the award was made";

(2) "[t]he party against whom the award is invoked was not given proper notice of the appointment of the arbitrator or of the arbitration proceedings or was otherwise unable to present his case";

(3) "[t]he award deals with a difference not contemplated by or not falling within the terms of the submission to arbitration, or it contains decisions on matters beyond the scope of the submission to arbitration";

(4) "[t]he composition of the arbitral authority or the arbitral procedure was not in accordance with the agreement of the parties, or, failing such agreement, was not in accordance with the law of the country where the arbitration took place"; or

(5) "[t]he award has not yet become binding on the parties, or has been set aside or suspended by a competent authority of the country, in which, or under the law of which, that award was made."

A competent authority in a country where recognition and enforcement of the arbitral award is sought may also refuse recognition or enforcement if it finds (1) the subject matter is not capable of settlement by arbitration under the law of that country; or (2) recognition or enforcement would be contrary to the public policy of that country.

Unlike the Domestic FAA, the Convention Act does not expressly authorize a U.S. court to vacate an arbitral award falling under the Convention. Instead, the Convention contemplates that a party can ask a competent authority in the country in which, or under the law of which, the award was made, to set aside or suspend the award. The Convention does not specify grounds for setting aside or suspending the award. The court under whose law the arbitration was conducted has been allowed to apply the law of its country to a motion to set aside or suspend the award.

Finally, article VII(1) provides that the Convention shall not "deprive any interest[ed] party of any right he may have to avail himself of an arbitral award in the manner and to the extent allowed by the law or the treaties of the country where such award is sought to be relied upon." The Convention Act, however, provides no express means of enforcing article VII(1) except through section 201, which recognizes that the Convention is to be enforced in U.S. courts in accordance with the Convention Act.

NOTE ON EXPANDING GROUNDS TO VACATE ARBITRATION AWARDS

In a domestic law arbitration case, *Hall Street Associates v. Mattel*, 552 U.S. 576 (2008), the U.S. Supreme Court considered the issue whether the parties to an arbitration agreement can validly by contract expand the grounds for vacating arbitration awards beyond those listed in the domestic Federal Arbitration Act, 9 U.S.C. §10 (2006). In *Hall Street*, the parties by contract added legal error as a ground for vacating an arbitration award. The Supreme Court ruled that disputing parties may not expand the grounds for vacating an award beyond those listed by statute. *Hall Street*, 552 U.S. at 581. Although the Supreme Court did not address the application of the *Hall Street* holding to disputes involving international commercial arbitration, the decision is notable for the Court's concern that the enforcement of contracts to expand the grounds for vacating awards would transform arbitration into a mere prelude for long and expensive litigation, exactly what arbitration is designed to prevent.

Negotiating and Structuring International Arbitration Transactions, Using Model Arbitration Clauses, and Practical Matters in Arbitration

Arbitration is now the most common and most effective means to resolve international business disputes. For this reason, most international business contracts contain an arbitration clause as the exclusive forum for dispute resolution.

DRAFTING THE ARBITRATION CLAUSE

The arbitration clause of the contract will be the basis upon which the arbitration is conducted. Accordingly, this clause should be drafted with care. The arbitration clause should be worded to fit the parties' intentions and the particular character of the business venture involved. For example, the parties may want a fast-track arbitration schedule that reduces the time and costs of any arbitration; they may prefer a multi-tiered arbitration clause that ensures that certain other options for dispute settlement have been exhausted before resort to arbitration; or they may want an arbitration clause that excludes class arbitrations. If the business contract is with a state, the arbitration clause should waive sovereign immunity.

A relatively simple arbitration clause is the Model Clause recommended by the International Centre for Dispute Resolution of the American Arbitration Association (AAA):

> Any controversy or claim arising out of or relating to this contract or the breach thereof, shall be determined by arbitration administered by the International Centre for Dispute Resolution in accordance with its International Arbitration Rules.

Alternatively, a more extensive arbitration clause may be desirable such as the following provision recommended by the International Chamber of Commerce:

> All disputes arising in connection with the present contract shall be finally settled under the Rules of Conciliation and Arbitration of the International Chamber of Commerce as presently in force, by one or more arbitrators appointed in accordance with said rules.
>
> The place of arbitration shall be _____, and the law applicable to arbitration procedure shall be determined by referring to the law of the place of arbitration. The arbitrator(s) shall determine the matters in dispute in accordance with the law of _____. The _____ language shall be used throughout the arbitral proceedings.
>
> The parties agree that the award of the arbitrator(s): shall be the sole and exclusive remedy between them regarding any claims, counter-claims, issues, or accountings presented or pled to the arbitrator(s); that it shall be made and shall promptly be payable in U.S. dollars [or alternative currency] free of any tax, deduction or off-set; and that any cost, fees, or taxes incident to enforcing the award shall, to the maximum extent permitted by law, be charged against the party resisting such enforcement.
>
> The award shall include interest from the date of any damages incurred for breach or other violation of the contract, and from the date of the award until paid in full, at a rate to be fixed by the arbitrator(s) but in no event less than the London Interbank Offering Rate (LIBOR) per annum quoted for the corresponding period of _____ in the London Interbank Market of United States dollars [or alternative currency] for immediately available funds.
>
> All notices by one party to the other in connection with the arbitration shall be in writing and shall be deemed to have been duly given or made if delivered or mailed by registered air mail, return receipt requested, or by telex, to the following addresses: [addresses of the parties].

In most cases a comprehensive and detailed arbitration clause is best because such a clause gives guidance to the parties and answers the sometimes difficult questions that arise once there is a dispute.

THE ARBITRATION FORUM AND PROCEDURE

A fundamental point of choice will be whether to specify an *ad hoc* arbitration forum or to employ one of the recognized international arbitration institutions, such as the London Court of Arbitration, the International Chamber of Commerce (ICC), or the American Arbitration Association (AAA). The advantage of choosing an established forum for arbitration is to have institutional support for the proceedings. An organization such as the ICC will provide administration, procedural rules, technical expertise, support staff and facilities. Of course, this institutional aid is somewhat expensive so the parties to a business contract may want to choose *ad hoc* arbitration. *Ad hoc* arbitration is also private and is typically less expensive. Either institutional arbitration or *ad hoc* arbitration may be enforced through the New York Convention.

If the parties choose *ad hoc* arbitration, the arbitration clause must spell out in detail such matters as the mechanism for selecting the arbitrators, the procedural rules that will be used, and any other matters that govern the arbitration. The parties are free to select a single arbitrator or a panel of arbitrators by agreement or by some other method. A common method is to have a panel of three arbitrators, one selected by each party and the third by agreement of the two chosen by the parties. A mechanism for selecting alternates should be included in case one or more arbitrators selected cannot serve for some reason.

It is particularly important to designate the rules by which the arbitration will be conducted. In the case of an *ad hoc* arbitration, parties commonly select the Rules of the United Nations Commission on International Trade Law (UNCITRAL). The UNCITRAL Rules were revised and reissued in 2010, and are available at *http://www.uncitral.org.*

SCOPE OF THE ARBITRATION

The parties should decide the scope of the arbitration they desire at the time the arbitration clause is drafted. Here the question is: Do they wish to subject all questions and all disputes to arbitration or only selective issues? A well-drafted clause on the scope of the arbitration will prevent needless subsequent wrangling over "scope" issues. The parties should also consider the possible need for ancillary relief in connection with the arbitration, such as a temporary restraining order to prevent disposition of property and/ or security. Laws and arbitration rules vary on this point so the parties should authorize the arbitrators to grant judicially enforceable preliminary relief.

PLACE OF ARBITRATION AND APPLICABLE LAW

In addition to a choice of law clause in the contract selecting the law governing the contract, it is important that the arbitration provision itself designate the law applicable to the arbitration. This is because a host of legal issues may arise having to do with the interpretation of the arbitration provision. The arbitration clause should contain a choice of law clause that settles these questions. If no choice of law is designated for this, the law of the forum will likely be applied to decide these questions.

The parties should not neglect consideration of the option of having certain issues decided by the arbitrators as *amiable compositeurs,* on the basis of justice and equity without reference to any law. Certain issues in complex transactions such as mergers and acquisitions may be best decided this way especially if they have been overlooked in the company documents or company statutes.

The choice of a place for the arbitration is also important. The locale for the arbitration should be convenient for the parties and in a place where the law is clear and favorable to arbitration and where the state is a party to the New York Convention.

ADDITIONAL PRACTICAL MATTERS

A number of additional practical matters should be addressed in the arbitration provision:

- A separate "notice" provision from the notice provision in the contract.
- Provision on aspects of relief, such as the currency applicable to the payment of an arbitration award and whether pre- and post-judgment interest will be

payable and the rate of interest. Costs and attorneys' and expert fees should also be addressed. What is a "cost" of enforcement should be defined and the costs should be apportioned in some way.

- Discovery issues should be addressed.
- If a state is involved, there should be specific waiver of sovereign immunity. In *Triple A International, Inc. v. Democratic Republic of the Congo*, 721 F.3d 415 (6th Cir. 2013), the court ruled that a seller could not recover for military equipment sold to the Republic of the Congo because the state's purchase of military equipment did not fall within the commercial activity exception of the Foreign Sovereign Immunities Act (FSIA). It is important to realize as well that even if a sovereign is not immune from suit, there may be a problem attaching certain state funds that may be immune from collection. In *Export-Import Bank of Republic of China v. Grenada*, 876 F. Supp. 2d 263 (S.D.N.Y. 2012), taxes owed by airlines were ruled to be immune from attachment to satisfy an arbitration award. Compare *Blue Ridge Investments, LLC v. Republic of Argentina*, 902 F. Supp. 2d 367 (S.D.N.Y. 2012), where the court confirmed an arbitration award against a State on grounds of waiver under the FSIA. On appeal to the Second Circuit, the Court affirmed the district court's ruling under the FSIA citing the Arbitral Award Exception in that Act, which reads in relevant part as follows:

> [a] foreign state shall not be immune from the jurisdiction of courts of the United States or of the States in any case in which the action is brought to confirm an award made pursuant to an agreement to arbitrate, if the agreement or award is or may be governed by a treaty or other international agreement in force for the United States calling for the recognition and enforcement of arbitral awards. 28 U.S.C. §1605(a)(6).

902 F. Supp. 2d at 375. The Court of Appeals also upheld the district court's ruling confirming the arbitral award and denying immunity on the basis of implied waiver, holding that Argentina waived immunity by becoming a Party to the ICSID Convention. *See Blue Ridge Investments, LLC v. Republic of Argentina*, 735 F.3d 72 (2d Cir. 2013). For a discussion of ICSID and enforcement of ICSID arbitration awards, see Chapter Six, pp. 365-366, 386-387.

NOTES AND QUESTIONS

1. Careful consideration should go into the drafting of the arbitration clause. We only highlight a few of the more obvious matters. A checklist of considerations may include the following:

- Broad or narrow clause?
- Location
- Language
- Notice provisions
- Substantive law
- Rules of evidence and extent of discovery
- Arbitrators
- Procedures
- Confidentiality

- Consolidation of claims
- Interim measures
- Waiver of sovereign immunity
- Currency
- Costs and interest
- Finality

2. The choice of law is obviously important. If the parties fail to make a choice, the arbitrator may follow the law of the forum country or may use applicable conflicts of law principles to choose the law. The latter is the solution mandated by the Rome Convention (Article 13) and the UNCITRAL rules (Article 33.1).

3. As for arbitral forums and procedures, parties generally prefer to go to institutions such as the International Chamber of Commerce and the American Arbitration Association. Why? In arbitration, parties may choose a national law, but they may also choose to apply the *lex mercatoria* (law merchant). Another option is to choose "justice and fairness" (*ex aequo et bono*). Why may these options be desirable in a particular case? Consider the following comment about how the use of the *lex mercatoria* in a case involving very convoluted and complex conflict of laws issues:

> [W]e managed to find our way to what I believe was a principled and technically correct solution [to the conflict of laws issue]. I cannot be certain, however, whether we decided first on the solution and then found a way to achieve it, or whether we set out on a truly unguided journey and ended up with the right results.
>
> My feeling is that wholly neutral principles of conflict of laws are an illusion, but that an understanding of reasonable behavior and expectations of major commercial enterprises can be defined with a fair degree of precision, focusing on such issues as the customs of the particular trade, justified expectations of the parties in the light of the prior and current communications between them, the obligation of good faith dealings, and evidence of reliance. The suggestion is that whether or not the two parties before the tribunal had concluded a contract could and probably should have been decided by reference to *lex mercatoria*, rather than by elaborate exercises in comparative conflict of laws.

Andreas F. Lowenfeld, *Lex Mercatoria: An Arbitrator's View*, 6 Arb. Int'l 133, 139-140 (1990).

B. Enforcing the Agreement to Arbitrate

PROBLEM 8-1

Jones works for New Age Products, Inc., a California subsidiary of a People's Republic of China state-owned enterprise in the fiber-optics industry. As a senior executive, Jones spends six months of the year in Beijing and the remainder of the year in San Francisco. When Jones was recruited by New Age, Jones was delighted by the opportunity and signed the standard, nonnegotiable employment contract used by New Age, which provided for settlement of all employment-related claims by arbitration in Beijing. When passed over for a promotion, Jones files a claim in the federal district court for the Northern District of California under Title VII, claiming discrimination on the basis of sex, age, and race. New Age moves to dismiss the claim on the basis of the forum selection clause, arguing that the Title VII claim should be resolved by arbitration in Beijing. In opposing the motion to dismiss, Jones argues that (1) the vital interests of the United States as embodied in Title VII cannot be fully vindicated if the case is decided by a panel of private arbitrators in China and (2) Title VII and the federal antidiscrimination laws that are part of the basic democratic system of the United States are profoundly inconsistent with China's communist system and authoritarian state, which does not give adequate recognition to individual freedom and protection against invidious discrimination. What is the result? Consult *Mitsubishi* below.

Mitsubishi Motors Corp. v. Soler Chrysler-Plymouth, Inc.
United States Supreme Court, 1985
473 U.S. 614

Justice BLACKMUN delivered the opinion of the Court.

The principal question presented by these cases is the arbitrability, pursuant to the Federal Arbitration Act, and the Convention on the Recognition and Enforcement of Foreign Arbitral Awards (Convention), of claims arising under the Sherman Act, 15 U.S.C. §1 *et seq.*, and encompassed within a valid arbitration clause in an agreement embodying an international commercial transaction.

I

Petitioner–cross-respondent Mitsubishi Motors Corporation (Mitsubishi) is a Japanese corporation which manufactures automobiles and has its principal place of business in Tokyo, Japan. Mitsubishi is the product of a joint venture between Chrysler International, S.A. (CISA), a Swiss corporation registered in Geneva and wholly owned by Chrysler Corporation, and Mitsubishi Heavy Industries, Inc., a Japanese corporation. The aim of the joint venture was the distribution through Chrysler dealers outside the continental United States of vehicles manufactured by Mitsubishi and bearing Chrysler and Mitsubishi trademarks. Respondent–cross-petitioner Soler Chrysler-Plymouth, Inc. (Soler), is a Puerto Rico corporation with its principal place of business in Pueblo Viejo, Guaynabo, Puerto Rico.

On October 31, 1979, Soler entered into a Distributor Agreement with CISA which provided for the sale by Soler of Mitsubishi-manufactured vehicles within a designated area, including metropolitan San Juan. On the same date, CISA, Soler, and Mitsubishi entered into a Sales Procedure Agreement (Sales Agreement) which, referring to the Distributor Agreement, provided for the direct sale of Mitsubishi products to Soler and governed the terms and conditions of such sales. Paragraph VI of the Sales Agreement, labeled "Arbitration of Certain Matters," provides:

> "All disputes, controversies or differences which may arise between [Mitsubishi] and [Soler] out of or in relation to Articles I-B through V of this Agreement or for the breach thereof, shall be finally settled by arbitration in Japan in accordance with the rules and regulations of the Japan Commercial Arbitration Association."

Initially, Soler did a brisk business in Mitsubishi-manufactured vehicles. In early 1981, however, the new-car market slackened. Soler ran into serious difficulties in meeting the expected sales volume, and by the spring of 1981 it felt itself compelled to request that Mitsubishi delay or cancel shipment of several orders. About the same time, Soler attempted to arrange for the transshipment of a quantity of its vehicles for sale in the continental United States and Latin America. Mitsubishi and CISA, however, refused permission for any such diversion, citing a variety of reasons, and no vehicles were transshipped. Attempts to work out these difficulties failed. Mitsubishi eventually withheld shipment of 966 vehicles.

The following month, Mitsubishi brought an action against Soler in the United States District Court for the District of Puerto Rico under the Federal Arbitration Act and the Convention.[1] Mitsubishi sought an order, pursuant to 9 U.S.C. §§4 and 201, to compel arbitration in accord with VI of the Sales Agreement. Shortly after filing the complaint, Mitsubishi filed a request for arbitration before the Japan Commercial Arbitration Association.

Soler denied the allegations and counterclaimed against both Mitsubishi and CISA. It alleged numerous breaches by Mitsubishi of the Sales Agreement, raised a pair of defamation claims, and asserted causes of action under the Sherman Act, 15 U.S.C. §1 *et seq.*; the federal Automobile Dealers' Day in Court Act, 70 Stat. 1125, 15 U.S.C. §1221 *et seq.*; the Puerto Rico competition statute, P.R. Laws Ann., Tit. 10, §257 *et seq.* (1976); and the Puerto Rico Dealers' Contracts Act, P.R. Laws Ann., Tit. 10, §278 *et seq.* (1978 and Supp. 1983). In the counterclaim premised on the Sherman Act, Soler alleged that Mitsubishi and CISA had conspired to divide markets in restraint of trade. To effectuate the plan, according to Soler, Mitsubishi had refused to permit Soler to resell to buyers in North, Central, or South America vehicles it had obligated itself to purchase from Mitsubishi; had refused to ship ordered vehicles or the parts, such as heaters and defoggers, that would be necessary to permit Soler to make its vehicles suitable for resale outside Puerto Rico; and had coercively attempted to replace Soler and its other Puerto Rico distributors with a wholly owned subsidiary which would serve as the exclusive Mitsubishi distributor in Puerto Rico.

After a hearing, the District Court ordered Mitsubishi and Soler to arbitrate each of the issues raised in the complaint and in all the counterclaims save two and a portion of a third. With regard to the federal antitrust issues, it recognized that the Courts of Appeals, following *American Safety Equipment Corp. v. J.P. Maguire & Co.*, 391 F.2d 821 (2d Cir. 1968), uniformly had held that the rights conferred by the antitrust laws were "'of a character inappropriate for enforcement by arbitration,'" quoting *Wilko v. Swan*, 201 F.2d 439, 444 (2d Cir. 1953), *rev'd*, 346 U.S. 427 (1953). The District Court held, however, that the international character of the Mitsubishi-Soler undertaking required enforcement of the agreement to arbitrate even as to the antitrust claims. It relied on *Scherk v. Alberto-Culver Co.*, 417 U.S. 506, 515–520 (1974), in which this Court ordered arbitration, pursuant to a provision embodied in an international agreement, of a claim arising under the Securities Exchange Act of 1934 notwithstanding its assumption, *arguendo*, that *Wilko, supra*, which held nonarbitrable claims arising under the Securities Act of 1933, also would bar arbitration of a 1934 Act claim arising in a domestic context.

---

1. The complaint alleged that Soler had failed to pay for 966 ordered vehicles; that it had failed to pay contractual "distress unit penalties," intended to reimburse Mitsubishi for storage costs and interest charges incurred because of Soler's failure to take shipment of ordered vehicles; that Soler's failure to fulfill warranty obligations threatened Mitsubishi's reputation and goodwill; that Soler had failed to obtain required financing; and that the Distributor and Sales Agreements had expired by their terms or, alternatively, that Soler had surrendered its rights under the Sales Agreement.

[A]fter endorsing the doctrine of *American Safety,* precluding arbitration of antitrust claims, the Court of Appeals concluded that neither this Court's decision in *Scherk* nor the Convention required abandonment of that doctrine in the face of an international transaction. Accordingly, it reversed the judgment of the District Court insofar as it had ordered submission of "Soler's antitrust claims" to arbitration. Affirming the remainder of the judgment, the court directed the District Court to consider in the first instance how the parallel judicial and arbitral proceedings should go forward.

II

At the outset, we address the contention raised in Soler's cross petition that the arbitration clause at issue may not be read to encompass the statutory counterclaims stated in its answer to the complaint. Soler reasons that, because it falls within the class for whose benefit the federal and local antitrust laws and dealers' Acts were passed, but the arbitration clause at issue does not mention these statutes or statutes in general, the clause cannot be read to contemplate arbitration of these statutory claims.

We do not agree, for we find no warrant in the Arbitration Act for implying in every contract within its ken a presumption against arbitration of statutory claims. The Act's centerpiece provision makes a written agreement to arbitrate "in any maritime transaction or a contract evidencing a transaction involving commerce . . . valid, irrevocable, and enforceable, save upon such grounds as exist at law or in equity for the revocation of any contract." 9 U.S.C. §2.

Accordingly, the first task of a court asked to compel arbitration of a dispute is to determine whether the parties agreed to arbitrate that dispute. The court is to make this determination by applying the "federal substantive law of arbitrability, applicable to any arbitration agreement within the coverage of the Act." *Moses H. Cone Memorial Hospital,* 460 U.S. at 24. And that body of law counsels

> "that questions of arbitrability must be addressed with a healthy regard for the federal policy favoring arbitration. . . . The Arbitration Act establishes that, as a matter of federal law, any doubts concerning the scope of arbitrable issues should be resolved in favor of arbitration, whether the problem at hand is the construction of the contract language itself or an allegation of waiver, delay, or a like defense to arbitrability."

Moses H. Cone Memorial Hospital, 460 U.S. at 24-25.

There is no reason to depart from these guidelines where a party bound by an arbitration agreement raises claims founded on statutory rights. Some time ago this Court expressed "hope for [the Act's] usefulness both in controversies based on statutes or on standards otherwise created," *Wilko v. Swan,* and we are well past the time when judicial suspicion of the desirability of arbitration and of the competence of arbitral tribunals inhibited the development of arbitration as an alternative means of dispute resolution. Of course, courts should remain attuned to well supported claims that the agreement to arbitrate resulted from the sort of fraud or overwhelming economic power that would provide grounds "for the revocation of any contract." 9 U.S.C. §2. But, absent such compelling considerations, the Act itself provides no basis for disfavoring agreements to arbitrate statutory claims by skewing the otherwise hospitable inquiry into arbitrability.

That is not to say that all controversies implicating statutory rights are suitable for arbitration. Just as it is the congressional policy manifested in the Federal Arbitration Act that requires courts liberally to construe the scope of arbitration agreements covered by that Act, it is the congressional intention expressed in some other statute on which the courts must rely to identify any category of claims as to which agreements to arbitrate will be held unenforceable. For that reason, Soler's concern for statutorily protected classes provides no reason to color the lens through which the arbitration clause is read. By agreeing to arbitrate a statutory claim, a party does not forgo the substantive rights afforded by the statute; it only submits to their resolution in an arbitral, rather than a judicial, forum. It trades the procedures and opportunity for review of the courtroom for the simplicity, informality, and expedition of arbitration. We must assume that if Congress intended the substantive protection afforded by a given statute to include protection against waiver of the right to a judicial forum, that intention will be deducible from text or legislative history.

In sum, the Court of Appeals correctly conducted a two-step inquiry, first determining whether the parties' agreement to arbitrate reached the statutory issues, and then, upon finding it did, considering whether legal constraints external to the parties' agreement foreclosed the arbitration of those claims.

III

We now turn to consider whether Soler's antitrust claims are nonarbitrable even though it has agreed to arbitrate them. In holding that they are not [arbitrable], the Court of Appeals followed the decision of the Second Circuit in *American Safety Equipment Corp. v. J.P. Maguire & Co.*, 391 F.2d 821 (1968).

At the outset, we confess to some skepticism of certain aspects of the *American Safety* doctrine. As distilled by the First Circuit, the doctrine comprises four ingredients. First, private parties play a pivotal role in aiding governmental enforcement of the antitrust laws by means of the private action for treble damages. Second, "the strong possibility that contracts which generate antitrust disputes may be contracts of adhesion militates against automatic forum determination by contract." Third, antitrust issues, prone to complication, require sophisticated legal and economic analysis, and thus are "ill-adapted to strengths of the arbitral process, *i.e.*, expedition, minimal requirements of written rationale, simplicity, resort to basic concepts of common sense and simple equity." Finally, just as "issues of war and peace are too important to be vested in the generals, . . . decisions as to antitrust regulation of business are too important to be lodged in arbitrators chosen from the business community—particularly those from a foreign community that has had no experience with or exposure to our law and values." *See American Safety*, 391 F.2d, at 826–827.

Initially, we find the second concern unjustified. A party resisting arbitration of course may attack directly the validity of the agreement to arbitrate. Moreover, the party may attempt to make a showing that would warrant setting aside the forum-selection clause—that the agreement was "[a]ffected by fraud, undue influence, or overweening bargaining power"; that "enforcement would be unreasonable and unjust"; or that proceedings "in the contractual forum will be so gravely difficult and inconvenient that [the resisting party] will for all practical purposes be deprived of his day in court." *The Bremen.* But absent such a showing—and none was attempted here—there is no basis for assuming the forum inadequate or its selection unfair.

Next, potential complexity should not suffice to ward off arbitration. In any event, adaptability and access to expertise are hallmarks of arbitration. The anticipated subject matter of the dispute may be taken into account when the arbitrators are appointed, and arbitral rules typically provide for the participation of experts either employed by the parties or appointed by the tribunal. Moreover, it is often a judgment that streamlined proceedings and expeditious results will best serve their needs that causes parties to agree to arbitrate their disputes; it is typically a desire to keep the effort and expense required to resolve a dispute within manageable bounds that prompts them mutually to forgo access to judicial remedies.

For similar reasons, we also reject the proposition that an arbitration panel will pose too great a danger of innate hostility to the constraints on business conduct that antitrust law imposes. International arbitrators frequently are drawn from the legal as well as the business community; where the dispute has an important legal component, the parties and the arbitral body with whose assistance they have agreed to settle their dispute can be expected to select arbitrators accordingly. We decline to indulge the presumption that the parties and arbitral body conducting a proceeding will be unable or unwilling to retain competent, conscientious, and impartial arbitrators.

We are left, then, with the core of the *American Safety* doctrine—the fundamental importance to American democratic capitalism of the regime of the antitrust laws. Without doubt, the private cause of action plays a central role in enforcing this regime. The importance of the private damages remedy, however, does not compel the conclusion that it may not be sought outside an American court.

There is no reason to assume at the outset of the dispute that international arbitration will not provide an adequate mechanism. To be sure, the international arbitral tribunal owes no prior allegiance to the legal norms of particular states; hence, it has no direct obligation to vindicate their statutory dictates. The tribunal, however, is bound to effectuate the intentions of the parties. Where the parties have agreed that the arbitral body is to decide a defined set of claims which includes, as in these cases, those arising from the application of American antitrust law, the tribunal therefore should be bound to decide that dispute in accord with the national law giving rise to the claim. And so long as the prospective litigant effectively may vindicate its statutory cause of action in the arbitral forum, the statute will continue to serve both its remedial and deterrent function.

Having permitted the arbitration to go forward, the national courts of the United States will have the opportunity at the award-enforcement stage to ensure that the legitimate interest in the enforcement of the antitrust laws has been addressed. The Convention reserves to each signatory country the right to refuse enforcement of an award where the "recognition or enforcement of the award would be contrary to the public policy of that country." Art. V(2)(b). While the efficacy of the arbitral process requires that substantive review at the award-enforcement stage remain minimal, it would not require intrusive inquiry to ascertain that the tribunal took cognizance of the antitrust claims and actually decided them.

As international trade has expanded in recent decades, so too has the use of international arbitration to resolve disputes arising in the course of that trade. The controversies that international arbitral institutions are called upon to resolve have increased in diversity as well as in complexity. Yet the potential of these tribunals for efficient disposition of legal disagreements arising from commercial relations has not yet been tested. If they are to take a central place in the international legal order, national courts will need to "shake off the old judicial hostility to arbitration," *Kulukundis Shipping Co. v. Amtorg Trading Corp.*, 126 F.2d 978, 985 (2d Cir. 1942), and also their customary and understandable unwillingness to cede jurisdiction of a claim arising under domestic law to a foreign or transnational tribunal. To this extent, at least, it will be necessary for national courts to subordinate domestic notions of arbitrability to the international policy favoring commercial arbitration.

Accordingly, we "require this representative of the American business community to honor its bargain," *Alberto-Culver Co. v. Scherk*, 484 F.2d 611, 620 (7th Cir. 1973) (Stevens, J., dissenting), by holding this agreement to arbitrate "enforce[able] . . . in accord with the explicit provisions of the Arbitration Act."

The judgment of the Court of Appeals is affirmed in part and reversed in part, and the cases are remanded for further proceedings consistent with this opinion.

It is so ordered.

NOTES AND QUESTIONS

1. After the *Mitsubishi* case, agreements to arbitrate are routinely enforced in U.S. courts. Will it be possible to avoid enforcement by making a public law claim? If not, is this good policy?

2. A refusal to compel arbitration by a lower court is appealable. *See* 9 U.S.C. §8.

3. There is a split of authority whether pre-award attachment can be ordered by a court. *Compare I.T.A.D. Associates, Inc. v. Podar Bros.*, 636 F.2d 75 (4th Cir. 1981) (no), *with Carolina Power & Light Co. v. Uranex*, 451 F. Supp. 1044 (N.D. Cal. 1977) (yes). What is the proper answer? Is this a reason for covering the matter of provisional measures in the arbitration clause?

C. Judicial Review and Enforcement of the Award

A party who has obtained a foreign arbitration award must enforce the award in a U.S. court. We examine how this is done in the following materials.

PROBLEM 8-2

A U.S. seller/shipper asks a shipping office in Louisiana to arrange a charter party with the *M/V Liberty*, a vessel owned by a New Orleans corporation, for the transport of goods to Marseilles, where the U.S. buyer/distributor will display them at a trade fair. The contract of carriage contains a clause providing for arbitration of all disputes at the International Chamber of Commerce in Paris, but as the parties were in haste the seller/shipper never reads or signs the contract. The shipper then delivers the goods to the M/V Liberty in exchange for a bill of lading, which contains a standard provision printed on the back of the form stating, "All provisions of the contract of carriage, if any, are hereby incorporated in this agreement." After a dispute later arises between the shipper and the carrier over damage to the cargo, the carrier files for arbitration in Paris and obtains an arbitral award declaring that it is not liable to the shipper for damage. The shipper does not appear in Paris. Later, the shipper files an action in federal district court in New Orleans against the carrier for damage to the cargo but the carrier asserts the Paris arbitral judgment as collateral estoppel on the issue of liability. The carrier argues that the award is entitled to recognition in the court under Chapter 2 of the Federal Arbitration Act implementing the New York Convention. The shipper argues the arbitral award is not entitled to recognition under the convention because there was never a written agreement between the parties to arbitrate and because no international parties were involved. France and the United States are parties to the New York Convention. What is the result? See *Polytek* below.

PROBLEM 8-3

Pursuant to an arbitration agreement, DeLuxe, a British company, sought an arbitration before the International Chamber of Commerce in Paris against Beijing Chemicals Factory (BCF), a Chinese company, for breach of a joint venture agreement to manufacture and sell laundry detergent in China. DeLuxe won an award from the arbitration panel in Paris and then brought an action against BCF in a federal district court under the Federal Arbitration Act to confirm the arbitral award. BCF moves to dismiss the action on the ground that the proper procedure is for DeLuxe to first confirm the arbitral award in a French court in Paris, the place of arbitration, and then to seek to enforce the judicial order confirming the award against BCF in France, the United Kingdom, or China. However, as the United States has no connection to the arbitration, the federal district court has no subject matter jurisdiction over the action to confirm the arbitral award. What is the result? Are there any other jurisdictional issues? The United Kingdom, France, China, and the United States are all parties to the New York Convention. *See Glencore Grain Rotterdam B.V. v. Shivnath Rai Harnarain Co.*, 284 F.3d 114 (9th Cir. 2002).

Polytek Engineering Co., Ltd. v. Jacobson Companies
United States District Court, District of Minnesota, 1997
984 F. Supp. 1238

ROSENBAUM, District Judge.

Plaintiff, Polytek Engineering Co., Ltd. ("Polytek"), asks this Court to confirm a $1,700,367.41 foreign arbitral award granted in its favor, pursuant to Article III of the Convention on the Recognition and Enforcement of Foreign Arbitral Awards and 9 U.S.C. §§201-208. The award was issued on May 26, 1997, by an arbitration panel of the Chinese International Economic and Trade Arbitration Commission ("CIETAC"). The arbitral award was rendered against defendant Jacobson, Inc. ("Jacobson") on a finding that Jacobson breached its contract with Polytek. The Court heard oral argument on October 3, 1997.

I. BACKGROUND

Polytek Engineering Co., Ltd., is a Hong Kong organized corporation with its principal place of business in Hong Kong. Defendant Jacobson, Inc., is a Minnesota corporation with its principal place of business in this state. For the purposes of this motion, the parties agree that Jacobson has never had staff, property, assets, or personnel outside of the United States.

In 1992, Polytek began negotiating with Hebei Import & Export Corp. ("Hebei"), based in the People's Republic of China, to sell rubber recycling equipment for a factory in China's Hebei Province. In November 1992, Polytek contacted Jacobson, a manufacturer of this type of equipment. After this initial contact, however, Polytek and Jacobson forestalled entry into a formal purchase agreement until Polytek concluded its contract with Hebei. In April 1993, Polytek entered into a contract with Hebei to sell the equipment (the "Hebei Contract"). Polytek then turned to Jacobson to obtain the equipment needed to satisfy the Hebei Contract.

To begin its purchase of the rubber recycling equipment, Polytek sent a one-page U.S. $865,000 equipment Purchase Order to Jacobson, dated May 10, 1993. The Purchase Order requested:

> One Set—Rubber Recycling Equipment including spare parts for two years; special tools; commissioning and training charges. For detail specification and terms, please refer to the attached contract.

The Purchase Order contained a section titled "Remarks," which provided that: "All the terms and conditions should conform with the main contract attached." Attached to the Purchase Order was a copy of the Hebei Contract.

Section 19 of the Hebei Contract contained the following arbitration clause:

> All disputes in connection with this contract or the execution thereof shall be settled through friendly negotiations. In case no settlement can be reached through negotiations, the case should then be submitted for arbitration to the Arbitration Commission of the China Council of the Promotion of International Trade[2] in accordance with the rules and procedures promulgated by the said Arbitration Commission. The arbitration shall take place in Beijing, China and the decision of the Arbitration Commission shall be final and binding upon both parties; neither party shall seek recourse to a law court or other authorities to appeal for revision of the decision. The arbitration fee shall be borne by the losing party.

(Polytek Pet., Exh. A).

Subsequent to Polytek's submission of the May 10, 1993, Purchase Order, Polytek and Jacobson discussed the irrevocable letter of guarantee or standby letter of credit, as required by the Hebei Contract. The parties agreed Jacobson would provide a standby letter of credit to Polytek, and Polytek would send Jacobson a deposit. Based upon its agreement with Polytek, Jacobson manufactured and shipped the recycling equipment to China and received payment from Polytek as specified in the Purchase Order.

In May 1995, Hebei claimed the Jacobson equipment failed to conform to contract specifications, and began a CIETAC arbitration proceeding against Polytek, its seller. On March 29, 1996, the arbitration tribunal awarded Hebei a total of U.S. $1,266,933.85 and 4,762,132.56 RMB, and ordered Polytek to collect the equipment at its cost.

Thereafter, on April 3, 1996, Polytek began its own CIETAC arbitration against Jacobson in Beijing, China, claiming Jacobson breached the Hebei Contract attached to the May 10, 1993, Purchase Order. Polytek claimed Jacobson supplied equipment which did not conform to contract specifications. Jacobson initially ignored the notice given by CIETAC, but ultimately replied to the Chinese arbitral forum in November 1996. Jacobson's reply denied CIETAC's jurisdiction over the matter and the existence of any arbitration agreement between Polytek and Jacobson. CIETAC considered the issue of jurisdiction prior to examining the case on the merits, and, on December 23, 1996, CIETAC issued a decision finding jurisdiction was proper.

---

2. Now known as the Chinese International Economic and Trade Arbitration Commission.

Upon rendering its decision, CIETAC wrote to both parties advising them it would hear the trade dispute on March 17, 1997. Jacobson did not appear at the hearing. CIETAC then notified Jacobson that the hearing had taken place and requested objections or further responses by April 20, 1997. CIETAC received nothing from Jacobson. CIETAC issued its decision on May 26, 1997, awarding Polytek U.S. $1,700,367.41, and ordering Jacobson to dismantle and collect the recycling equipment at its own expense.

II. DISCUSSION

A. THE CONVENTION

Chapter 2 of the Federal Arbitration Act grants federal courts the power to affirm foreign arbitral awards. This Chapter enables the Convention on the Recognition and Enforcement of Foreign Arbitral Awards ("Convention"), to which the United States is a signatory. *See* 9 U.S.C. §201. A court must "confirm the award unless it finds one of the grounds for refusal or deferral of recognition or enforcement of the award specified in the . . . Convention." 9 U.S.C. §207.

The Convention compels a court to conduct the following limited, four-part inquiry when deciding whether to confirm an award:

1.   Is there an agreement in writing to arbitrate the subject of the dispute?
2.   Does the agreement provide for arbitration in the territory of the signatory of the Convention?
3.   Does the agreement arise out of a legal relationship whether contractual or not, which is considered as commercial?
4.   Is a party to the agreement not an American citizen, or does the commercial relationship have some reasonable relation with one or more foreign states?

The Court does not consider the last three of these questions to be in serious dispute. The answer to the second question is simple: If the Hebei Contract is part of the Polytek/Jacobson agreement, there is a contract to arbitrate. And if the Hebei Contract is part of the agreement, it provides for arbitration in China, a signatory to the Convention. *See* 9 U.S.C. §201.

The third question asks whether some form of contract or legal contractual relationship existed between Polytek and Jacobson. Both Polytek and Jacobson stipulated in their pleadings that theirs was a legal and contractual relationship. The parties do not deny the commercial nature of the transaction.

As to the fourth question, Polytek is certainly one of the parties to the agreement. It is not an American corporation, and its commercial relationship with Jacobson relates to China, a foreign country. The fourth question is satisfied.

It is the first question— "Is there an agreement in writing to arbitrate the subject of the dispute?"—to which the Court now turns.

B. AN AGREEMENT IN WRITING TO ARBITRATE

The Convention defines an agreement in writing as an "arbitral clause in a contract or an arbitration agreement, signed by the parties or contained in an exchange of letters or telegrams." Convention, Art. II, para. 2, 9 U.S.C. §201. Jacobson claims it never agreed to Chinese arbitration, nor did it manifest an intent to do so.

The Chinese arbitration clause lies within Section 19 of the Hebei Contract attached to Polytek's May 10, 1993, Purchase Order. The Purchase Order twice refers to the attached Hebei Contract, and includes the statement: "All the terms and conditions should conform with the main contract." For the reasons set forth below, the Court finds Section 19 of the Hebei Contract, attached as it was to the Purchase Order, satisfies Article II's definition of an "agreement in writing."

The parties' behavior relative to this Purchase Order and attachment lends credence and support to this determination. Polytek and Jacobson had conducted preliminary negotiations in November, 1992, but waited until April, 1993—until the Hebei Contract was completed—before entering into their own purchase and manufacture agreement. Jacobson's president, Ivar W. Sorensen, sent a facsimile message to Polytek, dated February 24, 1993, stating: "We hope that you will be able to finish up the contract work this week [with Hebei], as planned. From our discussion, my understanding is that you will then issue us a Polytek Purchase Order, with the official contract attached." The manager responsible for the negotiation on behalf of Polytek, Lau Yiu Chung Reddy, faxed a reply to Mr. Sorensen's message on March 2, 1993, stating: "We'll issue a purchasing order with the contract as attachment to you within this week."

While the exact date the Purchase Order was delivered is in dispute, the date of its arrival is irrelevant. There is no question it arrived and was the document which governed the Polytek / Jacobson relationship. The parties' subsequent conduct decisively illustrates the Hebei Contract's direct influence on each party's transactional behavior.

On May 18, 1993, Mr. Lau asked Jacobson to provide an irrevocable letter of guarantee or a standby letter of credit, as required by Section 10 of the Hebei Contract. Mr. Sorensen declined to provide a standby letter of credit on behalf of Jacobson. After further correspondence, Polytek and Jacobson agreed to a deposit and a standby letter of credit arrangement satisfactory to both sides. This behavior shows that the parties were directly aware of, and were influenced in their contract performance by, the Hebei Contract far beyond the confines of specifications for the manufacture and delivery of rubber recycling equipment.

While Mr. Sorensen indicated initial disagreement with the letter of credit requirement, neither he nor anyone on Jacobson's behalf indicated any problem with the arbitration provision in Section 19 of the Hebei Contract. Mr. Sorensen wrote Polytek on July 21, 1993, indicating "the contract date, . . . will be the date we confirm receipt of the [Polytek] deposit." (Lau's Decl., Exh. 27). Mr. Sorensen then sent a facsimile, dated July 23, 1993, confirming Jacobson's receipt of Polytek's deposit and the commencement of the contract.

All terms of the agreement, with the exception of the compromised change concerning the letter of credit, were thereby adopted, confirming Jacobson's compliance with the Polytek Purchase Order and attached Hebei Contract. Thus, this Court finds that an "agreement in writing," as contemplated by the Convention, existed between Polytek and Jacobson.

C. CHALLENGING ENFORCEMENT OF AN ARBITRATION AWARD

Article V of the Convention governs a party's challenge to enforcement of an arbitration award. The challenging party must prove: 1) it was under an incapacity at the time the agreement was made; 2) the arbitration agreement was not valid under the law which the parties have subjected it, or under the law of the country where the award was made; 3) the party was not given proper notice of the proceeding; 4) the award concerned an issue which did not fall within the arbitration agreement; 5) the arbitration panel was invalid; or 6) the award has not yet become final. See Convention, Art. V, para. 1, 9 U.S.C. §201.

Jacobson does not argue that it falls under these criteria. Its attack on the arbitral award is restricted to its challenge to the claimed contract to arbitrate. An arbitration award may also be refused if "the subject matter of the difference is not capable of settlement by arbitration under the law of [this] country; or the recognition or enforcement of the award would be contrary to the public policy of [this] country." Convention, Art. V, para. 2, 9 U.S.C. s 201. Neither of these elements has been demonstrated to the Court. And again, this is not the thrust of Jacobson's argument.

III. Conclusion

For the reasons set forth above, it is ordered that:

1. The May 26, 1997, arbitration award issued by the China International Economic and Trade Arbitration Commission is recognized as binding and enforceable, pursuant to the Convention on the Recognition and Enforcement of Foreign Arbitral Awards and 9 U.S.C. §§201–208.
2. Defendant Jacobson shall pay plaintiff Polytek the sum of U.S. $1,700,367.41, plus interest at the rate of nine percent (9%), as specified in the arbitration award.
3. Defendant Jacobson shall dismantle and collect the rubber recycling equipment at its own expense.

Stolt-Nielsen SA v. AnimalFeeds Int'l Corp.
United States Court of Appeals, Second Circuit, 2008
548 F.3d 85

SACK, Circuit Judge:

Respondent-Appellant AnimalFeeds International Corp. ("AnimalFeeds") alleges that Petitioners-Appellees Stolt-Nielsen SA, Stolt-Nielsen Transportation Group Ltd., Odfjell ASA, Odfjell Seachem AS, Odfjell USA, Inc., Jo Tankers BV, Jo Tankers, Inc., and Tokyo Marine Co. Ltd. (collectively "Stolt-Nielsen") are engaged in a "global conspiracy to restrain competition in the world market for parcel tanker shipping services in violation of federal antitrust laws." AnimalFeeds seeks to proceed on behalf of a class of "[a]ll direct purchasers of parcel tanker transportation services globally for bulk liquid chemicals, edible oils, acids, and other specialty liquids from [Stolt-Nielsen] at any time during the period from August 1, 1998, to November 30, 2002."

AnimalFeeds initially filed suit in the United States District Court for the Eastern District of Pennsylvania on September 4, 2003. That action was transferred to the District of Connecticut pursuant to an order of the Judicial Panel on Multidistrict Litigation. In the District of Connecticut, Stolt-Nielsen moved to compel arbitration. The district court denied the motion but we reversed, holding that the parties' transactions were governed by contracts with enforceable agreements to arbitrate and that the antitrust claims were arbitrable.

The parties then entered into an agreement stating, among other things, that the arbitrators "shall follow and be bound by Rules 3 through 7 of the American Arbitration Association's Supplementary Rules for Class Arbitrations (as effective Oct. 8, 2003)."

Rule 3 provides:

> Upon appointment, the arbitrator shall determine as a threshold matter, in a reasoned, partial final award on the construction of the arbitration clause, whether the applicable arbitration clause permits the arbitration to proceed on behalf of or against a class (the "Clause Construction Award"). The arbitrator shall stay all proceedings following the issuance of the Clause Construction Award for a period of at least 30 days to permit any party to move a court of competent jurisdiction to confirm or to vacate the Clause Construction Award. . . .

In construing the applicable arbitration clause, the arbitrator shall not consider the existence of these Supplementary Rules, or any other AAA rules, to be a factor either in favor of or against permitting the arbitration to proceed on a class basis.

Pursuant to the Class Arbitration Agreement, AnimalFeeds, together with several co-plaintiffs not parties to this appeal, filed a demand for class arbitration. An arbitration panel was appointed to decide the Clause Construction Award.

The arbitration panel was required to consider the arbitration clauses in two standard-form agreements known as the Vegoilvoy charter party and the Asbatankvoy charter party.[3] Both agreements unambiguously mandate arbitration but are silent as to whether arbitration may proceed on behalf of a class.

The arbitration panel, tasked with deciding whether that silence permitted or precluded class arbitration, received evidence and briefing from both sides. AnimalFeeds and its co-plaintiffs argued that because the arbitration clauses were silent, arbitration on behalf of a class could proceed. Stolt-Nielsen's position was that because the arbitration clauses were silent, the parties intended not to permit class arbitration. On December 20, 2005, the arbitration panel issued a Clause Construction Award deciding that the agreements permit class arbitration. The panel based its decision largely on the fact that in all twenty-one published clause construction awards issued under Rule 3 of the Supplementary Rules, the arbitrators had interpreted silent arbitration clauses to permit class arbitration. The panel acknowledged that none of those cases was decided in the context of an international maritime contract. It said that it was nonetheless persuaded to follow those clause construction awards because the contract language in the cited cases was similar to the language used in the charter parties, the arbitrators in those cases had rejected contract-interpretation arguments similar to the ones made by Stolt-Nielsen in this case, and Stolt-Nielsen had been unable to cite any arbitration decision under Rule 3 in which contractual silence had been construed to prohibit class arbitration.

Stolt-Nielsen petitioned the district court to vacate the Clause Construction Award. The court granted the petition, concluding that the award was made in manifest disregard of the law. According to the district court, the arbitrators "failed to make any meaningful choice-of-law analysis." They therefore failed to recognize that the dispute was governed by federal maritime law, that federal maritime law requires that the interpretation of

---

3. "A charter party is a specific contract, by which the owners of a vessel let the entire vessel, or some principal part thereof, to another person, to be used by the latter in transportation for his own account, either under their charge or his." *Asoma Corp. v. SK Shipping Co.*, 467 F.3d 817, 823 (2d Cir. 2006); *see also* Thomas J. Schoenbaum, Admiralty & Maritime Law §11-1, at 2 (4th ed. 2004) ("The charter party is . . . a specialized form of contract for the hire of an entire ship, specified by name.").

charter parties is dictated by custom and usage, and that Stolt-Nielsen had demonstrated that maritime arbitration clauses are never subject to class arbitration. Because these clearly established rules of law were presented to the panel and the panel failed to apply them, the district court held, the Clause Construction Award must be, and was, vacated.

II. Grounds for Vacating an Arbitration Award

"It is well established that courts must grant an arbitration panel's decision great deference." *Duferco Int'l Steel Trading v. T. Klaveness Shipping A/S*, 333 F.3d 383, 388 (2d Cir. 2003). The Federal Arbitration Act ("FAA"), 9 U.S.C. §1 *et seq.* (2006), allows vacatur of an arbitral award:

> (1) where the award was procured by corruption, fraud, or undue means;
>
> (2) where there was evident partiality or corruption in the arbitrators, or either of them;
>
> (3) where the arbitrators were guilty of misconduct in refusing to postpone the hearing, upon sufficient cause shown, or in refusing to hear evidence pertinent and material to the controversy; or of any other misbehavior by which the rights of any party have been prejudiced; or
>
> (4) where the arbitrators exceeded their powers, or so imperfectly executed them that a mutual, final, and definite award upon the subject matter submitted was not made.

Id. at §10(a). We have also recognized that the district court may vacate an arbitral award that exhibits a "manifest disregard" of the law. *Duferco*, 333 F.3d at 388.

III. Stolt-Nielsen's "Manifest Disregard" Claim

A. LEGAL STANDARDS

The party seeking to vacate an award on the basis of the arbitrator's alleged "manifest disregard" of the law bears a "heavy burden." *GMS Group, LLC v. Benderson*, 326 F.3d 75, 81 (2d Cir. 2003). "Our review under the [judicially constructed] doctrine of manifest disregard is 'severely limited.' " *Duferco*, 333 F.3d at 399.

In this light, "manifest disregard" has been interpreted "clearly [to] mean[] more than error or misunderstanding with respect to the law." *Merrill Lynch, Pierce, Fenner & Smith, Inc. v. Bobker*, 808 F.2d 930, 933 (2d Cir. 1986). "We are not at liberty to set aside an arbitration panel's award because of an arguable difference regarding the meaning or applicability of laws urged upon it." *Id.* at 934.

In the context of contract interpretation, we are required to confirm arbitration awards despite "serious reservations about the soundness of the arbitrator's reading of th[e] contract." *Westerbeke Corp.*, 304 F.3d at 216 n.10 (2d Cir. 2002). "Whether the arbitrators misconstrued a contract is not open to judicial review." *Berhardt v. Polygraphic Co. of Am.*, 350 U.S. 198 (1956). "Whatever arbitrators' mistakes of law may be corrected, simple misinterpretations of contracts do not appear one of them." *I/S Stavborg v. Nat'l Metal Converters, Inc.*, 500 F.2d 424, 432 (2d Cir. 1975).

There are three components to our application of the "manifest disregard" standard.

First, we must consider whether the law that was allegedly ignored was clear, and in fact explicitly applicable to the matter before the arbitrators. An arbitrator obviously cannot be said to disregard a law that is unclear or not clearly applicable. Thus, misapplication of an ambiguous law does not constitute manifest disregard.

Second, once it is determined that the law is clear and plainly applicable, we must find that the law was in fact improperly applied, leading to an erroneous outcome. We will, of course, not vacate an arbitral award for an erroneous application of the law if a proper application of law would have yielded the same result. In the same vein, where an arbitral award contains more than one plausible reading, manifest disregard cannot be found if at least one of the readings yields a legally correct justification for the outcome. Even where explanation for an award is deficient or non-existent, we will confirm it if a justifiable ground for the decision can be inferred from the facts of the case.

Third, once the first two inquiries are satisfied, we look to a subjective element, that is, the knowledge actually possessed by the arbitrators. In order to intentionally disregard the law, the arbitrator must have known of its existence, and its applicability to the problem before him. In determining an arbitrator's awareness of the law, we impute only knowledge of governing law identified by the parties to the arbitration. Absent this, we will infer knowledge and intentionality on the part of the arbitrator only if we find an error that is so obvious that it would be instantly perceived as such by the average person qualified to serve as an arbitrator.

Duferco, 333 F.3d at 389–390.

B. THE EFFECT OF *HALL STREET* ON THE "MANIFEST DISREGARD" DOCTRINE

We pause to consider whether a recent Supreme Court decision, *Hall Street Associates, LLC v. Mattel, Inc.,* 552 U.S. 576, 128 S. Ct. 1396 (2008) affects the scope or vitality of the "manifest disregard" doctrine.

Although the "manifest disregard" doctrine was not itself at issue, the *Hall Street* Court nonetheless commented on its origins:

> The *Wilko* Court . . . remarked (citing FAA §10) that "[p]ower to vacate an [arbitration] award is limited," and went on to say that "the interpretations of the law by the arbitrators in contrast to manifest disregard [of the law] are not subject, in the federal courts, to judicial review for error in interpretation.

Hall Street, 128 S. Ct. at 1403 (quoting *Wilko,* 346 U.S. at 436–437).

> Maybe the term "manifest disregard" was meant to name a new ground for review, but maybe it merely referred to the §10 grounds collectively, rather than adding to them. Or, as some courts have thought, "manifest disregard" may have been shorthand for §10(a)(3) or §10(a)(4), the subsections authorizing vacatur when the arbitrators were "guilty of misconduct" or "exceeded their powers."

Id. at 1404. The Court declined to resolve that question explicitly, noting instead that it had never indicated, in *Wilko* or elsewhere, that "manifest disregard" was an independent basis for vacatur outside the grounds provided in section 10 of the FAA. *See id.*

In the short time since *Hall Street* was decided, courts have begun to grapple with its implications for the "manifest disregard" doctrine. Some have concluded or suggested that the doctrine simply does not survive. Others think that "manifest disregard," reconceptualized as a judicial gloss on the specific grounds for vacatur enumerated in section 10 of the FAA, remains a valid ground for vacating arbitration awards. We agree with those courts that take the latter approach.

[W]e view the "manifest disregard" doctrine, and the FAA itself, as a mechanism to enforce the parties' agreements to arbitrate rather than as judicial review of the arbitrators' decision. We must therefore continue to bear the responsibility to vacate arbitration awards in the rare instances in which "the arbitrator knew of the relevant [legal] principle, appreciated that this principle controlled the outcome of the disputed issue, and nonetheless willfully flouted the governing law by refusing to apply it."

Westerbeke, 304 F.3d at 217.

C. ANALYSIS OF STOLT-NIELSEN'S "MANIFEST DISREGARD" CLAIM

[I]n light of our conclusion that the "manifest disregard" doctrine survives *Hall Street*, we must instead decide whether the district court's finding of "manifest disregard" was correct.

1. Review of the District Court's Opinion

According to the district court, the arbitration panel went astray when it "failed to make any meaningful choice-of-law analysis." *Stolt-Nielsen*, 435 F. Supp. 2d at 385. Because the arbitrators failed to recognize that the dispute was governed by federal maritime law, the district court reasoned, they ignored the "established rule of maritime law" that the interpretation of contracts "is . . . dictated by custom and usage." *Id.* at 385–386. Even under state law, the arbitral panel was required to interpret contracts in light of "industry custom and practice." *Id.* at 386. The district court concluded that, had the arbitration panel followed these well-established canons, "the [p]anel would necessarily have found for Stolt, since, as the [p]anel itself noted, Stolt presented uncontested evidence that the clauses here in question had *never* been the subject of class action arbitration." *Id.* Had the district court been charged with reviewing the arbitration panel's decision *de novo*, we might well find its analysis persuasive. But the errors it identified do not, in our view, rise to the level of manifest disregard of the law.

a. Choice of Law. First, the arbitral panel did not "manifestly disregard" the law in engaging in its choice-of-law analysis. The "manifest disregard" standard requires that the arbitrators be "fully aware of the existence of a clearly defined governing legal principle, but refuse[] to apply it, in effect, ignoring it." *Duferco*, 333 F.3d at 389. "In determining an arbitrator's awareness of the law, we impute only knowledge of governing law identified by the parties to the arbitration." *Id.* at 390.

Stolt-Nielsen's brief to the arbitration panel referred to choice-of-law principles in a single footnote without citing supporting case law. It then assured the panel that the issue was immaterial:

Claimants argue that the law of New York governs these contracts. . . . We believe, to the contrary, that because these are federal maritime contracts, federal maritime law should govern. The Tribunal need not decide this issue, however, because the analysis is the same under either.

This concession bars us from concluding that the panel manifestly disregarded the law by not engaging in a choice-of-law analysis and expressly identifying federal maritime law as governing the interpretation of the charter party language.

b. Federal Maritime Rule of Construction.   Second, the arbitration panel did not manifestly disregard the law with respect to an established "rule" of federal maritime law. Indeed, Stolt-Nielsen cites no decision holding that a federal maritime rule of construction specifically precludes class arbitration where a charter party's arbitration clause is silent. To the contrary, during oral argument before the arbitration panel, counsel for Stolt-Nielsen conceded that the interpretation of the charter parties in this case was an issue of first impression.

Stolt-Nielsen's challenge to the Clause Construction Award therefore boils down to an argument that the arbitration panel misinterpreted the arbitration clauses before it because the panel misapplied the "custom and usage" rule. But we have identified an arbitrator's interpretation of a contract's terms as an area we are particularly loath to disturb. *See Westerbeke*, 304 F.3d at 214 ("The arbitrator's factual findings and contractual interpretation are not subject to judicial challenge, particularly on our limited review of whether the arbitrator manifestly disregarded the law."); *id.* at 222 (holding that "vacatur for manifest disregard of a commercial contract is appropriate only if the arbitral award contradicts an *express* and *unambiguous* term of the contract or if the award so far departs from the terms of the agreement that it is not even arguably derived from the contract" (emphases added)).

As for whether the panel misapplied the "custom and usage" rule, we have held that "the misapplication . . . of . . . rules of contract interpretation does not rise to the stature of a 'manifest disregard' of law." *Amicizia Societa Navegazione v. Chilean Nitrate & Iodine Sales Corp.*, 274 F.2d 805, 808 (2d Cir. 1960), *cert. denied*, 363 U.S. 843 (1960). And determinations of custom and usage are findings of fact, which federal courts may not review even for manifest disregard.

[The Second Circuit considered and rejected the argument that the arbitration panel manifestly disregarded New York State law. This part of the opinion is omitted.]

Conclusion

For the foregoing reasons, the judgment of the district court is reversed and the cause remanded to the district court with instructions to deny the petition to vacate.

———————————

The decision by the Second Circuit in *Stolt-Nielsen* held that the arbitration panel did not act in manifest disregard of the law and reversed the district court order vacating the arbitration award. Stolt-Nielsen, the petitioner below, appealed to the United States Supreme Court, which issued the following opinion:

Stolt-Nielsen SA v. AnimalFeeds International Corporation
Supreme Court of the United States, 2010
559 U.S. 662

Justice ALITO delivered the opinion of the Court.

Petitioners contend that the decision of the arbitration panel must be vacated, but in order to obtain that relief, they must clear a high hurdle. It is not enough for petitioners to show that the panel committed an error—or even a serious error. "It is only when an arbitrator strays from interpretation and application of the agreement and effectively dispenses his own brand of industrial justice that his decision may be unenforceable." In that situation, an arbitration may be vacated under section 10(a)(4) of the [Federal Arbitration Act] on the ground that the arbitrator exceeded his powers, for the task of an arbitrator is to interpret and enforce a contract, not to make public policy. In this case we must conclude that what the arbitration panel did was simply to impose its own view of sound policy regarding class arbitration.[4]

***

While the interpretation of an arbitration agreement is generally a matter of state law, the FAA imposes certain rules of fundamental importance, including the basic precept that arbitration "is a matter of consent, not coercion." [T]he FAA provides, in pertinent part, that a "written provision in any maritime transaction" calling for the arbitration of a controversy arising out of such transaction "shall be valid, irrevocable, and enforceable, save upon such grounds as exist at law or in equity for the revocation of any contract." 9 U.S.C. sec. 2. Under the FAA, a party to an arbitration agreement may petition a United States district court for an order directing that "arbitration proceed in the manner provided for in such agreement." Sec. 4. Consistent with these provisions, we have said on numerous occasions that the central or "primary" purpose of the FAA is to ensure that "private agreements to arbitrate are enforced according to their terms."

Whether enforcing an agreement to arbitrate or construing an arbitration clause, courts and arbitrators must "give effect to the contractual rights and expectations of the parties." This is because an arbitrator derives his or her powers from the parties' agreement to forego the legal process and submit their disputes to private dispute resolution.

We think it is also clear from our precedents and the contractual nature of arbitration that parties may specify *with whom* they choose to arbitrate their disputes.

From these principles, it follows that a party may not be compelled under the FAA to submit to class arbitration unless there is a contractual basis for concluding that the party agreed to do so. In this case, however, the arbitration panel imposed class arbitration even though the parties concurred that they had reached "no agreement" on that issue. The critical point, in the view of the arbitration panel, was that petitioners did not "establish that the parties to the charter agreements intended to *preclude* class arbitration." The panel's conclusion is fundamentally at war with the foundational FAA principle that arbitration is a matter of consent.

An implicit agreement to authorize class-action arbitration . . . is not a term that the arbitrator may infer solely from the fact of the parties' agreement to arbitrate. This is so because class-action arbitration changes the nature of arbitration to such a degree that it cannot be presumed the parties consented to it by simply agreeing to submit their disputes to an arbitrator. In bilateral arbitration parties forego the procedural rigor and appellate review of the courts in order to realize the benefits of private dispute resolution: lower costs, greater efficiency and speed, and the ability to choose expert adjudicators to resolve specialized disputes. But the relative benefits of class-action arbitration are

---

4. We do not decide whether "manifest disregard" survives our decision in *Hall Street Associates, L.L.C. v. Mattel, Inc.*, 552 U.S. 576, 585 (2008), as an independent ground for review or as a judicial gloss on the enumerated grounds for vacatur set forth in 9 U.S.C. sec. 10. Animal Feeds characterizes that standard as requiring a showing that the arbitrators "knew of the relevant [legal] principle, appreciated that this principle controlled the outcome of the disputed issue, and nonetheless willfully flouted the governing law by refusing to apply it." Assuming, *arguendo*, that such a standard applies, we find it satisfied for the reasons that follow.

much less assured, giving reason to doubt the parties' mutual consent to resolve disputes through class-wide arbitration.

For these reasons, the judgment of the Court of Appeals is reversed, and the case is remanded for further proceedings consistent with this opinion.

[Three Justices (Ginsburg, Stevens, and Breyer) filed a dissenting opinion that would have affirmed the decision of the Court of Appeals.]

NOTES AND QUESTIONS

1. *The Supreme Court's Decision.* Are you surprised at the grounds the Supreme Court used to decide the *Stolt-Nielsen* case? Why did the Court avoid the "manifest disregard" issue? Do you agree that the issue was as simple as Justice Alito's opinion makes it out to be?

2. *Grounds for Vacating an Arbitration Award.* Courts reviewing an arbitration award must exhibit great deference to the decision of the arbitrators. The FAA §10(a) allows vacation of an arbitration award on four grounds:

   (1) Where the award was procured by fraud, corruption, or undue influence;
   (2) Where there was evident partiality or corruption in the arbitrators;
   (3) Where the arbitrators were guilty of misconduct in refusing to postpone the hearing, upon sufficient cause shown, or in refusing to hear evidence pertinent and material to the controversy; or of any other misbehavior by which the rights of any party have been prejudiced; or
   (4) Where the arbitrators exceeded their powers, or so imperfectly executed them that a mutual, final, and definite award upon the subject matter submitted was not made.

Federal Arbitration Act, 9 U.S.C. §10(a) (2012). Which of these, if any, did the Supreme Court employ?

3. *Manifest Disregard of the Law.* What is the status of "manifest disregard of the law" as grounds for vacating an arbitration award? The Supreme Court addressed this in a footnote on p. 618, *supra.*

III.   Litigation

We now turn to an examination of the traditional method of resolving international business disputes: court-based litigation. Note that some of the issues discussed below such as forum selection clauses and choice of law may also apply in arbitration. Keep in mind as you review these materials how litigation compares with arbitration, discussed in the previous section.

International litigation comprises many issues and problems that are similar to but distinct from litigation in the national context. Within the space limitations of this chapter, we treat in some detail several important aspects of international litigation: (1) choice of forum; (2) choice of law; (3) jurisdiction; (4) evidence and discovery; and (5) recognition and enforcement of judgments.

At the outset we wish to emphasize a major difference between international arbitration and international litigation as dispute settlement methods: While international arbitration is dominated by the New York Convention and international standards, there is no corresponding wide-ranging international treaty on litigation issues. Thus, national courts tend to decide international litigation issues by reference to national laws. This factor alone makes international litigation somewhat unpredictable.

We will see that there are a modicum of international agreements that govern certain aspects of international litigation, but there is no overarching agreement analogous to the New York Convention. Many efforts have been made to negotiate a broad-based convention on international litigation, but these efforts have come to naught. The latest effort by the Hague Conference on Private International Law produced a draft Convention on Jurisdiction, Recognition and Enforcement of Foreign Judgments in Civil and Commercial Matters in 2003, but no agreement on this text was possible.

The materials that follow cover the issues primarily from the viewpoint of the American-based lawyer, but we wish to outline first the very important effort in the European Union, 28 nations, in which international legislation has been adopted on international litigation as part of the EU project to create a European Judicial Area that will operate somewhat the same as the 50-state United States. The EU has accordingly issued obligatory regulations on choice of law, jurisdiction, and recognition and enforcement of judgments that apply to international litigation within the 28 member states of the EU.

The jurisdiction and recognition of judgments law of the EU is known as the "Brussels Regime" of international private law. The latest version of the Brussels Regime is the so-called Recast Regulation, Regulation 1215/2012 of the European Parliament and of the Council of 12 December 2012 on Jurisdiction and the Recognition and Enforcement of Judgments in Civil and Commercial Matters, 2012 O.J. (L351/1) (EU) (Brussels I), which is reprinted in the Documents Supplement to this book. The Recast Regulation, which will become effective in 2015, is the successor regulation to the original Brussels I Regulation, Council Regulation 44/2001 of 22 December 2000 on Jurisdiction and the Recognition and Enforcement of Judgments in Civil and Commercial Matters 2001 O.J. (L 012) (EC). This regulation, in turn, is the successor to the 1968 Brussels Convention on Jurisdiction and the Enforcement of Judgments in Civil and Commercial Matters, Sept. 27, 1968, 8 I.L.M. 229. The Recast Regulation embodies several general rules:

- The Brussels Regime applies when the defendant in any litigation in the EU is domiciled in the EU.
- The Brussels Regime applies to parties domiciled outside the EU in any matter where EU member state courts have exclusive jurisdiction or where the parties to an agreement select an EU forum.
- The Brussels Regime respects as a general rule the autonomy of the parties to a commercial agreement and their right to contract as to the applicable forum for dispute settlement.
- In the absence of a choice of forum agreement, the general rule requires suit to be filed in the country of domicile of the defendant.
- A judgment rendered in any EU member state is automatically recognized and enforced without any special procedure.
- A separate regulation, Brussels II, Council Regulation 2201/2003 of 27 November 2003 Concerning Jurisdiction and the Recognition and Enforcement of Judgments in Matrimonial Matters and the Matters of Parental Responsibility, 2003 O.J. (L 338) (EC), applies to family law matters.

The EU also has extensive rules governing choice of law. This might be termed the "Rome Regime" because the regulations are:

(1) Regulation 593/2008 of 17 June 2008 on the Law Applicable to Contractual Obligations (Rome I), 2008 O.J. (L 177/6) (EC).
(2) Regulation 864/2007 of 11 July 2007 on the Law Applicable to Non-Contractual Obligations (Rome II), 2007 O.J.(L 199) (EC).
(3) Council Regulation 1259/1210 of 20 December 2010 Implementing Enhanced Cooperation in the Area of the Law applicable to Divorce and Legal Separation (Rome III), 2010 O.J. (L 343/10) (EU).

For international business transactions the Rome I Regulation is most relevant. (We include Rome I in the Documents Supplement.) The Rome I Regulation is the successor to the EC Convention on the Law Applicable to Contractual Obligations (1980). The most important rules on choice of law in the EU are:

- The parties to a commercial agreement are free to choose the law applicable to their contract.
- In the absence of agreement on a choice of law, the law applicable will be the law of the country most closely connected to the contractual obligations.
- There are special rules for contracts for the carriage of goods and passengers, consumer contracts, insurance and employment contracts.

The Brussels and Rome Regulations are subject to interpretation in particular cases by the Court of Justice of the European Union. *See, e.g.,* Case C-133/08, *Intercontainer Interfrigo SC (ICF) v. Balkenende Oosthuizen BV,* 2009 E.C.R. I-09687 (in a preliminary ruling case the Court declared that the law applicable to a charter party is the law of the country where the carrier has its principal place of business only where the main purpose of the contract is not merely to make available a means of transport but the actual carriage of goods).

With this background we now turn to U.S. law on these matters.

A.   Choice of Forum

A preliminary consideration in any business litigation is the choice of the court in which to commence the action. Increasingly, this issue is decided in advance by agreement by the parties. But are these agreements always enforceable?

PROBLEM 8-4

A U.S. company buys an electric generator from a seller in a South American country under a sales contract providing that all disputes under the contract are governed by U.S. law and that the courts of the seller "will have venue over all disputes." The U.S. buyer installs the generator in its manufacturing plant, but when a problem with the generator develops, the plant is shut down for several weeks, causing the U.S. buyer to miss delivery on certain goods that the company was to produce for a major client. Failure to meet the order has cost the U.S. company $500,000 in lost sales. The U.S.

buyer sues the seller in federal district court based upon diversity for the faulty generator and for $500,000 in damages. The seller appears and moves to dismiss the action on
the basis of the forum selection clause in the contract. In opposing the motion, the U.S.
buyer argues:

(1) There is no language providing for exclusive jurisdiction in the sellers' courts so
    an action can also be brought in U.S. courts;
(2) State law governs in cases of diversity jurisdiction and the relevant state has
    strong policies in favor of disregarding forum selection clauses;
(3) U.S. courts are far more familiar with handling complex contract cases of the
    type involved in this case and have a far greater expertise applying complex U.S.
    contract law, here the Uniform Commercial Code;
(4) All issues of proof concerning the faulty generator and lost sales are located in
    the United States and it would be seriously inconvenient to introduce this evi-
    dence in a foreign court in a foreign language;
(5) Courts of the foreign country do not recognize consequential damages even when
    they apply foreign law. The refusal to recognize consequential damages is based
    on the grounds of local public policy. The buyer would be severely prejudiced if it
    were limited to the replacement cost or repair of the faulty generator; and
(6) A recently issued decree in the South American country places a $500,000 maxi-
    mum limit on all damage awards issued by its courts in favor of foreign plaintiffs
    against domestic companies.

Review each of these arguments and discuss whether any of them will allow the U.S.
buyer to proceed in its litigation in the United States despite the forum selection clause.
Consult *The Bremen* and *Gita* below.

M/S Bremen v. Zapata Off-Shore Co.
United States Supreme Court, 1972
407 U.S. 1

Mr. Chief Justice BURGER delivered the opinion of the Court.

We granted certiorari to review a judgment of the United States Court of Appeals
for the Fifth Circuit declining to enforce a forum-selection clause governing disputes
arising under an international towage contract between petitioners and respondent. The
circuits have differed in their approach to such clauses. For the reasons stated hereafter,
we vacate the judgment of the Court of Appeals.

In November 1967, respondent Zapata, a Houston-based American corporation,
contracted with petitioner Unterweser, a German corporation, to tow Zapata's ocean-
going, self-elevating drilling rig *Chaparral* from Louisiana to a point off Ravenna, Italy, in
the Adriatic Sea, where Zapata had agreed to drill certain wells.

Zapata had solicited bids for the towage, and several companies including Unterweser
had responded. Unterweser was the low bidder and Zapata requested it to submit a contract, which it did. The contract submitted by Unterweser contained the following provision, which is at issue in this case:

"Any dispute arising must be treated before the London Court of Justice."

In addition the contract contained two clauses purporting to exculpate Unterweser from liability for damages to the towed barge.[5]

After reviewing the contract and making several changes, but without any alteration in the forum-selection or exculpatory clauses, a Zapata vice president executed the contract and forwarded it to Unterweser in Germany, where Unterweser accepted the changes, and the contract became effective.

On January 5, 1968, Unterweser's deep sea tug *Bremen* departed Venice, Louisiana, with the *Chaparral* in tow bound for Italy. On January 9, while the flotilla was in international waters in the middle of the Gulf of Mexico, a severe storm arose. The sharp roll of the *Chaparral* in Gulf waters caused its elevator legs, which had been raised for the voyage, to break off and fall into the sea, seriously damaging the *Chaparral*. In this emergency situation Zapata instructed the *Bremen* to tow its damaged rig to Tampa, Florida, the nearest port of refuge.

On January 12, Zapata, ignoring its contract promise to litigate "any dispute arising" in the English courts, commenced a suit in admiralty in the United States District Court at Tampa, seeking $3,500,000 damages against Unterweser *in personam* and the *Bremen in rem*, alleging negligent towage and breach of contract. Unterweser responded by invoking the forum clause of the towage contract, and moved to dismiss for lack of jurisdiction or on *forum non conveniens* grounds, or in the alternative to stay the action pending submission of the dispute to the "London Court of Justice." Shortly thereafter, in February, before the District Court had ruled on its motion to stay or dismiss the United States action, Unterweser commenced an action against Zapata seeking damages for breach of the towage contract in the High Court of Justice in London, as the contract provided. Zapata appeared in that court to contest jurisdiction, but its challenge was rejected, the English courts holding that the contractual forum provision conferred jurisdiction.

In the meantime, Unterweser was faced with a dilemma in the pending action in the United States court at Tampa. The six-month period for filing action to limit its liability to Zapata and other potential claimants was about to expire, but the United States District Court in Tampa had not yet ruled on Unterweser's motion to dismiss or stay Zapata's action. On July 2, 1968, confronted with difficult alternatives, Unterweser commenced an action to limit its liability in the District Court in Tampa. That court entered the customary injunction against proceedings outside the limitation court, and Zapata refiled its initial claim in the limitation action.

It was only at this juncture, on July 29, after the six-month period for filing the limitation action had run, that the District Court denied Unterweser's January motion to dismiss or stay Zapata's initial action. In denying the motion, that court relied on the prior decision of the Court of Appeals in *Carbon Black Export, Inc. v. The Monrosa*, 254 F.2d 297 (5th Cir. 1958), *cert. dismissed*, 359 U.S. 180 (1959). In that case the Court of Appeals had held a forum-selection clause unenforceable, reiterating the traditional view of many American courts that "agreements in advance of controversy whose object is to

---

5. The General Towage Conditions of the contract included the following:

1. . . . [Unterweser and its] masters and crews are not responsible for defaults and/or errors in the navigation of the tow.

2. . . .

   b) Damages suffered by the towed object are in any case for account of its Owners.

In addition, the contract provided that any insurance of the *Chaparral* was to be "for account of" Zapata. Unterweser's initial telegraphic bid had also offered to "arrange insurance covering towage risk for rig if desired." As Zapata had chosen to be self-insured on all its rigs, the loss in this case was not compensated by insurance.

oust the jurisdiction of the courts are contrary to public policy and will not be enforced." 254 F.2d at 300–301. Apparently concluding that it was bound by the *Carbon Black* case, the District Court gave the forum-selection clause little, if any, weight. Instead, the court treated the motion to dismiss under normal *forum non conveniens* doctrine applicable in the absence of such a clause, citing *Gulf Oil Corp. v. Gilbert* (1947). Under that doctrine "unless the balance is strongly in favor of the defendant, the plaintiff's choice of forum should rarely be disturbed." The District Court concluded: "the balance of conveniences here is not strongly in favor of [Unterweser] and [Zapata's] choice of forum should not be disturbed."

Thereafter, on January 21, 1969, the District Court denied another motion by Unterweser to stay the limitation action pending determination of the controversy in the High Court of Justice in London and granted Zapata's motion to restrain Unterweser from litigating further in the London court. The District Judge ruled that, having taken jurisdiction in the limitation proceeding, he had jurisdiction to determine all matters relating to the controversy.

On appeal, a divided panel of the Court of Appeals affirmed, and on rehearing *en banc* the panel opinion was adopted, with six of the 14 *en banc* judges dissenting. As had the District Court, the majority rested on the *Carbon Black* decision, concluding that "at the very least" that case stood for the proposition that a forum-selection clause "will not be enforced unless the selected state would provide a more convenient forum than the state in which suit is brought." From that premise the Court of Appeals proceeded to conclude that, apart from the forum-selection clause, the District Court did not abuse its discretion in refusing to decline jurisdiction on the basis of *forum non conveniens.*

We hold, with the six dissenting members of the Court of Appeals, that far too little weight and effect were given to the forum clause in resolving this controversy. For at least two decades we have witnessed an expansion of overseas commercial activities by business enterprises based in the United States. The barrier of distance that once tended to confine a business concern to a modest territory no longer does so. Here we see an American company with special expertise contracting with a foreign company to tow a complex machine thousands of miles across seas and oceans. The expansion of American business and industry will hardly be encouraged if, notwithstanding solemn contracts, we insist on a parochial concept that all disputes must be resolved under our laws and in our courts. Absent a contract forum, the considerations relied on by the Court of Appeals would be persuasive reasons for holding an American forum convenient in the traditional sense, but in an era of expanding world trade and commerce, the absolute aspects of the doctrine of the *Carbon Black* case have little place and would be a heavy hand indeed on the future development of international commercial dealings by Americans. We cannot have trade and commerce in world markets and international waters exclusively on our terms, governed by our laws, and resolved in our courts.

Forum-selection clauses have historically not been favored by American courts. Many courts, federal and state, have declined to enforce such clauses on the ground that they were "contrary to public policy," or that their effect was to "oust the jurisdiction" of the court. Although this view apparently still has considerable acceptance, other courts are tending to adopt a more hospitable attitude toward forum-selection clauses. This view, advanced in the well-reasoned dissenting opinion in the instant case, is that such clauses are prima facie valid and should be enforced unless enforcement is shown by the resisting party to be "unreasonable" under the circumstances. We believe this is the correct doctrine to be followed by federal district courts sitting in admiralty.

The argument that such clauses are improper because they tend to "oust" a court of jurisdiction is hardly more than a vestigial legal fiction. It appears to rest at core on historical judicial resistance to any attempt to reduce the power and business of a particular court and has little place in an era when all courts are overloaded and when businesses once essentially local now operate in world markets. It reflects something of a provincial attitude regarding the fairness of other tribunals. No one seriously contends in this case that the forum-selection clause "ousted" the District Court of jurisdiction over Zapata's action. The threshold question is whether that court should have exercised its jurisdiction to do more than give effect to the legitimate expectations of the parties, manifested in their freely negotiated agreement, by specifically enforcing the forum clause.

There are compelling reasons why a freely negotiated private international agreement, unaffected by fraud, undue influence, or overweening bargaining power, such as that involved here, should be given full effect. In this case, for example, we are concerned with a far from routine transaction between companies of two different nations contemplating the tow of an extremely costly piece of equipment from Louisiana across the Gulf of Mexico and the Atlantic Ocean, through the Mediterranean Sea to its final destination in the Adriatic Sea. In the course of its voyage, it was to traverse the waters of many jurisdictions. The *Chaparral* could have been damaged at any point along the route, and there were countless possible ports of refuge. That the accident occurred in the Gulf of Mexico and the barge was towed to Tampa in an emergency were mere fortuities. It cannot be doubted for a moment that the parties sought to provide for a neutral forum for the resolution of any disputes arising during the tow. Manifestly much uncertainty and possibly great inconvenience to both parties could arise if a suit could be maintained in any jurisdiction in which an accident might occur or if jurisdiction were left to any place where the *Bremen* or Unterweser might happen to be found. The elimination of all such uncertainties by agreeing in advance on a forum acceptable to both parties is an indispensable element in international trade, commerce, and contracting. There is strong evidence that the forum clause was a vital part of the agreement, and it would be unrealistic to think that the parties did not conduct their negotiations, including fixing the monetary terms, with the consequences of the forum clause figuring prominently in their calculations. Under these circumstances, as Justice Karminski reasoned in sustaining jurisdiction over Zapata in the High Court of Justice, "[t]he force of an agreement for litigation in this country, freely entered into between two competent parties, seems to me to be very powerful."

Thus, in the light of present-day commercial realities and expanding international trade we conclude that the forum clause should control absent a strong showing that it should be set aside. Although their opinions are not altogether explicit, it seems reasonably clear that the District Court and the Court of Appeals placed the burden on Unterweser to show that London would be a more convenient forum than Tampa, although the contract expressly resolved that issue. The correct approach would have been to enforce the forum clause specifically unless Zapata could clearly show that enforcement would be unreasonable and unjust, or that the clause was invalid for such reasons as fraud or overreaching. Accordingly, the case must be remanded for reconsideration.

We note, however, that there is nothing in the record presently before us that would support a refusal to enforce the forum clause. The Court of Appeals suggested that enforcement would be contrary to the public policy of the forum under *Bisso v. Inland Waterways Corp.*, 349 U.S. 85 (1955), because of the prospect that the English courts would enforce the clauses of the towage contract purporting to exculpate Unterweser from liability for damages to the *Chaparral.* A contractual choice-of-forum clause should be held unenforceable if enforcement would contravene a strong public policy of the forum in which suit is brought, whether declared by statute or by judicial decision. It is clear, however, that whatever the proper scope of the policy expressed in *Bisso*, it does not reach this case. *Bisso* rested on considerations with respect to the towage business strictly in American waters, and those considerations are not controlling in an international commercial agreement. Speaking for the dissenting judges in the Court of Appeals, Judge Wisdom pointed out:

> "[W]e should be careful not to overemphasize the strength of the [*Bisso*] policy. . . . [T]wo concerns underlie the rejection of exculpatory agreements: that they may be produced by overweening bargaining power; and that they do not sufficiently discourage negligence. . . . Here the conduct in question is that of a foreign party occurring in international waters outside our jurisdiction. The evidence disputes any notion of overreaching in the contractual agreement. And for all we know, the uncertainties and dangers in the new field of transoceanic towage of oil rigs were so great that the tower was unwilling to take financial responsibility for the risks, and the parties thus allocated responsibility for the voyage to the tow. It is equally possible that the contract price took this factor into account. I conclude that we should not invalidate the forum selection clause here unless we are firmly convinced that we would thereby significantly encourage negligent conduct within the boundaries of the United States." 428 F.2d at 907–908.

The judgment of the Court of Appeals is vacated and the case is remanded for further proceedings consistent with this opinion.

Gita Sports Ltd. v. SG Sensortechnik GmbH & Co. KG
United States District Court, Western District of North Carolina, 2008
560 F. Supp. 2d 432

WHITNEY, District Judge.

Plaintiff is a North Carolina corporation involved in the wholesale sales of racing bicycles and related equipment. Defendant is a German corporation doing business in North Carolina and is the manufacturer of Ergomo, a mobile performance measuring instrument. Pursuant to a written agreement between the parties, the Sales Exclusive Supply Agreement ("Agreement"), Plaintiff became the exclusive distributor of Ergomo Pro, Ergomo Spin, Ergomo parts and accessories, and any future Ergomo products within the United States and Canada. The parties entered into the Agreement on December 5, 2005; it took retroactive effect on November 1, 2005, and was to expire on December 31, 2008. According to Plaintiff's Complaint, 21 percent of Defendant's products were returned for service and repairs during the 2006–2007 fiscal year. The rate of services and repairs for the current fiscal year is 31 percent. Under the Agreement, Defendant was to replace faulty products within thirty (30) days of being notified that they were faulty. Defendant has allegedly failed to meet its obligations to repair its faulty products. On November 7, 2007, Plaintiff received a termination notice from Defendant for not meeting the minimum purchase amount required. In December of 2007, Defendant made certain statements that allegedly have been harmful to Plaintiff's reputation. In addition, Defendant allegedly has been selling Ergomo products through other North American distributors, despite the fact that the original term for the exclusive distributorship has not yet expired.

More important to the instant motion are the following clauses from the Agreement: "(1) The place of fulfillment and court of venue is Mörfelden-Walldor[;] (2) The laws of the Federal Republic of Germany are solely applicable to this exclusive supply agreement." The Agreement, including these forum-selection and choice-of-law clauses, was written in English.

ANALYSIS

The parties have vigorously argued and briefed the following issues: (1) whether the forum-selection clause is mandatory or permissive; and (2) if mandatory, whether the forum-selection clause is valid. The second inquiry is more complex than it first appears, in that the parties have suggested three alternative bases for determining validity: (a) the *Bremen, Carnival Cruise,* and *Stewart* line of Supreme Court cases and their progeny; (b) North Carolina law; or (c) German law, be it (i) domestic German law or (ii) European Community law. These issues will be addressed in turn.

A. MANDATORY OR PERMISSIVE

A forum-selection clause can be either mandatory—providing the designated forum with exclusive jurisdiction over any disputes—or permissive—providing the designated forum with jurisdiction over the parties, but not necessarily exclusive jurisdiction. *Scotland Memorial Hosp., Inc. v. Integrated Informatics, Inc.,* 2003 WL 151852 at 3–4 (M.D.N.C. 2003). As a general rule, a forum-selection clause "will not be enforced as a mandatory selection clause without some further language that indicates the parties' intent to make jurisdiction exclusive." *Id.* at 4. A crucial distinction between a mandatory clause and a permissive clause "is whether the clause only mentions jurisdiction or specifically refers to venue." *Id.*

In *Scotland Memorial,* the forum-selection clause stated, "venue will be the courts in Atlanta, Georgia." *Id.* The court noted, "Although language such as 'exclusive' or 'sole' is not used, the specific reference to the venue indicates mandatory language. . . . [T]he language of the contract deals with an exact venue and indicates specific intent." *Id.* Based on this reference to a specific venue, the court concluded that the forum-selection clause was mandatory.

In this case, the forum-selection clause states, "The place of fulfillment and court of venue is Mörfelden-Walldor." Just as in *Scotland Memorial,* the parties have clearly and specifically designated a forum, Mörfelden-Walldor, Germany, as the court of venue. The clause does not say that the parties consent to jurisdiction in Mörfelden-Walldor, but rather that Mörfelden-Walldor *is* the court of venue. The Court will not construe this clause to be anything other than what it plainly is: a forum-selection clause that specifically states the exclusive court of venue. The clause is, therefore, mandatory, and must be enforced if it is valid.

B. VALIDITY

A mandatory forum-selection clause designating an international forum must result in dismissal of the case if the clause is valid. The parties have briefed three possible standards under which validity may be determined.

1. Federal or State Law

In the seminal case of *M/S Bremen v. Zapata Off-Shore Co.,* 407 U.S. 1 (1972), the Supreme Court took a situation in which "[f]orum-selection clauses have historically not been favored by American courts," *id.* at 9, and replaced it with one in which "such clauses are prima facie valid and should be enforced unless enforcement is shown by the resisting party to be 'unreasonable' under the circumstances," *id.* at 10. The Court applied the same reasoning to a forum-selection clause in a form contract between a cruise line and individual consumers in *Carnival Cruise Lines, Inc. v. Shute*, 499 U.S. 585 (1991). The Court added that the clause must be "reasonable" and pass "judicial scrutiny for fundamental fairness." *Id.* at 595. The United States Court of Appeals for the Fourth Circuit has summarized the test for reasonableness thusly:

> Choice of forum and law provisions may be found unreasonable if (1) their formation was induced by fraud or overreaching; (2) the complaining party "will for all practical purposes be deprived of his day in court" because of the grave inconvenience or unfairness of the selected forum; (3) the fundamental unfairness of the chosen law may deprive the plaintiff of a remedy; or (4) their enforcement would contravene a strong public policy of the forum state.

Allen v. Lloyd's of London, 94 F.3d 923, 928 (4th Cir. 1996) (*quoting Bremen*, 407 U.S. at 18). Because *Bremen* dealt with federal question jurisdiction, there was some confusion as to whether the same analysis would apply in a case involving diversity of citizenship. The Supreme Court answered this question affirmatively in *Stewart Organization, Inc. v. Ricoh Corp.*, 487 U.S. 22 (1988). However, the Court in *Stewart* based its ruling on an interpretation of 28 U.S.C. §1404(a) and the jurisprudential axiom that "a district court sitting in diversity must apply a federal statute that controls the issue before the court and that represents a valid exercise of Congress' constitutional powers." *Id.* at 27. This reasoning in *Stewart* tied to the application of a federal statute, left open the issue of which law to apply when there was no guiding federal statute, such as when a motion is made to dismiss pursuant to Rule 12(b)(3). Lower courts have struggled with this question, and there has been no definitive word from the Fourth Circuit. [T]he majority of circuits — all those to address the issue except the Third Circuit — have accepted the proposition that federal law ought to apply. *See ADT Sec. Services, Inc. v. Apex Alarm, LLC*, 430 F. Supp. 2d 1999, 1201–1204 (D. Colo. 2006) (discussing the majority view among the circuits and holding that "the Supreme Court's rationale will apply with equal force to procedural questions arising under Rule 12(b)(3) and similar provisions; where Congress has authored a statute or authorized a Rule on point, federal law controls"). The Court finds the reasoning of the cases applying federal law to be persuasive.

Accordingly, the Court will apply the federal standard from the *Bremen, Carnival Cruise*, and *Stewart* line of cases as embodied by *Allen*'s four-factor test. If an analysis of *Allen*'s factors results in a determination that the forum-selection clause is valid, this case must be dismissed.

(i) Fraud or Overreaching. There are no allegations that the forum-selection clause was the result of fraud or overreaching. Indeed, both parties are sophisticated business entities dealing in arms-length, international transactions.

(ii) Grave Inconvenience; Day in Court. Both Plaintiff's and Defendant's experts agree that there are several procedural differences between United States district courts and German courts, including differences in discovery, witness presentation, and the general presentation of evidence. Regarding Germany's procedural differences, the Court agrees with the many courts who have ruled that "Germany has a civilized legal system [and that] [n]one of the circumstances mentioned by the plaintiff . . . indicate that plaintiff could not maintain an action in Germany." *Mackley v. Gruner & Jahr A.G. & Co.*, 1995 WL 417069 at

1 (S.D.N.Y. 1995). Despite the procedural differences of the German courts—differences that are inevitable in any legal system that is not our own—the Court is in accord with the other courts who have considered this issue in concluding that Germany has a fair and civilized legal system.

Similarly, courts are in agreement that the expense of litigation is insufficient to invalidate a forum-selection clause, especially in a diversity case. Thus, Plaintiff's contention that it would be inconvenient or costly to transport witnesses and litigate in Germany is insufficient to demonstrate unreasonableness. It would be just as costly and inconvenient for Defendant to litigate in this Court; even more so, in fact, because Defendant would be deprived of the benefit that it presumably bargained and paid for under the Agreement.

(iii) Fundamental Unfairness. Plaintiff contends that certain remedies available in this Court would be unavailable in a German court. For example, Plaintiff observes that neither treble damages under N.C. Gen. Stat. §75-16 nor punitive damages are available in Germany. This argument, however, must fail for the same reason that the previous argument failed. German law is certainly different from North Carolina law, but that does not mean that Plaintiff will be deprived of "*a* remedy," *Allen*, 94 F.3d at 928 (emphasis added), even if it is not the same remedy that North Carolina law would afford. Nor do the inevitable legal differences between the different systems mean that German law is fundamentally unfair. Indeed, just as courts have held that a German forum does not deprive a party of its day in court, they have held that German law is fair. Accordingly, the Court is of the opinion that a German court applying German law would not be fundamentally unfair to Plaintiff's case.

(iv) Strong Public Policy of Forum State. North Carolina has a well recognized and strong public policy against forum-selection clauses. N.C. Gen. Stat. §22B-3 provides that "any provision in a contract entered into in North Carolina that requires the prosecution of any action . . . that arises from the contract to be instituted or heard in another state is against public policy and is void and unenforceable." Defendant has two arguments for the inapplicability of §22B-3. First, Defendant argues that §22B-3 refers to another "state," not to foreign nations, and that it is therefore inapplicable in an international context. Second, Defendant argues that under German law contract formation was completed in Germany, not North Carolina, and that North Carolina's public policy is therefore irrelevant. The Court, however, believes the final disposition of these issues to be unnecessary. The *Allen* factors do not represent an elemental test, with the satisfaction of each element being a necessary condition. Rather, the factors are just that: factors meant to inform the Court as to the clause's reasonableness. Having already determined that the first of the *Allen* factors is inapplicable and the other two favor enforcement of the clause, the fourth factor is not dispositive. In *Allen* itself, the Fourth Circuit enforced the forum-selection clause even though it violated the applicable public policy. *Allen*, 94 F.3d at 928. Even assuming the applicability of North Carolina's strong public policy, the balance of the *Allen* factors favors enforcement of the clause.

Having determined that there was no fraud or overreaching in this case, that Plaintiff will not be gravely inconvenienced or denied its day in court, and that Germany as a forum and German law are not fundamentally unfair, the Court holds that the forum-selection clause is valid notwithstanding North Carolina's strong public policy against forum-selection clauses.

2. The Klaxon *Principle*

The Court has already determined that federal law applies to the determination of validity and that under federal law the forum-selection clause is valid. Nevertheless, the outcome would be the same under an application of North Carolina law. Under the long-standing *Klaxon* principle, a federal court sitting in diversity must apply the substantive law of the forum state, including its choice-of-law rules. *Colgan Air, Inc. v. Raytheon Aircraft Co.*, 507 F.3d 270, 275 (4th Cir. 2007) (*citing Klaxon Co. v. Stentor Elec. Mfg. Co.*, 313 U.S. 487, 496–497 (1941)). Because the predominant factor of the Agreement is the sale of goods — the Ergomo and its related products — the choice-of-law rule that applies is N.C. Gen. Stat. §25-1-301. That section provides that "when a transaction bears a reasonable relation to this State and also to another state or nation the parties may agree that the law either of this State or of such other state or nation shall govern their rights and duties." The transaction in this case clearly bears a reasonable relation to Germany; much of the contract formation took place in Germany, Defendant is a resident of Germany, and much of the contract performance was to take place in Germany. Thus, the parties were within the ambit of §25-1-301 when they agreed that "[t]he laws of the Federal Republic of Germany" shall govern their rights and duties. In addition, North Carolina courts interpret forum-selection clauses on the basis of the law applicable to the contract as a whole. Thus, even if a state law analysis applied, North Carolina's conflicts principles would lead to the application of German law.

As Professor Hay has stated in his expert report, interpretation and application of the forum-selection clause would be governed by the law that a German court would apply to this case: European Community ("EC") law. Because Defendant is an EC party and the case is international in nature, EC law governs the Agreement. *Id.* According to Professor Hay, the forum-selection clause is mandatory because EC law provides that when "the parties, one or more of whom are domiciled in a Member State, have agreed that a court of the courts of a Member State are to have jurisdiction to settle any disputes . . . that court shall have jurisdiction." *Id.* at 4 (*quoting* Brussels-I Regulation Art. 23(1)). This rule is applicable "even if the plaintiff is domiciled in a non-member country." *Id.* Professor Michaels does not address the application of EC law, but rather concludes that the forum-selection clause is not mandatory under domestic German law. Professor Michaels's analysis, however, is largely based upon his focus on the "place of fulfilment" language, which the Court has already found unpersuasive. The Court is persuaded by the expert report of Professor Hay that the forum-selection clause is mandatory under either EC law or domestic German law.

Furthermore, Professor Hay demonstrates that the forum-selection clause is valid under EC law. That law's only requirement that is relevant to this case — that the agreement be in writing — is satisfied by the Agreement. *Id.* at 7–8. Thus, the forum-selection clause is both mandatory and valid under either the application of federal law or North Carolina's conflicts principles, which lead to the application of German law.

[The court granted the defendant's motion to dismiss based upon the forum selection clause.]

NOTES AND QUESTIONS

1. Like most cases decided after *The Bremen*, *Gita* upheld the choice of forum clause. What are the criteria for their validity set out by the Supreme Court? For a rare case

refusing to uphold a choice of forum clause, see *McDonnell Douglas Corp. v. Islamic Republic of Iran*, 758 F.2d 341 (8th Cir. 1985).

2. The Supreme Court has reaffirmed and expanded the holding in *The Bremen*. In *Carnival Cruise Lines, Inc. v. Shute*, 499 U.S. 585 (1991), the Court upheld a forum selection clause printed on the back of a passenger ticket issued by a cruise line. As long as a passenger cannot prove bad faith, fraud, or overreaching by the cruise line, such clauses will be upheld. Similarly, in *Vimar Seguros y Reaseguros, S.A. v. M/V Sky Reefer*, 515 U.S. 528 (1995), the Supreme Court upheld a forum selection clause contained in a bill of lading issued by a sea carrier for the shipment of goods.

3. *The Bremen* was a case that arose under the Admiralty Jurisdiction Clause of the U.S. Constitution and the corresponding statute, 18 U.S.C. §1333. *Stewart Organization, Inc. v. Ricoh Corp.*, 487 U.S. 22 (1988), discussed in *Gita*, held that the same approach applies in cases based upon diversity jurisdiction. The *Bremen* holding has been uniformly followed in non-admiralty cases in federal and state courts.

PROBLEM 8-5

In a contract for the sale of a collating machine to a U.S. buyer, a Japanese seller inserts a clause that expressly incorporates the regulations of a Japanese business organization that promulgates model contract provisions for incorporation by parties. The regulations contain a forum selection clause providing that, in case of a dispute, all lawsuits must be brought in the same locale as the seller's principal place of business, which is in Osaka. The U.S. buyer's sales department manager signed the contract but the U.S. buyer can show that no one in the U.S. organization read the clause or knew about or had even heard of the Japanese organization. The buyer also argues that the regulations were in Japanese and that no one at the buyer's organization reads or understands Japanese. The buyer further argues that the Japanese seller was well aware that Americans generally lack knowledge of foreign languages and that the Japanese seller's insertion of the clause was an underhanded attempt to sneak the forum selection clause into the contract and amounts to fraud. Under these circumstances, it would be unjust to hold it to the forum selection clause. What is the result? *See Paper Express Ltd. v. Pfankuch Maschinen, GmbH*, 972 F.2d 753 (7th Cir. 1992).

PROBLEM 8-6

In a contract for the sale of goods between a U.S. buyer and an Italian seller, the contract contains the following clauses:

> This agreement shall be construed according to the laws of Italy.
> All disputes arising between the parties shall come within the jurisdiction of the competent Italian courts.

When a dispute arises, the U.S. buyer brings an action in a U.S. federal district court. The Italian seller moves to dismiss on the basis of the forum selection clause. What is the result? *See John Boutari & Son, Wines & Spirits, S.A. v. Attiki Importers & Distributors Inc.*, 22 F.3d 51 (2d Cir. 1994). What change would you make to the clause above to achieve the intent of the Italian seller?

PROBLEM 8-7

Alex, a U.S. citizen, accepted employment some years ago at Loomberg, LP, a privately-held, international financial software, mass media, and data analysis company headquartered in New York City, as a producer of special projects. After stints in Loomberg's Tokyo and New York offices, Alex was assigned to Loomberg's London office, where he has worked for over six years. Upon accepting this assignment, Alex executed an employment contract with Loomberg that identified London as Alex's "normal place of business." This contract also provided that English law governed the agreement and that "all disputes arising hereunder shall be subject to the exclusive jurisdiction of the English courts." Throughout his career at Loomberg, Alex has received strong performance reviews and he was frequently promoted. In 2015, Alex was named to head Loomberg's television operations in Europe, the Middle East, Africa, and Asia.

Several months ago, Alex informed his superiors at Loomberg that he had been subjected to physical abuse by his same-sex domestic partner. Alex thereupon sought treatment from Loomberg's occupational health-care provider and was referred to a psychologist. Alex then took several weeks' unscheduled leave from his employment. When Alex returned to work, his colleagues expressed concern that he was did not seem well. Alex then took several weeks of medical leave. During his absence, the managers of Loomberg made a review of the company's business and removed Asia from Alex's responsibilities. Two months ago, when Alex informed the company that he was ready to return to work, he was told that Loomberg had reorganized the company and that Alex's position had been eliminated. Shortly thereafter, Alex's employment was formally terminated by Loomberg.

Alex filed suit in federal court in the Southern District of New York against Loomberg seeking damages and attorneys' fees for wrongful termination of employment. He also alleges (1) discrimination on the basis of disability in violation of the Americans with Disability Act, 42 U.S.C. §§12101–12213 and (2) discrimination on the basis of sexual orientation in violation of New York State law and the New York City Human Rights Code. The defendants moved to dismiss based upon improper venue. You are a lawyer advising Alex and are asked the following questions: (1) What law governs the enforceability of the forum selection clause in this case? (2) Is the choice of law clause valid? If so, does English law govern the question whether Alex's claims "arise under" the employment contract? (3) Is the forum selection clause enforceable? What is the result? *See Martinez v. Bloomberg, LP*, 740 F.3d 211 (2d Cir. 2014).

NOTE ON THE HAGUE CONVENTION ON CHOICE OF COURT AGREEMENTS

An important new Convention was concluded on June 30, 2005 at the Twentieth Session of the Hague Conference on Private International Law: the Hague Convention on Choice of Court Agreements. This Convention is not yet in force, but it is designed to serve as the litigation counterpart to the landmark New York Arbitration Convention, which provides for the international recognition and enforcement of choice of court agreements as well as enforcement of judgments stemming from such agreements. If widely adopted, the Choice of Court Convention will substantially expand not only the international recognition of choice of forum clauses, but also the recognition and enforcement of judgments rendered in cases litigating international business contracts. The Convention applies with respect to international business-to-business agreements that designate a single court or the courts of a single country for the resolution of disputes (this is the meaning of the term "exclusive choice of court agreement"). The Convention does not apply to certain other types of contracts, such as those involving a consumer, purely domestic agreements, contracts of employment, intellectual property (except copyright), and the carriage of goods.

Article 5 of the Convention states that the court or courts of state parties designated in an exclusive choice of court agreement shall have jurisdiction to decide the dispute.

Article 6 requires courts other than those of the chosen state to dismiss or suspend the proceeding.

Selected portions Articles 8 and 9, which govern the recognition and enforcement of judgments, read as follows:

Article 8   Recognition and enforcement

1. A judgment given by a court of a Contracting State designated in an exclusive choice of court agreement shall be recognised and enforced in other Contracting States in accordance with this Chapter. Recognition or enforcement may be refused only on the grounds specified in this Convention.

2. [T]here shall be no review of the merits of the judgment given by the court of origin. The court addressed shall be bound by the findings of fact on which the court of origin based its jurisdiction, unless the judgment was given by default.

3. A judgment shall be recognised only if it has effect in the State of origin, and shall be enforced only if it is enforceable in the State of origin.

Article 9   Refusal of recognition or enforcement

Recognition or enforcement may be refused if—

(a) the agreement was null and void under the law of the State of the chosen court, unless the chosen court has determined that the agreement is valid;

(b) a party lacked the capacity to conclude the agreement under the law of the requested state;

(c) the document which instituted the proceedings or an equivalent document, including the essential elements of the claim, [did not give the defendant notice];

(d) the judgment was obtained by fraud in connection with a matter of procedure;

(e) recognition or enforcement would be manifestly incompatible with the public policy of the requested State . . . ;

In addition, Article 22 of the Convention provides an additional option: Parties to the Convention may declare that their courts will recognize and enforce judgments given by courts of other parties that are designated even in a *non-exclusive* choice of court agreement. These rules are designed to enhance predictability in international trade and business.

B.   Choice of Law

In an international business dispute decided by litigation or arbitration, when the parties have not chosen an applicable law, choice of law questions must be resolved under general choice of law approaches developed by courts or under an applicable statute or treaty;

where the parties have provided for a law by contract, the issue becomes whether a court will uphold the choice of law clause. The following sections deal with both situations.

1. Choice of Law Approaches

Choice of law rules in contract disputes applicable in the absence of agreement by the parties are relatively easy to articulate, but difficult and unpredictable to apply. Three approaches are in use in the United States.

First, the *lex loci* (the applicable law is the place of the contract) rule is the traditional approach under the Restatement (First) of Conflict of Laws (1931, withdrawn 1971). But what is the place of the contract? Where the initial offer was made? Where the last essential act occurred? In this day of electronic communication, applying this rule is a search for a will-o'-the-wisp. And a meaningless search at that. But this rule is still followed by about 15 states. *See, e.g., Sturiano v. Brooks,* 523 So. 2d 1126 (Fla. 1988).

A second approach is the "most significant relationship test" of the Restatement (Second) of Conflict of Laws §188 (1971). This test seeks to balance the diverse interests and expectations of the parties involved in the dispute. Seven factors are important in determining a significant relationship: (1) the needs of the interstate and international systems; (2) the relevant policies of the forum; (3) the policies of interested states; (4) the expectations of the parties; (5) the basic policies underlying the particular field of law; (6) the certainty, predictability, and uniformity of the result; and (7) the ease of applying the law. In applying these factors, the court will consider the place of contracting; the place of negotiation of the contract; the place of performance; the location of the subject matter of the contract; and the domicile, residence, nationality, place of incorporation, and place of business of the parties. *See, e.g., Citizens First Bank v. Intercontinental Express, Inc.,* 713 P.2d 1097 (Or. Ct. App. 1986). Clearly, this is a flexible test, but one that maximizes uncertainty.

A third approach followed in a few states is "governmental interest analysis." This method requires the court to make a preliminary analysis of the interests of the involved states and a determination of whether the conflict is a true conflict, an apparent conflict, or a false conflict. The last is one where it will be determined that, in reality, only one state has an actual, legitimate interest. If there is only an apparent conflict, the court may be able to resolve it by interpretation. If there is a true conflict, the court will apply the law of the forum with the greatest interest in the dispute. *See, e.g., Clemco Indus. v. Commercial Union Ins. Co.,* 665 F. Supp. 816 (N.D. Cal. 1987), *aff'd,* 848 F.2d 1242 (9th Cir. 1988). The following case is an example of a false-conflict situation.

Amco Ukrservice v. American Meter Co.
United States District Court, Eastern District of Pennsylvania, 2004
312 F. Supp. 2d 681

DALZELL, District Judge.

[The full background facts of this case are set out in Chapter Three on pp. 177-181. Plaintiffs Amco Ukrservice and Prompriladamco are two Ukrainian corporations that brought an action against defendant American Meter Company, a Pennsylvania company in the business of manufacturing utility meters. Plaintiffs claim that defendant breached two joint venture agreements under which American Meter agreed to supply meters to plaintiffs for sale in the republics of the former Soviet Union. In its defense, American Meter moved for summary judgment, arguing that the joint venture agreements were unenforceable under either the Convention on Contracts for the International Sale of Goods or Ukrainian law. In the first part of its opinion, the federal district court rejected American Meter's argument that the CISG applied to the joint venture agreements (see pp. 180-181, *supra*) and then in the portion of the opinion below turned to the issue of whether the joint venture agreements were unenforceable under Ukrainian law. In order to make that determination, however, the court had to first decide whether Pennsylvania or Ukrainian law applied to the joint venture agreements. As the court was sitting in diversity jurisdiction, the court followed the mandate of *Klaxon Co. v. Stentor Electric Mfg. Co., Inc.*, 313 U.S. 487 (1941), and applied Pennsylvania choice of law rules to decide whether Pennsylvania or Ukrainian law applied to the case.]

1. THE PENNSYLVANIA CHOICE-OF-LAW REGIME

In *Griffith v. United Air Lines, Inc.*, 203 A.2d 796, 805 (Pa. 1964), the Pennsylvania Supreme Court adopted a flexible choice of law rule that "permits analysis of the policies and interests underlying the particular issue before the court." Our Court of Appeals has explained that the *Griffith* "methodology combines the approaches of both [the Restatement (Second) of Conflict of Laws] (contacts establishing significant relationships) and 'interest analysis' (qualitative appraisal of the relevant States' policies with respect to the controversy)." *Melville v. American Home Assurance Co.*, 584 F.2d 1306, 1311 (3d Cir. 1978).

In applying *Griffith*'s hybrid approach, we begin with an "interest analysis" of the policies of all interested states and then, based on the results of that analysis, proceed to characterize the case as a true conflict, false conflict, or unprovided-for case. A true conflict exists "when the governmental interests of both jurisdictions would be impaired if their law were not applied." *Lacey*, 932 F.2d at 187 n.15. On the other hand, there is a false conflict "if only one jurisdiction's governmental interests would be impaired by the application of the other jurisdiction's law." *Id.* at 187.

2. SOURCES OF LAW

While the plaintiffs and American Meter agree that ordinary breach of contract principles would govern the plaintiffs' claims under Pennsylvania law, they dispute whether the joint venture agreements are invalid under Ukrainian law and, if so, what governmental interests any invalidating laws would serve. We therefore begin with a discussion of Pennsylvania's interest in this action and then turn to the more difficult problems that Ukrainian law presents. Finally, after we have isolated any applicable statutory provisions, we will consider Ukraine's interest in their enforcement.

(A) PENNSYLVANIA LAW

At the threshold, we note that American Meter has disputed whether Pennsylvania has any interest at all in the enforcement of the joint venture agreements because they were negotiated in Ukraine, written in the Ukrainian language, and provide for the creation of Ukrainian corporations. This argument does not withstand close scrutiny because the record amply demonstrates the important contacts between Pennsylvania and both the parties to the joint venture agreements and the obligations those agreements created.

All of the American Meter employees who hatched the Ukrainian project worked from corporate headquarters in Horsham, Pennsylvania, and most important of all, the parties to the joint venture agreements contemplated that American Meter would oversee the project, extend credit, and arrange for the shipment of goods from its offices here.

Not only does Pennsylvania have significant contacts with both the parties and the joint ventures, but enforcement of the joint venture agreements would advance the Commonwealth's general interests. As American Meter grudgingly concedes, the vindication of contractual parties' legitimate expectations creates a stable business environment and thereby helps the Commonwealth achieve its commercial potential. Finally, although American Meter asserts that the plaintiffs' claims for damages are too speculative, it does not dispute that, as an abstract proposition, the joint venture agreements create enforceable obligations under Pennsylvania law.

(B) UKRAINIAN LAW

American Meter contends that the joint venture agreements are invalid under three separate statutory schemes and that each advances identifiable and significant state interests.

1. "Regulations on the Supply of Industrial Goods" (1988)

On July 25, 1988, the USSR Council of Ministers promulgated "Regulations on the Supply of Industrial Goods," which remained effective in Ukraine after the collapse of the Soviet Union pursuant to a general reception statute that the Verkovna Rada, the Ukrainian Parliament, enacted in 1991. Under Paragraph 19 of the Regulations, a contract for the supply of goods must identify the goods to be delivered, the time of delivery, and their price, quantity, and quality. American Meter's Ukrainian legal expert has opined that the Regulations were still in force in 1998 and that the joint venture agreements are invalid because their supply provisions lack the terms detailed in Paragraph 19. The plaintiffs' legal expert, however, contends that the Regulations have no relevance here because they were enacted to regulate the Soviet Union's internal market and, in any event, never applied to joint venture agreements.

Although American Meter solicited a supplemental affidavit from its Ukrainian expert, he declined to challenge the plaintiffs' expert's views on the Regulations. In view of the fact that the plaintiffs' contentions appear to have textual support—and in the absence of a counter-argument from American Meter—we must conclude that the plaintiffs' view carries the day on this issue and that the Regulations are inapplicable here.

2. "Provisions on the Form of Foreign Economic Agreements" (1995)

American Meter's legal expert has also brought to our attention the "Provisions on the Form of Foreign Economic Agreements," which the Ukrainian Ministry of Foreign Economic Relations and Trade enacted in 1995. The Provisions' preamble states that they "are applicable when concluding sale (purchase) agreements on goods (services, performance of work) and barter agreements among Ukrainian and foreign economic subjects irrespective of their property form and type of activities."

Agreements governed by the Provisions must, inter alia, identify the goods to be sold and specify their quantity and quality. American Meter contends that the joint venture agreements are invalid under the Provisions because they manifestly do not satisfy these requirements. However, as the plaintiffs' legal expert has contended, the Provisions offer no textual support for American Meter's position. Indeed, the text of the Provisions suggests that they do not regulate joint venture agreements and were instead enacted to regularize contracts for the sale of goods and provision of services.

Finally, the plaintiffs' construction of the Provisions gains support from the framers' apparent intention that they be read in pari materia with Ukraine's Foreign Economic Activities Law ("FEAL"). Because the FEAL recognizes joint venture agreements, it is improbable that the Foreign Ministry intended the 1995 enactment to invalidate such agreements, which create long-term relationships and are unlikely to contain price, quantity, and delivery terms that would be sufficiently precise to satisfy the Provisions.

In view of this textual evidence, we conclude that although the Provisions would likely govern a particular sales contract executed pursuant to a joint venture agreement, they do not bear on the validity of the joint venture agreement itself.

3. Foreign Economic Activity Law (1991)

Finally, American Meter invites us to consider whether the Ukrainian courts would invalidate the joint venture agreements under Article 6 of the FEAL. At the time the parties entered into these agreements, Article 6 required any contract between a Ukrainian entity and a foreign entity to be executed by two representatives of the Ukrainian signatory, and neither [of the plaintiff Ukrainian corporations] complied with this rule.

Ukraine's two-signature rule was the final incarnation of a policy with deep roots in the history of the Soviet command economy. According to a Stalin-era decree, any contract between a foreign entity and a Soviet foreign trade organization ("FTO") that was executed in Moscow required the signatures of the FTO's chairman or deputy as well as a person possessing the chairman's power of attorney. Contracts executed abroad required the signatures of two persons with powers of attorney.

Whatever its purpose may have been, one might have thought that the two-signature rule would have disappeared after 1990 along with the other legal trappings of the Soviet economy. [However, the two signature rule was formally enshrined in Ukrainian law in 1991 and then formally repealed in 1999.]

Apparently, however, the lower courts [show] willingness to invoke the two-signature rule in cases involving contracts executed before the repeal. In 2001, for example, Judge Zyrnov of the Kyiv City Commercial Court relied upon the rule to nullify a lease and credit agreement between a Ukrainian corporation and Fortis Bank of the Netherlands, despite the fact that the Bank had rendered performance.

Predicting another judicial system's resolution of an issue is always a perilous business, but we must conclude there is at least a possibility that a Ukrainian court would invalidate the joint venture agreements on the ground that the Ukrainian parties did not comply with the two-signature rule.

3. CHARACTERIZATION OF THE CONFLICT OF LAW PROBLEM

Our conclusion that the courts of Pennsylvania and Ukraine might diverge in their treatment of the joint venture agreements merely poses the conflict of law problem without resolving it. In order to determine whether this case involves a false or true conflict, we must first determine what, if any, governmental interests the two-signature rule advances.

American Meter contends that Ukraine has an interest in the retroactive enforcement of the rule because it protects Ukrainians who enter into contracts with foreigners and promotes certainty, predictability, and uniformity in commercial relationships. American Meter's "argument from paternalism" would bear close scrutiny if we were resolving this conflict of law problem in 1992. After all, the plaintiffs' legal expert had stated that the Verkovna Rada included the rule in the FEAL as a sop to legislators who opposed economic liberalization, and perhaps its proponents believed that requiring two signatures on contracts would protect Ukrainian naïfs from more commercially sophisticated (and capitalism-hardened) foreigners. Now that the Verkovna Rada has repealed the two-signature rule, however, we cannot conclude on the record before us that its continued enforcement advances any current social, political, or economic interest of Ukraine. Turning to American Meter's "argument from commercial certainty," we note that this articulation of Ukraine's interest in the rule remains plausible despite the repeal. A hard-and-fast policy that all foreign economic agreements executed between the enactment of the FEAL and the statute's 1999 amendment must comply with the two-signature rule would—like any bright-line rule—have the advantage of letting parties know exactly where they stand. But as the recent decisions of the SACU and Kyiv Commercial Court underscore, the difficulty with this argument is that the two-signature rule is not so much a bright-line rule as it is a controversial repository of judicial discretion that allows courts to invalidate contracts for any reason—or perhaps for no reason at all. Under these circumstances, we cannot discern how the two-signature rule advances any of the procedural or commercial advantages that Ukraine would derive from a predictable body of law governing the validity of contracts.

To summarize, we have concluded that Pennsylvania and Ukraine both have significant relationships with the parties and the transactions. Moreover, we have found that Pennsylvania has a general interest in the enforcement of contracts, and it goes without saying that this interest would be compromised if a Pennsylvania corporation could defeat the expectations of its trading partners in the manner American Meter has proposed here. Finally, we have concluded that American Meter has not identified any governmental interest of Ukraine in the continued enforcement of the repealed two-signature rule.

Because our analysis reveals that Pennsylvania's interest would be harmed by applying Ukraine's law, but that no identified Ukrainian interest will be impaired by enforcing these contracts, this case presents a false conflict. Under the Pennsylvania choice-of-law regime, Pennsylvania law therefore governs the plaintiffs' claims, and American Meter is not entitled to summary judgment on the ground that the contracts are invalid under Ukrainian law.

Defendant's motion for summary judgment is denied.

NOTES AND QUESTIONS

1. In the *Amco* case, what was the purpose of the two-signature rule? Why was this requirement repealed?

2. In the *Amco* case, the court found that the issue was a false conflict because, although both Pennsylvania and Ukraine have significant interests, the enforcement of Pennsylvania law and Pennsylvania's interest would not harm any identified significant interest in Ukraine. Do you think that a court in Ukraine would agree with this analysis?

3. Conflict of laws questions may involve true conflict of laws in the sense that if both laws apply to the legal issue at hand, conflicting answers arise. A second possibility is that the conflict may be a false conflict, as in the *Amco* case. A third possibility is that, in a conflicts situation, the laws of both states may apply because the legal issues at hand are

different. The latter case is called by the French term, *depéçage*. The broadest definition of *depéçage* is that the laws of different states are applied to govern different issues in the same case. For example, a contract for the sale of goods may be governed by England; but the contract may use finance sourced from the United States, in which case the governmental interest analysis may dictate that American law controls the financing issues. Should the court in the *Amco* case have applied *depéçage*? For an illuminating study of *depéçage*, see Willis L. M. Reese, *Depéçage: A Common Phenomenon in Choice of Law*, 73 Colum. L. Rev. 58 (1973). *Depéçage* often arises by the agreement of the parties to an international contract, the topic of the next section.

2. Choice of Law Clauses

The parties are, of course, free to insert choice of law clauses in international contracts, which are now widely upheld and seldom litigated. The Uniform Commercial Code, §1-105(1),[6] also specifically authorizes choice of law clauses. Nevertheless, interesting issues sometimes arise.

PROBLEM 8-8

An Ohio company enters into a contract with a German towing company for the towage of a rig owned by the Ohio company from the United States to Argentina. The contract provides that all disputes arising out of the contract are governed by the laws of France. In a subsequent lawsuit for damage to the rig brought by the Ohio company in an Ohio court, the German defendant argues that the issue of risk of loss should be determined by French law pursuant to the contract's choice of law clause. Assume that under French law the risk of loss is on the Ohio company. The Ohio company objects to the use of French law on the grounds that it has no connection with the parties or the transaction. How would this case be resolved under Restatement §187 below?

PROBLEM 8-9

A French company sends an application for a credit card to an Ohio consumer providing for a card with a 60 percent annual interest rate. The credit card contract provides that it is governed by the laws of country Z. Assume that both Ohio and France have laws against usury but that Z does not. In a lawsuit brought by the consumer in an Ohio court against the French company over the amount of a credit card bill, the consumer objects to the application of Z's law on the grounds that it has no connection with the parties or the transaction. How should the Ohio court decide this issue? What if the French company set up a subsidiary in Z for the purpose of serving as the entity on the credit card contract? See Restatement §187 below.

---

6. UCC §1-105(1) provides as follows:

   Except as provided hereafter in this section, when a transaction bears a reasonable relation to this state and also to another state or nation the parties may agree that the law either of this state or of such other state or nation shall govern their rights and duties. Failing such agreement this Act applies to transactions bearing an appropriate relation to this state.

The Restatement (Second) of Conflict of Laws (1971)

Section 187. Law of the State Chosen by the Parties

(1) The law of the state chosen by the parties to govern their contractual rights and duties will be applied if the particular issue is one which the parties could have resolved by an explicit provision in their agreement directed to that issue.

(2) The law of the state chosen by the parties to govern their contractual rights and duties will be applied, even if the particular issue is one which the parties could not have resolved by an explicit provision in their agreement directed to that issue, unless either:

(a) The chosen state has no substantial relationship to the parties or the transaction and there is no other reasonable basis for the parties' choice, or

(b) Application of the law of the chosen state would be contrary to a fundamental policy of a state which has a materially greater interest than the chosen state in the determination of the particular issue and which, under the rule of Section 188 [relating to the most significant contacts], would be the state of the applicable law in the absence of an effective choice of law by the parties.

(3) In the absence of a contrary indication of intention, the reference is to the local law of the state of the chosen law.

NOTES AND QUESTIONS

1. Can you explain why no substantial relationship of the state of the chosen law is required in Problem 8-8 and Restatement (Second) of Conflicts of Laws §187(1) but is required under Problem 8-9 and §187(2)?

2. Is the Restatement approach too restrictive? In contrast to the U.S. approach, Article 3 of the Rome Convention on the Law Applicable to Contractual Obligations (1980), the applicable law in the European Union, allows parties to a contract to freely choose the applicable law even if the law chosen has no connection with either the parties or the subject matter of the contract.

3. It may be dangerous to simply select a governing law without proper knowledge and planning. In *Volt Info. Sci., Inc. v. Bd. of Trs. of Leland Stanford Junior Univ.*, 489 U.S. 468 (1989), the parties chose California law and provided that any dispute would be settled by arbitration. When a dispute arose and litigation was filed in California state courts, however, there was no authority under California law that arbitration was exclusive, and the Supreme Court ruled that the selection of California law included California, not federal, arbitration law, and arbitration was stayed pending resolution of the related litigation in the California state courts.

4. How does the attorney prove foreign law in a U.S. court? This question was addressed in *In re Arbitration Between: Trans Chem. Ltd. & China Nat'l Mach. Imp. & Exp. Corp.*, 978 F. Supp. 266, 275 (S.D. Tex. 1997) as follows:

> In determining Chinese law the court is not bound by the evidence presented by the parties or by the Federal Rules of Evidence. Pursuant to Fed. R. Civ. P. 44.1 "[t]he court, in determining foreign law, may consider any relevant material or source, including testimony, whether or not submitted by a party or admissible under the Federal Rules of Evidence. The court's determination shall be treated as a ruling on a question of law."

Rule [44.1] permits the court to consider any material that is relevant to a foreign-law issue, whether submitted by counsel or unearthed by the court's own research, and without regard to its admissibility under the rules of evidence.

C. Jurisdiction

1. International Law

Jurisdiction is a term with many meanings, especially in the international context. In international law, jurisdiction is an aspect of sovereignty. Every sovereign state has the authority to exercise ultimate control over persons and properties in the national sphere through its legislature, police force, and courts. This formulation posits three types of jurisdiction: prescriptive, adjudicative, and enforcement. We examine all three types of jurisdiction in this section beginning with the most important, prescriptive jurisdiction, which refers to the power of states to prescribe or enact laws that are valid and have binding authority over their objects. In international law, prescriptive jurisdiction is based on three principles:

(1) *Territoriality.* States have power to prescribe binding laws over all persons, property, and conduct within their territorial boundaries;
(2) *Nationality.* States can enact binding laws covering their nationals wherever in the world;
(3) *Effects.* States have prescriptive jurisdiction over persons (other than their own nationals), property, and conduct located in other states when these persons, property, or conduct cause substantial effects within the prescribing states.

The first two principles are well accepted, but the last principle is controversial. Another issue is that states must have limits to avoid interference with the legitimate exercise of prescriptive jurisdiction by other states. Consider the following summary of international jurisdiction from the U.S. perspective.

Kathleen Hixson, Extraterritorial Jurisdiction Under the Third Restatement of Foreign Relations Law of the United States
12 Fordham Int'l L.J. 127, 132–137 (1988)

B. BASES OF JURISDICTION TO PRESCRIBE

The bases of jurisdiction in the Restatement Second draw upon traditional principles of international law that have found general acceptance abroad; these bases of jurisdiction include territory and nationality. As an offshoot of the traditional territoriality principle, section 18 recognizes the more controversial "effects" doctrine, wherein a state may have prescriptive jurisdiction over conduct occurring outside its territory that causes an effect within.[7] The effects doctrine is limited to rare circumstances when conduct is

---

7. *See* Restatement Second, §18. The effects doctrine receives the following treatment in the Restatement Second:

> A state has jurisdiction to prescribe a rule of law attaching legal consequences to conduct that occurs outside its territory and causes an effect within its territory, if either
>
> (a) the conduct and its effect are generally recognized as constituent elements of a crime or tort under the law of states that have reasonably developed legal systems, or
>
> (b) (i) the conduct and its effect are constituent elements of activity to which the rule applies; (ii) the effect within the territory is substantial; (iii) it occurs as a direct and foreseeable result of the conduct outside the territory; and (iv) the rule is not

generally recognized as a crime; the effect within the territory is direct, substantial, and foreseeable; and the rule is consistent with the principles of justice in states that have reasonably developed legal systems.

The Restatement Third enumerates bases of jurisdiction to prescribe in section 402.[8] Within this section, the second and third subsections outline the "nationality" and "protective" principles of jurisdiction. Subsection (1) deals with the principle of territoriality under three approaches: two of these allow a right to prescribe with respect to conduct within the territory or the status of persons or things present within the state; the third allows a state to prescribe law with respect to "conduct outside its territory that has or is intended to have substantial effect within its territory." Although the Restatement Third takes a traditional approach to territorial jurisdiction generally, this last subsection substantially relaxes the more stringent requirements on the effects doctrine found in the Restatement Second. While the Restatement Second requires direct, substantial, and foreseeable effects under the Restatement Third the effect need not be actual, but merely intended. Actual but unintended effects would also be sufficient to support jurisdiction. And finally, the Restatement Third eliminates the requirement that the conduct in question be generally recognized as a crime in the international community.

C. LIMITATIONS ON JURISDICTION

Both the Restatement Second and the Restatement Third recognize that conflict may arise when two states concurrently exercise jurisdiction. The Restatement Second approaches this problem, in section 40, as one of the proper exercise of enforcement jurisdiction. While the first prerequisite to enforcement jurisdiction is valid prescriptive jurisdiction, the impact of enforcement jurisdiction is then further ameliorated by section 40. Where the assertion of concurrent jurisdiction by two or more states might require inconsistent conduct, section 40 requires a state to consider in good faith moderating its enforcement jurisdiction. This consideration is stated as an express requirement of international law.

The Restatement Third provides for conflict resolution in section 403 under the heading "Limitations on Jurisdiction to Prescribe."[9] This section states, first, the so-called "rule of reason," which is the foundation of the Restatement Third balancing test. Under

---

inconsistent with the principles of justice generally recognized by states that have reasonably developed legal systems.

8. Restatement Third, §402.
   Subject to §403, a state has jurisdiction to prescribe law with respect to
   (1) (a) conduct that, wholly or in substantial part, takes place within its territory;
   (b) the status of persons, or interests in things, present within its territory;
   (c) conduct outside its territory that has or is intended to have substantial effect within its territory;
   (2) the activities, interests, status, or relations of its nationals outside as well as within its territory; and (3) certain conduct outside its territory by persons not its nationals that is directed against the security of the state or against a limited class of other state interests. *Id.*

9. Restatement Third, §403. Section 403 reads:
   (1) Even when one of the bases for jurisdiction under §402 is present, a state may not exercise jurisdiction to prescribe law with respect to a person or activity having connections with another state when the exercise of such jurisdiction is unreasonable.
   (2) Whether exercise of jurisdiction over a person or activity is unreasonable is determined by evaluating all relevant factors, including, where appropriate:

this rule, a state may not exercise prescriptive jurisdiction over persons or things having connections with other states where the exercise of such jurisdiction is unreasonable. Reasonableness, in this provision, is to be measured by evaluating all relevant factors, including certain nonexclusive factors listed in subsection (2). Where the prescriptions by two or more states are both reasonable, but conflict nonetheless, each state must evaluate its own, as well as the other state's interest and should defer to the other state if that state's interest is clearly greater.

In this area, the Restatement Third has taken perhaps the most radical departure from the Restatement Second. First, under the Restatement Second, the good-faith weighing of interests is presented as a requirement of international law. Under the Restatement Third, however, a state "has an obligation" to evaluate, but "should" defer if the other state's interest is "clearly" greater. The actual moderation of jurisdiction is presented more as an exercise of deference based on principles of comity.

Second, the Restatement Third places less emphasis on territoriality. Instead, it focuses on elements such as the nature of the activity, the effect on the regulating state, and the interests of both the regulating and territorial states, which interests are measured by the amount of regulation generally exercised. These factors are far more difficult to quantify than the narrowly defined factors of the Restatement Second. Thus, they open the door to a substantially broader interpretation of extraterritorial jurisdiction.

Finally, the Restatement Third limitations turn on the concept of reasonableness. This leaves open to the courts the interpretation of the meaning of reasonableness.

NOTES AND QUESTIONS

1. The whole thrust of the Restatement (Third) compared to the Restatement (Second) was to greatly expand concepts of U.S. jurisdiction. Why was this the case? In which areas of law does the United States have an interest in expanding its influence?

(a) the link of the activity to the territory of the regulating state, *i.e.*, the extent to which the activity takes place within the territory, or has substantial, direct, and foreseeable effect upon or in the territory;

(b) the connections, such as nationality; residence, or economic activity, between the regulating state and the person principally responsible for the activity to be regulated, or between that state and those whom the regulation is designed to protect;

(c) the character of the activity to be regulated, the importance of regulation to the regulating state, the extent to which other states regulate such activities, and the degree to which the desirability of such regulation is generally accepted;

(d) the existence of justified expectations that might be protected or hurt by the regulation;

(e) the importance of the regulation to the international political, legal, or economic system;

(f) the extent to which the regulation is consistent with the traditions of the international system;

(g) the extent to which another state may have an interest in regulating the activity; and

(h) the likelihood of conflict with regulation by another state.

(3) When it would not be unreasonable for each of two states to exercise jurisdiction over a person or activity, but the prescriptions by the two states are in conflict, each state has an obligation to evaluate its own as well as the other state's interest in exercising jurisdiction, in light of all the relevant factors, Subsection (2); a state should defer to the other state if that state's interest is clearly greater.

Does the Restatement (Third) comport with or depart from international law in its expansive notion of jurisdiction?

2. Consider the "effects" doctrine. To the consternation of other countries, U.S. courts often invoke the effects doctrine as a justification for the exercise of extraterritorial jurisdiction in the fields of antitrust, securities, and criminal law. Does the effects doctrine go too far?

3. To combat U.S. extraterritorial jurisdiction, many states have enacted "blocking" statutes that allow authorities to prohibit the production of evidence or compliance with U.S. legal requirements considered inappropriate. *See, e.g.*, Protection of Trading Interests Act, 1980, c. 11 (U.K.).

2. Adjudicative Jurisdiction: Subject Matter and Territorial Jurisdiction

Adjudicative jurisdiction refers to the power of courts over (1) the subject matter of a dispute and (2) persons or property involved in a dispute. The former is called subject matter jurisdiction and the latter is termed territorial jurisdiction. These concepts are embodied in the national law of each country and are rooted in concepts of order and fundamental fairness.

"Subject matter jurisdiction" refers to the authority of a particular court to decide a given dispute and assigns various subject matters by law to the appropriate courts. In the United States, subject matter jurisdiction is particularly important in maintaining the federal system; thus, the subject matter jurisdiction of the federal courts is generally limited to cases involving a federal question of law, admiralty, and litigation between persons domiciled in different states. In nations such as France and Germany, certain courts are assigned specialty subject matters, such as administrative law cases or labor law cases.

"Territorial jurisdiction" is the most important jurisdiction concept concerning private international business contracts and transactions. Of course, this topic is important to the domestic as well as the international litigant. In the landmark case of *International Shoe Co. v. State of Washington*, 326 U.S. 310, 316 (1945), the Supreme Court decided that, as an element of constitutional due process, a defendant must have certain minimum contacts with the state of the judicial forum to be subject to the state's adjudicative powers. In *Shaffer v. Heitner*, 433 U.S. 186, 212 (1977), the Supreme Court held that the ownership of property alone in the forum state cannot justify jurisdiction without minimum contacts as required by *International Shoe*. Nevertheless, a so-called quasi-in-rem case based on property ownership can still be brought consistent with due process if the maintenance of property, such as a bank account, constitutes minimum contacts. *See, e.g., Banco Ambrosiano, S.P.A. v. Artoc Bank & Trust Ltd.*, 62 N.Y.2d 65, 71–74 (N.Y. 1984).

Most international business litigation in the United States will concern state-created causes of action in state court or in federal court on the basis of diversity of citizenship. Although these cases will be under state jurisdictional rules, most states provide by statute or judicial interpretation that the jurisdiction of their courts extends to the limits permitted by due process under the U.S. Constitution. Thus, the same constitutional analysis will generally apply to both state and federal law claims in the United States.

Of course, each state or group of states will have its own international jurisdictional rules. In the EU, most international business contracts are subject to two conventions, the Brussels Convention on Jurisdiction and the Enforcement of Judgments in Civil and Commercial Matters (1968), Brussels I, discussed *supra*, p. 620 (applicable between member states), and the almost identical Convention on Jurisdiction and the Recognition and Enforcement of Judgments in Civil and Commercial Matters (New Lugano Convention), Oct. 30, 2007, 2007 O.J. (L 339) (entered into force 2010). These two conventions provide that a natural person or a company can be sued in contract in the state of domicile or in the place of performance of the obligation. Non-EU individuals and companies are subject to much more liberal jurisdiction under national laws that differ from state to state. *See generally* Samuel Cohen, *The EEC Convention and U.S. Law Governing Choice of Law for Contracts, with Particular Emphasis on the Restatement Second: A Comparative Study*, 13 Md. J. Int'l L. & Trade 223 (1989).

Many states, including France, Germany, Switzerland, and the United Kingdom, allow suit to be brought *in personam* based on the fact that a defendant owns tangible or intangible assets in the jurisdiction. *See, e.g., Derby & Co., Ltd. v. Weldon*, [1989] 2 W.L.R. 276 (A.C.) (Eng.). Such property-based jurisdiction goes beyond what would be permitted under U.S. due process standards.

In this section, we examine two cases that explore the outer limits of U.S. due process standards in litigation against foreign defendants.

PROBLEM 8-10

Nippon Electronics (NE) is a major Japanese manufacturer of household electronic goods such as flat screen high-definition televisions; handheld tablet and mobile phones; digital cameras; and CD and DVD players. NE sells products that reach the U.S. market in several ways.

(1) Each year, NE participates in a trade fair in Tokyo where eager buyers come from around the world. A purchaser from South Korea buys a large quantity of DVD players for sale in the Korean market; however, as the Korean buyer is unable to sell all of the goods in Korea, the buyer sells the surplus quantities to a distributor in Illinois. A little girl receives some burns on her arms and legs when the DVD player malfunctions as she is inserting a disk. Her mother brings an action against NE in Illinois state court in Chicago.

(2) At the trade fair in Tokyo, NE also sells an order of plasma screens manufactured to specifications to a Sacramento computer company, which incorporates the screens into its state-of-the-art laptop computers back in its California factory. When the screens prove to be defective, the Sacramento computer company sues NE for breach of warranty and breach of contract in California state court.

(3) NE keeps a small office in Texas where it stores some accounting and financial records. Once a month, a representative from NE's Tokyo office flies to Texas en route to NE's subsidiary in Canada and stops in the Texas office for two days to update the records and issue checks. A U.S. tourist from Texas travels to Tokyo and purchases an NE radio and audiocassette recorder and player at the trade fair. The tourist complains about a loss of hearing when the audio player emits a loud and unexpected static noise. When the tourist returns home, he files an action against NE in Texas state court.

(4) Suppose that NE was later acquired by Western Electronics (WE), a large diversified U.S. multinational company based in California, with many foreign subsidiaries. One of NE's new tablet computers is shipped to France where a malfunction causes an injury to a consumer. Although NE does not ship directly to California, a small percentage of NE's tablet computers are distributed in California by other affiliates of WE. The plaintiff uses both WE and its subsidiary NE in a federal court in California.

Discuss whether the courts in each of these instances have jurisdiction over NE. Consult *Asahi, Goodyear,* and *Glencore* below.

Asahi Metal Indus. Co., Ltd. v. Superior Court
United States Supreme Court, 1987
480 U.S. 102

Justice O'CONNOR announced the judgment of the Court.

This case presents the question whether the mere awareness on the part of a foreign defendant that the components it manufactured, sold, and delivered outside the United States would reach the forum State in the stream of commerce constitutes "minimum contacts" between the defendant and the forum State such that the exercise of jurisdiction "does not offend 'traditional notions of fair play and substantial justice.'" *International Shoe Co. v. Washington,* 326 U.S. 310, 316 (1945), quoting *Milliken v. Meyer,* 311 U.S. 457, 463 (1940).

I

On September 23, 1978, on Interstate Highway 80 in Solano County, California, Gary Zurcher lost control of his Honda motorcycle and collided with a tractor. Zurcher was severely injured, and his passenger and wife, Ruth Ann Moreno, was killed. In September 1979, Zurcher filed a product liability action in the Superior Court of the State of California in and for the County of Solano. Zurcher alleged that the 1978 accident was caused by a sudden loss of air and an explosion in the rear tire of the motorcycle, and alleged that the motorcycle tire, tube, and sealant were defective. Zurcher's complaint named, *inter alia,* Cheng Shin Rubber Industrial Co., Ltd. (Cheng Shin), the Taiwanese manufacturer of the tube. Cheng Shin in turn filed a cross-complaint seeking indemnification from its codefendants and from petitioner, Asahi Metal Industry Co., Ltd. (Asahi), the manufacturer of the tube's valve assembly. Zurcher's claims against Cheng Shin and the other defendants were eventually settled and dismissed, leaving only Cheng Shin's indemnity action against Asahi.

California's long-arm statute authorizes the exercise of jurisdiction "on any basis not inconsistent with the Constitution of this state or of the United States." Cal. Civ. Proc. Code Ann. §410.[10] (West 1973). Asahi moved to quash Cheng Shin's service of summons, arguing the State could not exert jurisdiction over it consistent with the Due Process Clause of the Fourteenth Amendment.

In relation to the motion, the following information was submitted by Asahi and Cheng Shin. Asahi is a Japanese corporation. It manufactures tire valve assemblies in Japan and sells the assemblies to Cheng Shin, and to several other tire manufacturers, for use as components in finished tire tubes. Asahi's sales to Cheng Shin took place in Taiwan. The shipments from Asahi to Cheng Shin were sent from Japan to Taiwan. Cheng Shin bought and incorporated into its tire tubes 150,000 Asahi valve assemblies in 1978; 500,000 in 1979; 500,000 in 1980; 100,000 in 1981; and 100,000 in 1982. Sales to Cheng Shin accounted for 1.24 percent of Asahi's income in 1981 and 0.44 percent in 1982.

---

10. Authors' Note: Both the United States and Japan are signatories to the Hague Convention.

Cheng Shin alleged that approximately 20 percent of its sales in the United States are in California. Cheng Shin purchases valve assemblies from other suppliers as well, and sells finished tubes throughout the world.

In 1983 an attorney for Cheng Shin conducted an informal examination of the valve stems of the tire tubes sold in one cycle store in Solano County. The attorney declared that of the approximately 115 tire tubes in the store, 97 were purportedly manufactured in Japan or Taiwan, and of those 97, 21 valve stems were marked with the circled letter "A," apparently Asahi's trademark. Of the 21 Asahi valve stems, 12 were incorporated into Cheng Shin tire tubes. The store contained 41 other Cheng Shin tubes that incorporated the valve assemblies of other manufacturers. An affidavit of a manager of Cheng Shin whose duties included the purchasing of component parts stated: "'In discussions with Asahi regarding the purchase of valve stem assemblies the fact that my Company sells tubes throughout the world and specifically the United States has been discussed. I am informed and believe that Asahi was fully aware that valve stem assemblies sold to my Company and to others would end up throughout the United States and in California.'" An affidavit of the president of Asahi, on the other hand, declared that Asahi "'has never contemplated that its limited sales of tire valves to Cheng Shin in Taiwan would subject it to lawsuits in California.'" *Ibid.* The record does not include any contract between Cheng Shin and Asahi.

Primarily on the basis of the above information, the Superior Court denied the motion to quash summons, stating: "Asahi obviously does business on an international scale. It is not unreasonable that they defend claims of defect in their product on an international scale."

The Court of Appeal of the State of California issued a preemptory writ of mandate commanding the Superior Court to quash service of summons. The court concluded that "it would be unreasonable to require Asahi to respond in California solely on the basis of ultimately realized foreseeability that the product into which its component was embodied would be sold all over the world including California."

The Supreme Court of the State of California reversed and discharged the writ issued by the Court of Appeal. The court observed: "Asahi has no offices, property or agents in California. It solicits no business in California and has made no direct sales [in California]." Moreover, "Asahi did not design or control the system of distribution that carried its valve assemblies into California." Nevertheless, the court found the exercise of jurisdiction over Asahi to be consistent with the Due Process Clause. It concluded that Asahi knew that some of the valve assemblies sold to Cheng Shin would be incorporated into tire tubes sold in California, and that Asahi benefited indirectly from the sale in California of products incorporating its components. The court considered Asahi's intentional act of placing its components into the stream of commerce—that is, by delivering the components to Cheng Shin in Taiwan—coupled with Asahi's awareness that some of the components would eventually find their way into California, sufficient to form the basis for state court jurisdiction under the Due Process Clause.

We granted certiorari, and now reverse.

II

A

The Due Process Clause of the Fourteenth Amendment limits the power of a state court to exert personal jurisdiction over a nonresident defendant. "[T]he constitutional touchstone" of the determination whether an exercise of personal jurisdiction comports with due process "remains whether the defendant purposefully established 'minimum contacts' in the forum State." *Burger King Corp. v. Rudzewicz*, 471 U.S. 462, 474 (1985), quoting *International Shoe Co. v. Washington.*

Most recently we have reaffirmed the oft-quoted reasoning of *Hanson v. Denckla*, that minimum contacts must have a basis in "some act by which the defendant purposefully avails itself of the privilege of conducting activities within the forum State, thus invoking the benefits and protections of its laws." *Burger King*, 471 U.S. at 475. "Jurisdiction is proper . . . where the contacts proximately result from actions by the defendant *himself* that create a 'substantial connection' with the forum State." *Ibid.*, quoting *McGee v. International Life Insurance Co.* (emphasis in original).

Applying the principle that minimum contacts must be based on an act of the defendant, the Court in *World-Wide Volkswagen Corp. v. Woodson* rejected the assertion that a consumer's unilateral act of bringing the defendant's product into the forum State was a sufficient constitutional basis for personal jurisdiction over the defendant. It had been argued in *World-Wide Volkswagen* that because an automobile retailer and its wholesale distributor sold a product mobile by design and purpose, they could foresee being haled into court in the distant States into which their customers might drive. The Court rejected this concept of foreseeability as an insufficient basis for jurisdiction under the Due Process Clause. The Court disclaimed, however, the idea that "foreseeability is wholly irrelevant" to personal jurisdiction, concluding that "[t]he forum State does not exceed its powers under the Due Process Clause if it asserts personal jurisdiction over a corporation that delivers its products into the stream of commerce with the expectation that they will be purchased by consumers in the forum State." The Court reasoned:

> When a corporation "purposefully avails itself of the privilege of conducting activities within the forum State," *Hanson v. Denckla*, it has clear notice that it is subject to suit there, and can act to alleviate the risk of burdensome litigation by procuring insurance, passing the expected costs on to customers, or, if the risks are too great, severing its connection with the State. Hence if the sale of a product of a manufacturer or distributor . . . is not simply an isolated occurrence, but arises from the efforts of the manufacturer or distributor to serve, directly or indirectly, the market for its product in other States, it is not unreasonable to subject it to suit in one of those States if its allegedly defective merchandise has there been the source of injury to its owners or to others.

In *World-Wide Volkswagen* itself, the state court sought to base jurisdiction not on any act of the defendant, but on the foreseeable unilateral actions of the consumer. Since *World-Wide Volkswagen*, lower courts have been confronted with cases in which the defendant acted by placing a product in the stream of commerce, and the stream eventually swept defendant's product into the forum State, but the defendant did nothing else to purposefully avail itself of the market in the forum State. Some courts have understood the Due Process Clause, as interpreted in *World-Wide Volkswagen*, to allow an exercise of personal jurisdiction to be based on no more than the defendant's act of placing the product in the stream of commerce. Other courts have understood the Due Process Clause and the above-quoted language in *World-Wide Volkswagen* to require the action of the defendant to be more purposefully directed at the forum State than the mere act of placing a product in the stream of commerce.

The reasoning of the Supreme Court of California in the present case illustrates the former interpretation of *World-Wide Volkswagen*. The Supreme Court of California held that, because the stream of commerce eventually brought some valves Asahi sold Cheng Shin into California, Asahi's awareness that its valves would be sold in California was sufficient to permit California to exercise jurisdiction over Asahi consistent with the requirements of the Due Process Clause. The Supreme Court of California's position was consistent with those courts that have held that mere foreseeability or awareness was a constitutionally sufficient basis for personal jurisdiction if the defendant's product made its way into the forum State while still in the stream of commerce.

Other courts, however, have understood the Due Process Clause to require something more than that the defendant was aware of its product's entry into the forum State through the stream of commerce in order for the State to exert jurisdiction over the defendant. In the present case, for example, the State Court of Appeal did not read the Due Process Clause, as interpreted by *World-Wide Volkswagen*, to allow "mere foreseeability that the product will enter the forum state [to] be enough by itself to establish jurisdiction over the distributor and retailer." In *Humble v. Toyota Motor Co.*, 727 F.2d 709 (8th Cir. 1984), an injured car passenger brought suit against Arakawa Auto Body Company, a Japanese corporation that manufactured car seats for Toyota. Arakawa did no business in the United States; it had no office, affiliate, subsidiary, or agent in the United States; it manufactured its component parts outside the United States and delivered them to Toyota Motor Company in Japan. The Court of Appeals, adopting the reasoning of the District Court in that case, noted that although it "does not doubt that Arakawa could have foreseen that its product would find its way into the United States," it would be "manifestly unjust" to require Arakawa to defend itself in the United States.

We now find this latter position to be consonant with the requirements of due process. The "substantial connection" between the defendant and the forum State necessary for a finding of minimum contacts must come about by an action of the defendant purposefully directed toward the forum State. The placement of a product into the stream of commerce, without more, is not an act of the defendant purposefully directed toward the forum State. Additional conduct of the defendant may indicate an intent or purpose to serve the market in the forum State, for example, designing the product for the market in the forum State, advertising in the forum State, establishing channels for providing regular advice to customers in the forum State, or marketing the product through a distributor who has agreed to serve as the sales agent in the forum State. But a defendant's awareness that the stream of commerce may or will sweep the product into the forum State does not convert the mere act of placing the product into the stream into an act purposefully directed toward the forum State.

Assuming, *arguendo*, that respondents have established Asahi's awareness that some of the valves sold to Cheng Shin would be incorporated into tire tubes sold in California, respondents have not demonstrated any action by Asahi to purposefully avail itself of the California market. Asahi does not do business in California. It has no office, agents, employees, or property in California. It does not advertise or otherwise solicit business in California. It did not create, control, or employ the distribution system that brought its valves to California. There is no evidence that Asahi designed its product in anticipation of sales in California. On the basis of these facts, the exertion of personal jurisdiction over Asahi by the Superior Court of California exceeds the limits of due process.

B

The strictures of the Due Process Clause forbid a state court to exercise personal jurisdiction over Asahi under circumstances that would offend "'traditional notions of fair play and substantial justice.'" *International Shoe Co. v. Washington,* quoting *Milliken v. Meyer.*

We have previously explained that the determination of the reasonableness of the exercise of jurisdiction in each case will depend on an evaluation of several factors. A court must consider the burden on the defendant, the interests of the forum State, and the plaintiff's interest in obtaining relief. It must also weigh in its determination "the interstate judicial system's interest in obtaining the most efficient resolution of controversies; and the shared interest of the several States in furthering fundamental substantive social policies." *World-Wide Volkswagen.*

A consideration of these factors in the present case clearly reveals the unreasonableness of the assertion of jurisdiction over Asahi, even apart from the question of the placement of goods in the stream of commerce.

Certainly the burden on the defendant in this case is severe. Asahi has been commanded by the Supreme Court of California not only to traverse the distance between Asahi's headquarters in Japan and the Superior Court of California in and for the County of Solano, but also to submit its dispute with Cheng Shin to a foreign nation's judicial system. The unique burdens placed upon one who must defend oneself in a foreign legal system should have significant weight in assessing the reasonableness of stretching the long arm of personal jurisdiction over national borders.

When minimum contacts have been established, often the interests of the plaintiff and the forum in the exercise of jurisdiction will justify even the serious burdens placed on the filing defendant. In the present case, however, the interests of the plaintiff and the forum in California's assertion of jurisdiction over Asahi are slight. All that remains is a claim for indemnification asserted by Cheng Shin, a Taiwanese corporation, against Asahi. The transaction on which the indemnification claim is based took place in Taiwan; Asahi's components were shipped from Japan to Taiwan. Cheng Shin has not demonstrated that it is more convenient for it to litigate its indemnification claim against Asahi in California rather than in Taiwan, or Japan.

Because the plaintiff is not a California resident, California's legitimate interests in the dispute have considerably diminished. The Supreme Court of California argued that the State had an interest in "protecting its consumers by ensuring that foreign manufacturers comply with the state's safety standards." The State Supreme Court's definition of California's interest, however, was overly broad. The dispute between Cheng Shin and Asahi is primarily about indemnification rather than safety standards. Moreover, it is not at all clear at this point that California law should govern the question whether a Japanese corporation should indemnify a Taiwanese corporation on the basis of a sale made in Taiwan and a shipment of goods from Japan to Taiwan.

World-Wide Volkswagen also admonished courts to take into consideration the interests of the "several States," in addition to the forum State, in the efficient judicial resolution of the dispute and the advancement of substantive policies. In the present case, this advice calls for a court to consider the procedural and substantive policies of other *nations* whose interests are affected by the assertion of jurisdiction by the California court. In every case, however, those interests, as well as the Federal interest in Government's foreign relations policies, will best served by a careful inquiry into the reasonableness of the assertion of jurisdiction in the particular case, and an unwillingness to find the serious burdens on an alien defendant outweighed by minimal interests on the part of the plaintiff or the forum State. Considering the international context, the heavy burden on the alien defendant, and the slight interests of the plaintiff and the forum State, the exercise of personal jurisdiction by a California court over Asahi in this instance would be unreasonable and unfair.

III

The judgment of the Supreme Court of California is reversed, and the case is remanded for further proceedings not inconsistent with this opinion.

It is so ordered.

Goodyear Dunlop Tires Operations, S.A. v. Brown
United States Supreme Court, 2011
131 S. Ct. 2846

Justice GINSBURG delivered the opinion of the Court.

This case concerns the jurisdiction of state courts over corporations organized and operating abroad. We address, in particular, this question: Are foreign subsidiaries of a United States parent corporation amenable to suit in state court on claims unrelated to any activity in the forum state?

A bus accident outside Paris that took the lives of two 13-year old boys from North Carolina gave rise to the litigation we here consider. Attributing the accident to a defective tire manufactured in Turkey at the plant of a foreign subsidiary of the Goodyear Tire and Rubber Company (Goodyear USA), the boys' parents commenced an action for damages in a North Carolina state court; they named as defendants Goodyear USA, an Ohio Corporation, and three of its subsidiaries organized and operating, respectively, in Turkey, France, and Luxembourg. Goodyear USA, which had plants in North Carolina and regularly engaged in commercial activity there did not contest the North Carolina court's jurisdiction over it; Goodyear USA's foreign subsidiaries, however, maintained that North Carolina lacked adjudicatory authority over them.

A state court's assertion of jurisdiction exposes defendants to the State's coercive power, and is therefore subject to review for compatibility with the Fourteenth Amendment's Due Process Clause. *International Shoe Co. v. Washington*, 326 U.S. 310 (1945). Opinions in the wake of the pathmarking *International Shoe* decision have differentiated between general or all-purpose jurisdiction, and specific or case-linked jurisdiction. *Helicopteros Nacionales de Colombia, SA v. Hall*, 466 U.S. 408, 414 nn. 8, 10 (1984).

A court may assert general jurisdiction over foreign (foreign sister-state or foreign country) corporations to hear any and all claims against them when their affiliations with the State are so "continuous and systematic" as to render them essentially at home in the forum State. Specific jurisdiction, on the other hand, depends on an "affiliation between the forum and the underlying controversy," principally, activity or an occurrence that takes place in the forum State and is therefore subject to the State's regulation. In contrast to general, all-purpose jurisdiction, specific jurisdiction is confined to adjudication of "issues deriving from, or connected with, the controversy that establishes jurisdiction."

Because the episode-in-suit, the bus accident, occurred in France, and the tire alleged to have caused the accident was manufactured and sold abroad, North Carolina courts lacked specific jurisdiction to adjudicate the controversy. [Thus, the question is:] Were the foreign subsidiaries nonetheless amenable to general jurisdiction in North Carolina courts? Confusing or blending general and specific jurisdictional inquiries, the North Carolina courts answered yes. Some of the tires made abroad by Goodyear's foreign subsidiaries, the North Carolina Court of Appeals stressed, had reached North Carolina through "the stream of commerce"; that connection, the Court of Appeals believed, gave

North Carolina courts the handle needed for the exercise of general jurisdiction over the foreign corporations.

A connection so limited between the forum and the foreign corporation, we hold, is an inadequate basis for the exercise of general jurisdiction. Such a connection does not establish the "continuous and systemic" affiliation necessary to empower the North Carolina courts to entertain claims unrelated to the foreign corporation's contacts with the State.

In contrast to the parent corporation, Goodyear USA, which does not contest the North Carolina court's personal jurisdiction over it, petitioners [the foreign corporations] are not registered to do business in North Carolina. They do not design, manufacture, or advertise their products in North Carolina. And they do not solicit business in North Carolina or themselves sell or ship tires to North Carolina customers. Even so, a small percentage of petitioners' tires (tens of thousands out of tens of millions manufactured between 2004 and 2007) were distributed within North Carolina by other Goodyear USA affiliates. These tires were typically custom ordered to equip specialized vehicles such as cement mixers, waste haulers, and boat and horse trailers. Petitioners state, and respondents do not here deny, that the type of tire involved in the accident, a Goodyear Regional RHS tire manufactured by Goodyear Turkey, was never distributed in North Carolina.

Since *International Shoe*, this Court's decisions have elaborated primarily on circumstances that warrant the exercise of specific jurisdiction, particularly in cases involving "single or occasional acts" occurring or having their impact within the forum State. As a rule in these cases, this Court has inquired whether there was "some act by which the defendant purposefully availed itself of the privilege of conducting activities within the forum State, thus invoking the benefits and protection of its laws." *See, e.g., World-wide Volkswagen Corp. v. Woodson*, 444 U.S. 286 (1980) (Oklahoma court may not exercise personal jurisdiction "over a nonresident automobile retailer and its wholesale distributor in a products liability action, when the defendants' only connection with Oklahoma is the fact that an automobile sold in New York to New York residents became involved in an accident in Oklahoma"); *Burger King Corp. v. Rudzewicz*, 471 U.S. 462 (1985) (franchisor headquartered in Florida may maintain breach-of-contract action in Florida against Michigan franchisees, where agreement contemplated ongoing interactions between franchisees and franchisor's headquarters); *Asahi Metal Industry Co. v. Superior Court*, 480 U.S. 102 (1987) (Taiwanese tire manufacturer settled product liability action brought in California and sought indemnification there from Japanese valve assembly manufacturer; Japanese company's "mere awareness . . . that the components it manufactured, sold, and delivered outside the United States would reach the forum state in the stream of commerce" held insufficient to permit California court's adjudication of Taiwanese company's cross-complaint).

In only two decisions postdating *International Shoe* has this Court considered whether an out-of-state corporate defendant's in-state contacts were sufficiently "continuous and systematic" to justify the exercise of general jurisdiction over claims unrelated to those contacts. *Perkins v. Benguet Consol. Mining Co.*, 342 U.S. 437 (1952) (general jurisdiction appropriately exercised over Philippine corporation sued in Ohio, where the company's affairs were overseen during World War II); and *Helicopteros*, 466 U.S. 408 (helicopter owned by Colombian crashed in Peru; survivors of U.S. citizens who died in the crash, the Court held, could not maintain wrongful-death actions against the Colombian corporation in Texas, for the corporation's helicopter purchases and purchase-linked activity in Texas were insufficient to subject it to Texas court's general jurisdiction) [.]

The North Carolina court's stream-of-commerce analysis elided the essential difference between case-specific and all-purpose (general) jurisdiction. Flow of a manufacturer's products into the forum, we have explained, may bolster an affiliation germane to *specific* jurisdiction. But ties serving to bolster the exercise of specific jurisdiction do not warrant a determination that, based on those ties, the forum State has *general* jurisdiction over a defendant. Measured against *Helicopteros* and *Perkins*, North Carolina is not a forum in which it would be permissible to subject petitioners to general jurisdiction.

Reversed.

Glencore Grain Rotterdam B.V. v. Shivnath Rai Harnarain Co.
United States Court of Appeals, Ninth Circuit, 2002
284 F.3d 1114

TROTT, Circuit Judge.

This case arises out of a series of eleven contracts under which Glencore Grain, a Netherlands corporation with its principal place of business in Rotterdam, agreed to purchase approximately 300,000 tons of rice from Shivnath Rai, a manufacturer and exporter of rice incorporated in India with its principal place of business in New Delhi. The contracts called for the delivery of rice at the Port of Kandla, India.

A dispute arose between the parties concerning the delivery of rice and was submitted to arbitration before the London Rice Brokers' Association ("LRBA"). In its written decision from July 1997, the LRBA ruled in favor of Glencore Grain, awarding it roughly $6.5 million; including interest, the award exceeded $7 million. Shivnath Rai did not challenge the decision in England, where the award became final and remains enforceable, nor did Shivnath Rai pay up.

In July 2000, Glencore Grain filed an application in the federal district court for the Northern District of California, seeking confirmation of the arbitral award under the [Convention on the Recognition and Enforcement of Foreign Arbitral Awards]. Shivnath Rai filed a motion to dismiss on six different grounds, including the absence of personal jurisdiction.

In its motion opposing dismissal, Glencore Grain submitted evidence of Shivnath Rai's minimum-contacts with California and with the United States as a whole to justify the exercise of personal jurisdiction. Glencore Grain provided evidence of the following shipments of rice by Shivnath Rai: a 1987 shipment into the Port of Los Angeles; seven shipments through East Coast ports from 1993 to 1995; and fifteen shipments into the Port of San Francisco from March 1999 to March 2000. In addition, Glencore Grain submitted documents indicating that Alok Mohan, President of Asian Brands, Inc., located in Union City, California, served as Shivnath Rai's sales agent for its rice sales throughout the United States. Glencore Grain contended that these contacts supported the exercise of either specific or general jurisdiction over Shivnath Rai.

Unswayed, the district court dismissed the action for lack of personal jurisdiction. In rejecting the general jurisdiction argument, the district court reasoned: "[p]etitioner has not asserted that Respondent conducts any business in the [United States] except through this sales agent [i.e., Asian Brands, Inc.]." In addition, the district court refused to exercise specific jurisdiction because "[Glencore Grain] nowhere asserts that the cause of action arises out of or relates to [Shivnath Rai's] activities within the forum."

This timely appeal followed.

The District Court Lacked Jurisdiction over Shivnath Rai

A. JURISDICTION UNDER RULE 4(K)(1)(A) AND THE CALIFORNIA LONG-ARM: SHIVNATH RAI LACKS MINIMUM CONTACTS WITH CALIFORNIA

Constitutional due process is satisfied when a non-resident defendant has "certain minimum contacts with [the forum] such that the maintenance of the suit does not offend 'traditional notions of fair play and substantial justice.'" *Int'l Shoe*, 326 U.S. at 316, (quoting *Milliken v. Meyer*, 311 U.S. 457, 463 (1940)). Depending on the nature of a foreign defendant's contacts with the forum, a federal court may obtain either specific or general jurisdiction over him. A court exercises specific jurisdiction where the cause of action arises out of or has a substantial connection to the defendant's contacts with the forum. Alternatively, a defendant whose contacts are substantial, continuous, and systematic is subject to a court's general jurisdiction even if the suit concerns matters not arising out of his contacts with the forum.

i. Specific Jurisdiction Is Not Proper over Shivnath Rai

Our Circuit applies a three-part test to evaluate the propriety of exercising specific jurisdiction: (1) whether the defendant purposefully availed himself of the privileges of conducting activities in the forum, (2) whether the claim arises out of or results from the defendant's forum-related activities, and (3) whether the exercise of jurisdiction is reasonable. Glencore Grain's suit fails to clear the second hurdle.

We apply a "but for" test to assess whether Glencore Grain's claims "arise out of" Shivnath Rai's forum conduct: Glencore Grain must show that it would not have been injured "but for" Shivnath Rai's contacts with California. The contracts giving rise to this dispute were negotiated abroad, involved foreign companies, and required performance (i.e., delivery of rice) in India. In short, Glencore Grain's claim does not arise out of conduct directed at or related to California. Thus, due process forbids the exercise of specific jurisdiction.

ii. General Jurisdiction Is Not Proper over Shivnath Rai

We consider, next, the nature of Shivnath Rai's contacts to see whether they constitute the kind of continuous and systematic general business contacts that "approximate physical presence." *Bancroft & Masters, Inc. v. Augusta Nat'l Inc.*, 223 F.3d 1082, 1086 (9th Cir. 2000). Such contacts were found to exist in *Perkins v. Benguet Consol. Mining Co.*, 342 U.S. 437, 448 (1952); the Supreme Court has summarized the circumstances that permitted the exercise of general jurisdiction over the defendant foreign corporation in that case:

> During the Japanese occupation of the Philippine Islands, the president and general manager of a Philippine mining corporation maintained an office in Ohio from which he conducted activities on behalf of the company. He kept company files and held directors' meetings in the office, carried on correspondence relating to the business, distributed salary checks drawn on two active Ohio bank accounts, engaged an Ohio bank to act as transfer agent, and supervised policies dealing with the rehabilitation of the corporation's properties in the Philippines. In short, the foreign corporation, through its president, "[had] been carrying on in Ohio a continuous and systematic, but limited, part of its general business[.]"

Helicopteros, 466 U.S. at 414–415 (quoting *Perkins*, 342 U.S. at 438).

Here, Shivnath Rai's contacts with California amount to the presence of an independently employed sales agent who imports and distributes Shivnath Rai's rice, a 1987 rice shipment into Los Angeles, and the fifteen San Francisco shipments from March 1999 to March 2000. There is no evidence that Shivnath Rai owns property, keeps bank accounts, has employees, solicits business, or has designated an agent for service of process in California. Though Shivnath Rai has exported considerable rice through the Port of San Francisco, these contacts seem to "constitute doing business *with* California, but do not constitute doing business *in* California. This is because engaging in commerce with residents of the forum state is not in and of itself the kind of activity that approximates physical presence within the state's borders." *Bancroft & Masters*, 223 F.3d at 1086. Put another way, while it is clear that Shivnath Rai has stepped through the door, there is no indication that it has sat down and made itself at home.

The idea of the foreign defendant making himself at home in the forum was critical in *Perkins*, where the foreign defendant had set up most aspects of its operations in the forum state. Shivnath Rai's San Francisco shipments pale in comparison to the transplanted business operations in *Perkins*. Further, no employee of Shivnath Rai was alleged to have ever stepped foot in California. Granted, Shivnath Rai's sales agent is located in the forum, but it is uncontested that this sales agent, Alok Mohan of Asian Brands, is neither employed by Shivnath Rai nor at liberty to contract on its behalf. Asian Brands's presence, then, does not appreciably magnify Shivnath Rai's California presence under our general jurisdiction analysis. In sum, Shivnath Rai's contacts with California make it, at most, a visitor to the forum; the "physical presence" necessary for an assertion of general jurisdiction requires more. Accordingly, the district court properly refused to exercise general jurisdiction.

iii. The Exercise of Personal Jurisdiction over Shivnath Rai Would Be Unreasonable

Even assuming that Shivnath Rai had the requisite minimum contacts to support the exercise of general jurisdiction, this Court must analyze whether the assertion of jurisdiction is reasonable. *Asahi Metal Indus. Co. v. Superior Court*, 480 U.S. 102, 113 (1987).

To assess the reasonableness of exercising jurisdiction, we consider seven factors identified by the Supreme Court in *Burger King*:

(1) the extent of a defendant's purposeful interjection into the forum state's affairs; (2) the burden on the defendant of defending in the forum; (3) the extent of conflict with the sovereignty of the defendant's home state; (4) the forum state's interest in adjudicating the dispute; (5) the most efficient judicial resolution of the controversy; (6) the importance of the forum to the plaintiff's interests in convenient and effective relief; and (7) the existence of an alternative forum.

Even a cursory glance at the factors reveals the unreasonableness of exercising jurisdiction in this case.

(1) Assuming that Shivnath Rai's regular shipments into San Francisco constituted "systematic and continuous" contacts, the extent of its *purposeful interjection* is slight for the reasons given in the previous section.

(2) The burden on Shivnath Rai to defend suit in California appears great, given that it is incorporated in India, owns no property in the forum, and has no employees or persons authorized to act on its behalf there. Moreover, its potential witnesses and evidence are likely half a world away.

(3) As for the potential conflict with India's sovereignty, this Court has noted: "Where, as here, the defendant is from a foreign nation rather than another state, the sovereignty barrier is high and undermines the reasonableness of personal jurisdiction." *Leonis,* 1 F.3d at 852.

(4) The underlying dispute involves foreign parties concerning a contract that was executed in England, that called for rice to be delivered in India, and which provided for English arbitration in the event of a dispute. California's interest in adjudicating this suit appears slight.

(5) The "most efficient resolution" factor "involves a comparison of alternative forums." *Id.* Two alternative forums are readily apparent: (1) India, where a parallel lawsuit is currently pending, and (2) England, where the arbitration award was rendered, is final, and may be sued upon.

(6) Given the foregoing analysis, it is unsurprising that Glencore Grain's interests would seem better served by bringing the action in a different forum. Glencore Grain has provided no evidence that California is particularly convenient for it, a Dutch company. Absent any evidence of assets in the California forum against which Glencore Grain could enforce its award, we find Glencore Grain's interest in "convenient and effective" relief is frustrated, not promoted, by bringing suit there.

(7) As noted above, an alternative forum exists in India where proceedings concerning this same arbitration award are currently pending. Moreover, English courts are also available.

The reasonableness calculus clearly compels the conclusion that the exercise of personal jurisdiction over Shivnath Rai would be unreasonable.

CONCLUSION

Personal jurisdiction must be based on a defendant's person or property. Glencore Grain failed to identify any property of or conduct by Shivnath Rai that might serve as the basis for the court's jurisdiction over it; even if Shivnath Rai's conduct supported the exercise of jurisdiction, that exercise would be unreasonable given the circumstances of this case. Accordingly, the district court properly dismissed this action.

Affirmed.

NOTES AND QUESTIONS

1. Due process allows the courts to extend personal jurisdiction over a defendant on two separate grounds: (1) on the basis of contacts directly related to the transaction in question, if the nature of the contacts with the jurisdiction are sufficient so that extending jurisdiction is deemed reasonable; (2) on the basis of contacts unrelated to the transaction in question if those contacts are "continuous and systematic." Which of these two tests is most important with respect to international business activities?

2. What different considerations are there for personal jurisdiction in tort and in contract actions? What can be done to maximize the possibility of personal jurisdiction when drafting an international business contract?

3. On the same day the Supreme Court handed down the *Goodyear Tires* case, the Court also decided *J. McIntyre Machinery Ltd. v. Nicastro,* 131 S. Ct. 2780 (2011). This case involved

a products liability suit filed by Nicastro, a worker who injured his hand in New Jersey while working on a J. McIntyre machine manufactured in England where J. McIntyre operates its business. There was no evidence that J. McIntyre specifically targeted the New Jersey market; it sold its machines on consignment through a U.S. distributor. Nonetheless, the New Jersey Supreme Court, applying the "stream-of-commerce" doctrine of jurisdiction, ruled that there was personal jurisdiction because J. McIntyre knew or reasonably should have known that its products, which are distributed through a nationwide distribution system, may be sold in any of the 50 states including in New Jersey. The Supreme Court majority (Justice Kennedy) reversed the New Jersey Supreme Court, holding that "the placement of a product into the stream of commerce, without more, is not an act of the defendant purposefully directed toward the forum state." The Court further stated that "it is the defendant's [purposeful] actions, not his expectations, that empowers a State's courts to subject him to judgment." 131 S. Ct. at 2788. Justice Ginsburg, joined by Justices Kagan and Sotomayor, dissented on the grounds that, although no general jurisdiction existed over the defendant, specific jurisdiction was present because J. McIntyre targeted the U.S. market as a whole through its distributor and through extensive advertising and attendance at trade shows. Furthermore, its U.S. sales were "good" and it sold several different lines of products in the United States. Justice Ginsburg's opinion distinguished the *Asahi* case: "Asahi, unlike McIntyre, did not itself seek out customers in the United States, it engaged no distributor to promote its wares here, it appeared at no trade shows in the United States, and, of course, it had no Web site advertising its products to the world. Moreover, Asahi was a component-part manufacturer with little control over the final destination of its products once they were delivered into the stream of commerce." 131 S. Ct. at 2803. Justice Ginsburg also observed that "the Court's judgment puts United States plaintiffs at a disadvantage in comparison to similarly situated complainants elsewhere in the world. . . . The European Union Regulation on Jurisdiction and the Recognition and Enforcement of Judgments provides for the exercise of specific jurisdiction 'in matters relating to tort in the courts for the place where the harmful event occurred.'" *Id.*

Which view is correct? Do you agree with the Supreme Court majority's state-by-state test for due process and personal jurisdiction? Suppose McIntyre was sued because its products violated a federal statute; would there be personal jurisdiction in federal court? In Washington DC? In New Jersey? In the United States, federal admiralty law recognizes admiralty jurisdiction in federal court and the application of the general maritime law (a type of federal common law) in products liability claims in admiralty jurisdiction. Suppose the McIntyre machine had been an appurtenant part of a vessel on navigable waters and that Nicastro had sued McIntyre in New Jersey federal court in admiralty jurisdiction and pleaded the general maritime law as the substantive basis of his complaint? What result?

3. Sovereign Immunity

While the previous section examined territorial jurisdiction in U.S. courts, this section turns to an issue of subject matter jurisdiction that is important in international business transactions. In international business, state sovereign immunity may preclude a court from exercising jurisdiction over a defendant. Sovereign immunity accrues not only to a state itself but also to business entities that are owned by or instrumentalities of a state. Under the law of the United States, the exclusive way of suing an entity with sovereign immunity is under the Foreign Sovereign Immunities Act of 1976, 28 U.S.C. §§1602–1611 (2006). The FSIA retains the traditional international law approach that a foreign sovereign is immune from jurisdiction in U.S. courts unless one of the exceptions to immunity found in the FSIA applies.

PROBLEM 8-11

AB-Shanghai Brewing, Ltd., is a joint venture in China formed by AB Industries, a Milwaukee, Wisconsin company, the Shanghai Brewing Company, a state-owned enterprise, and the Shanghai Bureau of Light Industry, a government entity. The ownership structure of the joint venture is as follows: Shanghai Brewing owns 30 percent of the joint venture, Shanghai Light Industries owns 30 percent of the joint venture, and AB Industries owns 40 percent. AB-Shanghai's beer is imported into the United States where a consumer in Ohio drinks the beer and is injured. The victim sues AB Industries and AB-Shanghai Brewing, Ltd., in the United States, but AB-Shanghai argues that it is entitled to foreign sovereign immunity on the ground that it is "an instrumentality" of the Chinese government and is therefore not subject to the jurisdiction of the U.S. courts. Plaintiff's lawyer counters that the joint venture is not under the control of the PRC government as Article 7 of the Joint Venture Law provides that "a joint venture has the right to independently conduct business operation and management within the scope prescribed by Chinese laws and regulations." As the law clerk for the judge presiding over the case, you are asked to answer two questions: (1) Does the joint venture qualify as an agent or instrumentality of a foreign state and (2) is the joint venture entitled to foreign sovereign immunity from jurisdiction in U.S. courts? See *Arbitration Between TCL & CNMC* below and the following note on the doctrine of restrictive immunity.

In re Arbitration Between: Trans Chem. Ltd. & China Nat'l Mach. Import & Export Corp.
United States District Court, Southern District of Texas, 1997
978 F. Supp. 266

LAKE, District Judge.

[This case involved litigation brought by Trans Chemical Ltd. (TCL) to enforce an arbitration award of over $9.4 million against China National Machinery Import & Export Corp. (CNMC), a Chinese company. The award was enforced by the court under the terms of the New York Convention on the Recognition and Enforcement of Foreign Arbitral Awards. The court had to deal with issues under the FSIA.]

JURISDICTION UNDER THE FOREIGN SOVEREIGN IMMUNITIES ACT

The FSIA provides that "[s]ubject to existing international agreements to which the United States [was] a party at the time of the enactment of this Act a foreign state shall be immune from the jurisdiction of the courts of the United States and of the States except as provided in sections 1605 to 1607 of this chapter." 28 U.S.C. §1604. Under 28 U.S.C. §1330(a) "[t]he district courts shall have original jurisdiction without regard to amount in controversy of any nonjury civil action against a foreign state as defined in section 1603(a) of this title as to any claim for relief *in personam* with respect to which the foreign state is not entitled to immunity under sections 1605–1607 of this title or under any applicable international agreement." 28 U.S.C. §1330(a). "Sections 1604 and 1330(a) work in tandem: §1604 bars federal and state courts from exercising jurisdiction when a foreign state *is* entitled to immunity, and §1330(a) confers jurisdiction on district courts to hear suits brought by United States citizens and by aliens when a foreign state is *not* entitled to immunity." *Argentine Republic v. Amerada Hess Shipping Corp.*, 488 U.S. 428, 434 (1989) (emphasis in original).

TCL alleges that CNMC is an "agency or instrumentality of a foreign state" within the meaning of the FSIA. 28 U.S.C. §1603 provides a detailed definition of an "agency or instrumentality of a foreign state":

> (a) A "foreign state," except as used in section 1608 of this title, includes a political subdivision of a foreign state or an agency or instrumentality of a foreign state as defined in subsection (b).
> (b) An "agency or instrumentality of a foreign state" means any entity—
> (1) which is a separate legal person, corporate or otherwise, and
> (2) which is an organ of a foreign state or political subdivision thereof, or a majority of whose shares or other ownership interest is owned by a foreign state or political subdivision thereof, and
> (3) which is neither a citizen of a State of the United States . . . nor created under the laws of any third country.

TCL bears the burden of showing jurisdiction under the FSIA.

The parties do not dispute that CNMC satisfies the first and last elements of §1603(b). CNMC is a corporation organized under the laws of the People's Republic of China ("China") and is not a citizen of a State of the United States or created under the laws of a third country. Their dispute focuses on the second element. CNMC argues that after its 1992 corporate reorganization it is no longer state-owned by the Chinese government as required by §1603(b)(2). CNMC also argues that the court should require TCL to prove, pursuant to *Edlow Int'l v. Nuklearna Elektrarna Krsko (NEK)*, 441 F. Supp. 827 (D.D.C. 1977), that CNMC discharges a governmental function or that the Chinese government exercises direct control over CNMC's operations in a manner indicating that it owns a controlling interest in CNMC.

Based on the court's analysis of Chinese law and CNMC's documents the court concludes that Chinese industrial enterprises "owned by the whole people," including CNMC, are "state-owned," with proprietary rights exercised by the State Council on behalf of the state. Because CNMC is state-owned the court also concludes that CNMC is an agency or instrumentality of the People's Republic of China within the meaning of 28 U.S.C. §1603(b)(2). Professor Rui's opinion that the 1988 Industrial Enterprises Law somehow converted "ownership by the whole people" from "state ownership" into a form of "social ownership" is not supported by Chinese law. The Constitution, the Civil Law, and the Industrial Enterprises Law and its implementing regulations do not refer to a separate category of "social property" or "social ownership," and do not distinguish between "government property" and "social property."

CNMC argues that adherence to the strict majority ownership test of 28 U.S.C. §1603(b)(2) would render virtually every enterprise in China an agency or instrumentality of the Chinese government under the FSIA. To avoid this result CNMC argues that the court should apply the *Edlow* analysis to determine whether CNMC is an organ of the Chinese government or whether the Chinese government actually exercised control over its operations. In this case, however, the court is not faced with the dilemmas faced by the court in *Edlow*. Private enterprises clearly exist in China, and the Chinese government is encouraging their growth. A Chinese private enterprise would not be an agency or instrumentality of the Chinese state under the FSIA. Moreover, the evidence of state ownership of CNMC in this case goes well beyond the naked presumption based on socialist political ideology offered by the plaintiff in *Edlow*. Because Chinese law makes it clear that CNMC remained a state-owned industrial enterprise even after its 1992 reorganization, the court concludes that an analysis under *Edlow* is unnecessary, even if such an analysis were relevant. CNMC is an agency or instrumentality of the People's Republic of China because it is owned by the Chinese state.

DOES THE COURT HAVE JURISDICTION OVER CNMC UNDER AN EXCEPTION TO IMMUNITY?

The court's conclusion that CNMC is an agency or instrumentality of China does not end the court's inquiry under the FSIA. As a foreign state CNMC is entitled to sovereign immunity from suit in the United States unless the relationship or transaction at issue falls within one of the FSIA's exceptions to immunity enumerated in 28 U.S.C. §1605(a). Section 1605(a) provides in relevant part:

> (a) A foreign state shall not be immune from the jurisdiction of courts of the United States or of the States in any case— . . .
> (6) in which the action is brought, either to enforce an agreement made by the foreign state with or for the benefit of a private party to submit to arbitration all or any differences which have arisen or which may arise between the parties with respect to a defined legal relationship, whether contractual or not, concerning a subject matter capable of settlement by arbitration under the laws of the United States, or to confirm an award made pursuant to such an agreement to arbitrate, if (A) the arbitration takes place or is intended to take place in the United States, (B) the agreement or award is or may be governed by a treaty or other international agreement in force for the United States calling for the recognition and enforcement of arbitral awards, (C) the underlying claim, save for the agreement to arbitrate, could have been brought in a United States court under this section or section 1607, or (D) paragraph (1) of this subsection is otherwise applicable.

If one of these exceptions to sovereign immunity applies the court has subject matter jurisdiction.

TCL alleges that the court has jurisdiction under §1605(a)(6)(A) over its claim to confirm the arbitral award pursuant to the FAA. CNMC does not challenge this allegation, and the court agrees that it has jurisdiction over the FAA claim under this subsection.

Section 1605(a)(6) also supplies jurisdiction over TCL's claim under the New York Convention. Section 1605(a)(6)(B) allows the court to exercise jurisdiction over CNMC if the arbitration award "is or may be governed by a treaty or other international agreement in force for the United States calling for the recognition and enforcement of arbitral awards." The Convention falls squarely within the terms of this exception. TCL's claim under the Convention is thus excepted from the immunity provided to CNMC under §1604.

NOTE ON RESTRICTIVE IMMUNITY

The FSIA adopts the doctrine of restrictive immunity under international law, which holds that a state is immune with regard to sovereign or public acts but not with regard to private acts. Section 1605(a) enumerates six types of claims for which there is no immunity from jurisdiction: A foreign state is amenable to jurisdiction in the United States if (1) the foreign state has waived its immunity, (2) the action is based on commercial activity carried on in the United States or having a direct effect in the United States, (3) the action concerns rights in property taken in violation of international law, (4) the action concerns rights in immovable property located in the United States, (5) the action involves a claim for damages under certain circumstances caused by the tortious activity of the foreign state, and (6) the action is brought in connection with an arbitration agreement with a foreign state. These exceptions may cover non-maritime as well as maritime claims. Section 1605(b), however, speaks specifically to maritime claims, stating that "[a] foreign state shall not be immune from the jurisdiction of the courts of the United States in any case in which a suit in admiralty is brought to enforce a maritime lien against a vessel or cargo of the foreign state, which maritime lien is based upon a commercial activity of the foreign state."

4. The Act of State Doctrine

Disputes in international business can also implicate the act of state doctrine, a judicially created doctrine of deference under which U.S. courts will dismiss the case because they refuse to examine and adjudicate the legality of the acts of a foreign state.

PROBLEM 8-12

While vacationing in Costa Rica, Jones receives a flyer under his hotel door advertising certificates of deposit issued by the Costa Rican branch office of Mid-America Bank, an Ohio banking corporation, payable in 12 months at 50 percent interest at Mid-America's office in Costa Rica. Jones immediately heads down to the nearest branch and buys $500,000 worth of certificates. When Jones returns to Ohio, he reads in the local paper that the Costa Rican government has nationalized the Mid-America branch in Costa Rica and has repudiated the obligation under the certificates. Jones sues Mid-America in Ohio for $750,000, the face amount of the certificates plus the interest due. Mid-America moves to dismiss the case on the basis of the act of state doctrine. What is the result? See *Optopics Laboratories* and Fogade below.

Optopics Lab. Corp. v. Savannah Bank of Nigeria, Ltd.
United States District Court, Southern District of New York, 1993
816 F. Supp. 898

SAND, District Judge.

This case is brought by Optopics Laboratories Corporation, a Delaware corporation, as assignee of Ashford Laboratories, Inc., against Savannah Bank of Nigeria, Ltd. for non-payment on a letter of credit issued by defendant. Jurisdiction is found under 28 U.S.C. §1330, which provides that district courts shall have original jurisdiction over non-jury civil actions against a foreign state, and also under the Foreign Sovereign Immunities Act. Currently before the Court are cross-motions for summary judgment. Because we find that no genuine issues of material fact are in dispute and that plaintiff is entitled to payment on the Letter of Credit as a matter of law, plaintiff's motion for summary judgment is granted. Defendant's motion for summary judgment is denied.

FACTUAL BACKGROUND

The material facts surrounding the transaction at issue in this lawsuit are undisputed. In October 1982, Ashford Laboratories, Inc. ("Ashford"), a New Jersey corporation, contracted to sell to a Nigerian importer, Mabson Pharmaceuticals, Ltd. ("Mabson"), cold capsules for $32,265. In order to effect payment, Mabson applied for an irrevocable letter of credit with defendant, a government owned bank, Savannah Bank of Nigeria (the "Bank"). On the reverse side of the Application are printed certain "General Terms & Conditions," including one which will be discussed in further detail below, which reads: "This Letter of Credit is subject to the usual terms and conditions operating in the center where the Credit be established."

Subsequent to the submission of the Application to the Bank by Mabson, Bank America International ("Bank America") advised Ashford that a letter of credit known as L-82493 in the amount of $32,265, payable in New York, in United States dollars, had been established by the defendant in Ashford's favor. The Letter of Credit is a two-page document, and is dated November 1, 1982. The Letter of Credit provides that it is subject to the Uniform Customs and Practice for Documentary Credits, 1974 Revision, International Chamber of Commerce Publication No. 290 (the "UCP").

After the Letter of Credit was established and in reliance thereon, Ashford shipped the pharmaceuticals to Mabson. Ashford presented conforming documents in strict compliance with the Letter of Credit on or about November 30, 1982. Each document specifically identified in the Letter of Credit was submitted by Ashford.

The Bank approved the Letter of Credit for payment on December 20, 1982. Both the Application and the Letter of Credit made clear that due to Nigeria's foreign exchange controls, a Form M would have to be filed by the importer, Mabson, through the defendant. A Form M is an application directed to the Central Bank to purchase foreign exchange. Defendant complied with this requirement on January 20, 1983, with the request that "the Foreign Currency should be paid to Bank of America, New York." The record suggests that Mabson also complied with related procedures regarding the Form M.

The Bank failed to pay on the Letter of Credit, claiming that it was unable to remit United States dollars to Bank America due to the failure of the Central Bank of Nigeria to provide foreign exchange. A June 8, 1983 cable from the Bank advised Bank America that it could negotiate the documents for the Letter of Credit but that Bank America would not be reimbursed by defendant until foreign exchange cover was made available. Similar cables were sent by defendant to Bank America on February 21, 1984, and January 15, 1985. Bank America, justifiably, has not negotiated the payment of the Letter of Credit. Significantly, the defendant has admitted that it would like to pay the Letter of Credit, and has offered to do so in Naira, the Nigerian currency. Plaintiff has rejected that offer.

Sometime subsequent to defendant's acceptance of the Letter of Credit, the Government of Nigeria engaged in a program to reschedule the payment of foreign debt, referred to as the "refinancing exercise." Defendant contends that as part of that refinancing exercise, Nigeria required, as a condition to payment on the Letter of Credit, that Ashford submit a claim form to Chase Manhattan Bank. Defendant further avers that at least as early as April 15, 1985, Ashford received a document entitled "The Central Bank of Nigeria—Circular dated 18th April, 1984," which gave notice that creditors must lodge claims with Chase Manhattan Bank to have debts paid by the Central Bank. Ashford never submitted any such claim form. Defendant asserts that due to Ashford's failure to submit the required document, the conditions of the Letter of Credit were not strictly complied with and the Bank is not required to honor the Letter of Credit.

Two other sets of facts should be noted at this point. In a letter to Mabson dated October 5, 1990, defendant acknowledged receipt of payment from Mabson for the Letter of Credit, and stated that "[w]e have not been able to remit same to the exporters [i.e., Ashford] due to a non-provision of the required foreign exchange cover by the Central Bank of Nigeria." This indicates both that refusal to release funds is not due to any withholding of the money by the bank's customer, and furthermore, that the reason for the refusal is non-provision of foreign exchange, as stated in the cables to Bank America, and not any failure on Ashford's part to strictly comply with the terms of the Letter of Credit.

ACT OF STATE

Defendant argues that the Nigerian exchange controls are governmental policy, and that any adjudication by this Court would be an interference with a sovereign act of state. Although we find that the act of state doctrine is not implicated, it is a claim which is of the utmost seriousness and will be addressed fully.

The act of state doctrine recognizes both that the laws of nations as applied within their own borders are sovereign and should not be passed upon by our courts, and that the judiciary must be restrained from rendering decisions which will affect the United States' foreign policy, a sphere of power constitutionally assigned to the executive and legislative branches. "The act of state doctrine declares that a United States court will not adjudicate a politically sensitive dispute which would require the court to judge the legality of the sovereign act of a foreign state." *International Ass'n of Machinists v. OPEC*, 649 F.2d 1354, 1358 (9th Cir. 1981), *cert. denied*, 454 U.S. 1163 (1982).

A prerequisite for the application of the act of state doctrine is that the act in question is one which takes effect entirely within the boundaries of the sovereign nation. Where this is not the case, our courts will give extraterritorial effect to the law of another nation, based on comity, only where it does not conflict with the laws and policies of the United States.

Defendant ignores a number of Second Circuit cases which indicate the nature of the pertinent inquiry in determining whether the application of Nigeria's exchange control regulations to the Letter of Credit takes place entirely within the boundaries of Nigeria.

In *Allied Bank Int'l v. Banco Credito Agricola*, 757 F.2d 516 (2d Cir. 1985), the plaintiff brought an action to recover on promissory notes issued by three Costa Rican banks wholly owned by the Government of Costa Rica, which were payable in United States dollars, in New York. The banks defaulted on the notes solely due to the Costa Rican government's suspending all external debt payments. The court explained that the primary concern in applying the act of state doctrine is whether "adjudication would embarrass or hinder the executive in the realm of foreign relations," and that the rule is to be applied flexibly on a case by case basis. 757 F.2d at 521.

The Second Circuit in *Allied* held that the applicability of the act of state doctrine depends on the situs of the debt, defined as the right to receive repayment from the banks in accordance with the loan agreements. The court viewed the Costa Rican government's actions in extinguishing plaintiff's right to receive payment as a "taking," and reasoned that if the taking occurred within the foreign sovereign's territory, then the act of state doctrine would prohibit the courts of this country from adjudicating the matter. The court said that locating the debt "depends in large part on whether the purported taking can be said to have 'come to complete fruition within the dominion of the [foreign] government.'" 757 F.2d at 521.

In applying that standard, the *Allied* court held that "Costa Rica could not wholly extinguish the Costa Rican banks' obligation to timely pay United States dollars to Allied in New York. Thus the situs of the debt was not Costa Rica." 757 F.2d at 521. The court proceeded to state that Costa Rica's

> interest in the contracts at issue is essentially limited to the extent to which it can unilaterally alter the payment terms. Costa Rica's potential jurisdiction over the debt is not sufficient to locate the debt there for the purposes of the act of state doctrine analysis.

757 F.2d at 522.

The *Allied* court further stated that "acts of foreign governments purporting to have extraterritorial effect . . . should be recognized by the courts only if they are consistent with the law and policy of the United States." 757 F.2d at 522. Because the United States would not condone the Costa Rican government's attempt to change unilaterally the terms of the contracts, the court did not give effect to the Costa Rican directives.

Two other Second Circuit cases employ the same analysis and reach the same result. In *Braka v. Bancomber*, 762 F.2d 222 (2d Cir. 1985), a case decided after *Allied*, the plaintiffs, United States citizens, purchased peso and dollar certificates of deposits from a Mexican bank, with the principal and interest payable in Mexico. Subsequently, the Mexican government decreed that all domestic obligations would be paid in pesos and at a devalued exchange rate. Plaintiffs then filed suit in federal district court in New York. The court held that the situs of the debt was Mexico, since the Mexican decree could wholly extinguish the plaintiffs' rights within the dominion of the foreign government. The act of state doctrine therefore barred plaintiffs' recovery.

In *Garcia v. Chase Manhattan Bank, N.A.*, 735 F.2d 645 (2d Cir. 1984), plaintiffs sued over the proceeds of two certificates of deposit which were issued by Chase's Cuba branch prior to the time Cuba seized the assets of the bank. The CDs provided that they were redeemable at any Chase branch worldwide. The Court found that the situs of the debt was wherever it could be collected, and therefore the acts of the Cuban government could not wholly extinguish the plaintiffs' rights. The act of state doctrine was therefore inapplicable.

The application of *Allied*, *Braka*, and *Garcia* to the case before this Court is clear. The "taking" is plaintiff's right to receive the proceeds of the Letter of Credit in United States dollars at a bank in New York. The act of the Nigerian government in refusing to provide the foreign exchange to defendant is not enough to wholly extinguish the Nigerian bank's obligation to pay on the Letter of Credit in New York. Therefore, the situs of the debt is not Nigeria, and the act of state doctrine is not implicated. Furthermore, because the Nigerian government's attempt to unilaterally modify a private letter of credit contract is against the law and policy of the United States, this Court will not enforce the Nigerian policy extraterritorially.

In response to this caselaw, defendant appears to place reliance on last year's Supreme Court decision in *Republic of Argentina & Banco Central de la Republica Argentina v. Weltover, et al.*, 504 U.S. 607 (1992). That case however did not address the act of state doctrine at all, but instead dealt with the Foreign Sovereign Immunities Act ("FSIA"), the application of which has not been seriously challenged in this action. *Weltover* makes clear that the FSIA would not bar plaintiff here, as the acts of the defendant clearly fall within the commercial activity exception in the statute and have a direct effect in the United States.

For the foregoing reasons, we find that the act of state doctrine is inapplicable and does not bar plaintiff's suit against the bank.

[Turning to the letter of credit issues, the court held that Ashford had strictly complied with the terms of the letter of credit and was entitled to payment from Savannah Bank and entered judgment in favor of the plaintiff.]

FOGADE v. ENB Revocable Trust
United States Court of Appeals, Eleventh Circuit, 2001
263 F.3d 1274

CARNES, Circuit Judge.

[In early 1994, Venezuela suffered a financial crisis precipitated by the collapse of Venezuela's largest bank. A number of Venezuelan banks were forced to seek assistance from the Fondo de Garantia de Depositós y Protección Bancaria (FOGADE), a Venezuelan government agency similar to the Federal Deposit Insurance Corporation, which provides financial assistance to Venezuelan depository institutions. Among those banks seeking assistance was Bancor, a stock corporation, a majority of whose shares was owned by Corpofin, another bank. Three individuals—Juan Santaella, Julio Leanez, and Oscar Zamora, the defendants in this case—were minority shareholders of Bancor and sat on Bancor's board. These same individuals were also minority shareholders and members of the board of Corpofin. Between March and June of 1994, Bancor received $300 million in financial assistance from FOGADE. On the grounds that Bancor had not repaid its debts or increased its capital, FOGADE caused Bancor to be "intervened," a process similar to placing a company in receivership. In September 1994, upon discovering that Corpofin had large unguaranteed debts with Bancor, FOGADE also placed Corpofin in receivership. As part of the intervention process, FOGADE also removed Santaella, Leanez, and Zamora from the boards of Bancor and Corpofin and appointed new directors. In October 1995, the Venezuelan government ordered Bancor to be liquidated. Corpofin remained in receivership.

Corpofin's intervenor subsequently discovered that on May 9, 1994, one day prior to their removal from Corpofin's board, defendants caused Corpofin to engage in a series of transactions that transferred all of Corpofin's ownership of shares of Eastern National Bank (ENB), a U.S. bank chartered in Miami, to several business entities, including the ENB revocable trust, which were directly controlled by defendants. The shares of ENB were worth $30 million but Corpofin received only $870,000 for the shares. On May 9, 1994, Corpofin owed Bancor $16.5 million, which would have been satisfied out of the shares of ENB shares that Corpofin owned.

Plaintiffs FOGADE and Corpofin brought suit in the federal district court for the Southern District of Florida, alleging that the individual defendants and their business entities unlawfully misappropriated ENB shares, which took place primarily in Miami. The district court granted summary judgment in favor of plaintiffs and ordered the shares of ENB be returned to Corpofin. Defendants appealed to the Eleventh Circuit Court of Appeals.]

THE ACT OF STATE ISSUES

Defendants asserted a large number of affirmative defenses [in the district court]. On appeal, defendants have pursued only one of the theories they asserted in their affirmative defenses. In essence, defendants contend that FOGADE illegally confiscated all of their financial interests in Venezuela, including their interest in Corpofin, and then, by causing Corpofin to pursue defendants' ownership interests in Eastern National Bank, sought to extend that unlawful confiscation into U.S. territory. Specifically, defendants argue FOGADE is guilty of confiscation and mismanagement of Corpofin and Bancor and assert RICO, conspiracy, fraud, reclamation of shares, unjust enrichment, accounting, waste, and breach of fiduciary theories. Plaintiffs respond before us, as they did in the district court, that the act of state doctrine bars consideration of the lawfulness of the Venezuelan government's intervention through FOGADE of Corpofin.

The district court agreed with plaintiffs that under the act of state doctrine the intervention of Corpofin must be deemed valid and cannot be subject to review in a United States court. Relying on *Banco Nacional de Cuba v. Sabbatino*, 376 U.S. 398 (1964), the district court concluded that:

> [w]hether FOGADE and others violated Venezuelan law in committing the alleged acts is irrelevant; "the Judicial Branch will not examine the validity of a taking of property within its own territory by a foreign sovereign government . . . even if the complaint alleges that the taking violates customary international law."

Defendants' primary challenge to that reasoning and conclusion is based upon the legislative overruling of *Sabbatino* by passage of the so-called "Second Hickenlooper Amendment," 22 U.S.C. §2370(e)(2). The Second Hickenlooper Amendment provides, in relevant part:

> Notwithstanding any other provision of law, no court in the United States shall decline on the ground of the federal act of state doctrine to make a determination on the merits . . . in a case in which a claim of title or other right to property is asserted . . . based upon (or traced through) a confiscation or other taking after January 1, 1959, by an act of [] state in violation of the principles of international law. . . .

22 U.S.C. §2370(e)(2). Thus, defendants argue that the district court should not have applied the act of state doctrine to dismiss their counterclaims because plaintiffs' intervention of Corpofin constituted a confiscation of property in violation of the principles of international law.

The Second Hickenlooper Amendment did overrule, at least with respect to confiscations of property, the *Sabbatino* decision to the extent that it held that the act of state doctrine would apply without regard to whether a foreign state's actions violated international law. The question is how the act of state doctrine and *Sabbatino*, as modified by the Second Hickenlooper Amendment, apply here.

The Second Hickenlooper Amendment has three requirements that must be met before it applies. The Amendment requires: (1) a claim of title or other right to property; (2) based upon or traced through a confiscation or other taking; (3) in violation of international law. 22 U.S.C. §2370(e)(2). Here, the parties do not dispute that the first requirement is met, because the Venezuelan-controlled Corpofin has asserted a claim of right to the shares of ENB. Regarding the second requirement, defendants argue that Corpofin's alleged ownership interest in ENB is "based upon" Venezuela's intervention of Corpofin, which, defendants contend, was an "illegal confiscation or other taking." As for the third requirement, defendants argue that Venezuela's confiscation of Corpofin without payment of compensation to the individual defendants constituted a violation of international law.

Even assuming that FOGADE's intervention of Corpofin constituted a "confiscation or other taking" (the second requirement), we are not persuaded that it was carried out in violation of international law (the third requirement). As a rule, when a foreign nation confiscates the property of its own nationals, it does not implicate principles of international law. None of the decisions that the defendants rely upon are to the contrary. They involve misappropriations by foreign governments of property that belonged to citizens of other countries. Because Venezuela's act of intervening Corpofin, a Venezuelan corporation owned entirely by Venezuelan nationals, does not violate international law, the Second Hickenlooper Amendment does not preclude application of the act of state doctrine.

Seeking to avoid this result, defendants attempt to shift the focus away from the plaintiffs' act of intervening Corpofin to their alleged "extraterritorial confiscation" of ENB, which, defendants stress, was at all times located in the United States. In other words, defendants want to collapse the plaintiffs' intervention of Corpofin and their subsequent "confiscation" of the ENB shares into one long drawn out act, arguing that the intervention of Corpofin was "for the sole purpose of confiscating the ENB shares."

Confiscations by a foreign state of property located in the United States, even if the property belongs to one of the foreign state's own nationals, implicates principles of international law. Moreover, a foreign state's expropriations occur in the jurisdiction in which they are perfected. Defendants' position is that the plaintiffs' actions about which they complain were not perfected in Venezuela with the intervention of Corpofin, but in this country when the ENB shares were "confiscated" by means of this lawsuit. That confiscation, the defendants argue, constituted a violation of international law, thereby precluding application of the act of state doctrine.

We disagree. As previously noted, the Second Hickenlooper Amendment provides that a federal court must not decline on act of state grounds to address the merits in a case when a party asserts a claim of right "*based upon* . . . a confiscation or other taking . . . by an act of state in violation of the principles of international law. . . ." 22 U.S.C. §2370(e)(2) (emphasis added). Thus, the claim to property must be "based upon"—that is, must be derivative of—an act of state that is in violation of international law.

Here the plaintiffs' claim of right to the ENB shares is "based upon" FOGADE's intervention of Corpofin and the defendants' contention that the plaintiffs obtained the ENB shares illegally is also "based upon" FOGADE's intervention of Corpofin. If the plaintiffs legitimately controlled FOGADE, the defendants would have no argument that plaintiffs acted illegally in taking control of ENB. The premise of defendants' position that FOGADE would not have standing to sue on behalf of Corpofin is that FOGADE unlawfully intervened it. So, everything turns on FOGADE's intervention of Corpofin. Thus, the defendants must show that the alleged confiscation of Corpofin was in violation of international law, not that the plaintiffs' subsequent and successful attempt to recapture the ENB shares through Corpofin was. As we have already explained, however, the intervention of Corpofin was purely domestic (to Venezuela) in nature, and does not violate international law. Therefore, because FOGADE's intervention of Corpofin, upon which Corpofin's claim to ENB is based, was not in violation of international law, the Second Hickenlooper Amendment does not apply to preclude the application of the act of state doctrine to defendants' affirmative defenses questioning the standing of plaintiffs to sue because of the alleged illegality of the intervention of Corpofin.

NOTES AND QUESTIONS

1. The act of state doctrine reached a fever pitch of political controversy when in *Banco Nacional de Cuba v. Sabbatino*, 376 U.S. 398 (1964), discussed in the FOGADE case,

the Supreme Court invoked it to refuse to disturb a nationalization of property in Cuba by the Castro government despite the fact there was a clear violation of international law.

2. In *Optopics Lab. v. Savannah Bank*, why did the plaintiffs reject the offer of the Savannah Bank to pay in Nigerian currency? Savannah Bank also asked Bank America to negotiate the documents for the letter of credit. Why did Bank America refuse? The court rejected the use of the act of state doctrine as a defense to payment by Savannah Bank and entered judgment for the plaintiff, but now the plaintiff has a practical problem. What must plaintiff do to collect?

PROBLEM 8-13

Vost Chemical Corporation is a Delaware corporation with its principal offices in New York. Three months ago, Vost entered into an agreement with the Jiang Trading Company (JTC), a Chinese company located in Shanghai, China, for the sale of styrene monomer, a raw material used in the production of automobiles, computers, and a variety of other products. The sales contract required that the styrene had to be delivered in Shanghai and that Vost had to transport and bear the risk of loss of the goods to the port of Shanghai and was obligated to place the goods at the disposal of the buyer, who was responsible for import clearance. To secure payment, JTC obtained an irrevocable letter of credit for the full price of the goods ($1.2 million) from the Shanghai branch of the Bank of China, the government central bank. No place of payment was designated for the letter of credit, but as the Bank of China has a branch office in New York and regularly made payments on its letter of credit business there, Vost assumed that it would submit the documents through that New York branch bank and receive payment there.

Vost shipped the styrene by ocean carrier and forwarded all necessary documents to complete the transaction to the New York branch of the Bank of China, asking that payment be made through the New York branch to Vost's bank account in New York.

The styrene arrived safely in Shanghai. However, when it was passing through Customs, the cargo was seized by the Chinese Bureau of Customs for nonpayment of past tariff obligations by JTC. As a result, the Bank of China notified Vost that the documents were inadequate, and it was refusing payment on the letter of credit. Advise Vost.

5. *International Comity and* Forum Non Conveniens

Another judicially created doctrine used by courts to refuse jurisdiction based upon discretionary concerns is the doctrine of "*forum non conveniens.*" This doctrine can be particularly important in business litigation brought by foreign plaintiffs against U.S. companies. Most of the witnesses and evidence may be located in a foreign country; U.S. courts may dismiss the action on the grounds that the lawsuit should be brought in a foreign forum.

DeYoung v. Beddome

United States District Court, Southern District of New York, 1989
707 F. Supp. 132

Mukasey, District Judge.

[Plaintiffs, individual shareholders of Dome Petroleum Limited (Dome), a Canadian producer of oil and natural gas, brought an action in federal district court to challenge a proposed acquisition of Dome by Amoco Canada Petroleum Company (AC), a Canadian subsidiary of Amoco Corporation (Amoco), an Indiana corporation with its headquarters in Chicago. Both of the Amoco entities were named as defendants in the case along with two individuals, Beddome and MacDonald, officers and directors of Dome. Plaintiffs alleged various state law business tort claims against both the individual and corporate defendants and in addition alleged claims as part of a class action brought on behalf of Dome shareholders that the defendants failed to comply with disclosure requirements of §14(a) of the Securities and Exchange Act, 15 U.S.C. §78n(a). Prior to filing the lawsuit in the United States, the plaintiffs had filed a previous action in a Canadian court against the defendants challenging the acquisition on similar grounds under Canadian law, including lack of adequate disclosure. The Canadian action was still pending when the plaintiffs filed the second action in the United States. After the U.S. lawsuit was filed, the Canadian court entered judgment in favor of the defendants, finding that disclosure was adequate. Before the federal district court were the defendants' motions to dismiss the action on the basis of *forum non conveniens* and international comity.]

For the reasons set forth below, I grant the motion to dismiss based on international comity. Accordingly, I do not reach the other grounds for dismissal asserted by defendants.

Hilton v. Guyot, 159 U.S. 113 (1895) provides the basis for applying the doctrine of international comity in federal courts, and defines it as

> the recognition which one nation allows within its territory to the legislative, executive, or judicial acts of another nation, having due regard both to international duty and convenience, and to the rights of its own citizens, or of other persons who are under the protection of its laws.

159 U.S. at 164, 16 S. Ct. at 143.

It is essential that the foreign proceeding or judgment not offend laws or public policy of the forum jurisdiction, or violate the rights of its citizens. Here it is significant that the foreign jurisdiction involved is Canada, "a sister common law jurisdiction with procedures akin to our own." *Clarkson Co. v. Shaheen,* 544 F.2d 624, 630 (2d Cir. 1976). In fact, the procedures adopted by the Court of Queens Bench in Alberta under the CBCA, and affirmed by the Court of Appeal, would seem to be if anything more protective of the rights of the shareholder plaintiffs in this case than procedures they might expect to encounter in this country. Against these considerations plaintiffs place in the balance their claim under Section 14(a) of the Securities Exchange Act, 15 U.S.C. §78n(a) (1981), and Rule 14a-9 promulgated thereunder, and argue that we should not risk compromise of federally protected rights by relegating these plaintiffs to Canadian courts that might not protect them. Furthermore, they argue that the Canadian court's decision should not be accorded comity here because it did not necessarily decide issues of full disclosure.

Although plaintiffs assert that Canadian law is less advantageous to them than the law that would be applied were the case to remain in this Court, they have made no showing that Canadian law does not afford them a cause of action to pursue their claims there.

Rather, plaintiffs' main objection to Canadian case law governing securities class actions and derivative actions seems to be that it does not permit contingent fee arrangements. But even if I were to assume *arguendo* that Canadian procedures are less favorable to the plaintiff than those in this Court, including particularly the unavailability of contingent fees in Canada, such factors have been found, in the context of *forum non conveniens,* not persuasive. There is no reason to accord that minor failing any greater weight in applying principles of international comity.

Accordingly, Canadian law provides causes of action that are the same in all significant respects as those available under United States law. Plaintiffs could have sought relief in Canadian courts, and may still do so, provided of course that Canadian principles of collateral estoppel would not bar such a suit.

Whether the prior judgment satisfies all the requirements of collateral estoppel under Canadian law need not be decided here, however. That decision is best left to the Canadian courts. Nevertheless, I find that the issue of full disclosure was sufficiently considered by the Canadian court so as to invoke international comity principles. Although plaintiffs vigorously dispute this question, my review of the Canadian proceedings convinces me that the issue of full disclosure was actually decided by the Canadian court. I have already described the procedures by which the Canadian court ensured that the corporation provided shareholders with full disclosure. In addition, in its July 14, 1988 judgment, the court specifically stated that it was "satisfied that in the Notice of Special Meeting, Notice Concerning Application and Information Circular and Proxy Statements of Dome dated April 26, 1988 Dome has provided the shareholders of Dome with full, true and plain disclosure of all material facts surrounding the Plan of Arrangement as regards the shareholders of Dome in accordance with the Interim Order." Order at 2. Those are the same disclosure documents challenged in the actions at bar.

When motions to dismiss were first filed, I found compelling defendants' arguments to dismiss on grounds of *forum non conveniens*. Although in the interim the Canadian court's decision has altered the dispositive issue here to one of comity, principles of *forum non conveniens* would support the result here. As defined in *Gulf Oil Corp. v. Gilbert*, 330 U.S. 501 (1947) and summarized in *Reyno*, 454 U.S. at 241 n.6, the criteria that doctrine provides for choosing between available forums relate to the private interests of the litigants — primarily convenience in gaining access to documents and witnesses for discovery and trial, and the public interest — including the "local interest in having localized controversies decided at home; the interest in having the trial of a diversity case in a forum that is at home with the law that must govern the action; the avoidance of unnecessary problems in conflict of laws, or in the application of foreign law; and the unfairness of burdening citizens in an unrelated forum with jury duty." *Id.*

[A] plaintiff's choice of forum weighs far less heavily in a case such as this where plaintiffs sue strictly in a representative or derivative capacity. Plaintiffs in such a case have only a small direct interest in a large controversy in which there are many potential plaintiffs, usually in many potential jurisdictions. In such a case, the plaintiffs who actually sue, like Messrs. Beddome and Katz, do not claim to be witnesses to anything other than their ownership of an interest in the dispute and their desire, and that of their lawyers, to represent others similarly situated. Such a case will often turn on events that occurred in a jurisdiction other than where the plaintiff lives, on evidence to be sought from witnesses and documents in such other jurisdiction, and on the law of such other jurisdiction.

Four of the five defendants in this case are domiciled in Canada. The acts of Dome's board challenged by plaintiffs took place in Canada. The agreement being challenged was negotiated between two Canadian corporations, and signed, in Canada. The underlying Dome documents are located in Canada. Indeed, the only location outside Canada where the parties have plausibly suggested any documents might be found is Chicago, where Amoco has its headquarters.

At oral argument, plaintiffs' counsel hypothesized that investment and commercial bankers in New York "controlled and made the decisions, and that is when those decisions were made." There is not a single allegation in either complaint to that effect, and not one of those unspecified bankers has been named as a defendant in either action.

To the contrary, the gravamen of both complaints is that Dome stockholders are being injured by the misconduct of Dome's board, aided and abetted by Amoco and AC. To the extent that the alleged misconduct involves rejecting bids from likely suitors, the only two identified in the complaints, whose representatives presumably would testify to the advantage they offer over AC, are Trans Canada Pipelines Limited and Imperial Oil Limited—both Canadian entities.

Plaintiffs note also that Dome's transfer agent, the Bank of New York, distributed to stockholders certain interim reports regarding the Dome-AC deal. But even if those reports played some role in the alleged impropriety, there is no suggestion that witnesses whose testimony bears on the content of the reports are to be found in New York. The transfer agent's role in their distribution is utterly insignificant in any evaluation of where the lawsuit should proceed.

Where the plaintiffs' substantive contribution to the litigation and the evidence to be found in this jurisdiction are both nil, where no potential witness in the litigation who may be unwilling to attend a trial is subject to this Court's process, and where discovery of third parties in Canada (*e.g.* Trans Canada and Imperial) would have to be conducted by cumbersome letters rogatory, it is downright perverse to argue that there is anything close to equal convenience in trying this case here or in Canada, modern communications notwithstanding. The public interest factors present here weigh, if possible, even more heavily in favor of having this case decided in Canada. There is little doubt that, applying New York choice of law rules, *Klaxon Co. v. Stentor Elec. Mfg. Co.*, 313 U.S. 487 (1941), Canadian law would govern the common law claims relating to corporate governance of Dome that are at the heart of both complaints. Dome, a Canadian corporation that conducts its operations in Canada, is that country's second largest producer of natural gas and third largest producer of crude oil. Under the governmental interest test that prevails to determine choice of law in New York, Canadian law would control issues of corporate governance here. That would compel this Court to apply an unfamiliar body of law, a prospect that argues strongly for dismissal.

Again, the interest of Canada in having controversies relating to one of its major corporations decided at home is substantial. That consideration, as well, supports dismissal. In this case, Canada's government and courts have already taken an active role over the subject matter of this dispute. Two agencies of the Canadian government approved the transaction, and the Court of Queen's Bench of Alberta, in Calgary, determined, after four days of hearings, just how Dome was to go about securing the approval of its creditors and shareholders before the proposed deal with AC could be consummated. Notably, two-thirds approval by stockholders was necessary before the transaction could be effected. As mentioned above, litigation was commenced in the Canadian courts to challenge the transaction. Finally, the Canadian courts have found that Dome fully disclosed all pertinent information to shareholders and that the transaction was fair. It would be highly intrusive for this Court to involve itself in a matter that has so heavily engaged the attention of both the executive and judicial authorities of Canada.

In addition, although this Court's unfamiliarity with Canadian law extends also to docket conditions in Canadian courts and the parties have offered us no proof on the subject, docket congestion in this Court is a persistent affliction. That, too, is a factor to consider in deciding whether to accept a case that can be litigated elsewhere.

In sum, I find that considerations of international comity mandate dismissal here. Moreover, this result is fully in accord with principles of *forum non conveniens*. Accordingly, defendants' motions for summary judgment are granted, and the complaints are dismissed.

So ordered.

NOTES AND QUESTIONS

1. Why did the plaintiffs bring a second action in the United States?

2. The *forum non conveniens* determination is up to the "sound discretion" of the trial court. It is a "balancing" determination based on a combination of so-called public interest factors and private interest factors. Did the court in *DeYoung* make the right decision?

3. How does the "comity" determination differ from *forum non conveniens*? Can you isolate the comity factors that are responsible for the court's decision? Is this doctrine even more flexible than *forum non conveniens*?

4. Sometimes *forum non conveniens* considerations become entangled with additional matters. What happens if the matter involves a business contract that contains a forum selection clause? In *GDG Acquisitions, LLC v. Government of Belize*, 749 F.3d 1024 (11th Cir. 2014), GDG, a Florida limited liability company, sued the government of Belize in federal district court in Florida for payments under a Master Lease for telecommunications equipment, alleging that Belize owed over $14 million in unpaid lease payments. The Master Lease contained a forum selection clause providing that all disputes relating to the lease had to be brought in a "court of competent jurisdiction" in Florida. Belize moved to dismiss based on: (1) foreign sovereign immunity; (2) *forum non conveniens*; and (3) international comity. The district court granted the motion to dismiss on the grounds of *forum non conveniens* and international comity because the dispute was essentially between two Belizean interests. 935 F. Supp. 2d at 1351–1353. The district court did not address the impact of the forum selection clause issue. On the *forum non conveniens* issue, the district court relied upon the Supreme Court's decision in *Sinochem Int'l Co. v. Malaysia Int'l Shipping Corp.*, 549 U.S. 422, 425 (2007) ("A district court . . . may dispose of an action by *forum non conveniens* dismissal, bypassing questions of subject matter and personal jurisdiction, when considerations of convenience, fairness, and judicial economy so warrant."). On appeal, the Court of Appeals for the Eleventh Circuit vacated the district court's decision and remanded the case. The Court of Appeals held that the district court should not have dismissed the case without considering the impact of the forum selection clause, specifically: (1) Was it mandatory or permissive? and (2) can the presumption of validity of the forum selection clause be overcome? *See* 749 F.3d at 1028–1029 ("When parties agree to a forum-selection clause, they waive the right to challenge the preselected forum as inconvenient or less convenient for themselves or their witnesses, or for their pursuit of the litigation. A court accordingly must deem the private-interest factors to weigh entirely in favor of the preselected forum. As a consequence, a district court may consider arguments about public-interest factors only. Because those factors will rarely defeat a transfer motion, the practical result is that the forum-selection clauses should control except in unusual cases.") (quoting *Atlantic Marine Constr. Co. v. U.S. Dist. Court for the W. Dist. of Texas*, 134 S. Ct. 568, 582 (2013)).

5. *International comity*. In the *GDG Acquisitions* case, as stated in the previous note, the district court granted the motion to dismiss on additional grounds of international comity, which is "an abstention doctrine that reflects the extent to which the law of one nation, as put in force in its territory . . . shall be allowed to operate within the dominion of another nation." *Hilton v. Guyot*, 159 U.S. 113, 163 (1895). Most often international comity is applied retrospectively to determine whether to give effect to the judgment of a foreign tribunal or to defer to parallel foreign proceedings. For retrospective international comity, the courts consider: (1) whether the foreign court is competent; (2) whether the foreign judgment is fraudulent; and (3) whether the foreign judgment violates American standards or public policy, decency, and justice. *See Ungaro-Benages v.*

Dresdner Bank AG, 379 F.3d 1227, 1238 (11th Cir. 2004). The *GDG Acquisitions* case was a rare application of international comity prospectively. The Court of Appeals ruled that prospective international comity must be evaluated by: (1) the strength of the interest of the government of the United States; (2) the strength of the interest of the foreign government; and (3) the adequacy of the alternative forum. *GDG Acquisitions*, 749 F.3d at 1030. Based on its analysis of these factors, the Court of Appeals held that the district court had abused its discretion. The major error that the court found was that the Master Lease unambiguously selected Florida law to govern the dispute. 749 F.3d at 1032. The Court of Appeals accordingly vacated the district court's judgment and remanded the case.

6. Service of Process

In a business litigation brought in a U.S. court, how does the plaintiff serve court papers on a defendant located in a foreign country? The following case deals with this issue.

Conax Florida Corp. v. Astrium Ltd.
United States District Court, Middle District of Florida, 2007
499 F. Supp. 2d 1287

WILSON, United States Magistrate Judge.

The plaintiff, Conax Florida Corporation, is headquartered in St. Petersburg, Florida. It specializes in the design and manufacture of pyrotechnic valves ("pyrovalves") that are used in satellites. Defendant Astrium Limited is an English company with its principal place of business in the United Kingdom. It builds and maintains satellites for civil and military communications.

In 2000, the defendant contacted the plaintiff regarding the purchase of pyrovalves for its Eurostar 3000 commercial telecommunication satellites. The parties had previously developed a relationship when the defendant purchased from the plaintiff pyrovalves for its aerospace industry satellites.

On July 24, 2000, the defendant gave the plaintiff in Florida an Authorization to Proceed and work order to manufacture pyrovalves for its Eurostar 3000 satellites. In March 2001, the defendant sent a team of employees to the plaintiff's facility in Florida in order to advance from the work authorization to the final contract. The parties reached in Florida an oral agreement, which was subsequently placed in writing and signed by the defendant in England. The parties' Subcontract for Pyrotechnic Valves ("Subcontract") was then executed by the plaintiff in Florida.

The defendant agreed to purchase from the plaintiff 406 pyrovalves, which were to be manufactured in four batches between April 2001 and June 2005. The Subcontract afforded the defendant full access to the plaintiff's facilities in order to observe, inspect, examine, and evaluate the plaintiff's work.

Accordingly, approximately every other month throughout the term of the Subcontract the defendant's representatives traveled to the plaintiff's facility in St. Petersburg, Florida, to oversee the manufacturing and testing of the pyrovalves. Additionally, the defendant brought its customers to Florida to tour the plaintiff's facility.

By June 2005, three of the four batches of pyrovalves had been manufactured and successfully tested. However, on June 28, and June 29, 2005, during the testing of the fourth batch of pyrovalves, both parties observed cracking in the valves. Additionally, further examination of earlier batches of pyrovalves also showed cracking. The defendant's representatives subsequently visited the plaintiff's facility several times to investigate with the plaintiff the cause of the cracking.

Thereafter, a dispute arose regarding the scope of the plaintiff's liability under the contract for the nonconforming pyrovalves. Thus, in October 2005, the defendant claimed damages of approximately 24.5 million euros (which is in excess of thirty million United States dollars). The plaintiff argues that this demand is excessive and is unrelated to the measure of damages contemplated in the Subcontract.

With regard to disputes, the Subcontract provides:

> In the event of any dispute arising out of the terms of this Subcontract, the Parties shall undertake to make every reasonable effort to reach an amicable settlement. Failing such settlement, a controversy or claim arising out of or relating to this Subcontract may be finally settled by arbitration in accordance with the rules then in effect of the International Chamber of Commerce.

After the parties investigated liability, they communicated on settlement issues, without success. The parties subsequently agreed to mediate this dispute on December 15, 2006, in Florida.

On December 12, 2006, Francesco P. Giobbe, defendant's counsel, traveled from France to Tampa to attend the mediation conference. The parties attended the mediation, but it ended in an impasse.

At the conclusion of the mediation, the mediator advised defense counsel to remain in the conference room. Thereafter, plaintiff's counsel entered the room with a process server and gave Giobbe a copy of the summons and complaint filed in this case. Unbeknownst to the defendant, the plaintiff had filed this lawsuit in Pinellas County Circuit Court the previous day, December 14, 2006.

The plaintiff's complaint concedes that its pyrovalves failed, but it disputes the scope of its liability. The plaintiff seeks a declaratory judgment that its liability for the failed pyrovalves does not extend beyond their repair, replacement, or a refund to the defendant of the amount received by the plaintiff for the nonconforming valves.

After removing this lawsuit from state court, the defendant filed its Motion to Quash Service of Process and to Dismiss for Lack of Personal Jurisdiction, or Alternative Motion to Stay Proceedings and Compel Arbitration.

II.

Under §48.031(1)(a), Fla. Stat, a party may effectuate service of process by "delivering a copy of it to the person to be served with a copy of the complaint, petition, or other initial pleading or paper. . . ." The plaintiff contends that it complied with this provision when it served Giobbe, the defendant's corporate representative, in Tampa on December 15, 2006, following the failed mediation.

The defendant argues that the plaintiff's service of process upon Giobbe is insufficient because the plaintiff accomplished service by luring him into Florida under the guise of settlement negotiations, which is a tactic prohibited by Florida law. Thus, in *Citrexsa S.A. v. Landsman*, 528 So. 2d 517 (Fla. Dist. Ct. App. 1988), service of process was quashed after the defendants, who traveled from Mexico to Florida to attend a settlement conference, were served with process prior to the mediation. The court found that the plaintiffs' conduct demonstrated that they "never intended to participate in good faith settlement negotiations, and that their agreement to participate in the settlement conference was merely an artifice to serve" the defendants.

In sum, there is a substantial dispute as to whether the plaintiff's actions in effecting personal service of process constitute bad faith. Its resolution would require an evidentiary hearing involving the disturbing circumstance of testimony from the lawyers involved in the mediation process. However, this issue need not be resolved and, therefore, no evidentiary hearing is necessary, because, as discussed below, the plaintiff properly effected substitute service upon the defendant pursuant to §§48.161 and 48.181, Flat. Stat.

The plaintiff contends that it effected service upon the defendant in accordance with §§48.161 and 48.181, Flat. Stat. In this regard, it explains:

> Three copies of process . . . were mailed certified mail, return receipt requested, as required, to the Secretary of State. A notice of service and a copy of the process were sent both to a company representative at [the defendant's] registered office in the United Kingdom and to its U.S. Attorney by certified mail, return receipt requested.

The defendant does not dispute that it received a copy of the summons and complaint through the mail. Rather, it argues that service of process by mail is not authorized by The Convention on the Service Abroad of Judicial and Extrajudicial Documents in Civil or Commercial Matters ("The Hague Convention"), which governs international service of judicial documents.

Article 10(a) of the Hague Convention specifies that the Convention shall not interfere with "the freedom to send judicial documents by postal channels directly to persons abroad" if the state of destination does not object. Since the United Kingdom has not objected to Article 10(a), the plaintiff contends that service of process by mail pursuant to §§48.161 and 48.181, Flat. Stat., is not inconsistent with the Hague Convention's requirements. However, the defendant argues that the plaintiff's reliance on Article 10(a) is misplaced because Article 10(a) applies only to documents sent *after* service of process is effected.

The crux of this issue is whether "freedom to send judicial documents" includes service of process. This is a matter on which federal courts disagree. One line of cases holds that the phrase "send judicial documents" does not include "service of process," but rather encompasses documents sent only after service of process is effected. *See Nuovo Pignone, SpA v. Storman Asia M/V*, 310 F.3d 374, 384 (5th Cir. 2002); *Bankston v. Toyota Motor Corp.*, 889 F.2d 172, 174 (8th Cir. 1989). These courts hold that, if Article 10(a) were intended to permit an additional method of process service, the word "service," as it is used liberally in other provisions, would have been chosen instead of "send." *Id.*

On the other hand, several federal courts hold that Article 10(a) does include service of process by mail, reasoning that "send judicial documents" encompasses "service of process." *Brockmeyer v. May*, 383 F.3d 798, 802 (9th Cir. 2004); *Ackermann v. Levine*, 788 F.2d 830, 838–840 (2d Cir. 1986).

As discussed in *Brockmeyer* service of process by mail "is consistent with the purpose of the Convention to facilitate international service of judicial documents." *Brockmeyer v. May, supra*, 383 F.3d at 802. Further, this interpretation is shared by commentaries, including the official report of the Hague Convention.

In particular, the United States Government, through the State Department, wrote a letter to the Administrative Office of the United States Courts on this issue, stating, in pertinent part:

> We . . . believe that the decision of the Court of Appeals in *Bankston* is incorrect to the extent that it suggests that the Hague Convention does not permit as a method of service of process

the sending of a copy of a summons and complaint by registered mail to a defendant in a foreign country.

In addition, this position is shared by several other member countries of the Hague Convention.

I find more persuasive those decisions, particularly *Brockmeyer*, that hold that Article 10(a) is applicable to service of process. Therefore, consistent with those decisions construing Article 10(a) of the Hague Convention to permit service of process by mail if the state law provides such an option, and the receiving country does not object, I find that the plaintiff's service of process upon the defendant in accordance with §§48.161 and 48.181, Flat. Stat., does not violate the Hague Convention. Notably, the defendant does not contend that the plaintiff failed to comply with those provisions of Florida law. Accordingly, the plaintiff has properly effected service of process upon the defendant.

***

The defendant has alternatively moved for a stay of proceedings in this case and to compel arbitration pursuant to the Federal Arbitration Act ("FAA"). It relies upon the arbitration clause in the parties' agreement which states, in pertinent part:

> In the event of any dispute arising out of the terms of this Subcontract, the Parties shall undertake to make every reasonable effort to reach an amicable settlement. Failing such settlement, a controversy or claim arising out of or relating to this Subcontract may be finally settled by arbitration in accordance with the rules then in effect of the International Chamber of Commerce.
>
> . . .
>
> The location of the arbitration shall be in London, England and the arbitration shall be held in English. Each party shall bear its own expenses in participating in the arbitration process.

Based on this provision, the defendant commenced arbitration proceedings in England. The plaintiff opposes arbitration, arguing that it is optional.

[The court upheld the arbitration clause requiring London arbitration and stayed the action, directing the parties to proceed with arbitration.]

NOTES AND QUESTIONS

1. In *Conax*, the court did not reach the issue of whether the service of the complaint and summons on the defendant's counsel in the United States was effective. Why not? If the court did reach the issue, would the service have been effective? What do you think of the conduct of the plaintiffs on how service was effected?

2. In order to facilitate service of process outside the United States, Rule 4(f) was added to the Federal Rules of Civil Procedure in 1993. Rule 4(f) states as follows:

> (f) *Service upon Individuals in a Foreign Country.* [S]ervice upon an individual . . . may be effected in a place not within any judicial district of the United States:
>> (1) by any internationally agreed means reasonably calculated to give notice, such as those means authorized by the Hague Convention on the Service Abroad of Judicial and Extrajudicial Documents; or
>> (2) if there is no internationally agreed means of service or the applicable international agreement allows other means of service, provided that service is reasonably calculated to give notice:

(A) in the manner prescribed by the law of the foreign country . . . ; or

(B) as directed by the foreign authority in response to a letter rogatory or letter of request; or

(C) unless prohibited by the law of the foreign country, by

(i) delivery to the individual personally of a copy of the summons and the complaint; or

(ii) any form of mail requiring a signed receipt, to be addressed and dispatched by the clerk of the court to the party to be served; or

(3) by other means not prohibited by international agreement. . . .

Is it a good policy to search for unilateral methods to serve process or is it better to rely on diplomatic channels?

3. In *Cupp v. Alberto-Culver USA, Inc.*, 308 F. Supp. 2d 873 (W.D. Tenn. 2004), the court stated that service of process abroad by sending a U.S. mail registered letter to the legal department of a French corporation was "questionable." Citing Fed. R. Civ. P. 4(f), the court further stated that (1) the Hague Convention applied and (2) the Hague Convention sets forth procedures for service of process that do *not* include sending documents through the U.S. mail. The court noted that there is a "split of authority" among U.S. federal courts concerning the proper interpretation of the Hague Convention "as to whether Article 10(a) allows service of process abroad by regular mail." The court concluded that the cases holding that service by registered U.S. mail does not comply with the Convention are "persuasive." For a case finding that service by registered mail does not violate the Convention, see *Ackermann v. Levine*, 788 F.2d 830, 839–840 (2d Cir. 1986). For contrary authority, see *Bankston v. Toyota Motor Corp.*, 889 F.2d 172, 174 (8th Cir. 1989).

4. Courts have commented variously on the meaning of Fed. R. Civ. P. 4(f)(3). In *Cascade Yarns, Inc. v. Knitting Fever, Inc.*, No. C10-861RSM, 2011 U.S. Dist. LEXIS 35761, at *4–5 (W.D. Wash. Mar. 18, 2011), the court stated that this provision is "neither a last resort nor extraordinary relief . . . [but] merely one means among several which enable service of process on an international defendant." The court indicated approval of such methods as publication, ordinary mail, e-mail, and delivery to a defendant's attorney. But the court in *Kexuan Yao v. Crisnic Fund, SA*, No. SACV 10-1299 AG (JCGx), 2011 U.S. Dist. LEXIS 97358, at *12–15 (C.D. Cal. Aug. 29, 2011), ruled that service by e-mailing a link to copies of the summons and complaint was insufficient.

7. Jurisdiction over Parent and Affiliated Companies

In international business litigation, an important issue is whether jurisdiction over a subsidiary or affiliate will justify jurisdiction over a parent or another affiliate located in a foreign country. We examine this issue in the materials below.

PROBLEM 8-14

Chapman is an Ohio Corporation headquartered in Cleveland. It is engaged in the business of developing, purchasing, fabricating, and selling industrial machine products. In 2015, Chapman developed a process by which it could make a unique, abrasion-resistant steel plate (AR plate) for use in some of its machine products. Because manufacturing costs in the United States would be very expensive, Chapman looked for and found a steel mill in Galatz, Romania, that could produce the AR plate to Chapman's specifications, using the Chapman process.

Because of Romanian economic and legal regulations, however, Chapman could not book orders with the Galatz mill directly; the transaction had to be structured through the Galatz mill's European trading partner, Kirchfeld AG, a German corporation located in Essen, Germany. Kirchfeld AG has partnered with the Galatz mill to sell its products to the European Union. Using Kirchfeld as an intermediary would enable the Galatz mill to obtain payment in euros from Kirchfeld, thus complying with Romanian regulations.

Accordingly, Chapman booked an order for 10,000 steel plates per month with Kirchfeld USA, a wholly-owned subsidiary of Kirchfeld AG. Kirchfeld USA is a California corporation headquartered in Los Angeles and serves as the exclusive conduit for handling all of Kirchfeld AG's business in North America. For the first six months of this business arrangement, all was fine. The steel arrived by ship in Cleveland; Kirchfeld USA invoiced Chapman, who paid the invoice in dollars. When the seventh shipment arrived, however, Chapman discovered some problems. Over 500 AR plates were missing, and the remaining plates were made of lower-grade steel, contrary to Chapman's specifications. Chapman's investigation disclosed that the missing plates may have been consigned in Germany, by mistake or on purpose, to a German competitor. Kirchfeld USA, however, denies all responsibility, and, in an e-mail to Chapman, states that Chapman must pay the invoice as usual, and look to Kirchfeld AG, the Galatz mill, or the carrier of the AR plates for an explanation and liability. What advice do you have for Chapman? Consult *Itel Containers* below.

Most cases holding that jurisdiction over a foreign subsidiary provides jurisdiction over the parent in a U.S. court find the following factors: (1) the parent is highly involved in the day-to-day operations of the subsidiary; (2) key personnel work for both the parent and the subsidiary or are regularly rotated between the two; (3) the parent uses the subsidiary as a conduit through which the parent makes a significant number of sales; (4) the parent uses the foreign subsidiary to perform services, such as transportation or distribution, that the parent would otherwise have to perform; (5) the parent and the subsidiary do not distinguish between the two entities in advertising or promotional materials; (6) the parent and subsidiary fail to observe corporate formalities in their dealings with each other; (7) the parent and subsidiary are both involved in the conduct in question, i.e., an international price fixing arrangement.

By contrast, cases in which jurisdiction over the parent is rejected occurs when the parent and subsidiary observe corporate formalities or where the parent behaves as an investor, giving advice, support, and monitoring the subsidiary lightly, but does not get involved in the day-to-day affairs of the subsidiary. Consider these factors in light of the following case.

Itel Containers Int'l Corp. v. Atlanttrafik Express Serv. Ltd.
United States Court of Appeals, Second Circuit, 1990
909 F.2d 698

Kearse, Circuit Judge.

[In 1984, Sea Containers Ltd. (SCL), which was engaged in the business of selling and leasing cargo containers and related equipment to ocean liners, decided to purchase a shipping line (the AES line) and its two carriers. Because SCL did not want to openly compete with its customers, SCL caused to be organized and incorporated a separate legal entity, Atlanttrafik Express Service Ltd. (AES Ltd.), under the laws of England for purpose of buying and serving as the holding company of the AES liner service. Another company, Atlanttrafik Express Service Inc. (AES Inc.), was formed as a wholly-owned subsidiary of AES Ltd. to operate the liner service. SCL advanced the funds to AES Ltd. to purchase the AES line and made loans to AES Ltd. to finance its operations. Five vessels that were owned or leased by other SCL subsidiaries were then leased or subleased to AES Ltd.

Plaintiffs Itel Containers International Corporation (Itel), Flexi-Van Leasing Inc. (Flexi-Van), and plaintiffs Textainer Inc. and Textainer Special Equipment Ltd. (collectively Textainer) were also in the business of leasing cargo containers to ocean carriers and had leased equipment to the AES line prior to its sale to AES Ltd. When they learned of SCL's involvement in the imminent purchase of the AES line by AES Ltd., they attempted to obtain SCL's guarantee on leases of equipment to the AES line that were being renegotiated, extended, or were being assigned by the AES line to AES Ltd. SCL refused to give its guarantee and the plaintiffs eventually entered into leases directly with AES Ltd.

In 1985, AES Ltd. encountered serious financial difficulty and went into liquidation in England. With AES Ltd. in bankruptcy, plaintiffs brought an action in the federal district court for the Southern District of New York to recover payment on the equipment rentals from SCL. The district court ruled that SCL had no liability for the debts of AES Ltd. and the plaintiffs brought this appeal.]

A. The Claims Against SCL

Plaintiffs advance three theories in support of their contention that SCL is liable for the damages that resulted when AES Ltd. ceased doing business and thereby breached the container leases. They contend that SCL should have been found liable (1) as a joint venturer with AES Ltd., or (2) as AES Ltd.'s principal, or (3) for such abuse of the corporate form as to warrant piercing the corporate veil. We find no merit in any of these arguments.

1. THE JOINT VENTURE THEORY

Under New York law, which applies to this case, a joint venture "is in a sense a partnership for a limited purpose, and it has long been recognized that the legal consequences of a joint venture are equivalent to those of a partnership." *Gramercy Equities v. Dumont*, 72 N.Y.2d 560, 565 (1988). Thus, for example, one coventurer will be bound by a lease signed by another coventurer, even if the first neither signed nor assented to the lease. Plaintiffs contend that the district court should have found that SCL and AES Ltd. were joint venturers in operating the AES line and that, under the above principles, SCL was liable for the container leases signed by AES Ltd. We conclude that the district court properly found that SCL was not party to a joint venture.

In order to form a joint venture, (1) two or more persons must enter into a specific agreement to carry on an enterprise for profit; (2) their agreement must evidence their intent to be joint venturers; (3) each must make a contribution of property, financing, skill, knowledge, or effort; (4) each must have some degree of joint control over the venture; and (5) there must be a provision for the sharing of both profits and losses. All of these elements must be present before joint venture liability may be imposed. At least two elements were lacking in the present case.

The district court found that SCL did not intend to engage in a joint venture. Plaintiffs have pointed to no evidence to the contrary, and the record fully supports the view that SCL purposely used layers of corporations so that its involvement with the AES line would be remote. Thus the second element listed above was not present. Further, the court found that SCL chose to operate through corporations in order to limit its losses to the amounts it was willing to advance in loans. Though SCL plainly hoped to share in whatever profits the AES line produced, there was no indication that it expected to share in the losses except as a lender to AES Ltd. Thus, the fifth element also was not present. Accordingly, assuming that the AES line was properly to be considered the "venture," the findings of the district court preclude the conclusion that it was an SCL joint venture.

Further, we note that the district court correctly found that AES Ltd. itself was not a joint venture because it was a corporation. A joint venture and a corporation are mutually exclusive ways of doing business. Though business associates may be treated as partners vis-à-vis one another even when they operate through a corporation, the corporate form is to be respected in dealings with third parties.

2. THE AGENCY THEORIES

Plaintiffs also contend that SCL should have been held liable on the leases as a principal for which AES Ltd. was the agent. Though they assert that there was an express agency relationship, their argument appears to rely to a greater extent on the proposition that there was an implied agency.

An express agency is created "by written or spoken words or other conduct of the principal which, reasonably interpreted, causes the agent to believe that the principal desires him so to act on the principal's account." *Restatement (Second) of Agency* §26 (1958) ("*Restatement*"). Whether such an agency is formed depends on the actual interaction between the putative principal and agent, not on any perception a third party may have of the relationship.

Plaintiffs point to various activities of SCL that might perhaps have been thought by others to establish an agency relationship in some respect. There was no evidence, however, that SCL actually authorized AES Ltd. to act as its agent or that it in any way led AES Ltd. to believe AES Ltd. was so authorized. SCL made clear from the start its intention to utilize the corporate form for AES Ltd. so as to limit SCL's liability. SCL did provide financing to AES Ltd., but AES Ltd. was meant to, and did, operate independently. SCL chose not to be a shareholder, and no SCL employee sat on AES Ltd.'s Board of Directors. The record simply would not have supported a finding that SCL authorized AES Ltd. to act on its behalf.

Implied agency, in contrast, depends not on the actual relationship between principal and agent but on the reasonable conclusion of a third party, derived from actions of the principal, that the person acting has authority to do so from the principal. "[A]pparent authority to do an act is created as to a third person by written or spoken words or any other conduct of the principal which, reasonably interpreted, causes the third person to believe that the principal consents to have the act done on his behalf by the person purporting to act for him." *Restatement* §27. Thus, in order to determine whether there was implied authority, the court must focus on the acts of the principal in relation to the third party.

Though plaintiffs argue that the actions of SCL reasonably led them to believe that SCL was AES Ltd.'s principal, the record refutes their claims. Under New York law, "[o]ne who deals with an agent does so at his peril, and must make the necessary effort to discover the actual scope of authority." *Ford v. Unity Hospital*, 32 N.Y.2d at 472. Whatever the possibility that some of SCL's actions may have given outsiders the impression that AES Ltd. was running the AES line on behalf of SCL, the scope of any such implied authority plainly could not be deemed to have extended to the one set of AES Ltd. actions that is pertinent here, *i.e.*, the execution of the container leases. Both Itel and Flexi-Van, in the course of negotiating the leases with AES Ltd., communicated directly with SCL in an attempt to get SCL to take responsibility for the leases. SCL flatly refused to do so. Neither these plaintiffs nor Textainer (which does not appear to have communicated with SCL when negotiating its leases) point to any action by SCL that they could reasonably have interpreted as authorizing AES Ltd. to enter into the leases on behalf of SCL.

We conclude that the record belies plaintiffs' contentions that SCL actually or impliedly authorized AES Ltd. to enter into the container leases as agent for SCL.

3. THE CORPORATE VEIL

Finally, plaintiffs contend that SCL should have been held liable for AES Ltd.'s debts on the theory that SCL's control over AES Ltd. constituted an abuse of the corporate form that justified piercing the corporate veil. The district court, in rejecting this claim, stated that to succeed on such a theory, plaintiffs would have to show, *inter alia*, (a) that SCL's control over AES Ltd. and/or AES Inc. had been so complete that the latter companies had no separate existence, and (b) that SCL had used that domination to perpetrate a fraud on plaintiffs. Though New York law allows the corporate veil to be pierced *either* when there is fraud *or* when the corporation has been used as an alter ego, we find no basis for reversal.

In *Gartner v. Snyder*, 607 F.2d 582, 586 (2d Cir. 1979), we noted that

> [b]ecause New York courts disregard corporate form reluctantly, they do so only when the form has been used to achieve fraud, or when the corporation has been so dominated by an individual or another corporation . . . , and its separate identity so disregarded, that it primarily transacted the dominator's business rather than its own and can be called the other's alter ego.

Similarly, in *Kirno Hill Corp. v. Holt*, 618 F.2d 982, 985 (2d Cir. 1980), we stated:

> The prerequisites for piercing a corporate veil are . . . clear . . . : [the defendant] must have used [the corporation] to perpetrate a fraud or have so dominated and disregarded [the corporation's] corporate form that [the corporation] primarily transacted [the defendant's] personal business rather than its own corporate business.

Mere use of the corporate form to avoid liability is insufficient to warrant piercing the veil.

The district court's rejection of plaintiffs' claim was consistent with these principles, for the court not only found that plaintiffs had failed to show any fraud by SCL but also found that they had failed to show sufficient control and domination by SCL of AES Ltd. or of AES Inc. to make either of them SCL's alter ego. These findings are not clearly erroneous.

The record shows that AES Inc. was responsible for the everyday affairs of the AES line and that SCL did not interfere. AES Ltd. observed the corporate formalities, including holding board meetings. [P]laintiffs did not show that SCL dominated AES Inc. or AES Ltd. or used its position to have its own loans to AES Ltd. repaid in preference to those of other AES Ltd. creditors. For example, the record includes evidence that AES Ltd. refused, despite SCL's importuning, to give preferential treatment to SCL containers; that in a dispute over whether to retain the president of AES Inc., SCL's view was overruled; and that when AES Ltd. received a $6 million payment from the former owner of the AES line to close a shortfall in the represented working capital, the money was used to pay off some of AES Ltd.'s outstanding bills, including bills from plaintiffs, but no part of the payment was used to reduce the amount owed to SCL.

In sum, we conclude that plaintiffs have presented no tenable theory for holding SCL liable for the debts of AES Ltd. The district court properly dismissed the claims against SCL.

NOTES AND QUESTIONS

1. In light of the foregoing criteria, what steps can or should a parent company take to minimize the possibility of a lawsuit and liability?

2. Compare the factors discussed by the court in *Itel Containers* with the factors enumerated on p. 678. Is there any distinction between the factors necessary for jurisdiction over the foreign parent and the factors necessary for liability?

3. In 2014, the Supreme Court revisited the due process question presented in the *Goodyear Tires* case (considered earlier in this chapter at pp. 651-653) in the context of whether actions of a foreign subsidiary could be attributed to a multinational corporation, Daimler AG, doing business in the United States under the aegis of a U.S. subsidiary company, Mercedes Benz USA, a Delaware limited liability company. In *Daimler AG v. Bauman*, 134 S. Ct. 746 (2014), the Court considered whether due process considerations permitted an Alien Tort Statute case to be brought against a German parent company for actions allegedly done by its Argentine subsidiary in Argentina. The Ninth Circuit ruled in favor of personal jurisdiction over Daimler, on the basis that Daimler through its U.S. subsidiary had contacts that were continuous and systematic with California so as to subject Daimler to general jurisdiction, because Mercedes Benz USA should be treated as Daimler's agent for jurisdictional purposes. *Bauman v. DaimlerChrysler Corp.*, 644 F.3d 909, 920-924 (9th Cir. 2011). The Supreme Court reversed (Justice Sotomayor concurring), ruling that even if Mercedes Benz USA's contacts in California were attributable to Daimler, there is no basis to subject Daimler to general jurisdiction in California for acts committed by its Argentine subsidiary. The Supreme Court, however, notably refused to rule on the main question—whether Mercedes Benz USA's contacts were in fact attributable to Daimler for general jurisdictional purposes. *See* 134 S. Ct. at 758-760. In dicta, however, the Court disapproved the agency theory and the idea that a foreign multinational can be subject to general jurisdiction solely because of the activities of its wholly-owned subsidiary. *See* 134 S. Ct. at 759. The Court also found that it had not been established that Daimler's own contacts with California were such that it could be subject to general jurisdiction in that state. *See* 134 S. Ct. at 760. The Court's opinion drew a blistering response from Justice Sotomayor, who stated in her concurring opinion that the Court should have ruled in favor of general jurisdiction over Daimler, and reversed only on the basis of the "unique circumstances" of this case. *See* 134 S. Ct. at 763-764.

PROBLEM 8-15

Xenos, an aggressive upstart U.S. computer software company, has established a wholly foreign-owned subsidiary in France to serve as Xenos's holding company for its intellectual property portfolio of patents and copyrights. Xenos assigns the entire portfolio to the French subsidiary, which then grants a license for all of the intellectual property rights back to Xenos for its use in the United States in exchange for royalties. Microtel, a well-established U.S. company and the market leader, brings an action against Xenos and its French subsidiary for breach of one of Microtel's patents in U.S. federal district court. Defendants move to dismiss the case on the grounds that (1) the federal district court has no *in personam* jurisdiction over the French subsidiary and that (2) as the subsidiary, the owner of the patents and copyrights, is an indispensable party without whom the lawsuit cannot proceed, the action should be dismissed against Xenos as well. Microtel argues that the federal district court has jurisdiction over the French subsidiary on the basis of the actions of Xenos, the parent in the United States. What is the result? Can you describe Xenos's strategy? Will it work? *See Dainippon Screen Mfg. Co., Ltd. v. CFMT, Inc.*, 142 F.3d 1266, 1271 (Fed. Cir. 1998).

8.   Conflicts of Jurisdiction: Multiple Proceedings in Different Forums

When there is litigation between international parties, the courts in more than one country may have jurisdiction. This means related lawsuits are often filed in more than one forum. This creates conflicts of jurisdiction and the possibility of competing or contradictory rulings in different forums with respect to the same or similar legal issues and parties. Such multiple proceedings take many forms. Among the most common are (1) the aggrieved party to an international transaction may file two lawsuits in two different forums in order to have "two bites of the apple"; (2) the defendant in one forum may file a related claim or a counterclaim against the other party in the defendant's home forum; (3) a party that is subject to ongoing public law or bankruptcy proceedings in one forum may pursue private-claim litigation in another forum; or (4) a party who is sued in a foreign forum may file suit in his home forum, seeking a negative declaratory judgment of nonliability in his home forum.

There are three possible judicial responses in one forum with regard to pending related litigation in another forum. First, a court may grant a motion to dismiss the case before it in whole or in part because of international comity in order to give primacy to the other forum. Second, a court may take a permissive approach and allow both cases to continue. Third, a court can issue an antisuit injunction against the continuance of the foreign litigation (the injunction is issued against a party not the foreign court).

Goss International Corp. v. Man Roland Druckmachinen AG
United States Court of Appeals, Eighth Circuit, 2007
491 F.3d 355

On December 3, 2003, a jury found Japanese-based Tokyo Kikai Seisakusho, Ltd. (TKS) liable to Goss International Corporation (Goss) under the Antidumping Act of 1916 (the 1916 Act), 15 U.S.C. §72 (repealed 2004), which made it unlawful for foreign persons to sell imported articles within the United States at a price substantially less than the actual market value or wholesale price at the time of exportation, with the intent of destroying or injuring an industry in the United States. The judgment, inclusive of statutory treble damages, attorney fees, and costs, amounted to more than $35,000,000.

During the pendency of TKS's appeal, Congress prospectively repealed the 1916 Act. Shortly thereafter the Japanese government passed "The Special Measures Law Concerning the Obligation to Return Profits Obtained pursuant to the Antidumping Act of 1916 of the United States, Law No. 162, 2004" (Special Measures Law), a clawback statute allowing Japanese nationals to sue for the recovery of any judgment entered against them under the 1916 Act.

On June 15, 2006, the district court granted Goss's motion for preliminary injunction prohibiting TKS from filing suit in Japan under the Special Measures Law. TKS paid the judgment in full, and the district court entered a satisfaction of judgment on June 21, 2006. On June 23, 2006, TKS filed this interlocutory appeal.

I. BACKGROUND

Goss and TKS both manufacture and supply newspaper printing presses and press additions. Goss was the major manufacturer of large printing presses in the United States for more than a century and enjoyed dominance in the United States printing press market into the late 1990s.

In the 1970s, TKS began selling its presses and press additions in the United States. By the 1980s, TKS obtained contracts with large United States newspapers, including the Wall Street Journal, the Washington Post, and the Newark Star-Ledger. Between 1991 and 2000, TKS began "dumping" its products, selling them in the United States at prices substantially below the market value of its similar products in Japan. During that period, TKS sold $125,000,000 worth of printing press additions in the United States. Goss, on the other hand, lost contracts because customers expected Goss to lower its prices to match TKS's prices. In 2000, Goss did not make a single printing press equipment sale.

In March 2000, Goss brought a civil action against TKS alleging violations of the 1916 Act. [This suit was successful resulting in the jury award of more than $35 million.]

On December 3, 2004, Congress repealed the 1916 Act. Because the repeal was prospective, it did not affect Goss's judgment. Japan considered the prospective repeal to be inconsistent with the United States' obligations under World Trade Organization (WTO) Agreements. Consequently, on December 8, 2004, Japan enacted the Special Measures Law, a clawback statute authorizing Japanese corporations and/or Japanese nationals to sue in Japanese courts for recovery of the full amount of any judgment . . . awarded under the 1916 Act. The Special Measures Law holds any wholly owned parent companies and subsidiaries of the party that prevailed under the 1916 Act jointly and severally liable. Goss Graphic Systems Japan, which is located in Tokyo, is a wholly-owned subsidiary of Goss.

On November 24, 2004, by stipulation of the parties, TKS agreed not to file a lawsuit under the Special Measures Law until after TKS exhausted its appeal under the antidumping law. On January 26, 2006, our court affirmed the jury verdict and damages award in the Antidumping action, and on June 5, 2006, the Supreme Court denied TKS's petition for writ of certiorari.

The same day the Supreme Court denied TKS's petition, TKS notified Goss of its intention to file suit under the Special Measures Law. Goss filed a motion for preliminary and permanent injunction to prevent TKS "from usurping the court's jurisdiction and frustrating the court's judgment. On June 15, 2006, the district court issued a preliminary antisuit injunction enjoining TKS from filing suit under the Special Measures Law. On June 19, 2006, TKS paid the judgment in full.

II. DISCUSSION

The propriety of issuing a foreign antisuit injunction is a matter of first impression in our circuit. Other circuits having decided the issue agree that "federal courts have the power to enjoin persons subject to their jurisdiction from prosecuting foreign suits." *Laker Airways, Ltd. v. Sabena Belgian World Airlines*, 731 F.2d 909 (D.C. Cir. 1984). The circuits are split, however, on the level of deference afforded to international comity in determining whether a foreign antisuit injunction should issue.

The First, Second, Third, Sixth, and District of Columbia Circuits have adopted the "conservative approach" under which a foreign antisuit injunction will issue only if the movant demonstrates (1) an action in a foreign jurisdiction would prevent United States jurisdiction or threaten a vital United States policy, and (2) the domestic interests outweigh concerns of international comity. *See e.g., Quaak v. Klynveld Peat Marwick Goerdeler Bedrijfsrevisoren*, 361 F.3d 11, 17 (1st Cir. 2004); *General Electric Co. v. Deutz AG*, 270 F.3d 144 (3d Cir. 2001); *Gau Shan Co. v. Bankers Trust Co.*, 956 F.2d 1349, 1355 (6th Cir. 1992); *China Trade & Dev. Corp. v. M.V. Choong Yong*, 837 F.3d 33, 35–36 (2d Cir. 1987). Under the conservative approach, "comity dictates that foreign antisuit injunctions be issued sparingly and only in the rarest of cases." *Gau Shan Co.*, 956 F.2d at 1354.

In contrast, the Fifth and Ninth Circuits follow the "liberal approach," which places only modest emphasis on international comity and approves the issuance of an antisuit injunction when necessary to prevent duplicative and vexatious foreign litigation and to avoid inconsistent judgments. *E&J Gallo Winery v. Andina Licores S.A.*, 446 F.3d 984 (9th Cir. 2006); *Kaepa, Inc. v. Achilles Corp.*, 76 F.3d 624 (5th Cir. 1996)[.] The Seventh Circuit similarly has indicated its agreement with the liberal approach. *Allendale Mutual Ins. Co. v. Bull Data Sys., Inc.*, 10 F.3d 425 (7th Cir. 1993).

We agree with the observations of the First Circuit that the conservative approach (1) recognizes the rebuttable presumption against issuing international antisuit injunctions, (2) is more respectful of international comity, (3) compels an inquiring court to balance competing policy considerations, and (4) acknowledges that issuing an international antisuit injunction is a step that should be taken only with care and with great restraint and with the recognition that international comity is a fundamental principle deserving of substantial deference.

We do not believe the rationale of those cases compels an injunction in the present case.

First, [in the antidumping case,] a verdict was entered for Goss, which we affirmed on appeal; TKS paid the judgment; and the district court lifted the stay of the *supersedeas* bond. No pending litigation, other than this appeal, remains in the United States courts. Thus the request for injunctive relief is not for the prevention of interdictory jurisdiction by the Japanese courts.

Second, in cases involving parallel litigation in foreign countries, once one court reaches a final judgment, the rule of comity for antisuit purposes is moot because there is no longer tension with the foreign country over concurrent jurisdiction.

Third, we disagree with the district court's assertion that Congress's decision to repeal the 1916 Act prospectively, rather than retroactively, may play a role in the decision to grant a foreign antisuit injunction to protect the court's jurisdiction or an important United States policy. Nothing in the repeal of the 1916 Act nor any principle of law aside from the doctrines of *res judicata* and collateral estoppel, which are inapplicable here, confers jurisdiction upon the court to maintain authority over the parties now that the judgment has been satisfied.

We are profoundly aware that a judgment in favor of TKS under the Special Measures Law would effectively nullify the remedy Goss legitimately procured in the United States courts. Although such a result is understandably objectionable to Goss, it does not threaten United States jurisdiction or any current United States policy. The propriety of the Special Measures Law, and TKS's action thereunder, are matters for the Japanese courts in the first instance. Any response by the United States, such as a blocking statute for protection against a judgment awarded under the Special Measures Law or trade sanctions against Japan, must come through authorized representatives of the United States Executive or Legislative branches, not the Judiciary. The resources of the Judiciary are inherently limited when faced with an affirmative decision by the political branches of the government to prescribe specific policies. In contrast, diplomatic and executive channels are, by definition, designed to exchange, negotiate and reconcile the problems which accompany the realization of national interests within the sphere of international association. These forums should and, we hope, will be utilized to avoid or resolve conflicts caused by contradictory assertions of concurrent prescriptive jurisdiction.

We vacate the district court's grant of a preliminary antisuit injunction and remand for dismissal of Goss's motion for injunctive relief.

NOTES AND QUESTIONS

1. Do you agree with the court? Is the "conservative approach" best? Suppose TKS had not paid the antidumping judgment; would the court's decision have been the same? Suppose Congress had not repealed the 1916 Act; should the court then grant the injunctive relief?

2. For scholarly consideration of these issues, see Daniel Tan, *Antisuit Injunctions and the Vexing Problem of Comity*, 45 Va. J. Int'l L. 285 (2005); Laura Eddleman Heim, *Protecting Their Own?: Pro-American Bias and the Issuance of Antisuit Injunctions*, 69 Ohio St. L.J. 701 (2008).

Finanz AG Zurich v. Banco Economico S.A.
United States Court of Appeals, Second Circuit, 1999
192 F.3d 240

STRAUB, Circuit Judge.

[This case involved a "forfaiting" transaction, which is a form type of arrangement for facilitating exports to debt-laden countries. Instead of paying cash for the imports, the importer issues promissory notes payable at some future date to the exporter. The exporter in turn sells the promissory notes to a third party, the forfaiter, who gives the exporter cash, usually at a substantial discount of the face value of the notes. In general, no party is willing to serve as a forfaiter unless the notes are guaranteed by a bank or other substantial guarantor. The importer arranges for the bank to guarantee the note to the forfaiter by providing an endorsement known as an "aval." The forfaiter then presents the notes to the bank at maturity for payment.

In this case, on May 2, 1995, a Brazilian importer Delba Comercio Importação e Exportação Ltda (Delba) issued six promissory notes with a face value of over $5.6 million payable in one year to forfaiter Deutsche Morgan Grenfell Trade Finance Ltd. (Morgan Grenfell). The notes were guaranteed by the Cayman Islands branch of Banco Economico S.A. (BESA). Each note stated, however, that it was payable at BESA's New York branch. In a subsequent telex to Morgan Grenfell, BESA's International Division confirmed that the Cayman Branch had guaranteed or "avalized" the notes and that they were payable in New York. On May 24, 1995, Morgan Grenfell sold three of the notes with a total face value of $3 million to Finanz AG Zurich on a non-recourse basis for $2.78 million.

On August 11, 1995, prior to the maturity date of the notes, Brazil's Central Bank caused BESA and all of its branches to be placed into "intervention" (similar to a receivership under U.S. law) and then liquidation, which is similar to a bankruptcy proceeding in the United States. As a result of the Central Bank's intervention, the U.S. Office of the Comptroller of the Currency (OCC) instituted cease-and-desist proceedings against BESA's New York branch, which was licensed by the OCC. The New York branch subsequently entered into an "amended consent order" with the OCC. The order established procedures under which the New York branch would maintain sufficient assets to pay off third-party liabilities and also provided that the branch would voluntarily liquidate and cease operations.

On May 2, 1996, Morgan Grenfell on behalf of Finanz presented the three notes for payment at the New York branch but payment was refused on the basis that the Cayman branch, not the New York branch, had the obligation to pay and that the New York branch served as the "paying agent" only of the Cayman branch. Pursuant to a notice published in the New York Times on May 16, 1997 by the liquidator of BESA describing a claims procedure for creditors, Finanz then filed a claim for the value of the notes in BESA's liquidation proceeding in Brazil.

On December 3, 1997, Finanz filed suit in a New York state court, seeking to recover on the promissory notes. The action was removed to federal district court on the grounds that as BESA was the real party in interest and BESA was an instrumentality of a foreign state, jurisdiction was governed by the Foreign Sovereign Immunities Act. BESA subsequently moved to dismiss the action on the grounds of international comity in deference to the Brazilian liquidation. The district court granted the motion and Finanz brought this appeal.]

DISMISSAL BASED ON INTERNATIONAL COMITY

We review a district court's decision to extend or deny comity to a foreign proceeding for abuse of discretion.

As the Supreme Court explained in *Hilton v. Guyot*, 159 U.S. 113 (1895), comity is "the recognition which one nation allows within its territory to the legislative, executive or judicial acts of another nation, having due regard both to international duty and convenience, and to the rights of its own citizens or of other persons who are under the protection of its laws." *Id.* at 164.

We have repeatedly noted the importance of extending comity to foreign bankruptcy proceedings. Since "[t]he equitable and orderly distribution of a debtor's property requires assembling all claims against the limited assets in a single proceeding," American courts regularly defer to such actions. *Id.* at 713–714. Nonetheless, we will afford comity to foreign bankruptcies only if those proceedings do not violate the laws or public policy of the United States, and if "the foreign court abides by 'fundamental standards of procedural fairness,'" *Allstate Life Ins. Co.*, 994 F.2d at 999.

Accordingly, in this case, deferral to the Brazilian extrajudicial liquidation of BESA is appropriate only if it does not violate United States public policy or principles of due process and fundamental fairness. Finanz argues that both are vitiated by the District Court's decision. Specifically, Finanz contends that (1) the extension of comity violates the United States interest in maintaining New York as a center of commerce and forfaiting; (2) deferral contravenes the United States policy of requiring Federal branches to satisfy all of their liabilities; (3) the Brazilian liquidation offends principles of due process because creditors are not given individualized notice of the bankruptcy; and

(4) the Brazilian procedures are fundamentally unfair because the debt is converted into Brazilian reals, thereby forcing the creditor to bear the risk of fluctuations in the value of currency. We consider each of these arguments in turn.

A. PUBLIC POLICY

Finanz first maintains that the District Court failed to consider that since New York is the location where the avals were to be paid, the United States has a special interest in ensuring that the debt remains recoverable in New York to maintain New York's status as a commercial and forfaiting center.

The fact that the forfaiting transaction here required payment in New York does not preclude the granting of comity. Indeed, we have rejected an analogous argument seeking the denial of comity to a foreign bankruptcy proceeding because an indenture agreement contained both a forum selection clause requiring that suit on a contract be brought in New York and a choice of law provision selecting New York law. *See Allstate Life Ins. Co.*, 994 F.2d at 1000 (noting that such clauses "do[]not preclude a court from granting comity where it is otherwise warranted"). We do not share Finanz's concern that, as a result of the District Court's decision, "forfaiters will doubt the efficacy of New York as a payment center" and will "choose to make these transactions payable in other commercial centers." Appellant's Brief at 21–22. While forfaiters may require payment in New York because they "expect [] . . . regularity in financial dealings," *A.I. Trade Fin., Inc. v. Petra Bank*, 989 F.2d 76, 78 (2d Cir. 1993), if they wish to ensure collection from the New York branch of an international financial institution in circumstances similar to those presented here, they should—and presumably do—take the additional precaution of having the New York entity itself act as a guarantor.

Finanz also asserts that affording comity to the Brazilian liquidation would violate the interest of the United States in enforcing the liabilities of a Federal branch regulated by the OCC. The New York Branch of BESA is currently in voluntary liquidation and is resolving claims of third-party creditors. Finanz is plainly correct that there is a strong United States policy of enforcing the obligations of a Federal branch such as the New York Branch and in ensuring that its liabilities are satisfied as part of its liquidation.

However, like the District Court, we trust the OCC to safeguard this policy interest when it enters into consent orders, and Finanz's argument therefore has merit only if the avals in this case can be deemed a liability of the New York Branch pursuant to the terms of the Amended Consent Order. The Amended Consent Order defines the "Aggregate Amount of Third Party Liabilities" that the branch must pay from its assets in the liquidation as, in pertinent part:

> any liabilities agreed to by the Branch with persons that are neither subsidiaries, Related Parties, Affiliates nor Institution-Affiliated Parties of the Branch or Bank, including checks issued by the Bank or any of its subsidiaries, Affiliates, Related Parties, or Institution-Affiliated Parties, which have been issued outside of the United States and may be presented to the Branch for payment. This term shall also include bankers' acceptances, standby or commercial letters of credit and any other contingent liabilities. This term shall not include . . . accrued expenses and amounts due and other liabilities to the head office of the Bank and any other branch . . . of the Bank or the Branch.

The District Court read this definition to include only those liabilities "agreed to by the Branch," and, since the avals were not liabilities "agreed to by the Branch," they were not its obligations under the Amended Consent Order. Finanz does not challenge the District Court's conclusion that the New York Branch did not "agree[] to" the avals. Instead, it relies upon the clause "checks issued *by the Bank* . . . , which have been issued outside of the United States and may be presented to the Branch for payment" (emphasis added). Finanz maintains that the word "checks" should be read to include "any other contingent liabilities," apparently because the next sentence in the definition states, "[t]his term shall also include . . . any other contingent liabilities." According to Finanz, since the Grand Cayman Branch affixed the avals and made them payable at the New York Branch, and the International Division of BESA "confirmed" these facts, the guaranties are contingent liabilities issued by BESA outside of the United States that may be presented to the New York Branch for payment.

However, we conclude that the District Court did not exceed its allowable discretion in reading the Amended Consent Order to include only those liabilities "agreed to by the Branch" within the definition of the New York Branch's third-party liabilities. The District Court's understanding of the Order comports with the plain language of the document. Thus, since the New York Branch did not "agree[] to" the avals, it cannot now be held liable for the notes under the terms of the Amended Consent Order.

In sum, we hold that the District Court did not exceed its allowable discretion in concluding that deferral to the Brazilian liquidation would not violate policy interests of the United States.

B. DUE PROCESS AND FUNDAMENTAL FAIRNESS

Finanz next asserts that affording comity to the Brazilian proceeding would violate due process because Brazilian law does not require individualized notice to creditors. To determine whether a foreign bankruptcy proceeding "abide[s] by fundamental standards of procedural fairness," *Cunard S.S. Co.*, 773 F.2d at 457, we have focused on several factors as "indicia of procedural fairness," including:

(1) whether creditors of the same class are treated equally in the distribution of assets; (2) whether the liquidators are considered fiduciaries and are held accountable to the court; (3) whether creditors have the right to submit claims which, if denied, can be submitted to a bankruptcy court for adjudication; (4) whether the liquidators are required to give notice to the debtor's potential claimants; (5) whether there are provisions for creditors meetings; (6) whether a foreign country's insolvency laws favor its own citizens; (7) whether all assets are marshaled before one body for centralized distribution; and (8) whether there are provisions for an automatic stay and for the lifting of such stays to facilitate the centralization of claims.

Allstate Life Ins. Co., 994 F.2d at 999. As it did in the District Court, Finanz argues that only the fourth factor is not satisfied. However, although the Brazilian proceeding apparently does not require individualized notice, Finanz received actual notice of the Brazilian proceeding from the general manager of the New York Branch and subsequently filed a timely claim. Accordingly, the District Court correctly concluded that there was no due process violation. Furthermore, we disagree with Finanz's contention that *this* action should not be dismissed in favor of the Brazilian liquidation proceeding, simply because *other* creditors might receive inadequate notice of this or another such proceeding.

Finally, we reject Finanz's argument that the Brazilian proceeding is fundamentally unfair because it requires the conversion of Finanz's claims into Brazilian reals. It may well be that this practice places the risk of currency fluctuation on Finanz. Nonetheless, the United States applies a similar practice in its bankruptcy proceedings, and it is not surprising that Brazil would utilize such a procedure to promote the orderly liquidation of claims. Of course, if the early conversion of a creditor's claims into foreign currency would render a debt unenforceable or valueless, we might have cause to conclude that a conversion procedure was fundamentally unfair. However, Finanz does not make this complaint, and that situation is not before us. Accordingly, we agree with the District Court that the conversion procedure in this case is not fundamentally unfair.

Ibeto Petrochemical Indus. Ltd. v. M/T Beffen
United States Court of Appeals, Second Circuit, 2007
475 F.3d 56

MINER, Circuit Judge:

On February 6, 2004, the Motor Tanker Ship Beffen departed Paulsboro, New Jersey, carrying a cargo of base oil for delivery to Lagos, Nigeria. A Bill of Lading for the shipment issued on that date indicated that the shipper was Chemlube International, Inc. ("Chemlube") and that the cargo was destined for delivery to Ibeto in Lagos. The Bill of Lading incorporated the Charter Agreement between Chemlube and Bryggen for carriage of the shipment aboard the Beffen as follows: "This shipment is carried under and pursuant to the terms of the Charter Party dated 31 December 2003 between Chemlube International, Inc. as Charterer and Bryggen Shipping and Trading A/S as Owner and all conditions and exceptions whatsoever thereto." The Charter Party Fixture incorporated the provisions of two other documents—the standard form "Asbatankvoy" Tanker Charter Party and the "Chemlube Terms" dated September 2002.

The Asbatankvoy provisions included the following:

> Any and all differences and disputes of whatsoever nature arising out of this Charter shall be put to arbitration in the City of New York or in the City of London whichever place is specified in Part I of this charter pursuant to the laws relating to arbitration there in force, before a board of three persons, consisting of one arbitrator to be appointed by the Owner, one by the Charterer and one by the two so chosen.

The Chemlube Terms included a provision for "arbitration to be in London, English law to apply."

The base oil shipment allegedly was contaminated with seawater when the Beffen arrived in the Port of Lagos on March 5, 2004. Ibeto, as receiver of the shipment, instituted an action against Bryggen and the Beffen in the Federal District Court of Nigeria on March 19, 2004. On a later visit to Nigeria, the Beffen was arrested by Ibeto. Security was posted for release of the vessel in the form of a bank guaranty issued by the Union Bank of Nigeria on July 8, 2004. It appears that, in December, 2004, Ibeto's claim for its loss was paid by the St. Paul Fire & Marine Insurance Company, which is now subrogated to the rights of Ibeto and is presently acting in the name of its subrogor. Settlement negotiations with the defendants thereafter were conducted. While negotiations were proceeding, according to Counsel for Ibeto, "out of an excess of caution and to protect the time for suit, arbitration was demanded in London and suit was commenced in New York."

[The district court determined that the provision for arbitration made part of the Charter Party through the Asbatankvoy Form and the Chemlube terms was binding on Ibeto as well as the defendants. The court accordingly directed the parties to proceed with arbitration in London and ruled that English law applied. The court also granted the defendants' motion to enjoin the lawsuit in Nigeria.]

The Anti-Foreign Suit Injunction

A. OF THE BASIS FOR THE INJUNCTION

Underlying its Order enjoining further proceedings in Nigeria was the District Court's determination that the controversy between the parties ought to proceed by way of arbitration and that "[p]ermitting the Nigeria litigation to continue may frustrate the general federal policy of promoting arbitration." *Ibeto*, 412 F. Supp. 2d at 292–293. Defendants contend that the anti-foreign suit injunction was not warranted because Ibeto did not contractually agree to arbitration with Bryggen in the first place.

While the Charter Party was entered into by Chemlube and Bryggen, its terms, including the provision for arbitration, were incorporated by reference in the Bill of Lading directing delivery from Chemlube to Ibeto in Lagos. According to the Bill of Lading, the shipment was "carried under and pursuant to the terms of the Charter Party dated 31 December 2003 between Chemlube International, Inc. as Charterer and Bryggen Shipping and Trading A/S as Owner and all conditions and exceptions whatsoever thereto." It was the Charter Party Fixture that incorporated the standard form Asbatankvoy Tanker Charter Party, which called for arbitration, and the Chemlube terms that provided for London as the place of arbitration and for the application of English law.

We long have held that "a broadly-worded arbitration clause which is not restricted to the immediate parties may be effectively incorporated by reference into another agreement." *Progressive Cas. Ins. Co. v. C.A. Reaseguradora Nacional De Venezuela*, 991 F.2d 42, 48 (2d Cir. 1993). According to this rule, a charter party provision for such arbitration is binding on the parties to a Bill of Lading that incorporates the Charter Party by reference. *Id.*

In the case before us, the Charter Party was specifically identified by date (December 31, 2003) and by the parties thereto (Chemlube as Charterer, Bryggen as Owner). That was more than sufficient to identify the relevant Charter Party (including the documents referred to in the Charter Party Fixture) and therefore to give effect to the incorporation of the arbitration clause under the provision incorporating "all conditions and exceptions whatsoever." The District Court's analysis comports with the general rule that "[w]here terms of the Charter Party are specifically incorporated by reference in the bill of lading, the Charter Party terms alone are to be looked to for the contract of the parties." 80 C.J.S. Shipping §89. And, although the District Court's direction to proceed with arbitration in London is not appealable (nor is the stay of this action pending that arbitration), *see* 9 U.S.C. §16(b)(1), (b)(2), we here note our agreement with the District Court's direction in light of Ibeto's challenge to arbitration as a basis for the anti-foreign suit injunction.

B. OF THE APPROPRIATENESS OF THE INJUNCTION AND ITS TERMS

Ibeto's challenge to the appropriateness of the District Court's injunction in regard to the action pending in Nigeria is properly before this Court. *See* 28 U.S.C. §1292(a)(1). Ibeto's contention that the injunction was inappropriate under the circumstances revealed in this case properly was rejected by the District Court. In issuing the injunction, the District Court carefully applied the test, set forth in *China Trade & Dev. Corp. v. M.V. Choong Yong*, 837 F.2d 33, 35–36 (2d Cir. 1987), for injunctions against suits in foreign jurisdictions.

Pursuant to the *China Trade* test,

[a]n anti-suit injunction against parallel litigation may be imposed only if: (A) the parties are the same in both matters, and (B) resolution of the case before the enjoining court is dispositive of the action to be enjoined. Once past this threshold, courts are directed to consider a number of additional factors, including whether the foreign action threatens the jurisdiction or the strong public policies of the enjoining forum.

In re Millenium Seacarriers, Inc., 458 F.3d 92, 97 n.4 (2d Cir. 2006).

The "threshold" described is clearly met in this case, for the parties are the same in this matter and in the Nigerian proceeding and the resolution by arbitration of the case before the District Court is dispositive of the Nigerian proceeding. The factors then to be considered under the *China Trade* test are the following:

(1) frustration of a policy in the enjoining forum; (2) the foreign action would be vexatious; (3) a threat to the issuing court's in rem or quasi in rem jurisdiction; (4) the proceedings in the other forum prejudice other equitable considerations; or (5) adjudication of the same issues in separate actions would result in delay, inconvenience, expense, inconsistency, or a race to judgment.

China Trade, 837 F.2d at 35.

In the *China Trade* case, we found that the factors having "greater significance" there were threats to the enjoining forum's jurisdiction and to its strong public policies. *Id.* at 36. Finding no such threats, we determined that the equitable factors of that case were "not sufficient to overcome the restraint and caution required by international comity." *Id.* at 37. Some courts and commentators have erroneously interpreted *China Trade* to say that we consider *only* these two factors.

Applying all the factors, the District Court found that the general federal policy favoring arbitration might be frustrated by the Nigerian litigation; widely disparate results might obtain because the Nigerian Courts would not apply the provisions of COGSA; a race to judgment could be provoked by the disparity; equitable considerations such as deterring forum shopping favor the injunction; and "it is likely that adjudication of the same issues in two separate actions would result in inconvenience, inconsistency, and a possible race to judgment." *Ibeto*, 412 F. Supp. 2d at 293. The District Court foresaw "considerable inconvenience" in the movement of witnesses between the two venues. *Id.* The District Court determined, however, that the threat to jurisdiction factor did not apply since "both courts have in personam jurisdiction over the parties." *Id.* We agree with the foregoing analysis of the District Court in applying the *China Trade* factors and add our observation that the policy favoring arbitration is a strong one in the federal courts. Accordingly, the injunction is fully justified in this case.

The foregoing having been said, we reiterate our understanding that due regard for principles of international comity and reciprocity require a delicate touch in the issuance of anti-foreign suit injunctions, that such injunctions should be used sparingly, and that the pendency of a suit involving the same parties and same issues does not alone form the basis for such an injunction. Having these caveats in mind, we think that the injunction in this case cuts much too broadly.

The learned District Court wrote only that "defendants' motion to enjoin the Nigerian action is granted." *Ibeto*, 412 F. Supp. 2d at 293. The injunction should be directed specifically to the parties, for it is only the parties before a federal court who may be enjoined from prosecuting a suit in a foreign country. Moreover, there is no need for the permanent injunction that the District Court seems to have issued. The parties need to be enjoined from proceeding in the courts of Nigeria only until the conclusion of the

London arbitration and the consequent resolution of the still-pending case in the District Court. The District Court should modify its injunction with a specificity consonant with this determination.

The appeal is dismissed in part, and the Order of the District Court is affirmed in part and modified in part, all in accordance with the foregoing. The case is remanded to the District Court for further proceedings as directed herein.

NOTES AND QUESTIONS

1. Are considerations of international comity and respect important in considering whether to issue antisuit injunctions? Consider the following:

> [A]ntisuit injunctions are destructive of foreign commerce. Antisuit injunctions deny foreign courts the right to exercise their proper jurisdiction [and] convey the message, intended or not, that the issuing court has so little confidence in the foreign court's ability to adjudicate a given dispute fairly and efficiently that it is unwilling even to allow the possibility.

Gua Shan Co., Ltd. v. Bankers Trust Co., 956 F.2d 1349, 1355 (9th Cir. 1992). Not only is it possible to obtain an antisuit injunction, but a plaintiff who believes that a potential defendant might bring an antisuit injunction can bring a preemptory "counter antisuit injunction," namely, an injunction issued by a court in Country A preventing a potential defendant from seeking an antisuit injunction in Country B against the plaintiff barring the plaintiff from adding the potential defendant to the litigation in Country A. When will this end? For an entertaining account of how a case involving a flurry of antisuit and counter antisuit injunctions in antitrust litigation involving Laker Airways, a British company, against a number of U.S. and British airlines in U.S. courts and courts in the United Kingdom, see Trevor C. Hartley, *Comity and the Use of Antisuit Injunctions in International Litigation*, 35 Am. J. Comp. L. 487 (1987).

2. *Dependable Highway Express v. Navigators Ins. Co.*, 498 F.3d 1059 (9th Cir. 2007), involved an insurance claim by a California company against an English insurer. When the insurer, Navigators, rejected the claim, the plaintiff filed suit in California state court. Navigators then filed suit in the High Court in London and obtained an antisuit injunction against Dependable (by default) on the grounds that the insurance contract provided for London arbitration. Navigators also removed the California case to federal court and filed a motion to dismiss the federal action in light of the English proceedings. The U.S. District Court granted a stay, acknowledging the English court's injunction and the London arbitration clause. The Ninth Circuit on appeal ruled that the district court's grounds for issuing the stay were erroneous because "we have received no indication that any arbitration proceedings have commenced in England." 498 F.3d at 1067. The Ninth Circuit also rejected affirming the stay on comity because of the incompleteness of the record: "[I]f the record were clear that the parties agreed to arbitration or if the District Court made such a determination, we would have little trouble upholding the stay on grounds of international comity." *Id.* at 1069.

3. Under the doctrine of abstention, courts in the international context sometimes dismiss or stay a case because of ongoing parallel proceedings in a foreign jurisdiction. This doctrine is highly discretionary. Factors applied include international comity concerns, fairness to litigants, and the efficient use of judicial resources. In *BDL Int'l v. Sodetal USA, Inc.*, 377 F. Supp. 2d 518 (D.S.C. 2005), the pendency of bankruptcy

proceedings in France was ruled not enough to stay contract litigation in the United States.

D. Evidence and Discovery

1. *Obtaining Evidence Abroad*

In international litigation in the United States, the lawyer will often be faced with obtaining documents and information that is located in countries outside the United States. A U.S. court order allowing discovery abroad is not enough to allow the lawyer to gather evidence outside the United States. At least where the other party is uncooperative, further action is necessary to get permission and to comply with the laws of the other state involved. In this respect, the Federal Rules of Civil Procedure are supplemented by the Hague Convention on the Taking of Evidence Abroad in Civil or Commercial Matters, Mar. 18, 1970, 23 U.S.T. 2555, 847 U.N.T.S. 241, which is reprinted in the Documents Supplement, and by possible bilateral agreements on mutual legal assistance known as "MLATs" (Mutual Legal Assistance Treaties). The United States maintains MLATs with many countries. *See In re Premises Located at 840 140th Avenue NE, Bellevue, Wash.*, 634 F.3d 557, 564 (9th Cir. 2011) (MLAT between the United States and Russia).

Rule 28(b) of the Federal Rules of Civil Procedure permits the taking of a deposition in a foreign country (a) under an applicable treaty; (b) under a letter of request; (c) on notice before a person authorized by law; (d) before a person commissioned by a foreign court.

PROBLEM 8-16

Sisco is an American computer software firm that believes that its products are being copied by Linosoft, an aggressive computer software firm with its headquarters in Brazil that is emerging as a major player in South America. Rather than bring an action in Brazil where Sisco believes that it has little chance of success, Sisco has decided to bring an action in the United States in the jurisdiction where Linosoft has a permanent U.S. office. Sisco is convinced that T.K. Suarez, the CEO of Linosoft, has been engaged in a systematic and widespread effort to copy Sisco's most valuable new products. As T.K. Suarez lives in Rio de Janeiro and there is no basis for jurisdiction over him, Sisco cannot require him to appear in the United States. However, Sisco's in-house lawyers believe that Suarez has information that is crucial to their case and they must obtain this information from him or they will have no chance of prevailing in the U.S. litigation. An in-house lawyer at Sisco has drafted the following document request: "Produce all documents relating to Sisco in your possession or in the possession of anyone in your company." The Brazilian Supreme Court has also recently issued a decree stating, "No documents relating to the computer industry shall be sent abroad in connection with any overseas litigation." The in-house lawyer calls your law firm and wishes to consult with you on the next steps that need to be taken to get these documents. The company lawyer is also concerned about the new decree and asks you what its intended purpose is and what, if anything, can be done to overcome it. What is your advice on how to proceed? Brazil is a party to the Hague Evidence Convention discussed in the *Tulip* case below. *See also* Restatement (Third) of Foreign Relations Law §442.

Tulip Computers Int'l B.V. v. Dell Computer Corp.
United States District Court, District of Delaware, 2003
254 F. Supp. 2d 469

JORDAN, District Judge.

I. INTRODUCTION

Presently before the Court are two motions by defendant Dell Computer Corporation ("Dell"). One of the motions requests international judicial assistance to take evidence from Mr. Gerardus Franciscus Duynisveld and the other motion requests international judicial assistance to take evidence from Mr. Frans Dietz. Both Mr. Duynisveld and Mr. Dietz are citizens of the Netherlands. Dell has filed these motions pursuant to Federal Rule of Civil Procedure 28(b)(2), and the Hague Convention on the Taking of Evidence Abroad in Civil or Commercial Matters ("Hague Evidence Convention" or "Convention"). Plaintiff Tulip Computers International B.V. ("Tulip") opposes the motions.

II. BACKGROUND

Tulip, a Dutch corporation with its principal place of business in the Netherlands, initiated this patent infringement lawsuit on November 24, 2000, asserting that Dell, a Delaware corporation with its principal place of business in Texas, is infringing its U.S. Patent No. 5,594,621 (issued Jan. 14, 1997) ("the '621 patent"). Dell answered Tulip's allegations of infringement on June 19, 2001, denying Tulip's claims of infringement and asserting the invalidity and unenforceability of the '621 patent. Discovery in the case closed on May 10, 2002. The parties completed briefing their pre-trial summary judgment motions by November 1, 2002. On December 9, 2002, the local magistrate judge issued a Report and Recommendation construing the contested '621 patent claim language. The magistrate judge has also issued Reports and Recommendations in this case addressing some of the parties' pre-trial summary judgment motions. The motions presently before the Court stem from a discovery dispute pre-dating the issue date of each of the magistrate judge's Reports and Recommendations.

III. DISCUSSION

A. THE HAGUE EVIDENCE CONVENTION

The Hague Evidence Convention serves as an alternative or "permissive" route to the Federal Rules of Civil Procedure for the taking of evidence abroad from litigants and third parties alike. The Convention allows judicial authorities in one signatory country to obtain evidence located in another signatory country "for use in judicial proceedings, commenced or contemplated." Hague Evidence Convention, Art. 1. The United States and the Netherlands are contracting states under the Hague Evidence Convention.

There are three available methods of taking evidence pursuant to the Convention:

(1) by a Letter of Request or "letter rogatory" from a U.S. judicial authority to the competent authority in the foreign state, (2) by an American or foreign diplomatic or consular officer or

agent after permission is obtained from the foreign state, and (3) by a private commissioner duly appointed by the foreign state.

Dell has opted to employ the first mechanism listed, *supra*, Letters of Requests. Pursuant to the Convention, a Letter of Request must provide the contracting state with specific information regarding the lawsuit and the information sought. The signatory state, upon receipt and consideration, "shall [then] apply the appropriate measure of compulsion" as is customary "for the execution of orders issued by the authorities of its own country." Hague Evidence Convention, Art. 10. Signatory states may refuse to execute a Letter of Request if the request "does not fall within the function of the judiciary" or if the "sovereignty or security" of the contracting state would be prejudiced but, execution "may not be refused solely on the ground that under its internal law the State of execution claims exclusive jurisdiction over the subject-matter of the action or that its internal law would not admit a right of action on it." Hague Evidence Convention, Art. 12.

The person to whom the discovery requests in a Letter of Request are directed has the right to "refuse to give evidence" to the extent that the person has a privilege under the law of the State of execution or the State of origin. Hague Evidence Convention, Art. 11. However, the Netherlands has stated that "[o]nly the court which is responsible for executing the Letter of Request shall be competent to decide whether any person concerned by the execution has a privilege or duty to refuse to give evidence under the law of a State other than the State of origin; no such privilege or duty exists under Dutch law." Hague Evidence Convention, Netherlands 2i, Art. 11.

The Netherlands has also adopted reservations to the Hague Evidence Convention pursuant to Article 23 of the Convention, which provides that "[a] Contracting State may at the time of signature, ratification or accession, declare that it will not execute Letters of Request issued for the purpose of obtaining pre-trial discovery of documents as known in Common Law countries." Hague Evidence Convention, Netherlands 2i. Thus, as implemented by the Netherlands, Letters of Request may not be acted upon if "issued for the purpose of obtaining pre-trial discovery of documents as known in Common Law countries." Hague Evidence Convention, Netherlands 2i, Art. 23.

B. THE PARTIES' ARGUMENTS

1. Dell's Position

Dell asserts that "[w]hile in the employment of Tulip, Mr. Duynisveld had knowledge of and participated in R & D activities that may be directly relevant to Dell's defenses in this case." (D.I. 458 at 2.) Similarly, Dell maintains that "[w]hile engaged by Tulip, Mr. Frans Dietz had knowledge of and participated in patent procurement activities that may be directly relevant to Dell's defenses in this case." (D.I. 459 at 2.) In particular, Dell contends that Mr. Duynisveld [and Mr. Dietz] may be able to provide information relating to "the validity of the '621 patent; the enforceability of the '621 patent; and the alleged infringement by Dell of the '621 patent." Dell contends, therefore, that since Mr. Duynisveld and Mr. Dietz are foreign nationals residing in the Netherlands and are not parties to the present litigation, discovery pursuant to the Hague Evidence Convention is proper.

Dell further asserts that the taking of evidence from these individuals compels proceeding under the Convention since all alternative efforts to obtain the evidence have failed. Dell contends that the Netherlands' reservations pursuant to Article 23 of the

Convention do not weigh against its requests. In addition, notes Dell, the parties have, during the course of this case, proceeded pursuant to the Convention to obtain evidence from other individuals. Moreover, argues Dell, Tulip's opposition is not well founded since the Dutch authorities will weigh the breadth of the evidence sought to assure compliance with the Convention and Netherlands judicial procedure. Dell contends that the documents and testimony sought are not privileged as Tulip maintains and, even if the evidence were privileged, it would first be returned to this Court, thus placing the Court in a position "to determine whether any applicable privilege prohibits the production of certain documents to Dell."

2. Tulip's Position

Tulip contends that the Court must apply a much higher standard than is applied in this country when ordering discovery, if the Court authorizes Dell's request to proceed pursuant to the Hague Evidence Convention, since use of the Convention raises issues of territoriality and comity. In particular, Tulip argues that Article 23 of the Convention prohibits the broad document inquiry sought by Dell because Dell's requests do not conform to the Netherlands' reservations with regard to Article 23, which may be characterized as prohibiting American-style discovery "fishing expeditions." In addition, asserts Tulip, the Court should deny Dell's requests because much of the evidence Dell seeks is privileged information. Moreover, maintains Tulip, the evidence sought is either irrelevant to the proceedings or constitutes inadmissible hearsay.

C. ANALYSIS

"A party which seeks the application of the Hague [Evidence] Convention procedures rather than the Federal Rules [of Civil Procedure] bears the burden of persuading the trial court []" of the necessity of proceeding pursuant to the Hague Evidence Convention. *Valois of Am., Inc. v. Risdon Corp.*, 183 F.R.D. 344, 346 (D. Conn. 1997). That burden is not great, however, since the "Convention procedures are available whenever they will facilitate the gathering of evidence by the means authorized in the Convention." *Aerospatiale*, 482 U.S. at 541. Factors relevant to the Court's decision include "considerations of comity, the relative interests of the parties including the interest in avoiding abusive discovery, and the ease and efficiency of alternative formats for discovery." *Madanes v. Madanes*, 199 F.R.D. 135, 141 (S.D.N.Y. 2001).

Resort to the Hague Evidence Convention in this instance is appropriate since both Mr. Duynisveld and Mr. Dietz are not parties to the lawsuit, have not voluntarily subjected themselves to discovery, are citizens of the Netherlands, and are not otherwise subject to the jurisdiction of the Court.

Tulip's arguments go more particularly to the scope of the discovery Dell seeks pursuant to the Hague Evidence Convention. The arguments do not justify wholly precluding Dell's efforts to acquire the evidence it seeks. Tulip's primary argument is that the evidence sought is privileged and Mr. Duynisveld and Mr. Dietz, therefore, should not be placed in a position to determine for themselves what information is or is not privileged in the case. Tulip contends, therefore, that in order to prevent an abuse of privilege the Court should deny Dell's requests *in toto*. The Court disagrees. Mr. Duynisveld and Mr. Dietz may avail themselves of the privilege provided in this country and in the executing country under Article 11 of the Convention. Presumably, they may also obtain counsel, if they wish, and Tulip will be free to express its own views on privilege and, if necessary, to seek this Court's opinion with respect to those views.

The Court is also not persuaded by Tulip's assertions with regard to the Netherlands reservations pursuant to Article 23 of the Convention as applied to Dell's proposed document requests. If Dell's document requests are overly broad under the law of the Netherlands, as Tulip maintains, then the requests will presumably be narrowed by the appropriate judicial authorities in the Netherlands before any documents are produced. The Court is content that such officials will make the appropriate determination under their own law.

Accordingly, it is hereby ordered.

That Dell's motions to approve requests for international judicial assistance, pursuant to the Hague Evidence Convention of 18 March 1970 on the taking of evidence in civil or commercial matters, to take evidence from Mr. Duynisveld and Mr. Dietz are granted.

NOTES AND QUESTIONS

1. The Hague Evidence Convention is not meant to be exclusive, but it may be the best practical means to obtain evidence located abroad. Courts will also, however, look to considerations of comity as specified in the Restatement (Third) of Foreign Relations of the United States, art. 442. In *Tiffany (NJ) LLC v. Qi Andrew*, 276 F.R.D. 143 (S.D.N.Y. 2011), the court weighed comity concerns and refused to order the production of documents that could lead to possible civil and criminal penalties under Chinese law. Instead the court ordered the parties to proceed under the Hague Convention. Thus, the Hague Convention is a useful tool to obtain documents or discovery with regard to sensitive matters. *See S.E.C. v. Stanford Int'l Bank, Ltd.*, 776 F. Supp. 2d 323, 337-339, 341-342 (N.D. Tex. 2011) (the foreign party would face significant hardship to produce documents under Swiss privacy law; parties must make request of Swiss government pursuant to the Hague Convention). In *In re TFT-LCD (Flat Panel) Antitrust Litigation*, No. M 07-1827 SI, 2011 WL 723571 (N.D. Cal. Feb. 22, 2011), the Special Master, in the face of privacy objections by the European Commission and Japan, ordered the production of documents for in camera review, ruling that such review alone would not violate privacy concerns. *Id.* at *1-2.

2. Under the Hague Evidence Convention, letters of request may be drafted broadly on the expectation that authorities in the country of request will narrow the request to eliminate privileged or inappropriate information. *See Pronova BioPharma Norge AS v. Teva Pharmaceuticals USA, Inc.*, 708 F. Supp. 2d 450, 453 (D. Del. 2010).

3. In some cases the U.S. court, after weighing considerations of comity, may come to the conclusion that ordering a party to produce documents located abroad is necessary because the Hague Evidence Convention will not be "effective" in the particular case. *See In re Air Cargo Shipping Servs. Antitrust Litig.*, 278 F.R.D. 51 (E.D.N.Y. 2010).

4. Letters Rogatory/Letters of Request may be issued to a non-party governmental corporation under the commercial exception to the Foreign Sovereign Immunities Act. *See Lantheus Medical Imaging, Inc. v. Zurich American Ins. Co.*, 841 F. Supp. 2d 769 (S.D.N.Y. 2012).

5. Taking a deposition in a foreign country is only possible by complying with all laws and regulations of the country in question. For example, Japan (a typical example) requires the following steps:

- A reservation request to *tokyoacs@state.gov* with complete information concerning the requesting party, the case name, and the preferred location

- Payment of the Reservation Fee
- A certified copy of the court order
- Application for a special deposition visa at the Japanese Embassy or Consulate in the United States
- A list of all participants and electronic equipment to be used

Japan requires U.S. attorneys to take depositions only at the U.S. Embassy or a U.S. consulate office in Japan. The U.S. attorney who complies with the rules will gain an appointment and the use of a deposition room in Tokyo or Osaka for the purposes of taking the deposition. Failure to comply with the rules may result in penalties and summary deportation.

2. Obtaining Evidence in the United States for Use in Foreign Courts

Federal district courts have the authority, under 28 U.S.C. §1782, to grant foreign litigants, without any requirement of reciprocity, special assistance in obtaining evidence in the United States for use in foreign courts.

In re Clerici
United States Court of Appeals, Eleventh Circuit, 2007
481 F.3d 1324

HULL, Circuit Judge:

This case involves the authority of federal district courts to assist in the production of evidence—here, sworn answers to written questions—for use in a foreign court. Appellant Patricio Clerici ("Clerici") appeals the district court's January 27, 2006 order denying his motion to vacate the district court's October 12, 2005 order granting the government's application, filed pursuant to 28 U.S.C. §1782, for judicial assistance to foreign tribunals. In its January 27, 2006 order, the district court appointed an Assistant United States Attorney to obtain sworn answers from Clerici to the questions posed in the Panamanian Court's letter rogatory. After review and oral argument, we affirm.

I. BACKGROUND

[In parts A and B of its opinion, the district court explained that Clerici, a Panamanian citizen who also resides in Miami, Florida, filed a civil lawsuit in 1998 against NoName Corporation ("NoName") and others in a Panamanian court. Clerici was able to obtain a judicial attachment of NoName's property in Panama. Clerici's lawsuit against NoName was eventually dismissed due to Clerici's failure to prosecute and the attachment was vacated. The dismissal of Clerici's case was affirmed by an appeals court in Panama. On April 27, 2001, NoName filed a lawsuit against Clerici in Panama claiming damages arising to NoName's reputation from Clerici's civil suit and the attachment proceeding. On September, 27, 2002, the Panamanian court issued an order against Clerici in an amount equivalent to $1,996,598.00 in damages and $294,589.70 in costs. NoName sought to enforce the judgment against Clerici's assets in Panama and using Panamanian civil procedure addressed a series of questions to Clerici concerning his real and personal property anywhere in the world, income, transfers, marital status, financial status (including bankruptcy), how he intended to pay the award of damages and costs, his nationalities, tax returns, and financial institutions with which Clerici had accounts.]

Because Clerici resided in the United States, NoName's petition suggested that the Panamanian Court obtain this evidence through the issuance of a letter rogatory.[11]

[T]he Panamanian Court issued a letter rogatory to the "Judicial Authorities of the City of Miami" requesting assistance with obtaining answers from Clerici, while under oath, to NoName's proposed questions. The Panamanian Court's letter rogatory stated that the evidence obtained "will be used in the civil process before this court," and the Panamanian Court cited as authority for its request the Inter-American Convention Regarding Letters Rogatory ("the Convention").

C. SECTION 1782 APPLICATION IN DISTRICT COURT

On October 11, 2005, the United States filed an *ex parte* application in the United States District Court for the Southern District of Florida, pursuant to 28 U.S.C. §1782, for an order appointing an Assistant United States Attorney as a commissioner for the purpose of obtaining the evidence requested by the Panamanian Court in its letter rogatory. Section 1782(a) provides that the district court where Clerici resides "may order him to give his testimony or statement . . . for use in a proceeding in a foreign . . . tribunal." 28 U.S.C. §1782(a). On October 12, 2005, the district court granted the government's §1782 application and appointed a commissioner "to take such steps as are necessary to obtain the evidence in conformity with the Letters Rogatory." The court-appointed commissioner then sent a letter to Clerici requesting that he sit for a deposition to answer the Panamanian Court's questions.

On December 27, 2005, Clerici filed a memorandum in opposition to the government's application. The district court construed Clerici's memorandum as a motion to vacate its previous order granting the §1782 application and appointing a commissioner. In the motion, Clerici asserted that NoName's judgment against him is invalid, is being challenged in Panama, and in any event, is unenforceable in Florida because it has not been domesticated. Clerici argued that the application should be denied because (1) the Panamanian Court's letter rogatory does not contain the necessary documentation under the terms of the Convention; and (2) §1782 cannot be used to enforce a foreign judgment pursuant to a letter rogatory. Clerici also argued that, even if §1782 authorized the requested assistance, the district court should, in its discretion, decline to grant judicial assistance because (1) the letter rogatory is an attempt to enforce a foreign judgment that has not been domesticated, and therefore, is unenforceable; and (2) the application is "unduly intrusive."

III. DISCUSSION

A. SECTION 1782

A district court has the authority to grant an application for judicial assistance if the following statutory requirements in §1782(a) are met: (1) the request must be made "by a

---

11. "A letter rogatory is the request by a domestic court to a foreign court to take evidence from a certain witness." *Intel Corp. v. Advanced Micro Devices, Inc.*, 542 U.S. 241, 248 n.1 (2004).

foreign or international tribunal," or by "any interested person"; (2) the request must seek evidence, whether it be the "testimony or statement" of a person or the production of "a document or other thing"; (3) the evidence must be "for use in a proceeding in a foreign or international tribunal"; and (4) the person from whom discovery is sought must reside or be found in the district of the district court ruling on the application for assistance. 28 U.S.C. §1782(a). If these requirements are met, then §1782 "authorizes, but does not require, a federal district court to provide assistance. . . ." *Intel*, 542 U.S. at 255.

Here, Clerici does not dispute that the Panamanian Court is a foreign tribunal or that he resides within the Southern District of Florida. Therefore, the first and fourth requirements for a proper request under §1782 are met.

As to the second statutory requirement—that the request must seek evidence—Clerici argues that the Panamanian Court is not seeking evidence, but rather is attempting to enforce its judgment through a §1782 request. We disagree because the Panamanian Court asked for assistance in obtaining only Clerici's sworn answers to questions regarding his assets and other financial matters. The district court recognized this key distinction and properly concluded that the request for assistance was limited to seeking evidence from Clerici, and therefore, was proper under §1782.

As to the third statutory requirement, we reject Clerici's contention that the requested evidence was not "for use in a proceeding" before the Panamanian Court. Here, there is a proceeding currently pending before the Panamanian Court that allows NoName or the Panamanian Court to question Clerici under oath about his properties, rights, credits, sustenance means, and other sources of income from the date of his court-ordered obligation. Had Clerici been residing in Panama, NoName or the Panamanian Court would have been able to interrogate Clerici directly with the questions proposed by NoName. Because Clerici was residing in Florida, however, the Panamanian Court issued a letter rogatory seeking international assistance in order to obtain this evidence. The Panamanian Court's letter rogatory itself stated that this evidence "will be used in the civil process before this court." Such a request is clearly within the range of discovery authorized under §1782 and comports with the purpose of the statute to provide assistance to foreign tribunals.

Because all four statutory requirements are met, the Panamanian Court's request for assistance in obtaining Clerici's sworn answers for use in the proceeding in Panama was proper under §1782 Accordingly, the district court had authority to grant the §1782 discovery application.

Even so, "a district court is not required to grant a §1782(a) discovery application simply because it has the authority to do so." *Intel*, 542 U.S. at 264 ("[A] district court's compliance with a §1782 request is not mandatory.") Once the prima facie requirements are satisfied, the Supreme Court in *Intel* noted these factors to be considered in exercising the discretion granted under §1782: (1) whether "the person from whom discovery is sought is a participant in the foreign proceeding," because "the need for §1782(a) aid generally is not as apparent as it ordinarily is when evidence is sought from a nonparticipant"; (2) "the nature of the foreign tribunal, the character of the proceedings underway abroad, and the receptivity of the foreign government or the court or agency abroad to U.S. federal-court judicial assistance"; (3) "whether the §1782(a) request conceals an attempt to circumvent foreign proof-gathering restrictions or other policies of a foreign country or the United States"; and (4) whether the request is otherwise "unduly intrusive or burdensome." *Id.* at 264–265. The Supreme Court in *Intel* added that "unduly intrusive or burdensome requests may be rejected or trimmed." *Id.* at 265.

Our review of the *Intel* factors reveals that none of the factors favors Clerici, and that the district court did not abuse its discretion in granting the §1782 application.

As to the first *Intel* factor, because Clerici is a party in the foreign proceeding, this factor normally would favor Clerici and suggest that §1782 assistance is not necessary. In this case, however, the first factor does not favor Clerici because Clerici has left Panama and the Panamanian Court cannot enforce its order against Clerici directly while Clerici is in the United States. Given the particular factual circumstances in this case, the first *Intel* factor does not favor Clerici.

As to the second and third *Intel* factors, there is nothing in the record to suggest that the district court should have declined to grant the §1782 application based on the nature of the foreign tribunal or the character of the proceedings in Panama, or that the Panamanian Court's request is merely an attempt to circumvent foreign proof-gathering restrictions. Rather, these factors all support the district court's decision to grant the §1782 application given that the foreign tribunal here is the Panamanian Court and the Panamanian Court itself issued the letter rogatory requesting assistance due to Clerici's presence in the United States.

Finally, as to the fourth *Intel* factor—whether the §1782 request is unduly intrusive—the district court's order granting the §1782 application specifically indicated that if Clerici wished to pursue his "unduly intrusive" argument, Clerici should file a motion to limit discovery. Clerici never did so and instead chose to appeal the grant of *any* discovery whatsoever. On appeal, as in the district court, Clerici does not identify the terms of the written request that are overly broad or assert how the scope of the request should be narrowed. Thus, we, like the district court, have no occasion to address the scope of the Panamanian Court's discovery request.

In sum, the district court had authority to grant the §1782 application, and Clerici has not shown that the district court abused its discretion in doing so.

AFFIRMED.

NOTES AND QUESTIONS

1. There is continuing conflict and controversy over carrying out American-style discovery in foreign countries. In *Societé Nationale Industrielle Aerospatiale v. United States District Court*, 482 U.S. 522 (1987), the Supreme Court held that the Hague Evidence Convention is neither the exclusive nor the required first option for discovery outside the United States. The Hague Convention is simply "one method of seeking evidence that a court may elect to employ." *Id.* at 540. The Supreme Court further stated that "American courts, in supervising pretrial proceedings, should exercise special vigilance to protect foreign litigants from unnecessary or unduly burdensome discovery. Objections to 'abusive' discovery that foreign litigants advance should therefore receive the most careful consideration." *Id.* at 547. Did the court in the *Tulip* case at p. 695 comply with this standard?

2. Many countries have passed "blocking statutes" under which government officials can prevent the production of documents or taking of evidence in certain cases. What is the impact of these blocking statutes? Consider the Restatement (Third) of Foreign Relations Law of the United States (1987), which provides in relevant part:

§442. *Requests for Disclosure: Law of the United States*

(1) (a) A court or agency in the United States, when authorized by statute or rule of court, may order a person subject to its jurisdiction to produce documents, objects, or other information . . . even if the information or the person in possession of the information is outside the United States.

(b) Failure to comply with an order to produce information may subject the person to whom the order is directed to sanctions, including dismissal of a claim or defense, or default judgment. . . .

(2) If disclosure of information located outside the United States is prohibited by a law, regulation, or order of a court or other authority of the state in which the information or prospective witness is located,

(a) a court or agency in the United States may require the person to whom the order is directed to make a good faith effort to secure permission from the foreign authorities to make the information available;

***

(c) a court or agency may . . . make findings of fact adverse to a party that has failed to comply with the order for production, even if that party has made a good faith effort to secure permission. . . .

E. Recognition and Foreign Enforcement of Foreign Judgments

A successful plaintiff who obtains a judgment against a U.S.-based defendant in a foreign court will need to enforce the foreign judgment in the United States. How is this done?

In the United States there are two distinct legal regimes relating to the recognition and enforcement of foreign court judgments. Many states have adopted the Uniform Foreign Money Judgments Recognition Act, 13 U.L.A. 263 (1986), which is set out and explained in this section. This Uniform Act adopts by statute principles of comity set out in the seminal case of *Hilton v. Guyot*, 159 U.S. 113, 227–229 (1885). States that have not adopted the Uniform Act and the federal government apply the *Hilton* comity principles as a matter of common law.

No general international treaty governs the recognition and enforcement of foreign court judgments (unlike arbitration where the New York Convention is applied by 149 parties). Thus, when it comes to recognition of foreign court judgments, each nation is on its own. The 2005 Convention on the Choice of Court Agreements, June 30, 2005, 44 I.L.M. 1294 (2005), which was concluded by the Hague Conference on Private International Law, however, provides an international system for recognizing and enforcing foreign court judgments. Under the Choice of Court Convention, the court chosen by parties to international commercial transactions must hear the case (unless the agreement between the parties is null and void under the law of that state) while courts in non-chosen states-parties to the Convention must both decline jurisdiction to hear the dispute and recognize and enforce any judgment issued by the chosen court. But the Choice of Courts Convention is not in force. While the United States has signed this Convention, it has not been ratified and no implementing legislation has been enacted. This matter is sensitive as it would expand the jurisdiction of the federal courts to recognize many foreign court judgments that are now left to state law.

We further examine enforcement of foreign judgments in the United States below.

PROBLEM 8-17

A group of MNEs with major commercial piracy problems in China has been persuaded by a U.S. law firm to sue the China Small Commodities City Group, Ltd. (CSCG, which is discussed in Chapter Seven; see pp. 543-551, *supra*), a major supplier of counterfeit products in China and around the world, in U.S. court. The MNEs have long been frustrated and angry about the lack of effective enforcement through the Chinese legal system and so the U.S. law firm has convinced them that an alternative is to sue the CSCG in a U.S. court. The U.S. law firm argues that the Chinese legal system is weak, is prone to local protectionism, and is notorious for damage awards that are ridiculously low by U.S. standards. Following this advice, the MNEs file suit in Texas against the CSCG, asserting jurisdiction on the basis that the CSCG has a relationship with an independent distributor in Texas. The U.S. law firm conducts extensive discovery, files a large number of motions, and assigns a large number of lawyers to conduct the trial (and, of course, receives very hefty legal fees from the MNEs). As a result, the MNEs recover a judgment against the CSCG for $50 million in damages and are ecstatic. However, as CSCG's property in the United States amounts to no more than $50,000, the MNEs are now wondering what to do with their judgment and have the following questions.

(1) Can this judgment be enforced against the CSCG in China? If so, what procedures must the judgment holders follow in China, which follows the general procedures in the international enforcement of judgments described in *Somportex* below?

(2) What standards or analysis will an international court use in determining whether to enforce a judgment? Assume that China will follow the general approach in *Somportex*.

(3) Can the CSCG argue that the U.S. judgment is not entitled to recognition in China because U.S. courts are clearly biased against China in intellectual property cases due to a negative general public perception and that it would be impossible for China to win in a piracy case brought by a U.S. plaintiff in a U.S. court? Is this a ground for refusal to recognize the judgment? Assume that China would follow the same approach on the recognition of foreign money judgments set forth in *Society of Lloyd's* following *Somportex*. Will the argument succeed? What must be shown?

(4) What are the chances of collecting on the $50 million judgment against CSCG in China?

(5) Is the strategy of suing the CSCG in the United States a good one?

Somportex Ltd. v. Philadelphia Chewing Gum Corp.
United States Court of Appeals, Third Circuit, 1971
453 F.2d 435, *cert. denied*, 405 U.S. 1017 (1972)

Aldisert, Circuit Judge.

Several interesting questions are presented in this appeal from the district court's order granting summary judgment to enforce a default judgment entered by an English court. To resolve them, a complete recitation of the procedural history of this case is necessary.

This case has its genesis in a transaction between appellant, Philadelphia Chewing Gum Corporation, and Somportex Limited, a British corporation, which was to merchandise appellant's wares in Great Britain under the trade name "Tarzan Bubble Gum." According to the facts as alleged by appellant, there was a proposal which involved the participation of Brewster Leeds and Co., Inc., and M.S. International, Inc., third-party defendants in the court below. Brewster made certain arrangements with Somportex to furnish gum manufactured by Philadelphia; M.S. International, as agent for the licensor of the trade name "Tarzan," was to furnish the African name to the American gum to be sold in England. For reasons not relevant to our limited inquiry, the transaction never reached fruition.

Somportex filed an action against Philadelphia for breach of contract in the Queen's Bench Division of the High Court of England. Notice of the issuance of a Writ of Summons was served, in accordance with the rules and with the leave of the High Court, upon Philadelphia at its registered address in Havertown, Pennsylvania, on May 15, 1967. The extraterritorial service was based on the English version of long-arm statutes utilized by many American states. Philadelphia then consulted a firm of English solicitors, who, by letter of July 14, 1967, advised its Pennsylvania lawyers:

> I have arranged with the Solicitors for Somportex Limited that they will let me have a copy of their Affidavit and exhibits to that Affidavit which supported their application to serve out of the Jurisdiction. Subject to the contents of the Affidavit, and any further information that can be provided by Philadelphia Chewing Gum Corporation after we have had the opportunity of seeing the Affidavit, it may be possible to make an application to the Court for an Order setting the Writ aside. But for such an application to be successful we will have to show that on the facts the matter does not fall within the provision of (f) and (g) [of the English long-arm statute].
>
> In the meantime we will enter a conditional Appearance to the Writ in behalf of Philadelphia Chewing Gum Corporation in order to preserve the status quo.

On August 9, 1967, the English solicitors entered a "conditional appearance to the Writ" and filed a motion to set aside the Writ of Summons. At a hearing before a Master on November 13, 1967, the solicitors appeared and disclosed that Philadelphia had elected not to proceed with the summons or to contest the jurisdiction of the English Court, but instead intended to obtain leave of court to withdraw appearance of counsel. The Master then dismissed Philadelphia's summons to set aside plaintiff's Writ of Summons. Four days later, the solicitors sought to withdraw their appearance as counsel for Philadelphia, contending that it was a conditional appearance only. On November 27, 1967, after a Master granted the motion, Somportex appealed. The appeal was denied after hearing before a single judge, but the Court of Appeal, reversing the decision of the Master, held that the appearance was unconditional and that the submission to the jurisdiction by Philadelphia was, therefore, effective. But the court let stand "the original order which was made by the master on Nov. 13 dismissing the application to set aside. The writ therefore will stand. On the other hand, if the American company would wish to appeal from the order of Nov. 13, I see no reason why the time should not be extended and they can argue that matter out at a later stage if they should so wish."

Thereafter, Philadelphia made a calculated decision: it decided to do nothing. It neither asked for an extension of time nor attempted in any way to proceed with an appeal from the Master's order dismissing its application to set aside the Writ. Instead, it directed its English solicitors to withdraw from the case. There being no appeal, the Master's order became final.

Somportex then filed a Statement of Claim which was duly served in accordance with English Court rules. In addition, by separate letter, it informed Philadelphia of the significance and effect of the pleading, the procedural posture of the case, and its intended course of action.

Philadelphia persisted in its course of inaction; it failed to file a defense. Somportex obtained a default judgment against it in the Queen's Bench Division of the High Court of Justice in England for the sum of £39,562.10 (approximately $94,000). The award reflected some $45,000 for loss of profit; $46,000 for loss of good will and $2,500 for costs, including attorneys' fees.

Thereafter, Somportex filed a diversity action in the court below, seeking to enforce the foreign judgment, and attached to the complaint a certified transcript of the English proceeding. The district court granted plaintiff's motion for summary judgment.

Appellant presents a cluster of contentions supporting its major thesis that we should not extend hospitality to the English judgment. First, it contends, and we agree, that because our jurisdiction is based solely on diversity, "the law to be applied . . . is the law of the state," in this case, Pennsylvania law. *Erie R.R. Co. v. Tompkins.*

Pennsylvania distinguishes between judgments obtained in the courts of her sister states, which are entitled to full faith and credit, and those of foreign courts, which are subject to principles of comity. *In re Christoffs Estate,* 411 Pa. 419, *cert. denied,* 375 U.S. 965 (1964).

Comity is a recognition which one nation extends within its own territory to the legislative, executive, or judicial acts of another. It is not a rule of law, but one of practice, convenience, and expediency. Although more than mere courtesy and accommodation, comity does not achieve the force of an imperative or obligation. Rather, it is a nation's expression of understanding which demonstrates due regard both to international duty and convenience and to the rights of persons protected by its own laws. Comity should be withheld only when its acceptance would be contrary or prejudicial to the interest of the nation called upon to give it effect.

Thus, the court in *Christoffs, supra,* 192 A.2d at 739, acknowledged the governing standard enunciated in *Hilton v. Guyot:*

> When an action is brought in a court of this country by a citizen of a foreign country against one of our own citizens . . . and the foreign judgment appears to have been rendered by a competent court, having jurisdiction of the cause and of the parties and upon due allegations and proofs, and opportunity to defend against them, and its proceedings are according to the course of a civilized jurisprudence, and are stated in a clear and formal record, the judgment is prima facie evidence, at least, of the truth of the matter adjudged; and it should be held conclusive upon the merits tried in the foreign court, unless some special ground is shown for impeaching the judgment, as by showing that it was affected by fraud or prejudice, or that by the principles of international law, and by the comity of our own country, it should not be given full credit and effect.

It is by this standard, therefore, that appellant's arguments must be measured.

Appellant's contention that the district court failed to make an independent examination of the factual and legal basis of the jurisdiction of the English Court at once argues too much and says too little. The reality is that the court did examine the legal basis of asserted jurisdiction and decided the issue adversely to appellant.

Indeed, we do not believe it was necessary for the court below to reach the question of whether the factual complex of the contractual dispute permitted extraterritorial service under the English long arm statute. In its opinion denying leave of defense counsel to withdraw, the Court of Appeal specifically gave Philadelphia the opportunity to have the factual issue tested before the courts; moreover, Philadelphia was allocated additional time to do just that. Three months went by with no activity forthcoming and then, as described by the district court, "[d]uring this three month period, defendant changed its strategy and, not wishing to do anything which might result in its submitting to the English Court's jurisdiction, decided to withdraw its appearance altogether." Under these circumstances, we hold that defendant cannot choose its forum to test the factual basis of jurisdiction. It was given, and it waived, the opportunity of making the adequate presentation in the English Court.

Additionally, appellant attacks the English practice wherein a conditional appearance attacking jurisdiction may, by court decision, be converted into an unconditional one. It cannot effectively argue that this practice constitutes "some special ground . . . for impeaching the judgment," as to render the English judgment unwelcome in Pennsylvania under principles of international law and comity because it was obtained by procedures contrary or prejudicial to the host state. The English practice in this respect is identical to that set forth in both the Federal and Pennsylvania rules of civil procedure. Fed. R. Civ. P. 12(b)(2) provides the vehicle for attacking jurisdiction over the person, and, in *Orange Theatre Corp. v. Rayherstz Amusement Corp.*, 139 F.2d 871, 874 (3d Cir. 1944), we said that Rule 12 "has abolished for the federal courts the age-old distinction between general and special appearances." Similarly, a conditional or "*de bene esse*" appearance no longer exists in Pennsylvania. A challenge to jurisdiction must be asserted there by a preliminary objection raising a question of jurisdiction. Pa. R.C.P. 1017(b)(1).

English law permits recovery, as compensatory damages in breach of contract, of items reflecting loss of good will and costs, including attorneys' fees. These two items formed substantial portions of the English judgment. Because they are not recoverable under Pennsylvania law, appellant would have the foreign judgment declared unenforceable because it constitutes an ". . . action on the foreign claim [which] could not have been maintained because contrary to the public policy of the forum," citing Restatement, Conflict of Laws, §445. We are satisfied with the district court's disposition of this argument:

> The Court finds that . . . while Pennsylvania may not agree that these elements should be included in damages for breach of contract, the variance with Pennsylvania law is not such that the enforcement "tends clearly to injure the public health, the public morals, the public confidence in the purity of the administration of the law, or to undermine that sense of security for individual rights, whether of personal liberty or of private property, which any citizen ought to feel, is against public policy."

Goodyear v. Brown, 155 Pa. 514, 518 (1893).

Finally, appellant contends that since "it maintains no office or employee in England and transacts no business within the country" there were not sufficient contacts there to meet the due process tests of *International Shoe Co. v. Washington*. It argues that, at best, "the only contact Philadelphia had with England was the negotiations allegedly conducted by an independent New York exporter by letter, telephone and telegram to sell Philadelphia's products in England." In *Hanson v. Denckla*, 357 U.S. 235, 253 (1958), Chief Justice Warren said: "The application of [the requirement of contact] rule will vary with the quality and nature of the defendant's activity, but it is essential in each case that there be some act by which the defendant purposely avails itself of the privilege of conducting business within the forum State, thus invoking the benefits and protection of its laws." We have concluded that whether the New York exporter was an independent contractor or Philadelphia's agent was a matter to be resolved by the English Court.

For the purpose of the constitutional argument, we must assume the proper agency relationship. So construed, we find his activity would constitute the "quality and nature of the defendant's activity" similar to that of the defendant in *McGee v. International Life Ins. Co.*, 355 U.S. 220 (1957), there held to satisfy due process requirements.

In sum, we find that the English proceedings met all the tests enunciated in *Christoffs, supra*. We are not persuaded that appellant met its burden of showing that the British "decree is so palpably tainted by fraud or prejudice as to outrage our sense of justice, or [that] the process of the foreign tribunal was invoked to achieve a result contrary to our laws or public policy or to circumvent our laws or public policy." *Christoffs, supra,* 192 A.2d at 739.

The judgment of the district court will be affirmed.

Society of Lloyd's v. Siemon-Netto
United States Court of Appeals, District of Columbia Circuit, 2006
457 F.3d 94

GARLAND, Circuit Judge.

Defendants Gillian and Uwe Siemon-Netto are two among the hundreds of "Names" [explained below] whom the Society of Lloyd's has sued for nonpayment of reinsurance premiums. The English High Court of Justice, Queen's Bench Division, entered money judgments in favor of Lloyd's against the Siemon-Nettos. Lloyd's then sued to enforce those judgments in the United States District Court for the District of Columbia. The district court granted summary judgment in favor of Lloyd's, and we now affirm.

I

A

The Parliament of the United Kingdom authorized the Society of Lloyd's to regulate a London insurance market through a series of Parliamentary Acts, known as the "Lloyd's Acts," passed between 1871 and 1982. In *Haynsworth,* the Fifth Circuit explained the structure of the Lloyd's market as follows:

> Lloyd's is a 300-year-old market in which individual and corporate underwriters known as "Names" underwrite insurance. The Corporation of Lloyd's, which is also known as the Society of Lloyd's, provides the building and personnel necessary to the market's administrative operations. The Corporation is run by the Council of Lloyd's, which promulgates "Byelaws," regulates the market, and generally controls Lloyd's administrative functions.
>
> Lloyd's does not underwrite insurance; the Names do so by forming groups known as syndicates. Within each syndicate, participating Names underwrite for their own accounts and at their own risk. . . .
>
> Names must become members of Lloyd's in order to participate in the market. Names must pass a means test to ensure their ability to meet their underwriting obligations, post security (typically, a letter of credit), and personally appear in London before a representative of the Council of Lloyd's to acknowledge their awareness of the various risks and requirements of membership, and in particular the fact that underwriting in the Lloyd's market subjects them to unlimited personal liability.

Haynsworth, 121 F.3d at 958–959.

B

Gillian and Uwe Siemon-Netto were among the Names who neither accepted their settlement offers nor paid the reinsurance premium for their outstanding underwriting liabilities. Nor did they take the opportunity afforded by the English courts to pursue separate fraud claims against Lloyd's.

On March 24, 1997, Lloyd's sued the Siemon-Nettos in England for breach of their contractual obligations to pay the reinsurance premiums. The English courts granted summary judgment against the Siemon-Nettos and on December 21, 1998, entered individual money judgments against Gillian Siemon-Netto for £280,055.72 and against Uwe Siemon-Netto for £87,109.97.

On July 15, 2003, Lloyd's filed suit against the Siemon-Nettos in the United States District Court for the District of Columbia, seeking recognition and enforcement of the English judgments under the District's Uniform Foreign Money Judgments Recognition Act of 1995 ("Recognition Act"), D.C. Code §15-381 *et seq.* Venue was based on the Siemon-Nettos' status as District residents and jurisdiction on diversity of citizenship.

II

Section 15-382 of the Recognition Act provides, in pertinent part, that "[e]xcept as provided in section 15-383," a "foreign-money judgment is enforceable in the same manner as the judgment of a sister jurisdiction which is entitled to full faith and credit." D.C. Code §15-382. Section 15-383 contains a list of specific exceptions, only one of which the Siemon-Nettos claim here:

A foreign-money judgment need not be recognized if: . . . (3) [t]he cause of action on which the judgment is based is repugnant to the public policy of the District of Columbia.

D.C. Code §15-383(b)(3). Concluding that none of the Siemon-Nettos' four affirmative defenses came within that exception, the district court struck them all as legally insufficient to bar enforcement of the English judgments.

As their first affirmative defense, the Siemon-Nettos contend that "the foreign-money judgment[s] obtained by Lloyd's in the courts of the United Kingdom [are] repugnant to the public policy of the District of Columbia and should not be recognized because the cause of action on which [they were] based conflicts with the public policy of the District of Columbia." The defendants list three grounds for finding repugnancy: (1) "a contract cannot be enforced against the party who did not knowingly assent to its terms"; (2) "the legislation on which the foreign cause of action was based (Lloyd's Act 1982) and [the] Reconstruction and Renewal Byelaw were unenforceable and voidable as a result of Lloyd's failure to satisfy the conditions imposed on it by the Parliament in exchange for the legislation"; and (3) "the Lloyd's Act 1982 constituted an unlawful delegation of legislative and governmental power to Lloyd's, a private business entity."

1. As their first ground, the defendants contend that the English judgments are repugnant to District public policy because they enforce a contract to which they did not assent. The contract at issue, they argue, is the Equitas reinsurance contract. That contract was not signed by them, but rather by the substitute agent appointed by Lloyd's to negotiate and sign for all Names who rejected the Reconstruction and Renewal (R & R) Plan. Recognition of such a contract, they insist, is repugnant to the general contract law principle that a contract requires mutual assent.

Section 15-383(b)(3) of the Recognition Act permits nonrecognition of a foreign judgment only if "the *cause of action* on which [it] is based" is repugnant to public policy. D.C. Code §15-383(b)(3)(b)(3) (emphasis added). A cause of action is the legal authority (here, English contract law) that permits a court to provide redress for a particular kind of claim (here, Lloyd's contention that the defendants breached their obligations to pay the reinsurance premiums). Accordingly, the dispositive question is whether the core principles of English contract law are repugnant to the public policy of the District of Columbia, not whether any particular application of that cause of action is repugnant.

That question is easily answered. As the district court noted, the Siemon-Nettos "have not suggested that English contract law principles differ substantively from those in the District of Columbia." Indeed, District of Columbia contract law, like American contract law in general, is historically derived from (and similar to) the English common law of contract. That being the case, it would be hard to regard the latter as repugnant to the former, and no federal court has done so.

The defendants do not suggest, for example, that English contract law principles permit parties to be bound to a contract without their consent. Rather, they contend only that this is the "practical effect" of the English judgments holding them responsible for a reinsurance contract they refused to sign. But even if we were to consider repugnancy on such an "as applied" basis, we still could not find the judgments repugnant to public policy, because the English court did not bind the Siemon-Nettos to a contract to which they did not assent. To the contrary, it held them to a contract to which they did assent: the General Undertaking.

When the Siemon-Nettos became Names, they (not their agents) personally signed a "standardized contract between Lloyd's and the individual Names" known as the General Undertaking. The Lloyd's Act 1982 specifically authorized Lloyd's to make Byelaws for the purpose of appointing substitute agents to bind Names, *see* Lloyd's Act, 1982, Sched. 2, §18(b), and such a "Substitute Agents Byelaw" was in existence when the defendants signed the General Undertaking. Thereafter, Lloyd's issued another series of Byelaws that authorized the appointment of "substitute agent[s] on behalf of Names specifically 'to execute the Reinsurance Contract for itself and on behalf of the Members.'" *Turner,* 303 F.3d at 328 n.3 (citing Lloyd's Byelaw No. 20 of 1983; Byelaw No. 82 of 1995; AUA9 Resolution of 1996).

It was no doubt risky for the defendants to agree to be bound by future Byelaws in this way. But the General Undertaking was no contract of adhesion. The Siemon-Nettos were investors who qualified for status as Lloyd's Names under a set of stringent criteria, and who presumably thought the upside potential was worth the downside risk. Regardless of whether we would reach the same disposition under District of Columbia contract law, we cannot say that the English courts' decision to bind the defendants under these circumstances is repugnant to the public policy of this jurisdiction.

2. The defendants' second ground for claiming that the English judgments are repugnant to District policy begins with their contention that the legislation (the Lloyd's Act 1982) that permitted Lloyd's to promulgate Byelaws — particularly the Byelaws that authorized Lloyd's to appoint substitute agents to execute the reinsurance contract on behalf of the Names — also imposed certain conditions on Lloyd's (i.e., the provision of better quality information to Names about the status of the Lloyd's market). The defendants argue that, because Lloyd's assertedly failed to satisfy those conditions, the Byelaws passed pursuant to that legislation "were unenforceable and voidable."

But the question of whether the Lloyd's Byelaws were valid under English law is itself a question of English — not District of Columbia — law. And it is a question that the English courts have already answered, concluding that the pertinent Byelaws are indeed valid. *See Society of Lloyd's v. Leighs,* [1997] C.L.C. 759 (Q.B.). We cannot reconsider that decision here. Certainly the defendants have pointed to nothing about the principles applied by the English courts in reaching that decision that would render repugnant the contractual cause of action on which Lloyd's judgments are based.

3. The third ground advanced by the defendants is their claim that "the Lloyd's Act 1982 [itself] constituted an unlawful delegation of legislative and governmental power to Lloyd's, a private business entity." But whether the Lloyd's Act constituted an "unlawful delegation" under English law is again a question that only the English courts can answer; in fact, it is a question that the act of state doctrine bars us from even asking. *See World Wide Minerals, Ltd. v. Republic of Kazakhstan*, 296 F.3d 1154, 1164 (D.C. Cir. 2002) (noting that the "act of state doctrine 'precludes the courts of this country from inquiring into the validity of the public acts a recognized foreign sovereign power committed within its own territory.'") (quoting *Banco Nacional de Cuba v. Sabbatino*, 376 U.S. 398, 401 (1964)). Moreover, there is once again nothing in the defendants' argument to support the only ground the defendants advance for nonrecognition of Lloyd's English judgments: that the contractual cause of action on which those judgments are based is repugnant to District policy.

In sum, we conclude that the district court committed no error in striking any of the Siemon-Nettos' affirmative defenses under Federal Rule of Civil Procedure 12(f).

***

At oral argument, counsel for the defendants made clear that the underlying basis of their defense is their belief that the English courts are biased in favor of Lloyd's: that is, that those courts have a "bias and prejudice in favor of Lloyd's under circumstances which make it impossible for a Name to win." The Recognition Act includes an exception for this kind of defense to a foreign judgment, but it requires proof that the "judgment was rendered under a system that does not provide impartial tribunals or procedures compatible with the requirements of due process of law." D.C. Code §15-383(a)(1).

The defendants do not assert that English courts fall within that category and could not prove it if they did. Indeed, the Siemon-Nettos' only evidence of the English courts' asserted "bias and prejudice" is that other Names in their position—whose arguments they believe had merit—lost their cases in those courts. But the fact that the Names' arguments did not prevail hardly establishes the partiality of the courts that heard them. Indeed, if it did, the fact that Names have lost similar (albeit not identical) cases in eight United States Courts of Appeals would require us to reach the same conclusion regarding American courts.

AFFIRMED.

NOTES AND QUESTIONS

1. The recognition and enforcement of foreign judgments in the United States is often a matter of state law. Selected provisions of the Uniform Foreign Money-Judgments Recognition Act, 13 U.L.A. 43 (2002), which has been adopted in many states, reads as follows in relevant part:

Section 4:

    (a) A foreign judgment is not conclusive if

        (1) the judgment was rendered under a system which does not provide impartial tribunals or procedures compatible with the requirements of due process of law;

        (2) the foreign court did not have personal jurisdiction over the defendant; or

        (3) the foreign court did not have jurisdiction over the subject matter.

    (b) a foreign judgment need not be recognized if

        (1) the defendant in the proceedings in the foreign court did not receive notice of the proceedings in sufficient time to enable him to defend;

(2) the judgment was obtained by fraud;

(3) the [cause of action or claim for relief] on which the judgment is based is repugnant to the public policy of this state;

(4) the judgment conflicts with another final and conclusive judgment. . . .

***

The court must also have territorial jurisdiction over the defendant. *See* Uniform Foreign Money-Judgments Recognition Act §5, *supra.*

2. *Recognizing and enforcing a foreign default judgment.* If a U.S. business is sued in a foreign court, should the U.S. business simply ignore the proceeding because it has no assets in the foreign country upon which a judgment can be levied? This tactic backfired in the case of *Syncrude Canada Ltd. v. The Highland Consulting Group, Inc.,* 916 F. Supp. 2d 620 (D. Md. 2013). In this case, Highland, energy consulting firms based in St. Michaels, Maryland, and Zug, Switzerland, were sued by Syncrude in Alberta, Canada. When the Highland entities did not appear, a default judgment was entered against them. Syncrude then filed suit in the district court in Maryland to enforce the default judgment. Although the recognition and enforcement of the judgment was governed by Maryland law, the federal court had jurisdiction on the basis of complete diversity of citizenship, 28 U.S.C. §1332(a) (2012) (but since diversity jurisdiction does not extend to foreign plaintiffs suing foreign defendants, the Swiss Highland entity was dismissed, 916 F. Supp. 2d at 624). In the district court, the Maryland Highland defendants contested recognition under the Maryland-enacted version of the Money Judgments Recognition Act on the basis that the service of process by the Alberta court was deficient and that it was against Maryland public policy to enforce a default judgment. *See id.* The court, however, ruled that service of process by registered mail was permissible under the Hague Service Convention, and that the default judgment was enforceable: "This court is hard-pressed to understand how a default judgment issued in a case where the defendants had actual knowledge of the suit yet refused to file any response is repugnant to federal or Maryland public policy." *See id.* at 624–628.

3. Certain nations have concluded international treaties to govern mutual recognition of their judgments. The most important is the Brussels Convention on Jurisdiction and the Enforcement of Judgments in Civil and Commercial Matters, Sept. 27, 1968, 8 I.L.M. 229 (the Brussels Convention). The Brussels Convention system was enlarged with the accession of new member states to the European Community/Union as well as a "parallel convention" known as the Convention on Jurisdiction and the Recognition and Enforcement of Judgments in Civil and Commercial Matters (New Lugano Convention), Oct. 30, 2007, 2007 O.J. (L 339) (entered into force, 2010). In December 2000, the Council of the European Union adopted a new regulation that replaces the Brussels Convention for all EU members except Denmark. *See* Council Regulation 44/2001 on Jurisdiction and the Recognition and Enforcement of Judgments in Civil and Commercial Matters, 2001 O.J. (L 12) 1. In 2012, the European Union issued an updated regulation on recognition and enforcement of EU judgments known as the Recast Regulation: Regulation 1215/2012 on Jurisdiction and the Recognition and Enforcement of Judgments in Civil and Commercial Matters, 2012 O.J. (L 351) 1, which will replace the foregoing legal instruments and become effective in January 2015. Under these legal rules, judgments rendered by courts in the 28-member EU are routinely recognized and enforced in other EU member states.

9 *Corporate Social Responsibility*

I. *Introduction*

The growth and importance of international business in the latter half of the twentieth century and the first part of the twenty-first raises many issues concerning the social responsibility of business to civil society. Corporate social responsibility (CSR) and business ethics are especially important in the international arena because of the rise of MNEs and the perception that they wield extraordinary power and influence. In fact, in terms of economic power, many MNEs have more annual revenues than the Gross Domestic Product of the majority of states of the world. MNEs usually operate through individual, linked companies so that they consist of a corporate group organized around a holding company and various subsidiary corporations. MNEs, of course, are subject to the national regulatory laws and policies of the countries in which they operate, but, because they are international, they may be able to organize their operations to avoid significant social responsibility within nations, and their economic and political power may allow them to pressure states into complying with their wishes. Opponents of globalization argue that powerful corporations are controlled by unscrupulous individuals who are driven purely by greed and profit, view themselves as above the law, and evade their responsibilities to their shareholders and the public. Developing countries in particular may be subject to their influence and control.

This is the perception of many, but is this borne out by the facts? Undoubtedly, there are abuses, but how widespread are they? Is avoidance of CSR the norm or the exceptional case? Furthermore, is it advisable for an MNE to shirk its CSR even if it has the opportunity? Are there reasons besides legal compulsion for an MNE to operate in a socially responsible way? Finally, what standards, guidelines, and procedures should an international company use to be socially responsible? Should it simply comply with the individual national requirements in each country in which it does business or should it adopt uniform minimum standards for all its operations? Although these issues may seem to be theoretical questions for an ivory tower far removed from the corporate boardroom, some recent developments provide clear indications that MNEs cannot ignore the concerns arising from CSR. The materials below set forth the major developments in this area.

In this chapter, we consider the international law norms that apply to international business as well as voluntary codes of conduct and other incentives and reasons why international business must today be very concerned with CSR.

We introduce these CSR concerns in a practical context in the problems below. To address these problems, consider the following articles by Professors Charney and Paust and the accompanying materials.

PROBLEM 9-1

Dresser, Inc., is a Texas company engaged in the highly competitive and labor-intensive athletic shoe and apparel industry. The CEO of Dresser comes to your law firm and says, "To survive in our business, we need to move our operations overseas and we need to find rock-bottom labor costs. I want a survey done of the world's labor laws and I want you to identify the country with the lowest level of protection and the fewest rights for workers so I can pay the lowest wages and earn the highest profits. Now I want to emphasize that this is 'no race to the bottom' as we do not want to do anything illegal. My strategy is to scrupulously follow the written laws of the country in which we are operating. My position is that so long as we are following local law to the letter and treating employees the same way they are being treated by their local employers, our conduct is lawful and we are protected. In fact, we should be commended for bringing jobs to the local economy." Is this a good strategy?

PROBLEM 9-2

NED Industries, Inc., is a major industrial company incorporated in Delaware and with headquarters in Chicago. NED is a world-class manufacturer of chemicals used in a variety of household and industrial applications. NED has subsidiary companies in Europe and Japan and is now considering selling its products as well as establishing manufacturing facilities in other areas.

NED's expansion plans target developing countries in Africa and South America. NED has a two-fold strategy of developing new export markets by an aggressive marketing campaign in these nations. When sales reach a certain volume, NED plans to establish subsidiary companies that will carry out manufacturing operations in several countries. Some of these operations may involve dangerous toxic chemicals. NED's founder and CEO, Ned Burner, is a colorful and idealistic personality who wants to be successful, but is conscious of his company's social responsibility to the countries in which he does business. He also does not want adverse publicity because it could cause NED economic harm. Burner comes to you, his general counsel, with the following questions:

(1) "I know that multinational companies like ours are subject to regulation by domestic legislation but are MNEs also subject to international legal norms that govern corporate behavior? If so, what types of norms might be applicable to our plans in Africa and South America?"

(2) "Explain whether you think we are better off or worse off if our company is subject to public international law norms rather than just subject to domestic regulation."

Jonathan I. Charney, Transnational Corporations and Developing Public International Law
1983 Duke L.J. 748, 762-769 (1983)

I. INTRODUCTION

Currently, one of the most significant developments in public international law is the apparent creation of law applicable to transnational corporations (TNCs). Although public international law has addressed international economic issues for some time, recently, in light of expanded TNC activity and increased third world leverage in international affairs, greater attention has been focused on the establishment of rules to govern TNC behavior. These developments are partly explained as an effort by the third world to increase its international power vis-à-vis the power of both the TNCs and the western developed world, with whom the TNCs are generally aligned, but there are also additional factors encouraging them. First, because one country usually cannot unilaterally regulate TNC power and behavior, even the western, developed countries have an interest in these developments. Second, TNCs themselves recognize the benefits of a uniform regulatory scheme that would avoid many of the difficulties produced by varying national requirements. Although these new rules will be aimed at TNCs, international practice has largely precluded TNCs from directly participating in this rule-making process.

There is evidence that TNCs have had international legal personality and have participated in the international legal system for some time. Examples of such participation include application of public international law to contracts with state entities and participation in dispute settlement forums established either by treaty or intergovernmental organizations. Some principles of public international law have become so widely accepted that they have been viewed as binding on the TNCs' international activities. Finally, TNCs advise international organizations when their interests are at stake and it is clear that they play a direct role in influencing national behavior on relevant international matters.

Some maintain that TNC activities are actually just a new form of western colonialism while others view the TNC as a more benign force that is ultimately subject to state control even without major new international initiatives. Regardless of which view is correct, the international community is moving toward greater international regulation of international business without allowing direct business participation.

There are strong arguments for expanding the role of TNCs in the international legal system. Nation-states aside, TNCs are the most powerful actors in the world today and to not recognize that power would be unrealistic. The international economy depends heavily on the services they provide and they have far greater influence and economic power than unorganized human beings or most other nongovernmental organizations. In fact, even the influence of intergovernmental organizations, which depends on the continued financial and political support of nation-state sponsors, cannot be compared to the power of many TNCs. This argument for increased TNC participation is further supported by the conclusion that the continued viability of the international legal system depends upon the close conformity of public international law to international realities.

Jordan J. Paust, Human Rights Responsibilities of Private Corporations
35 Vand. J. Transnat'l L. 801, 802–815 (2002)

Does human rights law reach private multinational corporations? Despite the lack of widespread early attention to private corporate liability for human rights deprivations, preferences of a few textwriters, and remarkable confusion, human rights law can reach private corporations. More generally, a private corporation as such is simply a juridic person and has no immunity under U.S. domestic or international law. In each nation-state, private corporations, like private individuals, are bound by domestic laws. Similarly, private corporations and entities are bound by international laws applicable to individuals. For example, in the United States and elsewhere, companies and other non-state associations and organizations have been found to have civil and criminal responsibility for various violations of international law, including human rights and related international proscriptions. In the United States, private companies have rights to sue under the Alien Tort Claims Act (ATCA) [28 U.S.C. §1350] and it is only logical and policy-serving that they can also be defendants under the ATCA. In fact, there have been express recognitions to that effect in U.S. cases. For example, in 1997, in *Doe v. Unocal Corp.*,[1] the Central District of California recognized that several human rights and other international law claims made by farmers from Burma against a private corporation and others were viable under the ATCA. These claims included claims of slave or "forced" labor, torture, violence against women, and other human rights violations and crimes against humanity that also occurred in complicity with Burmese military, intelligence groups, and police. Addressing universal jurisdiction through the ATCA and nonimmunity of corporate actors for cruel, inhumane treatment and slave or forced labor, the district court in *Iwanowa v. Ford Motor Co.* added: "No logical reason exists for allowing private individuals and corporations to escape liability for universally condemned violations of international law merely because they were not acting under color of law."[2] In 1907, an Opinion of the U.S. Attorney General recognized that a private U.S. company violated a treaty by diverting the Rio Grande through dredging activities.[3] The Attorney General noted that an International Water Boundary Commission "found . . . [t]hat the . . . Company . . . violated the stipulations of that treaty," and recognized that injuries included "damage to property," including injury to "riparian rights," and "[a]s to indemnity for injuries which may have been caused to citizens of Mexico, I am of the opinion that existing statutes provide a right of action and a forum. [T]he statutes [including the ATCA] thus provide a forum and a right of action."[4]

In *Burger-Fischer v. DeGussa AG. & DeGussa Corp.*, claims were made concerning the seizure of property and slave labor.[5] In *Bodner v. Banque Paribas*, the court found that claims against banks for looting, conversion, and withholding of assets of victims of the Nazi Holocaust in violation of human rights and other international law were actionable under the ATCA.[6] Alleged corporate involvement with prison labor also led to suits in *Ge v. Peng*[7] and *Doe v. The Gap, Inc.*[8] *Ge* was later dismissed, however, because, "[u]nlike *Kadic* and its progeny, . . . [the] case involves the use of forced prison labor in the production of soccer balls . . . [and] forced prison labor [according to the court] is not . . . proscribed by international law."[9] In *Jama v. U.S. I.N.S.*, the court found that violations of human rights prohibitions of cruel, inhuman, or degrading treatment by a private correctional corporation and its officers and employees acting under contract with the Immigration and Naturalization Services—which made the corporate officers "state actors"—were actionable under the ATCA.[10] In *Eastman Kodak Co. v. Kavlin*, the district court found that claims of arbitrary detention involving a Brazilian company and an individual owner thereof who allegedly conspired with local Brazilian officials were actionable under the ATCA.[11]

---

1. *Doe v. Unocal Corp.*, 963 F. Supp. 880 (C.D. Cal. 1997).
2. *Iwanowa v. Ford Motor Co.*, 67 F. Supp. 2d 424, 445 (D.N.J. 1999).
3. 26 Gp. Att'y Gen. 250, 251–54 (1907).
4. *Id.* at 251–53.
5. *Burger-Fischer v. DeGussa Ag. & DeGussa Corp.*, 65 F. Supp. 2d 248, 272–73 (D.N.J. 1999).
6. *Bodner v. Banque Paribas*, 114 F. Supp. 2d 117 (E.D.N.Y. 2000).
7. *Ge v. The Peng*, 1999 U.S. Dist. LEXIS 10834, at *6–7, *dismissed*, 2000 U.S. Dist. LEXIS 12711 (Aug. 28, 2000).
8. *Doe v. The Gap, Inc.*, No. CV99-77 (D. Haw. 1999).
9. *Ge v. Peng*, 2000 U.S. Dist. LEXIS 12711, at *18 (Aug. 28, 2000).
10. *Jama v. U.S. I.N.S.*, 22 F. Supp. 2d 353, 362–63 (D.N.J. 1998).
11. *Eastman Kodak Co. v. Kavlin*, 978 F. Supp. 1078, 1090–95 (S.D. Fla. 1997).

2. Trends in Decisions Outside the United States

Judicial decisions outside the United States have recognized human rights responsibilities of private persons, companies, and corporations. Japanese and German cases have recognized such forms of private responsibility, and there has been similar recognition by the European Court of Human Rights. More recently, the British House of Lords recognized that a private corporation's responsibilities under domestic employment law are "[s]ubject to observance of fundamental human rights. . . ."[12] In 1998, the Supreme Court of Canada recognized that it is possible "for a non-state actor to perpetuate human rights violations on a scale amounting to persecution" within the reach of the Refugee Convention and, more generally, that private actors can engage in human rights violations.[13]

Most human rights instruments speak generally of particular rights of each person or everyone without any mention of or limitation concerning which person or entities owe a corresponding duty. Thus, most duties are generally not limited to state actors and do reach private persons or entities. Moreover, violations of human rights recognized in particular treaties and customary international law often reach private perpetrators expressly or by implication. For example, the preamble to the Universal Declaration of Human Rights recognizes that the human rights proclaimed therein are "a common standard of achievement for all peoples . . . [including] every individual and every organ of society." Article 29, paragraph 1, affirms that "Everyone has duties to the community . . ."; Article 30 recognizes that no right of "any . . . group or person . . . [exists] to engage in any activity or to perform any act aimed at the destruction of any of the rights and freedoms set forth" in the Universal Declaration. Thus, there are correlative duties of groups and persons not to engage in acts aimed at the destruction of human rights set forth in the Declaration. Indeed, Article 30—like provisions in most major human rights instruments—contains an interpretive command that "[n]othing . . . be interpreted as implying for any State, group or person any right to engage in any activity or to perform any act aimed at the destruction of any of the rights and freedoms set forth herein." Because numerous human rights are set forth in the Declaration without any mention of "state" actors or any limitation to state actor duties or "color," the express and unavoidable interpretive command in Article 30 prohibits adding words or implying limitations that the drafters did not choose. Article 30 also should not be read so as to interpret particular human rights articles as if groups or persons can engage in any activity or perform any act aimed at the destruction of such rights, but state actors or those acting under "color"—and only such actors—cannot do so. The correlative reach of Article 30 is to "any" group or person.

The preamble to the International Covenant on Civil and Political Rights (ICCPR)[14] expressly affirms "that the individual, *having duties* to other individuals and to the community to which he belongs, *is under a responsibility* to strive for the promotion and observance of the rights recognized in the present Covenant."[15] Thus, at a minimum, individuals have duties to not violate human rights. Article 5, like Article 30 of the Universal Declaration,

---

12. *Johnson v. Unisys, Ltd.*, UKHL/13, ¶37 (22 March 2001) (Lord Hoffmann).

13. *Pushpanathan v. Canada*, [1998] 160 D.L.R. (4th) 193, 231, 1998 D.L.R. Lexis 512 (Can. 1998), also noting a related practice of Australia.

14. International Covenant on Civil and Political Rights, Dec. 19, 1966, 999 U.N.T.S. 171 (entered into force Mar. 23, 1976).

15. *Id.* pmbl. (emphasis added).

also affirms the lack of a right of "any . . . group or person . . . to engage in any activity or to perform any act aimed at the destruction of any of the rights and freedoms set forth" in the Covenant "or at their limitation to a greater extent than is provided,"[16] and thus impliedly affirms the duty of any group or person to not destroy or limit human rights.

Private duties are also expressly recognized in the preamble to and Articles 27 through 29 of the African Charter on Human and Peoples' Rights.[17] Article 17 of the European Convention for the Protection of Human Rights and Fundamental Freedoms contains a "group or person" provision similar to those in the Universal Declaration and the International Covenant.[18] It affirms the lack of a right of "any . . . group or person . . . to engage in any activity or perform any act aimed at the destruction of any of the rights or freedoms set forth . . . [in the European Convention] or at their limitation to a greater extent than is provided for in the Convention."[19] Thus, an implied correlative duty of any group or person exists to not destroy or limit such rights. Indeed, the authoritative European Court of Human Rights has expressly recognized that private "terrorist activities . . . of individuals or groups . . . are in clear disregard of human rights,"[20] therefore affirming that duties of private individuals and groups exist under human rights law.

The preamble to the American Declaration of the Rights and Duties of Man[21] acknowledges that "the fulfillment of duty by each individual is a prerequisite to the rights of all. Rights and duties are interrelated. . . ."[22] Articles XXIX through XXXVIII set forth several express duties of private actors. Indeed, the very title of the American Declaration is an express affirmation of private human rights duties. The American Convention on Human Rights[23] also contains express recognition that "[e]very person has responsibilities to . . . his community, and mankind,"[24] and Article 29(a) commands that the treaty not be interpreted to allow "any . . . group, or person to suppress the enjoyment or exercise of the rights and freedoms recognized . . . or to restrict them to a greater extent than is provided for" in the Convention.[25] Thus, an implied duty of groups and persons exists to not suppress or restrict human rights. The American Convention also contains express references to responsibilities of private companies.[26]

---

16. *Id.* art. 5, ¶ 1.

17. O.A.U. Doc. CAB/LEG/67/3 Rev. 5 (1981).

18. Convention for the Protection of Human Rights and Fundamental Freedoms, 213 U.N.T.S. 222, art. 17 (1950).

19. *Id.*

20. *Ireland v. United Kingdom,* 25 Eur. Ct. H.R. (ser. A) at 149 (1977).

21. O.A.S. Res. XX (1948), O.A.S. Off. Rec. OEA/Ser. L/V/I.4 Rev. (1965). The United States, and all states in the Americas, are bound by the American Declaration of the Rights and Duties of Man, which is now a legally authoritative indicia of human rights protected through Article 3(k) of the O.A.S. Charter, Apr. 30, 1948, 119 U.N.T.S. 3, 2 U.S.T. 2394, T.I.A.S. No. 2631, *amended by* the Protocol of Buenos Aires, Feb. 27, 1967, 21 U.S.T. 607, T.I.A.S. No. 6847.

22. O.A.S. Res. XX (1948), pmbl., O.A.S. Off. Rec. OEA/Ser. L./I.4 Rev. (1965).

23. American Convention on Human Rights, opened for signature Nov. 22, 1969, 144 U.N.T.S. 123 (1970) [hereinafter American Convention]. Although the United States signed but has not ratified the American Convention on Human Rights, the United States is obligated to take no action inconsistent with the major purposes of the Convention. *See* Vienna Convention on the Law of Treaties, May 23, 1969, art. 18(a), 1155 U.N.T.S. 331.

24. American Convention, *supra,* art. 32(1).

25. *Id.* art. 29(a).

26. *Id.* arts. 6(3)(a) ("shall not be placed at the disposal of any private party, company, or juridical person") and 14(3) ("company"). *See also id.* art. 29(a) ("group, or person") and art. 29(d) (incorporating the American Declaration—with its express recognition of private duties—by reference, as does the preamble to the Convention).

The authoritative Human Rights Committee created under the International Covenant on Civil and Political Rights has also recognized that states should report "the provisions of their criminal law which penalize torture and cruel, inhuman and degrading treatment or punishment, . . . *whether committed* by public officials or other persons acting on behalf of the State, or *by private persons.* Those who violate article 7, whether by encouraging, ordering, tolerating or perpetuating prohibited acts, must be held responsible."[27] The Human Rights Committee added that states have a duty to afford protection against such acts "*whether inflicted by people acting* in their official capacity, outside their official capacity or *in a private capacity*"[28] and "States must not deprive individuals of the right to an effective remedy."[29]

Professor Charney raises the important question of whether international companies are subject to international law norms. What are his answers? Does he believe that they should be? Professor Paust argues that international companies are increasingly subject to human rights norms in a variety of contexts and forums. How are their concerns reflected in decisions of U.S. courts? Consider the following case.

Doe I v. Wal-Mart Stores, Inc.
United States Court of Appeals, Ninth Circuit, 2009
572 F.3d 677

GOULD, Circuit Judge:

The appellants were among the plaintiffs in the district court and are employees of foreign companies that sell goods to Wal-Mart Stores, Inc. ("Wal-Mart"). They brought claims against Wal-Mart based on the working conditions in each of their employers' factories. These claims relied primarily on a code of conduct included in Wal-Mart's supply contracts, specifying basic labor standards that suppliers must meet. The district court dismissed the complaint for failure to state a claim under Federal Rule of Civil Procedure 12(b)(6). We have jurisdiction under 28 U.S.C. §1291, and we affirm.

Plaintiffs are employees of Wal-Mart's foreign suppliers in countries including China, Bangladesh, Indonesia, Swaziland, and Nicaragua. Plaintiffs allege the following relevant facts, which we take as true for purposes of this appeal:

In 1992, Wal-Mart developed a code of conduct for its suppliers, entitled "Standards for Suppliers" ("Standards"). These Standards were incorporated into its supply contracts with foreign suppliers. The Standards require foreign suppliers to adhere to local laws and local industry standards regarding working conditions like pay, hours, forced labor, child labor, and discrimination. The Standards also include a paragraph entitled "RIGHT OF INSPECTION":

To further assure proper implementation of and compliance with the standards set forth herein, Wal-Mart or a third party designated by Wal-Mart will undertake affirmative measures,

---

27. General Comment No. 20 [concerning violations of Article 7 of the Covenant on Civil and Political Rights] (1992), ¶13, *in* International Human Rights Instruments at 29–32, U.N. Doc. HRI/GEN/1 (1992) (emphasis added).

28. *Id.* ¶2 (emphasis added).

29. *Id.* ¶15 (emphasis added).

such as on-site inspection of production facilities, to implement and monitor said standards. Any supplier which fails or refuses to comply with these standards or does not allow inspection of production facilities is subject to immediate cancellation of any and all outstanding orders, refuse [sic] or return [sic] any shipment, and otherwise cease doing business [sic] with Wal-Mart.

Thus, each supplier must acknowledge that its failure to comply with the Standards could result in cancellation of orders and termination of its business relationship with Wal-Mart.

Wal-Mart represents to the public that it improves the lives of its suppliers' employees and that it does not condone any violation of the Standards. However, Plaintiffs allege that Wal-Mart does not adequately monitor its suppliers and that Wal-Mart knows its suppliers often violate the Standards. Specifically, Plaintiffs claim that in 2004, only eight percent of audits were unannounced, and that workers are often coached on how to respond to auditors. Additionally, Plaintiffs allege that Wal-Mart's inspectors were pressured to produce positive reports of factories that were not in compliance with the Standards. Finally, Plaintiffs allege that the short deadlines and low prices in Wal-Mart's supply contracts force suppliers to violate the Standards in order to satisfy the terms of the contracts.

Plaintiffs filed a class action lawsuit in California Superior Court in 2005 and Wal-Mart removed the case to federal court based on diversity of citizenship. Plaintiffs then filed an amended complaint in federal court, which is the complaint relevant here. Wal-Mart filed a motion to dismiss under Federal Rule of Civil Procedure 12(b)(6) for failure to state a claim. The district court granted the motion in a written order, and judgment was entered on March 27, 2008. Plaintiffs timely appealed.

***

Plaintiffs present four distinct legal theories, all of which aim to establish that the Standards and California common law provide substantive obligations that can be enforced by the foreign workers against Wal-Mart: (1) Plaintiffs are third-party beneficiaries of the Standards contained in Wal-Mart's supply contracts; (2) Wal-Mart is Plaintiffs' joint employer; (3) Wal-Mart negligently breached a duty to monitor the suppliers and protect Plaintiffs from the suppliers' working conditions; (4) Wal-Mart was unjustly enriched by Plaintiffs' mistreatment. Applying California law, we address each claim in turn.

A

We first address Plaintiffs' third-party beneficiary theory. The common law in California and elsewhere establishes that, as recited in the applicable Restatement (Second) of Contracts: "A promise in a contract creates a duty in the promisor to any intended beneficiary to perform the promise, and the intended beneficiary may enforce the duty." Restatement (Second) of Contracts §304 (1981). However, the Restatement also explains that a beneficiary is only "an intended beneficiary if recognition of a right to performance in the beneficiary is appropriate to effectuate the intention of the parties. . . ." Restatement (Second) of Contracts §302(1).

Plaintiffs argue that Wal-Mart promised the suppliers that it would monitor the suppliers' compliance with the Standards, and that Plaintiffs are third-party beneficiaries of that promise to monitor. Plaintiffs rely on this language in the Standards: "Wal-Mart will undertake affirmative measures, such as on-site inspection of production facilities, to implement and monitor said standards." We agree with the district court that this language does not create a duty on the part of Wal-Mart to monitor the suppliers, and does not provide Plaintiffs a right of action against Wal-Mart as third-party beneficiaries.

The language and structure of the agreement show that Wal-Mart reserved the right to inspect the suppliers, but did not adopt a duty to inspect them. The language on which Plaintiffs rely is found in a paragraph entitled "Right of Inspection," contained in a two-page section entitled "Standards for Suppliers." And after stating Wal-Mart's intention to enforce the Standards through monitoring, the paragraph elaborates the potential consequences of a supplier's failure to comply with the Standards — Wal-Mart may cancel orders and cease doing business with that supplier — but contains no comparable adverse consequences for Wal-Mart if Wal-Mart does not monitor that supplier. Because, as we view the supply contracts, Wal-Mart made no promise to monitor the suppliers, no such promise flows to Plaintiffs as third-party beneficiaries.

Plaintiffs alternatively argue that they are third-party beneficiaries of the suppliers' promises to maintain certain working conditions, and that Plaintiffs may therefore sue Wal-Mart. This theory fails because Wal-Mart was the promisee vis-a-vis the suppliers' promises to follow the Standards, and Plaintiffs have not plausibly alleged a contractual duty on the part of Wal-Mart that would extend to Plaintiffs.

Plaintiffs' allegations are insufficient to support the conclusion that Wal-Mart and the suppliers intended for Plaintiffs to have a right of performance against Wal-Mart under the supply contracts. *See* Restatement (Second) of Contracts §302(1). We therefore conclude that Plaintiffs have not stated a claim against Wal-Mart as third-party beneficiaries of any contractual duty owed by Wal-Mart, and we affirm the district court's dismissal of the third-party beneficiary contract claim.

B

We next address Plaintiffs' theory that Wal-Mart was Plaintiffs' joint employer, such that they can "sue Wal-Mart directly for any breach of contract or violation of labor laws." We conclude, to the contrary, that Wal-Mart cannot be considered Plaintiffs' employer on the facts alleged.

The key factor to consider in analyzing whether an entity is an employer is "the right to control and direct the activities of the person rendering service, or the manner and method in which the work is performed." *Serv. Employees Int'l Union v. County of L.A.*, 275 Cal. Rptr. 508, 513 (1990). "A finding of the right to control employment requires . . . a comprehensive and immediate level of 'day-to-day' authority over employment decisions." *Vernon v. State*, 10 Cal. Rptr. 3d 121, 132 (2004).

Here, Plaintiffs' allegations do not support the conclusion that Wal-Mart is Plaintiffs' employer. Plaintiffs' general statement that Wal-Mart exercised control over their day-to-day employment is a conclusion, not a factual allegation stated with any specificity. We need not accept Plaintiffs' unwarranted conclusion in reviewing a motion to dismiss. Plaintiffs allege specifically that Wal-Mart contracted with suppliers regarding deadlines, quality of products, materials used, prices, and other common buyer-seller contract terms. Such supply contract terms do not constitute an "immediate level of 'day-to-day'" control over a supplier's employees so as to create an employment relationship between a purchaser and a supplier's employees.

C

[The court next considered plaintiff's negligence claims brought under four distinct theories: third-party beneficiary negligence, negligent retention of control, negligent undertaking, and common law negligence. The court concluded that any negligence claim must be based on a duty that Wal-Mart owed to the Plaintiffs to monitor Wal-Mart's suppliers or to prevent the intentional mistreatment of Plaintiffs by the suppliers. In Part A and B, the court already found that Wal-Mart owed no such duty to the Plaintiffs and dismissed all of the negligence claims.]

D

We turn finally to Plaintiffs' claim of unjust enrichment. Plaintiffs allege that Wal-Mart was unjustly enriched at Plaintiffs' expense by profiting from relationships with suppliers that Wal-Mart knew were engaged in substandard labor practices. Unjust enrichment is commonly understood as a theory upon which the remedy of restitution may be granted. California's approach to unjust enrichment is consistent with this general understanding: "The fact that one person benefits another is not, by itself, sufficient to require restitution. The person receiving the benefit is required to make restitution only if the circumstances are such that, as between the two individuals, it is *unjust* for the person to retain it." *First Nationwide Sav. v. Perry*, 15 Cal. Rptr. 2d 173, 176 (1992) (emphasis in original).

The lack of any prior relationship between Plaintiffs and Wal-Mart precludes the application of an unjust enrichment theory here. Plaintiffs essentially seek to disgorge profits allegedly earned by Wal-Mart at Plaintiffs' expense; however, we have already determined that Wal-Mart is not Plaintiffs' employer, and we see no other plausible basis upon which the employee of a manufacturer, without more, may obtain restitution from one who purchases goods from that manufacturer. That is, the connection between Plaintiffs and Wal-Mart here is simply too attenuated to support an unjust enrichment claim.

In sum, we conclude that Plaintiffs have not stated a claim against Wal-Mart. Affirmed.

NOTES AND QUESTIONS

1. *Wal-Mart's Strategy.* The distinction between Wal-Mart's "right" of inspection and a "duty" of inspection was crucial to the outcome of this case. Why? Which did Wal-Mart have, a right or a duty? Why did Wal-Mart decide to use human rights standards for suppliers if Wal-Mart did not intend, according to the plaintiffs, to rigorously enforce these standards? Why didn't the plaintiffs just sue the suppliers in their home countries (including China, Bangladesh, Indonesia, Swaziland, and Nicaragua)? Would this be an effective strategy? Is international law making enough progress in applying international norms (including human rights) to multinational companies?

2. *MNEs as Subjects of International Law.* There is probably no reason why MNEs could not be considered subjects of international law, but at the present time individuals, including MNEs, are directly affected only exceptionally by international law norms. This is because states are still the primary international law subjects, and in most cases, international obligations are only derivative for individuals and companies. One important area in which derivative liability can attach to MNEs or other individuals is when MNEs or other individuals act under the "color" of state law. In such cases, individuals may then be subject to public international law norms that, by their terms, apply only to states and not individuals.

In certain areas, however, individuals, including business entities, are full international participants:

- Individuals can be subject to international criminal liability for international crimes such as genocide and crimes against humanity.
- Certain customary law and treaty-based human rights norms give rise to obligations enforceable against individuals.
- Certain treaty regimes, notably the Convention on Civil Liability for Oil Pollution Damage (1969 and Protocols 1992 and 2000), the Convention on Civil Liability for Damage Resulting from Activities Dangerous to the Environment (1993), and the Convention on Nuclear Safety (1994), provide for direct international liability of responsible individuals.
- Individuals are granted rights against states under certain international investment treaties (see Chapter Six at pp. 365-366).

3. *Extraterritorial Application of U.S. Law.* American companies operating in foreign countries must be aware that Congress has explicitly given many U.S. laws extraterritorial effect. Leading examples include the Americans with Disabilities Act, 42 U.S.C. §§12101–12213 (2006), 47 U.S.C. §225 (2006); Title VII of the Civil Rights Act of 1964 relating to discrimination in employment, 42 U.S.C. §2000e; and the Age Discrimination in Employment Act, 29 U.S.C. §§621–634 (2006). These laws apply to a foreign company that is owned or controlled by a U.S. company or person. A limited defense is available if the U.S. company can show that compliance with U.S. law would violate the foreign law of the country in which the workplace is located. But to assert this defense, the U.S. company must show that all possible steps were taken to obtain an exemption from the foreign law requirement.

4. *International Forums.* The question of the social responsibility of international business is addressed comprehensively in a number of international forums, such as the United Nations, but currently there are no binding laws on multinational companies. A number of voluntary codes and standards of conduct have been promulgated by various organizations. We consider the codes in the following section.

PROBLEM 9-3

Based on the readings so far, consider the following:

Zenos Industries, an Ohio company in the oil and gas business, has been offered a series of lucrative foreign investment projects with governments of countries in Southeast Asia. These governments are known as being repressive and are on watch lists of various nongovernmental organizations concerned with human rights abuses and environmental degradation and are subject to frequent criticism by international law experts that they do not comply with public international legal norms that apply to nation-states. Zenos's general counsel has the following concern: "We are aware that our partners are being criticized for not complying with public law norms that apply to nation-states in the areas of human rights and the environment, but we are a private company and, of course, our activities and actions do not involve state action. However, do we, as a private company, incur liability under norms of public international law applicable to nation-states only, just by doing business with a repressive government?

Does the nature of a foreign government become part of the business case in deciding whether to make a foreign investment in the country?"

II.   Codes and Standards of Conduct

There have been several efforts to develop generally applicable policies and standards to govern the activities of multinational enterprises. Perhaps the most prominent example of a *voluntary* code is the Organization for Economic Cooperation and Development Guidelines for Multinational Enterprises set forth below. (There is no legally binding code.) The following two problems involve some issues associated with the OECD guidelines.

PROBLEM 9-4

The aggressive CEO of an MNE has just learned about the OECD Guidelines for Multinational Enterprises set forth below. The CEO is puzzled though, because the guidelines are, by their terms, voluntary, and he has the following questions for your law firm: "I can understand why MNEs need to follow laws and other binding legal norms that create social obligations when they do business overseas. But why would I want to voluntarily adhere to a set of guidelines that seem to create an extensive list of social obligations that might have an impact on my bottom line? Can you make a business case (i.e., why it might actually help my bottom line) for why MNEs will want to adopt the OECD guidelines or any other voluntary codes that are being considered?"

PROBLEM 9-5

Hyde Industries is considering a very large foreign direct investment in an impoverished Southeast Asian nation. During a meeting between Hyde executives and officials of the host country, the Minister of Foreign Trade says, "We know that you are considering a number of countries for your investment but we are on the brink of social disaster and very badly in need of foreign capital. So I talked it over with the President and even though the laws do not provide for such exemptions, we would like to offer you several incentives: (1) a ten-year exemption from all pollution and environmental standards. We need industrialization very badly and we know that you can help us industrialize faster if we do not insist on strict environmental controls. We will also offer you (2) a five-year exemption from all local labor laws regarding your employees and we will offer you five years of 'free labor' from a group of young workers whom we will provide to you at our own expense. We'll take care of their health needs as well so you won't need to worry about that expense. And we will offer you (3) a five-year holiday from all local taxes."

When the Hyde officials return to the United States, the CEO calls you, the general counsel, and asks, "Should we accept these conditions? We didn't ask for them but they look pretty good to me." Assume that Hyde Industries is part of an industry group that has declared its intention to adhere to the OECD guidelines set forth below. Do these conditions violate any of these guidelines?

Organization for Economic Cooperation and Development: The OECD Guidelines for Multinational Enterprises, 2011[30]
I. Concepts and Principles

The Guidelines are recommendations jointly addressed by governments to multinational enterprises. They provide principles and standards of good practice consistent with applicable laws. Observance of the Guidelines by enterprises is voluntary and not legally enforceable.

II. General Policies

Enterprises should take fully into account established policies in the countries in which they operate, and consider the views of other stakeholders. In this regard, enterprises should:

1. Contribute to economic, social and environmental progress with a view to achieving sustainable development.
2. Respect the human rights of those affected by their activities consistent with the host government's international obligations and commitments.
3. Encourage local capacity building through close co-operation with the local community, including business interests, as well as developing the enterprise's activities in domestic and foreign markets, consistent with the need for sound commercial practice.
4. Encourage human capital formation, in particular by creating employment opportunities and facilitating training opportunities for employees.
5. Refrain from seeking or accepting exemptions not contemplated in the statutory or regulatory framework related to environmental, health, safety, labour, taxation, financial incentives, or other issues.
6. Support and uphold good corporate governance principles and develop and apply good corporate governance practices.
7. Develop and apply effective self-regulatory practices and management systems that foster a relationship of confidence and mutual trust between enterprises and the societies in which they operate.
8. Promote employee awareness of, and compliance with, company policies through appropriate dissemination of these policies, including through training programs.
9. Refrain from discriminatory or disciplinary action against employees who make bona fide reports to management or, as appropriate, to the competent public authorities, on practices that contravene the law, the Guidelines or the enterprise's policies.

---

30. Available at *http://www.oecd.org.*

10. Encourage, where practicable, business partners, including suppliers and sub-contractors, to apply principles of corporate conduct compatible with the Guidelines.

11. Abstain from any improper involvement in local political activities.

III. Disclosure

Enterprises should ensure that timely, regular, reliable and relevant information is disclosed regarding their activities, structure, financial situation and performance.

IV. Employment and Industrial Relations

Enterprises should, within the framework of applicable law, regulations and prevailing labour relations and employment practices:

1. a) Respect the right of their employees to be represented by trade unions and other bona fide representatives of employees, and engage in constructive negotiations, either individually or through employers' associations, with such representatives with a view to reaching agreements or employment conditions;

   b) Contribute to the effective abolition of child labour;

   c) Contribute to the elimination of all forms of forced or compulsory labour;

   d) Not discriminate against their employees with respect to employment or occupation on such grounds as race, colour, sex, religion, political opinion, national extraction or social origin, unless selectivity concerning employee characteristics furthers established governmental policies which specifically promote greater equality of employment opportunity or relates to the inherent requirements of a job period.

2. a) Provide facilities to employee representatives as may be necessary to assist in the development of effective collective agreements;

   b) Provide information to employee representatives which is needed for meaningful negotiations on conditions of employment;

   c) Promote consultation and co-operation between employers and employees and their representatives on matters of mutual concern.

3. Provide information to employees and their representatives which enables them to obtain a true and fair view of the performance of the entity or, where appropriate, the enterprise as a whole.

4. a) Observe standards of employment and industrial relations not less favorable than those observed by comparable employers in the host country;

   b) Take adequate steps to ensure occupational health and safety in their operations.

5. In their operations, to the greatest extent practicable, employ local personnel and provide training with a view to improving skill levels, in co-operation with employee representatives and, where appropriate, relevant governmental authorities.

6. In considering changes in their operations which would have major effects upon the livelihood of their employees, in particular in the case of the closure

of an entity involving collective lay-offs or dismissals, provide reasonable notice of such changes to representatives of their employees, and, where appropriate, to the relevant governmental authorities, and co-operate with the employee representatives and appropriate governmental authorities so as to mitigate to the maximum extent practicable adverse effects.

7. In the context of bona fide negotiations with representatives of employees on conditions of employment, or while employees are exercising a right to organize, not threaten to transfer the whole or part of an operating unit from the country concerned nor transfer employees from the enterprises' component entities in other countries in order to influence unfairly those negotiations or to hinder the exercise of a right to organize.

8. Enable authorized representatives of their employees to negotiate on collective bargaining or labour management relations issues and allow the parties to consult on matters of mutual concern with representatives of management.

V. Environment

Enterprises should, within the framework of laws, regulations and administrative practices in the countries in which they operate, and in consideration of relevant international agreements, principles, objectives, and standards, take due account of the need to protect the environment, public health and safety, and generally to conduct their activities in a manner contributing to the wider goal of sustainable development. In particular, enterprises should:

1. Establish and maintain a system of environmental management appropriate to the enterprise, including:
    a) Collection and evaluation of adequate and timely information regarding the environmental, health, and safety impacts of their activities;
    b) Establishment of measurable objectives and, where appropriate, targets for improved environmental performance, including periodically reviewing the continuing relevance of these objectives; and
    c) Regular monitoring and verification of progress toward environmental, health, and safety objectives or targets.

2. Taking into account concerns about cost, business confidentiality, and the protection of intellectual property rights:
    a) Provide the public and employees with adequate and timely information on the potential environment, health and safety impacts of the activities of the enterprise, which could include reporting on progress in improving environmental performance; and
    b) Engage in adequate and timely communication and consultation with the communities directly affected by the environmental, health and safety policies of the enterprise and by their implementation.

3. Assess, and address in decision-making, the foreseeable environmental, health, and safety-related impacts associated with the processes, goods and services of the enterprise over their full life cycle.

4. Consistent with the scientific and technical understanding of the risks, where there are threats of serious damage to the environment, taking also into account human health and safety, not use the lack of full scientific certainty as a reason for postponing cost-effective measures to prevent or minimize such damage.

5. Maintain contingency plans for preventing, mitigating, and controlling serious environmental and health damage from their operations, including accidents and emergencies; and mechanisms for immediate reporting to the competent authorities.

6. Continually seek to improve corporate environmental performance, by encouraging, where appropriate, such activities as:

   a) Adoption of technologies and operating procedures in all parts of the enterprise that reflect standards concerning environmental performance in the best performing part of the enterprise;

   b) Development and provision of products or services that have no undue environmental impacts; are safe in their intended use; are efficient in their consumption of energy and natural resources; can be reused, recycled, or disposed of safely;

   c) Promoting higher levels of awareness among customers of the environmental implications of using the products and services of the enterprise; and

   d) Research on ways of improving the environmental performance of the enterprise over the longer term.

7. Provide adequate education and training to employees in environmental health and safety matters, including the handling of hazardous materials and the prevention of environmental accidents.

8. Contribute to the development of environmentally meaningful and economically efficient public policy, for example, by means of partnerships or initiatives that will enhance environmental awareness and protection.

VI. COMBATING BRIBERY

Enterprises should not, directly or indirectly, offer, promise, give, or demand a bribe or other undue advantage to obtain or retain business or other improper advantage. Nor should enterprises be solicited or expected to render a bribe or other undue advantage.

VII. CONSUMER INTERESTS

When dealing with consumers, enterprises should act in accordance with fair business, marketing and advertising practices and should take all reasonable steps to ensure the safety and quality of the goods or services they provide.

VIII. SCIENCE AND TECHNOLOGY

Enterprises should:

1. Endeavor to ensure that their activities are compatible with the science and technology (S&T) policies and plans of the countries in which they operate and as appropriate contribute to the development of local and national innovative capacity.

2. Adopt, where practicable in the course of their business activities, practices that permit the transfer and rapid diffusion of technologies and know-how, with due regard to the protection of intellectual property rights.

3. When appropriate, perform science and technology development work in host countries to address local market needs, as well as employ host country personnel in an S&T capacity and encourage their training, taking into account commercial needs.

4. When granting licenses for the use of intellectual property rights or when otherwise transferring technology, do so on reasonable terms and conditions and in a manner that contributes to the long term development prospects of the host country.

5. Where relevant to commercial objectives, develop ties with local universities, public research institutions, and participate in co-operative research projects with local industry or industry associations.

IX. Competition

Enterprises should, within the framework of applicable laws and regulations, conduct their activities in a competitive manner. In particular, enterprises should:

1. Refrain from entering into or carrying out anti-competitive agreements among competitors:
   a. To fix prices;
   b. To make rigged bids (collusive tenders);
   c. To establish output restrictions or quotas; or
   d. To share or divide markets by allocating customers, suppliers, territories or lines of commerce.

2. Conduct all of their activities in a manner consistent with all applicable competition laws, taking into account the applicability of the competition laws of jurisdictions whose economies would be likely to be harmed by anti-competitive activity on their part.

3. Co-operate with the competition authorities of such jurisdictions by, among other things and subject to applicable law and appropriate safeguards, providing as prompt and complete responses as practicable to requests for information.

4. Promote employee awareness of the importance of compliance with all applicable competition laws and policies.

X. Taxation

It is important that enterprises contribute to the public finances of host countries by making timely payment of their tax liabilities.

NOTE ON IMPLEMENTATION OF THE OECD GUIDELINES FOR MULTINATIONAL ENTERPRISES

The OECD Guidelines are non-binding, but each OECD member has agreed to designate a National Contact Point (NCP), a government office responsible for ensuring the observance of the guidelines. *See* Org. for Econ. Co-operation and Dev. [OECD], *Decision of the Council on the OECD Guidelines for Multinational Enterprises*, C(2000)96/FINAL (June

27, 2000). The NCP for the United States, for example, is the Office of Investment Affairs, Bureau of Economic and Business Affairs, Department of State, Washington, D.C. 20520. On August 28, 2008, the United Kingdom's NCP issued a formal decision in response to a complaint lodged with them by a nongovernmental organization, Global Witness, against Afrimex, Ltd., a UK company doing business in Africa. The complaint set out breaches of the OECD Guidelines by Afrimex in relation to its activities in the Democratic Republic of the Congo (DRC). The UK NCP agreed with the allegations in its formal decision on the matter, stating that Afrimex had violated the guidelines by paying bribes to a rebel group and by purchasing metals from mines in the DRC that employ child and forced labor. *See Final Statement by the UK National Contact Point for the OECD Guidelines for Multinational Enterprises: Afrimex (UK) Ltd.* (August 28, 2008), available at *www.berr.gov.uk/ files/file47555.doc.* The UK NCP also made non-binding recommendations to Afrimex on how to improve its compliance with international human rights norms.

In this chapter, we have seen that there is no binding code of conduct for MNEs. Should there be one? There are about 77,000 MNEs with about 770,000 subsidiaries and suppliers. The question of a binding code was extensively considered by John Ruggie, the Special Representative of the United Nations Secretary General, who compiled a report at the request of the United Nations Economic and Social Council. His final report is entitled *Protect, Respect, and Remedy: A Framework for Business and Human Rights* and is contained in UN Human Rights Council, *Report of the Special Representative of the Secretary-General on the Issue of Human Rights and Transnational Corporations and Other Business Enterprises,* U.N. Doc. A/HRC/8/5 (Apr. 7, 2008) (*prepared by* John Ruggie) available at *http://www.ohchr. org/EN/Issues/TransnationalCorporations/Pages/Reports.aspx.* The Ruggie Report concludes that states have the primary responsibility to protect against abuses of human rights by corporations and private persons. The report also concludes that there can be no universal international law of corporate social responsibility and it is up to states to enforce local norms that safeguard internationally agreed upon human rights standards. What are the shortcomings of an approach that leaves it up to the government of each country to police its MNEs for violations? Are governments beholden to their MNEs?

In 2011, the UN Human Rights Council implemented the Ruggie Report by adopting UN Human Rights Council, *Guiding Principles on Business and Human Rights: Implementing the United Nations "Protect, Respect and Remedy" Framework,* U.N. Doc. A/HRC/17/31 (Mar. 21, 2011). This document identifies three pillars: (1) the state's duty to protect the human rights of its people; (2) the corporate responsibility to respect human rights; and (3) the need for more effective access to remedies for corporate abuses.

On February 6, 2012, the American Bar Association House of Delegates adopted Resolution 109, which formally endorsed the Ruggie Report and the OECD 2011 Guidelines for Multinational Enterprises. *Resolution 109,* AM. BAR ASS'N (Feb. 6, 2012), *http://www. americanbar.org/content/dam/aba/administrative/house_of_delegates/resolutions/2012_hod_ midyear_meeting_109.doc.*

NOTE ON THE "POLLUTER PAYS PRINCIPLE" AS THE BASIS OF ENCOURAGING MULTINATIONAL COMPANIES TO ENGAGE IN SUSTAINABLE DEVELOPMENT

A key issue in the twenty-first century is the concept of sustainable development. Given the right signals, businesses will incorporate the environmental costs of doing business into their internal calculation of costs and benefits. The Business Council for

Sustainable Development, a nonprofit organization, argues that the deterioration of natural resources and the environment inevitably leads to economic decline. At the same time, economic development that occurs without consideration of harmful side effects to the environment also causes serious damage. What is necessary, the Council says, is to create a long-term program of sustainable development, which is a system that encourages economic development but forces companies to consider the costs of pollution as part of their business decisions. Such a system will allow businesses to internalize the costs of pollution into their businesses' operations on the basis of market principles. The BCSD starts out with the "polluter pays principle," which requires the polluter to absorb all costs of pollution and remediation as the starting point for internalizing environmental costs:

> Three well-known mechanisms for internalizing environmental costs are analyzed in the report: government regulations (command and control), self-regulation, and economic instruments. The BCSD states that regulations are needed to create a basic regulatory framework in all countries. However, it feels that most countries rely too heavily on the command and control mechanism. Self-regulation could prove less costly than the other mechanisms but could also lead to the creation of cartels and protectionism. The third mechanism, economic instruments, receives the most favorable reviews. The BCSD characterizes economic instruments as those that involve government intervention in the form of taxes and charges, to create incentives or disincentives, for the purpose of changing behavior. In addition to being more cost efficient than government regulations, they provide the incentive for polluters to change to cleaner technologies rather than requiring the use of a specific technology, which, the report states, is often the case in command approaches.[31]

According the BCSD, the real advantage is not that the "polluter pays principle" forces companies to pay for damage caused by pollution but that these costs become internalized, i.e., environmental concerns become integrated into the business operations of the company so that pollution is viewed as a sign of inefficiency and lack of competitiveness. The BCSD argues integration can be done if companies have an organizational commitment to integrate environmental aspects into all of their activities and to establish a monitoring, evaluation, auditing, and reporting program in the area of sustainable development. If companies are forced to pay for damage caused by pollution, companies will begin to see sustainable development as a competitive advantage. Companies will develop cleaner, more efficient technologies that will avoid damage to the environment that must be remediated by the company. Pollution will become a sign of inefficiency in the marketplace as it results in wasted raw materials that are not sold in final products, damage to the environment, fines, and the expensive need to remediate the damage caused. Companies will compete with each other to see which can create safer, more environmentally responsible technologies. According to the BCSD, the imposition of the "polluter pays principle" on companies will result in more responsible corporate behavior as environmentally efficient behavior becomes a competitive advantage in the marketplace. Many U.S. companies appear to have accepted this view. For example, the electronic measurement equipment designer and manufacturer Agilent Technologies states on its web site that its commitment to conduct its business in an "environmentally sustainable manner . . . is consistent with our corporate objectives and is essential to continued business success." *Environmental Policy & Social Responsibility*, Agilent Technologies, *http://www.agilent.com/environment/environment.shtml.*

---

31. Anita Margrethe Halvorssen, Book Review: Change Course: A Global Business Perspective on the Development and the Environment by Stephen Schmidheiny with the Business Council for Sustainable Development, 4 Colo. J. Int'l Envtl. L. & Pol'y 241, 243–248 (1993).

PROBLEM 9-6

As part of an effort to take international environmental obligations seriously, Webb Industries, a publicly traded plastics manufacturer incorporated in Delaware with operations around the world, is considering various management changes. One plan under consideration is the appointment of a senior vice president in charge of global environmental responsibility to be located at the company's headquarters in Chicago. The new senior vice president would be in charge of setting company rules and policies and would oversee their implementation in all of Webb's subsidiaries and affiliates in the United States and abroad. Each subsidiary or affiliate would appoint a director of environmental compliance who would report directly to the vice president.

Webb's contemplated changes were prompted in part by recent problems within the company's global operations. The company has recently discovered that its wholly-owned subsidiary in Myanmar (formerly Burma) has been involved in an industrial accident that has caused serious damage to the local rainforests. As Webb has a strong relationship with the government of Myanmar, the government has told Webb that it is willing to control any news coverage of the damage if Webb is willing to repair the damage, estimated to be about $300 million. Webb's CEO wants to do "the right thing" by paying to fix the damage but also wants to prevent any reporting of the event and the adverse publicity that will result.

Webb wants your views on whether its environmental management plan is a good idea and whether it can prevent disclosure of the industrial accident. Consult the readings below.

Instituting a Corporate Environmental and Safety Management System

An environmental and safety management system is a continuing program and organizational structure designed to achieve explicit environmental and safety goals. Such a system involves, first, adopting company environmental and safety policies; second, implementation in all departments and corporate levels; third, monitoring and auditing compliance; fourth, making inspections and taking corrective actions; and finally continuing management oversight and review. An effective environmental and safety management system requires high-level corporate involvement and support, not only by company directors and officers but also by affiliated companies and corporate shareholders. In the case of operating subsidiaries, the support of parent organizations is crucial.

Many companies—some 250,000 world-wide—are participating in the most well-known global standard for environmental management systems (EMS) called ISO 14000. *See http://www.iso.org.* ISO stands for International Organization for Standardization in Geneva, which consists of representative committees from all over the world. The ISO established the ISO 14000 series of standards in 1996, which includes the ISO 14001 standard, which represents a core series of standards for environmental management. ISO 14001 sets out the core criteria for an environmental management system. ISO 14001 is a voluntary set of standards that do not state requirements for environmental quality, but rather map a framework a company can follow to set up an EMS. This framework, which is set out in the ISO publication, Environmental Management: The ISO 14001 Family of

International Standards (2010), available at *http://www.iso.org/home*, sets out the following criteria: (1) adoption of an environmental policy; (2) planning; (3) implementation and operation; (4) checking and corrective action; and (5) management review. Other standards in the ISO 14000 series deal with environmental labels, greenhouse gas emissions, product life-cycle assessment, environmental performance evaluation, and other matters. Participation in the ISO 14000 EMS is endorsed by the U.S. EPA, which on its web site has extensive information on adopting and developing an ISO EMS. See *http://www.epa.gov/ems/implement.htm.*

A major reason companies choose to participate in ISO 14000 is because, as a global standard, it is well known and ISO certification gains the company public relations value. The ISO, however, does not control or approve conformity assessment of EMSs. But compliance with ISO standards permits a company to seek third-party, external certification by recognized standardization organizations, such as Bureau Veritas (*http://www.bureau-veritas.com*) and ISO Quality Services (*http://www.isoqsitd.com*).

At this writing, the ISO 14000 series of standards is undergoing examination and revision. A new ISO 14001 revision is expected to be published in 2015.

Adopting and implementing an EMS has many advantages including economic benefits for a company. Some of the benefits are:

- Reduced raw material and natural resource use
- Reduced energy consumption
- Reduced waste generation
- Improved process efficiency
- Lower insurance costs

Thus, the institution and operation of an EMS typically increases a company's overall efficiency as well as its environmental performance. In preparation for launching an EMS certain steps should be taken. First, the company should define its EMS goals. These goals should be tailored to the operations and culture of the individual company. How and in what ways should the company seek to improve? At which locations? Are there priorities to consider? Second, the company should secure the approval of top management of the organization. In order to accomplish this, management must understand the reasons for adopting an EMS and its potential benefits as well as potential problems and the costs involved. Third, the person who will have overall responsibility for the EMS should be selected. He or she should be a systems-oriented person who enjoys the confidence of top management. Fourth, an EMS implementation team should be gathered including people with different expertise: finance, engineering, human resources, production, and services. This team should hold an initial meeting to discuss the organization's objectives for the EMS, the initial steps to be taken, and the various roles of team members. Fifth, this team should conduct a preliminary review of current compliance with environmental standards and an evaluation of existing systems, training, and procedures. Sixth, based on this preliminary review, the team can prepare a project plan, schedule, and budget. The plan and budget should be submitted both to employees and to management for discussion and approval.

Launching an EMS in a company typically involves the following steps and actions:

- *Adopting an environmental policy.* In order to adopt an environmental policy the EMS team should discuss and determine the impact of the particular company's operations and product on all aspects of the environment. What is the size and scope of the company's environmental footprint? The company should take into consideration the entire life-cycle of its products in this regard. The objectives of the EMS should be considered— the objective should be the control of environmental impacts in a cost-effective manner. The resultant set of environmental policies should be sent for approval to top management as well as set out in poster form and distributed to all employees.

- *Planning.* The planning element of an EMS involves setting particular objectives and targets to tackle identified environmental problems and creating an action plan to attain the objectives. The action plan may have multiple parts, such as a subplan to increase recycling, a subplan to improve energy efficiency, and a subplan to reduce greenhouse gas emissions.
- *Implementation and operation.* In the implementation phase, the action plan is implemented by the persons to whom responsibilities have been assigned.
- *Checking and corrective action.* The company should monitor and evaluate the meeting of set targets and objectives and should adopt corrective actions where necessary.
- *Management review.* Management should periodically review the EMS in order to evaluate its effectiveness and suitability and to suggest improvements.

With widespread adoption of EMS by transnational business entities, the consensus seems to be that EMS improves regulatory performance as well as overall performance of the business. Nevertheless, a transnational company should be aware of possible legal pitfalls and take them into consideration when designing an EMS. In large, complex business organizations, an EMS with active, in-depth involvement of parent and sibling corporations may lead to unintended liabilities of the enterprise as a whole. Thus, a well-designed EMS for a transnational company with many subsidiary operational entities should keep in mind the following principles:

- *Distinguish EMS policy from EMS implementation.* In *United States v. Bestfoods*, 524 U.S. 51 (1998), the Supreme Court drew a distinction between policy adoption and policy implementation when it comes to liability of parent corporations for the failings of subsidiaries. A parent company can articulate policies and goals but if it gets involved in the actual implementation of the policies and goals by the subsidiary, the parent might be held liable for the actions of the subsidiary. Thus, a parent transnational company may be able to require subsidiaries to adopt EMS and may assist in EMS policy development. But the parent should leave responsibility for implementation of EMS to the particular subsidiary entity involved. Subsidiaries and their personnel must know that they retain ultimate responsibility for their EMS and its success or failure.
- *Distinguish general monitoring from audits and inspections.* Parent companies can and should monitor the results of EMS and compliance efforts of their subsidiaries. This is considered normal shareholder activity. *E.g., Hinkle v. Delavan Industries, Inc.*, 24 F. Supp. 2d 819 (W.D. Tenn. 1998) (monitoring safety statistics does not constitute assumption of duty). Nevertheless, if a parent company or an affiliate company conducts detailed inspections or audits, there is danger that the parent becomes liable if something goes wrong.
- *Distinguish recommendations from requirements.* In order to safeguard the entire transnational enterprise from potential liability, the parent or affiliate company

should offer assistance and advice on EMS to an operating entity while making clear that this assistance and advice is a recommendation not a requirement.

- *Distinguish specific from overall responsibility.* If it becomes necessary because of unique technical expertise or some other problem for a parent company to assume certain operational responsibilities of a subsidiary, there should be clear documentation describing this involvement, why it is necessary, and the fact that it is limited in time and scope. The fact that the subsidiary retains specific responsibility for the matter concerned should be clearly set out.

With these safeguards, transnational business entities may benefit from the adoption of an EMS as well as similar systems to protect health and safety and other social obligations involved in their operations.

Environmental Liability Disclosure Obligations of Public Companies

For many years U.S. public companies have had disclosure obligations relating to environmental liability under the Securities Exchange Act of 1934 as amended. The most prominent of these disclosure obligations are:

- SEC Regulation S-K, Item 101: Description of Business (17 C.F.R. 229.101 (2014)), which requires the company to disclose material effects of complying or failing to comply with environmental requirements on capital expenditures, earnings, and the competitive position of the entity or its subsidiaries.
- SEC Regulation S-K, Item 103: Legal Proceedings (17 C.F.R. 229.103 (2014)), which requires the disclosure of any material pending legal proceedings to which the company is a party and a government authority is a party that may involve a monetary sanction in excess of $100,000. Legal proceedings that are material to the business or financial condition of the company or a claim for damages in excess of 10 percent of the assets of the company and its subsidiaries must also be disclosed.
- SEC Regulation S-K, Item 303: Management's Discussion and Analysis of Financial Condition and Results of Operations (17 C.F.R. 229.303 (2014)), which requires disclosure of environmental contingencies, such as known trends or demands, commitments, events, or uncertainties that may have a material effect on sales, revenues, or income from continuing operations. This includes the cost of environmental compliance.

In order to comply with these disclosure obligations, a company should institute and have in operation adequate internal systems to make appropriate determinations of these matters. The U.S. Environmental Protection Agency maintains an Enforcement and Compliance History Online (ECHO) web site (*www.epa.gov/echo/about_site.html*) that contains information related to inspections, violations, and enforcement actions and penalties for the past two years. State agencies have similar databases.

The Sarbanes-Oxley Act of 2002, Pub. L. No. 107-204, 116 Stat. 745 (codified in scattered sections of U.S.C. Titles 5, 11, 12, 15, 18, 28, 29, and 49 (2012)) enhances the requirement to comply with SEC disclosure and other obligations. Section 302 of

Sarbanes-Oxley requires that the CEO and CFO of a public company certify that SEC reports are accurate and materially complete and that the company has in place effective internal controls over financial reporting. Violation of this provision carries criminal penalties. Section 409 of Sarbanes-Oxley requires public companies to disclose, on an urgent basis, information on material changes to their financial condition or operations. Compliance with these enhanced disclosure obligations requires thorough cooperation and regular communications between senior business and environmental managers and outside environmental consultants and legal counsel.

NOTES AND QUESTIONS

1. *United Nations Global Compact.* In 2000, the Office of the Secretary General of the United Nations launched a new initiative to promote human rights, workers' rights, and protection of the environment by multinational corporations. The United Nations Global Compact consists of nine principles drawn from the UN Universal Declaration of Human Rights, the International Labour Organization's Declaration of Fundamental Principles and Rights at Work, and the Rio Declaration on the Environment and Development. Companies can join the UN Global Compact by addressing a letter from the chief executive officer to the Office of the UN Secretary General. The UN Global Compact is not regulatory in scope. A participating company agrees voluntarily to implement the nine principles and to publish an annual report on its achievements.

The nine principles are as follows:

Human Rights
Principle 1: Businesses should support and respect the protection of internationally
    proclaimed human rights within their sphere of influence, and
Principle 2: Make sure that they are not complicit in human rights abuses.
Labour Standards
Principle 3: Businesses should uphold the freedom of association and the effective
    recognition of the right to collective bargaining;
Principle 4: Eliminate all forms of forced and compulsory labour;
Principle 5: Eliminate child labour; and
Principle 6: Eliminate discrimination in respect of employment and occupation.
Environment
Principle 7: Businesses should support a precautionary approach to environmental
    challenges;
Principle 8: Undertake initiatives to promote greater environmental responsibility;
    and
Principle 9: Encourage the development and diffusion of environmentally-friendly
    technologies.

2. *Environmental Reporting and "Eco-Audits."* Voluntary programs modeled on the ISO 14001 model above and other voluntary environmental reporting and "eco-audits" are quickly becoming the norm among multinational companies. There are many national and industry-based voluntary codes of conduct. The European Union has adopted Regulation 1221/2009, 2009 O.J. (L 342) 1 (EC), which provides for voluntary eco-audits by participating companies that are willing to report on corporate environmental performance. *See also* Council Regulation 517/2013, 2013 O.J. (L 158) 1 (amending EC

Regulation 1221/2009). Are these eco-audits of conduct useful? What are their advantages and disadvantages? Should they be compulsory?

A GUIDE FOR THE PERPLEXED: CREATING A CSR PROGRAM FOR YOUR COMPANY

As the foregoing materials demonstrate, there is no shortage of voluntary international CSR standards or programs. The main problem for many MNE managers is not whether to create a CSR program, but which of the multitudes of international CSR guidelines, standards, and institutions to use in framing the company's own program. We have included material on the UN Global Compact Principles, the OECD's Guidelines, and the ISO 14001 program covering environmental management systems. Yet another program is the International Labor Organization's Tripartite Declaration of Principles Concerning Multinational Enterprises and Social Policy, which addresses employment practices, such as promotion equality of opportunity, job security, working conditions, safety and health, freedom of association, and training (details available at *www.ilo.org*).

An attempt to draw all these disparate programs and standards together is the International Organization for Standardization's (ISO) 26000 standard, which attempts to harmonize and incorporate all the existing CSR criteria into a useful whole. The ISO 26000 Social Responsibility Standard, which was promulgated in 2010, provides guidance on the underlying principles of social responsibility and suggests ways to implement corporate socially responsible conduct into existing organizational procedures and practices. (See *www.iso.org* for details.)

In any case, since every company is unique, most companies will wish to formulate their own version of CSR tailored to the needs and policies of their particular business. Some points to keep in mind in carrying out this task include:

- Should the program be issue specific or comprehensive in scope?
- Should the program have a national or a global framework?
- Does the program cover both legally required standards and measures as well as voluntary measures and are these two clearly distinguished?
- Is there a clear and good implementation plan?
- How will performance and achievement of goals be measured?
- Is there an adequate communication plan both internally and externally?

III.   Exporting Hazard: Legal and Ethical Considerations

Many developed countries "sell" and then export hazardous substances and wastes to developing countries where the wastes are buried. What are the legal and ethical dimensions of this business of "selling" waste to developing countries?

PROBLEM 9-7

Global Solutions, Inc. (GSI), a business consulting firm, is a strong proponent of responsible corporate behavior and believes that there has been too much criticism of

MNEs in the media. Recently, GSI has been hired to work on media and public relations for a group of chemical companies that have been accused of taking advantage of developing countries by setting up dangerous enterprises that would not be allowed at home. A spokesperson for GSI says, "First of all, the vast majority of companies in our industry just don't behave this way. There may be one or two rogue companies, but basically this is just corporate bashing. Second, while MNEs are often criticized for shirking their environmental responsibilities, some developing countries are actually contributing to this problem." Do you agree with GSI's statements? How might developing countries contribute to irresponsible behavior by MNEs? Consult the articles by Leonard and Bent below. If you were advising developing countries on how to deal with MNEs, what would you suggest?

H. Jeffrey Leonard, Confronting Industrial Pollution in Rapidly Industrializing Countries: Myths, Pitfalls, and Opportunities
12 Ecology L.Q. 779, 784–786, 800–801, 811 (1985)

Although there are many clear instances of American multinational corporations and their subsidiaries causing serious pollution problems in developing countries, most of the documented cases have involved discrete and declining types of industries. The most egregious examples of pollution by multinational corporations in the developing world have involved aging industries, industries that are difficult to re-equip, low technology operations such as mineral processing, and industries in which both production and demand are declining in the advanced countries.

In contrast, most high-technology multinational corporations building large integrated production plants today routinely use pollution control measures everywhere they locate. Most of these companies possess the technology and the knowledge to alleviate serious potential pollution problems and to operate modern efficient plants. As a result, some developing countries are beginning to require that incoming industries construct pollution-minimizing facilities that will not substantially exacerbate pollution problems.

Another reason why industrializing nations have some degree of latitude to drive hard bargains on pollution control is that most pollution control standards for industries in developing nations are set on a case-by-case basis. Thus, the stringency of environmental regulations for particular facilities varies according to the preferences of local or national officials, the amount of public pressure, and some rough calculation of the assimilative capacity of the local environment. Because of the ad hoc nature of this process, and the lack of national standards uniformly applied to foreign and domestic industries, most countries require multinational corporations to abide by stricter standards than those applied to locally owned industries.

Countries soliciting multinational corporations to build and operate production facilities can set technology and process constraints to which the multinational corporations must adhere if they wish to locate in the country. The costs to corporations of meeting these constraints and specific pollution control guidelines are often partly subsidized by various government grants and tax breaks. The remaining costs can be included in the companies' overall capital expenditure budgets for their projects. Only rarely will a company's investment decision turn on these incremental costs. If the country seems hospitable, and the long-range potential appears profitable, multinational firms may be quite willing to absorb the extra-capital costs of pollution control as the price of locating in the country.

In contrast, those countries that forbid multinational corporations from owning or operating plants on their soil for ideological or economic reasons, usually experience problems related to their own lack of expertise in pollution matters. Such countries still must often purchase foreign technology for their domestic plants. Technology importing nations have less room to bargain with foreign companies about pollution control than do countries that tolerate or encourage foreign investors.

Industrializing countries seeking to attract international capital must not only assess the immediate pollution problems that incoming industries might cause, but must also try to project the long-term environmental impacts of welcoming such industries. Such projections are difficult because there is seldom adequate information for informed judgment and because some industries at first appear much more environmentally benign than they eventually prove to be. Industrializing countries accepting new industries are therefore playing a sort of Russian roulette both because of their lack of advanced research capabilities, particularly with respect to environmental carcinogens, and because of deficiencies in information transfer from the more technically advanced nations.

Industrializing countries need not accept gross environmental damage by foreign firms as the price of economic development. Most multinational companies—whether American, European, or Japanese—are willing, when required, to take precautions to protect both workers' safety and the surrounding environment. A government that clearly and forthrightly outlines its minimum pollution control standards for foreign investors is likely to encounter few multinational firms that will withdraw from negotiations on this basis alone.

Maureen A. Bent, Exporting Hazardous Industries: Should American Standards Apply?
20 N.Y.U. J. Int'l L. & Pol. 777, 778–781 (1987)

Multinational corporations play a decisive role in the industrialization of developing countries. They design, construct and operate industrial facilities, and serve as a major conduit of technology transfers. Generally, technology exports to developing countries occur either as a result of intra-firm transfers or participation by multinational corporations and host countries in joint ventures. Where technology transfers occur in a joint venture setting, the host country often shares in the ownership and management of the enterprise. When the technology involved is relatively new, however, MNCs are usually reluctant to relinquish full control. In such cases, MNCs typically establish wholly- or majority-owned subsidiaries.

Since they wish to accelerate industrial development and attract high technology industry, developing countries frequently fail to challenge MNCs' demands to retain control over the technology that they seek to import. In fact, developing countries accord priority and grant preferential treatment to MNCs with more sophisticated technology. MNCs often benefit from liberal investment incentives, and host countries frequently relieve them of more stringent environmental and worker safety regulation. The nature of the parent-subsidiary and joint-venture relationship, as well as the developing countries' desire to attract sophisticated technology, provide MNCs with practically unfettered ability to "export" highly technical, and often hazardous, industries to lesser developed countries.

The United States is one of the leading source countries for foreign investment in the manufacturing industry in developing countries. A significant share of its investment was earmarked for the chemical industry, which accounted for 25.2 percent of the U.S. total foreign investments in 1980. Compared with the lower regulatory standards of developing countries, tougher U.S. environmental regulations may account for the significant presence of chemical industries in those countries. Although some industries seriously consider environmental regulations when determining plant location abroad, such regulations are only one of many factors weighed by U.S. manufacturing industries when determining plant location. Perhaps the driving force behind investments in manufacturing abroad is the ability of MNCs to obtain greater profits than they may otherwise make at home. MNCs maximize profits by taking advantage of limited, and often weakly enforced, environmental regulations in developing countries, as well as minimal requirements for investment in safety equipment to control potential hazards to workers and the general public, low employee wages and benefits, and weak taxation structures.

Whatever the reasons for the significant presence of MNCs in developing countries, one fact is clear: U.S. MNCs adhere to a double standard when operating abroad. The lack of stringent environmental regulations and worker safety standards abroad and the relaxed enforcement of such laws in industries using hazardous processes provide little incentive for MNCs to protect the safety of workers, to obtain liability insurance to guard against the hazard of product defects or toxic tort exposure, or to take precautions to minimize pollution of the environment. This double standard has caused catastrophic damage to the environment and to human lives.

If U.S. MNCs insist on exporting hazardous industries, measures should be taken to prevent or at least reduce the damage from accidents such as the Bhopal disaster. The most effective and expeditious means of achieving these ends would be to impose upon U.S. MNCs operating abroad the environmental and worker protection standards to which they are subjected when operating in the U.S.

Treaties Restricting Trade in Hazardous Materials

Three important and extensive treaties have been concluded for the purpose of restricting international trade in hazardous materials. The United States is not a party to any of these three treaty regimes.

- The Basel Convention on the Control of Transboundary Movements of Hazardous Wastes and Their Disposal, Mar. 22, 1989, 1673 U.N.T.S. 57 aims to "ensure that the management of hazardous wastes and other wastes including their transboundary movement and disposal is consistent with the protection of human health and the environment whatever their place of disposal." Basel Convention, Preamble. This Convention, which has been ratified by 181 parties, subjects trade in hazardous waste to a comprehensive control system based upon the principle of prior informed consent. Article 6 of the Convention states that a country can export hazardous waste only if it has obtained prior informed written consent from the importing country and all transit countries. Furthermore, trade in such materials is forbidden with non-parties unless agreements with non-parties have been concluded that do not derogate from the principles of environmentally sound management required by the Convention (Arts. 4 and 11). A party has the right to ban the entry of foreign hazardous waste entirely (Art. 4). An amendment to the Convention adopted in 1995 bans entirely the export of hazardous waste from OECD countries to non-OECD countries, but this amendment although ratified by 79 parties is not in force, though it is generally observed.

- The Rotterdam Convention on the Prior Informed Consent Procedure for Certain Hazardous Chemicals and Pesticides in International Trade, Sept. 10, 1998, 2244 U.N.T.S. 337 has the objective of protecting human health and the environment from certain hazardous chemicals. Annex III of the Convention lists the chemicals that are subject to the prior informed consent procedure. The exporting country is also responsible for labeling requirements that ensure the availability of information with regard to risks and hazards to human health and the environment (Art. 13). Exports of chemicals that are banned or severely restricted in the exporting state's territory are subject to special export notification requirements specified in Annex V of the Convention. A state may ban the import of Annex III chemicals entirely but must simultaneously prohibit or make subject to the same conditions import of the chemical from any other country and the domestic production of the chemical (Art. 10). The Rotterdam Convention currently has 154 parties.
- The Stockholm Convention on Persistent Organic Pollutants, May 22, 2001, 2256 U.N.T.S. 119, which is ratified by 179 parties, was concluded with the aim of the eventual elimination of eight types of dangerous organic chemicals and severely restricting eight such additional chemicals. Exportation of such chemicals is allowed only for their environmentally safe disposal or for a use specifically allowed under the agreement.

Organization for Economic Cooperation and Development: Council Recommendation on the Application of the Polluter-Pays Principle to Accidental Pollution
July 7, 1989 28 I.L.M. 1320, 1322–1324 (1989)

THE POLLUTER-PAYS PRINCIPLE . . .

3. [T]he "principle to be used for allocating the costs of pollution prevention and control is the so called Polluter-Pays Principle," [which] "means that the polluter should bear the expenses of carrying out the pollution prevention and control measures introduced by public authorities in Member countries, to ensure that the environment is in an acceptable state. In other words, the cost of these measures should be reflected in the çost of goods and services which cause pollution in production and/or consumption."

APPLICATION OF THE POLLUTER-PAYS PRINCIPLE

4. In matters of accidental pollution risks, the Polluter-Pays Principle implies that the operator of a hazardous installation should bear the cost of reasonable

measures to prevent and control accidental pollution from that installation which are introduced by public authorities in Member countries in conformity with domestic law prior to the occurrence of an accident in order to protect human health or the environment.

5. Domestic law which provides that the cost of reasonable measures to control accidental pollution after an accident should be collected as expeditiously as possible from the legal or natural person who is at the origin of the accident, is consistent with the Polluter-Pays Principle.

***

9. Public authorities of Member countries that "have responsibilities in the implementation of policies for prevention of, and response to, accidents involving hazardous substances" may take specific measures to prevent accidents occurring at hazardous installations and to control accidental pollution. Although the cost entailed is as a general rule met by the general budget, public authorities may with a view to achieving a more economically efficient resource allocation, introduce specific fees or taxes payable by certain installations on account of their hazardous nature (e.g., licensing fees), the proceeds of which are to be allocated to accidental pollution prevention and control.

10. One specific application of the Polluter-Pays Principle consists in adjusting these fees or taxes, in conformity with domestic law, to cover more fully the cost of certain exceptional measures to prevent and control accidental pollution in specific hazardous installations which are taken by public authorities to protect human health and the environment (e.g., special licensing procedures, execution of detailed inspections, drawing up of installation-specific emergency plans or building up special means of response for the public authorities to be used in connection with a hazardous installation), provided such measures are reasonable and directly connected with accident prevention or with the control of accidental pollution released by the hazardous installation. Lack of laws or regulations on relevant fees or taxes should not, however, prevent public authorities from meeting their responsibilities in connection with accidents involving hazardous substances.

11. A further specific application of the Polluter-Pays Principle consists in charging, in conformity with domestic law, the cost of reasonable pollution control measures decided by the authorities following an accident to the operator of the hazardous installation from which pollution is released. Such measures taken without undue delay by the operator or, in case of need, by the authorities would aim at promptly avoiding the spreading of environmental damage and would concern limiting the release of hazardous substances (e.g., by ceasing emissions at the plant, by erecting floating barriers on a river), the pollution as such (e.g., by cleaning or decontamination), or its ecological effects (e.g., by rehabilitating the polluted environment).

NOTE ON U.S. CONTROLS ON EXPORTS OF HAZARDOUS WASTES

Under U.S. law, all exports must satisfy the requirements of the Export Administration Act, which requires an export license (see Chapter Two at p. 134) and other documents. Exports require extensive documentation to support each transaction.

U.S. exporters are subject to additional requirements for shipments of hazardous chemicals, pesticides, and hazardous wastes. The Toxic Substances Control Act, 15 U.S.C. §§2601–2629 (2012) and the Federal Insecticide, Fungicide, and Rodenticide Act, 7

U.S.C. §§136–136y (2012) require that the exporter must notify the export to the government of the importing consignee. At least five other U.S. laws require some form of notice to importing countries when hazardous substances are being shipped to those countries. *See, e.g.,* Resource Conservation and Recovery Act, 42 U.S.C. §6938; 40 C.F.R. §§262.53, 262.83, 273.20, 273.40 (2013). For a detailed discussion of the various laws and regulations affecting the export of waste from the United States, see generally Jeffrey M. Gaba, *Exporting Waste: Regulation of the Export of Hazardous Wastes from the United States,* 36 Wm. & Mary Envtl. L. & Pol'y Rev. 405 (2012). Note that the bulk of U.S. export laws require notice to the importing country, not its consent. The purpose of the notice is to provide foreign governments with information on the U.S. regulatory controls imposed on certain chemicals and hazardous substances in the United States. Only the Resource Conservation and Recovery Act requires that the exporter obtain the express consent of importing countries to shipments of hazardous wastes. International criticism has been leveled at developing countries for their lax controls on the export of hazardous substances and wastes. International criticism has been leveled at developed countries for the lack of effective controls on exports of hazardous chemicals, pesticides, and hazardous wastes. Indeed, there has been a perception that developed countries use developing countries as a dumping ground for their hazardous waste. Proposals for more effective control include total export bans enforced by exporting countries, more complete information exchange, and requiring informed consent by importing countries as a condition of shipment of wastes to those countries. The international trend is toward greater disclosure of information but so far there has not been a general movement in favor of total export bans.

NOTES AND QUESTIONS

1. Since the United States is not a party to any of these three conventions, their provisions do not apply to companies exporting materials from the United States. However, multinational companies doing business outside the United States must comply with the conventions in most cases. Should the United States ratify these three treaties? Or are U.S. restrictions sufficient?

2. The polluter pays principle is not a rule of international law but is a principle of "soft law." Would you favor it as a hard international law rule?

IV.   *Liability for Industrial Accidents*

PROBLEM 9-8

Waste Solutions, Inc. (WSI) is a Texas company in the waste management field. For several years, it has been shipping garbage to landfills in South Carolina, but it has encountered increasing resistance from the local population. In looking for an alternative site, WSI has found that there is strong resistance from surrounding states as well. Because of the mounting resistance, WSI has begun negotiations with Z, a small impoverished developing country. WSI has now entered into a long-term contract to ship garbage to Z in exchange for generous payments to the government of Z. The Z government then simply dumps the untreated garbage in crudely made open-air dump sites near some large natural lakes. WSI's top management is very pleased with this solution as it relieves them of the headache of finding a suitable dump site in the United States, and Z government officials are happy because they are receiving payments from WSI. (Whether WSI needs to be concerned about where the payments are going is another issue; see Chapter Six, Part IV.) The CEO at WSI refers to this arrangement as "the classic win-win situation."

(1) Do any international laws prohibit the "sale" of garbage by WSI to Z? What norms, if any, apply?

(2) In response to a request from the Z government, WSI sets up a wholly foreign-owned subsidiary in Z to help the government treat the garbage before disposal. Later, it is discovered that the treatment of the garbage by the subsidiary leaves some toxic materials in the waste that seep into the nearby lakes and contaminate the water to the extent that it can no longer be used for drinking purposes unless the water undergoes expensive waste treatment. WSI's sharp in-house counsel has been scrupulously following corporate formalities in dealing with the subsidiary and has the paperwork and electronic records to prove it and all of the technicians in the subsidiary were expertly trained at WSI's corporate headquarters. Does WSI have any liability?

In addition to the readings so far, see the *Union Carbide* case, and the Divan and Rosencranz article discussing the *Bhopal* litigation.

Stephen C. McCaffrey, Accidents Do Happen: Hazardous Technology and International Tort Litigation
1 Transnat'l Law. 41, 48–51 (1988)

[In this article, Professor McCaffrey, taking the facts of the disaster at Bhopal, India, where 2,000 people were killed and 200,000 injured in an industrial disaster in 1984, examines the question of jurisdiction over the subsidiary and parent corporation in that case.]

Assertion of judicial jurisdiction over the subsidiary by local (in the *Bhopal* case, Indian) courts would present no problem in countries following either the civil or the common law system. However, the target defendant will probably be the parent company or foreign exporter of the hazardous technology, not only because the parent may have controlled the subsidiary, and may be responsible for, e.g., the defective design, process, or method of operation that led to the accident, but also—and perhaps chiefly—because the parent will have the deeper pocket. Further, as in the Bhopal litigation, plaintiffs may wish to sue the parent in order to obtain the most attractive forum. Finally, it may be that no local subsidiary was involved, in which case the foreign manufacturer or exporter may be the only available defendant.

If suit is brought against a foreign entity having no direct presence in the forum state, the question of jurisdiction over that entity is almost certain to be challenged, costing victims time and money. Even in the United States, which has shown perhaps the greatest readiness to "pierce the corporate veil," mere ownership of a majority or even all of the subsidiary's stock would probably not be enough by itself to allow the state in which the subsidiary is incorporated to assert jurisdiction over the parent. On the other hand, earlier reluctance of U.S. courts to reach a foreign parent through a local subsidiary has given way to a recognition that assertion of jurisdiction over the foreign parent is permissible where the parent so controls the subsidiary as to disregard its separate corporate existence. Obviously, however, this theory would not be available where it is claimed that plaintiff's injuries resulted from the foreign corporation's *failure* to exercise adequate supervision and control over a local subsidiary. Still, plaintiff in such a case could seek to hold the foreign corporation directly responsible if its failure to supervise were negligent (i.e., where it had breached a duty of supervision).

PROBLEM 9-9

Citizens for Corporate Accountability, a nonprofit organization, asks you to write a memorandum analyzing the infamous *Bhopal* industrial disaster case. You are to answer the following questions:

(1) Did Union Carbide Corporation's corporate structure play an important role in the outcome of this litigation?
(2) How important was the dismissal of the case in the United States on the grounds of *forum non conveniens*? The lawsuit was then relegated to the Indian courts. How did this affect the plaintiffs' prospects for meaningful relief? Was the Indian legal system efficient? Sophisticated?
(3) Why did the Indian government seek a pretrial award of damages? How would the Indian government enforce the award against Union Carbide Corporation (UCC), the defendant? Was UCC concerned about the damages award? Did the Indian government show a high level of legal skill in handling this case?
(4) Was the Indian government under pressure to resolve this case? Who was under greater pressure, the Indian government or UCC?
(5) Was the award of damages equitable and fair? Review in particular the award of damages for wrongful death. If the industrial disaster had occurred in the United States instead of India, what would have been the size of the award for wrongful death?
(6) Did UCC suffer serious adverse financial consequences from this incident, sufficient to deter similar conduct in the future?

To write your memorandum, consult the *Bhopal* case below and the following notes.

In re Union Carbide Corp. Gas Plant Disaster at Bhopal, India in December 1984
United States Court of Appeals, Second Circuit, 1987
809 F.2d 195

MANSFIELD, Circuit Judge.

This appeal raises the question of whether thousands of claims by citizens of India and the Government of India arising out of the most devastating industrial disaster in history—the deaths of over 2,000 persons and injuries of over 200,000 caused by lethal gas known as methyl isocyanate which was released from a chemical plant operated by Union Carbide India Limited (UCIL) in Bhopal, India—should be tried in the United States or in India. The Southern District of New York, John F. Keenan, Judge, granted the motion of Union Carbide Corporation (UCC), a defendant in some 145 actions commenced in federal courts in the United States, to dismiss these actions on grounds of *forum non conveniens* so that the claims may be tried in India, subject to certain conditions. The individual plaintiffs appeal from the order and the court's denial of their motion for a fairness hearing on a proposed settlement. UCC and the Union of India (UOI), a plaintiff, cross-appeal. We eliminate two of the conditions imposed by the district court and in all other respects affirm that court's orders.

The accident occurred on the night of December 2–3, 1984, when winds blew the deadly gas from the plant operated by UCIL into densely occupied parts of the city of Bhopal. UCIL is incorporated under the laws of India. Fifty and nine-tenths percent of its stock is owned by UCC, 22 percent is owned or controlled by the government of India, and the balance is held by approximately 23,500 Indian citizens. The stock is publicly traded on the Bombay Stock Exchange. The company is engaged in the manufacture of a variety of products, including chemicals, plastics, fertilizers and insecticides, at 14 plants in India and employs over 9,000 Indian citizens. It is managed and operated entirely by Indians in India.

Four days after the Bhopal accident, on December 7, 1984, the first of some 145 purported class actions in federal district courts in the United States was commenced on behalf of victims of the disaster. On January 2, 1985, the Judicial Panel on Multidistrict Litigation assigned the actions to the Southern District of New York where they became the subject of a consolidated complaint filed on June 28, 1985.

In the meantime, on March 29, 1985, India enacted the Bhopal Gas Leak Disaster (Processing of Claims) Act, granting to its government, the UOI, the exclusive right to represent the victims in India or elsewhere. Thereupon the UOI, purporting to act in the capacity of *parens patriae*, and with retainers executed by many of the victims, on April 8, 1985, filed a complaint in the Southern District of New York on behalf of all victims of the Bhopal disaster, similar to the purported class action complaints already filed by individuals in the United States. The UOI's decision to bring suit in the United States was attributed to the fact that, although numerous lawsuits (by now, some 6,500) had been instituted by victims in India against UCIL, the Indian courts did not have jurisdiction over UCC, the parent company, which is a defendant in the United States actions. The actions in India asserted claims not only against UCIL but also against the UOI, the State of Madhya Pradesh, and the Municipality of Bhopal, and were consolidated in the District Court of Bhopal.

By order dated April 25, 1985, Judge Keenan appointed a three-person Executive Committee to represent all plaintiffs in the pre-trial proceedings. It consisted of two lawyers representing the individual plaintiffs and one representing the UOI. On July 31, 1985, UCC moved to dismiss the complaints on grounds of *forum non conveniens*, the plaintiffs' lack of standing to bring the actions in the United States, and their purported attorneys' lack of authority to represent them. After several months of discovery related to *forum non conveniens*, the individual plaintiffs and the UOI opposed UCC's motion. After hearing argument on January 3, 1986, the district court, on May 12, 1986, 634 F. Supp. 842, in a thoroughly reasoned 63-page opinion granted the motion, dismissing the lawsuits before it on condition that UCC:

(1) consent to the jurisdiction of the courts of India and continue to waive defenses based on the statute of limitations,

(2) agree to satisfy any judgment rendered by an Indian court against it and upheld on appeal, provided the judgment and affirmance "comport with the minimal requirements of due process," and

(3) be subject to discovery under the Federal Rules of Civil Procedure of the United States.

On June 12, 1986, UCC accepted these conditions subject to its right to appeal them; and on June 24, 1986, the district court entered its order of dismissal. In September 1986 the UOI, acting pursuant to its authority under the Bhopal Act, brought suit on behalf of all claimants against UCC and UCIL in the District Court of Bhopal, where many individual suits by victims of the disaster were then pending.

In its opinion dismissing the actions the district court analyzed the *forum non conveniens* issues, applying the standards and weighing the factors suggested by the Supreme Court in *Piper Aircraft Co. v. Reyno*, 454 U.S. 235, 102 S. Ct. 252, 70 L. Ed. 2d 419 (1981). At the outset Judge Keenan concluded, in accordance with the Court's expressed views in *Piper* that, since the plaintiffs were not residents of the United States but of a foreign country, their choice of the United States as a forum would not be given the deference to which it would be entitled if this country were their home. Following *Piper*, the district court declined to compare the advantages and disadvantages to the respective parties of American versus Indian Laws or to determine the impact upon plaintiffs' claims of the laws of India, where UCC had acknowledged that it would make itself amenable to process, except to ascertain whether India provided an adequate alternative forum, as distinguished from no remedy at all. Judge Keenan reviewed thoroughly the affidavits of experts on India's law and legal system, which described in detail its procedural and substantive aspects, and concluded that, despite some of the Indian system's disadvantages, it afforded an adequate alternative forum for the enforcement of plaintiffs' claims.

As the district court found, the record shows that the private interests of the respective parties weigh heavily in favor of dismissal on grounds of *forum non conveniens*. The many witnesses and sources of proof are almost entirely located in India, where the accident occurred, and could not be compelled to appear for trial in the United States. The Bhopal plant at the time of the accident was operated by some 193 Indian nationals, including the managers of seven operating units employed by the Agricultural Products Division of UCIL, who reported to Indian Works Managers in Bhopal. The plant was maintained by seven functional departments employing over 200 more Indian nationals.

In short, the plant has been constructed and managed by Indians in India. No Americans were employed at the plant at the time of the accident. In the five years from 1980 to 1984, although more than 1,000 Indians were employed at the plant, only one American was employed there and he left in 1982. No Americans visited the plant for more than one year prior to the accident, and during the 5-year period before the accident the communications between the plant and the United States were almost nonexistent.

We are concerned, however, that as it is written the district court's requirement that UCC consent to the enforcement of a final Indian judgment, which was imposed on the erroneous assumption that such a judgment might not otherwise be enforceable in the United States, may create misunderstandings and problems of construction. Although the order's provision that the judgment "comport with the *minimal* requirements of due process" (emphasis supplied) probably it intended to refer to "due process" as used in the New York Foreign Country Money Judgments Law and others like it, there is the risk that it may also be interpreted as providing for a lesser standard than we would otherwise require. Since the court's condition with respect to enforceability of any final Indian judgment is predicated on an erroneous legal assumption and its "due process" language is ambiguous, and since the district court's purpose is fully served by New York's statute providing for recognition of foreign-country money judgments, it was error to impose this condition upon the parties.

We also believe that the district court erred in requiring UCC to consent (which UCC did under protest and subject to its right of appeal) to broad discovery of it by the plaintiffs under the Federal Rules of Civil Procedure when UCC is confined to the more limited discovery authorized under Indian law.

Basic justice dictates that both sides be treated equally, with each having equal access to the evidence in the possession or under the control of the other. Application of this fundamental principle in the present case is especially appropriate since the UOI, as the sovereign government of India, is expected to be a party to the Indian litigation, possibly on both sides.

For these reasons we direct that the condition with respect to the discovery of UCC under the Federal Rules of Civil Procedure be deleted without prejudice to the right of the parties to have reciprocal discovery of each other on equal terms under the Federal Rules, subject to such approval as may be required of the Indian court in which the case will be pending.

As so modified the district court's order is affirmed.

Shyam Divan and Armin Rosencranz, The Bhopal Settlement
1989 Envtl. Pol'y & L. 166, 166–169

A. Introduction

On February 14, 1989, the Indian Supreme Court cut the Gordian knot that the *Bhopal* case had come to resemble. That afternoon, the Court induced the Indian Government and the Union Carbide Corporation (Carbide) to accept its suggestion for an overall settlement of the claims arising from the Bhopal disaster. More than four years earlier, during the early hours of December 3, 1984, forty tons of highly toxic methyl-isocyanate (MIC) escaped into the atmosphere from Carbide's pesticide plant in Bhopal and killed over 2,500 people. Another 200,000 people, caught in the path of the dispersing gas, suffered injuries.

B. Summary of the Settlement

Under the settlement, Carbide agreed to pay U.S. $470 million[32] to the Indian Government on behalf of all the Bhopal victims in full and final settlement of all past, present and future claims arising from the Bhopal disaster. The entire amount had to be and was paid by March 31, 1989. In addition, to facilitate the settlement, the Supreme Court exercised its extraordinary jurisdiction and terminated all the civil, criminal and contempt of court proceedings that had arisen out of the Bhopal disaster and were pending in subordinate Indian courts.

C. India's Weak Institutional Framework

Almost any country's regulatory and redressive machinery would have been severely tested by a disaster of Bhopal's magnitude. In India, the challenge was particularly formidable. It quickly became apparent that the institutional framework both for immediate

---

32. In 1985, Carbide had paid U.S. $5 million to the International Red Cross for the relief and rehabilitation of the Bhopal victims.

and long term support to the Bhopal victims was remarkably weak. None of the government agencies knew how to contain the damage inflicted by the lethal gas. None had detailed information about the toxicological properties of MIC or the appropriate post-exposure treatment for the victims. Characteristic of an oblivious-to-safety culture, there was no disaster management plan at any level of government. As a result, the medical response to the disaster was entirely voluntary, unplanned and haphazard.

The dim prospect of early compensation under India's judicial system compounded the victims' immediate difficulties. Moreover, Indian lawyers are courtroom advocates, unaccustomed to the searching investigation and fact development that a case like Bhopal demanded. India has an undeveloped tort law. In the decade between 1975–84, there were only 56 non-motor vehicle cases reported in the All India Reporter. These cases, despite their straightforward nature, took an average of 12 years and 9 months from filing to decision. Significantly, average recoveries among the successful plaintiffs were very low—the Rupee equivalent of U.S. $950.

These weaknesses, together with the risks attending all complex litigation, made the Bhopal lawsuits eminently suitable for settlement. As the Supreme Court itself observed, "The tremendous suffering of thousands of persons compelled us to move into the direction of immediate relief which, we thought, should not be subordinated to the uncertain promises of the law."[33] Indeed, given the formidable obstacles in securing redress, few lawyers would have predicted that the victims would secure U.S. $475 million from Carbide in just four years.

D. The Bhopal Act

To ensure that claims arising out of the disaster were dealt with speedily, effectively and equitably, the Indian Parliament, in March, 1985, enacted the Bhopal Gas Leak Disaster (Processing of Claims) Act of 1985 (the Bhopal Act). The Bhopal Act conferred an exclusive right on the Indian Government to represent all claimants both within and outside India, and directed the Government to organize a plan for the registration and processing of the victims' claims.

E. How the *Bhopal* Case Reached the Indian Supreme Court

In April 1985, shortly after the enactment of the Bhopal Act, the Indian Government sued Carbide in the United States. The Government's preference for an American court stemmed from a lack of confidence in its own judicial system, the lure of large damages that an American jury might award, and its uncertainty about whether Carbide would submit to the jurisdiction of an Indian court. The American court, however, declined to try the Bhopal lawsuit, declaring that India was the more appropriate forum. Consequently, in September 1986, nearly two years after the tragedy, the Indian Government sued Carbide in the Court of the District Judge, Bhopal, for U.S. $3 billion in damages.

The Bhopal case reached the Indian Supreme Court through the separate appeals of Carbide and the Indian Government from the judgment of Justice Seth of the Madhya Pradesh High Court. In April, 1988, Justice Seth awarded interim damages of U.S. $192

---

33. Supreme Court of India, Order dated May 4, 1989 (setting out the reasons that persuaded the Court to make the February 14, 1989 Order for settlement in the Bhopal case), p. 24.

million on the basis of "more than a *prima facie* case having been made out" against the defendants. Carbide's lawyers claimed that the judgment was unsustainable because it amounted to a verdict without trial. The Indian Government appealed because Justice Seth reduced by 30 percent District Judge Deo's earlier interim payment award of U.S. $270 million.

Surveying the Bhopal litigation in December 1988, the five judge Supreme Court Bench must have been dismayed at the lack of progress in the principal lawsuit. The ineffectiveness of the Indian Government's maneuvers, combined with Carbide's apparent disregard for the victims, had dimmed the victims' hopes for early compensation. Proceedings in the original lawsuit before the Bhopal District Judge had stalled. Pre-trial matters such as "discovery" had yet to be addressed. Four years after the tragedy, the Government had still to finalize its list of authentic claimants.

Rather than proceeding rapidly with the trial of the original lawsuit and establishing a legal claim on Carbide's American assets with a determinative final judgment, the Government had preferred to pursue a risky short-cut. Encouraged by an early suggestion of Bhopal District Judge Deo, regarding an "interim" award," the Attorney General of India's main litigation strategy was the pursuit of such a pre-trial award. More than a year had been consumed in appeals from that award. In separate proceedings, additional efforts had been expended in a contempt of court action against Carbide, its Chairman and its lawyers. Indeed, there was little in the Government's handling of the Bhopal case that might have impressed the Supreme Court Judges with the Government's capacity to devise legal strategies and introduce reformed trial procedures that could bring the Bhopal lawsuit to a swift conclusion.

F. OPTIONS BEFORE THE SUPREME COURT

Eager to help the victims, the Supreme Court faced difficult choices. One option before the Court was to uphold the High Court's pre-trial judgment of U.S. $192 million. But American courts (which the Indian government would have had to enlist to enforce any interim award) have no experience with interim payments, and they would almost certainly have dismissed an Indian pretrial judgment as a denial of due process. So certain were Carbide's lawyers of the unenforceability of the Seth Judgment that they did not bother to obtain a stay of the U.S. $192 million award, pending the outcome of their appeal.

Alternatively, the Supreme Court could have struck down the interim award and urged the Government to pay some interim compensation until it secured a final judgment against Carbide. This course, although legally sound, seemed politically unfeasible. Temporarily relieving the multinational of its liability to compensate the victims would have marred the reputation of the Court in the eyes of the Indian public. Besides, it is unlikely that the Indian Government, in an election year, would have consented to pay interim compensation. Such payment could have been criticized as an interest-free loan and sell-out to the insensitive multinational.

Faced with these no-win options from the perspective of the Bhopal victims, the Supreme Court pressured the parties into settling the dispute. In the situation facing it, the Court did the best it could.

G. THE SETTLEMENT: AN EVALUATION

The basic analytical question is whether the settlement efficiently achieves the traditional tort goals of compensation, corrective justice and deterrence.

The Bhopal settlement is welcome because it obtains compensation efficiently: Future litigation costs have been avoided and compensation has been secured within five years of the disaster—a short time by Indian standards. Frequently, the compensation secured in mass tort cases is dwarfed by the transaction costs of litigation. Attorneys' fees may eat into more than one third of the total award. For example, one study of the asbestos trials in the United States concludes that litigation expenses consumed 63 percent of the recovery, leaving only 37 percent for victim relief.[34] The Bhopal settlement both contains transaction costs and cuts long years of expensive litigation. At the sluggish pace at which the Indian Government was proceeding in the case, it might have been 15 more years before the victims saw the colour of their money. By that time, the compensation—so urgently required by the impoverished and displaced victims—would have been meaningless. With the settlement, the victims should begin receiving compensation in a few months' time.

[1] COMPENSATION

The basis for the amount of U.S. $470 million suggested by the Supreme Court and accepted by the Indian Government and Carbide was disclosed by the Court in its post-settlement Order on May 4, 1989. During settlement negotiations, Carbide's best offer had been U.S. $426 million, while the Government's lowest demand was U.S. $500 million. The Court arrived at a middle figure of U.S. $470 million after estimating the amount of appropriate compensation due to the claimants for varying degrees of injury.

The settlement provides U.S. $44 million for the 3000 dead, U.S. $160 million for the 30,000 permanently disabled, U.S. $60 million for the 20,000 temporarily disabled and an additional U.S. $50 million for 2000 victims who suffered other serious injuries. The Court also set aside U.S. $16 million for specialized medical treatment, after-care and rehabilitation of the victims. The remaining U.S. $140 million was allocated to meet the claims of those with less serious injuries, such as those who lost personal belongings and livestock.

Under the Settlement, compensation for the deceased will average U.S. $14,600. This amount is nearly three times higher than what has been awarded in motor vehicles accident claims under Indian tort law. Moreover, the Supreme Court's May 4, 1989 order implies that the entire U.S. $470 million will go to the victims and that neither the Federal nor the Madhya Pradesh state government will be entitled to draw reimbursements from that amount, for litigation and rehabilitation expenditures incurred by them.

The U.S. $470 million settlement, with its immediate payment condition, compares favorably with Carbide's previous offer in March 1986, to pay U.S. $350 million over 5 to 7 years. Moreover, the March 1986 Carbide offer was made during proceedings before a U.S. District Court. The Bhopal victims were then represented by several American lawyers, who would have skimmed off as much as 40 percent of the $350 million in contingency fees. By contrast, the entire U.S. $470 million will now go to aid the victims.

Could a better settlement have been secured? From Carbide's standpoint, there was no imminent threat to its American assets—Justice Seth's pre-trial award was little more than a paper decree—and apparently there was no urgent need to settle. Apart from the Supreme Court's inducements, the only real pressures working on Carbide were the

---

34. J. Kakalik, P. Ebener, W. Felstiner, G. Haggstrom & M. Shanly, Variations in Asbestos Litigation Compensation and Expenses at XII–XIX (Rand Corp. 1984).

mounting legal costs and the continuing stain on its reputation. Carbide's officers do not seem to have been much moved by their company's bad publicity and they seem to have held fast to a sum that was relatively modest in terms of Carbide's total assets. Given the negligible progress in the original suit, it seems unlikely that the Indian Government could have secured more favorable terms that it did from the multinational.

[2] CORRECTIVE JUSTICE

Although the Supreme Court's orders do not ascribe liability to Carbide, the settlement implicitly establishes the multinational's accountability. Retributive or corrective justice requires that the tortfeasor not benefit from his or her action or negligence but instead be forced to compensate the victim. The settlement clearly achieves this end. Indeed, the Bhopal settlement is the first in a mass tort case where a multinational has paid for the actions of its local subsidiary. The settlement, therefore, is likely to strengthen the emergent norm of international law that transnational corporations are strictly liable for mishaps from hazardous activities conducted by their subsidiaries around the globe.

[3] DETERRENCE

The U.S. $470 million paid by Carbide to the Supreme Court in February, 1989, pursuant to the settlement, was more than double the corporation's U.S. $200 million insurance coverage. This amount seems large enough to deter foreign and domestic entrepreneurs from recklessly investing in hazardous technologies in India or, indeed, in developing countries generally. At the same time, by consenting to a settlement that will not severely deplete Carbide's assets, the Indian Government has signaled its willingness to permit new investments in hazardous industries, provided that the investors are willing to internalize the social costs resulting from their activities.

H. CONCLUSION

In the final analysis, the Supreme Court's statesmanship has secured more for the Bhopal victims than the Indian Government could have otherwise obtained, at least for the short term. As for the future, the Supreme Court must constitute an oversight machinery to ensure that the money actually reaches the victims. It must also issue directions for the speedy distribution of compensation.

NOTE ON THE BHOPAL SETTLEMENT AND ITS TORTUOUS AFTERMATH

Despite the 1989 settlement, litigation in both India and the United States has continued non-stop to this writing in 2014, with no end in sight.

Subsequent to the 1989 settlement, two important corporate changes occurred. In 1994, the Indian government approved UCC's sale of its 50.9 percent stake in UCIL, reportedly so that the proceeds of the sale could be used to build a hospital. The reorganized UCIL business now operates in India under the ironic name, Eveready Industries, Ltd. The second change occurred in 2001, when Dow Chemical Company acquired control of UCC in a stock-purchase transaction.

In the United States, a series of collateral class action and individual lawsuits were filed against UCC in New York federal courts asking for compensation under the Alien Tort Statute under nuisance laws, and under tort law asking for medical monitoring and environmental remediation of the Bhopal site. The plaintiffs focused on post-leak contamination and additional uncompensated injuries as the basis for these lawsuits. These cases bounced back and forth between the U.S. District Court and the U.S. Court of Appeals for the Second Circuit more than a score of times. Thus far the courts have denied relief, refusing to pierce the corporate veil between UCC and UCIL and upholding the validity of the 1989 settlement. *See Bano v. Union Carbide Corp.*, 273 F.3d 120 (2d Cir. 2001) and *Bano* case history, *http://www.earthrights.org/print/787; Sahu v. Union Carbide Corp.*, 475 F.3d 465 (2d Cir. 2007) and Summary Order of June 27, 2013, 528 F. App'x 96 (2d Cir. 2013), *aff'g* 2012 U.S. Dist. LEXIS 91066 (S.D.N.Y. June 26, 2012). But litigation in U.S. courts appears certain to continue as Indian activists have announced new efforts to hold not only UCC liable but also Dow Chemical as the successor owner of UCC. *See India: Court Decision Requires Dow Chemical to Respond to Bhopal Gas Tragedy*, AMNESTY INT'L (July 23, 2013), *http://www.amnesty.org/en/news/india-court-decision-requires-dowchemical-respond-bhopal-gas-tragedy-2013-07-23.*

Legal proceedings are continuing in India as well. On the civil side, the Indian Supreme Court has handled a series of filings by the Indian government as well as others to reopen the 1989 Bhopal settlement. Thus far the court has rejected all these petitions. *See SC Refuses to Re-Open Bhopal Gas Case*, LIVE MINT (May 11, 2011) *http://www.livemint.com/Politics/eqT2ZekjPbyDr7PP2eRi7O/SC-refuses-to-reopen-Bhopal-gas-case.html.* On the criminal side, in 2010, seven former executives of UCIL were convicted in the Bhopal district court of negligent homicide and given fines and jail sentences. Similar criminal charges are pending in Bhopal district court against UCC and its former CEO, Warren Anderson, who have refused to appear. The Indian government has filed a formal request for extradition with the U.S. State Department concerning these charges.

NOTES AND QUESTIONS

1. What is your opinion of the Bhopal settlement? Does it meet standards of corrective and distributive justice?

2. It appears that no UCC employee (and no American) was connected in any way with UCIL at the time of the Bhopal disaster. Moreover, UCIL and UCC were operated as independent legal entities. UCC management was clearly surprised, shocked, and dismayed by the disaster. But what do you make of the court's statement in the Bhopal case that for at least during the five-year period before the incident, communications between UCC and UCIL were "almost non-existent"? Is it wise policy for a multinational company that is a majority owner of a foreign company to allow it extreme autonomy? Should a parent company in such a case incur liability for inadequate supervision, training, and oversight of the foreign company?

3. What law is applicable to a disaster such as occurred in Bhopal, India in 1984? At present national law—the law of the host country—applies. Is this sufficient? Although the Bhopal incident did not have transboundary impact, an industrial accident that causes deaths, injuries, and destruction across national boundaries can easily be imagined. In fact, such accidents occurred at the ICMESA plant in Seveso, Italy in 1976, and at the Sandoz plant near Basel, Switzerland in 1986. These accidents provided the impetus for law-making initiatives in European countries. The European Union has adopted a series of "Seveso Directives" that require standards for prevention, preparedness, and

response to industrial accidents that apply in all 28 EU member states. The current Seveso Directive is Directive 2012/18/EU, 2012 O.J. (L 197) 1. In addition, the UN Economic Commission for Europe has adopted the 1992 Convention on the Transboundary Effects of Industrial Accidents, Mar. 17, 1992, 2105 U.N.T.S. 457 [hereinafter Helsinki Convention] (entry into force April 19, 2000, with 41 parties as of 2014), which adopts standards similar to the Seveso Directive for the wider European area. Two international instruments have been concluded that adopt international standards for liability of businesses involved in industrial accidents. The Convention on Civil Liability for Damage Resulting from Activities Dangerous to the Environment, June 21, 1993, 32 I.L.M. 1228 (1993) provides for recovery of damages from the parties responsible (persons or companies in control of the activity causing damage) for industrial accidents based on strict liability standards and including damages to the environment. In addition a Protocol on Civil Liability and Compensation for Damage Caused by the Transboundary Effects of Industrial Accidents on Transboundary Waters, May 21, 2003, available at *http://www. unece.org/fileadmin/DAM/env/civil-liability/documents/protocol_e.pdf* was adopted in 2003, as a joint protocol to the Helsinki Convention and the Convention on the Protection and Use of Transboundary Waters and International Lakes, Mar. 17, 1992, 1936 U.N.T.S. 269. However, neither convention allowing the recovery of damages is in force at present. Is it desirable to have international standards for damage liability and compensation in this area?

4. After conducting hearings on the Bhopal incident, the U.S. Congress in 1986 enacted the Emergency Planning and Community Right-to-Know Act (EPCRA), Pub. L. No. 99-499, 100 Stat. 1728 (codified at 42 U.S.C. §§11001–11050 (2012)). This law provides support for state and local government programs to inform the public and to have emergency plans in place to cope with possible industrial accidents. The EPCRA requires owners and operators of facilities in the United States that use hazardous substances (1) to notify local emergency planning committees of any releases of such substances, 42 U.S.C. §11004; (2) to cooperate with local and state officials to prepare emergency contingency plans, 42 U.S.C. §11003; (3) to make full disclosure regarding data and an inventory of chemicals being made or used, 42 U.S.C. §§11021–11023; and (4) to submit annual reports on safety and release of chemicals 42 U.S.C. §11021–11023. Thus, the Bhopal gas incident had a major impact in the United States.

V. The U.S. Alien Tort Statute

The Alien Tort Statute (ATS), codified at 28 U.S.C. §1350, is a legislative product of the very first Congress in 1789. Its current version reads as follows: "The District Courts shall have original jurisdiction of any civil action by an alien for a tort only, committed in violation of the law of nations." Although it may seem unlikely that U.S. corporations need to be concerned about such an ancient and obscure statute in their conduct of international business, recent decisions by U.S. courts indicate that issues concerning the ATS can be an important consideration in IBTs.

In the first 170 years of its existence, only one case was brought under the ATS, but recently, plaintiffs have begun to bring lawsuits under the ATS against MNEs engaged in international business. In the first wave of litigation, begun in the 1990s, the plaintiffs in ATS cases faced three hurdles:

(1) *Violation of International Law.* The ATS requires a tort committed in violation of the "law of nations" or public international law. Plaintiffs found it difficult to allege a violation based upon a specific treaty provision creating a binding legal obligation and courts were not hospitable to claims based upon customary international law, i.e., the practice of states (see Chapter One at pp. 28-29), on the grounds that custom was vague and ambiguous. *See Beanal v. Freeport-McMoran, Inc.,* 197 F.3d 161, 165 (5th Cir. 1999) (dismissing a complaint against a mining company for violations of human rights, environmental torts, genocide, and cultural genocide for failure to show violation of substantive international legal norm in a treaty or custom and for failure to plead with specificity).

(2) *State Action.* Nation-states, not private parties, are subjects of international law and a private party cannot be sued for a violation of international law unless state action or color of state action is involved. For a handful of crimes, such as slave trading, genocide, and war crimes, no state action is required and an individual can be held directly liable under international law. *See Tel-Oren v. Libyan Arab Republic,* 726 F.2d 774, 794-795 (D.C. Cir. 1984). However, most MNEs are not likely to engage in crimes of such a heinous nature. For all other violations, such as environmental torts, an individual, such as an MNE, is not liable unless it acts under the color of state action. But what is color of state action? Does an MNE need to partner with a government or does an MNE need to obtain explicit government authority to act? This could be a difficult standard to meet.

(3) Forum Non Conveniens. Plaintiffs who sued MNEs in U.S. courts for actions taken in foreign countries found that U.S. courts were often open to dismissing the case on the grounds of *forum non conveniens* (see Chapter Eight at pp. 668-671. The doctrine is one of judicial discretion allowing U.S. courts to decide that the lawsuit should be brought in a foreign court. U.S. courts weighed a number of factors: The plaintiffs were often foreign nationals and most of the witnesses and evidence were to be found overseas. The dismissal of the case, however, required a finding that an adequate foreign forum existed in which plaintiffs could assert their claims. U.S. courts were inclined to dismiss these cases even though plaintiffs alleged that foreign courts and governments were corrupt and that any meaningful relief was illusory. *See Aguinda v. Texaco, Inc.,* 303 F.3d 470, 477-478 (2d Cir. 2002) (upholding decision to dismiss action against Texaco for environmental damage in Ecuador and Peru on grounds of *forum non conveniens* despite allegations of corruption in Ecuadorian judicial system).

These considerations meant that only a small handful of cases were ever successfully brought under the ATS and none of them involved an MNE engaged in international business. Most of the cases involved actions taken by a foreign sovereign state during wartime or actions by an authoritarian government to suppress political dissent. *See Kadic v. Karadzic,* 70 F.3d 232, 241-243 (genocide and war crimes); *Filártiga v. Peña-Irala,* 630 F.2d 876, 878 (2d Cir. 1980) (state use of torture).

In 2004, in the landmark ATS case of *Sosa v. Alvarez-Machain,* 542 U.S. 692 (2004), the U.S. Supreme Court took a "no-nonsense" approach to the interpretation of the Act, whose implications are now being worked out by the lower courts. The *Sosa* case determined that the ATS "was intended as jurisdictional in the sense of addressing the power of the courts to entertain cases concerned with a certain subject." *Sosa,* 542 U.S. at 714. Thus, the Court (three Justices dissenting) concluded that Congress intended to create a private cause of action by passing the ATS; it was not intended to be "placed on the shelf" to await future legislative action.

But what is the contour of the cause of action created? Here, the Court concluded that the ATS furnishes "jurisdiction for a relatively modest set of actions alleging violations of the law of nations." *Id.* at 720. This may seem to be a truism, but the Court went on to state that this means a narrow set of common law actions "based on the present-day law of nations to rest on a norm of international character accepted by the civilized world and defined with specificity comparable to the features of the 18th century paradigms we have recognized." *Id.* at 725. The reference to "18th century paradigms" was threefold: violation of safe conduct, infringement of the rights of ambassadors, and piracy. The Court seemed to approve, or at least did not disapprove, the landmark 1980 case involving torture, *Filártiga v. Peña-Irala*, 630 F.2d 876 (2d Cir. 1980). In the *Sosa* case itself, which involved a claim by the plaintiff Alvarez based on wrongful arrest and abduction from Mexico in order that he could stand trial in the United States, the Court held there was no ATS cause of action since the norm advanced "expresses an aspiration that exceeds any binding customary rule having the specificity we require." *Sosa,* 542 U.S. at 738. It might be added that this was an easy determination since the Supreme Court in 1992, in *United States v. Alvarez-Machain,* 504 U.S. 655 (1992), had upheld the legality of this very seizure and abduction.

What is the future of the ATS for international business? Consider the following cases.

Abdullahi v. Pfizer, Inc.

United States Court of Appeals, Second Circuit, 2009
562 F.3d 163, *cert. denied,* 130 S. Ct. 3541 (2010)

PARKER, J.

This consolidated appeal is from the judgments of the United States District Court for the Southern District of New York dismissing two complaints for lack of subject matter jurisdiction under the Alien Tort Statute, 28 U.S.C. §1350 ("ATS"). . . .

BACKGROUND

A. PFIZER'S TROVAN TEST IN NIGERIA

On review of a district court's grant of a motion to dismiss, we assume as true the facts alleged in the complaints, construing them in the light most favorable to the appellants. The central events at issue in these cases took place in 1996, during an epidemic of bacterial meningitis in northern Nigeria. The appellants allege that at that time, Pfizer, the world's largest pharmaceutical corporation, sought to gain the approval of the U.S. Food and Drug Administration ("FDA") for the use on children of its new antibiotic, Trovafloxacin Mesylate, marketed as "Trovan." They contend that in April 1996, Pfizer dispatched three of its American physicians to work with four Nigerian doctors to experiment with Trovan on children who were patients in Nigeria's Infectious Disease Hospital ("IDH") in Kano, Nigeria. Working in concert with Nigerian government officials, the team allegedly recruited two hundred sick children who sought treatment at the IDH and gave half of the children Trovan and the other half Ceftriaxone, an FDA-approved antibiotic the safety and efficacy of which was well-established. Appellants contend that Pfizer knew that Trovan had never previously been tested on children in the form being used and that animal tests showed that Trovan had life-threatening side effects, including joint disease, abnormal cartilage growth, liver damage, and a degenerative bone condition. Pfizer purportedly gave the children who were in the Ceftriaxone control group a deliberately low dose in order to misrepresent the effectiveness of Trovan in relation to Ceftriaxone. After approximately two weeks, Pfizer allegedly concluded the experiment and left without administering follow-up care. According to the appellants, the tests caused the deaths of eleven children, five of whom had taken Trovan and six of whom had taken the lowered dose of Ceftriaxone, and left many others blind, deaf, paralyzed, or brain-damaged.

Appellants claim that Pfizer, working in partnership with the Nigerian government, failed to secure the informed consent of either the children or their guardians and specifically failed to disclose or explain the experimental nature of the study or the serious risks involved. The appellants also contend that Pfizer deviated from its treatment protocol by not alerting the children or their guardians to the side effects of Trovan or other risks of the experiment, not providing them with the option of choosing alternative treatment, and not informing them that the non-governmental organization Médecins Sans Frontières (Doctors Without Borders) was providing a conventional and effective treatment for bacterial meningitis, free of charge, at the same site.

The appellants allege that, in an effort to rapidly secure FDA approval, Pfizer hastily assembled its test protocol at its research headquarters in Groton, Connecticut, and requested and received permission to proceed from the Nigerian government in March 1996. Appellants also contend that the experiments were condemned by doctors, including one on Pfizer's staff at the time of the Kano trial. In 1998, the FDA approved Trovan for use on adult patients only. After reports of liver failure in patients who took Trovan, its use in America was eventually restricted to adult emergency care. In 1999, the European Union banned its use.

DISCUSSION

I. THE ALIEN TORT STATUTE

The Alien Tort Statute, 28 U.S.C. §1350, provides that "[t]he district courts shall have original jurisdiction of any civil action by an alien for a tort only, committed in violation of the law of nations or a treaty of the United States." Included in the Judiciary Act of 1789, the statute provided jurisdiction in just two cases during the first 191 years after its enactment. In the last thirty years, however, the ATS has functioned slightly more robustly, conferring jurisdiction over a limited category of claims.

We first extensively examined the ATS in *Filártiga v. Peña-Irala*, 630 F.2d 876 (2d Cir. 1980), where we held that conduct violating the law of nations is actionable under the ATS "only where the nations of the world have demonstrated that the wrong is of mutual, and not merely several, concern, by means of express international accords." Following *Filártiga*, we concluded that ATS claims may sometimes be brought against private actors, and not only state officials when the tortious activities violate norms of "universal concern" that are recognized to extend to the conduct of private parties—for example, slavery, genocide, and war crimes. This case involves allegations of both state and individual action. In *Flores v. Southern Peru Copper Corp.*, 414 F.3d 233 (2d Cir. 2003), we clarified that "the law of nations" in the ATS context "refers to the body of law known as customary international law," which "is discerned from myriad decisions made in numerous and

varied international and domestic arenas" and "does not stem from any single, definitive, readily-identifiable source." In *Flores*, we concluded that ATS jurisdiction is limited
to alleged violations of "those clear and unambiguous rules by which States universally
abide, or to which they accede, out of a sense of legal obligation and mutual concern."
Id. at 252. Applying this standard, we held that the appellants' claim that pollution from
mining operations caused lung disease failed to state a violation of customary international law. We reasoned that the "right to life" and the "right to health" were insufficiently
definite to constitute binding customary legal norms.

In 2004, the Supreme Court comprehensively addressed the ATS for the first time
in *Sosa v. Alvarez-Machain*, 542 U.S. 692 (2004). Justice Souter, writing for the majority,
clarified that the ATS was enacted to create jurisdiction over "a relatively modest set of
actions alleging violations of the law of nations." The Supreme Court confirmed that
federal courts retain a limited power to "adapt [] the law of nations to private rights" by
recognizing "a narrow class of international norms" to be judicially enforceable through
our residual common law discretion to create causes of action. *Id.* at 728–29. It cautioned,
however, that courts must exercise this power with restraint and "the understanding that
the door [to actionable violations] is still ajar subject to vigilant doorkeeping," permitting
only those claims that "rest on a norm of international character accepted by the civilized
world and defined with a specificity comparable to the features of the 18th-century paradigms [the Supreme Court has] recognized." *Id.* at 725, 729. These 18th-century paradigms consist of offenses against ambassadors, violations of the right to safe passage, and
individual actions arising out of piracy. The common theme among these offenses is that
they contravened the law of nations, admitted of a judicial remedy, and simultaneously
threatened serious consequences in international affairs. Lower courts are required to
gauge claims brought under the ATS against the current state of international law, but are
permitted to recognize under federal common law only those private claims for violations
of customary international law norms that reflect the same degree of "definite content
and acceptance among civilized nations" as those reflected in the 18th-century paradigms.
Id. at 732–33. The Supreme Court in *Sosa* also counseled that "the determination whether
a norm is sufficiently definite to support a cause of action should (and, indeed, inevitably
must) involve an element of judgment about the practical consequences of making that
cause available to litigants" in federal courts. In this way *Sosa* set a "high bar to new private
causes of action" alleging violations of customary international law.

Turning now to this appeal, and remaining mindful of our obligation to proceed
cautiously and self-consciously in this area, we determine whether the norm alleged
(1) is a norm of international character that States universally abide by, or accede to, out
of a sense of legal obligation; (2) is defined with a specificity comparable to the 18th-
century paradigms discussed in *Sosa*; and (3) is of mutual concern to States.

A. THE PROHIBITION OF NONCONSENSUAL MEDICAL EXPERIMENTATION ON HUMANS

Appellants' ATS claims are premised on the existence of a norm of customary international law prohibiting medical experimentation on non-consenting human subjects.
To determine whether this prohibition constitutes a universally accepted norm of customary international law, we examine the current state of international law by consulting
the sources identified by Article 38 of the Statute of the International Court of Justice
("ICJ Statute"), to which the United States and all members of the United Nations are

parties. Article 38 identifies the authorities that provide "competent proof of the content of customary international law." *Flores*, 414 F.3d at 251. These sources consist of:

a) international conventions, whether general or particular, establishing rules expressly recognized by the contesting states;

b) international custom, as evidence of a general practice accepted as law;

c) the general principles of law recognized by civilized nations;

d) ...judicial decisions and the teachings of the most highly qualified publicists of the various nations, as subsidiary means for the determination of rules of law.

Statute of the International Court of Justice, art. 38(1), June 26, 1945, 59 Stat. 1055, 1060, T.S. No. 993.

The appellants ground their claims in four sources of international law that categorically forbid medical experimentation on non-consenting human subjects: (1) the Nuremberg Code, which states as its first principle that "[t]he voluntary consent of the human subject is absolutely essential"; (2) the World Medical Association's Declaration of Helsinki, which sets forth ethical principles to guide physicians world-wide and provides that human subjects should be volunteers and grant their informed consent to participate in research; (3) the guidelines authored by the Council for International Organizations of Medical Services ("CIOMS"), which require "the voluntary informed consent of [a] prospective subject"; and (4) Article 7 of the International Covenant on Civil and Political Rights ("ICCPR"), which provides that "no one shall be subjected without his free consent to medical or scientific experimentation."

The district court found that "non-consensual medical experimentation violates the law of nations and, therefore, the laws of the United States" and cited the Nuremberg Code for support. It then noted that with the exception of the Nuremberg Code, these sources contain only aspirational or vague language lacking the specificity required for jurisdiction. It also determined that because the United States did not ratify or adopt any of these authorities except the ICCPR, and because even the ICCPR is not self-executing, none of them create binding international legal obligations that are enforceable in federal court. Finally, the district court concluded that the plaintiffs failed to provide a proper predicate for ATS jurisdiction because none of the sources independently authorizes a private cause of action and the inference of such a cause of action is a matter best left to Congress.

The district court's approach misconstrued both the nature of customary international law and the scope of the inquiry required by *Sosa*. It mistakenly assumed that the question of whether a particular customary international law norm is sufficiently specific, universal, and obligatory to permit the recognition of a cause of action under the ATS is resolved essentially by looking at two things: whether each source of law referencing the norm is binding and whether each source expressly authorizes a cause of action to enforce the norm. But *Sosa*, as we have seen, requires a more fulsome and nuanced inquiry. The district court also inappropriately focused its consideration on whether the norm identified by the plaintiffs is set forth in conventions to which the United States is a party, and if so, whether these treaties are self-executing or executed by federal legislation. While adoption of a self-executing treaty or the execution of a treaty that is not self-executing may provide the best evidence of a particular country's custom or practice of recognizing a norm, the existence of a norm of customary international law is one determined, in part, by reference to the custom or practices of many States, and the broad acceptance of that norm by the international community.

1. Universality

The appellants must allege the violation of a norm of customary international law to which States universally subscribe. The prohibition on nonconsensual medical experimentation on human beings meets this standard because, among other reasons, it is specific, focused and accepted by nations around the world without significant exception.

The evolution of the prohibition into a norm of customary international law began with the war crimes trials at Nuremberg. The United States, the Soviet Union, the United Kingdom and France "acting in the interest of all the United Nations," established the International Military Tribunal ("IMT") through entry into the London Agreement of August 8, 1945. According to the Charter, the IMT had the "power to try and punish persons who, acting in the interests of the European Axis countries, whether as individuals or as members of organizations, committed," among other offenses, war crimes and crimes against humanity. U.S. military tribunals effectively operated as extensions of the IMT. In August 1947, Military Tribunal 1 promulgated the Nuremberg Code as part of the tribunal's final judgment against fifteen doctors who were found guilty of war crimes and crimes against humanity for conducting medical experiments without the subjects' consent. Among the nonconsensual experiments that the tribunal cited as a basis for their convictions were the testing of drugs for immunization against malaria, epidemic jaundice, typhus, smallpox and cholera. Seven of the convicted doctors were sentenced to death and the remaining eight were sentenced to varying terms of imprisonment. The judgment concluded that "[m]anifestly human experiments under such conditions are *contrary to the principles of the law of nations* as they result from usages established among civilized peoples, from the laws of humanity, and from the dictates of public conscience." (emphasis added) The Code created as part of the tribunal's judgment therefore emphasized as its first principle that "[t]he voluntary consent of the human subject is absolutely essential."

The American tribunal's conclusion that action that contravened the Code's first principle constituted a crime against humanity is a lucid indication of the international legal significance of the prohibition on nonconsensual medical experimentation. As Justices of the Supreme Court have recognized, "[t]he medical trials at Nuremberg in 1947 deeply impressed upon the world that experimentation with unknowing human subjects is morally and legally unacceptable." *United States v. Stanley*, 483 U.S. 669 (1987) (Brennan, J., concurring in part and dissenting in part). Moreover, both the legal principles articulated in the trials' authorizing documents and their application in judgments at Nuremberg occupy a position of special importance in the development of bedrock norms of international law. United States courts examining the Nuremberg judgments have recognized that "[t]he universal and fundamental rights of human beings identified by Nuremberg—rights against genocide, enslavement, and other inhumane acts . . . —are the direct ancestors of the universal and fundamental norms recognized as *jus cogens*," from which no derogation is permitted, irrespective of the consent or practice of a given State. *Siderman de Blake v. Republic of Arg.*, 965 F.2d 699, 715 (9th Cir. 1992) (cited in *Sampson v. F.R.G.*, 250 F.3d 1145, 1150 (7th Cir. 2001)). Since Nuremberg, states throughout the world have shown through international accords and domestic law-making that they consider the prohibition on nonconsensual medical experimentation identified at Nuremberg as a norm of customary international law.

In 1955, the draft International Covenants on Human Rights was revised to add a second sentence to its prohibition of torture and cruel, inhuman or degrading treatment or punishment. The addition provided that "[i]n particular, no one shall be subjected without his free consent to medical or scientific experimentation involving risk, where such is not required by his state of physical or mental health." This prohibition became part of Article 7 of the ICCPR, which entered into force in 1976, and is legally binding on the more than 160 States-Parties that have ratified the convention without reservation to the provision. As the court mentioned in *Sosa*, the Universal Declaration of Human Rights and the ICCPR themselves could not establish the relevant, applicable rule of international law in that case. Nonetheless, the ICCPR, when viewed as a reaffirmation of the norm as articulated in the Nuremberg Code, is potent authority for the universal acceptance of the prohibition on nonconsensual medical experimentation.

In 1964, the World Medical Association adopted the Declaration of Helsinki, which enunciated standards for obtaining informed consent from human subjects. It provides that "subjects must be volunteers and informed participants in the research project." Although the Declaration itself is non-binding, since the 1960s, it has spurred States to regulate human experimentation, often by incorporating its informed consent require- ment into domestic laws or regulations. Currently, the laws and regulations of at least eighty-four countries, including the United States, require the informed consent of human subjects in medical research. The incorporation of this norm into the laws of this country and this host of others is a powerful indication of the international acceptance of this norm as a binding legal obligation.

The history of the norm in United States law demonstrates that it has been firmly embedded for more than 45 years and its validity has never been seriously questioned by any court. Congress mandated patient-subject consent in drug research in 1962. Tellingly, the sources on which our government relied in outlawing non-consensual human med- ical experimentation were the Nuremberg Code and the Declaration of Helsinki, which suggests the government conceived of these sources' articulation of the norm as a bind- ing legal obligation.

Additional international law sources support the norm's status as customary interna- tional law. The European Union embraced the norm prohibiting nonconsensual medical experimentation through a 2001 Directive passed by the European Parliament and the Council of the European Union. Since 1997, thirty-four member States of the Council of Europe have also signed the Convention on Human Rights and Biomedicine, a binding convention and a source of customary international law. It provides that the informed consent of human subjects is required for their involvement in medical research. The United Nations Educational, Scientific and Cultural Organization (UNESCO) adopted the Universal Declaration on Bioethics and Human Rights, which requires "the prior, free, express and informed consent of the person concerned" for research-oriented treatments.

This history illustrates that from its origins with the trial of the Nazi doctors at Nuremburg through its evolution in international conventions, agreements, declarations, and domestic laws and regulations, the norm prohibiting nonconsensual medical exper- imentation on human subjects has become firmly embedded and has secured universal acceptance in the community of nations.

2. Specificity

Sosa requires that we recognize causes of action only to enforce those customary international law norms that are no "less definite [in] content . . . than the historical para- digms familiar when [the ATS] was enacted." The norm prohibiting nonconsensual med- ical experimentation on human subjects meets this requirement. In *United States v. Smith*, 18 U.S. (5 Wheat) 153, 159–61 (1820), Justice Story found that "whatever may be the diver- sity of definitions, . . . all writers concur, in holding, that robbery or forcible depredations upon the sea . . . is piracy." We have little trouble concluding that a norm forbidding nonconsensual human medical experimentation is every bit as concrete—indeed even more so—than the norm prohibiting piracy that Story describes. The Nuremberg Code, Article 7 of the ICCPR, the Declaration of Helsinki, the Convention on Human Rights and Biomedicine, the Universal Declaration on Bioethics and Human Rights, the 2001 Clinical Trial Directive, and the domestic laws of at least eighty-four States all uniformly and unmistakably prohibit medical experiments on human beings without their consent, thereby providing concrete content for the norm.

3. Mutual Concern

Customary international law proscribes only transgressions that are of "mutual" concern to States— "those involving States' actions performed . . . towards or with regard to the other." *Flores*, 414 F.3d at 249 (differentiating matters of "mutual" concern from those of "several" concern, in which "States are separately and independently interested"). An important, but not exclusive, component of this test is a showing that the conduct in question is "capable of impairing international peace and security." Appellants have made both of these showings.

As we have seen, States throughout the world have entered into two express and binding international agreements prohibiting nonconsensual medical experimentation: the ICCPR and the Convention on Human Rights and Biomedicine. The entry of over 160 States into these agreements and the European Union's passage of the 2001 Clinical Trial Directive demonstrates that States have not only acted independently to outlaw large-scale, nonconsensual drug testing on humans, but they have also acted in concert to do so. The administration of drug trials without informed consent on the scale alleged in the complaints poses a real threat to international peace and security. Over the last two decades, pharmaceutical companies in industrialized countries have looked to poorer, developing countries as sites for the medical research essential to the development of new drugs. Pharmaceutical companies recognize the potential benefits of drug trials to poor nations and have sought to promote access to medicines and health care in underserved populations through philanthropy and partnership with governments and NGOs. This trend offers the possibility of enormous health benefits for the world community. Life-saving drugs can potentially be developed more quickly and cheaply, and developing countries may be given access to cutting edge medicines and treatments to assist under-resourced and understaffed public health systems, which grapple with life-threatening diseases afflicting their populations.

The administration of drug trials without informed consent on the scale alleged in the complaints directly threatens these efforts because such conduct fosters distrust and resistance to international drug trials, cutting edge medical innovation, and critical international public health initiatives in which pharmaceutical companies play a key role. This case itself supplies an exceptionally good illustration of why this is so. The Associated Press reported that the Trovan trials in Kano apparently engendered such distrust in the local population that it was a factor contributing to an eleven month-long, local boycott of a polio vaccination campaign in 2004, which impeded international and national efforts to vaccinate the population against a polio outbreak with catastrophic results. According to the World Health Organization, polio originating in Nigeria triggered a major international outbreak of the disease between 2003 and 2006, causing it to spread across west, central, and the Horn of Africa and the Middle East, and to re-infect twenty previously polio-free countries.

The administration of drug trials without informed consent also poses threats to national security by impairing our relations with other countries. Seven of the world's twelve largest pharmaceutical manufacturers—a group that includes Pfizer—are

American companies. Consequently, American companies are likely to be sponsors of medical experiments on human subjects abroad. As this case illustrates, the failure to secure consent for human experimentation has the potential to generate substantial anti-American animus and hostility.

B. STATE ACTION

A private individual will be held liable under the ATS if he "acted in concert with" the state, i.e., "under color of law." *Kadic*, 70 F.3d at 245. In making this determination, courts look to the standards developed for finding state action in claims brought under 42 U.S.C. §1983. Under §1983, state action may be found when "there is such a close nexus between the State and the challenged action" that seemingly private behavior "may be fairly treated as that of the State itself." *Brentwood Acad. v. Tenn. Secondary Sch. Athletic Ass'n*, 531 U.S. 288, 295 (2001). That nexus may exist "where a private actor has operated as a willful participant in joint activity with the State or its agents," *Gorman-Bakos v. Cornell Coop. Extension of Schenectady County*, 252 F.3d 545, 551–52 (2d Cir. 2001), or "acts together with state officials or with significant state aid," *Kadic*, 70 F.3d at 245. Pfizer meets this test.

The Appellants have alleged that the Nigerian government was involved in all stages of the Kano test and participated in the conduct that violated international law. They allege that the Nigerian government provided a letter of request to the FDA to authorize the export of Trovan, arranged for Pfizer's accommodations in Kano, and facilitated the nonconsensual testing in Nigeria's IDH in Kano. Despite overcrowding due to concurrent epidemics, the Nigerian government extended the exclusive use of two hospital wards to Pfizer, providing Pfizer with control over scarce public resources and the use of the hospital's staff and facilities to conduct the Kano test. Finally, in addition to assisting with the Kano test, Nigerian officials are alleged to have conspired to cover up the violations by silencing Nigerian physicians critical of the test and by backdating an "approval letter" that the FDA and international protocol required to be provided prior to conducting the medical experiment. At the pleading stage, these contentions meet the state action test because they adequately allege that the violations occurred as the result of concerted action between Pfizer and the Nigerian government.

For the foregoing reasons, we REVERSE the judgments of the district court and REMAND for further proceedings.

After this case Pfizer filed a Petition for Certiorari in the Supreme Court of the United States, which was denied in 2010. In 2011, the parties settled the case for an undisclosed sum. After the parties settled, the Supreme Court considered the application of the ATS in the following case.

Kiobel v. Royal Dutch Petroleum Company
United States Supreme Court, 2013
133 S. Ct. 1659

Chief Justice ROBERTS delivered the opinion of the Court.

[In this case the petitioners, Kiobel et al., Nigerian citizens residing in the United States, alleged that Royal Dutch Shell et al., two companies based in Europe, had aided and abetted the Nigerian government in committing human rights and environmental atrocities in Nigeria in violation of the law of nations. The Supreme Court initially granted certiorari on the question whether a corporation can incur liability under the ATS. But after oral argument on this question, the Court directed the parties to brief a different question: "Whether and under what circumstances the ATS allows courts to recognize a cause of action for violations of the law of nations occurring within the territory of a sovereign other than the United States."]

The question here is not whether petitioners have stated a proper claim under the ATS, but whether a claim may reach conduct occurring in the territory of a foreign sovereign. Respondents contend that claims under the ATS do not, relying primarily on a canon of statutory interpretation known as the presumption against extraterritorial application. That canon provides that "when a statute gives no clear indication of an extraterritorial application, it has none." *Morrison v. National Australia Bank, Ltd.*, 561 U.S. [247] (2010) [§10(b) of the Securities Exchange Act cannot provide the basis for a cause of action to allow foreign plaintiffs to sue foreign and American defendants in connection with securities traded on foreign stock exchanges]. This presumption "serves to protect against unintended clashes between our laws and those of other nations which could result in international discord" [citations omitted]. We typically apply this presumption to discern whether an act of Congress regulating conduct applies abroad [citations omitted]. [W]e think the principles underlying [this] canon of interpretation similarly constrain courts considering causes of action that may be brought under the ATS. Indeed, the danger of unwarranted judicial interference in the conduct of foreign policy is magnified in the context of the ATS, because the question is not what Congress has done but instead what courts may do.

[The Court's opinion points out that *Sosa v. Alvarez-Machain*, 542 U.S. 692, 713 (2004), ruled that while extraterritoriality is a "merits question," the ATS is "strictly jurisdictional," and there is no indication in the text that Congress intended the ATS to have extraterritorial reach. "[T]he fact that the text reaches 'any civil action' . . . [does] not rebut the presumption against extraterritoriality."]

Nor does the historical background against which the ATS was enacted overcome the presumption against application to conduct in the territory of another sovereign. Two notorious episodes involving violations of the law of nations occurred in the United States shortly before passage of the ATS. Each concerned the rights of ambassadors and each involved conduct within the Union. In 1784, a French adventurer verbally and physically assaulted Francis Barbe Marbois—the Secretary of the French Legion—in Philadelphia. The assault led the French Minister Plenipotentiary to lodge a formal protest with the Continental Congress and threaten to leave the country unless an adequate remedy were provided. And in 1787, a New York constable entered the Dutch ambassador's house and arrested one of his domestic servants. At the request of Secretary of Foreign Affairs John Jay, the Mayor of New York City arrested the constable in turn, but cautioned that because "neither Congress nor our [State] Legislature have yet passed any act respecting a breach of the privileges of Ambassadors," the extent of any available relief would depend on the common law. The two cases in which the ATS was involved shortly after its passage also concerned conduct within the territory of the United States. *See Bolchos*, 3 F. Cas. 810 [(D.S.C. 1795) (No. 1607)] (wrongful seizure of slaves from a vessel while in port in the United States); *Moxon*, 17 F. Cas. 942 [(D. Pa. 1793) (No. 9895)] (wrongful seizure in United States territorial waters).

The third example of a violation of a law of nations familiar to the Congress that enacted the ATS was piracy. Piracy typically occurs on the high seas, beyond the jurisdiction of the United States or any other country. Applying U.S. law to pirates, however, does not typically impose the sovereign will of the United States onto conduct occurring within the territorial jurisdiction of another sovereign, and therefore carries less direct foreign policy consequences. Pirates were fair game wherever found, by any nation, because they generally did not operate within any jurisdiction.

We therefore conclude that the presumption against extraterritoriality applies to claims under the ATS, and that nothing in the Statute rebuts that presumption. On these facts, all of the relevant conduct took place outside the United States. And even where the claims touch and concern the territory of the United States, they must do so with sufficient force to displace the presumption against extraterritorial application. Corporations are often present in many countries, and it would reach too far to say that mere corporate presence suffices.

[A concurring opinion was filed by Justice Kennedy. Justice Alito, with whom Justice Thomas joined, filed a concurring opinion holding that "a putative ATS cause of action will fall within the scope of the presumption against extraterritoriality—and will therefore be barred—unless the domestic conduct is sufficient to violate an international law norm that satisfies *Sosa*'s requirements of definiteness and acceptance among civilized nations." A third concurring opinion was filed by Justice Breyer, joined by Justices Ginsburg, Sotomayor, and Kagan, holding that the presumption against extraterritorial application is not a helpful tool to resolve the jurisdictional issue. Rather, Justice Breyer would look to jurisdictional concepts under international law as expounded in the Restatement (Third) of Foreign Relations Law of the United States, §§402 and 403. Justice Breyer would limit the jurisdiction of the ATS to cases "where (1) the alleged tort occurs on American soil; (2) the defendant is an American national; or (3) the defendant's conduct substantially and adversely affects an important American national interest, and that includes a distinct interest in preventing the United States from becoming a safe harbor for a torturer or other common enemy of mankind."]

NOTES AND QUESTIONS

1. The *Sosa* and *Kiobel* cases significantly cut back the application of the Alien Tort Statute. Is this a salutary development? How do you evaluate the three different interpretations of the ATS in the *Kiobel* case? There is a fundamental difference between Justices Roberts, Scalia, Kennedy, Alito, and Thomas, on the one hand, who focus on extraterritoriality— a "merits issue"—and Justices Breyer, Ginsburg, Sotomayor, and Kagan, on the other hand, who focus on jurisdiction. Which interpretation is best?

2. Apply the ruling in *Kiobel* to the *Abdullahi v. Pfizer case*. Did Pfizer's lawyers settle the case too soon?

3. What is the future of the ATS after *Kiobel*? The question seems to be: What does it take to overcome the presumption articulated in the Court's opinion?

4. The *Kiobel* opinion leaves many questions surrounding the ATS unanswered, such as: (1) whether corporations may incur liability; (2) the existence and scope of a requirement to exhaust local remedies; (3) the viability of aiding and abetting claims; (4) the liability of individual defendants; (5) the application of *forum non conveniens*; (6) the applicable

substantive law; and (7) the appropriate deference to the U.S. executive branch's policy in a particular case. These questions will need to be worked out by lower courts.

5. For six essays by leading commentators on the future of the ATS after *Kiobel*, see *Agora: Reflections on* Kiobel, 107 Am. J. Int'l L. 829–863 (2013). For a European perspective on *Kiobel* and its relationship to human rights concerns of transnational enterprises, see Nerina Boschiero, *Corporate Responsibility in Transnational Human Rights Cases: The U.S. Supreme Court Decision in* Kiobel v. Royal Dutch Petroleum, XLIX (2) Revista di Diritto Internazionale Privato e Processuale 249 (2013).

Table of Cases

Principal cases are indicated by italics.

Abdullahi v. Pfizer, Inc., 756, 765
A. Bourjois & Co. v. Katzel, 569, 570, 572
Ackermann v. Levine, 675, 677
Adams v. Lindsell, 191
ADT Sec. Servs., Inc. v. Apex Alarm, LLC, 628
Agawam Co. v. Jordan, 334
Aguinda v. Texaco, Inc., 755
Ahlstrom v. Commission, 456
Ahmadou Sadio Diallo, Case of (Republic of Guinea v. Democratic Republic of Congo (DRC)), 360, 361
Air Cargo Shipping Servs. Antitrust Litig., In re, 698
A.I. Trade Fin., Inc. v. Petra Bank, 688
Ajax Tool Works, Inc. v. Can-Eng Mfg. Ltd., 33
Alaska Textile Co. v. Chase Manhattan Bank, N.A., 247
Alberto-Culver Co. v. Scherk, 607
Allen v. Lloyd's of London, 628, 629
Allendale Mut. Ins. Co. v. Bull Data Sys., Inc., 685
Allied Bank Int'l v. Banco Credito Agricola, 663, 664
Allstate Life Ins. Co. v. Linter Grp. Ltd., 687, 688, 689
Alvarez-Machain; United States v., 756
Ambraco, Inc. v. Bossclip B.V., 110
Amco Ukrservice & Prompriladamco v. American Meter Co., 177, 634, 638, 639
American Bell International, Inc. v. Islamic Republic of Iran, 265, *269,* 280
American Home Assurance Co. v. Panalpina Inc., 109
American National Fire Insurance Co. v. Mirasco, Inc., 121
American Safety Equip. Corp. v. J.P. Maguire & Co., 603, 604, 605, 606
Amicizia Societa Navegazione v. Chilean Nitrate & Iodine Sales Corp., 617
Amoco Egypt Oil Co. v. Leonis Navigation Co., 656
Anglo-Iranian Oil Co. Case (United Kingdom v. Iran), 358
Anvil Knitwear v. Crowley American Transport, Inc., 111
ARA Libertad (Arg. v. Ghana), 422
Arbitration Between Trans Chemical Ltd. & China National Machinery Import & Export Corp., In re, 640, 658

Archer Daniels Midland Co. & ADM Rice v. JP Morgan Chase Bank, 280
Argentina v. Ghana, 422
Argentine Republic v. Amerada Hess Shipping Corp., 659
Asahi Metal Industry Co. v. Superior Court, 646, 652, 655, 657
Asante Techs. Inc. v. PMC-Sierra, Inc., 33
Asian Agric. Prods. Ltd. v. Republic of Sri Lanka, 363-364
Asoma Corp. v. SK Shipping Co., 613
Atlantic Marine Constr. Co. v. United States Dist. Court for the W. Dist. of Tex., 672
Attadis USA, Inc. v. Sea Star Line, 101
AZKO Chemie BV v. Commission, 441
Azteca Mill Co. v. United States, 158

Banco Ambrosiano, S.P.A. v. Artoc Bank & Trust Ltd., 644
Banco Espanol de Credito v. State St. Bank & Trust Co., 250
Banco Nacional de Cuba v. Sabbatino, 591, 666, 667, 711
Banco Nacional de Mexico S.A. v. Societe Generale, 265
Bancroft & Masters, Inc. v. Augusta Nat'l Inc., 654, 655
Banden Industrie Michelin v. Commission, 440
Bank of Montreal v. Federal Nat'l Bank & Trust Co., 249
Bankston v. Toyota Motor Co., 675, 677
Bano v. Union Carbide Corp., 753
Barcelona Traction, Light & Power Co., Case Concerning (The Barcelona Traction Case) (Belgium v. Spain), 359, 362
Bauman v. DaimlerChrysler Corp., 682
Bausch & Lomb, Inc. v. United States, 154
Baxter Healthcare Corp. of Puerto Rico v. United States, 150
BDL Int'l v. Sodetal USA, Inc., 693

Beanal v. Freeport-McMoran, Inc., 755
Beijing Metals & Minerals Imp./Exp. Corp. v.
    American Bus. Ctr., Inc., 185
Belgium v. Spain, 359-360
Berhardt v. Polygraphic Co. of Am., 614
Bestfoods v. United States (260 F.3d 1320), 160
Bestfoods v. United States (110 F. Supp. 2d 965), 161
Bestfoods; United States v., 734
Better Home Plastics Corp. v. United States, 152
Beyene v. Irving Trust Co., 248, 249, 250
BG Grp. PLC v. Republic of Arg., 366
Biddell Brothers v. E. Clemens Horst Co., 78, 81, 82
Bisso v. Inland Waterways Corp., 625, 626
Blue Ridge Invs., LLC v. Republic of Arg., 387, 600
Board of Governors, FRS v. Dimension Fin. Corp.,
    573
Bobbs-Merrill Co. v. Straus, 579, 580
Bodner v. Banque Paribas, 716
Boeing/McDonnell Douglas v. Commission, 456
Bolchos v. Darrel, 764
Boyd Motors, Inc. v. Employers Ins. of Wausau, 124
*BP Oil International, Ltd. v. Empresa Estatal Petroleos de
    Ecuador*, 208, *210*, 212
Braka v. Bancomber, 664
Brentwood Acad. v. Tennessee Secondary Sch.
    Athletic Ass'n, 763
Brockmeyer v. May, 675, 676
Burger-Fischer v. DeGussa AG & DeGussa Corp., 716
Burger King Corp. v. Rudzewicz, 648, 652, 655

Caemint Food, Inc. v. Lloyd Brasiliero Companhia de
    Navegacao, 116
Carapanayoti & Co. Ltd. v. E.T. Green Ltd., 216
Carbon Black Exp., Inc. v. The Monrosa, 623, 624
Carl Zeiss, Inc. v. United States, 150, 152
Carnival Cruise Lines, Inc. v. Shute, 627, 628, 631
Carolina Power & Light Co. v. Uranex, 607
Cascade Yarns, Inc. v. Knitting Fever, Inc., 677
*Cassis de Dijon Case (Rewe-Zentral AG v.
    Bundesmonopolverwaltung für Branntwein)*, *428*, 430
Cedar Petrochemicals, Inc. v. Dongbu Hannong
    Chem. Co., 185
Centros Ltd. v. Erhverus-og Selskabsstyrelsen, *431*, 432
Century Importers, Inc. v. United States, 155
Certain German Interests in Polish Upper Silesia
    (Chozów Factory Case), Case Concerning, 361
Chateau des Charmes Wines Ltd. v. Sabate USA Inc.,
    174, 198-199
Chemtura Corp. v. Government of Can., 396
Cheung v. United States, 31
China Trade & Dev. Corp. v. M.V. Choong Yong, 685,
    691, 692
Chorzów Factory cases, 361
Christoffs Estate, In re, 706, 707, 708
Citizens First Bank v. International Express, Inc., 634
Citrexsa S.A. v. Landsman, 674
Citrus Mktg. Bd. of Israel v. J. Lauritzen A/S, 114, 120
Clarkson Co. v. Shaheen, 669

Clemco Indus. v. Commercial Union Ins. Co., 634
Clerici, In re, 699
CMS Gas Transmission Co. v. Republic of Arg., 385,
    386
CNA Ins. Co. v. Hyundai Merch. Marine Co., Ltd.,
    109
Coalition to Preserve the Integrity of Am.
    Trademarks v. United States, 573
Colgan Air., Inc. v. Raytheon Aircraft Co., 630
Commercial Molasses Corp. v. New York Tank Barge
    Corp., 91
Commission of the European Cmtys. v. Tetra Laval
    BV, 455
*Comptoir d'Achat et de Vente Du Boerenbond Belge S/A v.
    Luis de Ridder Limitada (The Julia)*, *83*, 87, 88, 89
Conax Florida Corp. v. Astrium Ltd., *673*, 676
Courage Ltd. v. Crehan, 301
CSS Antenna, Inc. v. Amphenol-Tuchel Elecs.,
    GmbH, 194, 198
Cunard S.S. Co. v. Salen Reefer Servs. AB, 689
Cupp v. Alberto-Culver USA, Inc., 677
CVD Equip. Corp. v. Taiwan Indus. Glass Corp., 241,
    251

Daimler AG v. Bauman, 682
Dainippon Screen Mfg. Co., Ltd. v. CFMT, Inc., 683
Denbicare U.S.A., Inc. v. Toys "R" Us, Inc., 582
Dependable Highway Express v. Navigators Ins. Co.,
    693
Derby & Co. v. Weldon, 645
DeYoung v. Beddome, *668*, 672
*Dingxi Longhai Dairy, Ltd. v. Becwood Technology Group,
    LLC*, *220*
Doe v. *See name of opposing party*
Duferco Int'l Steel Trading v. T. Klaveness Shipping
    A/S, 614, 615, 616
Dynamics Corp. of Am. v. Citizens & S. Nat'l Bank,
    269

Eastman Kodak Co. v. Kavlin, 716
E. Clemens Horst Co. v. Biddell Bros., *81*
Edlow Int'l v. Nuklearna Elektrarna Krsko (NEK),
    659, 660
E & H Partners v. Broadway Nat'l Bank, 247
EIMSHIP USA, Inc. v. Atlantic Fish Mkt., 89
E&J Gallo Winery v. Andina Licores S.A., 685
*Elettronica Sicula S.p.A., Case Concerning (The ELSI
    Case) (United States v. Italy)*, *360*, 361
Elgie & Co. v. S.S. "S.A. Nederburg," 61
ELSI Case (United States v. Italy), *360*, 361
English, Scottish & Australian Bank, Ltd. v. Bank of
    S. Africa, 243
Equitable Trust Co. of N.Y. v. Dawson Partners, Ltd.,
    243
Erie R.R. Co. v. Tompkins, 167, 706
Export-Imp. Bank of Republic of China v. Grenada,
    600

Farrell Lines, Inc. v. Jones, 117
Feldman v. Mexico, 389, 395, 567
Fesco, Inc. v. Shone, 113
Filanto, S.P.A. v. Chilewich International Corp., 195, 198
Filártiga v. Peña-Irala, 755, 756, 757
Finanz AG Zurich v. Banco Economico S.A., 686
First Nationwide Sav. v. Perry, 722
Flores v. Southern Peru Copper Corp., 757, 758, 759, 762
FOGADE v. ENB Revocable Trust, 661, *665,* 667
Ford v. Unity Hosp., 680
Forestal Guarani S.A. v. Daros International, Inc., 187
Fossum v. Timber Structures, Inc., 207
Foster v. Neilson, 31

Gaon (Albert D.) & Co. v. Societé Interprofessionelle des Oleaginuex Fluides Alimentaires, 216
Gap, Inc.; Doe v., 716
Garcia v. Chase Manhattan Bank, N.A., 664
Gartner v. Snyder, 681
GATX Leasing Corp. v. DBM Drilling Corp., 263
Gau Shan Co. v. Bankers Trust Co., 685
GDG Acquisitions, LLC v. Government of Belize, 672, 673
Ge v. Peng, 716
General Elec. v. Commission, 457
Gita Sports Ltd. v. SG Sensortechnik GmbH & Co. KG, 622, 626, 630, 631
Glencore Grain Rotterdam B.V. v. Shivnath Rai Harnarain Co., 608, 646, *653*
GMS Grp., LLC v. Benderson, 614
Goodyear Dunlop Tires Operations, S.A. v. Brown, 646, *651,* 656, 682, 707
Gorman-Bakos v. Cornell Coop. Extension of Schenectady Cnty., 763
Goss International Corp. v. Man Roland Druckmachinen AG, 683
GPL Treatment, Ltd. v. Louisiana-Pacific Corp., 185, *186*
Gramercy Equities v. Dumont, 679
Great N. R. Co. v. O'Connor, 100, 101
Griffith v. United Air Lines, Inc., 635
Gruppo Essenziero Italiano, S.p.A. v. Aromi D'Italia, Inc., 182, 306
Gua Shan Co. v. Bankers Trust Co., 693
Gulf Oil Corp. v. Gilbert, 624, 670

Hall St. Assocs. LLC v. Mattel, Inc., 597, 615, 616, 618
Hanil Bank v. PT. Bank Negara Indonesia, 242, *246,* 249, 250
Hanson v. Denckla, 648, 707
Harris Corp. v. National Iranian Radio & Television, 269, *275,* 280
Hartford Fire Ins. Co. v. California, 456
Hawaii v. Ho, 163
Haynsworth v. The Corp., 708
Helen Kaminski, Pty. Ltd. v. Marketing Australian Prods., Inc., 180

Helicopteros Nacionales de Colombia, S.A. v. Hall, 651, 652, 653, 654
Hilton v. Guyot, 669, 672, 687, 703, 706
Hinkle v. Delavan Indus. Inc., 734
Hoffman-La Roche & Co. v. Commission, 441
Humble v. Toyota Motor Co, 649

Ibeto Petrochemical Industries Ltd. v. M/T Beffen, 690, 691, 692
ICI v. Commission, 456
Imperial Chem. Indus. Ltd. v. Commission of the European Cmtys., 300
Impuls I.D. Internacional, S.L. v. Psion-Teklogix Inc., 174
Indussa Corp. v. S.S. Ranborg, 109-110
In re. *See name of party*
Instituto Chemioterapico Italiano S.p.A. v. Commission, 440
Intel Corp. v. Advanced Micro Devices, Inc., 700, 701, 702
Intercontainer Interfrigo SC (ICF) v. Balkenende Oosthuizen BV, 621
International Ass'n of Machinists v. OPEC, 663
International Commodities Exp. Corp. v. American Home Assurance Co., 126
International Shoe Co. v. Washington, 590, 644, 646, 648, 650, 651, 652, 654, 707
Ireland v. United Kingdom, 718
I/S Stavborg v. National Metal Converters, Inc., 614
I.T.A.D. Assocs., Inc. v. Podar Bros., 607
Italy; United States v., 360
Itel Containers v. Atlanttrafik Express Service Ltd., 678, 682
Iwanowa v. Ford Motor Co., 716

Jama v. INS, 716
Jamaica Nutrition Holdings, Ltd. v. United Shipping Co., 117
Jazz Photo Corp. v. International Trade Comm'n, 584
J. Gerber & Co. v. S.S. Sabine Howaldt, 118
J.H. Rayner & Co., Ltd. v. Hambro's Bank, Ltd., 242, 250, 251
J. McIntyre Mach. Ltd. v. Nicastro, 656
John Boutari & Son, Wines & Spirits, S.A. v. Attiki Imps. & Distribs. Inc., 631
Johnson v. Unisys, Ltd., 717
John Wiley & Sons v. Kirtsaeng, 584
The Julia, 83, 87, 88, 89
JVC Co. of America v. United States, 150
J. Zeevi & Sons, Ltd. v. Grindlays Bank, 168

Kadic v. Karadzic, 716, 755, 763
Kaepa, Inc. v. Achilles Corp., 685
Kawasaki Kisen Kaisha Ltd. v. Regal-Beloit Corp. (The "K" Line Case), 96, 101, *102,* 109
Kay; United States v., 401, 403, 404, *405*

Kexuan Yao v. Crisnic Fund, 677
Kiobel v. Royal Dutch Petroleum Co., 763, 765, 766
Kirno Hill Corp. v. Holt, 681
Kirtsaeng v. John Wiley & Sons, Inc., 577, *580, 584*
Klaxon Co. v. Stentor Elec. Mfg. Co., 167, 175, 630, 635, 671
The "K" Line Case, 96, 101, *102,* 109
K Mart Corp. v. Cartier, Inc., 125, 570, *571,* 576, 577
Kozeny; United States v., 403, *419*
Kristinus v. H. Stern Com. e. Ind. S.A., 165, 167, 168, 175
Kulukundis Shipping Co. v. Amtorg Trading Corp., 606

Lacey v. Cessna Aircraft Co., 635
Laker Airways, Ltd. v. Sabena Belgian World Airlines, 685
Lanco International, Inc. v. Argentine Republic, 368, 374
Lantheus Med. Imaging, Inc. v. Zurich Am. Ins. Co., 698
Leonis. *See* Amoco Egypt Oil Co. v. Leonis Navigation Co.
Lever Bros. Co. v. United States, 571, *574,* 576, 577
LG&E Energy Corp. v. Argentine Republic, 380, 385
Liebo; United States v., 403
Luigi Bormioli Corp. v. United States, 158
Lykes Bros. S.S. Co.; United States v., 116

Mackley v. Gruner & Jahr A.G. & Co., 628
Madanes v. Madanes, 697
Mannesman Demag Corp. v. M/V Concert Express, 119
Marino Indus. Corp. v. Chase Manhattan Bank, N.A., 247, 249
Martinez v. Bloomberg, 632
Marvin Feldman v. Mexico, 389, 395, 567
Maurice O'Meara Co. v. National Park Bank of New York, 233, *236,* 241, 254
McDonnell Douglas Corp. v. Islamic Republic of Iran, 631
McGee v. International Life Ins. Co., 648, 707
Medical Marketing International, Inc. v. Internazionale Medico Scientifica S.r.l., 208
Medtronic, Inc. v. Mirowski Family Ventures, LLC, 334
Melville v. American Home Assurance Co., 635
Merck & Co. v. United States, 148
Merrill Lynch, Pierce, Fenner & Smith, Inc. v. Bobker, 614
Methanex Corp. v. United States, 396
Mexico v. Karpa, 395
Mexico v. Metalclad, 395
Microsoft Corp. v. Commission of the European Communities, 442, *445,* 450
Microsoft Corp.; United States v., 450
Mid-America Tire, Inc. v. PTZ Trading Ltd., 258, 265
Millenium Seacarriers, Inc., In re, 692

Miller v. Miller, 166
Milliken v. Meyer, 646, 650, 654
Mitsubishi Motors Corp. v. Soler Chrysler-Plymouth, Inc., 594, *602,* 607
Morgan v. Stokely-Van Camp, Inc., 185
The Mormacoak, 96
Morrison v. National Austl. Bank, Ltd., 764
Moses H. Cone Mem'l Hosp. v. Mercury Constr. Corp., 604
Moxon v. The Fanny, 764
M/S Bremen v. Zapata Off-Shore Co., 107, 605, *622, 627,* 628, 630, 631
Mutual Exp. Corp. v. Westpac Banking Corp., 248, 249

National Juice Prods. Ass'n v. United States, 161
New Braunfels Nat'l Bank v. Odiorne, 250
New Jersey Steam Navigation Co. v. Merchants' Bank of Boston, 91
NLRB v. Thalbo Corp., 418
NML Capital, Ltd. v. Republic of Arg., 522
Norcal/Crosetti Foods, Inc. v. United States, 163
Norfolk Southern Railway Co. v. Kirby, 96, *97,* 101, 102, 103, 104, 105, 107
North Am. Foreign Trading Corp. v. Mitsui Sumitomo Ins. USA, Inc., 127
North American Processing Co. v. United States, 149
Nuovo Pignone, SpA v. Storman Asia M/V, 675

Old Colony Trust Co. v. Lawyer's Title & Trust Co., 255
OLG Düsseldorf, 180
OLG Koblenz, 180
Oliver v. Dubai Bank Kenya Ltd., 240
Omega SA v. Costco Wholesale Corp., 584
Optopics Laboratories Corp. v. Savannah Bank of Nigeria, Ltd., 661, 668
Orange Theatre Corp. v. Rayherstz Amusement Corp., 707

Paper Express Ltd. v. Pfankuch Maschinen, GmbH, 631
The Paquete Habana, 31
Percheman; United States v., 31
Perkins v. Benguet Consol. Mining Co., 652, 653, 654, 655
Philip Morris Brands Sàrl v. Oriental Republic of Uruguay, 365
Piper Aircraft Co. v. Reyno, 670, 747
Polytek Engineering Co., Ltd. v. Jacobson Cos., 608
Premises Located at 840 140th Ave. NE, Bellevue, Wash., In re, 694
Prime Start Ltd. v. Maher Forest Products Ltd., 173, 175, 185, 207
Princesse D'Isenbourg et Cie. Ltd. v. Kinder Caviar, Inc., 172

Progressive Cas. Ins. Co. v. C.A. Reaseguradora Nacional De Venezuela, 691

Pronova BioPharma Norge AS v. Teva Pharms. USA, Inc., 698

Pronuptia de Paris GmbH v. Pronuptia de Paris, 343, 346, 347

Pushpanathan v. Canada, 717

Quaak v. Klynveld Peat Marwick Goerdeler Bedrijfsrevisoren, 685

Quality King Distributors, Inc. v. L'anza Research International, Inc., 577, 581, 582

Republic of Arg. v. NML Capital Ltd., 523

Republic of Arg. & Banco Cent. de la Republica Arg. v. Weltover, 644

Republic (of Ghana) v. High Court Accra, ex parte Attorney Gen., 522

Republic of Guinea v. Democratic Republic of Congo (DRC), 360, 361

Rewe-Zentral AG v. Bundesmonopolverwaltung für Branntwein (Cassis de Dijon Case), 428, 430

Robert C. Herd & Co. v. Krawill Mach. Corp., 99

Rollerblade, Inc. v. United States, 153

Rooney; United States v., 417

Royal & Sun Alliance, PLC v. Service Transfer, Inc., 109

Sabah Shipyard Sdn. Bhd. v. M/V Harbel Tapper, 96, 120

Sahu v. Union Carbide Corp., 753

St. Louis, I.M. & S.R. Co. v. Starbird, 105

St. Paul Guardian Ins. Co. v. Neuromed Med. Sys. & Support, GmbH, 33

Salini Costruttori S.p.A. v. Kingdom of Morocco, 365

Sampo Japan Ins. v. Union Pac., 101

Sampson v. F.R.G., 760

Scherk v. Alberto-Culver Co., 594, 603, 607

Scotland Mem'l Hosp., Inc. v. Integrated Informatics, Inc., 627

SEC v. Stanford Int'l Bank, Ltd., 698

Service Emps. Int'l Union v. County of L.A., 721

Shaffer v. Heitner, 644

Siderman de Blake v. Republic of Arg., 760

Sinochem Int'l Co. v. Malaysia Int'l Shipping Corp., 672

Smith; United States v., 761

Societé Nationale Industrielle Aerospatiale v. United States District Court, 697, 702

Society of Lloyd's v. Leighs, 710

Society of Lloyd's v. Siemon-Netto, 704, *708*

Society of Lloyd's v. Turner, 710

Solae, LLC v. Hershey Can., Inc., 199

Sompo Japan Ins. v. Union Pac. R. Co., 103

Somportex Ltd. v. Philadelphia Chewing Gum Corp., 704

Sosa v. Alvarez-Machain, 755, 758, 759, 761, 764, 765

Southern Int'l Sales Co. v. Potter & Brumfield Div. of AMF Inc., 306

Stanley; United States v., 760

Steel Coils, Inc. v. Captain Nicholas I M/V, 90

Steel Coils, Inc. v. M/V Lake Marion, 111, 113, *114,* 121

Stewart Org., Inc. v. Ricoh Corp., 627, 628, 631

Stichting Ter behartiging Van de Belangen Van Oudaandeelhouders in Het Kapitaal Van Saybolt International B.V. v. Schreiber, 403, 405, *413,* 422

Stolt-Nielsen SA v. AnimalFeeds International Corp. (559 U.S. 662), 617, 619

Stolt-Nielsen SA v. AnimalFeeds International Corp. (548 F.3d 85), 612, 616

Sturiano v. Brooks, 634

Success Universal Ltd. v. CWJ Int'l Trading Co., 241

Syncrude Can. Ltd. v. Highland Consulting Grp., Inc., 712

Sztejn v. J. Henry Schroder Banking Co., 241, 254, 255, 258, 265, 278

Tel-Oren v. Libyan Arab Republic, 755

Tetra Laval BV v. Commission of the European Communities, 452

Texport Oil Co. v. United States, 148

TFT-LCD (Flat Panel) Antitrust Litig., In re, 698

Tiffany (NJ) LLC v. Qi Andrew, 698

Torrington Co. v. United States, 158, 159

Tosco Corp. v. Federal Deposit Ins. Corp., 250

Trans Chemical Ltd. & China National Machinery Import & Export Corp., Arbitration Between, 640, *658*

Triple A Int'l, Inc. v. Democratic Republic of the Congo, 600

Tsakiroglu & Co. v. Noblee Thorl G.m.b.H., 215

Tulip Computers International B.V. v. Dell Computer Corp., 694, *695,* 702

Turner. *See* Society of Lloyd's v. Turner

UNCITRAL CLOUT Case 122, 181-182

UNCITRAL CLOUT Case 131, 181

UNCITRAL CLOUT Case 137, 186

Ungaro-Benages v. Dresdner Bank AG, 672-673

Unilex, D. 1993-3.4, 218-219

Unilex, D. 1995-1, 213

Union Carbide Corp. Gas Plant Disaster at Bhopal, India in December 1984, In re, 745, 752

United Brands Co. v. Commission of the European Communities, 442

United Kingdom v. Iran, 358-359

United Parcel Serv. v. Canada, 396

United States v. *See name of opposing party*

United Technologies International Pratt & Whitney Commercial Engine Business v. Malev Hungarian Airlines, 202, 205

Unocal Corp.; Doe v., 716

Urquhart Lindsay & Co., Ltd. v. Eastern Bank, Ltd., 233

Valois of Am., Inc. v. Risdon Corp., 697

Vernon v. State of Cal., 721

Vimar Seguros y Reaseguros, S.A. v. M/V Sky Reefer, 103, 109, 110, 594, 631

Viva Vino Imp. Corp. v. Farnese Vini S.r.l., 180

Voest-Alpine Trading USA Corp. v. Bank of China, 249, 250

Volt Info. Scis., Inc. v. Board of Trs. of Leland Stanford Junior Univ., 640

VWP of Am. v. United States, 157

Wal-Mart Stores, Inc.; Doe I v., 719

Ware v. Hylton, 31

Waterman S.S. v. United States Smelting Ref. & Mining Co., 119

Wena Hotels, Ltd. v. Arab Republic of Egypt, 374, 379

Westerbeke Corp. v. Daihatsu Motor Co., 614, 616, 617

Whitney v. Robertson, 31

Wilburn Boat Co. v. Fireman's Fund Ins. Co., 127

Wilko v. Swan, 603, 604, 615

Wood Pulp Case. *See* Ahlstrom v. Commission

World Wide Minerals, Ltd. v. Republic of Kazakhstan, 711

World-Wide Volkswagen Corp. v. Woodson, 648, 649, 650, 652

Zuniga v. United States, 158, 159, 160

Index

Abstention, doctrine of, 693-694
Accidents, industrial
   liability for, 743-754
Acquisitions. *See* Mergers and acquisitions (M&A)
Act of state doctrine, 661-668
   overview, 590-591
   Second Hickenlooper Amendment, 666-667
Adjudicative jurisdiction, defined, 644
Admiralty Jurisdiction Clause, 631
African Charter on Human and Peoples' Rights, 718
Age Discrimination in Employment Act
   exterritorial application of U.S. law, 723
Agency and distributorships, 285-307
   anticompetition issues, 287
   antitrust issues, 287
   CISG, 306-307
   competition law issues, 287
   control, 286-287
   European Union, 300-302
   Foreign Corrupt Practices Act, 287
   German Commercial Code, 296-299
   intellectual property issues, 289
   local and regional legal requirements, 296-307
   overview, 285
   sample distribution agreement, 291-296
   tax issues, 307
   termination issues, 287-288
   UCC, 306-307
Agreement on Trade Related Aspects of Intellectual Property Rights. *See* TRIPs
Agreement on Trade-Related Investment Measures. *See* TRIMs (Agreement on Trade-Related Investment Measures)
Agricultural Foreign Investment Disclosure Act, 426
Air transport, 91
Alien Tort Claims Act. *See* Alien Tort Statute
Alien Tort Statute, 682, 754-766
   Bhopal disaster, 753
   extraterritorial application of, 763-765
   forum non conveniens, 755, 765
   genocide, 755
   human rights violations, 755

   hurdles for plaintiffs to overcome, 754-755
   medical experimentation on non-consenting humans, 756-763
   overview, 716
   slave trading, 755
   state action, 755, 763
   torture, state use of, 755
   violation of international law, 755
   war crimes, 755
Alternative dispute resolution, 591-593
American Arbitration Association, 601
American Convention on Human Rights, 718
American Declaration of the Rights and Duties of Man, 718
Americans with Disabilities Act
   exterritorial application of U.S. law, 723
Amsterdam, Treaty of, 41
Antiboycott laws, 132-133
   Commerce Department, 132-133
   Treasury Department, 133
Antitrust issues
   agency and distributorships, 287
   Sherman Act
      anticompetition law, as, 300
      arbitration, 602-603
Appeals in arbitration, 607-619
Approach of book, 1-3
Arbitration, 593-619
   ad hoc arbitration, 598-599
   advantages of, 592
   American Arbitration Association, 601
   appeals, 607-619
   applicable law, 599
   Automobile Dealers' Day in Court Act, 603
   bills of lading, foreign arbitration clause in, 110
   choice of law clause, 599
   choosing arbitration, 593-601
   Convention on the Recognition and Enforcement of Foreign Arbitral Awards, 593-597, 602, 608-612
   drafting the arbitration clause, 597-598
   enforcing agreement to arbitrate, 601-607

Arbitration (*continued*)
    enforcing awards, 607-619
    Federal Arbitration Act, 593-619
    foreign arbitration clauses, in bills of lading, 110
    forum and procedure, 598-599
    forum selection clauses, in bills of lading, 109-110
    Inter-American Convention on International
        Commercial Arbitration, 594
    international commercial arbitration and U.S.
        courts, 594-597
    in International Center for the Settlement of
        Investment Disputes, 592
    in International Chamber of Commerce, 593, 598,
        601
    judicial review, 607-619
    law merchant, 601
    lex mercatoria, 601
    in London Court of Arbitration, 593, 598
    model clauses, 598
    negotiating and structuring international
        commercial transactions, 597-600
    New York Convention, 593-600, 602, 608-612, 620
    overview, 592
    Panama Convention Act, 594
    place of arbitration, 599
    procedure, 598-599
    Puerto Rico Dealers' Contracts Act, 603
    scope of arbitration, 599
    Securities Exchange Act, 603
    Sherman Act, 602-603
    in Stockholm Chamber of Commerce, 593
    UNCITRAL rules, 599, 601
    vacating awards, grounds for, 597, 619
        "manifest disregard of the law," 612-617, 618,
        619
Argentina
    sovereign debt collection, 521-522
ASEAN plus six, 38
Asia Pacific Economic Cooperation, 42-43
Association of Southeast Asian Nations (ASEAN), 38,
    42, 43
Attorneys in international business, 4-9
    challenges for, 7-8
    in-house lawyers, reporting structure for, 5
    issues faced by, 4
    multinational enterprises, role of counsel for, 4-6
Automobile Dealers' Day in Court Act
    arbitration, 603
    business format franchising, 335

Basel Convention on the Control of Transboundary
    Movements of Hazardous Wastes and Their
    Disposal, 740-741
Berne Convention for the Protection of Literary and
    Artistic Works, 312-313, 554
    copyright, 319-320
    protecting intellectual property rights, 554

Bhopal disaster, 744-754
    Federal Rules of Civil Procedure and, 748
    impact in United States, 754
Bhopal Gas Leak Disaster (Processing of Claims) Act
    of 1985, 749
Bills of exchange, 52-53
    check, 52
    note, 52
    sight bill, 52
    time bill, 52
    trade acceptance, 52-53
Bills of lading, 89-121
    Carriage of Goods by Sea Act, 97, 101, 102-109,
        111-113, 115-116
    choice of law, 109
    electronic, 63
    Federal Bill of Lading Act, 61, 63
    foreign arbitration clauses in, 110
    form, 62
    forum selection clauses in, 109-110
    functions of, 60-61
    hijacking disclaimer, 111-113
    negotiable vs. nonnegotiable, 65
    overview, 60-61
    Pomerene Act, 61
Biopiracy, 564-566
    Convention for Biological Diversity, 565-566
    WIPO role, 566
Blocked Persons List, 131
Bonded facilities, 148
Brands and commercial piracy, 527-528
Brazil and foreign direct investment, 492-521
    approach to FDI, 493-494
    background economic history, 494-496
    branch offices, 512
    business climate, 497-509
    business organizations, 509-513
    consortia, 513
    joint ventures, 512-513
    legal regime, 509-523
        applicability to FDI, 513-520
    limited liability companies, 510-511
    overview, 492-493
    policy objectives, 494
    Profits Remittance Law, 496-497, 514-520
    stock corporations, 511-512
    tax laws, 520-521
Bretton Woods Conference, 13
Bribery Convention (OECD), 403-404, 411-412
Brussels Convention on Jurisdiction and the
    Enforcement of Judgments in Civil and
    Commercial Matters
    enforcement and recognition of foreign
        judgments, 712
    jurisdictional issues, 644
Brussels Regime, 620, 621
Business Council for Sustainable Development,
    730-731

Business format franchising, 334-347
    overview, 334-336
    sample franchise agreement, 337-343

Canada
    Access to Medicines Act, 563
    medicines, compulsory licenses for production of,
        563
Carmack Amendment, 92, 96, 101, 102-109
    COGSA vs., 108-109
Carriage of goods. *See* Transport of goods
Carriage of Goods by Sea Act (COGSA), 94, 97, 101,
        102-110, 111-113, 115-121
    Carmack vs., 108-109
    exceptions to carrier liability, 120
Categorization of international business transactions, 1
CCL. *See* Commerce Control List
CFIUS. *See* Committee on Foreign Investment in the
        United States (CFIUS)
Chamber of Commerce. *See* International Chamber
        of Commerce
China
    advanced technology, 537-538
    commercial piracy in, 537-553
    counterfeiting in, 537-553
        costs of enforcement, 540
        court-ordered damages, 539
        enforcement, 539, 540
        payments to officials, 540
        size and scope of, explanations for, 537-538
    foreign direct investment in, 457-492, 537-538
        approval process, 466-468
        capital investment, 468
        economic system, 457-463
        Equity Joint Venture Law, 471-474
        establishment of joint venture, 466-492
        Implementing Regulations for Equity Joint
            Venture Law, 472-474
        joint ventures, 464, 466-492
        legal regime, 464-465
        management structure, 468
        overview, 457
        sample joint venture contract, 474-490
        wholly foreign-owned enterprises, 465
    free trade agreements, 38, 43
    Industrial Enterprises Law, 659
    rise of, 18-19
    trademark counterfeiting in, 537-553
        Administration of Industry and Commerce, 539
        cigarettes, 544
        costs of enforcement, 540
        court-ordered damages, 539
        criminal penalties for, 556
        deterrence, lack of, 538
        enforcement, 539, 540
        exports, 538-539
        foreign governments, responses by, 552

        MNEs, responses by, 552
        organized crime, role of, 543-544
        payments to officials, 540
        protectionism, role of, 544-551
        "Quality Brands Protection Committee," 552
        size and scope of counterfeiting, explanations
            for, 538-539
        state support of, 538
        Trademark Law, 539
Choice of forum, 621-633
    Admiralty Jurisdiction Clause, 631
    enforcement of judgments, 632-633
    overview, 588-589
    recognition of judgments, 632-633
Choice of law, 634-640
    approaches, 634-639
    CISG, applicability, 635
    clauses, 639
    Convention on the Law Applicable to Contractual
        Obligations, 168
    European Union rules, 621
    governmental interest analysis, 634
    international law context, 22-24
    lex loci, 634
    most significant relationship test, 634
    overview, 589
    Restatement (First) of Conflicts of Law, 634
    Restatement (Second) of Conflicts of Law, 167-168,
        634, 640
    sales contracts, 165-168
    UCC, 167, 639
CIF, 69, 70, 74-82
    documents of title, 82-87, 88
    UCC, 82
Cigarettes
    trademark counterfeiting, 544
CISG. *See* Convention on Contracts for the
        International Sale of Goods
Civil Rights Act of 1964, Title VII of
    exterritorial application of U.S. law, 723
Classification issues
    import trade, 137-140, 148-154
Clause Paramount, 108, 111
Codes of conduct, 719-722, 730
COGSA. *See* Carriage of Goods by Sea Act
Comity, 668-673
    conflict of laws, relationship to, 687-690
    international comity, 672-673
    overview, 588
    Securities Exchange Act, 669
Commerce Control List (CCL), 131, 134
Commerce Department
    antiboycott laws, 132-133
    Export Administration Regulations, 132-133
    overview, 45-46
Commercial Law Development Program, 46
Commercial letters of credit, 59. *See also* Letters of
        credit

Commercial piracy, 526-553
   access to materials and technology, 527
   benefits resulting from, 536
   biopiracy, 564-566
      Convention for Biological Diversity, 565-566
      WIPO role, 566
   categories, 529-537
   China, trademark counterfeiting in, 537-553
      Administration of Industry and Commerce, 539
      cigarettes, 544
      costs of enforcement, 540
      court-ordered damages, 539
      enforcement, 539, 540
      exports, 538-539
      foreign governments, responses by, 552
      MNEs, responses by, 552
      organized crime, role of, 543-544
      payments to officials, 540
      protectionism, role of, 544-551
      Trademark Law, 539
   copyright piracy, 529-532
   distribution networks, 536-537
   importance of trademarks and brands, 527-528
   International Trade Commission studies, 526
   levels of piracy, methods for determining, 535-536
   losses, methods for determining, 536
   overview, 526-553
   patent infringement, 534-537
      World Health Organization estimates, 535
   rise in, 526-528
   technology transfer through FDI, 528
   trademark counterfeiting, 532-534
      in China, 537-553
      International Chamber of Commerce estimates, 532
      Trademark Counterfeiting Act, 534
Commission on International Trade Law, 53, 94
   arbitration rules, 599
   CISG
      case law, 170-171
      formation of, 170
   conciliation rules, 592
   formation of contracts, 189
   overview, 26
Committee on Foreign Investment in the United States (CFIUS), 354, 422-423
Common carriers, types of, 90-91
Common Market for Eastern and Southern Africa, 37-38
Conciliation, 592
   UNCITRAL rules, 592
Conflict of laws, 683-694
   comity, relationship to, 683-686, 687-690
   due process considerations, 689-690
   injunctions, 691-694
   overview, 22-24
Consortia
   foreign direct investment in Brazil, 513
Contracts of affreightment, 89-97

cost, insurance, and freight (CIF), 86
   overview, 60
Convention Against Corruption, 404
Convention for Biological Diversity, 565-566
Convention for the Unification of Certain Rules for International Carriage by Air, 91
Convention on Civil Liability for Damage Resulting from Activities Dangerous to the Environment, 723, 754
Convention on Civil Liability for Oil Pollution Damage, 723
Convention on Combating Bribery of Foreign Public Officials in International Business Transactions, OECD, 403-404, 411-412
Convention on Contracts for the International Carriage of Goods Wholly or Partly by Sea, 94-95
Convention on Contracts for the International Sale of Goods (CISG), 66, 67, 69, 168-224
   acceptance of offer, 189-201
      UNIDROIT Principles of International Commercial Contracts, 201
   agency and distributorships, 306-307
   anticipatory breach and installment contracts, remedies, 224
   application, 171-224
   Article 1(1)(a), 172-173
   Article 1(1)(b), 173-176
   Article 79, 214-217, 217-219
   Article 95, 173-175
   basic features, 170
   buyer, remedies of, 222-224
   case law, 170-171
   choice of law, 173
   complex sales contracts, formation of, 201-206
   conforming goods, 207-212
   delivery by seller, 206-207
   distribution agreements, nonapplicability to, 182
   exclusions from coverage, 170, 182
   excused performance, 214-219
      Article 79, 214-217, 217-219
      delegation to third party, 217-219
   formation of, 170
   formation of contract, 189-206
      acceptance of offer, 190-201
      battle of forms, 200-201
      complex sales contracts, 201-206
      offer, 190
      revocation of offer, 190-191
      UNIDROIT Principles of International Commercial Contracts, acceptance of offer, 201
      withdrawal of offer, 190-191
   historical overview, 170
   interpretation, 183-189
   offer, 190
   overview, 168-169
   parol evidence rule, 184-185
   parties to the CISG, 169

payment by buyer, 212-214
performance under contract, 206-224
  Article 79, excused performance, 214-217, 217-219
  conforming goods, 207-212
  delegation to third party, excused performance, 217-219
  delivery by seller, 206-207
  excused performance, 214-219
  payment by buyer, 212-214
Principles of International Commercial Contracts, acceptance of offer, 201
remedies, 219-224
  anticipatory breach and installment contracts, 224
  buyer, of, 222-224
  seller, of, 220-222
revocation of offer, 190-191
scope, issues relating to, 176-183
seller, remedies of, 220-222
test of internationality, 172-173
UCC
  acceptance of offer, 191, 193, 197, 199
  complex sales contracts, formation of, 205
  conforming goods, 207
  offer, 191
  parol evidence rule, 185
  warranties, 207
UNCITRAL
  case law, 170
  formation of contract, 189
UNIDROIT
  formation of contract, 189
  Principles of International Commercial Contracts, acceptance of offer, 201
Convention on Independent Guarantees and Standby Letters of Credit, 267
Convention on Nuclear Safety, 723
Convention on Persistent Organic Pollutants, 741
Convention on the International Carriage of Goods by Road, 92
Convention on the Law Applicable to Contractual Obligations
sales contracts, choice of law, 168
Convention on the Prior Informed Consent Procedure for Certain Hazardous Chemicals and Pesticides in International Trade, 741
Convention on the Protection and Use of Transboundary Waters and International Lakes, 754
Convention on the Recognition and Enforcement of Foreign Arbitral Awards, 593-600, 602, 608-612
Convention on the Settlement of Investment Disputes Between States and Nationals of Other States
foreign direct investment, 358, 362-380
Convention on the Transboundary Effects of Industrial Accidents, 754

Convention on Transnational Bribery (OECD), 404
Copyright Act of 1976
copyrights, 318-319
first sale doctrine, 577-584
gray-market goods, 577-584
parallel imports, 577-584
Copyrights. See also Intellectual property rights
Copyright Act of 1976, 318-319
piracy, 529-532
technology transfer and licensing issues, 319-320
  Berne Convention for the Protection of Literary and Artistic Works, 319-320
  Copyright Act of 1976, 318-319
  international treaties, 319-320
  TRIPs, 319-320
Corporate social responsibility, 713-766
African Charter on Human and Peoples' Rights, 718
Alien Tort Statute, 716, 754-766
American Convention on Human Rights, 718
American Declaration of the Rights and Duties of Man, 718
Basel Convention on the Control of Transboundary Movements of Hazardous Wastes and Their Disposal, 740-741
Bhopal disaster, 744-754
  Federal Rules of Civil Procedure and, 748
codes and standards of conduct, 724-743
Convention on Civil Liability for Damage Resulting from Activities Dangerous to the Environment, 723, 754
Convention on Civil Liability for Oil Pollution Damage, 723
Convention on Nuclear Safety, 723
Convention on Persistent Organic Pollutants, 741
Convention on the Prior Informed Consent Procedure for Certain Hazardous Chemicals and Pesticides in International Trade, 741
eco-audits, 736-737
environmental management systems, 732, 737
environmental reporting, 736-737
European Convention for the Protection of Human Rights and Fundamental Freedoms, 718
European Court of Human Rights, 717, 718
extraterritorial application of U.S. law, 723
Federal Insecticide, Fungicide, and Rodenticide Act, 742
globalization, harmful effects of, 21
hazardous industries, exporting, 739-740
hazard, exportation of, 737-743. See also Hazardous waste exporting
Human Rights Committee, 719
human rights responsibilities, 715-719
industrial accidents, liability for, 743-754
International Covenant on Civil and Political Rights, 717-718, 719
international forums, 723
international law and transnational corporations, 714-715

Corporate social responsibility (*continued*)
International Standards Organization, 737
international tort litigation, 744
MNEs
code of conduct for, 730
creative capitalism, 21
social compact, 21
as subjects of international law, 722-723
OECD
Guidelines for Multinational Enterprises,
724-730
implementation of Guidelines, 729-730
polluter-pays principle, 741-742
overview, 713-724
polluter-pays principle, 730-731, 741-742, 743
program for CSR, creation of, 737
rapidly industrializing countries, industrial
pollution in, 738-739
Resource Conservation and Recovery Act, 743
Rotterdam Convention, 741
safety management systems, 732
Sarbanes-Oxley Act, 735-736
SEC regulations, 735
sustainable development, program of, 730-731
Toxic Substances Control Act, 743
United Nations
Global Compact, 736
Universal Declaration of Human Rights,
717-718
Corruption. *See* Bribery Convention; Foreign Corrupt
Practices Act
Cost, insurance, and freight (CIF), 69, 70, 74-82
documents of title, 82-87, 88
UCC, 82
Council of Europe
Criminal Law Convention on Corruption, 404
Council of Ministers, 41
Council of the European Union, 41
Counsel in international business, 4-9
challenges for international attorneys, 7-8
in-house lawyers, reporting structure for, 5
issues faced by, 4
multinational enterprises, role of attorneys, 4-6
Court of First Instance, 42
Court of International Trade, 45
Creeping expropriation, 367
Crisis, global financial, 44
Critical infrastructure, defined, 423
Cultural concerns, 9-12
in negotiating styles, 11
Customs Service
duties, determining, 148
gray-market goods, regulations, 570, 572-577
origin marking, 163
overview, 45
parallel imports, regulations, 570, 572-577
Customs unions, 37, 142, 364
examples, 37, 364

**Declaration on the TRIPs Agreement and Public
Health,** 561-564
**Declaratory judgment action regarding patent license
agreement**
burden of proof/persuasion, 334
Deposition in foreign country, 698-699
Disclosure obligations of companies, 735-736, 754
Discovery issues, 694-703
deposition-taking in foreign country, 698-699
Federal Rules of Civil Procedure, 694, 697
Hague Evidence Convention, 694-698
letters rogatory/letters of request, 698
overview, 593
production of documents, 698, 702-703
Restatement (Third) of Foreign Relations Law of
the United States, 694, 702-703
Dispute resolution, 587-712
act of state doctrine, 661-668
overview, 590-591
Admiralty Jurisdiction Clause, choice of forum,
631
affiliated companies, jurisdiction over, 677-683
alternative dispute resolution, 591-593
arbitration. *See* Arbitration
Brussels Convention on Jurisdiction and the
Enforcement of Judgments in Civil and
Commercial Matters, 644, 712
choice of forum, 621-633
overview, 588-589
choice of law, 634-640. *See also* Choice of law
approaches, 634-639
clauses, 639
governmental interest analysis, 634
lex loci, 634
most significant relationship test, 634
overview, 589
CISG, applicability, 635
comity, 668-673
conflict of laws, relationship to, 687-690
overview, 588
conciliation, 592
conflict of laws, 683-694
comity, relationship to, 683-686, 687-690
due process considerations, 689-690
injunctions, 691-694
discovery issues, 694-703
overview, 593
due process and jurisdiction, 647-651, 656-657
enforcement of foreign judgments, 703-712
evidentiary issues, 694-703
overview, 593
Federal Rules of Civil Procedure
discovery issues, 694, 697
evidentiary issues, 694, 697
service of process, 676-677
Foreign Sovereign Immunities Act, sovereign
immunity, 590-591, 657-661
commercial activity exception, 522, 698

forum non conveniens, 668-673
overview, 590-591
Hague Conference on Private International Law, recognition and enforcement of choice of court agreements and judgments, 632
Hague Convention on the Service Abroad of Judicial and Extrajudicial Documents service of process, 675-677
Hague Evidence Convention
discovery issues, 694-698
evidentiary issues, 694-698
international law and jurisdiction, 641-644
issues, overview of, 587-588
jurisdictional issues, 641-694. *See also* Jurisdictional issues
litigation, other than by, 591-593
Lugano Convention on Jurisdiction and the Recognition and Enforcement of Judgments in Civil and Commercial Matters, 644, 712
mediation, 592
national law and jurisdiction, 644-657
negotiation, 592
overview, 587-593
parent companies, jurisdiction over, 677-683
recognition of foreign judgments, 703-712
resolving issues by agreement, 592
Restatement (First) of Conflicts of Law, choice of law, 634
Restatement (Second) of Agency, jurisdiction over parent or affiliated companies, 680
Restatement (Second) of Conflicts of Law, choice of law, 634, 639-640
Restatement (Third) of Foreign Relations Law of the United States
discovery issues, 694, 702-703
evidentiary issues, 694, 702-703
Securities Exchange Act
comity, 669
forum non conveniens, 669
service of process, 673-677
overview, 593
sovereign immunity, 657-661
overview, 590-591
restrictive immunity, 660-661
subject matter jurisdiction, 644
territorial jurisdiction, 644-657
UCC, choice of law, 639
UNCITRAL conciliation rules, 592
Uniform Foreign Money-Judgments Recognition Act, recognition of foreign judgments, 711-712
Documents of title, 82-89
cost, insurance, and freight (CIF), 82-87, 88
Doha Declaration on TRIPs, 561-564
Doha Development Agenda, 37
Due process
conflict of laws, 689-690
jurisdictional issues, 647-651, 656-657
Duties

drawbacks, 148
refunds, 148

East Asia, rise of, 18-19
ECCN. *See* Export Control Classification Number
Eco-audits, 736-737
Economic Community of West African States, 37
Economic Espionage Act of 1996 (EEA), 133, 320-321
EEA. *See* Economic Espionage Act of 1996
Electronic bills of lading, 63
Electronic Signatures in Global and National Commerce Act, 66
E-mail
acceptance of offer, 191
FCPA jurisdiction, and nexus with interstate commerce, 402
service of process, 677
Emergency Planning and Community Right-to-Know Act (EPCRA), 754
Energy Charter Treaty, 358, 364, 366
Enforcement of foreign judgments, 620, 703-712
Brussels Convention on Jurisdiction and the Enforcement of Judgments in Civil and Commercial Matters, 712
Hague Conference on Private International Law, 632
Lugano Convention on Jurisdiction and the Enforcement of Judgments in Civil and Commercial Matters, 712
Environmental issues. *See also* Corporate social responsibility
Convention on Civil Liability for Damage Resulting from Activities Dangerous to the Environment, 723, 754
disclosure obligations of companies, 735-736, 754
hazardous industries, exporting, 739-740
hazardous waste exporting, 737-743. *See also* Hazardous waste exporting; Pollution
Basel Convention on the Control of Transboundary Movements of Hazardous Wastes and Their Disposal, 740-741
Convention on Civil Liability for Oil Pollution Damage, 723
Convention on Persistent Organic Pollutants, 741
Rotterdam Convention on the Prior Informed Consent Procedure for Certain Hazardous Chemicals and Pesticides in International Trade, 741
Stockholm Convention on Persistent Organic Pollutants, 741
U.S. controls on, 742-743
industrial accidents, liability for, 743-754
polluter-pays principle, 730-731, 741-742, 743
rapidly industrializing countries, industrial pollution in, 738-739
sustainable development, 730-731
Environmental management systems, 732, 737

Environmental reporting, 736-737
EPCRA. *See* Emergency Planning and Community
    Right-to-Know Act
E-Trade contracts, 66
EURATOM Treaty, 41
European Coal and Steel Community Treaty of 1951,
    41
European Commission, 41
European Community Patent Convention, 316
European Community Treaty, 40, 300
    Article 81, 300, 303, 304, 439, 456
        collusive conduct, 300
        exemptions, 301-302
        horizontal agreements, 300
        vertical agreements, 300
European Community Convention on the Law
        Applicable to Contractual Obligations, 621
European Convention for the Protection of Human
        Rights and Fundamental Freedoms, 718
European Council, 42
European Court of Human Rights, 717, 718
European Court of Justice, 42
European Economic Community, 427
European Judicial Area, 620
European Parliament, 42
European Patent Convention, 315-316
European Patent Office, 315-316
European Union, 40-42
    Brussels Regime, 620, 621
    choice of law, rules governing, 621
    competition law, 300-307, 439-457
    Court of Justice of, 621
    customs classification rules, 148
    as customs union, 37, 42
    E-Commerce Directive, 66
    economic terms, 42
    enforcement of judgments, 620
    European Judicial Area, creation of, 620
    executive branch, 41
    family law matters, 620
    foreign direct investment. *See* European Union,
        and foreign direct investment
    historical beginnings, 41
    industrial accidents, 753-754
    judicial system, 42
    law of, 42
    legislative body, 42
    management of, 42
    medicines, compulsory licenses for production of,
        563
    Recast Regulation, 620, 712
    recognition and enforcement of judgments, 620
    Rome Regime, 621
    Seveso Directives, 753-754
    structure, 40-41
    supranational institutions, 41
European Union, and foreign direct investment,
    427-457
    access to internal markets, 427-433

    competition law considerations, 439-457
        abuse of dominant position, 440-451
        categories of EU competition law, 439
        dominance, 440-451
        elements of proof, 440-441
        geographic market, 440
        merger regulation, 451-457
        product market, 440
        temporal market, 440
    employee co-determination in management issues,
        437-438
    establishment, 433-439
    extraterritorial application, 456-457
    in France, 435-436, 437
    in Germany, 436-437
    intellectual property, protection of, 433
    overview, 427
    protection of intellectual property, 433
    in United Kingdom, 437-438
Evergreen review, 423
Evidentiary issues, 694-703
    "blocking statutes," 702
    deposition-taking in foreign country, 698-699
    disclosure, requests for, 702-703
    discovery, American-style, in foreign countries, 702
    Federal Rules of Civil Procedure, 694, 697
    Hague Evidence Convention, 694-698
    letters rogatory/letters of request, 698
    obtaining evidence abroad for use in U.S. courts,
        694-699
    obtaining evidence in U.S. for use in foreign
        courts, 699-703
    overview, 593
    privileged information, 698
    production of documents, 698, 702-703
    Restatement (Third) of Foreign Relations Law of
        the United States, 694, 698, 702-703
Exon-Florio Amendment, 354, 426
Export Administration Act, 130, 132
Export Administration Regulations, 132-133
Export Control Classification Number (ECCN), 134
Export trade matters, 129-134
    antiboycott laws, 132-133
        Commerce Department, 132-133
        Treasury Department, 133
    Blocked Persons List, 131
    Commerce Control List, 131, 134
    Economic Espionage Act, 133
    Export Administration Act, 130, 132
    Export Administration Regulations, 132-133
    Export Control Classification Number, 134
    Foreign Corrupt Practices Act, 133-134
    Internal Revenue Code, 133
    International Emergency Economic Powers Act,
        131
    international trade law, 163-164
    International Traffic in Arms Regulations, 132
    Office of Antiboycott Compliance, 132
    Office of Foreign Assets Control, 131

Specially Designated Nationals, 131
Trading with the Enemy Act, 131
USA Patriot Act, 134
Expropriation
creeping expropriation, 367
current law, 361
Extraterritorial application of EU competition law,
456-457
Extraterritorial application of U.S. law, 723
Extraterritorial jurisdiction, 641-644, 763-765

FAA. *See* Federal Arbitration Act
FCPA. *See* Foreign Corrupt Practices Act
FDI. *See* Foreign direct investment
Federal Arbitration Act (FAA)
arbitration, 593-619
vacating arbitration awards, grounds for, 597, 619
Federal Bill of Lading Act, 63
Federal Insecticide, Fungicide, and Rodenticide Act,
742
Federal Rules of Civil Procedure
Bhopal disaster, 748
discovery issues, 694, 697
evidentiary issues, 694, 697
jurisdictional issues, 707
motion for summary judgment, 111
motion to dismiss, 720
protecting intellectual property rights, temporary
restraining orders, 557
service of process, 676-677
summary judgment, motion for, 111
FINSA. *See* Foreign Investment and National Security
Act of 2007 (FINSA)
First sale doctrine, 577-584
FOB, 68-70
Foreign arbitration clauses
in bills of lading, 110
Foreign Corrupt Practices Act (FCPA)
agency and distributorships, control issues, 286-287
China under, 540
enforcement of FCPA, emphasis on, 422
export trade matters, 133-134
foreign direct investment, 399-423
basic issues, 405-423
corrupt intent, 403
Criminal Law Convention on Corruption, 404
elements, 401-403
Inter-American Convention Against Corruption,
404
jurisdictional scope, 404
nexus with interstate commerce, 402
OECD, Convention on Combating Bribery of
Foreign Public Officials in International
Business Transactions, 403-404, 411-412
overview, 401-403
persons subject to FCPA, 402
persons to whom payments are made, 403
proscribed payments, 403

purpose of payments, 403
terrorism and, 422-423
United Nations Convention Against Corruption,
404
Foreign default judgment
recognition and enforcement of, 703-712
Foreign direct investment (FDI), 349-523
bilateral treaties, 362-387
fair and equitable treatment, 380-381
liability for breach of treaty obligations, 380-387
state of necessity, measures during, 381-387
in Brazil, 492-521. *See also* Brazil and foreign direct
investment
in China, 457-492. *See also* China
commercial piracy, 528
Convention on the Settlement of Investment
Disputes Between States and Nationals of
Other States, 358, 362, 365-380
decision to invest, 349-353
global competition concerns, 353
intellectual property concerns, 351-352
management and control concerns, 351
market penetration concerns, 351
research and development concerns, 352-353
defined, 350
economic development, role in, 356
Energy Charter Treaty, 358, 364, 366
in European Economic Community, 427
in European Union, 427-457. *See also* European
Union, and foreign direct investment
Exon-Florio Amendment, 426
Foreign Corrupt Practices Act, 399-423
Foreign Investment in Real Property Tax Act, 426
foreign sovereign debt collection, 521-523
in France, 435-436, 437
in Germany, 436-437
global competition concerns, 353
global trends, 14, 355-357
growth in FDI, 16, 355-356
intellectual property concerns, 351-352
International Centre for Settlement of Investment
Disputes, role of, 362-380
International Court of Justice, 358-362, 365, 366
international investment law, 357-399
International Investment Survey Act, 426
Iran-U.S. Claims Tribunal, 358, 366
management and control concerns, 351
market penetration concerns, 351
mergers and acquisitions, 353-354, 452-455
Multilateral Agreement on Investment, 397
Multilateral Investment Guarantee Agency, 366
multilateral treaties, 362-387
NAFTA, 358, 364, 387-397, 399
Overseas Private Investment Corporation, 387
overview, 3, 16-17, 349-351
recent growth in, 355-356
research and development concerns, 352-353
Restatement (Third) of Foreign Relations Law of
the United States, 361, 367

Foreign direct investment (FDI) (*continued*)
　transactional aspects, 423-521
　　in Brazil, 492-521
　　in China, 457-492
　　conceptual outline and checklist, 425-426
　　in European Union, 427-457
　　in France, 435-436, 437
　　in Germany, 436-437
　　overview, 423-425
　　in United Kingdom, 437-438
　　in United Kingdom, 437-438
　　United Nations Compensation Commission,
　　　366
　　World Trade Organization, role of, 397-399
Foreign Investment and National Security Act of
　2007 (FINSA), 422-423
Foreign Investment in Real Property Tax Act, 426
Foreign judgments, recognition and enforcement of,
　703-712
Foreign Sovereign Immunities Act (FSIA), 590-591,
　600, 658-661
Foreign subsidiary of U.S. corporation, jurisdiction
　over, 651-653, 682
Foreign trade zones, 148
Forum non conveniens, 668-673
　forum selection clause and, 672
　overview, 588, 623
　Securities Exchange Act, 669
Forum selection clauses
　in bills of lading, 109-110
　forum non conveniens and, 672
France
　employment laws, 436
　foreign direct investment in, 435-436, 437
　labor laws, 436
　legal system, overview of, 435
　national security review law, 354
Franchising, 334-347
　overview, 334-336
　sample franchise agreement, 337-343
Fraud exception to independence principle
　innocent third parties, 256-257
　overview, 253-255
　sources of law, 255-256
　UCC
　　innocent third parties, 256-257
　　not involving innocent third parties, 257-258,
　　　262-265
　　as source of law, 255-256
　Uniform Customs and Practice for Documentary
　　Credits
　　not involving innocent third parties, 262
　　silence on fraud issue, 255, 262
Free on board (FOB), 68-70
Free trade agreements (FTAs), 37-38, 364
Free Trade Area of the Americas, 43-44
Free Trade Areas, 142-145
FSIA. *See* Foreign Sovereign Immunities Act
FTAs. *See* Free trade agreements (FTAs)

GATS (General Agreement on Trade in Services),
　397, 398
GATT (General Agreement on Tariffs and Trade),
　397
　international trade law rules, 163-164
　marking, 162-163
　merchandise trade, 397
　overview, 13-14
　tariff negotiating rounds, 37-38
　WTO obligations, 35-37
General Agreement on Trade in Services. *See* GATS
　(General Agreement on Trade in Services)
General Inter-American Convention of 1920, 318
Germany
　commercial code, agency and distributorships,
　　296-299
　company law, 436
　corporate governance, 436
　employment law, 436-437
　foreign direct investment in, 456-458
　labor law, 436-437
　legal framework, 436
　national security review law, 354
　Takeover Law, 354
Global financial crisis, 44
Globalization, 20-22
Goods, trade in, 14-16
Gray-market goods, 566-585
　affiliated companies under common ownership,
　　569
　Copyright Act of 1976, 580-585
　Customs Service regulations, 570, 572-577
　defined, 567-568
　Lanham Act, 575-577, 584
　licensed manufacturing abroad, 569
　overview, 567-568
　Tariff Act of 1922, 570, 572
　Tariff Act of 1930, 570-572, 576, 577, 584
　U.S. law, 568-585
　U.S. owners of foreign trademarks, 569

Hague Conference on Private International Law
　enforcement and recognition of choice of court
　　agreements and judgments, 620, 632
Hague Convention on Choice of Court Agreements,
　632-633
Hague Convention on the Service Abroad of Judicial
　and Extrajudicial Documents
　service of process, 675-677
Hague Evidence Convention
　discovery issues, 694-698
　evidentiary issues, 694-698
Hague Rules, 94
Hague-Visby Rules, 90, 92-94, 95, 96
Hamburg Rules, 26
Harmonized Tariff Schedule, 137, 139-140, 148, 153,
　158
Hazardous industries, exporting, 739-740

Hazardous waste exporting, 737-743
  Basel Convention on the Control of
      Transboundary Movements of Hazardous
      Wastes and Their Disposal, 740-741
  Bhopal disaster, 744-754
    Federal Rules of Civil Procedure and, 748
  Convention on Persistent Organic Pollutants, 741
  Convention on the Prior Informed Consent
      Procedure for Certain Hazardous Chemicals
      and Pesticides in International Trade, 741
  disclosure responsibilities, 743
  Federal Insecticide, Fungicide, and Rodenticide
      Act, 743
  international tort litigation, 744
  polluter-pays principle, 741-742
  Resource Conservation and Recovery Act, 743
  Rotterdam Convention, 741
  Toxic Substances Control Act, 742
  U.S. controls on, 742-743
Helsinki Convention, 754
Hijacking disclaimer in bill of lading
  COGSA's effect on, 111-113
Himalaya Clause, 108, 111
Historical overview, 12-14
  disintegration of Soviet Union, effect of, 13
Horizontal agreement, 300
Human rights, 715-722
  African Charter on Human and Peoples' Rights,
      718
  American Convention on Human Rights, 718
  European Convention for the Protection of
      Human Rights and Fundamental Freedoms,
      718
  European Court of Human Rights, 717, 718
  international companies, responsibilities of,
      715-722
  International Covenant on Civil and Political
      Rights, 717-718, 719
  Universal Declaration of Human Rights, 717-718
Human Rights Committee, 719

ICSID. *See* International Center for the Settlement of
      Investment Disputes
"Imperial Clause," 167
Import trade matters, 134-164
  bonded facilities, 148
  case law, 148-163
  classification issues, 137-140, 148-154
  customs unions, 142
  duty drawbacks, 148
  foreign trade zone, 148
  free trade areas, 142-145
  international trade law, 163-164
  marking, 146-147, 160-163
  NAFTA, 142-146
  preferential duty programs, 146
  refunds of duties, 148
  rules of origin, 141-146, 146-147, 158-160

  tariffs, 137-140, 143-148
  temporary importation under bond, 148
  U.S.-Canada Free Trade Agreement, 143
  valuation issues, 141, 154-158
  WTO tariff rates, 147-148
Incoterms, 67-77
  chart, 70
  cost, insurance, and freight (CIF), 74-82
  "C" terms, 70
  documents of title, 82-87
    UCC, 82
  "D" terms, 69
  free on board (FOB), 68-70
  obligations of parties, 69
Independence principle, and letters of credit,
      232-241
  fraud exception
    innocent third parties, 256-257
    not involving innocent third parties, 262-265
    overview, 253-255
  UCC, fraud exception
    innocent third parties, 256-257
    not involving innocent third parties, 257-258
    sources of law, 255-256
  Uniform Customs and Practice for Documentary
      Credits, fraud exception, 241
    not involving innocent third parties, 262
    sources of law, 255-256
India
  Bhopal disaster, 744-754
  Bhopal Gas Leak Disaster (Processing of Claims)
      Act, 749
Industrial accidents, liability for, 743-754
Injunctions
  antisuit injunctions, 683-686, 693
  and conflict of laws, 691-694
Institute of London Underwriters, 127
Institutions, legal, 26-28. *See also specific institutions*
  Commission on International Trade Law. *See*
      Commission on International Trade Law
  International Chamber of Commerce. *See*
      International Chamber of Commerce
  International Institute for the Unification of
      Private Law. *See* International Institute for
      the Unification of Private Law
  UNCITRAL. *See* UNCITRAL
  UNIDROIT. *See* UNIDROIT
Institutions, regulatory, 33-47. *See also specific
      institutions*
  Americas, free trade in, 43-44
  Asia, free trade in, 42-43
  Asia Pacific Economic Cooperation, 42, 43
  Association of Southeast Asian Nations, 42, 43
  Commerce Department, 45
  Commercial Law Development Program, 46
  Court of International Trade, 45
  Customs and Border Control, 45
  developing countries, 44-45
  European Union, 40-42. *See also* European Union

Institutions, regulatory (*continued*)
Free Trade Area of the Americas, 43-44
International Trade Administration, 45
International Trade Commission, 46
NAFTA, 38-40
administration, 39-40
dispute settlement, 39-40
objectives, 39
OECD, 45
Office of Export Licensing, 46
Office of the U.S. Trade Representative, 46, 47, 552
overview, 33-34
preferential trade agreements, 37-38. *See also*
Preferential trade agreements
U.S. trade institutions and policy, 45-46
World Trade Organization, 35-37
creation, 35
decision making, 36
functions, 35-36
GATT obligations, 35
GATT tariff negotiating rounds, 35
structure, 35-36
Insurance
marine cargo insurance, 127. *See also* Marine
insurance
Intellectual property rights, 525-585
Agreement on Trade-Related Aspects of
Intellectual Property Rights. *See* TRIPs
Berne Convention for the Protection of Literary
and Artistic Works, 554
biopiracy, 564-566
Convention for Biological Diversity, 565-566
WIPO role, 566
commercial piracy, 526-553. *See also* Commercial
piracy
copyright piracy, 529-532
gray-market goods, 566-585. *See also* Gray-market
goods
medicines, access to, 558-564
Declaration on the TRIPs Agreement and Public
Health, 561-564
other unauthorized use, 559-560
overview, 525-526
parallel imports, 566-585. *See also* Parallel imports
Paris Convention, 554
patent infringement, 534-537
World Health Organization estimates, 535
Tariff Act of 1930, 556
temporary restraining orders and, 557
trademark counterfeiting. *See* Trademarks
transfer, 17-18
TRIPs, 553-566. *See also* TRIPs
WIPO role, 554
Inter-American Convention Against Corruption, 404
**Inter-American Convention on International
Commercial Arbitration,** 594
Internal Revenue Code, 133
**International Center for the Settlement of
Investment Disputes (ICSID)**
arbitration in, 592, 600
foreign direct investment, 362-380
ICSID Convention, 386-387
International Chamber of Commerce
arbitration in, 593, 598, 601
Incoterms, 67-77. *See also* Incoterms
overview, 27-28
trademark counterfeiting, estimates, 532
Uniform Customs and Practice for Documentary
Credits. *See* Uniform Customs and Practice
for Documentary Credits (UCP)
Uniform Rules for Demand Guarantees, 267
**International Convention Concerning the Carriage
of Goods by Rail,** 92
**International Convention for the Protection of
Industrial Property,** 312-313
patents, 314-315
International Court of Justice
Anglo-Iranian Oil Co. case, 358-359
Barcelona Traction case, 359-360
ELSI case, 360
foreign direct investment, 358-362, 366
International Covenant on Civil and Political Rights,
717-718, 719
**International Emergency Economic Powers
Act,** 131
**International Institute for the Unification of Private
Law**
formation of, 170
formation of contracts, 189
overview, 26-27
Principles of International Commercial Contracts,
171
acceptance of offer, 201
International Investment Survey Act, 426
International Monetary Fund (IMF), 13, 21, 98
International Standards Organization (ISO), 737
14001 program, 737
26000 standard, 737
International Standby Practices, 267
International Trade Administration, 45
International Trade Commission (ITC)
commercial piracy, studies, 526-527
exclusion orders, 556
overview, 46
International Trade Organization, 13
International Traffic in Arms Regulations, 132
Investment disputes
Convention on the Settlement of Investment
Disputes Between States and Nationals of
Other States, 358, 362-380
International Center for the Settlement of
Investment Disputes, 592, 600
Invoices, 53, 55
Iran-U.S. Claims Tribunal, 358, 366
ISO (International Standards Organization), 737
Italy
The ELSI case, 360
ITC. *See* International Trade Commission

Japan
deposition-taking in, 698-699
free trade agreements, 38, 43
Joint ventures
  Brazil, foreign direct investment in, 512-513
  China, foreign direct investment in
    Equity Joint Venture Law, 471-474
    Implementing Regulations for Equity Joint
      Venture Law, 472-474
    legal regime, 464-465
    sample joint venture contract, 474-490
Judicial review of arbitration, 607-619
Jurisdictional issues, 641-694
  act of state doctrine, 661-668
    overview, 590-591
  adjudicative jurisdiction, 644
  affiliated companies, jurisdiction over, 677-683
  Brussels Convention on Jurisdiction and the
    Enforcement of Judgments in Civil and
    Commercial Matters, 644, 712
  comity, 668-673
    conflict of laws, relationship to, 687-690
    overview, 588
  conflict of laws, 683-694
    antisuit injunctions, 683-686
    comity, relationship to, 683-686, 687-690
    due process considerations, 689-690
    injunctions, 691-694
  conflicts of jurisdiction, 685-694
  due process considerations, 647-651, 656-657
  extraterritorial jurisdiction, 641-644, 763-765
  Federal Rules of Civil Procedure, 707
    service of process, 676-677
  Foreign Sovereign Immunities Act
    sovereign immunity, 590-591, 657-661
  foreign subsidiary of U.S. parent corporation,
    651-653, 682
  forum non conveniens, 668-673
    overview, 588, 623
  Hague Convention on the Service Abroad of Judicial
    and Extrajudicial Documents, 675-677
  international law, 641-644
  Lugano Convention on Jurisdiction and the
    Enforcement of Judgments in Civil and
    Commercial Matters, 644, 712
  multiple proceedings in different forums, 683-694
  national law, 644-657
  overview, 589-590
  parent companies, jurisdiction over, 677-683
  Restatement (Second) of Agency, jurisdiction over
    parent or affiliated companies, 680
  Restatement (Second) of Foreign Relations Law of
    the United States, 641-642
  Second Hickenlooper Amendment, act of state
    doctrine, 666-667
  Securities Exchange Act
    comity, 669
    forum non conveniens, 669
  service of process, 673-677

  overview, 593
sovereign immunity, 657-661
  overview, 590-591
  restrictive immunity, 660-661
state court jurisdiction over foreign subsidiary of
  U.S. corporation, 651-653, 682
stream-of-commerce doctrine, 657
subject matter jurisdiction, 644
territorial jurisdiction, 644-657

Lanham Act
  gray-market goods, 575-577, 584
  parallel imports, 575-577, 584
  trademarks, 316-317
Law merchant
  arbitration, 601
  overview, 24, 29
Legal framework, 22-33. *See also specific acts,*
    conventions, and treaties
  categories of law, 28-30
  choice of law, 22-24
  Commission on International Trade Law, 26
  conflict of laws, 22-24
  domestic law, 30
    relationship of international law to, 30-32
  institutions, 26-28
  International Chamber of Commerce, 27-28
  International Institute for the Unification of
    Private Law, 26-27
  law merchant, 24, 29
  lex mercatoria, 24, 29
  overview, 22
  private international law, 23-24
  public international law, 23, 28-29
  regional supranational law, 29
  sources of law, 24-25
  UNCITRAL, 26
  UNIDROIT, 26-27
  uniform codes, 29-30
Letters of credit, 225-281
  basic features, 226-232
  electronic communications, 251-253
  form for commercial letter of credit, 59
  fraud exception to independence principle, 255
    innocent third parties, 256-257
    not involving innocent third parties, 262-265
    overview, 253-255
    UCC, 255-257
  independence principle, 232-241
  overview, 57-58, 225
  sources of law, 225-226
  standby letters of credit, 265-281
    Convention on Independent Guarantees and
      Standby Letters of Credit, 267
    injunctive relief, 265-280
    International Standby Practices, 267
    overview, 265-267
    sources of law, 267-268

Letters of credit (*continued*)
   strict compliance principle, 250-251
      electronic communications, 251-253
      minor spelling discrepancies, 251
   UCC
      fraud exception to independence principle, 255-
         258, 262-265
      innocent third parties, 256-257
      not involving innocent third parties, 257-258,
         262-265
      sources of law, 225-226, 255-256, 267-268
      standby letters of credit, 267-268
      strict compliance principle, 250-251
   Uniform Customs and Practice for Documentary
      Credits
      fraud exception to independence principle not
         involving innocent third parties, 262
      independence principle, 232
      silence on fraud issue, 255, 262
      sources of law, 225-226, 255-256
      standby letters of credit, 267-268
      strict compliance principle, 241-242, 247-248,
         249-250, 267
   Uniform Rules for Demand Guarantees, standby
      letters of credit, 267
Letters of inquiry, 54
Letters of request, 698
Letters rogatory, 698
Lex mercatoria
   arbitration, 601
   overview, 24, 29
Limited liability companies
   foreign direct investment in Brazil, 510-511
Lisbon, Treaty of, 42
Litigation. *See* Dispute resolution
London Court of Arbitration, 593, 598
Lugano Convention on Jurisdiction and the
      Enforcement of Judgments in Civil and
      Commercial Matters
   enforcement and recognition of foreign
      judgments, 712
   jurisdictional issues, 644

Maastricht Treaty on European Union, 40-41
Madrid Agreement Concerning the International
      Registration of Marks, 318
Marine insurance, 121-128
   Institute of London Underwriters, 127
Marine Insurance Act (English law), 127
Market of the South (Mercosur), 38, 44
Marking in import trade, 146-147, 160-163
Mediation, 592
Medicines, access to, 558-564
   Declaration on the TRIPs Agreement and Public
      Health, 561-564
   other use without authorization of right holder,
      559-560
Mergers and acquisitions (M&A), 353-354

   as abuse of dominant position, 451
   advantages, 353
   cross-border M&A, 353-354
   national security review of, 354
   triangular merger, 354
Modern forms and practices, 14-18
   foreign direct investment, 16-17
   goods, trade in, 14-15
   intellectual property transfer, 17-18
   services, trade in, 15-16
   technology transfer, 17-18
Money laundering, 134
Montreal Convention, 91
Multilateral Agreement on Investment, 397
Multilateral Investment Guarantee Agency, 366
Multimodal export transactions, 109
Multimodal import transactions, 102-109
Multimodal transport, 91, 102-109
Multinational enterprises (MNEs), generally, 1
   code of conduct for, 730
   counsel to, role of, 4-6
   creative capitalism, 21
   main business of, 5
   social compact, 21
   as subjects of international law, 722-723

NAFTA. *See* North American Free Trade Agreement
National security review
   of foreign direct investment, 423
   of mergers and acquisitions, 354
Negotiating styles
   cultural concerns in, 10
Negotiation, 592
New developments, 18-22
   China, rise of, 18-19
   East Asia, rise of, 18-19
   globalization, 20-21
   multinational enterprises, role of, 19-20
   South Asia, rise of, 18-19
New York Convention and arbitration, 593-600, 602,
      608-612, 620
Nice Agreement Concerning the International
      Classification of Goods and Services for the
      Purposes of the Registration of Marks, 317
Nice, Treaty of, 41
Non-establishment forms of international business,
      283-347
   agency and distributorships, 285-307. *See also*
      Agency and distributorships
   business format franchising, 334-347
      overview, 334-336
      sample franchise agreement, 337-343
   overview, 283-284
   patent license agreements, 322-334
      declaratory judgment action, 334
      EU Regulation No. 316/2014, 323, 330-334
      new technology produced by licensee, 334
      sample agreement, 324-333

technology transfer and licensing, 307-322. *See also*
Technology transfer and licensing
Non-Vessel Operating Common Carrier (NVOCC),
90-91
services of, 91
North American Free Trade Agreement (NAFTA), 38
administration, 39-40
dispute settlement, 39-40
foreign direct investment, 358, 364, 387-397, 399
import trade matters, 142-146
investment decisions and awards, review of, 395
marking, 160-163
objectives, 39
overview, 38
regional trade agreement, as example of, 387-397
rules of origin, 159-160
NVOCC. *See* Non-Vessel Operating Common Carrier
(NVOCC)

OECD. *See* Organization for Economic Cooperation
and Development
Office of Antiboycott Compliance, 132
Office of Export Licensing, 46
Office of Foreign Assets Control, 131-132
Office of the U.S. Trade Representative, 46, 47, 552
Organization for Economic Cooperation and
Development (OECD), 397
Convention on Combating Bribery of Foreign
Public Officials in International Business
Transactions, 403-404, 411-412
Convention on Transnational Bribery, 404
Guidelines for Multinational Enterprises, 724-730
overview, 45
polluter-pays principle, 741-742
Overseas Private Investment Corporation, 367

Panama Convention Act, 594
Parallel imports, 566-585
affiliated companies under common ownership,
569
Copyright Act of 1976, 580-584
Customs Service regulations, 570, 572-577
defined, 567-568
Lanham Act, 575-575, 584
licensed manufacturing abroad, 569
overview, 567-568
Tariff Act of 1922, 570, 572
Tariff Act of 1930, 570-572, 576, 577, 584
U.S. law, 568-585
U.S. owners of foreign trademarks, 569
Paramount, Clause. *See* Clause Paramount
"Pari passu" **clause,** 522
Paris Convention, 312-313
patents, 314-315
protecting intellectual property rights, 554
Parol evidence rule, 184-185
Patent and Trademark Office, 312, 314, 317

Patent Cooperation Treaty, 314-316
Patents. *See also* Intellectual property rights
importation of patented products
national exhaustion principle, 584
sale abroad first, bar on importation, 584
sale in U.S., then shipment abroad, 584
infringement, 534-537
World Health Organization estimates, 535
license agreements, 322-334
declaratory judgment action, 334
EU Regulation No. 316/2014, 323-324, 330-334
new technology produced by licensee, 334
sample agreement, 324-333
national exhaustion principle, 584
scope of, 334
technology transfer and licensing issues, 313-316
European Community Patent Convention, 316
European Patent Convention, 315-316
European Patent Office, 315-316
International Convention for the Protection of
Industrial Property, 312-313, 314-315
international treaties, 314-316
Patent Cooperation Treaty, 314-316
TRIPs, 313-314
WIPO role, 315
Petroleum Marketing Practices Act, 335
Pharmaceuticals, access to, 558-564
Declaration on the TRIPs Agreement and Public
Health, 561-564
other use without authorization of right holder,
559-560
Piracy, 526-553. *See also* Commercial piracy
biopiracy, 564-566
Convention for Biological Diversity, 565-566
WIPO role, 566
copyright piracy, 529-532
Pollution. *See also* Corporate social responsibility;
Environmental issues
Convention on Civil Liability for Oil Pollution
Damage, 723
Convention on Persistent Organic Pollutants, 741
polluter-pays principle, 741-742, 743
sustainable development, program of, 730-731
rapidly industrializing countries, industrial
pollution in, 738-739
Pomerene Act, 61, 63
POPs Convention, 741
Preferential duty programs, 146
Preferential trade agreements, 37-38
customs unions, 37
free trade agreements (FTAs), 37-38
Priority foreign country, 552
Private international law, 23-24
Pro forma invoices, 53, 55
Protection of Trading Interests Act, 644
Protocol on Civil Liability and Compensation for
Damage Caused by the Transboundary
Effects of Industrial Accidents on
Transboundary Waters, 754

Public international law, 23, 28-29
Puerto Rico Dealers' Contracts Act, 603
Purchase orders, 56

Racketeer Influenced and Corrupt Organizations Act (RICO), 551
Rail transport, 92, 108
Recognition of foreign judgments, 703-712
　Brussels Convention on Jurisdiction and the Enforcement of Judgments in Civil and Commercial Matters, 644, 712
　Hague Conference on Private International Law, 620, 632
　Lugano Convention on Jurisdiction and the Recognition and Enforcement of Judgments in Civil and Commercial Matters, 712
　Uniform Foreign Money-Judgments Recognition Act, 711-712
Regional supranational law, 29
Regional trade agreements
　NAFTA as example of, 387-397
Resource Conservation and Recovery Act, 743
Restatement (First) of Conflict of Laws
　choice of law, 634
Restatement (Second) of Agency
　jurisdiction over parent or affiliated companies, 680
Restatement (Second) of Conflict of Laws
　choice of law, 167-168, 634-635, 639-640
　　sales contracts, 168
Restatement (Second) of Contracts, 720, 721
Restatement (Second) of Foreign Relations Law of the United States
　jurisdictional issues, 641-642
Restatement (Third) of Foreign Relations Law of the United States
　discovery issues, 694, 698, 702-703
　evidentiary issues, 694, 698, 702-703
　foreign direct investment, 361, 367
　jurisdictional issues, 641-644, 765
RICO. *See* Racketeer Influenced and Corrupt Organizations Act
Road transport, 92
Rome, Treaty of, 40
　agency and distributorships, 343
　foreign direct investment, 427
Rome Convention on the Law Applicable to Contractual Obligations
　arbitration, 601
　choice of law, 640
Rome Regime, 621
Rotterdam Convention, 741
Rotterdam Rules, 95, 109, 110
Rules for Electronic Bills of Lading of the Comité Maritime International, 63
Rules of origin, 141-146, 146-147, 158-160

Safety management systems, 732
Sales contracts, 165-224

acceptance of offer, 190-201
anticipatory breach and installment contracts, remedies, 224
B2B E-Trade contracts, 66
buyer, remedies of, 222-224
case law, 170-171
choice of law, 165-168, 173
complex sales contracts, formation of, 201-206
conforming goods, 207-212
consideration, part performance as, 88-89
Convention on the Law Applicable to Contractual Obligations, choice of law, 168
delivery by seller, 206-207
electronic formation of, 66
excused performance, 214-219
　Article 79, 214-217, 217-219
　delegation to third party, 217-219
formation of contract, 189-206
　acceptance of offer, 190-201
　complex sales contracts, 201-206
　offer, 190
　revocation of offer, 190-191
forms, 54-56, 59
invoice, 53, 55
letter of inquiry, 53, 54
offer, 190
parol evidence rule, 184-185
part performance as consideration, 88-89
payment by buyer, 212-214
performance of contract, 206-224
　Article 79, excused performance, 214-217, 217-219
　conforming goods, 207-212
　delegation to third party, excused performance, 217-219
　delivery by seller, 206-207
　excused performance, 214-219
　payment by buyer, 212-214
Principles of International Commercial Contracts, acceptance of offer, 201
pro forma invoice, 53, 55
purchase order, 56
remedies, 219-224
　anticipatory breach and installment contracts, 224
　buyer, of, 222-224
　seller, of, 220-222
Restatement (Second) of Conflicts of Law, choice of law, 167-168
revocation of offer, 190-191
seller, remedies of, 220-222
UCC
　acceptance of offer, 193, 197, 199
　choice of law, 167
　complex sales contracts, formation of, 205
　conforming goods, 207
　offer, 191
　parol evidence rule, 185
UNCITRAL

case law, 170
formation of contract, 189
UNIDROIT
formation of contract, 189
Principles of International Commercial
Contracts, acceptance of offer, 201
Uniform Law for the International Sale of
Goods, 170, 189
Uniform Law on the Formation of Contracts for
the International Sale of Goods, 170, 189
Sales of goods, 49-281
bills of exchange, 52-53
bills of lading, 89-121. *See also* Bills of lading
commercial terms, 67-82
chart, 70
cost, insurance, and freight (CIF), 69, 70, 74-82,
89
interpretation of, 78-82
contracts, 165-224. *See also* Sales contracts
contracts of affreightment, 60, 89-97
cost, insurance, and freight (CIF), 69, 70, 74-82, 89
documents of title, 82-87, 88
E-Trade contracts, 66
expectations of parties, 49-50
export trade matters, 129-134. *See also* Export trade
matters
FOB, 68-70
freedom of contract, 89
free on board (FOB), 68-70
import trade matters, 134-164. *See also* Import trade
matters
Incoterms, 67-77. *See also* Incoterms
Institute of London Underwriters, 127
International Chamber of Commerce, Incoterms,
67-77
international context, 50-67
international trade law considerations, 128-164
overview, 128-129
letters of credit, 225-281. *See also* Letters of credit
marine insurance, 121-128
overview of transactions, 63-65
reputation of seller, ascertaining, 50
risks of nonperformance, 51-52
sales contracts, 165-224. *See also* Sales contracts
trade acceptance, 52-53
trade financing, 52-53
transport of goods, 89-95. *See also* Transport of goods
trustworthiness of seller, ascertaining, 50
UCC, cost, insurance, and freight (CIF), 82
Sarbanes-Oxley Act of 2002, 735-736
Scope of book, 1-3
SDNs. *See* Specially Designated Nationals
Second Hickenlooper Amendment, 666-667
Securities Exchange Act
arbitration, 603
comity, 669
forum non conveniens, 669
**Securities Exchange Commission regulations and
corporate social responsibility,** 735

Security review laws, 354, 423
Service of process, 673-677
e-mailing, 677
Federal Rules of Civil Procedure, 676-677
Hague Convention on the Service Abroad
of Judicial and Extrajudicial
Documents, 675
overview, 593
Services, trade in, 15-16
Seveso Directives, 753-754. *See also* European Union
Sherman Act
anticompetition law, as, 300
arbitration, 602-603
Shipping Act of 1984, 90
Social responsibility, 713-766. *See also* Corporate
social responsibility
South African Customs Union (SACU), 37
South Asia, rise of, 18-19
Sovereign debt collection, 521-523
Sovereign immunity, 657-661
Foreign Sovereign Immunities Act, 590-591, 600,
658-661
overview, 590-591
restrictive immunity, 660-661
Spain
Barcelona Traction case, 359-360
national security review law, 354
Specially Designated Nationals (SDNs), 131
Standby letters of credit, 265-281
Convention on Independent Guarantees and
Standby Letters of Credit, 267
injunctive relief, 265-280
International Standby Practices, 267
overview, 265-267
sources of law, 267-268
UCC as source of law, 267
Uniform Customs and Practice for Documentary
Credits, 267
Uniform Rules for Demand Guarantees, 267
State Department
International Traffic in Arms Regulations, 132
Stock corporations
foreign direct investment in Brazil, 511-512
Stockholm Chamber of Commerce, 593
**Stockholm Convention on Persistent Organic
Pollutants,** 741
Strict compliance principle and letters of credit
electronic communications, 251-253
minor spelling discrepancies, 251
UCC, 250-251
Uniform Customs and Practice for Documentary
Credits, 241-242, 247-248, 249-250, 267
Subject matter jurisdiction, 644
Sustainable development, 730-731

Tariff Act of 1922
gray-market goods, 570, 572
parallel imports, 570, 572

Tariff Act of 1930, 314
    gray-market goods, 570-572, 576, 577, 584, 585
    parallel imports, 570-572, 576, 577, 584, 585
    protecting intellectual property rights, 556
Tariffs, 137-140, 143-148
    rates, 147-148
Technology transfer and licensing, 307-322
    commercial piracy, 526-528
    copyright, 318-320
        Berne Convention for the Protection of Literary
            and Artistic Works, 319-320
        Copyright Act of 1976, 318
        international treaties, 319-320
        TRIPs, 319-320
    horizontal licensing, 309
    importance of technology transfer, 308-311
    international business, technology transfer in,
        309-310
    international legal system for intellectual property,
        312-322
    overview, 307-308
    patents, 313-316
        European Community Patent Convention, 316
        European Patent Convention, 315-316
        European Patent Office, 315-316
        International Convention for the Protection of
            Industrial Property, 312-313, 314-315
        international treaties, 314-316
        Patent Cooperation Treaty, 314-316
        TRIPs, 313
        WIPO role, 315
    related topics, 311
    trademarks, 316-318
        General Inter-American Convention of 1920,
            318
        international treaties, 317-318
        Lanham Act, 316-317
        Madrid Agreement Concerning the
            International Registration of Marks, 318
        Nice Agreement Concerning the International
            Classification of Goods and Services for
            the Purpose of the Registration of Marks,
            317-318
        TRIPs, 317
    trade secrets, 320-321
        international treaties, 321
    TRIPs, 321-322
    Uniform Trade Secrets Act, 320
    vertical licensing, 309
    world economic development and intellectual
        property, 310-311
Temporary restraining orders
    protecting intellectual property rights, 557
Territorial jurisdiction, 644-657
Terrorism
    anti-terrorist legislation, 134
    foreign direct investment and, 422-423
Torts
    exporting of hazardous waste, international tort
        litigation, 744

    products liability suit, 656-657
Toxic Substances Control Act, 742
Trade, channels of, 397
    investment, 397
    merchandise, 397
    services, 397
    technology, 397
Trade acceptance, 52-53
Trade Act of 1974, 552
Trade institutions and policy in the United States,
    45-46
Trademark Counterfeiting Act of 1984, 534, 551
Trademarks
    China, counterfeiting in, 537-553
        Administration of Industry and Commerce, 539
        cigarettes, 544
        costs of enforcement, 540
        court-ordered damages, 539
        enforcement, 539, 540
        exports, 538-539
        foreign governments, responses by, 552
        MNEs, responses by, 552
        organized crime, role of, 543-544
        protectionism, role of, 544-551
        Trademark Law, 539
    counterfeiting, 532-534
        in China, 537-553
        International Chamber of Commerce estimates,
            532
        Trademark Counterfeiting Act, 534
    technology transfer and licensing issues, 316-318
        General Inter-American Convention of 1920,
            318
        international treaties, 317-318
        Lanham Act, 316-317
        Madrid Agreement Concerning the
            International Registration of Marks, 318
        Nice Agreement Concerning the International
            Classification of Goods and Services for
            the Purpose of the Registration of Marks,
            317-318
        TRIPs, 317
Trade secrets
    international treaties, 321
    technology transfer and licensing issues, 320-321
    TRIPs, 321-322
    Uniform Trade Secrets Act, 320
Trading with the Enemy Act, 131
Transport of goods, 89-95
    by air, 91
    common carriage, 91
    hijacking disclaimer in bill of lading, 111-113
    liability, system of, 89-97, 97-101
    lost, damaged, or stolen cargo, 97-101, 111-113
    multimodal transport, 91, 102-109
    private carriage, 91, 95
    by rail, 92, 108
    by road, 92
    by sea, 92-95, 95-97, 101, 102-110, 111-113, 115-121
    by water, 92-95, 95-97, 101, 102-110, 111-113, 115-121

Treasury Department
antiboycott laws, 133
Treaty Establishing the European Community
agency and distributorships, 300
Treaty of Rome. *See* Rome, Treaty of; Treaty
Establishing the European Community
**TRIMs (Agreement on Trade-Related Investment
Measures),** 397-398
forbidden TRIMs, illustrative list, 398
**TRIPs (Agreement on Trade-Related Aspects of
Intellectual Property Rights),** 397
Berne Convention, protecting intellectual property
rights, 554
biopiracy, 564-566
Convention for Biological Diversity, 565-566
WIPO role, 566
copyright, 318-319
Declaration on the TRIPs Agreement and Public
Health, 561-564
Doha Declaration, 561-564
enforcement obligations, 555-558
failure to satisfy obligations, 556-557
generally, 555-557
International Trade Commission, exclusion
orders, 556
provisional measures, 557-558
Tariff Act of 1930, 556
temporary restraining orders, 557
medicines, access to, 563
overview, 313
Paris Convention, protecting intellectual property
rights, 554
patentable subject matter, 321
patents, 313-314
pharmaceuticals, access to, 558-564
Declaration on the TRIPs Agreement and Public
Health, 561-564
other use without authorization of right holder,
559-560
protecting intellectual property rights, 553-566
suspension of release by customs authorities,
555-556
technology trade, 397
trademarks, 317
trade secrets, 321
WIPO role, 554
WTO role, 553-554

UCC. *See* Uniform Commercial Code
UCP. *See* Uniform Customs and Practice for
Documentary Credits
Ukraine
Foreign Economic Activities Law, 637-638
Provisions on the Form of Foreign Economic
Agreements, 636-637
UNCITRAL
arbitration rules, 599, 601
case law, 170
CISG

case law, 170-171
formation of, 170
formation of contracts, 189
parties to, 169
conciliation rules, 592
formation of contracts, 189
overview, 26
UNIDROIT
acceptance of offer, 201
formation of contracts, 189
overview, 26-27
Principles of International Commercial Contracts,
171
Uniform codes, 29-30
Uniform Commercial Code (UCC)
agency and distributorships, 306-307
choice of law, 167, 639
CIF transaction, 82
CISG and
acceptance of offer, 192-194, 197, 199, 205-206
complex sales contracts, formation of, 205
conforming goods, 207
offer, 187
parol evidence rule, 185
letters of credit
fraud exception to independence principle,
255-258, 262-265
innocent third parties, 256-257
not involving innocent third parties, 257-258,
262-265
sources of law, 225-226, 255-256, 267-268
parol evidence rule, 184-185
sales contracts
acceptance of offer, 191, 197, 199
choice of law, 167
complex sales contracts, formation of, 205
conforming goods, 207
firm offer, 191
offer, 191
parol evidence rule, 184-185
standby letters of credit, sources of law, 267
strict compliance principle, 250-251
**Uniform Customs and Practice for Documentary
Credits (UCP)**
act of state doctrine, 662
fraud exception to independence principle
not involving innocent third parties, 262
sources of law, 255-256
independence principle, 232
sources of law, 225-226
standby letters of credit, sources of law, 267
strict compliance principle, 241-242, 247-248,
249-250, 267
Uniform Foreign Money-Judgments Recognition Act,
711-712
Uniform Law for the International Sale of Goods,
170, 189
**Uniform Law on the Formation of Contracts for the
International Sale of Goods,** 170, 189
Uniform Rules for Demand Guarantees, 267

Uniform Trade Secrets Act of 1979, 320
United Kingdom
   Anglo-Iranian Oil Co. case, 358-359
   Bribery Act, 404
   CISG, non-signatory to, 174, 192
   foreign direct investment in, 437-438
   national security review law, 354
   Protection of Trading Interests Act, 644
United Nations
   CISG. *See* Convention on Contracts for the
      International Sale of Goods
   Commission on International Trade Law. *See*
      Commission on International Trade Law
   Compensation Commission, 366
   Conference on Trade and Development, 44
   Convention Against Corruption, 404
   Convention on Contracts for the International
      Sale of Goods. *See* Convention on Contracts
      for the International Sale of Goods
   Convention on International Bills of Exchange
      and International Promissory Notes, 53
   Convention on Contracts for the International
      Carriage of Goods Wholly or Partially by Sea
      (Rotterdam Rules), 94-95
   Convention on the Use of Electronic
      Communications in International Contracts,
      66
   Global Compact, 736, 737
   UNCITRAL. *See* UNCITRAL
United States Trade Representative, 46, 47, 552
Uruguay Round, 37
USA Patriot Act, 134
U.S.-Canada Free Trade Agreement, 143
**U.S. Electronic Signatures in Global and National
   Commerce Act,** 66
U.S. Shipping Act of 1984, 90
U.S. Trade Act of 1974, 552

Valuation issues in import trade, 141, 154-158
Vertical agreement, 300
Vessel Operating Common Carrier (VOCC), 90-91

VOCC. *See* Vessel Operating Common Carrier
   (VOCC)
Vulture funds, 522

Warranties, 207
   express, 207
   implied, 207
Waste exporting. *See* Hazardous waste exporting
Watch list, 552
Water transport, 92-94
Wholly foreign-owned enterprises
   foreign direct investment in China, 465
WIPO. *See* World Intellectual Property Organization
World Bank, 13, 21, 44, 45, 365
World Health Organization
   patent infringement estimates, 535
World Intellectual Property Organization (WIPO)
   biopiracy, role in, 566
   patents, 315
   protecting intellectual property rights, role
      in, 554
World Trade Organization (WTO)
   creation, 35
   decision making, 36
   Dispute Settlement Body, 557
   dispute settlement process, 556-557
   foreign direct investment, role in, 397-399
   functions, 35-36
   GATS. *See* GATS (General Agreement on Trade in
      Services)
   GATT. *See* GATT (General Agreement on Tariffs
      and Trade)
   international trade law rules, 163-164
   marking, 162-163
   overview, 2, 35-37
   rules of origin, 160
   structure, 35
   TRIMs. *See* TRIMs (Agreement on Trade-Related
      Investment Measures)
   TRIPs. *See* TRIPs (Agreement on Trade-Related
      Aspects of Intellectual Property Rights)